S0-AQL-614

Business, Government, and Society

A Managerial Perspective, Text and Cases

Twelfth Edition

John F. Steiner

*Professor of Management
California State University,
Los Angeles*

George A. Steiner

*Harry and Elsa Kunin
Professor of Business and
Society and Professor of
Management, Emeritus, UCLA*

**McGraw-Hill
Irwin**

Boston   Burr Ridge, IL   Dubuque, IA   New York   San Francisco   St. Louis
Bangkok   Bogotá   Caracas   Kuala Lumpur   Lisbon   London   Madrid   Mexico City
Milan   Montreal   New Delhi   Santiago   Seoul   Singapore   Sydney   Taipei   Toronto

The McGraw·Hill Companies

McGraw-Hill
Irwin

BUSINESS, GOVERNMENT, AND SOCIETY:
A MANAGERIAL PERSPECTIVE, TEXT AND CASES
Published by McGraw-Hill/Irwin, a business unit of The McGraw-Hill Companies, Inc., 1221 Avenue of the Americas, New York, NY, 10020. Copyright © 2009, 2006, 2003, 2000, 1997, 1994, 1991, 1988, 1985, 1980 by The McGraw-Hill Companies, Inc.

All rights reserved. No part of this publication may be reproduced or distributed in any form or by any means, or stored in a database or retrieval system, without the prior written consent of The McGraw-Hill Companies, Inc., including, but not limited to, in any network or other electronic storage or transmission, or broadcast for distance learning.

Some ancillaries, including electronic and print components, may not be available to customers outside the United States.

This book is printed on acid-free paper.

1 2 3 4 5 6 7 8 9 0 DOC/DOC 0 9 8

ISBN 978-0-07-128357-1

MHID 0-07-128357-9

www.mhhe.com

We dedicate this book to the memory of
Jean Wood Steiner

Brief Table of Contents

Table of Contents

Preface

This twelfth edition continues a long effort to tell the story of how forces in business, government, and society shape our world. As always, since the last edition, a stream of events has dictated the need for wide, and sometimes deep, revision. Accordingly, we have updated every chapter to include new ideas, laws, personalities, and publications.

While current events move rapidly over the surface of our subject matter, the underlying principles and relationships at its core lie undisturbed. As in every edition, we adapt to the flow of ephemera, but we also continue the work of building insight into the basic nature of the discipline. So, while current events will play havoc with the look of this edition, we believe that discussions about the plain nature of business, government, and society interrelationships are stronger and will endure longer than in our previous volumes.

We carry on our effort to give more prominence to global and comparative aspects of the subject matter. More than in previous editions we focus on business activities, ideas, and civil society networks that span borders. Although we emphasize current events, we continue to provide historical background. Often, what is fresh in our memory is but the periodic display of an enduring phenomenon. We explain the ancient origins of the tension between wealth and virtue, discuss how great industries shaped nations, and study personalities from the past who have left a lasting imprint.

With this edition we also continue a strong and spirited collaboration between father and son extending now over 30 years.

THE CHAPTERS

The new edition brings many changes. Key updates and additions in the chapters include these.

- Chapter 4, "Critics of Business," contains a new section on the globalization of critics, which discusses progressive civil society, neoliberalism, and the global justice movement.
- Chapter 5, "Corporate Social Responsibility," is revised extensively to incorporate international developments, specifically, the rise of new global norms, civil regulation, soft law, and multistakeholder initiatives. This reflects rapid evolution in the practice of corporate social responsibility.
- Chapter 6, "Implementing Corporate Social Responsibility," now focuses more on management processes for carrying out responsibility strategies. It introduces a new model of implementation. It also discusses new market-driven styles of philanthropy.
- Chapter 7, "Business Ethics," updates students on the executive fraud prosecutions from turn-of-the-century scandals. It includes a new, extended discussion about the ethical dimensions of corporate culture.

- Chapter 9, "Business in Politics," now explains how business continues to dominate the political arena following the Abramoff scandals and recent reforms designed to limit both corporate lobbyists and corporate political donations.

- Chapter 10, "Regulating Business," is a new chapter that replaces two chapters in previous editions. It covers how regulation works, how it affects corporations, its costs and benefits, and its use in other nations.

- Chapter 11, "Multinational Corporations," is a fundamentally new chapter about the impact of MNCs in global markets, particularly in emerging economies, and the international codes intended to regulate their activities. It contains short case stories about Weatherford International, Drummond Company, and Wal-Mart and Mattel.

- Chapters 13 and 14, the two chapters on business and the environment, are revised to report advances in scientific understanding. There are new discussions of ecosystems and carbon markets.

- Chapter 18, "Corporate Governance," is rewritten to better explain evolving relationships of share owners, boards of directors, and management. It contains a new discussion of backdating and a more detailed analysis of executive compensation practices.

THE CASE STUDIES

Every chapter, except Chapter 1, concludes with a case study. The cases illustrate one or more central themes in the chapter. Three new cases are added to this twelfth edition.

- "David and Goliath at the WTO" tells how the tiny island nation of Antigua and Barbuda challenged the United States in the World Trade Organization. It hosts offshore Internet gambling businesses and argued that U.S. laws prohibiting most Internet gambling were an unfair trade barrier.

- "Harvesting Risk" is the story of a pesticide manufacturer in Los Angeles with a distinctive strategy. It buys the rights to older and more dangerous pesticides from big agrichemical companies that have moved on to more advanced, safer products. Then it makes big profits selling them in niche markets where they are still legal.

- "High Noon at Hewlett-Packard" takes readers into a boardroom power struggle over the proper role of directors. It invites discussion of the pretexting scandal and the downfalls of CEO Carly Fiorina and Chairman Patricia Dunn.

CHAPTER-OPENING STORIES

As in past editions, we begin each chapter with a true story about a company, a biographical figure, or a government action. Seven new stories appear in this edition.

- "The Bill & Melinda Gates Foundation." The Gates Foundation endowment is larger than the GDPs of 112 countries, but the problems it confronts are large too. Can the genius behind Microsoft make a dent in them?

- "'Today's verdict is a triumph of our legal system . . .'" Of all the executives put on trial in the corporate fraud scandals, Bernard Ebbers at WorldCom got the longest sentence—25 years—a retribution exceeding that given to mafia hit men and ordinary murders. Were his crimes that bad?

- "The Abramoff Scandals." This story unfolds the scandal in the stories of four men it consumed—Jack Abramoff and Representatives Tom DeLay (R-Tex.), Bob Ney (R-Ohio), and Randy "Duke" Cunningham (R-Calif.).

- "Annals of Regulation: The FCC and CBS." After exposure of Janet Jackson's breast in Super Bowl XXXVIII, the Federal Communications Commission gave CBS the maximum fine permitted by law for broadcast indecency. The story describes how the agency acted and raises the question of the fine's fairness.

- "The Commerce Railyards." Diesel exhaust from a complex of four railyards raises cancer risks for the population of Los Angeles. The story explains those risks and illustrates the small, unseen dangers of industrial pollution.

- "The Employment Non-Discrimination Act of 2007." For the first time, the House of Representatives passed a bill to give gays, lesbians, and bisexuals the same employment rights that other Americans were given in the Civil Rights Act of 1964. The bill has not yet become law. Should it?

- "Backdating with Dr. McGuire." Remarkably, Dr. William McGuire, the CEO of UnitedHealth Group, always seemed to receive option grants on days when his company's stock price hit quarterly and yearly lows. When a study published in *The Wall Street Journal* put the odds against picking these dates by chance at one in 200 million, forces were set in motion that ended Dr. McGuire's career.

SUPPORT MATERIALS FOR INSTRUCTORS

The *Online Learning Center*, at www.mhhe.com/steiner12e, includes sample course outlines, chapter objectives, case study teaching notes with answers to the case questions, term paper topics for each text chapter, and a test bank covering chapters and case studies, including multiple-choice, true/false, fill-in, and essay questions.

A set of *PowerPoint®slides* highlighting chapter topics is available for use in classroom lectures.

A *Computerized Test Bank* contains all the questions in the print test bank. It is a powerful system that allows tests to be prepared quickly and easily. Instructors can view questions as they are selected for a test; scramble questions and answers; add, delete, and edit questions; create multiple test versions; and view and save tests.

An *Online Learning Center* also features resources for both instructors and students. The site offers downloadable supplements for instructors, and interactive exercises and self-quizzes designed to enhance student understanding of text material. Go to www.mhhe.com/steiner12e.

Acknowledgments

We are indebted to the long line of authors, extending from ancient Athens to the present, who have tutored us. We extend thanks to the ranks of colleagues and friends within the Academy of Management who have joined us in our journey over the years. Where appropriate we cite their work.

For this edition, the following reviewers guided us in our revision with their insights about strengths and weaknesses in the text. They are

Carlos Alsua	*University of Alaska, Anchorage*
Ruby Barker	*Tarleton State University*
Richard Coughlan	*University of Richmond*
James J. Freiburger	*Southern New Hampshire University*
Marilyn Kaplan	*University of Texas at Dallas*
John Keiser	*SUNY College at Brockport*
Kelly M. Kilcrease	*Franklin Pierce College*
Steven Kreft	*Indiana University*
Karen Moustafa	*Indiana University/Purdue University Fort Wayne*
Diana Sharpe	*Monmouth University*
Ivan Vernon	*Cleveland State University*

At California State University, Los Angeles, we want to thank Robert Goldstone for opening the trails to new ideas. We also thank Alan Stein at the John F. Kennedy Memorial Library for enduring advice and assistance on the research process. Elsewhere, we thank Deborah F. Dubin of Washington University, St. Louis, and Andrew C. Gross of Cleveland State University for making important suggestions.

We are indebted to our outstanding editorial team, including sponsoring editor Dana Woo and editorial assistant Sara E. K. Hunter at McGraw-Hill/Irwin and Jodi Dowling, our project manager at Aptara Corporation. The skill and effort of each has left its imprint on the book. More important, their patience and faith made it possible. We also express gratitude to our copy editor Gretlyn Cline for attending to the details of the manuscript so diligently and well.

Finally, we are grateful to Deborah Luedy for her gracious and abundant support of our work. And we thank Isabel Heinmiller for volunteering to nourish the project in her generous, kindhearted way.

This edition, like all previous editions, is an improbable, momentary conquest of a cosmic mass of information. That it may have improved in quality since the last edition is possible because of the efforts of those named here.

John F. Steiner

George A. Steiner

About the Authors

John F. Steiner

is Professor of Management at California State University, Los Angeles. He received his B.S. from Southern Oregon University and received an M.A. and Ph.D. in political science from the University of Arizona. He has coauthored two other books with George A. Steiner, *Issues in Business and Society* and *Casebook for Business, Government, and Society.* He is also the author of *Industry, Society, and Change: A Casebook.* Professor Steiner is a former chair of the Social Issues in Management Division of the Academy of Management and former chair of the Department of Management at California State University, Los Angeles.

George A. Steiner

is one of the leading pioneers in the development of university curriculums, research, and scholarly writings in the field of business, government, and society. In 1983 he was the recipient of the first Sumner Marcus Award for distinguished achievement in the field by the Social Issues in Management Division of the Academy of Management. In 1990 he received the Distinguished Educator Award, given for the second time by the Academy of Management. After receiving his B.S. in business administration at Temple University, he was awarded an M.A. in economics from the Wharton School of the University of Pennsylvania and a Ph.D. in economics from the University of Illinois. He is the author of many books and articles. Two of his books received "book-of-the-year" awards. In recognition of his writings, Temple University awarded him a Litt.D. honorary degree. Professor Steiner has held top-level positions in the federal government and in industry, including corporate board directorships. He is a past president of the Academy of Management and cofounder of *The California Management Review.*

Chapter One

The Study of Business, Government, and Society

Exxon Mobil Corporation

ExxonMobil is the largest publicly traded international oil company. Although it is headquartered in Irving, Texas, and most people regard it as an American company, 69 percent of its sales, which were $366 billion in 2006, are in more than 200 other countries.[1] Its main business is discovering, producing, and selling oil and natural gas, and it has a long record of profiting more at this business than its rivals.

ExxonMobil cannot be well understood apart from its history. It descends from the Standard Oil Trust, incorporated in 1882 by John D. Rockefeller as Standard Oil of New Jersey. Rockefeller was a brilliant strategist and organizer who crushed competitors. He believed that the end of imposing order on a youthful, rowdy oil industry justified the use of ruthless means. As Standard Oil grew, Rockefeller's values defined the company's culture; that is, the shared assumptions, both spoken and unspoken, that animate its employees. If the values of a founder such as Rockefeller are effective, they become embedded over time in the organization. Once widely shared, they tend to be exceptionally long-lived and stable.[2] Rockefeller emphasized cost control, efficiency, centralized organization, and suppression of competitors. And no set of principles was ever more triumphant. Standard Oil once had more than 90 percent of the American oil market.

Standard Oil's power so offended public values that in 1890 Congress passed the Sherman Antitrust Act to outlaw its monopoly. In 1911, after years of legal battles, the trust was finally broken into 39 separate companies. After the breakup, Standard Oil of New Jersey continued to exist. Although it had shed 57 percent of its assets to create the new firms, it was still the world's largest oil company. Some companies formed in the

---

[1] Figures in this paragraph are from Exxon Mobil Corporation, Form 10-K 2006, filed with the Securities and Exchange Commission, February 28, 2007.

[2] See, for example, Edgar H. Schein, *The Corporate Culture Survival Guide* (San Francisco: Jossey-Bass, 1999), part one.

breakup were Standard Oil of Indiana (which was later renamed Amoco), Atlantic Refining (ARCO), Standard Oil of California (Chevron), Continental Oil (Conoco), Standard Oil of Ohio (Sohio), Chesebrough-Ponds (a company that made petroleum jelly), and Standard Oil of New York (Mobil). In 1972 Standard Oil of New Jersey changed its name to Exxon, and in 1999 it merged with Mobil, to form ExxonMobil.

Rockefeller's influence is buried in the passage of time, but ExxonMobil's actions remain consistent with his nature. It has a centralized and authoritarian culture. Cost control, capital productivity, and strict financial controls are emphasized in operations. Profit is an overriding goal, and projects must meet strict criteria for return on investment. Unlike Southwest Airlines or Google, where having fun is part of the job, performance pressure at ExxonMobil is so intense that it "is not a fun place to work."[3] Over many years it has consistently bettered industry rivals in its favorite measure, return on average capital employed, just like the old Standard Oil Trust. And competitors still find it a ferocious adversary. The company says simply that it "employs all methods of competition which are lawful and appropriate."[4]

ExxonMobil is a massive organizational force, shaping international markets, pushing against competitors, and influencing governments. However, today it exists in a more difficult environment than did Rockefeller's dominating trust. As in the old days, its power is contested and limited by the interplay of economic, political, and social forces. Only now those forces are more leveling.

Markets are more contested. ExxonMobil pumps only 8 percent of the world's daily output of oil and controls less than 1 percent of petroleum reserves. These figures are far lower than in the 1950s when Exxon was the largest of the Seven Sisters, a group of Western oil firms that dominated worldwide production and reserves, including the huge Middle East oil fields.[5] Now its largest competitors are seven state-owned oil companies, often called the "new Seven Sisters," whose output dwarfs that of yesteryear's titans.[6] The biggest, Saudi Aramco, is 3.5 times the size of ExxonMobil in daily output and has 32 percent of world reserves.[7]

The rise of these state-owned oil companies reflects a new resource nationalism in developing nations that want to recapture oil profits from foreign firms. Climbing crude oil prices since the late 1990s have made oil reserves more valuable, leading many countries to take over oil fields. This happened to ExxonMobil in Venezuela. It lost 2 percent of daily production in 2007 when the government seized projects valued at $4.5 billion.[8]

ExxonMobil is on a treadmill, constantly searching for new oil and natural gas supplies to compensate for declining production in existing fields. Output from a mature

[3] Fadel Gheit, a former employee and leading oil industry analyst, quoted in Geoff Colvin, "The Defiant One," *Fortune,* April 30, 2007, p. 88.

[4] See, for example, Exxon Mobil Corporation, Form 10-K 2006, p. 2.

[5] The Seven Sisters were Exxon, Mobil, Shell, British Petroleum, Gulf, Texaco, and Chevron.

[6] These new "seven sisters" are Saudi Aramco (Saudi Arabia), Gazprom (Russia), China National Petroleum Company (China), National Iranian Oil Company (Iran), Petróleos de Venezuela S.A. (Venezuela), Petrobras (Brazil), and Petronas (Malaysia).

[7] Government Accountability Office, *Crude Oil*, GAO-07-283, February 2007, fig. 9.

[8] Chris Kraul, "Exxon, Conoco Drop Venezuela Oil Projects," *Los Angeles Times,* June 27, 2007, p. C3.

field drops 5 to 8 percent a year. To maintain profitability the company pursues new reserves wherever they are located, taking political risks and abiding unrest and corruption. In Iran and Venezuela ExxonMobil's assets were appropriated. In Chad, Angola, Nigeria, and Equatorial Guinea, it paid dictators for access to oil. Indonesian troops guard its facilities against attacks by rebel forces.[9]

Governments are more powerful and relations with them more complex than in the past. ExxonMobil's operations are restricted by the laws and regulations of each country in which it does business. In the United States alone approximately 200 federal agencies and bureaus impose rules and standards on the company. Only a handful of these existed in Rockefeller's day. In foreign countries ExxonMobil faces import and export restrictions, production taxes, price controls, and regulations to protect nature. In 2006 it supported governments by paying $101 billion in taxes worldwide, a sum exceeding the combined revenues of Dell and Microsoft.

ExxonMobil also faces a demanding social environment. As a leader in the world's largest industry, it is closely watched by environmental, civil rights, labor, and consumer groups—some of which are actively hostile. For years the company has agitated environmentalists by rejecting the scientific case for global warming. Alone among major oil companies, it refuses to make significant investments in renewable energy sources such as ethanol, solar, wind, or tidal. A former CEO called such investments "a complete waste of money."[10] Energy from renewables is more expensive to produce than energy from oil, gas, and coal, which will be the dominant sources of energy far into the future. Therefore, ExxonMobil shuns renewables, which lack promise of satisfying its lofty return on capital standards.

ExxonMobil got a good public caning because for years it funded the research of groups that denied global warming. In 2006 Britain's scientific academy, the Royal Society, took the unprecedented step of writing to the company's management, asking that it stop "misinforming the public."[11] Then two senators, Olympia Snowe (R-ME) and John Rockefeller IV (D-WV), the great grandson of the company's founder, sent a letter to the CEO and members of its board of directors. They asked that ExxonMobil end its "climate change denial strategy" because it was adversely affecting the credibility of the United States in the international community."[12]

Such pressure led CEO Rex Tillerson to grant publicly that the world is warming. But he did not make any notable strategic changes.[13] His reversal of belief failed to satisfy critics, especially ExxposeExxon, a coalition of environmental groups that opposes the company's policies. The coalition includes Defenders of Wildlife,

---

[9] The company faces murder charges brought by villagers who claim it was complicit when government troops attacked area natives sympathetic to the rebels. See *Doe v. Exxon Mobil Corp.,* 473 F.3d 345 (2007).

[10] Lee Raymond, quoted in "The Unrepentant Oilman," *The Economist,* March 15, 2003, p. 64.

[11] David Adam, "Scientists Attack Climate Change Denial," *The Guardian Weekly,* September 29, 2006, p. 14.

[12] Quoted in Steven Mufson, "At Exxon Meeting, a Storm Outside but Calm Within," *Washington Post,* May 31, 2007, p. D2.

[13] Jeffrey Ball, "Exxon Softens Climate-Change Stance," *The Wall Street Journal,* January 11, 2007, p. A2.

Greenpeace, the Natural Resources Defense Council, the Sierra Club, and the Union of Concerned Scientists. This league of greens continues to hound the oil giant. Its banner outside the firm's 2007 shareholder's meeting read "No Planet, No Dividends."

As a corporate citizen ExxonMobil funds worldwide programs to benefit education, communities, health, nature, and the arts. Its largest contributions, about 25 percent of the total, go to higher education. Other projects range from a $13 million campaign to save the world's tigers from extinction, an appropriate project since the tiger is the company's brand symbol, to sponsorship of free poetry readings in Singapore, where the company owns a chemical plant. In 2006 ExxonMobil gave $139 million to such efforts. This is a large sum from the perspective of an individual. However, for ExxonMobil it was one-twenty-sixth of 1 percent of its $366 billion revenues, the equivalent of a person making $1,000,000 a year giving $385 to charity. Does this giving live up to the elegant example of founder John D. Rockefeller, the great philanthropist of his era?

The story of ExxonMobil raises central questions about the role of business in society. When is a corporation socially responsible? How can managers know their responsibilities? What actions are ethical or unethical? How responsive must a corporation be to its critics? This book is a journey into the criteria for answering such questions. As a beginning for this first chapter, however, the story illustrates a range of interactions between one large corporation and many nations and social forces. Such business–government–society interactions are innumerable and complicated. In the chapter that follows we try to order the universe of these interactions by introducing four basic models of the business–government–society relationship. In addition, we define basic terms and explain our approach to the subject matter.

WHAT IS THE BUSINESS–GOVERNMENT–SOCIETY FIELD?

business
Profit-making activity that provides products and services to satisfy human needs.

In the universe of human endeavor, we can distinguish subdivisions of economic, political, and social activity—that is, business, government, and society—in every civilization throughout time. Interplay among these activities creates an environment in which businesses operate. The business–government–society (BGS) field is the study of this environment and its importance for managers.

To begin, we define the basic terms.

Business is a broad term encompassing a range of actions and institutions. It covers management, manufacturing, finance, trade, service, investment, and other activities. Entities as different as a hamburger stand and a giant corporation are businesses. The fundamental purpose of every business is to make a profit by providing products and services that satisfy human needs.

government
Structures and processes in society that authoritatively make and apply policies and rules.

Government refers to structures and processes in society that authoritatively make and apply policies and rules. Like business, it encompasses a wide range of activities and institutions at many levels, from international to local. The focus of this book is on the economic and regulatory powers of government as they affect business.

society
A network of human relations composed of ideas, institutions, and material things.

idea
An intangible object of thought.

value
An enduring belief about which fundamental life choices are correct.

ideology
A bundle of values that creates a particular view of the world.

institution
A formal pattern of relations that links people together to accomplish a goal.

A *society* is a network of human relations that includes three interacting elements: (1) ideas, (2) institutions, and (3) material things.

Ideas, or intangible objects of thought, include values and ideologies. *Values* are enduring beliefs about which fundamental choices in personal and social life are correct. Cultural habits and norms are based on values. *Ideologies*—for example democracy and capitalism—are bundles of values that create a certain world view. They establish the broad goals of life by defining what is considered good, true, right, beautiful, and acceptable. Ideas shape every institution in a society.

Institutions are formal patterns of relations that link people together to accomplish a goal. They are essential to coordinate the work of individuals who have no personal relationship with each other.[14] In modern societies, economic, political, cultural, legal, religious, military, educational, media, and familial institutions are salient. There are multiple economic institutions including financial institutions, the corporate form, and markets. Collectively, we call these business.

Figure 1.1 shows how a range of institutions supports markets. Capitalism as an economic system shows wide variation in the nations where it exists because supporting institutions grow from unique historical and cultural roots. In developed nations these institutions are highly evolved and mutually supportive. Where they are weak, markets work in dysfunctional ways. An example is Russia, which introduced a market economy after the fall of communism.

Institutions that had evolved under Soviet political repression and state planning were ill-suited to support a free market. The story of labor is an example. In the old system workers spent lifetimes in secure jobs at state-owned firms. There was no unemployment insurance and, since few workers ever moved, housing markets were undeveloped. A free market economy requires a strong labor market, so workers can switch from jobs in declining firms to jobs in expanding ones. But in Russia the development of a labor market was arrested. The government did not yet provide unemployment benefits to idled workers, so there was no safety net. And housing markets were anemic. Company managers, out of basic humanity, were unwilling to lay off workers who got no benefits and who would find it difficult to move elsewhere.[15] As a result, restructuring in the new Russian economy was torpid. The lesson is that institutions are vital to markets.

Each institution has a specific purpose in society. The function of business is to make a profit by producing goods and services at prices attractive to consumers. A business uses the resources of society to create new wealth. This justifies its existence and is its priority task. All other social tasks—raising an army, advancing knowledge, healing the sick, or raising children—depend on it. Businesses must, therefore, be managed to make a profit. A categorical statement of this point comes from Peter Drucker: "Business management must always, in every decision and

---

[14] Arnold J. Toynbee, *A Study of History,* vol. XII, *Reconsiderations* (London: Oxford University Press, 1961), p. 270.

[15] Joseph E. Stiglitz, *Globalization and Its Discontents* (New York: W. W. Norton, 2002), p. 140.

FIGURE 1.1 How Institutions Support Markets

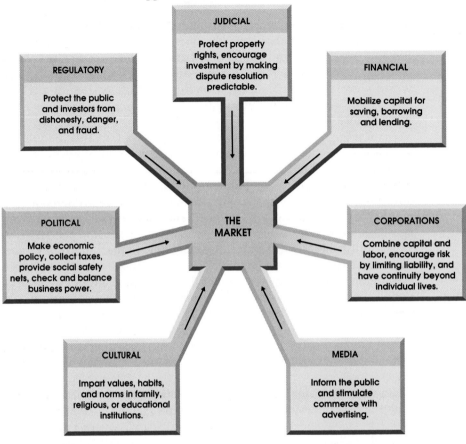

action, put economic performance first."[16] Without profit, business fails in its duty to society and lacks legitimacy.

material things
Tangible artifacts of a society that shape and are shaped by ideas and institutions.

The third element in society is *material things,* including land, natural resources, infrastructure, and manufactured goods. These shape and, in the case of fabricated objects, are partly products of ideas and institutions. Economic institutions, together with the extent of resources, largely determine the type and quantity of society's material goods.

The BGS field is the study of interactions among the three broad areas defined above. The primary focus is on the interaction of business with the other two elements. The basic subject matter, therefore, is how business shapes and changes government and society, and how it, in turn, is molded by political and social pressures. Of special interest is how forces in the BGS nexus affect the manager's task.

[16] *Management: Tasks–Responsibilities–Practices* (New York: Harper & Row, 1973), p. 40.

WHY IS THE BGS FIELD IMPORTANT TO MANAGERS?

To succeed in meeting its objectives a business must be responsive to both its economic and its noneconomic environment.[17] ExxonMobil, for example, must efficiently discover, refine, transport, and market energy. Yet swift response to market forces is not always enough. There are powerful nonmarket forces to which many businesses, especially large ones, are exposed. Their importance is clear in the two dramatic episodes that punctuate ExxonMobil's history—the 1911 court-ordered breakup and the 1989 *Exxon Valdez* oil spill.

In 1911 the Supreme Court, in a decision that reflected public opinion as well as interpretation of the law, forced Standard Oil to conform with social values favoring open, competitive markets. With unparalleled managerial genius, courage, and perspicacity, John D. Rockefeller and his lieutenants had built a wonder of efficiency that spread fuel and light throughout America at lower cost than otherwise would have prevailed. They never understood why this remarkable commercial performance was not the full measure of Standard Oil. But beyond efficiency, the public demanded fair play. Thus, the great company was dismembered.

In Alaska a sudden crisis changed ExxonMobil's political and social environments, leading to billions of dollars of sanctions. Today ExxonMobil operates its tanker fleet with extreme care. It has new environmental safeguards and randomly tests crew members for drugs and alcohol. Remarkably, it is now so disciplined that it measures oil spills from its fleet of tankers in teaspoons per million gallons shipped. In 2003 it reported losing less than one teaspoon per million gallons.[18]

Recognizing that a company operates not only within markets but within a society is critical. If the society, or one or more powerful interests within it, does not accept a company's actions, that firm will be punished and constrained. A basic agreement or *social contract* exists between the business institution and society. This contract defines the broad duties that business must perform to retain society's support. It is partly expressed in law, but it also resides in social values.

social contract
An underlying agreement between business and society on basic duties and responsibilities business must carry out to retain public support. It may be reflected in laws and regulations.

Unfortunately for managers, the social contract is not as clear-cut as are the economic forces a business faces, as complex and ambiguous as the latter often are. For example, the public believes that business has social responsibilities beyond making profits and obeying regulations. If business does not meet them, it may suffer. But precisely what are they? How is corporate performance measured? To what extent must a business comply with ethical values not written into law? When meeting social expectations conflicts with maximizing profits, what is the priority? Despite these questions, the social contract contains the expectations of society, and managers who ignore or violate it are courting disaster.

---

[17] For discussion of this distinction see Jean J. Boddewyn, "Understanding and Advancing the Concept of 'Nonmarket,'" *Business & Society,* September 2003.

[18] Exxon Mobil Corporation, "All Ahead Safe," *National Journal,* March 20, 2004, p. 888 (advertisement).

FOUR MODELS OF THE BGS RELATIONSHIP

Interactions among business, government, and society are infinite and their meaning is open to interpretation. Faced with this complexity, many people use simple mental models to impose order and meaning on what they observe. These models are like prisms, each having a different refractive quality, each giving the holder a different view of the world. Depending on the model (or prism) used, a person will think differently about the scope of business power in society, criteria for managerial decisions, the extent of corporate responsibility, the ethical duties of managers, and the need for regulation.

The following four models are basic alternatives for seeing the BGS relationship. As abstractions they oversimplify reality and magnify central issues. Each model can be both descriptive and prescriptive; that is, it can be both an explanation of how the BGS relationship does work and, in addition, an ideal about how it should work.

The Market Capitalism Model

The market capitalism model, shown in Figure 1.2, depicts business as operating within a market environment, responding primarily to powerful economic forces. There, it is substantially sheltered from direct impact by social and political forces. The market acts as a buffer between business and nonmarket forces. To appreciate this model, it is important to understand the history and nature of markets and the classic explanation of how they work.

Markets are as old as humanity, but for most of recorded history they were a minor institution. People produced mainly for subsistence, not to trade. Then, in the 1700s, some economies began to expand and industrialize, division of labor developed within them, and people started to produce more for trade. As trade grew, the market, through its price signals, took on a more central role in directing

FIGURE 1.2
The Market Capitalism Model

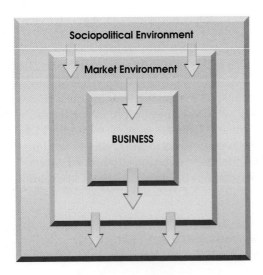

Full Production and Full Employment under Our Democratic System of Private Enterprise, ca. 1944, a crayon and ink drawing by Michael Lenson, an artist working for the Works Progress Administration Federal Art Project. Lenson focuses on the virtues of market capitalism. Source: The Library of Congress, Prints & Photographs Division, LC-USZC4-6568.

market economy
The economy that emerges when people move beyond subsistence production to production for trade, and markets take on a more central role.

capitalism
An economy in which private individuals and corporations own the means of production and, motivated by the desire for profit, compete in free markets under conditions of limited restraint by government.

the creation and distribution of goods. The advent of this kind of *market economy*, or an economy in which markets play a major role, reshaped human life.

The classic explanation of how a market economy works comes from the Scottish professor of moral philosophy Adam Smith (1723–1790). In his extraordinary treatise, *The Wealth of Nations*, Smith wrote about what he called "commercial society" or what today we call *capitalism*. He never used that word. It was adopted later by the socialist philosopher Karl Marx (1818–1883), who contrived it as a term of pointed insult. But it caught on and soon lost its negative connotation.[19] Smith said that the desire to trade for mutual advantage lay deep in human instinct. He noted that the growing division of labor in society led more people to try to satisfy their self-interests by specializing their work, then exchanging goods with each other. As they did so, the market's pricing mechanism reconciled supply and demand, and its ceaseless tendency was to make commodities cheaper, better, and more available.

The beauty of this process, according to Smith, was that it coordinated the activities of strangers who, to pursue their selfish advantage, were forced to fulfill the needs of others. In Smith's words, each trader was "led by an invisible hand to promote an end which was no part of his intention," the collective good of society.[20] Through markets that harnessed the constant energy of greed for the public welfare, Smith believed that nations would achieve "universal opulence." His genius was to demystify the way markets work, to frame market capitalism in moral terms, to extol its virtues, and to give it lasting justification as a source of human progress. The greater good for society came when businesses competed freely.

[19] Jerry Z. Muller, *The Mind and the Market: Capitalism in Modern European Thought* (New York: Knopf, 2002), p. xvi.
[20] Adam Smith, *The Wealth of Nations*, ed. E. Cannan (New York: Modern Library, 1937), Book IV, chap. II, p. 423. First published in 1776.

In Smith's day producers and sellers were individuals and small businesses managed by their owners. Later, by the late 1800s and early 1900s, throughout the industrialized world, the type of economy described by Smith had evolved into a system of *managerial capitalism*. In it the innumerable, small, owner-run firms that animated Smith's marketplace were overshadowed by a much smaller number of dominant corporations run by hierarchies of salaried managers.[21] These managers had limited ownership in their companies and worked for shareholders. This form of capitalism has now spread throughout the world. Nowhere does it work exactly like Smith's theory. Nevertheless, the market capitalism model continues to exist as an ideal against which to measure practice.

managerial capitalism
A market economy in which the dominant businesses are large firms run by salaried managers, not smaller firms run by owner-entrepreneurs.

laissez-faire
An economic philosophy that rejects government intervention in markets.

The model incorporates important assumptions. One is that government interference in economic life is slight. This is called *laissez-faire*, a term first used by the French to mean that government should "let us alone." It stands for the belief that government intervention in the market is undesirable. It is costly because it lessens the efficiency with which free enterprise operates to benefit consumers. It is unnecessary because market forces are benevolent and, if liberated, will channel economic resources to meet society's needs. It is for governments, not businesses, to correct social problems. Therefore, managers should define company interests narrowly, as profitability and efficiency.

Another assumption is that individuals can own private property and freely risk investments. Under these circumstances, business owners are powerfully motivated to make a profit. If free competition exists, the market will hold profits to a minimum and the quality of products and services will rise as firms try to attract more buyers. If one enterprise tries to increase profits by charging higher prices, consumers will go to a competitor. If one producer makes higher-quality products, others must follow. In this way, markets convert selfish competition into broad social benefits.

Other assumptions include these: Consumers are informed about products and prices and make rational decisions. Moral restraint accompanies the self-interested behavior of business. Basic institutions such as banking and laws exist to ease commerce. There are many producers and consumers in competitive markets.

The perspective of the market capitalism model leads to these conclusions about the BGS relationship: (1) government regulation should be limited, (2) markets discipline private economic activity to promote social welfare, (3) the proper measure of corporate performance is profit, and (4) the ethical duty of management is to promote the interests of shareholders. These tenets of market capitalism have shaped economic values in the industrialized West and, as markets spread, they do so increasingly elsewhere.

There are many critics of capitalism and the market capitalism model. As promised by its defenders, capitalism has created material progress. Yet there are trade-offs: It is argued that capitalism creates prosperity only at the cost of rising inequality. Karl Marx believed that owners of capital exploited workers and used imperialist foreign policies to spread markets. Others believe that markets erode virtue. The avarice, self-love, and ruthlessness that energize them are base values that drive out virtues such as love and friendship. Another

---

[21] Alfred D. Chandler, Jr., "The Emergence of Managerial Capitalism," *Business History Review,* Winter 1984, p. 473.

enduring fear is that markets place too much emphasis on money and material objects. Pope John Paul II, for example, cautioned against a "domination of things over people."[22] Critics see these problems as inherent to markets. Still other criticisms focus on the flaws that sometimes, perhaps inevitably, appear in them. Without correction they may reward conspiracies and monopoly. Also, the profit motive has led companies to pollute and plunder the earth.

All these criticisms of capitalism are pronounced today, but none are new. They represent a series of recurrent attacks that wind through the Western philosophical tradition. Adam Smith himself had some reservations and second thoughts. He feared both physical and moral decline in factory workers and the unwarranted idolization of the rich, who might have earned their wealth by unvirtuous methods. In his later years, he grew to see more need for government intervention. But Smith never envisioned a system based solely on greed and self-interest. He expected that in society these traits must coexist with restraint and benevolence.[23]

The ageless debate over whether capitalism is the best means to human fulfillment will continue.[24] Meanwhile, we turn our discussion to an alternative model of the BGS relationship that attracts many of capitalism's detractors.

The Dominance Model

The dominance model is a second basic way of seeing the BGS relationship. It represents primarily the perspective of business critics. In it, business and government dominate the great mass of people. This idea is represented in the pyramidal, hierarchical image of society shown in Figure 1.3. Those who subscribe

FIGURE 1.3
The
Dominance
Model

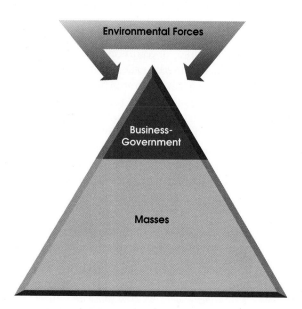

[22] Encyclical Letter, *Centesimus annus,* May 1, 1991, p. 16.

[23] *The Theory of Moral Sentiments,* ed. E. G. West (Indianapolis: Liberty Classics, 1976), pp. 70–72. Originally published in 1853.

[24] Muller, *The Mind and the Market: Capitalism in Modern European Thought,* pp. x–xiv.

to the model believe that corporations and a powerful elite control a system that enriches a few at the expense of the many. Such a system is undemocratic. In democratic theory, governments and leaders represent interests expressed by the people, who are sovereign.

Proponents of the dominance model focus on the defects and inefficiencies of capitalism. They believe that corporations are insulated from pressures holding them responsible, that regulation by a government in thrall to big business is feeble, and that market forces are inadequate to ensure ethical management. Unlike other models, the dominance model does not represent an ideal in addition to a description of how things are. For its advocates, the ideal is to turn it upside down so that the BGS relationship conforms to democratic principles.

In the United States, the dominance model gained a following during the late nineteenth century when large trusts such as Standard Oil emerged, buying politicians, exploiting workers, monopolizing markets, and sharpening income inequality. Beginning in the 1870s, farmers and other critics of big business rejected the ideal of the market capitalism model and based a populist reform movement called populism on the critical view of the BGS relationship implied in the dominance model.

populism
A political pattern, recurrent in world history, in which common people who feel oppressed or disadvantaged seek to take power from a ruling elite seen as thwarting fulfillment of the collective welfare.

Populism is a recurrent spectacle in which common people who feel oppressed or disadvantaged in some way seek to take power from a ruling elite that thwarts fulfillment of the collective welfare. In America, the populist impulse bred a sociopolitical movement of economically hard-pressed farmers, miners, and workers lasting from the 1870s to the 1890s that blamed the Eastern business establishment for a range of social ills and sought to limit its power.

This was an era when, for the first time, on a national scale the actions of powerful business magnates shaped the destinies of common people. Some displayed contempt for commoners. "The public be damned," railroad magnate William H. Vanderbilt told a reporter during an interview in his luxurious private railway car.[25] The next day, newspapers around the country printed his remark, enraging the public. Later, Edward Harriman, the aloof, arrogant president of the Union Pacific Railroad, allegedly reassured industry leaders worried about reform legislation, saying "that he 'could buy Congress' and that if necessary he 'could buy the judiciary.'"[26] It was with respect to Harriman that President Theodore Roosevelt once noted that "men of very great wealth in too many instances totally failed to understand the temper of the country and its needs."[27]

---

[25] "Reporter C. P. Dresser Dead," *New York Times*, April 25, 1891, p. 7. In fairness to Vanderbilt, the context of the remark is elusive. It came in response to questioning by a reporter who may have awakened Vanderbilt at 2:00 A.M. to ask, perhaps insolently, if he would keep an unprofitable route in service to the public. Vanderbilt's response was magnified far beyond a cross retort to become the age's enduring emblem of arrogant wealth. See "Human Factor Great Lever in Railroading," *Los Angeles Times*, October 20, 1912, p. V15; and Ashley W. Cole, "A Famous Remark," *New York Times*, August 25, 1918, p. 22 (letter to the editor).

[26] Quoted from correspondence of Theodore Roosevelt in Maury Klein, *The Life & Legend of E. H. Harriman* (Chapel Hill: University of North Carolina Press, 2000), p. 369.

[27] Ibid., p. 363.

This 1900 political cartoon illustrates a central theme of the dominance model, that powerful business interests act in concert with government to further selfish money interests. Although the cartoon is old, the idea remains compelling for many.
Source: © Bettmann/CORBIS

IN THE HANDS OF HIS PHILANTHROPIC FRIENDS.

The populist movement in America ultimately fell short of reforming the BGS relationship to a democratic ideal. Other industrializing nations, notably Japan, had similar populist movements. Marxism, an ideology opposed to industrial capitalism, emerged in Europe at about the same time as these movements, and it also contained ideas resonant with the dominance model. In capitalist societies, according to Karl Marx, an owner class dominates the economy and ruling institutions. Many business critics worldwide advocated socialist reforms that, based on Marx's theory, could achieve more equitable distribution of power and wealth.

In the United States the dominance model may have been most accurate in the late 1800s when it first arose to conceptualize a world of brazen corporate power and politicians who openly represented industries. However, it remains popular. Ralph Nader, for example, speaks its language.

> Over the past 20 years, big business has increasingly dominated our political economy. This control by corporate government over our political government is creating a widening "democracy gap." The unconstrained behavior of big business is subordinating our democracy to the control of a corporate plutocracy that knows few self-imposed limits to the spread of its power to all sectors of our society.[28]

[28] "Statement of Ralph Nader," in *The Ralph Nader Reader* (New York: Seven Stories Press, 2000), pp. 3 and 4.

FIGURE 1.4
The Counter-
vailing Forces
Model

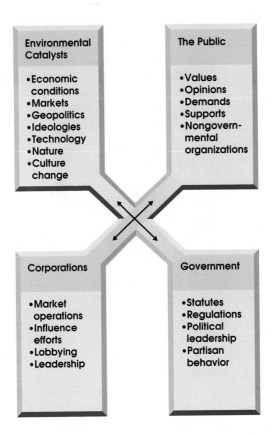

In recent years fear of transnational corporations has given the dominance model new life in a global context. Running for president in 2004, Nader tried "to rescue our public authorities from the corporate government of big business," particularly "large multinational corporations" that are "increasingly and pervasively replacing the sovereignty of the people."[29]

The Countervailing Forces Model

The countervailing forces model, shown in Figure 1.4, depicts the BGS relationship as a flow of interactions among the major elements of society. It suggests complex exchanges of influence among them, attributing dominance to none.

This is a model of multiple or pluralistic forces. Their strength waxes and wanes depending on factors such as the subject at issue, the power of competing interests, the intensity of feeling, and the influence of leaders. The counter-

---

[29] See "Ralph Nader Announcement of Candidacy: Toward a 'New Birth of Freedom' and Justice, "February 23, 2004, and "In the Spirit of the Common Good—A Request for Views" (undated), both at www.votenader.org.

vailing forces model reflects the BGS relationship in industrialized nations with democratic traditions. It differs from the market capitalism model, because it opens business directly to influence by nonmarket forces. Many important interactions implied in it would be evaluated as negligible in the dominance model.

What overarching conclusions can be drawn from this model?

1. Business is deeply integrated into an open society and must respond to many forces, both economic and noneconomic. It is not isolated from its social environment, nor is it always dominant.

2. Business is a major initiator of change in society through its interaction with government, its production and marketing activities, and its use of new technologies.

3. Broad public support of business depends on its adjustment to multiple social, political, and economic forces. Incorrect adjustment leads to failure. This is the social contract at work.

4. BGS relationships continuously evolve as changes take place in the main ideas, institutions, and processes of society.

The Stakeholder Model

The stakeholder model in Figure 1.5 shows the corporation at the center of an array of mutual relationships with persons, groups, and entities called *Stakeholders*. Stakeholders are those whom the corporation benefits or burdens by its actions and those who benefit or burden the firm with their actions. A large corporation has many stakeholders. These can be divided into two categories based on the nature of the relationship. But the assignments are relative, approximate, and inexact. Depending on the corporation or the episode, a few stakeholders may shift from one category to the other.

Primary stakeholders are a small number of constituents for which the impact of the relationship is immediate, continuous, and powerful on both the firm and the constituent. They are stockholders (owners), customers, employees, communities, and governments and may, depending on the firm, include others such as suppliers or creditors.

Secondary stakeholders include a possibly broad range of constituents in which the relationship involves less mutual immediacy, benefit, burden, or power to influence. Examples are activist groups, trade associations, and schools.

Exponents of the stakeholder model debate how to identify who or what is a stakeholder. Some use a broad definition and include, for example, natural entities such as the earth's atmosphere, oceans, terrain, and living creatures because corporations have an impact on them.[30] Others reject this broadening, since natural entities are represented by conventional stakeholders such as environmental groups. Some include competitors because, although they do not work to benefit

stakeholder
An entity that is benefitted or burdened by the actions of a corporation or whose actions may benefit or burden the corporation. The corporation has an ethical duty toward these entities.

primary stakeholders
Entities in a relationship with the corporation in which they, the corporation, or both are affected immediately, continuously, and powerfully.

secondary stakeholders
Entities in a relationship with the corporation in which the effects on them, the corporation, or both are less significant and pressing.

[30] See, for example, Edward Stead and Jean Garner Stead, "Earth: A Spiritual Stakeholder," *Business Ethics Quarterly,* Ruffin Series no. 2 (2000), pp. 321–44.

FIGURE 1.5
The
Stakeholder
Model

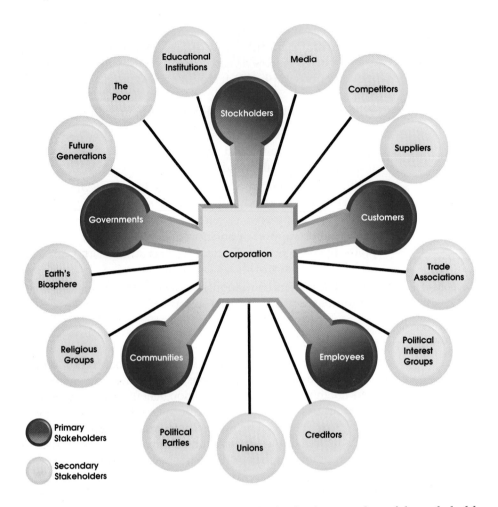

the firm, they have the power to affect it. At the furthest reaches of the stakeholder idea lie groups such as the poor and future generations. But in the words of one stakeholder advocate, "[s]takeholder theory should not be used to weave a basket big enough to hold the world's misery."[31] If groups such as the poor were included in the stakeholder network, managers would be morally obliged to run headlong at endless problems, taking them beyond any conceivable economic mission.

The stakeholder model reorders the priorities of management away from those in the market capitalism model. There, the corporation is the private property of those who contribute its capital. Its immediate priority is to benefit one group—the investors. The stakeholder model, by contrast, is an ethical theory of management in which the welfare of each stakeholder must be considered as an end.

[31] Max Clarkson, *A Risk-Based Model of Stakeholder Theory* (Toronto: The Centre for Corporate Social Performance & Ethics, 1994), cited in Robert Phillips, *Stakeholder Theory and Organizational Ethics* (San Francisco: Berrett-Koehler, 2003), p. 119.

Stakeholder interests have intrinsic worth; they are not valued only to the extent that they enrich investors. Managers have a duty to consider the interests of multiple stakeholders, and because of this, "the interests of shareowners . . . are not always primary and never exclusive."[32]

Stakeholder management, then, creates duties toward multiple constituents of the corporation—duties not emphasized in the practice of market capitalism, which tends toward domination of the environment and enrichment of shareowners. Management must raise its gaze above profits to see and respond to a spectrum of other values. One group of scholars, for example, urges that corporations "should adopt processes and modes of behavior that are sensitive to the concerns and capabilities of each stakeholder constituency."[33] The stakeholder model is intended to redefine the corporation. It rejects the shareholder-centered view of the firm in the market capitalism model as "ethically unacceptable."[34]

Not everyone agrees. Critics of the stakeholder model argue that it is not a realistic assessment of power relationships between the corporation and other entities. It seeks to give power to the powerless by replacing force with ethical duty, a timeless and often futile quest of moralists. In addition, it sets up too vague a guideline to substitute for the yardstick of profits for investors. Unlike traditional criteria such as return on capital, there is no single, clear, and objective measure to evaluate the combined ethical/economic performance of a firm. According to one critic, this lack of a criterion "would render impossible rational management decision making for there is simply no way to adjudicate between alternative projects when there is more than one bottom line."[35] In addition, the interests of stakeholders so vary that often they conflict with shareholders and with one another. With respect to corporate actions, laws and regulations protect stakeholder interests. Creating surplus ethical sensitivity that soars above legal duty is impractical and unnecessary.[36]

Some puzzles exist in stakeholder thinking. It is not clear who or what is a legitimate stakeholder, to what each stakeholder is entitled, or how managers should balance competing demands among a range of stakeholders. Yet its advocates are compelled by two arguments. First, a corporation that embraces stakeholders performs better. A corporation better sustains its wealth-creating function with the support of a network of parties beyond shareholders. Put bluntly by one advocate of the stakeholder perspective, "[e]xecutives ignore stakeholders at the peril of the survival of their companies."[37] Second, it is the ethical way to manage because stakeholders have moral rights that grow from the way powerful corporations affect them. Irrespective of academic debates, in practice many large

---

[32] James E. Post, Lee E. Preston, and Sybille Sachs, *Redefining the Corporation: Stakeholder Management and Organizational Wealth* (Stanford, CA: Stanford University Press, 2002), p. 17.

[33] Clarkson Centre for Business Ethics, *Principles of Stakeholder Management* (Toronto: Clarkson Centre for Business Ethics, 1999).

[34] Post, Preston, and Sachs, *Redefining the Corporation*, p. 16.

[35] John Argenti, "Stakeholders: The Case Against," *Long Range Planning,* June 1997, p. 444.

[36] Anant K. Sundaram, "Tending to Shareholders," *Financial Times,* May 26, 2006, p. 6.

[37] "R. Edward Freeman, "The Wal-Mart Effect and Business, Ethics, and Society," *Academy of Management Perspectives,* August 2006, p. 40.

corporations have adopted methods and processes to analyze their stakeholders and engage them. This trend is discussed in Chapter 6.

OUR APPROACH TO THE SUBJECT MATTER

Discussion of the business–government–society field could be organized in many ways. The following is an overview of our approach.

Comprehensive Scope

This book is comprehensive. It covers many subjects. We believe that for those new to the field seeing a panorama is helpful. Because there is less depth in the treatment of subjects than can be found in specialized volumes, we suggest additional sources in footnotes.

Interdisciplinary Approach with a Management Focus

The field is exceptionally interdisciplinary. It exists at the confluence of a fairly large number of established academic disciplines, each of which contributes to its study. These disciplines include the traditional business disciplines, particularly management; other professional disciplines, including medicine, law, and theology; the social sciences, including economics, political science, philosophy, history, and sociology; and, from time to time, natural sciences such as chemistry and ecology. Thus, our approach is eclectic; we cross boundaries to find insight.

strategic management
Actions taken by managers to adapt a company to changes in its market and sociopolitical environments.

The dominant orientation, however, is the discipline of management and, within it, the study of *strategic management,* or actions that adapt the company to its changing environment. To compete and survive, firms must create missions, purposes, and objectives; the policies and programs to achieve them; and the methods to implement them. We discuss these elements as they relate to corporate social performance, illustrating successes and failures.

Use of Theory, Description, and Case Studies

theory
A statement or vision that creates insight by describing patterns or relationships in a diffuse subject matter. A good theory is concise and simplifies complex phenomena.

Theories simplify and organize areas of knowledge by describing patterns or regularities in the subject matter. They are important in every field, but especially in this one, where innumerable details from broad categories of human experience intersect to create a new intellectual universe. Where theory is missing or weak, scholarship must rely more on description and the use of case method.

No underlying theory to integrate the entire field exists. Fortunately, the community of scholars studying BGS relationships is building theory in several areas. The first is theory describing how corporations interact with stakeholders. The second is theory regarding the ethical duties of corporations and managers. And the third is theory explaining corporate social performance and how it can be measured. Theory in this last area focuses on defining exactly what a firm does to be responsible in society and on creating scales and rulers with which to weigh and measure its actions. Scholarship in all three areas shows increasing sophistication and wider agreement on basic ideas.

Despite the lack of a grand theory to unify the field, useful theories abound in related disciplines. For example, there are economic theories about the impact of

TABLE 1.1
Select
Multinational
Corporations
with High
Percentages
of Sales,
Assets, and
Employees
Outside Home
Countries,
2005

Source: United
Nations Conference
on Trade and Devel-
opment, *World,
Investment Report,
2007* (New York and
Geneva: United
Nations, 2007), an-
nex A, table A.I.13.

Company	Sales	Assets	Employees
Nokia (Finland)	99%	65%	57%
Nestlé (Switzerland)	98	65	97
Honda (Japan)	80	74	87
ExxonMobil (United States)	69	69	63
McDonald's (United States)	66	65	78
Procter & Gamble (United States)	57	44	51

government regulation, scientific theories regarding industrial pollution, political theories explaining corporate power, and legal theories on subjects such as negligence applied by courts to corporations when, for example, industrial accidents occur. When fitting, we discuss such theories; elsewhere we rely on descriptions of events. We also use case studies at the end of each chapter to raise issues for discussion.

Global Perspective

Today global capitalism animates the planetary stage, creating movements of people, money, goods, and information that, in turn, beget conflicts as some benefit more and others less or not at all. Viewing any nation's economy or businesses in isolation from the rest of the world is myopic. Every government finds its economic and social welfare policies judged by world markets. Every corporation has a home country, but as shown in Table 1.1, many large multinational corporations have more sales, assets, and employees outside its borders than within. For now, global capitalism is ascendant. It brings unprecedented wealth creation and new material comforts. But it also imposes burdens on human rights and the environment, challenges diversity of values, and creates conflict with those who are fed upon in the lively predation or who stand aloof from the free market consensus. A fitting perspective on the BGS relationship must, therefore, be global.

Historical Perspective

history
The study of
phenomena
moving
through time.

History is the study of phenomena moving through time. The BGS relationship is a stream of events, of which only one part exists today. Historical perspective is important for many reasons. It helps us see that today's BGS relationship is not like that of other eras; that current ideas and institutions are not the only alternative; that historical forces are irrepressible; that corporations both cause and adapt to change; that our era is not unique in undergoing rapid change; and that we are shaping the future now. When appropriate, we examine the antecedents of current arrangements.

Chapter **Two**

The Dynamic Environment

Royal Dutch Shell PLC

Royal Dutch Shell is the world's second largest private energy company, operating in 130 countries. Each year it makes capital investments of between $15 and $19 billion, sums that are larger than the annual revenues of all but a few corporate behemoths.[1] With such large sums and payoffs that come only after years—even decades—risks are also large. Shell exists in an uncertain geopolitical environment stirred by forces it cannot dominate. Even a giant must bend to heedless fortune. Are its investments the right ones for the world of the future?

scenario
A plausible story of the future based on assumptions about how current trends might play out.

To find out, Shell convenes teams of elite scholars and staff that create alternate visions of this future called scenarios.[2] A *scenario* is a plausible story of the future based on assumptions about how current trends might play out. Carefully written scenarios challenge managers to think in original ways. They are mental wind tunnels that shift environmental forces around the form of the company to see how it "flies."

Scenarios were first used in the 1960s by scholars studying the idea of a nuclear war between Russia and the United States. With no historical precedent for an exchange of atomic bombs, they drew up riveting alternatives about how such a battle might advance.[3] In the 1970s, Shell pioneered the use of scenarios in corporate planning and they soon proved helpful. In 1971 its planners created a scenario in which oil-rich countries cut their oil exports to raise prices. Conventional wisdom at the time held this improbable. Nonetheless, thinking about the possibility changed Shell's strategy, and when an oil embargo surprised the world in 1973 it was the only major oil firm ready for the supply interruption. Shell's reward was higher profits than its competitors for years afterward. Shell then continuously used scenarios as a basis for its strategic thinking. In the 1990s, its planners formed a theory of change in the

---

[1] Royal Dutch Shell plc, Form 20-F (2005), p. 3.

[2] See Peter Cornelius, Alexander Van de Putte, and Mattia Romani, "Three Decades of Scenario Planning in Shell," *California Management Review,* Fall 2005.

[3] For example, Herman Kahn, *On Escalation: Metaphors and Scenarios* (New York: Praeger, 1965).

liberalization
An economic policy of lowering tariffs and other barriers to encourage trade.

global business environment caused by three dominant forces: globalization, technological change, and *liberalization* (meaning relaxation of trade restrictions and regulations). According to Shell, these forces made up "a rough, impersonal game, involving stresses and pressures akin to those of the Industrial Revolution."[4]

Until 2001, a series of scenarios created imaginary worlds that adapted differently to the three forces. Then, two occurrences created what Shell planners call "discontinuities," or unforecast events that alter ongoing, predictable trends. First, scandals produced a global wave of public mistrust focused on corporations and markets. These included not only the banner criminality at Enron, Worldcom, Adelphia, and Tyco in the United States, but also cheating at firms such as Parmalat in Italy, Vivendi in France, and Tokyo Electric Power in Japan. Second, terrorism, particularly the September 11 attacks, combined with upheavals in the Middle East to produce a security crisis.

To explore the effect of the twin crises of trust and security to the year 2025, Shell's planners built three new global scenarious.[5]

- In a *Low Trust Globalization* scenario the trend toward globalization continues. Strong economic growth in China, India, and Brazil dramatically raises world energy demand. But anxiety over security and suspicion of markets require Shell to operate in a climate of heavy regulation and public distrust. Coercive and complex government rules force more disclosure and more corporate responsibility. Nations enact new taxes to discourage pollution. Activist groups become more confrontational and litigious. Transnational corporations grow in size because spreading heavy regulatory costs over large operations is economical.

- *Open Doors* is a contrasting world of globalization and strong economic growth. In this scenario, security issues recede and trust in markets is restored. Shell does not face a climate of oppressive laws and regulation. Instead, a vibrant, global civil society emerges and, along with it, global norms of corporate social responsibility. Companies work cooperatively with stakeholders to promote a more just and sustainable world, even cooperating with governments in joint delivery of services such as education and health. Demand for oil grows, but new incentives to develop renewable sources of energy emerge also.

- The last scenario is *Flags*. The term "flags" is a metaphor for the multiple entities in a splintered world of values, causes, nations, religions, and global crusades. Splits within societies and nations deepen. Terrorism continues. Trust is low. Trade barriers rise as nations put security before economic growth. Globalization stalls. World energy demand is flat. Taxes on business rise. In a climate of deep distrust, activists and the media closely watch big firms such as Shell to ferret out wrongdoing. People become very cynical about voluntary corporate social responsibility. Agreement on international norms of corporate behavior is weak, so a patchwork of bridling national regulation grows.

Such story worlds may be more fantasy than prophecy. However, they show the importance that Shell places on understanding its dynamic external environment. In

---

[4] Shell International Limited, *Global Scenarios 1995–2020,* Public Scenarios PX96-2, 1996, p. 2.

[5] Shell International Limited, *The Shell Global Scenarios to 2025* (London: Shell Center, 2005).

what follows we present a framework for understanding the forces that animate this environment. First, we identify deep historical forces that create change and risk. Then, we identify key dimensions of the global business environment and describe major trends within them.

UNDERLYING HISTORICAL FORCES CHANGING THE BUSINESS ENVIRONMENT

historical force
An environmental force of unknown origin and mysterious action that provides the energy for events. The discussion divides this force, somewhat artificially, into nine separate but related forces causing distinct chains of events.

We believe that, in a broad sense, order can be found in the swirling patterns of current events; that there is a deep logic in the passing of history; and that change in the business environment is the result of elemental historical forces moving in roughly predictable directions. Henry Adams defined a *historical force* as "anything that does, or helps to do, work."[6] The work to which Adams refers is the power to cause events. Change in the business environment is the work of nine deep historical forces or streams of related events discussed below.

The Industrial Revolution

industrial revolution
Transforming changes that turn agricultural economies into industrial economies. This transformation occurs in the presence of certain economic, technological, political, and philosophical conditions.

The first historical force is the industrial revolution, a powerful force that grips the imagination of humanity. The term *industrial revolution* refers to transforming changes that turn simple economies of farmers and artisans into complex industrial economies. In thousands of years before the industrial takeoff of Great Britain in the late eighteenth century, there had been no widespread, sustained economic growth to raise living standards. The vast majority of the world's population was mired in poverty.

Industrial transformation requires specific conditions, including a sufficiency of capital, labor, natural resources, and fuels; ready transportation; strong markets; and ideas and institutions that support the productive blend of these ingredients. Britain came first because it was first to have the right mix of social, political, and economic supports. It was an open society that allowed social mobility and encouraged individual initiative. Its parliament embodied values of political liberty, free speech, and public debate. Perhaps consequently, Britain was the source of scientific advances and inventions such as the steam engine that liberated energy in the nation's massive coal deposits. Its climate supported agriculture and its island geography put it at the hub of sea routes for world trade.[7]

After Britain's takeoff, conditions for sustained economic growth arose in western Europe and the United States during the nineteenth century. Japan and Russia followed in the first half of the twentieth century, and other Asian nations, including Taiwan, South Korea, and China, followed in the second half. Industrialization continues to spread as less developed nations try to create the conditions for it.

Industrial growth remakes societies. It elevates living standards, alters life experience, and shifts values. Historically, material progress has been associated

[6] In the essay "A Dynamic Theory of History (1904)," in Henry Adams, *The Education of Henry Adams* (New York: Modern Library, 1931), p. 474; originally published in 1908.

[7] See Jeffrey Sachs, *The End of Poverty: Economic Possibilities for Our Time* (New York: Penguin Press, 2005), chapter 2.

FIGURE 2.1
World GDP Growth in 50-Year Intervals

Source: Bradford J. DeLong, "Estimating World GDP, One Million B.C.–Present," available at http://econ161.berkeley.edu.

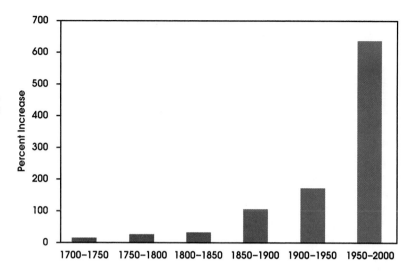

with moral progress; that is, in the words of one historian, it "fosters greater opportunity, tolerance of diversity, social mobility, commitment to fairness, and dedication to democracy."[8] Since institutions built on older ideas change more slowly than people's lives, industrialization generates huge strains in the social fabric even as it elevates civil life. The size and acceleration of economic growth in the twentieth century were astounding. The total amount of goods and services produced exceeded all that was produced in prior human history. As Figure 2.1 shows, output for just the half century from 1950 to 2000 exceeded all that came before. This growth continues today, generating enormous tensions in both developing and developed societies.

Inequality

From time immemorial, status distinctions, class structures, and gaps between rich and poor have characterized societies. Inequality is ubiquitous, as are its consequences—envy, demands for fair distribution of wealth, and doctrines to justify why some people have more than others. The basic political conflict in every nation, and often between nations, is the antagonism between rich and poor.[9]

As the industrial revolution accelerated the accumulation of wealth, it worsened the persistent problem of uneven distribution. Explosive economic growth widened the gap between rich and poor around the globe. Global income inequality is measured by the *Gini index*, a statistic in which 0 percent stands for absolute equality, that is, a theoretical situation in which everyone has the same income, and 100 percent represents absolute inequality, where one person has all the income. Using this measure, inequality becomes greater as the percentage figure rises toward 100.

Gini index
A statistical measure of inequality in which 0 is perfect equality (everyone has the same amount of wealth) and 100 is absolute inequality (a single person has all wealth).

[8] Benjamin M. Friedman, *The Moral Consequences of Economic Growth* (New York: Knopf, 2005), p. 4.
[9] Mortimer J. Adler, *The Great Ideas* (New York: Macmillan, 1992), pp. 578–79.

FIGURE 2.2
World Poverty and Income Inequality since 1820

Sources: François Bourguignon and Christian Morrisson, "Inequality among World Citizens: 1820–1992," *American Economic Review,* September 2002, table 1; UNDP, *Human Development Report 2005,* p. 4; and U.S. Census Bureau, "Total Midyear Population for the World: 1950–2050," April 2004.

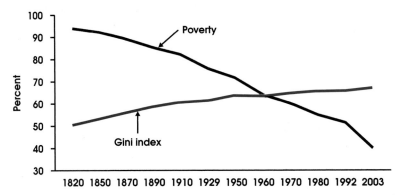

Figure 2.2 shows that by 1820, when the industrial revolution was spreading from England to western Europe, global income inequality was already very high. The Gini index of 50 percent in 1820 climbed to 61 percent in 1910, as economies in industrializing nations rapidly expanded. After that, the rise continued, but more slowly, as populous Asian countries holding the bulk of the world's poor began to industrialize and catch up. The Gini index reached 64 percent in 1950 and continued its decelerating rise to 67 percent in 2003.[10] This represents an extreme level of inequality across the world population, so high that it exceeds the inequality within any single nation. It reflects a situation in which the top 5 percent of people receive about 33 percent of all income and the bottom 5 percent receive 0.2 percent.[11] The cause of this striking gap is the diverging economic fortunes of nations.

Contrary to popular opinion, economic growth itself does not increase income inequality within modernizing nations. During industrialization the incomes of the poorest people rise in proportion to the rise in average income for the country as a whole.[12] The cause of most of the rise in world income inequality is a growing gap between the peoples of rich and poor nations, not a growing separation of rich and poor within nations.

Today about 2.6 billion people live in poverty, defined as an income of less than $2 a day.[13] This is more poor people than any time in history, an enormous pool of misfortune constituting 40 percent of the world population. Yet in 1820, near the beginning of the industrial revolution, 94 percent of the world's population lived in poverty. A great and steady retreat in the poverty percentage for almost two centuries, in the face of vaulting population growth, is testimony to the wealth-creating power of industrial development. Even as economic growth has widened

[10] Figures are from François Bourguignon and Christian Morrisson, "Inequality among World Citizens: 1820–1992," *American Economic Review,* September 2002, pp. 731–32; and United Nations Development Programme, *Human Development Report 2005* (New York: Oxford University Press, 2005), p. 55.

[11] Branko Milanovic, "Global Income Inequality: What It Is and Why It Matters," World Bank Policy Research Working Paper 3865, March 2006, p. 16.

[12] David Dollar and Aart Kraay, "Spreading the Wealth," *Foreign Affairs,* January/February 2002, p. 128.

[13] United Nations Development Programme, *Human Development Report 2007/2008,* p. 25.

FIGURE 2.3
Historical
World
Population
Growth and
Projections:
1 A.D. to 2300

Sources: U.S. Bureau
of the Census, "His-
torical Estimates of
World Population,"
available at www.
census.gov/ipc/
www/worldhis.
html; and United
Nations, *World
Population to 2300*,
table A1.

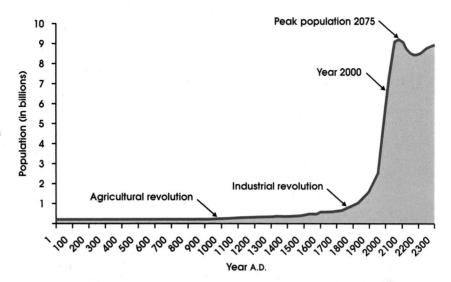

the gap between rich and poor, it has dramatically reduced the proportion of the poor in the total population.

Although the Gini index trend line in Figure 2.2 seems to rise only modestly over the years, it in fact represents a striking confluence of progress and tragedy. If world distribution of income had not become more unequal after 1820, economic growth would have reduced the number of people living in poverty today by an estimated 80 percent.[14] Instead, as the wealth gap between nations widened with each passing year, the distribution of income grew more unequal. Yet even as inequality worsened, the drop in the poverty trend line shows how economic growth has led to a continuous, sharp reduction in privation.

Inequality is resilient and, according to the United Nations, "truly staggering on a global scale."[15] It is perpetuated by social institutions such as caste, marriage, land ownership, law, and market relationships. Arrangements and rules in these institutions are resilient, creating sinkholes of unequal opportunity. The vast majority of the world's 2.6 billion poor people live in nations not yet transformed by industrial growth where entrenched inequities persist over generations. This situation creates expectations that ethical duties of global corporations include helping the poor and equitably distributing the fruits of commerce. The historical lesson of almost two centuries is that if capitalism is harnessed to create economic growth, the poor will benefit.

Population Growth

The basic population trend throughout human history is growth. As shown in Figure 2.3, world population inched ahead for centuries, then grew a little faster

[14] Bourguignon and Morrisson, "Inequality among World Citizens," p. 733. The $2-a-day figure represents what could be purchased in the United States for $2, not what could be purchased in local currency.

[15] World Bank, *World Development Report 2006: Equity and Development* (New York: Oxford University Press, 2005), p. 8.

The Human Development Index

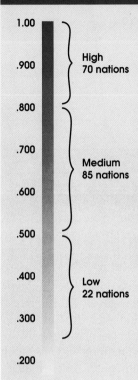

The Human Development Index (HDI) is a statistical tool used by the United Nations for measuring the progress of humanity. It is based on the theory that income alone is not an adequate measure of the standard of living, let alone a rich and fulfilling life. If this theory is correct, discussions of inequality based on income differences within and between nations do not give a complete picture of differences in human welfare.

The HDI is a scale running from 0 to 1, with 1 representing the highest human development and 0 the lowest. It measures the development of nations as an average of scores in three equally weighted categories.

- *Longevity,* or life expectancy at birth.
- *Knowledge,* or the adult literacy rate plus the ratio of students enrolled in school as a percentage of the population of official school age.
- *Income,* or gross domestic product per capita (in equivalent U.S. dollars).

Of the 177 nations in the 2005 Human Development Index, 70 have high index values of 0.800 or above, 85 are in the medium range with values of 0.500 to 0.799, and 22 fall in the low range with values below 0.499. Iceland is highest ranked with an index value of 0.968. Sierra Leone is lowest at 0.336. The United States ranks eighth with 0.948.[16]

Historical HDI index values show enormous increases in human welfare since the late nineteenth century, as a consequence mainly of declining mortality and economic growth. In 1870 the United States had an HDI value of 0.467, a score that today is equaled by Tanzania in the low human development category. In 1913 it had an HDI value of 0.730 that would today rank it slightly below Viet Nam deep in the medium human development category.[17]

Since 1950 the absolute gap between the highest- and lowest-rated countries has narrowed substantially, showing that inequality in living standards around the world, as measured by the HDI, is declining even while income inequality, as measured by per capita GDP, is rising. Thus, inequality is greater if measured only by monetary income and less if longevity and education, two traditional measures of a good life, are taken into consideration.

[16] United Nations Development Programme, *Human Development Report 2007/2008* (New York: United Nations Development Programme, 2007), pp. 234–37.

[17] Nicholas Crafts, "Globalization and Growth in the Twentieth Century," IMF working paper, WP/pp/44 (Washington, DC: International Monetary Fund, March 2000), pp. 6–7.

beginning about 1,000 years ago with the inception of large-scale crop cultivation. After eight more centuries, population growth began a rapid new acceleration in the late 1800s that turned into a skyrocketing rise through the twentieth century. It took until 1825 for the world population to reach 1 billion; then each billionth additional person was added faster and faster—first in 100 years, then in 35, then in 15, then in only 12.[18] This astonishing growth had two causes, both related to the industrial revolution. First, advances in water sanitation, hygiene, and scientific medicine reduced deaths from infectious disease, leading to rapid mortality decline. Second, mechanized farming expanded the food supply to feed record numbers.

[18] Clive Ponting, *A Green History of the World* (New York: Penguin Books, 1991), p. 240.

World population reached 6.6 billion in 2007 and it continues to rise, but growth is predicted to slow and, for the first time in recorded history, end. Figure 2.3 shows United Nations projections that the world population will grow to a peak of 9.2 billion in 2075, then decline over a century to 8.3 billion in 2175 before slowly rising back to 9 billion in 2300.[19] This is an intriguing preview of the distant future, but for the near future, in the years 2010 to 2050, rapid though slowing growth will characterize the business environment.

Growth will slow and eventually end as the world undergoes a transition from high to low fertility. In the initial stages of the industrial revolution economic progress encouraged population growth. Now this progress is a brake on fertility because having fewer children frees women to attend school, enter professions, and increase income. The world's total fertility rate, or the number of births per woman, dropped from 5.12 in 1950 to 2.65 in 2005 and is expected to drop as low

replacement fertility rate
The number of children a woman must have on average to ensure that one daughter survives to reproductive age.

as 2.05 by 2050.[20] This would be below the *replacement fertility rate* of 2.1 births per woman, calculated as the number of children a woman must have on average to ensure that one daughter survives to reproductive age. In theory, this number is sufficient to maintain a stable population. Fertility is declining on all continents, but the world average of 2.65 disguises wide variation. Fertility is lowest in a group of 44 developed nations averaging 1.56 and highest in a group of 148 less developed nations averaging 2.9. The extremes are captured by Hong Kong's low fertility rate of .94 as opposed to Niger's world high of 7.91.[21]

The world population is also aging. Its median age rose from 24 years in 1950 to 28 years now and it will rise faster up to 2050 when it is projected to be 38. Aging will be most rapid in developed nations where mortality rates are lowest. As with fertility, global age averages mask extremes. In Japan, the world's oldest population has a median age of 43 and a life expectancy of 82, far higher than in African nations such as Malawi, where the median age is 16 and life expectancy is only 40 years.[22]

Migration now plays a larger role in population dynamics than in the past. In the 1950s immigration was a negligible factor, leading to net population changes of no more than 5,000 a year in any nation. Today, about 2.6 million people a year migrate to developed countries. For the decade 2000 to 2010, the United States will take in more immigrants than any other nation, about 11.6 million. Mexico and China will lose the most people, 3.8 and 3.7 million, respectively.[23]

Falling fertility, low mortality, and migration will drive future population changes. About 95 percent of all growth to 2050 will occur in developing and less

[19] United Nations, *World Population to 2300* (New York: United Nations Department of Economic and Social Affairs, 2004), p. 2. Figures in this section are based on the medium variant of the 2004 revision of the population database.

[20] United National Department of Economic and Social Affairs, Population Division, *World Population Prospects: The 2004 Revision,* vol. III, *Analytical Report* (New York: United Nations, 2006), tables III.4 and III.9.

[21] Ibid., table III.1, III.2, and III.4.

[22] Ibid., tables II.3 and IV.2.

[23] Ibid., tables V.2.

developed countries, with only 5 percent in the developed world. Fertility will be lowest in Europe and by 2050 its population will fall 10 percent or by 75 million people, reducing it from 11 percent of the world's population to only 7 percent. In North America the population will grow by 32 percent, but due to declining fertility rates in the United States (from 2.04 in 2005 to 1.85 in 2050) this growth will come from immigration. Africa, which contains most of the world's least developed nations, will grow fastest. Despite elevated mortality from the HIV/AIDS epidemic, by 2050 it will add more than 1 billion people, an increase of 114 percent from 2005.[24]

These population trends have many implications. First, although overall world growth is slowing, it will be highest in less industrialized regions, further widening the wealth gap between high- and low-income countries. Second, growth will continue to strain the earth's ecosystems, especially as industrial activity spreads. Third, the West is in demographic decline compared with other peoples. Shrinking, aging populations may lead to lower GDP growth rates and put pressure on national welfare and pension policies.[25] In the future, growing non-Western populations will be stronger economically, militarily, and politically and will push to expand their influence. Although Western market values and business ideology seem ascendant now, they may be less widespread in the future as the numerical basis of Western civilization declines. In such ways will population trends alter the business environment and create new societal expectations for corporate behavior.

Technology

Throughout recorded history new technologies and devices have fueled commerce and reshaped societies. In the 1450s the printing press was an immediate commercial success, but its impact went far beyond the publishing business. Over the next 100 years the affordable, printed word reshaped European culture by creating a free market for ideas that undermined the doctrinal monopoly of the Catholic Church. Printed pamphlets spread Martin Luther's challenge to its scriptural dogma and brought on the Protestant Reformation. Galileo was placed under house arrest in Florence for holding heretical views about astronomy, but his theories prevailed because they were published in Protestant Holland. A Europe opened to the exchange of new ideas based on experience and observation was primed for the scientific revolution.

The invention of the steam engine in the late 1700s and its widespread use beginning in the early 1800s, along with increased use of the waterwheel and new iron-making methods, triggered the industrial revolution. As Figure 2.4 shows, this was the first of five waves of technological revolution. With each wave innovations spread, stimulating economic booms of increased investment, rising productivity, and output growth. The shortening of successive waves reveals faster innovation.

[24] United Nations Department of Economic and Social Affairs, Population Division, *World Population Prospects: The 2004 Revision*, vol. III, *Analytical Report*, table 1.

[25] Nicoletta Batini, Tim Callen, and Warwick McKibbin, "The Global Impact of Demographic Change," IMF Working Paper, WP/06/9, January 2006, pp. 3 and 13.

FIGURE 2.4 **Waves of Innovation since the Beginning of the Industrial Revolution**

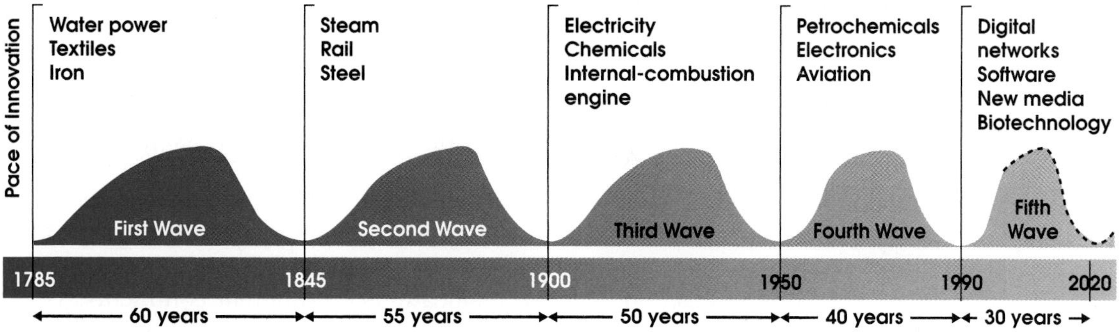

Water power Textiles Iron	Steam Rail Steel	Electricity Chemicals Internal-combustion engine	Petrochemicals Electronics Aviation	Digital networks Software New media Biotechnology
First Wave	Second Wave	Third Wave	Fourth Wave	Fifth Wave

1785 — 60 years → 1845 — 55 years → 1900 — 50 years → 1950 — 40 years → 1990 — 30 years → 2020

(Pace of Innovation)

Source: "A Survey of Innovation in Industry," *The Economist*, February 20, 1999, p. 8. Copyright © 1999 The Economist Newspaper, Ltd. All rights reserved. Further reproduction prohibited. Reprinted with permission.

New technologies foster the productivity gains that sustain long-term economic progress, and they promote human welfare. However, like the printing press, they also can agitate societies. For example, before the 1860s a transatlantic voyage on a sailing ship took a month, cost a year's wages for a European worker, and was risky. About 5 to 10 percent of passengers died due to sinkings and shipboard transmission of diseases. Then steamship technology cut the cost of passage by 90 percent and reduced travel time to one week, cutting mortality to less than 1 percent. As a result, European immigrants poured into the American east, creating labor gluts that led to wage depressions and fueling political movements against big companies, financiers, and the gold standard.[26] In this way, steamship technology strained American political stability.

During the rise of industrial societies over more than two centuries, technology has altered human civilization by stimulating economic and population growth to sustained rises unimaginable in previous recorded history. New things have created many benefits, including higher living standards and longer life spans, but because technology changes faster than human beliefs and institutions, it also imposes strains.

Globalization

globalization
The creation of networks of human interaction that span worldwide distances.

Globalization occurs when networks of economic, political, social, military, scientific, or environmental interdependence grow to span worldwide distances.[27] In the economic realm, globalization occurs when nations open themselves to foreign trade and investment, creating world markets for goods, services, and capital. The current rise of such a system began after World War II, when the victor nations lowered trade barriers and loosened capital controls. Over the next 50 years, international negotiations led more nations to open themselves to global

[26] Robert William Fogel, *The Fourth Great Awakening & The Future of Egalitarianism* (Chicago: University of Chicago Press, 2001), p. 54.
[27] Joseph Nye, Jr., "Globalization's Democratic Deficit," *Foreign Affairs,* July–August 2001, p. 2.

flows of goods, services, and investment until today no national economy of any significance remains isolated from world markets.

Today's economic globalization is the leading edge of a long trend. For thousands of years the human community has, in fits and starts, become more tightly knit. According to historians J. R. McNeill and William H. McNeill, in prehistoric times humans interacted in a loose worldwide web through which genes and inventions such as language and the bow and arrow were slowly exchanged by migrations between relatively isolated bands. Beginning about 12,000 years ago with the growth of agricultural societies, stable and expanding populations formed the first cities. Over time, these cities grew into nodes that tied regions together. Still, there was little interaction between civilizations on different continents. Then, about 500 years ago, China sponsored oceanic voyages to extend its power.[28]

Soon Portugal and Spain followed and over the next 250 years mariners connected even the most remote places to the great centers of civilization. By the late 1700s the world was knit together with the exchange of trade goods, currencies, and ideas. The consequences of this initial globalization are similar to those arising from the current globalization. Economic activity rapidly increased. Mines in Bolivia exported such quantities of silver that nations around the world adopted silver currencies, smoothing international trade. Trade expansion increased inequality among nations. Cultures changed, as when, for example, Spanish conquistadors introduced horses to the Plains Indians. Infectious diseases spread. In little more than a century microbes endemic to Europe killed 50 to 90 percent of the population of the Americas from Cape Horn to the Arctic.

Since this initial tying together of societies in the late 1700s, the trend toward integration has continued. Globalization has been accelerated by new technologies, particularly those based on electricity, but also sometimes slowed by national rivalries and wars.

Transnational corporations, especially a few hundred of the largest headquartered in developed nations, are the central forces of current economic globalization. Their rising levels of investment outside home countries make them the modern equivalents of the intrepid mariners who opened trade routes in the 1400s. Many of these firms have more resources than the governments of smaller nations. However, globalization complicates their management. By operating in many countries they multiply the number and kind of stakeholders to which they must respond. Their actions create strains and anxieties that lead to heightened expectations of responsible behavior. In addition, there is a strong anticorporate movement supported mainly by groups in rich nations that see the growing velocity of trade with alarm because it clashes with their values on the environment, human rights, and democracy. These groups seek to restrain and regulate the activities of transnational corporations and they have had some success.

nation-state
An international actor having a ruling authority, citizens, and a territory with fixed borders.

Nation-States

In the international arena, the *nation-state* is an actor formed of three elements, a ruling authority, citizens, and a territory with fixed borders. The modern nation-state

[28] *The Human Web* (New York: Norton, 2003), intro. and chap. VI.

system arose in an unplanned way out of the wreckage of the Roman Empire. The institution of the nation-state was well-suited for Western Europe, where boundaries were contiguous with the extent of languages. However, the idea was subsequently transplanted to territories in Eastern Europe, Southwest Asia, and the Middle East, partly by force of colonial empires and partly by mimicry among non-Western political elites for whom the idea had attained high prestige. Where it was transplanted, nations were often irrationally defined and boundary lines split historic areas of culture, ethnicity, religion, and language.

The nation-state is the unit of human organization in which individuals and cultural groups can influence their circumstances and future. This is its paramount function and the reason it has survived over centuries. Today the world is a mosaic of independent countries, and the dynamics of this system are a powerful force in the international business environment. Conflict between nations seeking to aggrandize wealth and power is frequent, though because of economic globalization its nature has changed.

In the past, nations increased their power by seizing territory. With more territory they acquired new natural resources, agriculture, and labor. Hence, in the 1930s Japan colonized South Asian countries to gain access to oil and bauxite. Now, however, the wealth of high-income nations is based on the operation of global corporations that use flows of capital and knowledge to provide goods and services in many nations. Seizing the headquarters or a few manufacturing facilities of one of these corporations would not enable the aggressor nation to take advantage of the value chain in the firm's worldwide operations, particularly where wealth creation was based on brainpower. So nations today increasingly prefer to aggrandize themselves through trade, where they can build wealth more efficiently than through traditional warfare designed to seize land and material resources.[29]

Even as world markets become new sources of national power, they also limit the power of regimes to control their economies. Freewheeling international competition penetrates borders. Nations have a choice. Either close borders to flows of goods, services, and capital, isolating their economies from the world, a move sure to stifle growth, or open borders, allowing free reign to disobedient market forces that quicken growth. No nation can choose isolation and still offer its citizens opportunity and prosperity. So governments are now deeply concerned about how international markets will interpret their domestic actions and policies.

An example is the fate of Mexico after it opened its economy to the North American market in the early 1990s. In 1994, when the government attempted to maintain the peso's value relative to the dollar, world markets rejected the move. Currency speculators attacked the peso and foreign investors pulled great sums of money out of the country. The peso collapsed. Its devaluation halved the life savings of average Mexican citizens and caused bankruptcies, inflation above 50 percent a year, and a 6 percent drop in GDP.[30] Soon similar speculation caused currency

---

[29] This thesis is elaborated in Richard Rosecrance, *The Rise of the Virtual State* (New York: Basic Books, 1999).

[30] Jeffry A. Frieden, *Global Capitalism: Its Fall and Rise in the Twentieth Century* (New York: Norton, 2006), p. 389.

devaluations and sell-offs in six East Asian countries, prompting the prime minister of Malaysia to say that he was "very scared about foreign capital."[31]

Market forces are just one force that penetrates nation-states and reduces their autonomy. Other forces are epidemics, climate change, terrorism, nuclear weapons, and potent ideas such as international norms of human rights.[32] As intractable global forces, particularly market power, undercut the ability of national governments to protect their citizens, corporations may be called on to assume more of the responsibility.

Dominant Ideologies

ideology
A set of reinforcing beliefs and values that constructs a worldview.

Thought shapes history. An *ideology* is a set of reinforcing beliefs and values that constructs a worldview. The industrial revolution in the West was facilitated by a set of interlocking ideologies, including capitalism, but also constitutional democracy, which protected the rights that allowed individualism to flourish; progress, or the idea that humanity was in upward motion toward material betterment; Darwinism, or Charles Darwin's finding that constant improvement characterized the biological world, which reinforced the idea of progress; social Darwinism, or Herbert Spencer's idea that evolutionary competition in human society, as well as the natural world, weeded out the unfit and advanced humanity; and the Protestant ethic, or the belief that sacred authority called for hard work, saving, thrift, and honesty as necessary for salvation.

Ideologies are more than the sum of sensory perception and rational thought. They fulfill the human need for concepts and categories of meaning that explain daily life. Ideologies in accord with experience and current conditions often spread widely. Their belief systems lead adherents to feel a collective identity and to follow common norms that direct social behavior, thereby promoting cooperation and stability. And they give institutions that represent them, such as churches, governments, and corporations, the power to interpret events and resolve human problems.[33]

Ideologies are highly competitive and locked in a constant Darwinian struggle. Vibrant pluralism of belief existed for most of recorded history, but many doctrines have perished with globalization. As ideas diffuse through trade, travel, missionary work, and conquest, they often clash. A centuries-old culling process in the marketplace of ideas has eliminated and marginalized many historical belief systems and favored the ascendancy of a few.[34] Hundreds of local religions, unable to compete with the world salvation religions, have gone extinct. Cultural styles in entertainment, dress, sports, and food now converge in urban societies. In the political sphere monarchy and dictatorship are fighting an end game against democracy. After two

---

[31] Mahathir Bin Mohamad, "Asian Economies: Challenges and Opportunities," *Vital Speeches of the Day,* October 15, 1997, p. 12.

[32] Philip Bobbitt, "The Market State," in Shell International Limited, *The Shell Global Scenarios to 2025,* p. 160.

[33] Michael Mann, *The Sources of Social Power,* vol. 1 (Cambridge, England: Cambridge University Press), 1986, pp. 20–23.

[34] J. R. McNeill and William H. McNeill, *The Human Web,* pp. 269–76.

centuries of contention, the economic ideology of capitalism has marginalized its rival socialism. This sifting of ideas accelerated in the twentieth century because of rising literacy and innovations that spread information, from magazines and radios in the early part of the century to jet aircraft and computers later.

Great Leadership

Leaders have brought both beneficial and disastrous changes to societies and businesses. Alexander imposed his rule over the ancient Mediterranean world, creating new trade routes on which Greek merchants flourished. Adolf Hitler of Germany and Joseph Stalin in the Soviet Union were strong leaders, but they unleashed evil that retarded industrial growth in their countries.

There are two views about the power of leaders as a historical force. One is that leaders simply ride the wave of history. "Great men," writes Arnold Toynbee, "are precisely the points of intersection of great social forces."[35] When oil was discovered in western Pennsylvania in 1859, John D. Rockefeller was a young man living in nearby Cleveland, where he had accumulated a little money selling produce. He saw an opportunity in the new industry. His remarkable traits enabled him to domineer over a rising industry that reshaped the nation and the world. Yet is there any doubt that the reshaping would have occurred nonetheless had Rockefeller decided to stick with selling lettuce and carrots?

A differing view is that leaders themselves change history rather than being pushed by its tide. "The history of the world," wrote Thomas Carlyle, "is at bottom the History of the Great Men who have worked here."[36] It was John Jacob Astor of the American Fur Company who established a presence in the wild lands of the American continent, exploring them, knitting them together, and thwarting the efforts of other nations to occupy them. The United States map might today be different absent the effects of Astor's singular lust for fur riches. It was James B. Duke of the American Tobacco Company whose solitary marketing genius turned cigarette smoking from a local custom confined largely to the American South into a worldwide health disaster continuing now for more than a century.

Cases and stories in this text provide instances for debate about the role of business leaders in changing the world.

Chance

Scholars are reluctant to use the notion of chance, accident, or random occurrence as a category of analysis. Yet some changes in the business environment may be best explained as the product of unknown and unpredictable causes. No less perceptive a student of history than Niccolò Machiavelli observed that fortune determines about half the course of human events and human beings the other half. We cannot improve on this estimate, but we note it. Its significance is that managers must be prepared for the most unprecedented events and have faith in Machiavelli's counsel that when such episodes arrive those who are ready will prevail, as fortune "directs her bolts

---

[35] *A Study of History,* vol. XII, *Reconsiderations* (London: Oxford University Press, 1961), p. 125.

[36] In "The Hero as Divinity," reprinted in Carl Niemeyer, ed., *Thomas Carlyle on Heroes, Hero-Worship and the Heroic in History* (Lincoln: University of Nebraska Press, 1966), p. 1. This essay was originally written in 1840.

where there have been no defenses or bulwarks prepared against her."[37] No doubt Machiavelli would think Shell's scenarios are praiseworthy.

SEVEN KEY ENVIRONMENTS OF BUSINESS

Figure 2.5 shows the seven most important environments affecting business today. In each one powerful forces create change in the relationships between businesses, governments, and societies. These forces are often related and major changes in one area rarely occur in isolation. Here we give thumbnail sketches of each key environment. We will dig more deeply into them throughout the book.

The Economic Environment

The economic environment consists of forces that influence market operations, including overall economic activity, commodity prices, interest rates, currency fluctuations, wages, competitors' actions, technology change, and government policies. Continuing long-term growth in output, consumption, and investment characterizes the global economic environment. World GDP increased 310 percent in the years between 1982 and 2005, rising from $10.9 trillion to $44.7 trillion.[38] Growth briefly slowed in 2001 and 2002 because of economic repercussions from the September 11, 2001, terrorist attacks and the sudden acute respiratory syndrome epidemic in Asia. However, after a rough patch of several years the world economy picked up again, led by recovery in the United States and rapid expansion in China

FIGURE 2.5
The Seven Key Environments of Business

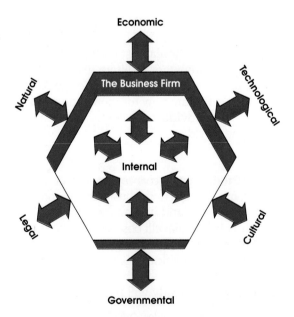

Economic

Natural

Technological

The Business Firm

Internal

Legal

Cultural

Governmental

---

[37] Niccolò Machiavelli, *The Prince,* trans. George Bull (New York: Penguin Books, 1961), chap. XXV, p. 73.
[38] United Nations Conference on Trade and Development, (UNCTAD) *World Investment Report 2006* (New York: United Nations, 2006), table I.2.

FIGURE 2.6
Worldwide
FDI Inflows:
1980–2005

Source: United
Nations Commis-
sion on Trade and
Development, *World
Investment Reports,*
various editions,
annex table B.1.

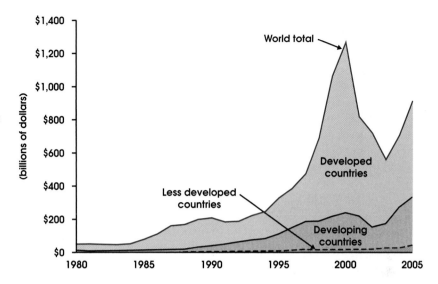

and India. Underlying this strong and continuing overall economic growth are two basic subtrends.

The first is rising trade. Three years after the end of World War II, in 1948, the global sum of all merchandise exported was $58 billion. In 2004 it was $10.2 trillion, an increase of 17,586 percent.[39] This spectacular rise has been enabled by a trading system created at the end of World War II. Nations within the system have been encouraged to lower tariffs and other trade barriers because other member nations promised to reciprocate this openness. The system has evolved into an institution called the World Trade Organization (WTO) that embodies an ongoing process of negotiation and *trade liberalization* in which 149 nations now participate. In addition, several hundred regional trade agreements promote freer exchange among countries that are parties to them.

The second subtrend underlying continued economic growth is a major expansion of foreign direct investment (FDI) by transnational corporations. *Foreign direct investment* is capital investment by private firms outside their home countries. Between 1982 and 2005, global FDI inflows (that is, corporate investments moving into foreign countries) rose from $59 billion a year to $916 billion, a 1,553 percent increase.[40] There are about 78,000 multinational corporations and, through FDI, they own or control about 778,000 foreign businesses. Many foreign affiliates are acquired by merger and acquisition and between 1997 and 2002 there was an unprecedented burst of cross-border merger activity both in the number of deals and in their dollar value.[41] Figure 2.6 shows the remarkable rise of FDI, the consequences of the post-2001 slowdown in the world economy and resumption of the

trade liberalization
A philosophy in which nations promote trade by easing restrictions, including both tariff and nontariff barriers. This philosophy, sometimes referred to as simply *liberalization,* is the bedrock of economic globalization.

foreign direct investment
Capital investment by private firms outside their home countries.

[39] World Trade Organization, *International Trade Statistics 2006* (Geneva: WTO, 2006), table II.2.
[40] UNCTAD, *World Investment Report 2006,* table I.2.
[41] For the six years of 1997 through 2002 there were 633 deals worth $2.4 trillion as compared to the previous six years, including 1991 through 1996, with 134 deals worth $290 billion, see UNCTAD, *World Investment Report 2003* (New York: United Nations, 2003), table I.7.

upward trend in 2003. It also reveals that most investment flows to and from developed nations.

Rising trade and consumer demand have rapidly expanded markets. To remain competitive, corporations have expanded with markets and restructured for efficiency. They invest to enter growing markets or to increase their power in established ones. Many multinational firms have restructured by creating "global factories" or "virtual corporations" in which production of goods or services takes place across geographically dispersed networks. These networks seek to duplicate at a global level the efficiencies of specialization and outsourcing often seen at the national level. They are now so extensive that nearly two-thirds of the world's exports move within them.

Since World War II, and especially since the early 1980s, the international economic environment has been favorable to growth and expansion of corporations. Growth remains robust due to a confluence of factors including high corporate profits, strong worldwide consumption, checked inflation, and low long-term interest rates. However, the International Monetary Fund (IMF) has warned that "surrounding the central scenario of robust growth, risks are weighted on the downside."[42] Years of expansion have created large trade imbalances for some nations, including the United States, and misalignment of currency exchange rates. Protectionist responses that raise trade barriers could limit future international economic integration and lead to stagnation. These are, warns the IMF, "the best of times but they are also the most dangerous of times."[43]

The Technological Environment

nanotechnology
Technology that is developed on the scale of a nanometer, which is one-billionth of a meter.

Today new scientific discoveries create a business environment filled with mind-boggling technology. For example, *nanotechnology* allows manipulation of objects the size of atoms. New materials and tiny machines invisible to the naked eye can be engineered at the molecular level. Semiconductor makers can now make microchips with components the size of one ten-millionth of a meter. When this ability is harnessed to practical manufacturing, it will create chips that operate on an atomic scale comparable to the photosynthesis process in plants. Users with such circuits could store all information in the Library of Congress in the space of a sugar cube.[44] Human genome mapping promises new biogenetic products that will cure intractable diseases. Fuel cells and methods of harnessing renewable energy may dramatically reduce use of fossil fuels.

wiki
A Web site open to collaborative editing by multiple individuals.

Digital telecommunications technology now creates a global network of computers, software, and electronic devices. This network has led to radical innovations such as open sourcing, which allows numbers of individuals to participate in the creation of complex knowledge products. *Wikis,* or Web sites open to collaborative editing by multiple or innumerable parties, have been used to create browsers, encyclopedias, dictionaries, and news sites.

[42] International Monetary Fund, *World Economic Outlook 2006: Globalization and Inflation* (Washington, DC: IMF, 2007), p. xii.

[43] Ibid., p. xii.

[44] Philip Bond, quoted in Ronald Bailey, "The Smaller the Better," *Reason,* December 2003, p. 47.

The wiki principle is an example of how an innovation can be both an opportunity and a threat. It releases an open, Darwinian process in which knowledge emerges from the common pool of humanity and survives the meticulous scrutiny of collective expertise rather than emanating from a single individual or small group to a passive audience. It promotes equality, but undermines hierarchical authority, and attacks old business models of software firms and publishers. In fact, novel technologies are minefields for established firms, which often focus on the immediate commercial possibilities of a technology and miss, or underestimate, its ultimate defiance of their existing business model. An example is Western Union, the dominant communications company of the nineteenth century, which was so confident in the telegraph that it rejected the telephone.

When Alexander Graham Bell invented the telephone in 1876, it had only a three-mile range. Western Union considered hooking telephones into its lines, but decided such a short-range device was just a toy. So Bell formed his own company. When engineers lengthened the range of the phone by using wires made of copper instead of iron, Western Union saw its mistake and rushed into the business with a phone device of its own. The mighty company used "every devious and underhanded method," including political pressure and bribes, to prevent towns and cities from adopting the Bell phone.[45] However, in 1878 it lost a patent infringement suit brought by Bell's company and had to drop the business.

The tiny Bell Telephone Company grew into AT&T, at one time in the twentieth century the world's largest corporation in revenues, a firm so creative that it gave birth to the transistor and the laser, so dominant that the U.S. government broke it up in 1984, so satisfied with success that it repeatedly failed to adapt. Stubbornly, it defined its business as providing voice conversation over wires, thus abiding with indifference as future competitors articulated new digital communication technologies such as wireless and cable networks, computers, and the Internet. Although AT&T is still a large corporation, it now scrambles through mergers and strategies, seeking a formula to restore past glory.

New technologies have unforeseen consequences for society when they are put in wide use for commercial gain. The cigarette-rolling machine was invented before the dangers of smoking were known. Manufacturing that mixed asbestos into hundreds of common materials came long before the morbid effects of asbestos fiber became clear. The World Wide Web is spreading into millions of lives before anyone has a full understanding of its implications for personal privacy. The lesson of the past is that corporations have an ethical duty to weigh carefully not only the strategic impact of technologies on their business models, but also the dangers they may impose on people.

The Cultural Environment

culture
A system of shared knowledge, values, norms, customs, and rituals acquired by social learning.

A *culture* is a system of shared knowledge, values, norms, customs, and rituals acquired by social learning. No universal culture exists, so the environment of a transnational corporation includes a variety of cultures, each with differing peoples, languages, religions, and values.

[45] Page Smith, *The Rise of Industrial America*, vol. 6 (New York: Penguin Books, 1984), p. 115.

On one level, this variation causes conflicts of business custom, and managers in foreign countries must absorb both subtle and striking differences in employee loyalty, group versus individual initiative, the place of women in organizations, ethical values, norms of giving and gratuities, attitudes toward authority, the meaning of time, and clothing worn in business settings. The consequences of cultural differences are often trivial, even humorous. Thus, a consulting firm that helps American managers avoid social blunders in foreign countries counsels them not to force the custom of name tags at business meetings on Europeans, who feel they are being treated as schoolchildren when wearing them.[46] However, consequences can be serious too. In France, the notion is widespread that American fast food causes obesity and, worst of all, is bad tasting and insults the refined French palate. President Jacques Chirac said that national ways of eating should be preserved in the face of an assault by cross-Atlantic invaders; and a minister of agriculture once said that the United States was "home to the world's worst food."[47] For McDonald's, these cultural feelings turned deadly. A mob wrecked one of its restaurants and another was bombed, killing an employee.

On a deeper level, although no uniform world culture exists, there is a fundamental divide between the culture of Western economic development and the rest of the world's cultural groupings. The culture of the advanced West promotes a core ideology of markets, individualism, and democratic government. It is sustained by Western nations that dominate international organizations, contain the most powerful corporations, and have the strongest militaries. However, although developing nations tend to adopt elements of Western culture, some nations and cultures have resisted its spread. Islamic nations and China see spreading Western values as a form of cultural aggression. They have resisted adopting them, particularly participatory forms of government.

Over the last half of the twentieth century, some cultural values in developed nations began to shift, creating changes in the global business environment. In these societies, beginning in the 1960s, traditional values based on historical realities of economic scarcity were transformed. In their place came what are called *postmodern values,* or values based on assumptions of affluence. For example, in older industrializing societies materialism was a dominant value. People sacrificed other values such as leisure time and environmental purity to make money and buy necessities, then luxuries. While consumption is still a powerful value in developed nations, their affluent citizens grow more concerned with quality of life and self-expression.

postmodern values
Values based on assumptions of affluence, for example, quality of life and self-expression.

The World Values Surveys, a series of surveys in 75 countries now spanning 25 years, show that the rise of postmodern values has uniformly shifted the social, political, economic, and sexual norms of rich countries. Despite some resistence in non-Western cultures, surveys show the rise of these norms in all modernizing nations. Among the Chinese public, for example, there is "surprisingly high" support

---

[46] Lalita Khosia, "You Say Tomato," *Forbes,* May 21, 2001, p. 36.

[47] John-Thor Dahlburg, "To Many French, Ugly American Is McDonald's," *Los Angeles Times,* April 22, 2000, p. A10.

for values linked to democracy.[48] And support for democratic ideals in eleven Muslim societies has grown to equal that in Western societies.[49]

Postmodern norms are a strong influence in the operating environments of multinational corporations. To illustrate, there is a powerful global movement to promote fundamental human rights by stamping out racism, sexism, authoritarianism, intolerance, and xenophobia. This movement is energized by West-dominated coalitions of individuals, advocacy groups, governments, and international organizations such as the United Nations. Similar and interrelated movements have risen to promote sustainable development and humanitarian assistance to poor regions. This global tide of morality, based on the postmodern values of developed nations, elevates expectations about the behavior of multinational corporations. Increasingly, they must follow proliferating codes and rules developed by moral reformers and must define their basic purposes as promoting human welfare above narrow profit making.

The Government Environment

Governments have simultaneously stimulated and constrained business. In this regard, two long-term global trends in government are central.

First, government activity has greatly expanded. One way of measuring this is by comparing a government's spending with the size of its economy. Around the world, the percentage of this spending has risen, from single digits in 1900 to an average of 29 percent in 2002.[50] In the United States, in 1913, spending was 8 percent of GDP, but by 2005 it had risen to 35 percent.[51] The percentages have risen highest, up to 40 percent and more, in European welfare states and are lower in developing countries, but broadly the trend is up because governments have taken on new functions. For one, they promote social welfare with a range of transfer payments to their citizens. This role grew in the twentieth century as many nations expanded their electorates. New voters included women and the less privileged, groups that voted to enlarge government assistance programs. Another source of government growth is expanded regulation of industries to protect citizens from abuses. In the United States, for example, there is today practically no aspect of business that governments cannot and will not regulate if the occasion arises and popular support exists. New laws, added to past laws, result in more constraints on business.

The second long-term trend is rising democratization. In 1900 no nation was a full *democracy* with multiparty elections and universal suffrage. The United States and Britain were close, but both lacked female suffrage, and the United States additionally lacked black suffrage in practice. Yet by 1950 there were 22 democracies

democracy
A form of government requiring three elements—popular sovereignty, political liberty, and majority rule.

[48] Ronald Inglehart, "Globalization and Postmodern Values," *Washington Quarterly,* Winter 2000, p. 19.

[49] Ronald Inglehart and Pippa Norris, "The True Clash of Civilizations," *Foreign Policy,* March/April 2003, pp. 64–66.

[50] United Nations Economic and Social Council, *Basic Data on Government Expenditure and Taxation* (New York: United Nations, 2004), table 3.

[51] International Monetary Fund, *World Economic Outlook 2000* (Washington, DC: IMF, May 2000), table 5.4; and Bureau of the Census, *Statistical Abstract of the United States, 2007,* 126th ed. (Washington, DC: Bureau of the Census, 2005), tables 419, 458, and 648.

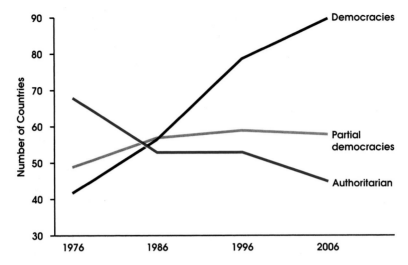

FIGURE 2.7
The Rise of Democratic Regimes

Source: Freedom House. Data is based on combined measures for democracy and civil liberty.

and by 2006 there were 90.[52] Figure 2.7 shows the dramatic rise—from 91 to 148—in the number of democratic and partially democratic regimes since 1975. Much of this rise came in the late 1980s and early 1990s after the breakup of the Soviet Union. When repressive socialist regimes no longer received external support from the Soviet bloc and the United States reduced its support for authoritarian regimes that were anticommunist, a wave of democratization swept Southeast Asia, Latin America, and Africa.

However, a more fundamental cause of expanding democracy is the rise of postmodern values in countries that have undergone socioeconomic growth. These values undermine hierarchical authority and shape expectations for more political participation and autonomy. Authoritarian regimes are now largely confined to nations with lagging economies, where traditional values have not evolved into aspirations for liberty and choice. For business, the consequence of more openness to popular majorities is that governments increasingly respond to public demands for corporate social performance and these demands reflect postmodern values promoting human rights, the environment, aesthetics, and ethics.

The Legal Environment

The legal environment consists of legislation, regulation, and litigation. Five enduring trends in this environment work to constrain business behavior. First, laws and regulations have steadily grown in number and complexity. Second, legal duties to protect the rights of stakeholders, such as employees, consumers, and the public, have expanded. These rights derive from the steady flow of laws and court decisions on, for example, discrimination, sexual harassment, advertising,

[52] Figures are from *Democracy's Century: A Survey of Global Political Change in the 20th Century* (Washington, DC: Freedom House, 2001), p. 2 and Figure 2.7; and Freedom House, *Freedom in the World: 2007* (Washington, DC: Freedom House, 2007), p. 2.

antitrust, the environment, product liability, and intellectual property. Third, globalization has increased the complexity of the legal environment by exposing corporations to international law and laws of foreign nations. In addition, advocacy groups promoting human rights and environmental causes push corporations to adopt so-called *soft law,* or voluntarily adopted codes of conduct that set forth rules for corporate behavior based on emerging international standards of conduct. These rules often exceed requirements in specific laws of nations. Fourth, although the requirements of ethical behavior and corporate social responsibility go beyond legal duty, they are continuously plucked from the voluntary realm and encoded into law. For instance, saving money by firing a long-time employee the week before he or she qualified for a pension was always ignoble. In 1974 the Employee Retirement Income Security Act made it illegal as well.

soft law
Voluntarily adopted codes of conduct setting forth rules about corporate behavior. Guidelines are often derived from emerging international conduct standards.

Finally, the law is constantly evolving. Because of technological change, for example, corporations need to anticipate emerging causes of liability. In this respect, the old *T. J. Hooper* case is still good reading for corporate counsel. On a sunny day in March 1928 the tugboat *T. J. Hooper* hauled a coal barge out to sea. Two days later it hit stormy weather off New Jersey, and the barge sank with its load of coal. The owners of the cargo sued, claiming that the tug was unseaworthy because it had no receiving radio. Lacking a radio, the *T. J. Hooper* missed a weather broadcast that caused other ships to put into harbor before the gale hit. Although no law required a radio and there was no industry custom of installing them, the eminent judge Learned Hand held that "there are precautions so imperative that even their universal disregard will not excuse their omission."[53]

The tug owners were found negligent and paid for the coal cargo because they had not adopted a cutting-edge technology. Moving ahead to the present, a parallel example is the existence of electrically charged table saw blades that can detect contact with a human finger and stop rotation within thousandths of a second.[54] No law or industry standard now requires manufacturers to use this technology, but its availability opens employers who do not use them to charges of negligence by workers who cut off fingers and hands.

The Natural Environment

Economic activity is a geophysical force with power to change the natural environment. Just as it has strained the ability of human institutions to adapt, so also has it sometimes overwhelmed the ability of ecosystems to cleanse and regenerate. Spectacular economic growth in the twentieth century came at a high cost to the planet. It depleted mineral resources, reduced forest cover, killed species, released artificial molecules, unbalanced the nitrogen cycle, and altered the chemistry of the earth's atmosphere enough to trigger climate change.

Two measures used by the World Wildlife Fund exhibit global trends for the overall burden of human activity on nature. *The Living Planet Index,* shown in Figure 2.8, combines in one measure thousands of population trends among terrestrial, freshwater, and marine vertebrate species. It fell by about 30 percent between

---

[53] *In re The* T. J. Hooper *et al.,* 60 F.2d 737 (1932), at 740.
[54] Melba Newsome, "An Edgy New Idea," *Time Inside Business,* May 2006, p. A16.

FIGURE 2.8 Measures of Human Impact on Nature

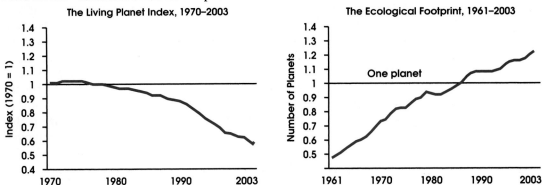

Source: From *Living Planet Report 2006*, World Wildlife Fund, www.panda.org. Copyright © 2007 WWF. Some rights reserved.

1970 and 2003.[55] This decline of biodiversity reflects deteriorating conditions in the forests, grasslands, deserts, savannahs, and freshwater and marine ecosystems that provide habitat for the world's species. A second indicator, the *Ecological Footprint*, also shown in Figure 2.8, measures human consumption of renewable natural resources. It is calculated as the total land area, in hectares, required to maintain worldwide human consumption of food, wood fiber, energy, and water. In the figure, the vertical axis shows the number of planets required to support ecological footprints of varying size. The horizontal line crosses at one planet, marking the earth's current biological capacity to support life. The trend line shows that the human ecological footprint moved beyond the earth's carrying capacity in the late 1980s and is now unsustainable. The overall human footprint is calculated to be 14.1 billion hectares, whereas the planet's life-carrying capacity is estimated to be only 11.3 billion hectares.[56] The implication is that the extent of natural resource use encouraged by global capitalism is unsustainable.

Attitudes about the relationship of economic activity to nature are now rapidly changing. When the twentieth century began, dominating and consuming nature was justified by a variety of doctrines, not the least being capitalism, which values nature as a production input. At its end, thinking moved toward preservation of nature. Managers must adapt to this changed thinking. With growing frequency environmental criteria enter into judgments of their performance.

The Internal Environment

In a corporation, the internal environment consists of four groups, as shown in Figure 2.9. Each group has different objectives, beliefs, needs, and functions that managers must coordinate to achieve overall company goals. In this process, a corporate culture that transcends the values of any single internal group is created.

[55] World Wide Fund for Nature, *Living Planet Report 2006* (Gland, Switzerland: WWF International, 2006), pp. 2–3.

[56] A hectare is an area of 10,000 square meters, equivalent to 2.47 acres.

FIGURE 2.9
A Depiction
of the Internal
Business
Environment

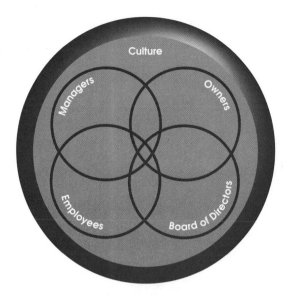

Forces in external environments have recently reduced the power of these internal groups. Managers are limited in their decisions by government and forced to accommodate a range of outside stakeholders having the power or claiming the right to influence them. Employees are losing power over management because of globalization of labor markets that puts them in competition with lower-wage workers elsewhere. In the United States, new financial regulations designed to protect shareholders from dishonest managers have given boards of directors more power and greater independence from top management. However, there is also some erosion of shareholder power by external groups demanding socially responsible actions that conflict with profit maximization.

CONCLUDING OBSERVATIONS

The environments of business have profound implications for managers. Figure 2.10 summarizes the chapter discussion by illustrating the dynamic interconnection of business with historical forces and current environments. The deep historical forces act to shape the seven key environments, while the actions of business constantly influence not only current environments but, in addition, the deeper course of history. As the arrow running from the corporation to the world in Figure 2.10 indicates, business is not simply a passive entity that moves with historical and environmental forces like a billiard ball reacting to impacts. On the contrary, although strongly constrained by its environment, business has a powerful capacity to shape society and change history in ways small and large.

For example, when Eastman Kodak wanted to display the speed of its fast film and Flashmatic shutter in 1940, it ran magazine ads showing pictures of "Kodak Moments" when people blew out candles on their birthday cakes. The ads so

FIGURE 2.10   The Dynamic Interaction of Historical Forces, Business Environments, and Corporate Actions

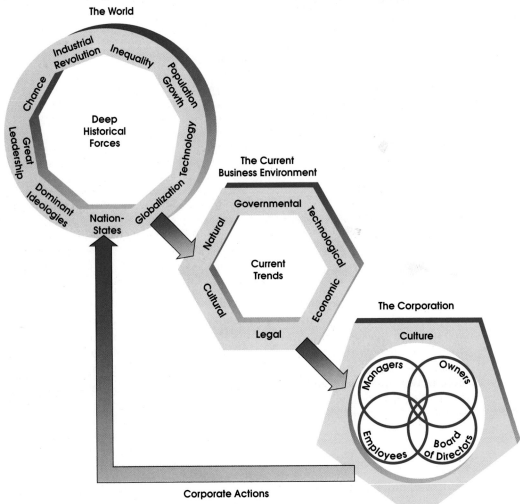

popularized this charming rite that it became universal among Americans.[57] In contrast to such a small cultural change, the story of the automobile illustrates how industries can rearrange whole societies. Perhaps no twentieth century industry created more intentional and unintentional change. It was a prime mover of the American economy and once accounted directly or indirectly for one of every eight jobs. It encouraged an expansive highway system, brought decline to the railroads, depleted oil reserves, created pollution, altered cities, entrenched the idea that status was conferred by ownership of material objects, and changed patterns of courtship and crime.

[57]James B. Twitchell, *Lead Us Not into Temptation* (New York: Columbia University Press, 1999), p. 26.

The American Fur Company

The American Fur Company was a relentless monopoly built in the climactic era of the fur trade. It was created in 1808 by John Jacob Astor, a striving German immigrant, in an environment so favorable that over vast North American territories it had more power than the fledgling American government. In its time, this company shaped the destiny of a young nation. It made Astor the richest American of his day. Yet by the 1830s its situation had so changed that it and the 300-year-old trade in furs collapsed.

ASTOR ARRIVES IN A YOUNG NATION

In 1763 Astor was born to a butcher and his wife in the German village of Waldorf. Young John Jacob found village life dull, so at the age of 15 he left for London, working four years there to save money for an ocean voyage to the New World. In 1783, at the age of 20, with no education, little money, and speaking poor English, he set sail on a merchant ship. During the long voyage, a fur trader taught him how to appraise and handle skins. These lessons gave Astor knowledge he needed for an occupation. He would soon show himself an apt student.

At this time, the fur trade on the North American continent was almost 300 years old. It had begun early in the sixteenth century after Spanish and French explorers made contact with native forest dwellers, and it soon included the British. The Europeans wanted beaver, martin, ermine, mink, otter, bear, deer, muskrat, wolf, racoon, and other animal skins for fashionable hats and clothing. The Native Americans, who had not yet entered the age of metal, were anxious to get even the simplest manufactured goods such as knives, mirrors, ornaments, and buttons. This simple mutual advantage proved durable over time.

Indians were the fur industry's production workers. Fur traders depended on them to trap animals, then negotiated with them to buy pelts in exchange for trinkets. Indian women skinned and prepared the hides. Overhead costs for traders were low. Instead of wages, Indians took trade goods worth a fraction of a fur's ultimate value. Since furs were light, they could be transported economically by mules, barges, and ships to eastern ports and thence to Europe. Profits were enormous.

Fur trading had transforming effects on society because it promoted settlement. Traders worked on the edges of Euro-American habitation. Over time, fur production in these frontier areas always declined. Populations of fur-bearing animals such as beaver, having slow breeding cycles, were steadily depleted. The reliability of Indian trappers fell as their tribal cultures buckled under the strains of new values and diseases. When productivity in an area declined, fur traders pushed over the horizon. In their wake came settlers using fresh maps and trails. Farms and towns sprouted. Indians were killed or dislodged. This unsentimental cycle of the fur trade, repeated over and over, generated waves of migration that settled much of the United States.

ASTOR ENTERS THE FUR BUSINESS

Astor made his way to New York where he got a job selling bakery goods. He invested most of his $2-a-week pay in small trinkets and in his spare time prowled the waterfront for Indians who might have a fur to trade. Within a year he picked up enough skins to take a ship back to London, where he established connections with fur-trading houses. This was a phenomenal achievement for an immigrant lad of 21 who had been nearly penniless on his arrival in America, and it revealed Astor's deadly serious and hard-driving personality.

Astor worked briefly with a fur dealer in New York City during which time he trekked into the forests of upstate New York to bargain for furs. He soon left his employer and by 1787 was working solely for himself. He demonstrated sharp negotiating skills in trading trinkets for furs and soon built up an impressive business. One neighbor said:

> Many times I have seen John Jacob Astor
> with his coat off, unpacking in a vacant yard
> near my residence a lot of furs he had bought
> dog-cheap off the Indians and beating them
> out, cleaning them and repacking them in

more elegant and salable form to be transported to England and Germany, where they would yield him 1,000 percent on the original costs.[1]

Astor made great profits and expanded his business but, like other Americans, he was blocked from harvesting furs in the forests of the Northwest Territory. The Northwest Territory was the huge unsettled area between the Ohio River and the Mississippi River bounded on the north by the Great Lakes. After the Revolutionary War, Great Britain ceded this area to the United States but continued to maintain forts and troops there because the American government was too weak to enforce its rights. British fur-trading companies exploited the area and incited Indians to attack American traders and settlers who dared enter.

This audacity pushed Congress near to declaring war. To avoid hostilities, England agreed to a treaty in 1794[2] that required removal of British troops and gave both British and Americans trading rights in the Northwest Territory. "Now," said Astor on hearing this news, "I will make my fortune in the fur trade."[3] But he was stunned when President George Washington proposed befriending the Indians by setting up government fur-trading posts to be run with benevolent policies. These posts would compete with Astor and other private traders. Congress approved the plan, which required that trade goods be sold at cost, prohibited the use of liquor, and ordered payment of fair prices for furs.

The government trading posts infuriated Astor, who moved quickly to undercut them. He saturated the territory with his agents, instructing them to buy every fur they could get their hands on before competitors did. He bought trade goods in huge quantities to lower the cost, and his agents paid for furs with these trinkets. And he allowed liquor to flow freely during trade negotiations, creating an advantage the government could not match.

Astor had great success with these tactics. The government lacked his nimbleness and commitment, and he outwitted other rivals. In less than 10 years he was the second-richest man in America

(after only Stephen Girard, the shipping magnate and banker). Having accumulated deep resources, the Astor juggernaut turned toward the West.

THE LOUISIANA PURCHASE

In 1803 the territory of the United States more than doubled with the Louisiana Purchase. President Thomas Jefferson agreed to purchase from France for $15 million approximately 800,000 square miles of land between the Mississippi River and the Rocky Mountains and running north from New Orleans to the forty-ninth parallel, which is now the Canada–U.S. boundary. At the time, little was known about the area called the Louisiana Territory. No accurate or complete maps existed; even its exact boundaries were vague. But Louisiana was beautiful in its mystery.

Some geographers thought it was largely an arid desert. Others predicted a lush, fertile land. Rumors of geological wonders, horrific animals, and strange natives circulated, including the story of a tribe of bow-hunting, man-hating female savages in which the archers had their right breasts removed to keep them from interfering with the bowstrings.[4]

Jefferson himself had a clear vision of how to use the new territory. In his 1803 message to Congress, he proposed to relocate into Louisiana eastern tribes getting in the way of American settlers, and over the next 50 years this occurred many times.[5] He also ordered an Expedition of Discovery headed by Meriwether Lewis and William Clark to explore on foot the unknown territory.

A primary purpose of the Lewis and Clark expedition was to determine the suitability of Louisiana for the fur trade. The adventurers set out on a round-trip march between St. Louis and the Pacific Ocean, going where no white American had gone before, and on their return in 1806 reported a wondrous land "richer in beaver and otter than any country on earth."[6] They also reported that most Indian tribes in

---

[1] A "Gentleman of Schenectady," quoted in John Upton Terrell, *Furs by Astor* (New York: Morrow, 1963), p. 55.

[2] The treaty was negotiated for the United States by John Jay and is known as Jay's Treaty.

[3] Terrell, *Furs by Astor*, p. 93.

[4] Ben Gilbert, *The Trailblazers* (New York: Time-Life Books, 1973), p. 18.

[5] For a list of 24 relocations, see Cardinal Goodwin, *The Trans-Mississippi West (1803–1853)* (New York: Appleton, 1922), plate following p. 88.

[6] Quoted in David J. Wishart, *The Fur Trade of the American West (1807–1840): A Geographical Synthesis* (Lincoln: University of Nebraska Press, 1979), p. 19, citing the original journals of the trip.

the territory were friendly to Americans and the fur trade. These discoveries were not lost on fur traders, among them John Jacob Astor.

THE AMERICAN FUR COMPANY IS BORN

The Lewis and Clark expedition was a catalyst for fur trading in the new territory. Beaver production in the Northwest Territory was already beginning to fall off. The North West Company, Astor's main competitor, began to move down from Canada, intent on harvesting the Louisiana Territory as rapidly as possible.

However, it would reckon with Astor, who wanted the prize himself. In his distant New York City study, Astor pored over maps of the fur-rich areas discovered by Lewis and Clark, hatching a vast and daring plan for a new company that would string trading posts over a 2,000-mile route.

In those days, state legislatures had exclusive power to create a company by issuing a charter that listed the conditions of its existence. So he approached the governor and legislature of New York seeking to charter a company to be known as the American Fur Company.

To sell the idea, he cloaked his mercenary scheme with a veil of patriotism. He argued that most of the furs taken from the Louisiana territory went to Canadians and British, thereby depriving America of trade revenue. His new company would drive the foreigners out. He would join with 10 or 12 other wealthy entrepreneurs to capitalize the new company, which would then issue stock to others. The new company would enhance U.S. security by establishing a strong presence of American citizens over unpopulated areas. And finally, Astor promised that his company would deal honestly with the Indians and drive out smaller, irresponsible traders. The legislators of New York, responding more to Astor's open pocketbook than to the credibility of his arguments, passed a charter setting up the American Fur Company. Soon President Jefferson wrote a letter to Astor giving his blessing to the new company also.

Astor proceeded to take on four partners and establish a board of directors as the charter required. However, he retained 99.9 percent of the stock, elected himself president, and subsequently declared dividends whenever he wanted to compensate himself. The partnership was a fiction; Astor never intended to share either the proceeds of the company or any portion of the fur trade that he could control.

In 1810 he made his first move. His ship, the *Tonquin,* sailed to the mouth of the Columbia River on the Pacific Coast and set up a trading post named Astoria. At this time, Britain and the United States contested the wild area known as Oregon territory, consisting of present-day Oregon and Washington. Astor got diplomatic support for his trading post by arguing that its presence established an American claim to the territory. Secretly, however, he hoped to form a new nation called Astoria and make himself king.

Meanwhile, he would make Astoria one end of a vise that would squeeze competitors out of the new fur areas. Furs taken in the west would come to Astoria and then be shipped to China, which was a major fur market, or to New York. By this time, Astor owned a fleet of ships with which to do this. The other end of the vise would be St. Louis. Furs from Astor's planned string of trading posts on the eastern slopes of the Rocky Mountains would come down the Missouri River system to St. Louis and from there go overland to New York or on to the port of New Orleans to be shipped to Europe. It was a megalomaniac scheme, and no one but Astor had both the nerve and the resources even to attempt it. But it was too grandiose. Only part of it was to work, and the rest worked only until the fur trade fell apart.

THE ROAD TO MONOPOLY

In 1813 Astor's plan suffered a great reversal when he was forced to sell Astoria to the British during the War of 1812. He sold out at a fraction of its value because British soldiers were in a position to seize it as a war prize. Without Astoria as a foothold in the Oregon territory, he was unable to compete with British and Canadian fur companies. And 61 of Astor's employees died pursuing the settlement, along with hundreds of natives they came in conflict with.[7] Unbowed, Astor later commissioned Washington Irving, the best-selling author of the day, to write a book about the intrepid adventurers and himself as the great mind behind them.[8]

[7] Axel Madsen, *John Jacob Astor: America's First Multimillionaire* (New York: Wiley, 2001), p. 163.

[8] *Astoria; or, Enterprise beyond the Rocky Mountains* (New York: The Century Co., 1909); originally published in 1839.

Despite the loss of Astoria, Astor nonetheless predominated. In 1816 his lobbying succeeded in getting Congress to pass a law forbidding foreigners from trading furs in U.S. territories. This prevented Canadian and British companies from operating in the Northwest Territory, and Astor immediately bought out their interests, giving him a monopoly in furs east of the Missouri River. Blocked from the Pacific Coast trade by the British presence, he turned his attention to the upper-Missouri fur trade.

Astor bided his time as other fur companies pioneered trading in the northern Great Plains and then, after discovery of rich valleys of beaver, in the Rocky Mountains. By 1822 Astor had established a presence selling trade goods and buying furs in St. Louis, but he waited as other companies sent expensive expeditions of traders and mountain men up the Missouri, absorbing heavy losses of men and money. Despite losses, these pioneering companies found tremendous reserves of beaver in Rocky Mountain valleys, mapped new routes, and discovered advantageous locations for trading posts.

Then he crushed the competition. In 1826 he merged with Bernard Pratte & Company, an established firm, using it as an agent. He bought out and liquidated another competitor, Stone, Bostwick & Company. In 1827 he broke the Columbia Fur Company by building his own trading posts next to every one of theirs, engaging in cutthroat price competition for furs, and plying Indians liberally with whiskey. His trappers shadowed its trapping parties to learn where the beaver were, then muscled in. Using similar tactics, he bankrupted Menard & Valle. Now, according to Astor's biographer Terrell:

> Competition on the Missouri River was all but nonexistent. What remained was inconsequential, and might have been likened to a terrier yapping at a bear. The bear lumbered on, ignoring the noise until it became aggravating. Then with the sudden swipe of a paw, the yapping was forever stilled.[9]

Astor made astonishing profits. He would buy, for example, a 10-pound keg of gunpowder for $2, or 20 cents a pound, in London and transport it to his trading posts using his ships. He paid himself a 2 percent

Portrait of John Jacob Astor. Source: © Stock Montage/ Getty Image.

commission for buying the trade goods, or $.04 cents on the keg of gunpowder. He paid himself a freight charge for carrying the gunpowder on his ship to New Orleans. From there the keg was transported up the Missouri using the inexpensive labor of his hired trappers and traders. The gunpowder was valued at $4 a pound to the Indians, who were not allowed to pay money for it but got it only by exchanging furs or on credit. In the 1820s Astor charged one 2-pound beaver skin for each pound of gunpowder, getting 10 skins weighing 20 pounds for the keg of gunpowder. These skins were transported back to London, where they were worth $7 a pound or $140. From the $140 Astor deducted a 5 percent commission, or $7, for brokering the sale of the furs. Astor also subtracted 25 percent, or $35 from the $140, for the estimated costs of transportation and wages.

All told, this left a net profit for the American Fur Company of $97.96, or 4,900 percent on the original $2 investment.[10] And Astor owned over 99 percent of the company's shares. This profitable arithmetic was repeated on a wide range of trade goods.

The value of trade goods lay not in their utility, but in Indian beliefs. Indians coveted them so much

---

[9] Terrell, *Furs by Astor,* p. 391.

[10] These calculations are based on figures in ibid., pp. 397–98.

that they considered whites foolish to exchange even the smallest trinkets for beaver skins that were abundant in the forests. The idea of material acquisition beyond basic needs was foreign to Indian cultures. The Arikaras, for example, believed that a person who had more possessions than needed to survive ought to give the excess to others. Offering money to Indians did not motivate them to trap and process furs; they were indifferent to accumulating currency.

Trade goods such as rifles, knives, clothing, blankets, beads, and trinkets were useful, making them attractive to the Indians, but native-made equivalents were often just as good. Trade goods, however, had mystical significance beyond their utility or monetary value. Their allure lay in magical, spiritual qualities. Indians believed that the future could be seen by looking in a reflection of the self. Because manufactured mirrors gave a clearer reflection than water they were a wondrous advance in prophecy. They thought guns had supernatural properties, because they created thunder, an event associated with the spiritual world. They thought pots and kettles were alive, because they rang or sang out when hit. Thus, Indians found supernatural qualities in trade goods that were lost on Europeans.[11]

Astor encouraged Indians to take trade goods on credit. As a result, some tribes—the Winnebagos, Sacs, Foxes, Cherokees, Chickasaws, and Sioux—were hopelessly mired in debt, owing the American Fur Company as much as $50,000 each. Since trinkets had sky-high markups, Astor could not lose much even if tribal debts grew, but indebtedness forced tribes to trade furs with him rather than with competitors.

His traders and trappers fared no better. He marked up trade goods heavily before selling them to traders. Often, traders were in debt to Astor or had mortgaged their trading posts to him and were forced to mark up goods heavily themselves before selling them to Indians and trappers.

Trappers employed by the American Fur Company were ruthlessly exploited. They worked unlimited hours in hazardous conditions and extreme weather, but when Astor achieved dominance in an area, he cut their salaries from $100 a year to $250 every three years. They had to buy trade goods and staples at markups that were higher than those

charged Indians to get furs. Whiskey costing $.30 a gallon in St. Louis was diluted with water and sold to them at $3 a pint. Coffee and sugar costing $.10 a pound was sold for $2 at trading posts up the Missouri. Clothing was marked up 300 to 400 percent.

Astor had contrived a lucrative, pitiless system that amplified his fortune by diminishing those caught in its workings. Though never venturing out West, he was in touch, working long hours, his shrewd mind obsessed with the most minor details and with squeezing out the smallest unnecessary expenses. In 1831 his son William estimated American Fur Company revenues of "not less than $500,000" yearly.[12] Astor was by now the richest man in America. He began to buy real estate in and around New York City.

ASTOR RACES ON

In the early 1830s it seemed nothing could slow Astor. Men who hated the American Fur Company started competing firms, but few lasted. Astor destroyed them by underbidding for furs and debauching the Indians with alcohol.

In 1832 Congress prohibited bringing alcohol into Indian territories, but the law was mostly ignored. Astor never favored using alcohol. It raised costs. However, many competitors saw inebriation as their only hope of seducing Indians with furs away from him. Astor, obsessed with defeating his rivals, let the spirits flow despite sad consequences.

Alcohol was unknown in native cultures; Indians developed a craving for it only after European traders introduced intoxication into fur price negotiations. Some thought that spirits occupied their bodies when they drank. Among Indians who took to whiskey, a new desire was created, a desire that motivated them to produce furs. A few tribes, notably the Pawnee, Crow, and Arikara, never imbibed. Most did, however, and some were so debilitated that their fur production fell and traders moved on.

Astor smuggled liquor as needed past Indian agents. He ordered construction of a still at the confluence of the Yellowstone and Missouri rivers, producing enough spirits to keep tribes in several states in a constant drunken state. Congress could not enforce its will because the federal government had almost no presence

[11] Richard White, "Expansion and Exodus," in Betty Ballantine and Ian Ballantine, eds., *The Native Americans: An Illustrated History* (Atlanta: Turner, 1993), chap. 14.

[12] Gustavus Myers, *History of the Great American Fortunes* (New York: Modern Library, 1936), p. 102; originally published in 1909.

in vast areas of the West. Statutes were meaningless where no authorities stood to enforce them. In Indian country, the only law was the will of leaders of trading companies and brigades of trappers who wore self-designed, military-style uniforms and could rob, cheat, and murder both Indians and whites with impunity. An 1831 report to Lewis Cass, Secretary of War, stated:

> The traders that occupy the largest and most important space in the Indian country are the agents and engagees of the American Fur Trade Company. They entertain, as I know to be the fact, no sort of respect for our citizens, agents, officers of the Government, or its laws or general policy.[13]

Government officials such as Cass were disinclined to thwart Astor in any case since they were frequently in his pay. Cass, who was the federal official in charge of enforcing the prohibition law, was paid $35,000 by the American Fur Company between 1817 and 1834.[14] At one time, Astor even advanced a personal loan of $5,000 to President James Monroe. Over the years, the Astor lobby achieved most of its objectives in Washington, DC, and state capitals, including heavy tariffs on imported furs and abolition of the government fur-trading posts so beloved to Washington and Jefferson. Under these circumstances, it is not surprising that the government failed to regulate the fur trade.

In 1831 Astor introduced a new technological innovation, the steamboat *Yellowstone,* which could travel 50 to 100 miles a day up the Missouri, transporting supplies to his posts. Keelboats used by competitors made only twenty miles upriver on a good day and exposed men pulling them with ropes from the bank to hostile Indian fire. Upriver Indians were awestruck by the *Yellowstone* and traveled hundreds of miles to see the spirit that walked on water. Some tribes refused to trade with the Hudson Bay Company any longer, believing that because of the *Yellowstone* it could no longer compete with the American Fur Company.

THE ENVIRONMENT OF THE FUR TRADE CHANGES

Although the American Fur Company was ascendant, unfavorable trends were building that would bring it down. Demand for beaver was falling as the fashion trends that made every European and American gentleman want a beaver hat waned. Silk hats became the new rage. Also, new ways of felting hats without using fibrous underhair from beaver pelts had developed, and nutria pelts from South America were entering the market.

These were not the only problems. In 1832 trade came to a near standstill during a worldwide cholera epidemic because many people thought the disease was spread on transported furs. Beaver populations were depleted by overtrapping. The fur companies made no conservation efforts; the incentive was rather to trap all beaver in an area, leaving none for competitors. In the 1820s the Hudson Bay Company tried to prevent Astor from moving into Oregon territory by exterminating beaver along a band of terrain to create a "fur desert" that would be unprofitable for Astor's trappers to cross.

Losses of human life rose as mountain men entered the shrinking areas where beaver were still abundant, leaving behind somewhat friendly Indians such as the Snake and Crow to encounter more hostile tribes such as the Blackfeet, who poisoned their arrows with rattlesnake venom and conducted open war against trappers.[15] One study of 446 mountain men actively trapping between 1805 and 1845 found that 182, or 41 percent, were killed in the occupation.[16]

Astor knew that the fur industry was doomed. Beaver pelts that had fetched $6 a pound in 1830 brought only $3.50 a pound by 1833. In that year he liquidated all his fur-trading interests. He spent the rest of his life accumulating more money in New York real estate. For a time, the American Fur Company carried on under new owners, but the industry environment continued to worsen. In 1837 the firm's steamboat *St. Peters* carried smallpox up the Missouri, killing more than 17,000 natives, and an agent observed that "our most profitable Indians have died."[17] By 1840 the firm had withdrawn from the Rocky Mountains and focused on buffalo robes, which remained profitable for some time.

[13] Report of Andrew S. Hughes, quoted in ibid., p. 99.

[14] Myers, *History of the Great American Fortunes,* p. 103.

[15] Trappers also attacked Blackfeet without provocation. See Osborne Russell, *Journal of a Trapper* (Lincoln: University of Nebraska Press, 1955), pp. 52, 86.

[16] William H. Goetzmann, "The Mountain Man as Jacksonian Man," *American Quarterly,* Fall 1963, p. 409.

[17] Jacob Halsey, a clerk at Fort Pierre, quoted in Wishart, *The Fur Trade of the American West,* p. 68.

ASTOR'S LAST YEARS

Astor lived on in New York, wringing immense profits from rents and leases as the city grew around his real estate holdings. By 1847 he had built a fortune of $20 million that towered above any other of that day. In 1998 this sum was estimated to be the equivalent of $78 billion, at the time more than the wealth of Microsoft's Bill Gates.[18] In his last years he was weak and frail and exercised by having attendants toss him up and down in a blanket. Yet despite his physical deterioration, he remained focused on getting every last penny from his tenants, poring over the rents for long hours behind the barred windows of his office.

Astor gave little to charity, and social critics attacked him for his stinginess. When he died in 1848, his major gift to society was $460,000 in his will for building an Astor Library. In addition, he left $50,000 to the town of Waldorf, Germany, his birthplace; $30,000 for the German Society of New York; and $30,000 to the Home for Aged Ladies in New York City. This totaled, in the words of one commentator, less than "the proceeds of one year's pillage of the Indians."[19] The rest of his wealth went to his heirs. As to how America felt about him, one obituary minced no words.

> No doubt he had many fine, noble qualities, but avarice seemed to hold an all-conquering sway. . . . [W]hat a vast amount of good he might have rendered the world! But how reverse is the case—he dies and no one mourns! His soul was eaten up with avarice. Charity and benevolence found not a congenial home in his cold and frigid bosom![20]

THE LEGACY OF THE FUR TRADE

For 300 years the fur trade shaped the economic, political, and cultural life of both native and European inhabitants of the raw North American continent. Its climactic era has often been depicted as a progressive and romantic period when trading posts represented "civilization which was slowly mastering the opposition of nature and barbarism."[21] According to historian Dan Elbert Clark:

> The fur traders, with all their faults and shortcomings, were the pathfinders of civilization. They marked the trails that were followed by settlers. They built trading posts where later appeared thriving towns and cities. They knew the Indians better than any other class of white men who came among them.[22]

The American Fur Company and its competitors greatly advanced geographical knowledge and blazed trails. The fur industry reinforced central American values such as rugged individualism, the frontier spirit, and optimism about the inevitability of progress. Yet there is also a dark side to the story. Traders undermined Indian cultures by introducing new economic motivations. Tribal societies were destroyed by alcohol, smallpox, and venereal disease. "The fur trade," according to Professor David J. Wishart of the University of Nebraska, "was the vanguard of a massive wave of Euro-American colonisation which brought into contact two sets of cultures with disparate and irreconcilable ways of life."[23]

The industry also left extensive ecological damage in its wake. It slaughtered animal populations and denuded riverside forest areas to get steamboat fuel. Astor's mentality of pillage set a destructive standard. Argues Wishart: "The attitude of rapacious, short-term exploitation which was imprinted during the fur trade persisted after 1840 as the focus shifted from furs to minerals, timber, land, and water."[24]

The American Fur Company, now largely forgotten, was the main actor in a global industry with enormous geopolitical power. The firm's operation was like a test-tube experiment on the social consequences of raw, unrestrained capitalism. It would be many years before the American nation gave thought to the lessons.

[18] This is the estimate of Michael Klepper and Robert Gunther in "The American Heritage 40," *American Heritage*, October 1998, p. 56.

[19] Myers, *History of the Great American Fortunes*, p. 149.

[20] "John Jacob Astor," *Appleton's Journal of Literature, Science and Art*, June 1, 1848, p. 116.

[21] Arthur D. Howden Smith, *John Jacob Astor: Landlord of New York* (Philadelphia: Lippincott, 1929), p. 131.

[22] Dan Elbert Clark, *The West in American History* (New York: Thomas Y. Crowell, 1937), p. 441.

[23] Wishart, *The Fur Trade of the American West*, p. 215.

[24] Ibid., p. 212.

Questions

1. How would you evaluate Astor in terms of his motive, his managerial ability, and his ethics? What lesson does his career teach about the relationship between virtue and success?

2. How did the environment of the American Fur Company change in the 1830s? What deep historical forces are implicated in these changes?

3. What were the impacts of the fur trade on society in major dimensions of the business environment, that is, economic, cultural, technological, natural, governmental, legal, and internal?

4. Who were the most important stakeholders of the nineteenth-century fur industry? Were they treated responsibly by the standards of the day? By the standards of today?

5. On balance, is the legacy of the American Fur Company and of the fur trade itself a positive legacy? Or is the impact predominantly negative?

6. Does the story of the American Fur Company hint at how and why capitalism has changed and has been changed over the years?

7. Do one or more models of the business–government–society relationship discussed in Chapter 1 apply to the historical era set forth in this case? Which model or models have explanatory power and why?

Chapter **Three**

Business Power

James B. Duke and the American Tobacco Company

On December 23, 1856, cries of new life swelled from a North Carolina farmhouse, their source a baby boy named James Buchanan Duke. The lad would have far more impact on the world than the failed president his name was intended to honor.

Soon, the Civil War displaced the Duke family from its land. On returning home in 1865 little James's father built a small factory to manufacture a brand of chewing tobacco named Pro Bono Publico (a Latin phrase meaning "for the public good"). James helped. He was a precocious, energetic boy who became the driving force behind the business.

By his late teens, James had visions of grandeur for the little factory. But the presence of a rival firm, the Bull Durham Co., thwarted them. Its chewing tobacco was so dominant that head-on competition was hopeless. Taking a major gamble, he committed the company to a then-novel product—the cigarette. This was a venturesome move, because at the time few people smoked them. Most tobacco users were rural men who associated cigarettes with degenerate dudes and dandies in big cities.

Nonetheless, in 1881 Duke brought 10 Russian immigrant cigarette rollers to his North Carolina factory and set them to work. Each made about 2,000 per day. At first there was no demand. Tobacco shops refused to order his Duke of Durham brand since customers never asked for them. But Duke was a merchandising genius. In Atlanta, he took out a full-page newspaper ad of a famous actress holding Duke cigarettes in her outstretched hand. This use of a woman to advertise cigarettes created a sensation and, along with it, demand. In St. Louis, Duke confronted extreme prejudice against cigarettes. Tobacco shop proprietors simply would not place orders. He had his agents hire a young, redheaded widow to call on the tobacconists, and she got 19 orders on her first day.

By this time a Virginia engineer, James Bonsack, had invented a machine capable of rolling 200 cigarettes per minute. He offered it first to the largest tobacco companies, but they turned him down, believing that smokers would reject newfangled, machine-rolled cigarettes. Duke saw the significance of the technology and jumped at it.[1] In 1883 he negotiated an exclusive agreement to operate the device and his competitors

---

[1] Patrick G. Porter, "Origins of the American Tobacco Company," *Business History Review,* Spring 1969, pp. 68–69.

Duke lured men to try his new cigarette brands by putting picture cards in packs. The first cards were stage actresses in poses that were provocative for that day. Later card series included Indian chiefs, perilous occupations, ocean and river steamers, coins, musical instruments, flags, fish, ships, and prize fighters. Source: Courtesy Emergence of Advertising in America, Special Collections Library, Duke University.

never recovered. With the new Bonsack machines, Duke simultaneously cut manufacturing costs from $.80 per thousand to $.30 and multiplied factory production by many times. [2]

To find new markets for this swollen output, Duke next went to New York City, where he rented a loft and set up a small cigarette factory. Then he moved to create demand. He was tireless, working twelve hours a day in the factory, then making the rounds of tobacco shops at night. He gave secret rebates and cash payments to friendly dealers. He hired people to visit tobacco shops and demand his new machine-rolled Cameo and Cross Cut brands. Immigrants were welcomed with free samples as they emerged from the New York Immigration Station to set foot in America for the first time. Ingeniously, he put numbered cards with glamour photos of actresses in his cigarette packs, encouraging men to complete a collection. Late at night he haunted the streets, picking up crumpled cigarette packs from sidewalks and trash cans, creating a crude sales count.

Overseas, Duke's minions were also at work. One great conquest was China. At the time a few Chinese, mostly older men, smoked a bitter native tobacco in pipes. Cigarettes were unknown. Duke sent experts to Shantung Province with bright leaf

[2] John K. Winkler, *Tobacco Tycoon: The Story of James Buchanan Duke* (New York: Random House, 1942), p. 56.

from North Carolina to cultivate a milder tobacco. His sales force hired "teachers" to walk village streets showing curious Chinese how to light and hold cigarettes. He installed Bonsak machines in four new manufacturing plants that soon ran 24 hours a day. And he unleashed on the Chinese a full range of promotional activities. At one time his cigarette packs contained pictures of seminude American actresses, which were a big hit with Chinese men. In this way, Duke turned China into a nation of smokers.

Back home his tactics wore down competitors. He carefully observed John D. Rockefeller's conquest of the oil industry and saw that Rockefeller's methods could be applied to the tobacco industry. In 1884, at the age of 26, he engineered a combination of his firm and other large firms into a holding company known as the American Tobacco trust. As president, Duke built the trust into a monopoly that controlled 98 percent of the domestic cigarette market by 1892, a year in which 2.9 billion cigarettes were sold.[3] Not content with domination alone, he worked tirelessly to expand the tobacco market. By 1903, more than 10 billion cigarettes were sold in the United States.[4] Over two decades his combination ruthlessly swallowed or bankrupted 250 firms until it dominated the cigar, snuff, and smoking tobacco markets too.

Duke used a simple method to strangle competitors. Instead of selling its output at wholesale prices, Duke's company "consigned" its products to dealers. The dealers had to pay full retail price for tobacco goods sent to them "on consignment" and do so within ten days of receipt. Three months later, the company paid the dealer a "commission," which was the dealer's profit. Dealers who sold competitors' brands were not eligible to receive this "commission," so they could not make a profit on the brands that the vast majority of their customers wanted. Duke used detectives to spy on dealers and enforce the scheme. Many dealers disliked this arrogant, coercive system, but they had to play along or wither away.

Duke's monopoly lasted until 1911, when the Supreme Court ordered it broken up.[5] Duke himself figured out how to divide the giant firm into four independent companies: Ligget & Myers, P. Lorillard, R. J. Reynolds, and a new American Tobacco Company. After the breakup he retired from the tobacco industry to start an electric utility, Duke Power & Light. He also gave money to a small North Carolina college, which became Duke University. He died of complications from pernicious anemia in 1925.

Duke's career illustrates the power of commerce to shape society. He made the cigarette an acceptable consumer product and spread it around the world. His monopoly destroyed rivals and defined the structure of the tobacco industry. Its influence checked the early efforts of antitobacco leagues to publicize health hazards. His bribes to legislators blocked antismoking laws. And, owing largely to Duke's ingenuity, growing tobacco trade revived the crippled post–Civil War southern economy. Eventually, he ran into a hard check on power when the Supreme Court dismantled his colossus, but his work endures in the roll call of smokers across 120 years.

---

[3] "Iron Heel of Monopoly," *New York Times,* December 28, 1892, p. 10.

[4] "The Caesar of Tobacco," *The Wall Street Journal,* June 27, 1903, p. 6.

[5] *United States v. American Tobacco Company,* 221 U.S. 106 (1911).

THE NATURE OF BUSINESS POWER

Business has tremendous power to change society, and the extent of this power is underappreciated. In past eras, companies in ascending industries changed societies by altering all three of their primary elements—ideas, institutions, and material things. This effect is visible in the stories of dominant companies such as the American Tobacco Company, the American Fur Company, and the Standard Oil Trust. The cumulative power of all business is a massive, irrepressible shaping force. In this chapter we explain the underlying dynamics of this power to change society. We then discuss its limits.

WHAT IS POWER?

power
The force or strength to act or to compel another entity to act.

Power is the force or strength to act or to compel another entity to act. In human society it is used to organize and control people and materials in order to achieve individual or collective goals. It exists on a wide spectrum ranging from coercion at one extreme to weak influence at the other. Its use in human society creates change. Although power is sometimes exerted to prevent change, such resistance is itself a force that alters history. There are many sources of power, including wealth, position, knowledge, law, arms, status, and charisma. Power is unevenly distributed, and all societies have mechanisms to control and channel it for wide or narrow benefit. These mechanisms, which are imperfect, include governments, laws, police, cultural values, and public opinion. Also, multiple, competing formations of power may check and balance each other.

business power
The force behind an act by a company, industry, or sector.

Business power is the force behind an act by a company, industry, or sector. The greater this force, the more the action creates change or influences the actions of other entities in society. Its basic origin is a grant of authority from society to convert resources efficiently into needed goods and services. In return for doing this, society gives corporations the authority to take necessary actions and permits a profit. This agreement derives from the social contract.

legitimacy
The rightful use of power. Its opposite is tyranny, or the exercise of power beyond right.

The social contract legitimizes business power by giving it a moral basis. *Legitimacy* is the rightful use of power. The power of giant corporations is legitimate when it is exercised in keeping with the agreed-upon contract.[6] The philosopher John Locke wrote that for governments the opposite of legitimacy is tyranny, defined as "the exercise of power beyond right."[7] Corporations breach the social contract, exercising "power beyond right," when they violate social values, endanger the public, or act illegally.

Business power is legitimate when it is used for the common good. The grounds of legitimacy vary between societies and over time. Child labor, once widespread in the United States, is no longer permitted, but it exists in other nations. As we will

[6] For an effort to stipulate social contract norms that should guide business behavior, see Thomas Donaldson and Thomas W. Dunfee, *Ties That Bind: A Social Contracts Approach to Business Ethics* (Boston: Harvard Business School Press, 1999).

[7] John Locke, *The Second Treatise of Government* (New York: Bobbs-Merrill, 1952), p. 112; originally published in 1690.

see in subsequent chapters, the definition of the common good that business must serve has expanded throughout American history and is now expanding globally.

LEVELS AND SPHERES OF CORPORATE POWER

Corporate actions have an impact on society at two levels, and on each level they create change. On the *surface level,* business power is the direct cause of visible, immediate changes, both great and small. Corporations expand and contract, hire and fire; they make and sell products.

On a *deep level,* corporate power shapes society over time through the aggregate changes of industrial growth. At this level, corporate power creates many indirect, unforeseen, and invisible effects. Multiple lines of events converge and interact in complex networks of cause and effect. At this deep level, the workings of corporate power are unplanned, unpredictable, and slow to appear, but they are far more significant. Corporate power "is something more than men," wrote John Steinbeck. "It's the monster. Men made it, but they can't control it."[8] This is a poetic but accurate description of business power at a deep level.

On both the surface and deep levels, business power is exercised in spheres corresponding to the seven business environments set forth in Chapter 2.

- *Economic power* is the ability of the corporation to influence events, activities, and people by virtue of control over resources, particularly property. At the surface level, the operation of a corporation may immediately and visibly affect its stakeholders, for example, by building or closing a factory. At a deeper level, the accumulating impact of corporate economic activity has sweeping effects. For example, over many years corporations have created enough wealth to raise living standards dramatically in industrialized nations.
- *Technological power* is the ability to influence the direction, rate, characteristics, and consequences of physical innovations as they develop. On a surface level, in 1914, assembly lines run by new electric motors allowed Henry Ford to introduce transportation based on the internal combustion engine. Using this method, he turned an expensive luxury of the rich into a mass consumer product. But at a deeper level, as the auto took hold in American society it created unanticipated consequences. One juvenile court judge in the 1920s called the automobile a "house of prostitution on wheels," something that the puritanical Henry Ford doubtless never intended to create.[9]
- *Political power* is the ability to influence governments. On the surface, corporations give money to candidates and lobby legislatures. On a deeper level, around the world industrialization engenders values that radiate freedom and erode authoritarian regimes.
- *Legal power* is the ability to shape the laws of society. On the surface, big corporations have formidable legal resources that intimidate opponents. On a

---

[8] *The Grapes of Wrath* (New York: Viking Press, 1939), p. 45.

[9] Frederick Lewis Allen, *Only Yesterday: An Informal History of the 1920s* (New York: Harper & Brothers, 1931), p. 100.

American Landscape, a 1930 oil painting, depicts Ford Motor Company's mighty River Rouge plant, which took in raw materials such as sand and iron ore at one end and turned out finished autos at the other. In its day, the plant was regarded as a wonder and people traveled from around the world to see it. Here artist Charles Sheeler evokes the power of business to change and shape society. On the surface, this vista seems to beautify and ennoble the architecture of production, making it seem almost pastoral. Yet on a deeper level the painting provokes anxiety. Factory buildings run nature off the scene, dominating a landscape that is now, but for the sky, entirely artificial. A tiny human figure in the middle ground is overwhelmed and marginalized by the massive complex; its movement limited and regimented by the surrounding industrial structure. Here, then, art reveals emotions and insights about business power. Other Sheeler paintings and photographs are open to the same interpretation. He never revealed his intentions, leaving art critics to debate whether he was, in fact, sanguine or dispirited about how business power was shaping the "American landscape." Source: Digital Image © The Museum of Modern Art/Licensed by SCALA/Art Resource, NY.

deeper level, the laws of the United States—including constitutional, civil, and criminal laws—have been shaped by the consequences of industrial activity.

- *Cultural power* is the ability to influence cultural values, habits, and institutions such as the family. John Wanamaker, founder of a department store chain and a master of advertising, started Mother's Day in the early 1900s. He ran full-page ads in the *Philadelphia Inquirer* about a woman mourning for her mother, creating the sentiment that gratitude for mothers should be expressed by a gift on a special day.[10] At a deeper level, the cumulative impact of ads has altered American society by reinforcing values selectively, for example, materialism over asceticism, individualism over community, or personal appearance over inner character.

- *Environmental power* is the impact of a company on nature. On the surface, a power plant may pollute the air; on a deeper level, since the seventeenth century, emission of gases in the burning of wood, coal, and oil to power industry has altered the chemistry of earth's atmosphere. One study found that since 1882 the Standard Oil Trust and its successor companies have contributed between 4.7 and 5.2 percent of worldwide carbon dioxide emissions.[11]

- *Power over individuals* is exercised over employees, managers, stockholders, consumers, and citizens. On the surface, a corporation may determine the work life and buying habits of individuals. At a deeper level, industrialism sets the pattern of daily life. People are regimented, living by clocks, moving in routes fixed by the model of an industrial city with its streets and sidewalks. Their occupation determines their status and fortune.

Activity in the economic sphere is the primary force for change. From this, change radiates into other spheres. The story of the railroad industry in the United States illustrates how an expanding industry with a radical new technology can change its environments.

THE STORY OF THE RAILROADS

When small railroads sprang up in the 1820s, most passengers and freight moved by horse and over canals. The railroad was a vastly superior conveyance and was bound to revolutionize transportation. Tracks cost less to build than canals and did not freeze in winter. Routes could be more direct. For the first time in history, people and cargo traveled overland faster than the speed of a horse. The trip from New York to Chicago was reduced from three weeks to just three days. And the cost of moving goods and passengers was less; in a day a train could go back and forth many times over the distance that a canal boat or wagon could traverse once.

The initial boom in railroading came at mid-century. In 1850 trains ran on only 9,021 miles of track, but by 1860 30,626 miles had been laid down. During that decade, 30 railroad companies completed route systems, which had significant consequences for the financial system. Tracks were expensive, and each of these enterprises was a giant for its day. Many needed $10 to $35 million in capital, and the smallest at least $2 million. Companies in other industries did not approach this size; only a handful of textile mills and steel plants required capitalization of more than $1 million.[12]

---

[10] Richard Wolkomir and Joyce Wolkomir, "You Are What You Buy," *Smithsonian*, May 2000, p. 107.

[11] Friends of the Earth International, *Exxon's Climate Footprint* (London: FOEI, January 2004), p. 5. See also Richard Heede, *Exxon Mobil Corporation Emissions Inventory: 1882–2002* (London: Friends of the Earth Trust Ltd., December 17, 2003).

[12] Alfred D. Chandler, Jr., *The Visible Hand: The Managerial Revolution in American Business* (Cambridge, MA: Belknap Press, 1977), pp. 83, 86, and 90.

The call for this much money transformed capital markets. The only place such huge sums could be raised was in large northeastern cities. Since interest rates were a little higher in Boston at the time, New York became the center of financial activity and has remained so to this day. Railroads sold bonds and offered stocks to raise capital, and a new investment banking industry was created. The New York Stock Exchange went from a sleepy place, where only a few hundred shares of stock might change hands each week, to a roaring market. Speculative techniques such as margin trading, short-selling, and options trading appeared for the first time. Later, the financial mechanisms inspired by railroad construction were in place when other industries needed more capital to grow. This changed American history by accelerating the industrial transformation of the late 1800s. It also put New York bankers such as J. P. Morgan in a position to control access to capital.

At first the railroads ran between existing trade centers, but as time passed and track mileage increased, they linked ever more points. The 30,626 miles of track in 1860 increased to 93,267 miles by 1880 and 167,191 miles by 1890.[13] This required enormous amounts of wood, and led to extensive clear-cuts where forests were harvested to make ties and stoke fires in early steam locomotives. A deeper consequence of extending the tracks was a society transformed.

Before tracks radiated everywhere, the United States was a nation of farmers and small towns held together by the traditional institutions of family, church, and local government. Since long-distance travel was time-consuming and arduous, these towns often were isolated. Populations were stable. People identified more with local areas than with the nation as a whole. Into this world came the train, a destabilizing technology powered by aggressive market capitalism.

Trains took away young people who might have stayed in rural society but for the lure of wealth in distant cities. In their place came a stream of outsiders who were less under the control of community values. Small-town intimacy declined, and a new phenomenon appeared in American life—the impersonal crowd of strangers. Trains violated established customs. Sunday was a day of rest and worship, so many churchgoers were angered when huffing and whistling trains intruded on services. But new capital accounting methods used by railroad companies dictated using equipment an extra day each week to increase return on investment. This imperative trumped devoutness. In early America, localities set their own time according to the sun's overhead transit, but this resulted in a patchwork of time zones that made scheduling difficult. An editorial in *Railroad Age* argued, "Local time must go."[14] For the convenience of the railroads, a General Time Convention met in 1882 and standardized the time of day, though not without resistence from holdouts who felt that "[s]urely the world ran by higher priorities than railroad scheduling."[15]

---

[13] Bureau of the Census, *Statistical Abstract of the United States,* 77th ed. (Washington, DC: Government Printing Office, 1956), table 683.

[14] Bill Kauffman, "Why Spring Ahead," *The American Enterprise,* April–May 2001, p. 50.

[15] Ibid., p. 50, quoting Michael O'Malley, *Keeping Watch: A History of American Time* (Washington, DC: Smithsonian Institution Press, 1996).

As the railroads grew, they spread impersonality and an ethic of commerce. Towns reoriented themselves around their train stations. Shops and restaurants sprang up nearby so that strangers would spend money before moving on. The railroads gave more frequent service to cities with commercial possibilities and bypassed small towns or let them wither from less frequent service. This speeded urbanization and the centralization of corporate power in cities. Rural areas were redefined. Once the cultural heartland, they now were seen as backward and rustic—places best used for vacations from urban stress.

The railroads also changed American politics. On the surface, their lobbyists could dominate legislatures. On a deeper level, the changes were more profound. Congress had always selected nominees before presidential elections, but now trains brought delegates to national party nominating conventions, changing the way candidates were picked. Trains enabled all sorts of associations to have national meetings, and the rails spread issues that might in an earlier era have remained local. The movement to give women the vote, for example, succeeded after Susan B. Anthony took trains to all parts of the country, spreading her rhetoric and unifying the cause.[16]

At first government encouraged and subsidized railroads. All told, federal and state governments gave them land grants of 164 million acres, an area equal to the size of California and Nevada combined.[17] But later the challenge was to control them. When Congress passed the Interstate Commerce Act in 1887 to regulate railroads, the approach of the statute, with all its strengths and weaknesses, set the example for regulating other industries later.

Many other changes in American society are traceable to the railroads. They were the first businesses to require modern management structures. The need for precise coordination of speeding trains over vast reaches caused railroads to pioneer professional management teams, division structures, and modern cost accounting—all innovations later adopted in other industries.[18] Railroads lay behind Indian wars. For the plains Indians, tracks that divided old hunting grounds were the main barrier to peace.[19] Thousands of laborers came from China to lay rail, and their descendants live on in communities along the lines. Railroads changed the language. The word *diner*, meaning a place to eat, appeared after the introduction of the Pullman Palace Car Company's first dining car in 1868. The expression "hell on wheels" originally described the raucous body of prostitutes, gambling cars, and saloons that rolled along with construction crews as tracks spread west. The phrase "off again, on again" derives from discussions about train derailments.[20] And social values changed. Big-city commercial values rumbled down the tracks, jolting traditions along rural byways.

[16] These and other social and political changes are treated at length in Sarah H. Gordon, *Passage to Union* (Chicago: Ivan R. Dees, 1996).

[17] Page Smith, *The Rise of Industrial America*, vol. 6 (New York: Viking Penguin, 1984), p. 99.

[18] Chandler, *The Visible Hand*, chap. 3.

[19] Smith, *The Rise of Industrial America*, p. 89.

[20] Rudolph Daniels, *Trains across the Continent: North American Railroad History*, 2d ed. (Bloomington: Indiana University Press, 2000), pp. 53 and 78.

FIGURE 3.1   Railroad Track Miles in Operation 1830–2005
The rise and decline of a powerful industry is reflected in the miles of track that trains have run on over the years.

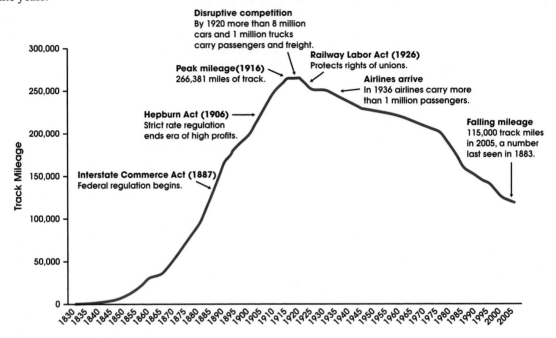

Source of data: *Statistical Abstract of the United States*, various editions 1878–2006.

As the track system swelled so did the power of railroads to shape the socio-political as well as the physical landscape. Figure 3.1 shows how track mileage fell after 1916, reflecting a decline in the fortunes of the industry. Government regulation matured, making rate hikes more difficult and strengthening the hand of unions. In addition, railroads came into competition with new transportation technologies, first autos, buses, and trucks, then aircraft. As the importance of rails receded, these emerging technologies gathered power to shape American life.

TWO PERSPECTIVES ON BUSINESS POWER

There is agreement that business has great power. There is considerable disagreement about whether its power is adequately checked and balanced for the public good. Views about business power cover a wide spectrum, but there are two basic and opposing positions.

On one side is the *dominance theory*, which holds that business is preeminent in American society, primarily because of its control of wealth, and that its power is both excessive and inadequately checked. Corporations can alter their environments in self-interested ways that harm the general welfare. This was the thesis of Karl Marx, who wrote that a ruling capitalist class exploited workers and dominated

dominance theory
The view that business is the most powerful institution in society, because of its control of wealth. This power is inadequately checked and, therefore, excessive.

pluralist theory
The view that business power is exercised in a society where other institutions also have great power. It is counterbalanced and restricted and, therefore, not excessive.

other classes. The dominance theory is the basis of the dominance model of the business–government–society relationship set forth in Chapter 1.

On the other side the *pluralist theory* holds that business power is exercised in a society in which other institutions such as markets, government, labor unions, advocacy groups, and public opinion also have great power. Business power is counterbalanced, restricted, controlled, and subject to defeat. Adam Smith was convinced that largely through market forces, business power could be disciplined to benefit society. The pluralist theory is the basis of the countervailing forces model in Chapter 1.

The Dominance Theory

In industrializing societies, business organizations grow in size and concentrate wealth. According to the dominance theory, business abuses the power its size and wealth confer in a number of ways. The rise of huge corporations creates a business elite that exercises inordinate power over public policy. Asset concentration creates monopoly or oligopoly in markets that reduces competition and harms consumers. Corporations wield financial and organizational resources unmatched by opposing interests. For example, they use campaign contributions to corrupt politicians, hire lobbyists to undermine the independence of elected officials, employ accountants and lawyers to avoid taxes, and run public relations campaigns that shape opinion in their favor.

Moreover, large corporations achieve such importance in a nation's economy that elected officials are forced to adopt probusiness measures or face public wrath. "If enterprises falter for lack of inducement to invest, hire, and produce," writes one advocate of the dominance theory, "members of the political elite are more likely than those of the entrepreneurial elite to lose their positions."[21] We will discuss further the growth in size and wealth of corporations and the presence of elites.

Corporate Asset Concentration

The idea that concentration of economic power results in abuse arose, in part, as an intellectual reaction to the awesome economic growth of the late nineteenth century. Until then, the United States had been primarily an agricultural economy. But between 1860 and 1890, industrial progress transformed the country. Statistics illustrating this are striking. During these 30 years, the number of manufacturing plants more than doubled, growing from 140,433 to 355,415; the value of what they made rose more than 400 percent, from $1.8 billion to $9.3 billion; and the capital invested in them grew 650 percent, from $1 billion to $6.5 billion.[22]

This growth did more than create wealth; it also concentrated it. At the end of the century, between 1895 and 1904, an unprecedented merger wave assembled dominant firms in industry after industry. Since then, there have been other great

[21] Charles E. Lindblom, *The Market System: What It Is, How It Works, and What to Make of It* (New Haven: Yale University Press, 2001), p. 247.

[22] Figures in this paragraph are from Arthur M. Schlesinger, *Political and Social Growth of the United States: 1852–1933* (New York: Macmillan, 1935), pp. 132–44.

merger waves, but this was the first. It made a definitive impression on the American mind, and its legacy is an enduring fear of big companies.

Merger waves are caused by changes in the economic environment that create incentives to combine. The main stimulus for the 1895–1904 wave was the growth of the transcontinental railroads, which reduced transportation costs, thereby creating new national markets. Companies rushed to transform themselves from regional operations to national ones. Combinations such as James Duke's American Tobacco Company gorged themselves, swallowing competitors. They crowded into formerly isolated markets, wiping out small family businesses. The story was repeated in roughly 300 commodities, including oil, copper, cattle, smelting, and such items as playing cards and tombstones. A 1904 study of the 92 largest firms found that 78 controlled 50 percent of their market, 57 controlled 60 percent or more, and 26 controlled 80 percent or more.[23]

At the time, the public failed to see the growth of huge firms as a natural, inevitable, or desirable response to the new economic incentives. Instead, it saw them as colossal monuments to greed. Companies of this size were something new. They inspired a mixture of awe and fear. In 1904, when the United States Steel Corporation became the first company with more than $1 billion in assets, people were astounded. Previously, such numbers applied in the realm of astronomy, not business.

In the twentieth century, corporations continued to grow in size, but the marked rise in asset concentration slowed and leveled off. By 1929 the 200 largest nonfinancial corporations in the United States (less than 0.7 percent of all nonfinancials) controlled nearly 50 percent of all corporate wealth. But by 1947 the nation's top 200 corporations had only 46 percent of corporate wealth, and this was reduced to 36 percent in 1996.[24] Although no continuing data series exists to provide a current figure, a recent study reveals that asset concentration in the top 200 firms on the Fortune 500 declined by 8 percent between 1995 and 2004.[25]

Because of the trend toward global production today the number of transnational firms and the scale of their activity has grown. There are approximately 78,000 transnationals, up from only about 34,000 as recently as 1990. Assets and sales of the largest of these firms are rising. Between 1990 and 2005, assets of the 100 biggest transnationals increased by 271 percent and sales by 213 percent.[26] However, despite

---

[23] John Moody, *The Truth about Trusts: A Description and Analysis of the American Trust Movement* (New York: Greenwood Press, 1968), p. 487; originally published in 1904.

[24] J. Fred Weston, Kwang S. Chung, and Juan A. Siu, *Takeovers, Restructuring, and Corporate Governance*, 2d ed. (Upper Saddle River, NJ: Prentice Hall, 1998), p. 116. These figures allow rotation of new firms into the top 200 firms. If the same 200 firms had been followed over the years, asset concentration would have fallen even faster.

[25] Edward Nissan, "Structure of American Business: Goods versus Services," *Southwestern Economic Review* (online), Spring 2006, table 1.

[26] United Nations Conference on Trade and Development (UNCTAD), *World Investment Report 2007* (New York: United Nations, July 2007), table I.10; and UNCTAD, *World Investment Report 1993* (New York: United Nations, July 1993), table I.11.

heightened global merger activity, the largest global firms do not show signs of concentrating international assets the way that large American firms have concentrated domestic assets. In fact, the foreign assets of the largest 100 transnationals fell from 13 percent of estimated global assets in 1999 to 11 percent in 2004.[27] And these 100 firms are still only a small part of world economic activity. For the decade 1990–2000, their economic activity as a share of world GDP grew from 3.5 percent to only 4.3 percent.[28]

Despite this, adherents of the dominance theory believe that the increasing size and financial power of global corporations will be converted into the same old abuses. But the link between market power and abuse remains to be seen. Larger transnational firms in many industries do not necessarily even have increased market power because they face formidable competitors, emerging competition from new industries, enlarged market boundaries, and more aggressive antitrust enforcement. In the sociopolitical dimension, these firms face growing global pressures to act responsibly.

Also, no corporation, no matter how large, is assured of prospering. Over time, poor management, competition, and technological change have continuously revised the roster of America's biggest companies. Of the 100 largest corporations in 1909, only 36 remained on the list until 1948. Between 1948 and 1958, only 65 of the top 100 held their place. Only 116 company names remained on the Fortune 500 list of industrial corporations from its inception in 1955 to 1994. By 2003 only 71 of the original 500 were still there.[29] Many firms dropped from the list were, of course, acquired by other firms. Among the 100 largest transnational corporations there were 28 American firms in 1990, but that number had declined to 25 by 2004.[30] The lesson is that, with a very few exceptions, the power of uncontrollable competitive forces exceeds the power of even the largest corporations to maintain their dominance.

Elite Dominance

Another argument that supports the dominance theory is that there exist a small number of individuals who, by virtue of wealth and position, control the nation. The members of this elite are alleged to act in concert and in undemocratic ways. There is a long history of belief in an economic elite dominating American society. In the debates preceding adoption of the Constitution in 1789, some opponents charged that the delegates were wealthy aristocrats designing a government favorable to their businesses. Later, farmers suspected the hand of an economic elite in

---

[27] Figures are from UNCTAD, *World Investment Report 2000* (New York: United Nations, 2000), p. 71; and UNCTAD, *World Investment Report 2006* (New York: United Nations, July 2006), p. 30.

[28] UNCTAD, *World Investment Report 2002*, box table IV.1.2. These figures are based on a value-added calculation (the sum of salaries, pretax profits, and depreciation and amortization) for TNCs.

[29] Figures in this paragraph are from Neil H. Jacoby, *Corporate Power and Social Responsibility* (New York: Macmillan, 1973), p. 32; John Paul Newport, Jr., "A New Era of Rapid Rise and Ruin," *Fortune*, April 24, 1989, p. 77; Carol J. Loomis, "Forty Years of the 500," *Fortune*, May 15, 1995, p. 182; and Julie Schlosser and Ellen Florian, "Fifty Years of Amazing Facts!" *Fortune*, April 5, 2004, p. 159.

[30] UNCTAD, *World Investment Report 2006*, p. 31.

The Rise and Decline of Powerful Corporations

In 1896 journalist Charles H. Dow created a list of 12 companies as an index of stock market performance. Each firm was a leader in an important industry and represented its fortunes. As America's industrial structure changed over the years, companies came and went; and the list, today called the Dow Jones Industrial Average Index, grew from 12 to 30. The most recent additions and deletions were made in 2008.

The leading firms in 1896 reflect a different world. Farming was much more important in the American economy, and four firms dealt in agricultural products. They included James B. Duke's American Tobacco Company, cotton and sugar producers, and a company that made livestock feed. Other firms represented the prominence of industrial technologies based on iron, lead, and coal. U.S. Leather made a product in the shadow of imminent obsolescence, leather belts used for power transmission in factories. General Electric, which made electric motors, was the technology company of that era. Chicago Gas and Laclede Gas Light Co. of St. Louis were utilities supplying natural gas for new gas streetlamps in cities. North American Co. ran streetcars.

1896		2008
American Cotton Oil	Alcoa	Home Depot
American Sugar Refining	American Express	IBM
American Tobacco	American International Group	Intel
Chicago Gas	AT&T	J. P. Morgan Chase
Distilling & Cattle Feeding	Bank of America	Johnson & Johnson
General Electric	Boeing	McDonald's
Laclede Gas Light	Caterpillar	Merck
National Lead	Chevron	Microsoft
North American	Coca-Cola	3M
Tennessee Coal & Iron	Citigroup	Pfizer
U.S. Leather	DuPont	Procter & Gamble
U.S. Rubber	ExxonMobil	United Technologies
	General Electric	Verizon Communications
	General Motors	Wal-Mart Stores
	Hewlett-Packard	Walt Disney

The 2008 list registers the rise of new technologies and sectors of the economy providing services and consumer products. General Electric is the only company that was on the 1896 list, and it was removed for nine years between 1898 and 1907. Of the other 11 original firms, 2 (American Tobacco and North American) were broken up by antitrust action, 1 (U.S. Leather) was dissolved, and 8 continue to operate as less important companies or as parts of other firms that acquired their assets.

As a biography of American industry, the index dramatizes the rise and fall of powerful companies and industries. Over more than a century, 100 different firms have been listed. The index teaches that dominance of even the largest firms is transient.

the probusiness policies of Alexander Hamilton, George Washington's secretary of the treasury, who had many ties to wealth and commercial power. Since the colonial era, charges of elitism have surfaced repeatedly in popular movements opposed to big business.

The modern impetus for the theory of elite dominance comes from the sociologist C. Wright Mills, who wrote a scholarly book in 1956 describing a "power elite" in American society. "Insofar as national events are decided," wrote Mills, "the power elite are those who decide them."[31] Mills saw American society as a pyramid of power and status. At the top was a tiny elite in command of the economic, political, and military domains. Mills was never specific about its numbers, but said it was small. Just below was a group of lieutenants who carried out the elite's policies. They included professional managers of corporations, politicians beholden to the elite for their election, and bureaucrats appointed by the politicians. The large base of the pyramid was composed of a mass of powerless citizens, including feeble groups and associations with little policy impact. This image of a pyramid corresponds to the dominance model in Chapter 1.

Mills did not see America as a democracy and thought that the elite simply used government "as an umbrella under whose authority they do their work."[32] Although he never stated that the economic segment of the elite was dominant over the political and military, he noted that "the key organizations, perhaps, are the major corporations."[33]

The Power Elite is a book in which there is more speculation than substantiation. It is based on cursory evidence. There is none of the statistical research that would be required to support such sweeping generalizations in a similar work of sociology today. Yet it contained a powerful new explanation of economic power and came out just as many American leftists were becoming disenchanted with Marxism. Mills's vision of a small ruling elite caught on and has been popular with the anticorporate left ever since. Mills would have been pleased. In correspondence, he once expressed indignation about the power of "the sons of bitches who run American Big Business."[34]

Scholars inspired by Mills have pressed the study of elites and are less reluctant to suggest business dominance. One is G. William Domhoff, who has for more than 30 years argued that an upper class dominates America through its control of corporations. He writes of "a general leadership group for the corporate community and the upper class, called the *power elite*," that consists of "members of the upper class who have taken on leadership roles in the *corporate community*."[35]

> [T]he owners and top-level managers in large companies work together to maintain themselves as the core of the dominant power group. Their corporations, banks, and

power elite
A small group of individuals in control of the economy, government, and military. The theory of its existence is associated with the American sociologist C. Wright Mills.

---

[31] C. Wright Mills, *The Power Elite* (New York: Oxford University Press, 1956), p. 18.

[32] Ibid., p. 287.

[33] Ibid., p. 283.

[34] In a letter to his parents quoted by John B. Judis, "The Spiritual Wobbly," *New York Times Book Review,* July 9, 2000, p. 9.

[35] G. William Domhoff, *Who Rules America: Power, Politics, & Social Change,* 5th ed. (New York: McGraw-Hill, 2006), pp. xiii and 103 (emphasis in the original).

agribusinesses form a corporate community that shapes the federal government on the policy issues of interest to it . . . [t]he power elite consists of those people who serve as directors or trustees in profit and nonprofit institutions controlled by the corporate community through stock ownership, financial support, or involvement on the board of directors.[36]

In an effort extending over 25 years political scientist Thomas R. Dye has tried to identify precisely which individuals constitute an American elite. Believing that power comes from leadership roles in corporations, government, and other large organizations, he defines a "national institutional elite" composed of

individuals who occupy the top positions in *the institutional structure of American society*. These are the individuals who possess the formal authority to formulate, direct, and manage programs, policies, and activities of the major corporate, governmental, legal, educational, civic, and cultural institutions in the nation. . . . For purposes of analysis we have divided American society into ten sectors: (1) industrial (nonfinancial) corporations, (2) banking, (3) insurance, (4) investments, (5) mass media, (6) law, (7) education, (8) foundations, (9) civic and cultural organizations, and (10) government. [37]

Applying this method, Dye identified 7,314 elite positions and found that they were held by 5,778 individuals (because some persons held more than one position). This is a much larger elite than that suggested by Mills, but it is still only about three-thousandths of 1 percent of the population.

Elites formed from some combination of wealth, ability, position, and social status are inevitable. Their existence is a challenge to the validity of democratic governance in that it divides citizens into a small number who rule and a vast majority who are ruled. But elites are not necessarily sinister, oppressive, or conspiratorial. They can be sources of talent and expert leadership. The American business elite comes from the ranks of top corporate executives and directors, and those who hold these positions do so based overwhelmingly on ability. Turnover is frequent. However, those selected at these rarified levels come from a narrow range of backgrounds. Every study of them finds that disproportionately they are male, white, and Christian; that they come from upper-class families; and that they graduate from a few prestigious universities. Evidence suggests that inclusion of blacks, Latinos, and women is based on their similarity in background and thinking to the existing elite.[38] In conclusion, the presence of an American elite, one perhaps dominated by business interests, troubles a nation with such a deep commitment to equality. Yet some argue that its actions are adequately checked and balanced. This view is taken up in the next section.

Pluralist Theory

pluralistic society
A society with multiple groups and institutions through which power is diffused.

A *pluralistic society* is one having multiple groups and institutions through which power is diffused. Within such a society no entity or interest has overriding power, and each may check and balance others. The countervailing forces model

---

[36] Ibid., pp. xi and 103.

[37] Thomas R. Dye, *Who's Running America? The Bush Restoration,* 7th ed. (Upper Saddle River, NJ: Prentice Hall, 2002), p. 8; emphasis in the original.

[38] Richard L. Zweigenhaft and G. William Domhoff, *Diversity in the Power Elite: Have Women and Minorities Reached the Top?* (New Haven: Yale University Press, 1998).

J. P. Morgan and the Panic of 1907

In the first decade of the twentieth century, J. P. Morgan (1837–1913), head of J. P. Morgan & Co. in New York, was often called the most powerful man in the country. He specialized in buying competing companies in the same industry and merging them into a single, monopolistic firm. He joined separate railroads into large systems. He combined smaller electrical concerns into General Electric in 1892 and then pulled a collection of manufacturers into the International Harvester Company, which started with 85 percent of the farm machinery market. In 1901 he created the first billion-dollar company when he merged 785 separate firms to form the United States Steel Company with capitalization of $1.4 billion.

Morgan and two of his close associates together held 341 corporate directorships. His power was very independent of government controls since at the time antitrust laws were little enforced, there was no national bank to regulate the money supply, and existing securities and banking laws were rudimentary. One awestruck biographer said that Morgan "was a God" who "ruled for a generation the pitiless, predatory world of cash."[39] His critics were less kind. Senator Robert W. La Follette once called him "a beefy, red-faced, thick-necked financial bully, drunk with wealth and power."[40]

In October 1907 panic swept Wall Street and stocks plummeted as frantic investors sold shares. Soon banks suffered runs of withdrawals and were on the verge of failure. Liquidity, or the free flow of money, was fast vanishing from financial markets, and the nation's banking system teetered on the verge of collapse. So influential was Morgan that he commanded the New York Stock Exchange to stay open all day on October 24 to maintain investor confidence. To support it, he raised $25 million of credit.

The federal government could do little to ease the crisis. President Theodore Roosevelt was off hunting bears in Louisiana, an ironic pursuit in light of the crashing stock market. Without a national bank, the government had no capacity to increase the money supply and restore liquidity. Powerless, Secretary of the Treasury George B. Cortelyou traveled to New York to get Morgan's advice.

On the evening of October 24, Morgan gathered members of the New York banking elite at his private library. He played solitaire while in another room the assembled bankers discussed methods for resolving the crisis. Periodically, someone came to him with a proposal, several of which he rejected. Finally, a plan was hatched in which $33 million would be raised to support the stock exchange and failing banks. Where would this money come from? The secretary of the treasury was to supply $10 million in government funds, John D. Rockefeller contributed $10 million, and Morgan the remaining $13 million.

This action stabilized the economy. Perhaps it demonstrates that elite power may be exercised in the common good. It should be noted, however, that the panic of 1907—and other panics of that era—came after Morgan and other titans of finance repeatedly choked the stock exchange with the colossal stock offerings needed to finance their new combinations.

Morgan was widely criticized for his role in ending the panic of 1907. Conspiracy theorists, suspicious of so much power resident in one man, attacked him. Upton Sinclair, for example, accused him of inciting the panic for self-gain, a wildly erroneous accusation. In 1912 Morgan was the focus of congressional hearings which concluded that he led a "money trust" that controlled the nation's finances and that this was bad for the nation. Death claimed him in 1913 just before Congress passed the Federal Reserve Act to set up a central bank and ensure that no private banker would ever again be sole caretaker of the money supply.

[39] John K. Winkler, *Morgan the Magnificent* (New York: Doubleday, 1950), p. 3; originally published in 1930.
[40] Jean Strouse, *Morgan: American Financier* (New York: Random House, 2000), p. x.

in Chapter 1 illustrates how, in such a society, business must interact with constraining forces in its environment. It may have considerable influence over some of them; but over most it has limited influence, and over a few none at all. Several features of American society support this thesis of pluralism.

First, it is infused with democratic values. Unlike many nations, America has no history of feudal or authoritarian rule, so there is no entrenched deference to an aristocracy of wealth. In colonial days, Americans adopted the then-revolutionary doctrine of natural rights, which held that all persons were created equal and entitled to the same opportunities and protections. The French aristocrat Alexis de Tocqueville, who toured America and wrote an insightful book about American customs in the 1830s, was forcibly struck by the "prodigious influence" of the notion of equality. Belief in equality, he wrote, ran through American society, directing public opinion, informing the law, and defining politics. It was, he wrote, "the fundamental fact from which all others seem to be derived." [41] Thus, in America laws apply equally to all. All interests have the right to be heard. To be legitimate, power must be exercised for the common good.

Second, America encompasses a large population spread over a wide geography and engaged in diverse occupations. It has a great mixture of interests, more than some other countries. Economic interests, including labor, banking, manufacturing, agriculture, and consumers, are a permanent fixture. A rainbow of voluntary associations (whose size, longevity, and influence vary) compete in governments at all levels.

Third, the Constitution encourages pluralism. Its guarantees of rights protect the freedom of individuals to form associations and freely to express and pursue interests. Thus, business is challenged by human rights, environmental, and other groups. The Constitution diffuses political power through the three branches of the federal government and between the federal and state governments and to the people. This creates a remarkably open political system.

In addition, business is exposed to constraining market pressures that force a stream of resource allocation decisions centered on cost reduction and consumer satisfaction, forces that can fell even the mighty. Henry J. Kaiser seemed unerring in business. The son of German immigrants, he worked his way up from store clerk to owner of 32 companies, including seven shipyards that launched one finished ship a day during most of World War II. When he started an auto company in 1945, nobody thought he could fail. Eager customers put down thousands of deposits before a single car was built.[42] But his cars, the Kaiser and the Frazier, were underpowered and overpriced, and the market eventually rejected them. The venture failed. Kaiser never got costs under control; he had to negotiate the prices of many parts with competing auto companies that made them. Toward the end, he built a model that was sold at Sears as the Allstate. This was a terrible mistake because it gave the car a low-quality image with consumers.

---

[41] Alexis de Tocqueville, *Democracy in America* (New York: New American Library, 1956), p. 26; originally published as two volumes in 1835 and 1850.

[42] Robert Sobel, "The $150 Million Lemon," *Audacity,* Winter 1997, p. 11.

FIGURE 3.2
Boundaries of
Managerial
Power

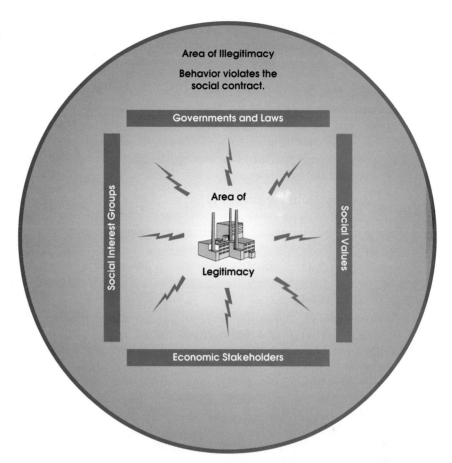

In sum, predictable and strong forces in a pluralistic, free market society limit business power. Wise managers anticipate that, despite having considerable influence on governments, markets, and public opinion, their power can be restricted, challenged, or shared by others. Overall, as illustrated in Figure 3.2, there are four major boundaries on managerial power.

1. *Governments and laws* in all countries regulate business activity. Governments are the ultimate arbiters of legitimate behavior and can act forcefully to blunt the exercise of corporate power that harms the public. Laws channel and restrict operations.

2. *Social interest groups* represent every segment of society and use many methods to restrain business, including product boycotts, lawsuits, picket lines, media campaigns, and lobbying for more regulation. Historically, labor has been the great antagonist and counterweight to business power, but also prominent in recent years are environmental, human rights, religious, consumer, and public interest groups.

3. *Social values* are transmitted across generations, reflected in public opinion, and embedded in the law. Managers internalize them in schools and churches.

Social values include norms of duty, justice, truth, and piety that can direct a manager's behavior as powerfully as laws. For example, in the 1960s shifting generational values gave film studios license to experiment with brazen nudity and violence, but Walt Disney never did. No financial incentive was enough to make him forsake his own values about the importance of morality, family life, and the small-town decency he saw in his Kansas boyhood. [43]

4. *Markets and economic stakeholders* impose strong limits. Stockholders, employees, suppliers, creditors, and competitors influence corporate decisions. The marketplace also registers the great waves of technological change that can sweep away even the largest corporations.

According to the theory of pluralism, these are the boundaries of managerial power. Just as in the solar system the planets move freely within but cannot escape their gravitational fields, so major corporations in American society move within orbits constrained by plural interests.

CONCLUDING OBSERVATIONS

In a recent poll, 77 percent of Americans felt that "[t]oo much power is concentrated in the hands of a few large companies."[44] Are they correct? The answer requires perspective and judgment. In this chapter we break down the idea of corporate power into patterns, categories, and theories to allow critical thinking. We explain how corporate power is a strong force for change and how, at a deep level, economic growth shapes society in sweeping, unplanned ways.

We also set forth two opposing perspectives. The dominance theory holds that inadequately restrained economic power is concentrated in large corporations and in the hands of a wealthy elite. The pluralist theory holds that many restraints in an open society control corporate power. These theories are locked in perpetual conflict. Both are molds into which varieties of evidence must be fitted. Both contain insights, but neither has a lock on accuracy. And both attract adherents based on inner judgments about whether market capitalism moves society in the right direction.

If corporate power remains generally accountable to democratic controls, society will accord it legitimacy. If rule by law and a just economy exist, corporate power will broadly and ultimately be directed toward the public welfare, this despite the habitual breakouts of deviltry that inflame critics.

[43] Richard Schickel, *The Disney Version,* 3d ed. (Chicago: Ivan R. Dee, 1997), p. 39.

[44] Princeton Survey Research Associates International, national adult survey, question ID USPSRA.051005A, R11M, May 10, 2005.

John D. Rockefeller and the Standard Oil Trust

This is the story of John D. Rockefeller, founder of the Standard Oil Company. It is the story of a somber, small-town boy who dominated the oil industry with organizational genius, audacity, and ruthless, methodical execution. He became the richest man in America and, for a time, the most hated.

Rockefeller's life spanned 98 years. At his birth Martin Van Buren was president and settlers drove covered wagons over the Oregon Trail. He lived to see Franklin Roosevelt's New Deal, watch the rise of the Nazi party in Germany, and hear Frank Sinatra and *The Lone Ranger* on radio.

The historical backdrop of this lifetime is an economy gripped by the fever of industrial progress. Rockefeller built his fortune in an era that lacked many of today's ethical norms and commercial laws, an era in which the power of a corporation and its founder could be exercised with fewer restraints.

THE FORMATIVE YEARS

John Davison Rockefeller was born on July 8, 1839, in a small village in southern New York. He was the second of six children and the oldest boy. His father, William Rockefeller, was an itinerant quack doctor who sold worthless elixirs and engaged in a wide variety of businesses. He was jovial, slick, and cunning and made enough money to keep the family in handsome style until he had to flee and live away from home to avoid arrest on a charge of raping a local woman. After that, he visited only in the dark of night. But he taught young John D. and his brothers lessons of business conduct, especially that sentimentality should not influence business transactions. "I cheat my boys every chance I get," he once said. "I want to make 'em sharp."[1]

John D.'s mother was a somber, religious woman who gave the children a strict upbringing, emphasizing manners, church attendance, and the work ethic. She preached homilies such as "Willful waste makes woeful want." And she taught charity to the children; from an early age John D. made regular contributions to worthy causes.

Young John D. was not precocious in school. In high school he was an uninspired student, little interested in books and ideas, but willing to work hard. He grew into a somber, intense lad nicknamed "the Deacon" by his classmates because he faithfully attended a Baptist church and memorized hymns. In the summer of 1855 he attended a three-month course at a business college in Cleveland, Ohio, and then set out looking for a job. In addition to his formal schooling, he carried the contradictory temperaments of his parents—the wily, self-assured

boldness of his father and the exacting, pietistic character of his mother. He internalized both, and the combination was to prove formidable. Here was a man with the precision of an accountant and the cunning of Cesare Borgia.

EARLY BUSINESS CAREER

Rockefeller's first job was as a bookkeeper at a Cleveland firm where he meticulously examined each bill submitted and pounced on errors. He also recorded every cent he earned and spent in a personal ledger. Its pages show that he was parsimonious and saved most of his $25-a-month salary but that he still gave generously to the Baptist church and the poor.

In 1859 he formed a successful partnership with two others in the produce business in Cleveland and proved himself an intense negotiator, described by an acquaintance as a person "who can walk right up on a man's shirt bosom and sit down."[2] The business boomed from supplying food to the Union army during the Civil War. Although in his early 20s at the time, the steady, unemotional lad was never touched by patriotic fervor. In those days, the law permitted any man of means to pay someone else to serve in his place, and this he did.

BEGINNINGS OF THE OIL BUSINESS

Profits from the produce business were high, and John D. looked around for a promising new investment. He soon found one—a Cleveland petroleum refinery in which he invested $4,000 in 1863. At the time, petroleum production and refining was an infant industry. A new drilling technology had led to an 1859 oil strike in nearby Pennsylvania, followed by a frenzied boom in drilling and refining.

Soon Rockefeller devoted himself full time to the oil business, and he began to apply his principles of parsimony. One basic principle was to avoid paying a profit to anyone. For example, instead of buying barrels and paying the cooper $2.50 each, Rockefeller set up his own barrel-making factory and made them for $.96. He purchased a forest to make staves from his own trees. Another basic principle was methodical

[1] David Freeman Hawke, *John D.: The Founding Father of the Rockefellers* (New York: Harper & Row, 1980), p. 13.

[2] Jules Abels, *The Rockefeller Billions* (New York: Macmillan, 1965), p. 35.

cost cutting. Lumber for barrel staves was kiln-dried before shipment to the cooperage plant. Water evaporated from the wood, making it lighter and lowering transportation costs.

Though obsessed with details and small economies, Rockefeller also proved aggressive in larger plans. He borrowed heavily from banks to expand the refinery. The risk scared his partners, so he bought them out. In 1865 he borrowed more to build a second refinery. Soon he incorporated an export sales company in New York, making the world his market.

DYNAMICS OF THE OIL INDUSTRY

During this early period, the new industry was in a chaotic state. A basic cause was overproduction in the Pennsylvania oil regions, which were the only source of crude oil. The price of crude fluctuated wildly, but was in long-term decline. Each drop in the price of crude oil encouraged construction of new refineries and by the late 1860s refining capacity was three times greater than oil production. This caused vicious price wars. Some refiners tried to stay in business by selling products at a loss to raise cash for continued debt payments. In doing so, they dragged down profit margins for all refiners.

Rockefeller had the insight to invest in large-scale refineries and, because he cut costs relentlessly, his refineries made money. Yet despite disciplined cost control, the market forces of a sick industry ate away at his net earnings. He believed it was time to "rationalize" the entire industry and stop destructive competition.[3] His method for doing this would be monopoly, his tactics hard-nosed.

ROCKEFELLER'S COMPETITIVE STRATEGIES

Rockefeller used a range of competitive strategies. He was a low-cost, high-volume producer. He used debt financing to expand. He attempted to make his refined petroleum products of high and consistent quality, since fly-by-night refiners turned out inferior distillates. Cheap kerosene with a low ignition point had burned many a home down after exploding in a

wick lamp. When he incorporated the Standard Oil Company of Ohio in 1870, the name suggested a "standard oil" of uniformly good quality. He engaged in vertical integration by making wooden barrels. As time when on, he also bought pipelines, storage tanks, and railroad tank cars.

Critical to his success, however, was the art of strong-arming the railroads. In this, Rockefeller was the master. Transportation costs paid to railroads were important to refiners, who shipped in crude oil and then shipped out products such as kerosene or lubricating oil. In the 1860s railroads were highly competitive and often altered shipping rates to attract business. No law prohibited this and published rates were only the starting point of negotiations.

Railroads often granted *rebates* to shippers; that is, they returned part of the freight charge after shipment. These rebates were usually secret and given in return for the guarantee of future business. Large volume shippers, including oil refineries, got the biggest rebates. Standard Oil was no exception.

At this time, Rockefeller has been described by biographers as a prepossessing man with penetrating eyes who drove a hard bargain. He would take the measure of a person with a withering stare, and few were his match. He was formidable in negotiations because he was invariably informed in detail about the other's business. And he was still a pious churchgoer who read the Bible nightly before retiring.

Late in 1870 Rockefeller hatched a brazen plan for stabilizing the oil industry at the refining level. In clandestine meetings, he worked out a rebate scheme between a few major refiners and the three railroads going into the Pennsylvania oil regions. They gave this scheme an innocent-sounding name, the South Improvement Plan. In it, the railroads agreed to increase published rates for hauling oil. Then Rockefeller's Cleveland refineries and a few others would get large rebates on each barrel shipped. For example, the regular rate between the oil regions and Cleveland would be $.80 a barrel and between Cleveland and New York $2.00 a barrel. It would cost a total of $2.80 per barrel for any other refinery in Cleveland to bring in a barrel of crude oil and ship a barrel of refined oil to New York for sale or export. Rockefeller and his accomplices, on the other hand, would be charged $2.80 but then get a rebate of $.90.

In addition, the refineries participating in the South Improvement Plan received *drawbacks*, or payments made on the shipment of oil by competitors! Thus,

[3] Ron Chernow, *Titan: The Life of John D. Rockefeller, Sr.* (New York: Random House, 1998), pp. 130 and 149–52.

Rockefeller would be paid $.40 on every barrel of crude oil his competitors shipped into Cleveland and $.50 on every barrel of refined oil shipped to New York. Under this venal scheme, the more a competitor shipped, the more Rockefeller's transportation costs were lowered. While competitors were charged $2.80 on the critical route (Pennsylvania oil regions–Cleveland–New York), Rockefeller paid only $1.00. Moreover, the railroads agreed to give the conspirators waybills detailing competitors' shipments; a better espionage system would be hard to find.

Why did the railroads agree to this plot? There were several reasons. First, it removed the uncertainty of cutthroat competition. Oil traffic was guaranteed in large volume. Second, the refiners provided services to the railroads including tank cars, loading facilities, and insurance. And third, railroad executives received stock in the participating refineries, giving them a stake in their success.

The consequences of the South Improvement Plan were predictable. Nonparticipating refiners faced bloated transportation costs and would be uncompetitive. They had two choices. Either they could sell to Rockefeller and his allies, or they could stand on principle and go bankrupt. When they sold, as they must, the flaw in industry structure would be corrected. Rockefeller intended to acquire them, then close them or limit their capacity. This would give him market power to stabilize the price of both crude oil and refined products. And the rebates would be a formidable barrier to new entrants.

THE CONSPIRACY PLAYS OUT

In February of 1872 the new freight rates were announced. Quickly, the full design was revealed, causing widespread, explosive rage in the oil regions. Although it broke no laws, it overstepped prevailing norms. People believed that since railroads got their right-of-ways from the public they had a duty to serve shippers fairly. Volume discounts might be justified, but this shakedown was extortionate. Producers and refiners in the oil regions boycotted the conspirators and the railroads.

Rockefeller, seen as the prime mover behind the South Improvement Plan, was vilified in the industry and the press. His wife feared for his life. Yet he never wavered. "It was right," he said of the plan. "I knew it as a matter of conscience. It was right between me and my God."[4] As journalist Ida Tarbell noted, Rockefeller was not squeamish about such business affairs.

> Mr. Rockefeller was "good." There was no more faithful Baptist in Cleveland than he. Every enterprise of that church he had supported liberally from his youth. He gave to its poor. He visited its sick. He wept with its suffering. Moreover, he gave unostentatiously to many outside charities. . . . Yet he was willing to strain every nerve to obtain himself special and unjust privileges from the railroads which were bound to ruin every man in the oil business not sharing them with him.[5]

Within a month, the weight of negative public opinion and loss of revenue caused the railroads to cave in. They rescinded the discriminatory rate structure. All appearances were of a Rockefeller defeat, but appearances deceived. Rockefeller had moved quickly, meeting one by one with rival refiners, explaining the rebate scheme and its salutary effect on the industry, and asking to buy them out. He offered the exact value of the business in cash or, preferably, in Standard Oil Company stock.

By the time the railroads reset their rates, Rockefeller had bought out 21 of his 26 Cleveland competitors. Some acquisitions were simply dismantled to reduce surplus capacity. He now dominated Cleveland, the country's major refining center, and controlled more than a quarter of U.S. capacity. In secrecy, he negotiated a new rebate agreement with the Erie Railroad. Of these actions, Ida Tarbell noted sardonically: "He had a mind which, stopped by a wall, burrows under or creeps around."[6] Regardless of methods, he had, indeed, corrected structural flaws in the oil industry. It would attract more capital. If any circumstance cast a shadow over this striking victory, it was that public opinion had turned against him. From then on, he was reviled as an unfair competitor, hatred of him growing apace with his burgeoning wealth. He never understood why.

[4] Peter Collier and David Horowitz, *The Rockefellers: An American Dynasty* (New York: New American Library, 1976), p. 11.

[5] Ida M. Tarbell, *The History of the Standard Oil Company,* vol. 1 (Gloucester, MA: Peter Smith, 1963), p. 43.

[6] Ibid., p. 99.

ONWARD THE COURSE OF EMPIRE

Rockefeller, now 33, was wealthy. Yet he drove on, compelled to finish a grand design, to spread his pattern over the industry landscape, to conform it to his vision.

He continued the strategy of horizontal integration at the refinery level by absorbing more and more of his competitors. As the size of Standard Oil increased, Rockefeller gained added leverage over the railroads. Like an orchestra conductor he played them against each other, granting shares of the oil traffic in return for rebates that gave him a decisive advantage.

Some competitors stubbornly clung to their businesses, partly out of hatred for Rockefeller. He made them "sweat" and "feel sick" until they sold.[7] The fleets of tank cars that he leased to railroads were often "unavailable" to ship feedstock and distillates to and from such refiners. Rockefeller concealed many of his acquisitions, disguising the full sweep of his drive to monopoly. These companies were the Trojan horses in his war against rival refiners. They seemed independent but secretly helped to undermine Standard's competitors. Often they were at the center of elaborate pricing conspiracies involving code words in telegrams such as "doubters" for refiners and "mixer" for railroad drawbacks. The phantoms bought some refiners who refused in principle to sell out to Standard Oil. Their existence confronted independents with a dark, mysterious force that could not be brought into the light and fought.

THE STANDARD OIL TRUST

By 1882 Rockefeller's company was capitalized at $70 million and produced 90 percent of the nation's refining output. Its main product, illuminating oil, was changing the way people lived. Before the sale of affordable illuminating oil of good quality, most Americans went to bed with darkness. They could not afford expensive candles or whale oil and feared using the unstable kerosene made by early, small refiners. With the rise of Rockefeller's colossus, they had reliable, inexpensive light and stayed up. Their lives, and the life of the nation, changed.

Rockefeller reorganized Standard Oil as a trust.[8] His purpose was to make state regulation more difficult. Soon other large companies followed his lead, adopting the trust form to avoid government restrictions. Inside Standard Oil, Rockefeller's organizing skills were extraordinary. Working with a loyal inner circle of managers, he directed his far-flung empire from headquarters at 26 Broadway in New York City. As he absorbed his competitors, so had he co-opted the best minds in the industry and much of Standard's success is attributable to this stellar supporting cast. Though dominant, Rockefeller delegated great responsibility to his managers. High-level committees controlled business operations. He circulated monthly cost statements for each refinery, causing fierce internal competition among their managers that led to high performance. He set up a network of informants around the globe. Critics called them spies, but they functioned as a well-organized information system. A perfectionist, he insisted on having a statement of the exact net worth of Standard Oil on his desk every morning. Oil prices always were calculated to three decimals. He was so dogged about efficiency and recycling that his Standard Oil plants might win environmental awards were they operating today. At night he prowled the headquarters turning down wicks in oil lamps.

His management style was one of formal politeness. He never spoke harshly to any employee. Once, when a manager leaked information to the press, Rockefeller said to his secretary: "Suggest to Mr. Blank that he would do admirably as a newspaper man, and that we shall not need his services after the close of this month."[9] Compared with other moguls of that era, he lived simply. He had two large estates, in Cleveland and New York, but neither was too ostentatious. He read the Bible daily, continued regular attendance at a Baptist church, and gave generously to charities.

Rockefeller's organizing skills were critical to his success. Discussions often focus on his ethics, but the

---

[7] Abels, *The Rockefeller Billions*, p. 35.

[8] A trust is a method of controlling a number of companies in which the voting stock of each company is transferred to a board of trustees. The trustees then have the power to coordinate the operations of all companies in the group. This organizing form is no longer legal in the United States.

[9] Quoted in "A Great Monopoly's Work: An Inner View of the Standard Oil Company," *New York Times*, February 27, 1883, p. 1.

key to Standard Oil's long-term domination lay elsewhere. The company was an immense, organized force opposed only by smaller, less united adversaries. Its success came from centralized, coordinated effort. Compromising methods, to the extent they were used, were of far less importance. [10]

EXTENDING DOMINATION

By the 1880s Standard Oil had overwhelming market power. Its embrace of refining activity was virtually complete, and it had moved into drilling, pipelines, storage tanks, transportation, and marketing of finished products. By now the entire world was addicted to kerosene and other petroleum products, and Standard's international sales grew.

Rockefeller's dominating competitive philosophy prevailed. His marketing agents were ordered to destroy independent suppliers. To suppress competition, his employees pioneered fanatical customer service. The intelligence-gathering network paid competitors' employees to pass information to Standard Oil. Railroad agents were bribed to misroute shipments. Standard workers climbed on competitors' tank cars and measured the contents. Price warfare was relentless. A stubborn competitor often found Standard selling kerosene to its customers at a price substantially below production cost.

Rockefeller himself was never proved to be directly involved in flagrant misconduct. He blamed criminal and unethical actions on overzealous subordinates. His critics thought the strategy of suffocating small rivals and policies such as that requiring regular written intelligence reports encouraged degenerative ethics among his minions.

Rockefeller saw Standard Oil as a stabilizing force in the industry and as a righteous crusade to illuminate the world. How, as a good Christian devoted to the moral injunctions of the Bible, was Rockefeller able to suborn such vicious behavior in commerce? One biographer, Allan Nevins, gives this explanation:

> From a chaotic industry he was building an efficient industrial empire for what seemed to him the good not only of its heads but of the general public. If he relaxed his general methods of warfare . . . a multitude of small competitors would smash his

empire and plunge the oil business back to chaos. He always believed in what William McKinley called "benevolent assimilation"; he preferred to buy out rivals on decent terms, and to employ the ablest competitors as helpers. It was when his terms were refused that he ruthlessly crushed the "outsiders." . . . It seemed to him better that a limited number of small businesses should die than that the whole industry should go through a constant process of half-dying, reviving, and again half-dying.[11]

THE STANDARD OIL TRUST UNDER ATTACK

Standard Oil continued to grow, doubling in size before the turn of the century and doubling again by 1905.[12] Eventually its very size brought a flood of criticism that complicated operations. Predatory monopoly was at odds with prevailing beliefs about individual rights and free competition. The states tried to regulate Standard Oil and filed antitrust suits against it. Overwrought muckrakers lashed out at Rockefeller. Because of him, wrote one, "hundreds and thousands of men have been ruined."[13] Rockefeller was the personification of greed in political cartoons. Politicians not suborned by his bribery lambasted him.

Rockefeller, by now the richest American, was shaken by public hatred. He hired bodyguards and slept with a revolver. Pinkerton detectives were present at church on Sundays to handle the gawkers and shouters who appeared. He developed a digestive ailment so severe that he could eat only a few bland foods, and upon his doctor's advice he stopped daily office work. By 1896 he appeared only rarely at 26 Broadway. Soon he was afflicted with a nervous disorder and lost all his hair.

As attacks on Rockefeller grew, the vise of government regulation tightened on his company. A swarm of lawsuits and legislative hearings hung about it. Finally, in 1911, the Supreme Court ordered its breakup under the Sherman Antitrust Act, holding that its monopoly position was an "undue" restraint on trade

---

[10] David M. Chalmers, ed., "Introductory Essay," in Ida M. Tarbell, *The History of the Standard Oil Company, Briefer Version* (Mineola, NY: Dover, 2003), pp. xvii–xviii.

[11] Allan Nevins, *Study in Power: John D. Rockefeller,* vol. 2 (New York: Scribner, 1953), p. 433.

[12] Ibid., app. 3, p. 478.

[13] Henry Demarest Lloyd, "Story of a Great Monopoly," *The Atlantic,* March 1881, p. 320.

that violated the "standard of reason."[14] The company was given six months to separate into 39 independent firms. The breakup consisted mainly of moving the desks of managers at 26 Broadway and was a financial windfall for Rockefeller, who received shares of stock in all the companies, the prices of which were driven up by frenzied public buying. Before the breakup kerosene sales had buoyed the company. However, just as electric light bulbs were replacing oil lamps, the automobile jolted demand for another petroleum distillate—gasoline. Rockefeller, who was 71 at the time of the breakup and would live another 26 years, earned new fortunes simply by maintaining his equity in the separate companies.

Rockefeller remained a source of fascination for the American public. As *The Wall Street Journal* noted, "[t]he richest man in a world where money is power is necessarily a fascinating object of study."[15] This being so, it was his enduring misfortune that muckraking journalist Ida Tarbell turned her gaze on him.

Tarbell wrote two unflattering character studies and a detailed, two-volume biography of Rockefeller, all serialized in the widely read *McClure's Magazine* between 1902 and 1905. Her unsentimental words were no less ruthless than the actions of the old man himself. Although admitting that Rockefeller and Standard Oil had some measure of "legitimate greatness," she was obsessed with his flaws. In one essay she found "something indefinably repulsive" in his appearance, writing that his mouth was "the cruelest feature of his face," and that his nose "rose like a thorn."[16] Such ad hominem attacks lacked merit but, in addition, Tarbell delved deeply into Rockefeller's career, producing narratives of exquisite detail. The thesis she conveyed to the public was that by his singular example, Rockefeller was responsible for debasing the moral tone of American business. She believed his story incited legions of the ambitious to use cold-blooded methods, teaching them that success justifies itself. Like the master, the junior scoundrels often cited biblical verse to support their actions.

Few public figures have a nemesis such as Ida Tarbell. Her relentless pen, along with others,

deprived him of some public adulation he may have craved and her scholarship permanently defined him. Her intricate period research cannot be duplicated and subsequent biographers, even more friendly ones, must go to it for insight. Rockefeller may or may not have deserved such a definitive hand. He called her a "poisonous woman." [17]

THE GREAT ALMONER

Since childhood Rockefeller had made charitable donations and, as his fortune accumulated, he increased them. After 1884 the total was never less than $100,000 a year, and after 1892 it was usually over $1 million and sometimes far more. In his mind, these benefactions were linked to his duty as a good Christian to uplift humanity. To a reporter he once said:

> I believe the power to make money is a gift from God—just as are the instincts for art, music, literature, the doctor's talent, yours—to be developed and used to the best of our ability for the good of mankind. Having been endowed with the gift I possess, I believe it is my duty to make money and still more money and to use the money I make for the good of my fellow-man according to the dictates of my conscience.[18]

Over his lifetime, Rockefeller gave gifts of approximately $550 million. He gave, for example, $8.2 million for the construction of Peking Union Medical College in response to the need to educate doctors in China. He gave $50 million to the University of Chicago. He created charitable trusts and endowed them with millions. One such trust was the General Education Board, set up in 1902, which started 1,600 new high schools. Another, the Rockefeller Sanitary Commission, succeeded in eradicating hookworm in the South. The largest was the Rockefeller Foundation, established in 1913 and endowed with $200 million. Its purpose was "to promote the well-being of mankind throughout the world." Rockefeller always said, however, that the greatest philanthropy of all was developing the earth's natural resources and employing people. Critics greeted his gifts with skepticism, thinking them atonement for years of plundering American society.

In his later years, Rockefeller lived a secluded, placid existence on his great Pocantico estate in

[14] *Standard Oil Company of New Jersey v. United States,* 31 U.S. 221. It was an 8–1 decision.

[15] "Incarnate Business," *The Wall Street Journal,* June 26, 1905, p. 1.

[16] Ida Tarbell, "John D. Rockefeller: A Character Study," *McClure's,* August 1905, p. 386.

[17] Chernow, *Titan: The Life of John D. Rockefeller, Sr.,* p. xxii.

[18] Quoted in Abels, *The Rockefeller Billions,* p. 280.

John D. Rockefeller at age 65. This photograph was taken shortly after a disease, generalized alopecia, caused him to lose his hair. Source: Library of Congress, Prints and Photographs Collection, LC-USZ62-123825.

New York, which had 75 buildings and 70 miles of roads. As years passed, the public grew increasingly fond of him. Memories of his early business career dimmed, and a new generation viewed him in the glow of his huge charitable contributions. For many years, he carried shiny nickels and dimes in his pockets to give to children and well-wishers.

On his 86th birthday he wrote the following verse.

> I was early taught to work as well as play,
> My life has been one long, happy holiday;
> Full of work and full of play—
> I dropped the worry on the way—
> And God was good to me every day.

He died in 1937 at the age of 97. His estate was valued at $26,410,837. He had given the rest away.

Questions

1. With reference to the levels and spheres of corporate power discussed in the chapter, how did the power of Standard Oil change society? Was this power exercised in keeping with the social contract of Rockefeller's era?

2. How does the story of Standard Oil illustrate the limits of business power? Does it better illustrate the dominance theory or the pluralist theory discussed in the chapter?

3. Did Rockefeller himself ever act unethically? By the standards of his day? By those of today? How could he simultaneously be a devout Christian and a ruthless monopolist? Is there any contradiction between his personal and business ethics?

4. In the utilitarian sense of accomplishing the greatest good for the greatest number in society, was the Standard Oil Company a net plus or a minus? On balance, did the company meet its responsibilities to society?

5. Did strategies of Standard Oil encourage unethical behavior? Could Rockefeller's vision have been fulfilled using "nicer" tactics?

Chapter Four

Critics of Business

Mary "Mother" Jones

In the early years of the twentieth century Mary Jones (1837–1930), known as Mother Jones, was one of the most notable women in America. Emerging from personal tragedy, she created a singular persona and hurled herself against big corporations and the capitalist system that sustained them. Hers was an era of great change, dissent, and conflict. It was the ideal stage for a defiant performance.

She was born in 1837 as Mary Harris in Cork, Ireland. When she was eight years old, a fungus blighted the nation's potato crop, causing a terrible famine. She emigrated with her family to Toronto and there grew up, graduated from a convent school, and became a schoolteacher. Eventually she moved to Memphis and married an iron molder named George Jones. Between 1862 and 1867 they had four children. She devoted herself to cooking, cleaning, and sewing for the family. Then yellow fever struck.

The deadly epidemic came in the fall of 1867. As mortality rose, rich families left town, leaving those who could not afford travel to become victims. The sounds of death carts taking bodies away filled neighborhoods. Mary Jones describes what happened to her.

> All about my house I could hear weeping and the cries of delirium. One by one, my four little children sickened and died. I washed their little bodies and got them ready for burial. My husband caught the fever and died. I sat alone through nights of grief. No one came to me. No one could.[1]

She nursed the sick until the plague ended, then returned to Chicago to set up a dressmaking business. She often worked for wealthy society matrons.

> I had ample opportunity to observe the luxury and extravagance of their lives. Often while sewing for the lords and barons who lived in magnificence on the Lake Shore Drive, I would look out of the plate glass windows and see the poor, shivering wretches, jobless and hungry, walking along the frozen lake front. The contrast of their condition with that of the tropical comfort of the people for whom I sewed was painful to me. My employers seemed neither to notice nor to care.[2]

[1] Mary Field Parton, ed., *The Autobiography of Mother Jones* (Chicago: C. H. Kerr, 1925), p. 12.

[2] Ibid., chap. 1, p. 13.

Several years passed, then in 1871 the Great Chicago Fire burned her business and left her destitute. After the fire she attended evening meetings of the Knights of Labor, an early union, and became engrossed in the fight of industrial workers for better wages and conditions. The perspective of class war began to dominate her view of society. She felt that workers were enslaved by corporate employers and by the corrupt politicians and judges who did their bidding. She believed that only by overthrowing capitalism could the laboring class end its bondage and usher in a new day of socialism, so she joined a small socialist political party.

For almost two decades Mary Jones worked in obscurity for labor causes and during this time she created the persona that would make her powerful and famous. Mary Jones became Mother Jones. The loss of her own family had freed her to take on another, to adopt the downtrodden. In an era when women had no vote, held no leadership positions, and received no encouragement to speak up, she would use this metaphor of motherhood to give her power.

She rose to prominence as an organizer for the United Mine Workers. Horrible working conditions prevailed in coal mines. Miners worked 10- and 12-hour days in damp, dusty, cramped, dangerous tunnels. Wages were so low that to get by mining families put their children to work. Boys as young as eight years old toiled six or seven days a week, some spending so many hours in cramped shafts that their bones grew irregularly and they could not stand straight as adults. Textile mills were built near mining towns to employ the miners' wives and daughters. The United Mine Workers wanted to unionize the miners, but the coal companies viciously resisted. Organizers were followed and observed. Miners who shook an organizer's hand were fired. Hired thugs beat up troublemakers. Companies had friendly judges convene lunacy hearings and commit prounion employees to asylums. The miners wanted unions, but they were intimidated.

In the late 1890s Mother Jones arrived in Pennsylvania coal country. At 60 years old she looked like a grandmother. She stood five feet tall with silver hair and sharp blue eyes. With great energy she worked the coal towns. She was an explosive orator with a vocal range from shrill cries to a forceful, low pitch that mesmerized listeners. She knew the miners' language and spoke in colorful terms, calling mine owners "a crew of pirates," "a gang of thieves," and "cowards." She called the men her "boys" and as their "mother" told them to stand up to the companies.

During a bitter strike in 1900 when some miners were losing their nerve she organized marches of the miners' wives. The women paraded to work sites wearing aprons, waving mops, and banging pans. Laughing company guards saw no danger from the comical processions and let them through, not realizing how Mother Jones had cleverly dramatized the role of aggrieved wives and mothers fighting for the welfare of their families. She scolded the men, telling them they were shamed if their wives stood up to the companies and they did not.

Mother Jones used ironic wit to puncture establishment pretensions. In 1902 she was arrested in West Virginia after the coal companies got an injunction against union organizing. In court, the judge suspended her sentence, but advised her that because she was a woman it would be "better far for her to follow the lines and paths which the Allwise Being intended her sex should pursue." She appreciated the advice, she said, adding that it was no surprise he was taking the company's side, since

Mary "Mother" Jones. Source: Library of Congress, Prints and Photographs Collection, LC-USZ62-7678.

experience had taught her that "robbers tend to like each other."[3] When asked by a Princeton professor to address his class, she brought with her a stooped and pale 10-year-old boy. "Here's a textbook on economics," she said. "He gets three dollars a week . . . [working] in a carpet factory ten hours a day while the children of the rich are getting higher education."[4] She had a favorite story for audiences: "I asked a man in prison once how he happened to get there. He had stolen a pair of shoes. I told him that if he had stolen a railroad he could be a United States Senator."[5]

Eventually, Mother Jones fell out with the United Mine Workers because she was more militant than its leadership. She became a lecturer for the Socialist Party, but in time she renounced socialism. She was a doer, not an ideologue, and she lacked patience with hairsplitting doctrinal debates among intellectuals who led comfortable lives. However, in 1905 she helped launch the International Workers of the World (IWW), a radical union dedicated to overthrowing American capitalism. By 1911 she had returned to the front lines in mining regions. Later, she marched with striking

---

[3] Gene R. Nichol, Jr., "Fighting Poverty with Virtue," *Michigan Law Review,* May 2002, p. 1661.

[4] Quoted in Marilyn Jurich, "The Female Trickster—Known as Trickstar—As Exemplified by Two American Legendary Women, 'Billy' Tipton and Mother Jones," *Journal of American Culture,* Spring 1999, p. 69.

[5] "Mother Jones Speaks to Coney Island Crowd," *New York Times,* July 27, 1903.

garment and streetcar workers in New York City. In 1916 she started a riot by two hundred wives of streetcar workers with an inflammatory speech, telling them: "You ought to be out raising hell."[6]

By the 1920s Mother Jones had grown disillusioned with unions. She quit the IWW saying it was more interested in symbolic displays than in concrete victories. Other unions had grown comfortable with the corporate establishment. She had contempt for union leaders motivated by their own status and importance in society and called John L. Lewis, president of the United Mine Workers, a "pie counter hunter."[7] She retired from public life, speaking out now and then, and died in 1930 at the age of 92.

Today Mother Jones is little remembered. Her time passed and the specific labor abuses that enraged her are mostly ended. Perhaps her invective is unmatched today. She defined "monster capitalism," as a "robber system" supported by the "national gang of burglars of Wall Street." The corporations she attacked had "snake brains"and were run by "idiots" and "commercial pirates." But her ideas live on. Although her life was unique in its tragedy and drama, her attacks were based on enduring values that recycle through time. We may forget Mother Jones, but we hear her in today's business critics. In this chapter we explore the birth and life of these values.

ORIGINS OF CRITICAL ATTITUDES TOWARD BUSINESS

There are two underlying sources of criticism of business, one ancient and the other modern. The first is the belief that people in business place profit before more worthy values such as honesty, truth, justice, love, piety, aesthetics, tranquillity, and respect for nature. The second is the strain placed on societies by economic development. During industrialization and later, when market economies grow large and complex, business has a range of problematic impacts on societies. We will discuss both fundamental sources of criticism. We begin in the ancient Mediterranean world.

The Greeks and Romans

agrarian society
A society with a largely agricultural economy.

The earliest societies were agrarian in nature. An *agrarian society* is a preindustrial society in which economic, political, and cultural values are based on agricultural experience. In these societies, most people worked the land for subsistence. No industrial centers or mass markets existed, so business activity beyond barter and exchange was a tiny part of the economy. The activities of merchants were often thought unprincipled because their sharp trading practices clashed with the traditional, more altruistic values of family and clan relations among farmers. Merchants typically had lower class status than officials, farmers, soldiers, artisans, and teachers.

The extraordinary civilizations of ancient Greece and Rome were based on subsistence agriculture. Economic activity by merchants, bankers, and manufacturers was limited. The largest factory in Athens, for example, employed 120 workers

[6] "Car Riot Started by 'Mother' Jones," *New York Times,* October 6, 1916, p. 1.
[7] Quoted in Elliot J. Gorn, Mother Jones: *The Most Dangerous Woman in America* (New York: Hill and Wang, 2001), p. 249.

making shields.[8] Commercial activity was greater in Rome, but it was still mainly an agrarian society. Perhaps because industry was so limited in both societies, inaccurate economic doctrines arose to explain commercial activity.[9] For example, the desire for riches was suspect due to the popular belief that the amount of wealth was fixed. If so, an individual accumulated wealth only by subtracting from the share of others. This is believable logic in an agrarian society because the land on which the economy is based is fixed in amount.

Philosophers moved into this realm of intellectual error, reasoning that profit seeking was an inferior motive and that commercial activity led to excess, corruption, and misery. Their views are of lasting significance because, as with many topics of discourse in Western civilization, they first defined the terms of debate over the ranking of profit relative to other values. In particular, both Plato and Aristotle articulated the fundamental indictment that casts an everlasting shadow over business.

Plato believed that insatiable appetites existed in every person. These could be controlled only by inner virtues painstakingly acquired through character development. The pursuit of money was one such appetite, and Plato thought that when people engaged in trade they inevitably succumbed to the temptation of excess and became grasping. In a society, as with an individual, wealth spawned evils, including inequality, envy, class conflict, and war. "Virtue and wealth," he argued, "are balanced against one another in the scales."[10] Rulers of the utopian society he conceived in *The Republic* were prohibited from owning possessions for fear they would be corrupted and turn into tyrants. So troubled was he about this that they were forbidden even to touch gold or silver.

Aristotle believed there was a benign form of acquisition that consisted of getting the things needed for subsistence. This kind of acquisition was natural and moderate. However, after trading and monetary systems arose, the art of acquisition was no longer practiced this simple way. Instead, merchants studied the techniques of commerce, figuring out how to make the greatest profit, seeking not the necessities, but unlimited pools of money. Aristotle thought this was a lower form of acquisition because it was activity that did not contribute to inner virtue.

For Aristotle, happiness is the ultimate goal of life. It comes to those who develop character virtues such as courage, temperance, justice, and wisdom. He called these virtues "goods of the soul" and held them superior to "external goods," which he defined as possessions and money. Aristotle believed that the amount of happiness a person gained in life was equal to the amount of virtue accumulated in the soul. Since material possessions beyond those needed for subsistence added nothing to the store of virtue in the soul, it followed that they contributed nothing to happiness; thus, it was a waste or "perversion" of any virtue to apply it toward the acquisition of excess. "The proper function of courage, for example, is not to produce money but to give confidence," he wrote.[11]

---

[8] Will Durant, *The Life of Greece* (New York: Simon & Schuster, 1939), p. 272.

[9] John Kenneth Galbraith, *Economics in Perspective* (Boston: Houghton Mifflin, 1987), pp. 9–10.

[10] *The Republic*, trans. F. M. Cornford (New York: Oxford University Press, 1945), p. 274.

[11] In *Politics*, trans. Ernest Barker (New York: Oxford University Press, 1962), book I, chap. X, § 17. See also book VII, chap. 1, §§ 1–10.

Thus, both Plato and Aristotle relegated the profit motive to the sphere of lower or base impulses, a place from which it would not escape for centuries and then only partially. Soon, Roman law would forbid the senatorial class from making business investments (and the law would be widely circumvented). Likewise, the Stoic philosophers of Rome, including Epictetus and Marcus Aurelius, taught that the truly rich person possessed inner peace rather than capital or property. "Asked, 'Who is the rich man?' Epictetus replied, 'He who is content.'"[12] These sages looked down on merchants of their day as materialists who, in pursuit of wealth, sacrificed character development. Of course, this did not deter the merchants from accumulating fortunes and neglecting the study of ideals. The scornful ethos of the philosophers, though potent enough to endure and to beget perennial hostility, has never had enough power to suppress the tide of commerce.

The Medieval World

During the Middle Ages, the prevailing theology of the Roman Catholic Church was intolerant of profit seeking. As the Christian religion arose, its early practitioners had been persecuted by the wealthy and corrupt ruling class of Rome. The Church, then, rejected a focus on wealth and sought special status for the poor. Saint Augustine, the towering figure of early Church doctrine, accepted the idea that material wealth was fixed in supply. To become rich, a person necessarily sinned by accumulation that violated the natural equality of Creation. Moreover, the love of material things was a snare that pulled the soul away from God.[13]

just price
A price giving a moderate profit; one inspired by fairness, not greed.

The Church's most definitive theologian, St. Thomas Aquinas, was greatly influenced by the ideas of Aristotle when he set forth Church canon about the ethics of profit making and lending money. Merchants were exhorted to charge a *just price* for their wares, a price that incorporated a modest profit just adequate to maintain them in the social station to which they were born. The just price stands in contrast to the modern idea of a *market price* determined by supply and demand without any moral dimension. Today we hear echoes of medieval theology when consumers complain that high prices for a scarce product are unjust. Catholicism also condemned *usury*, or the lending of money for interest. By the twelfth and thirteenth centuries, however, the money supply and economic activity had greatly expanded and interest-bearing loans were commonplace. "Commercial activity," notes historian Will Durant, "proved stronger than fear of prison or hell."[14] In time, the Church backed away from the dogma of just price and usury. It was a slow process. Church teaching making lending money for interest a sin was not officially renounced until 1917.

market price
A price determined by the interaction of supply and demand.

usury
The lending of money for interest.

Protestant ethic
The belief that hard work and adherence to a set of virtues such as thrift, saving, and sobriety would bring wealth and God's approval.

The Modern World

As business activity accelerated during the Renaissance, new theories arose to justify previously condemned practices. Two are of great importance. First, is the rise of the *Protestant ethic* in the sixteenth century. The Protestant reformers Martin

---

[12] *The Golden Sayings of Epictetus,* trans. Hastings Crossley, in Charles W. Eliot, ed., *Plato, Epictetus, Marcus Aurelius* (Danbury, CT: Grolier, 1980), p. 179.

[13] Saint Augustine, *The City of God,* trans. Gerald G. Walsh et al. (New York: Image Books, 1958), book XIX, chap. 17. This work was completed in A.D. 426.

[14] *The Age of Faith* (New York: Simon & Schuster, 1950), p. 631.

Luther and John Calvin believed that work was a means of serving God and that if a person earned great wealth through hard work it was a sign of God's approval. This confronted the Church's antagonism toward commerce with a new doctrine that removed moral suspicion of wealth. It contradicted the belief that pursuit of money corrupted the soul. Second, in 1776 Adam Smith published his theory of capitalism, writing that free markets harnessed greed for the public good and protected consumers from abuse. This defied the Church's insistence on the idea of a just price. Moreover, visible wealth creation in expanding economies forcefully countered the notion that only a more or less fixed amount of wealth existed in a society. These developments ended the domination of doctrines that made business activity seem faintly criminal and released new energies into commerce. But the broom of doctrinal reform failed to make a clean sweep, and many business critics clung to the old approbations of the Greek philosophers and of the Church.

In addition, just when old strictures were loosening, the industrial revolution created new tensions that reinforced critical attitudes about business. These new tensions arose as inventions and industries transformed agrarian societies and challenged traditional values with modern alternatives. During industrialization, rural, slow-paced, stable societies are swiftly and dramatically altered. They become urban and fast-paced. More emphasis is placed on material things and people's values shift. Wealth creation overwhelms self-restraint. Consumption supplants thrift and saving. Conquest of nature replaces awe of nature.

THE AMERICAN CRITIQUE OF BUSINESS

As societies modernize, the antiquarian values of Greece live on in the charges of critics who are troubled by these changes. Always, the fundamental critique is altered to fit current circumstances. We will see how this happened in the United States.

The Colonial Era

The American nation was colonized by corporations. The colonists who landed at Jamestown, Virginia, in 1606 were sponsored by investors in the London Company, who hoped to make a fortune by discovering gold in the New World. Instead, the colonists found a mild strain of native tobacco that caused a sensation in England (and became the basis for the plantation economy that would rise in the South). The Pilgrims who came in the *Mayflower* to Cape Cod, Massachusetts, in 1620 had fled persecution to set up a religious colony. But their voyage was financed by the Plymouth Company, whose backers sought to make a profit. To repay their debt and to buy manufactured goods they exported furs and forest products such as timber, tar, and turpentine. In this way the early colonists became lively traders.

As international trade in coastal regions expanded, settlers moved inland, creating a broad agrarian base for the economy. These frontier farms seethed with profit-oriented activity. Unlike European peasants, American farmers owned their land and this turned them into little capitalists. Most tried to make money by raising crops for market. Some were land speculators. Others built and ran grain mills and in other ways employed their capital like the traders and merchants in towns.

The popular theoretician of the rising capitalist spirit was Benjamin Franklin (1706–1790). Franklin began a business career at the age of 22 by opening a printing shop. He then bought several newspapers and retired rich at the age of 42. During travels in Europe he became acquainted with Adam Smith, who shared parts of the manuscript for *Wealth of Nations* with him. Franklin came to accept Smith's then-radical views on the superiority of laissez-faire markets. Writing prolifically, Franklin gave form to a new American business ethos.

In 1732 he published the first annual *Poor Richard's Almanack,* an eclectic book of facts, information, and self-help advice. Over many years the *Almanack* carried aphorisms and maxims about the road to success in business, a road open to all who practiced virtues such as hard work, thrift, and frugality. "The sleeping Fox catches no Poultry." "Lost Time is never found again." "Diligence is the Mother of Good Luck." "The Art of getting Riches consists very much in Thrift."[15]

Unlike the Old World theologians who taught that commercial success was slightly sinful, Franklin taught that God would approve the pursuit of self-interest and wealth. "God gives all things to Industry."[16] He made business activity synonymous with traditional virtues and released it from moral suspicion. His teaching resonated with the American condition and he became the prophet of a vibrant economy. Not surprisingly, his *Almanacks* were best sellers.

The Young Nation

The amalgam of a new land, a new people, and new thinking generated an early emphasis on business activity and material progress. Yet not everyone felt this was either inevitable or proper and dissent soon emerged. After independence in 1783 business interests were important in the new nation but not to the extent that they would be in time. There were few large companies. The economy was 90 percent agricultural, so the interests of farmers and planters dominated those of infant industry. A major debate arose over the direction of the economy, one that would define subsequent debate between business and its critics in America. It was played out in a bitter rivalry between two members of President George Washington's cabinet who differed both in temperament and ideas.

Alexander Hamilton (1755–1804), the first secretary of the treasury, was young, ambitious, brilliant, and inclined to action. He believed that industrial growth would increase national power and designed a grand scheme to promote manufacturing and finance. He was an arrogant, aloof leader who mistrusted the wisdom of common citizens. Having once said that "the people is a great beast," he favored rule by an economic elite.[17] Hamilton got Congress to approve his plans for taxation, debt financing, tariffs to protect infant industry, and creation of a national bank, setting a policy of industrialization in motion.

---

[15] Quotations are in *Poor Richard's Almanack,* 1749, and "The Way to Wealth," Preface to *Poor Richard Improved,* 1758, in Nathan G. Goodman, ed., *The Autobiography of Benjamin Franklin and Selections from his other Writings* (New York: Carlton House, 1932), pp. 198, 206, 207.

[16] Ibid., "The Way to Wealth," p. 207.

[17] Quoted in Vernon Louis Parrington, *Main Currents in American Thought,* vol. 1 (New York: Harcourt, Brace, 1958), p. 300; originally published in 1927.

He was opposed by Secretary of State Thomas Jefferson (1743–1826), one of America's most original and philosophical minds. Jefferson was a shy man who avoided conflict. His thinking achieved great depth, but he was less a man of action than Hamilton. His weakness as a manager is summed up in a revealing statement. "We can only be answerable for the orders we give, and not for their execution."[18] He had grown up in sparsely populated frontier areas of Virginia, never having seen a village of more than 20 houses until he was 18 years old. Awed by the common sense and resourcefulness of the settlers he knew, he formed the opinion that an agrarian economy of landowning farmers was the ideal social order.

Reading books as much as 15 hours a day, he gathered arguments to reinforce his convictions. According to Jefferson, America should aspire to spread farming over its immense, unsettled territory. He wrote that God placed "genuine virtue" in farmers, His chosen people. Manufacturing as an occupation "suffocates the germ of virtue," leads to venality, and corrupts the "manners and principles" of those who work at it.[19] He believed that an agrarian economy would prevent the rise of subservience to the wealthy and bring a state of equality, basic justice, and concern for the common good. Jefferson was well-read in Greek philosophy and it was no coincidence that he echoed the admonitions against commerce found in Plato and Aristotle. Even as he restated the Greeks, he laid the ground for more than two centuries of American business critics to follow.

Jefferson did not prevail. His agrarian ideal was fated to exist in the shadows of industrial growth. His theory of a nation of small farmers was somewhat nebulous and idealistic. As a policy it was no match for the more concrete design that Hamilton sold to Congress with great energy, a design that was surely more in tune with economic forces afoot in the young nation. With the support of business leaders, Hamilton carried out a bold, visionary program to stimulate the growth of manufacturing. His actions prepared the ground for the unexampled industrial growth that roared through the next century. He so angered Jefferson that the two rarely spoke even as they served together in George Washington's cabinet. Each had many followers and the conflict between their positions created not only the basis for subsequent criticism of business, but the basic cleavage that has prevailed in the American two-party system to the present.

1800–1865

The first half of the nineteenth century saw steady industrial growth. This aroused critics who clung to the values and life of the agrarian society that was fading before their eyes. Early in the century banking and manufacturing expanded. Markets were opened by tens of thousands of miles of new turnpikes. Completion of the 350-mile-long Erie Canal in 1825 inspired another 4,400 miles of canals to transport goods over water.[20] Railroads started to run in the 1830s. Immigrants arrived and cities grew. Business boomed.

[18] Letter to Baron F. W. von Stueben, March 10, 1781, quoted in Stanley Elkins and Eric McKitrick, *The Age of Federalism* (New York: Oxford University Press, 1993), p. 206.

[19] Quotes are from *Notes on Virginia,* in Adrienne Koch and William Peden, *The Life and Selected Writings of Thomas Jefferson* (New York: Random House, 1944), p. 280; first published in 1784.

[20] James Oliver Robertson, *America's Business* (New York: Hill and Wang, 1985), p. 81.

As the force of events put capitalism in control, agrarian romantics were pushed to the side, having only the power to object as cherished values were eroded. "Commerce," complained Ralph Waldo Emerson in 1839, "threatens to upset the balance of man and establish a new, universal Monarchy more tyrannical than Babylon or Rome."[21] Later, his friend Henry David Thoreau wrote to belittle a society in which this commerce smothered the poetry and grace of everyday life.

> This world is a place of business. What an infinite bustle! I am awakened almost every night by the panting of the locomotive. It interrupts my dreams. There is no sabbath. It would be glorious to see mankind at leisure for once. It is nothing but work, work, work. I cannot easily buy a blank-book to write thoughts in; they are commonly ruled for dollars and cents. . . . I think that there is nothing, not even crime, more opposed to poetry, to philosophy, ay, to life itself, than this incessant business.[22]

Among those who rejected capitalism, some tried to create alternative worlds. Beginning in the 1820s there was a frenzy of utopia building. Small bands of people who disdained the values prized in industrial society—materialism, competition, individualism, and tireless labor—built model communities intended to act as beacons for a better way. The largest was New Harmony, Indiana, founded in 1825 by Robert Owen (1771–1858), an English industrialist. Owen ran a large cotton mill in Scotland that had become a model for fair treatment of workers. Yet he believed that human values were corrupted by factory work and life in capitalist societies. He aspired to show that a society based on principles of equality, charity, cooperation, and moderation could flourish. At New Harmony money was abolished and the residents shared the fruits of communal labor.

Owen called his creation a "socialist" system and in the 1820s the term "socialism" first came into widespread use as a reference to Owen's philosophy. He started several other socialist communities and his ventures inspired others to form utopias based on socialist principles. More than 100 such communities appeared between 1820 and 1850.[23] A few were successful. The Oneida Community in New York lasted thirty-one years from 1848 to 1879. But most floundered, on average in less than two years.[24]

New Harmony emptied after only four years. Like other utopias it required businesslike activities for subsistence, but it attracted more loafers than skilled farmers and artisans who, in any case, could command higher material rewards in the outside world. After their initial zeal wore off, the sojourners tired of spartan living, regimentation, and rules to enforce cooperation. Most communes had programs to infuse socialist values into human natures tainted by capitalist schooling. Rarely did this work. One indication is that pilfering of supplies from common storehouses was common.

---

[21] Quoted from Emerson's *Journals,* vol. V, pp. 284–86, in Parrington, *Main Currents in American Thought,* vol. I, p. 386.

[22] "Life without Principle," *The Atlantic Monthly,* October 1863, pp. 484–85.

[23] W. Fitzhugh Brundage, *A Socialist Utopia in the New South* (Urbana: University of Illinois Press, 1996), p. 6.

[24] Joshua Muravchik, *Heaven on Earth: The Rise and Fall of Socialism* (San Francisco: Encounter Books, 2002), p. 51.

The agrarian and socialist communes failed utterly as alternatives to the bustling capitalism beyond their margins. Although a few new ones appeared as late as the 1890s, by the 1850s the idea had run its course. It failed in practice because it was based on romantic thinking, not on sustaining social forces. A series of withered utopias and a growing consensus on capitalist values adjourned the experiments. Socialism would return, but it awaited a new day and new ideas.

Populists and Progressives

At the end of the Civil War in 1865, America was still a predominantly rural, agrarian society of small, local businesses. But explosive industrial growth rapidly reshaped it, creating severe social problems in the process. Cities grew as farmers left the land and immigrants swelled slum populations. Corrupt political machines ran cities but failed to improve parlous conditions. Companies merged into huge national monopolies. These changes were the raw material of two movements critical of big business.

populist movement
A political reform movement that arose among farmers in the late 1800s. Populists blamed social problems on industry and sought radical reforms such as government ownership of railroads.

The first was the *populist movement*, a farmers' protest movement that began in the 1870s and led to formation of a national political party, the Populist Party, which assailed business interests until its decisive defeat in the presidential election of 1896. The movement arose soon after the Civil War, when farmers experienced falling crop prices. The declines were due mainly to overproduction by mechanized farm machinery and to competition from foreign farmers exploiting new transport technologies. Farmers overlooked these factors and blamed their distress on railroad companies, the largest businesses of the day, which frequently overcharged for crop hauling, and on "plutocrats" such as J. P. Morgan and other eastern bankers who controlled the loan companies that foreclosed on their farms.

In a typical tirade, Mary Lease, a populist orator who whipped up crowds of farmers at picnics and fairs, explained:

> Wall Street owns the country. It is no longer a government of the people, by the people and for the people, but a government of Wall Street and for Wall Street. The great common people of this country are slaves, and monopoly is the master. The West and South are bound and prostrate before the manufacturing East.[25]

To solve agrarian ills, the populists advocated government ownership of railroad, telegraph, and telephone companies and banks, a policy dagger that revealed their fundamental rejection of capitalism. They demanded direct election of U.S. senators, who at the time were picked by state legislatures corrupted with money from big business. And to ease credit they sought to abandon the gold standard and expand the money supply.

Historian Louis Galambos believes that despite the populist critique, there existed a great reservoir of respect for and confidence in business until the late 1880s.[26] After that, analysis of newspaper and magazine editorials shows mounting

[25] In John D. Hicks, *The Populist Revolt* (Minneapolis: University of Minnesota Press, 1931), p. 160.

[26] Louis Galambos, *The Public Image of Big Business in America, 1880–1940* (Baltimore: Johns Hopkins University Press, 1975), chap. 3. Galambos examined 8,976 items related to big business that were printed in newspapers and journals between 1879 and 1940, using content analysis to reconstruct rough measures of opinion among certain influential groups.

Was President McKinley the Wizard of Oz?

The Wonderful Wizard of Oz is one of the all-time best-selling children's books.[27] It was written by Lyman Frank Baum (1856–1919), an actor, salesclerk, and small-town newspaper editor who loved creating stories for children. On the surface, the book is a magical adventure in a fairyland where children are as wise as adults. However, the book has a deeper dimension. It is a parable of populism.[28]

The Wonderful Wizard of Oz satirizes the evils of an industrial society run by a moneyed elite of bankers and industrialists. "Oz" is the abbreviation for ounce, a measure of gold. It and the Yellow Brick Road allude to the hated gold standard. The main characters represent groups in society. Dorothy is the common person. The Scarecrow is the farmer. The Tin Woodsman is industrial labor. His rusted condition symbolizes factory closings in the depression years of the 1890s, and his lack of a heart hints that factories dehumanize workers. The Cowardly Lion is William Jennings Bryan, the defeated Populist Party candidate, whom Baum regarded as lacking sufficient courage. The

[27] L. Frank Baum (Chicago: Reilly & Britten, 1915), first published in 1900.

[28] The classic interpretation of symbolism is by Henry W. Littlefield, "The Wizard of Oz: Parable on Populism," *American Quarterly,* Spring 1964.

Wicked Witch of the East is a parody of the capitalist elite. She kept the munchkins, or "little people," in servitude. At the end of the Yellow Brick Road lay the Emerald City, or Washington, DC, where on arrival the group was met by the Wizard, representing the president of the United States. At the time Baum wrote the book, William McKinley was president, having defeated Bryan in 1896. Populists reviled McKinley because he had the backing of big trusts and he supported the hated gold standard.

At the conclusion, Dorothy melted the Wicked Witch of the East, the Wizard flew off in a balloon, the Scarecrow became the ruler of Oz, and the Tin Woodsman took charge of the East. This ending is the unrealized populist dream.

Baum's first motive was to be a child's storyteller, not to write political satire for adults. He never stated that the book contained populist themes, leading to debate over whether finding such symbolism is fair. Yet Baum lived in South Dakota while populism was emerging and he marched in Populist Party rallies. *The Wonderful Wizard of Oz* was written in 1898, at the height of ardor for reform. Therefore, it seems reasonable to think that Baum's tale was inspired by the politics of the day.

hostility toward large trusts. Soon the populists succeeded in electing many state and local officials, who enacted laws to regulate the railroads and provided the political groundswell behind creation of the Interstate Commerce Commission in 1887 to regulate railroads.

The populist movement was a diverse, unstable coalition of interests, including farmers, labor, prohibitionists, antimonopolists, silverites, and suffragists. These groups were held together for a time by a common, deep-seated hostility toward big companies. Ultimately, the populists failed to forge an effective political coalition and the movement was moribund after 1900 when William Jennings Bryan, the Populist Party's presidential candidate, was decisively defeated for a second time.

However, the populists refined a logic and lexicon for attacking business. They blamed adverse consequences of industrialization on monopoly, trusts, Wall Street, "silk-hatted Easterners," the soulless "loan sharks" and shameless "bloodhounds of money" who foreclosed on farms, and on corrupt politicians who worked as errand boys for the "moneybags" in a system of "plutocracy" (or rule by the wealthy).

Their criticisms were harsh and colorful. "The James Brothers and the Daltons were limited in their methods," thundered Mary Lease to a cheering crowd. "If they had operated on as large a scale as the millionaires of the country they could have built universities like Rockefeller. . . ."[29] In an essay on the virtues of farming as an occupation, Bryan wrote that for farmers "even the dumb animals are more wholesome companions than the bulls and bears of Wall Street."[30] Thomas Jefferson would likely have applauded.

It was, of course, too late for America to be a nation of farmers. This did not diminish the appeal of the populist message to large segments of the population. On the contrary, continued industrial growth has caused this message to resurface time and again up to the present, each time its vocabulary recycled and its content refined to fit current circumstances.

progressive movement
A turn-of-the-century political movement that associated moderate social reform with progress. Progressivism was less radical than populism and had wider appeal.

The second critical movement was the *progressive movement*, a broader reform effort lasting from about 1900 until the end of World War I in 1918. Fueled by wide moral indignation about social problems caused by industry, it had strong support from the urban middle class and professionals. Although a short-lived Progressive Party was formed and unsuccessfully ran Theodore Roosevelt for president in 1912, both the Democratic and Republican parties had powerful progressive wings. Unlike populism, progressivism was a mainstream political doctrine. Like populism, it was at root an effort to cure social ills by using government to control perceived abuses of big business.

Because of broad popular support, progressives were far more effective than populists in their reform efforts, and during their era a cleansing tide washed over business. "Turn the waters of pure public spirit into the corrupt pools of private interests," wrote Ernest Crosby, editor of *Cosmopolitan* magazine, "and wash the offensive accumulations away."[31] Progressives broke up trusts and monopolies, outlawed campaign contributions by corporations, restricted child labor, passed a corporate income tax, and regulated food and drug companies and public utilities. With the Seventeenth Amendment in 1913 requiring direct election of senators they completed part of the Populist agenda.

Socialists

socialism
The doctrine of a classless society in which property is collectively owned and income from labor is equally divided among members. It rejects the values of capitalism.

The full story of the Progressive movement's success lies in the counterpoint it provided to the socialist movement of that era. *Socialism* is a classless social system in which property is collectively owned and income from labor is equally and indiscriminately divided among members. When wealth is shared, want and conflict are eliminated. Socialism poses a revolutionary challenge to capitalist society because it requires a change in property relationships that destroys bedrock arrangements.

Although elements of socialist thinking are ageless, the originator of modern socialist doctrine is Francois-Noël Babeuf (1764–1797), a minor French official and writer who wanted to fulfill the promise of equality for all made during the French

[29] Quoted in "Furor over Mary Lease," *New York Times,* August 11, 1896, p. 3.
[30] "Farming as an Occupation," *Cosmopolitan,* January 1904, p. 371.
[31] "The Man with the Hose," August 1906, p. 341.

Art Young, a radical cartoonist of the Progressive era, had an impish ability to highlight the excesses of the industrial age. This cartoon, typical of many then drawn by Young and others, first appeared in 1912.

CAPITALISM

Revolution of 1789. He advocated seizing the possessions of the wealthy and giving them to the masses. Following this seizure, Babeuf envisioned a new communal economy. Private property would be abolished. Citizens would be required to work based on their trade or skill. The government would receive their output and distribute to everyone the basic material necessities of life. To eliminate individual desire for wealth and power, schools would teach egalitarian principles. Babeuf pushed for a violent overthrow of the French regime to achieve his vision and for this he was imprisoned, then beheaded in 1797. But his ideas took hold and circulated throughout Europe. One convert was Robert Owen, who was inspired to set up his tiny utopia in Indiana.

For a half century after Babeuf, socialist thought was splintered and muddied in a ferment of competing schools. Then, in 1848, Karl Marx (1818–1883) and his lifetime collaborator, Friedrich Engels (1820–1895), published *The Communist Manifesto* and put socialism on a new foundation.[32] Marx and Engels argued that the basis for socialism was an inevitable process of class struggle underlying and explaining the history of human society. Under capitalism the working class is exploited by the owners of capital, who pay low wages for dehumanizing work and then usurp for themselves the value of what workers toil to create. Marx often used metaphors in which capitalists became vampires and werewolves, sucking the lifeblood from labor.

Like Babeuf and others, Marx and Engels envisioned an equalitarian society that abolished private ownership of capital and instituted wealth-sharing among all members. Workers would no longer be alienated by miserable, meaningless labor. With class distinctions ended, people would live in harmony, their basic needs fulfilled. While Marx and Engels repeated many of the timeless criticisms of capitalism as characterized by barbaric competition, corruption of values by money, and meaningless work, they made socialism more compelling when they discovered a theory of history to explain it. Class warfare was the underlying dynamic that changed society. Workers in all nations had the duty to rise and overthrow the capitalist class. The last sentence of the *Manifesto* reads: "WORKINGMEN OF ALL COUNTRIES UNITE!"[33]

Meanwhile, in the United States of 1850 to 1900, rapid industrial growth was taking place within a coarse, little-regulated capitalist system that in many ways seemed to bear out the socialist's nightmare of exploitation. Child labor was widespread; factories injured and wore down workers; wealth and power were concentrated in great banks, trusts, and railway systems; inequality between rich and poor seemed obscene; and the masses suffered through financial panics and unemployment. Also, industrial growth was taking people away from agrarian occupations and creating a new class of employed Americans. In 1860 about 1.3 million people worked for the trusts, mines, and railroads, but by 1890 there were 4.3 million so occupied.[34] The rise of this new social class formed the soil in which labor unions could grow, and given widespread labor abuses, these unions might be attracted to socialism. As it turned out, this attraction would be limited.

As unions sprang up employers fought them. Most early unions were tied to single companies or locations. A few were radical and avowedly socialist, especially those with many European immigrants who brought Marxist thinking with them. The first big national union was the Knights of Labor, set up in 1869. Its constitution recognized exploitation of labor by owners of capital, but it called for

[32] According to Paul Sweezy, Marx chose to use the word "communist" rather than "socialist" because the meaning of the word "socialist" had become muddled. The term communist, in use for centuries to denote pooled property, more clearly conveyed his theory. See *Socialism* (New York: McGraw-Hill, 1949), pp. 8–9.

[33] Karl Marx and Friedrich Engels, *Manifesto of the Communist Party,* in Lewis S. Feuer, ed., *Marx & Engels: Basic Writings on Politics & Philosophy* (New York: Anchor Books, 1959), p. 41.

[34] Arthur M. Schlesinger, *Political and Social Growth of the United States: 1852–1933* (New York: MacMillan, 1935), p. 203.

reforms to protect labor rather than for overthrow of the capitalists. However, the union movement soon struck fear in the capitalist heart.

In the summer of 1877 a wave of violent strikes hit the railroads, then rolled on to other industries as it spread across the nation. Fighting and killing between strikers and the hired armies of employers was widespread. President Rutherford B. Hayes called his cabinet into a continuous session. He was so terrified that the country would fall to a workers' revolution that, rather than using federal troops to restore order in major cities, he gathered them in Washington, DC, to protect the government. The strikes eventually ran their course, and although there was never again such a violent cluster, from this time until the end of the century the number, size, and violence of strikes only increased.

In this climate of unrest, the socialist movement was surprisingly slow to blossom. The largest union, the American Federation of Labor, formed in 1886, disdained Marxism and elected to work with employers for higher wages and better working conditions. As time passed and the union movement grew, many workers still wanted radical change. They eventually found a home when the Industrial Workers of the World (IWW) was formed in 1905. The IWW proposed to represent all workers of both sexes and all races and in every industry in the fight to overthrow the capitalist system. Its platform was clear.

> We are here to confederate the workers of this country into a working-class movement that shall have for its purpose the emancipation of the working-class from the slave bondage of capitalism. . . . The aims and objects of this organization shall be to put the working-class in possession of the economic power, the means of life, in control of the machinery of production and distribution, without regard to the capitalist masters.[35]

Although the IWW was not as large as other unions, its unmitigated rejection of the system scared mainstream America and it was severely repressed. Laws were passed to prevent IWW members from speaking or assembling and it defied them, sometimes violently.

Working alongside the IWW was a young Socialist Party with growing power. It had been formed in 1901 with the avowed purpose of overthrowing capitalism. At the peak of its popularity in 1912 it had 118,000 members and its presidential candidate, Eugene V. Debs, got 6 percent of the popular vote. More than 1,000 socialists had been elected to state and local office.[36] This moment was the high mark of socialism in the United States. From then on, its appeal rapidly declined and it never recovered meaningful power.

There were four immediate reasons. First, because of its electoral successes the Socialist Party chose to make itself less radical to appeal to more voters. This breached socialist unity by alienating firebrand IWW leaders. Second, moderate reforms of the Progressive movement stole much of the socialists' thunder. Arguably, these reforms came only because the threat of growing socialist popularity put

---

[35] Quoted in Howard Zinn, *A People's History of the United States: 1492–Present,* rev. ed. (New York: HarperCollins, 2003), p. 330.

[36] Irving Howe, *Socialism and America* (New York: Harcourt, Brace, Jovanovich, 1985), p. 3.

pressure on the capitalist elite. Third, socialist unions made a huge tactical mistake (though not a doctrinal error) when they labeled World War I (1914–1918) an imperialist war and said that labor would refuse to shed its blood for wealthy capitalists. In 1917 the government put 101 leaders of the IWW on trial for violating sedition laws and all were convicted. Almost half of them got prison sentences of from 10 to 20 years. Others got shorter terms. This decapitated the IWW and crippled the socialist labor movement going forward. Fourth, as time passed the lot of most workers simply improved. Between 1897 and 1914 real wages rose 37 percent and the average sixty-hour workweek declined to fifty hours.[37] Again, the irony is that much of this improvement undoubtedly came out of fear of socialism.

The Great Depression and World War II

With the decline of socialism, capitalism had pushed back its most radical critics. After the triumph of progressive reforms, there was a period of high public confidence in big business during the prosperous, expansive 1920s. This rosy era ended abruptly with the stock market crash of 1929, and business again came under sustained attack. During the 1920s, the idea that American capitalism would bring perpetual prosperity had been widely accepted. The catastrophic depression of the 1930s disproved this and, in addition, brought to light much ineptness, criminal negligence, and outright fraud by prominent executives. There was a popular feeling that the economic collapse would not have occurred if business leaders had been more honest.

As the depression deepened, anger at business grew and the old rhetoric of populism reemerged. In the Senate, for example, Huey Long, a colorful populist Democrat from Louisiana who claimed to be the advocate of the poor against the rich, rose to condemn a "ruling plutocratic class."[38]

> The 125 million people of America have seated themselves at the barbecue table to consume the products which have been guaranteed to them by their Lord and Creator. There is provided by the Almighty what it takes for them all to eat: yea, more. . . . But the financial masters of America have taken off the barbecue table 90 percent of the food placed thereon by God, through the labors of mankind, even before the feast begins, and there is left on that table to be eaten by 125 million people less than should be there for 10 million of them.
>
> What has become of the remainder of those things placed on the table by the Lord for the use of us all? They are in the hands of the Morgans, the Rockefellers, the Mellons, the Baruchs, the Bakers, the Astors, and the Vanderbilts—600 families at the most either possessing or controlling the entire 90 percent of all that is in America. . . . I hope none will be horror-stricken when they hear me say that we must limit the size of the big man's fortune in order to guarantee a minimum of fortune, life and comfort to the little man.[39]

[37] Louis B. Wright et al., *The Democratic Experience: A Short American History* (Chicago: Scott Foresman, 1963), p. 302.

[38] *Congressional Record,* 73d Cong., 2d sess., 1934, p. 6081, speech of April 5.

[39] Radio speech broadcast March 7, 1935, inserted in the *Congressional Record,* March 12, 1935.

FIGURE 4.1
Production of .30 and .50 Caliber Machine Guns by General Motors: 1941–1944

Source: Based on data in James Truslow Adams, *Big Business in a Democracy* (New York: Scribner's Sons, 1945), p. 251.

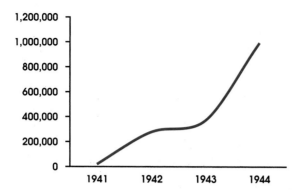

These remarks echo the ancient Greek view that wealth in a society is limited and the accumulation of one person is a taking from all others—that great material wealth reflects greed. Long used these views to gain moral authority for his radical proposals. In 1934 he introduced a plan to redistribute wealth by collecting annual taxes on corporate assets and large fortunes and then giving every family a $5,000 initial gift followed with a guaranteed annual income of $2,500. In a collapsed economy, this populist-like plan had tremendous appeal, and Long attracted millions of followers. However, he was assassinated before it could be enacted, leaving the milder reforms of President Franklin D. Roosevelt's New Deal to carry the day.

During World War II, support for business rebounded. Industry wrapped itself in patriotism, and its high output proved essential to Allied victory. For example, General Motors converted itself almost entirely to war production. The company made 3,600 war items, including ball-bearings, bullets, rifles, torpedoes, trucks, tanks, bombers, and fighter airplanes. In a remarkable effort, it doubled its output of war material between 1942 and 1944. Figure 4.1 shows the production record for one item, machine guns.

Because of similar efforts by many corporations, the war years washed away the populist/socialist/depression era image of the corporation as a bloated plutocracy. It was instead the source of miraculous industrial production. In a radio address President Franklin Roosevelt labeled American business the "arsenal of democracy" that would turn the tide against evil dictatorships that sought to control the world.[40] The wartime performance was spectacular and in a postwar poll, only 10 percent of the population believed that where "big business activity" was concerned "the bad effects outweighed the good."[41] This renascence of respect lasted into the 1960s before the populist seed again sprouted.

The Collapse of Confidence

Strong public support for business collapsed in the mid-1960s. The nation was growing more affluent, but four strong social movements—for civil rights, consumer rights, and the environment and against the Vietnam War—attacked business for

[40] Radio address, Washington, DC, December 29, 1940. U.S. Department of State, *Peace and War: United States Foreign Policy, 1931–1941* (Washington, DC: U.S. Government Printing Office, 1943), pp. 598–607.

[41] Burton R. Fisher and Stephen B. Withey, *Big Business as the People See It* (Ann Arbor: University of Michigan Microfilms, December 1951), p. xiii.

FIGURE 4.2
Percentage
of American
Public
Expressing "A
Great Deal of
Confidence"
in Leaders
of Major
Companies:
1966–2006

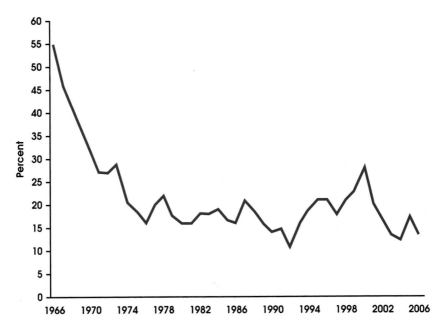

contributing to a range of social ills including racism and sexism, consumer fraud, dangerous and alienating work, political corruption, and war profiteering. These attacks coincided with a negative trend in public opinion toward business. While in 1968, 70 percent of Americans agreed that business tried to strike a fair balance between profits and the public interest, by 1970 the number had declined to 33 percent, and by 1976 to 15 percent. This astonishing drop of 55 points took only eight years.[42]

Scholars who studied the polls theorized that turmoil in American society in the 1960s created a "confidence gap," or a gap between public expectations about how corporations *should* act and public perceptions of how they actually *did* act. Such gaps are perennial. They widened during the populist and progressive eras and during the Great Depression years. This new gap has now persisted for almost 40 years and continues to define the climate of public opinion.

Figure 4.2 shows the long-term trend for the percentage of Americans expressing "a great deal of confidence" in "people in charge of running major companies." In 1966, 55 percent of the public expressed such confidence, but over the next decade the percentage fell to 16 percent. Since then the confidence trend has bumped along a low road for 30 years, recovering to 28 percent in 2000 near the peak of a great bull market, but sinking again to 12 percent in 2004 after a cluster of fraud scandals including the Enron Corporation bankruptcy.[43]

---

[42] Seymour M. Lipset and William Schneider, "How's Business: What the Public Thinks," *Public Opinion*, July–August 1978.

[43] Figures are based on Harris polls asking this question: "As far as people in charge of running . . . major companies . . . are concerned, would you say you have a great deal of confidence, only some confidence, or hardly any confidence in them?" See Harris Poll no. 22, "Overall Confidence in Leaders of Major Institutions Remains Steady," March 2, 2006, tables 1, 2A–2D, at www.harrisinteractive.com.

The steep fall of public trust after 1966 opened the door for reformers to increase government regulation dramatically. During the late 1960s and early 1970s liberals in Congress created powerful new laws and agencies to protect the environment, consumers, and workers. However, by the mid-1970s corporations had organized to fight back. They soon dulled the blade of reform with a multifaceted campaign that included lobbying to block new regulation and public relations to influence public opinion.

A new group, the Business Roundtable, was set up to coordinate lobbying by corporate CEOs. Although business was unsuccessful in restoring basic public trust, it did alter key attitudes. Corporations funded conservative think tanks and used advertising to spread the message that excessive government regulation imposed unnecessary costs and burdens on companies, reducing their competitiveness and weakening the American economy. With the election of Ronald Reagan in 1980 a tide of Republican conservatism swept through the federal government, frustrating liberal reformers whose ideology of using government to control business was diminished—even discredited.

The New Progressives

Out of this liberal defeat rose a new leftist movement with a new ideology. The new movement adopted the label "Progressive" after the turn-of-the-century movement that sought a broad range of social and political reforms. Both movements have in common the desire to restrain corporate power in the public interest, but major difference exist between them. The *old Progressives* had wings in both the Democratic and Republican parties, so a wide span of liberals and moderates often supported reforms. Support for the *new Progressives'* agenda comes entirely from the left.

Unlike the old Progressives, who wanted to enact reforms through government, the new Progressive left seeks to carry out more radical change through direct action. And while the old-timers applied new scientific, legal, and management theories of the day to smooth the harsh edges of capitalism, the obsession of the new Progressives has been attacks on large corporations and the values and laws that support them. Largely blocked from the avenue of reform legislation by conservative and antiregulatory trends, activists confront corporations directly, one-by-one, trying to alter their behavior, even in the absence of laws against what the corporations are doing. Some seek to abolish the corporate form rather than to reform or regulate it. Underlying this deep antipathy are three basic beliefs.

First, corporations have too much power. Those with huge revenues and assets have excessive economic power in markets. They use their wealth to undermine democracy by dominating governments and corrupting politicians. Like entrenched oligarchs, they are unaccountable to the public for their self-interested exercise of power.

Second, corporations have inordinate legal rights. In the colonial era the charters that authorized corporations carefully restricted them to ensure that they acted for the common welfare. For example, they defined the company's business and limited its existence to a stated number of years. Today, instead of restricting corporations, state charters are very permissive. They allow branching out to new

old Progressive
A reference to political and social reformers at the beginning of the twentieth century.

new Progressives
Members of left-leaning groups who advocate more radical corporate reforms than did the old Progressives. New Progressives seek to avoid being branded as liberals and try to take advantage of favorable connotations in the word progressive.

lines of business and grant the corporation perpetual life. Over the years legislatures, courts, and trade agreements have regularly added more rights, including the granting of "personhood" to corporate entities, entitling them to many constitutional rights of flesh-and-blood citizens.[44]

Third, corporations are inherently immoral. If often run or staffed by good people, the actions of these people are perverted by an implacable, master force, the very logic of the corporations itself. Corporations act to make money. They seek market expansion, sales growth, short-term financial results, and regulatory lenience. They value nature only as a production resource, workers only as costs, and human needs only as demand. Strong corporate cultures inculcate these values, pressuring and ultimately coercing the wills of even the most ethical employees, turning them into witting or unwitting agents of an antisocial institution.

The progressive network has no single leader, but in the United States a prominent figure and senior diplomat is Ralph Nader. Nader began his activist career more than 30 years ago by writing *Unsafe at Any Speed*, a book that attacked the auto industry for putting styling ahead of safety.[45] The popularity of the book helped Congress to pass auto safety legislation. Based on this success and his desire to seek change through government, Nader created more than 50 organizations to articulate consumer issues and lobby for protective laws. Over time, his hostility toward corporations has deepened and his desire to seek moderate reforms has lessened.

Announcing his candidacy for president of the United States in 2000, Nader said he was running to challenge "rampaging corporate titans," " runaway commercial imperatives," and "global corporations . . . astride our planet."[46] He declined to seek nominations as either a Republican or a Democrat because, he explained, both parties "feed at the same corporate trough."[47] Instead, he ran as a candidate for the Green Party, a global political movement that began as an antinuclear movement in Great Britain and New Zealand and has extended its platform to include main elements of the progressive agenda.

Although Nader got only 2.7 percent of the popular vote in 2000, he prevented Democrat Al Gore from winning the electoral votes of key states, allowing Republican George W. Bush, the more probusiness candidate, to win. In 2004 Nader again entered the presidential race, this time as an independent candidate, declaring that he represented "all Americans who wish to declare their independence from corporate rule and its expanding domination."[48] This time his impact was a faint two-tenths of 1 percent of the popular vote, making him insignificant in the outcome and leaving the nation, in his words, "a government of the Exxons, by the General Motors, for the DuPonts!"[49]

---

[44] For enumeration see Ted Nance, *Gangs of America: The Rise of Corporate Power and the Disabling of Democracy* (San Francisco: Berrett-Koehler, 2003), table 1.1.

[45] New York: Grossman, 1965.

[46] "Closing the Democracy Gap," *The Progressive Populist,* October 15, 2000, pp. 13 and 14.

[47] Ibid., p. 14.

[48] "Ralph Nader Announcement of Candidacy: Toward a 'New Birth of Freedom' and Justice," February 23, 2004, p.1.

[49] Quoted in Patricia Sheridan, "Ralph Nader," *Pittsburgh Post-Gazette*, July 4, 2005, p. C2.

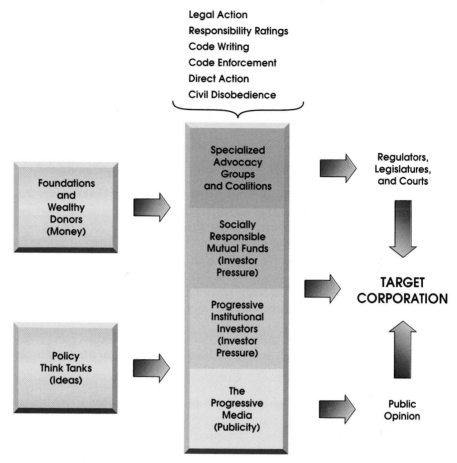

FIGURE 4.3
How the Progressive Network Attacks a Corporation

Source: Adapted from Jarol B. Manheim, *Biz-War and the Out-of-Power Elite* (Mahwah, NJ: Lawrence Erlbaum, 2004), fig. 10.2. Reprinted with permission of Laurence Erlbaum Associates, Publishers.

Legal Action
Responsibility Ratings
Code Writing
Code Enforcement
Direct Action
Civil Disobedience

Foundations and Wealthy Donors (Money)

Policy Think Tanks (Ideas)

Specialized Advocacy Groups and Coalitions

Socially Responsible Mutual Funds (Investor Pressure)

Progressive Institutional Investors (Investor Pressure)

The Progressive Media (Publicity)

Regulators, Legislatures, and Courts

TARGET CORPORATION

Public Opinion

The progressive left movement is highly articulated and specialized. It has a network structure that includes leftist philanthropic and legal foundations; research institutes; publications; mutual funds; pension funds; unions; and groups of environmental, human rights, and labor advocates. The fraternity is knit together not only by shared ideology, but by flows of funding, program sponsorships, shared directorships, overlapping membership, information exchange, and coalition agreements.[50] Entities in the movement are specialized, creating an organizational symbiosis. Some groups use lawsuits to challenge business; others engage in civil disobedience. Some write conduct codes for industries; others train inspectors to enforce them. Some rate corporations on their social performance; others form mutual funds to invest in more responsible companies. Figure 4.3 shows various parts of the progressive left and how they combine to fight corporate power.

[50] For details on network dynamics see Jarol B. Manheim, *Biz-War and the Out-of-Power Elite: The Progressive-Left Attack on the Corporation* (Mahwah, NJ: Lawrence Erlbaum, 2004), pp. 38–40.

Global Critics

Corporate power increasingly challenges its antagonists on the world stage. With expansion of the global economy transnational corporations have grown in size and number, their mazelike structures spilling over national borders, their initiative eluding local regulation, their managers decreeing life chances for millions. Progressives fear corporate trickery in a void of weak social control over global markets.

Seeds of reaction against corporate power have sprouted in the soil of a new international civic culture. Within the international arena there is eruptive growth of *nongovernmental organizations* (NGOs), or voluntary organizations that are not part of governments. There are now more than 40,000 international NGOs, almost 90 percent of them created since 1970.[51] The variety of NGOs that operate over national boundaries encompasses business, cultural, educational, environmental, human rights, social service, health, and religious actors. They animate a global zone of ideas, discourse, and action that has come to be called *civil society*. Although civil society is a vast churning of interests, it is dominated by individuals, NGOs, grass roots movements, and institutions with progressive values critical of corporations. These actors, linked by electronic communications, engage in advocacy and struggle over a leftist design that includes global income redistribution, sustainable development, gender equity, and protection of human and labor rights.

In the 1990s an *antiglobalism movement* evolved within civil society, its forces coalescing around resistance to a global economy directed by markets, corporations, trade agreements, and capitalist-dominated international financial institutions. The movement was animated by progressive-leaning actors including labor unions, human rights organizations, environmentalists, religious orders, farmers, socialists, indigenous people's movements, feminists, animal rights activists, Neo-Luddites,[52] and anarchists opposed to any overarching world order. It first achieved high visibility in 1999 when 50,000 activists gathered to protest World Trade Organization meetings in Seattle and street riots broke out. Two years later, at a *Group of Eight* summit in Genoa, Italy, as many as 100,000 came to protest as leaders of industrial nations met to discuss economic issues. Rioting led to the death of one activist.

Since then the movement has created less visible turbulence. Concerns about terrorism made street protests more difficult and protests against trade became awkward after the September 11, 2001, attacks on the World Trade Center, a symbol of free trade.[53] But outside the limelight it has proved durable, growing in numbers and connectivity.

The antiglobalism coalition encompasses diverse, sometimes inconsistent agendas, so ascribing to it a specific goal or platform is difficult. However, its membership

nongovernmental organization
A term for voluntary organizations that are not affiliated with governments.

civil society
A zone of ideas, discourse, and action that transcends national societies and focuses on global issues. It is dominated by progressive values.

antiglobalism movement
A coalition of groups united by opposition to economic globalization dominated by corporations and trade liberalization.

Group of Eight
An annual meeting where leaders of the large industrial democracies discuss political and economic issues.

---

[51] Michael Edwards, *Civil Society* (Cambridge, England: Polity Press, 2004). p. 23.

[52] The Luddites (1811–1816) were English textile workers who blamed unemployment and low wages on new steam-powered textile machines. The name comes from a mythical figure, Ned Ludd. They wrecked the machines and violently attacked their makers before being suppressed.

[53] Juliane von Reppert-Bismarch, "Activists Take the Fight Inside," *The Wall Street Journal*, December 15, 2005, p. A10.

neoliberalism
A term denoting both the ideology of using markets to organize society and a set of policies to free markets from state intrusion.

liberalism
The philosophy of an open society in which government does not interfere with rights of individuals.

economic liberalism
The philosophy that social progress comes when individuals freely pursue their self-interests in unregulated markets.

is united against the tyranny of *neoliberalism,* a term that encompasses both the philosophy and the specific practices on which current global economic expansion is based. To understand the meaning of neoliberalism, it is necessary to understand the history of the idea of liberalism.

Liberalism arose in Europe as a social philosophy in the 1500s. It promoted a free and open society in which the power of government to interfere with individual rights such as speech, association, conscience, and occupation was limited. Liberals had great faith in human reason and believed that this freedom would lead to social progress. For example, as freedom of speech allowed multiple opinions to be aired, truth would drive out falsehood. Liberalism proved compelling. It spread and today it defines the essence of a good society in much of the world.

One natural extension of liberalism was a philosophy of *economic liberalism* that sanctified the pursuit of individual self-interest in markets free from state interferences. It saw the market as another sphere of individual freedom. Liberals had faith that, like free speech, free markets would lead to positive social outcomes such as wealth creation and, ultimately, to human progress. Adam Smith's vision of *laissez-faire* capitalism defined this notion of economic liberalism.

Economic liberalism seized hold in the West. It was a critical ideology underlying the industrial revolution in England. Later, in the United States, it was used to justify the predatory capitalism of the 1800s and early 1900s that so aggravated Mary Lease, Mother Jones, and Huey Long. Then classical liberalism perished in the world depression of the 1930s. To end the depression and make economies perform for the public good governments decided to intervene in markets. Dropping the hands-off-the-market philosophy changed liberalism. It was no longer assumed that free markets always produced moral outcomes. They required state supervision. An era of growing market regulation followed. However, it was relatively short-lived, ending by the late 1970s when, in the opinion of the antiglobalists, corporate elites manipulated publics and governments to accept a new doctrine of free and expanding markets. This new doctrine came to be called neoliberalism.

To the antiglobalists, neoliberalism is the rebirth of the philosophy of economic liberalism coupled with a set of free-market economic policies including deregulation, privatization of state-owned enterprises, restrictions on labor unions, trade expansion, tax cuts, and reductions in the welfare state. Under the reign of neoliberalism, markets become the organizing principle for society. Corporate advertising makes our values more material. Corporations expand markets by, for example, expanding store hours, patenting genetic strains of crop seedlings, and running public services such as prisons for a profit. In neoliberal societies markets also guide personal lives. Individuals educate themselves to enhance their labor market value. They dress to please employers. They equate success in life with success in business. Neoliberal logic requires nations to tailor their economic policies to court foreign investors. On the international level undemocratic institutions—the World Trade Organization, the World Bank, and International Monetary Fund—enforce neoliberal policies on developing countries as the price of entering world markets. Overall, it is a pervasive, probusiness ideology that disgusts Progressives.

World Social Forum
The annual meeting of the antiglobalism movement.

The goals of the antiglobalism movement are elusive. Many in it find the anti-globalism label inaccurate. Few members reject globalization itself, and for this reason some prefer to call it the "global justice movement."[54] By whatever name, the brotherhood has come together each year since 2001 at a mass gathering called the *World Social Forum,* held in a developing country in January. The World Social Forum's charter states that it consists of "groups and movements of civil society that are opposed to neo-liberalism" and that these entities "are committed to building a planetary society directed toward fruitful relationships among Mankind and between it and the Earth."[55] But the movement is a cacophony of voices. According to one group of observers who attended a World Social Forum, the term neoliberalism was "little more than oratorical flypaper: an ugly, sticky mess to which everything the critics consider politically loathsome is made to stick in a single buzzing heap."[56] Yet the movement has goals including universal human and labor rights, income equity, equality of the sexes, democratic economic and political institutions, and sustainable development.

For now, debate and confrontation often center on the actions of transnational corporations seen as impeding progress toward a better world. The struggle against them excites many in the movement. Managers have come to fear clashes between market logic and the moral agenda of civil society. One estimate is that 6,000 of the world's 40,000 NGOs are of the variety that attack corporations.[57] A leading scholar within civil society issues the call to battle.

> [We are in] . . . a struggle between two globalizations grounded in sharply contrast-ing visions of human possibility—one imperial and the other democratic. It pits an alliance of state and corporate power devoted to a vision of global Empire against an alliance of people power devoted to a vision of Earth Community. Empire holds the edge in institutional power; Earth Community holds the edge in the moral power of the authentic cultural values of a mature consciousness.[58]

Global Activism

Activists, by definition, take action. Progressive elements have created unique webs of advocacy to correct perceived problems or abuses. An early example is the International Campaign to Ban Landmines, composed at its height of 800 groups in 50 countries. Activists from groups such as Human Rights Watch attacked corporations making antipersonnel mines. As a result, Raytheon stopped making mine components, and others, including Motorola, Hughes Aircraft, and General

[54] Naomi Klein, "Naomi Klein, Journalist," in Kate Holbrook, Ann S. Kim, Brian Palmer, and Anna Portnoy, eds, *Global Values 101* (Boston: Beacon Press, 2006), p. 117.

[55] World Social Forum India, *Charter of Principles,* 2006, at www.wsfindia.org.

[56] Matthew Sparke, Elizabeth Brown, Dominic Corva, Heather Day, Carolina Faria, Tony Sparks, and Kirsten Varg, "The World Social Forum and the Lessons for Economic Geography," *Economic Geography,* October 2005, p. 361.

[57] George Lodge and Craig Wilson, *A Corporate Solution to Global Poverty* (Princeton, NJ: Princeton University Press, 2006), p. 46.

[58] David C. Korten, *The Great Turning: From Empire to Earth Community* (Bloomfield, CT: Kumarian Press, 2006), p. 12.

Electric, quit selling parts used to make mines.[59] Similar advocacy networks have formed to fight sweatshop contracting by clothing makers and environmental abuses by energy and mining companies.

Such campaigns are not new. In the early 1800s a remarkably similar advocacy network led the global antislavery campaign.[60] In the 1970s international campaigns forced Nestlé and other infant-formula makers to change the way formula was sold in developing countries. And in the 1980s a fierce human rights coalition pushed foreign corporations out of very profitable markets in apartheid-era South Africa.[61]

Attacks on corporations marshal a range of devices that create pressure. Following is a list, hardly exhaustive, of tactics.

- *Consumer boycotts.* A boycott is a call to pressure a company by not buying its products and services. Perhaps the first global boycott, against white sugar, was called in 1792 by radical groups in England protesting brutal slavery in the British East Indies. It halved sugar sales in England and may have been crucial in ending the slave trade within the British Empire.[62] In recent years advocacy groups have called hundreds of boycotts. Here are some current examples. Friends of the Earth is boycotting Singapore Airlines because the government of Singapore threatened to jail violent protestors at World Bank meetings. A Belgian group, Mother Earth, is leading a coalition of 150 NGOs boycotting Altria Group, ExxonMobil, ChevronTexaco, PepsiCo, Coca-Cola, and McDonald's because they are big contributors to the Republican party in the United States. The groups are angry with President Bush for failing to act against climate change. A British NGO, Vegetarians International Voice for Animals is running a worldwide boycott of Adidas for using the skins of inhumanely killed kangaroos to make soccer boots.

- *Shareholder attacks.* In the United States and European nations rules permit shareowners of public companies to sponsor resolutions on which all stockholders may vote at annual meetings. Religious groups often lead in sponsoring resolutions in line with the progressive agenda. One group, the Interfaith Center on Corporate Responsibility, coordinates more than 200 religious orders and denominations that sponsor as many as 250 social responsibility proposals annually at shareholder meetings. Recent examples (with the percentage of the shareholder vote they received in 2006) are a proposal asking Ford Motor Company to reveal its lobbying activities to block higher fuel economy standards (7 percent) and a proposal calling on DuPont to cut its use of toxic chemicals (29 percent).

---

[59] Christina Del Valle and Monica Larner, "A New Front in the War on Land Mines," *BusinessWeek,* April 28, 1997, p. 43.

[60] Margaret E. Keck and Kathryn Sikkink, *Activists Beyond Borders* (Ithaca, NY: Cornell University Press, 1998), pp. 8–22.

[61] S. Prakash Sethi and Oliver F. Williams, *Economic Imperatives and Ethical Values in Global Business: The South African Experience and International Codes Today* (South Bend, IN: University of Notre Dame Press, 2001).

[62] "Sick with Excess of Sweetness," *The Economist*, December 23, 2006, p. 93.

Few social responsibility proposals have gotten a majority vote, but they create bad publicity and often lead to serious negotiations with management.

- *Harassment, ridicule, and shaming.* Essential Action, a group started by Ralph Nader, chartered a corporation named Licensed to Kill, Inc., in Virginia, stating in the charter that its work was to make and sell tobacco "in a way that each year kills . . . Americans."[63] Members of Essential Action then attended the annual shareholders meeting of Altria Group, whose Philip Morris subsidiary is the world's largest cigarette company. When the question and answer period came, an "executive" of Licensed to Kill invited Altria's CEO to join the new firm's board of directors, bringing his "experience in making a killing around the world."[64] The offer was declined.

  Forms of harassment are limited only by the imagination. Activists bring lawsuits based on clever charges such as racketeering. They disrupt the lives of executives and their families by picketing their homes, protesting at their children's schools, and interrupting services at their churches. They climb corporate buildings to unfurl banners. Some groups hand out mock awards to corporate targets. Corporate Accountability International regularly inducts corporations into its Hall of Shame. Each year on the eve of the World Economic Forum, advocacy groups meet to hand out "awards" to corporations nominated by NGOs around the world for exceptional irresponsibility. Past "winners" include Nestlé, Citigroup, Walt Disney, and Wal-Mart.

- *Codes of conduct.* Some advocacy groups develop codes of conduct that essentially enact progressive agendas. Corporations are pressured to sign on. If they sign, they often must submit to compliance monitoring done by specialized organizations with connections to activists. An example is Social Accountability 8000, a detailed code created by organizations in the worldwide campaign against sweatshop labor. The code sets forth principles for ethical treatment of workers. It requires corporate signers to be certified and then submit to periodic monitoring by examiners trained in code enforcement. An organization named Verité, with progressive ties, was set up to verify compliance.

- *Corporate campaigns.* A corporate campaign is a broad, sustained attack, usually by a coalition of groups, that mobilizes activists for coordinated warfare and employs a wide range of tactics.[65] The campaign depicts the firm as engaging in antisocial behavior to make a profit while representing the advocacy groups as moral crusaders for some universal truth. Transnational corporations have enormous financial resources, strong influence on governments, and trusted brand names. Activists typically have slender financing, little political influence, and low public recognition. However, a key source of strength is the tendency of the public to see environmental, religious, or human rights groups as selfless and acting for justice. Using this perception, activists seize the ethical

---

[63] "Articles of Incorporation, 2003." See www.licensedtokill.biz.

[64] Ibid., "Licensed to Kill Invites Altria CEO to Become an L2K Director!" 2003.

[65] For an extended discussion, see Jarol B. Manheim, *The Death of a Thousand Cuts: Corporate Campaigns and the Attack on Corporations* (Mahwah, NJ: Lawrence Erlbaum, 2001).

high ground and engage the corporation with an assault that might be likened to warfare because the action sometimes stretches or breaks the bonds of civility. A recent example is the campaign of ForestEthics to get Victoria's Secret, a subsidiary of Limited Brands, to stop using pulp from virgin Canadian forests in its catalogs. The company agreed to use recycled paper after enduring two years of a "Victoria's Dirty Secret" campaign that included store picketing by chain-saw wielding women in lingerie, civil disobedience in shopping malls, and shareholder meetings picketed by hecklers in bear costumes.

The activism of global civil society challenges traditional notions of democracy. Advocacy groups have limited memberships. Unlike representative legislatures, they are not accountable to a broad base of voters even as they claim that their ideas about everything from sustainable forests to healthy diets represent the public interest. They are unwilling to accept as responsible corporate behavior that which is guided merely by laws, trade agreements, or the choices of individual consumers in markets. Instead, they argue that since corporations have corrupted governments and manipulated consumers, they are justified in taking action to impose standards of "responsibility," "justice," "equity," and "rights" as defined by the progressive vision. This vision is not uncontroversial. Once into a campaign, progressive advocates tap the deep cynicism in public opinion to build anger against the corporate target. If the company capitulates and changes its policies, the activists have, in effect, appropriated its power and assets to further their policy agenda. And this may have been accomplished by an end run around formal institutions and regulators.

CONCLUDING OBSERVATIONS

We have narrated a history in which basic criticisms of business are repeated over and over. Each era brings new personalities, new targets, and some new issues, but the fundamental substance endures. The story is one of endless dialogue between critics and defenders of capitalism. Figure 4.4 shows two timelines that represent this dialogue. Imagine a dinner party at which Aristotle, Saint Augustine, Thomas Jefferson, and Ralph Nader sit at one table while Adam Smith, Benjamin Franklin, Alexander Hamilton, and Ronald Reagan sit at another. Now imagine the harmony among tablemates as contrasted with the gulf between the two groups.

There is no question that industrial capitalism is a historical force for continuous, turbulent social change; it is, as the economist Joseph Shumpeter wrote years ago, "a perennial gale of creative destruction" that strains institutions and challenges existing authority.[66] The defense of capitalism is that, for the most part, the changes it brings represent progress, a condition of improvement for humanity. All the while that critics have been objecting, it has steadily improved living standards for hundreds of millions of people. As against promoting greed and avarice,

---

[66] *Capitalism, Socialism and Democracy* (New York: Harper & Row, 1976), p. 143; originally published in 1942.

FIGURE 4.4   Timelines of Ideological Conflict

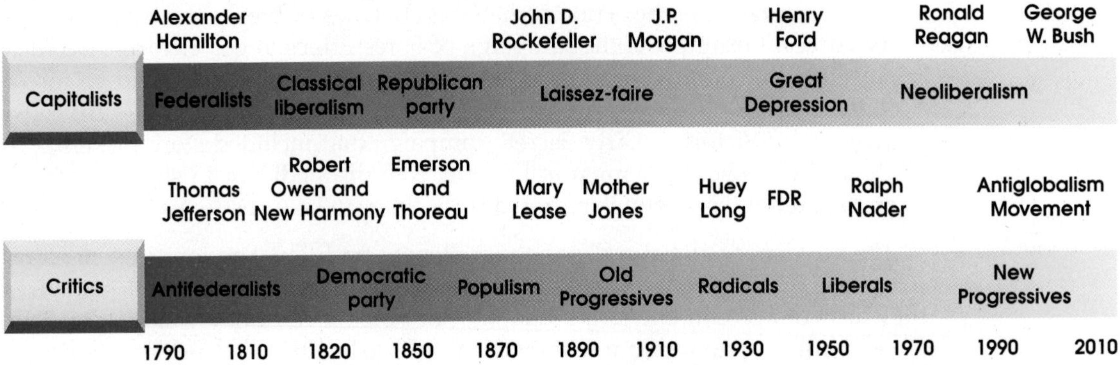

	Alexander Hamilton				John D. Rockefeller	J.P. Morgan		Henry Ford		Ronald Reagan	George W. Bush
Capitalists	Federalists	Classical liberalism	Republican party	Laissez-faire				Great Depression	Neoliberalism		

		Thomas Jefferson	Robert Owen and New Harmony	Emerson and Thoreau	Mary Lease	Mother Jones	Huey Long	FDR	Ralph Nader		Antiglobalism Movement
Critics	Antifederalists		Democratic party		Populism	Old Progressives		Radicals	Liberals		New Progressives

| 1790 | 1810 | 1820 | 1850 | 1870 | 1890 | 1910 | 1930 | 1950 | 1970 | 1990 | 2010 |

The two timelines show how a debate between business and its critics moves through American history. Each timeline represents the sweep of people and ideas associated with one side of this enduring debate.

it has promoted positive cultural values such as imagination, innovation, cooperation, hard work, and the interpersonal trust necessary to conduct billions of daily business transactions.

In the end, a broad spectrum of criticism is an important check on power. Legitimate criticism exists and demands attention. If criticism is properly channeled, it can preserve the best of the business institution and bring wide benefit. In Ralph Nader's words: "Whenever, in our nation's history, people successfully challenge the excessive power of commercial interests, whether over workers, child labor, minorities, consumers and the environment, the country became better and the economy stronger."[67]

Not all antiglobalists and Progressives reject capitalism. Many now believe that corporate-led economic development underlies social progress even as companies sometimes behave badly. They have come to accept that growing trade holds the potential for alleviating poverty. These critics now promote the doctrine of corporate social responsibility, the subject of our next two chapters.

[67] "Human Need Trumps Corporate Greed," *The Wall Street Journal*, October 25, 2000, p. A22.

A Campaign against KFC Corporation

War was declared on January 6, 2003. In a press release, People for the Ethical Treatment of Animals (PETA), a militant animal rights group, announced it was beginning a pressure campaign against KFC Corporation, the world's largest chicken restaurant chain. PETA held KFC responsible for the "cruel treatment" of poultry raised and slaughtered for its restaurants.[1]

It demanded that KFC force new, more humane practices on its suppliers. KFC responded with a statement dismissing "allegations made by PETA" and saying that its chickens were treated humanely.[2]

KFC does not raise any chickens. In the United States it buys them from 18 independent companies operating more than 50 chicken farms and slaughterhouses and pursues similar arrangements in other

[1] "Company Stonewalls on Animal Welfare Reforms," press release, People for the Ethical Treatment of Animals, January 6, 2003, available at www.peta.org.

[2] "KFC Denies PETA Claims," press release, KFC Corporation, January 7, 2003, available at www.kfc.com.

nations. PETA is angry about how chickens are handled by these suppliers, but their facilities are out of public view and make difficult targets. KFC, with its popular restaurants, is highly vulnerable to attack. By assaulting its brand image PETA hopes to make KFC use its market power as the world's largest purchaser of chickens to force reform on growers and slaughter plants. If this occurs, PETA will have harnessed a reluctant giant to accomplish its goals.

Going into the chicken war, PETA had a record of success. Its initial effort was a campaign against McDonald's in 1999. After less than a year of exposure to a boycott, restaurant demonstrations, and the group's mccruelty.com Web site the company succumbed, imposing stricter animal welfare standards on its suppliers as a condition for ending the assault. It forced changes on reluctant growers, including roomier cages for hens, surprise slaughterhouse inspections, and more effective stunning of chickens before killing them. After McDonald's capitulated, its smaller rivals followed. Burger King adopted animal welfare guidelines after a five-month campaign. Then Wendy's buckled. Safeway lasted only three months. Albertsons and Kroger's were subdued by campaigns of only one week each.

INITIAL SKIRMISHES

KFC learned of PETA's intentions in 2001, when Cheryl Bachelder, its president, received a letter from Bruce Friedrich, director of the group's restaurant campaigns. The letter asked why KFC, knowing of PETA's actions against its competitors, was doing "nothing at all" to improve the lives of chickens raised for its restaurants. Friedrich asked what KFC intended to do, offered to put the company in touch with animal welfare experts, and added "we are looking ahead to our next target."[3]

Over the next several weeks Friedrich had a series of phone calls and meetings with Bachelder and David Novak, CEO of KFC's parent corporation Yum! Brands. Yum! Brands was created in 1997 when PepsiCo spun off its KFC, Pizza Hut, and Taco Bell chains as a separate corporation. Subsequently, the new firm bought the Long John Silver's and A&W chains. Today, Yum! is the world's largest quick-service restaurant corporation with 35,000 restaurants worldwide. The KFC brand traces its origins to the Kentucky Fried Chicken franchise started by the avuncular Colonel Harlan Sanders in 1952. It has 14,500 restaurants in 100 countries and serves about 12 million customers every day.

The dialogue revealed a wide gulf between the company and its interlocutor. KFC told Friedrich that it included humane treatment guidelines in its poultry supplier contracts. He accused the company of using only inadequate industry standards permitting ghastly treatment of chickens and considering their welfare only at the point where deaths from abuse lowered profits. He stated that the suffering of chickens was an ethical issue going beyond financial considerations.[4] KFC said it would review its guidelines and promised to keep PETA informed.

In the months that followed, KFC took several actions. It convened an Animal Welfare Advisory Council composed of outside academic and industry experts. It began unannounced audits of growers and slaughterhouses. And it worked with industry associations to develop new poultry welfare guidelines. However, its efforts were unsatisfactory to PETA because they did not lead to specific, more radical changes including the following.

- *Gas killing.* KFC chickens are stunned by electrical shock before immersion in scalding water (to loosen feathers) and then exposed to mechanical blades that slit their throats. PETA believes that gas killing is preferable because it ensures that chickens are insensate before these painful procedures, whereas electrical stunning is less reliable.

- *Cameras in slaughterhouses.* Cameras would supplement audits and make oversight more reliable.

- *Mechanized chicken-catching.* Hand-catching crews gather KFC chickens from grower buildings. PETA believes that the crews treat the birds roughly and that mechanical catching systems are less likely to result in bruises and broken bones.

- *New genetic strains of chickens.* The chickens eaten in KFC restaurants, known as "broilers," are bred to gain weight rapidly over their brief lives. However, the "broiler breeders" used to produce the flocks of chickens slaughtered for restaurant meals live longer. They exhibit the rapid weight gain

[3] The letter is at www.kfccruelty.com/letter-042501.asp.

[4] Letter of May 14, 2001, from Bruce G. Friedrich to Jonathan D. Blum, senior vice president, Tricon Global Restaurants, at www.kfccruelty.com/letter-052401.asp. Yum! Brands was formerly named Tricon Global Restaurants.

characteristic of all broiler strains, but their skeletons and joints do not grow commensurate with their overall weight and they are prone to painful joint conditions as they age. PETA requested introduction of leaner genetic strains that did not exhibit skeletal deficiencies.

- *Elimination of forced growth.* Broiler strains bred for rapid weight gain under forced growth regimens suffer from metabolic pathologies and excess mortality. Slowing growth means longer upkeep of chickens before slaughter, but it reduces premature deaths.

- *More room for birds to move around.* PETA requests that KFC give its chickens at least two to three times more space per bird and give them sheltered areas and perches in the warehouselike buildings where they are raised.

- *Allowance for instinctive behavior of chickens.* PETA believes that birds raised in captivity suffer from chronic stress and boredom induced by suppression of natural behaviors. Among other measures, it suggests that they get whole green cabbages to peck and eat.[5]

Debate between the antagonists was dysfunctional. PETA addressed the corporation in the tone of a parent scolding an errant child. It was "extremely concerned" that the firm "has no interest in making real progress to stop animal cruelty," adding that "we have pressed you to take action on this issue, yet you have done nothing."[6] KFC, on the other hand, wrote to PETA "[i]n the spirit of open communications," but kept it at arms length, giving only brief and general information about conducting audits, holding meetings, and working on animal welfare standards with industry groups.[7] PETA believed that KFC was dragging its feet.

A LOOK AT PETA

PETA is dominated by its founder, Ingrid Newkirk, who became an animal rights activist after a formative experience. Living in Maryland in 1972, she was training to become a stockbroker. A neighbor moved, abandoning cats that soon bred litters of kittens nearby. She gathered them up and took them to a nearby animal shelter to be cared for. Yet a short time later she learned they had been killed. The episode changed her. With no desire to become a stockbroker remaining, she talked her way into a job at the shelter. Observing brutal treatment of animals, she began to arrive early in the morning to kill them in a humane way before others came. "I must have killed a thousand of them," she says, "sometimes dozens every day."[8]

From the shelter Newkirk moved on to work as a deputy sheriff on animal cruelty investigations, then headed a commission to control animal disease. She was inspired to form PETA after reading a book, *Animal Liberation,* by philosopher Peter Singer.[9] In the book, Singer argues that animals have moral rights. Moral rights are strong entitlements to dutiful treatment by others—in this case human beings. He asserts that the traditional, absolute dominion of humans over animals is an unfair exploitation. Because animals are living, sentient beings capable of suffering, their interests are entitled to equal consideration with human interests. In his words: "No matter what the nature of the being, the principle of equality requires that its suffering be counted equally with the like suffering . . . of any other being."[10] Thus, he argues, animals have an unalienable right to have their needs accommodated by humans. Denial of this right is speciesism, or the prejudicial favoring of one species over another. Speciesism, according to Singer, is an evil akin to racism and sexism because it restricts moral rights to one species just as racism and sexism have restricted them to one race or sex. The PETA Mission Statement, Exhibit 1, reflects the inspiration Newkirk found in this philosophy.

Newkirk has a combative attitude about animal rights. "The animals are defenseless," she says. "They can't talk back, and they can't fight back. But we can. And no matter what it takes, we always will."[11] After reading about a Palestinian bomb put on a donkey and detonated by remote control she wrote to Yasir Arafat requesting that innocent animals be left out of

---

[5] Letter of August 6, 2002, from Bruce G. Friedrich to Jonathan D. Blum, available at www.kfccruelty.com/letter-080602.asp.

[6] Ibid.

[7] Letter of July 17, 2002, from Jonathan Blum to Bruce G. Friedrich, available at www.kfccruelty.com/petakfc.asp.

[8] Quoted in Michael Specter, "The Extremist," *The New Yorker*, April 14, 2003, p. 56.

[9] New York: Avon Books, 1975.

[10] Ibid., p. 8.

[11] Quoted in Specter, "The Extremist," p. 54.

EXHIBIT 1 **PETA's** **Mission** **Statement** Source: Courtesy of People for the Ethical Treatment of Animals (PETA).	People for the Ethical Treatment of Animals (PETA), with more than 1.6 million members and supporters, is the largest animal rights organization in the world. PETA focuses its attention on the four areas in which the largest numbers of animals suffer the most intensely for the longest periods of time: on factory farms, in laboratories, in the clothing trade, and in the entertainment industry. We also work on a variety of other issues, including the cruel killing of beavers, birds and other "pests," and the abuse of backyard dogs. PETA works through public education, cruelty investigations, research, animal rescue, legislation, special events, celebrity involvement, and protest campaigns.

the Arab-Israeli conflict. Her will stipulates that when she dies the meat on her body is to be cooked for a human barbeque, her skin used to make leather products such as purses, and her feet made into umbrella stands.[12]

PETA is creative. Since most people give no thought to animal rights, its actions are designed to attract attention, even at the cost of offending some. Perhaps the mildest attention-getting tactic is the use of theater. For example, PETA demonstrators have dragged themselves down streets with their feet in leg traps to publicize the evils of fur trapping. Another tactic is that of the outrageous act. To protest pictures of women wearing fur in *Vogue*, activists went to the expensive Manhattan restaurant where its editor was having lunch and threw a dead racoon on her plate. Young ladies at county fairs are crowned as Pork Queens only to have pies thrown in their faces by PETA activists. The group has asked Wisconsin, the "Dairy State," to change its state beverage from cows' milk to soy milk.

PETA freely uses sexuality to get attention. When the American Meat Institute puts on its Annual Hot Dog Lunches for government officials in Washington, DC, former *Playboy* Playmates wearing bikinis made of lettuce hand out "veggie dogs" outside. It recruits celebrities to present its message. Fame and glamor attract. Their presence endows a view that might otherwise be disregarded with the celebrity's aura of success and legitimacy. PETA also uses the Internet well to get its message out. It has multiple Web sites for issues such as zoos, circuses, and animal testing. The network of sites is easy to navigate, informative in depth, and often entertaining. There are facts,

games, pictures video clips, humor, and celebrities. PETA makes a special effort to influence children. One comic brochure, "Your Mommy Kills Animals" shows a crazed woman wielding a bloody knife over a rabbit. "Ask your mommy," it suggests, "how many animals she killed to make her fur coat."[13]

All these tactics, and more, have been employed in the fight against KFC.

THE CHICKENS

At the center of the conflict are the chickens. Chickens are a species of the order Galliformes, which includes turkeys, pheasants, grouse, and partridges. Galliformes are heavy-bodied, short-duration fliers that feed on insects and seeds, nest on the ground, and hatch precocial (self-caring) young. They are social birds that communicate with each other and establish complex hierarchies in flocks.

The earliest wild chickens, members of the species *Gallus gallus*, inhabited jungles of southeast Asia. About 4,000 years ago they were domesticated. From Asia the domesticated chicken, *Gallus domesticus*, spread across the globe. In ancient Greece they were valued for the sport of cockfighting, and in imperial Rome prophets read the future in their entrails. Chickens had such a hold on the superstitious Romans that generals kept special flocks in the belief that their behavior could foretell victory or defeat in battle. In the hours before combat, hardened legionnaires crowded around these flocks seeking portents. As the legions marched, they spread *Gallus domesticus* across the empire. Centuries later, the earliest European settlers brought chickens to North America.

[12] Ibid., pp. 57, 58.

[13] At www.furissdead.com

In the United States, large-scale chicken production developed slowly. As late as the 1920s chicken farms had flocks of only about 500 free-ranging birds. Today the industry is highly specialized, with some farms in egg production and others raising broilers (or chickens slaughtered for meat; literally, chickens for broiling—or baking or frying). Flocks are now raised in long, windowless, buildings with automated equipment to maintain as many as 100,000 birds. Consumption of chicken has risen. In 1955 only a little more than 1 billion broilers were raised, or 6.5 chickens for each American; by 2005 there were 8.7 billion raised, or 30 per American.[14]

Chickens, like other animal species, adapted for survival in an ecological niche. In doing so, certain behaviors became instinctive. They live in flocks of approximately 10 and establish dominance hierarchies called pecking orders. The dominant bird in a flock can peck any other bird, and that bird will yield. Status in the pecking order is conveyed by sounds such as crowing or cackling, aggressive or passive postures, spacing, use of more or less desirable nesting sites, and running at or away from rivals. In mixed-sex flocks there are two pecking orders, one for cocks and one for hens, but the hen hierarchy is completely subordinate. All hens yield to even the lowest cock. This is a genetically predisposed trait essential for species survival because a cock will not mate with a dominating hen. Pecking orders have survival value. Once dominance is established, fighting ceases and energy is used in socially productive ways.

In nature, chickens are omnivorous, eating plants, insects, and small animals such as lizards. Hens are secretive and build hidden nests, preferably on the ground. During the day chickens spread out to forage, but at dusk they reduce the spaces between them. At night they often roost in trees. According to PETA, chickens are "inquisitive and interesting animals" and "as intelligent as mammals like cats, dogs, and even primates."[15] In nature, they are individuals with "distinct personalities" that "form friendships and social hierarchies, recognize one another, love their young, and enjoy a full life, dust-bathing, making nests, roosting in trees, and more."[16]

Life in high-density growing environments frustrates these natural behaviors. Cages or crowding prevent division into flocks with established pecking orders. Without a complete pecking order, individuals may not yield to threat displays, and physical attacks occur as birds compete over space, food, and water.[17] Weaker animals have no place to hide and may be assaulted repeatedly until they die. In addition, crowded chickens are unable to engage in a range of ordinary foraging, grooming, nesting, brooding, and roosting behaviors. Critics claim that such deprivation violates the right of an animal to satisfy its needs through natural behaviors.

THE CAMPAIGN

At the start of the campaign, PETA sought to inflict damage on the KFC brand and harass company executives. In the first months it conducted hundreds of demonstrations at KFC restaurants around the world. Protesters dressed like chickens and locked themselves in cages. They handed out "Buckets of Blood" containing "Psycho Col. Sanders" figures and toy chickens with slit throats. When Yum! Brands CEO David Novak appeared at the opening of a restaurant in Germany, two activists doused him with fake blood and feathers. According to campaign leader Friedrich: "There is so much blood on this chicken-killer's hands, a little more on his business suit won't hurt."[18]

KFC issued a statement calling the attacks "corporate terrorism" that "crossed the line from simply expressing their views to corporate attacks and personal violence."[19] In Paris, Ingrid Newkirk and celebrity Chrissie Hynde of The Pretenders led activists who stormed into a busy KFC restaurant at the noon hour. They smeared red paint symbolizing chicken blood on the front window and talked to customers until security guards threw them out. Outside, the protest blocked traffic on a boulevard for two hours. Back in the United States, PETA put up roadside billboards depicting Col. Sanders hacking a chicken with

[14] *Statistical Abstract of the United States 1956, 77*th ed., tables 1 and 857; and *Statistical Abstract of the United States 2007*, 127th ed., tables 2 and 842.

[15] "Chickens," at www.peta.org.

[16] "PETA Reveals Shocking Cruelty to Animals at KFC Factory Chicken Farm," press release, October 2, 2003, at www.peta.org.

[17] T. R. O'Keefe et al., "Social Organization in Caged Layers: The Peck Order Revisited," *Poultry Science*, July 1988, p. 1013.

[18] Quoted in Jay Nordlinger, "PETA vs. KFC," *National Review*, December 22, 2003, p. 28.

[19] Cited in "Animal Rights Activists Spray KFC Chief with Fake Blood and Chicken Feathers," The Associated Press State & Local Wire, June 23, 2003.

Yum! Brands CEO David Novak after being splattered with blood at a demonstration in Hanover, Germany, on June 23, 2003. Source: © AP Photo/PETA Deutschland.

a bloody knife under the slogan "Kentucky Fried Cruelty. We do chickens wrong."[20]

Although the main effort of the campaign went into publicly associating the KFC brand with cruelty toward chickens, another focus was on pressuring KFC and Yum! Brand executives at a personal level. After several months of the campaign KFC President Cheryl Bachelder failed to keep what Ingrid Newkirk though was a commitment to call her. So Newkirk phoned Bachelder at home on a Saturday evening. When Bachelder objected to being called at home, Newkirk responded with a letter that read, in part:

> Of course you would rather not be disturbed in the privacy of your own home, but the animals you torture and slaughter pay for that home with their misery and their very lives yet have nothing remotely like a life or even a nest of any kind. . . . It is merely an accident of birth that you are not one of them.[21]

Newkirk wrote to both Bachelder and CEO Novak at their homes in Louisville, Kentucky, posting the letters with their home addresses on PETA's kfccruelty.com Web site. It enlisted former Beatle Paul McCartney to write to Novak. His letter, which requested an end to "the egregious forms of abuse endured by chickens," ran as a full-page ad in the Louisville *Courier-Journal*. A KFC spokesperson responded that "PETA should follow one of Sir Paul's songs and just 'Let It Be.'"[22]

PETA also wrote to friends and neighbors of Yum! Brands and KFC executives, requesting to visit their homes and speak with them. Bachelder's home was picketed. Pickets also came on Sunday to the Louisville church attended by Novak and another top executive. Outside the service, PETA parked its "Reality TV" truck that displayed big-screen images of slaughterhouse abuses.[23] On Christmas Eve and Christmas Day 2003 Friedrich dressed up as Santa Claus and blocked a sidewalk outside the church. He also demonstrated at the home of a KFC senior vice president, leading to a conviction for trespass.[24]

In the first summer of the campaign, KFC President Bachelder flew to Norfolk, Virginia, for a meeting with Newkirk at PETA's headquarters. At the meeting, she agreed to install cameras in slaughterhouses that supply KFC chickens, to provide more stimulation for chickens, to use mechanized chicken-gathering equipment, and to increase the space for each bird. In return, PETA agreed to scale back its campaign for 60 days.[25] However, the agreement fell apart when Newkirk accused Bachelder of not following through.

As time went on, PETA rolled out its broad strategic inventory. It recruited a long list of celebrity supporters. Actress Pamela Anderson narrated video clips showing how chickens are abused. Ms. Anderson freely lent her sex appeal to the campaign by, for example, posing for billboards in a white satin bra.[26] His Holiness the Dalai Lama wrote to ask that KFC end plans to build a restaurant in Tibet. The Rev. Al

[20] "Finger-Lickin' Foul" "*Houston Press*, December 18, 2003, p. 2.

[21] Letter of March 24, 2003, from Ingred E. Newkirk to Cheryl Bachelder, available at www.kfcruelty.com/petakfc.asp.

[22] Mark Naegele, "McCartney Accuses KFC of Fowl Play," *Columbus Dispatch*, July 25, 2003, p. 2C.

[23] Scott Sonner, "PETA Steps Up Campaign against KFC Farm, Slaughter Practices," The Associated Press State & Local Wire, September 19, 2003.

[24] "Christmas Protests Net Conviction for PETA Exec," *Restaurant Business*, May 18, 2004, online at restaurantbiz.com.

[25] Wesley J. Smith, "PETA-Fried," *National Review*, July 11, 2003, p. 25.

[26] "Billboard Companies Refuse to Run PETA Ad," *The Globe and Mail*, February 2, 2006, p. S2.

Sharpton spoke out asking the black community to boycott KFC.

Taking advantage of Securities and Exchange Commission rules, PETA gained entry to the Yum! Brands 2003 annual shareholders meeting in Louisville. After activists spoke, CEO Novak called on the group to end its campaign, saying, "We don't want to be abused, just like you don't want the chickens to be abused." In 2004 PETA qualified a shareholder resolution asking for a company report on actions to reduce cruelty toward chickens. Only 7.6 percent of shareholders voted for it. When PETA introduced a similar resolution in 2006, it went down to defeat with only 9 percent voting in favor.

PETA sued Yum! Brands alleging false statements about treatment of chickens on its Web site. The company deleted the wording. In a bizarre show of dedication a PETA staff member changed his legal name from Chris Garnett to KentuckyFriedCruelty.com.[27] PETA has conducted a dozen undercover investigations at KFC supplier plants in the United States, Europe, and Asia documenting incidents of sickening animal abuse. Protests continue. There have been more than 10,000 all around the world, many with female activists wearing bikinis to get attention.[28]

A MUTED CORPORATE DEFENSE

Throughout the PETA campaign, KFC and Yum! Brands have tried to maintain a low media profile while working to elevate animal welfare standards. This reticence is characteristic of the animal agriculture, food, and restaurant industry generally when animal welfare becomes an issue. In mass growing and slaughter some pain for animals is inevitable. Altering production to address chicken discomfort, injury, and behavioral deprivation raises costs.

Most consumers are ignorant of factory farming methods and fail to entertain the link between a KFC meal and the life experience of the creature in it.

Despite PETA's efforts, there is no groundswell of public opinion for more humane treatment of chickens. Reacting to a protest going on outside a restaurant in Israel, a KFC customer said: "There's nothing to do. This is life and it is all part of the food chain. I have to eat."[29]

The vacuum of interest and concern sustains industry calculations balancing poultry welfare against costs. For example, industry guidelines that KFC helped develop and now follows stipulate that electrical "stunning should be effective at [a] minimum of 98% of birds in [a] 500-bird sample."[30] This standard may be defined as humane, but it is met even if 10 conscious chickens out of every 500 are plunged in a tank of scalding hot water to loosen their feathers before further "processing." Such compromises in chicken welfare to avoid higher costs are tacitly accepted by KFC diners, but difficult to defend in a media debate. PETA's greatest source of power is the desire of average people to think of themselves as humane and decent.[31] The impossibility of defending a standard that lets chickens be boiled alive makes cautious nonconfrontation a better policy than frontal attack on PETA.

In response to attacks, the company consistently makes these points. It complies with all laws in the more than 100 countries where it has restaurants. It is only a purchaser and does not own the animal farms and slaughterhouses where abuses may occur. It accepts that its size as a chicken buyer gives it responsibility and the power to lead in the humane treatment of chickens and it is taking action.

Since 2000 KFC has followed the Yum! Brands Animal Welfare Guiding Principles (Exhibit 2) and since 2004 it has implemented a more comprehensive set of KFC Poultry Welfare Guidelines covering breeding, chicken houses, catching, transport, holding, stunning, and slaughter. KFC calls these guidelines "industry leading," but PETA rejects them because they do not require the changes it demands. Yum! Brands set up an Animal Welfare Advisory Council composed of distinguished animal scientists and industry

[27] Dave Golowenski, "Activist Group Squawks over KFC's Treatment of Chickens," *The Columbus Dispatch*, January 8, 2006, p. 17C.

[28] For example, "Bikini Protester Ruffles Feathers," *Nelson Daily News* (British Columbia), May 4, 2006, p. 1; and Maria Levitov, "Bikini-Clad Activists Target KFC," *The Moscow Times*, August 2, 2006, and "Bare Boycott" *South China Morning Post*, November 6, 2006, p. 3.

[29] Yitzchak Mokitada, quoted in Jenny Merkin and Yael Wolynetz, "KFC Diners Remain Unflappable in Face of Chicken Cruelty Protest," *The Jerusalem Post*, July 4, 2006, p. 5.

[30] *FMI-NCCR Animal Welfare Program, June 2003 Report*, at www.fmi.org.p.2.

[31] Eric Dezenhall, *Nail 'Em* (Amherst, NY: Prometheus Books, 2003), p. 80.

EXHIBIT 2
Yum! Brands
Animal
Welfare
Guiding
Principles

Source: www.yum.
com (2004).

Food Safety: Above all else, we are committed to providing our customers with safe, delicious meals and ensuring that our restaurants are maintained and operated under the highest food safety standards. This commitment is at the heart of our entire operations and supply chain management, and is evident in every aspect of our business—from raw material procurement to our restaurant food preparation and delivery.

Animal Treatment: Yum! Brands believes treating animals humanely and with care is a key part of our quality assurance efforts. This means animals should be free from mistreatment at all possible times from how they are raised and cared for to how they are transported and processed. Our goal is to only deal with suppliers who provide an environment that is free from cruelty, abuse and neglect.

Partnership: Yum! Brands partners with experts on our Animal Welfare Advisory Council and our suppliers to implement humane procedures/guidelines and to audit our suppliers to determine whether the adopted guidelines are being met.

Ongoing Training and Education: Yum! Brands recognizes that maintaining high standards of animal welfare is an ongoing process. Training and education has and will continue to play a key role in our efforts. Yum! Brands will continue to work with experts to ensure our quality assurance employees and suppliers have the training and knowledge necessary to further the humane treatment of animals.

Performance Quantification & Follow-up: Yum! Brands' animal welfare guidelines are specific and quantifiable. Yum! Brands measures performance against these guidelines through audits of our suppliers on a consistent basis.

Communication: Yum! Brands will communicate our best practices to counterparts within the industry and work with industry associations such as the National Council of Chain Restaurants and the Food Marketing Institute to implement continuous improvement of industry standards and operations.

representatives from supplier companies. When the Council was set up, PETA recommended people acceptable to it as members and the company appointed four of them. In 2005 three of these panel members submitted to KFC a carefully prepared set of recommendations for promoting animal welfare. They suggested that consumers were becoming more conscious of humane treatment and the time had come to elevate standards for chickens. Their recommendations called for actions that would have satisfied all of PETA's demands.[32] At about this time PETA had suspended its campaign to engage in secret negotiations with KFC. After a series of meetings, it asked KFC to pledge it would carry out the panelist's recommenda-

tions, but it refused. Soon after, PETA renewed its campaign and two of the three resigned.

KFC STANDS FIRM

As the campaign moved into its fourth year, KFC stood firm. PETA's boycott seemed of little financial consequence. Yum! Brands does not break out sales by each of its restaurant chains, but its overall financial performance has been very strong. Between 2003 and 2005, revenue was up 12 percent and net income (a measure of profitability) was up 24 percent. Shareholders have fared well. If you had invested in Yum! Brands' on the day PETA announced its campaign, your shares would have risen 133 percent by its fourth anniversary, far exceeding a 52 percent rise in the S&P 500 over the same period.[33]

[32] "Animal Welfare Recommendations and Proposed Plan of action for Implementation at KFC Suppliers," memo from Dr. Iam Duncan, Dr. Temple Grandin, and Dr. Mohan Raj to Harvey Brownlee, Chief Operating Officer, KFC, March 11, 2005.

[33] January 6, 2003, to January 5, 2007.

During that time earnings per share rose 26 percent and the company would have increased your dividend by 48 percent.

Now and then KFC and Yum! let strong feelings about PETA show. At the beginning of the campaign a spokesperson promised that "just like the U.S. government we will not negotiate with corporate terrorists."[34] In 2004 Gregg Dedrick, who replaced Bachelder as president of KFC, said that PETA had "distorted the truth time and time again" in its "campaign of harassment, invasion of privacy and what I'd call 'corporate terrorism.'"[35] In 2006 a Yum! senior executive said, "we're not going to capitulate" giving as his reason that "PETA's ultimate goal is to end meat consumption."[36]

This comment points to an assumption, surely existing at KFC though unstated by the company, that meat eating is good. In this the company is supported by Richard Martin, editor of the industry magazine *Nation's Restaurant News*. Martin says PETA errs in its "rejection of the animal kingdom's remorseless food chain paradigm" and in its "repudiation of the worldwide acceptance of meat eating as a proper option for descendants of hunters. . . . "[37] This position is entirely at odds with the values of animal rights activists, including one who writes, "if we cannot imagine how chickens must feel . . . perhaps we should try to imagine ourselves placed helplessly in the hands of an overpowering extraterrestrial species, to whom our pleas for mercy sound like nothing more than bleats and squeals and clucks—mere 'noise' to the master race in whose 'superior' minds we are 'only animals.'"[38]

Questions

1. Do you support KFC Corporation or People for the Ethical Treatment of Animals in this controversy? Why?

2. What are the basic criticisms that PETA makes of KFC? Are they convincing? Are its criticisms similar to timeless criticisms of business mentioned in the chapter?

3. What methods and arguments has KFC used to support its actions? Is it conducting the best defense?

4. Is the range of PETA's actions acceptable? Why does the group use controversial tactics? What are its sources of power in corporate campaigns?

5. Is it proper for PETA to pressure KFC for change when the company is following the law and public custom? Does PETA represent so compelling a truth or enough people to justify attacks on, and perhaps damage to, major corporations supported by and supporting millions of customers, employees, and stockholders?

6. Do animals have rights? If so, what are they? What duties do human beings have toward animals? Does KFC protect animal welfare at an acceptable level?

---

[34] Paul Holmes, "If KFC Wants to Combat PETA, Using Similar Over-the-Top Rhetoric Isn't the Best Method," *PR Week*, April 5, 2004, p. 7.

[35] "Press Conference Comments by KFC President Gregg Dedrick," July 21, 2004, at www.kfc.com, p. 2.

[36] Jonathan Blum, senior vice president of public affairs, quoted in Tom Price, *Activists in the Boardroom: How Advocacy Groups Seek to Shape Corporate Behavior* (Washington, DC: Foundation for Public Affairs, 2006), p. 11.

[37] Richard Martin, "Game of Chicken: Critics Say Capitulation to PETA Will Worsen Animal Rights Reprisals," *Nation's Restaurant News*, July 28, 2003, p. 31.

[38] Karen Davis, "Animal Suffering Similar to Human Slaves," *Chicago Sun-Times*, September 6, 2005, p. 50.

Corporate Social Responsibility

Merck & Co., Inc.

Corporate social responsibility takes many forms. The following story stands out as extraordinary.

For centuries river blindness, or *onchocerciasis* (on-ko-sir-KYE-a-sis), has tortured humanity in tropical regions. Its cause is a parasitic worm that lives only in humans. People are infected with the worm's tiny, immature larvae when bitten by the female blackfly, which swarms near fast-moving rivers and streams. The larvae settle in human tissue and form colonies, often visible outside the body as lumps the size of tennis balls, where in adults grow up to two feet long. Mature adults live for 7 to 18 years coiled in these internal nodes, mating, and releasing tens of thousands of microscopic new worms. The offspring migrate back to the skin's surface, where they cause disfiguring welts, lumps, and discoloration along with a persistent itch that has driven many sufferers to suicide. Eventually, they move into the eyes, causing blindness. The cycle of infection is renewed when blackflies bite a person with onchocerciasis, ingesting tiny worms in the blood, then bite uninfected individuals, passing on the parasite.

People suffer in many ways. For Amarech Bitena of Ethiopia, the cost of river blindness is a broken heart. The parasites came in childhood. Now, at 25, her skin has become hard and dark, her vision blurred. She has not married. "When I think about the future," she says, "I feel completely hopeless. . . . My vision can't be restored. My skin is destroyed. I would have liked to be a doctor."[1] More than 18 million people have oncocerciasis, most in the river regions of some of the poorest African nations. About 500,000 have impaired vision and 270,000 are blind.[2] It affects 37 percent of the population of Cameroon and 14 percent in Nigeria.[3] It saps economies by enervating workers and driving farmers from fertile, riverside land.

---

[1] Claudia Feldman, "River Blindness: A Forgotten Disease," *The Houston Chronicle,* October 9, 2005, p. 5

[2] María-Globia Bañéż et al., "River Blindness: A Success Story under Threat?" *PloS Medicine,* September 2006, p. 1454.

[3] "River Blindness: Six Million Camaroonians Affected," *Africa News*, September 26, 2006; "20 Million Nigerians on Onchocerciasis Treatment," *Africa News*, January 19, 2007.

In countries ravaged by river blindness, the blind sometimes hold sticks and follow the lead of children. Merck commissioned this bronze sculpture for the lobby of its New Jersey headquarters, where top executives pass by each day. It symbolizes Merck's commitment to make medicine for the good of humanity. Because of Merck's unprecedented donation of a river blindness drug, such scenes are no longer common.
Source: Photo courtesy of Merck & Co., Inc.

Until recently, no practical treatment for river blindness existed, and little was being done. It is only one of many tropical diseases affecting millions in developing nations. Critics allege that big drug companies ignore these epidemics to focus on pills for the diseases of affluent people in developed nations. Years ago the World Health Organization began pesticide spraying to kill the blackfly, but it was a frustrating job. Winds carry flies up to 100 miles from breeding grounds. And scientists estimate that the breeding cycle must be suppressed for 14 years to stop reinfections.

In 1975 scientists at Merck & Co. discovered a compound that killed animal parasites. By 1981 they had synthesized it and marketed it for deworming dogs, cattle, sheep, and pigs. Ivermectin, as it was called, was a blockbuster hit and would be the best-selling veterinary drug worldwide for two decades. Merck's researchers had a strong hunch it also would be effective in humans against *Onchocerca volvulus*, the river blindness parasite.[4]

Merck faced a decision. It would be very expensive to bring a new drug to market and manufacture it. Yet people with the disease were among the world's poorest. Their villages had no doctors to prescribe it, no drug stores to sell it. Should Merck develop a drug that might never be profitable?

George W. Merck, son of the firm's founder and its leader for 32 years, once said: "We try never to forget that medicine is for the people. It is not for the profits. The profits follow, and if we have remembered that, they have never failed to appear."[5] This advice was still respected at Merck; it lived in the corporate culture. Merck's scientists were motivated by humanitarian goals and restraining them was awkward. The decision to go ahead was made. The cost would be $200 million.[6]

Clinical trials of ivermectin, confirmed its effectiveness. A single dose taken once a year dramatically reduced the population of the tiny worms migrating through the body and impaired reproduction by adult parasites, alleviating symptoms and preventing blindness.[7]

Eventually, it became clear that neither those in need nor their governments could afford to buy ivermectin. So in 1987 Merck committed itself to manufacture and ship it at no cost to where it was needed for as long as it was needed to control river

[4] David Bollier, *Merck & Company* (Stanford, CA: Business Enterprise Trust, 1991), p. 5.

[5] Roy Vagelos and Louis Galambos, *The Moral Corporation* (New York: Cambridge University Press, 2006), p. 171.

[6] Ibid., pp. 164 and 169.

[7] Mohammed A. Aziz et al., "Efficacy and Tolerance of Ivermectin in Human Onchocerciasis," *The Lancet*, July 24, 1982.

blindness. The company asked governments and private organizations to help set up distribution.

Since then, Merck has given away more than 1.4 billion tablets in 37 countries at a cost of $2.1 billion.[8] Estimates are that treatment has prevented 40,000 cases of blindness each year; returned to use 62 million acres of farmland, an area the size of Michigan; and added 7.5 million years of adult labor in national workforces.[9] A study of economic effects for two areas in Africa estimated $573 million in net benefits over 40 years.[10]

River blindness will not be eliminated soon. Infection rates have fallen, but the blackfly is so persistent and adult parasites in the body survive yearly doses of ivermectin. For now, the Merck program protects millions of people from new infection and blindness.

For a drug company to go through the new drug development process and then give the drug away was unprecedented. Merck's management believes that although developing and donating ivermectin has been expensive, humanitarianism and enlightened self-interest vindicate the decision. Still, not everyone gives Merck the highest praise. Erika Check, a biomedical writer for *Nature*, is reserved: "It is doubtful that the company would have ever created a drug for treating [river blindness] had it not been for their interest in manufacturing a profitable veterinary health medicine."[11]

Few corporations have such a singular opportunity to drive evil from human life and the mind-set to take advantage of it, but most firms today, through inspiration or under pressure, go beyond routine business to enrich society in some way. Merck's effort is a stellar example of old-fashioned philanthropy the way it has been done in America since the rise of big companies. In this chapter we define the idea of social responsibility and explain how it has expanded in meaning and practice over time. The next chapter explains more about how corporations carry out their social responsibilities.

THE EVOLVING IDEA OF CORPORATE SOCIAL RESPONSIBILITY

corporate social responsibility
The duty of a corporation to create wealth in ways that avoid harm to, protect, or enhance societal assets.

Corporate social responsibility is the duty of a corporation to create wealth in ways that avoid harm to, protect, or enhance societal assets. The term is a modern one. It did not enter common use until the 1960s, when it appeared in academic literature. If often goes by other names, including its abbreviation CSR, corporate citizenship, stakeholder management, and sustainability. Whatever it is called, there is no precise, operational meaning. It is primarily a political theory, not a management or

[8] H. R. Waters, J. A. Rehwinkel, and G. Burnham," Economic Evaluation of Ivermectin Distribution," *Tropical Medicine and International Health*, April 2004, p. A23. Total cost is based on an estimated cost of $1.50 per tablet.

[9] "The Merck Ivermectin Donation Program," at www.merck.com/cr/enabling_access/developin_world/ivermectin/.

[10] H. R. Waters et al., "Economic Evaluation of Mectizan Distribution," *Tropical Medicine and International Health,* April 2004, p. A16.

[11] "Letters: Erika Check Replies," *Foreign Policy,* September/October 2006, p. 16.

economic theory, because its central purposes are to control and legitimize the exercise of corporate power.

The fundamental idea is that corporations have duties that go beyond lawful execution of their economic function. Here is the reasoning. The overall performance of a firm must benefit society. Because of market imperfections, the firm will not fulfill all its duties, and may breach some, if it responds only to market forces. Laws and regulations correct some shortcomings, more in developed countries, fewer in the less developed. Beyond the law, firms must voluntarily take additional actions to meet their full obligations to society. What additional actions must they take? These have to be defined in practice by negotiation with stakeholders. In doing so there is often a struggle between corporations, their critics, and a range of stakeholders.

Advocates of social responsibility justify it with two basic arguments. First, it is a moral duty to promote social justice. A timeless moral principle is that power should be used fairly. Second, social responsibility has concrete benefits. It motivates employees and creates loyal customers. It leads to innovative products and strategies. It strengthens surrounding communities. It protects reputations and avoids regulation.

Opponents believe that corporate social responsibility is an unwarranted cost. It creates administrative expenses, distracts executives, confuses economic goals with other goals, and subtracts from social welfare when the corporation is less efficient.[12] Corporations are owned by shareholders and the primary fiduciary responsibility of managers is to maximize profits for them. Managers who take on social projects or charities do so with money from the shareholder's pockets, thereby cheating them. In addition, social justice has no definitive meaning and reasonable people, from progressives to conservatives, differ on what the corporation must do to promote it. The agenda of corporate social responsibility is centered in progressive ideology and based, therefore, on the goals of a movement that is at heart dubious of capitalism. Markets, not politics, should direct corporations. When markets fail, they should be corrected by the policies of representative government, not by unelected executives or by activists.

The political spectrum of beliefs about corporate responsibility is shown in Figure 5.1. On the left, progressives seek expansive exercise of social responsibility. Near the middle, but on the side of acceptance, are corporate managers, most of whom accept the idea as a practical necessity even as they often harbor doctrinal reservations. At the right are free market *libertarians*, advocates of laissez-faire who believe that the market allocates resources more efficiently than political pressures.

Years ago, most managers were on the right side of the spectrum with the libertarians. Why did they move left? As we will explain, the doctrine of corporate responsibility has evolved over time to require more expansive action by companies largely because stakeholder groups gained more power to impose their agendas, but also because the ethical and legal philosophies underlying it matured to support broader action by managers. The story of corporate social responsibility begins with Adam Smith.

libertarians
Those who believe in the maximum freedom, or liberty, to act or use property without interference by others, especially government.

[12] See, for example, "The Good Company: A Survey of Corporate Social Responsibility," *The Economist*, January 22, 2005.

FIGURE 5.1
The CSR
Spectrum

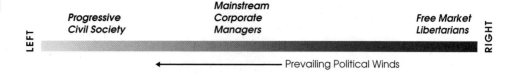

Social Responsibility in Classical Economic Theory
==

Throughout American history, classical capitalism, which is the basis for the market capitalism model in Chapter 1, has been the basic inspiration for business. In the classical view, a business is socially responsible if it maximizes profits while operating within the law, because an "invisible hand" will direct economic activity to serve the good of the whole.

This ideology, derived from Adam Smith's *Wealth of Nations,* is compelling in its simplicity and its resonance with self-interest. In nineteenth-century America, it was elevated to the status of a commandment. However, the idea that markets harness low motives and work them into social progress has always attracted skeptics. Smith himself had a surprising number of reservations about the market's ability to protect human welfare.[13] Today the classical ideology still commands the economic landscape, but, as we will see, ethical theories of broader responsibility have worn down its prominences.

The Early Charitable Impulse
============================

The idea that corporations had social responsibilities awaited the rise of corporations themselves. Meanwhile, the most prominent expression of duty to society was the good deed of charity by business owners.

Most colonial era businesses were very small. Merchants practiced thrift and frugality, which were dominant virtues then, to an extreme. Benjamin Franklin's advice to a business acquaintance reflects the penny-pinching nature of the time: "He that kills a breeding sow, destroys all her offspring to the thousandth generation. He that murders a crown, destroys all that it might have produced, even scores of pounds."[14] Yet charity was a coexisting virtue, and business owners sought respectability by giving to churches, orphanages, and poorhouses. Their actions first illustrate that although American business history can be pictured as a jungle of profit maximization, people in it have always been concerned citizens.[15]

Charity by owners continued in the early nineteenth century, and grew as great fortunes were made. Mostly, the new millionaires endowed social causes as individuals, not through the companies that were the fountainheads of their wealth.

---

[13] Jacob Viner, "Adam Smith and Laissez-Faire," *Journal of Political Economy*, April 1927.

[14] In "Advice to a Young Tradesman [1748]," in *The Autobiography of Benjamin Franklin and Selections from His Other Writings*, ed. Nathan G. Goodman (New York: Carlton House, 1932), p. 210. A crown was a British coin on which appeared the figure of a royal crown.

[15] Mark Sharfman, "The Evolution of Corporate Philanthropy, 1883–1952," *Business & Society,* December 1994.

Andrew Carnegie (1835–1919).
Source: Library of Congress, Prints and Photographs Collection, LC-USZ62-15566.

One of the earliest was Steven Girard, a shipping and banking tycoon. When he died in 1831, the richest person in the nation, he made generous charitable bequests in his will, the largest of which was $6 million for a school to educate orphaned boys from the first grade through high school.[16] This single act changed the climate of education in the United States because it came before free public schooling, when a high-school education was still only for children of the wealthy.

Following Girard, others donated generously and did so while still living. John D. Rockefeller systematically gave away $550 million over his lifetime. Andrew Carnegie gave $350 million during his life to social causes, built 2,811 public libraries, and donated 7,689 organs to churches. He wrote a famous article entitled "The Disgrace of Dying Rich" and argued that it was the duty of a man of wealth "to consider all surplus revenues . . . as trust funds which he is called upon to administer."[17]

However, Carnegie's philosophy of giving was highly paternalistic. He believed that big fortunes should be used for grand purposes such as endowing universities and building concert halls like Carnegie Hall. They should not be wasted by paying higher wages to workers or giving gifts to poor people; that would dissipate riches on small indulgences and would not, in the end, elevate the culture of a society. Thus, one day when a friend of Carnegie's encountered a beggar and gave him a quarter, Carnegie admonished the friend that it was one of "the very worst actions of his life."[18]

social Darwinism
A philosophy of the late 1800s and early 1900s that used evolution to explain the dynamics of human society and institutions. The idea of "survival of the fittest" in the social realm implied that rich people and dominant companies were morally superior.

In this remark, Carnegie echoed the doctrine of **social Darwinism,** which held that charity interfered with the natural evolutionary process in which society shed its less fit to make way for the better adapted. Well-meaning people who gave to charity interfered with the natural law of progress by propping up failed examples of the human race. The leading advocate of this astringent doctrine, the English philosopher Herbert Spencer, wrote the following heartless passage in a best-selling 1850 book.

---

[16] The school became known as Girard College, which one of the authors of this book, George Steiner, attended. It still exists in Philadelphia.

[17] Andrew Carnegie, *The Gospel of Wealth* (Cambridge, MA: Harvard University Press, 1962), p. 25; originally published in 1901.

[18] Quoted in Page Smith, *The Rise of Industrial America,* vol. 6 (New York: Penguin Books, 1984), p. 136.

Herbert Spencer (1820–1903). Spencer attempted a synthesis of human knowledge based on the unifying idea of evolution. When he visited the United States in 1882 a grand dinner attended by 200 leading Americans was held for him at Delmonico's in New York. Source: © Hulton-Deutsch Collection/ CORBIS.

ultra vires
A Latin phrase denoting acts beyond the powers given the corporation by law.

It seems hard that a laborer incapacitated by sickness from competing with his stronger fellows should have to bear the resulting privations. It seems hard that widows and orphans should be left to struggle for life or death. Nevertheless, when regarded not separately, but in connection with the interests of universal humanity, these harsh fatalities are seen to be full of the highest beneficence—the same beneficence which brings to early graves the children of diseased parents and singles out the low-spirited, the intemperate, and the debilitated as the victims of an epidemic.[19]

Spencer approved of some charity, though only when it raised the character and superiority of the giver. Still, the overall effect of Spencer's arguments was to moderate charity by business leaders and retard the growth of a modern social conscience.

More than just faith in markets and social Darwinism constrained business from undertaking voluntary social action. Charters granted by states when corporations were formed required that profits be disbursed to shareholders. Courts consistently held charitable gifts to be *ultra vires*, that is, "beyond the law," because charters did not expressly permit them. To use company funds for charity or social works took money from the pockets of shareholders and invited lawsuits. Thus, when Rockefeller had the humanitarian impulse to build the first medical school in China, he paid for it out of his own pocket; not a penny came from Standard Oil. Although most companies took a negative view of philanthropy, by the 1880s the railroads were an exception. They sponsored the Young Men's Christian Association (YMCA) movement, which provided rooming and religious indoctrination for rail construction crews. Yet such actions were exceptional.

As the twentieth century approached, classical ideology was still a mountain of resistance to expanding the idea of business social responsibility. A poet of that era, James Russell Lowell, captured the spirit of the day.

> Not a deed would he do
> Not a word would he utter
> Till he's weighed its relation
> To plain bread and butter.

Social Responsibility in the Late Nineteenth and Early Twentieth Centuries

Giving, no matter how generous, was a narrow kind of social responsibility often unrelated to a company's impacts on society. By the late 1800s it was growing apparent to the business elite that prevailing doctrines used to legitimize business defined its responsibilities too narrowly. Industrialization had fostered social problems and political corruption. Farmers were in revolt. Labor was increasingly

---

[19] Herbert Spencer, *Social Statics* (New York: Robert Schalkenbach Foundation, 1970), p. 289; first published in 1850.

violent. Socialism was at high tide. A growing number of average Americans began to question unfettered laissez-faire economics and the heartless doctrine of social Darwinism. Business feared calls for more regulation, was terrified of socialist calls for appropriation of assets, and sought to blunt the urgency of these appeals by voluntary action.

During the Progressive era, three interrelated themes of broader responsibility emerged. First, managers were *trustees,* that is, agents whose corporate roles put them in positions of power over the fate of not just stockholders, but of others such as workers, customers, and communities. This power implied a duty to promote the welfare of each group. Second, managers had an obligation to *balance* these multiple interests. They were, in effect, coordinators who settled competing claims. Third, many managers subscribed to the *service principle,* a near-spiritual belief that individual managers served society by making each business successful; if they all prospered, the aggregate effect would eradicate social injustice, poverty, and other ills. This belief was only a fancy reincarnation of classical ideology. However, many of its adherents conceded that companies were still obligated to undertake social projects that helped, or "served," the public.[20] These three interrelated ideas—trusteeship, balance, and service—expanded the idea of business responsibility beyond simple charity. But the type of responsibility envisioned was still paternalistic, and the actions of big company leaders often showed an underlying Scroogelike mentality.

One such leader was Henry Ford, who had an aptitude for covering meanness with a shining veneer of citizenship. In the winter of 1914 Ford thrilled the public by announcing the "Five-Dollar Day" for Ford Motor Co. workers. Five dollars was about double the daily pay for manufacturing workers at the time and seemed very generous. In fact, although Ford took credit for being big-hearted, the $5 wage was intended to cool unionizing and was not what it appeared on the surface. The offer attracted hordes of job seekers from around the country to Highland Park, Michigan. One subzero morning in January, there were 2,000 lined up outside the Ford plant by 5:00 A.M.; by dawn there were 10,000. Disorder broke out, and the fire department turned hoses on the freezing men.

The few who were hired had to serve a six-month apprenticeship and comply with the puritanical Ford Motor Co. code of conduct (no drinking, marital discord, or otherwise immoral living) to qualify for the $5 day. Many were fired on pretexts before the six months passed. Thousands of replacements waited outside each day hoping to fill a new vacancy. Inside, Ford speeded up the assembly line. Insecure employees worked faster under the threat of being purged for a younger, stronger, lower-paid new hire. Those who hung on to qualify for the $5 wage had to face greedy merchants, landlords, and realtors in the surrounding area who raised prices and rents.

Ford was a master of image. In 1926 he announced the first five-day, 40-hour week for workers, but with public accolades still echoing for this "humanitarian" gesture, he speeded up the line still more, cut wages, and announced a program

trustee
An agent of a company whose corporate role puts him or her in a position of power over the fate of not just stockholders, but of others such as customers, employees, and communities.

service principle
A belief that managers served society by making companies profitable and that aggregate success by many managers would resolve major social problems.

[20] Rolf Lunden, *Business and Religion in the American 1920s* (New York: Greenwood Press, 1988), pp. 147–50.

Inventor and industrialist Henry Ford (1863–1947). The public made him a folk hero and saw him as a generous employer. But he manipulated workers to lower costs.
Source: Library of Congress, Prints and Photographs Collection, LC-USZ62-111278.

to weed out less-efficient employees. These actions were necessary, he said, to compensate for Saturdays off. Later that year, Ford told the adulatory public that he had started a social program to fight juvenile delinquency. He proposed to employ 5,000 boys 16 to 20 years old and pay them "independence wages."[21] This was trumpeted as citizenship, but as the "boys" were hired, older workers were pitted against younger, lower-paid replacements.

A few business leaders, however, acted more consistently with the emerging themes of business responsibility. One was General Robert E. Wood, who led Sears, Roebuck and Company from 1924 to 1954. He believed that a large corporation was more than an economic institution; it was a social and political one as well. In the Sears *Annual Report* for 1936, he outlined the ways in which Sears was discharging its responsibilities to what he said were the chief constituencies of the company—customers, the public, employees, sources of merchandise supply, and stockholders.[22] Stockholders came last because, according to General Wood, they could not attain their "full measure of reward" unless the other groups were satisfied first. In thought and action, General Wood was far ahead of his time.

Nevertheless, in the 1920s and after that, corporations found various ways to support communities. Organized charities were formed, such as the Community Chest, the Red Cross, and the Boy Scouts, to which they contributed. In many cities, companies gave money and expertise to improve schools and public health. In the 1940s corporations began to give cash and stock to tax-exempt foundations set up for philanthropic giving.

1950–The Present

The contemporary understanding of corporate social responsibility was formed during this period. An early and influential statement of the idea was made in 1954 by Howard R. Bowen in his book *Social Responsibilities of the Businessman*.[23] Bowen said that managers felt strong public expectations to act in ways that went beyond profit-maximizing and were, in fact, meeting those expectations. Then he laid out the basic arguments for social responsibility: (1) managers have an ethical duty to consider the broad social impacts of their decisions; (2) businesses are reservoirs of skill and energy for improving civic life; (3) corporations must use power in keeping with a broad social contract, or lose their legitimacy; (4) it is in the enlightened self-interest of business to improve society; and (5) voluntary action may head off negative public attitudes and unwanted regulations. This book, despite being 50 years old, remains an excellent encapsulation of the current ideology of corporate responsibility.

---

[21] Keith Sward, *The Legend of Henry Ford* (New York: Rinehart & Company, 1948), p. 176.

[22] James C. Worthy, *Shaping an American Institution: Robert E. Wood and Sears, Roebuck* (Urbana: University of Illinois Press, 1984), p. 173.

[23] New York: Harper, 1954.

Not everyone accepted Bowen's arguments. The primary dissenters were conservative economists who claimed that business is *most* responsible when it makes money efficiently, not when it misapplies its energy on social projects. The best-known advocate of this view, then and now, is Nobel laureate Milton Friedman.

> There is one and only one social responsibility of business—to use its resources and engage in activities designed to increase its profits so long as it stays within the rules of the game, which is to say, engages in open and free competition, without deception or fraud. . . . Few trends could so thoroughly undermine the very foundations of our free society as the acceptance by corporate officials of social responsibility other than to make as much money for their stockholders as possible. This is a fundamentally subversive doctrine.[24]

Friedman argues that managers are the employees of a corporation's owners and are directly responsible to them. Stockholders want to maximize profits, so the manager's sole objective is to accommodate them. If a manager spends corporate funds on social projects, he or she is diverting shareholders' dollars to programs they may not even favor. Similarly, if the cost of social projects is passed on to consumers in higher prices, the manager is spending their money. This "taxation without representation," says Friedman, is wrong.[25] Furthermore, if the market price of a product does not reflect the true costs of producing it, but includes costs for social programs, then the market's allocation mechanism is distorted.

The opposition of Friedman and other adherents of classical economic doctrine proved to be a principled, rearguard action. In theory the arguments were unerring, but in practice they were inexpedient. At the time they were expressed there was a power struggle going on between corporations and critics seeking to control the excesses of capitalism and reduce externalities such as pollution. In this struggle, Friedman's position incited critics and invited retaliation and more regulation should the business community openly agree with it. Moreover, the idea that corporations could undertake expanded corporate social responsibility had enormous utility for business. If corporations volunteered to do more it would calm critics, forestall regulation, and preserve corporate legitimacy. Not surprisingly, Friedman's view was decisively rejected by business leaders, who soon articulated a vision of expanded duty. In 1971 the Committee for Economic Development, a prestigious corporate leadership group, published a bold statement of the case for expansive social responsibility. Society, said the report, has broadened its expectations outward over "three concentric circles of responsibilities."[26]

- An *inner circle* of clear-cut responsibility for efficient execution of the economic function resulting in products, jobs, and economic growth.
- An *intermediate circle* encompassing responsibility to exercise this economic function with a sensitive awareness of changing social values and priorities.

---

[24] *Capitalism and Freedom* (Chicago: University of Chicago Press, 1962), p. 133.

[25] "The Social Responsibility of Business Is to Increase Its Profits," *New York Times Magazine,* September 13, 1970.

[26] Committee for Economic Development, *Social Responsibilities of Business Corporations* (New York: CED, 1971), p. 11.

- An *outer circle* that outlines newly emerging and still amorphous responsibilities that business should assume to improve the social environment, even if they are not directly related to specific business processes.

Classical ideology focused solely on the first circle. Now business leaders argued that management responsibilities went further. The report was followed in 1981 by a *Statement on Corporate Responsibility* from the Business Roundtable, a group of 200 CEOs of the largest corporations. It said:

> Economic responsibility is by no means incompatible with other corporate responsibilities in society. . . . A corporation's responsibilities include how the whole business is conducted every day. It must be a thoughtful institution which rises above the bottom line to consider the impact of its actions on all, from shareholders to the society at large. Its business activities must make social sense.[27]

Friedmanism
The theory that the sole responsibility of a corporation is to optimize profits while obeying the law.

After these statements from top executives appeared, the range of social programs assumed by business expanded rapidly in education, the arts, public health, housing, the environment, literacy, employee relations, and other areas. However, although the business elite formally rejected *Friedmanism,* corporate cultures, which change only at glacial rates, still promoted a single-minded obsession with efficiency and financial results. The belief that a trade-off existed between profits and social responsibility was (and still is) widespread and visible in corporate actions.

BASIC ELEMENTS OF SOCIAL RESPONSIBILITY

The three elements of social responsibility are market actions, externally mandated actions, and voluntary actions. Figure 5.2 illustrates the relative magnitude of each, how it has changed over historical eras, and how change will progress if the trend toward expansion of the idea of corporate social responsibility continues. To be socially responsible, a corporation must fulfill its duties in each area of action.

Market actions are responses to competitive forces in markets. Such actions have always dominated and this will continue. When a corporation responds to markets, it fulfills its first and most important social responsibility. All else pales before its economic impact. Recently the giant Unilever Group cooperated with Oxfam International, a confederation of progressive NGOs fighting world poverty, to study the overall impact of its branch company in Indonesia. Oxfam is suspicious of corporations and had "ruthlessly challenged" Unilever's profit-seeking actions.[28] Yet the final report detailed a wondrous economic effect in a country where half the population lives below $2 a day.

Unilever Indonesia (UI) is the thirteenth-largest company in the country. Like its global parent, it sells personal and home products such as Kleenex, Pepsodent, and Lux soap, along with a variety of foods. Over five years ending in 2006, UI

---

[27] New York: Business Roundtable, October 1981, pp. 12 and 14.

[28] Jason Caly, *Exploring the Links Between International Business and Poverty Reduction: A Case Study of Unilever in Indonesia* (Eynsham, UK: Oxfam GB and Unilever PLC, 2005), p. 10.

FIGURE 5.2
Motives
for Social
Responsi-
bility and
Their
Evolving
Magnitudes

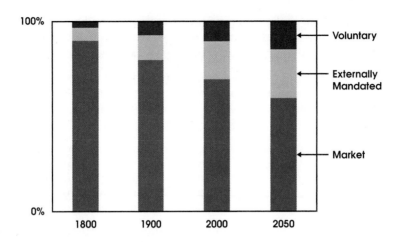

value chain
The sequence
of coordinated
actions that add
value to a prod-
uct or service.

made a net profit of $212 million. But the surprise was that its operations created total monetary value of $633 million along its *value chain*. A value chain is the sequence of coordinated actions that add value to a product or service. For Unilever it includes economic actors outside the corporation in both its backward supply chain and forward distribution channels.

Of the $633 million total, only 34 percent was captured by UI, the rest, most of it, went to others: 4 percent to farmers for their crops, 12 percent to several hundred suppliers, 6 percent to product distributors, and 18 percent to as many as 1.8 million retailers, among them tiny shops and street vendors selling "sachets," or small packets of Unilever products made especially for low-income consumers who could not afford regular sizes. From its share, UI put the majority back into the Indonesian economy, reinvesting 25 percent in its local business, giving 30 percent to the government in taxes, and paying 7 percent in dividends to Indonesian shareholders.[29] Unilever Indonesia employed about 5,000 workers, but the study found that the entire value chain created 300,764 full-time jobs, an important contribution in a nation with more than 9 percent unemployment.

Figures such as these illustrate how the greatest positive impact of a corporation on society is economic and why maximizing that impact is a corporation's greatest social responsibility. From the study, Oxfam concluded that tremendous potential for poverty alleviation existed in UI's routine profit-seeking actions. It absolved the company of draining Indonesian society by profiting on the backs of poor people, though it still needled the company, accusing it of using advertising to create demand for unessential products such as ice cream.

**civil
regulation**
Regulation by
nonstate actors
based on social
norms or stand-
ards enforced
by social or
market sanc-
tions.

Mandated actions are initiatives required either by government regulation or civil regulation. Government, or public, regulation is rooted in the authority of the state and its mandates are enforceable by law. Government mandates have multiplied rapidly over the past 75 years. *Civil regulation* is regulation by non-state actors based on social norms or standards enforced by social or market sanctions. Civil regulation, sometimes called private regulation, has many

[29] The other 38 percent was paid as dividends to overseas shareholders. Figures in this paragraph are from ibid., pp. 14, 82, and 83.

faces. It is imposed when activists, consumers, investors, lenders, shareholders, or employees make demands on a company and failure to comply will lead to reputational or financial damage. Such mandates are enforced by the power of the market, not the power of law.[30] As we will see later in this chapter, mandates based on civil regulation are now expanding rapidly in international operations.

The third element is *voluntary actions* that go beyond what is compelled by law, regulation, or other mandates. Some voluntary actions can be described as "legal plus" because they exceed required mandates. An example would be cutting pollution below legally permitted levels. Other actions are unrelated to mandates, but respond to public consensus. Charitable giving is an example. This helps the community, though it pales in importance compared to economic benefits from normal operations. Still other voluntary actions may be strategic initiatives where the firm seeks to profit from solving a social problem. Finally, a few companies have acted beyond public consensus in ways they believed were responsible. For example, Benetton Group once ran an anti-death-penalty ad campaign in the United States. Ads showing the faces of murderers on death row were intended to provoke debate on the death penalty. They did, but they also led Sears, Roebuck to drop Benetton clothing from its stores and ignited a boycott of Benetton outlets by relatives of murdered children.[31]

GENERAL PRINCIPLES OF CORPORATE SOCIAL RESPONSIBILITY

No universal rules for social responsibility apply to every company. However, the following broad principles are widely accepted by managers and others.

- *Corporations are economic institutions run for profit.* Their greatest responsibility is to create economic benefits. They should be judged primarily on economic criteria and cannot be expected to meet purely social objectives without financial incentives. Corporations may incur short-run costs on social initiatives that promise long-term benefits. And they should seek ways to solve social problems at a profit.
- *All firms must follow multiple bodies of law,* including (1) corporation laws and chartering provisions, (2) the civil and criminal laws of nations, (3) bodies of regulation that protect stakeholders, and (4) international laws. However, obeying the law is a minimum. Law is reactive and lags behind emerging norms and duties.
- *Managers must act ethically.* They must respect the law and, in addition, conform their behavior to ethical principles; model ethical values such as integrity, honesty, and justice; and set up codes, policies, and procedures to elevate behavior within the firm.

---

[30] David Vogel, "The Private Regulation of Global Corporate Conduct," Working Paper Series, University of California, Berkeley, Paper 34, 2006.

[31] Jerry Della Famina, "Benetton Ad Models Are Dressed to Kill Sales," *The Wall Street Journal*, March 20, 2000, p. A34.

external cost
A production
cost not paid by
a firm or its
customers, but
by members of
society.

- *Corporations have a duty to correct adverse social impacts they cause.* They should try to internalize *external costs*, or costs of production borne by society. A factory dumping toxic effluent into a stream creates costs such as human and animal disease that are imposed on innocents, not on the company or its customers.
- *Social responsibility varies with company characteristics* such as size, industry, products, strategies, marketing techniques, locations, internal cultures, and external demands. Thus, a global pharmaceutical company such as Merck has a far different impact on society than a local insurance company, so its responsibilities are different and greater.
- *Managers should try to meet legitimate needs of multiple stakeholders.* Although corporations have a fiduciary duty to shareholders, it is not legally required, or desirable or possible to manage solely in their interest. Consumers, employees, governments, communities, and other groups also have important claims on the firm.
- *Corporate behavior must comply with norms in an underlying social contract.* To understand this contract and how it changes, managers can study the direction of national policies and global norms as evidenced in legislation, regulations, treaties, trade agreements, declarations, and public opinion.[32]
- *Corporations should accept a measure of accountability toward society.* They should publicly report on their social performance in addition to their financial performance. This social reporting should cover major social impacts and, like financial reporting, be verifiable; that is, audited and checked by independent parties.

ARE SOCIAL AND FINANCIAL PERFORMANCE RELATED?

Scholars have done many studies to see if companies that are more socially responsible are also more profitable. Most support the thesis that social responsibility and profits go together. Yet many of them have mixed, inconclusive, or negative findings. A review of 95 such studies over 30 years found that a majority (53 percent) showed a positive relationship between profits and responsibility. However, 24 percent of them found no relationship, 19 percent a mixed relationship, and 5 percent a negative relationship.[33]

The inconsistency of results from study to study is not surprising given the difficult problems of method that researchers face. To begin, no fixed, neutral definition of social responsibility exists. Therefore, an objective ranking of corporations as more or less responsible is impossible. Many studies have used social responsi-

---

[32] An early argument for the importance of managing beyond, but in the direction of, laws and rules is Lee E. Preston and James E. Post, *Private Management and Public Policy: The Principle of Public Responsibility* (Englewood Cliffs, NJ: Prentice Hall, 1975).

[33] Joshua Daniel Margolis and James Patrick Walsh, *People and Profits: The Search for a Link between a Company's Social and Financial Performance* (Mahwah, NJ: Lawrence Erlbaum, 2001), p. 10. See also similar results in a review of 51 studies in Jennifer J. Griffin and John F. Mahon, "The Corporate Social Performance and Corporate Financial Performance Debate," *Business & Society*, March 1997.

bility ratings done by progressive analysts who evaluate companies based on whether they fulfill the social agendas of activists, Others rely on rankings of reputations for social responsibility made by executives of Fortune 500 companies, who have a more conservative perspective.

As opposed to the subjectivity of a corporation's social performance it might seem that financial performance can be gauged more objectively, but there are many ways to measure profitability. Should researchers use accounting measures such as net income or market measures such as stock price appreciation? Also, if social performance is defined as including economic performance, then any effort to separate the two elements to assess their relationship is doomed.

In the above review of 95 studies, the authors report that researchers drew on 27 different information sources to rate social performance and used 70 different methods to calculate financial performance. This makes it difficult to compare the findings of one study to the findings of others. However, a fresh analysis of 52 studies took advantage of a statistical technique that allows correlations in individual studies to be compared. The authors found that the overall correlation between social and financial performance was "moderately positive," rising to "highly positive" for some combinations of performance measures.[34] Still, confounding results persist. A recent study looked at companies that made *Business Ethics* magazine's annual list of 100 Top Corporate Citizens four years in a row. It found that most were less profitable than direct competitors in their industries, suggesting to the authors that "higher profitability is associated with less corporate social responsibility."[35]

Overall, the majority of academic studies find that companies rated as notably responsible are at least as profitable, and often more so, than companies rated as less responsible. However, the results are mixed and there are such significant methodological questions that reservations are warranted. The best conclusion is that socially responsible companies are at least as profitable as those less responsible. It is possible that they are more profitable, but there is no conclusive evidence for this. It is also possible that if socially responsible companies became less responsible their profits would rise.[36]

CORPORATE SOCIAL RESPONSIBILITY IN A GLOBAL CONTEXT

In the early twenty-first century the doctrine of corporate social responsibility is widely accepted in industrialized nations, particularly the United States, but also in Europe, Japan, Australia, and in a few developing nations such as India, Brazil, and the Philippines. It is often defined differently outside the

---

[34] Marc Orlitzky, Frank L. Schmidt, and Sara L. Rynes, "Corporate Social and Financial Performance: A Meta-Analysis," *Organization Studies*, vol. 24, no. 3 (2003).

[35] Arthur B. Laffer, Andrew Coors, and Wayne Winegarden, *Does Corporate Social Responsibility Enhance Business Profitability?* (San Diego: Laffer Associates, 2005), p. 5.

[36] See David Vogel's discussion in *The Market for Virtue* (Washington, DC: The Brookings Institution, 2005), chap. 2.

United States.[37] In Europe there is more emphasis on the rights of employees and environmental protection. In Japan it means paternalism toward workers and there is little tradition of philanthropy. In India it arose on the teaching of Mohandas Gandhi that those who accumulate wealth hold it in trust for society. There is no consensus on the meaning and extent of CSR from nation to nation. Now, in addition, recent trends provoke debate about the responsibilities of transnational corporations in their global activities.

Since the 1980s trade has increased as free markets spread and governments lower trade barriers. Dominant corporations have grown larger and more active. As they have, critics and observers perceive the exercise of too much power and too little restraint.

The perception that transnationals elude proper controls is rooted in a group of observations. First, international law is weak in addressing social impacts of business. It strongly protects commercial rights, but norms protecting labor, human rights, nature, indigenous cultures, and other social resources are little codified. Second, transnational corporations are subject to uneven regulation in developing nations, where institutions may be rudimentary and enforcement feeble. Some governments have overly bureaucratic agencies riddled with corruption. And some are undemocratic, run by elites that syphon off the economic benefits of foreign investment and neglect public needs. Third, in adapting to global economic growth, corporations have used strategies of joint venture, outsourcing, and supply chain extension that create efficiencies, but sometimes also distance them from direct accountability for social harms. And fourth, significantly more government regulation of transnational firms is unlikely. In developed nations conservative political tides run against it. Developing nations fear, correctly, that stricter rules will deter foreign investment.

Developed countries already have highly evolved, expertly enforced domestic regulations. Yet these do not apply outside their borders. In international law, *extraterritoriality* is the exercise of jurisdiction by one nation over actions that occur within the borders of another nation. Treaties that Western colonial nations forced on subject countries in the 1800s often gave them extraterritorial rights within a colonized country, so that the doctrine today has a bad taint. If the United States were to enforce the Clean Air Act on ExxonMobil facilities in African nations it would be regarded as an arrogant violation of sovereign rights, even if it led to cleaner air. Problems of gathering data or making inspections in distant countries make extension of domestic regulation impractical as well.

In a world where regulation is uneven, some corporations, such as Merck, have operated with high standards across nations. But some others have compromised their standards in permissive host country environments. By the early 1990s, critics of multinational corporations began calling for new standards of responsibility. One by-product of globalization was the growing number, international reach,

extraterritoriality
The application of one nation's laws within the borders of another nation.

---

[37] For a discussion of comparative "CSR regimes" see Rob Van Tulder with Alex van der Zwart, *International Business–Society Management: Linking Corporate Responsibility and Globalization* (London: Routledge, 2006), chap. 12.

and networking of nongovernmental organizations (NGOs). Many of these groups developed a close association with the United Nations which, besides its peace-keeping function, promotes international human rights and interests of poorer, developing nations. During the 1990s, coalitions of NGOs pushed for a series of conferences sponsored by the UN for member nations. Conferences were held on environmental sustainability (Rio de Janeiro, 1992), population (Cairo, 1993), human rights (Vienna, 1994), social development (Copenhagen, 1995), and gender (Beijing, 1995).

A defining moment came at the Rio conference on sustainability in 1992, when NGOs arrived demanding regulation of corporations. Their agenda failed, in part because the philosophy of economic liberalization driving the world economy was inhospitable to restrictions on business and in part because corporations and business groups that lobbied against regulation promoted an expanded, international doctrine of corporate social responsibility. NGOs, unable to secure the hard regulations they wanted, were forced to work with business groups in developing new responsibility doctrines.

soft law
Statements of philosophy, policy, and principle found in nonbonding international conventions that, over time, gain legitimacy as guidelines for interpreting the "hard law" in legally binding agreements.

In hindsight, these conferences led to several important changes in the operating environments of multinational corporations. First, they generated a series of declarations, resolutions, statements of principle, guidelines, and frameworks under UN auspices that shaped international standards for the conduct of both nations and corporations. These documents created what international legal scholars call *soft law*. In the realm of international law, "hard law," found mainly in treaties, creates binding rights, prohibitions, and duties. While "soft law" creates no binding obligations or duties for corporations, if its contents are widely accepted as expressing international norms it can over time become the basis for interpreting treaties. Second, the conferences provided occasions for NGOs to interact and develop influence strategies for confronting corporations. And third, they set the stage for further, this time global, expansion of the CSR ideology.

GLOBAL CORPORATE SOCIAL RESPONSIBILITY

The new, global dimension of CSR makes it the duty of a multinational corporation to voluntarily compensate for international and developing country regulatory deficits, It should do this by first, extending its home country standards outward to its foreign operations and to its supply chain, and second, by following a growing body of international norms despite their having no basis in law. This added dimension of CSR has put down strong roots because it has value across much of the CSR political spectrum. It appeals to activists as a substitute for the new regulatory laws they would prefer but cannot get and as a way to overcome the failure of weak governments to resist child labor, corruption, pollution, and poverty. It also appeals to enlightened corporations as a way to forestall more traditional and formal regulation and to placate belligerent NGOs. As a result, the world seethes with activity pushing the idea along.

Figure 5.3 shows the range of entities and elements in an evolving system of global CSR. This system, solidifying now out of a less mature patchwork, organizes

FIGURE 5.3
A Global
System of
CSR Activity

values, principles, rules, institutions, and tools in support of voluntary corporate actions. Simultaneously, it has grown into a framework of civil regulation that can often command corporate behavior. We illuminate its structure by discussing its elements as set forth in Figure 5.3, moving clockwise from the top right. In subsequent chapters we discuss some of them at greater length.

Development of Norms and Principles

norm
A standard that arises over time and is enforced by social sanction or law.

A *norm* is a standard that arises over time and, as agreement on it becomes widespread, it is enforced by social sanction or law. It is similar to a *principle*, which is a rule, natural law, or truth used as a standard to guide conduct. The norms and principles that direct global CSR are derived in part from timeless accretions of civilization, but international conventions to codify and interpret them are increasingly influential. The United Nations is a ringleader. An early codification of norms is the *Universal Declaration of Human Rights,* adopted by the UN in 1948, which spells out a "common standard" of "inalienable rights," that are specified in 30 articles.[38] The rights in this document are now widely accepted and it is the foundation for many

principle
A rule, natural law, or truth used as a standard to guide conduct.

[38] *Universal Declaration of Human Rights,* G.A. res. 217 A (III), UN Doc. A/810, December 10, 1948, Preamble.

corporate human rights policies. It requires, for example, equal rights for men and women, and businesses must meet this standard, often imposing it on suppliers in less developed nations where no legislation requires it.

A second milestone in the development of norms is the *Tripartite Declaration of Principles concerning Multinational Enterprises and Social Policy*, adopted by an organ of the UN in 1977. The Tripartite Declaration, so-called because unions, governments, and industry collaborated in its creation, came in response to the rising power of multinational corporations in the 1960s. It sets forth a long list of voluntary norms related to worker rights, for example, that multinational corporations should not offer wages and benefits less than those offered for comparable work elsewhere in a country.[39] Over the years, the Tripartite Declaration has been accepted as a foundational statement and it now is the basis for most international labor codes. As new norms solidify, additions are made. In 2006 a strongly worded new entry encouraged TNCs to act against child labor.

At the cutting edge of emerging norms is a recent compilation of *Norms on the Responsibilities of Transnational Corporations*, adopted by a subcommittee of the UN Human Rights Commission in 2003. In treatylike language it imposes a wide range of social obligations on transnational corporations. The corporation "shall not use forced or compulsory labour," "[n] or shall [it] . . . advertise harmful or potentially harmful products," and it "shall generally conduct [its] activities in a manner contributing to the wider goal of sustainable development."[40] It requires transnational corporations (TNCs) to adopt internal rules for compliance and submit to monitoring by the UN in which NGOs would participate. For now, legal scholars believe that there is no basis for imposing these duties on TNCs, and corporate interests oppose the *Norms*.[41] It is an exceptionally aggressive document that pushes past international consensus, but perhaps only for the moment.

Landmark statements of norms and principles such as these rise from the steady accumulation of hundreds of international charters, conventions, declarations, multilateral agency policies, and treaties on labor, human rights, corruption, the environment, and other issues which, by their sheer numbers, promote broad acceptance of progressive, developed-country values as universal norms. These norms are the basis for proliferating codes of conduct that target corporate behavior.

Codes of Conduct

codes of conduct
Formal statements of aspirations, principles, guidelines, and rules for corporate behavior.

Codes of conduct are formal statements of aspirations, principles, guidelines, and rules for corporate behavior. They arise from many sources. Corporations write them. In addition, there are hundreds of codes created by trade associations,

---

[39] *Tripartite Declaration of Principles concerning Multinational Enterprises and Social Policy,* 3rd ed. (Geneva: International Labour Office, 2001), p. 7, para. 33. First edition published in 1977.

[40] *Norms on the Responsibilities of Transnational Corporations and Other Business Enterprises with Regard to Human Rights,* U. N. Doc. E/CN.4/Sub.2/2003/12/Rev.2 (2003), secs. D.(5), F.(13), and G.(14).

[41] Larry Cata Backer, "Multinational Corporations, Transnational Law: The United Nations' Norms on the Responsibilities of Transnational Corporations as a Harbinger of Corporate Social Responsibility in International Law," *Columbia Human Rights Law Review,* Winter 2006.

NGOs, governments, and international organizations. Many codes result from collaborative processes with multiple parties. A large multinational corporation follows more than one code. It will have its own code and, in addition, will be a signatory of multiple codes developed by other actors, including specialized codes focused on labor, human rights, environmental protection, corruption, and other matters. Here are examples of codes from different sources.

- Samsung Electronics Company has a *Global Code of Conduct* based on five aspirational principles: legal and ethical behavior, a "clean organization culture" (which means a culture free of discrimination, sexual harassment, insider trading and similar misbehaviors), respect for stakeholders, care for the environment, and social responsibility. Detailed statements in each category give specific guidance to employees.[42]

- *The Electronics Industry Code of Conduct* was created in 2004 to protect workers in overseas plants that do computer assembly and component manufacturing. The 10-page code requires signatories to "go beyond legal compliance" in enforcing its standards for labor, health and safety, environmental protection, and ethical behavior. It explicitly incorporates standards in the Universal Declaration of Human Rights and other codifications of international norms.

- Amnesty International, a human rights NGO that claims 1.8 million members, believes that while only nations have a legal duty to secure basic human rights, corporations, because they are powerful organs of society, have a moral duty to do so as well. It has written a code entitled *Human Rights Principles for Companies,* in which corporate duties are listed.[43] The code's influence is limited.

- The Ethical Trading Initiative is an alliance of companies, unions, and NGOs based in the United Kingdom. It has a *Base Code* setting standards for working conditions in overseas supplier firms. Member companies agree to conform their own codes to the Base Code, apply the standards across their international supply chains, and allow independent monitoring for compliance.

No matter what the source of a code, the target is the corporation. A code's effectiveness depends on how the corporation carries it out. Codes written by corporations themselves often lack rigorous implementation. The Samsung code, for example, fails to assign responsibilities for oversight to any managers, sets no goals or measurable targets, and requires no reporting. Codes created by other parties may require companies to sign compliance agreements, but in the words of one critic, "these agreements are spineless" because they lack force of law.[44] Therefore, as the global CSR system matures, it produces ways of monitoring corporate performance and verifying code compliance.

[42] Samsung Electronics Co., *Global Code of Conduct* (Seoul, Korea: Samsung, 2006).

[43] Amnesty International, *Human Rights Principles for Companies,* January 1998, at http://web.amnesty.org/library at ACT 70/001/1998.

[44] Veronica Besmer, "The Legal Character of Private Codes of Conduct," *Hastings Business Law Journal,* Winter 2006, p. 286.

Reporting and Verification Standards

sustainability reporting
The practice of a corporation publishing information about its economic, social, and environmental performance.

There is growing demand for accurate information about CSR performance. This has led more companies to issue public reports that describe and measure their actions, a practice often called *sustainability reporting*. The reports take many forms. Information may be part of the annual report or appear in separate publications. It is costly for corporations to collect data and compile such reports, but they have benefits. They protect corporate reputation and they are a management tool that allows the company to measure performance and progress.

Two problems with sustainability reporting are, first, that defining and measuring social performance is difficult and, second, that the reports are not comparable from company to company. But uniformity is growing. A new international standard for sustainability reporting is the format set up by an organization in the Netherlands, the *Global Reporting Initiative* (GRI), which defines both specific data for measuring performance and procedures for compiling reports. Of an estimated 1,750 corporations that issue sustainability reports, almost 40 percent now follow the GRI protocol.[45]

Sustainability reporting is largely voluntary, but more is being mandated. For example, a new French law requires public companies to publish a series of sustainability indicators. Denmark and the Netherlands require companies in polluting industries to publish voluminous data on environmental impacts. Because of widespread cynicism about corporate honesty, institutions of independent verification have arisen. An NGO named the Institute of Social and Ethical Accountability has created a widely used "assurance standard," for independent parties that audit corporate sustainability reports. Reporting is further discussed in Chapter 6.

Labeling and Certification Schemes

Labels are symbols displayed on or with products to certify that the product, or its production process, meets a set of social responsibility criteria. Such schemes try to create social or environmental progress by influencing the market on the demand side. Criteria for labels are set by the labeling organization, which is often a cooperative project of industry, NGOs, unions, and sometimes governments. Certified companies usually must allow independent auditors to inspect and monitor their activities. Typically the process is funded with licensing fees paid by producers, importers, and retailers. Here are several examples from among dozens of such schemes.

- *The Kimberly Process Certification Scheme* is a device to stop the flow of rough diamonds from parts of Africa where sales to exporters have funded civil wars and rebellions. Its governing body consists of 71 member nations including all major diamond producing and importing nations and representatives from both the diamond industry and human rights NGOs. Governments are required to set up controls on diamond production. Companies export diamonds only in

---

[45] Based on an estimate of KPMG International in a 2005 survey, reported in Parliamentary Joint Committee on Corporations and Financial Services, *Corporate Responsibility: Managing Risk and Creating Value* (Canberra: Senate Printing Unit, Parliament House, 2006), p. 87.

sealed, tamper-proof containers accompanied by compliance certificates. Smuggling around the scheme is a nuisance, but after its inception the share of "blood diamonds" in world markets dropped from 15 percent to 0.2 percent.[46]

- *RugMark* is a blue and red label applied to carpets from factories in India, Nepal, and Pakistan that are free of child labor. It is run by a coalition of NGOs, rug importers, and UN agencies. Rug factories must agree to random inspections. If children are found the factories lose their right to use the label and the children are asked if they would like to go to school. With licensing fees from factories, importers, and retailers the foundation that runs RugMark set up six schools that are now filled with former child laborers. The scheme has removed thousands of children from rug factories.

fair trade
Payment of wages to small, marginal agricultural producers in developing nations sufficient to allow sustainable farming and labor practices.

- Many certifications promote *fair trade*, or the idea that small, marginal producers in Africa, Asia, and Latin America should be paid a "fair," that is, a stable, guaranteed, and sometimes above-market price for crops so they can make a living and engage in sustainable farming practices. Transfair USA, a coalition of development, religious, human rights, labor, and consumer groups, offers the *Fair Trade Certified* label on coffee exported to the United States. It audits transactions between farmers and companies that buy coffee beans. Its black and white label depicting a farmer in front of a globe certifies that coffee farmers have been paid a guaranteed minimum price.

Management Standards

management standard
A model of the methods an organization can use to achieve certain goals.

A *management standard* is a model of the methods an organization can use to achieve certain goals. The use of quality standards is widespread. Now, actors in the global CSR network have established standards for social responsibility or elements of social responsibility such as health and safety or environmental protection.

- The *Eco-Management and Audit Scheme* (EMAS) is a standard that rises above legal requirements for environmental performance in European nations that already have some of the strictest regulations in the world.[47] Companies that join this voluntary initiative must reduce emissions, energy use, and waste beyond legal requirements. They also agree to publish regular statements of their environmental performance and have them checked for accuracy by outside auditors. More than 3,000 companies in Europe participate. They are allowed to use the EMAS logo in ads that make green claims for products. EMAS is run by representatives of governments, industries, unions, and NGOs.

- The International Standards Organization (ISO), which has already created widely used international standards in other areas, for example, *ISO 9000* on quality and *ISO 14000* on the environment, is now working to write a broad, new social responsibility standard to be known as *ISO 26000*. The standard, which is due in two years, will be a set of guidelines modeled on best practices.

---

[46] Vivienne Walt, "Diamonds Aren't Forever," *Fortune*, December 11, 2006, p. 89.

[47] The standard is set forth in Regulation (EC) No. 761/2001 of the European Parliament and of the council, March 2001, *Official Journal of the European Communities*, April 24, 2001, p. L114/1.

Social Investment and Lending

Equity capital and borrowing are critical to corporate financial strategies. Actors in the international CSR movement, aware of this, have initiated efforts to affect capital markets. Several examples follow.

- Under the auspices of the United Nations, a coalition of institutional investors and civil society groups created a set of voluntary *Principles for Responsible Investment.* The principles require signatories to consider a company's environmental, social, and governance performance when they invest. Signatories also accept a duty to press corporations in the direction of responsible behavior and greater disclosure of data on their CSR performance. So far, funds representing more than $5 trillion in assets have signed on.[48]

- The *FTSE4Good Global Index* is intended to set the world standard for investors seeking "companies that meet globally recognized corporate responsibility standards." The index is created by a British company. Scanning a universe of about 2,000 companies on 23 world stock exchanges, it first excludes companies producing tobacco, nuclear weapons, major weapons systems, nuclear power, and uranium. From what remains, it includes companies that meet its somewhat stringent criteria for following a range of CSR codes and standards. When recently it developed more strict environmental criteria, 192 index corporations elected to improve their performance and another 85 that did not do enough were deleted.[49]

- The International Finance Corporation (IFC) is an agency of the World Bank. Its mission is to promote development and reduce poverty by funding projects for corporations. Since its founding in 1956 it has arranged $73 billion in funds for more than 3,300 corporations.[50] In 1998 it adopted a set of policies designed to safeguard indigenous peoples, labor, community health, and the environment on projects it funded. Pushed by civil society groups, it updated its standards in 2006, making them tougher. Now, corporations that seek IFC funding must meet new requirements to consult with civil society groups, monitor greenhouse gas emissions, and adopt CSR management systems.

Initiatives such as these threaten to raise the cost of capital for corporations that dodge evolving norms. Yet, so far, they harness relatively small amounts of money. At one mainstream investment firm, State Street Corporations, the Boston branch alone manages $5.2 trillion, more than the amount managed by all signatories of the UN's Principles for Responsible Investment.[51] State Street is not a signatory.

---

[48] "Signatories to the Principles for Responsible Investment," at http://www.unpri.org/signatories/, accessed February 7, 2007. UNCTAD, *World Investment Report 2006* (New York: United Nations, 2006), p. 234.

[49] "FTSE4Good Index Series," at http://www.ftse.com/Indeces/FTSE4Good_Index_Series/, accessed February 7, 2007.

[50] International Finance Corporation, "IFC Adopts New Environmental and Social Standards," press release, February 21, 2006.

[51] Keith Reed, "State Street to Acquire Investors' Financial," *The Boston Globe*, February 6, 2007, p. E1.

Government Actions

Governments advance corporate responsibility mainly with binding regulation, but they also actively promote voluntary actions. European nations lead. The European Commission and European Parliament generate a stream of communications and reports encouraging codes, labels, and forums. The Belgium government set up the *Belgium Social Label*, a brown and blue cartoon of a person with arms uplifted in exultation, presumably because the company that made the product saw to it that its entire production chain followed basic International Labor Organization standards.[52] The United Kingdom appointed a government Minister of Corporate Social Responsibility. Among other actions, the ministry supports an index ranking the top 100 British corporations on their overall responsibility.[53] The Australian legislature recently published a study of global CSR initiatives and recommended "greater uptake" of the idea by Australian companies.[54] One motive for government encouragement of CSR is to stimulate competitiveness in international markets. When the textile industry in Cambodia was no longer able to compete with Chinese manufacturers on low costs alone, the government promoted higher labor standards in an attempt to attract corporations interested in a responsible supply chain. A government official told companies that buying from Cambodia would "look good in your annual report."[55] The United States does far less than most European governments, but a recent study found 50 federal activities that could be classified as promoting CSR.[56] Most of these were awards or programs with tiny budgets.

Civil Society Vigilance

NGOs watch multinational corporations and police actions they see as departing from emerging norms. A campaign by experienced activists is unpleasant and, if it carries any element of validity, very dangerous to brand reputation. The abiding threat of attack inspires entry into various code, labeling, reporting, and standards schemes. Here are several instances.

- The force behind the Electronics Industry Code of Conduct is the Catholic Agency for Overseas Development. When the group issued a report on "computer factory sweatshops" and began a "Clean Up Your Computer" campaign, it galvanized Hewlett-Packard, IBM, Dell, and others in the industry to create a protective code of conduct.[57]

[52] For an overview of European activities see, European Commission, *ABC of the Main Instruments of Corporate Social Responsibility* (Luxembourg: Office for Official Publications of the European Communities, 2004).

[53] Business in the Community, *Corporate Responsibility Index 2006*, at www.bitc.org.uk.

[54] Parliamentary Joint Committee on Corporations and Financial Services, *Corporate Responsibility: Managing Risk and Creating Value*, p. xxiv.

[55] Halina Ward, *Public Sector Roles in Strengthening Corporate Social Responsibility: Taking Stock* (Washington, DC: World Bank Group, January 2004), p. 14.

[56] General Accountability Office, *Globalization: Numerous Federal Activities Complement U.S. Business's Global Corporate Social Responsibility Efforts*, GAO-05-744, August 2005.

[57] CAFOD, *Clean Up Your Computer: Working Conditions in the Electronics Sector* (London: CAFOD, January 2004); Peter Burrows, "Stalking High-Tech Sweatshops," *BusinessWeek*, June 19, 2006, p. 62.

- The *Voluntary Principles for Security and Human Rights* is a code with standards to prevent human rights abuses. It was established in a multiparty process convened by the United States and British governments that included companies and NGOs. Since the code was established, Amnesty International, one of the NGOs that participated in its drafting, has attacked the conduct of two signatories, Chevron and Shell, over their actions in Nigeria and claims the code lacks credibility.[58] The group is now negotiating to require annual compliance reports from companies.

- In 2000, the Rainforest Action Network (RAN) began a campaign against Citigroup, the largest U.S. bank, alleging that the bank's loans funded socially and environmentally disruptive pipelines, mines, dams, and other projects in developing countries. RAN was the sharp edge of a coalition of more than 100 NGOs. This coalition opposed bank lending that failed to take deforestation, pollution, and disruption of indigenous peoples into account. Three years of artful attack on the bank's reputation and harassment of its executives went by until Citigroup tired. Working with other banks it adopted industry lending guidelines based on environmental and social guidelines then in use by the World Bank. Today, largely due to pressure by RAN, 40 of the world's largest banks, making 80 percent of the world's private development loans, subscribe to these "voluntary" principles, now called the *Equator Principles*.[59] The principles divide projects into high, medium, and low social and environmental risk and compel borrowers to meet standards for ecological protection and consultation with native peoples.[60] In effect, this is a global environmental regulatory scheme for the banking, mining, forestry, and energy industries.

ASSESSING THE EVOLVING GLOBAL CSR SYSTEM

In sum, as multinational corporations grew in power with the expansion of global trade, a perceived deficiency in regulation was countered by action within civil society. NGOs, working through an omnipresent United Nations, gained power by fabricating soft law to raise expectations of corporate behavior and then attacked the reputations of noncompliant firms. As this unfolded over 20 years, regulatory power has flowed from nations to other actors, particularly to multiparty ventures that combine NGOs, UN agencies, unions, and businesses. These ventures have created novel organizations that promote and enforce corporate adherence to international CSR standards using tools such as codes, labels, audits, and certifications.

---

[58] Amnesty International, *Nigeria Ten Years On: Injustice and Violence Haunt the Oil Delta,* at http://web. amnesty.org/library at AFR 44/022/2005 (2005).

[59] International Finance Corporation, "IFC Adopts New Environmental and Social Standards," and Erik Assadourian, "The State of Corporate Responsibility and the Environment," *Georgetown International Environmental Law Review*, vol. 18 (2006), p. 575.

[60] Natasha Affolder, "Cachet Not Cash: Another Sort of World Bank Group Borrowing," *Michigan State Journal of International Law,* vol. 14 (2006).

No company can remain aloof from the emerging global CSR system. NGOs have emerged as "de facto regulators" imposing standards that some believe are "tougher than the legal requirements corporations face."[61] To advocates of more CSR the reality is "an emerging voluntary system of responsibility assurance" functioning to support enlightened corporations and to restore public trust in TNCs.[62] Others dislike what seems to be an emerging regime of civil regulation. They see the new system as undemocratic because it relies heavily for monitoring and compliance on NGOs that are self-constituted communities of belief, unelected and not clearly or formally representative even of their membership rolls, let alone of the people in developing countries affected by transnational corporations.[63] Yet despite some criticism and reluctance in the business community the trend is toward continued growth of the global CSR system. An important issue is whether or not the emerging system is the most appropriate way to regulate large corporations.

CONCLUDING OBSERVATIONS

Historically, corporations have been motivated primarily by profit, an orientation sanctioned in classical economic ideology. However, as they have grown in size and power they have been exhorted and pressured to alter this single-minded focus. This is because (1) the idea of corporate social responsibility has continuously expanded in meaning and (2) the power of stakeholders to define corporate duty has increased.

Whereas only a short time ago the norms and power equations of individual nations defined the responsibilities of corporations, the explosion of global trade and growth of global corporations created new standards and practices of social responsibility tied to global norms. The rise of these new standards and expectations is reflected in a proliferation of CSR initiatives that, combined, create the emerging outline of a new regulatory system. If history is any guide, the doctrine will continue to expand.

In this chapter, we focused on defining and explaining the idea of corporate social responsibility and its evolution. Figure 5.4 summarizes this evolution. In the next chapter we look at the management methods corporations use to implement CSR.

[61]Jeb Brugmann and C. K. Prahalad, "Cocreating Business's New Social Compact," *Harvard Business Review*, February 2007, pp. 82–83.

[62] Sandra Waddock, "Building the Institutional Infrastructure for Corporate Social Responsibility," Corporate Social Responsibility Initiative, Working Paper No. 32, John F. Kennedy School of Government, Harvard University, December 2006, p. 8.

[63] Larry Cata Backer, "Multinational Corporations, Transnational Law: The United Nations' Norms on the Responsibilities of Transnational Corporations as a Harbinger of Corporate Social Responsibility in International Law," *Columbia Human Rights Law Review*, Winter 2006, p. 386–88.

FIGURE 5.4 The Evolution of Corporate Social Responsibility

Although the term corporate social responsibility is of recent use, the idea it represents has been under construction for more than two centuries. This timeline shows how its elements evolved in the United States. The duty to serve society by making a profit has remained constant. Philanthropy, an early duty of business owners, is now expected of large corporations. Mandated duties grew with domestic regulation, then with the rise of civil regulation on an international scale. Finally, the theory of social responsibility changed from the cruel denials of Herbert Spencer to a doctrine of expansive duties. Now it is expanding to include broader duties in global commerce.

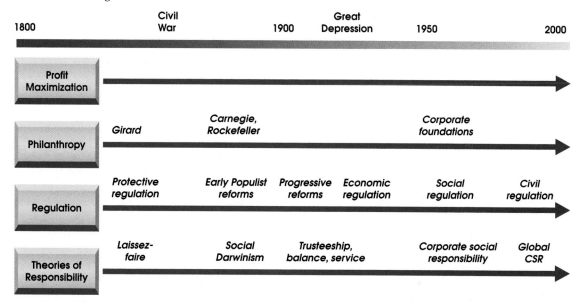

The Jack Welch Era at General Electric

In April 1981 John Francis "Jack" Welch, Jr., became chief executive officer of General Electric. He held the position for 20 years until retiring in September 2001. During that time, he transformed GE, taking a solidly profitable manufacturing company and turning it into an exceptionally profitable conglomerate dominated by service businesses. If you had invested $100 in GE stock when Welch took the reins and held it for 20 years, it would have been worth $6,749.

Welch is lauded for his creative management style and became a national business hero. A fawning *BusinessWeek* article called him "America's #1 Manager."[1]

Fortune magazine gushed that GE under Welch was "the best-managed, best-regarded company in America."[2] Yet the intense, aggressive Welch made fortunes for GE shareholders using methods that had mixed impacts on employees, unions, communities, other companies, and governments. As a result, not everyone sees the GE performance as a model for corporate social responsibility. Upon Welch's retirement, the *Multinational Monitor,* a progressive magazine founded by Ralph Nader, devoted an entire issue to making "The Case Against GE." The lead editorial branded Welch as a corporate titan opposed to rules

---

[1] John A. Byrne, "Jack: A Close-Up Look at How America's #1 Manager Runs GE," *BusinessWeek,* June 8, 1998, p. 91.

[2] Jerry Useem, "It's All Yours, Jeff. Now What?" *Fortune,* September 17, 2001, p. 64.

of society and said that his actions were "disastrous" for workers and communities.[3]

Did General Electric under Jack Welch carry out the full range of its duties to society? Did it fall short? Readers are invited to decide.

JACK WELCH RISES

Most top executives come from backgrounds of wealth and privilege. Jack Welch is an exception. He was born in 1935 to working-class Irish parents in a small Massachusetts town. His father was a quiet, passive man who endured as a railroad conductor punching tickets on commuter trains. Welch's mother was a dominating woman who caused her husband to wilt but instilled a powerful drive in her son. Welch was an outstanding student at the University of Massachusetts at Amherst and went on to get a doctorate in chemical engineering at the University of Illinois.

After graduating, he started working at a GE plastics factory in 1960. His tremendous energy and ambition were very apparent. He was so competitive in weekend softball games that his aggressive play alienated co-workers and he stopped going. After one year, he threatened to quit when he got the same $1,000 raise as everyone else. His boss cajoled him into staying and as the years and promotions flashed by he never again wavered.

As he rose, Welch exhibited a fiery temperament and expected those around him to share his intensity. He was blunt, impatient with subordinates, and emotionally volatile. He loved no-holds-barred discussions in meetings but frequently put people on the spot, saying, "My six-year-old kid could do better than that."[4] With every promotion, he sized up his new staff with a cold eye and purged those who failed to impress him. "I'm the first to admit," he says, "I could be impulsive in removing people during those early days."[5]

This was just preparation for the big leagues to come. GE had a polished corporate culture reflecting the eastern establishment values of its leadership over many decades. Welch did not fit. He was impatient, frustrated by the company's bureaucracy, and lacking in deference. With this mismatch GE might have re-

pulsed Welch at some point, but his performance was outstanding. Several times he got mixed reviews for a promotion, but because of exemplary financial results he was never blocked. In 1981 he took over as CEO of one of America's singular companies.

THE STORY OF GENERAL ELECTRIC

The lineage of General Electric goes back to 1879 when Thomas Alva Edison (1847–1931), with the backing of banker J. P. Morgan, started the Edison Electric Light Company to make light bulbs and electrical equipment. Although Edison was a great inventor, he was a poor manager and the company lost ground in the market for electrical equipment. So in 1892 Morgan took charge, engineering a merger with a competitor and plotting to reduce Edison to a figurehead in the new company.

Morgan disposed of Edison's top managers and dropped the word Edison from its name so that the firm became simply General Electric Company. Morgan sat as a commanding figure on the new company's board. Although Edison was also a director, he attended only the first meeting and never appeared again.[6]

After the merger, GE went on to build a near-monopoly in the incandescent bulb market. Over the years, other products emerged from the company. Early in the twentieth century, its motors worked the Panama Canal locks, powered battleships, and ran locomotives.[7] GE's research labs bred a profusion of new electrical appliances, including fans, toasters, refrigerators, vacuum cleaners, ranges, garbage disposals, air conditioners, and irons. At first these new inventions were very expensive, but as more people used them production costs fell and they became commodities within the reach of every family. By 1960 GE was credited with a remarkable list of other inventions, including the X-ray machine, the motion picture with sound, fluorescent lighting, the diesel-electric locomotive, the jet engine, synthetic diamonds, the hard plastic Lexan, and Silly Putty.[8]

---

[3] "You Don't Know Jack," *Multinational Monitor,* July–August 2001, p. 5.

[4] Jack Welch, *Jack: Straight from the Gut* (New York: Warner Books, 2001), p. 43.

[5] Ibid., p. 43.

[6] Thomas F. O'Boyle, *At Any Cost: Jack Welch, General Electric, and the Pursuit of Profit* (New York: Knopf, 1998), p. 55.

[7] For more on the history of GE see John Winthrop Hammond, *Men and Volts: The Story of General Electric* (Philadelphia: J. B. Lippincott, 1948).

[8] Thomas F. O'Boyle, "'At Any Cost' Is Too High," *Multinational Monitor,* July–August 2001, p. 41.

As it added manufacturing capacity to build these inventions, GE grew. By 1981, when Jack Welch took the reins, the company had $27 billion in revenues and 404,000 employees. It was organized into 50 separate businesses reporting to a layer of six sector executives at corporate headquarters in Fairfield, Connecticut, who in turn reported to the CEO. To make it run, a large and strong staff of researchers and planners created detailed annual plans setting forth revenue goals and other objectives for each business.

THE WELCH ERA BEGINS

Welch believes that managers must confront reality and adapt to the world as it is, not as they wish it to be. As he studied GE's situation in the early 1980s, he saw a corporation that needed to change. GE's manufacturing businesses were still profitable, but margins were shrinking. The wages of American workers were rising even as their productivity was declining. International competition was growing, particularly from the Japanese, who had cost advantages because of a weak yen. Although GE seemed healthy on the surface, ominous forces were gathering in the environment. In addition, Welch saw GE bloated with layers of bureaucracy that infuriated him by slowing decisions and frustrating change. The company, as currently operated, could not weather the competitive storms ahead. It would have to change.

Welch articulated a simple guiding vision. Every GE business would be the number one or number two player in its industry. If it failed this test it would be fixed, closed, or sold. In addition, Welch said that all GE businesses would have to fit into one of three areas—core manufacturing, technology, or services. Any business that fell outside these three strategic hubs was a candidate for sale or closure. This included manufacturing businesses that could not sustain high profit margins.

In the next five years, Welch executed his strategy by closing 73 plants, selling 232 businesses, and eliminating 132,000 workers from GE payrolls.[9] As he conformed GE to his vision, he also bought hundreds of other businesses large and small. Within GE businesses he eliminated jobs through attrition, layoffs, and outsourcing. In the largest acquisition of that period, Welch acquired RCA in 1985. RCA was a giant electronics and broadcasting conglomerate with a

Jack Welch (1935–). Source: © Bob Daemmrich/CORBIS.

storied history as the company that had developed radio technology. After paying $6.7 billion for RCA, Welch chopped it up, keeping NBC and selling other businesses one by one, in effect, destroying the giant company as an organizational entity. As jobs vanished, Welch got the nickname "Neutron Jack," comparing him with a neutron bomb that left buildings standing but killed everyone inside.

Welch also attacked the GE bureaucracy. One problem was its size. There were too many vice presidents, too many layers, and too many staffs with authority to review and approve decisions. A second problem was the bureaucratic mentality in which headquarters staff practiced a "superficial congeniality" that Welch interpreted as smiling to your face and getting you behind your back.[10] He demolished the hierarchy by laying off thousands of central staff in strategic planning, personnel, and other areas. Then he set out to change GE's culture by promoting the notion of a "boundaryless" organization, or one in which ideas were freely

---

[9] Frank Swoboda, "GE Picks Welch's Successor," *Washington Post*, November 28, 2000, p. E1.

[10] Welch, *Jack*, p. 96.

EXHIBIT 1
The Vitality
Curve

Source: *From Jack:*
Straight from The Gut
by Jack Welch with
John A. Byrne.
Copyright © 2001
by John F. Welch, Jr.
Foundation. By
permission of Grand
Central Publishing.
All rights reserved.

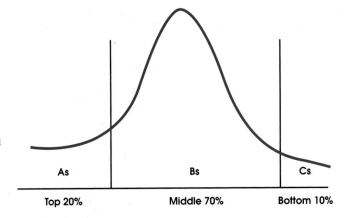

As   Bs   Cs

Top 20%   Middle 70%   Bottom 10%

exchanged so that organizational learning could rapidly occur. Welch compared GE to an old house:

> Floors represent layers and the walls functional barriers. To get the best out of an organization, these floors and walls must be blown away, creating an open space where ideas flow freely, independent of rank or function.[11]

Later, Welch introduced the practice of "workout" sessions in which employees in every GE business had an opportunity to confront their bosses to express frustration with bureaucratic practices and suggest more efficient alternatives. Managers in these sessions sat in front of a room filled with subordinates and had to agree or disagree on the spot to carry out suggestions. Thousands of such sessions were held to drive out the bureaucratic mentality. Welch also used Crotonville, the company's campuslike training center on the Hudson River, to meet with managers and instill his vision. He invited candid discussions, and gradually the company culture became more informal and open.

DIFFERENTIATION

Welch is convinced that having the right people in management positions is the single most important cause of success in a business. Early in his career, he developed a colorful vocabulary to differentiate between players. Inept managers were "turkeys" and "dinks," standouts were called "all-stars." As CEO he reinforced strategic initiatives with a system of "differentiation" that generously rewarded managers who achieved performance goals and got rid of

those who missed them. In this system, every year each GE business was forced to evaluate its managers and rank them on a "vitality curve" that differentiated among As, Bs, and Cs. The As were committed people, filled with passion for their jobs, who took initiative and exceeded performance goals. They had what Welch called "the four Es of GE leadership":

> very high *energy* levels, the ability to *energize* others around common goals, the *edge* to make tough yes-and-no decisions, and finally, the ability to consistently *execute* and deliver on their promises.[12]

The vitality curve was Darwinian. The As were the top 20 percent, Bs were the middle 70 percent, and Cs were the bottom 10 percent (see Exhibit 1). The As received salary increases, promotions, and stock options. Welch followed their careers closely. He kept large loose-leaf notebooks containing evaluations of the top 750 of GE's 4,000 managers. Bs were considered vital to the success of the company and were coached so that some would become As. Cs were not worth wasting time on and were dismissed. The process was repeated annually, and each time the bottom 10 percent had to go. The curve applied to every GE business. No business leader could claim that his or her group was an exception, though some tried. Filling the A, B, and C categories forced difficult decisions. If 20 managers were evaluated, 2 had to be placed at the bottom and their careers at GE ended. After several years of getting rid of low performers, the leaders of GE businesses resisted classifying anyone as a C, but Welch was relentless. If they didn't identify the bottom 10 percent, he refused to carry out stock option and salary recommendations

---

[11] Welch, *Jack*, p. 162.

[12] Welch, *Jack*, p. 158.

for the entire group until they did. In this way, the bar of performance was continually raised.

Welch compared people to plants. "If they grow, you have a beautiful garden," he said. "If they don't, you cut them out."[13] He disagreed with those who found the system heartless:

> Some think it's cruel or brutal to remove the bottom 10 percent of our people. It isn't. It's just the opposite. What I think is brutal and "false kindness" is keeping people around who aren't going to grow and prosper. . . . The characterization of a vitality curve as cruel stems from false logic and is an outgrowth of a culture that practices false kindness.[14]

AN ASSESSMENT OF THE WELCH YEARS

With Jack Welch at the helm GE sustained exceptionally high rates of profitability, and shareholders were enriched. Even with five stock splits, earnings per share rose from $.46 in 1981 to $1.07 in 2000, his last full year as CEO, and total return on GE shares averaged 21.5 percent.[15] In 2000 GE reported a net operating margin of 19 percent and earned 27 percent on invested capital.[16] These are high figures for a large multinational corporation.

Welch also reshaped GE. He continuously bought and sold businesses both large and small. During his last four years alone he made more than 400 acquisitions. One underlying reason for the increasing profitability of GE is that through this churning of businesses GE's center of gravity shifted from manufacturing to services. The GE he inherited earned 85 percent of its revenues from manufacturing; the GE he created got 70 percent of its revenues from services.[17]

The bulk of service revenue came from financial services, but manufacturing businesses also engage in services; for example, the company not only makes aircraft engines, it services them over their lifetimes.

Welch wrung profits from GE by creating a performance culture. Managers were energized. Plants grew more efficient. For instance, when Welch became CEO, GE's locomotive plant in Erie, Pennsylvania, needed 7,500 hourly employees to make 350 locomotives a year. By 2000 productivity had improved so much that only 4,000 workers could make 900 locomotives a year.[18]

The story of the Welch years has the elements of legend. An ambitious son of working-class parents rises through hard work to command a mighty company, inspire managers everywhere, and become rich along with other company shareholders. To reward Welch for the shower of wealth he created, in his last year the GE board awarded him a special bonus bringing his yearly compensation to $174 million.[19] At this time he held more than 22 million shares of GE stock and options worth almost $1 billion, as shown in Exhibit 2. This is astronomical compensation for one person, but his $972 million in stock is only two-thousandths of 1 percent of the $460 billion in equity value created during his tenure.

Exhibit 2 shows how directors shared in the GE equity windfall. When they joined the board, each outside (nonemployee) director was given 5,000 shares of GE stock and a $150,000 life insurance policy. Thereafter, each year directors were given $75,000, $2,000 for each of the 10 meetings they were required to attend, and options on 18,000 more shares of GE stock. If they retired at age 65 with five years of service, they were eligible to receive the $75,000 annual retainer for life. There were other rewards. One GE business sold diamonds and directors could buy them at cost for their personal use or for spouses. The year that Welch retired, the group purchased $975,595 worth of diamonds and must have looked very good at the kinds of parties to which laid-off workers were not invitied.[20]

While the board feted Welch, not everyone saw his leadership as something to admire or emulate. Early in his career, Welch was compared to a speedboat going down a narrow canal, leaving considerable

---

[13] Quoted in Carol Hymowitz and Matt Murray, "Raises and Praise or Out the Door—How GE's Chief Rates and Spurs His Employees," *The Wall Street Journal,* June 21, 1999, p. B1.

[14] Welch, *Jack,* p. 162. See also Jack and Suzy Welch, "The Case for 20-70-10," *BusinessWeek,* October 2, 2006, p. 108.

[15] Swoboda, "GE Picks Welch's Successor," p. E1; Julie Schlosser, "Jack? Jack Who?" *Fortune,* September 17, 2001, p. 52.

[16] General Electric Company, *GE Annual Report 2000* (Fairfield, CT: General Electric Company, 2001), p. 42.

[17] James Flanigan, "New Boss's Challenge: To Keep GE Together," *Los Angeles Times,* August 26, 2001, p. C1.

[18] "Dignity and Defiance: An Interview with John Hovis," *Multinational Monitor,* July–August 2001, p. 35.

[19] General Electric Company, *Notice of 2001 Annual Meeting* and *Proxy Statement,* March 9, 2001, pp. 22 and 27.

[20] Ibid., p. 14.

EXHIBIT 2   The 2001 GE Board of Directors: Market Value of Total Holdings in GE Stock (shaded entries are inside directors)

Director	Value	Director	Value
James I. Cash Professor, Harvard Business School	$3,719,059	Sam Nunn Former U.S. Senator from Georgia	$4,516,975
Silas S. Cathcart CEO, Illinois Tool Works(ret.)	$34,601,060	Roger S. Penske Chairman, Penske Corp.	$6,844,896
Paolo Fresco Chairman, Fiat	$111,700,043	Frank H. T. Rhodes President Emeritus, Cornell University	$10,931,672
Ann M Fudge Vice President, Kraft Foods	$1,667,828	Andrew C. Sigler CEO, Champion International (ret.)	$5,820,301
Claudio X. Gonzalez CEO, Kimberly-Clark de Mexico	$9,871,797	Douglas A. Warner Chairman, J. P. Morgan Chase & Co.	$8,323,021
Andrea Jung CEO, Avon Products	$2,733,352	Dennis. D. Dammerman Chairman, GE Capital	$187,238,259
Kenneth G. Langone CEO, Invamed Associates	$14,805,848	Jeffrey R. Immelt President, General Electric	$130,853,846
Rochelle B. Lazarus CEO, Ogilvy & Mather Worldwide	$877,690	John F. Welch, Jr. Chairman and CEO, General Electric	$972,022,731
Scott G. McNealy CEO, Sun Microsystems	$2,089,684	Robert Wright Vice Chairman of GE, President, NBC	$229,777,982
Gertrude Michelson Former Senior V.P., Macy's	$14,381,950		

Source: General Electric Company, *Proxy Statement*, March 9, 2001, p. 12. Total holdings include common stock, option holdings, deferred compensation, restricted stock units, and stock appreciation rights.

turbulence in its wake.[21] His detractors say that once Welch was at the master controls of GE he piloted the mammoth organization through global straits the same way. There is no denying that he created wealth. But what were the costs to people, communities, and society? The flaws in the Welch performance, according to critics, include the following.

LOSS OF JOBS

Early on, Welch was caricatured as a ruthless job cutter. When he became CEO in 1981, the corporate culture reinforced loyalty. People went to work at GE directly out of college, stayed for 40 years, retired in

communities of GE people, and attended GE alumni clubs until rigor mortis set in.

As Welch remodeled GE there were mass layoffs. Within a few years, one of every four employees was gone. Welch believed that the idea of loyalty in GE's culture retarded change, so he rooted it out. At meetings he told employees it was out of fashion. He instructed staff never to use the word *loyalty* in any company document, press release, or publication. He wanted all GE managers to prove their value every day and said people who knew they could be fired worked harder.

In the Welch years there was tumultuous change in the workforce. No total number exists for workers who lost jobs. When he took over there were 404,000 GE employees; when he left there were 313,000. In between, tens of thousands came and went. Union

[21]O'Boyle, *At Any Cost,* p. 59.

leaders estimate that in his last 15 years GE eliminated 150,000 jobs in the United States through layoffs, subcontracting, and outsourcing to foreign countries.[22] Welch expressed his feelings about these layoffs in his memoirs:

> Removing people will always be the hardest decision a leader faces. Anyone who "enjoys doing it" shouldn't be on the payroll and neither should anyone who "can't do it." I never underestimated the human cost of those layoffs or the hardship they might cause people and communities.[23]

Welch stressed globalization of production to lower costs. Many jobs still existed, but they left the United States. In 1985 the electrical worker's union had 46,000 members working at GE, but by 2001 the number had declined to 16,000. Ed Fire, the union's president, estimates that two-thirds of the 30,000 lost jobs were simply transferred to low-wage countries.[24] GE eliminated additional jobs in the United States by pressuring suppliers to migrate along with it. After moving production to Mexico, for example, GE Aircraft Engines held a conference for supplier companies and told them to cut costs by moving their facilities (and jobs) to Mexico's low-wage labor market or face inevitable loss of their GE business.[25] Says Fire:

> GE is the quintessential American corporation that has engaged in what has been referred to as the "race to the bottom"—finding the lowest wages, the lowest benefit levels and most intolerant working conditions. . . . I don't think they have given enough consideration to the consequences, particularly the human consequences, of the decisions they make. In my opinion, the decisions are designed too much to increase the company's profitability at the expense of the employees.[26]

A DEFECTIVE EVALUATION SYSTEM

The vitality curve rating method is flawed. Forced ranking hurts the morale of employees who are not placed on top. At first, GE ranked employees in five categories instead of three, but it was soon discovered that everyone who failed to land in the top category was demoralized. Hence, three categories were combined into one to create the "vital" 70 percent of Bs in the middle. Disheartening classifications as 2s, 3s, and 4s were abolished.

The system also hurts teamwork by pitting people against each other. It may encourage back-stabbing behavior. Its inflexibility produces unfair results when high-performing and low-performing units must classify managers the same way. The bottom 10 percent in an outstanding business may be better than middle- or top-ranked managers on a weaker team. If the axing of the bottom 10 percent goes on for many years, people who were once in the middle range may find themselves lopped off. Of course, the curve calls the recruiting system into question if recent hires are lost.

Forced ranking was just one source of pressure on GE managers, who were expected to meet high profit goals and knew that if there were too many mistakes or misjudgments Welch would get rid of them. His confrontational style reduced some to tears. He reportedly believed that overweight people were undisciplined. At GE businesses these people were hidden when he visited for fear they would catch Welch's eye and lose their jobs. One large manager trying to save his career had surgery to staple his colon.[27] Working at GE was also hard on marriages because of the long hours required to be a player. Welch himself divorced in 1987 and remarried in 1990.

Because of Welch's status as a management icon, his approach to forced ranking has spread widely, imposing the practice on many managers at other corporations. Sun Microsystems, for example, uses an identical 20-70-10 percent curve. Even small businesses have picked up the idea. The manager of a Fifth Avenue clothing store once took Welch aside and explained that he had 20 sales workers. "Mr. Welch," he asked, "do I really have to let two go?"

[22] "GE Fast Facts," GE Workers United, May 7, 2001, at www.geworkersunited.org/news/fast_facts.asp.

[23] Welch, *Jack*, p. 128.

[24] Ed Fire, president of the International Union of Electronic, Electrical, Salaried, Machine and Furniture Workers–Communications Workers of America, the Industrial Division of CWA, "Resisting the Goliath," *Multinational Monitor,* July–August 2001, p. 31.

[25] Robert Weissman, "Global Management by Stress," *Multinational Monitor,* July–August 2001, p. 20.

[26] Fire, "Resisting the Goliath," pp. 31 and 33.

[27] O'Boyle, *At Any Cost,* p. 76.

"You probably do," replied Welch, "if you want the best sales staff on Fifth Avenue."[28]

NO DIVERSITY AT THE TOP

Using the vitality curve Welch created a high-performance management team, but failed to create diversity. The year before Welch retired the *New York Times* reported that although women and minorities were 40 percent of its domestic workforce, white men dominated its top leadership. The paper ran a photo collage of the top 31 executives, including heads of the 20 businesses responsible for 90 percent of corporate earnings. All were male and all but one were white.[29]

Diversity was never a priority for Welch. Later, Welch would explain why not. "Winning companies are meritocracies . . . [that] practice differentiation" and "this is the most effective way for an organization of field the best team." "Quotas," he argues, "artificially push some people ahead, independent of qualifications" and that slows the rise of star performers, puts "unprepared people" into important jobs, and "doesn't do much for results."[30] Yet, in the subhead for its story the *Times* challenged Welch with this question: "Can Only White Men Run a Model Company?"

POLLUTION IN THE HUDSON RIVER

For 35 years several GE manufacturing plants in New York released polychlorinated biphenyls (PCBs) into the Hudson River. They followed permits that set release levels and stopped in 1977 when PCBs were outlawed because of evidence that they were toxic to humans and animals. There is widespread scientific agreement that PCBs cause cancer in test animals and probably cause cancer and a range of other illnesses in humans.

More than 100,000 pounds of PCBs released by GE still lay on the river bed. Although the biggest deposits were covered by new sediments, slowing their release into the river, fish were unsafe to eat and the chemicals gradually spread downstream from hot spots of contamination. PCBs are stable molecules that persist in the environment, and because they are fat soluble, they accumulate in human tissue. The GE plants released more than a million pounds of PCBs, and most of this had already floated down 200 miles of river to the ocean, from there migrating around the planet.

The Environmental Protection Agency (EPA) studied the river, concluding that dredging the bottom was necessary to remove the dangerous deposits. This would be extremely expensive, and GE was liable for the cost. GE objected. It sponsored studies showing that PCBs were not harmful to health, but these were rejected by the EPA and outside experts. It argued that removing the contaminated sediment would stir up embedded PCBs, doing more harm than good, but the EPA planned to monitor the dredging to prevent this.

GE undertook an extensive public relations campaign in the Hudson River region to convince the public that dredging would be an ineffective nuisance. It succeeded in dividing the public to such an extent that people began to shop only at stores where the owners supported their position and classmates teased children over their parents' views.[31] GE hired 17 lobbyists, including a former senator and six former House members, to fight an extended political battle against the cleanup.[32] After many years of delay, the EPA finally ordered dredging in 2001. The cost to GE was estimated at $460 million.[33]

THE GE PENSION FUND

During Welch's tenure the GE pension fund covered approximately 485,000 people, including 195,000 who were aheady retired. As the stock market rose in the 1990s, the fund also rose, and by 2001 it totaled $50 billion. Its liabilities, the future payments it must make to retirees, were only $29 billion, leaving a surplus of $21 billion. GE's retirees and their unions requested increased benefits and cost-of-living

[28] Welch, *Jack,* p. 434.

[29] Mary Williams Walsh, "Where G.E. Falls Short: Diversity at the Top," *New York Times*, September 3, 2000, sec. 3, pp. 1 and 13.

[30] Jack Welch with Suzy Welch, *Winning* (New York: HarperCollins, 2005), p. 346.

[31] John M. Glionna, "Dredging Up Ill Will on the Hudson," *Los Angeles Times,* October 1, 2001, p. A17.

[32] Charlie Cray, "Toxins on the Hudson," *Multinational Monitor,* July–August 2001, pp. 9–18.

[33] "Mrs. Whitman Stays the Course," *New York Times,* August 2, 2001, p. A20.

increases for pensioners, but the company rejected their demands. By law, it did not have to meet more than the original obligations.

Welch understood that there were several benefits in leaving the pension plan overfunded. First, it generated bottom-line profits. Under accounting rules, a company can put interest earned by the pension fund on the balance sheet as revenue, and during the Welch years these earnings increased GE's net by as much as 13.7 percent.[34] Second, these "vapor profits" increased the income of top GE executives, whose bonuses were tied to corporate profits. And third, the excess funding made it easier for GE to acquire companies with underfunded pension plans. This eased deal making, but involved sharing funds set aside for GE workers and retirees with people who got a windfall coming in after careers in other companies.

After being pressured by unions and pensioners, GE announced increases of 15 to 35 percent in 2000. But since 1965 prices had risen by 60 percent, so retirees were still losing ground.[35] Helen Quirini, 81, was part of a group protesting GE's failure to be more generous. After working 39 years at a GE factory, one year less than Welch's 40-year tenure, she retired in 1980 and was receiving $737 a month, or $8,844 a year. She believed that GE management was "out all the time trying to figure out how to screw us" using "accounting gimmicks."[36]

Welch's GE pension is $357,128 a month. Court documents filed in proceedings when Welch divorced his second wife in 2002 revealed that he spent an average of $8,982 a month on food and beverages, slightly more than Helen Quirini's yearly pension income.[37] A 1996 retention agreement between Welch and the GE board also granted him nonmonetary perquisites in retirement. He got lifetime use of a spacious apartment owned by GE at the Trump International Hotel and Tower on Central Park West in New York, including a cook, a housekeeper, and a wait staff plus flowers, laundry and dry cleaning, newspaper and magazine subscriptions, and front-row seats at sporting and entertainment events.[38] He was allowed unlimited use of GE's corporate jets. Criticism of these arrangements arose when they were detailed during the divorce. Although he felt there was nothing improper with them, he elected to pay GE "between $2 and $2.5 million a year" for continued use of the apartment and planes.[39]

CRIMINALITY AT GE

Pressure for performance tempts employees to cut corners. Welch knew this.

> If there was one thing I preached every day at GE, it was integrity. It was our No. 1 value. Nothing came before it. We never had a corporate meeting where I didn't emphasize integrity in my closing remarks.[40]

Yet during his tenure, GE committed a long string of civil and criminal transgressions. The *Multinational Monitor* compiled a "GE Rap Sheet," listing 39 law violations, court-ordered remedies, and fines in the 1990s alone.[41] Many are for pollution hazards from GE facilities. Others are for consumer fraud, including a $165,000 fine for deceptive advertising of light bulbs and a $100 million fine on GE Capital for unfair debt-collection practices. Still others are for defense contracting fraud, including a $69 million fine for diverting fighter contract funds to other purposes and other fines for overcharging on defense contracts.

Since GE is such a large company, technical violations of complex regulations and incidents of wrongdoing by individual managers are inevitable. The *Multinational Monitor* sees "a consistent pattern of violating criminal and civil laws over many years."[42] The key question is whether GE's malfeasance increased because of relentless performance pressure on its managers.

[34] Rob Walker, "Overvalued: Why Jack Welch Isn't God," *The New Republic,* June 18, 2001, p. 22. See *GE Annual Report 2000,* Notes to Consolidated Financial Statements, 6, "Pension Benefits."

[35] "GE Pension Fund Story: Workers Pay, GE Benefits," GE Workers United, April 1, 2001, at www.geworkersunited.org/pensions/index.asp?ID + 61.

[36] Vincent Lloyd, "Penny Pinching the Retirees at GE," *Multinational Monitor,* July–August 2001, p. 23.

[37] "Here's the Retirement Jack Welch Built: $1.4 Million a Month," *The Wall Street Journal,* October 31, 2002, p. A1.

[38] Geraldine Fabrikant, "G.E. Expenses for Ex-Chief Cited in Filing," *New York Times,* September 6, 2002, p. C1.

[39] Jack Welch, "My Dilemma and How I Resolved It," *New York Times,* September 16, 2002, p. A14.

[40] Welch, *Jack,* pp. 279–80.

[41] "GE: Decades of Misdeeds and Wrongdoing," *Multinational Monitor,* July–August 2001, p. 26.

[42] Ibid., p. 30.

ASSESSING THE SOCIAL RESPONSIBILITY OF GE

General Electric in the Welch years fulfilled its primary economic responsibilities to society. It was remarkably profitable. It paid taxes. Shareholders, including pension and mutual funds, were enriched. Many of its directors and managers became multimillionaires in GE stock.

In the Welch system, however, wealth was transferred from workers to shareholders. He insulated himself from the pain this caused, rationalizing that what he did was for the greater good.

> I believe social responsibility begins with a strong, competitive company, only a healthy enterprise can improve and enrich the lives of people and their communities. . . . That's why a CEO's primary social responsibility is to assure the financial success of the company. Only a healthy, winning company has the resources and the capability to do the right thing.[43]

During the Welch years, GE engaged in a broad range of philanthropy and community activity. In 2000 the GE foundation made $40 million in grants to colleges, universities, and nonprofit groups in the United States and worldwide. This was three-thousandths of 1 percent of GE's $12.7 billion in net earnings that year. On the other hand, the company pressured cities, counties, and states to lower taxes by threatening to

relocate operations, and this lowered budgets for schools. Through the Elfin Society, a community support group within GE, current and former GE employees volunteered 1 million hours of community service. Assuming eight-hour days and two weeks of vacation a year for all 313,000 employees, this was about one hour out of every 500 employee-hours worked and many hours were donated by retirees. As these figures illustrate, GE's community initiatives hardly distracted it from its profit obsession.

Questions

1. Corporate social responsibility is defined in Chapter 5 as the corporate duty to create wealth by using means that avoid harm to, protect, or enhance societal assets. Did GE in the Welch era fulfill this duty? Could it have done better? What should it have done?

2. Does GE under Welch illustrate a narrower view of corporate social responsibility closer to Friedman's view that the only social responsibility is to increase profits while obeying the law?

3. How well did GE comply with the "General Principles of Corporate Social Responsibility" set forth in the section of that title in the chapter?

4. What are the pros and cons of ranking shareholders over employees and other stakeholders? Is it wrong to see employees as costs of production? Should GE have rebalanced its priorities?

---

[43] Welch, *Jack,* pp. 381–82.

Chapter Six

Implementing Corporate Social Responsibility

The Bill & Melinda Gates Foundation

Growing up in Seattle, William H. Gates III was a slender, intense boy with a messy room and a dazzling mind. At age seven or eight he read the entire *World Book Encyclopedia*. At his family's church the minister challenged young congregants to earn a free dinner by memorizing the Sermon on the Mount, a passage covering Chapters 5, 6, and 7 in the Book of Matthew. At age 11 young Bill became the only one, in 25 years of the minister's experience, ever to recite every word perfectly, never stumbling, never erring.[1] Yet Christianity itself never attracted Gates. Years later he would remark that "there's a lot more I could be doing on a Sunday morning," an incongruous conviction for one who would become devoted to serving the poor.[2] His brilliance, however, was lasting.

At private Lakeside prep school he was a prodigy, often challenging his teachers in class. Obsessed with computers in their then-primitive form, he stayed up all night writing code, a routine that would stay with him. He also read biographies of great historical figures to enter their minds and understand how they succeeded. After high school he attended Harvard University hoping to find an atmosphere of exciting erudition. Instead, he grew bored and left to pursue his fascination with computers.

At age 19, Gates founded Microsoft Corporation with his Lakeside School friend Paul Allen. As its leader he was energetic, independent, and confrontational. He developed the reputation of a fanatical competitor willing to appropriate any technology and crush market rivals. He built a dominant business and by 1987, at age 31, he was a billionaire.

[1] James Wallace and Jim Erickson, *Hard Drive: Bill Gates and the Making of the Microsoft Empire* (New York: HarperBusiness, 1992), pp. 6–7.

[2] Garrison Keillor, "Faith at the Speed of Light," *Time,* July 14, 1999, p. 25.

Bill Gates at 31, already a billionaire.
Source: © Ed Kashi/CORBIS.

Microsoft's stock took flight, making more billions for Gates. However, even as he became the world's richest man he remained absorbed in running his corporation. He put little energy into charity, thinking it could wait until he grew old. But the world expected more. Requests for good deeds and contributions poured in. Gates responded with the help of his father, who worked in a home basement office handling his son's donations. In 1994, Gates formalized his giving by creating the William H. Gates Foundation and endowing it with $94 million. His father agreed to manage it from the basement. Eventually, this arrangement evolved into a new Bill & Melinda Gates Foundation, which included the name of his wife and was run by a professional staff from its new headquarters in Seattle.

A foundation is essentially an organization with a pool of money for giving to nonprofit and charitable causes. It is not taxed if it gives out at least 5 percent of its money each year. Bill Gates gave his foundation $16 billion in Microsoft stock in 2000. Since then he has given more. When his shares are sold to diversify the foundation's assets, the large capital gains in them are not taxed. And when the foundation's pool of money, or endowment, earns more money from interest and capital growth, these gains are untaxed as well.

Today, the Gates Foundation has an endowment of $33 billion, making it the world's largest. It has two parts. One part decides what projects to fund. So far, more than $13.4 billion has been given out. The other part manages the endowment by investing Gates' money to make it grow. The Gates are deeply involved in the foundation's work, which is based on a pair of "simple values" that inspire them. One is that "all lives—no matter where they are being led—have equal value," and the other is that "to whom much is given, much is expected." They focus the foundation on programs that (1) improve health and reduce poverty in developing nations, (2) bring computer technologies to public libraries, (3) improve education, and (4) help low-income families in the Seattle area.

The Gates Foundation's endowment is unprecedentedly large, more than the GDPs of 112 countries, so its goals are very ambitious. One is to correct market signals that cause modern medicine to neglect diseases of the poor, thus failing to value all lives equally. Pursuing this goal, the foundation has spent $3.8 billion on basic vaccinations for 90 percent of newborns in 70 countries with low GDPs. So far, this has prevented about 2.3 million deaths.[3] Another $278 million grant funds research on an AIDS vaccine.[4] And $68 million is being spent to develop

[3] Charles Piller, "Health Plan Focuses on Training Workers," *Los Angeles Times,* January 27, 2007, p. A7; GAVI Alliance, "Immunization Rates Hit Record High in Poor Countries," press release, January 26, 2007, at www.gavialliance.org.

[4] Thomas H. Maugh II, "Gates Foundation Donates $278 Million for AIDS Research," *Los Angeles Times,* July 20, 2006, p. A14.

vaccines for three parasitic diseases that infect 600 million people and kill 550,000 each year.[5]

In 2006 Bill Gates' friend Warren Buffet, chairman of Berkshire Hathaway and the world's second-richest man, decided to give most of his wealth away and made a bequest of 10 million shares of Berkshire Hathaway to the Gates Foundation. He believed that the two Gates were doing such a fine job that he could do no better and, rather than manage billions of dollars of giving on his own, he preferred to put his philanthropic funds in their hands. At the time, his gift was worth $31 billion, a sum that roughly doubles the Gates endowment. It will arrive in annual installments of 5 percent of the amount of the shares remaining with Buffett or his estate. The money will stop when neither Bill or Melinda Gates are there to direct the foundation. His bequest also requires that all of each year's gift be spent in that year on top of the 5 percent of its own endowment that the foundation is legally required to spend.

The Gates Foundation confronts enormous social problems. Poverty and disease defy solution. Spending large sums in poor nations is a challenge. Corruption diverts funds. Agencies lack capacity. When infant lives are saved by vaccination, more people seeking ordinary care burden understaffed national health care systems. Some nations struggle to provide even the most basic care due to shortages of doctors and nurses. Thus, children are saved from diphtheria only to die in large numbers from common diarrhea.[6] Improving education is another nightmare. After spending $1 billion over six years to make small high schools better, an analysis showed that attendance, graduation rates, and test scores on basic subjects were lower than at similar schools not funded by the Gates Foundation.[7]

Despite its remarkable good works and promise the Gates Foundation attracts critics. Since there is no government oversight as it spends remarkable sums it is called an elitist, antidemocratic institution subsidized by taxpayers (through its tax exemptions) but having no accountability to society for how it spends its money.[8] After Warren Buffett formally joins the foundation, its sole trustees will be Buffett and Bill and Melinda Gates, putting "more than $60 billion in tax-exempt assets under the control of members of just two families."[9]

And both Buffett and Gates have come in for their share of criticism. When Buffett announced that as a trustee he would not play an active role, he was called "a very poor model of philanthropic stewardship" for abdicating the duty of a donor to

---

[5] Marilyn Chase, "Gates Targets Three Diseases Plaguing the Developing World," *The Wall Street Journal*, September 14, 2006, p. A11.

[6] Laurie Garrett, "The Challenge of Global Health," *Foreign Affairs*, January/February 2007.

[7] The National Institutes of High School Transformation, *Evaluation of the Bill & Melinda Gates Foundation's High School Grants Initiative: 2001–2005 Final Report* (Washington, DC: American Institutes for Research, 2006), pp. 9–10.

[8] "Philanthropic World Voices Mixed Reaction on Buffett's Gift to Gates Fund," *Chronicle of Philanthropy*, July 20, 2006, p. 12, comment of Rick Cohen.

[9] Pablo Eisenberg, "The Gates-Buffett Merger Isn't Good for Philanthropy," *Chronicle of Philanthropy*, July 20, 2006, p. 33.

preside over his charitable giving.[10] Bill Gates remains the world's richest man and does not plan to put more of his money into the foundation until 2015. For that, philosopher Peter Singer accuses him of failing to live up to the principle that each life has equal worth. Singer notes that while Gates has given away at least $30 billion he still has more than $50 billion. He lives in a 66,000-square-foot house worth more than $100 million and in 1994 he spent $30.8 million on a handwritten book by Leonardo da Vinci. Asks Singer, "Are there no more lives that could be saved by living more modestly and adding the money thus saved to the amount he has already given?"[11]

The Bill & Melinda Gates Foundation illustrates one method for turning capitalist wealth to promotion of social good. Gates follows a long and growing tradition of wealthy entrepreneurs who have made fortunes, sometimes by compromising ethics, then later in life used their wealth for works of extraordinary benevolence. In this chapter we will expand on the subject of philanthropy. First, however, we look at how managers plan and carry out social responsibility efforts within their firms.

MANAGING THE RESPONSIVE CORPORATION

Corporations must and do undertake a range of social initiatives. Whatever management's opinion about corporate social responsibility (CSR)—its desirability and its affect on profits—companies must respond to multiple sources of pressure for social actions. There is no alternative. Figure 6.1 shows multiple sources of these pressures on corporations. Each source can generate many demands, some conflicting. We begin here a discussion about how CSR actions may be defined and implemented. First, we look at two elements that can determine the CSR orientation of a firm—its business model and its leadership.

FIGURE 6.1
Sources of Pressure for Social Responsibility

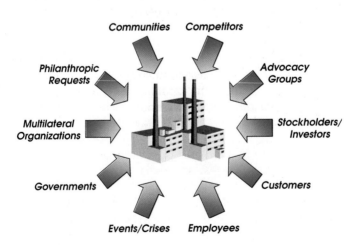

LEADERSHIP AND BUSINESS MODELS

business model
The underlying idea or theory that explains how a business will create value by making and selling products or services in the market.

Top management usually sets the tone for a company's social response. When founders or CEOs have a strong social responsibility philosophy, it is reflected throughout the organization. A few companies have been founded by progressive visionaries who made social initiatives central to their business model. A *business model* is the underlying idea or theory of how a business will create value by making and selling something in the market. The theory is validated if the business makes a profit.

A traditional business model is one in which the central strategy for creating value is based on meeting market demands. A progressive business model differs by defining a strategy that meets market needs by mitigating social problems. Usually, the value proposition is based on actions that would be considered voluntary responsibilities for more traditional companies. Anita Roddick conceived of The Body Shop as a beacon of ethical and social activism in a world darkened by capitalist greed. She saw cosmetics as "an industry dominated by men trying to create needs that don't exist" and she devoted herself to "harnessing commercial success to altruistic ideals."[12] Her business model predicted that women would buy from an honest company that used natural ingredients, made realistic product claims, and supported feminist and progressive causes. The company's ads encouraged women to accept their natural appearance. One read: "There are 3 billion women who don't look like supermodels and only 8 who do."

Progressive business models are rare, the basis of only a few companies. Other examples include Ben & Jerry's, the ice cream company founded to promote social causes such as world peace; Patagonia, Inc., a clothing firm that built environmental protection into its strategy; Stonyfield Farm, an organic yogurt maker; and Seventh Generation, which makes nontoxic household products. The validity of a business model is determined by profit or loss. These businesses have succeeded, at least for an extended time, though each has faced tensions between social missions and market realities. Several have suffered financial difficulties and been absorbed by larger firms run on more traditional business models.

In a second category are companies that, although based on traditional business models, have cultures emphasizing voluntary social responsibility in one or more dimensions. Bertelsmann AG, for example, was founded in 1835 to publish hymnals by Carl Bertelsmann, a Protestant inspired by the Great Awakening. He believed that the primary goal of his company should be to make society better. Bertelsmann shared half the firm's profits with employees and gave them pensions and other benefits long before other German companies. Bertelsmann has grown into the third-largest global media conglomerate owning, among other brands, BMG Music, Random House, and RCA, but it is still controlled by descendants of the founder. The family recently fired its chief executive, in part because he bought Napster, a business they believed was irresponsible.[13]

---

[12] Anita Roddick, *Business as Unusual* (London: Thorsons, 2000), pp. 97 and 172.

[13] Matthew Karnitschnig and Neal E. Boudette, "History Lesson: Battle for the Soul of Bertelsmann Led to CEO Ouster," *The Wall Street Journal,* July 30, 2002, p. A1.

FIGURE 6.2
A Spectrum of Responses to Social Demands

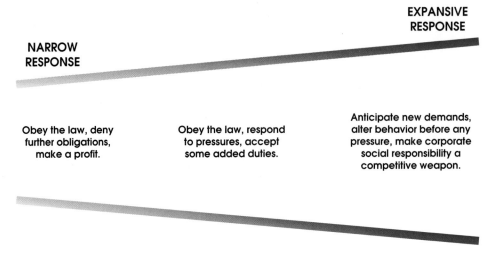

Obey the law, deny further obligations, make a profit.

Obey the law, respond to pressures, accept some added duties.

Anticipate new demands, alter behavior before any pressure, make corporate social responsibility a competitive weapon.

Companies in a third category, the most populous by far and including most of the largest transnational corporations, have no special founding impulse toward the progressive agenda. Their social performance is based on the response of their management teams to pressures in the business environment. Such companies vary in their reaction to these pressures across a spectrum of responses running from reluctance to enthusiasm. At the left of this spectrum (see Figure 6.2), companies focus on making a profit and resist demands to go beyond the minimum duty of obeying the law. For them, the extent of corporate responsibility is determined by the power of stakeholders over their behavior. In the middle, where perhaps most are located, companies accept social obligations and may work to mitigate adverse impacts on society before new laws and regulations are passed. And at the right, a few companies seek to be proactive by anticipating demands and resolving problems before they arise.[14]

A MODEL OF CSR IMPLEMENTATION

Companies can manage their responses to social pressures by moving through a process of CSR implementation. Figure 6.3 illustrates a model sequence or method for assessing the societal environment, defining responsibilities, creating a CSR strategy, and

FIGURE 6.3   **A Model Process of CSR Implementation**

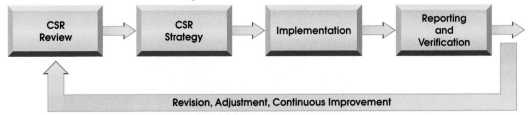

[14] Corporations may also evolve to a higher level of social response. See, for example, Phillip Mirvis and Bradley Googins, "Stages of Corporate Citizenship," *California Management Review,* Winter 2006, p. 115.

taking action. The sequence implied in this basic model is an ideal. It implies a more systematic approach than may exist in practice.[15] Beginning at the left with CSR assessment, we will discuss each stage and illustrate related company actions.

CSR Review

As a first step in implementing corporate social responsibility a corporation should assess its current situation and activities. No single formula for social responsibility fits all companies. It is necessary to review each business systematically, discovering a range of societal impacts and societal expectations unique to it. Discovery of these elements requires looking at factors such as its size, financial structure, products, production processes, employees, culture, geographic location, influence over supply chains, and leaders' views. The review should be wide ranging. It can begin with a definition of CSR to provide a focus. Then it might explore legal or regulatory requirements, inventory existing company CSR initiatives, and examine competitors' initiatives. Two other important steps are discovery of core values and engagement of stakeholders to reveal expectations in society.

Discovery of Core Values

Core values reside in documents setting forth the basic goals, values, and principles that guide decisions in the firm. Guiding standards may exist in multiple documents, including mission, vision, and values statements, charters, and codes of conduct. Social initiatives taken by the firm should harmonize with core goals and values. If these basic documents do not reference goals and values that facilitate CSR, support for action may be weak.

mission statement
A brief statement of the basic purpose of an organization.

For most organizations a key source of values is the *mission statement,* a document setting forth, with brevity, the basic purpose of the organization or company. The best ones define the business, differentiate it from competitors, explain relationships with stakeholders, and focus energy on critical activities and goals. If social responsibility is central to the company's mission, that should be reflected in its wording. The Ben & Jerry's mission statement sets forth a "social mission," which is "[t]o operate the company in a way that actively recognizes the central role that business plays in society by initiating innovative ways to improve the quality of life locally, nationally & internationally." The idea of "initiating innovative ways" led over the years to specific actions. The company planted trees to replace the wood used in its popsicle sticks and it donated a percentage of Peace Pops sales to fund research on world peace.

In the past, most mission statements centered on profits and products. Many still limit themselves to this narrow focus. AutoNation aspires "[t]o be America's best run, most profitable automotive retailer." News Corporation aspires to "the creation and distribution of top-quality news, sports and entertainment around

---

[15] The structure of this model is inspired by models and process standards elsewhere, including especially, Business Leaders Initiative on Human Rights et al., *A Guide for Integrating Human Rights into Business Management* (New York: Global Compact Office, February 2007); International Standards Organization, Task Group 6, Working Draft 2, chap. 7, "Guidance for Organizations on Implementing SR," http://isotc.iso.org; and Government of Canada, *Corporate Social Responsibility: An Implementation Guide for Canadian Business* (Ottawa: Public Works and Government Services Canada, March 2006).

the world." However, in recent years many companies have revised their missions to include a social purpose. PhilipMorris states its mission as "manufacturing and marketing the best quality tobacco products" but adds that in doing so it will "act in a way that is consistent with society's expectations of a responsible company."

Guiding documents have great power to inspire and direct decisions throughout even the largest corporations. Unilever distributes a one-page Code of Business Principles, unchanged except for translation into local languages, to each of its 206,000 employees. It sets standards that "everyone at Unilever follows, wherever they are in the world."[16] In Saudi Arabia, religious custom and civil regulation restrain women from accepting work outside the home. Yet one paragraph of the code commits Unilever to "diversity in a working environement where there is mutual trust and respect" and requires employment "on the sole basis of the qualifications and abilities needed for the work to be performed." It also requires "compliance with the laws and regulations of the countries in which we operate." Aspiring to meet these guiding principles, managers at a Saudi facility sought to employ local women. After some negotiations with authorities they received permission to do so, but on the condition that the women work in separate offices and this was carried out.[17]

stakeholder map
A diagram showing stakeholders and their relationship to the firm.

Engaging Stakeholders

Many companies now engage in dialogue with a range of stakeholders. Stakeholders can be identified on a *stakeholder map*, a diagram that sketches stakeholders in categories and depicts their relationship to the firm. Figure 6.4 shows a basic stakeholder

FIGURE 6.4
Basic Stakeholder Map

[16] Unilever, "Code of Business Principles," at www.unilever.co.uk.
[17] Speech by Niall Fitzgerald, "CSR: Rebuilding Trust in Business," London Business School, October 2, 2003.

FIGURE 6.5
Stakeholder
Map
Articulated
to Show
Government
Stakeholders

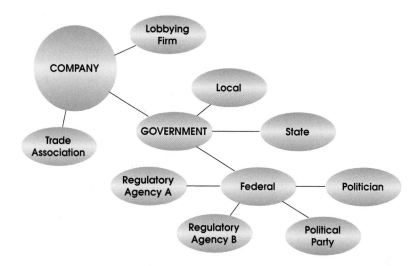

map with common stakeholder categories. This map is only a beginning. Figure 6.5 shows how just one category, government, might be articulated to render a more complete picture of the entities affected by or able to affect the firm.

With stakeholders identified by mapping, a plan of engagement is constructed. Stakeholders can be categorized by, for example, their orientation to the firm (confrontational, neutral, or supportive), their power to affect its business (high, medium, or low influence), or by their area of claims (feminists, environmentalists, or antipoverty groups).[18] These classifications help decide which methods of engagement are best, for example, surveys, private or public meetings, advisory panels, focus groups, workshops, and presentations.

Engaging with constituents has advantages. Mapping helps identify the corporation's sphere of influence. Dialogue can reveal gaps between company performance and stakeholder expectations. It may produce new ideas or information and it enhances the likelihood of spotting trends early. It can also build trust and ease tensions. Sometimes, engagement with stakeholders leads to cooperative efforts. As a result of reaching out to environmental groups, Federal Express worked with an activist group, Environmental Defense, to convert part of its truck fleet to hybrids. Those vehicles now carry the Environmental Defense logo on their sides.[19]

In conclusion, the result of the CSR review should be a company profile that defines the company's current situation with respect to CSR. When completed, it spells out core values related to CSR, where the firm has impacts on society, and what stakeholders expect of it. These insights can be used to develop a CSR strategy.

---

[18] For some suggested classifications see John F. Preble, "Toward a Comprehensive Model of Stakeholder Engagement," *Business and Society Review* vol. 110, no. 4 (2005); and Patrick Hughes and Kristin Demetrious, "Engaging with Stakeholders or Constructing Them?" *The Journal of Corporate Citizenship,* Autumn 2006.

[19] Claudia H. Deutsch, "Companies and Critics Try Collaboration," *New York Times,* May 17, 2006, p. G1.

CSR Strategy

strategy
A basic approach, method, or plan for achieving an objective.

The next stage in Figure 6.3 is the development of an overall strategy for corporate responsibility. A *strategy* is a basic approach, method, or plan for achieving an objective. A company with a strategy is like a traveler with a map showing the city of destination and a plan to reach it by taking the morning train. Like this traveler, a company defining its CSR strategy must first find an objective, or a vision of what it will achieve, then create a method for reaching it.

To establish its CSR objective a company can consider options suggested by the profile of its situation constructed in the prior CSR review stage. This profile can be analyzed to find the strengths and weaknesses in the company's social response and the threats and opportunities in its environment. Based on this analysis the company can list a range of possible social initiatives. At a minimum, these actions must meet legal requirements. Beyond that, voluntary actions can be listed. Then, a few actions should be given priority. These become the firm's strategic CSR objectives.

For large firms the task of setting priorities is complex. Multiple, sometimes conflicting, stakeholder demands exist. Along the value chain there are potential adverse impacts to correct. More broadly, difficult social problems in the firm's environment may demand attention. To which tasks should the firm assign priority? Companies must respond to some stakeholder demands or risk damage to their reputations and businesses. Ethical duty requires that where the firm has influence it should seek to mitigate value chain activities that damage society. Yet beyond such imperatives there are many options.

Porter and Kramer suggest an "essential test" for the worthiness of any additional social initiative, that is, "whether it presents an opportunity to create shared value—that is, a meaningful benefit for society that is also valuable to the business."[20] According to them, companies should distinguish between a wide range of generic social issues and a much narrower range of social issues that affect their competitive advantage. Generic social issues, such as the need to reduce crime, poverty, and disease, are important in society, but are not affected by and do not affect the company's business. Competitive social issues are those related to factors that influence success in the marketplace. The importance of issues to firms will vary according to their nature. Greenhouse gas emissions are a generic social issue for Tiffany's, but a competitive factor for General Motors and Toyota, which sell low-emission vehicles. Poverty may be a generic social issue for Lockheed, but a competitive issue for Unilever and Nestlé, which have begun to market small, inexpensive, single-use product packages.

An example of how a company can prioritize a social issue to competitive advantage is General Electric's "ecomagination" strategy. Ecomagination is a neologism created to denote concern for the environment and the imagination residing in GE's research labs. As a strategy, it is simultaneously a plan for revenue growth and a social program aimed at environmental issues or, in GE's words, "a commitment to imagine and build innovative solutions that benefit customers and society

---

[20] Michael E. Porter and Mark R. Kramer, "Strategy & Society," *Harvard Business Review,* December 2006, p. 84.

at large."[21] To implement its ecomagination strategy, GE will add $800 million to clean technology research and has set a target of $20 billion from new products by 2012.[22] The strategy is based on GE's belief that oil and gas depletion, global warming, and global shortages of clean water are not only social problems but business opportunities.

Implementation of CSR Strategy

To be carried out, the strategy must be translated into specific goals and performance objectives, embedded in policies and procedures, and supported by both the formal structure and the informal elements of corporate culture. If the organization structure, culture, and processes of a company are misaligned with its strategic social goals, those goals will be slighted. A range of actions that facilitate implementation will be discussed.

Organization Structure

An initial step in implementation is to create an effective CSR decision-making structure within the overall organization. Many companies create elements of formal structure at top management levels to provide leadership and organize decision making for social responsibility. Examples of companies with social responsibility committees on their boards of directors are Hasbro, Kellogg, and Occidental Petroleum. Below the board, a top executive can be assigned to oversee the action. A few corporations, including British Petroleum, General Motors, Nike, Time Warner, Wal-Mart, and Walt Disney have staff vice presidents of corporate social responsibility to coordinate their social initiatives.

However, the growing number of board committees and vice presidencies implies more centralization than usually exists in practice. At most companies CSR strategy is supplemental, and perhaps incidental, to core business strategies. Elements of CSR are isolated in separate parts of the organization. Charitable giving is in the company foundation. Human rights and diversity are often managed by the human resources staff. The code of ethics is in the legal department. Environmental health and safety may be in another area. In most corporations the CSR agenda is fragmented. To wit:

> Citizenship has many rooms but no home. Rarely is corporate citizenship organized across the business. Many organizational functions touch some piece of the elephant but each unit is generally responsible . . . to a particular part of citizenship. . . . [O]rganizational silos are created and frustrate any overall organization strategy where all units are pulling together around a common vision. . . .[23]

To centralize oversight a few companies, for example, Coca-Cola, Pfizer, and Time-Warner have formed cross-functional CSR committees made up of managers from different departments. Such organizational forms are still in the minority.

---

[21] General Electric Company, *GE 2006 Citizenship Report: Solving Big Needs* (Fairfield, CT: General Electric Company, 2006), p. 22.

[22] Ibid., p. 23.

[23] Bradley K. Googins and Steven Rochlin, "Corporate Citizenship Top to Bottom: Vision, Strategy, and Execution," in Marc J. Epstein and Kirk O. Hanson, eds. *The Accountable Corporation: Corporate Social Responsibility,* vol. 3 (Westport, CT: Praeger, 2006), p. 117.

Action Planning

Once a strategy and decision-making structure are in place a plan is still necessary to transform intent into action. An action plan sets forth the multitude of tasks that, together, will bring the strategy to fruition. Such tasks include revising or creating policies, budgeting resources, and assigning work.

An illustration of the effectiveness of an action plan is found within Novo Nordisk, a global pharmaceutical corporation with 24,000 employees in 79 countries. Late in the 1990s a human rights review led the company to decide that the focus of its social responsibility strategy would be fighting all forms of discrimination. The strategy had three parts. First, employees were trained in national laws and regulations against discrimination. Second, informal barriers to advancement within Novo Nordisk were identified and removed. Third, managers were encouraged to turn employee diversity into a business advantage. Each Novo Nordisk location set up an action plan to carry out the strategy. In South Africa, where physicians are predominantly white, the company sales representatives were white also. The action plan called for creating a diverse sales force and removing barriers to nonwhite sales representatives. Soon more than half the sales force was black and mixed-race. A strict policy was then required, excluding as customers doctors who dislike visits from nonwhite salespersons.[24]

Performance Goals, Timelines, and Targets

An effective action plan includes performance targets and timelines for their accomplishment. Examples of time-based, quantitative objectives, desirable for their clarity, are those set by General Electric for carrying out its ecomagination strategy. GE pledges to raise funding for clean technology research to $1.5 billion by 2010, increase revenues from ecomagination products and services to at least $20 million by 2010, and cut its greenhouse gas emissions by 1 percent by 2012.[25]

Performance Accountability

To create accountability for performance, incentives can be set up to encourage achievement of goals and targets. Social goals can be written into job descriptions so that performance evaluations, pay, and promotions are linked to them. Executive pay is linked to environmental performance at Alcoa, Dow Chemical, and Phillips Petroleum. At Coca-Cola and Texaco, which have suffered highly publicized discrimination suits, pay is linked to achieving diversity goals. At Alcoa between 2 and 30 percent of a manager's bonus, rising with the level of the manager, is tied to meeting CSR goals.[26]

Alignment of Strategy and Culture

Corporate culture must be aligned with strategic intent. Where the culture contains deep-seated, informal values that conflict with official CSR policies, those

[24] United Nations Development Programme, *Implementing the UN Global Compact: A Booklet for Inspiration* (Copenhagen: UNDP, 2005), pp. 11–12.

[25] General Electric Company, *GE 2006 Citizenship Report: Solving Big Needs*, p. 23.

[26] Parliamentary Joint Committee on Corporations and Financial Services, *Corporate Responsibility: Managing Risk and Creating Value* (Canberra: Senate Printing Unit, Parliament House, July 2006), p. 145.

policies are likely to be ignored. If managers who are highly productive but ignore social duties are promoted, it indicates that formal policy is inconsistent with underlying beliefs about requirements for career advancement. For example, at Timberland Co. executives promoted a program allowing employees to take one week a year at full pay to work at company-sponsored local charities. However, line managers felt pressured to meet production goals and resisted giving workers time off.[27]

Reporting and Verification

transparency
The state in which company social policies, processes, and actions are visible to external observers.

To complete the cycle of CSR implementation shown in Figure 6.3 companies can assess and report information about their social performance. Publishing such reports serves two main purposes. First, by informing stakeholders they create *transparency*; that is, they open the company to reveal the decisions, processes, and actions that define its impact on society. The opposite of transparency is opacity, or an inability to see inside the organization to know how it works and acts. Openness is increasingly necessary to protect a firm's reputation and establish trust with stakeholders. Reporting also allows managers to assess corporate social performance and measure overall progress toward strategic goals.

In the last decade a new wave of social reporting has risen. This followed an initial wave of social reports, called social audits to differentiate them from traditional financial audits, that came in the 1960s and 1970s. At the time, a few large firms, including Bank of America, Exxon, and Philip Morris, did widely publicized assessments of their social impacts. For a few years in the 1970s, Atlantic Richfield Company published an annual social balance sheet that candidly weighed the pluses and minuses of its social performance, a pioneering effort that ended when the company was acquired by British Petroleum. A 1974 survey found that 76 percent of 284 large companies did some form of social auditing.[28]

sustainability reporting
Documentation and disclosure of how closely corporate performance conforms to the goal of sustainable development.

Early interest in social auditing waned after a massive increase in environmental and social regulation hit business in the 1970s. New regulations contained strong reporting requirements that were, in effect, government-mandated social reports. However, as time passed, fewer new regulations were enacted, creating an information gap between what stakeholders want to know and what regulations require corporations to report. In the late 1990s voluntary social reporting again emerged as a useful tool for companies to address stakeholders.

sustainable development
Economic growth that meets the needs of the present without consuming social and environmental resources in a way that harms future generations.

The leading effort to create a new reporting format is the Global Reporting Initiative (GRI), an international organization of companies, NGOs, and government agencies that joined to develop uniform standards for *sustainability reporting*, or documentation and disclosure of how closely corporate performance conforms to the goal of *sustainable development*. Sustainable development is an ideal of economic growth that can "meet the needs of the present without compromising the

[27] Joseph Pereira, "Doing Good and Doing Well at Timberland," *The Wall Street Journal,* September 9, 2003, p. B1.

[28] John J. Corson and George A. Steiner, *Measuring Business's Social Performance: The Corporate Social Audit* (New York: Committee for Economic Development, 1974), pp. 24–25.

FIGURE 6.6
**The Prism
of the Triple
Bottom Line**

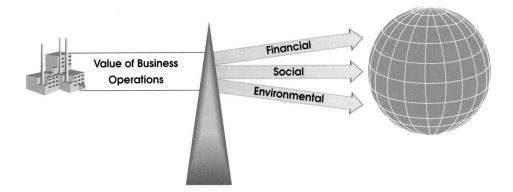

**triple bottom
line**
An accounting
of a firm's
economic,
social, and
environmental
performance.

ability of future generations to meet their own needs."[29] Using GRI guidelines, companies show how closely their operations conform to this idea by accounting for their performance on a *triple bottom line* of economic, social, and environmental results (see Figure 6.6). In 2006, about 950 corporations around the world used the GRI format for sustainability reports.[30]

The triple bottom line is a concept born in the progressive community of the late 1990s.[31] Its purpose is to appraise the overall impact of a firm's operations, by adding nonfinancial measures—social and environmental values—to traditional financial results. The idea rankles skeptics, who point out its limits as an accounting tool. There is no unit of measurement common to all three areas, leaving no way to compare results across financial and nonfinancial bottom lines. Even if social and environmental entries are ascribed a dollar amount, the calculation of that amount contains value judgments on which there is no agreement.[32] Economic conservatives dislike its implicit challenge to the primacy and totality of financial results that they see as essential to economic progress. Although such problems are a "colossal limitation" for critics, the triple bottom line has become the most accepted approach to CSR reporting, not because it is an elegant calculation, but because it can satisfy a range of demanding stakeholders.[33]

According to the GRI guidelines, a good social report meets certain criteria. Its content is useful to stakeholders—clear, timely, comparable to past reports, reliable, and verifiable. It should include a statement of management's CSR vision and strategy, an extensive factual profile of the company, a description of its governance structure and management policies for matters such as executive pay and

[29] Global Reporting Initiative, *Sustainability Reporting Guidelines,* ver. 3 (Amsterdam: GRI, 2000–2006), p. 3, citing World Commission on Environment and Development, *Our Common Future* (Oxford: Oxford University Press, 1987), p. 43.

[30] Global Reporting Initiative, "New Reporters: A Year in Review," press release, December 20, 2006, at http://www.globalreporting.org.

[31] Its earliest use is ascribed to John Elkington in *Cannibals with Forks: The Triple Bottom Line of 21st Century Business* (Oxford: Oxford University Press, 1997), chap. 3.

[32] Fred Robins, "The Challenge of TBL: A Responsibility to Whom?" *Business and Society Review,* March 2006, pp. 1–2.

[33] Ibid., p. 2.

GRI Indicators

Economic Performance Indicators
- Net revenues.
- Employee wages and benefits.
- International, national, and local taxes and penalties paid.
- Voluntary donations to communities.
- Number of jobs supported in the supply chain and distribution chain.

Environmental Performance Indicators
- Materials used by weight and volume.
- Percentage of materials used that are recycled input materials.
- Energy saved due to conservation and efficiency improvements.
- Percentage and total volume of water recycled and reused.
- Habitats protected or restored.
- Total greenhouse gas emissions by weight.

Social Performance Indicators
- Total hours of employee training on policies and procedures concerning aspects of human rights.
- Total number of incidents of discrimination and actions taken.
- Percentage of employees trained in the organization's anticorruption policies and procedures.
- Total value of financial and in-kind contributions to political parties and politicians.
- Total number of substantiated complaints regarding breaches of customer privacy.

Source: Global Reporting Initiative, *Sustainability Reporting Guidelines,* ver. 3 (Amsterdam: GRI, 2000–2006), Indicator Protocols.

stakeholder engagement, and data on a series of performance measures for each of the triple bottom lines.

Examples of recommended indicators are listed in the accompanying box. To standardize reporting, the GRI has developed approximately 140 such indicators, allowing company performance to be measured across time and in comparison with other companies.

assurance
Verification by audit that information in a corporate sustainability report is correct.

Finally, the GRI strongly suggests providing *assurance,* that is, verification that information in the report is correct. The most effective assurance is provided by independent, external auditors who examine the contents and certify its validity. However, despite the development of nonfinancial assurance standards, only about one-third of companies provide external verification of their reports.[34]

Around the world, corporate social responsibility reporting is becoming a mainstream activity. A 2005 survey by KPMG International of the largest 250 global corporations found that a majority, 52 percent, issued such reports, an increase of 16 percent over three years.[35] The most likely to report were Japanese (80 percent) and United Kingdom (72 percent) companies. In the United States there is still resistance to sustainability reporting based on costs of preparation and fear of lawsuits over the information in them. Only 32 percent of U.S. firms in the survey published reports, but

[34] *KPMG International Survey of Corporate Responsibility Reporting 2005* (Amsterdam: KPMG International, 2005), p. 7. There are two main assurance standards, the International Standard for Assurance Engagements (ISAE) 3000 and the AA1000 Assurance Standard (AA1000AS).

[35] *KPMG International Survey of Corporate Responsibility Reporting 2005,* p. 4.

Four Costly Errors of CSR Implementation

In practice, most companies fall short of the model process for CSR action set forth in this section because they make one of these errors.

1. They give no coherent, systematic thought to CSR.
2. They allow CSR strategy to be reactive by not aligning it with major social impacts, core competencies, or business strategies.

3. They fragment responsibility for CSR initiatives by assigning them to separate areas without central oversight.
4. They do not issue credible reports of CSR actions for stakeholders and fail the test of transparency.

pressure to report is growing. In 2007 a record 37 shareholder proposals requesting that companies issue such reports were introduced at annual meetings.[36]

CORPORATE PHILANTHROPY

philanthropy
Concern for the welfare of society expressed by gifts of money or property to the needy or to activities for social progress.

Philanthropy is concern for the welfare of society expressed by gifts of money or property to the needy or to activities for social progress. Large philanthropic contributions by American companies are a relatively recent thing. Until about 50 years ago courts held that corporate funds belonged to shareholders; therefore, managers had no right to give money away, even for noble motives. This restrictive doctrine made sense in the distant past when businesses were small and charity came mainly from their owners. However, as businesses grew and professional managers took control from their rich founders, the public started to expect giving from corporations too.

The first major break from narrow legal restrictions on corporate giving was the Revenue Act of 1935, which allowed charitable contributions to be deducted from taxable earnings up to 5 percent of net profits before taxes (raised to 10 percent in 1981). Still, the legality of corporate giving remained doubtful, and managers were tight with charity dollars because they feared stockholder suits. Eventually, the *A. P. Smith* case in 1953 (see the box) cleared away outdated rigidities in the law, freeing companies to be more generous. Now, corporations give $13 to $14 billion a year for worthy causes ranging from disaster relief to support for local orchestras. Conservative opponents of corporate social responsibility still argue that such giving is a theft, like Robin Hood stealing from stockholders and giving to the poor. However, opponents who believe it is "charity with other people's money" no longer receive support from the law.[37]

[36] Antonie Boessenkool, "Activists Push More Firms on Social Responsibility," *The Wall Street Journal,* January 31, 2007, p. B4D.
[37] "A Survey of Corporate Social Responsibility," *The Economist,* January 22, 2005, survey, p. 8.

A. P. Smith Manufacturing Company v. Barlow et al., 13 N.J. 145 (1953)

A. P. Smith was a New Jersey corporation set up in 1896. It made valves and hydrants. In 1951 the firm gave $1,500 to Princeton University's annual fund-raising drive. This was not its first charitable contribution. It gave to a local community chest fund and had donated to other nearby colleges.

These contributions were made in a legal environment clouded by inconsistency. On the one hand was the law of corporate charters. These charters were issued by states, and corporations were not allowed to act beyond the powers expressly granted in them. The assumption in the charters was that the corporation's duty was to maximize profits for shareholders. A. P. Smith's incorporation papers, like those of most firms at the time, did not grant specific authority to make charity gifts. On the other hand was a statute. New Jersey passed a law in 1930 giving its corporations the right to make such donations if they did not exceed 1 percent of capital.

Ruth Barlow and four other angry owners of common and preferred stock thought the company had no right to give away any amount of money, because it was rightfully theirs as shareholders. They sued and in due course a trial was held. Luminaries from the business community appeared as witnesses for A. P. Smith to assert the merits of corporate charity. A Standard Oil of New Jersey executive argued that it was "good business" to show the kind of citizenship the public demanded. A U.S. Steel executive said that maintaining universities was essential to preserving capitalism. Nevertheless, the judge ruled against A. P. Smith, saying that the company had acted beyond its legitimate power.

A. P. Smith appealed. In 1953 the Supreme Court of New Jersey overturned the lower court, holding that rigid interpretation of charters to restrict charitable giving was no longer fitting since, unlike the old days when corporations were small and had limited assets relative to individuals, they now had enormous assets and it was reasonable for the public to expect generosity from them.

The *Smith* case settled the legal question of whether corporations could give to charity. After it, the legal cloud of acting *ultra vires* dissipated, clearing the way for greater corporate giving.

Patterns of Corporate Giving

Charitable giving is now a traditional dimension of corporate social responsibility. Even so, most firms do not give a significant amount compared with their potential. In 2005, for example, corporations gave $13.8 billion, a large sum, but only 0.08 percent of worldwide sales and 1 percent of pretax earnings.[38] Since the 1950s, overall corporate contributions have been remarkably consistent, hovering around 1 percent of pretax earnings.[39] This is far less than the 10 percent that is tax deductible. The largest firms are more generous than smaller ones. A survey of 211 of the largest corporations and their foundations revealed that they gave 71 percent of all 2005 corporate giving and most of that came from a few of the largest companies, which gave more than 5 percent of pretax income.[40]

[38] Sophia A. Muirhead, *The 2006 Corporate Contributions Report* (New York: The Conference Board, 2006), p. 5.

[39] Paul Ostergard, "Should Corporations Be Praised for Their Philanthropic Efforts? Yes: A Golden Age," *Across the Board,* May–June 2001, p. 46.

[40] Muirhead, *The 2006 Corporate Contributions Report,* pp. 5 and 10.

FIGURE 6.7
Ten-Year Trend in Private Philanthropy: 1995–2005

Source: U.S. Census Bureau, *Statistical Abstract of the United States: 2006* (126th edition) Washington, DC, 2006, table 567 and Giving USA Foundation, "Charitable Giving Rises 6 Percent to More Than $260 Billion in 2005," News Release. June 19, 2006.

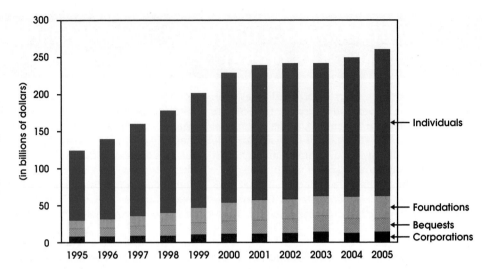

Corporate philanthropy is a small part of overall private philanthropy in the United States. In 2005 it was only 5.3 percent. Figure 6.7 displays the 10-year trend in giving and segments sources into their relative proportions. During this time overall giving rose from $124 billion to $260 billion. As the segmented bars reveal, individuals gave by far the largest proportion, followed by foundations, charitable bequests, and, finally, corporations (including corporate foundations). In the years shown, corporate giving rose from $7.3 billion to $13.8 billion, again showing consistency by staying between 5 and 6 percent of total giving.

Corporations that contribute do so in many ways, including cash, products, services, volunteered employee time, and use of facilities. Cash giving is only about 45 percent of all giving. Among the largest corporations, most giving, about 44 percent, goes to United Way campaigns and grants to health and human service agencies such as the American Red Cross and the American Cancer Society. Another 12 percent flows to education, and about 8 percent goes to civic and community recipients such as YMCA/YWCAs, housing programs, and urban development groups. The rest is splintered among other categories with the smallest sliver, less than 1 percent, going to environmental causes.[41]

altruism
The desire to give to, help, or improve others and society with no expectation of self-gain in return.

The basic motives for corporate giving are response to pressure, belief that it will bring monetary profit, desire for reputational gain, and *altruism* or selfless concern for the welfare of others. Much giving stems from a mixture of these. Although charitable actions are tax deductible, this is not a compelling motive, since many alternative uses of funds, for example advertising, are also tax deductible. Recent studies report that philanthropy is associated with better corporate reputations,[42] but not with financial performance.[43] Nevertheless, 66 percent of managers who

[41] Ibid., p. 9.

[42] Stephen Brammer and Andrew Millington, "Corporate Reputation and Philanthropy: An Empirical Analysis," *Journal of Business Ethics* 61 (2005).

[43] Bruce Seifert, Sara A. Morris, Barbara R. Bartkus, "Having, Giving, and Getting: Slack Resources, Corporate Philanthropy, and Firm Financial Performance," *Business & Society,* June 2004.

The Secretive George Feeney

George F. Feeney, 76, is one of the greatest living philanthropists. In a style reminiscent of the old television program "The Millionaire," he has given away hundreds of millions of dollars using cashier's checks that do not reveal his name.

Feeney is an Irish-American who was raised in a working-class New Jersey neighborhood. With a partner he founded the Duty Free Shoppers stores found in airports around the world. In 1984 he experienced a revelation. "I simply decided I had enough money," he told a reporter. Without even informing his business partner, he set up a foundation in Bermuda so it would not be subject to U.S. laws requiring disclosure of contributions. Then he irrevocably transferred his ownership interest in Duty Free Shoppers to the foundation. At the time, this was worth about $500 million; over the years, the foundation has had assets as high as $4.8 billion, making it one of the world's largest.

Feeney could now be worth more than $5 billion, but his personal assets are only about $5 million. According to a friend, he does not own a house or a car. He wears a $15 watch and carries his papers in a plastic bag instead of a briefcase. He prefers casual clothes, doubts the need for more than one pair of shoes, and calls himself a "shabby dresser."

Most of the foundation's gifts go to hospitals, universities, and mainstream charities around the world.

His passion for secrecy stems from a desire to live life without constant importuning from supplicants and from his belief in the teachings of Maimonides, a twelfth-century philosopher who taught that the highest form of giving was anonymous and selfless. Feeney's staff painstakingly seeks out and probes individuals, groups, and causes to find worthy beneficiaries. Unsolicited requests for money are always disqualified. Feeney sometimes attends staff meetings with potential recipients, who are not told the identity of the quiet observer.

Most foundations give away only limited amounts each year, allowing them to maintain large endowments over time. In 2002, when Feeney was 70 years old, he instructed his foundation to exhaust its remaining $4 billion over the next 15 years. He believed that this would prevent it from becoming focused on its own perpetuation rather than on solving social problems.

direct corporate contributions reported in a survey that they were trying to align giving with business objectives.[44] In the next section, we discuss this trend.

Strategic Philanthropy

With historical roots in religious teachings, the act of philanthropy presumes a selfless motive of giving out of moral duty to benefit the needy or to advance society. Traditionally, corporate philanthropy conformed to such ideals of altruism and magnanimity. Companies and their foundations gave to help the destitute while funding social goods such as education and the arts. Some self-benefit resided in these donations since the elevating deed often raised corporate reputations, created goodwill, or improved the economy by strengthening society.

As corporations gained experience with philanthropy, some concluded that the traditional approach of diffuse giving to myriad worthy causes was noble but flawed. Over time, the number of causes grew. As charity recipients proliferated,

[44] Sophia A. Muirhead, *Philanthropy and Business: The Changing Agenda* (New York: The Conference Board, 2006), p. 6.

the shrinking sums given to each had less and less impact. Executives and their spouses diverted funds into pet artistic and cultural projects unimportant to the firm's main stakeholders. Such a passive approach to philanthropy, often called *checkbook philanthropy,* lacked any underlying logic. Most large corporations continue to engage in heavy checkbook philanthropy. However, more and more convert their philosophy of giving from one of pure, if scattered and unplanned, generosity to one that aligns giving with commercial objectives. This is known as *strategic philanthropy,* or the alignment of a corporation's charitable strategy with its business strategy.

checkbook philanthropy
A traditional, passive form of corporate philanthropy characterized by donations to multiple worthy causes without any relationship to business strategy.

General Mills was a pioneer. The company set up a foundation in 1954 after the green light of the *A. P. Smith* decision. For many years it emphasized giving to prestigious cultural and arts programs in its Minneapolis headquarters area. In the late 1990s, however, it began to direct its support to projects helping families, children, and youth in 20 cities where it had facilities. This better matched charity giving with the concerns of average grocery shoppers who buy Cheerios and Betty Crocker cake mixes. There are many other examples.

strategic philanthropy
A form of corporate philanthropy in which charitable activities reinforce strategic business goals.

- Mattel donated $25 million to put its name on the children's hospital at UCLA, now called Mattel Children's Hospital. The company has no role in running the hospital, although it gives toys to patients. Adding the company name to the hospital increases brand recognition and contributes to a compassionate corporate image among toy buyers. These benefits reinforce the commercial goals of a toy company while also helping sick children.[45]

- Consumer research done by Washington Mutual shows that a key concern of its customers is the well-being of local schools. So it focuses multiple philanthropic actions on improving K–12 education in communities where it has branches. It gives money to schools. Local employees volunteer to assist teachers and refurbish buildings. It also connects initiatives to product offerings. Employees present financial literacy courses at schools. Children are encouraged to learn the virtue of saving by opening savings accounts.[46]

Not everyone approves of strategic philanthropy. The mixed motive of the corporation departs from the pure altruism depicted in religious parables about charity. One critic calls it "self-serving and self-interested," just "business by other means."[47] Defenders retort that looking behind good deeds to disparage the benefactor's motive is equally unworthy. In fact, there is a blend of motives. Intel spends $100 million a year giving to education. It has trained 3.5 million teachers around the world to use computers in schoolrooms. When asked if this program is "really altruism, or are you trying to sell more chips?" Intel Chairman Craig Barrett replied, "It is a mixture" that helps people but also "has to be good for business."[48]

---

[45] Julie Edelson Halpert, "Dr. Pepper Hospital? Perhaps, for a Price," *New York Times,* February 18, 2001, sec. 3, p. 1.

[46] Philip Kotler and Nancy Lee, *Corporate Social Responsibility* (New York: Wiley, 2005), pp. 24–33.

[47] Benjamin R. Barber, "Should Corporations Be Praised for Their Philanthropic Efforts? No: Always an Angle," *Across the Board,* May–June 2001, p. 49.

[48] "Intel Chairman Craig Barrett," *The American,* November/December 2006, p. 83.

Cause-Related Marketing

Cause-related marketing is a variant of strategic philanthropy in which charitable contributions are based on purchases of a product. It is used to link a brand to a social cause so that both benefit. Marketers use branding to differentiate products, especially mass-produced products that consumers might see as interchangeable commodities if they lacked brand attributes. Companies spend heavily to endow brands with these attributes so they can charge a price premium. Traditional branding creates attributes in two dimensions to influence buying decisions. One is an impression of the product's positive qualities directed to the logical mind. The other is the creation of an emotional association with the product that allows consumers to fulfill emotional needs by using it.

Consumer expectations of corporate social responsibility are expanding. Marketers have learned that if their brand is connected to a charitable cause a third attribute is created, one that appeals to the consumer's conscience. In cause-related marketing the corporation calculates that it will add this benevolent dimension to its brand while also doing a philanthropic good deed.

Cause-related marketing is a powerful sales tool. In a recent survey, 85 percent of consumers said that if price and quality were comparable, they would switch to a brand associated with a cause.[49] For example, Coca-Cola ran a six-week campaign in which it gave 15 cents to Mothers Against Drunk Driving for each carton of Coke sold at Wal-Mart stores. Its sales rose 490 percent, presumably at the expense of rival soft drinks.[50] Other examples follow.

- In the early 1990s American Express encountered restaurant owners who felt its card fees were too high. Enough restaurants refused the cards when they were tendered that, rather than face rejection, many cardholders chose to use a competing card instead. To counteract this, the company started a cause-related marketing campaign called "Charge Against Hunger" in which it donated $0.3 per transaction to nonprofit antihunger groups during the holiday months of November and December each year. The campaign created a clear link between using the card to pay for restaurant meals and fighting hunger. It raised $21 million in four years for donations to 600 antihunger groups. It also increased charge volume by 12 percent and raised the opinion of restaurant owners about the card.[51]

- Avon Products sells more beauty products than any other company. Most of its revenues come from direct sales through 5 million part-time, predominantly female sales representatives in 114 countries. In the early 1990s Avon's brand image was deteriorating because its direct-selling strategy carried an old-fashioned, down-market connotation. The company decided to use cause-related marketing to burnish its name. The vast majority of Avon's sales are to women. Research showed that the cause of fighting breast cancer struck a

---

[49]Cheryl V. Jackson, "In the Pink," *Chicago Sun-Times,* July 10, 2006, p. 57, referring to a Cone Corp. Citizen Survey.

[50]Amy Ellis Nutt, "Pink Isn't Always Green for Charities," *Times-Picayune,* October 22, 2006, p. 1.

[51] Shirley Sagawa and Eli Segal, *Common Interest, Common Good* (Boston: Harvard Business School Press, 2000), p. 15.

responsive chord in them, so Avon developed a line of affordable "pink ribbon" products and donated a specified amount from the purchase price to breast cancer research and treatment. Avon's brand has benefited so much that the cause-related "crusade" continues uninterrupted. Since 1992 Avon has collected more than $450 million for breast cancer research, detection, and treatment.[52]

Cause-related marketing raises big sums for worthy causes but, like other forms of strategic philanthropy, its mixture of altruism and self-interest attracts criticism. Skeptics note that companies pick causes based on research into what consumers care about, instead of research to find the most acute needs. Heart disease is the leading killer of women and the leading fatal cancer in women is lung cancer. However, because the fight against breast cancer resonates best with high-spending female consumers between the ages of 30 and 55, more than 300 companies copied Avon's marketing innovation. Other causes languish from this convergence.

There is plenty of cynicism about corporate motives. In current breast cancer campaigns Yoplait donates 10 cents per yogurt container, Everlast gives $1.25 from the sale of each $25 pair of boxing gloves, and Campbells's soup donates 3.5 cents per can after purchases of pink-labeled tomato and chicken soup. Yoplait makes consumers put their container lids in an envelope and return them by mail before it makes a contribution, imposing the cost of a stamp that exceeds the donation amount on people who have fewer than five lids. According to one breast cancer activist, "[w]omen's bodies and women's health are being used for corporate profit."[53] Corporations, however, do not see commercial interest as an ethically inferior motive and believe that concrete benefits to both companies and causes far outweigh the importance of abstract arguments about base motives.

New Forms of Philanthropy

Philanthropy can be inefficient compared with market-driven business activity. Large foundation offices and staffs create administrative expenses. Charities that get money may be wasteful or ineffective in their work. Monitoring them to measure performance is expensive. An emerging approach, which might be called the new philanthropy, seeks to increase productivity from charitable giving by bringing businesslike methods to the task. This approach has many names and dimensions. In "high-engagement philanthropy" the donor may set goals for the recipient charity and become involved in achieving them. In "venture philanthropy" givers fund the incubation of new charitable organizations with unique approaches to social problems.

Perhaps the most imaginative and exciting efforts of the new philanthropy are those that use the profit motive, efforts that have been called "philanthrocapitalism."[54] Here are some examples, all different, but having in common the use of market incentives.

[52] "Avon Breast Cancer Crusade," at www.avoncompany.com/women/avoncrusade/index.html, accessed March 6, 2007.

[53] Carly Weeks, "Ribbon Campaign Has Dark Twist," *The Gazette,* October 18, 2006, p. A12.

[54] "The Business of Giving: A Survey of Wealth and Philanthropy," *The Economist,* February 24, 2006, p. 8.

- Residents of urban slums in Mexico City struggle to add cement floors and rooms to their homes, often using inferior materials and taking years to complete projects. Cemex, a transnational cement corporation, now enters partnerships with nonprofit community groups that create a market for its cement. Unlike the big corporation, these nonprofits are trusted by poor homeowners, who follow instructions to pool money in savings clubs called *tandas*. When the sums are adequate, Cemex delivers small batches of concrete. So far, thousands of families have built additions this way. Cemex makes a small profit that it shares with the nonprofit groups to cover their operating expenses. In sum, rather than just give money away on housing, Cemex built a new market among previously ignored buyers, created an efficient form of action, and raised its brand image in Mexico.

- Red is a company cofounded by the celebrity musician Bono to fight the African AIDS epidemic. It licenses the brand name Product Red to business partners that use it on their own products, then pay back part of the profit to Red. Red keeps enough to pay for overhead costs and marketing the Red concept, then gives the rest to a foundation that buys AIDS drugs for Africans. American Express started a Red credit card and returns 1 percent of card purchases. The Gap returns 50 percent of profits from a line of Red clothing. The Red network is not a charity. It is a business model predicated on the theory that "the rich can consume their way to a better world for the poor."[55] So far, it has transferred more than $10 million from the pockets of affluent consumers to Africa.

- Before the initial public offering of Google, its founders, Larry Page and Sergey Brin, told investors that 1 percent of the equity and 1 percent of annual profits would be set aside for philanthropy. This work is done within an entity named google.org, which, with funding of about $1 billion, is a laboratory for social entrepreneurship. It contains a traditional, tax-exempt foundation that gives to charities, but it is small, holding only $90 million. The rest of the $1 billion is a taxable, for-profit corporation that invests in new businesses trying to make a profit by addressing poverty, disease, and global warming. It is now funding research on a car engine that will get 100 miles per gallon. Return on this investment, and others like it, goes back into google. org, where it can be reinvested in new initiatives. The underlying philosophy is that market discipline will focus Google's philanthropy on the most efficient efforts.

Over the last several decades the location of philanthropic wealth has shifted. Until the 1980s most of it was in New York foundations such as those started by Rockefeller, Ford, and Carnegie. In their day, these foundations were innovative in their own way, seeking to do great deeds by going to the root of social problems instead of scattering money to needy individuals as those before them had done. With the rise of new technology industries came fantastic new fortunes such as those of Gates, Page, Brin, and others. With 40 percent more institutional philanthropy

---

[55] Alan Beattie, "Spend, Spend, Spend," *Financial Times,* January 27, 2007, p. 18.

funding than New York, the center of gravity for American philanthropy is now on the West Coast, primarily in California and Washington.[56] And this shift has been accompanied by new approaches to philanthropy seeking to solve global problems by correcting market failures and applying the tools of capitalism. Time will tell what mark this makes on timeless, deep problems.

CONCLUDING OBSERVATIONS

Good intentions are worth little if not reflected in actions. If a corporation hopes to be socially responsible, it must follow up with the hard work of building its aspirations into its operations. To implement CSR strategies it must use the same managerial tools and levers used to implement business strategies. No CSR initiative of any significance will succeed without their application.

Corporate philanthropy is a basic, time-honored way to implement social responsibility. As corporations have shifted from more altruistic giving to a new style that aligns giving with business strategy, critics have attacked them for being too self-interested. However, strategic philanthropy is a promising development because it injects thinking about social responsibility into the strategic mainstream, a change for which apostles of CSR have been praying.

[56] Douglas McGray, "Network Philanthropy," *Los Angeles Times,* January 21, 2007, p. 14.

Marc Kasky versus Nike Inc.

Marc Kasky of San Francisco sees his world as a community and has a long history of caring about the others in it. He got his first lessons in business ethics from his father, who ran a car repair business.

> The customer would bring his car in and say there's something horribly wrong in my car: I think I need a new transmission. . . . My father would call them back an hour later and say, "Come get your car, there was a loose screw here and there; I fixed it. What does it cost? Nothing." I saw how that affected our family. It impressed me a great deal.[1]

After graduating from Yale University in 1969, he volunteered to work in poor Cleveland neighborhoods. Moving to San Francisco, he headed a nonprofit center for foundations that funded schools. He involved himself in civic and environmental causes. He also became an avid jogger and ran marathons.

[1] Quoted in Jim Edwards, "Taking It to the Big Guys," *Brandweek,* August 12, 2002, p. 1.

Over the years Kasky wore many pairs of Nike shoes and considered them a "good product."[2] But he stopped buying them in the mid-1990s after reading stories about working conditions in overseas factories where they were made. By then Nike, Inc., had become the main focus of the antisweatshop cause, accused of exploiting low-wage workers who made its shoes and clothing. The more Kasky read about Nike, the more convinced he was that it was not only victimizing workers, but lying about it too. Kasky sought the help of an old friend, Alan Caplan, an attorney who had

[2] Steve Rubenstein, "S. F. Man Changes from Customer to Nike Adversary," *San Francisco Chronicle,* May 3, 2002, p. A6. Kasky stated his ownership of Nike shoes in the interview for this article. However, his lawyer told the Supreme Court that he had "never bought any Nikes." *Nike v. Kasky,* No. 02-575, Oral Argument, April 23, 2003 (Washington, DC: Alderson Reporting Company, 2003), p. 30, lines 21 and 22. We give priority to Kasky's story, but this is a remarkable contradiction.

Marc Kasky. Source: © AP Photo/Denis Poroy.

achieved fame in progressive circles by bringing the suit that forced R. J. Reynolds to stop using Joe Camel in its ads.

With Caplan's help, Kasky sued Nike in April 1998 for false advertising, alleging it had made untrue statements about its labor practices. This was not Kasky's first lawsuit. Previously, he had sued Perrier over its claim to be "spring water" and Pillsbury Co. for labeling Mexican vegetables with the words "San Francisco style." Both suits were settled.[3] Nike sought dismissal of Kasky's suit, arguing that the statements he questioned were part of a public debate about sweatshops and protected by the First Amendment.

NIKE

Nike, Inc., is the world's largest producer of athletic shoes and sports apparel. It grew out of a handshake in 1962 between Bill Bowerman, the track coach at the University of Oregon, and Phil Knight, a runner he had coached in the 1950s. Knight had just received an MBA from Stanford University. In a term paper there he had written about competing against established

[3] Roger Parloff, "Can We Talk?" *Fortune,* September 2, 2002, p. 108.

athletic shoe companies by importing shoes made in low-wage Asian factories. Now he was ready to try it. He and Bowerman each put up $550 and Knight flew to Japan, arranging to import 300 pairs of Onitsuka Tiger shoes. After seven years, Knight and Bowerman decided to stop selling the Japanese company's brand and create their own. So they designed a shoe and subcontracted its production to a factory in Japan. By now Bowerman and Knight had incorporated and an employee suggested naming the company Nike, for the Greek goddess of victory. Knight paid a design student at Portland State University $35 to create a logo. She drew a "swoosh," which the company adopted. The elements of future market conquest were now in place and the company grew rapidly.

Nike succeeded by following two basic strategies. Its product strategy is to design innovative, fashionable footwear and apparel for markets in developed nations, then have the items manufactured by contractors in low-wage economies. This way Nike avoids the cost of building and running its own factories.

At first, most of its shoe production was done in Japanese factories (some shoes were made in the United States until 1980), but as wages rose in Japan it moved its contracts to plants in South Korea and Taiwan. When wages rose in these countries, Nike again shifted its production, this time to China, Indonesia, and Thailand, and later to Vietnam. Today almost 90 percent of its shoes are made in these four countries.

Its marketing strategy is to create carefully calculated brand images. Advertising campaigns associate the Nike brand name with a range of ideas. Prominent among these is the idea of sport. Endorsements by professional athletes and college teams endow the swoosh with a high-performance image. Campaigns with the "just do it" slogan add connotations of competition, courage, strength, winning, and high performance. Other advertising associates the brand with urban culture to make it "street cool." In this way Nike transforms shoes and T-shirts that would otherwise be low-cost commodities into high-priced, high fashion items that generate positive emotions when they are worn.

THE SWEATSHOP LABOR ISSUE

Nike grew rapidly. By 1980 when the company went public it had seized half the world's athletic shoe market. But the outsourcing and advertising strategies that propelled it to the top put it on a collision course with a force in its social environment. This force, the sweatshop issue, would gain power and cause considerable damage.

In 1988 an Indonesian union newspaper published a study of bad working conditions in a plant making Nike footwear.[4] Soon other critical articles appeared in the Indonesian press. The AFL-CIO decided to investigate how workers were being treated in plants that manufactured for American firms and sent an investigator named Jeffrey Ballinger to Indonesia. Ballinger focused on Nike contractors, gathering detailed information.

In 1992 he published a clever indictment of Nike in *Harper's Magazine* by exhibiting the monthly pay stub of an Indonesian woman named Sadisah who made Nike running shoes. Sadisah worked on an assembly line 10-and-a-half hours a day, six days a week, making $1.03 per day or about $0.14 an hour, less than the Indonesian minimum wage. She was paid only $0.02 an hour for 63 hours of overtime during the pay period. Her home was all she could afford, a rented shanty lacking electricity and plumbing. The Nikes that she made sold for $80 in the United States, yet the cost of her labor per shoe was only $0.12 cents. If anyone missed the point, Ballinger noted that the year before Nike had made a profit of $287 million and signed Michael Jordan to a $20 million advertising contract, a sum that Sadisah would have had to work 44,492 years to earn.[5]

Ballinger's article appeared with a flurry of other negative stories, but the issue did not immediately heat up. Nevertheless, Nike elected to show more responsibility for the welfare of foreign workers. In 1992 it adopted a "Code of Conduct" requiring its contractors to certify compliance with local minimum wage, child labor, health, safety, workers' compensation, forced labor, environmental, and discrimination laws. In 1994, it hired the accounting firm Ernst & Young to audit code compliance by making spot checks at factories.

These developments suggest that at some point CEO Philip Knight came to believe that even if Nike did not directly employ foreign workers it benefitted from their labor and so had an ethical duty toward their welfare. But Nike would not escape

damage from the issue. Negative stories about its contract factories grew more numerous.

Finally, the issue exploded after April 1996 congressional testimony by the leader of a human rights group, who said that clothing for Wal-Mart's "Kathie Lee" apparel line was made at a Honduran factory where children worked 14 hours a day. Daytime television viewers saw talk show host Kathie Lee Gifford reduced to tears as she responded. "You can say I'm ugly, you can say I'm not talented, but when you say that I don't care about children.... How dare you?"[6] Now the issue had emotional content for American consumers.

Soon after the Gifford spectacle antisweatshop activists decided to focus on Nike and attacks heated up. Nike was an industry leader. If it could be reformed, other clothing companies and retailers would fall into line. It was also vulnerable to a brand name attack. Progressive advocacy groups, including Global Exchange, the National Labor Committee, Press for Change, SweatshopWatch, and the Interfaith Center for Corporate Responsibility, joined forces to inform the public of what they saw as a gap between the inspiring images in Nike's advertising and the grim reality of its labor practices. This alarmed Nike because bad publicity could rub away the image magic that made its brand cool.

NIKE AT WAR WITH ITS CRITICS

The war over Nike's image would be fought in the media. An early skirmish came when Bob Herbert at the *New York Times* wrote the first of what became a year-long series of columns berating Nike. After describing a climate of atrocities in Indonesia, including government-condoned killings and torture, he accused Nike of using "the magnificent image of Michael Jordan soaring, twisting, driving, flying" to divert attention from its exploitation of Indonesian workers. "Nike executives know exactly what is going on in Indonesia. They are not bothered by the cries of the oppressed. It suits them. Each cry is a signal that their investment is paying off."[7]

Nike CEO Philip Knight quickly responded with a letter to the editor, citing ways that Nike worked with

---

[4] Cited in Jeffrey Hollender and Stephen Fenichell, What *Matters Most* (New York: Basic Books, 2004), p. 190.

[5] Jeffrey Ballinger, "The New Free-Trade Heel," *Harper's*, August 1992, pp. 46–47.

[6] Rob Howe et al., "Labor Pains," *People Magazine*, June 10, 1996, p. 58.

[7] Bob Herbert, "Nike's Bad Neighborhood," *New York Times*, June 14, 1996, p. A29.

EXHIBIT 1
Rise of Negative News Stories about Nike's Labor Practices, 1988–1999

Source: From S. Prakash Sethi, *Setting Global Standards,* 2003. Table 9.2. Reprinted with permission of John Wiley & Sons, Inc.

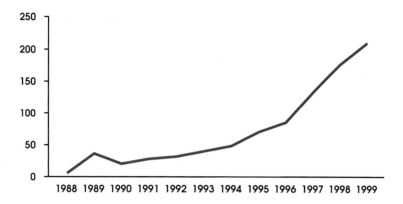

contractors to benefit workers, and noting that Nike paid "double the minimum wage" and "had an oversight system that works." He accused Herbert of trying to "sacrifice enlightenment for hype."[8] Herbert's response was a second column rebuking Nike for running theme ads about women's empowerment while most of its shoes were produced "by grossly underpaid women stuck in utterly powerless and often abusive circumstances."[9]

Over the next two years, negative stories about Nike appeared with increasing frequency. An inspection report by the human rights group Vietnam Labor Watch reported that young women working in a Nike factory were paid subminimum wages. A supervisor had forced 56 women to run twice around the 1.2-mile factory boundary under a hot sun for failing to wear regulation shoes. Twelve of them fainted and required hospitalization.[10] Gary Trudeau drew a series of *Doonesbury* cartoons based on these allegations.

Activists urged people to return Nike sneakers during "shoe-ins" at Niketown outlets. A disgruntled Ernst & Young employee leaked a confidential spot inspection report on a Vietnamese shoe factory. It showed violations of Vietnamese working hours law and found that 77 percent of the employees suffered respiratory problems from breathing toxic vapors at levels that violated both Vietnamese

and U.S. standards.[11] Another group, the Hong Kong Christian Industrial Committee, released a study of Nike factories in China documenting long work days, forced overtime, pay below minimum wages, and unsafe levels of airborne dust and toxic chemicals.[12] *The Oregonian*, the paper in Portland where Nike is headquartered, called Nike "an international human rights incident."[13]

Now Nike found itself at the center of a worldwide debate over sweatshops. The company countered its critics by expanding efforts to stop workplace abuses and by mounting a public relations campaign. At great expense it became the only shoe company in the world to eliminate the use of polyvinyl chloride in shoe construction, ending worker exposure to dangerous chlorine compounds. It revised its conduct code, expanding protections for workers. It set up a compliance department of more than 50 employees. Its staff members were assigned to specific Asian plants or to a region, where they trained local managers and did audits assessing code compliance.[14] Full compliance was elusive.

Working with Kathie Lee Gifford, other companies, and human rights groups, Nike helped to develop the Fair Labor Association code of conduct (see Chapter 11) and agreed to abide by its conditions. It hired Andrew Young, a former U.S. Ambassador to

[8] "Nike Pays Good Wages to Foreign Workers," *New York Times,* June 21, 1996, p. A26.

[9] "From Sweatshops to Aerobics," *New York Times,* June 24, 1996, p. A15.

[10] Vietnam Labor Watch, "Nike Labor Practices in Vietnam," March 20, 1997, available at www.saigon.com/ ~nike/reports/report1.html#summary; and Ellen Neuborne, "Nike to Take a Hit in Labor Report," *USA Today,* March 27, 1997, p. 1A.

[11] Steven Greenhouse, "Nike Shoe Plant in Vietnam Is Called Unsafe for Workers," *New York Times,* November 8, 1997, p. A1.

[12] *Kasky v. Nike,* 93 Cal. Rptr. 2d 856.

[13] Jeff Manning, "Nike's Global Machine Goes on Trial," *The Oregonian,* November 9, 1997, p. A1.

[14] S. Prakash Sethi, *Setting Global Standards* (New York: John Wiley & Sons, 2003), p. 167.

EXHIBIT 2
The Nike Code of Conduct

Source: www.Nike.com.

The Code of Conduct has been revised and articulated since its introduction in 1992. Listed below are its seven "core standards." Another document, the Code Leadership Standards, elaborates 51 specific labor, safety, health, and environmental standards. The Code is translated into local languages and today is posted in more than 900 contract factories making Nike products.

1. **Forced Labor.** The contractor does not use forced labor in any form—prison, indentured, bonded, or otherwise.

2. **Child Labor.** The contractor does not employ any person below the age of 18 to produce footwear. The contractor does not employ any person below the age of 16 to produce apparel, accessories or equipment. If at the time Nike production begins, the contractor employs people of the legal working age who are at least 15, that employment may continue, but the contractor will not hire any person going forward who is younger than the Nike or legal age limit, whichever is higher. To further ensure these age standards are complied with, the contractor does not use any form of homework for Nike production.

3. **Compensation.** The contractor provides each employee at least the minimum wage, or the prevailing industry wage, whichever is higher; provides each employee a clear, written accounting for every pay period; and does not deduct from employee pay for disciplinary infractions.

4. **Benefits.** The contractor provides each employee all legally mandated benefits.

5. **Hours of Work/Overtime.** The contractor complies with legally mandated work hours; uses overtime only when each employee is fully compensated according to local law; informs each employee at the time of hiring if mandatory overtime is a condition of employment; and on a regularly scheduled basis provides one day off in seven, and requires no more than 60 hours of work per week on a regularly scheduled basis, or complies with local limits if they are lower.

6. **Environment, Safety and Health (ES&H).** From suppliers to factories to distributors and to retailers, Nike considers every member of our supply chain as partners in our business. As such, we've worked with our Asian partners to achieve specific environmental, health and safety goals, beginning with a program called MESH (Management of Environment, Safety and Health).

7. **Documentation and Inspection.** The contractor maintains on file all documentation needed to demonstrate compliance with this Code of Conduct and required laws; agrees to make these documents available for Nike or its designated monitor; and agrees to submit to inspections with or without prior notice.

the United Nations, to visit Asian plants and write an inspection report. Young toured 12 factories over 15 days and found that conditions "certainly did not appear to be what most Americans would call sweatshops."[15] Nike purchased full-page editorial advertisements in newspapers to broadcast his generally favorable findings, saying that the report showed it was "operating morally" and promising to act on his recommendations for improvement.

[15] Dana Canedy, "Nike's Asian Factories Pass Young's Muster," *New York Times,* June 25, 1997, p. D2.

Finally, Nike ran a public relations counteroffensive. Unlike some rival firms that lay low, it chose to confront critics. It hired an experienced strategist to manage the campaign. Nike responded to every charge, no matter how small or what the source. Allegations were countered with press releases, letters to the editor, and letters to presidents and athletic directors of universities using Nike products. In these communications Nike sought to portray itself as a responsible employer creating opportunity for thousands of workers in emerging economies. CEO Knight expressed the Nike philosophy, saying, "This

At work in a Vietnam plant making Nike footwear.
Source: © Steve Rayner/CORBIS.

is going to be a long fight, but I'm confident the truth will win in the end."[16]

THE KASKY LAWSUIT

While Knight thought he was fighting for truth, Marc Kasky perceived something less noble— a fraud conducted to sell shoes and T-shirts. He believed that Nike knowingly deceived consumers, who relied on the company's statements for reassurance that their purchases did not sustain sweatshops. Under an unusual state law, any California citizen can sue a corporation on behalf of the public for an unlawful business practice. Kasky took advantage of this provision, alleging that Nike had engaged in negligent misrepresentation, fraud and deceit, and misleading advertising in violation of the state's commercial code. The code prohibits "any unlawful, unfair, deceptive, untrue or misleading advertising."[17]

In his complaint, Kasky accused Nike of using a "promotional scheme," including its code of conduct, to create a "carefully cultured image" that was "intended...to entice consumers who do not want to purchase products made in sweatshop . . . conditions."[18] He set forth six classes of misleading claims.

- In its Code of Conduct and in a "Nike Production Primer" pamphlet given to the media, Nike stated that its contracts prevent corporal punishment and sexual harassment at factories making Nike products. But the Vietnam Labor Watch report told of workers forced to kneel in the hot sun and described frequent complaints by female employees against their supervisors.

- In a range of promotional materials Nike asserted that its products were manufactured in compliance with laws and regulations on wages and overtime. But evidence from a report by the Hong Kong Christian Industrial Committee and the leaked Ernst & Young audit showed that plants in China and Vietnam violated such laws.

[16] Quoted in Tony Emerson, "Swoosh Wars," *Newsweek*, March 12, 2001, p. 35.

[17] The law is California's Unfair Competition Law, which is codified as §17200 (source of the quotation) and §17500 of the California Business & Professions Code. Kasky also alleged violations of California Civil Code §1572 (which defines fraud) and §1709 and §1710 (which define deceit).

[18] First Amended Complaint of Milberg, Weiss et al., *Kasky v. Nike,* Superior Court, San Francisco County, No. 994446, July 2, 1998, pp. 5, 6, and 10.

- At the Nike Annual Shareholder Meeting in 1997 CEO Knight said that the air in Nike's newest Vietnam shoe factory was less polluted than the air in Los Angeles. But the Ernst & Young report documented exposures to excessive levels of hazardous air pollutants.

- In his letter to the editor of the *New York Times,* Knight stated that Nike paid, on average, double the minimum wage to workers worldwide. But this is contradicted by data from pay stubs in the Vietnam Labor Watch report. He also said that Nike gave workers free meals, but an article in the *Youth Newspaper* of Ho Chi Minh City reported that workers paid for lunches.

- In its paid editorial ads discussing Andrew Young's report on its factories, Nike made the claim that it was "doing a good job" and "operating morally." But the report was deficient because it failed to address central issues such as minimum wage violations.

- In a press release Nike made the claim that it guaranteed a "living wage for all workers." But the director of its own Labor Practices Department had written a letter defining a "living wage" as income sufficient to support a family of four, then stating that the company did not ask contractors to raise wages that high.[19]

California unfair competition law did not require Kasky to own a pair of Nike sneakers or to claim personal damages. He did not need to show that anyone else had relied on Nike's claims or been injured by them. He did not even have to prove that Nike had lied on purpose. Under the law it would be enough if a court judged the statements false.

Kasky sought no monetary gain for himself. Instead, he asked for an injunction against further deception, a court-approved public information campaign forcing the company to correct misrepresentations, disgorgement of Nike profits from California sales, and payment of his legal expenses.

Instead, Superior Court Judge David A. Garcia threw the case out. There was no trial to decide whether any of the statements made by Nike were misleading. The judge simply accepted Nike's claim that the statements in question were part of an ongoing public debate and, therefore, entitled to broad protection.

COMMERCIAL SPEECH OR PROTECTED EXPRESSION?

Freedom of speech is a central value in American culture. It derives from a long philosophical tradition, exemplified in John Stuart Mill's classic essay *On Liberty.* Mill believed that freedom of opinion and expression were necessary to maintain a free society, the kind of society that could protect liberty and promote happiness. He wrote that a natural tendency existed to silence discomfiting, doubtful, or unorthodox views. But this is wrong, because no person is in possession of unerring truth.

Restricting debate deprives society of the opportunity to find new ideas that are more valid than prevailing ones. Even bizarre or incorrect comments should be valued. The former may contain partial truth and the latter make the truth more compelling because of its contrast to the falsehood. Censorship of any kind is wrong because no person, society, or generation is infallible. It is better to leave open many avenues for expression of views so that error and pretention can be opposed. Truth, said Mill, needs to be "fully, frequently, and fearlessly discussed."[20]

The First Amendment was intended to protect public debate that is critical to the functioning of democracy. It prohibits government from "abridging the freedom of speech, or of the press."[21] A complicating factor is the efforts of courts over many years to distinguish between commercial speech and other speech. Commercial speech, or advertising, receives less protection from restriction by government than speech in the broad marketplace of ideas. Ordinary speech, including political, scientific, and artistic expression, is entitled to strong protection. Laws restricting expression of opinion are regarded as invalid on their face and justified only in extreme circumstances. Commercial speech, however, is often restricted by federal and state laws to prevent consumer deception and fraud.

[19] Ibid., pp. 10–25.

[20] John Stuart Mill, *On Liberty,* ed. Currin V. Shields (Indianapolis: Bobbs-Merrill, 1956), p. 43. Originally published posthumously in 1907.

[21] The amendment originally applied only to actions by the federal government, but the Supreme Court has held that it also limits state government's infringement on speech.

Over many years, courts have struggled to come up with a clear definition of commercial speech.[22] The Supreme Court has defined it as "speech proposing a commercial transaction," but this still begs clarification.[23] An ad that said "Buy Nike shoes" would be commercial speech under this definition. But what about an ad picturing athletes with the statement "Just Do It," in which there is no literal sales proposal? Elsewhere in the same case, the Supreme Court also defined commercial speech as "expression related solely to the economic interests of the speaker and its audience."[24] Would Nike's statements on sweatshops meet this standard?

The focal point of Kasky's suit would become whether or not Nike's communications were, in fact, commercial speech. At a Superior Court hearing in early 1999, his lawyers argued that they were, therefore, they should be required to meet standards of truth and honesty enforced in California law. They were not entitled to the deference that would be given under the First Amendment to, for example, statements of political candidates or poets. Nike disagreed, saying that its statements about shoe and garment factories were part of a broader public debate and so were speech entitled to strong First Amendment protection.[25] The judge agreed with Nike and dismissed the case.[26] Kasky appealed, but a year later the appeals court rejected his argument again. Kasky then appealed to the California Supreme Court.

There he won. In a 4–3 decision the California Supreme Court held that Kasky's case should go to trial.[27] In reaching its decision, the majority created a novel, three-part definition of commercial speech and applied it to Nike's messages. For speech to be commercial it had to (1) come from a business, (2) be intended for an audience of consumers, and (3) make representations of facts related to products. Nike's statements fit each requirement. The majority conceded that commercial and noncommercial speech were intermingled in the communications, but argued that "Nike may not 'immunize false or misleading product information from government regulation simply by including references to public issues.'"[28] That put Nike in the position of a used car dealer falsely advertising "none of our cars has ever been in an accident," but evading prosecution for fraud by adding a political opinion such as, "our city should budget more for traffic safety."

Dissenting opinions revealed serious disagreement among the justices. Justice Ming Chin attacked the majority for unfairly tilting the playing field against Nike. "While Nike's critics have taken full advantage of their right to 'uninhibited, robust, and wide-open' debate," he wrote, "the same cannot be said of Nike, the object of their ire. When Nike tries to defend itself from these attacks, the majority denies it the same First Amendment protection Nike's critics enjoy."[29]

A second dissent came from Justice Janice R. Brown, who found Nike's commercial and noncommercial speech inseparable. In her view, "Nike's commercial statements about its labor practices cannot be separated from its noncommercial statements about a public issue, because its labor practices *are* the public issue."[30] She admonished the majority for creating a test of commercial speech that was unconstitutional because it made "the level of protection given to speech dependant on the identity of the speaker—and not just the speech's content."[31]

The consequences of the decision went far beyond Nike. Now any company doing business in California had to be careful about expressions of fact or opinion that reached consumers in the state. The sharpest and most ideological critics of a corporation could take issue with its statements, bring it to court, and force a trial about the accuracy of its claims. The

[22] Samuel A. Terilli, "*Nike v. Kasky* and the Running-But-Going-Nowhere Commercial Speech Debate," *Commercial Law and Policy* 10 (2005).

[23] *Central Hudson Gas & Electric Corp. v. Public Service Commission*, 447 U.S. 562 (1980).

[24] Ibid., at 561.

[25] Nike also asserted speech protections under Article I, section 2(a) of the California Constitution which reads: "Every person may freely speak, write and publish his or her sentiments on all subjects, being responsible for the abuse of that right. A law may not restrain or abridge liberty of speech or press."

[26] *Kasky v. Nike*, 79 Cal. App. 4th 165 (2000).

[27] *Kasky v. Nike*, 27 Cal. 4th 939 (2002).

[28] At 966, quoting *Bolger v. Youngs Drug Prods. Corp.*, 463 U.S. 68 (1983).

[29] At 970–971, quoting *Garrison v. Louisiana* 379 U.S. 75 (1964).

[30] At 980. Emphasis in the original.

[31] At 978.

decision was as unwelcome in the business community as it was unexpected. Nike would seek to overturn it.

IN THE UNITED STATES SUPREME COURT

Nike appealed to the United States Supreme Court, which accepted the case.[32] In its brief, Nike asked that the California Supreme Court's definition of commercial speech be struck down to remove its unconstitutional, chilling effect on public debate. Kasky argued once again that statements emanating from Nike's public relation's campaign fell into the category of free speech. He asserted that the First Amendment gave no shelter to false statements by a company about how its products were made.

Strangely, no decision would ever be made. The nine justices heard oral argument in April 2003. Then, late in June, they dismissed their consideration of the case as "improvidently granted."[33] In a brief opinion Justice John Paul Stevens said the Court had erred in accepting it before trial proceedings in California were finished. The Court would wait.

This view was not unanimous. Justices Anthony Kennedy, Stephen Breyer, and Sandra Day O'Connor dissented. They saw no reason to wait and hinted that they were ready to strike down any restriction on Nike's speech.

> In my view . . . the questions presented directly concern the freedom of Americans to speak about public matters in public debate, no jurisdictional rule prevents us from deciding these questions now, and delay itself may inhibit the exercise of constitutionally protected rights of free speech without making the issue significantly easier to decide later on . . . . [A]n action to enforce California's laws—laws that discourage certain kinds of speech—amounts to more than just a genuine, future threat. It is a present reality—one that discourages Nike from en-

gaging in speech. It thereby creates "injury in fact." Further, that injury is directly "traceable" to Kasky's pursuit of this lawsuit. And this Court's decision, if favorable to Nike, can "redress" that injury.[34]

SETTLEMENT AND AFTERMATH

With the Supreme Court dismissal, Kasky's specific charges against Nike could go to trial in California. The company would now be forced to defend the alleged misrepresentations about its labor practices. Its antagonists relished the prospect.

However, late in 2003 Kasky and Nike announced a settlement agreement. In return for Kasky dropping the case, Nike agreed to give $1.5 million to an industry-friendly factory monitoring group. It may have paid Kasky's legal fees. This was not a tough settlement for Nike.

Supporters on both sides were disappointed. Activists lost their grand show trial putting the corporate devil on display. Industry was disappointed that Nike did not stay the course because settlement left standing the California Supreme Court's broad definition of commercial speech. This definition still stands and only time will tell whether it chills corporate speech or fades into obscurity.[35]

More generally, the corporate community was aghast at the spectacle of a progressive activist humbling a giant corporation and it went after California's Unfair Business Competition Law. It backed a 2004 ballot proposition to amend the law, making it much harder for individuals like Kasky to sue. With heavy spending by big oil, tobacco, auto, insurance, and health care corporations, the proposition passed by a 59 to 41 percent margin.[36]

NIKE TURNS A NEW LEAF

Meanwhile, Nike was moving through a process of CSR review and implementation. In 2005 it published

---

[32] By now *Nike v. Kasky* had attracted considerable attention. The Court received 31 *amicus curiae*, or "friend of the court," briefs. Among these were briefs supporting Nike from the U.S. Chamber of Commerce, the Business Roundtable, several advertising associations, and large corporations, including ExxonMobil, Microsoft, and Pfizer. Kasky was supported by briefs from the attorneys general of 18 states and progressive advocacy groups such as Global Exchange, Public Citizen, and the Sierra Club.

[33] *Nike v. Kasky,* 539 U.S. 654 (2003), p*er curiam.*

[34] Ibid., at 667, 668.

[35] Its presence has been noted by activists. See, for example, Julia Fisher, "Note: Free Speech to have Sweatshops? How *Kasky v. Nike* Might Provide a Useful Tool to Improve Sweatshop Conditions," *Boston College Third World Law Journal,* Spring 2006.

[36] Carmen Balber, "Unfair Competition," *Multinational Monitor,* March/April 2005, p. 18.

a *Corporate Responsibility Report* stating three strategic CSR goals.[37] First, it would seek to create industry-wide, systemic change for the better in contractor shoe and apparel factories. Second, it would promote sustainability by eliminating toxic chemicals in shoe-making and by using more recycled materials. Third, it would improve society by promoting the idea of sport with its benefits of healthy exercise and keeping young people out of trouble.

Nike learned that its business processes and culture were in tension with the policies in its code for contractors. Many of its own actions triggered violations. Buyers, for example, were rewarded for meeting price, quality, and delivery date targets, giving them a financial incentive to push contractors hard, by that undermining code policies to limit work-weeks and hours in the factories. Nike products were often seasonal and ordered in response to rapidly shifting fashion trends. This had led Nike to adopt a low inventory policy, but in consequence its factories were often pressured to meet last-minute production goals. Sometimes their managers responded by cheating on labor guidelines. Changing Nike's internal processes to align them with its CSR goals meant slowing its reaction to consumer trends and risking loss of revenue. It also violated the spirit of Nike's aggressive procurement culture and met with resistence.[38]

Rather than penalize itself by adopting lone social responsibility guidelines in highly competitive markets, Nike decided to promote change within its industry, joining efforts with other leading companies, labor groups, and NGOs to create common factory labor codes. For example, it entered an experiment with Adidas-Salomon, the Gap, and six NGOs to develop a single code of conduct for contract factories in Turkey.[39]

Nike critics are giving the company a chance to make progress. It now engages in extensive dialogue with stakeholders. By doing this, it might not miss the rise of the next big CSR issue the way it missed the sweatshop issue.

Questions

1. What responsibility does Nike have for workers at the factories making its products? Has it carried out these responsibilities well? Should it do more?

2. Could Nike have better carried out its social programs to avoid or ease conflicts with advocacy groups? If so, what should it have done?

3. Should Nike be subject to false advertising lawsuits based on statements in editorial advertising, letters written by its executives, and press releases responding to issues raised by critics? Why or why not?

4. Did the California Supreme Court make the correct decision? Why or why not?

5. How should the line between commercial and noncommercial speech be drawn?

6. Should Nike have settled the case with Marc Kasky or should it have continued to fight?

[37] Nike, Inc., *FY04 Corporate Responsibility Report* (Beaverton, Oregon: Nike, April 2005).
[38] Simon Zadek, "The Path to Corporate Responsibility," *Harvard Business Review,* December 2004, p. 129–30.

[39] Joint Initiative on Corporate Accountability and Worker's Rights, "The Pilot Project in Turkey," at www.jo-in.org/pub/turkey.shtml.

Business Ethics

**"Today's verdict is a triumph
of our legal system . . ."**

Attorney General Alberto Gonzalez

September 27, 2006. At 9:00 A.M. on this Tuesday morning Bernard J. Ebbers, the former CEO of WorldCom, got into his car and left his home just outside Jackson, Mississippi. At 1:09 P.M. he arrived at a federal prison near Oakdale, Louisiana, drove through the gate, and surrendered himself to begin serving 25 years for securities fraud. The trip was about 200 miles, far enough to go from one life to another.

Of all the key defendants put on trial in a series of corporate finance scandals, Ebbers got the longest sentence. It was also the longest prison term in memory for a white-collar crime. There is no parole for a federal sentence. Time can be reduced up to 15 percent for good behavior, but even with this Ebbers will serve 21 years and 4 months. Since he was 65 when he entered prison, he would be 86 on his earliest

Former WorldCom chief Bernard Ebbers drives through the gates of a federal prison in Oakdale, Louisiana, to begin a 25-year sentence for his role in a massive accounting fraud. Source: © AP Photo/Rogelio V. Solis.

possible release date in 2028. However, he has a serious heart condition. Besides his freedom, Ebbers also lost his fortune. Once a billionaire, he has forfeited all assets except a home and $50,000 to be used by his wife.

Ebbers built WorldCom from a small telecommunications company into a global giant. It all started back in 1984 when he invested in a local long-distance phone company. Soon he was invited to manage it. He made it grow through a series of aggressive—even audacious—mergers. Eventually, it became a publicly traded corporation with annual revenues of $39 billion. As the company grew so did Ebbers's wealth, but his extravagant spending forced him to use all of his WorldCom stock as collateral for bank loans to pay his debts. If its price fell too far he would be bankrupt.

About this time the 1990s dot-com investment bubble burst. WorldCom's revenues declined and expenses for its world-spanning fiber optic network rose more than anticipated. According to later investigations, in 2000 Ebbers gave the first in a string of instructions to his chief financial officer to report false revenues and use accounting tricks to disguise rising expenses. The share prices held. However, internal auditors discovered the deceit and reported it to the Securities and Exchange Commission (SEC). The agency started an investigation. WorldCom's board of directors forced Ebbers to resign.

Soon the truth came out and WorldCom shares lost 90 percent of their value. In 2002 WorldCom set a record in failure, breaking Enron's previous total for the largest bankruptcy in American history. Although the company ultimately survived, 17,000 workers lost their jobs and investors lost billions.

Federal prosecutors charged Ebbers with nine counts of criminal conspiracy, securities fraud, and filing false documents with the SEC.[1] He refused to plead guilty, claiming that his chief financial officer had duped him. At his trial in 2005 he testified that he had no knowledge of the fraud.

> **Q:** Did you ever believe that any of the statements contained in those public filings were not true?
> **A:** No, sir.
> **Q:** Did you ever believe that WorldCom had reported revenue that it was not entitled to report?
> **A:** No, sir ....
> **Q:** Did you ever believe that WorldCom was putting out bad numbers in its financial statements in any way at all?
> **A:** No.[2]

Five of Ebbers's subordinates, including the chief financial officer, pled guilty and agreed to cooperate with prosecutors. They all testified against Ebbers, accusing him of not only knowing about the conspiracy, but also actively directing it. A jury convicted him on all counts. It was a big victory for federal prosecutors. "Today's verdict is a triumph of our legal system," lectured U.S. Attorney General Alberto Gonzalez.[3]

---

[1] *United States v. Bernard J. Ebbers,* Indictment, S3 02 Cr. 1144 (BSJ), 2004.

[2] *United States v. Bernard J. Ebbers,* 458 F.3d 124 (2006).

[3] Department of Justice, *Statement of Attorney General Alberto R. Gonzales on the Bernard Ebbers Conviction,* press release 05-122, March 15, 2005.

Ebbers "wept and sniffled" at his sentencing in 2005.[4] Victims of the fraud were invited to speak. One was a former WorldCom sales representative whose retirement money had evaporated from a company 401 (k) plan. "My life was destroyed by the greed of Bernard Ebbers," he said. "He can't ever repay me or the tens of thousands like me whose lives disintegrated in the blink of an eye."[5] Federal sentencing guidelines called for a sentence of 30 years based on the presence of certain aggravating factors. Direct losses to investors were estimated to be $2.2 billion, there were thousands of victims, and as a CEO Ebbers had abused a position of public trust. Judge Barbara Jones decided to subtract five years. She was moved by 170 letters from Ebbers's friends and neighbors asking for mercy. That left the sentence at 25 years. Ebbers requested further leniency because he suffers from cardiomyopathy, an inflammation of the heart. The judge rejected the relevance of this condition to sentencing. "Although I recognize . . . this is likely to be a life sentence for Mr. Ebbers," she said, "I find anything else would not reflect the seriousness of the crime."[6]

The judge recommended that Ebbers serve his time in a low-security facility. However, the Federal Bureau of Prisons bases assignments on the length of sentences, assuming that a long sentence signals its bearer is more likely to pose an escape risk and to endanger fellow inmates. Because Ebbers's sentence was 25 years, unprecedented for a white-collar crime, he was put in a medium-security facility. There, he lives with violence-prone inmates, sleeps in a cell rather than a dormitory, and encounters many locks and fences.

Ebbers still maintains his innocence.

Criminal sentences are intended to both punish individuals and deter future crime. Ebbers's sentence inspires rumination. Was it fair retribution for his actions? Was its harshness necessary to deter more accounting fraud? Was it fair that other WorldCom conspirators got much lighter sentences? The CFO who testified against Ebbers was sentenced to 5 years. The four other conspirators who pled guilty received sentences ranging from probation to one year. And how does Ebbers's 25 years compare with the sentences of violent criminals? It exceeds the recent 11-year sentence given to Anthony Megale, an underboss in New York's Gambino crime family. It exceeds the 20 years given to Salvatore Gravano, a Mafia hit man who confessed to 19 murders.[7] It exceeds the average of 24.2 years served by first-degree murderers in California.[8]

Ebbers is revealed now as unethical, a criminal, and deficient as a leader. In this chapter we add perspective to each of these dimensions. We begin by discussing the sources of ethical values in business, including truth telling, a basic virtue that Ebbers neglected. Then we discuss recent prosecutions of corporate crime. Finally, we look at factors shaping ethical climates in organizations and describe the managerial tools available to elevate behavior.

[4] Carrie Johnson, "Ebbers Gets 25-Year Sentence for Role in WorldCom Fraud," *Washington Post,* July 14, 2005, p. Al.

[5] Quoted in Leonard Greene and Richard Wilner, "Bawling Bernie Smacked," *The New York Post,* July 14, 2005, p. 3.

[6] Quoted in Carrie Johnson, "Ebbers Gets 25-Year Sentence for Role in WorldCom Fraud," p. Al.

[7] Andy Newman, "Mafia Turncoat Gets 20 Years for Running Ecstasy Ring," *New York Times,* September 7, 2002, p. 3.

[8] Department of Corrections and Rehabilitation, *Time Served on Prison Sentence* (Sacramento, CA: DCR, March 2006), table 1.

WHAT ARE BUSINESS ETHICS?

ethics
The study of good and evil, right and wrong, and just and unjust.

business ethics
The study of good and evil, right and wrong, and just and unjust actions in business.

Ethics is the study of what is good and evil, right and wrong, and just and unjust. *Business ethics,* therefore, is the study of good and evil, right and wrong, and just and unjust actions in business. Ethical managers try to do good and avoid doing evil. A mass of principles, values, norms, and thoughts concerned with what conduct *ought* to be exists to guide them. Yet in this vaporous mass, the outlines of good and evil are at times shadowy. Usually they are distinct enough, but often not. So, using ethical ideas in business is an art, an art requiring judgment about both the motivations behind an act and the act's consequences.

Discussions of business ethics frequently emphasize refractory and unclear situations, perhaps to show drama and novelty. Although all managers face difficult ethical conflicts, applying clear guidelines resolves the vast majority of them. The Eighth Commandment, for example, prohibits stealing and is plainly violated by taking tools home from work or theft of trade secrets. Lies in advertising violate a general rule of the Western business world that the seller of a product must not purposely deceive a buyer. This general understanding stems from the Mosaic law, the Code of Hammurabi, Roman law, and other sources and is part of a general ethic favoring truth going back at least 3,000 years.

Overall, ethical traditions that apply to business support truth telling, honesty, protection of life, respect for rights, fairness, and obedience to law. Some beliefs in this bundle of traditions go back thousands of years. Others, such as the idea that a corporation is responsible for the long-term health of its workers, have emerged more recently. In keeping with this long and growing ethical heritage, most business actions can be clearly judged ethical or unethical; eliminating unethical behavior such as bribery or embezzlement may be difficult, but knowing the rightness or wrongness of actions is usually easy.

This does not mean that ethical decisions are always clear. Some are troublesome because although basic ethical standards apply, conflicts between them defy resolution.

> Lockheed Aircraft Corp. made large campaign contributions to Japanese officials intended to influence the Japanese government to buy airplanes. This saved jobs for American workers. However, though such contributions were common in Japan and for the international aerospace industry overall, they violated U.S. business norms. Lockheed's actions are still debated.

Some ethical issues are hidden, at least initially, and hard to recognize.

> The A. H. Robins Co. began to market its Dalkon Shield intrauterine device through general practitioners while competitors continued to sell them only through obstetricians and gynecologists. This strategy was wildly successful in gaining market share for Robins and did not, initially, seem to raise ethical issues; but when dangerous health problems with the Shield started to appear, the general practitioners were slower to recognize them than the specialists. Robins's failure to make extra efforts in tracking the safety of the device then emerged as an ethical shortcoming.

Daniel Drew (1797–1879), speculator in railroad stocks and an exponent of the theory of amorality. Source: © Picture History/ Napoleon Sarony.

And some ethical issues are very subtle, submerged in everyday work-place behavior. Managers must often work in a world of uncertainty and act or pass judgment without complete knowledge of facts. The following case involves a commitment, a promise.

> A regional manager tells a factory manager that replacement equipment for a factory with production prob-lems due to breakdowns will be or-dered from this year's budget. At year's end, however, the equipment has not been ordered because, as the regional manager explains, "there just wasn't enough money left to do it." Is the factory manager entitled to expect the budget to be managed so that the commitment could be kept? Why was the commitment not kept? Poor plan-ning? Disguised withdrawal of coop-eration? Another reason?

TWO THEORIES OF BUSINESS ETHICS

There is an ageless debate about whether ethics in business may be more permis-sive than general societal or personal ethics. There are two basic views.

theory of amorality
The belief that business should be conducted without refer-ence to the full range of ethical standards, restraints, and ideals in society.

The first, the *theory of amorality*, is that business should be amoral, that is, conducted without reference to the full range of ethical standards, restraints, and ideals in soci-ety. Managers may use compromising ethics because competition distills their selfish actions into benefits for society. Adam Smith noted that the "invisible hand" of the market assures that "by pursuing his own interest [a merchant] frequently promotes that of the society more effectively than when he really intends to promote it."[9]

The apex of this view came during the latter half of the nineteenth century. It was widely believed that business and personal ethics existed in separate compartments, that business was a special sanctuary in which less idealistic ethics were permissi-ble.[10] Daniel Drew, who made a fortune in the 1860s by manipulating railroad stocks

---

[9] *The Wealth of Nations,* ed. Edwin Cannan (New York: Modern Library, 1937), p. 423; originally published in 1776. Smith also believed that merchants must abide by prevailing societal ethics.

[10] This was the conviction of social Darwinist Herbert Spencer, who believed in two sets of ethics. *Family ethics* were based on the principle of charity and benefits were apportioned without relation to merit. *State ethics* were based on a competitive justice and benefits were apportioned on the basis of strict merit. Family ethics interjected into business or government by well-meaning people were an inappropriate interference with the laws of nature and would slowly corrupt the workings of Darwinian natural selection. See "The Sins of Legislators," in *The Man versus the State* (London: Watts, 1940); originally published in 1884. Dual ethical perspectives have developed in other cultures, such as Slavic cultures, that assert one set of ethical standards for personal relationships and a second set that justifies less perfection for business matters. See Sheila M. Puffer, "Understanding the Bear: A Portrait of Russian Business Leaders," *Academy of Management Executive,* February 1994, p. 47.

James Cash Penney (1875–1971), son of a Baptist minister and an exemplar of the theory of moral unity.
Source: © Oscar White/CORBIS.

without scruple, summed up the nine-teenth-century compartmentalization of business decisions in these words:

> Sentiment is all right up in the part of the city where your home is. But downtown, no. Down there the dog that snaps the quickest gets the bone. Friendship is very nice for a Sunday afternoon when you're sitting around the dinner table with your relations, talking about the sermon that morning. But nine o'clock Monday morning, notions should be brushed aside like cobwebs from a machine. I never took any stock in a man who mixed up business with anything else. He can go into other things outside of business hours, but when he's in the office, he ought not to have a relation in the world—and least of all a poor relation.[11]

The theory of amorality has far less public acceptance today, but it lives on quietly. Many managers still allow competitive pressures to justify acts that would be wrong in private life. The theory of amorality releases them from feelings of guilt.

theory of moral unity Business actions are judged by the general ethical standards of society, not by a special set of more permissive standards.

The second basic ethical view is the *theory of moral unity,* in which business actions are judged by the general ethical standards in society, not by a special set of more permissive standards. Only one basic ethical standard exists, so business actions are judged by the same principles as actions in other areas of life.

Many managers take this position today, and some did even in the nineteenth century. An example is James Cash Penney. We remember Penney for building a chain of department stores, but his first enterprise was a butcher shop. As a young man, Penney went to Denver, where, finding the shop for sale, he wired his mother for $3,000 (his life savings) to buy it. The departing butcher shop owner warned him that his success depended on orders from a nearby hotel. "To keep the hotel for a customer," the butcher explained, "all you have to do is buy the chef a bottle of whiskey a week." Penney regularly made the gift and business was good, but he soon had second thoughts. Resolving no longer to do business that way, he stopped the bribe, lost the hotel's business, and went broke when the shop failed. He was 23 years old.

Penney later started the Golden Rule Department Store in Denver and always believed that principles of honesty led to its ultimate success. In contrast to the unsentimental lone wolf Daniel Drew, Penney reflects his focus on ethics in this little story.

---

[11] Quoted in Robert Bartels, ed., *Ethics in Business* (Columbus: Bureau of Business Research, Ohio State University, 1963), p. 35.

It seems that the manager of a chain store had run out of a certain line of goods and had appealed to the manager of another store in the chain for a share of the supply which this second man had on hand. This man consented—but sent some goods of poor quality which *he* had not been able to sell. He thought he was being very shrewd. But if I had the chance I would fire that man. He was not being square. He hadn't the instinct of fair dealing. You can't build a solid, substantial house with decayed planks, no matter what kind of a veneer is put over their rottenness. That man's action was rotten, even though it was veneered with temporary shrewdness.[12]

To J. C. Penney, and other exemplars of the theory of moral unity, desire to succeed is never an excuse to neglect principled behavior. Actions are not moral just because they make money. Ethical conflicts cannot be avoided simply because they arise in the course of business.

MAJOR SOURCES OF ETHICAL VALUES IN BUSINESS

reciprocity
A form of social behavior in which people behave supportively in the expectation that this behavior will be given in return.

Four great repositories of ethical values influence managers. They are religion, philosophy, cultural experience, and law (Figure 7.1). A common theme, the idea of *reciprocity,* or mutual help, is found in each of these value systems. This idea reflects the central purpose of ethics, which is to bind individuals into a cooperative social whole. Ethical values are a mechanism that controls behavior in business and in other areas of life. Ethical restraint is more efficient with society's resources than are cruder controls such as police, lawsuits, or economic incentives. Ethical values channel individual energy into pursuits that are benign to others and beneficial to society.

FIGURE 7.1
Major Sources of Ethical Values in Business

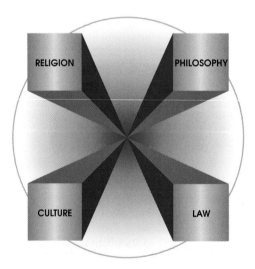

[12] J. C. Penney, "It Is One Thing to Desire—and Another to Determine," in Peter Krass, ed., *The Book of Business Wisdom* (New York: Wiley, 1997), p. 89. Reprinted from *American Magazine,* August 1919. Emphasis in the original.

Religion

The great religions, including the Judeo-Christian tradition prominent in American history, converge in the belief that a divine will reveals the nature of right and wrong behavior, including in business. Despite doctrinal differences, major religions agree on ideas forming the basic building blocks of ethics in every society. For example, the principle of reciprocity is found, encapsulated in variations of the Golden Rule, in Buddhism, Confucianism, Hinduism, Islam, Judaism, and Christianity. These religions also converge in emphasizing traits such as promise keeping, honesty, fairness, charity, and responsibility to others.

Christian managers often seek guidance in the Bible. Like the source books and writings of other main religions, the Bible was written in a premodern, agricultural society, and many of its ethical teachings require interpretation before they can be applied to problems in the modern workplace. Much of the ethical teaching in the Bible comes from parables. The parable of the prodigal son (Luke 15:11–32) tells the story of an unconditionally merciful father—an image applicable to ethical conflicts in corporate superior—subordinate relationships. The story of the rich man and Lazarus (Luke 16:19–31) teaches concern for the poor and challenges Christian managers to consider the less privileged, a fitting admonition in a world where billions of people survive on less than $1 a day.[13]

In Islam the Koran is a source of ethical inspiration. The Prophet Muhammad says that "Every one of you is a shepherd and everyone is responsible for what he is shepherd of."[14] In a modern context, the Muslim manager is like a shepherd and the corporation is like a flock. The manager has a duty to rise above self-interest and protect the good of the organization.

In the Jewish tradition, managers can turn to rabbinic moral commentary in the Talmud and the books of Moses in the Torah. Here again, ancient teachings are regarded as analogies. For example, a Talmudic ruling holds that a person who sets a force in motion bears responsibility for any resulting harm, even if natural forces intervene (*Baba Qamma* 60a). This is discussed in the context of an agrarian society in which a person who starts a fire is responsible for damage from flying sparks, even if nature intervenes with high winds. In an industrial context, the ethics lesson is that polluting companies are responsible for problems caused by their waste.[15] Another passage comments on a situation in which laborers have been hired to dig in a field, but a nearby river has overflowed, preventing the work (*Bava Metzia* 76b–77a). The Talmud counsels that if the employer knew the river was likely to overflow then the workers should be paid, but if the flood was unpredictable then the workers should bear the loss. This teaching may inform thinking about modern layoffs. In highly cyclical industries, workers can anticipate the

---

[13] See Oliver F. Williams and John W. Houck, *Full Value: Cases in Christian Business Ethics* (New York: Harper & Row, 1978), for discussion of these and other biblical sources of inspiration for managers.

[14] Quoted in Tanri Abeng, "Business Ethics in Islamic Context: Perspectives of a Muslim Business Leader," *Business Ethics Quarterly,* July 1997, p. 52.

[15] Moses L. Pava, *Business Ethics: A Jewish Perspective* (New York: Yeshiva University Press, 1997), pp. 72–73.

risk of layoffs, but in more stable industries management may bear greater responsibility for job security.[16]

Parables and stories in the literature of ancient worlds can seem so innocent as to have little value for modern managers. However, as one rabbinic scholar notes, "Our world has undergone tremendous technological changes, but the issues stay the same—egotism, jealousy, greed, among others."[17] Thus, the central wisdom remains. When Confucius told Chinese merchants that "He who acts with a constant view to his own advantage (*li*) will be much murmured against," he planted a speck of truth visible in the atmosphere of any era.[18]

Philosophy

A Western manager can look back on more than 2,000 years of philosophical inquiry into ethics. This rich, complex tradition is the source of many notions about what is right or wrong in business. Every age has added new ideas, but it is a mistake to regard the history of ethical philosophy as a single debate that, over centuries, has matured to bear the fruit of growing wisdom and clear, precise standards of conduct. Even after two millennia, there remains considerable dispute among ethical thinkers about the nature of right action. If anything, standards of ethical behavior were arguably clearer in ancient Greek civilization than they are now.

In a brief circuit of milestones in ethical thinking, we turn first to the Greek philosophers. Greek ethics, from Homeric times onward, were embodied in the discharge of duties related to social roles such as shepherd, warrior, merchant, citizen, or king. Expectations of the occupants of these roles were clearer than in contemporary America, where social roles such as those of business manager or employee are more vague, overlapping, and marked by conflict.[19]

Socrates (469–399 B.C.) asserted that virtue and ethical behavior were associated with wisdom and taught that insight into life would naturally lead to right conduct. He also introduced the idea of a moral law higher than human law, an idea that activists use to demand supralegal behavior from transnational corporations. Plato (428–348 B.C.), the gifted student of Socrates, carried this doctrine of virtue as knowledge further by elaborating the theory that absolute justice exists independently of individuals and that its nature can be discovered by intellectual effort. In the *Republic*, Plato set up a 50-year program for training rulers to rule in harmony with the ideal of justice.[20] Plato's most apt pupil, Aristotle, spelled out virtues of character in the *Nicomachean Ethics* and advocated a regimen of continuous learning to improve ethical behavior.[21]

---

[16] See Robert H. Carver, "If the River Stopped: A Talmudic Perspective on Downsizing," *Journal of Business Ethics* 50, 2004, pp. 144–45.

[17] Meir Tamari, quoted in Gail Lichtman, "Ethics Is Their Business," *The Jerusalem Post,* May 25, 2001, p. 13.

[18] *Analects,* book IV, chap. XII. Cited in Stephen B. Young, "The CRT *Principles for Business* as an Expression of Original Confucian Morality," *Caux Roundtable Newsletter,* Fall 2000, p. 9.

[19] Alasdair MacIntyre, *After Virtue: A Study in Moral Theory* (South Bend, IN: University of Notre Dame Press, 1981), p.115.

[20] Trans. F. M. Cornford (New York: Oxford University Press, 1945).

[21] *Nicomachean Ethics,* trans. Thomson, p. 51.

The Stoic school of ethics, spanning four centuries from the death of Alexander to the rise of Christianity in Rome, furthered the trend toward character development in Greek ethics. Epictetus (A.D. 50–100), for instance, taught that virtue was found solely within and should be valued for its own sake, arguing that this inner virtue was a higher reward than external riches or worldly success.

In business, the ethical legacy of the Greeks and Romans lives on in the conviction that virtues such as truth telling, charity, obeying the law, justice, courage, friendship, and the just use of power are important qualities. Today when a manager trades integrity for profit, we condemn this on the basis of the teachings of the ancient Mediterranean world.

Ethical thinking after the rise of Christianity was dominated by the great Catholic theologians St. Augustine (354–430) and St. Thomas Aquinas (1225–1274). Both believed that humanity should follow God's will; correct behavior in business and in all worldly activity was necessary to achieve salvation and life after death. Christianity was the source of many ethical teachings, including specific rules such as the Ten Commandments.

Christian theology created a lasting reservoir of ethical doctrine, but its command of ethical thought weakened during the historical period of intellectual and industrial expansion in Europe called the Enlightenment. Secular philosophers such as Baruch Spinoza (1632–1677) tried to demonstrate ethical principles with logical analysis rather than ordain them by reference to God's will. So also, Immanuel Kant (1724–1804) tried to find universal and objective ethical rules in logic. Kant and Spinoza, and others who followed, created a great estrangement with moral theology by believing that humanity could discover the nature of good behavior without reference to God. To this day, there is a deep divide between Christian managers who look to the Bible for divine guidance and other managers who look to worldly writing for ethical wisdom.

Other milestones of secular thinking followed. Jeremy Bentham (1748–1832) developed the idea of utilitarianism as a guide to ethics. Bentham observed that an ethical action was the one among all alternatives that brought pleasure to the largest number of persons and pain to the fewest. The worldly impact of this ethical philosophy is almost impossible to overestimate, because it validated two dominant ideologies, democracy and industrialism, allowing them first to arise and then to flourish. The legitimacy of majority rule in democratic governments rests in large part on Bentham's theory of utility as later refined by John Stuart Mill (1806–1873). Utilitarianism also sanctified industrial development by legitimizing the notion that economic growth benefits the majority; thus the pain and dislocation it brings to a few may be ethically permitted.

John Locke (1632–1704) developed and refined doctrines of human rights and left an ethical legacy supporting belief in the inalienable rights of human beings, including the right to pursue life, liberty, and happiness, and the right to freedom from tyranny. Our leaders, including business leaders, continue to be restrained by these beliefs.

A *realist school* of ethics also developed alongside the idealistic thinking of philosophers such as Spinoza, Kant, the utilitarians, and Locke. The realists believed that both good and evil were naturally present in human nature; human behavior

realist school
A school of thought that rejects ethical perfection, taking the position that human affairs will be characterized by flawed behavior and ought to be depicted as they are, not as we might wish them to be.

inevitably would reflect this mixture. Since good and evil occurred naturally, it was futile to try to teach ideals. Ideals could never be realized because evil was a permanent human trait. The realist school, then, developed ethical theories that shrugged off the idea of perfect goodness. Niccolò Machiavelli (1469–1527) argued that important ends justified expedient means. Herbert Spencer (1820–1903) wrote prolifically of a harsh ethic that justified vicious competition among companies because it furthered evolution—a process in which humanity improved as the unfit fell down. Friedrich Nietzsche (1844–1900) rejected the ideals of earlier "nice" ethics, saying they were prescriptions of the timid, designed to fetter the actions of great men whose irresistible power and will were regarded as dangerous by the common herd of ordinary mortals.

Nietzsche believed in the existence of a "master morality" in which great men made their own ethical rules according to their convenience and without respect for the general good of average people. In reaction to this master morality, the mass of ordinary people developed a "slave morality" intended to shackle the great men. For example, according to Nietzsche, the mass of ordinary people celebrate the Christian virtue of turning the other cheek because they lack the power to revenge themselves on great men. He felt that prominent ethical ideals of his day were recipes for timidity and once said of utilitarianism that it made him want to vomit.[22] The influence of realists on managers has been strong. Spencer was wildly popular among the business class in the nineteenth century. Machiavelli is still read for inspiration. The lasting influence of realism is that many managers, deep down, do not believe that ideals can be achieved in business life.

Cultural Experience

Every culture transmits between generations a set of traditional values, rules, and standards that define acceptable behavior. In this way, individuals channel their conduct in socially approved directions. Civilization itself is a cumulative cultural experience consisting of three stages; in each, economic and social arrangements have dictated a distinct moral code.[23]

For millions of generations in the *hunting and gathering stage* of human development, ethics were adapted to conditions in which our ancestors had to be ready to fight, face brutal foes, and suffer hostile forces of nature. Under such circumstances, a premium was placed on pugnacity, appetite, greed, and sexual readiness, since it was often the strongest who survived. Trade ethics in early civilizations were probably deceitful and dishonest by our standards, and economic transactions were frequently conducted by brute force and violence.

Civilization passed into an *agricultural stage* approximately 10,000 years ago, beginning a time when industriousness was more important than ferocity, thrift paid greater dividends than violence, monogamy became the prevailing sexual custom because of the relatively equal numbers of the sexes, and peace came to be valued over wars, which destroyed crops and animals. These new values were

---

[22] His exact words were "the general welfare is no ideal, no goal, no remotely intelligible concept, but only an emetic." In *Beyond Good and Evil* (New York: Vintage Books, 1966), p. 157; originally published in 1886.

[23] Will Durant and Ariel Durant, *The Lessons of History* (New York: Simon & Schuster, 1968), pp. 37–42.

codified into ethical systems by philosophers and founders of religions. So the great ethical philosophies and theologies that guide managers today are largely products of the agricultural revolution.

Two centuries ago, society entered an *industrial stage* of cultural experience, and ethical systems began to reflect an evolving institutional, intellectual, and ecological environment. Powerful forces such as global corporations, population growth, the capitalist ideology, constitutional democracy, new technology, and ecological damage have appeared. Industrialism has not yet created a distinct ethic, but rising postmodern values put stress on ethical values that evolved in ancient, agriculture-based worlds. Postmodern values alter people's judgments about good and evil. For example, the copious outpouring of material goods from factories encourages materialism and consumption at the expense of older, scarcity-based virtues such as moderation and thrift. The old truism that nature exists for human exploitation is less compelling when reexamined in a cloud of industrial pollution.

Ethical Variation in Cultures

Ethical values differ among nations as historical experiences have interacted with philosophies and religions to create diverging cultural values and laws. Where differences exist, are some cultures correct about proper business ethics and others wrong? There are two ways to answer this question.

The school of *ethical universalism* holds that in terms of biological and psychological needs, human nature is everywhere the same. Ethical rules are transcultural because behavior that fulfills basic human needs should be the same everywhere—for example, basic rules of justice must be followed. Basic justice might be achieved, however, by emphasizing group ethics or by emphasizing individual ethics, leaving room for cultural variation.

The school of *ethical relativism* holds that although human biology is everywhere similar, cultural experience creates widely diverging values, including ethical values. Ethical values are subjective. There is no objective way to prove them right or wrong as with scientific facts. A society cannot know that its ethics are superior, so it is wrong for one nation to impose standards on another.

We cannot settle this age-old philosophical debate. However, ethical variation is a practical and urgent issue. Because of globalization, corporations struggle with the question of how to apply conduct codes across cultures. If large multinationals vary behavior based on local customs, they open themselves to disturbing practices, for example, in countries that permit workplace discrimination against women. If, on the other hand, firms maintain absolute consistency of standards, they may offend local norms. Some flexibility seems appropriate.

What guidelines exist for companies that want flexibility in their conduct codes? Some scholars argue that at a high level of abstraction, the ethical ideals of all cultures converge to basic sameness. Thomas Donaldson and Thomas W. Dunfee see a deep social contract underlying all human societies. This contract is based on what they call *hypernorms,* or principles at the root of all human ethics. Examples are basic rights, such as rights to life and to political participation. These hypernorms validate other ethical norms, which can differ from nation to nation but still be consistent with the hypernorms. For example, many U.S. corporations prohibit

ethical universalism
The theory that because human nature is everywhere the same, basic ethical rules are applicable in all cultures. There is some room for variation in the way these rules are followed.

ethical relativism
The theory that ethical values are created by cultural experience. Different cultures may create different values and there is no universal standard by which to judge which values are superior.

hypernorms
Master ethical principles that underlie all other ethical principles. All variations of ethical principle must conform to them.

people from hiring their relatives. In India, however, tradition places a high value on supporting family and clan members, and some companies promise to hire workers' children when they grow up. Although these practices are inconsistent, neither violates any universal prohibition. They exist in what Donaldson and Dunfee call "moral free space" where inconsistent norms are permitted if they do not violate any hypernorms.[24]

Law

Laws codify, or formalize, ethical expectations. They proliferate over time as emerging regulations, statutes, and court rulings impose new conduct standards. Corporations and their managers face a range of mechanisms set up to deter illegal acts, punish offenses, and rehabilitate offenders. In particular, they face civil actions by regulatory agencies and private parties and criminal prosecution by governments. We will discuss these mechanisms to illustrate how legal controls and sanctions work.

Damages

compensatory damages
Payments awarded to redress concrete losses suffered by injured parties.

punitive damages
Payments in excess of a wronged party's actual losses. They are awarded to deter similar actions and punish a corporation that has exhibited malicious and willful misconduct.

In civil cases courts may assess damages, or payments for harm done to others by a corporation. *Compensatory damages* are payments awarded to redress concrete losses suffered by injured parties. *Punitive damages,* or payments in excess of a wronged party's actual losses, are awarded to deter similar actions and punish a corporation. In this way, they serve the same purposes as criminal penalties. Punitive damages may be awarded only if malicious and willful misconduct exists. For example, a regional manager for Browning-Ferris Industries ordered a district manager to drive a small competitor in Vermont out of business using predatory pricing. His instructions were: "Do whatever it takes. Squish him like a bug."[25] Subsequently, a jury awarded the competitor $51,146 in actual damages, then added $6 million in punitive damages.

Since the purpose of punitive damages is to punish and deter misconduct, they must be large enough to cause pain. Yet they raise many questions about fairness. There is no fixed standard for calculating their size and arbitrary sums may violate constitutional due process requirements. Given similar offenses, juries often assess higher damages against a big corporation than against a smaller one simply to make certain the penalty hurts. And sometimes the sums awarded are so large that they must be weighed against Eighth Amendment prohibitions against "excessive fines" and "cruel and unusual punishments."

The Supreme Court decided to rein in punitive damages in the case of an Alabama physician, Dr. Ira Gore, Jr., who bought a BMW automobile for $40,751 and drove it for nine months without noticing any problem. After an auto detailer told him that part of the car had been repainted, the owner found out that BMW North America was secretly repainting cars with shipping damage and selling them as new. Gore estimated his damages at $4,000 and sued, charging BMW with gross,

[24] Thomas Donaldson and Thomas W. Dunfee, "When Ethics Travel: The Promise and Peril of Global Business Ethics," *California Management Review,* Summer 1999, p. 61.

[25] *Browning-Ferris Industries v. Kelko Disposal,* 57 LW 4986 (1989).

oppressive, and malicious fraud. A jury awarded him $4 million in punitive damages—1,000 times his actual loss.

On appeal, the Supreme Court held that such a big award for retouching paint was unconstitutionally excessive.[26] (Subsequently, the Alabama Supreme Court reconsidered the case and awarded Gore only $50,000.)[27] Although the Court did not set up a precise ratio of punitive damages to compensatory damages for judges and juries to follow, in a subsequent case it suggested that a ratio greater than 4–1 is suspect and a ratio of 10–1 or higher probably cannot be justified.[28]

Criminal Prosecution of Managers and Corporations

Ethical ideals alone often fail and the police powers of the state must reinforce them. Managers can be prosecuted for criminal actions undertaken in the course of their employment. Corporations are also subject to criminal prosecution. They are criminally liable for corrupt actions or omissions of managers if those actions are intended to benefit the corporation.[29] To establish guilty intent when crimes have occurred, the law assumes that a corporation has the aggregate knowledge of all its employees.

Criminal prosecution of corporations and their employees is exceptionally difficult. The government must prove beyond a reasonable doubt that an executive either had specific knowledge of a crime and acted to abet it or realized the probable existence of a crime and consciously avoided inquiring into it. Unlike civil proceedings defendants do not have to produce information, so pretrial investigations can be lengthy and expensive. Corporate defendants often hire illustrious lawyers and outspend government prosecutors. When Royal Caribbean Cruise Lines was indicted for criminal violations of the Clean Water Act, it put together an all-star defense team including two former United States attorneys general. (It still lost the case.) Corporate crimes such as accounting frauds require prosecutors to educate lay juries about intricate financial transactions that even experienced judges find hard to follow. This was a problem in the trial of Richard Scruchy, former CEO of HealthSouth, who was tried on 36 counts of conspiracy, fraud, and money laundering. After sitting through five months of testimony, petrified jurors acquitted him of all wrongdoing.

The United States has recently gone through a cycle of corporate crime prosecutions. In 2002 President George W. Bush responded to public dyspepsia over a cluster of corporate frauds, including the Enron collapse, by setting up a Corporate Fraud Task Force.[30] "It included U.S. attorneys and agents from the Federal Bureau of Investigation and the Internal Revenue Service." It's purpose was to speed investigations, to prosecute managers and, in the President's words, "to

[26] *BMW of North America, Inc. v. Gore,* 116 S. Ct. 1589 (1996).

[27] *BMW of North America, Inc. v. Gore,* 701 So. 2d 507 Ala. (1997).

[28] *State Farm Mutual Automobile Insurance Company v. Campbell,* 123 S. Ct. 1513 (2003).

[29] The Supreme Court established this precedent for liability in *New York Central & Hudson River Railroad Co. v. United States,* 212 U.S. 481 (1909).

[30] Executive Order 13271 of July 9, 2002, 67 FR 46091 (2002).

reaffirm the basic principles and rules that make capitalism work: truthful books and honest people. . . ."[31]

A separate Enron Task Force was created to concentrate on the labyrinthine Enron fraud. To pierce the veil of culpability, its prosecutors methodically pressured lower-level managers into cooperating as witnesses. In return for guilty pleas and testimony against their former bosses, they received lighter sentences. It was ruthless work. To get the cooperation of former chief financial officer Andrew S. Fastow, prosecutors charged his wife Lea, a former assistant treasurer at Enron, with defrauding the company for personal enrichment.[32] Both Fastows then agreed to reduction of charges in return for his testimony. As managers caved in one-by-one, the task force moved up the chain of responsibility to the very top where former CEOs Kenneth L. Lay and Jeffrey K. Skilling maintained ignorance of any wrongdoing.

Eventually, the task force summited in a 17-week trial in which jurors convicted both Lay and Skilling on multiple counts of conspiracy and fraud. After inculpating testimony by almost two dozen former subordinates, jurors simply did not believe that Lay and Skilling lacked knowledge of any schemes.[33] Although Lay died of a heart attack before sentencing, Skilling was sentenced to 24 years and 4 months in prison. Because Andrew Fastow cooperated with the government, his sentence was only six years. Lea Fastow served five months in prison.

The government's record in prosecuting corporate crime is mixed, but probably deserves a thumbs up. The Enron Task Force was disbanded in 2006 after bringing criminal charges against 27 executives and obtaining 20 convictions. The larger Corporate Fraud Task Force has so far investigated more than 400 corporate fraud cases and obtained 1,236 convictions, including 214 presidents and chief executive officers, 53 chief financial officers, and 129 vice presidents.[34] It will continue to operate. There is plenty of work.

Such large conviction numbers are impressive, but most offenders have pleaded guilty. Corporate criminals remain extremely difficult to prosecute. When cases have gone to trial, as they have with the highest-level executives, prosecutors have struggled. A study of 17 major corporate fraud prosecutions since 2002, including Enron, shows that government prosecutors failed to convict most of the defendants. Of 46 executives, 20 were convicted but 11 were acquitted and juries deadlocked on 15 others.[35]

Sentencing, Fines, and Other Penalties

In 1991 the United States Sentencing Commission, a judicial agency that standardizes penalties for federal crimes, released guidelines for sentencing both managers

---

[31] "President Announces Tough New Enforcement Initiatives," Office of the Press Secretary, the White House, July 9, 2002, p. 2.

[32] *United States v. Lea W. Fastow,* Indictment, U.S.D.C., S. Dist. Texas, Cr. No. H-03.

[33] Lianne Hawf, "'How Could They Not See It?'" *Los Angeles Times,* May 26, 2006, p. A14.

[34] Department of Justice, "Prepared Remarks of Deputy Attorney General Paul J. McNulty at the Corporate Fraud Task Force Fifth Anniversary Event," Washington, DC, July 17, 2007, p. 1, at www.usdoj.gov/criminal/pr/press_releases/.

[35] Kathleen F. Brickey, "In Enron's Wake: Corporate Executives on Trial," *Journal of Criminal Law & Criminology,* Winter 2006, pp. 401–407. Convictions of K. Lay and J. Skilling are included in the figures.

TABLE 7.1
Longest
Prison
Sentences for
Executive
Fraud

Bernard J. Ebbers	CEO, WorldCom	25 years
Jeffrey K. Skilling	CEO, Enron	24 years, 4 months
Timothy Rigas	CFO, Adelphia Communications	20 years
John J. Rigas	CEO, Adelphia Communications	15 years
Sidney Wolff	CEO, Homestore	15 years
Sanjay Kumar	CEO, Computer Associates Int.	12 years
L. Dennis Kozlowski	CEO, Tyco International	$8\frac{1}{3}$–25 years*
Mark H. Swartz	CFO, Tyco International	$8\frac{1}{3}$–25 years*
Martin Grass	CEO, RiteAid	8 years
Andrew Fastow	CFO, Enron	6 years
Scott D. Sullivan	CFO, WorldCom	5 years

*Kozlowski and Swartz were sentenced by a New York state court and are eligible for parole after serving their minimum eight-year, four-month sentences. Other sentences are federal sentences with no parole.

and corporations. These guidelines are not mandatory, but most judges follow them.[36] When managers such as Lay, Skilling, and Fastow are convicted of a crime, their prison sentences are calculated based on a numerical point system. Calculations begin with a base score for the type of offense. Points are then added or subtracted because of enhancing or mitigating factors. A sentence for fraud, for example, begins with a base level of 6, then 15 factors are considered, including the number of victims and their losses. As losses to victims rise on a scale from $5,000 to $400 million or more between 2 and 30 points are added. As the number of victims rises from 10 to 250 or more between 2 and 6 points are added.[37] Downward adjustments are made if the manager has no criminal history or cooperated with authorities. The total is then translated into a prison sentence using a table. Besides prison terms, managers may also be fined, put on probation, given community service, asked to make restitution to injured parties, or banned from working as corporate officers or directors.

After the early-century fraud scandals, Congress increased fraud penalties when it passed the Sarbanes-Oxley Act of 2002. Since most of this fraud was perpetrated before passage of the law, the stricter guidelines did not apply in the headline trials of the time. Nevertheless, as Table 7.1 shows, the sentences for some top executives were lengthy, sometimes equaling the 20- to 25-year sentences usually reserved for violent career criminals. Such sentences result from the way that the sentencing guidelines add points based on the monetary sums involved in a fraud and the number of victims. The large numbers involved practically guarantee a draconian sentence for any executive of a public corporation who defrauds shareholders.

Corporations cannot be imprisoned, but they can be fined and their actions restricted. Criminal fines are intended to punish, to deter future lawbreaking,

[36] The constitutionality of sentencing guidelines was recently challenged. The Supreme Court agreed, by a narrow 5–4 majority, that their mandatory use violated the Sixth Amendment right to a trial by jury. However, it allowed judges to continue using them if they were considered advisory, not mandatory. See *United States v. Booker*, 125 S. Ct. 738 (2005).

[37] United States Sentencing Commission, *Guidelines Manual*, §2B1.1 (November 2006).

to cause disgorgement of wrongful gains, and to remedy harms where possible. As with the prison sentences of managers, judges base their calculation on a point system in the federal sentencing guidelines. The calculation begins with a fine range based on the seriousness of the offense, then adds or subtracts points based on aggravating or mitigating factors such as the degree of top-management involvement and cooperation during the investigation. If, for example, management "willfully obstructed" authorities, 3 points are added. Up to 5 points may be subtracted if top managers immediately reported the crime.[38]

A cynical public doubts that fines are large enough to hurt. The Environmental Protection Agency once threatened to impose a $27,500 fine on General Electric each day it failed to clean up toxic waste at a factory. It was the equivalent of trying to intimidate a person making $1 million a year with a fine of three cents a day. When GE paid the government $1.84 million in fines to settle a billing fraud case, it was the same as a $25 parking ticket for a person making $50,000 a year. Yet fines can also be devastating. Although the accounting firm Arthur Andersen was fined only $500,000 after its conviction for obstructing justice in the Enron investigation, the collateral effects of a criminal fine drove it out of business.

The largest fine ever levied is a $2.5 billion civil penalty by the Securities and Exchange Commission against WorldCom in 2003. The record for a criminal fine is $500 million. It was twice imposed. One was for an antitrust penalty on F. Hoffmann-LaRoche Ltd. in 1999.[39] The company had led a decade-long conspiracy between it and six other European and Japanese companies to cheat buyers of common vitamin supplements by allocating market shares and fixing prices. Schering-Plough Corp. was similarly fined in 2002 for unsafe drug manufacturing practices.[40] One problem with fines is that they can punish innocent employees and shareholders who may already have been victimized by management's criminal behavior. Corporate indictments and fines are frequent. In 2006, for example, 217 companies were charged with criminal offenses. Of these, 162 were fined. The mean fine was $4.7 million.[41]

Other methods for penalizing corporate crime exist. Courts have required advertisements and speeches to show contrition for wrongdoing. Some corporations pay their fines to charities, and their executives do community service. Many are forced to adopt internal compliance programs. Occasionally, a person from outside the company is appointed to monitor these efforts. Following a criminal conviction, both managers and corporations are subject to civil suits by parties such as shareholders who have been damaged. In these civil cases the burden of proof is lower than in a criminal case—a preponderance of the evidence—and the remedy sought is usually financial.

---

[38] Ibid., §8C2.5 at (e) and (g)(1).

[39] *U.S. v. F. Hoffmann-LaRoche Ltd.,* No. 3:99-CR-184-R (NDT), 1999.

[40] *U.S. v. Schering-Plough,* Consent Decree of Permanent Injunction, U.S.D.C., D.N.J., (2002).

[41] United States Sentencing Commission, *2006 Sourcebook on Federal Sentencing Statistics* (Washington, DC: USSC, 2006), table 52.

FACTORS THAT INFLUENCE MANAGERIAL ETHICS

Strong forces in organizations shape ethical behavior. Depending on how they are managed, these forces elevate or depress standards of conduct. We discuss here four prominent and interrelated forces that shape conduct: leadership, strategies and policies, organization culture, and individual characteristics (see Figure 7.2).

Leadership

The example of company leaders is perhaps the strongest influence on integrity. Not only do leaders set formal rules, but by their example they reinforce or undermine right behavior. Subordinates are keen observers and quickly notice if standards are, in practice, upheld or evaded. Exemplary behavior is a powerful tool available to all managers. It was well used by this executive.

> When Paul O'Neill arrived as CEO at Alcoa, a secretary put papers in front of him to join an expensive country club. His dues would be paid by the company. He was expected to join, because other senior executives could not continue their paid memberships unless the CEO was a member. Before signing, he looked into the club and realized that it had a discriminatory membership policy. He was urged just to go along and join, like others before him. Since he was new, he ought to wait a while before disturbing Alcoa custom. However, he refused to join. His thoughts were: "What excuse am I going to use six or twelve months from now? I've just discovered my principles? They were on vacation … when I first came?"[42] He then set up a policy against reimbursing executives for dues in discriminatory clubs.

A common failing is for managers to show by their actions that ethical duties may be compromised. For example, when managers give themselves expensive perks, they display an irreverence for the stewardship of money that rightly belongs to investors as owners, not to management. An executive at one large corporation describes how arrogant behavior sends the wrong signals.

FIGURE 7.2
Four Internal Forces Shaping Corporate Ethics

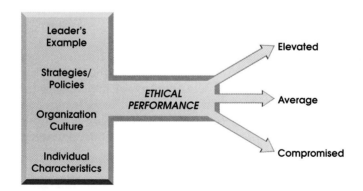

[42] Quoted in Linda K. Treviño and Katherine A. Nelson, *Managing Business Ethics: Straight Talk about How to Do It Right,* 4th ed. (New York: Wiley, 2007), p. 267, citing P. O'Neill, "O'Neill on Ethics and Leadership," speech at the Katz Graduate School of Business, University of Pittsburgh, 2002.

Too often through my career I've been at management dinners—no customers—and I see $600 bottles of wine being ordered. Think about the message that sends out through the whole organization. And don't ever think such attitudes don't spread and infect the whole firm. Leadership, after all, is about communicating values. And deeds trump words any day.

The message in that bottle is this: Some sales representative and a couple of technicians, supported by others, busted their butts to get that $600 to the bottom line. And their work, as evaluated by the guy who bought the wine, was worth a couple of tasty swallows.

If money is the way we keep track of the good things our employees accomplish for our customers, then who do we think we are spilling it?[43]

Many employees are prone to cynicism. Diverting blame for mistakes, breaking small promises, showing favoritism, and diversion of even trivial company resources for personal use are ill-advised—because if the leader does it, an opportunistic employee can rationalize his or her entitlement to do it also. According to Sherron Watkins, a whistleblower at Enron, Andrew Fastow was such a shrewdly observant subordinate. As Enron's chief financial officer, he created a warren of complex and deceitful investments that not only contributed nonexistent revenue, but diverted corporate funds into his and his wife's pockets. What inspired Fastow to act as he did? According to Watkins, it may have been the example set by CEO Ken Lay.

Ken Lay had Enron . . . use his sister's travel agency. That gave millions of dollars to that agency and it was a wretched travel agency. The service wasn't even good and I can speak to that because I have some horror stories about their travel scheduling. This went on for years and years and years. Now, if you take someone like Andy Fastow who does not appear to have a good sense of right-and-wrong, that's telling him that "hey, my partnerships are helping Enron meet their financial statement targets so why shouldn't I carve some out for myself because Ken Lay has been carving some out for his sister?"[44]

He also abused the corporate jet in really onerous ways. He moved a stepdaughter back and forth to France—furniture, not her! . . . [O]nce again that sent a message to executives that when you get to the top, the company is there for you versus you being there to serve the company.[45]

Strategies and Policies

A critical function of managers is to create strong competitive strategies that enable a company to meet its strategic objectives without encouraging ethical compromise. In companies with deteriorating businesses, managers have great difficulty meeting performance targets and may feel pressure to compromise ethical standards. Even in strong companies, strategies must be executed with policies that reinforce honest achievement. Of special concern are unrealistic performance goals that pressure those who must make them work.

[43] Betsy Bernard, President AT&T, "Seven Golden Rules of Leadership," *Vital Speeches of the Day,* December 15, 2002, p. 155.

[44] Sherron S. Watkins, "Ethical Conflicts at Enron: Moral Responsibility in Corporate Capitalism," *California Management Review,* Summer 2003, p. 17.

[45] Sherron Watkins, "Pristine Ethics," *Vital Speeches of the Day,* May 1, 2003, p. 435.

At Lucent Technologies CEO Richard McGinn made the company's shares rocket by promising 20 percent yearly sales growth. Twice he missed quarterly targets and each time the stock plummeted. He could not miss again. Warned by subordinates that fourth quarter sales might fall short, he "went ballistic."[46] Under intense pressure to meet the revenue goal, the sales force reacted. It first offered legitimate discounts to customers, but the goal was still unmet. Other tactics then emerged from the shadows. Customers were given credits toward future purchases and these were booked as revenue in the fourth quarter. Revenues were booked when products were sold to distributors, not final customers, an unoriginal trick known as "channel stuffing." Told again by the head of sales that the revenue target was hopeless, McGinn said he would not take no for an answer. Ultimately, the target was missed. McGinn was fired. Lucent had to report that $679 million in fourth quarter revenue was unallowable. One sales agent lost his job for falsifying sales documents. McGinn later rationalized that he "never asked anyone to do anything untoward."

Reward and compensation systems can also expose employees to ethical compromises.

Ads for the Laser Vision Institute stated a fee of $499 per eye for laser surgery, although small type warned that the "price may vary according to RX and astigmatism." When prospects arrived they did not see physicians at first, instead, they met with counselors who decided what type of surgery the person needed and collected a deposit. What patients did not realize was that the counselors worked on an incentive system. They made yearly base salaries of $40,000 but added to their income with bonuses paid when patients were upgraded to more expensive surgeries. For the $499 procedure they got a per-eye bonus of only $1. But the amount rose with the surgery's price—$2 for a $599 surgery, $6 for the $799 procedure, $16 for $999, and so forth, up to $40 for patients paying $1,599. To be eligible for these bonuses the counselors had to have a 75 percent close rate on people who came in. It is no surprise, then, that prospects were subjected to aggressive tactics similar to those faced by car buyers and that, in the end, 88 percent paid more than $499.[47] Eventually, customers sued over "bait and switch" tactics and the Federal Trade Commission ordered the company to stop making false claims.[48]

When companies adopt policies that put employees under pressure, they should build in strong ethical rules too. When the tide of money runs high, shore up the ethical dikes.

Corporate Culture

corporate culture
A set of values, norms, rituals, formal rules, and physical artifacts that exists in a company.

Corporate culture refers to a set of values, norms, rituals, formal rules, and physical artifacts that exists in a company. Corporate cultures are powerful and deep. In the words of one scholar, they are "like water around fish." They evolve as companies cope with recurring stresses in their competitive environments.

[46] Quotes in this paragraph are from Dennis K. Berman and Rebecca Blumstein, "Behind Lucent's Woes: All-Out Revenue Goal and Pressure to Meet It," *The Wall Street Journal,* March 29, 2001, pp. A1 and A8.

[47] Marc Borbely, "Lasik Surgery Sales Tactics Raise Eyebrows," *Washington Post,* September 4, 2001, p. A1.

[48] *Majka v. Laser Vision Institute,* Fla. Civ. Div., 13th Cir., No. 03 7291 Div. H. (2003); Agreement Containing Consent Order, *In re The Laser Vision Institute,* No. 022-3098 (2003).

Over time, attitudes and behaviors that solve problems and bring success are reinforced and become permanent parts of the culture. Often the influence of a founder is important and lasting. Henry Ford's early philosophy of brutal labor policies endured so strongly that more than 50 years after his death Ford Motor had to root out pervasive authoritarianism in its management ranks before it could adapt more flexible manufacturing methods to compete with Japanese rivals.

According to a pioneering researcher, Edgar Schein, a corporate culture can be understood by separating it into three levels and reflecting on their relationship.[49] The first level is one of *artifacts,* which include both physical expressions of culture and visible behaviors. Physical elements include ways of dressing, office layouts, and symbolic displays such as picture walls of former executives. Visible behaviors include patterns of interaction, for example, the use of first or last names as an indication of formality, and the kinds of decisions made.

At the second level are the organization's *espoused values,* that is, formal statements of belief and intention. Espoused values are found in documents such as mission statements, codes of ethics, and employee handbooks. They state what the organization officially stands for. Often, inconsistencies are observed between the physical and behavioral artifacts on the first level and the espoused policies on the second level.

When such inconsistencies arise they are explained by the hidden influence of a third cultural level of *tacit underlying values.* At this level reside the deep, shared assumptions in the organization's culture about how things really work. These are the unspoken, unwritten beliefs about the nature of the company and what behaviors bring success. Though often unarticulated, these silent assumptions are usually the cause of deviation from nice-sounding espoused values.

A simple example of such an inconsistency is a company with a mission statement that emphasizes teamwork, but in which a visible artifact, a prominently placed employee-of-the-month award plaque, seems to contradict the official emphasis on teamwork. This may indicate that at the level of tacit underlying assumptions employees understand individual achievement as the route to promotion despite the mission statement's endorsement of teamwork.

All corporate cultures have ethical dimensions. When the behavior of employees fails to match the values in a written ethics code, it can be a reflection of silent assumptions lying deep in the culture that confute the code. For example, recent graduates of the Harvard MBA program who were interviewed about the ethical atmosphere in their organizations revealed the strong presence of four informal but powerful "commandments" conveyed to them early in their careers.

> First, performance is what really counts, so make your numbers. Second, be loyal and show us that you're a team player. Third, don't break the law. Fourth, don't overinvest in ethical behavior.[50]

[49] Edgar H. Schein, *The Corporate Culture Survival Guide* (San Francisco: Jossey-Bass, 1999), pp. 15–20.
[50] Joseph L. Badaracco, Jr., and Allen P. Webb, "Business Ethics: A View from the Trenches," *California Management Review,* Winter 1995, p. 11.

These "commandments" clearly strain the spirit of any strong corporate ethics code. When the contradictions between espoused values and underlying tacit assumptions grow too wide trouble is not far ahead. The story of Fannie Mae illustrates the point.

> Franklin D. Raines was a suave and exceptionally talented manager who became CEO of Fannie Mae, the giant mortgage company. Fannie Mae had a strong Ethical Responsibility Policy that called for "a corporate culture characterized by openness, integrity, responsibility, and accountability."[51] Raines often espoused these values of honesty and openness in talks to employees.
>
> However, in his first few months on the job, he discovered that Fannie Mae would miss earnings per share (EPS) targets that triggered maximum executive bonuses. Raines told the firm's controller to prepare a list of "alternative" accounting methods and in a meeting with senior managers it was agreed to use them to meet the targets. This action overrode the advice of both internal and external auditors and sent the message to the organization that meeting EPS goals was what mattered, not the way they were met.
>
> Next Raines set in motion a five-year plan to double EPS from $3.23 to $6.46 and again tied bonuses to meeting yearly EPS goals. He pushed the plan hard. What happened to the culture is encapsulated in a speech to Fannie Mae's internal auditors by their boss.
>
>> Be objective, be fair but tough . . . [and] never compromise or dilute your conclusions. . . . By now every one of you must have 6.46 branded in your brains. You must be able to say it in your sleep, you must be able to recite it forwards and backwards, you must have a raging fire in your belly that burns away all doubts, you must live, breath and dream 6.46, you must be obsessed on 6.46. . . . Remember Frank has given us an opportunity to earn not *just* our salaries . . . but substantially over and above if we make 6.46. . . . It is our *moral obligation* to . . . have made tangible contributions to Frank's goals.[52]
>
> The mixed message in this speech typified the pervasive conflict between espoused values of openness and honesty and the tacit underlying assumption that meeting EPS targets in any way possible was the road to success. The result was years of questionable accounting. Eventually, probes by regulators forced Raines and other top executives to resign and the company had to restate $6.3 billion in earnings.[53]

Cultures are resilient. Observers are always puzzled when corporations with strong ethics programs founder. Why after years of formal effort to make Shell Oil a more responsible corporation was the CEO caught leading other executives in a conspiracy to lie about the company's oil reserves? Why was the CEO of Boeing, an experienced executive brought out of retirement to elevate the company's ethics, forced to resign over an affair with a subordinate? Why, after years of effort to elevate its ethics, did Chiquita Brand's top executives and board of directors

---

[51] Warren B. Rudman, ed., *A Report to the Special Review Committee of the Board of Directors of Fannie Mae* (Washington, DC: Paul, Weiss, Rifkind, Wharton & Garrison, February 23, 2006), p. 439.

[52] Quoted in Office of Federal Housing Enterprise Oversight, *Report of the Special Examination of Fannie Mae* (Washington, DC: OFHEO, May 2006), p. 42.

[53] Eric Dash, "Ex-Officers Sued by U.S." *New York Times,* December 19, 2006, p. 1.

covertly approve illegal bribes, not once, but many times?[54] One explanation is that these are simply perverse actions by a few bad apples. But a better explanation, insofar as humans can know the source of evils in their nature, likely lies deeper, in the persistence of contradictions in corporate cultures. As the story of Consolidated Edison illustrates, cultures are extremely resistant to change.

> After a steam explosion that killed three people and sprayed asbestos over a Manhattan neighborhood Consolidated Edison plead guilty to four federal environmental crimes. Only two weeks later in a state court it accepted guilt for 319 environmental violations over many years. It entered an agreement for broad reform "from the chairman to the lineman" and the court appointed a monitor to supervise its efforts during three years of probation.[55]
>
> Edison's leadership rolled out a program of environmental responsibility. A new senior vice president for environmental affairs was put in charge. Two high-level environmental committees were formed to review progress. Every employee was made personally responsible for environmental safety and encouraged to raise problems openly. Any worker had the power to stop a job immediately on seeing a problem.
>
> However, violations continued. More than a year later the court-appointed monitor reported that workers who spoke out were being intimidated. When one employee complained about pollutants leaking into the Hudson River, a supervisor called him a "snake" and a "troublemaker."[56] Another was transferred from his job. The monitor believed the company nurtured a "destructive corporate culture" that inhibited environmental responsibility.
>
> This was correct. Although the espoused values of Consolidated Edison had been quickly elevated, tacit underlying assumptions were much slower to change. For decades its workers shared the assumption that keeping power on was the top priority. They went to heroic lengths to fix problems, often ignoring formal procedures to speed the job. The work culture required unquestioned obedience to supervisors. Group loyalty was strong. No one confronted co-workers about environmental hazards and no one ratted outside the group. Anyone who did was ostracized.[57] These underlying values endured, leading to repeated violations of the new environmental policies.

Individual Characteristics

Despite the importance of culture, individuals still matter. Behavior is motivated by a mixture of situational incentives and internal disposition. In a corporation with a dreary ethical climate, corrupt leaders, and high pressure to achieve numbers, otherwise honest individuals may buckle. However, internal disposition can be strong enough to resist the powerful atmospheric influence of culture. All things being equal, having employees of high character is best.

---

[54] Department of Justice, "Chiquita Brands International Pleads Guilty to Making Payments to a Designated Terrorist Organization ... ," press release, March 19, 2007.

[55] Joe Sexton, "Con Edison Agrees to $9 Million Fine for Contamination," *New York Times,* November 16, 1994, p. A1.

[56] Dan Van Natta, Jr., "Con Ed Cited in Intimidation of Employees," *New York Times,* December 19, 1995, p. B1.

[57] Edgar H. Schein, *The Corporate Culture Survival Guide,* pp. 153–55.

Researchers have tried to discover what personal qualities are associated with ethical behavior. However, strong relationships are elusive. There are indications that higher ethics come with advancing age and longer work experience.[58] Some studies show that women are more ethical than men, but results are mixed.[59] No studies find men to be more ethically sensitive than women, but some show no difference. A few studies suggest that people with more education are more ethical, but others do not. Similarly, some studies find that religious belief leads to more ethical attitudes, but many others fail to discover any relationship.[60] There is considerable evidence that the company environment influences conduct. Individuals seem to act less ethically as corporations increase in size, but they tend to be more ethical where companies have codes of conduct.[61]

HOW CORPORATIONS MANAGE ETHICS

ethics program
A coordinated application of management methods to prevent lawbreaking and promote more ethical behavior.

In the past, it was assumed that right and wrong were matters of individual conscience. A few pioneers tried to elevate companywide ethics. In 1913 James Cash Penney introduced a conduct code in his department stores. His effort was a lonely one. Until the 1980s, most companies had more formal policies for managing petty cash than for elevating ethics. Since then, more and more companies have set up *ethics programs,* or coordinated applications of management methods designed to prevent lawbreaking and promote more ethical behavior. In general, these programs originated in scandal and they continue to grow from it. Although a few companies voluntarily adopted ethics management systems, more have put them in place after being ordered to by courts, and the vast majority now use them to meet expanding statutory and regulatory requirements.

In response to a run of billing frauds and cost overruns in the 1980s, military contractors started the Defense Industry Initiative, a project requiring firms to adopt ethics codes and train employees to obey laws. More scandal-spawned ethics programs came in the mid-1990s, when the federal government cracked down on hospitals and nursing homes for Medicare billing fraud. Corporations in the health care industry rushed to follow the defense industry model.

The need to manage ethics was driven home in the 1996 *Caremark* case. Caremark International, a health care company, was caught giving kickbacks to physicians who referred patients to its clinics. After being indicted, the company set up a compliance program, but it was too late to prevent a $250 million fine. Angry

---

[58] Terry W. Low, Linda Ferrell, and Phylis Mansfield, "A Review of Empirical Studies Assessing Ethical Decision Making in Business," *Journal of Business Ethics,* June 2000, p. 185.

[59] See the discussion in A. Catherine McCabe, Rhea Ingram, and Mary Conway Data-on, "The Business of Ethics and Gender," *Journal of Business Ethics,* March 2006.

[60] Gary R. Weaver and Bradley R. Agle, "Religiosity and Ethical Behavior in Organizations: A Symbolic Interactionist Perspective," *Academy of Management Review,* January 2002, p. 79.

[61] See, for example, Marshall Schminke, "Considering the Business in Business Ethics: An Exploratory Study of the Influence of Organizational Size and Structure on Individual Ethical Predispositions," *Journal of Business Ethics,* April 2001.

Seven Steps for an Ethics Program

The U. S. Sentencing Commission sets forth these seven steps as minimally required to prevent criminal behavior and promote an ethical corporate culture. For federal prosecutors and regulators they define an acceptable effort by managers to ensure that companies and their employees follow the law.

1. Establish standards and procedures.
2. Create high-level oversight.
3. Screen out criminals.
4. Communicate standards to all employees.
5. Monitor and set up a hotline.
6. Enforce standards, discipline violators.
7. Assess areas of risk, modify the program.

Source: *Guidelines Manual,* §8B2.1, effective November 1, 2004.

shareholders sued its directors for breach of duty because they had not set up an ethics program earlier and this omission had exposed the firm to a big fine. Caremark's directors narrowly escaped paying damages from their own pockets after a settlement. However, the judge who approved the settlement made it plain that if directors fail to set up management systems promoting lawful behavior they can be held liable for fines.[62]

Meanwhile, the United States Sentencing Commission in 1991 established the first sentencing guidelines. As previously explained, these guidelines set up systems of penalty and fine calculations for both managers and corporations. They allow major reductions in fines and penalties for companies with ethics programs. These reductions are a major incentive.

After the turn-of-the-century fraud scandals new regulatory compulsion for ethics programs was forthcoming. Congress created new requirements for anti-fraud mechanisms when it passed the Sarbanes-Oxley Act in 2002, including a code of ethics for financial officers, a mechanism for reporting illegal behavior, and protection for employees who reveal fraud. Both the Department of Justice and the Securities and Exchange Commission adopted guidelines on prosecuting corporations for crimes, taking the presence of legal compliance efforts into consideration. The New York Stock Exchange required that listed companies have in place a code of ethics and procedures to enforce it.[63]

While there is no standard format for ethics programs the U.S. Sentencing Commission's *Guidelines Manual* sets forth seven minimal steps that define a diligent effort (see the box). Many companies explicitly follow these steps and others create processes that meet their general requirements in a variety of ways. The seven steps provide a convenient framework for explaining the basic elements of corporate ethics programs.

---

[62] *In re Caremark International Inc. Derivative Litigation,* 698 A.2d 970 (1996).

[63] New York Stock Exchange, *Listing Manual,* §303 A. 10, "Code of Business Conduct and Ethics," last modified November 3, 2004. The NASDAQ Stock Market has adopted similar code of conduct requirements.

THE GE Code of Conduct

- Obey the applicable laws and regulations governing our business conduct worldwide.
- Be honest, fair and trustworthy in all your GE activities and relationships.
- Avoid all conflicts of interest between work and personal affairs.
- Foster an atmosphere in which fair employment practices extend to every member of the diverse GE community.

- Strive to create a safe workplace and to protect the environment.
- Through leadership at all levels, sustain a culture where ethical conduct is recognized, valued and exemplified by all employees.

Source: General Electric Company, *Integrity: The Spirit & the Letter of Our Commitment,* June 2005, p. 3.

1. *Establish standards and procedures to prevent and detect criminal conduct.* Companies meet this requirement with a variety of written documents. The centerpiece is often a short statement of guidelines at a high level of abstraction. An example is GE's (see the box). Most companies also set forth a more detailed code of conduct, often in a booklet of 20 to 50 pages in length. Some begin with a list of basic values such as honesty, integrity, fairness, respect for others, obedience to the law, citizenship, and responsibility that should characterize employee behavior. Then they set forth brief guidance in a range of problem areas, including conflict of interest, bribery, gifts, insider trading, antitrust violations, trade secrets, political contributions, and discrimination. These relatively brief treatments are backed by dozens of long and detailed corporate policy documents, so that the complete "code of ethics" of a large company may run hundreds of pages.

Conduct codes contain typical elements, introductions by CEOs, ways to report wrongdoing, tips for making ethical decisions, and disciplinary procedures. There is inexhaustible sameness in both the content and format of corporate codes. They are saturated with similar principles, cover much the same lists of ethical issues, and contain virtually identical guides for reporting concerns. Creativity comes at the margins. Dow Chemical's colorful *Code of Business Conduct: Integrity in Action* booklet contains simple cases in question and answer format. Here is an example from the section on accounting integrity.

Q: I ordered some software and my supervisor is asking me to record the charge against another expense category because our budget for software has been exceeded. What should I do?

A: Remind your supervisor that no one should knowingly make an incorrect record in the books and records of our company. If your supervisor persists, contact your supervisor's supervisor or the Office of Global Ethics and Compliance.

Codes are usually distributed to all employees, who may be asked to sign a form certifying compliance. Multinational companies translate them into multiple languages. Merck's *Values and Standards* booklet is written in 25 languages.[64] Statements in codes mean little without further steps to ensure fidelity to them. Enron had a typical "Code of Ethics" that was based on four principles—"respect, integrity, communication, and excellence"—but it was not well enforced.

2. *Give oversight of the program to the board of directors and assign responsibility for it to a high-level executive who, in turn, will assign day-to-day responsibility to a specific manager.* The *Guidelines Manual* requires that the board of directors exercise "reasonable oversight" over an ethics and compliance program, that one or more top executives take responsibility for it, and that specific managers be assigned day-to-day supervision. An example of a structure that meets these requirements is the Abbott Laboratories program shown in Figure 7.3. This structure is the result of a strengthened compliance effort coming after the FBI uncovered a 10-year fraud to cheat customers and Abbott paid $614 million in fines.[65]

At Abbott a vice president and chief ethics and compliance officer takes day-to-day responsibility for running the program. This ethics chief reports directly to Abbott's top executive, the chairman of the board and CEO, and also reports directly to the board of directors through periodic reports to its Public Policy Committee and annual reports to the full board. In addition, the ethics chief chairs a Business Conduct Committee that includes the heads of Abbott's business divisions, which are found in its four operating groups, and staff experts in ethics-related areas.

Below the ethics chief the program structure reaches down into the organization. Each business division has an ethics and compliance officer who reports to a divisional vice president of ethics and compliance, who in turn reports back to the corporate ethics chief. In this way the program parallels Abbott's operating structure. Note how a reporting chain for the ethics staff is created separately from the line chain of command all the way up to the board of directors. This separation is an important check and balance. If ethics officers reported only to division managers, without a separate ethics reporting channel, they would have less independence. Some companies have made this mistake.[66]

3. *Exclude individuals with a history of illegal or unethical conduct from positions of substantial authority.* Background checks for criminal records are inexpensive. Companies that fail to conduct them can be surprised, as was Smith & Wesson Holding Corp. on discovering that its chairman was the notorious "Shotgun Bandit" who had terrorized victims in a string of armed robberies years before.[67]

---

[64] Raymond V. Gilmartin, *Ethics and the Corporate Culture* (Waltham, MA: Bentley College Center for Business Ethics, November 10, 2003), p. 12.

[65] Department of Health and Human Services and Department of Justice, *Health Care Fraud and Abuse Control Program: Annual Report FY2004* (Washington, DC: HHS and DOJ, September 2005), p. 13.

[66] Notable is scandal-ridden Tyco International, which had general counsel charged with compliance oversight in business segments reporting to the segment managers. See Eric M. Pillmore, "How We're Fixing Up Tyco," *Harvard Business Review,* December 2003, pp. 100–01.

[67] Vanessa O'Connell, "How Troubled Past Finally Caught Up with James Minder," *The Wall Street Journal,* March 8, 2001, p. A1.

FIGURE 7.3   Oversight Structure of Abbott Laboratories' Ethics and Compliance Program

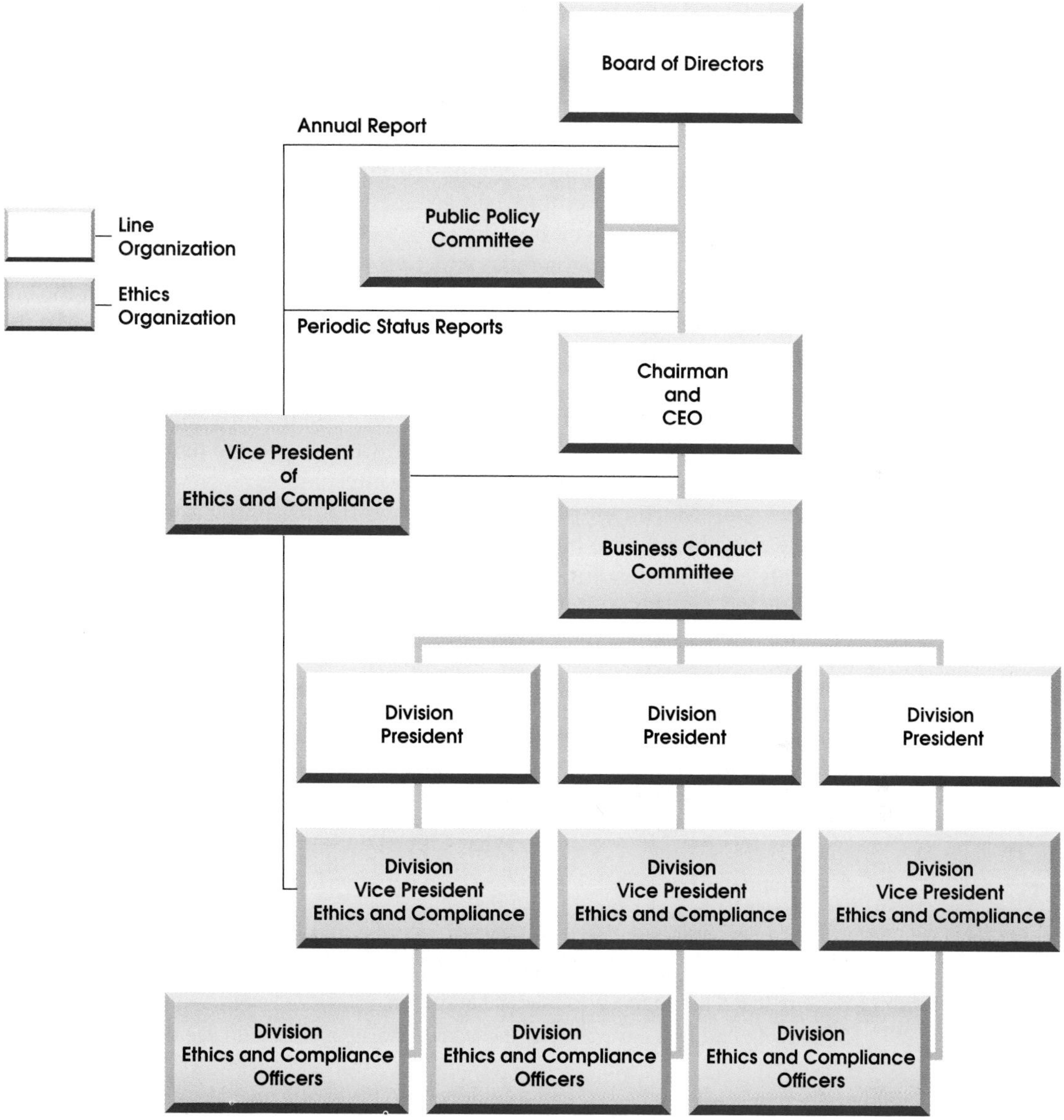

Companies also check for false claims about education and job experience on résumés. Is it possible to detect a corrupt disposition? Paper-and-pencil honesty tests are effective in screening out thieves among applicants for low-level positions. But it is unlikely that the attitudes about stealing that they measure are useful for appraising the inner character required for ethical leadership by higher-level managers.

Some psychologists believe that integrity can be tested in interviews. One expert recommends building rapport with the subject, then eliciting comments on ethical issues late in an interview. He suggests these inquiries. "Give me an example of an ethical decision you have had to make on the job." "Have you ever had to bend the rules or exaggerate a little bit when trying to make a sale?" and "Tell me about an instance when you've had to go against company guidelines or procedures to get something done."[68]

4. *Periodically communicate standards and procedures to all employees from the lowest up to the board of directors.* Companies emphasize ethics using everything from T-shirts to newsletters. At MCI every employee's security badge has the phrase "do the right thing" printed on it. However, training is the key to communicating ethics.

Generally, ethics training is most effective when company managers do it, not outsiders, and when it steers away from abstract philosophy to focus on the work lives of attendees. A few companies offer in-depth seminars lasting one to three days with discussion of policies and case studies. Briefer sessions are more typical. One-to-three hour yearly sessions in which employees see a video and discuss cases are common. Also popular are interactive sessions on a company Web site or intranet in which employees read short case studies and try to pick the correct or most ethical responses from multiple-choice alternatives.

At Lockheed Martin employees attend two-hour training sessions where they watch a video, then divide into small groups to discuss short cases. The groups are told to rate alternative solutions for each situation using an "Ethics Effect" meter that allows rating a character's actions on a five-point scale from "highly ethical" to "highly unethical." Here is an example.

> On his way to lunch, Charlie cuts his leg on a desk drawer that was not completely closed. Charlie's supervisor has been talking for weeks that the group's injury performance had been good but one more incident would break the Target Zero goal for the department. Chloe, a co-worker, notices that Charlie hurt himself. Charlie asks her not to say anything.

What Chloe Did:

1. Reminded Charlie that Target Zero is an initiative to achieve an accident-free workplace, not an initiative to underreport or ignore accidents. Charlie then reported the incident to his supervisor and sought medical attention. *(Highly Ethical)*
2. Reported the incident to their supervisor so he could report the incident and ensure that Charlie receives medical attention. *(Ethically Sound)*
3. Having had first aid training, she asked Charlie if she could see the wound. *(Gray Area)*
4. Kept the issue to herself and told nobody. *(Unethical)*
5. Talked to co-workers and said that Charlie's silence is proof that all the company wants are lower accident rates at the expense of employees. *(Highly Unethical)*[69]

5. *Monitor the organization for criminal conduct, and set up a system for reporting of suspicious conduct without fear of retaliation.* Monitoring entails collection of data related to illegal activity. For example, some companies require reports of unusual

[68] William C. Byham, "Can You Interview for Integrity?" *Across the Board*, March/April 2004, pp. 36–37.

[69] Lockheed Martin, *The 2005 Ethics Effect: Leader's Guide,* at www.lockheedmartin.com/ethicsawarenesstraining/, p. 5.

financial transactions. Ethical audits can also detect problems. HCA Healthcare Corp. conducts two-day ethical compliance audits to reveal strengths and weaknesses at its hospitals. Employees are interviewed randomly as auditors cover a 53-page checklist.

Most programs have 24-hour toll-free telephone and e-mail hotlines for anonymous reporting of problems. To protect users' identities, these hotlines are sometimes managed by outside parties. Many whistle-blowers are suspicious and fear revenge, so hotlines must be supported with strong policies against retaliation. On average, between 2 and 4 percent of employees use hotlines each year and these calls create an enormous amount of work for ethics offices. Many callers seek advice: "Would it be a conflict of interest for me to work in the evening?" Others have trivial complaints, such as "My supervisor came back an hour late from lunch." Allegations must be investigated; for instance, "I think one of my team members is harassing a co-worker." Although few calls reveal criminal wrongdoing, hotlines open a critical channel of communication for those who might be intimidated by speaking to superiors.

6. *Enforce standards by providing both incentives to reward compliance and discipline to deter criminal conduct.* It has been objected that doing the right thing should require no incentive, however, many companies link ethics to performance reviews, promotions, and compensation. This seems like a powerful incentive, but in practice it is often difficult to rate ethical performance. Tenet Healthcare tried to tie the bonuses of its top 800 managers to a numerical ethics score between −5 and +5, with each point changing the bonus by 5 percent. Managers felt humiliated, however, when they received negatives scores, called "dings" in company slang.[70]

At Boeing, compliance with the company's ethics code is part of every employee's evaluation. But according to a report on Boeing's ethics program, it almost never affects the outcome.

> Managers perceive pressure (often self-imposed) not to rate any employee as below average in ethics. There is also resistance against rating any employee above average, as that implies that other employees are not doing as well with ethical conduct. The strong tendency, therefore, is to award all employees an average score for this component, effectively rendering it meaningless.[71]

Written disciplinary policies are widespread. Discipline is usually based on factors such as seriousness of the violation, the organizational level or leadership role of the violator, extent of cooperation with the investigation, prior misconduct, and willfulness of the action. A progressive range of disciplinary options—counseling,

---

[70] Andrew W. Singer, "At Tenet Healthcare: Linking Ethics to Compensation" *Ethikos,* January–February 2001, pp. 4–5.

[71] Warren B. Rudman et al., *A Report to the Chairman and Board of Directors of the Boeing Company Concerning the Company's Ethics Program and Its Rules and Procedures for the Treatment of Competitors' Proprietary Information* (Washington, DC: Paul, Weiss, Rifkind, Wharton & Garrison LLP, November 3, 2003), p. 36.

oral reprimand, written reprimand, probation, suspension, salary reduction, termination—can be used as fits the case.

7. *If criminal conduct occurs, modify the program to prevent repeat offenses. Periodically assess the risks of criminal conduct and try to reduce them.* Unless lawbreaking is the isolated failure of one person, the program is not working. It should be modified by changing or adding elements, restructuring responsibilities, or reappraising the culture in which it operates.

Ethical risk assessment is an emerging art. The *Guidelines Manual* suggests that companies examine the nature of their business for risks, then take action to reduce them. General Electric, for example, formed a risk committee of its top executives that meets quarterly to assess changing global ethical standards. This committee then decides whether GE should alter existing standards or adopt new ones.[72]

ETHICS PROGRAMS: A STRONG FUTURE?

Almost all large, publicly traded companies now have a set of interrelated policies and procedures to enforce ethical standards. Do the programs work? Since their spread is so recent, it is difficult to say that they have reduced criminal and unethical behavior. There are conspicuous examples of failure. Enron had a state-of-the-art code of conduct. Tenet Healthcare, Boeing, and Chiquita Brands were once viewed as exemplars of broad ethics and compliance efforts, but were nonetheless scandalized. In such cases we suspect lack of earnestness. Some companies fail to make the necessary resources available for the program. Sometimes ethics program managers are marginalized and have little influence.[73] Top executives can undermine formal efforts by lack of strong leadership by example. In such cases silent assumptions deep in the corporate culture can work to undermine official intentions.

These efforts are young and there is still much to be learned about teaching ethics to an organization. Despite trying for more than two millennia to overcome individual malfeasance there is little progress. We should not be too hasty in hoping for better results with organizations. What is clear is that collective behavior will deteriorate unless managers use the ethics and compliance tools at their disposal.

CONCLUDING OBSERVATIONS

The business environment is rich in sources of ethical values. Yet strong forces in both markets and corporations act to depress behavior. Managers can use a range of methods to discourage transgression and encourage high ethics. Likewise, individuals have a range of principles with which to enrich their ethical thinking and powerful methods with which to make ethical decisions. In the next chapter we take a closer look at individual decisions.

---

[72] Ben W. Heineman, Jr., "Avoiding Integrity Land Mines," *Harvard Business Review,* April 2007, p. 104.

[73] "Corporate Crime and Prosecution: An Interview with Win Swenson," *Multinational Monitor,* November/December 2005, p. 72.

The Trial of Martha Stewart

From indictment to sentencing, the case of Martha Stewart was a matter of intense public interest. Some thought that her misdeeds, if any, were slight. Cynics believed that in the wake of corporate scandals the government was prosecuting a celebrity for a minor infraction to show it was tough on business crime. An indignant *Wall Street Journal* complained that innocent employees and shareholders of Martha Stewart Living Omnimedia were paying the price for the government's zeal.[1] Feminists argued that she was picked on for being a successful woman. "It's hard to imagine a male in precisely this spot," said Mary Becker, a DePaul University law professor. "Targeting a successful woman is very consistent with dominant cultural values."[2]

Others believed that her prosecution was justified. "I don't buy any of it," wrote Scott Turow, a criminal defense lawyer and the author of best-selling legal fiction. "What the jury felt Martha Stewart did—lying about having received inside information before she traded—is wrong, really wrong."[3]

This is the story.

DECEMBER 27

On the morning of Thursday, December 27, 2001, Douglas Faneuil was on duty at the mid-Manhattan office of Merrill Lynch. Faneuil, 24, who had been in his job only six months, assisted a stockbroker named Peter Bacanovic. It was two days after Christmas and Bacanovic was on vacation. Staffing was thin and Faneuil expected a slow day with light trading.

Soon Faneuil took a call from Aliza Waksal. Aliza was the daughter of Samuel Waksal, cofounder of ImClone Systems, a biopharmaceutical company. She wanted to sell her ImClone shares. Faneuil executed the order and by 9:48 A.M. her 39,472 shares had been sold for $2,472,837. Then Faneuil had a call from Samuel Waksal's accountant requesting that another 79,797 shares held in his Merrill Lynch account be transferred

to Aliza's account and then sold. The call was followed by a written direction saying that making the transfer and sale that morning was imperative.

Faneuil sought help on the transfer and called Peter Bacanovic in Florida. Bacanovic, 39, was an old friend of Waksal's. He had worked at ImClone for two years before coming to Merrill Lynch and he handled the personal accounts of Waksal and his daughter. When Bacanovic learned that the Waksals were selling, he instructed Faneuil immediately to call another of his clients, Martha Stewart, while he remained on the line.

Bacanovic, who was active in New York social life, first met Martha Stewart in the mid-1980s when they were introduced by her daughter Alexis. Stewart was one of his most important clients. He handled her pension and personal accounts. He also handled accounts for her company, Martha Stewart Living Omnimedia, Inc. Two years earlier, he had directed part of the firm's initial public offering and now he administered both its 401(k) and employee stock option accounts.

At 10:04 A.M. Faneuil dialed Stewart, but reached her administrative assistant Ann Armstrong, who said that Stewart was on an airplane. Bacanovic left a brief message, asking Stewart to call back when she became available. In her phone log, Armstrong wrote "Peter Bacanovic thinks ImClone is going to start trading downward." Bacanovic instructed Faneuil that when Stewart called back he should tell her that the Waksals were selling all their shares. At this time ImClone was priced at $61.53 a share.

This instruction from Bacanovic bothered Faneuil. Merrill Lynch had a written policy (see Exhibit 1) that required its employees to hold client information in strict confidence. But he was very busy and working under a sense of urgency, handling calls from the Waksals, and making calls to Merrill Lynch staff in several offices arranging the transfer of Sam Waksal's shares.

Several hours later, Stewart's plane landed in San Antonio to refuel. She went into the airport and on her cell phone called Ann Armstrong to check for messages. At 1:39 P.M. she phoned Merrill Lynch, reaching Faneuil, who told her that Sam Waksal and his daughter had sold all of their shares. She asked for the current price of ImClone. Faneuil

[1] "The Trials of Martha," *The Wall Street Journal,* February 13, 2004, p. A12.

[2] Quoted in Jonathan D. Glater, "Stewart's Celebrity Created Magnet for Scrutiny," *New York Times, sec.* 1, p. 1.

[3] Scott Turow, "Cry No Tears for Martha Stewart," *New York Times,* May 27, 2004, p. 29.

EXHIBIT 1
Client
Information
Privacy Policy

Merrill Lynch protects the confidentiality and security of client information. Employees must understand the need for careful handling of this information. Merrill Lynch's client information privacy policy provides that—

...

- Employees may not discuss the business affairs of any client with any other employee, except on a strict need-to-know basis.
- We do not release client information, except upon a client's authorization or when permitted or required by law.

quoted approximately $58 a share. Stewart told him to sell all 3,928 shares she owned.

She hung up and immediately put in a call to Sam Waksal. The two were close friends who had been introduced by Stewart's daughter Alexis in the early 1990s. Unable to reach him, she left a message that his assistant took down as "Martha Stewart something is going on with ImClone and she wants to know what."[4] By 1:52 P.M. Stewart's ImClone shares had been sold at an average price of $58.43, for a total of approximately $228,000.

THE PUZZLE OF THE WAKSAL TRADES

What *was* going on with ImClone? For almost 10 years Waksal had put ImClone's resources into the development of a promising new colon cancer drug named Erbitux. Two months earlier, ImClone had submitted a licensing application for approval of Erbitux to the Food and Drug Administration (FDA). On December 26, Waksal learned from an ImClone executive that, according to a source within the FDA, on December 28 ImClone would receive a letter rejecting the Erbitux application. When the FDA's action was publicly announced ImClone's share price was sure to plummet.

Waksal was in possession of material insider information. It was material because any reasonable investor would find it important in deciding to buy or sell ImClone stock. It was insider information because it was not yet known to the public. Since the FDA application was so critical, ImClone's general counsel had declared a "blackout period" after December 21 when employees should not trade ImClone

[4] Complaint, *Securities and Exchange Commission v. Martha Stewart and Peter Bacanovic,* 03CV 4070 (NRB)(S.D.N.Y.), June 4, 2003, p. 7.

shares. The purpose of the "blackout" was to guard against illegal insider trading.

Despite being informed of the "blackout" and despite possessing knowledge of the law with respect to insider trading, Waksal elected to sell. This was exceptionally foolish. His motive was to escape the unpleasant consequences of debt. He had obligations of $75 million, most of which was margin debt secured by shares he owned in ImClone. Servicing this debt was costing him $800,000 a month. He knew that if ImClone's share price slipped very far many of his shares would be sold, dramatically lowering his net worth. He also tipped family and friends to sell on December 27. Besides his daughter Aliza, his father Jack sold 135,000 shares, his sister Patti sold 1,336 shares, and another daughter, Elana, sold 4,000 shares. Besides family members, Waksal tipped an investment adviser who sold all of her 1,178 shares on December 27 and passed the tip to a physician on one of ImClone's advisory boards, who sold more than $5 million in shares—all he owned—on the same day.

On Friday, December 28, the FDA faxed ImClone a "refusal to file" letter at 2:55 P.M. Later in the afternoon, after the market closed with ImClone trading at $55.25 a share, the company issued a press release disclosing the FDA's action. On December 31, the next trading day, ImClone opened at $45.39 a share. If Martha Stewart had waited until then to sell her shares, she would have gotten about $178,292 or $49,708 less than she received by selling on the afternoon of December 27. ImClone closed on December 31 at $46.46. It had dropped about 16 percent on the news of the FDA's action.

AN UNSETTLED AFTERMATH

Four days later a supervisor at Merrill Lynch contacted Faneuil to question him about the ImClone trades. Afterwards, Faneuil called Bacanovic, who was still vacationing in Florida. Bacanovic told him that Martha Stewart sold her shares because of a pre-arranged plan to reduce her taxes. He told Faneuil about a December 20 telephone call in which he and Stewart had gone down a list of the stock holdings in her account and decided which ones to sell at a loss to balance out capital gains from other sales during 2001. Soon, however, Faneuil had a call from Eileen DeLuca, Martha Stewart's business manager, who demanded to know why the ImClone shares had been sold, since the sale had resulted in a profit that disrupted her tax-loss selling plan. Again he called Bacanovic. This time, Bacanovic told him that Stewart had sold because they had a preexisting agreement to sell ImClone if the price fell below $60 a share.

Merrill Lynch had called the Securities and Exchange Commission (SEC) to report suspicions of insider trading in ImClone. On January 3, 2002, attorneys at the SEC called Faneuil to interview him about the events of December 27. Faneuil told them that Stewart had sold because the price of ImClone fell below $60 a share. He did not tell them that he had conveyed news about the Waksals' sales to her. On January 7, SEC attorneys interviewed Bacanovic on the telephone. He told them that he spoke to Martha Stewart on the day she traded and recommended that she sell based on their preexisting $60 sell agreement.

On January 16, Martha Stewart and Peter Bacanovic had a breakfast meeting. Their conversation is unrecorded. According to Faneuil, after the meeting Bacanovic told him, "I've spoken to Martha. I've met with her. And everyone's telling the same story. . . . This was a $60 stop-loss order. That was the reason for her sale. We're all on the same page, and it's the truth."[5] In at least five subsequent conversations Bacanovic reassured Faneuil of the need to stick to this story. If he did, Bacanovic promised to give him extra compensation.

On January 30, in response to a request for documents by SEC investigators, Bacanovic turned over the worksheet that he said was used in his December 20 tax sale conversation with Martha Stewart. The worksheet was a single-page printout listing approximately 40 securities in her account and noting the number of shares and the purchase price. On the worksheet, near the entry for ImClone, the notation "@60" appeared.

On January 31, Martha Stewart had a lengthy conversation with a criminal attorney. Following the conversation she went to her assistant Ann Armstrong asking to see the telephone log. Sitting at Armstrong's computer, she changed Bacanovic's December 27 phone message from "Peter Bacanovic thinks ImClone is going to start trading downward," to "Peter Bacanovic re imclone."[6] Then, thinking better of it, she told Armstrong to restore the original wording and left.

INTERVIEWS

On February 2, Martha Stewart was interviewed in New York by attorneys from the SEC, the Federal Bureau of Investigation (FBI), and the U.S. Attorney's Office. Asked to explain her ImClone transaction, she said that she and Bacanovic had decided to sell if ImClone fell below $60 a share. On December 27 she had spoken to Bacanovic, who told her it had fallen below $60 and inquired if she wished to sell. She had assented, in part, because she was on vacation and did not want to worry about the stock market. She did not recall speaking to Faneuil on that day. She denied knowledge of the December 27 phone message from Bacanovic, even though only two days before she had gone to her assistant's computer to alter its wording. According to one attorney present, at the end of the interview Stewart asked in a "curt, annoyed" tone, "Can I go now? I have a business to run."[7]

On February 13, Bacanovic was subpoenaed by the SEC to testify under oath in New York. He reported a December 20 phone call with Stewart in which he recommended the sale of ImClone if it fell below $60. The worksheet he turned over to the agency had notes of this conversation. He also stated that he had not discussed the matter of the ImClone stock sale with Stewart since December 27. Yet records of calls between Bacanovic's and Stewart's cell phones show that by this time they had spoken often, including once on the day of Stewart's interview in New York. The content of their conversations is unrecorded.

[6] Matthew Rose and Kara Scannell, "Dramatic Flourishes at Stewart, Tyco Trials," *The Wall Street Journal,* February 11, 2004, p. C1.

[7] Thomas S. Mulligan, "Jurors Hear of Attempt by Stewart to Alter Phone Log," *Los Angeles Times,* February 11, 2004, p. C7.

[5] Brooke A. Masters, "Stewart Ordered Sale, Says Witness," *Washington Post,* February 5, 2004, p. E1.

On March 7, Douglas Faneuil was interviewed by SEC attorneys and an FBI agent. Details of this session have not been made public, but his subsequent indictment alleges that he failed to fully and truthfully disclose all he knew about the events of December 27.[8] Following the interview, Bacanovic offered Faneuil an extra week of vacation and paid airfare for a trip as a reward for sticking to Bacanovic's script.[9]

On April 10, Stewart was interviewed again on the telephone by investigators from the SEC, FBI, and U.S. Attorney's Office. She told them that she had spoken with Bacanovic on December 27, but she could not remember if Bacanovic had mentioned the Waksals. She said again that the two had set up a $60 sell order on ImClone.

TURMOIL

After these interviews, government investigators continued with the painstaking work of gathering, verifying, and interpreting details. Meanwhile, the main actors in the ImClone trades struggled in the backwash from their actions. In late May, Samuel Waksal resigned as the CEO of ImClone. In early June, the Associated Press broke the story that Martha Stewart had sold ImClone the day before the FDA's decision on Erbitux, setting off a three-week decline in the share price of Martha Stewart Living Omnimedia from $19.01 to $11.47. Merrill Lynch suspended Peter Bacanovic without pay.

When Waksal was arrested and charged with criminal insider trading on June 12, shares in Stewart's company fell 5.6 percent. Waksal would eventually plead guilty to insider trading charges, receive a prison sentence of 87 months, and pay a fine of $4 million, which covered civil penalties for insider trading by members of his family. The family members were forced to disgorge the profits from their trades, with interest, and the two other tippees—the investment adviser and the physician, paid disgorgement of profits, interest, and civil fines totaling $112,000 and $2.7 million, respectively.

Stewart issued a statement after the close of trading in which she said that she and her broker had agreed on a $60 sell order in October 2001, that he had called her on December 27 and told her ImClone was trading under $60, and that she had told him to sell in

line with their prior understanding. She denied having any nonpublic information at the time. Later in the month she repeated this story at a conference for securities analysts and investors. Her intent was to halt the decline in her company's shares. At this time she held 61,323,850 shares, so she suffered paper losses of more than $462 million in the three-week share price decline.

Douglas Faneuil's conscience bothered him. In late June he went to a manager at Merrill Lynch and volunteered what he believed was the complete and accurate story of December 27 and its aftermath. Subsequently, he spoke again to government investigators, who then subpoenaed both Stewart and Bacanovic to testify at an investigative hearing. This time, both declined, invoking their Fifth Amendment privilege against self-incrimination. Faneuil pled guilty to a misdemeanor charge of accepting money from Bacanovic in return for not informing federal investigators of illegal conduct. Merrill Lynch fired Bacanovic.

INDICTMENTS

It took the government a year and a half, but on June 4, 2003, in a "coordinated action," both the U.S. Attorney's Office and the SEC filed indictments against Martha Stewart and Peter Bacanovic.

The U.S. Attorney's Office filed a criminal complaint with multiple counts under the basic charges of, first, conspiracy, and second, obstruction of justice and making false statements.[10] The two were charged with conspiring to conceal evidence that Bacanovic had provided nonpublic information about ImClone to Stewart. And they were accused of lying to government attorneys to hamper their investigation. In addition, only Martha Stewart was charged with securities fraud. The charge was that she had made a series of false statements about her innocence to mislead investors and prop up her company's share price. Conviction on all counts could bring a maximum of 30 years in prison and a fine of $2 million. Bacanovic alone was additionally charged with perjury for altering the worksheet that listed Stewart's stocks by adding "@60" near ImClone to fool investigators. He faced a maximum of 25 years in prison and a $1.25 million fine.

---

[8] Misdemeanor Information, *United States v. Faneuil,* 02 Cr. 1287, S.D.N.Y. (2002), pp. 7–8.

[9] Ibid., p. 8.

[10] *United States v. Martha Stewart and Peter Bacanovic,* 03 Cr. 717 (MGC)(S.D.N.Y.), 2003.

In its separate civil action, the SEC charged Stewart and Bacanovic with insider trading.[11] It sought disgorgement of illegal gains and the imposition of a fine. In addition, it sought to bar Stewart from acting as a director or officer of a public company.

Martha Stewart's lawyers immediately issued a statement challenging the government's case. "Martha Stewart has done nothing wrong," they said. They accused the government of making an "unprecedented" interpretation of the securities laws when it charged her with fraudulent manipulation simply because she spoke out publicly to maintain her innocence. And they questioned the government's motive for the other charges, raising themes that would course through the media during the subsequent trial.

> Is it for publicity purposes because Martha Stewart is a celebrity? Is it because she is a woman who has successfully competed in a man's business world by virtue of her talent, hard work and demanding standards? Is it because the government would like to be able to define securities fraud as whatever it wants it to be?[12]

A week later, Martha Stewart went to the FBI's Manhattan office for processing. She was given a mug shot, fingerprinted, and released without bail. She also resigned her positions as director and chief creative officer of Martha Stewart Living Omnimedia, taking on the nonofficer position of founding editorial director. She continued to receive her annual salary of $900,000 and in 2003 she was awarded an additional $500,000 bonus.

THE TRIAL OPENS

On January 20, 2004, Martha Stewart and Peter Bacanovic appeared in the Manhattan courtroom of the Hon. Miriam Goldman Cedarbaum, a federal district court judge with 18 years bench experience. They entered pleas of not guilty and jury selection for a trial began. Potential jurors were given 35 pages of questions designed to detect biases. One question was, "Have you ever made a project or cooked a recipe

from Martha Stewart?"[13] After interviews by attorneys for all sides in Judge Cedarbaum's office, a jury of eight women and four men was picked.

The trial began on January 27. The lead prosecutor was Assistant U.S. Attorney Karen Patton Seymour. In her opening argument she told the jury that Martha Stewart sold ImClone after a "secret tip" from Bacanovic that the Waksals were selling. Then, she and Bacanovic tried to cover it up. Stewart's motive, she argued, was a desire to protect her "multimillion dollar business empire." Seymour pointed out that every $1 decline in the price of Martha Stewart's company decreased her net worth by $30 million. "Ladies and gentlemen," she said, "lying to federal agents, obstructing justice, committing perjury, fabricating evidence and cheating investors in the stock market—these are serious federal crimes."[14]

In his opening argument Stewart's attorney, Robert G. Morvillo, pronounced her "innocent of all charges" and tried to offer reasonable explanations for her actions. He pointed out that the ImClone shares she sold were less than 1 percent of her net worth. He told the jury that December was a busy month for her and she gets worn out. When she called Faneuil about the trade she was in a noisy airport on her cell phone and thought she was talking to Bacanovic. She had no way of knowing that insider trading was taking place. "How," he asked, "was she supposed to figure out the broker, who has always been honorable, was asking her to commit a crime?" If, indeed, she had been told that Waksal and his daughter were selling, it meant that Merrill Lynch was making the sales, which it would not do if it believed them to be illegal.

Morvillo explained that Stewart and Bacanovic had established a $60 sell agreement the week before her trades. And he called Stewart's alteration of her assistant's entry in the phone log "much ado about nothing." He said that she was changing it "to be consistent with what she recalled," but then quickly realized that her change "might be misconstrued." He concluded his lengthy opening statement by asking the jury to "decide the case based upon what is correct and just."[15]

---

[11] *Securities and Exchange Commission v. Martha Stewart and Peter Bacanovic,* 03 CV 4070 (NRB)(S.D.N.Y), 2003.

[12] Robert G. Morvillo and John J. Tigue, "Press Statement," June 4, 2003, at www.marthatalks.com/trial.

[13] Thomas S. Mulligan, "Stewart Case Poses Challenges for All Parties as Trial Begins Today," *Los Angeles Times,* January 20, 2004, p. C1.

[14] Kara Scannel and Matthew Rose, "Early Sparks at the Stewart Trial," *The Wall Street Journal,* January 28, 2004, p. C1.

[15] Quotations of Morvillo are from "Opening Argument on Behalf of Martha Stewart," January 27, 2004, at www.marthatalks.com/trial.

TESTIMONY

Key witnesses for the government were Helen Glotzer, an SEC attorney, and Catherine Farmer, an FBI agent. Both had been present at interviews of Stewart and Bacanovic and both testified about apparent false statements they made, including Stewart's denial that she spoke with Faneuil on December 27 and her denial that she knew that the Waksals were selling.

The government's star witness, however, was Douglas Faneuil. Under questioning by Seymour, Faneuil described his morning phone call to Bacanovic on December 27. On learning that the Waksals were selling Bacanovic said: "Oh my God, you've got to get Martha on the phone!" Faneuil said that he then asked Bacanovic, "Can I tell her about Sam? Am I allowed to?" "Of course," replied Bacanovic, "That's the whole point."[16] When Martha Stewart called in that afternoon, she asked, "What's going on with Sam?" Faneuil said that he told her, "We have no news about the company, but we thought you might like to act on the information that Sam is selling all his shares." He described her end of the conversation as a series of "clipped demands." Faneuil also recounted how Bacanovic had tried to pull him into a cover-up. He described a scene at a coffee shop near their office in which he told Bacanovic, "I was on the phone. I know what happened." In response Bacanovic put an arm around him and said, "With all due respect, no, you don't."[17]

During cross-examination Bacanovic's attorney, David Apfel, tried to tarnish Faneuil as an unreliable witness. He called Faneuil an admitted liar who had changed his story seeking leniency from prosecutors. He brought out Faneuil's use of recreational drugs. And he introduced e-mail messages by Faneuil to show that he disliked Martha Stewart and might have held a grudge against her. One read: "I just spoke to MARTHA! I have never, ever been treated more rudely by a stranger on the telephone." Another was: "Martha yelled at me again today, but I snapped in her face and she actually backed down! Baby put

Ms. Martha in her place!!!"[18] Faneuil also testified about a time when he put Martha Stewart on hold. When he came back on the line she threatened to pull her account from Merrill Lynch unless the hold music was changed. This colorful testimony sometimes made the jurors laugh.

Faneuil's testimony took 13 hours over six days. On his last day he was cross-examined by Stewart's attorney Morvillo, who tried to depict him as overwhelmed by the rush of events on December 27. He pointed out that Faneuil had taken 75 phone calls on that day, and some e-mails. He questioned why his memory of Stewart's call was sharp, in contrast to some other calls about which he was less clear. He got Faneuil to admit that he suspected the Waksals of insider trading, but said nothing to Bacanovic.

Following Faneuil, several other prosecution witnesses gave notable testimony. Stewart's administrative assistant Ann Armstrong was called to testify about how Stewart altered the message of Bacanovic's call. Taking the stand, she began to sob. After getting a glass of water from the defense table she tried to resume, but could not. Judge Cedarbaum recessed the trial to the next day, when Armstrong recounted how Stewart first altered, then instructed her to restore, the wording of the phone message.

Maria Pasternak was a friend who had been traveling with Martha Stewart on December 27. Pasternak related conversations with Stewart at a resort in Los Cabos over the following days. She said Stewart told her that the Waksals were trying to sell all their shares in ImClone and that she had sold all her shares. She testified that Stewart remarked, "Isn't it nice to have brokers who tell you those things?" But under cross-examination she vacillated about the clarity of her recall. The judge instructed jurors to disregard the remark.

An expert ink analyst with the U.S. Secret Service was called for his analysis of Bacanovic's tax sale worksheet. Larry Stewart, who is not related to Martha Stewart, testified that tests he conducted showed two pens had been used on the worksheet. All the notations on it, except "@60," were made by a "cheap" Paper Mate pen. The "@60" was written with a second, unidentified pen. The second pen did not match any of 8,500 ink samples on record, so Stewart concluded that it was either foreign or very

[16] Brooke A. Masters, "Broker's Aide Says He Was Told to Tip Off Stewart," *Washington Post*, February 3, 2004, p. E1.

[17] Testimony quoted in Constance L. Hays, "Witness Describes Stewart Cover-Up," *New York Times*, February 5, 2004, p. C4.

[18] Brooke A. Masters, "Broker's Assistant, Stewart Clashed," *Washington Post*, February 5, 2004, p. E1.

rare.[19] This was important evidence for the prosecution, which argued that the "@60" had been added only after December 27, when the defendants constructed a cover-up.

After the prosecution finished its case, Martha Stewart's lawyers elected to use a minimal defense. They called only one witness, a former Stewart lawyer and note-taker at the February 4 meeting with investigators, who testified for only 15 minutes. There was much speculation about whether Martha Stewart would take the stand in her own defense. If she did, prosecutors would push her, try to trap her in inconsistencies and provoke her temper. If she did not, the intense curiosity of the jurors to learn what she could say to them would be unfulfilled. In the end, she did not take the stand.

Late in the trial Judge Cedarbaum accepted a motion by Stewart's lawyers to dismiss the government's allegations of securities fraud. This charge had met with wide skepticism from the beginning. How could a defendant exercise her right to speak out in self-defense if doing so could be construed as criminal manipulation of share prices? In dismissing the charge Cedarbaum said that, given the evidence, no reasonable juror could find her guilty beyond a reasonable doubt.[20]

After the defense called its single witness, there had been 27 witnesses during 19 days of testimony. Closing arguments came on March 2. Prosecutor Michael Schachter told the jurors that Stewart and Bacanovic believed they would never be caught. But the mistakes they made trying to deceive left a trail of damning inconsistencies. He carefully listed the contradictions in their stories. Bacanovic's lawyer gave a closing argument trying once again to undermine the credibility of Douglas Faneuil's testimony.

In his closing argument for Martha Stewart, Morvillo began by ridiculing the conspiracy charge, saying that the events alleged by the government amounted to "a confederation of dunces."[21] Nobody, "he argued," could have done what Peter Bacanovic and Martha Stewart are alleged to have done and done it in a dumber fashion." He asked the jurors to consider that if the two had really conspired they would have been much more consistent in their stories. Their inconsistencies were a sign of innocence. This was a dangerous argument, because it conceded some contradictions in testimony.

Morvillo then made the case for Stewart's innocence. She had no evidence that anything was wrong with the trade. She had no reason to suspect that Waksal would behave so foolishly as to trade in front of the FDA announcement during a blackout period. She had a preexisting agreement with her broker to trade ImClone if it fell below $60. She could not hear well enough on the phone to know she was talking to Faneuil, not Bacanovic. The amount of the trade was too small to tempt jeopardizing her future. Her change in Ann Armstrong's telephone log was insignificant. Faneuil was an untrustworthy witness. Finally, he explained that she did not take the stand because she twice testified on the record at investigative hearings two years before and "her recollection [of the events] hasn't gotten any better." He concluded with this.

> This has been a two-year ordeal for this good woman. It's an ordeal based on the fact that she trusted her financial advisor not to put her in a compromising position. It's an ordeal based on the fact that she voluntarily submitted to a government interview. And it's an ordeal that is in the process of wiping out all the good that she has done, all her contributions, all her accomplishments. . . . [M]artha Stewart's life is in your hands. . . . I ask you to acquit Martha Stewart. I ask you to let her return to her life of improving the quality of life for all of us. If you do that, it's a good thing.[22]

THE VERDICT

The jury deliberated for 14 hours over three days. On March 5 one female juror wept as the verdicts were announced. Stewart and Bacanovic were each found guilty on four counts of lying and conspiring to lie to conceal the fact that she had been tipped with insider information. However, the jury could not agree that the government had proved beyond a reasonable doubt its allegation that Stewart and Bacanovic fabricated the $60 sale agreement and it acquitted them on those counts.

Jurors described their deliberations as calm. They had found Faneuil credible and gave much weight to

[19] Matthew Rose and Kara Scannell, "Stewart Trial Gets Testimony of a Broker's Tip," *The Wall Street Journal*, February 20, 2004, p. C3.

[20] *United States v. Martha Stewart and Peter Bacanovic*, 305 F. Supp. 2d 368, February 27, 2004.

[21] "Closing Argument on Behalf of Martha Stewart," March 2, 2004, at www.marthatalks.com/trial, p. 1.

[22] Ibid., p. 10.

Martha Stewart outside the Manhattan courthouse after hearing the verdict. Source: © AP Photo/Julie Jacobson.

his testimony. Ann Armstrong was also an important witness because she cried. "We feel that she knew that something was wrong," said the forewoman. Jurors were also suspicious of the January 16 breakfast meeting between Stewart and Bacanovic and they felt cynical about Stewart hiring a criminal defense lawyer even before she was contacted by government investigators. They put little stock in the "conspiracy of dunces" argument. "We felt that she was a smart lady who made a dumb mistake," said the forewoman.[23]

A juror named Chappell Hartridge characterized the verdict as "a victory for the little guys who lose money in the market because of these kinds of transactions."[24] After looking into Hartridge's background, Stewart's legal team believed he had not been completely honest on his jurors' questionnaire. When asked about contacts with law enforcement, he did not disclose an arrest for assaulting a former girlfriend, being sued, and several other problems. Arguing that they would have exercised a challenge to keep Chappell off the jury had they known, her

lawyers moved for a new trial. Judge Cedarbaum ruled that the allegations were little more than hearsay and there was no evidence that bias in Chappell affected the verdict.[25]

Meanwhile, prosecutors had filed a criminal complaint against Larry Stewart, the ink expert who testified at the trial. Stewart was accused of perjury for saying that he had conducted the ink tests after a coworker came forward saying that, in fact, she had done them. Again Stewart's attorneys filed a motion for retrial. Again Cedarbaum denied the motion, because "there was no reasonable likelihood that this perjury could have affected the jury's verdict, and because overwhelming independent evidence supports the verdict. . . ."[26] Subsequently, Larry Stewart was tried and acquitted of perjury based on evidence that his co-worker had a history of harassment.[27]

SENTENCING

On July 16, 2004, Martha Stewart appeared before Judge Cedarbaum. Addressing the judge, she appealed for leniency, saying, "Today is a shameful day. I ask that in judging me, you remember all the good I've done and the contributions I've made." Prosecutor Seymour countered, arguing that Stewart was "asking for leniency far beyond" that justified for "a serious offense with broad implications" for the justice system. Judge Cedarbaum responded, "I believe that you have suffered, and will continue to suffer, enough."[28] Her sentence was five months imprisonment followed by five months of home confinement. She was fined $30,000. This set of penalties was at the lenient end of what could have been imposed under federal sentencing guidelines and showed that Judge Cedarbaum was using the discretion she had to avoid a harsh sentence.

After the sentencing, Martha Stewart emerged from the courthouse to read another statement. "I'm just very, very sorry that it's come to this, that a small

[23] Kara Scannell, Matthew Rose, and Laurie P. Cohen, "In Stewart Case, Reluctant Jurors Found Guilt after Skimpy Defense," *The Wall Street Journal*, March 8, 2004, p. A1.

[24] Constance L. Hays, "Martha Stewart Seeks New Trial, Saying a Juror Lied," *New York Times*, April 1, 2004, p. C3.

[25] *United States v. Martha Stewart and Peter Bacanovic*, 317 F. Supp. 2d 426, May 5, 2004.

[26] *United States v. Martha Stewart and Peter Bacanovic*, 323 F. Supp. 2d 606, July 8, 2004.

[27] "Jurors Acquit Stewart Witness," *Los Angeles Times*, October 6, 2004, p. C3.

[28] Thomas S. Mulligan, "Stewart Gets 5 Months in Prison, Then Delivers a Plug for Her Firm," *Los Angeles Times*, July 17, 2004, p. A4.

personal matter has been able to be blown out of all proportion, and with such venom and such gore—I mean, it's just terrible."[29]

At a separate hearing that day, Peter Bacanovic received a nearly identical sentence of five months in prison, five months of home confinement, and a $4,000 fine. A week later Daniel Faneuil appeared before Judge Cedarbaum. Tearfully, he apologized for his actions. His cooperation with federal prosecutors saved him from going to prison. His sentence was a $2,000 fine.

On October 8, Martha Stewart reported to a minimum-security prison camp in West Virginia to begin her incarceration. She had appealed her case, but the appeal was expected to take two years. Therefore, she elected to serve her sentence. Doing so would end much of the speculation and tumult affecting both her and her company.

She served her time. In prison she worked in the garden and cleaned the warden's office for 12 cents an hour. She disliked the food but made some friends among the other women. She gave them yoga lessons and a seminar on entrepreneurship. Her last day of home confinement (extended three weeks due to a violation that was not publicly revealed) ended on September 1, 2005. Meanwhile, she had hired a team of public relations experts to plan her image restoration. Its members interviewed hundreds of Americans and learned that her supporters wanted to see her reconnect with family. She picked her activities carefully and turned down interviews where she might be questioned on her conviction and prison term.[30]

In 2006 a federal appeals court turned down her request to overturn her conviction.[31] Then she settled with the SEC, which had brought a civil case of insider trading against her in 2003. In the settlement, she neither admitted nor denied guilt. She agreed to a five-year ban on serving as an officer or director of her company and a $195,081 fine. In the same settlement, Bacanovic agreed to a fine of $75,645.[32] Her legal troubles were finally over with the end of court-ordered probation in March 2007.

Questions

1. Did Martha Stewart commit the crime of insider trading when she sold her ImClone shares on December 27, 2001?

2. Did the U.S. Attorneys and the Securities and Exchange Commission use good judgment in indicting Martha Stewart? Do you believe that her indictment was based on evidence of a serious crime, or do you believe that prosecutors consciously or unconsciously had additional motives for pursuing the case?

3. Do you agree with the jury that she was guilty beyond a reasonable doubt of the conspiracy and obstruction of justice charges?

4. Was her punishment, including both imprisonment and fines, appropriate? Were the punishments of Peter Bacanovic and Douglas Faneuil appropriate?

---

[29] Ibid., p. A1.

[30] Patricia Sellers, "Remodeling Martha," *Fortune,* November 14, 2005, p. 114.

[31] *U.S. v. Martha Stewart and Peter Bacanovic,* 2006 U.S. App. LEXIS 271.

[32] See Securities and Exchange Commission, Litigation Release No. 19794, *SEC v. Martha Stewart and Peter Bacanovic,* 03 Civ. 4070 (RJH) (S.D.N.Y.), August 7, 2006.

Chapter 8

Making Ethical Decisions in Business

Realtors in the Wilderness

In ancient times the Gunnison River flowed through what is now western Colorado, carrying abrasive particles and debris, scouring the hard rock as it went to form a deep canyon 50 miles long. This spectacular cut in the earth reaches depths of 2,800 feet and at one point is just 40 feet wide. It is so narrow that sunlight shines on the floor only an hour a day, hence its name—Black Canyon.

In 1999 this geologic marvel became a national park, entitling it to uncompromising protection from human intrusion. However, just before the park was created, a group of investors in a limited partnership called TDX bought 112 acres of private land on the south side of the canyon. Small, privately owned tracts such as this in national parks and monuments are called inholdings. Property rights to inholdings were acquired long ago, before federal protections were put on the land. Most are homesteads or mining claims dating back to the late 1800s. Today they total less than 0.5 percent of park and wilderness acres. By law, the government cannot seize them or buy them back without the owners' consent. Nor can it restrict owners' rights to develop or mine or their property.

Using a local realtor named Tom Chapman, TDX bought its Black Canyon holding for $80,000.[1] Soon Chapman created a brochure advertising lots for the construction of luxury homes. Then a billboard rose on the site of the lots along the main road into the monument: "For Sale. Forty-acre building sites. Beautiful canyon views. World-class sunsets."[2] Chapman asked $4,500 an acre for the lots, an amount that would return a 630 percent to TDX investors.

Environmentalists were enraged. Houses would be visible from canyon outlooks, marring the atmosphere of wildness and natural splendor. At night their lights would intrude on the wild blackness. The park superintendent filed a lawsuit to halt development, but its legal basis was thin and the National Park Service told him to negotiate with Chapman instead. So far, the land has been subdivided and one house has been built. The National Part Service continues trying to buy the land, but so far it

[1] Bobby MaGill, "Black Eye for Black Canyon," *The Daily Sentinel,* December 27, 2006, p. 1.
[2] Richard Miniter, "Real Estate Broker from Hell," *Reader's Digest,* February 2001, p. 114.

cannot meet the asking price. In the meantime, the investors pay property taxes of only $45 a year.

In a prior foray into Black Canyon in 1984, when it was a national monument, Chapman represented a client who had been offered $200 an acre by the National Park Service for an inholding. To raise the offer, he picked part of his client's land, a highly visible area on the canyon's rim, and threatened to build a subdivision. After he brought in a bulldozer, the agency caved in and paid $510 an acre to buy the land and halt construction.

Eight years later Chapman and TDX bought 240 acres of inholdings in the West Elk Wilderness of Colorado for $4,000 per acre. When the U.S. Forest Service said it could not afford to buy the land, Chapman started to build a lodge. Since there was no road access into the island of property, work commenced with the roar of helicopters flying building materials over the surrounding forest. To stop destruction of the wild, the Forest Service offered to swap the TDX inholding for 107 acres of public land near Telluride, Colorado. That parcel was near a ski resort, and after the swap TDX sold it for $4.2 million, giving the investors a 438 percent profit. Chapman's share was about $1 million.[3]

This coercive tactic has been used repeatedly. It works because once virgin areas are developed, the wilderness is gone. Property rights are fundamental in America, and long-standing federal law protects inholders from interference. Yet Chapman and TDX are criticized for extorting money that could be used for the welfare of pristine lands and their visitors. While the speculators profit, national parks and monuments are severely underfunded, rangers get low pay, and lands deteriorate. Their tactics have been called immoral, unethical, and outrageous. Chapman, however, defends them.

> I will never apologize for being a capitalist because capitalism is what created the cornucopia of goods and services that we enjoy in this country. Everybody, everybody wants to sell something for more than they paid. It's all American. Unless of course you own property in a wilderness area or in a national park or a national forest. Then all of a sudden you are a greedy capitalist, a profiteer. . . . Why should capitalism be removed from wilderness areas?[4]

The story reveals an ethically complex situation. The speculators exercise basic property rights, but rights are not absolute. Their methods resonate with free market values, but markets exhibit flaws. In a just world, laws and rules are fair. When inholders pay taxes on their property but cannot use it as they wish or sell it for current market value, that seems unfair. However, extortionate land deals create lavish profits for a few, while foreclosing alternative uses of money that benefit many more.

In this chapter we set forth a wide range of principles and methods for making ethical decisions. These include principles great and small, character development, simple procedures that corporations suggest to their employees, and practical tips. Use of these devices makes ethical thinking more sophisticated. In themselves they do not resolve ethical issues. Judgment is still required. If you owned a pocket of land in

---

[3] Jason Blevins, "Real Estate Broker Defends Wilderness Tactics," *The Denver Post,* August 13, 2000, p. M1.
[4] Ibid.

a national park, would you threaten to build a subdivision of homes? If you decided to do that, would you feel comfortable explaining why on television? What are the rules when there is no definitive law? The material in this chapter can help to answer such questions.

PRINCIPLES OF ETHICAL CONDUCT

We begin with a compendium of ethical principles—some ancient, some modern. There are dozens, if not hundreds, of such principles in the philosophical and religious traditions of East and West.

From a larger universe, we set forth 14 principles that every manager should know and think about. (See the nearby box and discussion that follows.) The 14 principles here are fundamental guides or rules for behavior. Each of them has strengths and weaknesses. Some were created to be universal tests of conduct. Others have a more limited reach and apply only in certain spheres of human relations. Some are ideals. Others accommodate balancing of interests where perfection is elusive. A few invite compromise and can be used to rationalize flawed behavior. One principle, might equals right, is a justification for ignoble acts, but we include it here because it has been a basis of ethical reasoning since time immemorial.

These principles distill basic wisdom from 2,000 years of ethical thought. To the extent that they offer ideas for thinking about and resolving ethical dilemmas, they are not vague abstractions but useful, living guides to analysis and conduct.[5] We present them alphabetically.

The Categorical Imperative

categorical imperative
Act only according to that maxim by which you can at the same time will that it should become a universal law.

The *categorical imperative* (meaning, literally, a command that admits no exception) is a guide for ethical behavior set forth by the German philosopher Immanuel Kant in his *Foundations of the Metaphysics of Morals,* a tract published in 1785. In Kant's words: "Act only according to that maxim by which you can at the same time will that it should become a universal law."[6]

In other words, one should not adopt principles of action unless they can, without inconsistency, be adopted by everyone. Lying, stealing, and breaking promises, for example, are ruled out because society would disintegrate if they replaced truth telling, property rights, and vow keeping. Using this guideline, a manager faced with a moral choice must act in a way that he or she believes is right and just for any person in a similar situation. Each action should be judged by asking: "Could this act be turned into a universal code of behavior?" This quick *test of universalizability* has achieved great popularity.

test of universalizability
Could this act be turned into a universal code of behavior?

[5] T. K. Das asked business executives to rank the favorability of these principles for use in business decisions in "How Strong Are the Ethical Preferences of Senior Business Executives," *Journal of Business Ethics,* January 2005. Among the 14 ethical principles discussed in this chapter, the most positive ranking was given to the Golden Rule and the most negative to the Conventionalist Ethic.

[6] Immanuel Kant, *Foundations of the Metaphysics of Morals,* trans. Lewis White Beck (Indianapolis: Bobbs-Merrill, 1969), p. 44; written in 1785.

Fourteen Ethical Principles

The Categorical Imperative   Act only according to that maxim by which you can at the same time will that it should become a universal law.

The Conventionalist Ethic   Business is like a game with permissive ethics and any action that does not violate the law is permitted.

The Disclosure Rule   Test an ethical decision by asking how you would feel explaining it to a wider audience such as newspaper readers, television viewers, or your family.

The Doctrine of the Mean   Virtue is achieved through moderation. Avoid behavior that is excessive or deficient of a virtue.

The Ends–Means Ethic   The end justifies the means.

The Golden Rule   Do unto others what you would have them do unto you.

The Intuition Ethic   What is good or right is understood by an inner moral sense based on character development and felt as intuition.

Might-Equals-Right Ethic   Justice is the interest of the stronger.

The Organization Ethic   Be loyal to the organization.

The Principle of Equal Freedom   A person has the right to freedom of action unless such action deprives another person of a proper freedom.

The Proportionality Ethic   A set of rules for making decisions having both good and evil consequences.

The Rights Ethic   Each person has protections and entitlements that others have a duty to respect.

The Theory of Justice   Each person should act fairly toward others in order to maintain the bonds of community.

The Utilitarian Ethic   The greatest good for the greatest number.

Kant was an extreme perfectionist. He walked the same route each day at the same time, appearing at places along the route so punctually that neighbors set their clocks by him. Before leaving his house he attached strings to the top of his socks and connected them to a spring apparatus held by his belt. As he walked, the contraption would pull the slack out of his socks. To no one's surprise, his ethical philosophies are perfectionist also, and that is their weakness. Kant's categorical imperative is dogmatic and inflexible. It is a general rule that must be applied in every specific situation; there are no exceptions. But real life challenges the simple, single ethical law. If a competitor asks whether your company is planning to sell shirts in Texas next year, must you answer the question with the truth?

conventionalist ethic
Business is like a game with permissive ethics and any action that does not violate the law is permitted.

The Conventionalist Ethic

This is the view that business is analogous to a game and special, lower ethics are permissible. In business, people may act to further their self-interest so long as they do not violate the law. The *conventionalist ethic*, which has a long history, was popularized some years ago by Albert Z. Carr in *Business as a Game*.[7] "If an executive allows himself to be torn between a decision based on business considerations

[7]Albert Z. Carr, *Business as a Game* (New York: New American Library, 1968).

and one based on his private ethical code," explained Carr, "he exposes himself to a grave psychological strain."[8]

Business may be regarded as a game, such as poker, in which the rules are different from those we adopt in personal life. Assuming game ethics, managers are allowed to bluff (a euphemism for lie) and to take advantage of all legal opportunities and widespread practices or customs. Carr used two examples of situations in which game ethics were permissible. In the first, an out-of-work sales agent with a good employment record feared discrimination because of his age—58. He dyed his hair and stated on his résumé that he was 45. In the second, a job applicant was asked to check off magazines he read, but decided not to check off *Playboy, The Nation,* or *The New Republic.* Even though he read them, he did not want to be labeled controversial. He checked bland magazines such as *Reader's Digest* instead.[9]

The conventionalist ethic is criticized by those who make no distinction between society's ethics and business ethics. They argue that commerce defines the life chances of millions and is not a game to be taken lightly. As a principle, the conventionalist ethic is a thin justification for deceptive behavior at the office.

The Disclosure Rule

disclosure rule
Test an ethical decision by asking how you would feel explaining it to a wider audience such as newspaper readers, television viewers, or your family.

Using the *disclosure rule,* a manager faced with an ethical dilemma asks how it would feel to explain the decision to a wider audience. This simple idea appears in many company ethics codes. It is stated in Baxter International's *Global Business Practice Standards* in tests of ethics that are set forth in two questions.

- What will my manager, supervisor, co-workers, or family think about what I plan to do? (The "Others" Test)
- If what I do is reported in a newspaper, or on television, will I be proud of my actions? (The "Press" Test)[10]

This rule screens out base motives such as greed and jealousy, which are unacceptable if disclosed, but it does not always give clear guidance for ethical dilemmas in which strong arguments exist for several alternatives. Also, an action that sounds acceptable if disclosed may not, upon reflection, always be the most ethical.

The Doctrine of the Mean

doctrine of the mean
Virtue is achieved through moderation. Avoid behavior that is excessive or deficient of a virtue.

This ethic, set forth by Aristotle in the *Nicomachean Ethics* and sometimes called the *golden mean,* calls for virtue through moderation.[11] Right actions are found in the area between extreme behaviors, which are labeled as excess on the one hand and deficient on the other. Facing an ethical decision, a person first identifies the ethical virtue at its core (such as truthfulness) and then seeks the mean or moderate course of action between an excess of that virtue (boastfulness) and a deficiency of it (understatement).

---

[8] "Is Business Bluffing Ethical?" *Harvard Business Review,* January–February 1968, p. 149.

[9] Carr, *Business as a Game,* p. 142.

[10] Deerfield, IL: Baxter International Inc., 2006, p. 43.

[11] *Nicomachean Ethics,* trans. J. A. K. Thomson (New York: Penguin Books, 1982), book II, chap. 6.

At ITT, Harold Geneen pushed managers to extraordinary personal sacrifices. Their time, energy, loyalty, and will were bent to corporate purposes. Obsessive work led to remarkable business successes. During his tenure earnings increased for an incredible 58 consecutive quarters. And 130 of the managers he trained went on to take top positions at other companies.[12] Yet, it also led to personal difficulties such as marital problems. While the work of ITT was constructive and ethical, its demands led some to sacrifice a balanced life.[13] To Aristotle, this would have been wrong.

The doctrine of the mean is today little recognized, but the underlying notion of moderation as a virtue lingers in Western societies. The doctrine itself is inexact. To observe it is simply to act conservatively, never in the extreme. The moderate course and specific virtues such as honesty, however, are defined as aspects existing between and defined in relation to polar extremes. What they are is open to wide interpretation.

The Ends–Means Ethic

ends–means ethic
The end justifies the means.

This principle is age-old, appearing as an ancient Roman proverb, *existus acta probat*, or "the result validates the deeds." It is often associated with the Italian philosopher Niccolò Machiavelli. In *The Prince* (1513), Machiavelli argued that worthwhile ends justify efficient means, that when ends are of overriding importance or virtue, unscrupulous means may be employed to reach them.[14] When confronted with a decision involving an ethically questionable act, a person should ask whether some overall good—such as the survival of a country or business—justifies cutting corners.

In the 1980s Oracle Corporation grew rapidly. To get this growth, founder and CEO Lawrence J. Ellison pressed his sales managers to double revenues every year. Methods used by the frenzied sales force were watched less closely than its ability to hit targets. In 1993 the Securities and Exchange Commission fined Oracle for overstating earnings by double-billing customers, invoicing companies for products never sold, and violating accounting standards by recording sales revenue before it was received.[15] However, by then Oracle had crushed its early competition in the relational database market. Today Oracle is a $14.4 billion corporation and Ellison is a billionaire. Oracle employs 56,100 people and has made many of them millionaires. Its software makes governments, businesses, and universities more productive. It pays taxes in 60 countries. It has a wide range of social responsibility programs. Did belief in this end result justify the competitive tactics used to build the company?

Any manager using unscrupulous means concedes the highest virtue and accepts the necessity of ethical compromise. In solving ethical problems, means may be as important, or more so, than ends. In addition, the process of ethical character development can never be furthered by the use of expedient means.

---

[12] Alvin Moscow, "Introduction," in Harold Geneen, *Managing* (New York: Avon Books, 1984), pp. 5 and 13.

[13] Manuel Velasquez and Neil Brady, "Catholic Natural Law and Business Ethics," *Business Ethics Quarterly,* March 1997, p. 95.

[14] Niccolò Machiavelli, *The Prince,* trans. T. G. Bergin, ed. (New York: Appleton-Century-Crofts, 1947); written in 1513 and first published in 1532.

[15] Mike Wilson, *The Difference between God and Larry Ellison* (New York: William Morrow, 1997), p. 239.

The Golden Rule

Golden Rule
Do unto others as you would have them do unto you.

An ideal found in the great religions and in works of philosophy, the *Golden Rule* has been a popular guide for centuries. Simply put, it is: "Do unto others as you would have them do unto you." It includes not knowingly doing harm to others. A manager trying to solve an ethical problem places him- or herself in the position of another party affected by the decision and tries to figure out what action is most fair from that perspective.

practical imperative
Treat others as ends in themselves, not as means to other goals. This principle prohibits selfish manipulation of other people.

A related principle called the *practical imperative* was set forth by Immanuel Kant. It is: "Act so that you treat humanity, whether in your own person or in that of another, always as an end and never as a means only."[16] This principle admonishes a manager to treat employees as ends in themselves, not to manipulate them simply as factors of production for the self-interested ends of the company.

Around 1900, when E. H. Harriman owned the Southern Pacific railroad, train accidents killed between 5,000 and 6,000 people a year. One day on an inspection tour, his train hit a rough section of track and nearly derailed because a work crew had neglected to post a flagman. Instead of firing the crew chief, Harriman insisted on firing the whole crew. A top executive spoke up, arguing it was cruel to punish them all. "Perhaps," responded Harriman, "but it will probably save a lot of lives. I want every man connected with the operation to feel a sense of responsibility. Now, everybody knew that the man hadn't gone back with the flag."[17] Harriman used this crew of workers to send a message to all other crews. The workers were not treated as individuals; they were punished en masse to signal others in the company.

test of reversibility
Would you be willing to change places with the person or persons affected by your actions?

A manager may comply with both the practical imperative and the Golden Rule by using the *test of reversibility*, that is, by asking if he or she would change places with the person affected by the contemplated action. A problem with the Golden Rule is that people's ethical values differ, and they may mistakenly assume that their preferences are universal. In addition, it is primarily a perfectionist rule for interpersonal relations. So applying it in business life where the interests of individuals are subordinated to the needs of the firm is sometimes hard.

The Intuition Ethic

intuition ethic
What is good or right is understood by an inner moral sense based on character development and felt as intuition.

The *intuition ethic,* as defined by philosophers such as G. E. Moore in his *Principia Ethica* (1903), holds that what is good is simply understood.[18] That is, people are endowed with a moral sense by which they intuitively know the difference between right and wrong. The solution to an ethical problem lies in what you sense or understand to be right.

Most people facing an ethical conflict have an emotional, gut reaction that occurs before reason illuminates the specific problem in logical terms. The situation just bothers them, even if they are not sure why. Something is wrong. This ethical intuition is not simply ungrounded self-judgment. A person's ethical instincts are the product of socialization, role expectations, and character development. Every-

[16] Kant, *Foundations of the Metaphysics of Morals,* p. 54.

[17] Quoted in Maury Klein, *The Life & Legend of E. H. Harriman* (Chapel Hill: University of North Carolina Press, 2000), p. 266.

[18] New York: Cambridge University Press, 1948; reprint.

one carries a lifetime of moral lessons that can well up as strong emotions. Though fallible, intuition is usually accurate.

Some companies recognize the intuition ethic in their conduct codes and offer it as a general guideline for employees. At Cummins Inc., for example, employees are told to ask, "Do I feel uncomfortable with this particular course of action? If the answer is yes, don't do it."[19] When employees at Dow Chemical Company face an ethical decision they are told to ask: "What feels right or wrong about the situation or action?"[20]

Drawbacks exist. The approach is subjective. Self-interest may be confused with ethical insight. No standard of validation outside the individual is used. It is unpersuasive to others for a manager to say, "It's wrong because I just think so." Also, intuition may fail to give clear answers.[21]

The Might-Equals-Right Ethic

might equals right
Justice is the interest of the stronger.

The classic statement of this ancient ethic is that of Thracymachus (thră-sĭm-ă-cŭs), an Athenian teacher of rhetoric who argued with Socrates that justice is "nothing but what is the interest of the stronger."[22] No era since has been without both its expression and its practice. In business this thinking is expressed in some competitive strategies and marketing tactics. What is ethical is what a stronger individual or company has the power to impose on a weaker one. When faced with an ethical decision, people should seize what advantage they are strong enough to take, without regard for lofty sentiments.

In the 1860s Ben Holladay, owner of the Overland Stage Line, perfected a competitive strategy based on overbearing power. He entered new routes with lowball coach fares, subsidizing this service with profits from monopoly routes, waiting until local competitors failed. In 1863 a small stage line between Denver and Central City in Colorado charged $6 per run. Holladay put an elegant new Concord Coach with a leather interior on the line and charged only $2. The competitor soon folded, then Holladay replaced the new stagecoach with a primitive vehicle resembling a freight wagon and raised the fare to $12.

The weakness of the might-equals-right ethic lies in its confusion of ethics with force. Exercising power is different than acting from ethical duty. An ethical principle that can be invalidated by its foundation (e.g., physical force) is not consistent, logical, or valid. Might equals right is not a legitimate approach in civilized settings. It invites retaliation and censure, and it is not conducive to long-term advantage. Seizure by power violates the bedrock ethical duty of reciprocity on which all societies are based.

The Organization Ethic

Simply put, this principle is: "Be loyal to the organization." It implies that the wills and needs of individuals are subordinate to the overall welfare of the organization

---

[19] *Cummins Code of Business Conduct* (Columbus, IN: Cummins Inc., 2007), p. ii.

[20] Dow Chemical Company, *Code of Business Conduct* (Midland, MI: Dow, September 2006), p. 2.

[21] For an excellent discussion of intuition in managers' decisions, see Joseph L. Badaracco Jr., *Defining Moments* (Boston: Harvard Business School Press, 1997), chap. 4.

[22] Francis MacDonald Cornford, *The Republic of Plato* (New York: Oxford University Press, 1966), p. 18.

(be it a corporation, government, university, or army). A member should act consistent with the organization's goals. This ethic leads to cooperation and mutual trust.

Many employees have such deep loyalty to an organization that it transcends self-interest. Some Americans jeopardize their health and work excessively long hours without pay out of devotion to the employer. In Asian societies, which have strong collectivist values, identification with and commitment to companies is exceptionally strong. In Japan, workers are so afraid of letting down their work group or employer that they come to work despite broken limbs and serious ailments. This behavior is so common that a word for death from overwork, *karoshi*, has entered the Japanese language.

organization ethic
Be loyal to the organization.

The ethical limits of obedience are reached when duty to the organization is used to rationalize wrongdoing. The Nuremberg trials, which convicted Nazis of war crimes, taught that Western society expects members of organizations to follow their conscience. Just as no war criminal argued successfully that taking orders in a military chain of command excused his behavior, so no business manager may claim to be the helpless prisoner of corporate loyalties that crush free will and justify wrongdoing.

> You are sailing to Rome (you tell me) to obtain the post of Governor of Cnossus. You are not content to stay at home with the honours you had before; you want something on a larger scale, and more conspicuous. But when did you ever undertake a voyage for the purpose of reviewing your own principles and getting rid of any of them that proved unsound?
>
> **Source:** Epictetus, *The Discourses* (circa. A.D. 120).

The Principle of Equal Freedom

principle of equal freedom
A person has the right to freedom of action unless such action deprives another person of a proper freedom.

This principle was set forth by the philosopher Herbert Spencer in his 1850 book *Social Statics*. "Every man may claim the fullest liberty to exercise his faculties," said Spencer, "compatible with the possession of like liberty by every other man."[23] Thus, a person has the right to freedom of action unless such action deprives another person of a proper freedom. Spencer believed this was the first principle of ethical behavior in society because only when individual liberty was protected against infringement by others could human progress occur.

To use the principle, a person asks if an action will restrict others from actions that they have a legitimate right to undertake. Most people know the colloquial version: "Your right to swing your fist ends where my nose begins."

The principle of equal freedom lacks a tiebreaker for situations in which two rights conflict. Such situations require invocation of some additional rule to decide which right or freedom has priority. Ethically permissible management decisions may abridge the rights of some parties for the benefit of others. For example, all employees have broad privacy rights, but management invades them when it hires undercover detectives to investigate theft.

---

[23] New York: Robert Schalkenbach Foundation, 1970, p. 69; first published in 1850.

The Proportionality Ethic

**proportion-
ality**
A set of rules
for making
decisions
having both
good and evil
consequences.

Proportionality, an idea incubated in medieval Catholic theology, applies to decisions having both good and evil consequences. For instance, a maker of small-caliber, short-barreled, handguns that are irreverently called Saturday Night Specials has a dual impact on society. It makes available cheap, easily concealable weapons for criminals. Yet it also creates a supply of affordable self-defense weapons for poor people in crime-ridden areas who cannot buy high-quality handguns costing $1,000 and more. In this and similar cases, where a manager's action has a good effect but also entails a harm, the idea of proportionality fits.

**principle of
proportion-
ality**
Managers
can risk pre-
dictable, but
unwilled,
harms to peo-
ple after weigh-
ing five factors:
type of good
and evil, proba-
bility, urgency,
intensity of
influence, and
alternatives.

A classic formulation of proportionality into a specific principle is Thomas M. Garrett's *principle of proportionality.* It states that managers are responsible for the consequences when they create situations leading to both good and evil effects. The principle allows them to risk predictable, but unwilled, harms to people (for example, innocent victims being shot by handguns) if they correctly weigh five factors.

First, managers must assess the *type of good and evil* involved, distinguishing between major and minor forms. Second, they should calculate the *urgency* of the situation. For example, would the firm go out of business unless employees were laid off? Third, they must estimate the *probability* of both good and evil effects. If good effects are certain and risks of serious harm are remote, an action is more favorable. Fourth, the *intensity of influence* over effects must be considered. In considering handgun injuries, for instance, manufacturers might assume that criminal action was an intervening force over which they had no control. Fifth, the existence of *alternatives* must be considered. If, for instance, an advertisement subtly encourages product misuse, the most ethical action might be to change it. Garrett believed that taking these five factors into consideration would reveal fully the ethical dimension of a decision.[24]

**principle of
double effect**
When both
good and evil
consequences
result from a
decision, a
manager has
acted ethically
if the good
outweighs the
evil, if his or
her intention is
to achieve the
good, and if
there is no bet-
ter alternative.

An alternative formulation of the idea of proportionality is the *principle of double effect,* which is that in a situation from which both good and evil consequences are bound to result, a manager will act ethically if (1) the good effects outweigh the evil, (2) the manager's intention is to achieve the good effects, and (3) there is no better alternative.[25]

These are intricate principles, requiring consideration of many factors. They force a manager to think about and weigh these factors in an organized way.

The Rights Ethic

rights ethic
Each person
has protections
and entitle-
ments that oth-
ers have a duty
to respect.

Rights protect people against abuses and entitle them to important liberties. A strong philosophical movement defining *natural rights,* or rights that can be inferred by reason from the study of human nature, grew in Western Europe during the Enlightenment as a reaction against medieval religious persecutions. Over time, many such rights were given legal status and became *legal rights.*

[24] Thomas M. Garrett, *Business Ethics* (New York: Appleton-Century-Crofts, 1966), p. 8.

[25] This is a simple version of the principle of double effect. For fuller treatment, see Lawrence Masek, "The Doctrine of Double Effect, Deadly Drugs, and Business Ethics," *Business Ethics Quarterly,* April 2000, pp. 484–87.

natural rights
Protections and entitlements that can be inferred by reason from the study of human nature.

Basic rights that are now widely accepted and protected in Western nations include the right to life; personal liberties such as expression, conscience, religious worship, and privacy; freedom from arbitrary, unjust police actions or unequal application of laws; and political liberties such as voting and lobbying. In Eastern societies, especially those transfused by the collectivist values of ancient Chinese culture, there is far less recognition of individual rights.

Rights imply duties. Because individuals have rights, many protected by law, other people have clear duties to respect them. For example, management should not permit operation of a dangerous machine because this would deprive workers of the right to a safe workplace. This right is based on the natural right to protection from harm by negligent actions of others and is legally established in common law and the Occupational Safety and Health Act. If some risk in operating a machine is unavoidable, workers have the right to be given an accurate risk assessment.

legal rights
Protections and entitlements conferred by law.

Theories of rights have great importance in American ethical debates. A problem caused by our reverence for rights is that they are sometimes stretched into selfish demands or entitlements. Rights are not absolute and their limits may be hard to define. For example, every person has a right to life, but industry daily exposes people to risk of death by releasing carcinogens into the environment. An absolute right to life would require cessation of much manufacturing activity (for example, petroleum refining). Rights, such as the right to life, are commonly abridged for compelling reasons of benefit to the public.

The Theory of Justice

theory of justice
Each person should act fairly toward others in order to maintain the bonds of community.

A *theory of justice* defines what individuals must do for the common good of society. Maintaining the community is important because natural rights, such as the right to life, are reasonably protected only in a well-kept civil society. A basic principle of justice, then, is to act in such a way that the bonds of community are maintained. In broad terms, this means acting fairly toward others and establishing institutions in which people are subject to rules of fair treatment. In business life, justice requires fair relationships within the corporate community and establishment of policies that treat its members fairly.

In society, a person's chances for justice are determined by basic economic and political arrangements. The design of institutions such as business corporations and political constitutions has a profound effect on the welfare and life chances of individuals. A contemporary philosopher, John Rawls, has developed an influential set of principles for the design of a just society. Rawls speculates that rational persons situated behind a hypothetical "veil of ignorance" and not knowing their place in a society (i.e., their social status, class position, economic fortune, intelligence, appearance, or the like) but knowing general facts about human society (such as political, economic, sociological, and psychological theory) would deliberate and choose two rules to ensure fairness in any society they created. First, "each person is to have an equal right to the most extensive basic liberty compatible with a similar liberty for others," and second, "social and economic inequalities are to be arranged so that they are both (a) reasonably expected to be to everyone's advantage, and (b) attached to positions and offices

FIGURE 8.1
Three Spheres
of Justice

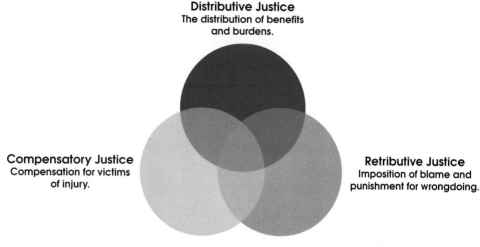

Distributive Justice
The distribution of benefits
and burdens.

Compensatory Justice
Compensation for victims
of injury.

Retributive Justice
Imposition of blame and
punishment for wrongdoing.

**distributive
justice**
The benefits
and burdens of
company life
should be dis-
tributed using
impartial
criteria.

**retributive
justice**
Punishment
should be even-
handed and
proportionate to
transgressions.

**compensatory
justice**
Victims should
receive fair
compensation
for damages.

**utilitarian
ethic**
The greatest
good for the
greatest
number.

open to all."[26] In general, inequality would only be allowed if it would make better the lot of the most disadvantaged members of the society.

The impartiality and equal treatment called for in Rawls's principles are re-
splendent in theory and may even inspire some business decisions, but they are
best applied to an analysis of broad societal issues. Acting justly in daily business
life, on the other hand, requires the application of maxims that more concretely
define justice. Managers can find such guidelines in three basic spheres of justice,
as shown in Figure 8.1.

Distributive justice requires that the benefits and burdens of company life be
distributed using impartial criteria. Awarding pay raises based on friendship
rather than performance criteria is unfair. All laws, rules, and procedures should
apply equally to each employee. *Retributive justice* requires punishment to be evenhanded and proportionate to transgressions. A cashier should not be fired for
stealing $5 if an executive who embezzled $10,000 is allowed to stay on the job and
pay it back. And *compensatory justice* requires fair compensation to victims. A corporation that damages nearby property must restore it to its original state; one
that hurts a customer must pay damages. The general idea of fairness in such maxims of justice supports orderly communities and organizations in which people
secure human rights and meet human needs.

The Utilitarian Ethic

The *utilitarian ethic* was developed between the late eighteenth century and the
mid-nineteenth century by a line of English philosophers, including Jeremy
Bentham and John Stuart Mill. The principle of utility, on which this ethic is based,
is that actions that promote happiness are right and actions that cause unhappi-
ness are wrong. The utilitarians advocated choosing alternatives that led to the
greatest sum of happiness or, as we express the thought today, the greatest good
for the greatest number.

[26] John Rawls, *A Theory of Justice* (Cambridge, MA: Harvard University Press, 1971), pp. 60–71.

Do Men and Women Reason Differently about Ethics?

Professor Lawrence J. Kohlberg of Harvard University became famous for research showing that from childhood on people pass through six stages of moral development.[27] These stages begin with utter selfishness and rise to the use of ethical principles. According to Kohlberg, not everyone gets to the highest, or principled-reasoning, stage—the moral development of most people is arrested at a middle stage.

To create and test his theory, Kohlberg measured changes over more than 20 years in the ethical thinking of 84 boys. Others who built on his work soon discovered that women, in particular, were unlikely to get to the higher stages. What was the reason? Were women less ethical than men? Professor Carol Gilligan, a colleague of Kohlberg's at Harvard, tried to answer these questions by studying the moral thinking of 144 men and women ranging in age from six to sixty.[28]

Gilligan learned that men and women approached ethical reasoning from different perspectives. The men in her studies grew to see themselves as autonomous, separate individuals in a competitive, hierarchical world of superior–subordinate relationships. As a result, male ethical thinking stressed protection of individual rights and enforcement of principled rules to channel and control aggression. The women, on the other hand, tended to see a world of relationships rather than individuals, a world in which people were interconnected in webs rather than arrayed in dominance hierarchies. Women did not think using abstract rules and principles that set sharp boundaries on behavior; they focused on the importance of compassion, care, and responsibility in relations with others. They were not ethically stunted; they just thought differently than men.

Kohlberg built his stages on the way ethical reasoning developed in men. Gilligan's work, however, indicated the existence of an equally valid but different developmental process in women. Based on her research, a *care ethic* exists; that is, a person should have compassion for others, avoid hurt in relationships, alleviate suffering, and respect the dignity of others. The care ethic is violated in business by, for example, cruelty toward subordinates, exploitation of consumers, deceit in relationships, or focus on individual performance that is indifferent toward the welfare of co-workers.

If Gilligan is correct, men emphasize rules, individual rights, and duties that can be fixed impartially; women emphasize caring and accept an intuitive emotional instinct as a valid criterion for behavior. However, even if this marked contrast exists, it seems to disappear in business. Studies of managers, as opposed to studies of young adults and students, fail to show gender differences in ethical decision making.[29]

[27] See, for example, Lawrence Kohlberg, "The Cognitive-Development Approach to Moral Education," in Peter Scharf, ed., *Readings in Moral Education* (Minneapolis: Winston Press, 1978).

[28] Carol Gilligan, *In a Different Voice* (Cambridge, MA: Harvard University Press, 1982).

[29] See Donald Robin and Laurie Babin, "Making Sense of the Research on Gender and Ethics in Business: A Critical Analysis and Extension," *Business Ethics Quarterly*, October 1997; and A. Catherine McCabe, Rhea Ingram, and Mary Conway Data-on, "The Business of Ethics and Gender," *Journal of Business Ethics*, March 2006.

In making a decision using this principle, one must determine whether the harm in an action is outweighed by the good. If the action maximizes benefit, then it is the optimum choice over other alternatives that provide less benefit. Decision makers should try to maximize pleasure and reduce pain, not simply for themselves but for everyone affected by their decision. Utilitarianism facilitates the comparison of the ethical consequences of various alternatives in a decision. It is a popular principle. Cost-benefit studies embody its logic and its spirit.

The major problem with utilitarianism is that in practice it has led to self-interested reasoning. Its importance in rationalizing the social ills of capitalism can hardly be overestimated. Since the 1850s it has been used to argue that the overall benefits of manufacturing and commerce are greater than the social costs. Since the exact definition of the "greatest good" is subjective, its calculation has often been a matter of expediency. A related problem is that because decisions are to be made for the greatest good of all, utilitarian thinking has led to decisions that permit the abridgment of individual or minority group rights. Utilitarianism does not properly relate individual and community ends in a way that protects both.[30]

REASONING WITH PRINCIPLES

The use of ethical principles, as opposed to the intuitive use of ethical common sense, may improve reasoning, especially in complex situations. Say a bank teller pockets $20 at the end of the day. The person's supervisor strongly feels that stealing is wrong and fires the teller. Ethical common sense is all that is needed in this situation, but the following situation defies a simple solution.

> I was working as a manager in a division that was going to be closed. The secret clock was ticking away to the surprise mass layoff. Then a co-worker approached. He was thinking of buying a house. Did I think it was a good time to get into real estate?
>
> The man's job was doomed and I knew it. But spilling the secret, I believed, would violate my integrity as a corporate officer and doom the company to a firestorm of fear and rumor. There was no way to win and no way out.
>
> I considered it my fiduciary responsibility to the business to keep my mouth shut, and yet here was this person coming for advice as a friend and a business acquaintance and I had material information that would affect him. For someone with a sense of empathy and sympathy, which I like to think I have some of, it was very, very hard.
>
> In the end I swallowed my anguish and kept silent. The man bought the house and lost his job. The secret held. But now 10 years later I have many times relived the story and second-guessed what I did that day.[31]

This is a vexing situation, and one created by the complexities of modern organizational life. The last paragraph finds the narrator alerted by the intuition ethic to the presence of an ethical conflict. Something in the situation causes anguish. In this predicament, however, simple moral homilies such as "tell the truth" or "be fair" are insufficient to resolve conflicts. Let us apply to this case three ethical principles, each of which offers a distinct perspective—utilitarianism, the rights ethic, and the theory of justice.

[30] See, for example, Mortimer Adler, *Desires: Right and Wrong* (New York: Macmillan, 1991), p. 61. John Stuart Mill's famous essay "Utilitarianism" deals directly and brilliantly with these and other criticisms. It is reprinted in Mary Warnock, ed., *Utilitarianism and Other Writings* (New York: New American Library, 1962), pp. 251–321.

[31] Paraphrased and quoted from Kirk Johnson, "In the Class of '70, Wounded Winners," *The New York Times,* March 7, 1996, p. A12.

The *utilitarian* ethic requires the manager to calculate which course of action, among alternatives, will result in the greatest benefit for the company and all workers. A frank response here will disrupt operations. People would resign, take days off, work less efficiently, and engage in sabotage. Keeping the secret will cause hardship for a single employee about to buy a house and perhaps others in a similar situation. On balance, the manager must protect the broader welfare of customers, stockholders, and remaining employees.

From the standpoint of *rights,* the employee is entitled to the truth and the manager has a duty to speak honestly. On the other hand, rights are not absolute. The corporation has the competing right to protect its property, and this right must be balanced against the right of an employee to straight talk. In addition, the manager, in effect, promised to keep the layoff confidential and has a duty of promise keeping.

In *justice,* corporations are required to promote fair, evenhanded treatment of employees. Distributive justice demands the impartial distribution of benefits and burdens. It would be partial to signal the layoff to one worker and not others.

Based on the application of utility, rights, and justice, the manager's decision to remain silent is acceptable. Some judgment is required in balancing rights, but the combined weight of reasoning with all three principles supports the manager's decision. Yet the manager's intuition was not wrongly aroused. The situation required, by commission or omission, a lie, and it violated the practical imperative by treating the employee as expendable while achieving a corporate goal. So both good and evil result from the resolution of this situation. In such cases, application of the principle of double effect is apppropriate. Here the welfare of the company outweighs the welfare of one employee, the manager's intention is not to hurt the employee but to help the company, and no better alternative presents itself (it is possible that the manager could be wishy-washy and evasive; however, this raises suspicion in the employee and, in any case, avoids resolution of the ethical dilemma). So the principle of double effect reconfirms the manager's action.

CHARACTER DEVELOPMENT

virtue ethic
Ethical behavior stems from character virtues built up by habit.

Character development is a source of ethical behavior separate from the use of principled reasoning. The theory that character development is the wellspring of ethical behavior can be called the *virtue ethic.* It originated with the Greek philosophers. Aristotle wrote that moral virtue is the result of habit.[32] He believed that by their nature ethical decisions require choice, and we build virtue, or ethical character, by habitually making the right choices. Just as we learn to play the piano through daily practice, so we acquire virtues by constant practice, and the more conscientious we are, the more accomplished we become. In a virtuous person ethical behavior comes from inner disposition, not from obeying external rules or applying abstract principles. Plato identified four fundamental traits— justice, temperance, courage, and wisdom—and these have come to be called the

---

[32] *Nichomachean Ethics,* trans. Thomson, p. 91.

cardinal virtues
The four most basic traits of an ethical character— justice, temperance, courage, and wisdom. They were identified by Aristotle.

cardinal virtues. Numerous other virtues have been mentioned over the years, including prudence, reverence, charitableness, hopefulness, and integrity.[33]

Application of the virtue ethic requires conscious effort to develop a good disposition by making right decisions over time. Then acts are generated by inner traits ingrained from repetition and reflect the disposition of a virtuous character. When Sholom Menora, CEO of Tri-United Technologies, moved out of Chicago, he sent a check for $25 to the city, believing that over the years he had neglected to feed parking meters from time to time.[34] This act reveals a trait of obsessive integrity, not the application of an abstract, high-level ethical principle.

The idea of acting from virtue does not require rejection of the ethical principles explained earlier in the chapter. Virtuous individuals might be more sophisticated in their principled reasoning.

PRACTICAL SUGGESTIONS FOR MAKING ETHICAL DECISIONS

There are practical steps to better define and resolve ethical problems in business. Here are some suggestions.

First, learn to think about ethics in rational terms using ideas such as universalizability, reversibility, utility, proportionality, or others. Such ideas enhance the ability to see ethical problems clearly and to create solutions.

Second, consider some simple decision-making tactics to illuminate alternatives. The philosopher Bertrand Russell advocated imaginary conversations with a hypothetical devil's advocate as an antidote for certitude. Write an essay in favor of a position and then a second opposed to it. Seek out a more experienced, ethically sensitive person in the company as an adviser. This person can be of great value in revealing the ethical climate of the firm or industry.

Use a two-column balance sheet to enter pros and cons for various alternatives, crossing out roughly equal considerations until a preponderance is left on one side or the other. Balance sheets organize information and discipline scattered, emotional thinking. Also, the process of entering all relevant factors sometimes brings new or unconscious considerations to light.

critical questions approach
A method of ethical reasoning in which insight comes from the answers to a preexisting, structured set of questions.

Another tactic is the *critical questions approach.* Ask yourself a series of questions about the ethical implications of an action. This approach is popular in corporations. If the questions are properly structured, answering them requires employees to consider key policies, principles, and relationships. The Raytheon conduct manual, for example, sets forth a list of 24 critical questions to figure out "the right thing to do."[35] Here is a similar, but shorter, list used at Lockheed Martin.

[33] Dennis J. Moberg, "The Big Five and Organizational Virtue," *Business Ethics Quarterly,* April 1999, p. 246.

[34] "Chicago Businessman Does Right by Jewish Law," *Ha'aretz,* October 6, 2000.

[35] Raytheon Company, *Standards of Business Conduct: Guidelines for Action* (Concord, MA: Office of Business Ethics and Compliance, August 2001), p. 4.

Quick Quiz—When in Doubt, Ask Yourself

- Are my actions legal?
- Am I being fair and honest?
- Will my actions stand the test of time?
- How will I feel about myself afterward?
- How will it look in the newspaper?
- Will I sleep soundly tonight?
- What would I tell my child to do?
- How would I feel if my family, friends, and neighbors knew what I was doing?

If you are still not sure what to do, ask . . . and keep asking until you are certain you are doing the right thing.[36]

These critical questions are shorthand for a variety of approaches to ethical reasoning. Some invoke basic maxims such as "obey the law" and "tell the truth." Others summon up the disclosure ethic and the intuition ethic.

Third, sort out ethical priorities early. Serious ethical dilemmas can generate paralyzing stress. However, clear values reduce stress by reducing temptation and easing conscience as a source of anxiety. For example, when being honest means sacrificing a sale, it helps to clarify in advance that integrity is more important than money.

Fourth, be publicly committed on ethical issues. Examine the workplace and find sources of ethical conflict. Then tell co-workers about your opposition to padding expense accounts, stealing company supplies, price fixing, or other actions that might become issues. Colleagues will be disinclined to approach you with corrupt intentions, and public commitment forces you to maintain your standards or suffer shame.

Fifth, set an example. This is a basic managerial function. An ethical manager creates a morally uplifting workplace. An unethical manager can make money, but he or she (and the company) pay the price—and the price is the person's integrity. Employees who see unethical behavior by their supervisor always wonder when that behavior will be directed at them.

Sixth, thoughts must be translated into action, and ethical deeds often require courage. Reaching a judgment is easier than acting. Ethical stands sometimes provoke anger in others or cost a company business, and there are personal risks such as job loss.

Seventh, cultivate sympathy and charity toward others. The question "What is ethical?" is one on which well-intentioned people may differ. Marcus Aurelius wrote: "When thou art offended by any man's fault, forthwith turn to thyself and reflect in what like manner thou dost err thyself; for example, in thinking that money is a good thing, or pleasure, or a bit of reputation, and the like."[37] Reasonable managers differ with respect to such matters as the rightness of outsourcing or genetic testing of workers.

Ethical perfection is illusory. We live in a morally complex civilization with endless rules, norms, obligations, and duties that are like road signs, usually pointing

---

[36] Lockheed Martin Corporation, *Setting the Standard: Code of Ethics and Business Conduct* (Bethesda, MD: Office of Ethics and Business Conduct, April 2006), p. 47.

[37] *The Meditations of Marcus Aurelius Antoninus,* trans. George Long (Danbury, CT: Grolier, 1980), p. 281; originally written circa A.D. 180.

Warning Signs

Lockheed Martin gives this list of phrases to all employees, telling them that when they hear one they are coming up on an ethical problem.

- "Well, maybe just this once."
- "No one will ever know."
- "It doesn't matter how it gets done as long as it gets done."
- "It sounds too good to be true."
- "Everyone does it."

- "Shred that document."
- "We can hide it."
- "No one will get hurt."
- "What's in it for me?"
- "This will destroy the competition."
- "We didn't have this conversation."

Source: Lockheed Martin, *Setting the Standard,* April 2006, p. 51. Reprinted with permission.

in the same direction but sometimes not. No decision ends conflicts, no principle penetrates unerringly to the Good, no manager achieves sainthood. There is an old story about the inauguration of James Canfield as president of Ohio State University. With him on the inaugural platform was Charles W. Eliot, president of Harvard University for 20 years. After receiving the mace of office, Canfield sat next to Eliot, who leaned over and whispered, "Now son, you are president, and your faculty will call you a liar." "Surely," said Canfield, "your faculty have not accused you of lying, Dr. Eliot." Replied Eliot, "Not only that, son, they've proved it!"

CONCLUDING OBSERVATIONS

There are many paths to ethical behavior. Not all managers appreciate the repertoire of principles and ideas that exist to resolve the ethical problems of business life. By studying ideas in this chapter, a person can become more sensitive to the presence of ethical issues and more resolute in correcting shortcomings. In addition, these principles and guidelines are applicable to ethical issues raised by the case studies throughout the book. We encourage referring to this chapter for conceptual tools.

Short Incidents for Ethical Reasoning

The following situations contain ethical conflicts. Try to define the ethical problems that exist. Then apply ideas, principles, and methods from the preceding two chapters to resolve them.

A CLOUDED PROMOTION

As chairman of an accounting firm in a large city, you were prepared to promote one of your vice chairmen to the position of managing partner. Your decision was based on a record of outstanding performance by this person over the eight years she has been with the firm. A new personnel director recently insisted on implementing a policy of résumé checks for hirees and current employees receiving promotions who had not been through such checks. Unfortunately, it was discovered that although the vice chairman claimed to have an MBA from the University of Michigan, she dropped out before completing her last 20 units of course work. Would you proceed with the promotion, retain the vice chairman but not promote her, or fire her?

THE ADMIRAL AND THE THIEVES

When Admiral Thomas Westfall took command of the Portsmouth Naval Shipyard, theft of supplies was endemic. It was a standing joke that homes in the area were painted gray with paint stolen from the Navy. Admiral Westfall issued an order that rules related to supply practices and forbidding theft would be strictly enforced. Within a few days, two career petty officers were apprehended carrying a piece of Plexiglas worth $25 out of the base. Westfall immediately fired both of them and also a civilian storeroom clerk with 30 years' service, who lost both his job and his pension. According to Westfall, "the fact that I did it made a lot of honest citizens real quick." Did the admiral act ethically?

SAM, SALLY, AND HECTOR

Sam, Sally, and Hector have been laid off from middle-management positions. Sam and Hector are deeply upset by their misfortune. They are nervous, inarticulate, and docile at an exit meeting in the personnel department and accept the severance package offered by the company (two weeks' pay plus continuation of health benefits for two weeks) without questioning its provisions. Sally, on the other hand, manifests her anxiety about job loss by becoming angry. In the exit meeting, she complains about the inadequacy of the severance package, threatens a lawsuit, and tries to negotiate more compensation. She receives an extra week of pay that the others did not get. Has the company been fair in its treatment of these employees?

A PERSONALITY TEST

You are asked by a potential employer to take a psychological profile test. A sample segment includes the items shown in the table at the bottom of the page.

Because you have read that it is best to fit into a "normal" range and pattern of behavior, and because it is your hunch that the personnel office will weed out unusual personalities, you try to guess which answers are most appropriate for a conservative or average response and write them in. Is this ethical?

AL

The CEO of a midwestern manufacturing company tells the following story.

> I was looking over recent performance reviews in the household products division and one thing that struck me was the review of a star sales rep named Al. I know Al because he handles our Wal-Mart account. Al had the highest annual sales for the past five years and last year nearly doubled the next highest rep's total. The sales manager's written evaluation was highly laudatory as expected, but cautioned Al to adhere strictly to discount policy, shipping protocol, and billing protocol. I got curious.
>
> A conversation with the division manager revealed that Al ingratiated himself with workers on the loading dock, socializing with them, sending them birthday cards, and giving them small gifts such as tickets to minor-league ball games. The loading dock supervisor complained that Al was requesting and sometimes getting priority loading of trucks for his customers despite the formal first-in, first-out rules for shipping orders. Second, Al had given several customers slightly deeper discounts than authorized, although the resulting orders were highly profitable for the company. And finally, late in December, Al had informally requested that one

	Yes	No	Can't Say
It is difficult to sleep at night.			
I worry about sexual matters.			
Sometimes my hands feel disjointed from my body.			
I sometimes smell strange odors.			
I enjoyed dancing classes in junior high school.			
Not all of my friends really like me.			
Work is often a source of stress.			

big account delay payment on an order by a week so that the commission would be counted in the next year. This would have gotten him off to a running start had not an accountant for the purchaser paid promptly and written to Al's manager in refusing the request.

The division head stuck up for Al. I didn't press or request that any action be taken. Did I do the right thing?

How would you answer the CEO's question?

A TRIP TO SEA WORLD

A sales representative for a large manufacturer of consumer electronics equipment headquartered in Los Angeles, California, has courted a buyer from a nationwide chain of 319 retail stores for over a year. At company expense the buyer was flown to Los Angeles from Trenton, New Jersey, with his spouse, for a three-day sales presentation. The company is paying all expenses for this trip and for the couple to attend a Los Angeles Dodgers baseball game and dine at fine restaurants.

During the second day of meetings, the buyer discusses a one-year, $40 million order. The chain that the buyer represents has not sold the company's products before, but once it starts, reorders are likely. At dinner that evening, the buyer mentions that he and his wife have always wanted to visit Sea World in San Diego. While they are in southern California and so close, they would like to fly down. It is clear that he expects the company to pay for this trip and that he will delay making a commitment for the $40 million order until he gets a response.

The company has already spent $2,200 for the buyer's trip to Los Angeles. The San Diego excursion would cost about $500. The marketing manager estimates that the company can make a 9 percent gross profit on the sale. The sales representative stands to receive a .125 percent commission over base salary.

What should the sales representative do?

MARY AND TOM

Mary P., an aerospace engineer, tells about a difficult career experience in which her friend Tom plays a central role.

My friend Tom and I are employed by Republic Systems Corporation. We started about the same time after graduating from engineering school five years

ago. The company does a lot of defense work, mostly for the Air Force, and it's big. Tom and I worked on project teams doing tests to make sure that electonics shipped to customers met specifications. We have very similar backgrounds and job records, and there has always been a little competition between us. But neither one of us pulled ahead of the other on the corporate ladder. That is until last winter.

At that time, we were assigned a special project to modify the testing protocol on certain radar components. The success of the projects was critical; it had to be done before Republic bid for two more years on its big radar systems contract. About 40 percent of our people work radar.

We rolled up our sleeves and put in long hours. After a month, though, Tom volunteered to be on a companywide task force developing a new employee privacy policy. Privacy is a big deal to Al Manchester, our CEO.

Tom continued to work with me, but he gradually put more and more of his energy into the privacy project. I had to start taking up some of the slack. He enjoyed the task force meetings. They met in the dining room at the Kenthill Country Club and he could hobnob with Al and some of the other big shots. He worked overtime to impress them.

We finally finished the testing project and it was a success. But toward the end I did the lion's share of it. One day, Tom made me angry by ending a capacitor test at 94 hours instead of the 100 hours you really have to have for validity. He did it because he was late for a privacy task force meeting. Overall, I guess Tom helped a lot, but he didn't do his share all the way through.

Last month the assistant manager of the radar project left the company and Tom and I both applied for the position. It was a pay raise of several grades and meant getting a lot of recognition. They chose Tom. The announcement in the company newsletter said that he was a "strong team player" and mentioned both the testing project and the privacy task force as major accomplishments.

I don't think it was fair.

Was Tom fair to Mary? Was Tom's promotion fair to Mary? Was the company wrong to promote Tom?

THE HONDA AUCTION

Dave Conant co-owned and managed Norm Reeves Honda in Cerritos, California. Naturally, he worked closely with Honda marketing executives to get cars for his dealership. One day, one of these executives, Dennis Josleyn, the new zone sales manager, approached him, asking him to submit a bid on 64 company cars. These were near-new cars previously driven by corporate executives or used to train mechanics. Company policy called for periodic auctions in which Honda dealers submitted competitive bids, and the high bidder got the cars to sell on its lot. It was Josleyn's job to conduct the auction.

"I want you to submit bids on each car $2,000 below wholesale market value," Joselyn told Dave Conant.

Conant dutifully inspected the 64 cars and submitted the asked-for bids. Meanwhile, Josleyn busied himself creating fake auction papers showing that other Honda dealers bid less than Conant. Of course, others bid near the wholesale price, so their bids were higher. Completing the phony auction, Josleyn announced the winner—Conant's dealership. The next day he showed up there and handed Conant an envelope.

"I have a little invoice for you," he said.

Conant went to his office, opened it, and found a bill for $64,000 payable to an ad agency co-owned by Josleyn and his brother. The message was clear. Josleyn wanted a 50–50 split with the dealer on the $2,000 windfall each car would bring, so he was billing Conant for half the extra $128,000 the entire batch of cars would bring in.

Conant faced a decision. If the invoice was paid, the dealership would make a $64,000 windfall. If he refused to pay, the cars would be rerouted to a dealer who was a "player" and future shipments of new Hondas might be slower. He decided to pay the invoice. In his own words: "I believed I had no choice. If I hadn't paid the amount, I would have incurred the wrath of Dennis Josleyn and possibly some of the other Honda gods, and I believe they would have taken our store down."[1]

Conant was not alone. Honda dealers around the country faced a dilemma. After investing large sums to build new showrooms and facilities and hire employees, they soon found themselves having to choose between two paths. If they gave bribes and kickbacks to Honda executives, they secured a copious flow of cars and made a fortune. On average, a favored dealer made almost $1,000,000 a year in personal income. However, if they stayed clean, no matter how modern their dealership and well trained its sales force, they received fewer cars and less profitable models. If they went bankrupt, and many did, the Honda executives arranged for less scrupulous owners to take over their dealerships. Many an honest dealer short on cars drove across town to see a rival's lot packed with fast-selling models in popular colors. Over time, it also became clear that the highest Japanese executives at Honda knew what was going on but chose to do nothing.

Did Conant make the right decision? What would you do in his position?

THE TOKYO BAY STEAMSHIP COMPANY

The Tokyo Bay Steamship Company operated a tourist ship between Tokyo and the volcanic island of Oshima 50 miles offshore. It also had a restaurant on the island. It was a modest business until February 1933, when Kiyoko Matsumoto, a 19-year-old college student, committed suicide by jumping into the crater of the volcano, which bubbled with molten lava. Ms. Matsumoto left a poetic suicide note and, through newspaper stories, the Japanese public became obsessed with her story.

Soon other Japanese emulated Ms. Matsumoto. In the next 10 months, 143 people threw themselves into the crater. Many more came to watch. One Sunday in April, for example, 31 people tried to jump; 25 were restrained, but 6 succeeded. People crowded around the edge of the crater waiting for jumpers. Shouts of "Who's next?" and "Step right this way. Lots of room down in front" could be heard.[2]

The Tokyo Bay Steamship Company capitalized on the volcano's popularity. It increased its fleet to 30 ships and added 19 more restaurants. Meanwhile, the Oshima police chief met the boat and tried to weed out potential suicides using a crude behavioral profile (was someone too happy or too sad?). A police officer stood at the rim of the volcano. The Japanese government made purchase of a one-way ticket to Oshima a crime. Many suicides were prevented; others succeeded. Twenty-nine people who were stopped at the volcano killed themselves by jumping into the ocean on the return boat to Tokyo.

In the meantime, Tokyo Bay Steamship company prospered. Its shares rose on the Tokoyo exchange. But did it meet basic standards of ethics?

---

[1] Quoted in Steve Lynch, *Arrogance and Accords: The Inside Story of the Honda Scandal* (Dallas: Pecos Press, 1997), p. 106.

[2] "Profits in Suicide," *Fortune*, May 1935, p. 116.

WOMEN AT IBM

In the spring of 1935 Thomas Watson, chairman of IBM, received a letter from Anne van Vechten, a 21-year-old college student at Bryn Mawr College who was friendly with his daughter. Watson agreed to meet her and discuss career opportunities in business. At the meeting she asked him why IBM did not hire women for professional careers.

Watson thought she had raised a good question. Soon van Vechten and 24 other young women were hired and enrolled for six weeks at the IBM school in Endicott, New York. This was a pleasant surprise to the 67 male sales and engineering candidates who arrived for the same training.

Watson was an intense autocrat who built IBM from a small calculating machine company, in part by creating a strong culture based on perfecting sales methods and absolute loyalty to the company. The six-week course would train these future IBM leaders in the IBM way. One way the culture was transmitted was through the songs employees sang. Watson composed many of them and hired a company band to play them. There was even one about women in the company.

"To Our IBM Girls"

(To the tune of "They're Style All the While")

They've made our IBM complete and worthwhile.
They work and they smile—so sweetly they smile.
Tall, short, thin, and stout girls—they win by a mile
With heavenly styles all the while.[3]

Source: From Songs of the IBM in Kevin Maney, *The Maverick and His Machine,* Wiley & Sons, 2003, p. 160. Reprinted with permission of John Wiley & Sons, Inc.

At the end of the six weeks, Watson threw a great dinner party for the students, where they mingled with IBM executives. Then, by tradition, the graduates went to IBM field offices where managers would assign them positions. But field managers refused to put the women in customarily male positions.

Watson had doted on these women. He was enraged and fired all 67 men in the class. If the men were not available, the field offices would have to accept the women or leave positions vacant. The men, many of whom had graduated from top colleges, were stunned at being thrown on the street while the nation was still in the grips of the Great Depression.

Did Watson make a good decision?

[3] From "Songs of the IBM," in Kevin Maney, *The Maverick and His Machine* (New York: John Wiley & Sons, 2003), p. 160. Copyright © 2003 John Wiley & Sons, Inc. This material is used by permission of John Wiley & Sons, Inc.

Columbia/HCA

Imagine injecting a shot of adrenaline into a lazy giant. This is what happened when one aggressive corporation brought business discipline to a health care industry unaccustomed to the rigors of market competition. It ran hospitals for a profit—a big profit. Yet its success was also its undoing. As its star rose, jealous competitors, nervous regulators, and guardians of traditional values in medicine gathered. When their moment arrived, they gave it a beating so severe that its management grew timid and its methods fell into disrepute, lying dormant now, awaiting resurrection.

HCA, as the corporation is now called, is still the nation's largest hospital chain. It owns 170 hospitals and 113 outpatient centers. At its peak it owned 318 hospitals, but it remains a dominating presence, with annual revenues exceeding those of Coca-Cola, Merck, or McDonald's.

RISING COSTS CHANGE AMERICA'S HEALTH CARE SYSTEM

The story is best begun by explaining long-term changes in the complex, chaotic tangle of entities and processes that is the U.S. health care system. Rising costs drive these changes. In 1950, health care in America consumed only 4.4 percent of GDP, but by 2006 that figure had risen to 16 percent, the highest of any nation.[1] Despite this massive spending, 45 million people who still lack health insurance have only limited access to care. And the system is characterized by tremendous inefficiency and poor service.

[1] Marc Kaufman and Rob Stein, "Record Share of Economy Spent on Health Care," *Washington Post,* January 10, 2006, p. A1.

The origins of rising expenditures lie in the years after World War II when the federal government began to fund medical studies. This, along with research in companies, led to a steady stream of new machines, drugs, and treatments that increased the expense of medical intervention. As medical care began to cost more, demand for health insurance rose, and in the 1960s most Americans enrolled in health plans, most of which were paid for by employers. These plans usually allowed people unlimited access to doctors and hospitals if they met small annual deductibles and co-payments. Insurers paid claims one by one on a fee-for-service basis. Financial incentives to limit treatment costs that had existed when patients themselves paid vanished when insurance became widespread.

In 1965 the federal government set up Medicare to pay hospitalization and other expenses for people over 65 and, sharing expenses with the states, set up the Medicaid program to finance care for the poor. The two programs covered most people who were not in employer-sponsored plans. In effect, government gave every citizen access to medical treatment, and health care soon came to be seen as an entitlement. These government programs increased demand for medical services and, of course, expenditures climbed.

As costs rose, so did pressures to reduce them. By the early 1980s Medicare and Medicaid payments strained government budgets. Private employers and insurance companies complained loudly that paying for employee health care sapped productivity and held down wages. Hospital expenses were the primary reason; it was in hospitals that dazzling new machines and procedures escalated costs out of control.

MEDICARE CHANGES ITS BILLING PROCEDURE

To combat rising hospital costs, Medicare in 1983 changed its reimbursement method. Instead of paying one by one for each inpatient treatment and procedure, it now gave the hospital a lump sum based on one of 470 categories, or "codes," into which patients' illnesses were classified. The single payment that Medicare would make was based on the underlying costs of each hospital and the average severity of specific maladies. This coding system was intended to lower Medicare payouts by giving hospitals

an incentive to cut the costs of treatment, and they did so.

When the 470 illness categories—or *diagnosis-related groups* (DRGs)—were introduced, the average length of hospitalizations shortened. There were cost savings in shortening patients' stays, but within two years Medicare payments began to creep up again. The incentive for hospitals was to spend less on patients and cut short their stays. However, shorter hospital stays led to a big rise in outpatient procedures and follow-up care, as many Medicare patients walked from hospital rooms to outpatient clinics for treatments.

The DRG system, which still functions, is terribly complex. The coding procedure is a labyrinth of rules covering more pages than the notoriously intricate Internal Revenue Code.[2] A small army of consultants exists to help hospitals digest it, and specialized software is used to ensure that Medicare is billed maximum rates. Despite their complexity, the rules have never been clear and cannot be made so. This is because the diagnosis of an illness by a physician is somewhat subjective. Moreover, the maladies of patients and the treatments they need often defy standard definitions. So no set of codes can ever neatly classify all illnesses and the range of their severities.

This shortcoming leads to a cat and mouse game between hospitals and the federal government in which hospitals routinely engage in *upcoding*, or interpreting the illnesses of patients in such a way that they fall into higher-paying DRG codes. Upcoding is so common in the industry that for most of the 1980s and 1990s Medicare payments were adjusted downward in anticipation of inflated billings from hospitals.[3]

THE RISE OF MANAGED CARE

While the government struggled to hold down Medicare payments with its complicated billing code, insurance companies and employers tried to hold down their costs by implementing a philosophy of health care delivery that has come to be called *managed care*. Managed care reduces nonessential and

[2] Uwe E. Reinhardt, "Medicare Can Turn Anyone into a Crook," *The Wall Street Journal*, January 21, 2000, p. A18.
[3] Holman W. Jenkins, Jr., "A Hospital Chain's Lemonade Man," *The Wall Street Journal*, May 24, 2000, p. A27.

marginally beneficial medical treatment by limiting reimbursement for it, causing it to be rationed.

Although managed care takes many forms, the primary form is the *health management organization,* or HMO. An HMO is an organization that includes an insurer and a network of physicians, hospitals, and services such as labs. Corporations enter contracts with HMOs under which they pay a fixed monthly or annual fee per employee in return for a full range of medical care. To compete for the business of employers, HMOs must control their costs, and they do so by limiting access to expensive specialists and treatments. The idea of managed care swiftly carried the day. As recently as the late 1980s, about 70 percent of insured employees were in older fee-for-service plans, but by the late 1990s, almost 85 percent of them were in some kind of managed care plan.[4]

The rise of managed care and the imposition of DRGs by Medicare made cost cutting the hammer of change. Both physicians and hospitals had to slash fees and discount services. This led to striking alterations in the medical industry. Physicians who had been solo practitioners were forced into HMOs to maintain full waiting rooms. Their traditional authority and the sanctity of the doctor–patient relationship were circumscribed in managed care where treatment decisions could be second-guessed by insurance bureaucrats who approved payments.

Merger waves swept through all parts of the system, including insurers, managed care organizations such as HMOs, and hospitals. These mergers were attempts to lower per-unit costs by achieving economies of scale and to get power over pricing by controlling a larger share of the market.

Both the profit and the not-for-profit entities that provide health care feel competitive forces, and both are forced to respond. Even tax-exempt hospitals must reduce their costs or risk catastrophic loss of the paying patients who subsidize their charitable work. These competitive forces in the health care industry led to the predatory incarnation of HCA known as Columbia/HCA Healthcare Corporation, a name the company later shed in the hope of restoring its reputation with the public.

THE RISE OF A PREDATOR

Columbia/HCA was the inspiration of a brilliant and hardworking entrepreneur named Richard L. Scott. As a boy growing up in Kansas City he watched his parents struggle with family finances. His father was a truck driver. His mother worked as a hostess at a Chinese restaurant and a clerk at J. C. Penney's to augment the family budget. Their money battles motivated him. "My goal was I wanted to do something good and not have to live paycheck to paycheck," he recalls.[5]

In 1977 Scott graduated from law school and joined a Dallas law firm, where he worked on acquisitions and public offerings for health care corporations. After 10 years of this, Scott, who was no shrinking violet, decided that he wanted to run his own company. He startled the industry by lining up financing and offering $3.9 billion to buy Hospital Corporation of America, then the nation's largest hospital company. Its directors rejected the bid, laughing at Scott. Here was a suitor, a relative unknown, whose only direct business experience was running two donut shops in college, stepping up to take charge of a mighty company, like a guy who flies model planes on weekends taking the controls of a Boeing 747.

Then, late in 1987 a Texas investor agreed to back Scott in starting a new hospital company. At the time, the hospital industry was ailing. Because of the introduction of DRGs by Medicare and the rise of managed care, both the number and length of hospital stays had declined. There was an oversupply of hospital beds. Many facilities could not cover costs and faced bankruptcy. Scott, however, had a penetrating vision of the industry in which he saw opportunity, not stagnation, and he got off to a running start. Setting up a Dallas office for the new company he named Columbia Hospital Corporation, he wrote 1,000 letters to hospitals around the country offering to buy them. Mostly, the answer was no, but eventually he bought two weak-performing El Paso hospitals.

With the two hospitals in hand, Scott began to inject the strategies that he would use to revolutionize the industry. First, he gave local physicians part ownership of the hospitals. Physicians are the source of patients for a hospital: no patient can be admitted

---

[4] Brian O'Reilly, "What Really Goes on in Your Doctor's Office?" *Fortune,* August 17, 1998, p. 166; and Mindy Charski, "A Healthy Trend Ends," *U.S. News & World Report,* September 28, 1998, p. 60.

[5] Quoted in M. C. Moewe, "Ex-Columbia Chief Helps Grow Solantic," *Jacksonville Business Journal,* April 14, 2006, p. 1.

without a doctor's signature. When physicians have an equity interest in a local hospital, they have a financial incentive to refer patients there. Second, he consolidated the El Paso market by buying a third hospital nearby and closing it. This reduced the number of beds available, raising demand for the remaining beds in Scott's hospitals. And third, he used the hospitals he owned as hubs to which he began attaching other health services, including a psychiatric hospital, diagnostic centers, and a cancer-treatment center. He planned to make money referring insured persons back and forth within a network of services owned by Columbia.[6]

Scott soon bought more hospitals. The pickings grew easier, because across the country, independent hospitals were floundering under the twin strains of an oversupply of beds and capped payments from insurers and Medicare. Scott promised the owners and trustees of stand-alone hospitals that he would take their struggling facilities and make them efficient cogs in his Columbia system.

While Scott rapidly bought individual hospitals, Columbia also expanded by acquiring other chains. In 1990 Columbia went public, and its successful offering and rising share price gave Scott more capital with which to finance acquisitions. Between 1990 and 1994 Columbia absorbed five competing hospital chains, bringing in 199 more hospitals and 96 surgical centers.[7] One of the chains was Hospital Corporation of America (HCA), whose directors had laughed off Scott's offer only three years before. After the HCA merger in 1994, the company's name became Columbia/HCA.

HOW COLUMBIA/HCA WORKED

As Scott took over hospitals, he wrung money from them by applying a hard-nosed business discipline exceeding anything ever seen in hospital management. He was a genius at coaxing efficiencies from a corporate system. Some of his methods were praiseworthy; others danced near ethical boundaries; all of them gamed the incentives in the industry environment to maximum advantage.

Because of Columbia/HCA's size and strong balance sheet, when it took over a hospital, it refinanced the facility's debt with cheaper capital. With the savings on debt service that this created, the corporation made the hospital more attractive by making cosmetic appearance changes, modernizing equipment, and installing a sophisticated information system. Rigorous cost cutting then took place.

Since the hospital was now in the large Columbia/HCA system, it could take advantage of the discounts and just-in-time deliveries that Scott demanded from suppliers. Columbia/HCA became the world's largest buyer of medical supplies, and Scott was an expert at squeezing vendors. Often, however, the staff had to use lower-quality items that cost less. At Good Samaritan Hospitals in Santa Clara County, California, nurses complained that the gloves the company bought were weaker and more likely to tear than those they had used previously and that the valves for chest tubes lacked open/shut indicators.[8]

Staff cuts also trimmed costs, and after Columbia/ HCA takeovers there were fewer nurses and administrators and more part-time workers. This sometimes led to deteriorating patient care. At Columbia Sunrise Hospital in Las Vegas, the ratio of staff to patients fell 20 percent.[9] Nurses in critical-care units reported that it took more than six hours to get the results of urgent blood tests that should have been reported in minutes. In a poll of workers at the hospital, 44 percent believed that staffing cuts had increased medication errors and 4 percent attributed one or more patient deaths to understaffing.[10]

Scott moved in his own managers and pushed them to perform. Hospital administrators were focused on quarterly earnings and given ambitious targets, typically revenue growth of 15 percent to 40 percent per year. He used a system of "scorecards" that showed the performance of each hospital in multiple areas. For example, part of each scorecard had a "case-mix index" to track the relative proportion of patients with illnesses that were highly reimbursed under Medicare's coding system. Administrators

[6] Sandy Lutz and E. Preston Gee, *Columbia/HCA—Healthcare on Overdrive* (New York: McGraw-Hill, 1998) pp. 70–73.

[7] Robert Kuttner, "Columbia/HCA and the Resurgence of the For-Profit Hospital Business," *New England Journal of Medicine,* August 1, 1996, p. 362.

[8] Ibid.

[9] David R. Olmos, "Do Profits Come First at Vegas Hospital?" *Los Angeles Times,* September 26, 1997, p. A1.

[10] Diane Sosne, "The Truth about Hospitals That Exist to Make Money," *Seattle Times,* July 11, 1997, p. B5.

were supposed to raise the index number.[11] Much of a hospital manager's pay was based on a salary bonus plan, and 90 percent of the bonus came from meeting short-term financial goals. In the mid-1990s a typical hospital manager had an annual salary of $150,000 but could earn up to $1 million with bonus and stock options.[12] This far exceeded the compensation of managers in not-for-profit hospitals.

The Columbia/HCA system included unsparing discipline—managers who missed their targets were abruptly replaced. Some hospitals had three or four new heads in a year. Many managers resigned when the pressure became too much or when they felt they were compromising their values. One chief administrator who left a Florida hospital had been asked to put a sign in the emergency room saying that patients' green cards would be inspected. Under federal law, no patient can be released from an emergency room until his or her condition is stabilized and so anyone who comes in must be seen. The sign was an effort to scare away to some competing hospital illegal immigrants with no health insurance or ability to pay.[13]

Columbia/HCA tried to increase revenues as well as cut costs. One way was by creating incentives for doctors. Giving them equity in the hospitals was a central tactic, and many Columbia/HCA hospitals were 15 to 20 percent physician-owned. A *New York Times* investigation examined referral patterns of 62 physicians in two Columbia/HCA hospitals in Florida and found that after investing in these facilities, the doctors as a group referred more patients to them and fewer to competitors.[14] Sometimes Columbia/HCA also owned the physicians' practices. During its expansion, it purchased 1,400 practices and provider networks to funnel in patients. There were other incentives. On slow weekends at Sunrise Medical Center in Las Vegas, doctors who admitted the most patients won Caribbean cruises.[15]

Another method of raising revenues was aggressive Medicare billing. As it grew, Columbia/HCA got more than 30 percent of its revenues from Medicare and became Medicare's largest single claimant. A team of *New York Times* investigative reporters studied the results of zealous billing at Cedars Medical Center in Miami.[16] Because Medicare pays a fixed amount for any patient in a given disease category, a hospital gets more if patients are coded in high-reimbursement categories. For example, in DRG 79, which is the code for upper respiratory treatments, there are four categories of pneumonia. The highest-paid category is complex respiratory infection, for which Cedars would be reimbursed $6,800 per case. The lowest-paid category is simple pneumonia, which was reimbursed at $3,150 per case.

Studying records, the *Times* reporters learned that before being taken over by Columbia in 1992, Cedars billed 31 percent of pneumonia cases as complex respiratory infections. After the takeover, complex respiratory infections rose to 93 percent of cases. Meanwhile, a county hospital across the street billed only 28 percent of its cases as complex respiratory infection. Years later, when the company was accused of illegally upcoding, or increasing payments by billing in higher categories than justified, it would argue that the billing at Cedars and other hospitals was not fraudulent; it simply reflected greater mastery of Medicare's complex coding rules than competitors could develop.

Scott introduced bold marketing. Unique to the industry was a sales force that prospected for new business. He also started a national branding campaign with television and print ads designed to fix the Columbia/HCA name and logo in the public mind so that when Americans needed a hospital they would seek out Columbia/HCA, just as when they wanted a hamburger, they looked for a McDonald's restaurant.

RESISTANCE AND CRISIS

As time went by, Scott's strategies became widely known and discussed. His methods abraded idealistic social values, built up over many generations, in which slighting treatment to save money is wrong.

[11] Lucette Lagnado, "Blowing the Whistle on Columbia/HCA: An Interview with Marc Gardner," *Multinational Monitor,* April 1998, p. 18.

[12] Michele Bitoun Blecher, "Rough Crossings," *Hospitals & Health Networks,* October 5, 1997, p. 40.

[13] Ibid.

[14] Martin Gottlieb and Kurt Eichenwald, "High Stakes Investments: Health-Care Giant Offers Its Doctors a Share of Hospitals," *Sun-Sentinel,* April 13, 1997, p. 1G.

[15] Olmos, "Do Profits Come First at Vegas Hospital?" p. 1G.

[16] Martin Gottlieb, Kurt Eichenwald, and Josh Barbanel, "Health Care's Giant: Powerhouse under Scrutiny," *The New York Times,* March 28, 1997, p. A1.

Competitors spoke against him. Labor unions resented his staff cutbacks and worked to undermine him. Soon resistance to new hospital acquisitions grew. In 1995 alone, Columbia/HCA had to back out of 30 pending deals when state regulators and civic groups that Scott's opponents had lobbied rose in opposition.

Nevertheless, the company prospered. Its growth showed in the rise of annual revenues from $4.9 billion in 1990 to $20 billion in 1996. Over this time, net profits averaged 7 percent a year, an excellent return that was 15 to 20 percent higher than at competing chains.

By then, Columbia/HCA was not only the largest hospital chain in the country but the largest home care operation as well, with 590 facilities in 30 states. Home care was critical in Scott's strategy to develop a continuum of services. One attraction of it was that Medicare payments for home care were more generous than were payments for hospital stays. Scott required hospital administrators to capture for Columbia/HCA facilities 85 percent of discharged patients needing home care.[17]

While Columbia/HCA grew, Scott became wealthy. He held 9.4 million shares and by 1996 had an annual salary exceeding $2 million. At this high point, however, the fall was near.

Entering 1997 Scott drove hard. He rose in the morning for 5:00 A.M. workouts and 6:00 A.M. strategy sessions. He worked frenetically and pushed those around him to do the same. Initiatives, policies, and directives spewed from him rapid-fire. Colleagues were fatigued by both his demands and the company's skyrocketing growth.

Then in March, federal authorities began a sweeping investigation into Medicare billing fraud at Columbia/HCA. Agents raided its hospitals in El Paso and removed billing documents. A federal grand jury in Florida indicted three executives for submitting false cost reports and claims. Soon federal agents served search warrants at 35 other facilities and issued subpoenas for all kinds of billing records.

These investigations punctured Columbia/HCA's stock price, stiffened resistance to acquisitions, foreshadowed friction with regulators, and threatened crippling fines. Yet Scott seemed unaware of the danger.

On the day the FBI raided 35 facilities and the company's shares tumbled 12 percent, he appeared on CNN and assured listeners that "government investigations are matter-of-fact in health care."[18]

A media obsession grew. Investigative reports ran in newspapers and on television, all built on horror stories about the effects of money incentives in Columbia/HCA hospitals. The company was strangely silent. Scott refused to respond; indeed, he seemed not to sense a crisis, but members of the Columbia/HCA board of directors did. In late July they summoned him to a meeting and forced his resignation. He got a $10 million severance package.

NEW COURSE IN A SEA OF TROUBLES

Another board member, Thomas Frist, Jr., was picked to succeed Scott. Frist quickly backed away from Scott's more aggressive strategies. He ended annual bonuses for hospital administrators, undid the equity relationships of physicians in hospitals, sold the home health care business, stopped the national branding campaign, changed billing procedures, and increased audits and compliance reports on Medicare billings. He also created the post of senior vice president of corporate ethics, compliance, and corporate responsibility. Soon a new, warm "Mission and Values" statement was adopted (see the box). And eventually, he changed the firm's name. The new name, HCA, Inc., dropped the word Columbia, disowning Scott's legacy.

Downdrafts from the investigations hit hard. Patients were frightened away. With Frist's approval, 40 hospitals dropped Columbia/HCA from their names. Revenues and net income fell. Share prices dived from a high of $45 in 1997 to a low of $17 in 1998. Acquisitions were typically financed with stock, but with share prices falling, the pending acquisition of another health care company was canceled. Hospital takeovers were shelved and construction of new hospitals stopped. Over the next several years, Frist sold more than 100 hospitals.

The assault by government was relentless. The Internal Revenue Service assessed $267 million in

---

[17] Lucette Lagnado, Anita Sharpe, and Greg Jaffe, "How Columbia/HCA Changed Health Care, for Better or Worse," *The Wall Street Journal,* August 1, 1997, p. A4.

[18] Lutz and Gee, *Columbia/HCA—Healthcare on Overdrive,* p. 135.

HCA, Inc., Mission and Values Statement
Above all else, we are committed to the care and improvement of human life. In recognition of this commitment, we will strive to deliver high quality, cost-effective healthcare in the communities we serve. In pursuit of our mission, we believe the following value statements are essential and timeless.

- We recognize and affirm the unique and intrinsic worth of each individual.
- We treat all those we serve with compassion and kindness.
- We act with absolute honesty, integrity and fairness in the way we conduct our business and the way we live our lives.
- We trust our colleagues as valuable members of our healthcare team and pledge to treat one another with loyalty, respect, and dignity.

Source: Reprinted courtesy of HCA, Inc.

back taxes for wrongful deductions the company had made. Whistle-blowers emerged from within and filed lawsuits under the False Claims Act, which allows workers to bring fraud charges against employers on behalf of the U.S. government and receive part of any monetary settlements. In 2000, HCA pled guilty to criminal charges and agreed to pay $840 million in criminal fines, civil restitution, and other penalties to settle Medicare fraud charges. It agreed to $745 million in civil penalties while not admitting wrongdoing. In addition, it accepted a $95 million criminal fine, pleading guilty to fraudulent pneumonia upcoding, false billing, and giving kickbacks to physicians for referring patients.[19] In 2003 the whistle-blower lawsuits were settled when HCA agreed to another $631 million in civil penalties and damages. Nine former employees received a total of $152 million as their share. In addition, the company paid a $250 million settlement to Medicare and Medicaid. Overall, it handed over more than $1.7 billion.[20]

These huge sums seemed to signal that HCA's management and culture were rife with fraud. Would executives go to jail? Remarkably, the government indicted only five midlevel managers on charges of criminal fraud. Of these, only two were convicted and their convictions were overturned in a unanimous U.S. appeals court ruling. The court found the Medicare rules so unclear that the way the two managers had interpreted them seemed as reasonable as the way the government prosecutors did.[21]

The dearth of successful prosecutions suggests that the government could not find strong evidence of criminal intent. Scott was never accused of any wrongdoing and never sued. One lawyer who spent seven years scrutinizing HCA documents on a civil case commented that he could never reach a conclusion about Scott's knowledge of any wrongdoing.[22]

As part of its 2000 criminal plea, HCA signed an agreement requiring it to set up an ethics and compliance program to be overseen by the Department of Justice until 2009. This program includes training for all employees, a network of compliance managers throughout the company, hotlines, and ethical audits. Among other changes, HCA now requires employees in its billing offices to submit questions about coding to physicians on a written form. The forms are closely audited.

The slow torture by investigation and prosecution of HCA petrified the health care industry. Companies pulled back from aggressive Medicare billing. Instead of upcoding, the industry lobbied for higher payments

[19] "HCA—The Health Care Company & Subsidiaries to Pay $840 Million in Criminal Fines and Civil Damages and Penalties," U.S. Department of Justice press release, December 14, 2000.

[20] "Largest Health Care Fraud Case in U.S. History Settled: HCA Investigation Nets Record Total of $1.7 Billion," U.S. Department of Justice press release, June 26, 2003.

[21] *United States v. Robert W. Whiteside and Jay A. Jarrell,* 285 F3d 1352 (2002).

[22] Peter Chatfield of the law firm Phillips and Cohen, quoted in Moewe, "Ex-Columbia Chief Helps Grow Solantic," p. 1.

and in 2000 Congress responded by raising reimbursements in the DRG codes. Whereas in the past Congress had squeezed payments in anticipation of upcoding, it now made them more generous to compensate for the extant wave of timidity. Either way, costs continued to rise.

WHITHER CORPORATE HEALTH CARE?

Rick Scott's vision of corporate-delivered, profit-conscious health care lies tattered. His company goes on, a maverick now rendered obedient. Were Scott's strategies inherently wrong, or were they appropriate but badly executed?

Scott applied market solutions to intractable problems growing in the health care system for half a century. The central problem was then, and remains, rising costs. Scott imposed the for-profit corporate form on the delivery of medical services and worked it to every advantage, ruthlessly seeking savings and efficiencies. Obscured in the controversy is the fact that the formula often succeeded, elevating hospital performance to the advantage of patients and communities as well as investors.

For example, when the company took over Cape Fear Memorial Hospital in Wilmington, North Carolina, in 1995, it made $1 million in improvements. A year later, admissions were up 6 percent, babies delivered up 40 percent, unpaid care to charity patients up 12 percent, and staffing up almost 25 percent.[23] Moreover, other hospitals in the area were forced to discipline their costs or Columbia/HCA would have underbid them for the business of local employers. This dampened medical cost inflation. However, story lines such as this were less newsworthy than claims that Columbia/HCA was killing patients with its miserly ways, so the public mostly heard and read about scandal, not achievement.

Nurses' unions that stood to lose members in staff cuts opposed Scott. Federal and state regulators who stood to lose power if free market forces grew stronger opposed him. And critics with traditional values opposed him, wanting to believe that unlimited, universal health care delivered by physicians in the mold of the old-fashioned, avuncular TV doctor Marcus Welby was a realistic, affordable option. They were suspicious

of business methods in the vicinity of life and death decisions. Among them was Pope John Paul II, who, after the El Paso raids, said that "the centrality and dignity of the human person are ignored and trampled on . . . when healthcare is regarded in terms of profit and not as a generous service."[24]

While the HCA prosecutions have pushed Scott's methods into the background, the market forces they thrived on remain. Costs keep rising. Payers resist price inflation. Government still distorts health care markets by setting prices for nearly $400 billion of health care each year, supporting its invasion with a thicket of rules forming perhaps the nation's single most confusing body of regulation. Although companies fear exploiting the ambiguities in these rules, they continue to exist. In any case, if these forces remain strong in health care markets, and they will, aggressive strategies based on efficiency at some point must again emerge.

WHITHER SCOTT AND HCA?

After Columbia/HCA, Scott started a venture capital firm in Florida, investing successfully in a variety of businesses, including a cable channel, a software company, and a plastics manufacturer. Nine years elapsed before he first allowed an interview touching on his resignation. "It clearly was hard," he said, "I built it from scratch. . . . You just go on, go do something."[25]

At heart, Scott remains a health care entrepreneur. Today he is chairman and majority owner of Solantic, a chain of retail health clinics. You can walk into one of his clinics located in a Florida Wal-Mart without an appointment and choose from a range of services, including physicals, X-rays, and blood tests. Physicians are present. A digital display keeps you informed of the waiting time. The company's Web site states: "We will strive to provide services in the most efficient way possible so we can provide fair prices to our customers. We will not waste money and will always look for ways to lower our expenses/costs so we can lower our prices."[26] Scott's strategy is to undercut traditional hospitals and doctors offices with low prices and prompt, friendly service. So far there

[23] Blecher, "Rough Crossings," p. 40.

[24] Quoted in "News at Deadline," *Modern Healthcare*, July 7, 1997, p. 4.

[25] Quoted in Moewe, "Ex-Columbia Chief Helps Grow Solantic," p. 1.

[26] http://www.solantic.com/values.asp

are 13 of these walk-in clinics with plans for 40 by 2009 and, eventually, 1,000. Will Scott rise with a visionary business model once again?

In 2006 HCA was taken private in a $33 billion buyout by its management and three private equity firms. At the time, it was the largest private buyout ever. Ordinarily such deals suggest that the investors believe a company is undervalued. By taking it private they avoid shareholder pressures and some securities regulations. In their absence, management can change the business, introducing new strategies and efficiencies. If successful, the value of the business grows. Then the investors can sell it back to public shareholders, making a large profit. Will HCA's new owners reintroduce elements of Scott's strategies?

Questions

1. Is a market-driven approach valid for the health care industry? Do you support or oppose trade-offs between care quality and efficiency?

2. Is health care a basic right? Can it be limited if the cost of providing unlimited treatment is prohibitive? If so, should it be regarded as a commodity and limited by market mechanisms, or should it be rationed by government regulation? If not, how can the nation pay for it?

3. How should the strategies behind HCA's rise to prominence be assessed? Were they fundamentally flawed, ethically wrong, and unworkable? Or were they appropriate and workable in the industry environment but badly carried out?

4. On balance, did HCA use health care resources more efficiently than competitors, or did it compromise care by shifting costs to patients and staff and moving the savings to executive salaries, dividends, and acquisitions?

5. HCA experienced terrible difficulties. Could they have been prevented? If you could go back in time, replace Rick Scott, and run the company, at what point would you choose to arrive and what changes would you make to salvage the good and prevent the bad?

Chapter Nine

Business in Politics

The Abramoff Scandals

In 2003 a *Washington Post* reporter began looking at the web of artifice spun by a lobbyist named Jack Abramoff. Her stories led the nation's Capitol into one of its periodic scandals.[1] Like others before it, this one was a blend of systemic problems and individual dishonesty.

The scandal unfolds in the stories of four men it consumed. We begin not with Abramoff, but with Congressman Tom DeLay (R-Tex.), who created the political climate in which Abramoff flourished.

Rep. Tom DeLay (R-Texas)

K Street Project
A political machine built to promote Republican domination by aligning the lobbying industry with Republican causes.

DeLay was first elected to the House of Representatives in 1984 from the suburbs of Houston. He joined an inner circle of conservatives working to bring Republicans to power. When the party took control in 1994, he became majority whip, and later, majority leader. From these powerful positions he built a political machine called the *K Street Project* that pressured lobbyists, trade associations, and corporations to support the Republican party. Its purpose was to protect the new Republican majority and promote a conservative legislative agenda.

Here is how the K Street Project worked. DeLay compiled lists of campaign contributions and called lobbyists to his office, telling them that if they supported Democrats they would not have access or influence in the House. He pressured trade associations to hire more Republican lobbyists, even recommending names. "We're just following the old adage of punish your enemies and reward your friends," he said.[2] It worked. After 1994, lobbying firms, trade groups, and corporations all hired more Republicans and gave more campaign contributions to Republican lawmakers.[3] Over the years 29 members of DeLay's staff moved from his office to jobs in the lobbying industry, representing about 350 corporations at one time or another.[4]

---

[1] Deborah Howell, "Getting the Story on Jack Abramoff," *Washington Post,* January 15, 2006, p. B6.

[2] Quoted in Thomas B. Edsall, "Lobbyists' Emergence Reflects Shift in Capital Culture," *Washington Post*, January 12, 2006, p. A1.

[3] Matthew Continetti, *The K Street Gang* (New York: Doubleday, 2006), p. 47.

[4] Ibid., p. 53.

earmark
A provision in a bill allocating a specific sum for a specific project.

To reward "friends" DeLay loosened constraints on the use of earmarks. An *earmark* is a provision in a bill allocating a specific sum for a specific project in a member's district. The earmark may direct that work be done by a particular company. This departs from standard appropriations that send money to an agency that then decides how to spend it. In the past, Congress had been wary of the potential for corruption in earmarks and only the most senior lawmakers used them in a limited way. But DeLay encouraged their more frequent use to reward loyal lobbyists. The number of earmarks skyrocketed, from 892 worth $2.6 billion in 1992 to 13,997 worth $27.3 billion in 2005.[5]

DeLay, who once ran a pest control company, ruled with an iron fist, and earned the nickname "The Hammer." As his machine rolled on, the tone in Washington changed. He disdained compromise with Democrats. Politics became more partisan and bare knuckled. Barriers between legislators and lobbyists wore away and with them ethical standards. As standards faded, the connection between campaign contributions and favors grew tighter. Earmarks became a "currency of corruption."[6]

DeLay's politics invited, almost required, ethical compromise and some obliged. The House ethics committee rebuked DeLay four times, once for example, for pressuring the Electronics Industry Association to hire a Republican as its top executive. Yet as scandals involving associates swirled around him, he declared innocence. Finally, he resigned in 2006 after being indicted in Texas for misuse of campaign funds. While he denied any crimes, his K Street strategy had beckoned corruption. Others may have added a second, essential ingredient—dishonesty. One was Jack Abramoff.

Jack Abramoff

Just when DeLay began to put his imprint on Washington politics in the mid-1990s, a young Jack Abramoff began his career as a lobbyist. Abramoff came from a wealthy family. There was one early hint of trouble; he was disqualified while running for president of his Beverly Hills elementary school. A teacher caught him serving hot dogs at a campaign party, in violation of school rules. However, he went on to become a star athlete at Beverly Hills High School. In college he turned into a fervent conservative. After graduation he worked as a political activist and when he made influential Republican friends, including Tom DeLay, he decided to enter lobbying.

His first clients were Mississippi Choctaws who wanted to build a casino. He expanded to represent several tribes on gaming issues. Then he picked up other clients, including factory owners in Saipan and Russian oil tycoons. As a lobbyist, his style was to lavish attention and favors on lawmakers. It violated House rules for a member to accept more than $100 a year in gifts or meals from a lobbyist and more than

---

[5] Thomas E. Mann and Norman J. Ornstein, *The Broken Branch* (New York: Oxford University Press, 2006), p. 177.

[6] Peter H. Stone, *Heist* (New York: Farrar, Straus and Giroux, 2006), p. 182, quoting Rep. Jeff Flake (R-Arizona).

$50 at one time. To get around this prohibition, Abramoff asked his clients to pay large sums, sometimes millions of dollars, to tax-exempt conservative groups run by close friends. Under his direction these groups then paid for the meals and trips he arranged for legislators, contributed to their political committees, bought office space for their campaigns, and sometimes paid their wives for "consulting" services. Such payments by nonprofit organizations were in themselves legal, but not when the organization was simply a conduit used to obscure Abramoff and his clients as their source. In addition, without the knowledge of his clients, the groups diverted millions of dollars in secret kickbacks to Abramoff.

Abramoff gave campaign contributions to at least 20 members of Congress. Most went to Republicans. In return, he sought earmarks and favors for clients. He was well known to DeLay, who called him "one of my closest and dearest friends."[7] He gave DeLay $70,000 in legal campaign contributions over the years and DeLay took several trips paid for by Abramoff's groups. DeLay's staff received cash, sports tickets, and golf trips in return for helping his clients. Eventually, two DeLay aides pleaded guilty to conspiracy on bribery charges.

Abramoff fell quickly after his actions became known. In 2006 he pleaded guilty to fraud in a deal to buy floating casinos in Florida and is now serving a prison term of 5 years and 10 months. In a separate prosecution of his lobbying crimes he pleaded guilty to fraud, tax evasion, and conspiracy to bribe a public official and faces another sentence of 9½ to 11 years. At one time the FBI had 48 agents assigned to investigate his schemes, leading to other indictments, resignations, and widespread fear among lawmakers and their staffs. One estimate is that the Abramoff scandal cost Republicans 16 seats in the 2006 midterm elections, enough to give the Democrats a majority and control of the House.[8]

Bob Ney (R-Ohio)

One lost seat was that of Rep. Bob Ney, a five-term representative from eastern Ohio. Ney was first elected to the House in 1994, when Republicans took control. During his five terms Ney came under Abramoff's spell. He accepted free trips, including a golfing trip to Scotland on a private jet, worth $170,000. He took frequent free meals at a Washington, DC, restaurant owned by Abramoff and accepted tickets to concerts and sports events. The lobbyist gave him $31,500 in campaign contributions. Ney did legislative favors at Abramoff's request, inserting earmarks in bills to benefit companies and Indian tribes.[9] In an unrelated relationship, Ney also accepted trips and cash from a Syrian industrialist in return for efforts to influence trade policy.

Eventually, he pleaded guilty to conspiracy to commit fraud and bribery and to filing false documents that failed to reveal the value of his gifts. In 2007 a federal court

---

[7] Kirsten Mack, "DeLay Mails 8-Page Letter to Rally His GOP Troops," *The Houston Chronicle*, February 10, 2006, p. B2.

[8] This is the estimate of White House political advisor Karl Rove, noted in Susan Schmidt, "Abramoff Is to Begin Sentence Today," *Washington Post*, November 15, 2006, p. A6.

[9] Jonathan Riskind and Jack Torry, "Ney Admits Taking Bribes," *The Columbus Dispatch*, September 16, 2006, p. A1.

sentenced him to 30 months in prison. "I'd like to apologize to my family, my friends and my constituents," he said. "I have caused them tremendous heartache."[10]

Rep. Randy "Duke" Cunningham (R-California)

Flying Phantoms from the *USS Constellation* Randy Cunningham became the first ace of the Vietnam War, downing five enemy MiGs, three in one day. Later he taught at the Navy's "top gun" pilot school. After retiring from the Navy, he was elected to the House in 1990 from a district near San Diego.

As a fighter pilot he displayed courage and mental agility. As a Representative he was a buffoon. He was prone to verbal gaffes, emotional, and volatile. He got into shoving matches with colleagues and once Capitol police were called to break up a fight he had started.

Cunningham was also corrupt to an unprecedented degree. He accepted $2.4 million in cash, mortgage payments, antique furniture, Oriental rugs, yachts, and a Rolls-Royce automobile from two defense contractors. They even paid for his daughter's graduation party at a Washington hotel. In return, he used his position on powerful appropriations and intelligence committees to earmark contracts worth $230 million for the two companies. He put what prosecutors later called a "bribe menu" on his congressional stationery. One entry, for example, stated that the price of $1 million of federal funding was $50,000.[11]

In 2006 he pleaded guilty to tax evasion and conspiracy to commit fraud and bribery. "No man has ever been more sorry," he told the judge, who responded, "You undermined the opportunity and option for honest politicians to do a good job."[12] His sentence was eight years, four months in federal prison, the longest ever for a member of Congress.

From left to right are Rep. Tom DeLay (R-Texas, lobbyist Jack Abramoff, Rep. Bob Ney (R-Ohio), and Rep. Randy "Duke" Cunningham (R-California). Sources: © Harris County Sheriff department/epa/CORBIS, © Carlos Barria/Reuters/CORBIS, © AP Photo/Bill Haber, © Earl S. Cryer/ZUMA/CORBIS.

[10] Jack Torry, "Two-and-a-Half Year Prison Sentence for Ney," *The Columbus Dispatch*, January 20, 2007, p. A1.

[11] Sonya Geis and Charles R. Babcock, "Former GOP Lawmaker Gets 8 Years," *Washington Post,* March 4, 2006, p. A1.

[12] Randal C. Archibold, "Ex-Congressman Gets 8-Year Term in Bribery Case," *New York Times*, March 4, 2006, p. A1.

Cunningham was not a central figure in the Abramoff scandals. His is the timeless story of ordinary greed, but not a separate story, because he flourished in the same loose Capitol atmosphere as Abramoff. The recent Washington scandals teach that the arena in which business must pursue its political goals can be highly compromising. It is notable that Fortune 500 corporations were never directly implicated in the wrongdoing. Yet over these years, as in the past, they dominated the political arena with huge expenditures for lobbying and campaign donations. No other interest has more potency than business. In this chapter we will explain how business exercises political influence. Our discussion begins with the basic structure of American government.

THE OPEN STRUCTURE OF AMERICAN GOVERNMENT

federal system
A government in which powers are divided between a central government and subdivision governments. In American government, the specific division of powers between the national and state governments is set forth in the Constitution.

Business seeks and exercises political power in a government that is extraordinarily open to influence. Its power is exercised on constitutional terrain created by the Founding Fathers more than 200 years ago. The Constitution of the United States, as elaborated by judicial interpretation since its adoption in 1789, establishes the formal structure and broad rules of political activity. Its provisions create a system predisposed to a certain pragmatic, freewheeling political culture in daily political life.

Several basic features of the Constitution shape American politics. Each stands as a barrier to the concentrated power that the Founders feared would lead to tyranny. Each has consequences for corporate political activity.

First, the Constitution sets up a *federal system,* or a government in which powers are divided between a national government and 50 state governments. This structure has great significance for business, particularly for large corporations with national operations. These corporations are affected by political actions at different levels and in many places.

supremacy clause
A clause in the Constitution, Article VI, Section 2, setting forth the principle that when the federal government passes a law within its powers, the states are bound by that law.

The *supremacy clause* in the Constitution stipulates that when the federal government passes a law within its powers, that law preempts, or takes precedence over, state laws on the same subject. For example, Congress passed the Telecommunications Act of 1996 to speed the growth and lower the cost of cell phone use. Later, San Diego County passed a zoning law that set height, color, and camouflage requirements for cellular towers to reduce their "visual impact." Sprint sued, claiming that the law raised costs and slowed the expansion of its wireless network and was, therefore, in conflict with the Telecommunications Act. A federal court agreed and ordered the county to stop enforcing the tower requirements.[13]

The federal system has many implications for the regulation of business. Sometimes business prefers federal regulation, so it must follow one law instead of as many as 50 different state laws. In the 1960s, for instance, several states tried to pass laws requiring health-warning labels on cigarette packs. If states had been allowed one by one to require labels, the tobacco companies would have had to

[13] *Sprint Telephony PCS v. County of San Diego,* 479 F.3d 1061 (2007).

separation of powers
The constitutional arrangement that separates the legislative, executive, and judicial functions of the national government into three branches, giving each considerable independence and the power to check and balance the others.

print specially worded cigarette packs for sale in each state. So they supported a bill in Congress that, when passed, preempted that area of regulation and required a uniform warning label across the country. Unlike the tobacco industry, the insurance industry fights regulation, preferring instead oversight by state insurance commissions. Insurance companies are big employers and heavy campaign contributors in many states. They tend to receive gentle treatment from these commissions and fight all efforts to pass national regulations.

Second, the Constitution establishes a system of *separation of powers,* under which the basic functions of government—legislative, executive, and judicial—are set up in three branches of the federal government. Each branch has considerable independence and has the power to check and balance the others. The states mimic these power-sharing arrangements in their governments. For business, it is significant that the actions of one branch do not fully define policy. For example, if Congress passes a law despite business opposition, corporations can lobby regulatory agencies in the executive branch to get favorable application of its provisions or they can go to the judicial branch to challenge its constitutionality.

judicial review
The power of judges to review legislative and executive actions and strike down laws that are unconstitutional or acts of officials that exceed their authority.

Third, the Constitution provides for *judicial review* by giving judges the power to review legislative and executive actions and to strike down laws that are unconstitutional or acts of officials that exceed their authority. A classic example of judicial review came in the spring of 1952 when a steelworkers' strike threatened to stop steel production while hard-pressed U.S. troops in Korea were desperate for supplies and equipment. To support the war effort, President Harry Truman issued an order for the government to take control of and run the steel industry. Steel companies sued to stop him and the Supreme Court held that Truman had exceeded his constitutional powers.[14]

The government structure created by the Constitution is open. It diffuses power, creates multiple points of access, and invites business and other interests to attempt influence. Because no single, central authority exists, government action often requires widespread cooperation between levels and branches of government that share power. This characteristic also makes the system particularly vulnerable to blockage and delay. When important actions require the combined authority of several elements of government, special interests can block action by getting a favorable decision at only one juncture. To get action, on the other hand, an interest such as business must successfully pressure many actors in the political equation. Thus, there has developed a style in the American system, in which interests are willing to bargain, compromise, and form temporary alliances to achieve their goals rather than stand firm on rigid ideological positions.

First Amendment
An amendment to the Constitution added in 1891 as part of the Bill of Rights. It protects the rights of free speech, a free press, freedom to assemble or form groups, and freedom to contact and lobby government.

The *First Amendment* is an additional element of the Constitution critical to business. It protects the right of business to organize and press its agenda on government. In its elegantly archaic language is stated the right "to petition the Government for a redress of grievances." The First Amendment also protects rights of free speech, freedom of the press, and freedom of assembly—all critical

---

[14] *Youngstown Sheet & Tube Co. v. Sawyer,* 343 U.S. 579. The basis for the Court's ruling was that Congress had once considered giving presidents the power to seize industries in similar circumstances but had not done so.

for pressuring government. Without these guarantees, the e-mail campaigns, speeches, editorials, and ads that business orchestrates could be suppressed. Imagine how different the system would be if the public, agitated by a corporate scandal, could pressure Congress to restrict the lobbying rights of some industry. While corporate speech is expansive, it is restricted in one area. The Supreme Court years ago defined monetary campaign contributions as a form of speech and allowed them to be limited because of fears that corporate money corrupts elections.[15]

A HISTORY OF POLITICAL DOMINANCE BY BUSINESS

Though not ordained in the Constitution, the preeminence of business in politics is an enduring fact in America. The Revolutionary War of 1775–1783 that created the nation was, according to some historians, fought to free colonial business interests from smothering British mercantile policies.[16] The Founders who drafted the Constitution were an economic elite. John Jay and Robert Morris, for example, were among the wealthiest men in the colonies. It comes as no surprise that the government they designed was conducive to domination by business interests. The noted historian Charles Beard argued that the Constitution was an "economic document" drawn up and ratified by propertied interests, for their own benefit.[17] His thesis is controversial, in part because it trivializes the importance of philosophical, social, and cultural forces in the politics of constitutional adoption.[18] Yet the record since adoption of the Constitution in 1789 is one of virtually unbroken business ascendancy.

Laying the Groundwork

Business interests were important in the new nation but did not dominate to the extent that they soon would. There were few large companies. The economy was 90 percent agricultural, so farmers and planters were a major part of the political elite. Their interests balanced and checked those of infant industry. The fledgling government was a tiny presence. Economic regulation was virtually nonexistent. Nevertheless, under the leadership of Secretary of the Treasury Alexander Hamilton the new government was soon turned toward the promotion of industry. With the support of business leaders, Hamilton pursued his visionary policies, laying the groundwork for the unexampled industrial growth that roared through the next century. As the young nation's economy expanded, so also did the political power of business.

---

[15] *Buckley v. Valeo,* 424 U.S. 1 (1976).

[16] See, for example, Clarence L. Ver Steeg, "The American Revolution Considered as an Economic Movement," *Huntington Library Quarterly,* August 1957.

[17] Charles Beard, *An Economic Interpretation of the Constitution of the United States* (New York: Macmillan, 1913).

[18] See, for example, Robert E. Brown, *Charles Beard and the Constitution* (Princeton: Princeton University Press, 1956); and Forrest McDonald, *We the People: The Economic Origins of the Constitution* (Chicago: University of Chicago Press, 1963).

Ascendance, Corruption, and Reform

During the nineteenth century, commercial interests grew in strength. When the Civil War between 1861 and 1865 decimated the power base of southern agriculture, a major counterweight to the power of northern industry vanished. In the period following the war, big business dominated state governments and the federal government in a way never seen before or since. It was a time of great imbalance, in which economic interests faced only frail obstacles.

Companies commonly manipulated the politics of whole states. West Virginia and Kentucky were dominated by coal companies. New York, a number of midwestern states, and California were controlled by railroads. Montana politics was engineered by the Anaconda Copper Mining Company. In Ohio, Texas, and Pennsylvania, oil companies predominated; the noted critic of Standard Oil, Henry Demarest Lloyd, wrote that "the Standard has done everything with the Pennsylvania legislature, except refine it."[19]

Business was also predominant in Washington, DC. Through ascendancy in the Republican party, corporations had decisive influence over the nomination and election of a string of probusiness Republican presidents from Ulysses S. Grant in 1868 to William McKinley in 1900.[20] In the Congress, senators were suborned by business money; some even openly represented companies and industries. One observer noted that in 1889,

> a United States senator . . . represented something more than a state, more even than a region. He represented principalities and powers in business. One senator, for instance, represented the Union Pacific Railway System, another the New York Central, still another the insurance interests of New York and New Jersey. . . . Coal and iron owned a coterie from the Middle and Eastern seaport states. Cotton had half a dozen senators. And so it went.[21]

Under these circumstances, corruption was rampant. Grant's first term, for example, was stained by the famous "whiskey ring" scandals in which liquor companies cheated on their taxes and a member of Grant's cabinet solicited bribes in exchange for licenses to sell liquor to Indian tribes. In Grant's second term, the Crédit Mobilier Company gave members of Congress shares of its stock to avoid investigation of its fraudulent railroad construction work.

The soaring political fortunes of business in the post–Civil War era invited reaction. A counterbalancing of corporate power began that continues to this day. Late in the century, farmers tried to reassert agrarian values through the Populist party. They foundered, but not before wresting control of several state legislatures from corporations and forcing through legislation to control the railroads, the biggest companies of that day. More important, the populist movement was the beginning of a long-lived democratic reform tradition opposed to big business power.

---

[19] "The Story of a Great Monopoly," *The Atlantic,* March 1881, p. 322.

[20] The exception was the election of the Democrat and reformer Grover Cleveland in 1884. But even Cleveland had strong business supporters, Andrew Carnegie and James J. Hill among them. His administration never threatened business interests.

[21] William Allen White, *Masks in a Pageant* (New York: Macmillan, 1928), p. 79.

THE BOSSES OF THE SENATE.

Nineteenth-century political cartoonist Joseph Keppler (1838–1894) was a critic of big business who particularly resented the ascendancy of moneyed interests in politics. This cartoon appeared in the magazine *Puck* on January 23, 1889. Source: © CORBIS.

Two other formidable business adversaries emerged. One was organized labor, which was destined to be the strongest single element opposing industry over the following century. The other was the powerful Anti-Saloon League, which advocated prohibition of alcohol. Like labor, the Anti-Saloon League became a strong national adversary of business. Brewers and distillers were not its only adversaries. Big corporations in many industries worked against prohibition because they opposed the principle and onset of more government regulation.

After 1900, reforms of the progressive movement curtailed overweening corporate power. For example, the Seventeenth Amendment in 1913 instituted the direct election of senators by voters in each state. Corporations fought the amendment. Before, state legislatures had chosen senators, a practice that invited corrupting influence by big companies. For example, in 1884 representatives of Standard Oil called members of the Ohio legislature one by one into a back room where $65,000 in bribes was handed out to obtain the election of Henry B. Payne to the Senate. One witness saw "canvas bags and coin bags and cases for greenbacks littered and scattered around the room and on the table and on the floor . . . with something green sticking out."[22]

[22] Quoted in Henry Demarest Lloyd, *Wealth Against Commonwealth* (New York: Harper, 1898), pp. 377–78.

Big business also fought suffrage for women. The battle was led by liquor companies that feared women would vote for prohibition. However, there was broader fear of women voters. It was widely believed by businessmen that women would vote for radical and socialist measures. The powerful Women's Christian Temperance Union, which had as many as 10,000 local chapters by 1890, frightened business by standing against liquor, child labor, and income inequality. Yet after adoption of the Nineteenth Amendment in 1920 giving women the vote, no strong shifts in voting patterns appeared.

The great political reforms of the progressive era were reactions to corruption in a political system dominated by business. It would be a mistake, however, to conclude that because of reforms and newly emerged opponents, the primacy of economic interests had been eclipsed. While business was more often checked after the turn of the century, it remained preeminent. Corruption continued. In 1920 Warren G. Harding, a backroom candidate picked by powerful business interests at a deadlocked Republican nominating convention, was elected president. His vice president was Calvin Coolidge, the rabidly antilabor ex-governor of Massachusetts. Harding's administration was so beset by scandals in which officials accepted money for granting favors to corporations that Congress was considering impeaching him when he died of a stroke in 1923. The worst scandal involved Secretary of the Interior Albert B. Fall, who accepted bribes from oil company executives in return for the right to pump oil from government reserves in Teapot Dome, Wyoming. The Teapot Dome affair came to light only after Harding's death, but so besmirched his reputation that it was eight years before his grand tomb in Marion, Ohio, could be dedicated.

Business Falls Back under the New Deal

By the time Harding was officially laid to rest, the stock market had crashed and catastrophic economic depression racked the country. Conservative business executives argued that the depression would correct itself without government action. After the election of Franklin D. Roosevelt in 1932, corporations fought his efforts to regulate banking and industry, strengthen labor unions, and enact social security. Against social security, for example, business lobbyists argued that children would no longer support aging parents, that the required payroll tax would discourage workers and they would quit their jobs, and that its protection would remove the "romance of life." Leaders of DuPont, General Motors, Standard Oil, U.S. Steel, J. C. Penney, Heinz, and other firms formed the anti-Roosevelt American Liberty League to campaign against "unconstitutional" and "socialistic" New Deal measures.

Many executives hated Roosevelt. They said that he was bringing communism to the United States and called him names such as "Stalin Delano Roosevelt."[23] But business had lost its way. Corporate opposition to New Deal measures ran counter to public sentiment. It became ineffective and was sometimes disgraceful. In 1935, for example, utility lobbyists sent Congress 250,000 fake letters and telegrams in a

---

[23] William Manchester, *The Glory and the Dream,* vol. 1 (Boston: Little, Brown, 1973), p. 126.

losing effort to stop a bill. Subsequently they ran a whispering campaign saying Roosevelt was insane.

Much New Deal legislation was profoundly egalitarian and humanitarian and reasserted the tradition of agrarian idealism. Because business lacked a positive philosophy for change, its political power was greatly diminished. According to Edwin M. Epstein, "corporate political influence reached its nadir during the New Deal."[24] Roosevelt was hurt by all the hate and felt that through his major New Deal programs, he had saved capitalism in spite of the capitalists.

The New Deal was a political sea change born out of the Great Depression. One lasting legacy of the era was the philosophy that government should be used to correct the flaws of capitalism and control the economy so that prosperity would no longer depend solely on unbridled market forces.[25] Government would also be used to create a "welfare state" to protect citizens from want. Whereas, in the past, government had kept its hands off corporations, now it would actively use interest rates, regulation, taxes, subsidies, and other policy instruments to control them. Whereas, in the past, most domestic spending had been for infrastructure programs that promoted business, spending would increasingly focus on social programs such as social security. These changes laid the groundwork for an increasingly large, powerful, and activist federal government.

Postwar Politics and Winds of Change

In the 1940s, industry's patriotic World War II production record and subsequent postwar prosperity quieted lingering public restiveness about corporate political activity. During the 1950s, corporations once again predominated in a very hospitable political environment. In the years between 1952 and 1960, Dwight D. Eisenhower was a probusiness president with a cabinet dominated by political appointees from business. A probusiness conservative coalition of southern Democrats and Republicans in Congress ensured legislative support. Corporations could promote their policy agendas by influencing a small number of leaders. Charls E. Walker, an official in the Eisenhower administration and later a business lobbyist, recalls how only four men shaped economic policy.

> These four officials were President Eisenhower, Treasury Secretary Robert Anderson, Speaker of the House Sam Rayburn, and Senate majority leader Lyndon B. Johnson. These four men would get together every week over a drink at the White House and the President would say, "I think we ought to do this or that." Then Mr. Sam or LBJ might say, "Well, that's a real good idea; send it up and we'll get it through." And they would. They could deliver because at that time they had great influence in Congress, partly because of the seniority system.[26]

---

[24] *The Corporation in American Politics* (Englewood Cliffs, NJ: Prentice Hall, 1969), p. 31.

[25] For the story of how this philosophy developed during the New Deal years, see Alan Brinkley, *The End of Reform: New Deal Liberalism in Recession and War* (New York: Knopf, 1995).

[26] Quoted in Gene E. Bradley, "How to Work in Washington: Building Understanding for Your Business," *Columbia Journal of World Business,* Spring 1994, p. 53.

However, changing political trends soon led business into more sophisticated methods of political intervention. During the 1960s and 1970s, national
politics became dominated by a liberal reform agenda. New groups rose to
defy corporations, internal reforms made Congress more openly democratic
and responsive to business's foes, business was bridled with expensive new
regulatory schemes, and government swelled with new tiers of authority. Business suffered unaccustomed defeats at the hands of public interest groups and
agency staffs in government, defeats that encouraged more aggression from
companies.

THE RISE OF ANTAGONISTIC GROUPS

During the late 1960s, the climate of pressure politics changed with the rise
of new groups focused on consumer, environmental, taxpayer, civil rights,
and other issues. Some, including Ralph Nader's Public Citizen, the Natural
Resources Defense Council, and the Consumer Federation of America, grew
to have many members and enough power to push an agenda of corporate
regulation.

The presence of these groups changed the political arena for business. A decade
earlier, corporations had dominated Washington politics with quiet, behind-the-
scenes influence over key leaders. Now they faced hostile groups that used a favorable climate of public opinion to wrest control of the policy agenda away from
business. The result was a remarkable period, lasting roughly from the late 1960s
to the late 1970s, during which the antagonists of business pressured Congress to
enact one massive regulatory program after another.

The rise of groups hostile to business is part of a broader trend in which new
groups of all kinds, including business groups, have been stimulated by growth of
government. Government growth is reflected by fast-rising federal spending. In
1960 the federal budget was $92 billion. By 1980 it reached $591 billion, an increase
of more than 600 percent, and by 2006 it was $2.7 trillion.[27] Figure 9.1 shows this
rise of federal spending and extends back to 1900. As government grows, interest
groups proliferate around policy areas. By the 1990s there were an estimated
23,000 organized interests, roughly 400 percent more than in the 1950s.[28] Of course,
many of these new groups represented business.

The heyday of the public interest movement was short-lived. By the late 1970s
business interests had mobilized to fight in more sophisticated ways and never
again would the movement win great victories, although it remains an institutionalized enemy of business.

---

[27] Bureau of the Census, *Statistical Abstract of the United States: 2007,* 126th ed. (Washington: DC,
January 2007), table 458 and historical tables.

[28] Burdett A. Loomis and Allan J. Cigler, "Introduction: The Changing Nature of Interest Group Politics,"
in Cigler and Loomis, *Interest Group Politics,* 5th ed. (Washington, DC: Congressional Quarterly Press,
1998), p. 11.

FIGURE 9.1 **Growth of the Federal Budget: 1900–2005**

The tremendous spending increase shown is a key measure of government's growth. This growth made government more complex, caused proliferation of interest groups, and increased its impact on industries, markets, and competition. Historically, growth of government is the major stimulant to political activity by business. Throughout the period shown here, progressives and liberals used government more and more to solve social problems and regulate business. As they built government bigger with expensive programs, they simultaneously strengthened the incentive for corporations to influence it.

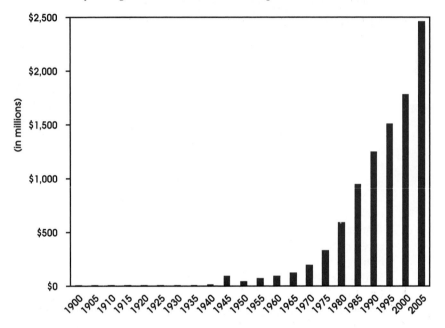

DIFFUSION OF POWER IN GOVERNMENT

Another change in the climate of politics, besides new groups and expanding business advocacy, has been the diffusion and decentralization of power in Washington, D.C. Three major reasons for this are (1) reforms in Congress, (2) the decline of political parties, and (3) increased complexity of government.

Traditionally, a few party leaders and powerful committee chairs ran the House and Senate autocratically. But the stubborn resistance of southern Democrats to civil rights legislation in the 1960s eventually led in 1974 to an uprising of junior legislators, who passed procedural reforms to democratize Congress, taking power from the party leaders and spreading it widely. After 1974, subcommittees could hold hearings on any subject they wished; they developed large staffs and often became small fiefdoms of independent action. Instead of an institution dominated by a few leaders, one observer described Congress as "like a log floating down a river with 535 giant ants aboard, and each one thinks he or she is steering."[29]

[29] Bradley, "How to Work in Washington," p. 55.

Now business lobbyists had to contact nearly every member of a committee or subcommittee to get support for a measure, rather than just the chair. A veteran lobbyist mused about the change this way. "On a tax issue if you had the agreement of the chairman of Ways and Means, you could go out and play golf," but "these days you can't rest easy unless you've worked all the members."[30]

Other changes also eroded party authority. The media, particularly television, began to supplant the parties as a source of information about candidates. Using television, more and more politicians bypassed their parties and spoke directly to voters. More television advertising increased the cost of elections. In the past, Senate and House members who were loyal to party leaders could count on substantial campaign funds from their parties. After 1974, however, increasingly independent legislators appealed directly to corporations and interests for contributions. And the corporations and interests were happy to oblige. In the background, the electorate grew more educated and independent than in past eras. More people split their ballots and used decision cues other than party labels. For all these reasons, the power of parties has ebbed over time.

An additional cause of power diffusion is the growth in size and complexity of the federal government. Washington today is a maze of competing power centers, including elected officials, congressional committees, cabinet departments, regulatory agencies, political parties, courts, interest groups, and lobbying firms. Relations among these power centers continuously shift as partisan tides, personal ambitions, power struggles, and emerging issues glide across the political landscape.

The sum of government activity has growing significance to business, and so corporations are far more politically active than in past eras. The expanded size and scope of government mean that its actions can be critical to company operations. Many bills passed by Congress directly affect earnings. Legislation affects taxes, interest rates, import/export rules, antitrust policy, defense spending, regulatory compliance costs, health care costs, the dollar exchange rate, uses of information, and much more.

THE UNIVERSE OF ORGANIZED BUSINESS INTERESTS

Literally thousands of groups represent business. What follows is a summary of this universe.

peak association
A group that represents the political interests of many companies and industries.

The most prominent groups are *peak associations* that represent many companies and industries. Their strength lies in representing a large expanse of the business community. One weakness is that some issues divide their members, so they lobby aggressively only on broad issues that unite diverse company interests.

The largest and most powerful peak association is the U.S. Chamber of Commerce, which was founded in 1912. The Chamber is a federation of 3,000 local and state chapters, 830 trade associations, and 3 million companies, 96 percent of which have fewer than 100 employees. Next largest is the National Association

---

[30] Charls E. Walker, quoted in Jill Abramson, "The Business of Persuasion Thrives in Nation's Capital," *New York Times,* September 29, 1998, p. A23.

of Manufacturers (NAM), founded in 1895, which, as the name suggests, represents manufacturers. It has a membership of 12,000 companies and 350 trade associations. Both the Chamber and the NAM carry a conservative business agenda to Congress and the public. They concentrate on causes that unite their diverse members, such as reducing regulation and lowering health care costs for employers.

Two other peak associations have more unified memberships. The National Federation of Independent Businesses (NFIB), founded in 1943, represents 600,000 small businesses, most with five or fewer employees and less than $500,000 a year in sales. It is the most conservative and least bipartisan of the major business groups. It pursues a lobbying agenda of easing compliance with government rules, reducing taxes, and keeping a lid on the minimum wage. Most of its campaign contributions go to Republicans. The president of the Chamber once said, "I love the NFIB, the way they get out there on the edge, like when they said, 'Get rid of the IRS.' They make us sound reasonable."[31] The Business Roundtable is the organization that speaks for big business. It was founded in 1972 and consists of about 160 CEOs whose companies pay dues to support it. Each year it confines its advocacy to a few issues critical to the largest multinational corporations. The Roundtable's great strength is that its member CEOs are its lobbyists. They go to Washington carrying its message directly to lawmakers.

trade association
A group representing the interests of an industry or industry segment.

Besides these peak associations, more than 6,000 *trade associations* represent companies grouped by industry. Virtually every industry has one or more such associations. Illustrative are the American Boiler Manufacturers Association, the Soap and Detergent Association, the Institute of Makers of Explosives, the Indoor Tanning Association, and the National Turkey Federation. Beyond lobbying for the industries they represent, these trade groups also act as early warning systems in Washington for companies, hold training conferences, set industry standards, and publish data. Trade associations of powerful industries, such as the American Petroleum Institute, have deep financial resources and are among the most influential players in Washington. Corporations with diversified business lines often belong to many trade associations.

Washington office
An office in Washington, DC, set up by a corporation and staffed with experts in advocating the firm's point of view to lawmakers and regulators.

More than 700 corporations have staffs of government relations experts in Washington. These *Washington offices* are set up mainly by big companies. General Electric, for example, has a staff organized into teams that specialize in lobbying for the needs of GE's business segments. Some specialize in contacting Republicans; others work with Democrats. The office also gives GE managers information about how events in Washington affect their operations.

Most firms supplement their Washington offices by hiring lobbyists from independent lobbying firms. Between 1998 and 2004, for example, GE hired more than 60 outside lobbying firms, paying them fees of $94 million.[32] There are dozens of independent lobbying firms in Washington, DC. The most prominent ones employ former top officials, ex-legislators, and ex-congressional staff members from both

---

[31]Quoted in Jeffrey H. Birnbaum, "Power Player," *Fortune Small Business,* October 2001, p. 56.

[32] Figures are based on data compiled by the Center for Public Integrity, "Lobby Watch: General Electric Co.," at www.publici.org.

political parties to offer a potent mix of access, influence, and advice. Few small firms can afford to have Washington outposts, so they work through trade associations or hired lobbyists.

coalition
A combination of business interests—including corporations, trade associations, and peak associations—united to pursue a political goal.

Business interests also form *coalitions* to create broader support. There are dozens of business coalitions in Washington at any given time. These groupings of instant allies are ephemeral. Most form around a single issue and break up when that issue loses urgency. The advantage of membership in a coalition is that lobbying with allies can enhance impact. Sometimes, allies in one coalition find themselves on opposite sides in another.

Business gains strength when it is united, but there is chronic disunity. Long-standing tensions exist between domestic and foreign firms, truckers and railroads, manufacturers and retailers, and raw material producers and end-product manufacturers. To illustrate, for years the American Sugar Alliance, which represents sugar growers and refiners, has fought to preserve federal price supports on raw cane and beet sugar.[33] Big corporations such as Mars and Coca-Cola oppose it, because higher sugar prices raise the cost of manufacturing candy, cookies, and soft drinks. More recently, a schism has developed between big technology companies and big pharmaceutical firms. A Coalition for Patent Fairness, which includes Microsoft, Cisco Systems, and Apple, is pushing Congress to narrow patent rights and protect technology firms from swarms of patent lawsuits. It is opposed by the big drugmakers who fear that weaker patent protection would threaten their monopolies on lucrative drugs.[34]

LOBBYING

There are two broad areas of business involvement in politics. One is government relations, or lobbying, in which business influences policy by contacting government officials. The other is electoral activity, in which business works to elect or defeat candidates. The two areas intertwine. In this section we discuss lobbying. In the following section we discuss electoral activity.

lobbying
Advocating a position to government.

Lobbying is advocating a position to government. A lobbyist is the person who presents the position of a corporation, interest group, or trade association to legislators or officials. The word carries negative connotations, and business lobbyists are often caricatured as pleading selfish interests, ignoring the public interest, and corrupting officials. Sainthood escapes the profession. There are a few dishonest lobbyists such as Jack Abramoff, who incline the public to cynicism. However, most lobbyists work honestly and their craft is an essential political art, the exercise of which lubricates the machinery of representative government.

Lobbyists channel and articulate the voices of interests in the great sweep of American pluralism. In doing so, they bring information to government. For example, members of Congress and their staffs operate under conditions of uncertainty.

---

[33] Eamon Javers, "Lobbyists Who Want Nothing," *BusinessWeek*, January 22, 2007, p. 72.
[34] Kate Ackley, "Tech Sector Rides High in 110th, *Roll Call*, February 1, 2007; Bill Swindell, "Coalitions Size Up, Stake Positions on Patent Reform Bill, *CongressDaily*, April 19, 2007.

They cannot investigate each of 20,000 or more bills introduced every session or the thousands of issues swirling in the political arena. Lobbyists provide critical intelligence to lawmakers, reducing this uncertainty. First, they can define and explain the contents of a bill or the key points of an issue. Recently Congress has worked to regulate new technologies that its most senior members struggle to understand. Lobbyists rush to educate them. Second, they can clarify political implications of a bill. Will it contribute to global warming, cause inflation, create jobs? How are the lawmaker's colleagues voting on it? Is it likely to pass? And third, they can explain electoral implications, or how segments of voters in the lawmaker's district or state feel about an issue.[35] According to the former chief of staff of two Senate committees, the best lobbyists are effective because they are good at this informational role.

> Good lobbyists tell you something you don't know—say, why teaching hospitals need more money for doctor training. They tell you what they think you should do about it, how to pay for it and, most important, who opposes it and why. They know their opposition is going to be lobbying you too, so they don't say anything that can be proved wrong in your next meeting.[36]

Lobbyists could try to mislead a lawmaker with bias and falsehood, but this is counterproductive. A former member of Congress explains the consequences.

> There is a proper term for a lobbyist who lies or misleads or distorts, and that proper term is *former lobbyist.* When you are dealing with each other . . . the truth is your . . . real capital. Once you mislead, once you exaggerate, once you fail to give an accurate picture, you'll never be allowed in the office again.[37]

A lobbyist who lacks integrity loses access to the very people he or she earns a living by influencing. In addition, effective lobbyists must defend their proposals based at least in part on public benefit, since legislators and regulators, as a rule, cannot justify acting simply to promote corporate self-interest. The exception is small provisions that mean something primarily, and perhaps only, to the industry or company sponsoring them. Lobbyists have been called the "detail men and women" of government.[38] They have little power over broad liberal and conservative tides and major issues to which the public is attentive. But backstage they orchestrate the small, precise details that determine how great political shifts play out.

In Washington today, legislators are receptive to lobbyists. They often form coalitions of them to help pass bills. In Congress, both parties have regular meetings with corporate lobbyists. Every other Tuesday top Republican lobbyists meet with Republican senators. On Mondays top Democratic lobbyists meet with high-ranking

[35] Anthony J. Nownes, *Total Lobbying* (New York: Cambridge University Press, 2006), pp. 26–28.

[36] Lawrence O'Donnell, "Good Lobbyists, Good Government," *Los Angeles Times,* January 13, 2006, p. B11.

[37] Quoted in Michael Watkins, Mickey Edwards, and Usha Thakrar, *Winning the Influence Game: What Every Business Leader Should Know about Government* (New York: Wiley, 2001), p. 173; emphasis in original.

[38] Nownes, *Total Lobbying,* p. 208.

staff of senators and representatives.[39] In these meetings lobbyists, legislators, and staff exchange information. The congressional leaders seek advice on how to get their legislation passed and ask lobbyists for tactical help. The lobbyists learn about strategy and cultivate relationships.

Lobbying Methods

contact lobbying
Direct interaction with government officials or staff in meetings, phone calls, or e-mail.

The art of persuasion admits of many approaches. Direct contact with officials, sometimes called *contact lobbying,* is the gold standard. Presenting the client's case in a face-to-face meeting is often the most effective way to get action. Access to decision makers is a precious commodity. Members of Congress typically have appointments booked at 5- to 10-minute intervals. An unwritten rule is that campaign contributions entitle the corporations or lobbyists who make them to access. A Texas legislator explains how he thinks about situations in which two lobbyists want to talk to him.

> One [is] a person you've never seen before [and] the other person helped "bring you to the dance" [i.e., contributed money to your campaign]. Who are you going to listen to? You come back to your office and there are 30 phone messages. You go through, you recognize five of them because they helped bring you to the dance. Which five are you going to return your calls to?[40]

Lobbyists often meet with a legislator's staff or committee staff. Working with staff they sometimes draft legislation. They testify at rule-making hearings in agencies and committee hearings in the House and Senate. During markup sessions when bills are put together it is common practice for them to catch a legislator's eye and give a thumbs-up or thumbs-down signal as amendments come to a vote. Unless they are former senators or representatives, they are not allowed on the floor of either chamber, but they can stand in hallways and confer with passing lawmakers. And sometimes the hallways are crowded. Former Senator David L. Boren (D-Oklahoma) writes about the press of supplicants.

> On several occasions when we were debating important tax bills, I needed a police escort to get into the Finance Committee hearing room because so many lobbyists were crowding the halls, trying to get one last chance to make their pitch to each Senator. Senators generally knew which lobbyist represented the interests of which large donor.[41]

background lobbying
Indirect lobbying activity designed to build friendly relations with officials and staff.

Most advocacy work is done away from legislative chambers. Lobbyists read documents, monitor agency actions, generate research, and write policy analyses to support their positions. Much additional time is spent on *background lobbying,* when lobbyists cultivate relationships rather than present a direct case. Corporations and groups sponsor fundraisers for senators and representatives,

---

[39] Jeffrey H. Birnbaum, "Lawmakers, Lobbyists Keep in Constant Contact," *Washington Post,* June 28, 2004, p. EI; and Jeffrey H. Birnbaum, "GOP Freezes Jobs List, a Vestige of the K Street Project," *Washington Post,* January 26, 2006, p. A2.

[40] Anonymous quotation in Knownes, *Total Lobbying,* p. 81. Brackets in original.

[41] Quoted in *McConnell v. FEC,* 124 S. Ct. 751.

FIGURE 9.2
Paths of
Pressure
A corporation
can directly
lobby for its
interests or
it may lobby
indirectly with
a grassroots
campaign
aimed at the
public or
certain groups
and interests
within the
public. It may
be assisted in
both efforts
by indepen-
dent lobbying
firms.

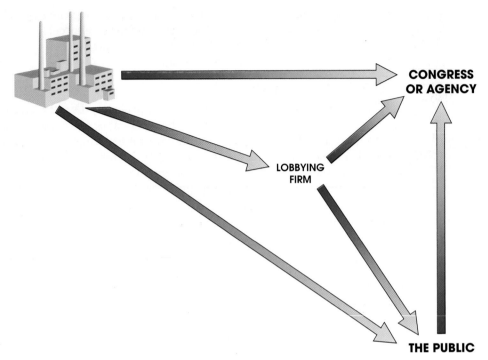

CONGRESS
OR AGENCY

LOBBYING
FIRM

THE PUBLIC

work in their campaigns, buy meals for them and their staffs, and otherwise
cultivate good feelings. Wal-Mart lobbyists recently held an evening reception
in a room just off the Senate floor to celebrate the completion of a documentary
film about female senators. Wal-Mart sponsored the film by giving a $150,000
grant to its producer, Nicole Boxer, the daughter of Senator Barbara Boxer
(D-California).[42]

Business lobbyists also try to influence decisions by having their customers,
employees, or other constituents, including the public, pressure officials for action.
These efforts are called *grassroots lobbying*. Seeing this support assures a lawmaker
that the corporation is not simply asking for special treatment. Grassroots efforts
often require multiple actions. Public relations skills are applied to get favorable
media coverage of issues. Opinion polls are used to measure public attitudes. Advertising campaigns are launched to shape opinion. Efforts are made to get people
to visit, call, or send e-mails and letters to their representatives if they agree with
the company's position.

Major lobbying efforts now resemble political campaigns in the way they combine a broad range of methods, including direct contact, public relations, legal
support, polling, policy analysis, and grassroots work (see Figure 9.2). The need
for this spectrum of skills has led to a merger wave in which large Washington

grassroots
lobbying
The technique
of generating
an expression
of public, or
"grassroots,"
support for the
position of a
company or
lobbyist.

---

[42] Jeffrey H. Birnbaum, 'Wal-Mart, the Democrats' New Friend," *Washington Post,* April 3, 2007, p. A21.

lobby firms absorb smaller firms that specialize in just one aspect of lobbying. The larger firm can then offer one-stop "full service" to client corporations.

Regulation of Lobbyists

Lobbyists are only loosely regulated. Restraints on them are suspect because the First Amendment protects both the right of speech and the right of citizens to contact government officials. Still, at the federal level there are three sources of constraint on their activities.

First, the Lobbying Disclosure Act of 1995 requires lobbyists to register with Congress and both they and their clients must fill out forms twice yearly showing their fees (if above $6,000) and expenditures (if above $24,500). The disclosures far underreport activity because (1) only lobbyists who spend more than 20 percent of their time lobbying Congress or executive branch officials must register and (2) the definition of lobbying in the act is very narrow, covering only personal or written contact with officials and excluding an important range of other influence activities. Nevertheless, this law makes some activity visible that would otherwise remain hidden.

Second, in 1995 both the House and the Senate adopted rules to prevent the appearance of impropriety. These rules were filled with loopholes and after the Abramoff scandals both chambers passed revisions to toughen them.[43] New rules now bar accepting most meals or any gift of more than nominal value, including trips and rides on corporate jets. But the rules are widely regarded as lax. As just one example, there are 23 exemptions to the House's meal ban. One is the so-called "toothpick rule." Although lobbyists cannot take a legislator to a restaurant—not even a McDonald's—every evening trade associations sponsor lavish receptions overflowing with food. Lawmakers are permitted to attend if there are no forks with the food! According to the House Ethics Committee, if forks were present, the receptions would be meals.

Third, it is illegal for public officials to give or receive a bribe or gratuity in return for undertaking an official act. However, the crime of bribery can be hard to define and prosecute. Usually, a bribe is something of value, given with a corrupt intent to influence or purchase an official act. Whether something is or is not a bribe depends heavily on context and situation. The exchange of money or a gift must be closely linked in time with a pending official act, be earmarked for a particular action, or be part of a pattern of exchanges associated with performance of official acts.[44] A campaign contribution, unless it involves a clear *quid pro quo,* that is, an exchange of the contribution for a specific action, is not a bribe.[45] Therefore, ordinary contributions given to curry general favor, even if very large, are not prosecuted. To avoid signs of bribery political etiquette requires that lobbyists and lawmakers speak about campaign contributions and legislative favors in separate

[43] See House Resolution 6, 110 Cong. 1st Sess., January 5, 2007, amending Rules of the House of Representatives and S. 1, the Legislative Transparency and Accountability Act of 2007.

[44] United States Department of Justice, *Criminal Resource Manual* (Washington, DC: DOJ, looseleaf with multiple dates), title 9 §2041, "Bribery of Public Officials," October 1997.

[45] See *United States v. Brewster,* 506 F.2d. 62 (1974).

conversations. When lobbyists give legislators meals, trips, rounds of golf, and other favors they do not engage in criminal bribery unless a tight, specific link to official favors exists. Naturally, such links are elusive and bribery convictions are rare.

Limits on campaign contributions also restrain lobbyists. We now discuss the presence and limits on business money in elections.

THE CORPORATE ROLE IN ELECTIONS

In the first presidential campaign, George Washington did little campaigning and spent only £39 on "treats" for the voters.[46] Since then, the length and cost of campaigns for federal offices—president, vice president, senator, and representative—have soared. In the 1999–2000 election cycle, total campaign spending for federal races was $3 billion, a large sum, but one that should be kept in perspective. It was less than the cost of an aircraft carrier and less than the nation spent on video games.

Efforts to Limit Corporate Influence

Throughout the nineteenth century, companies gave money directly to candidates. As companies grew and large trusts emerged the amounts given grew also. Eventually, excess invited reaction. After the Civil War, business money went disproportionately to the Republican party, which promoted the doctrine of laissez-faire economics. Corporate giving peaked in the presidential campaigns of William McKinley. The election of 1896 matched the probusiness Republican McKinley against the radical populist William Jennings Bryan, who ran as the Democratic candidate. Bryan, a spellbinder on the stump, terrified eastern bankers by advocating an end to the gold standard, a radical change that they opposed.

McKinley's campaign manager, Marcus Hanna, capitalized on their fright by establishing recommended levels of dollar contributions to the McKinley campaign. He assessed .25 percent of the assets of each bank from the trembling financiers and, overall, raised about $3.5 million.[47] This inflated McKinley's campaign funding to double that of any prior election and he was victorious.

In 1900 Bryan again ran against McKinley, this time on a platform of breaking up trusts. So Hanna assessed big trusts such as Standard Oil and U.S. Steel amounts based on their assets. He raised a new record sum, estimated as high as $7 million, an astronomical amount for that day. If the estimate is correct, it was not exceeded until the election of 1960 when both John F. Kennedy and Richard Nixon raised approximately $10 million each. McKinley won again, by an even larger margin.

Hanna believed his assessment scheme elevated the ethics of fundraising above the borderline bribery and petty extortion that had long characterized it. Companies did not give wanting special favors in return; instead, each put in a fair amount and in return would share in the general economic prosperity of a McKinley administration.

---

[46] James V. DeLong, "Free Money," *Reason*, August–September 2000, p. 42.

[47] See Herbert Croly, *Marcus Alonzo Hanna: His Life and Work* (New York: Macmillan, 1912), p. 220. A grateful McKinley engineered Hanna's appointment to the U.S. Senate.

In fact, the success of Hanna's formula created public hostility toward corporate money as the greatest threat of corruption in American elections. An effort at reform was inevitable and it came after the election of 1904, when Republican Theodore Roosevelt, who campaigned as a reformer, was embarrassed by his opponent, Democrat Alton B. Parker, for taking large cash contributions from corporations.

federal elections
Elections for president, vice president, senator, and representative. The 435 representatives are elected every two years, the president and vice president every four years, and the 100 senators every six years (with one-third of the senators up for election biennially). Elections are held on the first Tuesday after the first Monday of November in even-numbered years.

Progressive reformers sought to derail the business juggernaut. In 1907 they passed the Tillman Act, making it a crime for banks and corporations to directly contribute to candidates in *federal elections,* and this is still the law today.[48] The law was sponsored by Senator Benjamin R. "Pitchfork Ben" Tillman (D-S. Carolina). Tillman was not an idealist seeking fair elections. His purpose was to stop the gusher of corporate money flowing to the Republican party, breaking its dominance. He was a racist with a vicious hatred of the Republicans who had freed the slaves and given them the right to vote in his state. He bragged on the Senate floor about riding with vigilantes and shooting blacks at polling places. Tillman simply capitalized on the sentiment of the day to pursue his darker motive.

Tillman's venom is now a historical artifact. What endures from the era is fear of corporate money in politics. American political culture is shaped by egalitarian ideals. Large campaign contributions from business strained popular belief in a rough equality among interests. The Tillman Act was the first of many efforts to protect the electoral system from lopsided corporate influence. But money, especially corporate money, plays an essential role in funding elections. It is a resource that can be converted to power. Candidates use it to persuade voters. Contributors use it to buy access, influence, and favors. Because money is elemental, new sources and methods of giving arise when old ways are foreclosed.

After 1907 the spirit of the Tillman Act was quickly and continuously violated. Forbidden from giving directly, companies found clever, indirect ways to funnel dollars into campaigns. They loaned money to candidates and later forgave the debts, paid lavish sums for small ads in political party booklets, assigned employees to work for campaigns, and provided free services such as rental cars and air travel. Since the Tillman Act did not limit individual contributions, wealthy donors stepped in. These "fat cats," who included corporate executives, legally gave unlimited sums. And many companies gave salary bonuses to managers for use as campaign contributions. The history of election law after the Tillman Act has been one of trying to limit corporate influence by shutting off the range of these indirect methods for giving. But, as we will see, as each channel is blocked a new one quickly appears.

The Federal Election Campaign Act

In the years following the Tillman Act, Congress added to the body of election law from time to time, requiring candidates to disclose contributions, prohibiting elected officials from using federal employees in their campaigns, and barring direct contributions from labor unions to candidates.[49] Besides being riddled with

---

[48] Its formal title is Act of January 26, 1907, 2 U.S. Code §441b.

[49] The laws were, respectively, the Publicity Act of 1910, the Federal Corrupt Practices Act of 1925, the Hatch Act of 1939, and the War Disputes Act of 1943 (a temporary measure made permanent by the Taft-Hartley Act in 1947).

loopholes, none of these measures limited the influence of what continued to be the main source of campaign funding—corporations.

In 1968, Republican Richard Nixon outspent his Democratic opponent Hubert Humphrey largely because of contributions from wealthy business magnates. One was W. Clement Stone, an insurance company executive, who set a record by giving $2.2 million to Nixon through a maze of committees. Angry Democrats passed the Federal Election Campaign Act (FECA) of 1971 to stiffen disclosure requirements on campaign contributions and expenditures. Immediately after its passage, the election of 1972 again made corporate money in politics a major reform issue. Investigations related to the Watergate scandals found that 21 corporations had violated the Tillman Act by giving direct contributions totaling $842,000 to the Nixon campaign.

In reaction to this illegality, Congress extensively amended the FECA in 1974 (the first of five amending acts over a decade). As revised, the FECA curbed wealthy donors by placing ceilings on both campaign contributions and expenditures. Instead of giving as much as they wanted, individuals could contribute only $1,000 per election to a candidate and only $25,000 a year in total to any combination of candidates or political committees. The Tillman Act's prohibition on direct corporate contributions continued. In an attempt to put more enforcement power behind election law, the amendments created a new regulatory agency, the Federal Election Commission. The intent of the amendments was to limit corporate influence. However, over the 30 years that the legal framework remained in force it failed to do so. There were three reasons.

First, in 1976 the Supreme Court severely compromised the law's design for controlling campaign money. In *Buckley v. Valeo*, the Court held that giving and spending money in political campaigns are forms of expression protected by the guarantee of free speech in the First Amendment.[50] The Court upheld the FECA's *contribution* limits, saying that the government had a legitimate interest in avoiding corruption and the appearance of corruption that unlimited contributions invited. But it struck down *expenditure* limits as too great a restraint on political speech. This badly compromised the law's ability to limit campaign spending.

Second, the proliferation of interest groups caused by the growth of government created more organized interests to fund campaigns. Because the FECA—even after the *Buckley* decision—limited individual contributions, the era of fat cats seemed to be over, though as we will see, only temporarily. So corporations raced to set up devices called political action committees (PACs), which could legally contribute to candidates in their name. The number of PACs grew rapidly, and with them the sums of money entering politics.

Third, corporations and lobbyists adapted to the new FECA regime by learning how to exploit, avoid, and live with its regulations. Their machinations over 30 years paralleled those that followed the Tillman Act in 1907 and showed again that political money is like water in a stream; dammed up in one place, it flows around and over in another. The two most important maneuvers around the spirit

[50] 421 U.S. 1.

FIGURE 9.3
Contributions
to Candidates
by Corporate
and Labor
Political
Action
Committees
in Two-Year
Election
Cycles:
1986–2004

Source of data: FEC.

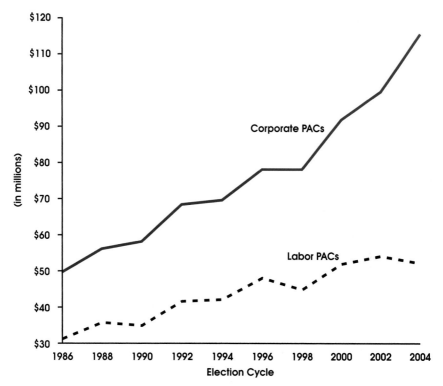

of the law were (1) the use of political action committees and (2) the rise of soft money used for issue advertising.

Political Action Committees

political action committee
A political committee carrying a company's name formed to make campaign contributions. The money it gives to candidates comes from individual employees, not from the corporate treasury.

When Congress limited individual contributions, it left open a loophole permitting corporations to set up *political action committees,* or political committees carrying a company's name. These committees make campaign contributions, not with corporate money, but with money put in by employees. Although corporations previously had not formed PACs, unions had used them since the 1940s to support prolabor candidates and already had more than 200. When the new FECA contribution limits went into effect in 1974, corporations started forming PACs too. The number rose steadily, peaking at 1,816 PACs in 1988, then slowly declining and stabilizing at around 1,600. The primary reason for the decline was that some companies felt harassed and degraded by politicians who pressured them with solicitations for money.

Other interests also use PACs and in 2006 there were 4,210 in all, including 1,621 corporate PACs, 283 union PACs, and 935 trade association PACs.[51] As Figure 9.3 shows, despite stability in numbers, contributions by corporate PACs more than doubled between 1986 and 2004. Union PACs still do not contribute as much as corporate PACs did almost two decades ago.

[51] "Semiannual PAC Count—2000–2006," *Federal Election Commission Record,* September 2006, p. 10.

How PACs Work

To start a PAC, a corporation must set up an account for contributions, a "separate segregated fund," to which it cannot legally donate 1 cent (because of the prohibition since 1907 of direct corporate giving). Corporate PACs get their funds primarily from contributions by employees. Executives and managers can be solicited in person or by mail. Many corporations suggest giving amounts based on a percentage of salary, usually .25 to 1 percent of annual salary. Some encourage enrollment in monthly paycheck deduction plans. Hourly employees can be solicited only twice a year, and then only by mail to their homes. It is illegal for companies to coerce PAC contributions. However, many employees feel subtle pressure to contribute and they resent the solicitations.

Money in a PAC is spent based on decisions made by PAC officers, who must be corporate employees. Their decisions are aligned with corporate political goals. Currently, PACs are allowed to give up to $5,000 per election to candidates, but most contributions are smaller ones of $500 to $2,000. In 2008 a $2,000 contribution was less than one-hundredth of 1 percent of the cost of an average Senate race and less than one-tenth of 1 percent of the cost of an average House race. Company lobbyists know that even these minor contributions create an expectation of access, or a hearing of the corporation's position, after the candidate is elected.

There are no dollar limits on the overall amounts that PACs may raise and spend. Most corporate PACs contribute less than $50,000 during a two-year *election cycle*, although in 2006 a handful contributed more than $2 million to candidates and about two dozen gave more than $1,000,000.[52]

election cycle
The two-year period between federal elections.

Soft Money and Issue Advertising

As PAC spending increased, another way emerged for corporations and wealthy executives to bypass contribution limits. In 1979 Congress passed a seemingly innocent amendment to the FECA to help state and local parties by suspending limits and prohibitions on contributions to them. These contributions came to be called *soft money,* or money that is unregulated as to source or amount under federal election law. Soft money stands in contrast to *hard money*, which is money raised and spent under the strict contribution limits and rules in federal election law (as shown in Figure 9.5). Anyone could give soft money directly to the parties. It was anticipated that it would be used for minutiae such as yard signs, posters, and local brochures. Soon, however, the national parties began to collect large sums of soft money and transfer them to state parties, which used the money in inventive ways, not to buy lawn signs, but to promote the election of federal candidates.

soft money
Money that is unregulated as to source or amount under federal election law.

hard money
Money raised and spent under the strict contribution limits and rules in federal election law.

Although corporations are barred from contributing to federal campaigns, a series of advisory opinions by the Federal Election Commission opened the door for them to give unlimited soft money contributions to the national parties. The national parties then disbursed the money to state and local parties. Corporations and executives began to give rising sums. Figure 9.4 shows how soft money receipts

[52] Federal Election Commission, News Release, "PAC Financial Activity Increases," August 30, 2006, attachment, "Top 50 Corporate PACs by Disbursements through June 30, 2006.

FIGURE 9.4
Soft Money
Receipts by
Democratic
and
Republican
National Party
Committees—
1992–2002
Election
Cycles

Source: Federal Election Commission.

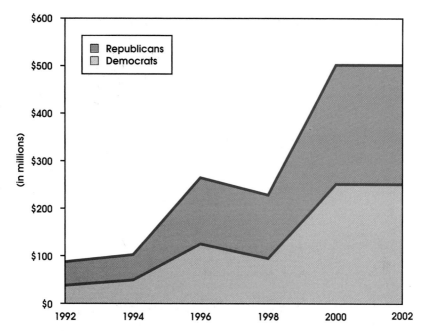

balloned from $87 million to $495 million in a decade. Corporations were virtually unrestrained. AT&T, the largest soft money donor in the 2002 election cycle, gave $2.3 million to the Republican party and $1.5 million to the Democratic party.[53]

Most of the flood came after 1996, when the Supreme Court held that soft money could be used for a certain kind of political ad aimed at influencing federal races.[54] The Court distinguished between *issue advocacy,* which presents a political view or comment on an electoral race, and *express advocacy,* which suggests the election or defeat of a candidate using specific words such as "vote for," "defeat," or "support." Soft money could be used for issue ads that tiptoed around direct electioneering by avoiding the use of these words, even if the intent to support or oppose a candidate was clear to voters.

Within a few years most soft money was buying issue ads on television. Corporations wrote big checks to the national Democratic and Republican parties, which forwarded the money to state and local parties, which used it to pay for thinly disguised electioneering targeted at federal races.

**issue
advocacy**
Advertising
that focuses on
issues in a federal election
but does not
specifically
advocate election or defeat of
a candidate.

**express
advocacy**
Political advertising that
expressly
advocates
election or defeat of a federal
candidate
using specific
words to that
effect.

Reform Legislation in 2002

By the election of 2000, the spectacle of corporations giving soft money in unlimited amounts mocked the spirit of election law. Finally, after strong public reaction to the news that Enron had manipulated elected officials with big soft

[53] Common Cause, "Top Soft Money Donors," www.commoncause.org. Figures include contributions by the corporation, its subsidiaries, and its executives.
[54] *Colorado Republican Federal Campaign Committee v. FEC,* 116 S. Ct. 2390 (1996).

FIGURE 9.5
Contribution
and Expenditure Rules
in Federal
Elections

Prohibitions, Limits, and Unlimited Areas

Corporations

- Prohibited from contributing to federal candidates using corporate accounts
- $10,000 to state political party committees where permitted by state law for registering and turning out voters
- May set up a political action committee (PAC) to make contributions within limits set forth below
- Unlimited direct contributions to 501c and 527 organizations

Individuals

- $2,300* per election[†] to candidates
- $5,000 per year to political action committees
- $10,000 per year combined limit to state and local party committees
- $28,500* per year to national party committees
- $108,200* total to all sources combined per two-year election cycle as follows: $42,700 per cycle to candidates and $65,500 per cycle to national parties and PACs (of which no more than $42,700 per cycle can go to PACs)
- Unlimited contributions to 501(c) and 527 organizations
- Unlimited expenditures to own campaign if running for office[†]
- Unlimited independent expenditures on behalf of or against candidates or causes

Political
Action
Committees

- $5,000 per election[†] to candidates and their committees
- $5,000 per year combined limit to state and local parties
- $15,000 per year to national party committees
- $5,000 per year to other political committees
- Unlimited independent expenditures

*These limits are indexed for inflation. Figures are for the 2007–2008 election cycle.
[†]Primary elections, general elections, special elections, and nominating conventions or caucuses are all separate elections, and individuals or committees may contribute up to the legal limit in each.
[‡]When House and Senate candidates contribute to their own campaigns in amounts exceeding certain thresholds (House, $350,000; Senate $300,000 plus $0.08 times the voting age population in the state) the individual and party contribution limits for their opponents are raised. This is called the "Millionaire's Amendment."

money contributions, Congress passed the Bipartisan Campaign Reform Act of 2002 (BCRA).[55] This new reform tried to limit the use and influence of soft money contributions by corporations, unions, and wealthy individuals. These are its central provisions.

- National parties are prohibited from raising or spending soft money.
- Corporations can give unlimited amounts of soft money to advocacy groups for issue advocacy, but during blackout periods beginning 30 days before primary elections and 60 days before general elections these groups cannot use that money for broadcast issue ads that refer to a federal candidate (newspaper, magazine, and Internet ads are permitted). Soft money from individuals can still be used. Only ads funded by hard dollars (that is, dollars contributed under federal election law as set forth in Figure 9.5) can run during the blackouts.
- Contribution limits for individuals are more than quadrupled and are indexed for inflation. The new limits, shown in Figure 9.5 as currently in effect, let

[55] The BCRA is sometimes called the McCain–Feingold Act after Senators John McCain (R-Arizona) and Russell Feingold (D-Wisconsin), its congressional sponsors. Technically, it is a set of amendments to the Federal Election Campaign Act of 1971.

individuals give $2,300 per election to federal candidates and up to $108,200 per two-year election cycle.

The main purpose of the new law is to end the use of soft money for issue ads run just before elections. National parties can no longer receive or spend it. The ban on its use by advocacy groups, for example, the Chamber of Commerce or the Sierra Club, shortly before elections is intended to prevent corporations from turning to these groups as a substitute for soft money gifts to the parties. The higher individual contribution limits are intended to make it easier for parties and candidates to raise significant sums of hard money from many individuals, thereby compensating for the loss of soft money.

The consequences of BCRA reforms are hard to predict and will take many years to play out. They have not interrupted the long-term rise of overall spending. Spending in the 2004 elections was estimated at $3.9 billion, higher than the $3 billion estimated for the 2000 presidential election cycle.[56] Shifts in contribution patterns more than compensated for the loss of almost $500 million in soft money denied to the national parties. Most important, hard money contributions, both from PACs and individuals, went way up. In addition, new nonprofit organizations that operated outside federal election laws arose to take in soft money. Rising expenditures are a historical constant and will continue. One prediction is that the 2008 election cycle will see expenditures of $5 billion.[57]

Despite the absolute ban on corporate contributions to federal candidates since the 1907 Tillman Act and the subsequent century of efforts by reformers to limit business influence, corporations inject large sums into elections. How do they do it? Here are the basic paths for both hard and soft dollars.

- *Political action committees.* Corporate PACs raise unlimited amounts of hard money that can be contributed to candidates, other political committees, and political parties in amounts as specified in Figure 9.5. As mentioned, some corporate PACs disburse millions of dollars during an election cycle.

- *Individual contributions.* Corporate executives contribute hard money up to the individual contribution limits shown in Figure 9.5. They contribute to candidates in state and local races according to state law. And they contribute soft money to the 501(c) and 527 nonprofit groups described below.

bundling
Fund-raising by an individual who solicits multiple contributions for a candidate, then "bundles" the checks and passes them on.

- *Executive bundlers. Bundling* occurs when an individual solicits contributions for a candidate, then "bundles" them together and passes them on. Each contribution falls within legal limits, but the total of a big "bundle" far exceeds them. The model was created by President George W. Bush in his 2004 campaign, the first in which wealthy individuals no longer could write large soft money checks. He asked them to become bundlers instead. There were three named categories. Pioneers pledged to raise $100,000 by getting 100 others to write a $1,000 check to Bush for president. Jack Abramoff and Ken Lay were Pioneers. Rangers raised $200,000 and Super Rangers $300,000. An estimated 385 bundlers, most of them

[56] Opensecrets.org, "04 Elections Expected to Cost Nearly $4 Billion," press release, October 21, 2004, p. 4.

[57] This is the prediction of Michael Toner, former chairman of the Federal Election Commission, quoted in Paul Bedard, "2008 Shocker: It Will Cost $5 Billion," *U.S. News & World Report,* April 23, 2007, p. 16.

corporate executives, raised more than $200 million for President Bush.[58] The bundlers met their targets by calling friends and, often, by writing fundraising letters to subordinates in their homes. Other candidates copied the technique, including all major presidential candidates since. No disclosure of bundling is required, so the names of corporate bundlers remain unknown.

- *501(c) tax-exempt groups.* After the BCRA groups set up under section 501(c) of the tax code took on new importance as channels for soft money. When electioneering is not their primary activity, Section 501(c) groups are regulated only under tax laws by the IRS. They can engage in issue advertising and get-out-the-vote drives without registering as a political committee with the Federal Election Commission. This means that they can take in soft money without having to reveal their contributors. There are many probusiness 501(c) groups formed under the tax code as civic and business leagues. An example is Americans for Job Security, a group funded by 500 corporations, trade associations, and wealthy executives. In 2006 it ran $1.6 million of issue ads supporting probusiness congressional candidates in four states.[59]

- *527 groups.* Groups organized under section 527 of the tax code are "political organizations" set up primarily to influence elections. If these groups advocate the election or defeat of specific candidates they must register with the Federal Election Commission and follow hard money guidelines in raising and spending money.[60] However, if they engage only in issue advocacy they can take in unlimited amounts of soft money from any source to run issue ads that may influence elections. Many companies contribute to them. In 2006, for example, Wal-Mart gave $743,055 to 527s and Pfizer gave $372,000.[61] Much spending by 527 groups is unreported, but one estimate of the total in 2004 was $424 million.[62]

- *Trade associations.* Corporations can make unlimited payments to trade associations as dues. Because trade associations are also organized under section 501(c) they are allowed to use this money for lobbying and electioneering, if political activity is not their major purpose. So, for example, in 2004 PhRMA, the trade association that represents big pharmaceutical corporations, collected $184 million in dues and spent $66 million on lobbying and political expenditures.[63]

---

[58] Thomas B. Edsall, Sarah Cohen, and James V. Garibaldi, "Pioneers Fill War Chest, Then Capitalize," *Washington Post,* May 16, 2004, p. Al; Craig L. McDonald, "Lobbyists Aren't the Campaigns' Only Bundlers," *Roll Call,* February 8, 2007.

[59] Stephen R. Weissman and Kara D. Ryan, *Soft Money in the 2006 Election and the Outlook for 2008* (Washington, DC: Campaign Finance Institute, 2007), p. 25.

[60] Federal Election Commission, "527 Organizations Pay Civil Penalties," *FEC Record,* January 2007, p. 1.

[61] Figures are reported by the Center for Political Accountability and based on data from the National Institute on Money in State Politics; see "Transparency Reports," at the National Institute on Money in State Politics, at www.politicalaccountability.net.

[62] Weissman and Ryan, *Soft Money in the 2006 Election and the Outlook for 2008,* p. 2.

[63] Bruce F. Freed and Jamie Carroll, *Hidden Rivers* (Washington, DC: Center for Political Accountability, 2006), p. 11.

FIGURE 9.6
When the
flow of
political
money into
elections
is blocked
by reform,
the money
flows around
the barrier
through
loopholes
in the
regulations.
In the long
run, each
milestone
effort to stem
the tide has
failed.

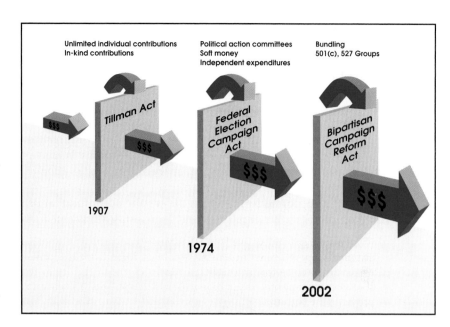

- *State and local elections.* Direct corporate contributions to federal candidates are illegal, but almost half the states and many cities allow corporate contributions to state and local candidates. Corporations are not required to report their giving at these levels and reporting by candidates and parties varies, so the total is unknown. But it is large. To give a few examples, in 2006 state-level contributions totaled $957,000 for Wal-Mart, $614,000 for Union Pacific, $500,000 for Microsoft, and $265,000 for Boeing.[64] These figures include both contributions from corporate treasuries and corporate PACs and are likely incomplete.

In sum, although corporations may not use money from their treasuries for making contributions to federal candidates, there are many other channels through which corporate money influences federal, state, and local elections. Figure 9.6 summarizes the futile, century-old effort to suppress corporate money in politics. As the figure shows, each time reformers set up new legal barriers, business finds a way around them. In the next section, we develop some perspective on business's influence.

TENSION OVER CORPORATE POLITICAL EXPRESSION

In America, there is a historic fear that business will corrupt officeholders. More than a century after the McKinley elections radiated corporate financial power, the nation has made only limited progress in controlling the spectacle. Why not more?

[64] Center for Political Accountability, "Transparency Reports," at www.politicalaccountability.net.

The answer lies in the tension between two strong values in the American political system, freedom of speech and political equality.

Government regulation to silence speech, including corporate speech, goes against the grain of the First Amendment, which gives expansive protection to free expression and debate. In *Buckley,* the Supreme Court held that a money contribution is a form of speech entitled to First Amendment protection. Therefore, restrictions of campaign donations by any group or interest, including corporations, are constitutionally suspect. Yet since 1907, legal restraints on corporate giving have been permitted to ensure political equality in elections. The Supreme Court has held that these speech restrictions on corporations are permitted for two reasons.

First, the corporate form, which allows the accumulation of immense wealth based on success in economic markets, is an unfair advantage in the political arena.

> [T]he resources in the treasury of a business corporation … are not an indication of popular support for the corporation's political ideas. They reflect instead the economically motivated decisions of investors and customers. The availability of these resources may make a corporation a formidable political presence, even though the power of the corporation may be no reflection on the power of its ideas.[65]

Second, the Court recognizes a "compelling governmental interest" in preventing corruption or the appearance of corruption in elections."[66] The presence of unlimited corporate cash, even if there is no overt corruption, undermines perceptions of integrity on which democratic elections depend for their legitimacy. So the Court finds it permissible to balance the right of free speech against the importance of maintaining elections free of both the appearance and reality of corruption. Figure 9.7 illustrates this fundamental vision of election law.

However, not everyone agrees. Conservatives on the court refuse to accept this balancing. Justice Antonin Scalia dissented in a recent election law case, saying it was "a sad day for freedom of speech" when the government could muzzle corporations, "the voices that best represent the most significant segments of the economy and the most passionately held social and political views."[67] Also dissenting, Justice Clarence Thomas accused the Court majority of allowing "what can only be described as the most significant abridgment of the freedoms of speech and association since the Civil War."[68]

The dissenters have repeatedly argued that corporations have the right to unlimited speech, that they should be able to make campaign contributions and spend as much money as they wish. Prohibiting corporate funds in elections is, in the words of Justice Scalia, "incompatible with the absolutely central truth of

---

[65] *Federal Election Commission v. Massachusetts Citizens for Life,* 479 U.S. 257 (1986), from the opinion by Justice William J. Brennan, Jr.

[66] *Austin v. Michigan Chamber of Commerce,* 58 LW 4373 (1990).

[67]*McConnell v. FEC,* 124 S. Ct. 720, 226.

[68] Ibid., at 730.

FIGURE 9.7   **The Fundamental Vision of Election Law**
The challenge to the courts and to Congress with respect to election law is to balance the guarantee of free speech in the First Amendment against an implied duty to maintain elections free of corruption and the appearance of corruption.

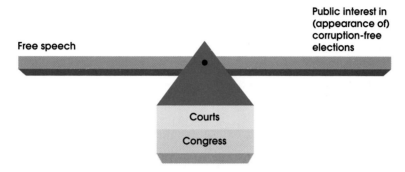

the First Amendment: that government cannot be trusted to assure, through censorship, the 'fairness' of political debate."[69] He and other conservatives on the court trust the ability of the public to judge the validity of corporate arguments and to withdraw support from politicians who succumb to corporate influence and sell out the public interest. If the conservatives prevail, the central purpose of federal election law—to limit corporate influence—would be rejected.

CONCLUDING OBSERVATIONS

Clearly, business retains its historically dominant position among interests. There is a significant imbalance of resources between corporate interests and other interests such as poor people, environmentalists, and consumer advocates. Labor can sometimes match the political muscle of business, but often not. However, an equal or greater imbalance has existed since the end of the colonial era, and business is today forced to deal with more, and stronger, opposing interests than in the past.

The rise of soft money and refinements in lobbying methods create a perception that corporate money is undermining the independence of officials. However, specific evidence of deep corruption, as opposed to periodic and healthy exposures of lawbreaking, is not forthcoming. In part because of disclosure rules, American politics is cleaner than the politics of most other nations and cleaner than in past eras.

The challenge for American society is to balance the First Amendment right of corporations to free political expression against the societal interest of maintaining corruption-free elections and government decisions. So far, our society has successfully maintained a rough, if not perfect, balance.

[69] Dissenting in *Austin,* 58 LW 4379.

Westar Goes to Washington

How does politics really work? For outsiders, the process is mostly opaque. Its hidden action and overwhelming complexity invite cynicism and simplistic judgments. The Westar story is a rare opportunity to look inside Washington and focus on a single instance of corporate influence. It is not clear if the story is typical. Its lessons for a working democracy are uncertain.

METAMORPHOSIS OF A COMPANY

Until the mid-1990s, Western Resources was a staid public utility providing retail electric service to about 640,000 people in Kansas. As a utility with a monopoly over its service area it was overseen by the Kansas Corporation Commission, which regulated the rates it could charge. The Federal Energy Regulatory Commission had jurisdiction over its wholesale electricity transactions and its transmission lines. It was a tight web of constraint.

Given their regulatory environments, energy utilities often have had conservative, plodding strategies. But when a climate of deregulation arose in the 1980s and early 1990s, arguments for allowing them greater strategic freedom gained strength. In this environment, John Hayes, the CEO of Western Resources, adopted an adventurous diversification strategy. He wanted to expand out from the regulated utility business into nonregulated businesses with potentially higher profits.

Looking for assistance, he hired a Wall Street merger wizard named David Wittig. He might as well have brought in Willie Sutton, but that is getting ahead of the story. Wittig seemed ideal for the job. He grew up in a small town on the wheat-covered Kansas plains, graduated with honors from the University of Kansas, and went on to become a star investment banker in New York. His picture once appeared on the cover of *Fortune* magazine.[1]

At Hayes's invitation, Wittig returned to Kansas to head corporate strategy at the utility. His job was to acquire other companies, taking Western Resources down the path of growth and diversification. Wittig

soon bought an equity interest in an Oklahoma natural gas company. Then, for tax reasons, he created a new holding company named Westar Capitol that was owned by Western Resources. Its purpose was to acquire and hold interests in nonutility businesses. Working through Westar, he took on equity interests in an overseas power plant builder; two home burglar alarm companies; and several paging companies.

Wittig used debt financing for these investments and the borrowing was approved by the Kansas Corporation Commission. The Commission did not regulate the holding company and its diverse businesses. But it had the authority to approve or restrict actions of any kind that affected Western Resource's electricity ratepayers. When Hayes retired in 1999, Wittig was appointed president, passing over several of Western's senior managers.

SPLITTING THE COMPANY

Adversity soon strained Wittig's strategy. The stock market fell, halting a planned merger between Western Resources and another utility. One of the burglar alarm companies had losses. The paging company investments declined in value. Western Resources had $3.2 billion in debt and its investments were foundering. Its share price fell and its debt rating sank. The Kansas Corporation Commission was alarmed. It imposed close supervision and disallowed more borrowing for further acquisitions.

Wittig seethed under the restrictions. He wanted to wheel and deal. Relations with regulators grew hostile. Rethinking the strategy, he hatched a plan to separate Western Resources, which he renamed Westar Energy, from the holding company Westar Capitol, which he had renamed Westar Industries. Each would become a separate, publicly traded company. In theory, this could maximize the market value of both new companies. The utility's shares would no longer be depressed by poorly performing investments in the holding company. And when the nonregulated businesses were unchained from oversight by the Kansas Corporation Commission their shares would be more attractive.

Since the borrowing needed to finance Wittig's acquisitions was secured by the utility company's cash flow and assets, the utility would be left with

---

[1] The cover story was "Wall Street's Overpaid Young Stars," *Fortune,* November 24, 1986.

most of the debt. When the holding company broke away, its balance sheet would be clean. At the time of the split, Wittig planned to jump from the utility and take charge of the other company, where he could escape the bonds of utility regulation. The utility's ratepayers would be left to face the debt he had run up.

There was one obstacle. The holding company held equity shares of its businesses, much like a mutual fund. If it became an independent, publicly traded company, it would be subject to regulation under the Investment Company Act of 1940, a depression-era law regulating mutual funds and other public companies that bought and held securities. To protect consumers from investment fraud, the law severely limits debt financing, transactions with subsidiaries, and even incentive compensation for managers. Its requirements are incompatible with the needs of operating companies. They would block the execution of an aggressive strategy.

There was a way to avoid Investment Company Act regulation. That was to apply for classification of Westar as an exempt holding company under the Public Utility Holding Company Act of 1935 (PUHCA). Its Section 3 allowed companies structured like Westar to qualify for such an exemption. There was one problem, however, Congress was about ready to do away with this statute. An energy bill, H.R. 4, which had recently been introduced in the House of Representatives, would repeal it in order to further deregulate the public utility industry. If H.R. 4 was enacted, Westar would no longer have a legal basis to exempt itself from inconvenient and undesirable Investment Company Act regulation. Wittig decided to make sure that even if the PUHCA was taken off the books, a Westar Industries spinoff would still be spared this oppression.

CALLING ON CONGRESS

Aside from occasional contact with the Kansas congressional delegation, Westar had no political strategy. So early in 2001, it hired a small Washington, DC, lobbying firm named Governmental Strategies Inc. (GSI). GSI represents energy companies. It advertises itself as helping clients to "extract real dollar value from . . . [the] legislative and regulatory process," and promises that a client's "expectations for investment in federal advocacy should match those for any other business investment. There must be a

real return."[2] It has four lobbyists, all former congressional staff members having extensive contacts with lawmakers and regulators.

Richard H. Bornemann was the GSI lobbyist who took the lead for Westar. In June he met with Rep. Joe Barton (R-Texas). Years before, Bornemann had worked with Barton as a young staff member on a House committee. Now Barton was in a key position to help Bornemann's client Westar. Barton was an expert in energy law who chaired the subcommittee that was considering H.R. 4, a massive energy bill. Barton worked closely with his friend and House colleague Rep. W. J. "Billy" Tauzin (pronounced TOE-zan) (R-Louisiana), the chairman of the House Committee on Energy and Commerce through which H.R. 4 had to move.

A provision to repeal the PUHCA was debated but not included as H.R. 4 passed in the House and went over to the Senate for consideration. But Barton, who had a conservative ideology and favored deregulation, was writing another energy bill, H.R. 3406, that would repeal the PUHCA. In the fall of 2001 he circulated a discussion draft of this bill to members of his subcommittee. In it, as Section 125, was a provision to exempt Westar from the Investment Company Act if the PUHCA was repealed (see Exhibit 1). If the bill passed, an independent Westar Industries would be free of Investment Company Act shackles.

Section 125 was soon noticed. Democrats on Barton's subcommittee read it and became uneasy when they found out that the Securities and Exchange Commission (SEC) had granted a similar exemption to Enron, allowing it to avoid scrutiny of deals implicated in its astonishing bankruptcy.

Early in 2001, Reps. John D. Dingell (D-Michigan) and Edward J. Markey (D-Massachusetts) wrote a letter to the SEC asking it to explain the consequences of the Westar provision if it became law.[3] The SEC responded that the loophole it created might be a big one. Hundreds of companies could transform themselves into unregulated mutual funds—a potential disaster for consumers.[4]

---

[2] "About GSI," at www.govstrat.com/public/about/about_main.php.

[3] Letter from John D. Dingell and Edward J. Markey to Harvey L. Pitt, January 30, 2002.

[4] Letter from Harvey L. Pitt (with attached memorandum from Paul F. Roye) to John D. Dingell and Edward J. Markey, February 13, 2002.

EXHIBIT 1   The Westar Energy Provision

This is the initial wording inserted in a discussion draft of H.R. 3406, the Electric Supply and Transmission Act, by Rep. Barton on September 21, 2001. Note that the name Westar nowhere appears in the text. Wording in paragraph (a) refers to "a person," in keeping with the legal standing of a corporation as a person under the law. Because of objections that the exemption created by this section could apply to many corporations, later versions were reworded to narrow down the type of "person" it applied to until only Westar Industries was covered. The word "grandfather," in paragraph (a), is used in legislation to signify an exemption granted to parties based on their situation before passage of a statute. Parties meeting the criteria are "grandfathered out" of having to comply with new rules.

SEC. 125. EFFECT ON INVESTMENT COMPANY ACT REGULATION

(a) GRANDFATHER OF EXISTING HOLDINGS—A person that, on December 31, 2001—

   (1) was an affiliate of a holding company, and

   (2) held investment securities in one or more companies engaged directly or indirectly in the electric or gas utility business, or other permitted business activities for a registered holding company and its subsidiaries,

shall not be treated as being an investment company under section 3(a)(1)(C) of the Investment Company Act of 1940 (15 U.S.C. 80a–3(a)(1)(C)) on the basis of investment securities issued by companies in which such person held such investment securities as of such date.

At the next subcommittee hearing on the bill, Rep. Markey confronted a surprised utility executive who was testifying by asking him whether he intended to start a mutual fund if the bill passed. The puzzled executive said no, that was not his business. "And that's good," Markey said, adding that others in the industry might be more inclined to take advantage of the exemption. " . . . [W]e know that Mr. Lay and Mr. Skilling would have taken advantage of it."

Rep. Barton responded to Markey's provocation with surprisingly little commitment to the provision he had inserted. It was put in "for a company or companies in the midwest," he said, and "if it is controversial, we will take it out in its entirety."[5] Barton did not seem ready to fight for Westar.

"A SEAT AT THE TABLE"

For Westar the action in Washington was heating up. The House was working on a bill that contained its special exemption. The Senate was now moving to pass a version of H.R. 4 that repealed the PUHCA. It was a situation with possibilities, but Westar was only a minor player in a grand legislative game. If it wanted

to shape events, it needed more influence. Its hired lobbyist, Richard Bornemann, had a plan to get it.

On April 22, Bornemann sent a confidential plan to Westar entitled "Federal Elections Participation," with "recommendations for beginning to develop a significant and positive profile for the Company's federal presence." Westar, he wrote, needed "a committee and leadership-based approach to Capitol Hill" and advised that there were "high 'up-front' costs" to get it. Bornemann then explained what the strategy involved.[6]

First, there were hard money contributions. Reps. Tauzin and Barton were working to secure the election and reelection of some "key allies and friends" in 2002. Bornemann recommended contributing $1,000 to eight of these candidates. He also advised giving contributions in eight other House races and one Senate race. Second, Westar would make soft money contributions. Bornemann wrote that "the most beneficial way to spend corporate dollars" was with the House Leadership. That meant "joining the fold, so to speak, of House Majority Leader Tom DeLay (R-Texas)."[7] For $25,000 someone from Westar could attend an upcoming weekend of golf that DeLay was hosting for energy industry executives. The

---

[5] Quotations in this paragraph are from a Hearing before the Subcommittee on Energy and Air Quality of the Committee on Energy and Commerce, *The Effect of the Bankruptcy of Enron on the Functioning of Energy Markets,* 107th Congress, 2nd Session, February 13, 2002, pp. 140–41.

[6] "CONFIDENTIAL MEMORANDUM" from Richard Bornemann to Douglas Lawrence, April 23, 2002, p. 1.

[7] Ibid., p. 3.

EXHIBIT 2
Recommended Contributions List

Source: "CONFI-DENTIAL MEMO-RANDUM" from Richard Bornemann to Douglas Lawrence, April 23, 2002.

Rep. John Shimkus (R-IL)	$1,000	Rep. Billy Tauzin (R-LA)	$5,000*
Rep. Sam Graves (R-MO)	$1,000	Rep. Joe Barton (R-TX)	$4,000†
Rep. Anne Northup (R-KY)	$1,000	Rep. Mike Oxley (R-OH)	$2,000‡
Rep. Shelley M. Capito (R-WV)	$1,000	Rep. Richard Burr (R-NC)	$2,000
Rep. Felix Grucci (R-NY)	$1,000	Tom Young for Congress	$5,000
Rep. Bob Simmons (R-CT)	$1,000	Rep. John Sununu (R-NH)	$3,000
Rep. Tom Latham (R-IA)	$1,000	Sen. Tim Johnson (D-SD)	$2,500
Rep. Robin Hayes (R-NC)	$1,000	Sen. Tom DeLay (R-TX)	$25,000
		Total	$56,500

*To Tauzin's Bayou Leader PAC.
†Includes $2,000 to Joe Barton Committee and $2,000 to Barton's Texas Freedom Fund PAC.
‡Includes $1,000 to Oxley for Congress Committee and $1,000 to Oxley's Leadership 2000 PAC.

price would be a $25,000 contribution to one of De-Lay's political action committees.

Almost all the politicians on Bornemann's list were Republicans. He was hooking Westar's fate to the Republican majority in Congress. The reason for each contribution was carefully explained in the memo. The contribution to Tom Young for Congress, for example, was recommended because Young was a member of Senator Richard Shelby's (R-Alabama) staff running for a House seat in Alabama. Shelby, a member of the Senate Energy Committee, wanted Young elected. Another contribution went to Rep. Tom DeLay (R-Texas). As Majority Leader DeLay was a powerful force. With the cooperation of key Republicans, it was unnecessary to contribute to Democrats, and perhaps unwise. DeLay pressured lobbyists to support Republicans and those who worked with Democrats might be punished. The full list of contributions is shown in Exhibit 2.

On April 26 the Senate passed an amended version of H.R. 4 that repealed the Public Utilities Holding Company Act.[8] Since the House and Senate bills differed, a joint conference committee of Representatives and Senators was set up to resolve differences between the versions. In mid-June, each chamber appointed conferees. Among those from the House were Reps. DeLay, Barton, Oxley, and Tauzin from Bornemann's list.

Westar executed the contributions strategy. Although the company itself could at that time contribute the $25,000 in soft money, under federal election law the $31,500 in contributions to candidates had to come from individuals. So Wittig authored a donation

scheme in which Westar officers wrote checks to the candidates in amounts proportionate to their annual compensation. The plan was explained in a May 17 memo, in which Douglas Lawrence, vice president of public affairs, set forth the "budget for our Washington efforts regarding the Federal Energy Bill and its impact on our financial restructuring plan."[9] Each executive was assigned one or more candidates and a specific dollar amount. The "suggested" total each would contribute is listed in Exhibit 3.

Lawrence explained the strategy in greater detail to Douglas Lake, senior vice president of Westar, who sent an e-mail with some questions. Lake had been asked to write a check for $2,500 to Tom Young's Alabama campaign and wanted to know why Young was important to the company. He also wondered what the connection was to Tom DeLay from Texas. Lawrence explained it.

> Right now, we are working on getting our grandfather provision on PUHCA repeal into the Senate version of the energy bill. It requires working with the Conference Committee to achieve. We have a plan for participation to get a seat at the table, which has been approved by David. . . . DeLay is the House Majority Leader. His agreement is necessary before the House Conferees can push the language we have in place in the House bill. Tom Young is Senator Shelby's Chief of Staff who is running for the House in Alabama. Shelby is a member of the Senate Energy Committee. . . . He is our anchor on the Senate side. He's made a substantial request of us for supporting Young's campaign.[10]

[8] Amended to substitute language of S.517, *Congressional Record,* pp. S3688-S3788, April 25, 2002.

[9] "Suggested Campaign Contributions," memorandum from Douglas Lawrence to Westar officers, May 17, 2002, p. 1.

[10] E-mail from Douglas Lawrence, "Re: Campaign Contributions," May 20, 2002.

EXHIBIT 3
Expected
Contribution
Amounts

Name	Amount
David Wittig	$3,450.00
Doug Lake	$2,500.00
Doug Sterbenz	$1,150.00
Paul Geist	$977.50
Dick Dixon	$690.00
Jo Hunt	$517.50
Doug Lawrence	$345.00
Lee Wages	$345.00
Bruce Akin	$345.00
Larry Irick	$345.00
Peggy Loyd	$345.00
Caroline Williams	$345.00

When the executives wrote their checks, they gave them to Lawrence, who forwarded them to the candidates. If anyone was disinclined to give to one candidate, another one was assigned. There were no threats of retribution, but some officers felt pressured.[11] The check writing went forward and within two months most of the contributions were made.

On, June 2, executives from five energy companies came together at The Homestead, a golf resort in Hot Springs, Virginia, for the fundraiser organized by Rep. Tom DeLay. Douglas Lawrence attended for Westar. The price of attendance was a soft money contribution of $25,000 to $50,000 to Texans for a Republican Majority PAC, a political action committee set up by DeLay to work for the election of Republican state legislators in his home state. Westar paid the $25,000 minimum.

DeLay had previously arranged a seat on the energy bill conference committee. He now was hosting 15 to 20 executives from companies affected by the bill.[12] On Sunday evening, before cocktails and dinner, DeLay spoke to the attendees and, as Lawrence recalled, invited them to express any interests they had in federal energy legislation. Lawrence advised DeLay that Westar needed a safe harbor provision if the PUHCA was repealed.

The event was set up to encourage interaction between DeLay, several members of his staff, and the energy executives. During a round of golf the following day, Lawrence shared a cart with one of DeLay's staff members, told him of Westar's interest, and later gave him a briefing book on the special provision in H.R. 4. At lunch, Lawrence was able to restate the company's needs to DeLay. After the event, Lawrence believed he had made "significant progress" because "contributions . . . were successful in opening the appropriate dialogue."[13]

PROGRESS

Late in June, the House-Senate conferees met. The group met only once more over the summer. The versions of the bill to be reconciled were both hundreds of pages long and discussion did not reach the subject of PUHCA repeal. In August, Bornemann attended two more Tex-Cajun fundraisers. Westar also hired another lobbyist, Marianne K. Smythe, a former SEC lawyer. As required by law, she registered in the Senate Office of Public Records as a Westar lobbyist, putting down that she was hired to advocate "an exemption from [the] Investment Company Act for [a] Single Company." Her job was to reword the Westar provision so that it indisputably applied only to Westar. This was an effort to counter the argument that it would unleash hundreds of unregulated mutual funds.

With the conferences under way, Westar was ready to continue its investment in the political process. Rep. Tauzin planned a fundraiser in Louisiana and the contributions schedule called for a $5,000 contribution.

[11] Westar Energy, Inc., *Report of the Special Committee to the Board of Directors*, April 29, 2003, p. 344.

[12] In addition to Westar, the companies were El Paso Electric, Mirant Energy, Reliant Energy, and Williams Energy.

[13] Letter to Rep. Tom DeLay from Reps. Joel Hefley and Alan B. Mollohan, October 8, 2004, p. 2.

EXHIBIT 4
Contribution Amounts for Tauzin Fundraiser

Name	Amount
David Wittig	$1,500.00
Doug Lake	$1,000.00
Doug Sterbenz	$500.00
Paul Geist	$425.00
Dick Dixon	$300.00
Jo Hunt	$225.00
Doug Lawrence	$150.00
Lee Wages	$150.00
Bruce Akin	$150.00
Larry Irick	$150.00
Peggy Loyd	$150.00
Caroline Williams	$150.00
Kelly Harrison	$150.00

Wittig again set out a formula for contributions from his management team (in Exhibit 4).

An accompanying memo from Lawrence reaffirmed the need for everyone's participation and explained Rep. Tauzin's importance.

> Right now we have made significant progress with . . . Tom DeLay. . . . The contributions made in the first round were successful in opening the appropriate dialogue. Now, as the conference committee begins meeting, Representative Tauzin will play a key role. Beyond serving on the conference committee, Representative Tauzin as chairman of the full committee is extremely influential in the decision to maintain the House position on our provision.[14]

Bornemann attended Tauzin's fundraiser. Tauzin recognized him and had his staff throw him out. Tauzin felt that Bornemann had deceived him years before about a railroad bill and since then had banned him from his office.[15] It is unclear whether anyone at Westar ever learned what happened, but Bornemann was still working for Westar when he arranged a July meeting with Rep. Barton. At the meeting, Marianne Smythe gave a PowerPoint presentation about the reworded grandfather clause. Soon Barton circulated the draft of a House offer to the Senate conference committee on H.R. 4, and it contained the Westar provision. The new wording, now more lengthy, narrowed the Investment Company Act exemption by restricting it to companies with ownership and incorporation characteristics matched only by Westar.[16]

On September 19, the House conferees met to discuss H.R. 4. and Rep. Markey introduced an amendment to strike the Westar provision. He was supported by his Democratic colleague Rep. John Dingell. Debate ensued.

> MARKEY: Now, we are told that this is only a special interest provision that is aimed at benefitting a single company. . . . This company reportedly claims that they need an exemption from the Investment Company Act because of their holdings, but I see no reason why we should give it to them. . . . They should not be wasting our time with a legislative fix. The fact that they are doing so raises some alarm bells to me as to what their real motivation might be. . . . Please support the Markey amendment to block this attempt at circumventing the legitimate oversight responsibilities of the Securities and Exchange Commission.
>
> BARTON: The chair would recognize himself in mild opposition to the Markey amendment. We have been round and round on this. . . . The reason I put it in is because this company is in a unique situation. . . . [A]t the appropriate time I think that this would be a subject that we could work [on] together with our colleagues in the Senate.
>
> DINGELL: But it is interesting to note that any company which could structure itself to be roughly the same as Western Resources could come in under that loophole and then could function . . . as a mutual fund . . . totally without any scrutiny, totally

---

[14] Douglas Lawrence, "Re: Campaign Contributions," memorandum of June 25, 2002, p. 1.

[15] Juliet Eilperin, "Westar Lobbyist's Role Detailed," *Washington Post,* June 10, 2003, p. A4.

[16] "Proposed House Offer," H.R. 4, Subtitle A, Section 156, July 19, 2004, pp. 45–47.

without any protection for the investors. . . . [W]e have no assurances that this splendid loophole is not going to be available to any number of smart rascals, MBAs and others on Wall Street so that they can skin the American investors in the most scandalous and outrageous ways.

BARTON: . . . [I]t does just deal with just one company. It does not deal with potentially hundreds of companies. . . .

MARKEY: All in all, a really, really nice exemption from the laws which you would think somebody would be requesting in 1928, right before the 1929 crash, not in year 2002. . . . I think it's a terrible, terrible thing for us to be doing.[17]

A vote was taken. The committee divided along party lines, with its six Democrats voting "aye" and its eight Republicans voting "nay." Markey's amendment failed. The grandfather clause stayed in the bill.

The next week, on September 25, Bornemann arranged a meeting for Wittig and Lawrence in DeLay's Capitol Hill office. It lasted only 10 to 15 minutes. Wittig presented DeLay with another briefing book on the grandfather clause.

"THINGS ARE GRIM"

The stars were aligned for Westar, but then came a sudden reversal of fortune. On September 27, John Wine, chair of the Kansas Corporation Commission, wrote Rep. Markey opposing the Westar provision. Wine informed Markey that the Commission had prohibited Westar Energy from splitting itself into two companies because the plan misallocated more than a billion dollars of debt to its electric utility operations.[18] Westar was fighting this ruling. The Westar provision, he wrote, "would have the effect of removing an important obstacle to Westar splitting its companies and leaving non-utility debt with the utility companies."[19]

On the same day, Westar filed a form 8-K with the Securities and Exchange Commission. Companies must file 8-K reports to announce important changes and events. The filing announced that Westar had been subpoenaed by the United States Attorney in Topeka, Kansas, for information about improper use of company airplanes.[20] Eventually, the federal grand jury investigation behind this subpoena would reveal that Wittig was using his position to loot Westar. But only a hint of the scandal to come existed at this time.

Still, Rep. Markey had enough to kill Westar's legislative hopes. He wrote to the co-chairs of the energy bill conference committee, Rep. Tauzin and Sen. Jeff Bingaman (D-New Mexico), urging that the Westar provision be excised from H.R. 4.

> It is not too late for my Republican colleagues to reverse . . . [their] earlier decision to grant Westar a new, ill-advised legal loophole. This company is under federal investigation and the state commission with regulatory authority over this company has come out strongly in opposition to the provision, as well as the underlying business transaction it is aimed at advancing. Accordingly, I strongly urge the House Republican conferees to reconsider their support for this ill-considered loophole and I urge the Senate conferees to resist adoption of this Enron-like loophole.[21]

That afternoon, Doug Lawrence sent a pessimistic e-mail to Wittig. It implied contact with Rep. DeLay's office and reveals his impression that a deal to support Westar had existed.

> Things are grim in DC. The DeLay staff has asked us to release people from their commitment to support our provision. The Wine letter has killed us, it has been circulated along with last week's 8-K. . . . At this point my recommendation is to release them. . . .[22]

KANSAS POSTSCRIPT

Wittig was in trouble. Within weeks federal prosecutors charged him in a bank fraud scheme back in Kansas. He was forced to resign as CEO. Eventually, a jury convicted him of submitting false documents to a

[17] Condensed from stenographic minutes, "House-Senate Joint Conference on H.R. 4, Securing America's Future Energy Act of 2001," September 12, 2002, pp. 107–19.

[18] State Corporation Commission of the State of Kansas, "Order for Western Resources to Permanently Halt Restructuring," Docket No. 01-WSRE-949-GIE, July 20, 2001.

[19] Letter from John Wine to Edward J. Markey, September 27, 2002, p. 1.

[20] Westar Energy, Inc., Form 8-K, September 27, 2002.

[21] Letter from Edward J. Markey to Billy Tauzin and Jeff Bingaman, September 30, 2002, p. 4.

[22] E-Mail from Douglas Lawrence to David Wittig, "Subject: Washington DC," September 30, 2002, 2:45 P.M.

Topeka bank to raise his line of credit and he was sentenced to four years and three months in prison.[23]

Meanwhile, evidence emerged that Wittig had also defrauded Westar. An investigation by the board of directors concluded that Wittig, sometimes conspiring with Douglas Lake, his second in command, had exploited his position for personal gain.[24] Twice Wittig tricked the board of directors into approving acquisitions in which he had an undisclosed financial interest. And because of stock compensation awards he had cajoled the board into approving, he stood to make as much as $65 million from the split of Westar into two companies, even as he left the utility business saddled with $3 billion in debt. His use of company airplanes revealed extreme arrogance. After joining Westar he purchased two corporate jets, set up a "flight department," and hired six pilots. Then he used the airplanes for personal trips. He took his children to summer camp, his friends to sporting events, and his family on vacation. He also charged the company for a $6 million remodeling of his home.

Wittig and Lake were eventually indicted on charges of conspiracy to defraud Westar, but federal prosecutors have had trouble convicting them. A first trial resulted in a hung jury. On retrial they were convicted on all counts charged. Wittig was sentenced to 18 years and Lake to 15 years. But an appeals court reversed convictions and disallowed a retrial on most counts.[25] Now the government is retrying the two executives on several remaining counts.

WASHINGTON, DC, POSTSCRIPT

Tom DeLay had political enemies. One was Rep. Tom Bell (D-Texas), who was defeated for reelection when the Texas State Legislature redrew congressional district lines based on a plan masterminded by DeLay. Boundaries were shifted to pack Democratic voters into as few districts as possible, thereby increasing the number of districts with Republican majorities. Bell was defeated in the primary in his redrawn district and blamed DeLay.

When Bell learned of Westar's political contributions he filed a complaint against DeLay with the House ethics committee. He accused DeLay of "illegal solicitation of political contributions from corporations such as Westar Energy in return for official action benefitting such corporations." He demanded an investigation into whether DeLay had violated criminal bribery laws in Title 18 of the United States Code (in Exhibit 5).[26]

DeLay denied any exchange of favors for money, saying, "It never ceases to amaze me that people are so cynical."[27] Bell also charged DeLay with using his political action committee to funnel illegal corporate contributions, including Westar's $25,000 soft money contribution, to state legislators in Texas, violating Texas election law. DeLay denied this, saying that the soft money was legally expended on administrative expenses, not on campaign contributions.

The Standards and Official Conduct Committee never made a formal investigation. Instead, Rep. Joel Hefley (R-Colorado), its chairman, and Rep. Alan B. Mollohan (D-West Virginia), its ranking minority member, looked into the charges and recommended that the committee send DeLay a "letter of admonition." The two senior members accepted DeLay's denial of trading favors for contributions. But they were suspicious about the July 2002 energy company fundraiser attended by Westar. Since it was held just when a major energy bill was coming to conference and DeLay had just gotten himself appointed to the conference committee, it created an improper appearance. The letter from the committee admonished him on this point.

> . . . [A] member may not make any solicitation that may create even an appearance that, because of a contribution, a contributor will receive or is entitled to either special treatment or special access to the Member in his or her official capacity. . . . In the same vein, a Member should not participate in a fundraising event that gives even an appearance that donors will receive or are entitled to either special treatment or special access. . . . [T]he energy company fundraiser . . . created such an appearance.[28]

[23] After Wittig had served 13 months in federal prison an appeals court struck down his sentence as excessively harsh. He was resentenced to 2 years. See *United States v. Wittig*, 474 F. Supp. 2d 1215 (D. Kan., 2007).

[24] Westar Energy, Inc., *Report of the Special Committee to the Board of Directors*, pp. 3–4.

[25] *United States v. Lake*, 472 F.3d 1247 (10th Cir. 2007).

[26] Chris Bell, M.C., Complainant; Tom DeLay, M.C., Respondent, *Complaint*, U.S. House of Representatives, Committee on Standards of Official Conduct, 108th Congress, 1st Session, June 15, 2004, p. 2.

[27] Eilperin, "Westar Lobbyist's Role Detailed," p. A4.

[28] Letter from Joel Hefley and Alan B. Mollohan to Tom DeLay, October 6, 2004, p. 1.

EXHIBIT 5
United States
Code, Title 18,
§201(b)(1)(2)

BRIBERY OF PUBLIC OFFICIALS
(b) WHOEVER—
(1) directly or indirectly, corruptly gives, offers or promises anything of value to any
public official, or offers or promises any public official or any person who has
been selected to be a public official to give anything of value to any other person
or entity, with intent—
(A) to influence any official act; or
(2) being a public official . . . , directly or indirectly, corruptly demands, seeks, receives, accepts, or agrees to receive or accept anything of value personally or
for any other person or entity, in return for:
(A) being influenced in the performance of any official act;
. . . shall be fined under this title or not more than three times the monetary
equivalent of the thing of value, whichever is greater, or imprisoned for not more
than fifteen years, or both, and may be disqualified from holding any office of
honor, trust, or profit under the United States.

The Committee postponed consideration of Bell's charges against DeLay's political action committee because Westar and other corporate contributors had been indicted for violation of Texas election laws.[29] It decided to let the legal proceedings run their course.

After the Committee on Standards of Official Conduct rebuked DeLay, there were calls for his resignation as Majority Leader. Minority Leader Nancy Pelosi (D-California) called him "unfit to lead the party."[30] But House Speaker Dennis Hastert (R-Illinois) came to his defense, saying "Tom DeLay is a good man."[31] DeLay declared himself absolved of wrongdoing, since the committee had chosen not to formally sanction him.

Questions

1. Examine again in Exhibit 5 the wording of §201(b)(2) in Title 18 of the United States Code.

[29]*Texas v. Westar Energy, Inc.,* Criminal Action No. 9-04-0579, D.C. Travis County, Tex. (2004).
[30] "Tom DeLay Reprimanded for Violating House Rules," *Foster Electric Report,* October 13, 2004, p. 1.
[31] Ibid.

Did Reps. DeLay, Barton, or Tauzin engage in criminal bribery? Reexamine the wording of §201(b)(1). Did Wittig, Lawrence, or Bornemann commit criminal acts of bribery? If not, were there errors of judgment?

2. Is there any difference between what these contributors and lawmakers did and daily practice in Washington, DC? Where should the line be drawn?

3. Should the House Standards and Official Conduct Committee have imposed a stronger sanction on Rep. DeLay? If so, what penalty was deserved?

4. Was Westar's strategy for political action appropriate? If not, what would be a better strategy?

5. Is a strategy of political influence based on the exchange of favors inherently corrupt? Or is it a constructive way to make the complicated trade-offs necessary in a democracy?

6. Did Westar or any of its officers violate the letter or spirit of federal campaign finance laws as they existed at the time (before the new rules of the Bipartisan Campaign Reform Act took hold)? If so, what was the violation?

Chapter Ten

Regulating Business

Annals of Regulation: The FCC Fines CBS

Super Bowl XXXVIII was the most-watched television program of 2004. For CBS, a subsidiary of the international media conglomerate Viacom, the game created products, intervals of commercial time so valuable that 30 seconds sold for more than $2 million. MTV, another Viacom subsidiary, was paid to create a live halftime concert with Janet Jackson, Justin Timberlake, and other celebrity entertainers.

At halftime the score was New England 14 and Carolina 10. President Bush turned off his set at the White House and went to bed. On the West Coast, your authors retired from the television for intellectual discourse. As the remaining audience watched, Jackson and Timberlake sang a duet in which he tore off part of her top, exposing her right breast to the cameras.

The exposure was accidental, the moment fleeting. Yet the corporation had unwittingly aroused a powerful adversary. As public complaints flooded in, CBS, and its parent Viacom, became the subjects of file number EB-04-IH-0011 at Federal Communications Commission (FCC) headquarters in Washington, D.C.

The FCC is an independent regulatory commission, modeled after the old state commissions that regulated railroads. It is headed by a five-member commission. Each commissioner is appointed by the president, who also names one of them to be its chairman. Commissioners serve staggered five-year terms. No more than three of the five can be of one political party. The commissioners preside over 1,900 regulators working in Washington and at 19 outposts around the country.

The FCC was created by Congress in the Communications Act of 1934 when President Franklin D. Roosevelt called for an agency to bring order to the nation's airwaves. Today, it oversees communication by radio, television, wire, cable, and satellite. It licenses broadcasters and assigns radio frequencies. To carry out its duties it writes rules and regulations directing the behavior of regulated parties. These have the force of law.

The day after the Super Bowl the FCC sent a formal letter of inquiry to CBS noting many public complaints about "indecent material" at halftime. People complained that the show contained "'crude,' 'inappropriate,' 'lewd' and 'sexually explicit' dancing and song lyrics, culminating in [Ms. Jackson] exposing her breast to the camera."[1] More specifically, the lyrics of one Janet Jackson song, "All for You," narrated the account of

---

[1] FCC, *Notice of Apparent Liability for Forfeiture,* File No. EB-04-IH-0011, September 22, 2004, p. 2.

Janet Jackson and Justin Timberlake after a split-second baring of her breast. A record 540,000 complaints came to the Federal Communications Commission after the Super Bowl XXXVIII halftime show. Source: © AP Photo/David Phillip.

a woman who saw a man with a "nice package" that she wanted to "ride . . . tonight." Singer Nelly repeatedly grabbed his crotch, and used profane, sexually suggestive lyrics. Kid Rock sang about "bastards from the IRS." Finally, in the duet "Rock Your Body" Justin Timberlake sang "gonna have you naked by the end of this song" and other suggestive lyrics as he rubbed his body against Janet Jackson's and, ultimately, ripped the clothing from her breast.

CBS defended itself by arguing it had not approved and had no advance warning of the exposed breast.[2] Both entertainers sent declarations that they had, at the last minute, decided to reveal a lacy red bra and the action just went awry. Timberlake's statement blamed the incident on a "wardrobe malfunction," gifting the English language with a neologism for mistakes ranging from the halftime incident to a man's open fly or the clash of plaid on stripes.[3] According to CBS, Jackson's breast was revealed for only 19/32 of a second and "the event became recognizable as nudity to

[2] CBS Broadcasting Inc., *Opposition to Notice of Apparent Liability for Forfeiture,* File No. EB-04-IH-0011, November 5, 2004.

[3] Louisa Pearson, "Thank Our Lucky Stars 'n' Stripes the Morality Police Are Watching Out for Us," *The Scotsman,* February 5, 2004, p. 16.

most people only because they actively searched for images after the fact."[4] CBS also noted its advance precaution against the broadcast of offensive material in having a five-second audio delay, but said it would begin a five-minute delay for similar telecasts in the future.

The FCC prohibits and penalizes the broadcast of indecent material. Its power comes from language in the Communications Act of 1934 codified in a section of the United States criminal code reading, "[w]hoever utters any obscene, indecent, or profane language by means of radio communication shall be fined...."[5] This authority is reworded to include television broadcasting in a rule adopted by the FCC in 1995 that reads, "no licensee of a radio or television broadcast station shall broadcast on any day between 6 A.M. and 10 P.M. any material which is indecent."[6] This rule has the force of law. However, neither the law nor the rule defines indecency. So in 2001 the FCC attempted to clarify exactly what broadcasters can and cannot air in a 27-page guidance document.[7]

In late 2004 the FCC sent CBS a notice informing the network of its decision to impose a $550,000 fine and explaining why it considered the broadcast indecent. It defined indecent speech as "language that, in context, depicts or describes sexual or excretory activities or organs in terms patently offensive as measured by contemporary community standards for the broadcast medium."[8] To be offensive in context, the material had to meet three criteria. First, it had to be explicit or graphic and the halftime show's song lyrics and images were considered to be so. Second, the material must dwell on or repeat at length descriptions of sexual or excretory organs or activities and the show's many references to sexual activity met this requirement. Third, the material must appear to pander to or be used to titillate or shock the audience. The commission felt that this was the case.

The FCC is forced to be tentative in its censorship of indecency, because the First Amendment protects the free speech of artists. Even indecent speech of a sexual or profane nature enjoys some constitutional protection. However, the FCC believed that here the broadcast confronted adults and children "in the privacy of the home, where the individual's right to be left alone plainly outweighs the First Amendment rights of an intruder."[9] One of every five children in America watched the Super Bowl. Even if most adults tolerated the show, CBS had a duty to avoid "offensive sexual material unsuitable for children."[10]

Although CBS might have been surprised by Janet Jackson's uncovered breast, the FCC believed it was forewarned about the nature of the halftime entertainment. CBS

[4] FCC, *Order on Reconsideration,* File No. EB-04OIH-0011, May 31, 2006, p. 5.

[5] 18 U.S.C. §1464, "Broadcasting Obscene Language."

[6] 47 C.F.R. §73.3999(b); 60 FR 44439, August 28, 1995. The Public Telecommunications Act of 1992 and an appeals court decision, *Action for Children's Television v. FCC,* 58 F. 3d 654 (D.C. Cir. 1995), established a "safe harbor" for indecent material in the hours between 10 P.M. and 6 A.M.

[7] FCC, *In the Matter of Industry Guidance On the Commission's Case Law Interpreting 18 U.S.C. §1464 and Enforcement Policies Regarding Broadcast Indecency,* File No. EB-00-IH-0089.

[8] FCC, *Notice of Apparent Liability for Forfeiture,* p. 5.

[9] Ibid., p. 12.

[10] Ibid., p. 13.

officials had monitored the script, song lyrics, and two rehearsals in which the indecent material was unchanged from the later broadcast. The $550,000 total fine was arrived at by fining each of the 20 Viacom-owned stations in the CBS network the statutory maximum of $27,500 for airing indecent material. Stations in the CBS network not owned by Viacom were not fined because the FCC held that they had no advance warning of what was coming in the broadcast.

CBS appealed the fine, but the FCC rejected the appeal.[11] CBS then paid the fine, but appealed it in a federal court. Because of the incident, Congress raised the maximum fine for airing indecency to $325,000.[12] Had that been in effect during the Super Bowl, CBS could have been fined $6,500,000.

This small drama is one of thousands of similar, but less well known, interactions of regulator and regulated that occur every year as a growing federal regulatory apparatus struggles to control excess, exuberance, and crime in the nation's commerce. In this chapter we discuss the reasons for government regulation, its rise, its legal basis, how it is carried out, its costs and benefits, and what it means in the rest of the world.

REASONS FOR GOVERNMENT REGULATION OF BUSINESS

Two circumstances justify regulation of the private sector, first, when flaws appear in the market that lead to undesirable consequences and, second, when sufficient social or political reasons for regulation exist.

Flaws in the Market

When functioning perfectly, the competitive market mechanism determines which of society's resources can be used most efficiently in producing goods and services that people want. It yields the "best" answer to questions of what should be produced, when, and how. Although highly efficient, the free market is not flawless. Some market failures that justify regulation are these.

- *Natural monopoly.* When a firm can supply the entire market for a good or service more cheaply than a combination of smaller firms, it has a natural monopoly. Examples are local public utilities that, without government regulation, could restrict output and raise prices without fear of competition.

- *Destructive competition.* When companies dominate an industry, they may engage in unfair or destructive competition. They may, for example, cut prices until competitors leave the market, then raise prices. Large firms may conspire to fix prices. Without laws to make such behavior illegal, consumers can be harmed.

externalities
Costs of production borne not by the enterprise that causes them but by society.

- *Externalities. Externalities* are costs of production borne not by the enterprise that causes them but by society. For example, a factory that dumps waste into a river pollutes the water. It costs the factory nothing, but the community will have to

---

[11] FCC, *Order on Reconsideration*.

[12] In the Broadcast Decency Enforcement Act of 2006, which amended the FCC's basic authority, the Communications Act of 1934.

pay dearly for the cleanup. Competition inhibits the factory from reducing its waste because buying expensive pollution control equipment would put it at a cost disadvantage to its competitors. Regulation can force all factories to bear the cost. The same principle applies to a wide range of similar external costs, from worker safety practices to jet noise.

- *Inadequate information.* Competitive markets operate more efficiently when producers and consumers have enough information to make informed choices. To the extent that such information is not available, government finds justification for regulating the knowledge in question. Thus, regulators require that consumers be told about product quality, warranty, and content; employees be warned of work hazards; and investors be given accounting data.

Social and Political Reasons for Regulation

Social regulation is used to promote the broad public interest. Some regulation is also adopted to help politically powerful special interests. The two kinds of regulation can blend when the public interest is defined in ways that benefit some interests at the expense of others. Some objectives that justify social and political regulations are these.

- *Socially desirable goods and services.* Regulation is used to ensure production of safe products. For example, the Department of Agriculture sets standards for and inspects foods entering the production process. The Department of Transportation requires seat belts and air bags in vehicles.
- *Socially desirable production methods.* Some regulations stop firms from making products in harmful ways, for example, by exposing workers to danger or by releasing pollutants. Regulation is also used to protect civil rights at work. The Equal Employment Opportunity Commission enforces rules prohibiting sexual harassment and workplace discrimination.
- *Resolution of national and global problems.* As the nation grew, the federal government took on more responsibility to solve national problems not resolvable by state and local governments or individuals. Examples are regulation of railroads, banks, and natural resources.
- *Regulation to benefit special interests.* Some regulations protect special interests that have the political strength to pressure lawmakers for favorable laws and rules. Many such regulations apply narrowly to single companies, but industries such as the steel industry and big agricultural sectors such as cotton, peanuts, sugar cane, and tobacco benefit from protectionist rules and subsidies.

WAVES OF GROWTH

Regulation grew from the beginning. It inched ahead in the nation's first century, when laissez-faire economic doctrines restrained government controls. It sped up and barreled ahead in the second century, as a consensus for controlling markets emerged. Figure 10.1 shows that volume growth in regulation displays a wavelike

FIGURE 10.1   Historical Waves of Government Regulation of Business

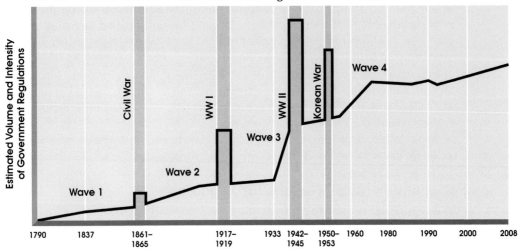

pattern, with successive waves triggered by popular demand for action to solve particular problems.

After each burst of activity, the rate of regulation levels off or declines. But the long trend is relentlessly up. Except after wars, drops have been small. Most wartime controls have been lifted with the end of hostilities. The "scale" to the left of Figure 10.1 is our estimate of the relative volume and impact of federal regulation of business. Though it is only an estimate, with all the limitations of such a measure, it adds some perspective on regulatory growth. Following are highlights of events in each wave.

Commerce Clause
A clause in Article I, Section 8 of the Constitution that gives Congress the power "To regulate Commerce with foreign Nations, and among the several States, and with the Indian Tribes."[13] It has been interpreted to give the federal government wide power to regulate business.

Wave 1: The Young Nation

In the dawn of its creation the federal government was tiny and regulation was a modest function. However, the basis for aggressive regulation existed in the United States Constitution. In particular, Article I, Section 8 gave Congress wide powers, including the power "to regulate Commerce . . . among the several States." This key phrase in the *Commerce Clause*, would eventually become the legal grounds for imposing extensive regulation on business. But that was far in the future.

At first regulation was predominately promotional for business. The government gave vast financial subsidies and huge grants of land to private interests for the building of turnpikes, canals, and railroads. These actions facilitated the building of a much needed infrastructure. There were also tariffs to protect "infant" industries.

[13] Other powers in Article I, Section 8 also gave a basis for the exercise of federal power over business. They include the power to provide for "the general welfare of the United States," to levy and collect taxes, to provide for the common defense, to borrow money, to establish bankruptcy laws, to promote science and useful arts by granting patents, and "[t]o make all Laws which shall be necessary and proper for carrying into Execution the foregoing Powers. . . ."

As the years passed, a few offices that performed regulatory functions were established, including the Patent and Trademark Office (1836), the Copyright Office (1870), and the Bureau of Fisheries (1871), but they also were primarily promotional. The exception was the Comptroller of the Currency, set up in 1863 to charter and regulate national banks. It was the first federal agency exercising control-like regulation and is today the oldest such agency.

Since there was little restrictive federal regulation in this era there was little resistance to it by business. However, the states were sometimes jealous of the prerogative to regulate and from time to time clashed with the federal government. The Supreme Court eventually resolved these clashes in two milestone 1819 decisions, establishing the supremacy of federal law over state law. In one case it struck down a tax levied by Maryland on the federal Bank of the United States.[14] In another it struck down a New York regulation on steamboats in the Hudson River as interfering with federal powers over commerce granted in the Commerce Clause.[15] These decisions confirmed the supremacy of federal law over state law and laid more groundwork for extensive federal regulation in later eras.

Wave 2: Confronting Railroads and Trusts

By the 1860s the railroads had grown into a large, aggressive presence. Late in the decade Massachusetts set up a state railroad commission, consisting of three commissioners and a small staff. Its purpose was to be a permanent arena for legal resolution of the conflicts that continuously arose over trains.[16] Other states soon copied this innovation. However, as railroad routes grew to span the continent it made less and less sense for state entities to regulate them. So in 1887 Congress built the prototype of the modern federal regulatory authority when it created the Interstate Commerce Commission (ICC). The ICC shifted railroad regulation from the states to the federal government. It was an *independent regulatory commission* run by five commissioners serving staggered six-year terms who were nominated by the president and confirmed by the Senate. The president was to designate one commissioner as chair. No more than three of the five were to be of any one political party.

independent regulatory commission
A regulatory agency run by a small group of commissioners independent of political control.

By the 1880s large, dominant trusts in many industries grew by absorbing competitors, colluding in cartels, and choking competition in other ways. The public was offended. When state laws against monopolistic practices proved ineffective, Congress passed the Sherman Antitrust Act in 1890. In 1914 it set up a second independent regulatory commission, the Federal Trade Commission (FTC), further to define and prohibit unfair means of competition. The FTC was modeled after the ICC, headed by five commissioners serving seven-year terms, no more than three from one party. Congress also passed more regulations in other areas and by the early 1930s there were seven more new federal agencies and commissions regulating business.[17]

---

[14] *McCulloch v. Maryland,* 4 Wheaton 316 (1819).

[15] *Gibbons v. Ogden,* 9 Wheaton 316 (1819).

[16] Thomas K. McCraw, *Prophets of Regulation* (Cambridge, MA: The Belknap Press, 1984), see chap. 2.

[17] *Federal Regulatory Directory,* 12ed (Washington, DC: CQ Press, 2006), p. 5.

These steps marked a significant increase in both the volume and force of regulation and now business began to fight for its freedom. Its biggest ally turned out to be the Supreme Court. Early in the era the Court seemed to clear the way for more regulation. It upheld state laws regulating railroads and in one 1877 decision made the seminal, sweeping, and noble statement that "When private property is devoted to a public use, it is subject to public regulation."[18] But soon the Court began to slow and limit regulation in decisions that, beneath the legal language, glowed with conservative economic philosophies of the day. For example, in 1905 it refused to allow a state law limiting bakers to 10 working hours a day because the law unreasonably meddled with the liberty of the bakers and their employers to make a contract on working conditions.[19] When Congress passed a 1916 law taxing products made by factories using child labor, the Court struck it down, saying that the power to regulate commerce extended only to the movement of goods in interstate transportation, not to their production in factories.[20] A national crisis would be required to enlighten such cramped reasoning. It arrived in the 1930s.

Wave 3: The New Deal

When Franklin D. Roosevelt was elected in 1932, the economy was sunk in depression. The gross national product had fallen from $103 billion in 1929 to $58 billion in 1932. Roosevelt proposed the New Deal, a series of programs to bring "Relief, Recovery, and Reform." Congress responded by passing new economic regulations pushed by the new president. As a result, the federal government for the first time assumed responsibility for stimulating business activity out of a depression. It undertook to correct a wide range of abuses in the nation's economic machinery, amassing more far-reaching laws to this end in a shorter time than ever before or since.

The Supreme Court, filled with aging, conservative justices, was still a roadblock. It struck down as beyond federal power a series of regulations designed to relieve the economic catastrophe. In 1936 it unanimously struck down the National Industrial Recovery Act, a centerpiece of Roosevelt's recovery program that regulated activity in many industries. It was unconstitutional, said the justices, because the Commerce Clause did not give the federal government power to regulate business activity within the states, which is where most of the NIRA's regulations applied. Again, the Court thought that government could only regulate *interstate* commerce, which it defined as the movement of products across state lines. Otherwise, said the Court, "there would be virtually no limit to federal power, and for all practical purposes we should have a completely centralized government."[21]

Roosevelt was outraged. Since his election in 1932 he had not had a chance to appoint even a single justice. In 1936 he was reelected in a landslide and believed that the Supreme Court was out of step with the mandate given him by American voters.

---

[18] *Munn v. Illinois,* 94 U.S. 113 (1877), at 130.
[19] *Lochner v. New York,* 198 U.S. 45 (1905).
[20] *Hammer v. Dagenhart,* 247 U.S. 251 (1918).
[21] *A. L. A. Schechter Poultry Corp. v. United States,* 295 U.S. 495 (1935), at 548.

"Man Controlling Trade" is one of two monumental limestone sculptures outside the Federal Trade Commission building in Washington, DC. At the ceremony for laying the building's foundation, President Roosevelt directed the commission "to insist on a greater application of the golden rule to the conduct of corporations."[24] The allegorical sculpture depicting a muscular man restraining a wild horse symbolizes the power of government regulation to restrain exuberant markets. It was completed by artist Michael Lantz in 1942. Just as its art deco style fits the New Deal era, so does the message it represents.
Source: © Elliot Teel.

executive agency
A regulatory agency in the executive branch run by a single administrator.

At the time, six of the nine justices were more than 70 years old. None suggested plans to retire. So Roosevelt sent Congress a scheme to change the Court by appointing one new justice for every justice over age 70, up to a membership of 15. This scheme would have allowed him to appoint enough pro–New Deal justices to overcome the deadweight of the Court's aging conservatives. However, it was never acted upon.

Right away, the Court got the message. In its first decision in 1937 it surprised everyone by reversing its position on the commerce clause, upholding the new National Labor Relations Act that regulated labor organizing. The justices said that the federal government could order a Pennsylvania steel plant to allow unionizing because the plant shipped steel out of the state in interstate commerce.[22] From then on, the Court saw factories and other business facilities as within a "stream of commerce" and held that the commerce clause gave the government power to regulate them.[23] This opened a door and new federal regulations rushed through it. The Court's changed constitutional interpretation is a good lesson that broad wording often ends up meaning what those with the most power want it to.

Wave 4: Administering the Social Revolution

There was little new regulation in the 1940s and 1950s. Then, in the late 1960s and early 1970s, a groundswell of interest in improving the quality of life created the fourth wave of government regulation. The result was a sudden burst of new controls designed to achieve broad social objectives.

The outpouring came in approximately 100 new statutes imposing regulation of consumer protection, environmental quality, workplace safety, and energy production.[25] There were several new independent commissions—the Equal Employment Opportunity Commission (1964) to protect civil rights in the workplace, the Consumer Product Safety Commission (1972) to protect the public from unsafe products, and the Nuclear Regulatory Commission (1974) to regulate nuclear facilities.

However, most of the new authorities went to a different kind of agency, the *executive agency,* or an agency within the executive branch run by a single administrator. This person is nominated by the president and confirmed by the Senate, but unlike the commissioners in independent commissions, who can be removed only for cause (such as incompetence or violating the law) agency heads can be

---

[22] *National Labor Relations Board v. Jones & Laughlin Steel Corp.,* 301 U.S. 1 (1937).

[23] Ibid., at 36.

[24] Franklin D. Roosevelt, "Address at the Cornerstone Laying Ceremonies for the New Federal Trade Commission Building," July 12, 1937, in John Woolley and Gerhard Peters, *The American Presidency Project* [online]. Santa Barbara, CA: University of California (hosted), Gerhard Peters (database), at www.presidency.ucsb.edu/ws/?pid=15436.

[25] *Federal Regulatory Directory,* p. 5.

removed by the president for any reason. These agencies are, therefore, exposed to more political winds than the independent commissions. Examples of executive agencies are the Environmental Protection Agency (1970), the Occupational Health and Safety Administration (1970), and the National Highway Traffic Safety Administration (1970).

deregulation
The removal or substantial reduction of the body of regulation covering an industry.

In this era, the voluminous buildup of regulations to achieve social objectives existed simultaneously with a *deregulation* movement that focused on removing or streamlining older economic regulations. While economic regulation was welcomed during the Great Depression as necessary to make markets work fairly, subsequent prosperity brought renewed faith in the efficiency of markets free from government interference. The objective of the movement was to cut regulations that limited competition within industries so that the free market could work.

In the first such experiment in 1976 all regulation of routes and fares was removed from the airlines. Financial institutions, cable television, and natural gas followed. Then railroads, trucking, and shipping were deregulated, leaving the original model of regulatory authority, the Interstate Commerce Commission, with so little to do that it was eventually abolished in 1995. Most deregulation seemed to benefit consumers, bringing more competition and lower prices, but not all of it ended happily. Reduction in federal oversight of the savings and loan industry led to corruption and fraud costing taxpayers more than $100 billion.

War Blips

As Figure 10.1 shows, wars have brought sudden increases in government controls. During the Civil War, there was little control over production and prices, but the North created a National Bank to help finance the war, and this had lasting impact on the financial system. World War I witnessed the introduction of substantial controls over industry, but the war ended before the controls began to bite. The federal government exercised complete control over the economy during World War II and to a lesser but still substantial extent during the Korean War. After both wars, the wartime controls were completely abandoned. No comparable increase in regulation came during the Vietnam War or the two Gulf wars, although the war on terrorism declared by President George W. Bush led to creation of the Department of Homeland Security with extensive regulatory powers.

HOW REGULATIONS ARE MADE

regulation
The effort by governments to achieve economic or social outcomes by directing the behavior of citizens, groups, and corporations.

Regulation is the effort by governments to achieve economic or social outcomes by directing the behavior of citizens, groups, and corporations. In the United States, federal regulation is carried out by rules created in a mazelike process that follows complex guidelines. Figure 10.2 shows a simplified, visual overview of this process, which we will describe.

Regulatory Statutes

All federal regulation originates in an act of Congress. When a bill containing regulatory authority has been passed by both houses of Congress and signed by

FIGURE 10.2
The
Regulatory
Process

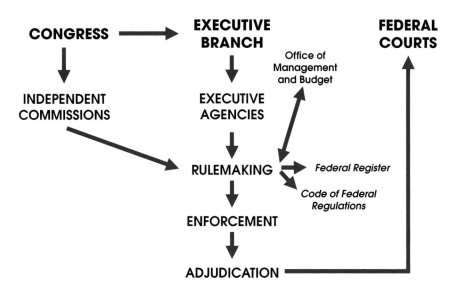

the president, that new statutory authority is assigned to a regulatory agency, either an independent commission or an executive branch agency. This agency then creates binding rules to implement provisions of the new law. Statutes rarely contain all the specific rules needed to assure that their intended purpose is achieved. It is the job of the agency to develop the necessary body of more detailed regulation. Some statutes give broad grants of authority to the implementing agency. The Federal Reserve Act of 1913, for example, gave the Federal Reserve Board complete authority to set interest rates. The Clean Air Act of 1970 granted the Environmental Protection Agency the authority to set and enforce air quality standards adequate to protect public health "allowing an adequate margin of safety."[26] The phrase "an adequate margin" allows the EPA to define how much of a specific pollutant can be emitted by factories and vehicles. Other statutes, however, are very specific. The Department of Transportation has little leeway in setting weight limits for trucks because Congress legislated an equation to calculate exact legal weights based on number of axles and their distance apart.[27]

Early in the New Deal era, Congress in its rush passed regulatory laws written with spacious and even vague wording. This capacious language was challenged by companies growing restive with the blizzard of rules emanating from bureaucrats in Washington. Business argued that delegating so much legislative power to the executive branch was unconstitutional. Congress's duty to make the laws could not be delegated to unelected drones in agencies. The Supreme Court resolved this issue, holding that broad delegation of legislative power to regulators

[26] Clean Air Act, as amended 1990, Title I, Part A, §109(B)(b)(1).
[27] "Vehicle weight limitations—Interstate System," 23 U.S.C. §127(a).

in the executive branch was constitutional, but only if Congress put clear principles and guidelines for using that power into the enabling statutes.[28]

Although the trend today is toward more specific laws, the great bulk of federal regulation is still created and administered in agencies based on broad grants of authority. This is inevitable, because Congress depends on the technical and scientific expertise of regulators to carry out its policies. Despite some early reticence, federal courts generally allow considerable leeway when agencies undertake to fill in the blanks in rulemaking.[29] However, as we will see, the courts keep a tight rein on regulators.

Rulemaking

rule
A decree developed by an agency to implement a law passed by Congress.

Regulatory agencies promulgate rules that have the force of law. A *rule* is a decree developed by an agency to implement a law passed by Congress."[30] There are many types of rules. For example, some rules command a business to do something or stop doing something. Some rules ask only for information, some set prices, some set standards for business to meet, some license business activity, some prescribe how standards set by government will be met, and some subsidize business.

Rules are created in a complex, formal rulemaking process. The process is designed to protect the public from arbitrary and capricious acts of government. Its basic steps were set forth in the Administrative Procedures Act in 1946, but since then more and more requirements have been added, making the process more rigid and cumbersome.[31] Rulemaking for lesser regulations can be completed in several months, but major rules can take years to complete. In what follows, we describe the basic steps.

Federal Register
A daily government publication containing proposed rules, final rules, and notice of other actions by federal regulatory agencies.

When an agency decides to promulgate a rule it may already have gone through a long process of research, deliberation, and contact with affected parties. When a rule is drafted the agency issues a Notice of Proposed Rulemaking and publishes it in the *Federal Register.* The *Federal Register* is a daily publication of the federal government started during the New Deal years as an official source for all agency rules and regulations. It is published every working day and has never missed a day since its first issue on March 14, 1936. Publication of a proposed rule opens a period of time, usually 60 to 90 days, during which the public can comment to the

[28] *Panama Refining Co. v. Ryan,* 293 U.S. 388. The Court did strike down some New Deal laws, wholly or in part because they delegated too much power to the executive branch. See, for example, *A. L. A. Schechter Poultry Corp. v. United States,* 295 U.S. 495 (1935) striking down the National Industrial Recovery Act in which Justice Benjamin Cardozo saw "delegation running riot" (at 553).

[29] See, for example, *Whitman v. American Trucking Associations,* 531 U.S. 457, upholding the EPA's right to fill in meaning to phrases in the Clean Air Act Amendments of 1990.

[30] The legal definition of a rule in the Administrative Procedure Act of 1946, 5 U.S.C. II §551(4), is "an agency statement . . . designed to implement, interpret, or prescribe a law or policy."

[31] In addition to guidelines in executive orders discussed later in this section, the most important of these additional requirements include environmental impact statements, if required under the National Environmental Policy Act of 1969; analysis of impacts on small businesses as required in the Regulatory Flexibility Act of 1980; minimization of paperwork under the Paperwork Reduction Act of 1995; appraisal of impacts on states and cities as required by the Unfunded Mandates Act of 1995; and following data guidelines set up under the Information Quality Act of 2000.

FIGURE 10.3
Annual Page Count in the *Federal Register*: 1936 to 2006

Source: Annual *Federal Register* pages published at www.llsdc.org/sourcebook/docs/fed-reg-pages.pdf.

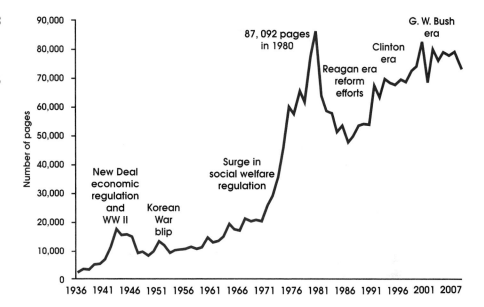

agency. For rules affecting business, comments usually come from lobbyists, corporate lawyers, and trade associations; however, anyone can submit a comment. A Web site, www.government.reg, was recently set up to centralize and simplify the act of commenting.

Newly proposed rules are also sent by agencies to the Office of Management and Budget (OMB), a White House group that provides central oversight of regulation for the president. If the proposed rule is defined as a "major rule," that is, a rule that will have an annual impact of $100 million or more on the U.S. economy, it must be accompanied by an analysis that details its full impact on the economy and society, including monetary costs and benefits. Such analyses can be big hurdles for agencies. They are time consuming and expensive. For example, when the EPA decided to require new emission controls on diesel locomotives the regulatory analysis took years and finally weighed in at 1,568 pages.[32] We will discuss OMB oversight more in the next section.

After the comment period ends the agency may reconsider and rewrite the draft regulation to incorporate public comments and advice from the Office of Management and Budget. Then it prints the final rule in the *Federal Register*. The rule usually takes effect 30 to 60 days after this printing.

Code of Federal Regulations
Annually revised, bound volumes that compile final rules and effective regulations from all federal agencies.

Pages in the *Federal Register* are a crude gauge of regulatory activity. By law it prints all proposed and final rules, executive orders, and notices of agency meetings and hearings. Figure 10.3 shows how the rise and fall of *Federal Register* pages reflect long-term regulatory growth interrupted by fleeting corrections.

After publication in the *Federal Register* final regulations are codified in another government publication, the *Code of Federal Regulations*. The *Code* is di-

[32] *Final Regulatory Analysis: Control of Emissions from Nonroad Diesel Engines,* EPA420-R-04-007 (Washington, DC: EPA Office of Transportation and Air Quality, May 2004).

vided into 50 titles containing final and effective regulations from all federal agencies. The titles are divided into volumes, chapters, parts, and sections with all rules from an agency generally found in one title or subpart of a title. For example, regulations from the EPA are contained in Title 40, "Protection of the Environment," covering 31 volumes with three chapters and 817 sections. Each title in the *Code* is updated and republished each year.[33] In print, it covers 158,183 pages in more than 236 volumes, costs $1,389 for a full set, and grows with every revision.

Even if corporations followed each regulation as it appeared in the *Federal Register* and the *Code of Federal Regulations* full compliance would still elude them. This is because, in addition to regulations, agencies issue even larger volumes of *guidance* in documents such as memoranda, circulars, compliance manuals, and advisory opinions. Such guidance is intended as clarification for regulated parties. In reality, it often changes and adds to existing rules. The agency's motive may be to assist the regulated, or it may be to bypass the increasingly petrified rulemaking process. A federal appeals court once explained how billows of guidance arise.

guidance
Information in nonbinding documents intended to clarify official regulations.

> Congress passes a broadly worded statute. The agency follows with regulations containing broad language, open-ended phrases, ambiguous standards and the like. Then as years pass, the agency issues circulars or guidance or memoranda, explaining, interpreting, defining and often expanding the commands in the regulations. One guidance document may yield another and then another and so on. Several words in a regulation may spawn hundreds of pages of text as the agency offers more and more detail regarding what its regulations demand of regulated entities. Law is made, without notice and comment, without public participation, and without publication in the *Federal Register* or the *Code of Federal Regulations*.[34]

Although guidance is not supposed to be legally binding, the regulated ignore it at their peril. Its volume is astounding. When a congressional committee asked three agencies to submit guidance documents from a three-year, nine-month period it received 1,225 documents from the National Highway Traffic Safety Administration, 3,374 from the Occupational Safety and Health Administration, and 2,653 totaling 96,906 pages from the EPA.[35] Trying to control guidance practices President George W. Bush in 2007 issued Executive Order 13422 requiring executive branch agencies to submit "significant" guidance documents, defined as those with an annual impact of $100 million or more, to the OMB for review.[36] Even if this helps, it will remain nearly impossible for any corporation acting in good faith fully to comprehend all that regulators require of it. It will be thwarted by a bewildering mass of instructions growing at a fantastic rate.

[33] The *Code of Federal Regulations* is published in printed volumes and on the Government Printing Office Web site at www.gpo.gov/nara/cfr/.

[34] *Appalachian Power Company v. Environmental Protection Agency,* 341 U.S. App. D.C. 46 (2000), at 1020.

[35] Committee on Government Reform, *Non-Binding Legal Effect of Agency Guidance Documents,* 106th Congress, 2d Session, H. Rep. 106-1009, October 26, 2000, p. 5.

[36] 72 FR 2763, January 23, 2007.

Presidential Oversight

In the past presidents have sought control over regulatory agencies, but met with little success. Theodore Roosevelt first suggested that independent regulatory commissions be supervised by cabinet secretaries. FDR repeated this proposal. In 1949 former President Herbert Hoover, then head of a blue-ribbon commission to review government regulation, again made the suggestion. No action was taken, but absent such formal authority recent presidents have discovered other ways to impose their will.

President Reagan took office in 1980 determined to stem the rising tide of regulation. He declared an initial moratorium on new regulations, created a task force on regulatory relief under Vice President George H. W. Bush, and cut agency budgets. He also issued Executive Order 12291 in 1981 giving the Office of Management and Budget authority to review existing and current rules to request changes if they were inconsistent with the administration's philosophy.[37] The order, which was a broad enactment of regulatory reform, required all new rules to meet a test in which they represented the greatest "net benefit" among alternative approaches. Major rules, those with an annual economic impact of $100 million or more, had to be supported by massive analytical studies, including formal analysis of costs and benefits. Early in the Reagan years, the output of new regulations sharply declined. His effort to take control, particularly by requiring centralized review, was unprecedented and would be continued. However, regulation itself was irrepressible, and by the end of his second term in 1988, growth had resumed.

The George H. W. Bush administration (1988–1992) focused more on foreign events than on domestic issues, including regulation, yet it continued the mandates in Executive Order 12291 and made one additional effort to slow regulatory growth. President Bush appointed Vice President Dan Quayle to head a new Council on Competitiveness, giving the group authority to review existing and proposed regulations. It rejected and repealed a modest number of rules, most because they imposed costs and inefficiencies on corporations.

President Bill Clinton, although he was a moderate Democrat less opposed in principle to regulatory power than his immediate predecessors, responded to pressure from Republicans in Congress by continuing efforts to control regulatory excess. In 1993 he issued Executive Order 12866, which replaced Reagan's earlier order but retained the requirements of centralized review.[38] In addition, Clinton asked agencies to consider nonregulatory alternatives to rules and to write regulations in simple, easily understood language. Vice President Al Gore was appointed to head a working group of regulatory agency heads, which invented an ambitious but ultimately quixotic plan to end "regulatory overkill" by eliminating many outdated, overlapping, and unnecessary regulations.[39] Despite this, agencies busied themselves with new rules up to the last days of the Clinton administration.

---

[37] "Improving Government Regulations," 46 FR 13193, February 17, 1981.

[38] "Regulatory Planning and Review," 58 FR 51735, October 4, 1993.

[39] Albert Gore, *Creating a Government That Works Better & Costs Less, Report of the National Performance Review* (Washington, DC: Government Printing Office, September 7, 1993), p. 32.

President George W. Bush came into office in 2001 committed to reasserting control. On taking office he imposed an immediate 60-day delay on 3,512 pages of new regulations agencies had submitted to the *Federal Register* on the last Friday of the Clinton presidency.[40] Although most of these rules eventually went into effect, he checked regulators in other ways. He set about naming agency heads who sympathized with his desire to reduce regulatory burdens. The Office of Management and Budget continued to follow oversight procedures in Clinton's executive order, but with tougher approval procedures. The net result was a small drop in new regulation early in Bush's presidency followed by resumed, though slower, growth.

In sum, presidents have used many devices to limit and direct regulation. Restraints have included executive orders, moratoriums, favorable appointments of agency administrators, budget cutting, and central review of regulations in the White House. While independent regulatory commissions are legally aloof from control by executive order and centralized review, since the Reagan administration they have been asked by the Office of Management and Budget voluntarily to submit major new regulations for review and most of the time they do. While central oversight of agencies is now well entrenched, they continue to pour forth more rules. Much of the reason lies within the agencies themselves.

> As anyone who has worked on regulatory issues knows, government agencies are not staffed with objective bureaucrats. The sympathies and paths to career advancement and outside pressures tend to go in one direction, toward more regulation.[41]

Congressional Oversight

Congress has many ways to influence and control regulatory agencies. Besides passing or amending laws it approves presidential nominees as head regulators and approves agency budgets. Committees in both Houses have jurisdiction over specific areas of regulation and may request information from agencies and summon regulators to testify at hearings. For example, the House Energy and Commerce Committee has jurisdiction over consumer protection, telecommunications, air quality, energy, and food and drug safety. Its current chairman, Rep. John Dingell (D-Mich.) is feared by regulators for his tenacious oversight of their agencies. Yet, overall, committee oversight is inconsistent, sometimes nonexistent. Jurisdiction over agencies often lies with several or more committees whose actions are not coordinated. Also, committees lack sufficient staff to investigate agency actions in depth.

In 1996 Congress added to its oversight capacity by passing the Congressional Review Act. This law mandates that most new rules cannot go into effect until 60 days after they have been sent to Congress for review. If, within that time, a resolution of disapproval is introduced, passed by both Houses, and signed by the president the rule is nullified. Since the law was passed, 37 joint resolutions of disapproval have been introduced, but only one passed—a rejection of an ergonomics rule from OSHA.[42]

---

[40] Cindy Skrzycki, "'Midnight Regulations' Swell Register," *Washington Post,* January 23, 2001, p. E1.

[41] Ike Brannon, "Treating the Unserious Seriously," *Regulation,* Winter 2005–2006, p. 51.

[42] Government Accountability Office, *Federal Rulemaking: Perspectives on 10 Years of Congressional Review Act Implementation,* GAO-06-601T, March 30, 2006, p. 3.

In sum, congressional oversight is an important influence on agency actions. However, the check that exists in theory is used in practice less often.

Challenges in the Courts

As they enforce rules, agencies are beset by conflicts with regulated parties. Formal conflicts are resolved in two ways. First, the Administrative Procedure Act requires each agency to set up an adjudication process leading to trial before an administrative law judge. Second, if the judge's decision fails to resolve the dispute, federal courts can review agency actions.

Usually, federal courts defer to the judgment of agencies when their rules are based on reasonable interpretations of statutes. The case that solidified this deference arose when a rule on factory pollution from the Environmental Protection Agency provoked environmental groups. A section of the Clean Air Act Amendments of 1977 required the EPA to cut emissions from "stationary sources" of air pollution at industrial plants. It issued a regulation that put all single emission sources at a plant under an imaginary plantwide "bubble" and required that total emissions within the bubble be reduced. This allowed companies to meet plantwide emission limits by cutting emissions more from some sources than others based on control costs. Angry environmentalists claimed that the statute's mandate to control "stationary source" pollution required permits and reductions for each stack, oven, engine, and valve, not a plantwide aggregate of sources.

In *Chevron v. National Resources Defense Council* the Supreme Court set the guiding precedent on deference to regulatory agencies. It held that a court should look first to see if a statute's direct wording revealed congressional intent. If it did not, as was the case here, then the court should decide whether the agency had made a "permissible" interpretation of wording. Unless the agency's interpretation was "arbitrary, capricious, or manifestly contrary to the statute," it should be held "reasonable" and "permissible."[43] This 1984 decision created the *Chevron doctrine,* or the general rule that courts should defer to agency rules that are based on reasonable interpretations of ambiguous statutes. Citing the *Chevron* doctrine, the courts now reject most challenges to agency rules.

Chevron doctrine
The general rule that federal courts should defer to agency rules that are based on reasonable interpretations of ambiguous statutes.

Although the standard for judging agency actions is a lenient one, judicial oversight is vigilant. Congress has given federal courts the power to hold unlawful agency actions that are arbitrary, capricious, unconstitutional, in excess of agency jurisdiction, or unsupported by evidence.[44] In this sampling of cases, rules were rejected for the following reasons.

- *The agency misinterpreted congressional intent.* General Dynamics and a labor union agreed that, henceforth, only workers who were already age 50 or older would get health benefits when they retired. However, the deal violated an EEOC rule prohibiting age-related discrimination of any kind against workers over age 40. The Supreme Court struck down the agency's rule saying that "beyond reasonable doubt" its underlying authority, the Age Discrimination in

---

[43] *Chevron U.S.A v. Natural Resources Defense Council*, 467 U.S. 837 (1984).

[44] The scope of judicial review comes under the authority of the Administrative Procedures Act and is set forth in 5 U.S.C. §706(2)(A).

Employment Act of 1967, was never intended by Congress to prohibit favoring the old over the young. Congress intended only to stop discrimination against older workers in favor of younger ones.[45]

- *The agency lacked convincing evidence for its action.* When the Environmental Protection Agency banned commercial uses of asbestos a federal appeals court struck down the rule because it was not based on "substantial evidence." The main problem was that the agency's cost-benefit studies never evaluated the risks of substitute materials likely to be used in place of asbestos.[46]

- *The agency ignored guidelines in the law.* The Energy Policy Act of 1992 directed the EPA to set human health standards for disposal of nuclear waste at a Yucca Mountain, Nevada, site. The statute directed the agency to base its standards on data from the National Academy of Sciences (NAS), which predicted high levels of radiation peaking after 100,000 years and lasting 2 to 17 million years Eventually, the EPA promulgated a standard that protected a hypothetical person living near the site for 10,000 years. Opponents of the site challenged this standard for ignoring the NAS prediction that radiation danger would be greatest in tens of thousands to 100,000 years. The EPA argued it had acted reasonably because regulating more than 10,000 years in the future was unrealistic. However, a federal appeals court held that the EPA had ignored its statutory mandate and struck down the rule.[47]

Finally, courts may force reticent agencies to act. Environmental groups petitioned the EPA to regulate auto emissions of gases implicated in global warming, including carbon dioxide. The EPA refused, saying that carbon dioxide did not fit the definition in the Clean Air Act of an "air pollutant" as "any physical, chemical, biological, [or] radioactive ... substance" posing a danger to people.[48] However, the Supreme Court held that the definition was "unambiguous" in including "any" airborne substance that threatened public health and welfare, including natural molecules such as carbon dioxide.[49] It ordered the EPA to initiate regulatory actions. This case illustrates the power of the judiciary to force a reticent agency to act.

THE COSTS AND BENEFITS OF REGULATION

Accumulating regulation has significant impact on everyone, especially business, that would be hard to exaggerate. One way of analyzing this impact is to measure and compare both the benefits of regulation and its costs. Comprehensive data for calculating the net benefit (or cost) of regulation, that is, its benefits minus its costs, does not exist. Both benefits and costs are difficult to measure in precise

---

[45] *General Dynamics Land Systems v. Cline,* 540 U.S. 581 (2004).

[46] *Corrosion Proof Fittings v. EPA,* 947 F.2d 1201 (1991).

[47] *Nuclear Energy Institute v. EPA,* 362 U.S. App. D.C. 204 (2004).

[48] 42 U.S.C. §7602(g).

[49] *Massachusetts v. EPA,* 127 S.Ct. 1438 (2007).

FIGURE 10.4
Total Administrative Costs of Regulation: 1960–2007

Source: From Susan Dudley and Melinda Warren, *Moderating Regulatory Growth: An Analysis of the U.S. Budget for Fiscal Years 2006 and 2007,* table A-5.

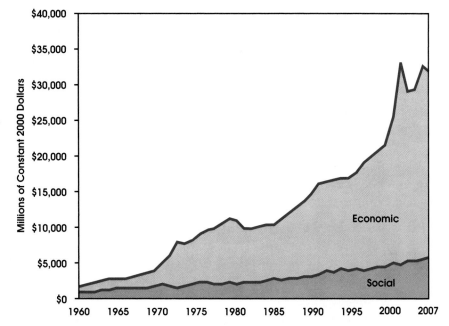

and comparable ways. Also, the benefits and costs of regulation usually go to different parties, turning calculation of net benefit into a political question. Government subsidies to farmers, for example, create a benefit by raising farmer's incomes. The cost falls on taxpayers.

The Regulatory Burden

We can measure or characterize the burden of regulation in many ways. One important measure is total dollar cost. A study of the overall compliance burden calculated that the total cost of federal regulation was $876 billion in 2000 or 8.6 percent of GDP.[50] A follow-up study calculated that by 2004 total cost had risen to $1.1 trillion or 11 percent of GDP.[51] One main finding of these studies is that small businesses bear a disproportionately large share of the regulatory burden. In 2004 the cost per employee at firms with fewer than 20 employees was $7,647 compared with only $5,282 at firms with 500 or more employees.[52]

Another measure of the burden is the cost of administering the regulatory process. The growth of this cost since 1960 is shown in Figure 10.4. The assumption, of course, is that the more budgeted for the regulatory agencies the more regulations

[50] W. Mark Crain and Thomas D. Hopkins, *The Impact of Regulatory Costs on Small Firms* (Washington, DC: Small Business Administration, SBAHQ-00-R-0027, 2001), p. 3. Figures in this paragraph are in 2001 dollars.

[51] W. Mark Crain, *The Impact of Regulatory Costs on Small Firms* (Washington, DC: Small Business Administration, SBHZ-03-M-0522, 2005), p. 4.

[52] Ibid., p. 5.

FIGURE 10.5
**If Agencies
Were Planets**
The size of
regulatory
agencies is
shown here
relative to
their fiscal
year 2007
budgets.

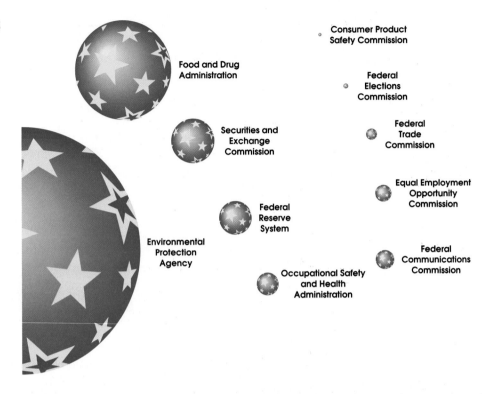

they create and the heavier is the burden borne by business. Two trends are visible
in Figure 10.4. One is the upward total expenditure trend, rising from $2.5 billion
in 1960 to an estimated $37.8 billion in 2007.[53] The other is that most of the growth in
expenditure has been for social regulation.

Figure 10.5 adds a second perspective on regulatory costs showing that some
agencies have much larger budgets than others. Agency budgets are a rough indication of the extent of regulatory activity within them and, in turn, of the compliance costs they create.

Other costs of regulation are also large but are indirect and much more difficult
to quantify. These include the impact of regulation on employment, productivity,
and innovation. An extreme but telling example is the decision of the Food and
Drug Administration to order a moratorium on the use of silicone gel breast implants in 1992. This decision led to the bankruptcy of Dow Corning, loss of more
than 1,000 jobs, evaporation of shareholder equity, and dampening of research into
new uses of silicone body parts. Eventually, medical research exonerated silicone,
but not before a robust industry had been crippled. In another example, the Securities and Exchange Commission has slowed the growth of an innovative financial
product, the exchange-traded fund. ETFs must be submitted to the SEC for approval

[53] Susan Dudley and Melinda Warren, *Moderating Regulatory Growth: An Analysis of the U.S. Budget for
Fiscal Years 2006 and 2007,* Mercatus Center and Weidenbaum Center, May 2006, p. 2006, table A2.
Figures are in constant 2000 dollars. The chart does not sum social and economic regulations.

before they begin trading on exchanges. Their journey is slow, taking up to five years, because ETFs are novel financial instruments that the agency's bureaucrats subject to an unusually complicated approval process.[54]

Benefits of Regulations

Measuring the benefits of federal regulation is far more difficult than calculating costs. At an aggregate level, business could not operate and society could not prosper without certain types of regulation. Regulation has reduced discrimination, improved the environment, prevented monopoly, freed competition, prevented corruption, strengthened the banking system, cut workplace fatalities, helped the elderly, controlled communicable diseases, and much more. These benefits are enormous and incalculable.

When proposals for new "major" rules are made to the OMB, they must be accompanied by estimates of benefits and costs. Critics of regulation believe that agencies sometimes bias their assumptions and calculations in favor of the rule. However, the studies often provide needed discipline. Here is one example.

By studying aircraft accidents the Federal Aviation Administration (FAA) concluded that more passengers and crew would survive crash landings if seats could withstand forces 16 times the force of gravity before collapsing rather than the existing 9 times the force of gravity. It wrote a rule requiring all seats in new airplanes to meet this standard beginning in 2009. It calculated the cost of stronger seats at $35 million between 2009 and 2034, but the benefits in lives saved and injuries averted were much greater, $79 million. Still more lives could be saved if the FAA required the airlines to retrofit existing passenger planes with stronger seats, but the agency's benefit-cost analysis showed that the cost would be $512 million, far greater than even the most optimistic benefit estimates. Therefore, the FAA finalized the rule without a retrofitting requirement.[55] Absent the benefit-cost study it might have imposed a net cost on society.

While the net benefits of specific rules can be clear, estimates of aggregate benefits of regulation to society have little credibility given the mushiness of the available data. A partial effort is that of the Office of Management and Budget to calculate total benefits and costs of 95 "major" regulations it reviewed over the period 1995 to 2005. During this time benefits were $94 billion to $449 billion, far greater than costs that were $37 billion to $44 billion. This left a net benefit (benefits minus costs) of $57 to $405 billion.[56] If these estimates are accurate, the benefits of major rules over a decade may be more than 10 times greater than their costs. Unfortunately, the figures provide little grounds for a similarly sanguine assumption regarding regulation in the aggregate.

[54] Duja Gullapalli, "Growth of Hot Investment Tool Slowed by Bureaucratic Backlog," *The Wall Street Journal,* June 17–18, 2006, p. A1.

[55] Cindy Skryzcki, "FAA Updates Rule on Airline Seats," *Washington Post,* October 18, 2005, p. D1.

[56] Office of Management and Budget, *Draft 2006 Report to Congress on the Costs and Benefits of Federal Regulations* (Washington, DC: OMB, April 13, 2006), p. 5.

REGULATION IN OTHER NATIONS

In varying form, quantity, and quality regulation of business exists in every national economy and in the global economy. It is a basic institution underlying markets and, as the following anecdotes suggest, it can support or impair them.

Tawanda owns a restaurant in Zimbabwe. Business has declined and she needs to lay off three workers, but under the country's labor laws if she does she must pay each between 4 and 10 years' salary. So instead of reducing her payroll, Tawanda abandons the business and flees across the border to Malawi. Meanwhile, five thousand miles to the east in Singapore, Chek takes a call and learns she has lost a major account with her small advertising agency. That afternoon she lays off the account representative and two graphic artists, paying each four weeks' salary as required by law.[57]

Fabien has a shop in Bujumbura, Burundi, where he sells bicycles imported from China. His shipments come through a Tanzanian port. It takes 50 days to get pre-arrival approvals at the port, 8 days of handling after arrival, 15 more days to process customs documents, and 30 days on trains before the shipment reaches Burundi's border. Then border inspection takes 12 days. Finally, after a barge trip the goods are subject to additional inspection on arrival in Bujumbura. Overall, the bicycles require 124 days, 19 documents, and 55 signatures to come from the port to Fabien's shop.[58] Meanwhile, four thousand miles to the north, Franziska also imports Chinese-made bicycles to sell at her shop in Berlin, Germany. It takes her only six days, four documents, and one signature to get all the needed approvals. After the bicycles are unloaded at a French port, their inland journey to Franziska's shop takes just two days.

Poorer countries generally have heavier regulations on business. They tend to be badly enforced and subject to corruption. The result is that people in business choose to operate underground. In Bolivia, for example, more than 80 percent of private business activity takes place underground. Workers have no paid vacations or maternity leave. Small businesses have difficulty getting credit, and enforcing contracts is hard. The infrastructure deteriorates because underground businesses pay no taxes, limiting government revenue. Businesses try to remain small in the hope of avoiding inspectors and tax collectors, crimping economic growth.

In 2004 the World Bank began an ambitious, long-term study to catalog, classify, compare, and evaluate regulations in every nation. This study, now in its fifth year and covering 175 nations, focuses on 10 dimensions of economic regulation: starting a business, obtaining licenses, employing workers, registering property, getting credit, protecting investors, paying taxes, trading across borders, enforcing contracts, and closing a business.

Early in the study, the World Bank made four basic findings.

- Regulation varies widely around the world.
- Poor countries regulate business the most. And heavier regulation brings bad outcomes, including delays, higher costs, more corruption, lower productivity, and less investment.

[57] World Bank, *Doing Business 2007: How to Reform* (Washington, DC: World Bank, 2006), pp. 20, indicator table, p. 85.

[58] World Bank, *Doing Business 2006: Creating Jobs* (Washington, DC: World Bank, 2005), p. 53, indicator table, p. 104.

FIGURE 10.6
Ease of Doing Business Rankings
The table lists the best and the worst regulatory environments for doing business in 175 economies. Calculations are based on the sum of average percentile rankings on 10 measures of performance indexed by the World Bank.

Source: World Bank, Doing Business 2008 (Washington DC: World Bank, 2007), table 1.2.

Top 10	Bottom 10
1. Singapore	169. Niger
2. New Zealand	170. Liberia
3. United States	171. Eritrea
4. Hong Kong, China	172. Venezuela
5. Denmark	173. Chad
6. United Kingdom	174. Burundi
7. Canada	175. Congo, Rep.
8. Ireland	176. Guinea-Bissau
9. Australia	177. Central African Republic
10. Iceland	178. Congo, Dem. Rep.

- Rich countries regulate business in a consistent manner. Poor countries do not. Rich countries regulate less on all aspects of business activity.
- Developed countries engage in continuous regulatory reform to improve the business environment. There is much less reform in developing countries.[59]

The study concluded that the same principles of effective regulation worked well in both rich and poor nations. It set forth five "principles of good regulation."

- Simplify and deregulate in competitive markets.
- Focus on enhancing property rights.
- Expand the use of technology (particularly the Internet and information systems).
- Reduce court involvement in business matters.
- Make reform a continuous process.[60]

Research shows a strong correlation between regulation that follows these principles and overall economic growth.[61] This holds true even among developed nations, where those with the least burdensome regulations exhibit faster GDP growth.[62] Thus, the World Bank concludes that reform can lead to accelerating growth. It ranks each nation in ease of doing business. This ranking, which is revised yearly, has inspired many reforms. Figure 10.6 lists the top 10 and bottom 10 nations.

---

[59] World Bank, *Doing Business 2004: Understanding Regulation* (Washington, DC: World Bank and Oxford University Press, 2004), pp. xiii–xvii and pp. 83–90.

[60] Ibid., p. 92.

[61] See, for example, Simeon Djankov, Caralee McLiesh, and Rita Ramalho, *Regulation and Growth* (Washington, DC: World Bank, March 17, 2006).

[62] Giuseppe Niccolette and Stefano Scarpetta, "Regulation, Productivity, and Growth: OECD Evidence," World Bank Policy Research Paper 2944, January 2003.

REGULATING THE GLOBAL ECONOMY

Investments, production, goods, and services move across borders in the global economy. All these activities are subject to regulation in one or more national economies. However, critics complain that transnational operations elude adequate regulation. Here the critics focus mainly on social regulation. The heaviest economic regulation is found in poor and developing nations, but these are the same nations that have fewer protections for workers, consumers, and the environment.

While poorer nations are counseled to have strong social regulations, when their governments are dominated by elites that exploit the status quo they make little progress. Therefore, social protections in the global economy are often imposed by the developed world. They are imposed in many ways. Treaties protect natural resources such as migratory birds. Trade agreements between developed and developing nations now contain protections for workers and the environment. Progressive groups, governments, and corporations form networks of *civil regulation* in which participants agree to follow codes of conduct. Civil regulation, which was discussed in Chapter 5, is most often based on global norms and designed to ensure labor rights and mitigate environmental impacts of business. All these initiatives are forms of social regulation.

civil regulation
Regulation by nonstate actors based on social norms or standards enforced by social or market sanctions.

Finally, local regulation can have worldwide effect in a global economy. The premier example is the impact of environmental regulations adopted in the European Union (EU). The 25-country EU single market is approximately equal to the U.S. market in GDP and share of global merchandise trade. For global producers of goods and services, such a market is too large to ignore and so EU standards affect production and design around the world.

For example, when the EU banned lead solder and five other substances in electronics, Coherent, Inc., a company that makes medical lasers, spent two years redesigning its products to be compliant. Although it is an American corporation that makes its products in California, 28 percent of its sales are in EU countries.[63] A new EU law requires that between 2007 and 2016 companies supply basic toxicity information on 30,000 chemicals now used in commerce and prove that 1,500 chemicals suspected of causing serious human illness are safe. The law applies to only chemicals in any product sold within the EU market. However, because large chemical companies and manufacturers in non-EU nations cannot afford to sacrifice revenues from the 480 million consumers in EU nations the European Parliament has, in effect, legislated a global regulation.

CONCLUDING OBSERVATIONS

Federal regulation of business has expanded over time. There have been ups and downs, but the basic direction has been up, with respect to both volume and complexity. Early growth was in economic regulation. Recent growth has been mainly in social regulation. Successive efforts of presidents over the past 40 years have

---

[63] Evelyn Iritani, "Europe Pushes Tech into Detox," *Los Angeles Times,* April 22, 2006, p. C1.

not succeeded in slowing the expansion, but have produced needed reforms including centralized review, simplification, benefit-cost analysis, and deregulation of some industries. The cost of federal regulation to industry and consumers is huge, but is offset by many benefits to society as a whole, individuals, companies, and industries.

The FDA and Tobacco Regulation

On August 10, 1995, President Bill Clinton held a White House media event announcing a big regulatory initiative. Behind a podium in the East Room he spoke to the press and to a group of children assembled for the occasion.

> Today I am announcing broad executive action to protect the young people of the United States from the awful dangers of tobacco. Today, and every day this year, 3,000 young people will begin to smoke; 1,000 of them ultimately will die of cancer, emphysema, heart disease and other diseases caused by smoking. That's more than a million vulnerable young people a year being hooked on nicotine that ultimately could kill them.
>
> Therefore, by executive authority, I will restrict sharply the advertising, promotion, distribution and marketing of cigarettes to teen-agers . . . . We need to act, and we must act now, before another generation of Americans is condemned to fight a difficult and grueling personal battle.[1]

The president's announcement came because the Food and Drug Administration (FDA), reversing a long-held position, had decided to regulate nicotine as a drug. This is the story of that reversal and of the subsequent effort to get the regulations implemented.

THE FOOD AND DRUG ADMINISTRATION

The Food and Drug Administration is a federal regulatory agency with headquarters in Washington, DC, and field offices around the country. Its origins lie in the progressive era of the early 1900s when reformers agitated to protect the public from adulterated foods and unsafe drugs.

In 1906 Congress passed the Pure Food and Drug Act to ban adulterated or misbranded foods, drinks, and drugs from interstate commerce. The new law went to a small agency within the Department of Agriculture which grew into the present-day FDA. After more than 100 people died from a patent medicine called elixir of sulfanilamide in 1937, Congress passed the Food, Drug, and Cosmetics Act of 1938, greatly extending the FDA's authority. It received the power to regulate medical devices and the safety of new drugs and to inspect production facilities of regulated products. Since then, more than 30 additional laws and amendments have broadened its powers.

THE QUESTION OF AUTHORITY TO REGULATE TOBACCO

In early America, smoking was mostly confined to southern states, but during the Civil War, Union troops occupying the South picked up the habit and brought it home with them, creating national demand for smoking tobacco. In the century following the Civil War, smoking became widely accepted, and by the 1950s, the majority of men and about one-third of women smoked.

From the beginning, however, suspicion of adverse health effects hung over cigarettes. Suspicion turned into realization in 1964, when the Surgeon General of the United States published a report on accumulated medical research. The report warned of a strong association between smoking and lung cancer.[2] It stated, for example, that death rates for male smokers were 170 percent those of male nonsmokers, and that mortality increased with the number of cigarettes smoked.

---

[1] Reuters, "Teen-agers and Tobacco: Excerpts from Clinton News Conference on His Tobacco Order," *New York Times,* August 11, 1995, p. A18.

[2] Department of Health, Education, and Welfare, *Smoking and Health: Report of the Advisory Committee to the Surgeon General of the Public Health Service* (Washington, DC: Government Printing Office, 1964).

Following the surgeon general's landmark report, damning medical evidence continued to accumulate. As it did, pressure was put on the FDA to regulate tobacco. Many people wondered why an agency set up to protect public health from dangerous products failed to ban a product that killed 400,000 Americans a year. Because of the Delaney Amendment of 1953, the FDA was required to ban any food containing a substance that caused cancer in humans or animals, no matter how small the amount or danger. As a result, the agency at one time banned saccharine, though the substance posed only a slight theoretical risk with ingestion of massive amounts requiring superhuman gluttony. Yet it never outlawed cigarettes.

In 1977 a coalition of groups led by Action on Smoking and Health filed a citizens' petition with the FDA requesting the agency to assert jurisdiction over tobacco. The petition was based on the statutory authority given to the FDA by the Food, Drug, and Cosmetics Act of 1938. Nowhere does the act mention tobacco. Instead, it sets forth general definitions of "drug" and "device" and empowers the agency to decide which substances and objects fall into those categories. In the statute, the term "drug" means:

(A) articles recognized in the official United States Pharmacopoeia, official Homoeopathic Pharmacopoeia of the United States, or official National Formulary, or any supplement to any of them; and (B) articles intended for use in the diagnosis, cure, mitigation, treatment, or prevention of disease in man or other animals; and (C) articles (other than food) intended to affect the structure or any function of the body of man or other animals; and (D) articles intended for use as a component of any article specified in clause (A), (B), or (C).[3]

The statute defines a "device" as:

[A]n instrument, apparatus, implement, machine, contrivance, implant, in vitro reagent, or other similar or related article, including any component, part, or accessory, which is . . . intended to affect the structure or any function of the body of man or other animals, and which does not achieve its primary intended purposes through chemical action within or on the body of man or other

animals and which is not dependent upon being metabolized for the achievement of its primary intended purposes.[4]

Action on Smoking and Health requested that the FDA define cigarettes as a "device" containing the "drug" nicotine, thereby giving it the authority to restrict their sale. It also requested that cigarettes be sold only through pharmacies. The FDA rejected the petition. It argued that the law allowed classifying a substance as a drug only when the manufacturer made a health claim for the product or intended it to be used as a drug. Since the tobacco companies did not make health claims for cigarettes or state an intent that nicotine be used for its pharmacological effects in the body, the agency had no statutory authority.

In addition, it argued that Congress had known for many years that the FDA did not classify tobacco as a drug. If Congress had wanted to, it could have amended the law to clarify that tobacco fell under the agency's jurisdiction. However, it never did so, although it had regulated tobacco in other ways, for example, by requiring warning labels on cigarette packs.

Action on Smoking and Health was disappointed. The group strongly believed that nicotine was a drug under any literal or commonsense reading of the 1938 law. It appealed the rejection of its petition but lost when a federal court agreed with the FDA, holding that a regulatory agency was entitled to "substantial deference" in the reading of those laws it is in charge of administering.[5] There matters stood for many years.

NEW LEADERSHIP UNDER DAVID KESSLER

The FDA, bred of nineteenth-century progressive outrage, is a reformist creation that thrives in an atmosphere of correction. While the consumer movement rode high in the 1960s and 1970s, the agency's powers steadily expanded. Then, following the election of President Ronald Reagan in 1980, the political atmosphere changed. Like other federal agencies, the FDA found its budget squeezed and its staff cut as

---

[3] 21 U.S.C. 321(g)(1). This citation references Title 21 of the *Code of Federal Regulations,* where all statutes that give the FDA its authority are codified along with the rules and regulations the agency has adopted. Section 321 is found in Chapter 9, Subchapter II.

[4] 21 U.S.C. 321(h)(3).

[5] *Action on Smoking and Health v. Harris,* 655 F.2d 237 (1980).

the Reagan administration tried to reduce regulation of business. With fewer resources, it grew less aggressive, and its staff felt deflated. Consumer advocates were disappointed by its loss of zeal.

However, in 1990 a new era dawned when President George Bush appointed David Kessler as commissioner. Kessler, then 39, was a Republican with a JD from the University of Chicago Law School and an MD from Harvard Medical School. He was dynamic, and he intended a new regime of vigorous enforcement. Immediately, he set to the task by confiscating 24,000 cartons of Procter & Gamble's Citrus Hill orange juice, which the company had labeled as "fresh" even though it was made from concentrate. The business community soon learned that it once again faced an energetic watchdog.

One day Jeff Nesbit, associate commissioner for public relations, approached Kessler to suggest that the time was right for regulating tobacco. Although Kessler did not know it then, Nesbit's father, a smoker, was in the hospital dying of cancer. Kessler was noncommittal, but he called a staff meeting to discuss the idea. Intense debate broke out. Some staffers thought that taking on the tobacco industry was a losing game. It invited reprisals from Congress and from conservative elements in the Bush White House. Others saw tobacco regulation as a righteous cause. How could anyone say with a straight face that the agency upheld its mission to protect public health when it pounced on mislabeled orange juice and ignored cigarettes? One attorney said that cigarette regulation was so important she was willing to devote the rest of her career to the cause if necessary.[6]

STUDY AND RESEARCH

The meeting revealed that the agency was divided, and Kessler remained noncommittal. A small interdepartmental group was formed to give the idea more study. Eventually, a member of this group, an attorney named David Adams, approached Kessler with an idea. Adams pointed out that tobacco companies could vary nicotine levels in cigarettes. Their manipulation of nicotine might be evidence that cigarettes were a product intended to have a druglike effect on the body. If so, the agency could satisfy legal criteria for regulating the nicotine in tobacco as a drug.

David A. Kessler (1951–), commissioner of the Food and Drug Administration from October 1990 to February 1997. Source: © AP Photo/Gene J. Puskar.

Kessler now saw a way to bring cigarettes within the agency's jurisdiction. Under the definition of a drug in the 1938 law, a manufacturer had to intend that its product "affect the structure or any function of the body." The FDA had always rejected cigarette regulation because the tobacco companies made no health claims in their ads. However, if the agency could prove that the companies knew nicotine was addictive and supplied it to satisfy smokers' cravings, then the criteria of intent in the 1938 act's definition of a drug could be met.

The immediate problem for Kessler was that no one in the agency knew much about cigarettes. Did the tobacco industry intentionally manipulate nicotine levels? The manufacturing processes of many industries are well known, but the tobacco industry had a history of secrecy about its methods. Lawsuits by smokers had made companies wary. Departing employees were asked to sign confidentiality agreements subjecting them to adverse consequences if they revealed information about research or production. Cleverly, the companies put lawyers in charge of operations, then claimed that information and documents were protected by the attorney-client privilege. Furthermore, since the FDA had no jurisdiction over tobacco, it had no legal authority to inspect cigarette factories or to require disclosure of data about tobacco products.

---

[6] This was Catherine Lorraine of the general counsel's office. David Kessler, *A Question of Intent* (New York: Public Affairs, 2001), p. 34.

By this time, the tobacco companies were aware that the FDA intended to pursue tobacco regulation. They were not about to help. Therefore, the agency started an investigation on its own to prove that nicotine levels were being manipulated, first to addict smokers, then to satisfy their cravings.

One avenue of inquiry was library research. Kessler and staff members immersed themselves in literature about smoking and tobacco. When the agency tried to get articles from a tobacco collection at North Carolina State University, it ran into resistance from a librarian who felt that the FDA was going to hurt the southern economy. Kessler sent a young intern to the campus with instructions to carry a backpack and look like a student. The intern subsequently found valuable material.

Informants were critical sources of information. The agency's Office of Criminal Investigations was soon in touch with "Deep Cough," a former R. J. Reynolds manager who described how the company created a slurry from old tobacco scraps, added nicotine, and then put this reconstituted tobacco into cigarettes. There were many informants. "Philip," a former research director at Philip Morris, told FDA investigators that a process to remove all nicotine from tobacco existed. "Cigarette" had done lab research with rats at Philip Morris, once writing a paper about how the animals became addicted to nicotine and pushed levers in their cages to get more. "Saint," a chemical engineer at Philip Morris, described a technique she had developed that removed carcinogens from tobacco. The company had abruptly and without explanation stopped her research.

The identities of these informants were concealed to protect them from reprisals by their former employers for violating confidentiality agreements. Contacts with them were often bizarre and frequently involved clandestine meetings. Once Kessler even borrowed a voice synthesizer from the Central Intelligence Agency to disguise his identity in phone conversations with informants, but it sounded so strange that he elected not to use it.

Information from informants had to be verified before it could be taken as factual. For example, "Macon," an employee of Brown & Williamson, revealed that the company had genetically engineered a high-nicotine tobacco plant known as Y–I. FDA investigators searched for a patent on the plant but could not find one. "Macon" remembered that Y–I had been field tested by a "Farmer Jones" in North

Carolina. Investigators laughed at the name "Farmer Jones," but they eventually found a small farm owned by an L. V. Jones and verified its use for an experimental tobacco crop. "Macon" also believed that large quantities of Y–I were growing in Brazil. An investigator was assigned to examine customs forms stored in large warehouses and after considerable searching came upon an invoice showing that Brown & Williamson had imported almost 500,000 pounds of Y–I from Brazil.

A team from the FDA also visited cigarette plants owned by Philip Morris, R. J. Reynolds, and Brown & Williamson. It received carefully scripted briefings and facility tours. The visit to Brown & Williamson's manufacturing plant in Macon, Georgia, was particularly frosty. The team's hosts had received information about its two prior visits to the other companies, including information that one team member was a "bully," another was "aggressive" and "underhanded," and a third a "zealot."[7] As the team questioned Brown & Williamson representatives during the morning, the atmosphere became hostile. A lengthy lunch break was called during which the FDA team was separated from its hosts for lunch. After lunch, the team was rushed through the cigarette factory and in the end had little to show for the day.

However, after more than three years, the investigative, legal, and scientific research done by the tobacco working group had uncovered extensive evidence of intent by manufacturers to manipulate nicotine as a drug. They now knew that tobacco firms had conducted research into the addictive qualities of nicotine, that they blended tobacco to manipulate nicotine content in cigarettes, and that cigarette paper and filter material was engineered to control nicotine doses to the smoker. Moreover, informants and documents from tobacco companies made publicly available by disgruntled employees suggested that tobacco advertising had been designed to attract new smokers. Kessler felt that the time had come to compose tobacco regulations.

WRITING REGULATIONS

Although the tobacco investigation had produced enough data to justify writing new regulations, the consequences of such regulations were disturbing. In Kessler's words: "Once the FDA classified nicotine as

7 Ibid., p. 180.

a drug, the tobacco companies would be required to file an application that showed cigarettes to be safe and effective; since they would be unable to do so, we would have to ban them."[8] However, with 50 million addicted smokers, a ban was politically untenable. The cigarette companies would tell smokers that government prohibition had robbed them of their freedom. A black market for cigarettes was inevitable. The agency would put itself on a collision course with elected officials and a powerful, vindictive tobacco lobby.

To escape the dilemma, Kessler decided to classify cigarettes as medical devices. The FDA had the authority to regulate a wide range of medical products such as tongue depressors, breast implants, and X-ray equipment. It could put restrictions on the sale and advertising of cigarettes if they were classified as devices made with the intention of delivering the drug nicotine to users. Kessler believed that this way the agency could regulate cigarettes without banning them, as it did with medical devices that posed risks. It could start with limited restrictions and tighten them in the future.

Kessler also believed that nicotine addiction began as a pediatric disease. Children and teenagers who experimented with tobacco got hooked. They continued smoking over many years, often a lifetime. Adults who smoked did so not because of measured decisions they made—what the industry called free choice—but because of unthinking, impulsive decisions made by a teenager years before. Therefore, he elected to design regulations to reduce the incidence of this pediatric disease. Adult smoking would not be affected. The FDA would only restrict the industry's ability to target youth in its advertising and marketing.

In the summer of 1995, Kessler set up a rule-making team to draft text for a proposed rule in the *Federal Register*. After four months of hard work, a draft regulation was ready.

PLAYING POLITICS

Since the FDA is housed in the Department of Health and Human Services, Kessler needed the approval of Secretary Donna Shalala before going further. At a meeting in late November 1994, he outlined key provisions in the draft to Shalala and her staff.

[8] Ibid., p. 266.

- Advertising in publications with more than 15 percent or more than 2 million under-18 readers would be limited to black-and-white text only and include warnings such as: "ABOUT 1 OUT OF 3 KIDS WHO BECOME SMOKERS WILL DIE FROM THEIR SMOKING." Pictures and cartoon figures would be prohibited.
- Outdoor advertising within 1,000 feet of a school would be banned.
- The use of cigarette brand names on nontobacco items such as T-shirts and hats would be prohibited.
- Cigarette brand names could no longer be used to sponsor sports events.
- Vending machines would be banned. Tobacco could be sold only in face-to-face transactions.
- Tobacco companies would be made to conduct FDA-approved public education campaigns to counteract their image from advertising among those under 18.
- If underage smoking had not declined by 50 percent five years after the rules went into effect, additional restrictions would be invoked.

Shalala was favorably impressed with the general content and told Kessler to work with her staff on a final draft. But Kessler soon discovered that her staff thought the regulations were a political blunder. Believing that he had Shalala's support, he decided to circumvent the staff and take the next step, which was getting White House approval.

Even though he was a Republican, Kessler had been reappointed as FDA head in 1992 by President Bill Clinton, a Democrat. Yet Kessler was barely acquainted with Clinton, having talked to him only once at a White House dinner. He did not have enough weight to call and schedule a meeting on his own. In fact, Clinton was worried about tobacco regulation. He believed that the two issues of tobacco and gun control had cost the Democrats control of the House of Representatives in the 1994 midterm elections. He and powerful members of his staff thought that reaction against tobacco regulation in key southern states might cost him a second term in the upcoming 1996 election.

Kessler approached Abner Mikva, an old law school acquaintance, who was an attorney on Clinton's staff. He asked Mikva to discuss with Clinton the potential public health benefits of restricting tobacco advertising

and marketing. From Mikva he learned that the tobacco companies were also lobbying the White House
to forestall FDA regulation. Next, working through another acquaintance, he got an appointment with Vice
President Al Gore, who was widely known to support
tobacco regulation. Kessler's meeting with Gore lasted
only five minutes, but the vice president made a strong
appeal to Clinton on behalf of the FDA.

Ultimately, the breakthrough in the battle for Clinton's support came because of Dick Morris, a shadowy figure who gave Clinton political advice based
on public opinion polls. It was because of the presence and influence of Morris that Clinton had gotten
the reputation of taking policy positions based on
polling rather than principle. With tobacco, that reputation would prove accurate. Morris took polls in
five southern states that were key to Clinton's reelection. The results showed large majorities were enthusiastic about regulations to reduce youth smoking.
Morris advised the president that support of the FDA
regulation was a winning position.

Soon Clinton met with Secretary Shalala and Kessler to discuss the proposed regulations. A month later,
Kessler was back in the East Room listening to Clinton
announce that tobacco regulation would go forward.

The next day, Friday, August 11, 1995, the FDA
published its proposed rule in the *Federal Register.* It
was a massive entry starting on page 44,314 and ending 473 pages later on page 44,787. The proposed
rule, entitled "Regulations Restricting the Sale and
Distribution of Cigarettes and Smokeless Tobacco
Products to Protect Children and Adolescents," covered 139 typical pages of small type in triple columns.
The rest of the entry was a reproduction of the document the FDA had written to justify regulating cigarettes as a device containing the drug nicotine.[9] This
part covered the remaining 334 pages.

In the proposed rule, the FDA estimated that its
regulations would prevent more than 60,000 deaths
and produce net monetary benefits of $28 to $43 billion
in lower medical costs, productivity gains, and hedonic
values. It estimated an annual record-keeping burden
on the industry of 1.2 million hours, increased annual
costs of $227 million per year, and a revenue decline of
4 percent in 10 years.

After a proposed rule is published in the *Federal
Register,* there is by law a comment period during
which the agency must consider and respond to sub-
stantive comments from the public. The tobacco industry chose to take advantage of this requirement
by swamping the FDA with more than 710,000 comments, including a 2,000-page comment with 45,000
pages of supporting documents. Many were generated by form letters sent out by the industry.[10] Working from a rented warehouse, the FDA staff
painstakingly answered each one.

It took 12 months, but on August 28, 1996, the final
rule appeared in the *Federal Register.* Although no major changes were made in the regulations, the agency
responded to various written comments, swelling the
entry to 922 pages.[11] More than four years had passed
since Kessler first convened a staff meeting to discuss
the prospects of regulating tobacco.

TO THE COURTS

Immediately the tobacco industry, joined by advertisers and tobacco retailers, filed suit in a federal district court in North Carolina to stop implementation
of the rule. It challenged the FDA with three main
arguments. The first was that the agency lacked jurisdiction over tobacco products because Congress
had never given it a specific grant of authority. FDA
attorneys responded that as a point of law it was
wrong to claim a product was excluded because it
had not been named in the Food, Drug, and Cosmetics Act of 1938. Congress had defined drugs and devices, leaving it up to the agency to determine what
products fit these definitions. Under the *Chevron*
doctrine, the agency was entitled to deference in its
reading of the statute.[12] The second argument by the
industry was that cigarettes did not fit the definition
of a drug or device because manufacturers made no
health claims about them. The FDA responded that
its research on nicotine manipulation confirmed the
classification was appropriate. The third argument
was that the proposed restraints on advertising violated the industry's First Amendment guarantee of
free speech. The FDA argued that the restrictions

---

[9] The title of this document is *Nicotine in Cigarettes and
Smokeless Tobacco Products Is a Drug and These Products
Are Nicotine Delivery Devices under the Federal Food, Drug,
and Cosmetics Act.*

[10] Kessler, *A Question of Intent,* pp. 336–37.

[11] 61 FR 44396–45318 (1996).

[12] *Chevron U.S.A. Inc. v. Natural Resources Defense Council,*
467 U.S. 837 (1984).

met legal guidelines for advertising restrictions as set forth previously by the U.S. Supreme Court.[13]

In its decision, the district court rejected the industry's first two arguments, upholding the restrictions on sales in the FDA rule. However, it concluded that the advertising restrictions were unconstitutional.[14] This was a win for the FDA. It left intact the agency's power to regulate tobacco.

Both sides appealed the decision, hoping for a complete victory. The appeals court reversed the district court, and the tobacco industry emerged triumphant. In a 2–1 decision, the court ruled that Congress had never intended to give the FDA jurisdiction over tobacco. Therefore, the agency had exceeded its powers.[15] The FDA appealed to the U.S. Supreme Court.

ENDGAME IN THE SUPREME COURT

On March 21, 2000, the Supreme Court, in a 5–4 decision, invalidated the FDA's tobacco rule. The justices divided into the conservative and liberal groups that have characterized many of the Court's decisions related to government regulation of business.[16] Associate Justice Sandra Day O'Connor, often regarded as a swing vote, joined with conservatives William Rehnquist, Antonin Scalia, Clarence Thomas, and Anthony Kennedy to build a five-member majority. She also wrote for the majority.

In her opinion, Justice O'Connor stated that although tobacco was one of the nation's most troubling public health problems, the FDA had no jurisdiction over it. She argued that if the FDA held that nicotine was a drug and cigarettes were a device to deliver that drug to the body, it would have to ban them. The Food, Drug, and Cosmetics Act of 1938 required that any drug or device regulated by the FDA had to be, in the language of the law, "safe" and "effective." Since the FDA had shown cigarettes to be an extremely dangerous health risk in its final rule, it would be required by law to prohibit tobacco companies from marketing them.

However, said O'Connor, a cigarette ban would violate the clear intent of Congress. She pointed out that in 1929 and in 1963 bills were introduced to give the FDA authority over tobacco. They were not passed. Instead, the lawmakers had passed six statutes regulating tobacco since 1965.[17] Collectively, these laws established a framework of regulation and showed that Congress rejected prohibition in favor of more limited regulation. O'Connor summed up the majority opinion this way.

> By no means do we question the seriousness of the problem that the FDA has sought to address. The agency has amply demonstrated that tobacco use, particularly among children and adolescents, poses perhaps the single most significant threat to public health in the United States. Nonetheless, no matter how "important, conspicuous, and controversial" the issue . . . an administrative agency's power to regulate in the public interest must always be grounded in a valid grant of authority from Congress.[18]

The dissenting opinion was written by Justice Stephen G. Breyer, who was joined by Justices John Paul Stevens, David Souter, and Ruth Bader Ginsburg. Justice Breyer began the dissent by pointing out that the purpose of the Food, Drug, and Cosmetics Act of 1938 was to protect public health. Since cigarettes posed a clear danger to public health, the statute had to be interpreted in a way that was "consistent with [this] overriding purpose."[19] Breyer thought the literal wording of the law gave the FDA authority to classify cigarettes as "devices" that delivered the "drug" nicotine and then to regulate their sale and use.

Rejecting the reasoning of the majority that Congress had chosen not to ban tobacco, he pointed out

---

[13] The definitive test of the constitutionality of commercial speech restraints imposed by government is set forth in *Central Hudson Gas & Electric Corp. v. Public Service Commission,* 447 U.S. 557 (1980).

[14] *Coyne Beahm, Inc. v. Food and Drug Administration,* 966 F. Supp. 1374 (1997).

[15] *Brown & Williamson v. Food and Drug Administration,* 153 F.3d 155 (1998).

[16] See, for example, *Adarand v. Pena,* the case study in Chapter 17.

[17] These are the Federal Cigarette Labeling and Advertising Act of 1965, the Public Health Cigarette Smoking Act of 1969, the Alcohol and Drug Abuse Amendments of 1983, the Comprehensive Smoking Education Act of 1984, the Comprehensive Smokeless Tobacco Health Education Act of 1986, and the Alcohol, Drug Abuse, and Mental Health Administration Reorganization Act of 1992.

[18] *Food and Drug Administration v. Brown & Williamson,* 529 U.S. 120, at 152.

[19] 529 U.S. 162.

that nowhere in any law was there specific language denying the FDA authority over tobacco or denying the agency a right to ban tobacco products. "[O]ne can just as easily infer," he wrote, "that Congress did not intend to affect the FDA's tobacco-related authority at all."[20] Breyer believed that the FDA had made a reasonable interpretation of the 1938 law in light of its "overall health-protecting purpose" and that, under the *Chevron* doctrine, the agency was entitled to broad deference.

POSTSCRIPT

Early in 1997 David Kessler resigned as FDA administrator to become dean of the Yale University School of Medicine. Even after leaving, he still had an obsessive interest in tobacco regulation. He often sat late at night poring over tobacco company documents in his garage, still working out the issues. The Court's holding pained him. In his own words: "The decision that could have saved hundreds of thousands of lives had been lost by a single vote."[21]

Although the tobacco industry staved off FDA regulation, it did not escape restrictions. In 1998 tobacco companies agreed to pay $246 billion over 25 years to settle suits by state attorneys general seeking to recover billions of Medicaid dollars paid out to treat smokers' illnesses. As a condition of settlement, they also agreed to advertising restrictions, notably bans on billboards, cartoon figures, event sponsorships, and the use of logos on promotional items.

After the settlement, the tobacco companies raised wholesale prices of cigarettes to compensate for their payments to the states. In effect, the settlement became a national tax on smokers. One of its purposes was to reduce smoking. As part of the settlement the industry agreed to pay for $25 million of antismoking ads each year for 10 years. However, these ads were pitted against industry marketing expenditures reaching $15 billion a year toward the end of that period.[22] The percentage of adult smokers fell slightly, from 24 percent in 1999 to 21 percent by 2004 and has

remained stable since then.[23] The states were supposed to fund smoking cessation programs with part of the annual payments they received, but by 2007 less than 3 percent was used for that purpose.[24] States had become addicted to tobacco money. About 17 percent was used for treating smoking-related illnesses and the rest supported other budget items, from education to highway construction.

If a bipartisan coalition in Congress has its way, the FDA will still have a chance to regulate the tobacco industry. However, it will not get the forceful police power envisioned by Kessler. Not long after the Supreme Court decision ended the FDA's quest, Philip Morris, the largest U.S. tobacco company, concluded that some form of new federal regulation was inevitable and perhaps desirable. It negotiated with supporters of tobacco regulation in Congress and the result was a regulatory bill that passed the Senate in 2004, but failed to pass in the House.

In 2007 this bill, the Family Smoking Prevention and Tobacco Control Act, was reintroduced. In it, Congress would give the FDA authority to regulate tobacco companies, but not to regulate tobacco as a drug or tobacco products as devices. The agency would get the power to prohibit adulterated and misbranded tobacco products. It could require larger warning labels and lists of ingredients on cigarette packs. It could act to reduce nicotine content and prohibit flavors and spices that might appeal to children. It could regulate advertising and promotion to prevent underage appeals. Finally, the bill requires premarket approval by the FDA for every new tobacco product. No new cigarette brand could be marketed unless the agency found it to be "appropriate for the public health."

If passed, the new regulations would accomplish important public health goals, mainly reducing ads that appeal to children and assuring that new "safer" cigarettes the industry wants to introduce really are safer. However, although the FDA could prohibit the introduction of new cigarette brands, it would not

[23] Centers for Disease Control and Prevention, "Percentage of Adults Who Were Current, Former, or Never Smokers: 1965–2004," "Tobacco Use Among Adults—United States, 2005," at http://www.cdc.gov/tobacco/data_statistics/tables/adult/table_2.htm; *Morbidity and Mortality Weekly Report*, Centers for Disease Control, October 27, 2006, p. 1145.

[24] Alan Blum, Testimony before the Senate Committee on Health, Education, Labor, & Pensions, *The Need for FDA Regulation of Tobacco Products*, 110th Congress 1st Session, February 22, 2007, p. 6.

[20] 529 U.S. 163.

[21] Kessler, *A Question of Intent*, p. 384.

[22] Andrew Martin, "Trying Again for a Bill to Limit Tobacco Ads," *New York Times*, February 16, 2007, p. 1.

have the power to take existing brands off the market. Thus, it would be an agency charged with protecting public health yet required to allow the sale of a product containing 4,000 poisons and 40 carcinogens.[25]

Philip Morris supports the bill. The company has 51 percent of U.S. cigarette sales. Its Marlboro brand alone accounts for 41 percent. The new law would raise the costs of regulatory compliance for smaller competitors. Its advertising restrictions and the need for new product approval by the FDA would make it nearly impossible for any competitor to introduce new brands to compete with its high-name-recognition brands. And it would shield the company from fraud lawsuits if it marketed its lethal products according to FDA rules. Some supporters of tobacco regulation believe that this measure is better than no regulation at all, but it obviously is a compromise.

[25] Ibid., p. 8.

Questions

1. Do you agree with the Food and Drug Administration that nicotine can be classified as a drug and that cigarettes can be classified as devices under the definitions in the Food, Drug, and Cosmetics Act?

2. Did the FDA make any legal or political errors that defeated its efforts to regulate tobacco?

3. Do you agree with the decision of the U.S. Supreme Court? Why or why not?

4. Do you believe that the story reveals flaws in American government and the regulatory process, or do you believe that the story reveals a system that, despite faults, is ultimately responsive and just?

5. Should Congress enact FDA regulation of tobacco products even if it adds to the competitive advantage of Philip Morris?

Chapter Eleven

Multinational Corporations

The Coca-Cola Company

Coca-Cola was invented in 1886 by a pharmacist named John S. Pemberton. After failing with a drugstore, he experimented with soft drink formulas until he found one that pleased him. At the suggestion of a friend he named it Coca-Cola, after two of its ingredients, namely, "coca," the dried leaf of a South American shrub, and "cola," an extract of the kola nut. Pemberton persuaded a soda fountain in Atlanta to sell it and the new drink was an immediate hit. When Pemberton died two years later, Asa G. Candler got ownership of the formula for $2,300. Candler formed the Coca-Cola Company in 1892 to produce the drink that the public had begun to call "Coke."[1]

Today, the Coca-Cola Company is an international giant. It has $21 billion in assets outside the United States, about 60 percent of its total assets. It is the world's largest manufacturer of nonalcoholic beverages, selling 1 out of every 10 in 200 countries. It posts 83 percent of its employees in a foreign country.

Coca-Cola makes only a small percentage of the finished beverages sold under its brand names. Its basic worldwide strategy is to expand by licensing other bottlers to make and sell its brands. About 25 percent of Coke products are made by independent bottlers in which Coke has no ownership. Another 58 percent are made by bottlers partly owned by Coca-Cola. It typically has about one-third of the equity in these bottlers, an amount usually sufficient to give it control. The company's organization structure reflects its global business. It divides the world into six regional operating groups—Africa, Asia, the European Union, Latin America, North America, and the Middle East.

Multinational corporations are a critical source of capital for less developed economies. When a giant MNC invests heavily in a poor country the effects can ripple through its economy and create jobs, taxes, and new prosperity. Coca-Cola, however, is typical of global manufacturing giants in that the great bulk of its investment flows

---

[1] Hannah Campell, *Why Did They Name It?* (New York: Ace Books, 1964), pp. 63–64.

to the richest nations. In 2006, for example, it made capital investments of $1.4 billion with 85 percent going to the United States and Europe.

The company has transformed itself from a single-product firm into a producer and marketer of beverages favored by local consumers. The beverage portfolio encompasses 400 brands from which come more than 2,600 beverage products.[2] This large number is the result of efforts to satisfy consumer preferences in foreign markets. For example, in the Asia Pacific area, the company has developed many new brands to reflect consumer tastes. In Japan, it replaces about 20 percent of its products each year, introducing as many as 200 new variations.[3] Its brands also change tastes. In Japan, its Georgia Coffee is consumed by traditional tea drinkers. In Africa and the Middle East it turned fruit-flavored sodas such as Fanta Apple and lemon-flavored Limca into big sellers.

Around the world 1.4 billion Coca-Cola brand drinks are sold daily. But a large number of satisfied customers has not insulated the company from vicious critics. Coca-Cola is a dominant worldwide brand and its commercial activity cannot be separated from foreign political attitudes toward the power and presence of the United States. Like other American companies such as Nike, McDonald's, and Kentucky Fried Chicken, it is a target for critics who resent U.S. influence.

In India, for example, environmental activists released data purporting to show that the company's soft drinks contain unsafe pesticide residues. Coca-Cola produced laboratory data certifying the safety of its products. Others pointed out that milk and tea bottled in India contain much higher levels of pesticides than Coke and nearly all of the country's groundwater has higher pesticide residues. Nevertheless, several Indian states prohibited Coke sales and one of its political parties called for a nationwide ban. Its members smashed bottles and staged mock funerals to express their outrage. "We are continuously challenged because of who we are," said Atul Singh, CEO of Coca-Cola India.[4]

In Columbia, a widow backed by activist lawyers accused Coca-Cola of complicity in the murder of a union leader at a bottling plant. This charge has persisted despite a court's dismissal of the case for lack of evidence that the company had any knowledge of, or control over, events at the independently owned plant.[5] In the United States Ray Rogers, a legendary labor activist, launched his "Killer Coke" campaign, justified because ". . . Coca-Cola is a world of lies, deceptions, corruption, gross human rights and environmental abuses!"[6] The company rejects the allegations in this campaign. Nevertheless, some colleges have banished Coke on campus.

One way that Coca-Cola protects its brand is to set rising standards for corporate citizenship. It planted 120,000 trees in Kenya and is spending $6 million to plant 30 million trees in Mexico. If any of the 60,000 African workers for Coke and its bottlers, or their family members, contract HIV/AIDS, it provides medical coverage. It builds playgrounds in the Ukraine and organized thousands of volunteers to clean parks in

---

[2] The Coca-Cola Company, *2006 Annual Review.*

[3] Melanie Warner, "New Course for Coke's Sinking Fortunes," *New York Times,* April 5, 2005, p. C1.

[4] Brian Bremner and Nandini Lakshman, "India: Behind the Scare over Pesticides in Pepsi and Coke," *BusinessWeek,* September 4, 2006, p. 43.

[5] *In re Sinaltrainal Litigation,* 474 F. Supp. 2d 1273 (2006).

[6] Dean Foust and Geri Smith, "'Killer Coke' or Innocent Abroad?" *BusinessWeek,* January 23, 2006, p. 46.

Russia. It has global programs to reduce its energy use and replace the water it takes from nature to bottle Coke.

Along with other multinational corporations Coca-Cola has tried to fit into emerging schemes of civil regulation that promote responsibility in less developed economies. To protect against accusations of human rights abuse it is awash in codes. It has adopted a "Workplace Rights Policy," a "Human Rights Statement," and "Supplier Guiding Principles." It recently joined the Business Leaders Initiative on Human Rights, a group of 16 large corporations that support the Universal Declaration of Human Rights in their businesses. As a signatory of the United Nations Global Compact it pledges to follow a set of 10 aspirational principles on labor rights, human rights, environmental protection, and fighting corruption. A statement on its Web site reads: "It's not enough to conduct business responsibly: we endeavor to go beyond this by improving the lives of those who are touched in some way by our business. Our efforts don't have an end date—corporate responsibility is an ongoing journey. It will continue to evolve as long as we exist."[7]

In this chapter we discuss the nature of multinational corporations, their strategies for internationalization, the impacts of their foreign investment, and their efforts to show responsibility using a range of devices, from voluntary codes of conduct through collaborations with multiple stakeholders. Elements of the Coca-Cola story illustrate all these themes.

THE MULTINATIONAL CORPORATION

multinational corporation
An entity headquartered in one country that does business in one or more foreign countries.

The *multinational corporation* (MNC) is an entity headquartered in one country, its home country, that does at least part of its business in one or more foreign, or host, countries. The universe of MNCs is one of exceptional diversity. Most are private enterprises, but some are cooperatives or state-owned. A few MNCs have the majority of their assets, sales, or employees in foreign countries. Most are primarily domestic businesses with some foreign activity. Some global giants have made a visible impact for good or ill in foreign societies. Most MNCs are only medium or small in size and hardly make a ripple. The oldest, largest, and most-powerful ones are based in rich countries. However, those based in China, India, Malaysia, South Africa, and other developing countries now challenge the global leaders, especially in emerging markets.

MNCs also vary widely in their organizational structures and operations. In general, however, there are five tiers of internationalization as shown in Figure 11.1. These tiers are not stages, though they might be for a given MNC. Rather, they represent alternate ways to extend business activity into foreign markets. Each tier is best seen as a theory, model, or ideal. Many of the largest MNCs defy categorization. They have so much structural and strategic variation that they simultaneously use the methods in all five tiers.

1. Export sales to foreign countries.
2. Establishment of foreign sales offices.

---

[7] The Coca-Cola Company, "Overview," http://the coca-colacompany.com/citizenship/overview.html.

FIGURE 11.1
Five Tiers of
Internation-
alization

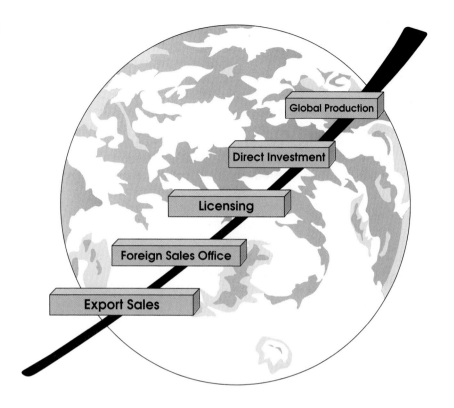

3. Licensing franchises, brands, the use of patents, or technology to foreign firms that make or sell the MNC's products. For example, McDonald's restaurants outside the United States are franchises run by foreign entrepreneurs. Coca-Cola licenses foreign bottlers to make almost all of its beverages in some 200 countries.

4. Direct investment to buy or create facilities in another country for producing in local markets. Such facilities may become hubs for regional or global sales. The company operates as a group of country-based business units or subsidiaries.

5. Global production in which a value chain spans two or more countries. Work on one or more tasks—research, design, manufacturing, logistics, distribution, marketing, sales, or support services—that would be confined to a single country in the fourth tier model now is done in two or more countries. Organization and control of these cross-border processes are centralized in the parent company's headquarters.

Companies have strategic reasons for moving across these tiers. Through much of the last century firms limited themselves to the first four tiers. Before World War II, only a handful of large companies such as Ford Motor, Singer, and Bayer, had moved into the fourth tier by operating foreign production facilities. Most manufacturers exploited foreign consumer markets through exports and foreign sales offices. The bulk of foreign investment was made in poor countries by multinationals engaged in plantation agriculture, mining, or petroleum extraction.[8]

After World War II the situation changed for manufacturers. Strong feelings of nationalism in many countries led to the rise of trade barriers for protecting domestic firms from import competition. Particularly in Europe, rising tariffs made export sales less profitable. Rather than exit large and lucrative domestic markets there, American manufacturers shifted strategies and set up subsidiaries within them. Thus, they moved from one of the first three tiers into the fourth tier. These new foreign subsidiaries often operated very independently of their parent firms, making distinctive products and assuming strong local identities.[9]

liberalization
The economic policy of lowering tariffs and other barriers to encourage trade and investment.

By the end of the century, however, the strategic advantages of this fourth tier model were less compelling. One reason was the spread of *liberalization,* or the economic policy of lowering tariffs and other barriers to encourage trade and investment. As trade barriers fell it became easier for corporations to move components, products, and services across borders. Also, revolutionary changes in information technology and telecommunications made new forms of global production possible. What ensued was fierce global competition stemming from the adoption of border-spanning production systems. To lower costs and speed output, MNCs created far-reaching networks of suppliers and foreign affiliates. Using new technologies they integrated work across geographic boundaries. As they did, they moved into the fifth tier of internationalization, where their strategic thinking was less influenced by national boundaries.

Today companies with international operations are given many names. They can be called simply international or global. A less preferred name is multidomestic. Most often they are called either multinational or transnational. These names are used loosely, but they occasionally signify diverging beliefs about the nature of these corporations. Sometimes those using the name multinational mean to imply that these companies have erased national allegiances, becoming itinerant firms that move investment and activity from nation to nation in search of profits. The name transnational is sometimes intended to suggest that rather than becoming stateless entities, large global firms are best understood as invariably and unalterably national companies that have simply extended their reach over borders. The distinction is impractical. There are so many variations of MNCs that either definition fails if applied to the whole universe. Therefore, in this book, we prefer the traditional and long-standing name multinational used loosely and interchangeably with transnational, global, and international.

A Look at Multinational Corporations

transnational corporation
As defined by the United Nations, a parent entity that controls the assets of affiliated entities in foreign countries.

Multinational corporations have flourished so spectacularly that if they were a natural species scientists would inspect their environment for the explanation. One trend is a rapid rise in numbers. The United Nations calculates that today there are 77,000 *transnational corporations,* which it defines as parent entities that control assets of affiliated

---

[8] Jeffry A. Frieden, *Global Capitalism* (New York: Norton, 2006), p. 293.

[9] Geoffrey G. Jones, "Nationality and Multinationals in Historical Perspective," Working Paper 06-052, Harvard Business School, 2005, p. 23.

FIGURE 11.2
The Dominance of the Largest Transnational Corporations

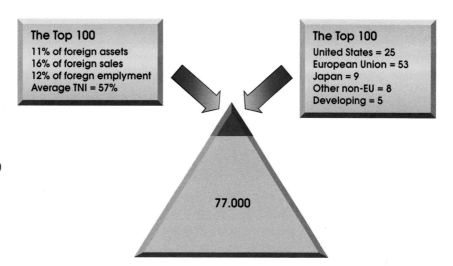

The Top 100
11% of foreign assets
16% of foreign sales
12% of foregn emplyment
Average TNI = 57%

The Top 100
United States = 25
European Union = 53
Japan = 9
Other non-EU = 8
Developing = 5

77.000

According to the United Nations, there are now 77,000 transnational corporations. Of these, the largest 100 nonfinancial corporations are 13 percent of the total number but have a disproportionately great impact on the global economy. All but 13 are from the United States, the European Union (EU), and Japan.

Data: United Nations Conference on Trade and Development, *World Investment Report 2006* (New York: United Nations, 2006), pp. 30, 33, and annex table A.1.4.

entities such as branches, subsidiaries, and joint ventures in foreign countries. It further estimates that these parent TNCs control 770,000 such foreign affiliates.[10] This is more than double the 37,000 TNCs in the United Nations' first estimate of their numbers back in 1991 and more than seven times the 10,700 estimated to exist in 1969.[11]

If the largest firms are any indication, transnational firms have also grown in size. In the decade from 1995 to 2005, the assets, sales, and employment of the largest 100 transnational firms increased by 113 percent, 45 percent, and 23 percent, respectively. As they have grown, a larger part of their activities has become international. During the same decade, the foreign assets, foreign sales, and foreign employment of these top 100 firms grew faster than their overall growth, rising 178 percent, 70 percent, and 27 percent, respectively.[12] On average, each of these big firms operates in 40 countries.

Figure 11.2 sketches the universe of TNCs and hints at the dominance of these 100 biggest firms. Their dominance reflects the commanding position in the global economy of the United States, the European Union, and Japan, which are home to 87 of the top 100. Table 11.1 shows several dimensions of these firms–their sales, assets, and rank on an index of internationalization that will be explained in the next section. Only about 20,000 TNCs, less than 3 percent, originate in developing countries. Although they too are growing rapidly, they are far less significant in

[10] United Nations Conference on Trade and Development, *World Investment Report 2006* (New York and Geneva: United Nations, 2006), "Methodological Notes: Definitions and Sources," p. 1. Figures are for 2004. This definition assumes control of affiliates through equity stakes. It excludes nonequity forms of asset control such as management contracts and franchise agreements.

[11] The 1990 estimate is from United Nations Conference on Trade and Development, *World Investment Report 1993* (New York: United Nations, 1993), table I.6. The 1969 estimate is extrapolated from data in fn. 7 and table I.6.

[12] United Nations Conference on Trade and Development, *World Investment Report 1997* (New York: United Nations, 1993), pp. 28 and 34; and United Nations Conference on Trade and Development, *World Investment Report 2006,* table I.13. Figures are based on an annual list of nonfinancial companies ranked by foreign assets.

TABLE 11.1 **Three Top 10 Rankings of TNCs**

Rankings by revenues, foreign assets, and the transnationality index give three perspectives on nonfinancial transnational corporations. Revenues figures are for 2006, foreign assets and transnationality are for 2004.

Sources: "Global 500," *Fortune*, July 23, 2007, p. 131; UNCTAD, *World Investment Report 2006*, annex table A.I.11.

Rank	Revenues*		Foreign Assets*		Transnationality	TNI
1	Wal-Mart Stores	$351	General Electric	$449	Thompson Corp.	97.3%
2	ExxonMobil	347	Vodafone Group	248	CRH	94.5
3	Royal Dutch Shell	319	Ford Motor	179	Nestlé	93.5
4	BP	274	General Motors	180	Vodafone Group	87.1
5	General Motors	207	BP	174	Alcan	85.6
6	Toyota Motor	204	ExxonMobil	154	Ahold	85.6
7	Chevron	201	Royal Dutch Shell	135	Philips Electronics	84.0
8	DaimlerChrysler	190	Toyota Motor	130	Nortel Networks	83.2
9	ConocoPhillips	172	Total	123	Unilever	82.8
10	Total	168	France Télécom	99	Astrazeneca	81.3

*Revenues and assets are rounded off in billions of dollars.

the global economy. The combined foreign assets of the largest 50 TNCs from developing countries are less than the foreign assets of General Electric.

How Transnational Is a Corporation?

One way of gauging the largest TNCs is by measuring the degree to which they have extended critical elements of their operations into foreign countries. Corporations vary in a range of international dimensions. These include the ratio of domestic to foreign operations; the number of foreign countries entered; the size of foreign direct investment; the geographic span of operations; the extent of global integration in the production chain; and the extent of national diversity among shareholders, employees, managers, and directors. Since TNCs differ greatly in these dimensions, no single measure can capture the definitive meaning of "transnational."

transnationality index (TNI)
The average of three ratios: foreign assets to total assets, foreign sales to total sales, and foreign employment to total employment.

Yet measures have been created. The most widely used is the *transnationality index*, or the TNI, used by the United Nations to rank corporations based on the relative importance of their domestic and foreign operations. The TNI is calculated as the average of three ratios: (1) foreign assets to total assets, (2) foreign sales to total sales, and (3) foreign employment to total employment.

In Table 11.2 we look at the TNI index for two of the largest 100 multinational corporations, General Electric, a diversified conglomerate headquartered in the United States, and Philips Electronics of the Netherlands, a global manufacturer of electrical and electronic equipment.

Although GE ranks first in assets among the largest 100 nonfinancial TNCs, it ranks 70th in its transnationality score. Philips, on the other hand, ranks 47th in assets, but ranks seventh in its TNI score, making it one of the most internationalized of the largest MNCs. Although Philips is a much smaller company, the foreign elements of its operations are a larger proportion of its total operations than

TABLE 11.2   **Calculating the Transnationality Index for GE and Philips**

Data: United Nations Conference on Trade and Development, *World Investment Report 2006,* chap. 1 annex, annex table A.1.11. Figures are for 2004.

General Electric		Ratio	Philips Electronics		Ratio
Foreign assets	$ 448,901		Foreign assets	$ 30,330	
Total assets	750,507	59.8%	Total assets	41,848	72.5%
Foreign sales	56,896		Foreign sales	36.155	
Total sales	152,866	37.2%	Total sales	37,646	96.0%
Foreign employees	142,000		Foreign employees	134,814	
Total employees	307,000	46.3%	Total employees	161,586	83.4%
	TNI score = 47.8%			**TNI score** = 84%	

are those at GE. One reason is that Philips has a much smaller domestic market in the Netherlands than does GE in the United States. It must expand its business into other nations to grow. Its foreign sales are 96 percent of all sales, compared with only 37 percent of all sales for GE.

In the eyes of some corporate critics, it is possible for an MNC to become too transnational. Eventually, some MNCs are said to be stateless in a pejorative sense, meaning that not only do foreign operations dominate strategy, but they structure themselves to elude national controls. This stateless incarnation is more theoretical than operational. The typical MNC remains national rather than international.

Corporations are formed under national incorporation laws. In the United States, for example, each company must be chartered by a state. Most employees at company headquarters are home-country nationals. Boards of directors are dominated by home-country majorities. It is still rare for top executives to be foreign citizens. Most shareholders are usually in the home country. Record keeping is done in the home country currency. These ties are part of the culture of the company, which is not easily modified. Finally, in many fifth-tier companies there is a strong trend toward more centralized authority rather than more "statelessness."[13] Sprawling global production networks require a strong, controlling hand at headquarters.

For all these reasons, escaping its nationality of origin is awkward for an MNC. Most remain national firms with international operations. Even Canada's Thomson Corporation, although 98 percent of its sales and 97 percent of its assets are outside the home country, is not likely to move its headquarters. Despite these generalizations, a few MNCs find strategic advantage in escaping at least some home-country bonds. Consider Weatherford International.

Breaking the Bonds of Country: Weatherford International

Weatherford International makes machinery used for oil and natural gas drilling and provides services to energy companies ranging from flushing pipes on drill rigs to cooking meals for crews. It was founded in 1976 in Texas and until the 1990s it operated mostly in the United States. Then, it decided to expand into oil

[13] Geoffrey G. Jones, "The Rise of Corporate Nationality," *Harvard Business Review,* October 2006, p. 21.

fields around the world. Today it has offices and plants in 100 countries. Foreign sales are 44 percent of its total $4.2 billion revenues and 39 percent of its assets are outside the United States.

Weatherford was incorporated in Delaware in 1976. Although its headquarters are in Houston, Texas, it could legally have chartered itself in any state. It may have picked Delaware because incorporation laws there are written to be business-friendly. In 2002, however, Weatherford decided to restructure and incorporate in Bermuda. It did so to get several advantages. Corporate taxes are lower. Bermuda also makes it harder for U.S. shareholders to sue directors and makes hostile takeovers much more difficult.

Weatherford's headquarters remains in Houston. Seven of its eight directors are Americans. One is a British citizen. It operates as a group of subsidiaries under a parent holding company in Bermuda. In keeping with its globalization strategy it has built, bought, and invested in 307 foreign subsidiaries.[14] Its ownership in these businesses ranges from 20 to 100 percent. Even the lower percentage is enough to give Houston headquarters either a strong voice or, when ownership is highly fragmented, full control when it wishes to exercise management authority.

One of its subsidiaries, Weatherford Oil Tool Middle East, is a sales and distribution facility in the United Arab Emirates. It rents drilling equipment to companies working oil fields in Sudan. The United States imposes sanctions against Sudan because of government-backed genocide in the Darfur region. These sanctions prohibit business transactions by U.S. firms or U.S. citizens with Sudan. Specifically, they forbid "all transactions by U.S. persons relating to Sudan's petroleum or petrochemical industries, including, but not limited to, oil field services. . . ."[15] In response to U.S. sanctions against several countries, including Sudan, Weatherford adopted a formal compliance policy that includes this statement.

> It is Weatherford's general policy that no U.S. incorporated or based affiliate of the Company, and no U.S. citizen or resident, officer or employee (wherever located) may participate in, approve, or facilitate any transaction involving [Sudan] or with any entity known to be owned, controlled or organized in [Sudan].[16]

Still, Weatherford Oil Tool Middle East maintains an office in Khartoum, the capital of Sudan. If they are autonomous, foreign subsidiaries of U.S. corporations can do business in countries from which their U.S. parent firms are barred. Weatherford maintains that neither its Houston headquarters nor any U.S. employee is involved with the Khartoum sales office, which takes all its instructions from the Dubai subsidiary.[17] Sanctions law permits this parsing of the organization.[18]

---

[14] Weatherford International Ltd., *Form 10-K*, February 23, 2007, exhibit 21.1.

[15] Executive Order 13412, "Blocking Property of and Prohibiting Transactions with the Government of Sudan," 71 FR 61369, October 17, 2006, sec. 2.

[16] Weatherford International Ltd., *Sanctions Compliance Policy*, §3.00, undated, at www.weatherford.com.

[17] Vivienne Walt, "A Texas Outfit in Sudan," *Fortune*, August 6, 2007, p. 18.

[18] See 31 CFR, ch. V, Office of Foreign Assets Control, Department of the Treasury, part 538, "Sudanese Sanctions Regulations."

Trade sanctions are enforced by the Department of the Treasury, but it has jurisdiction only over U.S. corporations and their executives. If federal regulators ever raise questions about the sales in Sudan, the company could provide answers through one of its directors, Nicholas Brady, a former secretary of the treasury.

FOREIGN DIRECT INVESTMENT

foreign direct investment
Funds invested by an MNC in one nation for starting, acquiring, or expanding an enterprise in another nation.

portfolio investment
The limited, speculative purchase of stocks and bonds in a foreign company by individuals or mutual funds.

The single measure that best captures the activity and power of MNCs is the amount of capital they inject into foreign economies. This capital is called *foreign direct investment,* or FDI, and is measured as the dollar value of funds invested by a parent corporation for starting, acquiring, or expanding an enterprise in a foreign nation. FDI stands in contrast to *portfolio investment,* or the purchase of stocks and bonds of a foreign company by individuals or mutual funds. Compared with FDI, portfolio investment is limited and speculative. Unlike FDI, it does not confer any degree of control over the company and it can be a short-term investment sold anytime. FDI is the financial process by which a corporation takes partial or total control of foreign assets with the intention of having a long-term presence. Usually, this is measured as an investment of 10 percent or more in a foreign enterprise.

FDI can come in the purchase of property such as factories, mines, or real estate; as reinvested earnings; or from the transfer of funds within a corporation to a subsidiary in a foreign country. Almost all FDI is made by transnational corporations, although a tiny fraction comes from individual entrepreneurs and about 1 percent comes from private equity and hedge funds. Annual flows of FDI from parent MNCs to foreign subsidiaries have increased dramatically, rising from $202 billion in 1990 to $916 billion in 2005, an increase of 354 percent. These annual flows elevated the total assets of foreign subsidiaries from $6 trillion to $46 trillion, an increase of 665 percent over the same period.[19]

Corporations make foreign direct investments for many reasons. Three are most common. First, they seek access to new markets. After World War II, for example, European countries had high tariffs on imported goods. Since European markets were lucrative, many American companies jumped over the tariff walls by starting European subsidiaries. Second, companies in nations with small domestic markets enter foreign markets to grow. Nestlé began in the 1860s as a powdered milk company in Switzerland. Now 85 percent of its assets are in other countries. Only 2 percent of its sales are within Switzerland. And third, competitive pressures lead to foreign investment. Companies create more efficient value chains and lower their costs by moving some operations across borders. By doing so they can use low-wage workers, own sources of critical material, and acquire skills that confer advantages over competitors in, for example, advertising, branding, logistics, or the use of new technologies.

As shown in Figure 11.3, the great bulk of FDI circulates within the developed world. The most recent data shows that 59 percent of annual world FDI went into developed nations and all but 4 percent of this 59 percent went into European

---

[19] United Nations Conference on Trade and Development, *World Investment Report 2006,* table I.2.

FIGURE 11.3
The
Distribution
of FDI: 2005

Source: WIR 2006,
annex table B.1.
Figures are for 2005.

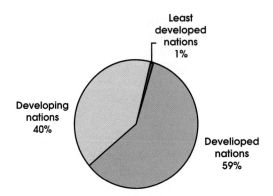

Least
developed
nations
1%

Developing
nations
40%

Develioped
nations
59%

Union countries and the United States. Developing nations took in 40 percent of worldwide FDI, with just three nations—China, India, and Brazil—receiving almost one-third of that. Although MNC investment can promote economic development, the group of 50 least developed countries took in only 1 percent of global FDI.[20] As a result, these nations suffer from capital shortages. They are unattractive to investment for a variety of reasons including weak currencies, political instability, the presence of trade barriers, bad regulatory climates, corruption, unskilled workforces, deficient infrastructure, and tiny domestic markets.

FDI in Less Developed Countries

Although multinational corporations invest the vast majority of their capital in developed nations, they do make investments in less developed countries (LDCs), and even though such investments are limited, they can be significant within local economies. In fact, annual flows of FDI into these nations are at least 10 times as great as development aid from the international community.[21] MNCs are for-profit entities. Their primary motive for investing in LDCs is getting an adequate return on capital invested. In seeking this return they may have many positive effects. Initially, the parent corporation injects capital into local economies. It may build or buy facilities, contract with local suppliers, and create jobs. If the local subsidiary is integrated into the TNC's international production network, it links the local economy to subsidiaries in other geographic areas and to international markets. It may bring new management skills and technologies to the host country. If conditions are right, FDI can stimulate growth of a local economic "ecosystem."

These positive effects have caused a new willingness by developing nations to court FDI. Many have altered their trade and investment policies to become more attractive to MNCs. Other actors in the international community have moved from a hostile attitude toward MNCs to embrace a new pragmatism about the promise of FDI. In the third world and among activist groups, deep suspicion has been shifting to calculated acceptance.

[20] Ibid., annex table B.1. Data is for 2005.
[21] Stephen D. Cohen, *Multinational Corporations and Foreign Direct Investment* (New York: Oxford University Press, 2007), p. 183.

Negative effects of FDI are also visible. They are the basis of enduring fear of MNC power by critics. In 1974 two authors of a popular book, *Global Reach,* wrote that "a few hundred" multinational corporations "are making daily business decisions which have more impact than those of most sovereign governments."[22] As accelerating trade liberalization produced a more global economy in the 1990s, critics expressed more anxiety over corporate power. A leading progressive intellectual, David C. Korten, argued that power on earth was being "transferred from national governments . . . to transnational corporations . . . which by their nature serve only the short-term interests of citizens."[23] A 2002 manifesto of progressive theorists noted that "several hundred global corporations and banks" held "a concentration of economic and political power that is increasingly unaccountable to governments, people, or the planet."[24] Such statements shaped the mood that hurled activists against MNCs.

To say that MNCs are so powerful is artful. Their economic and social power comes primarily from the impact of FDI. And although FDI is growing, and growing faster than domestic investment, the output of all foreign subsidiaries of all MNCs was only about 10 percent of world GDP in 2005.[25] So the economic activity generated by foreign direct investment is small compared with overall economic activity. The social impact of this investment, both positive and negative, cannot be measured as precisely, but should not be vastly exaggerated. The power of transnational corporations is closely connected to their foreign investments and cannot too greatly exceed this base. The world's largest corporations may arguably wield excessive power, but their transnational activities are insufficient in themselves to constitute the excess.

Still, negative economic and social effects of FDI exist. First we discuss potentially negative economic effects. Although competition from a new foreign affiliate can stimulate higher productivity in local firms, it can also overwhelm them and, in a lax regulatory climate, come to monopolize the domestic market. Some governments restrict FDI in sensitive business sectors. India, for example, allows only minority foreign ownership in its telecommunications industry. In China, foreign affiliates employ approximately 10 percent of the national labor force. To slow growing foreign influence, a recent law allows officials to reject foreign acquisition of Chinese companies if it threatens "economic security."[26]

Multinational corporations have been criticized for repatriating profits back to home countries, so that local residents get limited benefit from their presence. In Africa, global mining and energy firms own much of the continent's vast stores of

---

[22] See, for example, Richard J. Barnet and Ronald E. Müller, *Global Reach: The Power of the Multinational Corporations* (New York: Simon and Schuster, 1974), p. 15.

[23] David C. Korten, "The Limits of the Earth," *The Nation,* July 15/22, 1996, p. 16. See also Korten's book, *When Corporations Rule the World* (San Francisco: Kumarian Press and Barrett-Koehler, 1995).

[24] The International Forum on Globalization, *Alternatives to Economic Globalization* (San Francisco: Barrett-Koehler, 2002), p. 17.

[25] United Nations Conference on Trade and Development, *World Investment Report 2006,* p. 10.

[26] Deborah Solomon, "Foreign Investors Face New Hurdles across the Globe," *The Wall Street Journal,* July 6, 2007, p. A1.

oil, natural gas, gold, diamonds, uranium, copper, and platinum. Yet, using intrafirm money transfers, much of the economic value they generate is moved out of African nations. The production taxes and royalties these MNCs pay to African governments are often pocketed by corrupt elites. Critics say this kind of FDI amounts to a "recolonization" that leaves average citizens as poor as they were before its arrival.[27]

Even without making direct investments within a nation, powerful MNCs can shake its economy. For example, about 30 large supermarket and food corporations are now the gatekeepers in global markets for agricultural produce. Buyers for Wal-Mart, Carrefour, Royal Ahold, Tesco, and other companies seek low price, rapid delivery, and uniform quality when they buy fruits and vegetables. Their intense pressure pushes low prices all the way back to small farmers growing crops for export. When the big European supermarket chains had a price war on bananas in 2002, prices to growers dropped by one-third, hurting small growers and plantation workers throughout the Caribbean. Because big corporate buyers demand rapid delivery and uniform quality, they prefer to contract with a few big export companies rather than with multitudes of small farmers. In the last decade, most of Kenya's small farmers were driven from their livelihoods as more and more produce was purchased from large farms owned by export companies. So, although Wal-Mart and the others made no direct investment in the Kenyan economy, their market power reshaped its agricultural sector.[28]

The economic impact of multinational corporations is often accompanied by social impacts. Especially in developing and less developed countries where social regulation is rudimentary, these can be negative. Recurrently there are charges that mining and drilling facilities in unpopulated areas harm the environment and disrupt native peoples. MNCs in manufacturing are accused of exploiting factory workers. And MNCs selling consumer products such as entertainment, fast food, and apparel are suspected of tainting local cultural values with Western indulgence and materialism.

The widespread belief among progressive activists that multinational corporations have too much power led to the emergence of the global CSR system described at length in Chapter 5, a complex, interacting web of norms, standards, codes, labels, audits, and certifications standing as a bulwark against crimes of greed. No large MNC can remain aloof from this emerging system of civil regulation. Its rising net harnesses them to make sure that FDI inflows in poorer countries have a constructive impact. We now discuss additional elements of this global CSR system.

Alien Tort Claims Act
A 1789 law permitting foreign citizens to litigate alleged violations of international law in U.S. federal district courts.

The Alien Tort Claims Act

There are indications that some MNCs have compromised their standards in permissive host-country environments. Many reports are accusations by progressive left critics. The docket of cases brought under a singular law, the *Alien Tort Claims Act,*

[27] Jeffrey Gogo, "Vast Mineral Wealth Sparks New 'Scramble for Africa,'" *The Herald* (Zimbabwe), February 27, 2007, p. 1.

[28] United Nations Development Programme, *Human Development Report 2005* (New York: UNDP, 2005), pp. 142–43.

opens a window into allegations of the most serious kind. This law allows foreign citizens to bring civil actions in U.S. courts against corporations for violating international law anywhere in the world. Not only American MNCs, but those of any nation can be sued.

The original intent of the Alien Tort Claims Act, an old law passed in 1789, was to bring justice to pirates on the high seas.[29] Long in disuse, it was rediscovered by progressive and labor movement lawyers who saw it as a way to prosecute MNCs for crimes anywhere in the world. Since the early 1990s there have been more than 60 such lawsuits. So far, none have led to judgments against a corporation. Most have been dismissed. One case was settled before trial. Others are in pretrial stages and, as we will explain, one case has come to trial.

Some suits allege human rights abuses. In current litigation, Indonesian villagers accuse ExxonMobil of directing Indonesian soldiers to kidnap, rape, and murder villagers near a natural gas field, then providing bulldozers to help the troops dig mass graves.[30] In Nigeria, where protests against oil drilling on tribal lands are numerous, Chevron is charged with facilitating the government's repression of native activists. When it supplied helicopters to government troops they flew to a Chevron drilling rig and shot at native protestors occupying it, killing, two and wounding others. Another time, Chevron trucked government forces to villages near its oil fields where they killed four people.[31]

Many of these suits derive from alleged labor abuses. Relatives of 23 people killed and tortured in Argentina during the years of its military dictatorship have sued DaimlerChrysler. They accuse its Mercedes Benz subsidiary of collaborating with the regime by identifying union leaders who were then abducted, tortured, and killed.[32] Adults and children 6 through 16 years of age working at a Firestone Rubber Plantation in Liberia have sued Bridgestone Corporation. The workers believe that through unfair labor practices the Japanese company has turned them into "modern day slaves, forced to work by the coercion of poverty."[33]

Along with labor and human rights violations some suits allege environmental crimes. Residents of Papua New Guinea say that as Rio Tinto worked a gold mine on the island of Bougainville it forced natives to toil in "slavelike" conditions and dumped 200,000 tons of waste rock into waterways each day. The damage caused massive pollution that sickened the island's residents.[34] In another case, DynCorp. is accused of erratic herbicide spraying in Colombia that missed targeted cocaine and heroin fields, hitting a town where it made 89 percent of the people sick and killed four.[35]

---

[29] The entirety of this statute is a brief clause in the Judiciary Act of 1789 providing that "the district courts shall have original jurisdiction of any civil action by an alien for a tort only, committed in violation of the law of nations or a treaty of the United States."

[30] *Doe v. ExxonMobil Corporation,* 473 F.3d 345 (2007).

[31] *Bowoto v. Chevron Corp.,* No. C 99-02506 SI, U.S.D.C. N.D. Cal. (2006).

[32] *Bauman v. DaimlerChrysler AG,* No. C-04-00194 RMW, U.S.D.C., N.D. Cal., (2007).

[33] *Roe v. Bridgestone Corporation,* No. 1:06-cv-0627-DFH-JMS (2007), p. 17.

[34] *Sarei v. Rio Tinto Ltd.,* 456 F.3d 1069 (2006).

[35] *Arias v. Dyncorp,* No. 01-1908 (RWR), U.S.D.C., D. Col. (2007).

In such cases, MNCs or their subsidiaries operated under lax regulation, in climates of low standards, or in collaboration with repressive governments. Even under loose regulation, do MNCs commit such crimes? So far, only one Alien Tort Claims Act case has come to trial. The defendant was Drummond Company, a coal mining firm headquartered in Birmingham, Alabama.

Drummond Company on Trial

Widows of three murdered union leaders in Colombia sued Drummond for ordering the deaths of their husbands, who were union leaders engaged in heated contract negotiations with the company. In the suit, they alleged that Drummond had violated international human rights laws and a U.S. law, the Torture Victims Protection Act.[36]

Drummond was founded in 1935 to mine coal in Alabama. The company gradually moved across tiers of internationalization. First, it began exporting coal from its Alabama mines to Europe. Then it made its first direct foreign investment by building a mine in northeast Colombia. When Drummond entered Colombia in the late 1980s, it was aware of the country's violence. A shadowy, ongoing civil war persists between the country's government, Marxist guerillas, and right-wing paramilitary groups. Nevertheless, it put $1 billion into its La Loma mine, creating a huge facility that ships 25 million tons of coal to Europe and the United States each year.[37] To run the mine, Drummond created a wholly owned subsidiary headquartered in Alabama.

In 2001, paramilitaries pulled two La Loma union leaders from a company bus taking workers home at the end of their shift. Witnesses said the paramilitaries identified the two by name, forced them to show identification, and told both men that they had a problem with Drummond. Outside the bus, in view of its passengers, they shot one victim several times in the head. The other was abducted and found dead several hours later. He had been tortured, then shot in the head. Five months later, a third union leader was kidnaped from a public bus on his way home from work, tortured, and shot twice in the head.

In 2007 the case came to trial in Alabama. Several witnesses testified that Drummond made covert payments to local paramilitaries for security services and secretly employed their members. One former paramilitary said that the president of Drummond's Colombia subsidiary had met with one of the private army's leaders, paying him $200,000 to "neutralize" the first two union leaders. This and other evidence was hearsay and circumstantial. Much testimony came from former paramilitaries who submitted affidavits from Colombia jails. Drummond denied all the allegations and questioned the honesty of witnesses with criminal histories. One of its lawyers argued that, "Nobody at Drummond . . . believes that the rules don't apply to them just because they are doing business in Colombia."[38]

---

[36] *Complaint, Rodriquez v. Drummond,* CV-02-BE-0665-W, U.S.D.C. N. Dist. Ala. (March 2002). See also *Rodriquez v. Drummond,* 256 F. Supp. 2d 1250 (2003).

[37] Juan Forero, "U.S. Firm on Trial in Colombia Slayings," *Washington Post,* July 13, 2007, p. A12.

[38] Quoted in Kyle Whitmire, "Suit in U.S. over Murders in Colombia," *New York Times,* July 13, 2007, p. A4.

In the end a federal jury returned a verdict of not guilty, clearing Drummond. The verdict was a huge setback for proponents of Alien Tort Claims Act litigation. However, more cases under this unusual law are pending. A trial victory against a corporation would lead to a new flurry of litigation. The presence of these suits is a troubling hint of criminal activity by some of the largest MNCs.

INTERNATIONAL CODES OF CONDUCT

international codes of conduct
Voluntary, aspirational statements by MNCs that set forth standards for foreign operations.

International codes of conduct are aspirational statements of principles, policies, and rules for foreign operations that a multinational corporation voluntarily agrees to follow. The first such code to engage a large number of corporations was the *Sullivan Principles.*

In 1977 the Rev. Leon Sullivan, a Baptist minister and civil rights activist who sat on General Motors' board of directors, set forth six broad principles for the conduct of MNCs in South Africa. At the time, South African law decreed an elaborate system of *apartheid,* or separation of the races, in which the civil rights of black, Indian, and mixed-race citizens were restricted by a government of *Afrikaners,* descendants of white Europeans who had settled that part of Africa more than 300 years earlier. Human rights activists around the world charged MNCs that invested in South Africa with complicity in a repressive, racist regime. General Motors, which was the largest employer of blacks in South Africa, sold vehicles to the police and the military. Polaroid, for a time, sold the film used for pictures in official passbooks the government used to classify citizens by race and restrict their movements.

Sullivan Principles
A 1977 code of conduct that required multinational corporations in South Africa to do business in a nondiscriminatory way.

Reverend Sullivan rose to prominence as a civil rights activist and minister at a large Baptist church in Philadelphia. In 1971 General Motors put him on its board of directors and he became the first black director of a major U.S. corporation. As a director he led GM to hire more black workers and set up more black dealerships. But when he would argue that GM should leave South Africa to protest racism there, other directors were unconvinced. In time, they even began turning in their seats to show him their backs.[39] It was a trip to South Africa, however, that pushed him into more direct action. Years later, he told a reporter what happened.

> When I was getting on the plane to go home, the police took me to a room and told me to remove my clothes. A man with the biggest .45 I'd ever seen said, "We do to you what we have to."
>
> I stood there in my underwear, thinking, "I'm the head of the largest black church in Philadelphia and I'm on the board of directors of General Motors. When I get home, I'll do to you what I have to."[40]

The Sullivan Principles required MNCs in South Africa to integrate workplaces, provide equal pay, and promote nonwhites to supervisory roles. In effect, they turned

[39] Claudia Levy, "Civil Rights Crusader Leon Sullivan Dies," *Washington Post,* April 26, 2001, p. B7.
[40] Quoted in Jan Hoffman, "A Civil Rights Crusader Takes On the World," *New York Times,* November 3, 1999, p. B2.

Reverend Leon H. Sullivan (1922–2001), The Sullivan Principles demonstrated that codes of conduct could promote corporate responsibility.
Source: © Bettmann/CORBIS.

foreign corporations into civil disobedients, since these requirements violated South African employment law. This was an early instance when a code called on MNCs to enforce international norms in a host country. Additionally, companies were to improve housing, schools, and health care for nonwhite workers and their families.

The principles remained in place until a change in government ended apartheid in 1994. During this time more than 100 firms became signatories and spent $350 million to carry out their commitments.[41] The results were mixed. The principles helped overcome apartheid, but failed to satisfy global antiapartheid activists whose vicious attacks and domestic boycotts drove many signatory corporations out of South Africa. Coca-Cola, for example, argued that as a signatory it could have a constructive presence in South Africa. However, activists believed that the very presence of Coca-Cola, no matter how principled its operations, gave the regime legitimacy. They called a boycott. As black consumers emptied Coke bottles onto the streets around its Atlanta headquarters, the company sold its facilities to South African entrepreneurs.

The Sullivan Principles inspired subsequent efforts to codify standards of conduct for corporations. Code making exploded in the 1990s as a response to the expanding activity of MNCs. Today there are hundreds of conduct codes, sets of principles, and standards of operation for MNCs. Most of these are voluntary codes written by companies, but there are other sources including industries, governments, and nongovernmental organizations. Many codes result from collaborative

[41] Oliver F. Williams, "Shaping a High-Trust Society: The Crucial Role of Codes of Conduct," *Business Ethics Quarterly* 14, no. 2 (2004), p. 342.

processes involving multiple parties. The overall structure of this code-based civil regulation of CSR was discussed in Chapter 5. Here we will elaborate on the nature of codes created by and for MNCs.

Corporate Codes

Corporate codes of conduct set forth aspirations and principles of action for operations in emerging economies. Such codes are usually adopted in response to activist attacks, critical media reports, or general concern for maintaining an MNC's legitimacy. Their contents promise behavior that overcomes the charges of critics and so they vary in focus.

Certain kinds of foreign investment are lightning rods for pressure campaigns. MNCs in the extractive industries of oil, natural gas, and mining operate in the most marginal, troubled societies, where they coexist with repressive regimes and come in contact with indigenous peoples. Freeport–McMoRan Copper & Gold adopted a code entitled "Social Relationships and Development" that says it will work to understand, employ, and protect the rights of indigenous peoples. British Petroleum, Caterpillar, Shell, Talisman, Total, and Unocal have international codes.

MNCs in the apparel and toy industries were targeted by progressive and union activists during antisweatshop campaigns. In these industries loss of brand reputation among consumers is disastrous and companies obsessively cultivate brand images. Adidas, Disney, The Gap, Levi Strauss, Mattel, Reebok, and Wal-Mart now have codes focused on labor and human rights practices in their global supply chains. All companies that promote consumer brands are vulnerable to brand attacks. To protect its brand, Starbucks has both Coffee Sourcing Guidelines that set forth environmentally friendly growing practices for coffee farms and a Supplier Code of Conduct designed to prevent human rights, labor, and environmental abuses elsewhere along the supply chain.

Rolls-Royce, an especially venerable brand, has a code of conduct for its "supplier/partners" to set forth "minimum" ethical, human rights, and labor standards for contractors in countries with "different legal and cultural environments." The Rolls-Royce code contains a *snowball clause,* or a requirement that contractors use their power over firms in their own supply chains. This clause, which is frequently used by powerful MNCs at the center of large supply networks, extends the reach of a code.

A few companies invest heavily to make their codes work. The Gap has a vendor compliance department with 45 employees monitoring application of a Code of Vendor Conduct in suppliers around the world. At Nike, a staff of 80 checks on supplier compliance with its code of labor and environmental practices. Many other firms undertake extensive activity related to their codes. Yet, to be effective codes must satisfy attentive stakeholders. Some activists and academics are critical of self-policed efforts. They note that many companies do not pledge compliance with international norms such as those set forth in the *Universal Declaration of Human Rights.* They believe that although codes set forth high-minded intentions, fulfilling them in daily practice is a low priority. In the words of one expert on code enforcement, "codes are viewed as a necessary evil and an

---

snowball clause
A clause in a conduct code requiring or exhorting the corporation to use its power over contractors to make them comply with code standards.

Universal Declaration of Human Rights
A declaration recognizing the "equal and inalienable rights of all members of the human family" adopted by the United Nations General Assembly in 1948. It contains 30 articles that catalog basic human rights. It is not legally enforceable but has status as a benchmark in judicial proceedings.

inconvenient nuisance, which should be handled with minimum cost and as little effort as possible."[42]

Most companies reject rigorous monitoring by outsiders and simply check on themselves, a practice not designed to instill trust in those with a cynical view of corporate behavior, precisely the audience the code is intended to reassure. Even where self-monitoring occurs, it is often undisclosed or reported only in company-written reports. But such reports are not, in the language of academics, "transparent." That is, the facts cannot be independently verified outside the company. Stories about Wal-Mart and Mattel teach a lesson about transparency.

Wal-Mart and Mattel

Since 2002 Wal-Mart has audited factories that make its products. Enforcement of its Standards for Suppliers on thousands of factories around the world is a big effort run from the company's Arkansas headquarters. The standards cover worker hours, pay, health and safety, and rights to unionize. They forbid discrimination and child labor. Part of the contract with every Wal-Mart vendor is an agreement to uphold the standards and submit to regular compliance audits. In a recent year, for example, Wal-Mart's auditors did 16,700 inspections of 8,873 factories, with 26 percent being unannounced.

Factories are rated using a color code. A green coding is given to factories with low-risk violations, yellow is for medium-risk violations, orange is for high-risk violations, and red indicates such severe violations that the factory is permanently barred as a Wal-Mart supplier. Four orange ratings in a row over two years disqualify a factory for one year. Green facilities are audited every two years. Yellow and orange ones are audited every three months. Overall, Wal-Mart's inspectors rated 5 percent of the factories green and the rest were fairly evenly divided between yellow and orange. Only 2 percent were given a one-year disqualification and only 0.2 percent were dropped because of a red rating.[43]

Wal-Mart's costly, well-organized code compliance effort, disclosed in some detail, failed to satisfy international labor activists, who generated a class action lawsuit on behalf of workers in six countries alleging its enforcement was negligent. According to the complaint, Wal-Mart audits are not credible.

> Wal-Mart's system limits factory inspections to those conducted by internal Wal-Mart auditors, or relies upon consultants paid for by Wal-Mart. . . . Wal-Mart's code enforcement is a closed loop: Wal-Mart adopts the code, monitors the code, and reports on whether code compliance has been achieved—in the absence of meaningful transparency and in the absence of any independent, external mechanisms for enforcing the code.[44]

---

[42] S. Prakash Sethi, *Setting Global Standards: Guidelines for Creating Codes of Conduct in Multinational Corporations* (New York: Wiley, 2003), pp. 83–84.

[43] Figures in this paragraph are from Wal-Mart's *2006 Report on Ethical Sourcing* (Bentonville, AR: Wal-Mart Stores, Inc., 2007), p. 3.

[44] First complaint, *Doe v. Wal-Mart,* CA Sup Ct., L. A. Cty, No. CV 05-7307 (2005), para. 42. The case was dismissed.

By Wal-Mart's own admission, it continues to contract with yellow and orange factories having code violations. In the suit, foreign workers seek damages for low pay and injuries in locations where Wal-Mart has failed to enforce its standards. Here is a sampling of allegations. In Swaziland and Indonesia, workers in factories rated yellow and red were denied full pay and forced to do unpaid overtime. In Shenzhen, China, a factory withholds the first three months of each worker's wages and refuses to pay it if the employee ever quits. A female worker in this plant was slapped repeatedly by her supervisor for missing her quota. One blow made her nose bleed. In Chaka, Bangladesh, a pregnant sewing machine operator was kicked so hard in the stomach by a supervisor that her daughter was born with a bruise.

It is an open question whether a company as large as Wal-Mart can extend its standards through such a geographically dispersed supply chain with almost 10,000 links. However, no matter how great its effort, it cannot win the approval of global labor activists while it acts alone to enforce its code. The experience of Mattel confirms the advantages of greater transparency.

In 1997, five years after Wal-Mart started its factory inspections, Mattel was the first toy company to create a code of conduct. Its Global Manufacturing Principles set standards for "fair and safe working conditions and environmental protection." Like Wal-Mart, Mattel audits the factories where its products are made, but it is less thorough. Once every two years it visits 11 plants in 5 countries that it owns, operates, or manages. Twice a year it evaluates the 75 contract factories in China, India, and Brazil that make about half its toys and dolls.

However, it has only recently begun audits of another 3,000 factories around the world making products with Mattel logos and characters under contract for licensees. In a recent three-year period, about half its contract factories had "highly critical findings" and it audited less than 1 percent of factories doing license work.[45] In 2004 an investigative report in the *Los Angeles Times* found widespread code violations in Mattel's contract factories. Interviews with workers turned up stories of poor ventilation, excessive working hours, no bathroom breaks, coached lies to Mattel auditors, and a worker who was stabbed after making a complaint.[46] In 2007 Mattel was forced to recall more than a million toys made by a contract factory in Foshan, China, because of lead in their paint. It disqualified the factory from further contracts for code violations. Soon after, the owner, who lived in a small room at the factory, hung himself.[47]

Yet, despite the failures and shortcomings of the Mattel code, it has not been attacked by activists. Unlike Wal-Mart, Mattel allows independent audits of its global factories by the International Center for Corporate Accountability (ICCA), a nonprofit group that helps MNCs create and monitor conduct codes. Both Mattel and the ICCA post these audits on their Web sites. Neither Mattel nor Wal-Mart will succeed altogether in the noble and insurmountable task of imposing Western

---

[45] Figures in this paragraph are from Mattel's *2007 Global Citizenship Report* (El Segundo, CA: Mattel, Inc., 2007), p. 10.

[46] Abigail Goldman, "Sweat, Fear and Resignation Amid All the Toys," *Los Angeles Times,* November 26, 2004, p. A1.

[47] David Barboza, "Scandal and Suicide in China," *New York Times,* August 23, 2007, p. A1.

labor norms in developing countries. Arguably, Wal-Mart is the higher achiever; however, Mattel's commitment to independent verification has made its code more successful than Wal-Mart's in safeguarding its brand reputation.

Industry Codes

When an industry is besieged by critics, it sometimes creates an industrywide code. The argument for doing this is that companies in the industry face similar competitive forces and external pressures. Therefore, to create a level playing field in which no company is disadvantaged by costly social responsibility standards, a common code is desirable. In addition, a single code avoids the disorder of multiple codes. An unspoken advantage is that the industry-backed organization that executes the code will be lenient with member companies. Industries most likely to have international codes are those in which companies have sensitive brand images or have been the targets of pressure campaigns. So, industries with codes include the electronics, toy, tea, sporting goods, carpet, apparel, chemical, sugar, and mining and metals industries. Here are two examples.

- After two deadly fires in Asian toy factories the toy industry in 1995 created a Code of Business Conduct. Like Mattel's pioneering code, which it is closely modeled on, it requires factories to comply with core labor norms and to pass an exhaustive occupational health and safety checklist. So far, about 150 toy brands, including Mattel, have signed on. The code is managed by the International Council of Toy Industries, which accredits independent auditors. These auditors then certify that factories meet code requirements. Factories must comply with detailed standards for labor rights and worker health and safety. For a toy manufacturer to comply, each year one of its officers must sign a statement that it makes toys only in factories that pass code inspections. Its contracts for toy batches must say that failure to pass an audit is grounds for cancellation. About 70 to 80 percent of all toys are made in China. The work is spread out over 6,000 to 10,000 factories with approximately 3 million workers, mainly young women from rural backgrounds.[48] Yet most toys are sold in the United States, Europe, and Japan. One aim of the code is to assure Western consumers that their toys are made in decent conditions. Another purpose is to create a uniform audit system for factories so they do not bear the burden of dozens of inspections by various toy companies and retailers throughout the year.

- Mining scars the earth and yields waste. Some of the most lucrative mines are in poor countries wracked by violence and run by corrupt, despotic governments. In such settings, a handful of giant mining MNCs attract lightning-fast censure from activists over the smallest traces of pollution, human rights abuse, or collusion with tyrants. To maintain the legitimacy of the industry, the International Council on Mining and Metals, composed of 16 dominant mining MNCs, created a new code of ethical, social, and environmental responsibility. The code consists

---

[48] Reinhard Biedermann, "From a Weak Letter of Intent to Prevalence: The Toy Industries' Code of Conduct," *Journal of Public Affairs,* August–November 2006, pp. 199, 202.

of 10 basic principles, for example, to "maintain ethical business practices," to "uphold fundamental human rights," and to "contribute to conservation of bio-diversity."[49] Each of these 10 principles is amplified by explanatory statements—40 in all. Members, including Alcoa, Anglo-American, BHP Billiton, Mitsubishi Materials, and Rio Tinto, agree to report publicly their performances using Global Reporting Initiative indicators (see Chapter 5). Each company must allow third-party auditors to verify its claims.

Industry codes are attacked as loose and lax compared with traditional government regulation. They invite minimum performance. According to one critical observer, the mining and metals industry principles "are primarily inspirational in character" and "lack specificity" and in that are "similar to scores of other such codes."[50] The toy industry code is very specific on criteria for factory inspections, but it contains no sanctions for toy makers that fail to use only code-certified facilities. In fact, the code itself states that its purpose is "to establish a standard of performance . . . not to punish."[51] Neither code has enforcement procedures or sanctions for noncompliance. However, even if standards are not policed, their presence invites NGO critics to find gaps between aspiration and achievement. Industries will need to make their codes more credible or they will lose their ability to protect member MNCs from accusations of social irresponsibility.

Other Codes

There are many other international social responsibility codes for corporations set forth by a wide range of entities. These codes vary so much by subject, genesis, signatory parties, implementation, and credibility that their universe defies parsimonious categories. To give a feeling for the variety of codes, we offer brief descriptions of a few other noteworthy specimens.

- The Caux Round Table Principles for Business are global guidelines for socially responsible and ethical behavior based on ethical ideas in the great religions. They were written by a small group of business leaders from Japan, Europe, and the United States at meetings in the alpine hamlet of Caux, Switzerland, and published in 1994. There is a short preamble followed by seven general principles and six more specific principles for treatment of stakeholders. Their general purpose is to reinforce capitalism by making it moral.[52] Their impact is largely inspirational.

---

[49] International Council on Mining & Metals, *ICCM Sustainable Development Framework: ICCM Principles* (London, ICCM, no date), pp. 2 and 3.

[50] S. Prakash Sethi, "The Effectiveness of Industry-Based Codes in Serving Public Interest: The Case of the International Council on Mining and Metals," *Transnational Corporation,* December 2005, p. 84.

[51] International Council of Toy Industries, *Code of Business Practices,* §3(a), at http://www.icti-care.org/resources/codeofbusinesspractices.html.

[52] Steven Young, *Moral Capitalism: A Guide to Using the Caux Round Table Principles for Business* (San Francisco: Berrett-Koehler, 2003), chap. 6.

- A Code of Ethics on International Business for Christians, Muslims, and Jews was published in 1993 as a result of five years of dialogue between leaders and theologians of the three faiths. It sets forth an ethical framework for commerce built on four principles that the religions hold in common: justice, mutual respect, stewardship of God's creation, and honesty. The principles are accompanied by guidelines explaining the corporation's social role, the nature of ethical policies, and duties toward owners and employees. The code was designed to encourage reflection and is not administered.

- The Business Charter for Sustainable Development is a set of 16 broadly worded principles about protecting and conserving the natural environment. It was launched by the International Chamber of Commerce (ICC) in 1991. The principles, for example, call for putting environmental management "among the highest corporate priorities," for using "legal regulations as a starting point" and for applying "the same environmental criteria internationally." The ICC has more than 100,000 corporate members from about 130 nations and promotes an agenda of free markets, trade expansion, and self-regulation. About 2,300 companies have signed onto the charter's principles. The ICC provides no guidelines for implementing them and does no enforcement. It sees the standards as a framework for building environmental management systems that incorporate other, more actionable codes, for example, the International Organization for Standardization's 14000 and 14001 standards for certifying the environmental performance of facilities.

- The OECD Guidelines for Multinational Enterprises is the only comprehensive global code of corporate conduct endorsed by governments. The OECD, or the Organisation for Economic Co-operation and Development, is a group of 30 nations in Europe and North America formed in 1961. Its main purpose is to boost economic growth of its members by expanding trade. However, the guidelines emphasize that corporations must act responsibly if global economic progress is to be sustainable. Ten non-OECD nations have adopted the guidelines, bringing the number of countries to 40, including those that are home to nearly all of the 100 largest MNCs. The guidelines consist of 11 general policies (see the box) supplemented with detailed guidance statements. Complaints about violations are sent to an MNC's home country government which must try to mediate a settlement.

multilateral code
A code of conduct set up by several groups of stakeholders, including one or more corporations.

- The Free Labor Association (FLA) Workplace Code of Conduct is an example of a *multilateral code,* which is one based on a cooperative effort between MNCs and stakeholder groups. The FLA code consists of nine principles that cover basic international labor standards. These principles are backed by more detailed monitoring procedures. It applies to factories that make products for 17 well-known apparel and footwear companies that back the FLA, including Adidas, Eddie Bauer, Nike, and Nordstrom. It also covers factories that make apparel under license for 200 colleges and universities that are FLA members. The FLA is run by a board with members from MNCs, human rights groups, labor unions, and universities. It trains the groups that make factory inspections and publishes the compliance records of members' factories in an annual report.

The OECD Guidelines for Multinational Enterprises

GENERAL POLICIES

Enterprises should take fully into account established policies in the countries in which they operate, and consider the views of other stakeholders. In this regard, enterprises should:

1. Contribute to economic, social and environmental progress with a view to achieving sustainable development.

2. Respect the human rights of those affected by their activities consistent with the host government's international obligations and commitments.

3. Encourage local capacity building through close co-operation with the local community, including business interests, as well as developing the enterprise's activities in domestic and foreign markets, consistent with the need for sound commercial practice.

4. Encourage human capital formation, in particular by creating employment opportunities and facilitating training opportunities for employees.

5. Refrain from seeking or accepting exemptions not contemplated in the statutory or regulatory framework related to environmental, health, safety, labour, taxation, financial incentives, or other issues.

6. Support and uphold good corporate governance principles and develop and apply good corporate governance practices.

7. Develop and apply effective self-regulatory practices and management systems that foster a relationship of confidence and mutual trust between enterprises and the societies in which they operate.

8. Promote employee awareness of, and compliance with, company policies through appropriate dissemination of these policies, including through training programmes.

9. Refrain from discriminatory or disciplinary action against employees who make *bona fide* reports to management or, as appropriate, to the competent public authorities, on practices that contravene the law, the *Guidelines* or the enterprise's policies.

10. Encourage, where practicable, business partners, including suppliers and sub-contractors, to apply principles of corporate conduct compatible with the *Guidelines*.

11. Abstain from any improper involvement in local political activities.

Source: Organisation for Economic Cooperation and Development, *The OECD Guidelines for Multinational Enterprises: Revision 2000* (Paris, France, OECD, 2000). Reprinted with permission.

THE UNITED NATIONS GLOBAL COMPACT

The single most conspicuous effort to promote MNC social responsibility and to harness FDI for economic development is the Global Compact. It was first proposed in a 1999 speech by UN Secretary-General Kofi Annan, who challenged leaders of global corporations to collaborate with UN agencies, labor unions, NGOs, and governments in embracing a set of "universal values."[53] He called on MNCs to implement a set of 10 principles (see the box) based on rights

---

[53] The UN agencies that participate are the Office of the High Commissioner for Human Rights, the International Labour Office, the United Nations Environment Programme, the United Nations Development Programme, the United Nations Organization for Industrial Development, and the United Nations Office on Drugs and Crime.

The Global Compact Principles

Human Rights

1. Businesses should support and respect the protection of internationally proclaimed human rights; and
2. Make sure that they are not complicit in human rights abuses.

Labour Standards

3. Businesses should uphold the freedom of association and the effective recognition of the right to collective bargaining;
4. The elimination of all forms of forced and compulsory labour;
5. The effective abolition of child labour; and
6. The elimination of discrimination in respect of employment and occupation.

The Environment

7. Businesses should support a precautionary approach to environmental challenges;
8. Undertake initiatives to promote greater environmental responsibility; and
9. Encourage the development and diffusion of environmentally friendly technologies.

Anti-Corruption

10. Businesses should work against all forms of corruption, including extortion and bribery.

These principles are derived from the Universal Declaration of Human Rights (1948), the Rio Principles on Environment and Development (1986), the International Labor Organisation's Fundamental Principles on Rights at Work (1998), and the UN Convention Against Corruption.

and norms in international agreements made under UN auspices over the years.

The Global Compact is administered by an office housed in the United Nations Secretariat. Participation by all parties is voluntary. Although its nature is evolving, it retains two central purposes: (1) to promote corporate responsibility in MNCs, and (2) to form cooperative networks of its participants for solving the problems of economic globalization. By 2008 there were about 5,000 participants. Of these, 3,700 were corporations, a number including many subsidiaries of large MNCs. This is a large number, and more than any other global CSR initiative, but less than 5 percent of the total number of MNCs.

The Global Compact reflects a new consensus about MNCs within the United Nations. After its founding in 1945, the UN became dominated by poorer and less developed countries, many of them newly independent former colonies of Western powers. Collectively, these nations weighted it with an animus against the West and toward aggressive MNCs seen as carriers of Western economic and cultural imperialism. At first this critical perspective led the UN to promote regulation of MNCs. But by the late 1990s global free market forces were so irrepressible that international investment defined the tenor of the times. Moreover, a central mission of the UN is to promote economic development and it also had become clear that international aid, by itself, was not bringing robust economic growth to underdeveloped nations. Within the UN there was rising appreciation of the positive role that FDI could play in development. The Global Compact was designed to bring MNCs into the fold of those promoting a just and sustainable world economy.

At first, the Global Compact was slow to take off. Companies, especially the largest MNCs, were skeptical of the need for another code and feared being sued by NGOs for abridging the 10 principles. Cynical NGOs saw it as toothless because fidelity to the principles was not enforced. They believed that MNCs indulged in *bluewashing*, a word that references the color of the UN flag, a worldwide symbol of peace and justice. In bluewashing, the prestige of the UN is exploited by insincere corporations that sign onto the Global Compact principles but fail to fulfill their spirit. To combat this perception, corporations are now required to issue a report of their actions in support of the principles at least once a year. Those that fail for two years in a row are declared inactive. In fact, more than 600 companies have been delisted for silence about their progress.[54] Time and experience have eased both MNC and NGO fears, but not erased them. American corporations remain wary of lawsuits and are only 5 percent of participating MNCs.[55] Influential NGOs such as Greenpeace and Amnesty International remain skeptical.

bluewashing
The act of a corporation cloaking its lack of social responsibility by insincere membership in the UN Global Compact.

Corporations volunteer to join the Global Compact. Those that do, agree to write the 10 Global Compact principles into their mission statements, use them to guide strategy, apply them in daily operations, and extend them over their spheres of influence to subsidiaries, partners, and suppliers. They must report concrete examples of their progress on a UN Web site.[56] These reports, called *communications on progress* in Global Compact jargon, display a wide range of CSR activity. The Global Compact does not evaluate or judge them. It is not a binding code with compliance requirements. Rather, it is a forum for convening MNCs and other parties to form collaborative efforts and to share best practices.

communication on progress
A report from a corporation about its actions in support of the 10 Global Compact principles.

Here is a sampling of actions reported by Global Compact participants.

- In Africa power grids do not reach many impoverished areas. Without electricity children do not study in the evening and productive work stops with nightfall. ABB Group of Switzerland, which makes power station equipment, started a rural electrification program in Tanzania. Working with the World Wildlife Fund and local governments, it donates generators so that desert hamlets can have electricity. New businesses spring up when power goes on. New homes are built, and children are doing better in school.[57]

- Water-borne bacteria cause 2.2 million deaths each year from diarrheal disease. GlaxoSmithKline set up a program of hygiene for schoolchildren. In Bangladesh, Kenya, Nicaragua, Peru, and Zambia it collaborates with NGOs and health ministries to teach simple lessons about water use, including hand washing,

---

[54] "335 Companies Delisted as Part of Quality Drive," *Compact Quarterly* 2006, no. 4, www.unglobalcompact.org.

[55] Carol Stephenson and Paul Beamish, "When It Comes to Doing Good, We Can Do Better," *The Globe and Mail*, June 4, 2007, p. B2.

[56] The Web site is www.unglobalcompact.org/COP/index.html.

[57] *ABB Annual Report 2006: Sustainability Review* (Zurich: ABB Group, 2007), p. 28.

cleaning latrines, and wearing shoes or sandals in toilet areas. Children transfer new sanitation principles to their homes. The program will reach more than 1 million children by 2010.[58]

- Volkswagen South Africa, a subsidiary of the German carmaker, has a plant in Eastern Cape province. In the surrounding area 25 percent of adults are infected with the HIV virus. Volkswagen has responded with an HIV/AIDS prevention and management program in collaboration with a local physician's group, the workers' union, the provincial health department, and a German government ministry. Volkswagen pays each HIV-positive plant worker two allowances, one for medical treatment and one for antiretroviral drugs. It gives free testing for all workers and hands out as many as 17,000 condoms a month by means of vending machines. It also funds education programs for everyone in the surrounding area.[59] Volkswagen estimates that the annual cost of this program exceeds $1.5 million.[60]

- For decades the Brantas River in East Java was polluted by the waste of riverside residents. Poor water quality caused serious health problems and killed fish. A nearby Unilever factory that took water from the river bore high treatment costs. Unilever adopted four villages along the river, reorganized waste collection, and educated residents. It planted trees on the river's banks and released small fish that could grow and provide a livelihood for local fishermen. Rather than work alone, Unilever created a coalition of local businesses, environmental groups, schools, and government agencies to help the effort and named a full-time employee to lead it.[61]

These meritorious actions show the promise of the Global Compact. There are many similar stories. However most participating MNCs report less ambitious or less specific accomplishments. A typical communication on progress lists the 10 principles on a chart, with references to pages in a company sustainability report where actions said to be undertaken in support of a particular principle are discussed. It is not clear that the activities referenced are undertaken to further the principles or for unrelated reasons. And many activities, such as setting up a committee to investigate the company's performance with respect to X, Y, or Z responsibility, may or may not have significance.

The 10 principles themselves are very general and best characterized as "aspirational precepts rather than operational standards."[62] Although the Global Compact can delist companies for lack of reporting, it cannot penalize them for failing to abide by any interpretation of the principles. The actions of two signatories

[58] GlaxoSmithKline, *PHASE: A Simple Hand-Washing Programme That Saves Lives* (Brentford, Middlesex: GSK, 2007).

[59] Volkswagen AG, *One Plus One Equals Three: Corporate Social Responsibility at Volkswagen* (Wolfsburg, Germany: Volkswagen AG, 2006), pp. 35–36.

[60] Cláudio Bruzzi Boechat et al., "Volkswagen in the Global War against HIV/AIDS," Global Compact Learning Forum Case Study, January 13, 2004, annex 3.

[61] "Brantas River Project, Indonesia," Case Description, May 6, 2003, at www.unglobalcompact.org.

[62] Edwin M. Epstein, "The Good Company: Rhetoric or Reality?" *American Business Law Journal,* Summer 2007, p. 215.

illustrate this. Although principle 3 requires "recognition of the right to collective bargaining," the Australian mining company BHP Billiton requires new employees to sign individual employment contracts.[63] Principle 2 prohibits "complicity in human rights abuses." Yet signatory Deutsche Bank held the central bank funds for the government of Turkmenistan when that country was controlled by a repressive dictator.[64]

Such shortcomings engender continued skepticism about the Global Compact summed up by a member of Greenpeace International who argues that its principles are "too vague to be meaningful and fail to be clearly defined and enforced."[65] On the other hand, the Compact is rapidly evolving and expanding. Its principles contain the potent seed of ideals. An ideal with momentum, which the Global Compact now has, generally works to elevate behavior and shame laggards.

CONCLUDING OBSERVATIONS

Multinational corporations are highly variable entities. They vary in size, strategy, geographic reach, industrial sector, number of foreign affiliates, and extent of foreign direct investment. All these variables interact with unique forces in more than 200 host economies—poor, developing, and advanced—making generalization about MNC behavior difficult.

It is too great a leap to argue that MNCs dominate and define the global economy. They are better understood as entities reacting to forces of globalization along with governments, NGOs, and international agencies. They can be understood as reacting to change and opportunity with an inner business logic. In the next chapter, we will discuss forces of globalization in more depth.

While MNCs are still feared for their power and still act badly at times, the progressive community now has more appreciation of the need to bring them into the fold of cooperation with governments and NGOs to fight evils such as poverty, climate warming, and terrorism. MNCs now also face a rising network of codes of conduct and collaborative schemes to advance corporate citizenship. It is too early to say these new forces have caused a big increase in MNC responsibility. However, it is now impossible for the most powerful MNCs to avoid joining at least some of these corporate responsibility schemes. When they do, their actions will be compared to the principles, reporting standards, and UN-generated "universal" norms that drive arrangements such as the Global Compact. To retain long-term legitimacy, they will have to show acceptable performance.

---

[63] Surya Deva, "Global Compact: A Critique of the U.N.'s 'Public–Private' Partnership for Promoting Corporate Citizenship," *Syracuse Journal of International Law & Commerce,* Fall 2007, p. 131.

[64] Ivar Simensen and Hugh Williamson, "The Problem with Warm Words," *Financial Times,* May 10, 2007, p. 16.

[65] Daniel Mittler, quoted in John Zarocostas, "Global Compact Integrity Pressed," *The Washington Times,* July 9, 2007, p. A13.

Union Carbide Corporation and Bhopal

On December 3, 1984, tragedy unfolded at the Union Carbide pesticide plant in Bhopal, India. Water entered a large tank where a volatile chemical was stored, starting a violent reaction. Rapidly, a sequence of safety procedures and devices failed. Fugitive vapors sailed over plant boundaries, forming a lethal cloud that moved with the south wind, enveloping slum dwellings, searing lungs and eyes, asphyxiating fated souls, scarring the unlucky.

Bhopal is the worst sudden industrial accident ever in terms of human life lost. Death and injury estimates vary widely. The official death toll set forth by the Indian government for that night is 4,037, with an additional 60,000 serious injuries. Greenpeace has put the death toll at 16,000, with an estimated 500,000 injured.[1]

The incredible event galvanized industry critics. "Like Auschwitz and Hiroshima," wrote one, "the catastrophe at Bhopal is a manifestation of something fundamentally wrong in our stewardship of the earth."[2] Union Carbide was debilitated and slowly declined as a company after the incident. The government of India earned mixed reviews for its response. The chemical industry changed, but according to some, not enough. And the gas victims endure a continuing struggle to get compensation and medical care.[3]

UNION CARBIDE IN INDIA

Union Carbide established an Indian subsidiary named Union Carbide India Ltd. (UCIL) in 1934. At first the company owned a 60 percent majority interest, but over the years this was reduced to 50.9 percent. Shares in the ownership of the other 49.1 percent traded on the Bombay Stock Exchange. This ownership scheme was significant because although UCIL operated with a great deal of autonomy, it gave the appearance that Union Carbide was in control of its operations. By itself, UCIL was one of India's

largest firms. In 1984, the year of the incident, it had 14 plants and 9,000 employees, including 500 at Bhopal. Most of its revenues came from selling Eveready batteries.

Union Carbide decided to build a pesticide plant at Bhopal in 1969. The plant formulated pesticides from chemical ingredients imported to the site. At that time, there was a growing demand in India and throughout Asia for pesticides because of the "green revolution," a type of planned agriculture that requires intensive use of pesticides and fertilizers on special strains of food crops such as wheat, rice, and corn. Although pesticides may be misused and pose some risk, they also have great social value. Without pesticides, damage to crops, losses in food storage, and toxic mold growth in food supplies would cause much loss of life from starvation and food poisoning, especially in countries such as India. Exhibit 1 shows a Union Carbide advertisement from the 1960s that describes the company's activities in India.

The Bhopal plant would supply these pesticides and serve a market anticipated to expand rapidly. The plant's location in Bhopal was encouraged by tax incentives from the city and the surrounding state of Madhya Pradesh. After a few years, however, the Indian government pressured UCIL to stop importing chemical ingredients. The company then proposed to manufacture methyl isocyanate (MIC) at the plant rather than ship it in from Carbide facilities outside the country. This was a fateful decision.

Methyl isocyanate, CH_3NCO, is a colorless, odorless liquid. Its presence can be detected by tearing and the burning sensation it causes in the eyes and noses of exposed individuals. At the Bhopal plant it was used as an intermediate chemical in pesticide manufacture. It was not the final product; rather, MIC molecules were created, then pumped into a vessel where they reacted with other chemicals. The reaction created unique molecules with qualities that disrupted insect nervous systems, causing convulsions and death. The plant turned out two similar pesticides marketed under the names Sevin and Temik.

In 1975 UCIL received a permit from the Ministry of Industry in New Delhi to build an MIC production

[1] "Has the World Forgotten Bhopal?" *The Lancet,* December 2, 2000, p. 1863.

[2] David Weir, The Bhopal Syndrome (San Francisco: Sierra Club Books, 1987), p. xii.

[3] Kim Fortun, Advocacy After Bhopal (Chicago: University of Chicago Press, 2001).

EXHIBIT 1

Union Carbide Advertisement This ad appeared in *Fortune* magazine in April 1962.

Source: Photo courtesy of Union Carbide Corporation.

Science helps build a new India

Oxen working the fields . . . the eternal river Ganges . . . jeweled elephants on parade. Today these symbols of ancient India exist side by side with a new sight—modern industry. India has developed bold new plans to build its economy and bring the promise of a bright future to its more than 400,000,000 people. ▷ But India needs the technical knowledge of the western world. For example, working with Indian engineers and technicians, Union Carbide recently made available its vast scientific resources to help build a major chemicals and plastics plant near Bombay. ▷ Throughout the free world, Union Carbide has been actively engaged in building plants for the manufacture of chemicals, plastics, carbons, gases, and metals. The people of Union Carbide welcome the opportunity to use their knowledge and skills in partnership with the citizens of so many great countries.

A HAND IN THINGS TO COME   **UNION CARBIDE**

WRITE *for booklet B-3 "The Exciting Universe of Union Carbide", which tells how research in the fields of carbons, chemicals, gases, metals, plastics and nuclear energy keeps bringing new wonders into your life. Union Carbide Corporation, 270 Park Avenue, New York 17, N.Y.*

unit at the Bhopal plant. Two months before the issuance of this permit, the city of Bhopal had enacted a development plan requiring dangerous industries to relocate in an industrial zone 15 miles away. Pursuant to the plan, M. N. Buch, the Bhopal city administrator, tried to move the UCIL pesticide plant and convert the site to housing and light commercial use. For reasons that are unclear, his effort failed, and Buch was soon transferred to forestry duties elsewhere.

The MIC unit was based on a process design provided by Union Carbide's engineers in the

United States and elaborated by engineers in India. The design required storage of MIC in big tanks. An alternative used at most other pesticide plants would have been to produce small amounts of MIC only as they were consumed in pesticide production. The decision to use large storage tanks was based on an optimistic projection that pesticide sales would grow dramatically. Since an Indian law, the Foreign Exchange Regulation Act of 1973, requires foreign multinationals to share technology and use Indian resources, detailed design work was done by an Indian subsidiary of a British firm. Local labor using Indian equipment and materials built the unit.

In 1980 the MIC unit began operation under UCIL's management. During the five years of design and construction, densely populated shantytowns sprang up nearby, inhabited mainly by impoverished, unemployed people who had left rural areas seeking their fortunes in the city. A childlike faith that the facility was a benevolent presence turning out miraculous substances to make plants grow was widespread among them.

In fact, when the MIC unit came on line the plant began to pose higher risk to its neighbors; it now made the basic chemicals used in pesticides rather than using shipped-in ingredients. One step in the manufacture of MIC, for example, creates phosgene, the lethal "mustard gas" used in World War I. The benighted crowd by the plant abided unaware.

In 1981 a phosgene leak killed one worker, and a crusading Indian journalist wrote articles about dangers to the population. No one acted. A year later, a second phosgene leak forced temporary evacuation of some surrounding neighborhoods. Worker safety and environmental inspections of the plant were done by the state Department of Labor, an agency with only 15 factory inspectors to cover 8,000 plants and a record of lax enforcement.[4] Oversight was not vigorous.

Meanwhile, the Indian economy had turned down, and stiff competition from other pesticide firms marketing new, less expensive products reduced demand for Sevin and Temik. As revenues fell, so did the plant's budget, and it was necessary to defer some maintenance, lessen the rigor of training, and

[4] Sheila Jasanoff, "Managing India's Environment," *Environment,* October 1986, p. 33.

lay off workers. By the time of the incident, the MIC unit operated with six workers per shift, half the number anticipated by its designers.

UNION CARBIDE'S RELATIONSHIP WITH THE BHOPAL PLANT

What was the organizational relationship of Union Carbide Corporation in the United States to its subsidiary, Union Carbide India Ltd., and ultimately to the Bhopal plant? How much direction and control did the corporate parent half a world away in Danbury, Connecticut, exercise over the facility?

The Bhopal plant fit into the Union Carbide management hierarchy as shown in the chart in Exhibit 2. Although Carbide employees from the United States managed the plant in its early years, in 1982, under pressure from the government, it was turned over to Indian managers. The experience of colonial rule in India created a strong political need for leaders to put on shows of strength with foreign investors. Indians felt a burning desire to avoid any appearance of subjugation and demanded self-sufficiency. This is what had led to passage of the law requiring foreign investors to use Indian firms and workers in certain ways—and to put pressure on Union Carbide to turn the plant completely over to its Indian subsidiary.

The Bhopal plant was but one of 500 facilities in 34 countries in the Union Carbide Corporation universe. There was no regular or direct reporting relationship between it and Union Carbide's headquarters in Danbury, Connecticut. At the request of UCIL, employees of Union Carbide had gone to India twice to perform safety inspections on the plant. Other than those occasions, managers in the United States had received information or reporting about the plant only infrequently and irregularly when major changes or capital expenditures were requested. Thus, the Bhopal plant was run with near total independence from the American corporation. In litigation to determine where victims' lawsuits should be tried, a U.S. court described its autonomy in these words:

> . . . [Union Carbide Corporation's] participation [in the design and construction of the plant] was limited and its involvement in plant operations terminated long before the accident . . . . [It] was constructed and managed by Indians in India. No Americans were employed at the plant at the time of

EXHIBIT 2
Union
Carbide's
Organization
Structure as
Related to the
Bhopal Plant

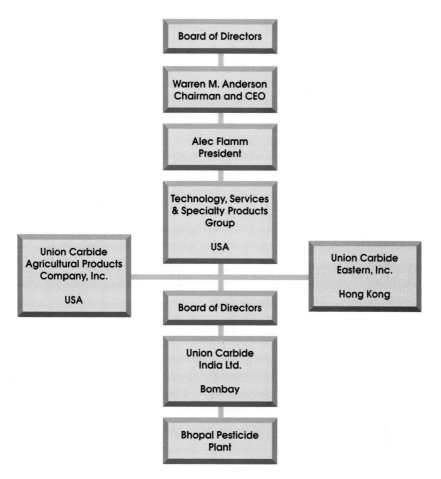

the accident. In the five years from 1980 to 1984, although more than 1,000 Indians were employed at the plant, only one American was employed there and he left in 1982. No Americans visited the plant for more than one year prior to the accident, and during the 5-year period before the accident the communications between the plant and the United States were almost nonexistent.[5]

Thus, the Bhopal plant was run by UCIL with near total independence from the American corporation. Despite this, shortly after the gas leak Chairman Warren M. Anderson said that Carbide accepted "moral responsibility" for the tragedy.

[5] *In re Union Carbide Corporation Gas Plant Disaster at Bhopal*, 809 F.2d 195 (1987), at 200.

THE GAS LEAK

On the eve of the disaster, tank 610, one of three storage tanks in the MIC unit, sat filled with 11,290 gallons of MIC. The tank, having a capacity of 15,000 gallons, was a partly buried, stainless steel, pressurized vessel. Its purpose was to take in MIC made elsewhere in the plant and hold it for some time until it was sent to the pesticide production area through a transfer pipe, there to be converted into Sevin or Temik.

At about 9:30 P.M. a supervisor ordered an operator, R. Khan, to unclog four filter valves near the MIC production area by washing them out with water. Khan connected a water hose to the piping above the clogged valves but neglected to insert a slip blind, a device that seals lines to prevent water leaks into adjacent pipes. Khan's omission, if it occurred, would have violated established procedure.

Because of either this careless washing method or the introduction of water elsewhere, 120 to 240 gallons of water entered tank 610, starting a powerful exothermic (heat building) reaction. At first, operators were unaware of the danger, and for two hours pressure in the tank rose unnoticed. At 10:20 P.M. they logged tank pressure at 2 pounds per square inch (ppsi). At 11:30 P.M. a new operator in the MIC control room noticed that the pressure was 10 ppsi, but he was unconcerned because this was within tolerable limits, gauges were often wrong, and he had not read the log to learn that the pressure was now five times what it had been an hour earlier.

Unfortunately, refrigeration units that cooled the tanks had been shut down for five months to save electricity costs. Had they been running, as the MIC processing manual required, the heat from the reaction with the water might have taken place over days instead of hours.

As pressure built, leaks developed. Soon workers sensed the presence of MIC. Their eyes watered. At 11:45 someone spotted a small, yellowish drip from overhead piping. The supervisor suggested fixing the leak after the regular 12:15 A.M. tea break. At 12:40 the tea break ended. By now the control room gauge showed the pressure in tank 610 was 40 ppsi. In a short time it rose to 55 ppsi, the top of the scale. A glance at the tank temperature gauge brought more bad news: The MIC was 77° F, 36° higher than the specified safety limit and hot enough to vaporize. Startled by readings on the gauges, the control room operator ran out to tank 610. He felt radiating heat and heard the concrete over it cracking. Within seconds, a pressure-release valve opened and a white cloud of deadly MIC vapor shot into the atmosphere with a high-decibel screech.

Back in the control room, operators turned a switch to activate the vent gas scrubber, a safety device designed to neutralize escaping toxic gases by circulating them through caustic soda. It was down for maintenance and inoperable. Even if it had been on line, it was too small to handle the explosive volume of MIC shooting from the tank. A flare tower designed to burn off toxic gases before they reached the atmosphere was also off line; it had been dismantled for maintenance and an elbow joint was missing. Another emergency measure, transferring MIC from tank 610 to one of the other storage tanks, was fore-

closed because both were too full. This situation also violated the processing manual, which called for leaving one tank empty as a safeguard.

At about 1:00 A.M. an operator triggered an alarm to warn workers of danger. The plant superintendent, entering the control room, ordered a water spraying device be directed on the venting gas, but this last-resort measure had little effect. Now most workers ran in panic, ignoring four emergency buses they were supposed to drive through the surrounding area to evacuate residents. Two intrepid operators stayed at the control panel, sharing the only available oxygen mask when the room filled with MIC vapor. Finally, at 2:30, the pressure in tank 610 dropped, the leaking safety valve resealed, and the venting ceased. Roughly 10,000 gallons of MIC, about 90 percent of the tank's contents, was now settling over the city.

That night the wind was calm, the temperature about 60°, and the dense chemical mist lingered just above the ground. Animals died. The gas attacked people in the streets and seeped into their bedrooms. Those who panicked and ran into the night air suffered higher exposures.

As the poisonous cloud enveloped victims, MIC reacted with water in their eyes. This reaction, like the reaction in tank 610, created heat that burned corneal cells, rendering them opaque. Residents with cloudy, burning eyes staggered about. Many suffered shortness of breath, coughing fits, inflammation of the respiratory tract, and chemical pneumonia. In the lungs, MIC molecules reacted with moisture, causing chemical burns. Fluid oozed from seared tissue and pooled, a condition called pulmonary edema, and its victims literally drowned in their own secretions. Burned lung tissue eventually healed, creating scarred areas that diminished breathing capacity. Because MIC is so reactive with water, simply breathing through a wet cloth would have saved many lives. However, people lacked this simple knowledge.

UNION CARBIDE REACTS

Awakened early in the morning, CEO Warren M. Anderson rushed to Carbide's Danbury, Connecticut, headquarters and learned of the rising death toll. When the extent of the disaster was evident, a senior management committee held an emergency meeting. They decided to send emergency medical supplies, respirators, oxygen (all Carbide products), and an American doctor with knowledge of MIC to Bhopal.

The next day, Tuesday, December 5, Carbide dispatched a team of technical experts to examine the plant. On Thursday, Anderson himself left for India. However, after arriving in Bhopal, he was charged with criminal negligence, placed under house arrest, and then asked to leave the country.

With worldwide attention focused on Bhopal, Carbide held daily press conferences. Christmas parties were canceled. Flags at Carbide facilities flew at half-mast. All of its nearly 100,000 employees observed a moment of silence for the victims. It gave $1 million to an emergency relief fund and offered to turn its guest house in Bhopal into an orphanage.

Months later, the company offered another $5 million, but the money was refused because Indian politicians trembled in fear that they would be seen cooperating with the company. The Indian public reviled anything associated with Carbide. Later, when the state government learned that Carbide had set up a training school for the unemployed in Bhopal, it flattened the facility with bulldozers.

CARBIDE FIGHTS LAWSUITS AND A TAKEOVER BID

No sooner had the mists cleared than American attorneys arrived in Bhopal seeking litigants for damage claims. They walked the streets signing up plaintiffs. Just four days after the gas leak, the first suit was filed in a U.S. court; soon cases seeking $40 billion in damages for 200,000 Indians were filed against Carbide.

However, the Indian Parliament passed a law giving the Indian government an exclusive right to represent victims. Then India sued in the United States. Union Carbide offered $350 million to settle existing claims (an offer rejected by the Indian government) and brought a motion to have the cases heard in India. Both Indian and American lawyers claiming to represent victims opposed the motion, knowing that wrongful death awards in India were small compared with those in the United States. However, in 1986 a federal court ruled that the cases should be heard in India, noting that "to retain the litigation in [the United States] . . . would be yet another example of imperialism, another situation in which an established sovereign inflicted its rules, its standards and values on a developing nation."[6] This was a victory

for Carbide and a defeat for American lawyers, who could not carry their cases to India in defiance of the government.

In late 1986 the Indian government filed a $3.3 billion civil suit against Carbide in an Indian court.[7] The suit alleged that Union Carbide Corporation, in addition to being majority shareholder in Union Carbide India Ltd., had exercised policy control over the establishment and design of the Bhopal plant. The Bhopal plant was defective in design because its safety standards were lower than similar Carbide plants in the United States. Carbide had consciously permitted inadequate safety standards to exist. The suit also alleged that Carbide was conducting an "ultrahazardous activity" at the Bhopal plant and had strict and absolute liability for compensating victims regardless of whether the plant was operating carefully or not.

Carbide countered with the defense that it had a holding company relationship with UCIL and never exercised direct control over the Bhopal plant; it was prohibited from doing so by Indian laws that required management by Indian nationals. In addition to the civil suit, Carbide's chairman, Warren Anderson, and several UCIL executives were charged with homicide in a Bhopal court. This apparently was a pressure tactic, since no attempt to arrest them was made.

On top of its legal battle, Carbide had to fight for its independence. In December 1985, GAF Corporation, which had been accumulating Carbide's shares, made a takeover bid. After a suspenseful month-long battle, Carbide fought off GAF, but only at the cost of taking on enormous new debt to buy back 55 percent of its outstanding shares. This huge debt had to be reduced because interest payments were crippling. So in 1986 Carbide sold $3.5 billion of assets, including its most popular consumer brands—Eveready batteries, Glad bags, and Prestone antifreeze. It had sacrificed stable sources of revenue and was now a smaller, weaker company more exposed to cyclical economic trends.

INVESTIGATING THE CAUSE OF THE MIC LEAK

In the days following the gas leak, there was worldwide interest in pinning down its precise cause. A team of reporters from the *New York Times* interviewed plant workers in Bhopal. Their six-week

---

[6] *In re Union Carbide Corporation Gas Plant Disaster,* 634 F. Supp. 867 (S.D.N.Y. 1986).

[7] *Union of India v. Union Carbide Corp. and Union Carbide India Ltd.,* Bhopal District Court, No. 1113 (1986).

investigation concluded that a large volume of water entered tank 610, causing the accident.[8] The *Times* reporters thought that water had entered when R. Khan failed to use a slip blind as he washed out piping. Water from his hose simply backed up and eventually flowed about 400 feet into the tank. Their account was widely circulated and this theory, called the "water washing theory," gained currency. However, it was not to be the only theory of the accident's cause.

Immediately after the disaster, Union Carbide also rushed a team of investigators to Bhopal. But the team got little cooperation from Indian authorities operating in a climate of anti-Carbide popular protest. It was denied access to plant records and workers. Yet the investigators got to look at tank 610 and took core samples from the bottom residue. These samples went back to the United States, where more than 500 experimental chemical reactions were undertaken to explain their chemical composition. In March 1985 Carbide finally released its report. It stated that entry of water into the tank caused the gas release, but it rejected the water washing theory.

Instead, Carbide scientists felt the only way that an amount of water sufficient to cause the observed reaction could have entered the tank was through accidental or deliberate connection of a water hose to piping that led directly into the tank. This was possible, because outlets for compressed air, nitrogen, steam, and water were stationed throughout the plant. The investigators rejected the water washing hypothesis for several reasons. The piping system was designed to prevent water contamination even without a slip blind. Valves between the piping being washed and tank 610 were found closed after the accident. And the volume of water required to create the reaction—1,000 to 2,000 pounds—was far too much to be explained by valve leakage.

The Carbide report gave a plausible alternative to the water washing theory, but within months an investigation by the Indian government rejected it. This study, made by Indian scientists and engineers, confirmed that the entry of water into the MIC tank caused the reaction but concluded that the improper washing procedure was to blame (see Exhibit 3).

There matters stood until late 1985, when the Indian government allowed Carbide more access to plant records and employees. Carbide investigators sought out the plant's employees. More than 70 interviews, and careful examination of plant records and physical evidence, led them to conclude that the cause of the gas leak was sabotage by a disgruntled employee who intentionally hooked a water hose to the tank.

Here is the sequence of events on the night of December 2–3 that Carbide set forth. At 10:20 P.M. the pressure gauge on tank 610 read 2 ppsi. This meant that no water had yet entered the tank and no reaction had begun. At 10:45 the regular shift change occurred. Shift changes take half an hour, and the MIC storage area would have been deserted. At this time, an operator who had been angry for days about his failure to get a promotion stole into the area. He unscrewed the local pressure indicator gauge on tank 610, hooked up a rubber water hose, and turned the water on. Five minutes would have sufficed to do this.

Carbide claimed to know the name of this person, but it has never been made public. Its investigative team speculated that his intention was simply to ruin the MIC batch in the tank; it is doubtful that this worker realized all that might happen. The interviews revealed that the workers thought of MIC chiefly as a lacrimator, a chemical that causes tearing; they did not regard it as a lethal hazard.

Now the plot thickens. A few minutes after midnight, MIC operators noted the fast pressure rise in tank 610. Walking to the tank, they found the water hose connected and removed it, then informed their supervisors. The supervisors tried to prevent a catastrophic pressure rise by draining water from tank 610. Between 12:15 and 12:30 A.M., just minutes before the explosive release, they transferred about 1 metric ton of the contents from tank 610 to a holding tank. Water is heavier than MIC, and the transfer was made through a drain in the tank's bottom; thus, the supervisors hoped to remove the water. They failed, and within 15 minutes the relief valve blew.

The investigators had physical evidence to support this scenario. After the accident, the local pressure gauge hole on tank 610 was still open and no

---

[8] The team wrote a series of articles. See Stuart Diamond, "The Bhopal Disaster: How It Happened," *New York Times,* January 28, 1985; Thomas J. Lueck, "Carbide Says Inquiry Showed Errors but Is Incomplete," *New York Times,* January 28, 1985; Stuart Diamond, "The Disaster in Bhopal: Workers Recall Horror," *New York Times,* January 30, 1985; and Robert Reinhold, "Disaster in Bhopal: Where Does Blame Lie?" *New York Times,* January 31, 1985.

EXHIBIT 3
Two Theories Clash on Water Entry into MIC Tank

According to the water washing theory of the Indian government, water was introduced through a hose into bleeder A at filter pressure safety valve lines. As the hose kept running, water proceeded through the leaking valve in that area and rose up into the relief valve vent header line (RVVH). It took a turn at the jumper line, B, and moved into the process vent header line (PVH), filling it in the reverse direction all the way to the slip blind, C. When PVH was completely filled, water rose at line D and proceeded into MIC storage tank 610.

On February 8, 1985, two months after the leak, India's Central Bureau of Investigation drilled a hole in the PVH line at point E to drain any water left in the line. No water emerged. Carbide says this fact alone disproves the water washing theory. The fact that various valves in the pathway to the tank were closed also disproves the theory, according to Carbide.

Carbide espouses an alternative theory: The company says it has proof that water was introduced by a "disgruntled employee" who removed pressure gauge F, attached a hose to the open piping, and ran water into the MIC tank. Gas then escaped through a rupture disk and proceeded through the RVVH and out the vent gas scrubber.

Source: Courtesy of Union Carbide.

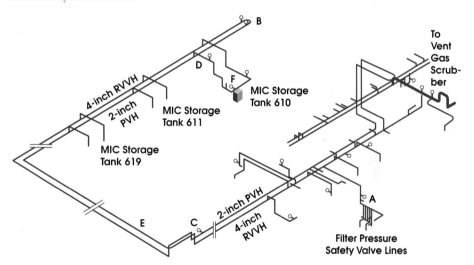

plug had been inserted, as would have been normal for routine maintenance. When the MIC unit was examined, a crude drawing of the hose connection was found on the back of one page from that night's log book. Also, operators outside the MIC unit told the investigation team that MIC operators had told them about the hose connection that night. In addition, log entries had been falsified, revealing a crude cover-up effort. The major falsification was an attempt to hide the transfer of contents from tank 610.

Why did the supervisors and operators attempt a cover-up? The Carbide investigators gave this explanation.

Not knowing if the attempted transfer had exacerbated the incident, or whether they could have otherwise prevented it, or whether they would be blamed for not having notified plant management earlier, those involved decided on a cover-up. They altered logs that morning to disguise their involvement. As is common in many such incidents, the reflexive tendency to cover up simply took over.[9]

[9] Ashok S. Kalelkar, "Investigation of Large-Magnitude Incidents: Bhopal as a Case Study," paper presented at the Instititution of Chemical Engineers conference on Preventing Major Chemical Accidents, London, England, May 1988, p. 27.

EXHIBIT 4

A Breakdown of the $470 million Settlement
The settlement was based on calculations about the number and size of payments in a range of categories.

Source: Kim Fortun, *Advocacy after Bhopal* (Chicago: University of Chicago Press, 2001), p. 38.

Amount	Medical Categorization
$ 43,500,000	$14,500 payments for 3,000 deaths
50,000,000	$25,000 payments for up to 2,000 victims with injuries of "utmost severity"
156,000,000	$5,200 payments to 30,000 permanently disabled
64,300,000	$3,215 payments to 20,000 temporarily disabled
140,600,000	Amount to cover 150,000 minor injuries, future injuries, property damage, commercial loss, and other claims
15,600,000	Medical treatment and rehabilitation of victims
$470,000,000	Total settlement

A SETTLEMENT IS REACHED

The theory of deliberate sabotage became the centerpiece of Carbide's legal defense. However, the case never came to trial. In 1989 a settlement was reached in which Carbide agreed to pay $470 million to the Indian government, which would distribute the money to victims (see Exhibit 4). In return, India agreed to stop all legal action against Carbide, UCIL, and their executives. India agreed to this settlement, which was far less than the $3.3 billion it was asking for, because a trial and subsequent appeals in the Indian court system would likely have taken 20 years.

Carbide paid the settlement using $200 million in insurance and taking a charge of $.43 per share against 1988 net earnings of $5.31 per share. Victims' groups were upset because they thought the settlement too small, and they challenged it. In 1991 the Indian Supreme Court rejected these appeals but permitted reinstatement of criminal proceedings against Warren Anderson and top managers at UCIL.[10] An arrest warrant for Anderson on manslaughter charges was issued in India in 1992, but it has never been served. A criminal trial of several UCIL managers began in 1989 and has now dragged on in India for more than 15 years with no end in sight. Only half of several hundred scheduled witnesses have been called.

The Indian government was slow and inefficient in distributing settlement funds to gas victims. In 1993, 40 special courts began processing claims, but the activity was riddled with corruption. Healthy people bribed physicians for false medical records with which they could get compensation. Twelve court officials were fired for soliciting bribes from gas victims who sought payments. More than 569,000 claims have been paid, including 14,824 death claims, with average compensation about $1,300. Ninety percent of all claims were settled for $550, the minimum allowed.[11] Because the claims process moved at a glacial pace for years, the settlement money accrued interest and after all claims were paid $325 million remained. The government wanted to use the interest to clean up soil contamination at the plant. But in 2004 the Indian Supreme Court ordered it distributed to the victims and families of the dead in amounts proportioned on the basis of claims already paid.[12]

POSTSCRIPT

In the wake of Bhopal, Congress passed legislation requiring chemical companies to disclose the presence of dangerous chemicals to people living near their plants and to create evacuation plans. The chemical industry's trade association adopted a program of more rigorous safety standards that all major firms now follow.

[10] *Union Carbide Corp. v. Union of India,* AIR 1992 (S.C.) 248.

[11] Paul Watson, "Cloud of Despair in Bhopal," *Los Angeles Times,* August 30, 2001, p. A6; and Government of Madhya Pradesh, "Claim and Compensation," http://www.mp.nic.in/bgtrrdmp/facts.htm.

[12] "Compensation for Bhopal Victims," *New York Times,* July 20, 2004, p. A6.

In 1994 Union Carbide sold its 50.9 percent equity in UCIL to the Indian subsidiary of a British company for $90 million. It gave all of this money to the Indian government for a hospital and clinics in Bhopal. After the sale, the company had no presence or current legal obligations in India. Nevertheless, Bhopal had destroyed it. As it exited India, it was a smaller, less resilient company. Forced to sell or spin off its most lucrative business, it grew progressively weaker. In 1984, the year of the gas leak, Carbide had 98,400 employees and sales of $9.5 billion; by 2000 it had only $5.9 billion in sales and 11,000 employees. The end came when it merged with Dow Chemical Co. in 2001 and its workforce suffered the bulk of cost-reduction layoffs.[13]

The Bhopal plant never reopened. Chemical waste at the site has contaminated the groundwater. In 1998 the state government took over the plant and developed cleanup plans, but its efforts have been blocked by lawsuits. Each year on the anniversary of the gas leak, people return to repaint graffiti on plant walls that still stand. "HANG ANDERSON" is an example.[14]

Activists among the gas victims, motivated by anger or vengeance and supported by groups such as Greenpeace and Amnesty International, keep demanding justice.[15] Survivors complain of chronic medical conditions including headaches, joint pain, shortness of breath, and psychiatric problems. They have filed a stream of lawsuits in the United States seeking to overturn the $470 million settlement, accusing Union Carbide of human rights violations, and trying to hold it responsible for cleaning up groundwater pollution at the plant site. All their efforts have failed.[16] Had they succeeded, Dow Chemical would have been obligated to pay the judgments.

In 2004 the United States denied a request by the Indian government to extradite Warren Anderson on charges of "culpable homicide not amounting to murder." Anderson, who is now in his mid-80s, has dropped from public view. In the unlikely event he is ever extradited, he would face a long trial and could be sentenced to 20 years in an Indian prison.

When Dow Chemical absorbed Union Carbide it became the new target of Bhopal victims and activists. They demand that Dow pay for cleaning up the contaminated plant site and further compensate injured survivors. Because the company denies any legal responsibility for Bhopal, it is the target of hunger strikes, demonstrations, and unfriendly shareholder resolutions.

Typical of large corporations, Dow has many social responsibility initiatives. It is a Global Compact signatory. At a Dow shareholder's meeting an activist with a hostile resolution for action on behalf of victims tried to embarrass its CEO.

> Dow asserts that it has embarked on an unprecedented campaign of responsibility and accountability for the world's most pressing problems . . . . How does Dow reconcile their public commitments to humanity, clean water, and ethical behavior with the decision to let people drink poisoned water in Bhopal?[17]

Despite the passage of time, Bhopal does not fade away. The library bookshelf on it keeps growing.[18] It has been the subject of at least six films, including a drama that became a box office hit in India. A tendentious book of reality fiction based on Bhopal became a best seller in Europe.[19] Told as a tragedy, the story seems to touch basic emotions. A Canadian critic reviewing a play on Bhopal found it badly written and acted, but nevertheless "a touching tale of human suffering" raising "such imposing themes as the relative worth of a human life and the intersection of greed and development in the Third World."[20]

[12] "Compensation for Bhopal Victims," *New York Times,* July 20, 2004, p. A6.

[13] Susan Warren, "Cost-Cutting Effort at Dow Chemical to Take 4,500 Jobs," *The Wall Street Journal,* May 2, 2001, p. A6.

[14] Daniel Pearl, "An Indian City Poisoned by Union Carbide Gas Forgets the Past," *The Wall Street Journal,* February 12, 2001, p. A17.

[15] See the International Campaign for Justice in Bhopal, at http://bhopal.net.

[16] *See, most recently, Bano v. Union Carbide and Warren Anderson, 198 Fed. Appx. 32 (2006).*

[17] Amnesty International USA, "Update from the Dow Annual Shareholder Meeting: May 10, 2007," http://www.amnestyusa.org, quoting Neil Sardana.

[18] A recent addition is Themistocles D'Silva, *The Black Box of Bhopal: A Closer Look at the World's Deadliest Industrial Disaster* (Victoria, BC: Trafford Publishing, 2006).

[19] Dominique Lapierre and Javier Moro, *Five Past Midnight in Bhopal* (New York: Warner Books, 2002).

[20] Kamal Al-Solaylee, "Bhopal: A Chemical and Theatrical Disaster," *The Globe and Mail,* October 25, 2003, p. R17. The play is Rahul Varma, *Bhopal* (Toronto: Playwrights Canada Press, 2006).

Questions

1. Who is responsible for the Bhopal accident? How should blame be apportioned among parties involved, including Union Carbide Corporation, UCIL, plant workers, governments in India, or others?

2. What principles of corporate social responsibility and business ethics are applicable to the actions of the parties in question?

3. How well did the legal system work? Do you agree with the decision to try the lawsuits in India? Were victims fairly compensated? Was Carbide sufficiently punished?

4. Did Union Carbide handle the crisis well? How would you grade its performance in facing uniquely difficult circumstances?

5. Does Dow Chemical Company have any remaining legal liability, social responsibility, or ethical duty to address unresolved health and environmental claims of Bhopal victims?

6. What lessons can other corporations and countries learn from this story?

Chapter Twelve

Globalization

McDonald's Corporation

Imagine an apparatus so colossal that it casts a shadow over 100 countries. At the back moves a stream of farmers pouring potatoes and lettuce through an opening, while beside them a line of cows, pigs, and chickens glides in and disappears. Inside, a uniformed crew of 465,000 works levers and buttons. In front, a torrent of 602 meals a second, day and night, flies into unceasing waves of humanity. A side door opens and bags of money drop out. Vents release bursts of paper, polystyrene, and other waste. On top, the stars and stripes snap and weave against the sky. As you watch, the great machine expands and quickens.

It all started in 1948 when brothers Richard and Maurice "Mac" McDonald built several hamburger stands with golden arches in Southern California. One day a traveling salesman named Ray Kroc came by selling milkshake mixers. The popularity of their $0.15 hamburgers impressed him, so he bought the world franchise rights and stretched the golden arches across the globe.

By 2007 McDonald's had 31,700 restaurants in 118 countries. More than half of them are outside the United States and these account for 62 percent of revenues.[1] The golden arches are so ubiquitous that a British magazine, *The Economist*, regularly publishes a "Big Mac Index" using the price of a Big Mac in foreign currencies to assess exchange-rate distortions.[2]

McDonald's is not one of the very largest multinational titans in revenues. Its $22 billion in 2006 sales were only about 6 percent of ExxonMobil's. However, it is a brand titan. According to *BusinessWeek*, it has the world's eighth most valuable brand, in part because of its "ability to cross geographic and cultural borders."[3] The golden arches are familiar to more people than the Christian cross.[4] Sixty-nine percent of three-year-old children recognize them, more than can state their own name.[5] After Santa Claus, the company's clown, Ronald McDonald, is the

---

[1] McDonald's Corporation, Form 10-K, February 26, 2007.

[2] See, for example, "Big Mac Index," *The Economist*, July 7, 2007, p. 162.

[3] "The Top 100 Brands," *BusinessWeek*, August 6, 2007, p. 59.

[4] Eric Schlosser, *Fast Food Nation* (Boston: Houghton Mifflin, 2001), p. 4.

[5] Jonathan Freedland, "The Onslaught," *The Guardian*, October 25, 2005, p. 8.

second-most-recognized person by children of the world.[6] And in Beijing, almost half the children under age 12 believe that McDonald's is a Chinese company.[7]

There are many perspectives on McDonald's. For some it inspires spacious reasoning. A prominent journalist popularized a "Golden Arches Theory of Conflict Prevention" based on the observation that countries with McDonald's restaurants have never gone to war with each other.[8] A social critic finds profound meaning in the spread of "McDonaldization," a powerful force of global change based on principles of "efficiency, calculability, predictability, and control."[9]

In developing nations, the arrival of a McDonald's signals modernization. It is often among the first foreign retail corporations to enter, and acts as "the canary in the coal mine of economic success" because it appears when disposable income rises and there is promise of sustained growth.[10] For many consumers in emerging economies the Big Mac signals a connection with world culture, "an imagined global identity that they share with like-minded people."[11]

For leftists and jihadists McDonald's symbolizes perceived evils of globalization, capitalism, America, and the West. Its restaurants have been targets of violence in more than a dozen countries. Protestors in Santiago, Chile, and Guatemala City attacked local McDonald's to protest visits by President George W. Bush. Within hours after U.S. bombers began to pound Afghanistan in 2001, angry Pakistanis damaged its restaurants in Islamabad. And in 2006, after European newspapers published cartoons depicting the Prophet Mohammad, mobs ransacked restaurants in Islamabad and Lahore.

In fact, McDonald's does transfer American cultural values and practices. A group of anthropologists documented its influence on east Asian cultures. They found that in Hong Kong and Taiwan the company's clean restrooms and kitchens set a new standard that elevated expectations throughout the country. In Hong Kong, children's birthdays had traditionally gone unrecognized, but McDonald's introduced the practice of birthday parties in its restaurants, and now birthday celebrations are widespread in the population. In Japan, *tachigui*, a centuries-old taboo against standing while eating, lost its strength after McDonald's opened restaurants in Tokyo with no tables or seats.[12]

On the other hand, many foreign customs are resistant to broad change based on what people eat for lunch. Most of McDonald's international restaurants are franchises, run as local businesses. The entrepreneurs who run them adapt to local custom. In France the restaurants modify their food and decor for French tastes, selling the French soft drink Orangina and lining walls with art posters.[13] In Japan the company adds

[6]"Big Mac's Makeover," *The Economist,* October 16, 2004, p. 64.

[7]Randall E. Stross, "The McPeace Dividend," *U.S. News & World Report*, April 1, 2002, p. 36.

[8]Thomas L. Friedman, *The Lexis and the Olive Tree* (New York: Farrar Straus Giroux, 1999), chap. 10.

[9]George Ritzer, *The Globalization of Nothing* (Thousand Oaks, CA: Pine Forge Press, 2004), pp. 82–83.

[10]Jonah Goldberg, "The Specter of McDonald's," *National Review,* June 5, 2000, p. 30.

[11]Douglas B. Holt, John A. Quelch, and Earl L. Taylor, "How Global Brands Compete," *Harvard Business Review*, September 2004, p. 71.

[12]James L. Watson, ed., *Golden Arches East: McDonald's in East Asia* (Stanford, CA: Stanford University Press, 1997), pp. 103, 134, 178–79.

[13]"Burger and Fries à la Française," *The Economist,* April 17, 2004, p. 60.

At a shopping mall in Riyadh, Saudi Arabia, women line up at the "ladies" sign and men at the "gentlemen's" sign. The mall is patrolled by Saudi religious police who enforce segregation of the sexes.
Source: © AP Photo/Hasan Jamali.

shrimp burgers to its menu. In Taiwan it serves rice burgers, made with beef or crispy chicken, lettuce, and cabbage between two toasted rice "patties." At the world's largest McDonald's in Beijing, managers fly the Chinese flag and serve green pea pies. In Saudi Arabia, McDonald's restaurants close five times each day for prayers. Eating zones for men and women are segregated.

globalization
Growth in networks of economic, political, social, military, scientific, or environmental interdependence to span worldwide distances.

The McDonald's story illustrates the complexity of globalization. A small, local, typically American business swelled into a far-flung multinational corporation with a radiant brand. It spread American business and cultural values, shaping both national cultures and an amorphous world culture. Yet its restaurants everywhere adapt to local tastes and customs.

In this chapter we discuss globalization, explaining how it affects people, corporations, nations, and governments. We also discuss related topics, including trade and trade agreements and the pervasiveness of corruption in the global economy. Throughout, we offer contrasting perspectives on the changes wrought by globalization.

WHAT IS GLOBALIZATION?

Globalization occurs when networks of economic, political, social, military, scientific, or environmental interdependence grow to span worldwide distances. Economic globalization refers to the development of an increasingly integrated commercial system based on free markets in which nations are open to foreign trade and investment. Globalization is a multifaceted phenomenon and observers see different elements in it. Some economists define it as the integration of economic systems. Political scientists may see it as a process that creates diffusion of national political authority through large trade blocs and the power of MNCs. Sociologists may see it as a process that erodes national cultures. Globalization is a controversial term because of such differences in perspective.

Some observers see today's globalization as nothing new. It has its roots, they point out, in the growth of huge trading companies in the sixteenth century. Other observers say today's globalization is far different from anything in the past. Bosworth and Gordon observe that global integration in recent years far exceeds that of the past "in degree, intensity, speed, volume, and geographic reach.[14] So rapid has been the change that some analysts speak of it as a revolution.

Major Forces in Expanding Globalization

Forces behind the extraordinary pace of globalization are economic, political, social, cultural, and technological as shown in Figure 12.1. Here are a few illustrations:

- Technological advances have significantly increased the speed and reduced the costs of communications. In 1930, for example, the cost of a one-minute telephone call to London from New York was about $245. In 1990 it was $3.32. Today a comparable communication over the Internet is virtually instantaneous and costs less not only to London but around the world.
- Transportation costs and delivery schedules of goods have been substantially reduced.
- The combined output of developing countries has shown a spectacular growth. In 2006 the combined output of the developing countries was about half the total world GDP. *The Economist* concludes that the developing economies " . . . will provide the biggest boost to the world economy since the industrial revolution."[15]
- There has been spectacular growth in world trade.
- There has been an explosive growth in the amount of money floating around the world to finance trade, acquire foreign assets, and speculate.
- Both developed and developing countries have been receptive to free market ideas.

Benefits of Globalization

Many economists point out that never before in human history has there been anything approaching the economic progress that most people of the world have witnessed and enjoyed in today's globalization. Jeffry A. Frieden, Stanfield Professor of International Peace at Harvard University, writes, "[t]he international economy

---

[14]Barry Bosworth and Philip H. Gordon, "Managing a Globalizing World," *Brookings Review,* Fall 2001, p. 3. For discussion of types and definitions of globalization see Martin Wolf, *Why Globalization Works* (New Haven and London: Yale University Press, 2005), pp. 14–16.

[15]"A Survey of the World Economy," *The Economist,* September 16, 2006, p. 3.

FIGURE 12.1 Main Forces in Globalization

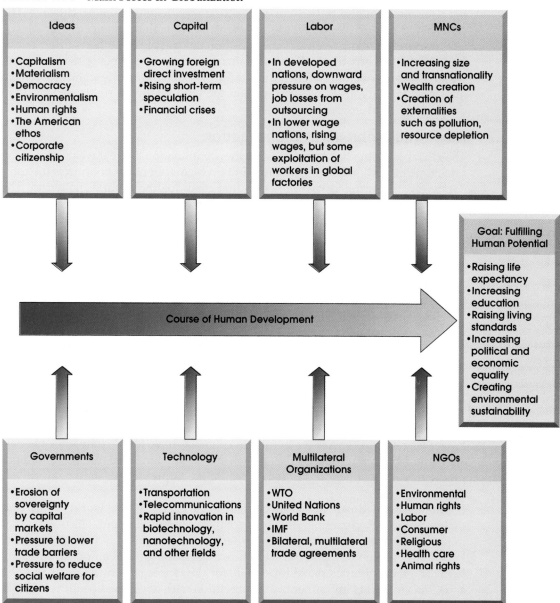

has enabled countries to develop, alleviate poverty, improve social conditions, lengthen life spans and carry out social and political reform."[16]

In the 1950s South Korea and Taiwan were " . . . miserably poor countries whose very survival was in question: in the 1990s they graduated into the ranks of the

[16]Jeffry A. Frieden, *Global Capitalism* (New York: W. W. Norton, 2006), p. 473.

world's advanced industrial nations."[17] Nokia reinvented itself from a producer of boots in rural Finland to the world's leading mobile telephone producer.[18] The purchasing power of the average person today in the advanced countries is 10 times greater than a century ago. Millions of people have been lifted out of comparative poverty to middle-class status. Consumers have benefited from more variety, lower cost, and higher quality of products. Working conditions have improved for millions of workers around the world. Human rights, especially in developing countries, have improved.

Flaws and Problems in Globalization

The global economy has made possible the accumulation of great wealth but at the same time has exhibited serious flaws and problems. Of major concern is the comparatively uncontrolled vast pool of liquid cash floating around the world. The danger to world stability of these funds was confirmed by the financial crisis in Southeast Asia beginning in 1997.

Starting in Thailand, the crisis spread almost immediately to Indonesia, Malaysia, the Philippines, and South Korea. In 1998 the Russian financial system collapsed and countries in Latin America also came under intense financial pressure. In these countries the financial systems, laws, ideas, and institutions did not keep pace with the rapid spread of globalization.

protectionist
A proponent of trade barriers designed to shield domestic producers from foreign competition.

Politicians and their constituents have become increasingly *protectionist*, that is, proponents of trade barriers designed to shield domestic producers from foreign competition. Today powerful interests lobby governments to put taxes, tariffs, quotas, and legislated rules in place to protect them from cross-border market forces. An illustration is demand for tariffs that shelter U.S. rice, cotton, and peanut farmers from exposure to commodity prices determined by global supply and demand.

Thousands of factories have been shut and tens of millions of manufacturing jobs have been lost in the United States and Europe because of global competition. Lower wages paid to workers in foreign countries have lured companies to operate there. Lower wages have also attracted U.S. consumers to buy more foreign-produced commodities. Too little has been done to provide a safety net for these displaced workers.

Thomas E. Friedman, in a best-selling book, argues that "the world is flat," and that is profoundly changing the global competitive environment. His point is that in far-off corners of the globe, such as Bangalore, it is possible to find the skills, knowledge, technology, and infrastructure to level the global competitive playing field. These capabilities make it possible for developing countries such as India and China to attract investments in competition with developed countries. This is not a new finding but his breezy style of writing offers a colorful perspective.[19]

The inequality of bargaining positions in trade disputes between the developed and undeveloped countries is an important flaw in globalization. It has led to the

---

[17]Ibid.

[18]Ibid.

[19]Thomas L. Friedman, *The World Is Flat: A Brief History of the Twenty-First Century* (New York: Farrar Straus and Giroux, 2005).

failure of trade meetings where countries meet to negotiate agricultural policies. The ministerial meeting of the World Trade Organization in Seattle in 1999, for example, illustrates the problem. The same fate befell world trade talks in Doha in 2006. Joseph E. Stiglitz, a Nobel Laureate and professor of economics at Columbia University, encapsulated the basic stumbling block in trade talks as follows: "The Western countries have pushed poor countries to eliminate trade barriers, but kept up their own barriers, preventing developing countries from exporting their agricultural products and so depriving them of desperately needed export income."[20] The Western countries, particularly the United States, continue stubbornly to subsidize agricultural products and maintain high tariffs to protect farmers while pressuring the developing countries to reduce their tariff barriers.

Critics of Globalization

The above flaws attract critics. They complain, for example, critics complain that there is no significant control of the trillions of dollars sloshing around the world with the potential of another crisis similar to that of the 1990s. Globalization has widened the income gap between rich and poor countries. This consequence of globalization assails universal norms of fairness and needs to be corrected, say the critics. The developing countries have lost some sovereignty which, among other things, prevents them from exercising the necessary control over their economic affairs.

The characteristics and quality of critics of globalization span a wide spectrum. Raucous crowds that greeted the delegates to the Third Ministerial Conference of the World Trade Organization in Seattle in 1999 stand at one end. Both organized and unorganized groups shot their arrows at the WTO, the World Bank, the International Monetary Fund, capitalism, and globalization. Tens of thousands of unruly demonstrators rioted and fought with police. Ralph Nader is a leader among activist critics. He says "the essence of globalization is a subordination of human rights, labor rights, consumer rights, environmental rights [and] democracy rights to the imperative of global trade and investment."[21]

At the other end of the spectrum are scholars such as Joseph Stiglitz who analyze the shortcomings of globalization and make policy recommendations to correct them. These scholars raise different questions about the future of globalization. One group asks "has globalization gone too far?"[22] They say "no" if policymakers act wisely. Another group asks: "Has globalization passed its peak?" They say "yes" but it is not likely to "unravel completely."[23]

Martin Wolf, a professor at Oxford University, is one of the most optimistic scholars in this field. He asserts that most of the criticisms are flawed. He writes,

[20]Joseph E. Stiglitz, *Globalization and Its Discontents* (New York: Norton, 2002), p. 6.

[21]Ralph Nader, from a transcript of *Globalization and Human Rights*, a PBS program, www.pbs.org/globalization/proloug.html.

[22]Dani Rodik, *Has Globalization Gone Too Far?* (Washington, DC: Institute for International Economics, 1997).

[23]Rawi Abdelal and Adam Segal, "Has Globalization Passed Its Peak?" *Foreign Affairs,* January/February, 2007, p. 103.

"The reason for rejecting most, though not all, of the charges of the critics is not that the world is perfect, but that it would be worse if they had their way. They would throw away half a century of progress in reconstructing a liberal international economic order."[24] Jagdish Bhagwati, a professor at Columbia University, in his book *In Defense of Globalization*, says globalization may need a few changes to smooth out some of its rough edges but it is the most powerful force today for social good.[25]

EXPANDING TRADE AGREEMENTS

free trade agreement
A treaty in which two or more nations agree to reduce or eliminate barriers, opening their borders to freer mutual trade.

A rapid increase in the number of trade agreements has been a major force in globalization. By 2007 there were more than 5,500 preferential trade agreements, including 241 *free trade agreements* in which two or more nations agree to reduce or eliminate barriers, opening their borders to freer mutual trade. These agreements, which are being negotiated with greater frequency, increase global competition and accelerate world trade. Nearly all countries are partners in at least one trading club. The United States, for example, participates in free trade agreements with 15 nations (see the box). Eleven of these have been implemented since 2000.

United States Free Trade Agreements

The official position of the United States is advocacy of free trade. It supports the opening of country, regional, and global markets. In 2008 it was a participant in free trade agreements with the following nations. Trade with these nations accounted for 43 percent of U.S. exports in 2006. Agreements with four other nations—Peru, Panama, Colombia, and South Korea—are pending.

- Australia
- Bahrain
- Central America Free Trade Agreement
  Dominican Republic
  El Salvador
  Guatemala
  Honduras
  Nicaragua
- Chile
- Israel
- Jordan
- Morocco
- North American Free Trade agreement (NAFTA)
  Canada
  Mexico
- Oman
- Singapore

Source: Office of the United States Trade Representative.

[24]Martin Wolf, *Why Globalization Works* (New Haven and London: The Yale University Press, 2005), p. 11.
[25]Jagdish Bhagwati, *In Defense of Globalization* (New York: Oxford University Press, 2004).

Most preferential trade agreements are bilateral, but some cover massive economic and population blocks. We will discuss two of these—the European Union (EU) and the North American Free Trade Agreement (NAFTA).

The European Union (EU)

On March 25, 1957, six European countries—France, West Germany, Italy, Luxembourg, Belgium, and the Netherlands—signed a treaty to establish the European Economic Community. The fundamental objective of this organization was to prevent a recurrence of Europe's devastating wars such as World War I and World War II. In 1993 this initial grouping was transformed into the European Union (EU). Many national laws and policies affecting trade were annulled and replaced with hundreds of new rules and regulations concerning such matters as health, the environment, competition, national security, and product quality standards. A milestone was reached in 1999 when the EU adopted a uniform currency, the euro. By 2008 there were 27 member states, as shown in Figure 12.2, with a total population of 490 million and a GDP of $15.7 trillion. By both measures, the EU is larger than the United States with its 301 million people and GDP of $13 trillion.

The achievements of the EU have far exceeded the expectations of the six original members. Besides establishing a union of nations that could reduce the likelihood of major wars, the 50th anniversary in 2007 looked back on significant successes in the most important areas of national interests. In mind is substantial economic growth for many nations, the removal of trade and human movement barriers among the member nations, financial stability of the union, and the development of standard rules that promote national integration. A milestone was reached in 2004 when the leaders of the 25 nations then in the union signed a 50-article EU constitution in Rome, in the meeting hall where the forerunner of the EU was formed 47 years before. The old constitution was comfortable for the original 6 nations but not for the 27 current members.

In recent years the EU economy has been sluggish. Its reinvigoration will require major reforms to make labor markets more flexible, trim too generous welfare payments, resolve difficult immigration policies, and stimulate industrial competition among the member nation states.[26]

Charles A. Kupchan, professor of International Affairs at Georgetown University, an observer of the EU, has identified major forces undermining the EU's foundations. First, he says, the member states are "squeezed from above by the pressures of competitive markets and from below by an electorate clinging to the comforts of the past and fearful of the future."[27] Second, "a combination of the EU's enlargement and the influx of Muslim immigrants has diluted traditional European identities and created new social cleavages."[28] Third, the populations of the member nations are becoming increasingly self-centered and concerned more about their interests than those of the EU community. And fourth, the EU lacks the kind of strong leadership needed to reinvigorate the union.

[26] "Fit at 50," *The Economist,* March 17, 2007, p. 13.
[27] Charles A. Kupchan, "Europe Turns Back the Clock," *Los Angeles Times,* May 30, 2006, p. B13.
[28] Ibid.

FIGURE 12.2   The European Union

Source: http://www.nationsonline.org/oneworld/europe_map.htm.

Hundreds of conflicting rules must be erased before the union will function harmoniously. For example, member nations are concerned about laws that allow movement of workers throughout the Union, so they are adopting measures to restrain unwanted immigration. In Sweden, for example, the Swedish Immigration Board is responsible for reviewing visa applications and will not grant a visa without a written offer of employment in Sweden. Denmark will permit entry of new workers only if they have jobs. Accounting standards differ among countries. There is no agreement on a uniform shape for electrical plugs.

Many businesses in newly joined nations face serious problems in complying with the rules and requirements found in some 80,000 pages of EU laws. Hygiene, safety, and quality standards, for example, may force some farmers out of business. Krystof Siediecki, a farmer in Poland, has followed the centuries-old farming custom of keeping his 12 pigs and 7 cows in the same building. He has always arranged for the waste of these animals to seep into the land behind his barn. Under newly applicable EU regulations he is obliged to build a septic tank for the animal waste but there is insufficient land for it. Mr. Siediecki expects to stop farming.[29]

Many individuals in the Union are unhappy. A survey published by the *Financial Times* in London reported that 44 percent of those responding said life has become worse since their nation joined the EU. Twenty percent believed bureaucracy was its defining characteristic.[30] Some observers think the EU will not succeed in completing the most-needed reforms.[31] Charles Kupchan seems cautiously optimistic in his conclusion: "Europeans must face the reality that they have reached a watershed moment. Unless they urgently revive the project of political and economic union, one of the greatest accomplishments of the twentieth century will be at risk."[32]

The North American Free Trade Agreement (NAFTA)

NAFTA includes the United States, Canada, and Mexico. The first step in its formation was taken in 1987 when the United States and Canada signed the Canada–United States Free Trade Agreement. In 1994 that agreement was extended to Mexico. By linking the United States, Canada, and Mexico, NAFTA created the world's largest trading bloc at that time. Today NAFTA unites in a single market countries with 443 million people and a combined GDP of $15.4 trillion.

A major objective of the agreement was to increase trade among the three nations. That has happened. As shown in Figure 12.3, at the beginning in 1994 exports between Mexico and the United States were approximately equal. Thereafter, exports have risen for both countries, with fastest growth for U.S. exports. On the other hand, from the very beginning U.S. exports to Canada have been less than imports and that gap has grown. As with Mexico, trade has grown for both countries. In l994 U.S. imports from Canada were $48 billion and exports were $44 billion. In 2007 U.S imports were $313 billion and exports were $249 billion.[33]

Labor unions in the United States opposed NAFTA from the beginning. They are concerned about the movement of American industry to Mexico to take advantage of the lower wages paid Mexican workers. Particularly hard hit has been the textile industry in the United States. Some analysts have concluded that while jobs

---

[29]Christopher Rhoads and Marc Champion, "As Europe Expands, New Union Faces Problems of Scale," *The Wall Street Journal,* April 29, 2004.

[30]Jeffrey Fleishman, "At 50, EU Faces an Identity Crisis," *Los Angeles Times,* March 25, 2007, p. A9.

[31]For example, Hans Geser, "Why the EU Cannot Succeed," *World Society and International Relations,* July 2000.

[32]Charles A. Kupchan, "Europe Turns Back the Clock," p. B13.

[33]U.S. Bureau of the Census, "Foreign Trade Statistics," at www.census.gov, accessed March 5, 2008.

FIGURE 12.3
U.S. Trade
with Mexico
1985–2006

Source: Bureau of
the Census.

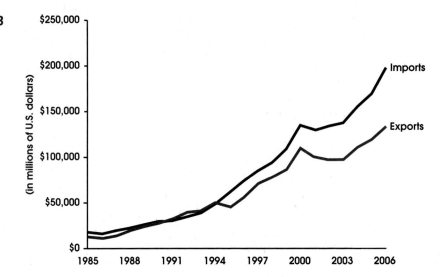

have been lost to Mexico, roughly an equal number of jobs have been created in the United States in the production of exports to Mexico. Others conclude that the net balance is more jobs lost than gained. The Carnegie Endowment for International Peace concluded that NAFTA produced a net gain of 270,000 U.S. jobs.[34] In Mexico the number of farm jobs declined from 9.5 million to 6.7 million in 2004 and continued to decline after that.[35] These are far from the optimistic numbers for job growth in the U.S. and Mexico projected by sponsors of the agreement.

However, for workers on both sides of the border there are individual losses and gains. Clearly, as U.S. companies have moved into Mexico, workers in the United States have suffered. When Green Giant and other food processing plants closed their doors in Watsonville, California, the town lost about 4,000 jobs, a serious problem for the community.[36] In Mexico hundreds of farm workers have been forced to seek jobs in the United States. Francisco Herrera Sanchez has a small grocery store in Tlachinola. The meager receipts of his store, he says, reflect a major decline in the local farm worker labor force. "The riches are up there," he says referring to the United States. "Here there is nothing, not even music. Just silence, like a dead man hanging." Sanchez lamented that "something is wrong."[37] The reason, which he did not understand, is that NAFTA accelerated an existing exodus of farm workers, many to the United States, and the treaty opened wide Mexican markets to subsidized U.S. farm products, such as corn.

Other important problems in the operation of NAFTA have arisen. One concerns trucking. The treaty specifies that Mexican trucks will have free access to

---

[34]Cited in Business Roundtable, *NAFTA: A Decade of Growth* (Washington DC: Business Roundtable, February 2004), p. 2.

[35]Mala Dickerson, "Placing Blame for Mexico's Ills," *Los Angeles Times,* July 1, 2006, p. C1.

[36]Evelyn Iritani, "U.S. Reaps Bittersweet Fruit of Merger," *Los Angeles Times,* January 19, 2004, p. A1.

[37]Marla Dickerson, "Placing Blame for Mexico's Ills," *Los Angeles Times,* July 1, 2006, p. C1.

American markets, but from the beginning there have been restrictions put on the movement of these trucks in the United States. Some justifications advanced for restrictions are that Mexican companies operate below U.S. safety standards, have poor safety records, and do not test drivers for drugs and alcohol. To settle this issue the U.S. Department of Transportation issued rules allowing Mexican truckers to begin operating in the United States. However, activists, unions, and trucking companies blocked them, arguing that U.S. environmental laws require the government to determine the health impact posed by these trucks before they begin operating on American highways.

A federal court examined the questions posed by the opposition, ruling that the government violated federal environmental laws when it issued rules that allowed Mexican carriers to haul cargo throughout the lower United States.[38] The case was appealed and the Supreme Court ruled unanimously in 2004 that the government could open U.S. highways to Mexican trucks without first doing an environmental study.[39] Despite bitter opposition, the Department of Transportation launched a pilot program allowing about 100 Mexican trucking companies full access to American highways.[40]

Assessments of NAFTA are polarized. Global Trade Watch, a division of Ralph Nader's Public Citizen watchdog group, prepared an early "report card" to assess the performance of NAFTA in a number of areas, such as job creation, agriculture, environment, public health, wage levels, and others. It stated that "on each of the issues examined, the only fair grade for NAFTA is a failing one."[41] The group reassessed NAFTA on its 10th anniversary in 2004. Once again, NAFTA flunked. Its analysis blamed NAFTA for "over 1.5 million Mexican farm livelihoods destroyed," a 20 percent decline in wages for Mexico's manufacturing workers, loss of more than 9 million jobs, stagnating blue-collar wages in the United States, and inflationary food prices in all three nations.[42]

Not surprisingly, however, an evaluation by the Business Roundtable, a group of CEOs representing some of the largest MNCs, is positive. Its evaluation, in brief, is as follows: "As expected NAFTA has had a net positive impact on U.S. output of goods and services. . . . As expected NAFTA has increased U.S. exports to Canada and Mexico. . . . As expected NAFTA has not appreciably increased U.S. imports from Canada and Mexico. . . . As expected, NAFTA's impact on employment has been positive."[43]

---

[38]*Public Citizen v. Department of Transportation*, 316 F.3d 1002 (2003).

[39]*Public Citizen v. Department of Transportation*, 124 S.Ct. 2204 (2004).

[40]Sean Lengell, "Mexican Trucks to Enter U.S. Soon Despite Strong Resistance," *The Washington Times*, September 7, 2007, p. A3.

[41]Public Citizen Global Trade Watch, *Report Card*, December 1998, www.citizen.org/ptrade/nafta/reports/5Years.htm.

[42]Public Citizen, *NAFTA at Ten Series*, 2004 at www.citizen.org/publications, "The Mexican Economy, Agriculture and Environment," p. 1; "U. S. Workers' Jobs, Wages and Economic Security," pp. 2–3; and "U.S., Mexican and Canadian Farmers and Agriculture," p. 1, 2004

[43]Business Roundtable, *NAFTA: A Decade of Growth* (Washington DC: Business Roundtable, February 2004), pp. 20–21.

Other Trade Agreements

The world is honeycombed with special trade agreements ranging from the largest, such as the EU, to arrangements between only two countries, such as between Mexico and Israel or between Chile and Korea. None are as large and structured as the EU and NAFTA. There are a few others of note and some of promise. Mercado Comun del Sur (Mercosure), for example, is an agreement negotiated in 1991 among Argentina, Brazil, Paraguay, and Uruguay. It was later joined by Chile and Bolivia. It is South America's largest trade bloc. In the 1990s it stimulated economic growth but creeping economic barriers and bickering among the members have prevented it from becoming a strong union.

The Asia–Pacific Economic Cooperation (APEC) group was formed in 1989. Today it has 21 members, including the United States, China, and Japan. Included also are rich Singapore and repressive Burma.[44] It is so beset with controversy that one commentator calls it "a tangled bowl of noodles." The organization is primarily a forum for the discussion of many political and social problems in the area, apart from trade.

The Association of South East Asian Nations (ASEAN) was formed in 1967 by five countries—the Philippines, Indonesia, Malaysia, Singapore, and Thailand. It has 34 countries today. The basic aims of the founders were acceleration of economic growth, social progress, cultural development among its members, and the promotion of regional peace. Many organizations and activities have developed under the umbrella of ASEAN, such as the ASEAN Students Exchange Programme and the ASEAN Work Programme on HIV/AIDS.[45]

GLOBALIZATION AND THE EROSION OF STATE SOVEREIGNTY

Some believe that forces of globalization substantially erode the sovereignty of nations. Others do not think so. How is this difference explained?

Part of the answer depends on what is meant by sovereignty. Sovereignty is a complex abstraction. It can refer to the ability of a state to control economic activities within and across its borders. It may also refer to the ultimate possession of political authority. Also, one's view of this question depends on the size and power of a specific country. So, the simplistic answer to the question is "it depends."[46]

Nation-State Sovereignty Has Been Eroded

Many observers see substantial erosion. For example, Kenichi Ohmae, a Japanese management consultant, believes we are witnessing the end of the nation-state.[47] He, and other members of this school of thought, argue that governments have

---

[44]Alan Beattie, "A Complex Curse: East Asia Exposes the Limits of the Regional World Trade," *Financial Times,* November 13, 2006.

[45]Kofi Annan, "Overview: Association of Southeast Asian Nations," Association of Southeast Asian Nations, February 16, 2000, p. 3.

[46]For an excellent analysis see Stephen D. Cohen, *Multinational Corporations and Foreign Direct Investment* (New York: Oxford University Press, 2007), pp. 233–44.

[47]Kenichi Ohmae, *The End of the Nation State* (New York: Free Press, 1995).

lost their traditional role because market forces overwhelm the economic powers of nation-states to determine economic, political, cultural, and social affairs.[48] This is inevitable, they say, as globalization expands.[49]

There are many examples of governments yielding traditional powers to newly powerful market forces. As noted, many European governments have been willing, indeed eager, to join the EU and waive their economic powers. Many free trade agreements also bind members to decisions that override domestic rules and regulations. Participation in multilateral organizations such as the World Trade Organization and the International Monetary Fund also brings restrictions of sovereign powers. Many developing countries yield to the investment potential of large MNCs and grant them concessions on taxes, environmental regulations, and labor laws. MNCs flex their economic muscle around the world. So much so that at least one observer concludes that "[t]he ability of sovereign nations to control the behavior and impact of MNCs increasingly is in doubt."[50]

Global market forces clearly have eroded nation-state sovereignty. A good example is the financial crisis of the 1990s in Southeast Asia in which governments felt helpless to prevent the wreckage created by abrupt and voluminous capital withdrawals. To make their industries competitive in global markets, governments must attract capital and technology. This cannot be done, they know, if too much restraint is placed on the free flow of money. The competitiveness imperative amounts to an infringement on state authority.

Nation-State Sovereignty Has Not Been Seriously Eroded

Opposed to the above beliefs are those who acknowledge that some government power has been yielded to cross-border market forces, but not much. All nations, small and large, have the authority and power to block the entrance of a subsidiary of a large global company into their country or to deny demands of an MNC for concessions. A good example is the EU's rejection of a proposed merger between General Electric and Honeywell, two powerful MNCs. Although the U.S. Department of Justice approved the merger, the two global giants had to accept the EU decision or not do business in the EU. Small and economically distressed countries, desperate for foreign investments, are more inclined to modify laws and regulations to meet foreign investor's demands. On the other hand, both developed and developing countries can force foreign investors to comply with their demands. It depends on how eager a foreign investor is to do business in their country. For example, as a price for China's purchase of airplanes it can demand some technology transfer.

In Sum

Robert Gilpin, an emeritus professor at Princeton University, points out that "despite the significance of globalization, it has not replaced the state, national

---

[48] Others in this school are Walter B. Wriston, *The Twilight of Sovereignty: How the Information Revolution Is Transforming Our World* (New York: Scribners, 1992); and Susan Strange, *The Retreat of the State: The Diffusion of Power in the World Economy* (Cambridge, UK: Cambridge University Press, 1996).

[49]Thomas L. Friedman *The Lexus and the Olive Tree: Understanding Globalization*.

[50]Stephen D. Cohen, *Multinational Corporations and Foreign Direct Investment, p. 238.*

differences, and politics as the really important determinants of domestic and international affairs."[51] There has been some erosion of national sovereignty among nations. In small, impoverished countries it has been significant and often welcomed. In the large wealthy countries it has been generally accepted as part of globalization. On the whole, says Stephen Cohen, "[t]he idea of a serious diminution of sovereignty caused specifically by multinationals is a hard sell."[52]

EROSION OF CULTURES

culture
A system of shared knowledge, values, norms, customs, and rituals acquired by social learning.

Officials from 19 countries met in Ottawa, Canada, in 1998 to discuss the growing impact throughout the world of U.S.-produced movies, television shows, music, and other entertainment. Their purpose was to decide what to do to protect their cultures from this infusion of American values. In Canada, for instance, the vast majority of movies, CDs, books, and magazines are American and the bulk of Internet content is U.S.-generated. "Market forces, left to their own devices," said Sheila Copps, the minister of Canadian heritage, "would have made the entire Canadian broadcasting system a U.S. subsidiary,"[53] This raises a question. Is the issue the alteration of *culture* or commercial self-interest?

The rapid, global spread of American culture is one significant trend within globalization. American music, movies, and television are so enjoyed and desired that they find their way to even the most remote regions. They influence the tastes, lives, and aspirations of people in virtually every nation. American consumer product brands such as Coca-Cola, Levi's, Marlboro, McDonald's, and KFC command a price premium over local brands. Teenagers everywhere wear baseball caps of American teams. American Internet content is available wherever computers are found. All this is conveyed in English, a language used universally.

Yet, throughout the world there is resentment about the transmission of certain Western cultural values. The French for years have sought to reject the entry of English words and phrases into their language. Members of the French Académie Français cringe at the use by the general population of such expressions as *le hotdog.* The French government identified 3,000 English words that should be expunged from their language. It did not happen. Many nations—for example, France, Canada, China, and Singapore—have passed laws designed to control and prevent the dissemination of American culture. As one observer notes, "These governments are the heirs of King Canute, the infamous monarch who set his throne at the sea's edge and commanded the waves to go backward."[54]

While governments are seriously concerned about the influence of American culture on their populations, their peoples express positive attitudes about the

[51]Robert Gilpin, *The Challenge of Global Capitalism* (Princeton, NJ: Princeton University Press, 2000), p. 312.
[52]Stephen D. Cohen, *Multinational Corporations and Foreign Direct Investment,* p. 249.
[53]Roger Ricklefs, "Canada Fights to Fend off American Tastes and Tunes," *The Wall Street Journal,* September 24, 1998, p. B1.
[54]David Rothkopf, quoted in Robert Gilpin, "In Praise of Cultural Imperialism? Effects of Globalization on Culture," *Foreign Policy,* June 22, 1997, p. 38.

matter. Majorities of people in European countries enjoy American music, television, films, and consumer brands but dislike the spread of American ideas. Middle Eastern populations seem to dislike American ideas, music, and televison, but do favor American technology.[55]

There is much ambivalence about the impact of U.S. cultural exports on other cultures. Around the world, shrill rhetoric from activists and intellectuals damn the United States, while ordinary people flock to see the violence and sexuality in American-made films. French critics blast McDonald's for the "pernicious" impact of its fast-food philosophy on the country's traditional leisurely way of eating, while French citizens, indifferent to the menace, fill its restaurants.

Entertainment and the sale of American consumer products are not the only forces spreading new cultural values around the world. Economic forces of globalization have encouraged massive migration of peoples. In Germany, for example, the demand for workers brought a long influx of Turkish workers who, of course, brought with them their culture, some aspects of which infiltrated into German society. In the United States recent Latin American immigrants have influenced American language and music. Throughout the world, globalization has stirred migrations of workers, leading to the diffusion of ethnic, religious, and cultural values.

A major question, is how much does the spread of cultures around the world really changes the core values of peoples? This was addressed by Samuel P. Huntington in his seminal book on civilizations.[56] He points out that much cultural diffusion is faddish and does not alter underling values. There are core cultural values in societies that are not easily changed. For example, he says, use of the English language in the world is more a convenient means of intercultural communication than a force to change core values.

There seems little doubt that globalization has significantly influenced the flow of values. Some forces, such as technological innovations (e.g., computers, biotechnology, and pharmaceuticals), may have more lasting impact. However, it is difficult to reject the thesis of Huntington and others that the core cultures of peoples are not easily and significantly changed.

FREE TRADE VERSUS PROTECTIONISM

free trade
The flow of goods and services across borders unhindered by government-imposed restrictions such as taxes, tariffs, quotas, and rules.

Free trade, or the flow of goods and services over borders unhindered by government-imposed restrictions, has been the official policy of the United States throughout most of its history. In practice, however, there have always been significant deviations from that policy. In recent years, the United States has taken the lead in creating international agencies to advance free trade among nations. At the same time, protectionist pressures have increased in the United States and in most other nations. Why free trade? Why protectionism?

[55]Robert Kunzig, "French Kiss-Off," *U.S. News & World Report,* December 16, 2002, p. 42.

[56]Samuel P. Huntington, *The Clash of Civilizations and the Remaking of World Order,* (New York: Simon & Schuster, 1996.).

Why Free Trade?

The case for free trade is comparatively simple. By virtue of climate, labor conditions, raw materials, capital, management, or other considerations, some nations have an advantage over others in the production of particular goods. For example, Brazil can produce coffee beans at a much lower cost than the United States. Coffee beans could be grown in hothouses in the United States, but not at a price equal to that which Brazilians can charge and make a profit. But the United States has a distinct advantage over Brazil in producing pharmaceuticals. Resources will be used most efficiently when each country produces that for which it enjoys a cost advantage. Gain will be maximized when each nation specializes in producing those products for which it has the greatest economic edge. This is what economists call the *law of comparative advantage.* It follows that maximum gain on a worldwide basis will be realized if there are no impediments to trade, if there is free competition in pricing, and if capital flows are unrestricted.

It is not always easy, however, to see just where a nation has a comparative advantage. At the extremes the case is clear, but not in the middle range. Differences in monetary units, rates of productivity of capital and labor, changes in markets, or elasticities of demand, for instance, obscure the degree of advantage one nation may have over another at any time. Nevertheless, it is argued that free trade will stimulate competition, reward individual initiative, increase productivity, and improve national well-being. It will enlarge job opportunities and produce for consumers a wider variety of goods and services at minimum prices and with higher quality.

This is the theory. In practice, all countries have set up restraints on imports to protect their industries. What are the main pressures for and against free trade?

law of comparative advantage
Efficiency and the general economic welfare are optimized when each country produces that for which it enjoys a cost advantage.

Pressures for Protectionism

Most domestic businesses, whether engaged in foreign trade or not, feel pressures from foreign competitors with better products and lower prices. Many seek and get protection from the government. This is *protectionism*, and it exists in the trade history of all nations. In the United States three major justifications are often given for protectionist measures.

First, the United States has large trade deficits that must be reduced. In 1975 the United States enjoyed a small trade surplus (the difference between total exports and total imports of goods and services). Since then have been growing. The deficit for 2007 was $712 billion. The largest trade deficit with any country was with China at $256 billion. This was almost three times the deficit with Japan of $83 billion. The next largest was with Canada at $64 billion. Protectionists are concerned about the persistence and size of the deficits, believing they are detrimental and should be eliminated. One way they assert, is to discourage excessive imports and encourage exports.

Second, protectionists want to shield industries from foreign competition. For example, foreign competitors have penetrated the U.S. market with products such as textiles, steel, shoes, motorcycles, dolls, luggage, automobiles, and television sets. A significant result, say protectionists, is loss of jobs. The sting of global competition is not always constructive and healthy for the nation.

protectionism
The doctrine that government should protect business interests from foreign competitors.

Third, trade barriers in foreign countries restrict American imports to them. These barriers also cost Americans jobs. If nations refuse to remove them then the United States should retaliate.

The Politics of Protectionism

Protectionism is not solely an economic issue. There is a significant political dimension. For example, President George W. Bush made expanding free trade is one of his highest priorities. In a speech before the Council of the Americas, he said: "When we negotiate for open markets we are providing new hope for the world's poor . . . and when we promote open trade we are promoting political freedom."[57]

Why then did he support substantial restrictions on imports of steel in his first major trade initiative? His staff explained that the decision followed a thorough examination of the problems of the steel industry and help was justified. For example, the industry today employs one-fifth the number of steelworkers it did in 1980, production has slumped, steel mills have closed, and the financial strength of the industry has declined. This is a result, the industry claims, of lower-priced imports from many different countries. Another reason for the president's decision is that the industry and its unions have political strength. They are heavy contributors to political campaigns, and their workers' votes can spell the difference between winning or losing electoral votes in critical states, such as Pennsylvania, Ohio, and West Virginia.

Free Trade Responses to Protectionism

Free traders advance many arguments against protectionism. One main argument is the logic for free trade as explained above. Another is that a major cause of the rise in world trade is the widespread reduction in tariff barriers. Former Senator Phil Gramm argued that impediments or hindrances to free trade are "immoral." "They limit my freedom," he said. "If I want to buy a shirt in China, who has the right to tell me as a free person that I can't do it?"[58] Antiprotectionists are fond of quoting John Stuart Mill, a famous nineteenth-century economist and philosopher who reportedly said, "Trade barriers are chiefly injurious to the countries imposing them."[59]

Joseph Stiglitz and Andrew Charlton, in their book *Fair Trade for All,* conclude that rich countries should reduce tariff barriers and poor ones should be allowed to maintain them until reduction is comfortable.[60] They argue that the underdeveloped countries do not have the infrastructure and institutions to open their markets to free trade. In developing countries the transportation systems are often

---

[57] Reported by Joseph Kahn, "Bush Moves against Steel Imports: Trade Tensions Are Likely to Rise, *The New York Times,* June 6, 2001, p. 1.

[58] Quoted in Gerald F. Seib and John Harwood "Disparate Groups on Right Join Forces to Make Opposition to China's Trade Status a Key Issue," *The Wall Street Journal,* June 10, 1997, p. A20.

[59] John Stuart Mill, *Essays on Some Unsettled Questions of Political Economy,* 2d ed. (New York: Augustus M. Kelley, 1968), p. 38. Originally published in 1874.

[60] Joseph E. Stiglitz and Andrew Charlton, *Fair Trade for All* (New York: Oxford University Press, 2005).

primitive, the banking institutions are fragile, the educational systems are elementary, and there is substantial unemployment. In brief, they are unable to take advantage of a world of free trade. Each country, therefore, should be allowed to move to free trade on a timetable suitable to its situation. Furthermore, the richer nations should help the poorer nations strengthen their institutions so they can move gradually to open markets.

Unfortunately, this is more theory than reality. The stumbling block is political. Trade ministers of developed countries say in private, "Our congresses and parliaments have tied our hands. We cannot tame the special interests. We live in democracies, and that is part of the price one has to pay for democracy . . . [T]he democracies of the developing countries replied: 'We too live in democracies. Our democracies are demanding that we sign a fair trade agreement. If we return with another agreement as unfair . . . we will be voted out of office. We too have no choice.'"[61] Agricultural issues have traditionally been the major impediment to trade agreements. Less developed countries want Western nations to remove their subsidies to agriculture. They want to maintain their tariffs on foreign agricultural products to protect their farmers. For political reasons both sides are inflexible.

U.S. Deviation from Free Trade Policy

Despite strong free trade rhetoric and the steady lowering of tariff and other trade barriers, the United States protects industries from foreign competition. Over the years, it has raised tariffs, imposed quotas, and prohibited the import of various products. There are hundreds of examples of deviation from free trade theory and policy that have added to the crazy quilt of world trade impediments. Here are some examples.

"buy American" laws
Laws that require or seek to influence governments and agencies to purchase U.S.-made goods and services rather than foreign-made goods and services.

Trade records are marbled with *"buy American" laws.* The Federal Buy American Act of 1933, still in force, requires federal agencies to pay up to a 6 percent differential for domestically produced goods. Many states have similar laws covering a wide range of products. The Merchant Marine Act prohibits foreign vessels from plying domestic waterways. The Passenger Vessel Services Act requires ships going from one U.S. port to another to be U.S. flagged, U.S. built, and U.S. crewed.

U.S. tariffs have declined significantly in recent years, but there are many exceptions. For example, we have high tariffs on imports of sugar, peanuts, certain types of glassware, textiles, motorcycles, and steel. At the same time, we have given duty-free status to hundreds of products to foster economic development for many LDCs by increasing their trade with the United States. While the total value of products involved is not great in terms of total U.S. trade, it can be very important to developing countries.

Tariff Barriers in Other Countries

Despite the benefits of free trade, all nations have some trade barriers. There is no doubt that tariffs levied on imported products have generally been cut, especially in the developed countries, but nontariff barriers have increased. Examples of

---

[61] Ibid, pp. vi–vii.

nontariff barriers are excessive delays in inspections of imported products; unreasonable technical standards for product characteristics, such as size, quality, health, and safety; practices that inhibit consumer purchases of foreign goods and services; and quotas. Such barriers are illustrated by the following.

China has reformed its trade practices to meet the standards of the World Trade Organization, which it joined, but it still imposes substantial barriers. It has quotas on imports of many products such as watches, automobiles, steel, textiles, wheat, corn, rice, cotton, and vegetable oils. Ineffective enforcement of intellectual property rights is a major trade problem with China. The EU bans U.S. beef and livestock treated with hormones, poultry treated to reduce bacterial risks, and genetically engineered products. Japan restricts U.S. imports of meat, poultry, vegetables, and fruit products. Rice imports are virtually banned. Taiwan also restricts imports of rice. Korea imposes high duties and maintains a variety of nontariff barriers on agricultural and fishery products. India maintains a broad range of trade restrictions. While NAFTA has led to a doubling of U.S. exports to Mexico, that country retains substantial trade restrictions on products such as meat, poultry, vegetables, and fruits. Brazil imposes high tariffs on information technology products that double the costs of personal computers. Brazil also virtually prohibits importation of many products, including automobiles.[62]

Classical Free Trade versus Reality

The reality is that the global economy is a mixture of free trade and protectionism. It always has been. Furthermore, classical free trade theory based on comparative advantage has lost much validity for a large part of world trade. Many of the assumptions of the seventeenth and eighteenth centuries, upon which the theory is based, no longer are valid in today's world.

competitive advantage of nations
A phrase coined by Professor Michael Porter identifying a nation as having a cluster of similar producers which gives the nation a special advantage over other countries.

Professor Michael Porter of the Harvard Business School has formulated a major modification of classical theory to fit the modern world. He calls it *competitive advantage of nations*. Porter asks: Why does a nation achieve global superiority in one industry? He answers that it is because "industrial clusters" are formed in the nation. These clusters are composed of firms and industries that are mutually supporting, innovative, competitive, low-cost producers, and committed to meeting demanding consumer tastes.

Why is it, he asks, that Switzerland, a landlocked country with few natural resources, is a world leader in the production of chocolates? Why is Italy a world leader in producing quality shoes? Why is Japan, a country whose economy was in shambles after World War II, a global leader in making low-cost, mass-produced, good quality high-technology products?

Porter's answer lies in a congeries of factors that go beyond natural resources. Among the factors are a sizable demand from sophisticated consumers, an educated and skilled workforce, intense competition in the industry, and the existence of related and supporting suppliers. Government plays a part, but not a major

---

[62] These illustrations are taken principally from "2003 Inventory of Trade Barriers," *USTR Releases* (Washington, DC U.S. Trade Representative, April 1, 2003).

one. Porter's theory is convincingly and amply illustrated in a major research project on the subject.[63] Classical theory is still valid for many products. Porter's work modernizes it to better fit the current reality of trade among nations in a broad range of products.

CORRUPTION

According to Water Kaegi, a history professor at the University of Chicago, corrupt officials in Byzantium in the eleventh century, were blinded and castrated.[64] In some ancient countries, in the early Roman republic for instance, the death penalty was imposed on judges who accepted bribes.[65] The death penalty, although rare in today's world, is not unknown. For example, Zheng Xiaoyu, head of China's version of the U.S. Food and Drug Administration, was executed in 2007 for accepting bribes valued at more than $850,000.[66]

Cultural differences, practices, and laws among the many countries where MNCs do business create extremely difficult moral, ethical, and legal problems. The way in which business is conducted around the world sometimes entangles U.S. companies in a complex web of influence, politics, customs, and subtle business arrangements. Companies have found in many LDCs, and even in some highly industrialized countries, that to do business it is necessary to make a variety of payments. This is not new.

What Is Corruption?

corruption
The debasement of integrity for money, position, privilege, or other self-benefit. It undermines markets by substituting bribery for honest competition based on price, quality, and service.

There is no consensus about a definition of *corruption;* there is more agreement about types of corruption. At one end of a possible spectrum is what might be called petty corruption or "grease" payments. These are bribes involving small amounts of money made to facilitate action by a low-level employee. They range from tips for services rendered to "requests" for money to get someone to do their regular duties, such as unloading articles off ships or clearing incoming products through customs. These small bribes are often called "lubrication bribes," "honest graft," "tokens of appreciation," "contributions," and so on. The practice is widely accepted around the world as legitimate for services rendered. These payments are often justified as offsets to low salaries. At the other end of the spectrum are extortion and outrageous bribery.

Between the extremes the lines of demarcation for distinguishing the probably acceptable and legitimate from the clearly unethical are not always clear. Suppose, for example, the normal practice in a country is for an import expediter to charge a moderate commission for services. However, the person involved not only charges a somewhat higher than customary fee, but also has close ties to a government

---

[63] Michael E. Porter, *The Comparative Advantage of Nations* (New York: Free Press, 1990).

[64] Quoted in Nelson D. Schwartz, "Bribes and Punishment," *The New York Times,* July 15, 2007, p. WK14.

[65] Ibid.

[66] David Barboza, "A Chinese Reformer Betrays His Cause, and Pays," *The New York Times,* July 13, 2007, p. A8.

agency buying the imported item. When is the payment "normal," and when does it become tainted with bribery? Paying a tax collector to reduce a company's tax load would be a clear example of bribery. Expensive jewelry given to an official's spouse would be considered bribery if the official could grant important favors to the giver. Paid vacations and free air travel, lavish entertainment, and, of course, cash given to a high political official would be forms of bribery.

offsets
Actions taken by a foreign corporation, at the recommendation of the government purchaser, to spend substantial sums of money to produce a good or service in exchange for the purchase.

A different problem in identification of bribery is *offsets*, which have become popular in the international arms trade. For example, in exchange for purchasing military hardware from Boeing, Northrop Grumman, and Lockheed Martin, the United Arab Emirates pressed the contractors to spend millions of dollars on a variety of activities to create jobs and improve the well-being of its population. These companies financed medical centers, built a shipyard, helped to clean up oil spills, and started a laser-printer recycling business. U.S. arms makers have helped the Dutch to export yarn and missile parts. Offsets can be part of an agreement to bring investment to a country. Contractors dislike offsets but they are essential for doing business in many countries.[67]

Costs and Consequences of Corruption

The dollar costs of "tips" for services rendered are usually small compared with the value of products involved. Such gratuities are readily accepted as routine. Bribes, however, can be very expensive. Foregoing bribery can also can be costly in terms of business lost to competitors. One study concluded that 43 percent of 350 MNCs based in seven countries said they failed to win new business in the last five years because a competitor had paid a bribe. In five of the countries studied respondents said there had been a noticeable increase in companies believing they lost business to bribery in the previous five years.[68]

Beyond individual company losses to competitors who bribe there are larger and more significant costs to corruption. For example, it undermines efforts to fight poverty. The United Nations describes an expansive range of additional costs.

> Corruption undermines democratic institutions, retards economic development and contributes to government instability. Corruption attacks the foundation of democratic institutions by distorting electoral processes, perverting the rule of laws, and creating bureaucratic quagmires whose only reason for existence is the soliciting of bribes. Economic development is stunted because outside direct investment is discouraged and small businesses within the country often find it impossible to overcome the "start-up costs" required because of corruption.[69]

Corruption varies significantly among countries. Every year Transparency International (TI), a civil society organization formed to fight worldwide corruption,

---

[67] "Offsets in Defense Trade and the U.S. Subcontractor Base," Department of Commerce, Bureau of Industry and Security, Office of Strategic Industries and Economic Security, August 2004, p. iii.

[68] Control Risks Group Limited and Simmons & Simmons, "International Business Attitudes to Corruption—Survey 2006," Amsterdam and Abu Dhabi, 2007.

[69] United Nations Office on Drugs and Crime, "UNODC and Corruption," at www.unodc.org/unodc/en/corruption/under.html, July l, 2007.

FIGURE 12.4
Transparency International's Indexes of Corruption

Source: Reprinted from Transparency International's Indexes of Corruption. Copyright © 2007 Transparency International: *The Global Coalition Against Corruption.* Used with permission. For more information, visit http://www. transparency.org.

The Corruption Perceptions Index: 2007		The Bribe Payers Index: 2006	
Top 10	Bottom 10	Top 10	Bottom 10
1. Denmark	172. Afghanistan	1. Switzerland	21. South Korea
1. Finland	172. Chad	2. Sweden	22. Saudi Arabia
1. New Zealand	172. Sudan	3. Australia	23. Brazil
4. Singapore	175. Tonga	4. Austria	24. South Africa
4. Sweden	175. Uzbekistan	5. Canada	25. Malaysia
6. Iceland	177. Haiti	6. UK	26. Taiwan
7. Netherlands	178. Iraq	7. Germany	27. Turkey
7. Switzerland	179. Myanmar	8. Netherlands	28. Russia
9. Canada	179. Somalia	9. Belgium	29. China
9. Norway	186. Laos	9. United States	30. India

publishes indexes of corruption. Figure 12.4 shows two of its rankings. The table on the left ranks the most and least corrupt countries in the world. It is based on surveys that assess the perceptions of experts. The United States ranked 20th on this index. The table on the right shows the top 10 and bottom 10 countries in Transparency International's most recent index of bribe paying by corporations in exporting countries. This index is based on a survey of thousands of business people in 125 countries. Although the most developed nations rank at the top, Transparency International believes that their firms "still routinely pay bribes."[70]

An examination of national rankings on both indexes suggests that there is less corruption in developed countries than in underdeveloped ones, a conclusion that corroborates the point that corruption inhibits economic growth. A related observation is that corruption is strongly associated with poverty. "Corruption," as former UN Secretary-General Kofi Annan once said, "hurts the poor disproportionately by diverting funds intended for development, undermining a government's ability to provide basic services, feeding inequality and injustice, and discouraging foreign investment and aid."[71]

Business Anticorruption Practices and Procedures

A study of 165 companies by The Conference Board concluded that " . . . anticorruption practices and procedures have become significantly more widespread, detailed and sophisticated than in 2000."[72] This development reflects the growth of international treaties and codes formed to fight corruption. Very important are the UN Global Compact, the UN Convention Against Corruption, the International Chamber of Commerce Rules of Conduct to Combat Extortion and Bribery, the Transparency

[70] Transparency International, "Leading Exporters Undermine Development with Dirty Business Overseas," *Press Release,* October 4, 2006.

[71] Quoted in United Nations Office on Drugs and Crime, "UNODC and Corruption," July 1, 2007.

[72] The Conference Board, *Resisting Corruption, an Ethics and Compliance Benchmarking Survey*, Research Report R 1397-06-RR, 2007, p. 6.

International Business Principles for Countering Bribery, and the Organisation for Economic Co-operation and Development (OECD) Anti-Bribery Convention.

The Foreign Corrupt Practices Act

In the United States, the Foreign Corrupt Practices Act (FPCA) of 1977 has spurred businesses to be more concerned about corrupt practices. This statute makes it both a civil and a criminal offense to bribe an official of a foreign government or ministry, or a member of a foreign political party or candidate for office. It defines the act of bribery as making or offering to make a payment of money or anything of value with the "corrupt intent" to influence any official act or decision in favor of a company's business. In 2001 Titan Corp., a defense contractor headquartered in San Diego, ordered its agent in Benin to contribute $2 million toward the reelection of that country's president. Its intent was to get the government's consent for raising fees on a wireless telephone network it was building there.[73] After being caught, Titan paid criminal and civil penalties totaling $28.4 million, including disgorgement of illegal gains, the largest fine ever for violation of the FCPA.

The law applies to the actions of U.S. corporations anywhere in the world. Even if foreign managers or subsidiaries pay bribes without informing managers on U.S. soil, the company will still be guilty of violating the FCPA. Otherwise, U.S. managers could simply ask to be kept in purposeful ignorance. It is also illegal to pay "commissions" to foreign consultants with the knowledge that the payments will be forwarded to prohibited recipients as bribes. Dow Chemical paid a $325,000 fine when the FBI discovered that a "fifth tier"subsidiary making pesticides in India paid $39,700 for Indian regulators to speed up registration of its products and made other bribes totaling $200,000 over many years.[74]

Foreign corporations and their managers can be prosecuted if they pay bribes or take action to facilitate foreign bribes while in U.S. territory. For unlawful acts, companies can be fined up to $2 million and up to twice the pecuniary gain they derived. Individual managers face fines of up to $1 million and five years in jail. The law also prohibits falsifying books and records to conceal corruption and violators of this section can be fined up to $25 million.

The FCPA contains an exception for facilitating or "grease" payments intended only to expedite "routine governmental action."[75] This allows companies to operate in business cultures where small bribes are needed to move cargo from docks, obtain permits or licenses, connect utilities, facilitate inspections, and expedite other ordinary services. Note that in the law illegal bribes are not defined by their size, but by their purpose and the recipient. Even the smallest bribe to a government official, given with the intent to corrupt, is illegal; theoretically, a larger sum given for obtaining a minor permit could be exempt from prosecution.

Bribes paid by managers of one corporation to managers of another are not illegal under the FCPA, although they likely violate fraud statutes in most nations. However, if the bribe is given to a manager of a state-owned corporation, the recipient is

---

[73] Office of the United States Attorney, Southern District of California, untitled news release, March 1, 2005.

[74] Organisation for Economic Co-operation and Development, "Steps Taken by the United States to Implement and Enforce the Convention on Combating Bribery of Foreign Public Officials in International Business Transactions," at www.oecd.org, June 13, 2007.

[75] 15 U.S.C. §78dd-1(b), January 2, 2006.

legally a "foreign official, because employed by the government." Several executives and managers of ITXC Corp., a company that provides Internet phone calls, learned this the hard way. Over five years, between 1999 and 2004 they paid bribes totaling $266,000 to employees of state-owned telecommunications companies in three African countries to retain business. Now one of them is serving 18 months in prison and has paid a $7,500 fine. The two others await sentencing.[76]

Corporate Policies on Corruption Prevention

Most large corporations have formal policies against corrupt payments. The Conference Board found that anticorruption statements of the major corporations tend to be comparable. The table below contains the major content of anticorruption statements as found by The Conference Board. Notwithstanding the directness of these statements implementation is not without its ambiguities. The study listed the principal difficulties of implementation as follows:

• Differing cultural views about what kind of behavior constitutes corruption.
• Difficulties in monitoring agent behavior for compliance.
• Local attitudes that behavior is justified because the "the competition does it."
• Difficulty in distinguishing between locally sanctioned lavish gift practices and bribes.
• Difficulties in monitoring, contracting, and procurement.
• Operation(s) in a particular country.[77]

Anticorruption Statement Content (N = 146)	
The anticorruption statement has:	*Percent*
Precise description and labeling of corrupt practices and explanation of how they can undermine company business	55%
Discussion of structure and producers that support the company's anticorruption policy	54
Justification for universal applicability of the program	47
Clear acknowledgement that adherence to anticorruption policies may result in lost business opportunities	41
Distinctions between different kinds of corruption	40
Statement of supplier status with regard to anticorruption policy	32
Case study example of specific ethics dilemmas that typically arise in global business practice	32
Statement of joint venture partner status with regard to anticorruption policy	16
Canvas of global/regional anticorruption initiatives	12

Source: *Resisting Corruption,* The Conference Board, 2006, p. 19.

[76] Department of Justice, "Two Former Executives of ITXC Corp Plead Guilty and Former Regional Director Sentenced in Foreign Bribery Scheme," *Media Release*, July 27, 2007.

[77] The Conference Board, *Resisting Corruption, an Ethics and Compliance Benchmarking Survey,* p. 27.

The Conference Board asked respondents to name the measures that they found most effective in their anticorruption programs. Here they are in descending order of importance.

- A detailed statement of company anticorruption policies.
- A required follow-up report if questionable practices have been disclosed.
- Group sessions with local managers in which actual or potential corruption statements are discussed.
- A requirement that employees sign a statement of adherence to anticorruption policies.
- An annual requirement that country managers must report questionable practices.[78]

Despite international, national, and corporate efforts at eradication, corruption and bribery endure. In 2007 the U.S. government collected more than $100 million from corporations in foreign bribery cases.[79] Companies from EU nations continue to pay bribes and prosecution varies. Great Britain has never brought a bribery prosecution resulting in conviction. France, Japan, and Italy have only recently begun to prosecute bribery cases. Only a decade ago, they allowed their corporations to deduct foreign bribes from taxes.

CONCLUDING OBSERVATIONS

Globalization is a revolutionary phenomenon. It has created enormous wealth for people all over the world. At the same time, it has led to exploitation, dislocation, and suffering for some who have yet to experience its benefits. It has changed business–government–society relationships in profound ways. On balance, there seems to be little question that the forces of globalization are beneficial and promise rising benefits. To achieve this promise, however, important reforms are necessary.

[78] Ibid. p. 28.
[79] Carrie Johnson, "U.S. Targets Bribery Overseas," *Washington Post,* December 5, 2007, p. D1.

David and Goliath at the WTO

In 1996 Jay Cohen had a lucrative job in San Francisco trading options and derivatives. However, he wanted to start his own business and make more money. So, he and two friends set up an Internet sports betting site on the island nation of Antigua and Barbuda. The business was successful, perhaps too successful, luring Americans to bet online and provoking opponents of gambling. Prosecuted by his own country, Cohen turned to the tiny nation that embraced his business for help. Eventually, that nation challenged the United States at the World Trade Organization. To everyone's surprise, it prevailed.

We begin the story in the balmy Caribbean, about 1,300 miles to the southeast of Florida.

ANTIGUA AND BARBUDA

Antigua and Barbuda consists of two small islands. Antigua (an-TEE-ga) is the larger with 108 square miles and is more developed. Barbuda (bar-BOO-duh) is smaller with 63 square miles. The two low-lying islands of limestone and coral are separated by 25 miles of ocean. Admiral Horatio Nelson once sheltered his men-of-war in their harbors. Today, the little country has a population of 69,500 and a GDP of about $900 million.

The major industry in Antigua and Barbuda is tourism, but in 1994 the government created a free trade zone for bookmakers, allowing them to operate tax free. It expected that gambling activity would create jobs for Antiguans, who suffer from chronically high unemployment. All an online gambling company needed to set up shop was a government license that cost $100,000. The government used this revenue to fund computer training schools for native Antiguans so they could acquire skills needed to work in the online betting parlors.[1] Gambling is now second only to tourism as an employer.

JAY COHEN'S MISADVENTURE

When Jay Cohen and his partners, all American citizens, founded World Sports Exchange Ltd. (WSE), they became one of about 25 gambling businesses in Antigua that ran telephone and online betting. The major market for these businesses, including Cohen's, was bettors in the United States. WSE thrived. Customers set up accounts by making credit card payments, wiring money, or sending cashier's checks. Then they used passwords to access their accounts by telephone or online and place bets on football, basketball, baseball, soccer, and other sports. Within two years, WSE had 2,000 customers. In one 15-month period it collected approximately $5.3 million in funds wired from the United States. Its profits came from taking a 10 percent commission on each bet.

Like other gaming companies in Antigua, WSE operated with a sense of legitimacy. Since it was licensed by the government, it was open about its operations, even advertising in American sports magazines and newspapers. "People are more comfortable with us than with the illegal bookmakers," Cohen said, "They know that when they win, we pay."[2]

Meanwhile, opponents of gambling in the United States were galvanized by what they saw as brazen flaunting of U.S. laws against gambling. They thought that Internet gambling sites flourishing where the trade winds blew, would seduce teenagers, ruin compulsive gamblers, and undermine American morality. In addition, major sports leagues demanded that WSE and other offshore operators remove team names and links to official league Web sites.

Soon FBI agents started a sting operation. As part of it, an agent placed a $300 bet on a hockey game through WSE. In 1998 federal prosecutors charged 14 offshore gambling site operators with illegal use of interstate phone lines to place bets. Jay Cohen was one of them and he was shocked. "We're licensed to do what we do here by a sovereign government," he told one reporter.[3]

Cohen volunteered to return to the U.S., convinced that its laws did not apply to his business in Antigua and Barbuda and believing that common sense was on his side. He was so wrong. Federal officers arrested him on his arrival. He was charged with eight counts of violating the Wire Wager Act of 1961 (the Wire Act) part of which reads:

> Whoever being engaged in the business of betting knowingly uses a wire communication facility for the transmissions in interstate or foreign commerce of bets or wagers or information assisting in the placing of bets or wagers on any sporting event or contest, or for the transmission of a wire communication which entitles the recipient to receive money or credit as a result of bets or wagers, or for information assisting in the placing of bets or wagers, shall be fined under this title or imprisoned for more than two years, or both.[4]

Cohen argued that his business was a foreign corporation engaged in legal activities in Antigua where its headquarters was located. All business operations were conducted outside the U.S. Based on the advice

---

[1] Brett Pulley, "With Technology, Island Bookies Skirt U.S. Law," *The New York Times,* January 31, 1998, p. A1.

[2] Quoted in ibid., p. A1.

[3] Quoted in Benjamin Weiser, "*14 Facing Charges in First U.S. Action on Internet Betting,*" *The New York Times,* March 5, 1998, p. A1.

[4] 18 U.S.C. § 1084.

Jay Cohen in a 2003 photograph taken at Nellis Federal Prison Camp in Nevada. Source: Aaron Mayes/Las Vegas Sun. Photo Courtesy of Las Vegas Sun.

of an attorney he consulted, he believed he had acted in good faith. Furthermore, the statute did not apply, he thought, to the Internet which was not yet invented when it was written. Prosecutors argued that Cohen was violating the plain provisions of the Wire Act. And his license to operate in Antigua was no defense because the Wire Act made bets over phone lines illegal unless gambling was legal in both the place of origin for bets and the place of their destination. They even charged him with an additional count of aiding and abetting violations of the Wire Act because even after his arrest he did not try to stop his company's American operations and continued to receive a salary.

Cohen's arguments failed to persuade a jury, which convicted him on every count. In 2002 he was found guilty and sentenced to 21 months in jail. He wound up at a federal prison camp in the desert near Las Vegas.[5] Subsequent appeals were rejected.[6] He served 17 months at the prison camp and was released in 2004 on two years of probation.

Meanwhile, Cohen's partners continued to operate WSE.[7] Although they live in the shadow of an FBI criminal indictment, they cannot be arrested on foreign soil and Antigua refuses to extradite them.

Enjoying the clement weather and graceful beaches of their tropical headquarters, these refugees have built WSE into what its Web site describes as "one of the largest Internet sportsbooks in the world" and "the recognized leader in the online gaming industry."[8]

ENTER THE WORLD TRADE ORGANIZATION

Jay Cohen learned that the action of the United States government in his case might violate world trade rules. This knowledge led him to get Antigua and Barbuda to initiate a complaint to the World Trade Organization (WTO). Thus began what was seen at first as the fruitless struggle of a tiny Caribbean island against the world's dominant superpower.

The WTO was established in 1995 by 94 nations (now 144) to replace the treaty system of international trade that developed after World War II. The role of the WTO is to administer and extend the scheme of trade liberalization built over a 50-year period under this older system.

An important function of the WTO is to adjudicate trade disputes between nations. These disputes are handled under a set of rules and procedures that sets forth an elaborate system of stages and timetables, as shown in Exhibit 1. The first step is the consultation stage, in which members are given 60 days to resolve their dispute through discussions. If the parties cannot resolve their differences, an impartial panel of experts is formed to adjudicate the dispute. Panels are composed of three members, each an expert in the subject area of the dispute. They are chosen from lists of eligible participants and agreed upon by all parties. Panel members must act independently and may not receive instructions from their governments about the dispute.

Countries involved in a dispute can appeal a panel decision to a seven-member standing appellate body. Its members are appointed by the WTO for four-year terms. They cannot be officials of any government and must be broadly representative of the WTO membership.

[5] Paul Blustein, "Against All Odds," *Washington Post,* August 4, 2006, p. D1.

[6] *United States v. Cohen,* 260 F.3d 68 (2001).

[7] Wayne Coffey, "An Offshore Thing," *New York Daily News,* March 26, 2000.

[8] World Sports Exchange, "About Us," at http://www.wsex.com/.

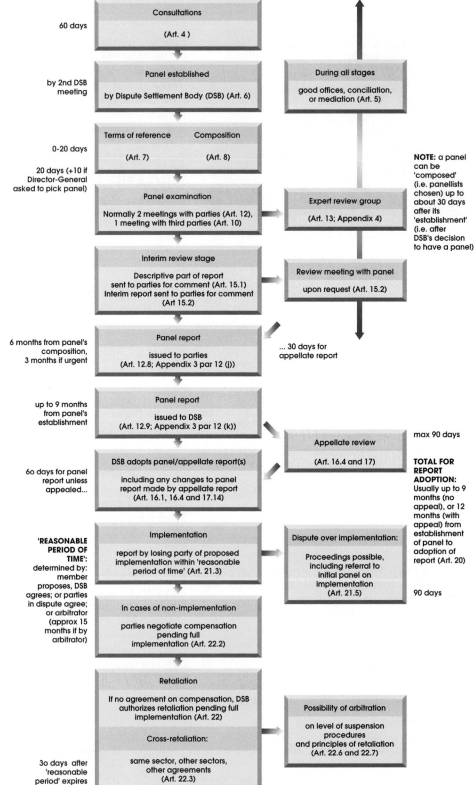

EXHIBIT 1
The WTO Dispute Settlement Process

Source: Reprinted with permission of WTO Publications.

60 days

Consultations

(Art. 4)

by 2nd DSB meeting

Panel established

by Dispute Settlement Body (DSB) (Art. 6)

During all stages

good offices, conciliation, or mediation (Art. 5)

0-20 days

Terms of reference   **Composition**

(Art. 7)   (Art. 8)

20 days (+10 if Director-General asked to pick panel)

Panel examination

Normally 2 meetings with parties (Art. 12), 1 meeting with third parties (Art. 10)

Expert review group

(Art. 13; Appendix 4)

NOTE: a panel can be 'composed' (i.e. panellists chosen) up to about 30 days after its 'establishment' (i.e. after DSB's decision to have a panel)

Interim review stage

Descriptive part of report sent to parties for comment (Art. 15.1) Interim report sent to parties for comment (Art 15.2)

Review meeting with panel

upon request (Art. 15.2)

6 months from panel's composition, 3 months if urgent

Panel report

issued to parties (Art. 12.8; Appendix 3 par 12 (j))

... 30 days for appellate report

up to 9 months from panel's establishment

Panel report

issued to DSB (Art. 12.9; Appendix 3 par 12 (k))

Appellate review

(Art. 16.4 and 17)

max 90 days

60 days for panel report unless appealed...

DSB adopts panel/appellate report(s)

including any changes to panel report made by appellate report (Art. 16.1, 16.4 and 17.14)

TOTAL FOR REPORT ADOPTION: Usually up to 9 months (no appeal), or 12 months (with appeal) from establishment of panel to adoption of report (Art. 20)

'REASONABLE PERIOD OF TIME': determined by: member proposes, DSB agrees; or parties in dispute agree; or arbitrator (approx 15 months if by arbitrator)

Implementation

report by losing party of proposed implementation within 'reasonable period of time' (Art. 21.3)

Dispute over implementation:

Proceedings possible, including referral to initial panel on implementation (Art. 21.5)

90 days

In cases of non-implementation

parties negotiate compensation pending full implementation (Art. 22.2)

Retaliation

If no agreement on compensation, DSB authorizes retaliation pending full implementation (Art. 22)

Cross-retaliation:

same sector, other sectors, other agreements (Art. 22.3)

Possibility of arbitration

on level of suspension procedures and principles of retaliation (Art. 22.6 and 22.7)

30 days after 'reasonable period' expires

THE ANTIGUA AND BARBUDA COMPLAINT

In 2003 the government of Antigua and Barbuda started the dispute process by requesting the WTO to form a dispute settlement panel. There followed a series of efforts by the two nations to settle their differences. They were unable to agree and the dispute process went on. The debate between Antigua and the U.S. flew back and forth like a shuttlecock and over time led to thousands of pages of documents in which lawyers on both sides argued fine nuances and different interpretations of laws.

Antigua said the U.S. took " . . . the unequivocal position that the provision of gambling and betting services by operators in Antigua to persons in the U.S. is illegal and in all instances violated United States law. The U.S. had further adopted a series of federal and state measures and taken actions to prevent operators in Antigua from offering these services to persons in the U.S. (including imprisonment of at least one person related to an Antiguan service supplier)."[9] This violated a commitment of the United States in a treaty named the General Agreement on Trade in Services (GATS), which was ratified by all WTO nations in 1995. GATS commits the United States to open its borders to trade in a wide range of services, including "recreational services." This phrase includes gambling, argued Antigua.

Antigua stated that its enterprises operate legally and under this treaty commitment they should have free access to U.S. consumers. Also, and apart from violating its legal commitment, the U.S. is hypocritical because it allows gambling in casinos, bingo parlors, card clubs, race tracks, and state lotteries. Horse racing bets can legally be placed through U.S.-based Internet sites, for example, Youbet.com in Pennsylvania, and Xpressbet.com in California. Existence of these practices makes the U.S. moral argument ring hollow.

THE UNITED STATES RESPONSE

The United States thought it had a strong defense on both legal and moral grounds. It claimed that operators in Antigua and Barbuda plainly violated its domestic laws prohibiting the use of phone wires for gambling. Federal laws also made it illegal to accept a sports wager from the United States in any foreign country. Three specific statutes were identified, namely, the Wire Act, the Travel Act, and the Gambling Business Act. State laws also prohibit illegal betting by wire. These laws banning interstate gambling had been in existence for decades and predated the WTO. The U.S. also alleged a sovereign right to ban goods and services that harmed its social fabric.

Unfortunately, when the GATS treaty was drafted in 1995, the U.S. failed to clarify that the market access provision did not extend to gambling. This oversight was buried until eight years later when Antigua launched its complaint. The U.S. argued that it never meant to open its market to cross-border gambling and it should not now be forced to do so.

The U.S. has obligations "to protect public morals [and] to maintain public order." It has generally prohibited or tightly restricted "gambling or betting services" for reasons of public morality, including the protection of minors and other vulnerable groups. There is evidence that Internet gambling is rapidly increasing in the U.S., creating growing numbers of teenage gambling addicts. This is a legitimate concern to Americans and a danger to public morals.

THE PANEL'S DECISION

In late 2004 the WTO panel hearing the case released its report.[10] The ruling favored Antigua and Barbuda. In its decision, the panel held that application of U.S. gambling laws to offshore Internet gambling establishments was contrary to the market access treaty obligations entered into by the United States under GATS. These restrictions, it concluded, constituted an "arbitrary and unjustifiable discrimination" and were a "disguised restriction on trade."[11] It agreed with Antigua and Barbuda that the phrase "other recreational services (except sporting)" in the treaty should be interpreted as including "gambling and betting services." Therefore, domestic gambling restrictions in federal and state laws were an unfair trade barrier to foreign businesses.

---

[9] "Before the Panel of the World Trade Organization on United States—Measures Affecting the Cross-Border Supply of Gambling and Betting Services," WTDS285, First Submission of Antigua and Barbuda, Executive Summary, October 8, 2003.

[10] World Trade Organization, "United States—Measures Affecting the Cross-Border Supply of Gambling and Betting Services: Report of the Panel," WT/DS285R, November 10, 2004.

[11] Ibid., p. 270.

The panel agreed that the U.S. denied offshore gambling operators the same freedom as domestic enterprises. It affirmed that the gambling enterprises of Antigua were lawful enterprises and entitled to enter the U.S. gambling market. Finally, the panel agreed that the restrictive gambling laws in question were designed to protect public morals, but ruled that the U.S. had failed to make a case that they were necessary.

The United States rebuffed the panel's decision. A statement issued by the Office of the United States Trade Representative had this to say.

> This panel report is deeply flawed. In 1995 the [United States] clearly intended to exclude gambling from U.S. services commitments. . . . Throughout our history, the United States has had restrictions on gambling . . . [i]t defies common sense that the United States would make a commitment to let international gambling operate within our borders.[12]

THE APPELLATE BODY'S DECISION

The U.S. appealed to the WTO standing Appellate Body (SAB), which in early 2005 upheld most of the dispute panel's decision.[13] It upheld the panel's finding that the U.S. acted inconsistently by barring cross-border Internet gambling while allowing domestic gambling companies to take Internet bets. However, it reversed the lower panel's holding on the necessity of the U.S. laws for protecting public morals. It concluded that the laws could, indeed, be justified to protect the American public from the growth of immoral behavior.

Nonetheless, it still agreed with the lower panel's finding that the U.S. violated terms of the GATS treaty requiring it to give equal access to foreign operators. It found particular significance in the Interstate Horseracing Act, which allows domestic betting services to take remote bets over the wires but prohibits foreign operators from accepting the same bets. In such circumstances, the moral justification raised by the U.S. lacked force and consistency and could not prevail.

ANTIGUA ASKS FOR SANCTIONS

So, the Antiguan David had prevailed over the United States Goliath. Now what? To comply with the decision the United States would be required to take one of two actions. It could change its laws to permit cross-border betting with foreign gambling services. Or it could change its laws to ban all domestic gambling over phone lines or the Internet. Neither was likely to occur.

Instead, the United States tried an end run around the ruling. It declared that it withdrew from the section of the GATS treaty requiring equal access of foreign gambling companies in its domestic market. In 2007 the WTO rejected this action, saying it did not constitute compliance.[14]

Under WTO rules if the losing party in a dispute fails to comply with the decision, it must offer compensation to the aggrieved party or accept retaliation. Retaliation requires imposing trade sanctions equivalent to the harm suffered by the complaining country.

Antigua and Barbuda estimated an economic harm of $3.4 billion a year from lost gambling revenues. The U.S. believed that this figure was too high and suggested that $500,000 was more appropriate. Following Antigua's lead, seven other WTO member nations—Japan, India, Canada, Australia, Costa Rica, Macao, and the European Union nations—piled on. They asked that the United States be forced to open other domestic markets as compensation for closing off its Internet gambling market to companies within their borders.[15]

Trade sanctions often take the form of raising tariffs on imports from the noncomplying country. How does a speck of a nation such as Antigua and

[12] The Office of the United States Trade Representative, "Statement from USTR Spokesman Richard Mills Regarding the WTO Gambling Dispute with Antigua and Barbuda," November 10, 2004, at www.ustr.gov.

[13] World Trade Organization, "United States—Measures Affecting the Cross-Border Supply of Gambling and Betting Services: Report of the Appellate Body, WT/DS285/AB/R, AB-2005-1, April 7, 2005.

[14] World Trade Organization, "United States—Measures Affecting the Cross-Border Supply of Gambling and Betting Services: Recourse to Article 21.5 of the DSU by Antigua and Barbuda—Report of the Panel," WT/DS285/RW, March 30, 2007.

[15] Lorraine Woellert, "A Web Gambling Fight Could Harm Free Trade," *BusinessWeek,* August 13, 2007.

Barbuda, whose trade with the U.S. is microscopic, conduct a retaliation? The Antiguans have asked the WTO for the right to retaliate by reproducing and exporting copyrighted entertainment material from the U.S. This would allow businesses on the islands to copy and sell $3.4 billion worth of music and films. Of course, such an idea is offensive to the U.S. recording companies and film studios whose products might be copied.[16]

Meanwhile, the United States has passed a new law intended to blight the cross-border gambling business. The Unlawful Internet Gambling Enforcement Act of 2006 prohibits banks and credit card companies from processing financial transactions with gaming sites anywhere in the world, including electronic credit card transactions, wire transfers, and paper checks. When the law passed, some of the largest gaming sites, such as PartyPoker.com announced they would no longer accept wagers from Americans. World Sports Exchange, however, continued to accept wagers by U.S. customers.[17]

GAMBLING IN THE UNITED STATES

Gambling has an uneven history in the United States. It has gone through cycles of great popularity followed by rejection and prohibition. Today strong forces in favor and opposed are locked in a contest of uncertain outcome. A central focus of their duel is Internet gambling.

In the colonial years the English settlers considered gambling harmless. The English Crown permitted lotteries to raise money for companies. In fact, the Virginia Company of London financed its Jamestown colony with a lottery. Soon the colonists were holding their own lotteries, using them to finance public works such as street paving and harbor construction. Even churches, which would later become hostile to gambling, were built with lottery funds. So were buildings at Harvard and Yale.

Gradually, however, taxation superseded lotteries for public funding. By the 1860s only Delaware, Missouri, and Kentucky held state-authorized lotteries.

State laws prohibited other forms of gambling as opposition by moralists grew.

Interest in gambling renewed at the turn of the century and states began to reauthorize it. A popular illegal game in the 1930s was the Irish sweepstakes. Ireland sold tickets smuggled into the United States. The proceeds were presumably used to finance hospitals in Ireland. This was not challenged by the government. Gambling became increasingly popular and today the country is awash with it. And with the Internet, Americans gamble around the world from the comfort of their homes.[18]

Internet gambling attracts special ire from anti-gambling forces—including law enforcement organizations, church groups, conservative family welfare groups, and sports leagues. They argue that it is powerfully addictive and will lead to bankruptcies, destruction of families, criminal activity, and a culture of betting that corrupts athletes. Those who want stronger laws to regulate or ban gambling are especially alarmed by the attraction of Internet gambling for young people, particularly young males. They believe that adolescents used to spending hours on video games are enticed by sophisticated gaming sites. Without the maturity to predict the consequences they are lured into a destructive habit.

A recent survey-based estimate is that at least once a month 35,000 males aged 14 to 17 gamble online along with 850,000 males aged 18 to 22. Among the latter group, frequency of gambling doubled in 2006. Among women ages 18 to 22, 35 percent reported monthly gambling (as opposed to 56 percent of similarly aged males).[19]

THE UNLAWFUL INTERNET GAMBLING ENFORCEMENT ACT OF 2006

As mentioned, in 2006 Congress reinforced U. S. rejection of the WTO's rulings by passing the Unlawful Internet Gambling Enforcement Act (UIGEA).

[16] Paul Blustein, "Against All Odds."

[17] " W.T.O. Sanctions against U.S. Are Urged," *The New York Times,* June 21, 2007, p. 12.

[18] "Brief History of Internet Gambling," http://www.unc.edu/-dismatthe/background.html; and James Oliver, "Internet Gambling; Will History Repeat Itself?" *Cyberlaw 2001,* March 29, 2001.

[19] The Annenberg Public Policy Center, "More Than I Million Young People Use Internet Gambling Sites Each Month," October 2, 2006.

Passage of the UIGEA culminated a 10-year effort by its supporters. In the past, powerful special interests had blocked it. These included race track owners, Indian tribes with casinos, parimutuel gaming interests, and the legal online gaming industry. In 2006, however, these voices were muted by scandals involving lobbyist Jack Abramoff, notably, those in which he had brokered corrupt favors for tribal gaming interests. Public outrage subdued the pro-gambling lobby.

The statute begins with the usual statements of findings and purpose. Congress finds that Internet gambling is a growing cause of debt collection problems for banks and credit card companies. Therefore, "new mechanisms for enforcing gambling laws on the Internet are necessary.'" This is followed by definitions, for example, to "bet or wager" is " . . . risking something of value on the outcome of a contest, sporting event or 'a game subject to chance.' "

The statute makes it illegal "to place, receive, or otherwise knowingly transmit a bet or wager by any means which involves the use, at least in part, of the Internet," when the bet violates any law in the state where it is initiated or received. Existing Internet gambling, such as betting on horse races, is allowed to continue.

The muscle of the new law is its effort to stop the flow of gambling payments. "No person engaged in the business of betting or wagering may knowingly accept, in connection with the participation of another person, in unlawful Internet gambling," credit through the use of a credit card, an electronic fund transfer, a check, or "the proceeds of any other form of financial transaction." Those who assist the transmission of, or receive, funds relating to prohibited Internet gambling may be prosecuted.

ARGUMENTS FOR THE UIGEA

Congress did not give birth to the new law without debate. The most open disagreement emerged during floor debate in the House of Representatives over an early version of the bill. In this section we extract arguments of the bill's proponents. In the next section we set forth some arguments by opponents.[20]

Representative James Leach (R-Iowa), a persistent voice for antigambling laws, told this story. "John Kindt, a professor of business at the University of Illinois at Urbana-Champaign calls the Internet 'crack cocaine for gamblers.' There are no needle marks, he says. There is no alcohol on the breath. You just click the mouse and lose your house. These comments could not be more apropos than for Greg Hogan, Jr., a 19-year-old Lehigh University class president and chaplain's assistant from Barberton, Ohio. This pastor's son gambled away $7,500 playing online Texas Hold'Em, then confessed to robbing a bank to try to recover his losses. His life is ruined. Never before has it been so easy to lose so much money, so quickly, at such a young age. Internet casinos are proliferating. Soon they will be ubiquitous."[21]

Later in the debate, Leach lamented that "[w]hile Congress has failed to act, the illegal Internet gambling industry has boomed. This year, Americans are projected to spend more than $6 billion to unregulated, offshore, online casinos, half the $12 billion that will be bet worldwide on Internet gambling. FBI and Justice Department experts have warned that Internet gambling sites are vulnerable to be used for money laundering, drug trafficking and even terrorist financing. Further, these sites evade rigorous U.S.-based regulations that control gambling by minors and problem gamblers and ensure the integrity of the games."[22]

Representative Spencer Bachus (R-Ala.) noted that "[t]he negative effects of gambling have been widely documented. All too often, gambling results in addiction, bankruptcy, divorce, crime and moral decline. Internet gambling magnifies the destructiveness of gambling by bringing the casino into your home. . . . Internet gambling has been linked to terrorists and organized crime."[23]

Representative Joseph Pitts (R-Iowa) said, "[g]ambling online is unique. No casinos, horse tracks or betting parlors are required. All one needs

---

[20] See also *Internet Gambling Prohibition Act of 2006,* Hearing before the Subcommittee on Crime, Terrorism, and Homeland Security of the Committee on the Judiciary, House of Representatives, 109th Congress, 2nd Session, April 5, 2006.

[21] *Congressional Record,* July 11, 2006, p. H4984.

[22] Ibid., p. H4984.

[23] Ibid., p. H4987.

is a computer, a credit card, and Internet access. With that, players are able to play 24 hours a day from the privacy of their homes. Minors are easily able to defy age requirements if they wish to play. And the online environment and credit card payment system combine to promote addiction, bankruptcy, and crime."[24]

ARGUMENTS AGAINST THE UIGEA

Here are some arguments made by opponents of Internet gambling restrictions.

Representative Barney Frank (D-Mass.), chairman of the Financial Services Committee, opposed what he believed was an unworkable infringement on freedom of choice. "Are we going to go back to Prohibition? Prohibition didn't work for alcohol; it didn't work for gambling. When people abuse a particular practice, the sensible thing is to try to deal with the abuse, not outlaw it. . . . In areas where we need to act together to protect the quality of our life, in the environment, in transportation, in public safety, we abstain; but in those areas where individuals ought to be allowed to make their own choices, we intervene. . . . Now, people have said, well, some students abuse it. We should work to try to diminish abuse. But if we were to outlaw for adults everything that college students abuse, we would all just sit home and do nothing. The fundamental principle of the autonomy of the individual is at stake today."[25]

Echoing Frank, Representative Ronald Paul (R-Tex.) agreed that a prohibition on Internet gambling would fail. ". . . [O]nce you make something illegal, whether it is alcohol or whether it is cigarettes or whether it is gambling on the Internet, it doesn't disappear because of . . . increased demand. All that happens is, it is turned over to the criminal element. So you won't get rid of it."[26]

Representative Robert Scott (D-Vir.) said he opposed the bill, " . . . because it does not prohibit Internet gambling; it only tries to prohibit running an Internet gambling operation. But because of the nature of the Internet, it is probably unlikely to do that, and that is because even if we are successful in closing down business sites in the United States or in countries we can get to cooperate, it will be ineffective because it will have no effect on those operations run outside the reach of the Department of Justice."[27]

Representative Scott was concerned about the burdensome expense and administrative efforts required of financial institutions that would be called on to identify funds destined for gambling. He noted that the legislation prohibits the use of credit cards in paying off gambling debts. " . . . [T]his will create an enforcement nightmare for financial institutions because it requires them to stop and look for illegal Internet gambling transactions. It is hard to identify those transactions, because they are not going to be identified as an illegal Internet transaction. . . . With some Internet gambling operations being legal, how would the financial institution distinguish between what is legal and what is illegal? . . . Over 85 foreign countries allow some form of gambling online, and that number is likely to grow as well. So what governments are likely to cooperate with us in prosecuting businesses that they authorize to operate?"[28]

Representative Shelley Berkely (D-Nev.) also focused on impracticality. "Despite the misinformed and misguided claims of this bill's supporters it would neither prohibit Internet gaming nor increase enforcement capabilities of the United States government. Instead, passing this bill will do the exact opposite. The millions of Americans who currently wager online will continue to use offshore Web sites out of the reach of U.S. law enforcement. . . . I continue to be astounded by the Members of this body who constantly rail against an intrusive federal government; and yet when it comes to gaming, they are the first, the first to call for government intrusion." "Supporters of this bill," she continued, "argue that online gaming is a great danger to society and our youth because some people gamble too much. . . . By that logic, the next piece of legislation we should be considering is banning online shopping."[29]

---

[24] Ibid., p. H4990.

[25] Ibid., p. H4985.

[26] Ibid., p. H4986.

[27] Ibid., p. H4986.

[28] Ibid., p. H4995.

[29] Ibid., p. H4996.

Questions

1. Was Jay Cohen's conviction justified?

2. Do you concur with the decisions of the World Trade Organization in the dispute between Antigua and Barbuda and the United States?

3. Should the United States comply with the WTO's decision? If so, what should it do?

4. Should Antigua and Barbuda be allowed to retaliate against the United States by exporting copyrighted entertainment material equal to the damages it has suffered?

5. Do you support the Unlawful Internet Gambling Enforcement Act of 2006? Was Congress justified in passing this law after the WTO's rulings about illegal trade barriers?

6. To what extent should the U.S. regulate gambling? Should gambling be banned?

Industrial Pollution and Environmental Policy

The Indian Health Service Solves a Mystery

Daniel Schultz, a surgeon at the Santa Fe Indian Hospital in New Mexico, was puzzled and alarmed when, in an 18-month period in 1984 and 1985, he diagnosed three cases of malignant mesothelioma in Indians from a nearby pueblo. An investigation of a state tumor registry revealed two more cases from this pueblo in 1970 and 1982, for a total of five cases over 15 years. On average, the victims were 65 years old and lived only 3.8 months after diagnosis.[1]

Malignant mesothelioma is an incurable tumor in the lining of the chest cavity that is virtually always caused by exposure to asbestos. It has a latency period of 40 to 50 years. Five cases of this unusual cancer in a pueblo of 2,000 Indians was roughly 1,000 times the number predicted over 15 years by standard mortality tables. Normally, five cases could be expected in a city of two million. Samples of lung tissue from the three cases in the Indian Hospital revealed the presence of all three types of asbestos used in commerce—chrysotile, amosite, and crocidolite. The Indians had been exposed to airborne asbestos fibers. But how? Schultz called in Richard J. Driscoll, an environmental health officer with the Indian Health Service (IHS), a small agency in the Department of Health and Human Services. Driscoll, along with colleagues from the IHS, set out to do some detective work to learn how asbestos exposure was occurring.

Immediately, the investigators ran into a problem. The Indians were reluctant subjects. They had a superstitious belief that fatal illness was explained by the presence of evil in its victims. They believed that people who discussed disease were wishing it on others and inviting additional sickness. The Indians also disliked attention and interference from outsiders because they wanted to keep their native culture and ways intact. Tribal elders finally agreed to discuss possible causes of asbestos exposure. Here is the story that emerged.

In the 1930s, a brick-manufacturing plant was built in the vicinity of the pueblo. A small private railroad was started to shuttle between the plant and a nearby main line

---

[1] Richard J. Driscoll, Wallace J. Mulligan, Daniel Schultz, and Anthony Candelaria, "Malignant Mesothelioma: A Cluster in a Native American Pueblo," *The New England Journal of Medicine,* June 2, 1988, p. 1437.

of the Santa Fe Railroad, and a steam locomotive operated on it. When the boiler and pipe insulation on the locomotive needed replacement, workers discarded the old asbestos insulation near the tracks, where it was found by members of the tribe and brought back to the pueblo. It was put to many uses. Asbestos pads were used for worktable insulation by silversmiths making Indian jewelry. Dancers at religious festivals scraped and pounded their deer-hide leggings with crumbling wads of pipe insulation to whiten them, releasing clouds of floating asbestos fibers. Gradually the Indians found more and more uses for asbestos, and the trackside scrap was supplemented by tribe members in construction work who scavenged at their job sites for more.

The investigators discovered that four of the five mesothelioma victims had been silversmiths and that all five had been active participants in ceremonial dances. The Indians were reluctant to give up their asbestos; selling it had become a cottage industry in the pueblo. When the investigators went door to door, they found that Indian families were hoarding asbestos in bags, pots, and jars. It was hard to get them to part with it, but they found that by emphasizing the harm it could cause to children, most of it could be confiscated.

The story of what happened to the Indians in the pueblo is analogous to what has happened to large populations in industrial societies. In both cases, dangerous substances with useful qualities promised better living. In both cases, elevated exposure to these substances predated adequate knowledge of their harmful effects. And in both cases, it was only after substantial exposures had occurred and sickness began to appear that government agencies mobilized to protect public health.

In this chapter we discuss the nature of industrial pollutants and the practices and social philosophies that allowed them to darken skies, poison waters, and despoil land. We then discuss how, in the United States beginning in the 1970s, massive regulatory programs developed to control industrial pollution. We explain the current operation of these programs, how they affect corporations, and how well they work.

POLLUTION

pollution
The presence of substances in the environment that inconvenience or endanger.

Pollution is the presence of substances in the environment that inconvenience or endanger humans. Much of it comes from natural sources. Forest fires release particles and toxic metals such as mercury into the atmosphere. Water picks up asbestos as it flows over rocks, gravel, and sand. Natural background radiation in North America is about 300 millirem a year, the equivalent of 50 chest X-rays. Tons of oil seep from fissures in the ocean floor.

Human activity adds more contaminants. For millions of years, hunter-gatherer bands generated little pollution. However, a gradual revolution in agricultural methods beginning about 10,000 years ago led to more settled societies in which populations grew and people gathered in cities. Wherever they lived, the primary pollution problem was gases and particles from indoor fuel combustion for cooking and heating. Significant death and disease rates are associated with exposure to the smoke of animal dung, wood, and charcoal, although this was unknown in those days.

Eventually, because of the Industrial Revolution, cities grew crowded with workers. Spatially confined urban ecosystems were overwhelmed by concentrated pollution. City air was a haze of particles and gases from the innumerable wood or coal fires required for daily life and work. A worse problem was huge amounts of human and animal waste. Few homes had lavatories. Primitive sewers were not flushed with water. Dead animals, dung from beasts of burden, and entrails from butcher shops littered streets.[2]

Water plant technology, widely introduced only in the late 1800s, eventually ensured sanitary water supplies, but not soon enough to prevent a high death toll from waterborne disease. By this time, contaminants from fossil-fuel combustion and manufacturing activity were a serious, added problem.

Most industrial pollution simply adds to background levels of natural substances, so that human exposures to metals, organic and inorganic compounds, radiation, and particles reach artificially high levels. For example, nearly all Americans carry elevated levels of cadmium in their bodies and about 5 percent carry levels high enough to cause kidney damage and decreased bone density. Cadmium is a soft, bluish metal released into the environment by smelting, petroleum refining, and waste incineration. It settles onto soil and is taken up by plants, then enters the food supply.[3]

The rise of synthetic chemistry since the 1940s has led to the creation and dispersal of persistent, complex artificial molecules used in plastics, pesticides, solvents, coolants, flame retardants, adhesives, cookware, and other products. The average person carries many of these substances in his or her tissues. One study detected 150 industrial chemicals, most of which did not exist 75 years ago, in the tissues of nine people. Their exposures could have come from any of 11,700 commercial products containing the chemicals.[4]

disability adjusted life year (DALY)
A statistical measure combining in one number years lost to premature mortality and years lived with disability. One DALY equals one lost year of healthy life.

Industrial activity both harms human health and disturbs natural ecology. We will briefly discuss its impact in each area.

Human Health

Disease caused by industrial pollution is significant, but far less significant than disease caused by older, nonindustrial forms of pollution. Table 13.1 shows the estimated burden of disease caused by air, water, and land pollution. This burden is calculated in *disability-adjusted life years,* or DALYs. DALYs combine in a single measure years of life lost because of premature death and years of life lived with a disability. One DALY equals one lost year of healthy life.

[2] Clive Ponting, *A Green History of the World* (New York: St. Martin's Press, 1992), p. 354.

[3] Centers for Disease Control and Prevention, *Third National Report on Human Exposure to Environmental Chemicals* (Atlanta: National Center for Environmental Health, July 2005), pp. 26–30.

[4] Joseph W. Thornton et al., "Biomonitoring of Industrial Pollutants: Health and Policy Implications of the Chemical Body Burden," *Public Health Journal,* July–August 2002, p. 315.

TABLE 13.1
Health Risks Posed by Major Sources of Environmental Pollution

Source: Kseniya Lvovsky, "Health and Environment," World Bank, draft working paper, Washington, DC, April 2000, p. 4.

Environmental Health Risk	Percent of DALYs	
	Less Developed Countries	Developed Countries
Water supply and sanitation	7%	1%
Indoor air pollution	4	0
Urban air pollution	2	1
Agricultural chemicals and industrial waste	1	2.5
All pollution-related causes	**14**	**4.5**

As the table shows, exposure to pollution is estimated to produce 14 percent of the disease burden in less developed nations but only 4.5 percent in developed ones. Most of this burden in developing nations is attributable to the age-old risks of unsanitary water and indoor combustion of wood and coal.[5] Urban air pollution from factories and vehicles and pollution from pesticides and toxic waste—the by-products of modern industry—are responsible for only 3 percent of DALYs in developing nations and 3.5 percent in developed ones. Clearly, when nations industrialize, far from creating a deadly blizzard of pollution, they instead greatly reduce the overall burden of disease by lowering exposures to lethal nonindustrial pollutants. The main advances are access to water unpolluted by feces and the transition in homes from dirty solid fuels to electricity.

ecosystem
An animated, interactive realm of plants, animals, and microorganisms inhabiting an area of the nonliving environment.

ecosystem services
The productivity of natural ecosystems in creating food and fiber and in regulating climate, water, soil, nutrients, and other forms of natural capital.

The Biosphere

Industrial activity also impinges on the biosphere, the slender margin atop the earth's surface that supports life, a space "so thin it cannot be seen edgewise from an orbiting spacecraft."[6] The biosphere is home to multiple ecosystems. An *ecosystem* is an animated, interactive realm of plants, animals, and microorganisms inhabiting an area of the nonliving environment. Ecosystems may be tiny and short-lived, such as a pond in the hollow of a tree trunk, or as vast and enduring as the tropical forest that hosts it.

Ecosystems provide services that support human well-being. These *ecosystem services* are benefits that humanity derives from the dynamic work of nature. Ecosystems produce food, fiber, and water. They regulate climates; control flooding, pests, and disease; purify water; create soil; and cycle nutrients. Coral reefs, for example, absorb carbon, stabilize seabeds, provide plant and fish habitats, and nurture biodiversity. Ecological services are given away by nature, but if they were priced one estimate is that they would equal world GDP, estimated at $57 trillion in 2008.[7]

[5] Kirk R. Smith, Sumi Mehta, and Mirjam Maeusezahl-Feuz, "Indoor Air Pollution from Household Use of Solid Fuels," in Majid Ezzati et al., eds., *Comparative Quantification of Health Risks*, vol. 1 (Geneva: World Health Organization, 2004), chap. 18.

[6] E. O. Wilson, "Hotspots: Preserving Pieces of a Fragile Biosphere," *National Geographic*, January 2002, p. 86.

[7] Edward O. Wilson, "That's Life," *The New York Times*, September 6, 2007, p. A25; International Monetary Fund, *World Economic Outlook 2007* (Washington, DC: IMF, October 2007), table A1.

Human economic and industrial activity capitalizes on ecosystem services. Recently, the United Nations commissioned a four-year effort by 1,300 scientists to study world ecosystems. Their report, *The Millennium Ecosystem Assessment*, finds that broad ecosystems are now degraded and under pressure.[8] Over the past two centuries remarkable advances in human well-being, including better nutrition, longer lives, and more material welfare, were achieved by exploiting ecosystem services. Sometimes this exploitation has damaged the ecosystem and reduced its capacity to continue providing services. Forests, for example, have been badly managed. While at the dawn of humanity they covered 12.4 billion acres, they are now reduced to 7.4 billion acres and still shrink an estimated 23 million acres a year.[9] World forests provide about 5,000 commercial products, but as they shrink they are less able to support species diversity or regulate hydrological cycles.

The causes of ecosystem strain are multiple and complex, but they center on accelerating economic activity. Today ideologies of affluence support rising per capita consumption and spur global trade that exploits distant ecosystems. Pollution and waste increase. This creates a danger of exceeding natural limits and thresholds. For example, living coral reefs host intricate interactions among thousands of species. When they are bathed by even small amounts of pollution from nearby coastal cities, they undergo a rapidly cascading series of negative changes, ultimately becoming overgrown with algae. Already, about 20 percent of the world's coral reefs have been destroyed.[10] Similarly, when an area of habitat is reduced past a threshold point that a species requires to survive, the species is irreversibly doomed though it may be decades before the last member dies. The lesson is that economic activity is not now always, but must ultimately become, sustainable. Otherwise, deterioration in ecosystem services will limit human well-being.

INDUSTRIAL ACTIVITY AND SUSTAINABILITY

Today there are nations on every continent with ambitious development plans that put industry before environmental protection. Poor nations house the vast majority of the 2.6 billion people with purchasing power of less than two U.S. dollars per day.[11] Their leaders see industrial growth as the only practical way of raising living standards and building national power. If these populous, underdeveloped nations take the path of the environmentally destructive eighteenth and nineteenth century industrial revolution in Europe, the United States, and Japan, the resulting pollution and resource depletion could lead to ecological disaster.

[8] Rashid Hassan, Robert Scholes, and Neville Ash, *Ecosystems and Human Well-being: Current State and Trends,* vol. 1 (Washington, DC: Island Press, 2006).

[9] Ibid., pp. 16, 18, 588.

[10] Ibid., p. 515.

[11] United Nations Development Programme, *Human Development Report 2007/2008* (New York: Palgrave Macmillan, 2007), p. 25.

FIGURE 13.1
The
Environmental
Kuznets
Curve

Source: Adapted
from Håkan Nord-
ström and Scott
Vaughan, *Trade and
Environment* (Geneva:
WTO Publications,
1999), p. 48.

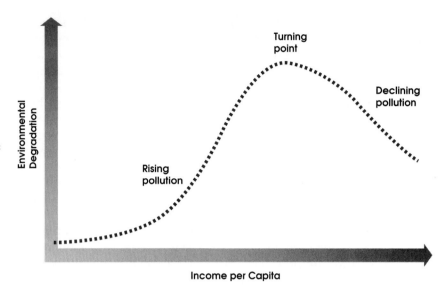

**sustainable
development**
Nonpolluting
economic
growth that
raises standards
of living without
depleting the
net resources of
the earth.

**environmental
Kuznets curve**
An inverted
U-shaped curve
illustrating
that as gross
domestic
product rises in
emerging econ-
omies pollution
goes through
stages of rapid
increase, lev-
eling off, and
decline.

Much interest today is focused on the notion of *sustainable development,* that is, nonpolluting economic growth that raises standards of living without depleting the net resources of the earth. However, the modern industrial revolution, as it is currently unfolding in developing nations, bears little resemblance to this ideal. In fact, at least in its early stages, it promises to exceed the old-time industrial revolu- tions in generating pollution and depleting resources. The new industrialization is faster. Economic growth rates in countries such as Korea, Thailand, and China have compressed the transformation into less than two decades rather than the 100 years and more it took England and the United States. As growth skyrockets, a range of modern industries quickly appears, creating more varied and dangerous pollutants than were typical of eighteenth and nineteenth century factories.

However, there is evidence that environmental quality in growing economies does not follow a path of long-term deterioration as in the old industrial revolu- tion model. Studies suggest that developing economies now follow a sequence in which pollution rises in the early stages of growth when incomes are low. As per capita gross domestic product continues to rise, pollution reaches a peak and eventually decreases, even as GDP continues to rise. This phenomenon can be represented as an inverted U-shaped curve, known as an *environmental Kuznets curve,*[12] illustrated in Figure 13.1.

Researchers studying more than 50 countries found, for example, that there was a rapid rise of sulfur dioxide emissions in the cities of countries undergoing economic development. Sulfur dioxide, a by-product of coal and oil combustion, is closely associated with industrialization. But this rise slowed and eventually leveled off when per capita GDP, measured as purchasing power parity with U.S.

[12] Simon Kuznets won the 1971 Nobel prize in economics for his studies of economic growth. He also said that, in addition to environmental quality, income inequality followed an inverted U-shaped relationship during development, first worsening, then leveling off, then declining.

dollars, reached about $4,000. After that, emissions began to decline even as incomes continued to rise. Particle emissions leveled off somewhat later, at a per capita GDP of around $8,000, and three measures of water quality based on oxygen demand caused by organic pollutants leveled off at a per capita GDP of $7,500. Waterborne concentrations of the heavy metal arsenic stabilized at $4,900 and began to decline at $10,000.[13]

These findings support the existence of an inverted U pattern for these pollutants. Although not all studies have arrived at the same figures and not all pollutants studied trace an inverted U pattern, there is general support for the theory.[14]

Many factors explain the environmental Kuznets curve. To begin, as countries industrialize, their economies change in composition. Early on, less capital-intensive agricultural and food processing sectors dominate. Pollution from them is quantitatively less and less toxic than from industries that come later. In the middle stages of industrialization, enough capital has accumulated to bring in more polluting industries such as cement, chemicals, and rubber. Other polluters that need even more capital and technical skill, including basic metals, paper and printing, and machinery soon follow.[15] As the economy matures, however, the last structural shifts expand much cleaner technology and service industries.

Even as pollution rises, growth is bringing other changes. With greater affluence there is more education. Shifts in cultural values occur as the population ascends from poverty. Preserving environmental quality and protecting public health assume higher priority.[16] Pressures rise for corporations, particularly highly visible MNCs, to use cleaner technologies. With development governments tend to grow stronger and more democratic. They are increasingly responsive to citizen demands for pollution reduction. Regulatory agencies experience an influx of more technically skilled personnel. These factors all underlie the pollution reductions observed coming with continued GDP growth.

If the environmental Kuznets curve predicts the future, more economic growth will not necessarily lead to steadily increasing levels of pollution. The view that development inevitably brings ruinous degradation is rooted in the historical experience of the West. Modern growth can be much cleaner.

Although sustainable development is a useful philosophy, and as we will see, some nations and corporations attempt to approach it in practice, the broad global reality bears little resemblance to the sustainable idea. Still, current fascination with sustainability suggests a shift in thinking about the relationship between industry and ecosystems. In the next section we discuss ideas that arose to support industrialization, then explain how they are now being challenged.

---

[13] Gene M. Grossman and Alan B. Krueger, "Economic Growth and the Environment," *Quarterly Journal of Economics,* May 1995 p. 353. Data are from the Global Environmental Monitoring System, a joint project of the World Health Organization and the United Nations Environmental Programme.

[14] Bruce Yandle, "Environmental Turning Points, Institutions, and the Rise to the Top," *The Independent Review,* Fall 2004.

[15] Richard M. Auty, "Pollution Patterns during the Industrial Transition," *The Geographic Journal,* July 1997, p. 206.

[16] Hoon Park, Clifford Russell, and Junsoo Lee, "National Culture and Environmental Sustainability: A Cross-National Analysis," *Journal of Economics and Finance,* Spring 2007.

IDEAS SHAPE ATTITUDES TOWARD THE ENVIRONMENT

What is the proper relationship between business and nature? In the past, and to some extent still, Western values that regard nature as an adversary to be conquered have legitimized industrial activity. These values were incubated in ancient Mediterranean society. Eventually they appeared in biblical text, giving them religious sanction and magnifying their influence. In the story of creation in Genesis, God creates first nature and then man and afterward instructs man on how to relate to nature.

dualism
The theory that humans are separate from nature because they have the power of reason and, unlike plants and animals, souls.

> Be fruitful and multiply, and replenish the earth and subdue it; and have dominion over the fish of the sea, and over the fowl of the air, and over every living thing that moveth upon the earth. (1:28)

This Judeo-Christian view laid the foundation for the conviction in Western civilization that humans were both separate from and superior to the natural world. It also incorporated the idea that humans must exercise wise stewardship over their dominion, but until recently the stewardship idea languished as a minor theme.

When Church dogma began to lose its primacy during the Renaissance in Europe, secular philosophers did not reject the biblical doctrine of human superiority to nature but reinforced it with their own worldly thinking. Within the comparatively short span of 150 years, four new ideas appeared that, combined, determined how nature would be regarded and treated during the coming industrial revolution.

progress
The belief that history is a narrative of improvement in which humanity moves from lower to higher levels of perfection.

The theory of *dualism* held that humans were separate from nature. The French philosopher René Descartes (1596–1650) believed that nature operated like a machine, according to fixed laws that humans could study and understand. Humans were separate from nature and other living organisms because they alone had the power of reason and, unlike plants and animals, had souls. Descartes's perspective laid the foundation for modern experimental science but also established a dualism reinforcing the Judeo–Christian idea that humans were superior to and apart from nature.

capitalism
An economy in which private individuals and corporations own the means of production and, motivated by the desire for profit, compete in free markets under conditions of limited restraint by government. In this economy, nature is valued primarily as an input into the production process.

The Renaissance brought improved living conditions, growth of cities, inventions, and the birth of industries. Such events kindled great optimism in European intellectuals who wrote about the idea of *progress,* or the belief that history was a narrative of improvement in which humanity moved from lower to higher levels on an inevitable march to perfection. This idea rejected the pessimism of previous civilizations that had looked back on past golden eras. Charles Darwin's theory of evolution supported the idea of progress in the popular mind. As industry expanded, the exploitation of nature for human welfare was soon entwined with the notion of progress.

Then, during the early years of the industrial revolution in England, powerful doctrines of economics and ethics arose, which in additional ways justified the exploitation of nature. The theory of *capitalism,* based on principles set forth by Adam Smith in 1776, valued nature primarily as a commodity to be used in wealth-creating activity that increased the vigor, welfare, and comfort of society. As a practical matter, early capitalism in action largely ignored environmental damage. This tendency still exists. For example, the gross domestic product, the accounting system of capitalism, rises when goods and services are produced but does not fall when pollution damage occurs. Thus, the GDP rose because of the *Exxon Valdez* oil spill, adding the millions of dollars spent by Exxon on the cleanup but not subtracting the costs of dead animals and degraded shoreline.

utilitarianism
The ethical philosophy of the greatest good for the greatest number.

Finally, the doctrine of *utilitarianism,* or "the greatest good for the greatest number," arrived in England simultaneously with the rise of capitalism. It also was used to justify economic activity that assaulted nature. Industry made the utilitarian argument that, although pollution was noxious, the economic benefits of jobs, products, taxes, and growth outweighed environmental costs and were the "greatest good." Utilitarianism was an ethical worldview that rationalized the destructive side effects of commerce. It blinded Western societies to alternative, but less exploitive, views of nature.

In Eastern civilization, the values of Buddhism, Confucianism, and Taoism placed stronger emphasis on the interconnection of people and nature. They supported a more humble, less domineering role for humanity. However, their main impact was on interpersonal relations. Industrialization in Asia has been as destructive of the environment as in the West.

New Ideas Challenge the Old

land ethic
A theory that humans are part of an ethical community that includes not only other human beings but all elements of the natural environment. It implies an ethical duty to nature as well as to humanity.

In the second half of the twentieth century, an alternative, nonexploitive environmental ethic emerged. Naturalist Aldo Leopold pioneered the revised worldview. His seminal statement of a new *land ethic* in a 1949 book, *A Sand County Almanac,* inspired others to rethink traditional ideas about the man–nature relationship. He wrote:

> All ethics so far evolved rest upon a single premise: that the individual is a member of a community of interdependent parts. . . . The land ethic simply enlarges the boundaries of the community to include soils, waters, plants, and animals, or collectively: the land. . . . In short, a land ethic changes the role of *Homo sapiens* from conqueror of the land-community to plain member and citizen of it. It implies respect for his fellow members and also respect for the community as such.[17]

For Leopold, the conventional boundaries of ethical duty were too narrow. Expansion was merited to include not only duties toward fellow humans but also duties to nonhuman entities in nature, both living and nonliving.

deep ecology
A theory that rejects human domination of nature and holds that humans have only equal rights with other species, not superior rights. Human interference with nature is now excessive and must be drastically reduced.

In the early 1970s, a more radical form of this land ethic came from Norwegian philosopher Arne Naess. Naess argued that Leopold and mainstream environmentalists were too shallow in their thinking because they were conciliatory with the industrial-age worldview. Naess said there were "deeper concerns" than how to compromise the protection of nature with ongoing economic activity. His position came to be called *deep ecology.* Naess argued that human domination of nature should cease. Philosophies of domination should be replaced by a "biospheric egalitarianism" in which all species had equal rights to live and flourish. Nature should no longer be valued only as inputs for factories as in capitalist economics because it has an intrinsic value that must not be compromised. In short, Naess rejected the four traditional ideas about the man–nature

[17] Aldo Leopold, *A Sand County Almanac* (New York: Ballantine, 1970), pp. 239–40.

relationship that support industrial activity. He concluded that the present level of human interference in nature was excessive and detrimental and that drastic changes were needed.[18]

The views of Naess and other philosophers who share his thinking inspired anti-corporate environmental groups. Some, such as Earth First! and the Environmental Liberation Front, believe that extreme measures, including disregard for the law, are warranted by the moral obligation to end destruction of nature.

speciesism
Bias by humans toward members of their own species and prejudice against members of other species.

Other new philosophies justify the expansion of rights to nonhuman entities. For example, philosopher Peter Singer popularized the idea of *speciesism*, or "a prejudice or attitude of bias toward the members of one's own species and against those of members of other species," that is analogous to racism or sexism.[19] The racist and sexist believe that skin color and sex determine people's worth; the speciesist believes that the number of one's legs or whether one lives in trees, the sea, or a condominium determines one's rights. Traditionally, when *Homo sapiens* compete for rights with plants and animals, the latter have lost. Singer argues that humans, though superior in important ways, are simply one species among many. And the others have intrinsic value independent of any economic usefulness to *Homo sapiens.*

Singer's arguments, like those of Naess, challenge the age-old view of human dominance and undermine the human-centered morality of industrial development—unless such development occurs in a way that respects nature. Recently, Singer has argued that because of modern scientific insights, traditional ethical values about the environment no longer conform to basic tenets of fairness. New ethical rules are needed. Our values evolved when the atmosphere, the forests, and the oceans seemed to be unlimited resources. Now, he writes, we know that "[b]y driving your car you could be releasing carbon dioxide that is part of a causal chain leading to lethal floods in Bangladesh."[20] Traditional values—for example, the sanctity of private property in capitalism—fail to impose adequate duties to protect assets that belong to all humanity.

ENVIRONMENTAL REGULATION IN THE UNITED STATES

The dominant approach to industrial pollution control in the United States has been to pass laws that strictly regulate emissions, effluents, and wastes. Before the 1970s there was little environmental regulation; but by the 1960s the public had become frightened of pollution, and a strong popular mandate for controlling it emerged. As a result, during what came to be called the "environmental decade" of the 1970s, Congress passed a remarkable string of new laws, creating a broad statutory base for regulating industry.

---

[18] Naess's basic arguments are in "The Shallow and the Deep, Long-Range Ecology Movement: A Summary," *Inquiry,* Spring 1973; and "A Defense of the Deep Ecology Movement," *Environmental Economics,* Fall 1984.

[19] Peter Singer, *Animal Liberation* (New York: Avon, 1975), p. 7.

[20] Peter Singer, *One World: The Ethics of Globalization* (New Haven, CT: Yale University Press, 2002), pp. 19–20.

Although more laws have been passed since the 1970s, the ones from that decade still form the basic regulatory framework. Most have been reauthorized and amended, some several times, and some of these revisions, such as the Clean Air Act Amendments of 1990, are so extensive that they fundamentally alter the statute. To illustrate, the Clean Air Act passed in 1970 was 50 pages, but when Congress amended it in 1990 it ballooned to 800 pages. These 800 pages rolled out 538 specific requirements for new rules, standards, and reports.

The Environmental Protection Agency

The Environmental Protection Agency (EPA) is an executive branch regulatory agency. It was created in 1970 to consolidate environmental programs scattered throughout the federal government. Its mission is to protect human health and to preserve the natural environment. Although a few other agencies administer environmental laws, the EPA enforces more than 30 statutes making up the overwhelming bulk of regulation in this area. In 2008 it had more than 17,000 employees and a budget of $4.9 billion, making it larger and better funded than the Department of State. It is the largest regulatory agency aside from the Department of Homeland Security.

When Congress passes an environmental law, EPA employees write the detailed, specific rules and standards needed to make it work. According to one study, between 1981 and 1999 the agency issued more than 2,700 regulations, 115 of which had an economic impact of $100 million or more.[21] The EPA can enforce these rules directly on corporations, but laws permit delegating enforcement to the states. State regulators, acting with federal funding and following EPA guidelines, now do most of the enforcement of the nation's environmental laws.

Although the EPA remains an aggressive agency imbued with a sense of mission, it suffers from work overload. And since its founding it has been whipsawed by competing interests. Environmentalists and Democrats in Congress sometimes criticize its actions as too little. Industry and its Republican allies, on the other hand, incline to see many actions as too strong, imposing an unreasonable regulatory burden.

PRINCIPAL AREAS OF ENVIRONMENTAL POLICY

There are three media for pollution: air, water, and land. Here we give a brief overview of regulations that protect them from degradation. In each area, we describe laws, basic problems, central concerns for business, and progress.

Air

Air pollution is best described as a set of complex interrelated problems, each requiring different control measures. The Clean Air Act, most recently amended in 1990, is the primary air quality statute. Although this law permits the use of some market incentives, these provisions depart from its core philosophy, which is to

[21] General Accounting Office, *Environmental Protection: Assessing the Impacts of EPA's Regulations through Retrospective Studies,* GAO/RCED-99-250, September 1999, p. 3 and fn. 4.

impose inflexible, draconian, command controls. We now discuss regulation of different air pollution problems.

National Air Quality

The Clean Air Act requires the EPA to set national standards that limit pollution from substances harmful to public health and the environment. These standards are supposed to be set without regard for cost and must provide an "adequate margin of safety" that protects even the most sensitive people. To do this, the EPA has set standards to curb emissions of six substances, called *criteria pollutants*, that are the primary threat to air quality because they are emitted in large quantities:

criteria pollutants
Six natural substances released in large quantities that cause substandard air quality—carbon monoxide, nitrogen dioxide, sulfur dioxide, ozone, particulates, and lead.

- *Carbon monoxide* (CO) is a gas produced from incomplete combustion of carbon in fuels such as gasoline. Its largest source is vehicle emissions. High concentrations of CO reduce the oxygen carrying capacity of the blood and may aggravate cardiovascular disease.

- *Nitrogen dioxide* (NO_2) is a gas resulting from oxidation in the atmosphere of nitrogen oxide (NO), a pollutant formed during high temperature combustion. It comes mainly from vehicle exhaust and fuel combustion in industry. It is a lung irritant and aggravates respiratory disease.

- *Sulfur dioxide* (SO_2) is a colorless gas that comes primarily from the burning of fossil fuels, which releases trapped sulfur compounds. Two-thirds of SO_2 is emitted by electric utilities burning coal and oil. SO_2 contributes to acid rain and fine particle pollution. It is a lung irritant that triggers asthma attacks and is associated with heart attacks and cancer.

- *Ozone* (O_3) molecules are not directly emitted by industrial processes or vehicles. Instead, they form in the air by chemical reactions between nitrogen dioxide and carbon-based molecules known as *volatile organic compounds* (VOCs), gases that vaporize from a wide range of liquid or solid carbon-based compounds including petroleum fuels, solvents, paints, adhesives, pesticides, and waxes. These airborne reactions are promoted by the energy in sunlight, which is why urban smog is worse on sunny days. Industry accounts for about half of all VOC emissions and vehicles for the other half. Some VOCs, including benzine, toluene, vinyl chloride, and xylenes cause cancer. Ozone is a bluish gas that irritates the lungs, and high concentrations damage lung tissue. Near ground level, ozone is considered a pollutant. High in the atmosphere, however, naturally occurring ozone absorbs solar radiation, making life possible on earth.

volatile organic compounds
Gases that evaporate from liquid or solid carbon-based compounds such as gasoline or floor wax. In sunlight they react with other pollutants to form urban smog.

condensibles
Small particles formed in the atmosphere by photochemical reactions of gases found in urban smog.

- *Particulate matter* (PM) is composed of small particles suspended in the air. These particles are released by industrial activity and combustion. Coal-burning power plants emit massive numbers of particles because fly ash is not completely removed from stack gases by existing control methods. Diesel exhaust is filled with small carbon particles that can remain airborne for several days. Some particles, called *condensibles*, are created in the atmosphere by reactions of precursor gases including NO_2, SO_2, VOCs, and ammonia. The EPA regulates particles that are 10 micrometers in size, about one-seventh the diameter of a human hair, or smaller. Industry emits only about 15 percent of these particles, labeled PM_{10}. Most come from dust raised by the wind. Particulates pose the greatest health risks of all the criteria pollutants. They are associated with respiratory and cardiovascular disease. Hospitalizations and near-term death rates for infants, the elderly, and the infirm rise during smog episodes primarily because of the inhalation of these small particles. The World Health Organization estimates that each year PM_{10} in outdoor urban air is responsible for about 800,000 deaths worldwide.[22] Recently, the EPA introduced standards for very small particles of 2.5 micrometers or less, called $PM_{2.5}$, which are especially dangerous to human health because they go more deeply into the airways. The majority of $PM_{2.5}$ are condensibles.

- *Lead* (Pb) is a metal that causes seizures and mental retardation. With the elimination of leaded gasoline years ago, the problem of lead in urban air has ended. Airborne lead is now a danger only in a few areas near lead smelters and battery plants.

parts per million (ppm)
The number of molecules of a chemical found in 1 million molecules of a particular gas, liquid, or solid. It can otherwise be expressed as the ratio of the molecules of a certain chemical to the total number of molecules in a gas, liquid, or solid.

For each criteria pollutant, the EPA sets standards for maximum concentrations. The CO standard, for example, is 9 *parts per million* (ppm) averaged over eight hours, or 35 ppm in one hour. This standard is largely met. More than 90 percent of 244 monitoring sites across the nation register 4 ppm or lower. The ozone standard, on the other hand, is far lower, only 0.08 ppm over 8 hours and 0.12 ppm for one hour. Despite being more than 100 times less than the CO standard, the 8-hour ozone standard is not met. More than 90 percent of monitoring sites record an average of 0.10 ppm.

As shown in Table 13.2, industrial activity is the source of only one-quarter of aggregate criteria pollutant emissions. By far, the largest industrial sources of criteria pollutants are coal-fired power plants. Industry is the largest source of only SO_2 and lead, and lead emissions, which have been reduced by 99 percent since 1970, are no longer a national problem.

TABLE 13.2
Estimated National Emissions of Criteria Pollutants by Source: 2006 (in thousands of short tons)

Substance	Industry[a]	Vehicles[b]	Other[c]	Total
Carbon monoxide	9,227	78,028	13,297	100,552
Nitrogen oxides	7,421	10,622	183	18,226
Sulfur dioxide	13,065	616	89	13,770
Volatile organic compounds	8,841	6,174	2,368	17,383
Particulates (PM_{10})[d]	2,812	480	15,128	18,420
Particulates $(PM_{2.5})$[e]	1,860	400	2,314	4,574
Lead[f]	3.6	0.6	0.03	4.23
Totals	41,369.6	95,920.6	31,065	168,355
Percentages	**25%**	**57%**	**18%**	**100%**

[a]Includes industrial fuel combustion and industrial processes.
[b]Includes aircraft.
[c]Includes, *inter alia*, residential wood burning, agricultural burning, forest wildfires, structural fires, and (for particulates) fugitive dust.
[d]Figures include condensable PM, or particles formed in the atmosphere from reactions of precursor gases.
[e]$PM_{2.5}$ is included in PM_{10} and not added into totals.
[f]Figures are for 2000.

Sources: EPA, *National Emissions Inventory Air Pollutant Emissions Trends Data: Current Emissions Trends Summaries,* http://www.epa.gov/ttn/chief/trends/, July 2007; for lead, *National Air Quality and Emissions Trends Report, 2003,* table A-3.

[22] United Nations Environmental Programme, *Global Environmental Outlook 4* (Nairobi: Kenya, UNEP, 2007), p. 45.

FIGURE 13.2 Declining Emissions of Criteria Pollutants: 1970–2005

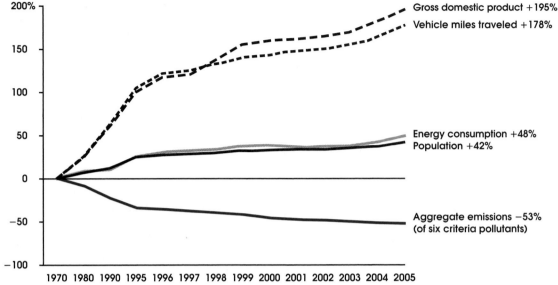

Source: Adapted from EPA, *FY 2006 Performance and Accountability Report*, EPA-190-R-06-002, p. 44.

To suppress criteria pollutants, the Clean Air Act mandates a range of expensive actions including emissions controls on power plants, factories, smelters, and vehicles. Since controls began early in the 1970s, emissions have dropped more than 50 percent. Figure 13.2 shows how remarkable this reduction is, since it was achieved in an uphill battle against growth of the activities that generate emissions.

Hazardous Air Pollutants

hazardous air pollutants
Chemical emissions that pose a health risk of serious illness such as cancer or birth defects with even small inhalation exposures.

Besides controlling the six criteria pollutants, the Clean Air Act mandates control of *hazardous air pollutants*. Hazardous air pollutants, sometimes called air toxics, cause cancer and other serious health effects such as brain damage or birth defects. The EPA has identified 650 air toxics. Examples are benzine, toluene, formaldehyde, and xylenes, which come mostly from vehicles; and arsenic, chromium, dioxin, mercury, and hydrochloric acid which come from industry. Combined emissions are between 4 and 5 million tons per year, only a fraction of 1 percent of the six criteria pollutants, but the EPA estimates that even this amount poses a lifetime cancer risk of 25 in 1 million for residents of American cities.[23]

Large industrial sources such as electric utilities, oil refineries, chemical plants, steel mills, and paper plants are responsible for about 20 percent of air toxics releases. Of the remainder, about 41 percent come from vehicles, 30 percent from a range of small sources such as dry cleaners and gas stations, and 9 percent from fires.

The Clean Air Act requires the EPA to set emission standards for 187 air toxics at levels that prevent disease and requires industry to use the "maximum achievable

[23] Environmental Protection Agency, *Performance and Accountability Report: Fiscal Year 2006*, EPA 190-R-06-002, November 2006, p. 45.

maximum achievable control technology
A performance standard used by the EPA to control emissions of hazardous air pollutants. It requires control of toxic air emissions at least equal to that achieved by the top 12 percent of sources in the industry.

control technology" to comply. In practice, *maximum achievable control technology* is emissions control equal to the control achieved by the best-performing 12 percent of sources in the industry. So far, the agency has set standards for 174 industries. For example, the melting furnaces in iron and steel foundries emit hazardous air pollutants such as nickel, lead, chromium, and manganese. A recent proposed rule limits these furnaces to 0.06 pounds of toxic metal air emissions per ton of metal melted (approximately one pound for every 17 tons melted).[24]

Although hazardous air emissions have been reduced about 65 percent since 1993, much of the decline is due to voluntary cuts by companies that do not wish to report high emissions levels publicly and to reformulation of gasoline and diesel fuel intended mainly to cut criteria pollutant emissions. The EPA's air toxics program is underfunded. It is now years behind on meeting most of its Clean Air Act deadlines.[25] Within the agency it has low priority and action is taken mainly in response to lawsuits by environmentalists. Meanwhile, most Americans are exposed to cancer risks from these dangerous air pollutants far greater than the agencies' goal of 1 in 1 million over a lifetime.

Acid Rain

acid rain
Deposition of acids formed when sulfur and nitrogen compounds undergo chemical reactions in the atmosphere and return to earth in rain, hail, snow, fog, and dry fallout of acidic particles.

Acid rain is the deposition, in various forms of moist and dry precipitation, of highly acidic compounds from the atmosphere. It is caused primarily by two airborne pollutants, sulfur dioxide and oxides of nitrogen (NO_x). In the atmosphere, these gases undergo chemical reactions and return to earth as acids that alter the pH of water, degrading lakes and forests and causing buildings to deteriorate. Both also contribute to formation of the small airborne particles that cause regional haze and adversely affect human health.

When Congress amended the Clean Air Act in 1990, it responded to public alarm about acid rain by requiring the EPA to reduce emissions of these two key precursor substances. Profligate emissions of SO_2 and NO_x coming from coal-fired electric power-generating plants in the Northeast and Midwest were blamed for degrading sensitive eastern lakes and forests found downwind of emission plumes. Coal combustion releases large amounts of both gases. About two-thirds of the SO_2 in the United States comes from electric utilities and there are effective, though extremely expensive, methods for removing it from boiler exhaust streams. Electric utilities are responsible for only about one-third of the nation's NO_x but control equipment is less effective.[26]

The EPA set up separate programs to reduce emissions of the two precursor gases. To control SO_2, it set a goal of capping aggregate emissions from power plants at 8.95 million tons per year by 2010. Rather than strictly regulating each plant and boiler, it issued permits to emit SO_2 equal to emissions in 1995, then slowly began reducing the number of permits until their number would limit

[24] Environmental Protection Agency, "National Emission Standards for Hazardous Air Pollutants for Iron and Steel Foundries Area Sources; Proposed Rule," 72 FR 52983, September 17, 2007.

[25] Government Accountability Office, *Clean Air Act: EPA Should Improve the Management of Its Air Toxics Program,* GAO-06-669, June 2006, pp. 15–21.

[26] Environmental Protection Agency, "Acid Rain Program: Nitrogen Oxides Emission Reduction Program," 61 FR 67112, December 19, 1996.

FIGURE 13.3
Emission
Trends for
Electric Power-
Generating
Plants in the
Acid Rain
Program

Source: Environ-
mental Protection
Agency, 2007.

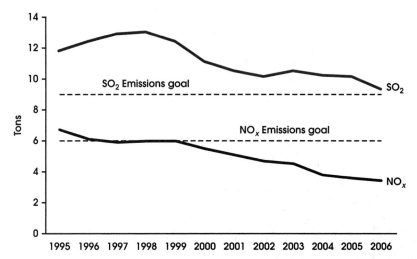

emissions equal to the annual goal of 8.95 million tons. Companies can reduce their emissions either as fast as or faster than the emissions permits are retired, or they can buy permits from other companies in an open market. This approach, which harnesses economic incentives to reduce pollution, is called "cap-and-trade." How it works is discussed in more detail in the next chapter.

To control NO_x emissions the agency resorts to traditional command-and-control regulation, setting emission limits for each boiler on the basis of its heat output. A facility can comply with these limits for individual boilers or it can average emissions from two or more boilers to meet averaged limits. At the start of the program, the EPA set a goal of limiting NO_x emissions to 6 million pounds per year by 2010 and this goal has been exceeded.

Figure 13.3 shows how aggregate emissions for 1,213 regulated power plants have fallen since the start of the acid rain program in 1995. As a result, the acidity of deposition in the eastern United States has declined by 30 percent. Lakes, rivers, and streams in three of four eastern regions studied by the EPA are less acid. The exception is southern Appalachian streams, which continue to grow more acidic.[27] In addition, atmospheric sulfate has been reduced by 27 percent, bringing better air quality and enormous public health benefits. One estimate is that by 2010 particulate reductions will be the cause of avoiding 17,000 deaths, 22,800 nonfatal heart attacks, and 12,130,300 workdays lost to illness. Reductions in ozone, which is formed in photochemical reactions between SO_2 and volatile organic compounds, will prevent an additional 700 deaths and 785,500 lost school days each year.[28] Overall, acid rain regulation is estimated to cost $3.5 billion a year by 2010 yet predicted to have annual health and ecosystem benefits worth $142 billion.[29]

[27] Environmental Protection Agency, *Acid Rain Program 2005 Progress Report*, EPA-430-R-06-015, October 2006, table 6.

[28]Lauraine G. Chestnut and David M. Mills, "A Fresh Look at the Benefits and Costs of the U.S. Acid Rain Program," *Journal of Environmental Management*, vol. 77 (2005), tables 3 and 4.

Indoor Air Pollution

Indoor air in developed nations is contaminated by a mixture of pollutants. These include asbestos, radon, tobacco smoke, combustion by-products from cooking, chlorine compounds released as gases from chlorinated water, formaldehyde from pressed wood in cabinets, biological contaminants such as mite dust, and vapors from air fresheners, cosmetics, glues, paints, dry-cleaned clothing, and household insecticides.

Indoor pollutants are dangerous because Americans spend 80 to 90 percent of their lives indoors, where concentrations of a dozen common organic pollutants can be 2-to-10 times greater than outdoors.[30] Another dangerous pollutant that builds up indoors is *radon*, a colorless, odorless, radioactive gas commonly found in soils. It seeps from the ground into homes, building up to unnaturally high concentrations in confined spaces. Radon emits beta and gamma radiation that penetrates human tissue and causes an estimated 7,000 to 30,000 deaths yearly.[31] At the high end this is more than 10 times the estimated number of cancer deaths from all toxic chemical emissions by industry.

> **radon**
> An inert, colorless, odorless gas found in soil and rock formations. It is a naturally occurring decay product of uranium.

More than 20 years ago the EPA ranked indoor air as one of the top five human health risks, but since then it has done little about mitigation. Congress has never authorized EPA inspectors to invade homes and offices with air-sampling equipment, forms, and ticket books. Beyond spending on research that is modest and sporadic in relation to the risks posed, the agency has a voluntary radon measurement program and publishes information to educate the public. Meanwhile, the health problem grows worse as more tightly sealed, energy-efficient buildings trap indoor pollutants.

Ozone-Destroying Chemicals

While ozone in urban smog is regarded as a pollutant, ozone in the stratosphere screens out ultraviolet energy harmful to living tissue. Ozone (O_3) is a molecule of three oxygen atoms that forms naturally during chemical reactions with oxygen in the presence of sunlight. About 90 percent of all ozone forms in the stratosphere, which begins at 6 to 10 miles above earth and rises to about 31 miles. Even in its peak band high in the stratosphere it exists in very low concentrations of about 12,000 ozone molecules for every 1 billion air molecules. Yet it forms a critical barrier, reducing penetration of ultraviolet wavelengths in sunlight to levels that permit life on earth.

Emissions of manufactured gases containing chlorine and bromine threaten this delicate barrier. Examples of major sources are chlorofluorocarbon refrigerants,

---

[29] Testimony of Brian McLean, before the Committee on Energy and Commerce, Subcommittee on Energy and Air Quality, U. S. House of Representatives, 110th Congress 1st Session, March 29, 2007, p. 7.

[30] These figures are based on the EPA's Total Exposure Assessment Methodology (TEAM) studies reported in American Lung Association et al., *Indoor Air Pollution for Health Professionals* (Washington, DC: Government Printing Office, 1994), EPA 402-R-94-007, at www.epa.gov.iaq.

[31] Department of Health and Human Services, Agency for Toxic Substances and Disease Registry, "Case Studies in Environmental Medicine: Radon Toxicity," ATSDR-HE-CS-2001-0006 (2001), p. 1.

**chlorofluoro-
carbons**
A family of
gases contain-
ing the ele-
ments chlorine,
fluorine, and
carbon used as
refrigerants,
aerosol propel-
lants, foams,
and solvents.
They are inert
and exception-
ally stable, but
break down in
the upper
atmosphere
in ozone-
consuming
reactions.

halons in fire extinguishers, solvents such as carbon tetrachloride, and pesticides containing methyl bromide. When released into the lower atmosphere they persist and eventually rise into the stratosphere, where they are converted by chemical reactions into more reactive gases that destroy ozone. In the catalytic processes that these reactive gases unleash, a single chlorine or bromine atom can destroy hundreds of ozone molecules.

Many ozone-depleting gases are extremely long-lived. *Chlorofluorocarbons* (CFCs), for example, are large, tough molecules that defy natural breakdown processes. Typically, they survive 50 to 100 years in the atmosphere, and in one case 1,700 years.

In high latitudes, the ozone layer has thinned as much as 30 percent because of the action of these industrial gases. This exposes planetary life and ecosystems to more ultraviolet radiation, causing excess skin cancers, eye cataracts, weakened immune systems, lowered crop yields, and reduction of phytoplankton in oceans. Even the highest levels of ozone in urban smog are inadequate to protect humans from this radiation damage.

In 1987 a treaty called the Montreal Protocol set timetables to phase out worldwide use of 96 ozone-depleting chemicals. To meet treaty obligations, the United States and other developed nations have already phased out production of the most destructive gases. Developing nations, however, have not met more extended timetables given them for ceasing production and consumption. Compliance is difficult for several reasons. Substitutes for some chemicals, including CFCs, are more expensive and many businesses in poor and transitional countries cannot afford the cost of conversion. Economic growth in Asia has led to increased use of CFCs. Around the world, a thriving black market in CFCs exists to avoid taxes and penalties imposed by governments.

Despite such problems, the treaty seems to be working. A scientific panel recently reported that concentrations of ozone-depleting gases in the troposphere have declined since peaking in the mid-1990s and the depletion of stratospheric ozone observed since 1980 has been arrested, though not reversed. Ozone concentrations are now stable. Atmospheric scientists predict that ozone concentrations in the upper atmosphere will return to their 1980 levels between 2050 and 2075.[32] The EPA estimates that this will reduce terrestrial radiation enough to save 6.3 million lives in the United States alone that would otherwise have been lost to malignant skin cancers.[33] Without the treaty, scientists estimate that by 2050 only 30 percent of the ozone layer would be left in higher latitudes and increased radiation would cause more than 20 million additional skin cancers worldwide.[34]

[32] World Meteorological Organization, *Scientific Assessment of Ozone Depletion: 2006,* Global Ozone Research and Monitoring Project, Report No. 50, February 2007, chap. 6.

[33] Environmental Protection Agency, *Achievements in Stratospheric Ozone Protection: Progress Report,* EPA-430-R-07-001, April 2007, p. 7.

[34] United Nations Environmental Programme, *Backgrounder: Basic Facts and Data on the Science and Politics of Ozone Protection* (Nairobe, Kenya: UNEP, October 5, 2001), p. 5.

FIGURE 13.4

Atmospheric Concentrations of Greenhouse Gases: 1750–2005

This chart shows observed concentrations of six greenhouse gases, including CO_2. Other gases are measured in terms of their CO_2 equivalents, or the amount of CO_2 that would have the same global warming potential. This is usually expressed as the number of tons of CO_2 that would have to be emitted to have the same potential for global warming as another gas. For example, 1 ton of methane is equal to 21 tons of CO_2, 1 ton of nitrous oxide is equal to 310 tons of CO_2, and 1 ton of HFC-23 (one of the fluorinated gases) is equal to 11,700 tons of CO_2. The CO_2 equivalent is expressed in parts per million, or the ratio of CO_2 molecules to air molecules.

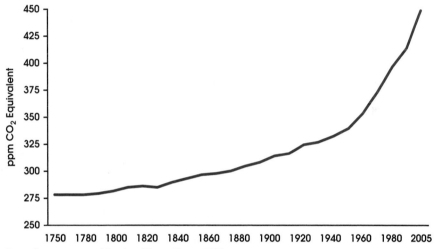

Source: Intergovernmental Panel on Climate Change, 2007.

Greenhouse Gases

greenhouse gases
Atmospheric gases that absorb energy radiated from the earth, preventing it from being released into space.

The industrial revolution led to rising emissions of a group of gases, called *greenhouse gases*, that trap heat in the atmosphere instead of allowing it to radiate into space. These gases include carbon dioxide, methane, nitrous oxide, and fluorinated gases such as those used in refrigerants and fire extinguishers. Electrons in the atoms of greenhouse gas molecules are excited by the energy in infrared wavelengths of outgoing terrestrial radiation, causing atmospheric heating. Without them more of the energy from incoming solar radiation in ultraviolet wavelengths would radiate back into space and the earth would cool.

In their preindustrial atmospheric concentrations greenhouse gases were part of a natural mechanism keeping a stable balance between heat buildup and heat loss so that global mean average temperature remained steady. Since the industrial revolution, however, human activity has raised atmospheric concentrations of these gases, as shown in Figure 13.4. The predominant greenhouse gas is carbon dioxide, which makes up about 85 percent of greenhouse gas emissions. Between 1750 and 2005, CO_2 resident in the earth's atmosphere rose from about 280 to 379 parts per million. Carbon dioxide is a product of complete combustion of carbon. Wood and fossil fuel combustion have released such huge amounts of carbon that natural processes of carbon absorption by oceans and forests are overwhelmed. Thus, more carbon remains in the atmosphere as CO_2.

Between 1850 and 2005 mean global surface temperature has warmed an estimated 0.76° Celsius (1.4°F). The oceans have absorbed 80 percent of this warming with average temperatures increasing to depths of 3,000 meters (9,800 feet). As oceans have warmed, the water has expanded, causing a global rise of 0.17 meter (about 6.7 inches) through the twentieth century. A scientific consensus has formed that these changes are caused by greenhouse gas emissions and added warming of 1.8° to 4.0° Celsius (3.2° to 7.2° F) and sea level rises of .18 to .59 meters (7 to 23 inches) will follow by 2100.[35] This warming is expected to cause unprecedented climate change that will disrupt ecosystems.

The major effort to slow global warming is an international treaty, the Kyoto Protocol, which went into effect in 2005. It requires industrial nations to cut emissions of primary greenhouse gases an average of 5 percent below 1990 levels by 2012. The United States is not a party to the Kyoto Protocol. Tremendous political opposition to participation exists because U.S. greenhouse gas emissions are rising and mandatory reductions would hurt the economy. Opponents say that American consumers would bear a heavy cost and more American jobs would move overseas.

Of the 175 other countries that ratified the Kyoto Protocol, most are not required to reduce CO_2 emissions. Developing nations, including big polluters such as China, India, Mexico, Brazil, and Nigeria, are not committed to emissions reductions under the treaty because of their fear that cuts would derail economic growth. They argue that the historical emissions of developed nations have caused most of the warming and that richer countries can better afford the costs of emission reduction. Since they are not subject to restrictions, and the United States refuses to act, the entire burden of saving earth's climate falls on 36 more industrialized nations, including those of the European Union. And, despite reduction efforts, their overall CO_2 emissions keep rising.

Without Kyoto participation, the main action of the United States is an initiative announced by President Bush in 2002 to reduce the *emissions intensity* of greenhouse gases 18 percent by 2012. Emissions intensity is the amount of greenhouse gases emitted per unit of economic output, measured as tons of emissions per million dollars of GDP. This "ambitious" project is built on a collection of more than two dozen voluntary programs, subsidies, and tax incentives designed to promote energy efficiency.[36] These range from weatherization assistance for low-income families to loan guarantees for nuclear energy plants to research on new technologies that improve air traffic flow so airliners burn less fuel.[37]

Because of growing energy efficiency, emissions intensity is already projected to fall almost 19 percent by 2012, so the goal of an 18 percent reduction from 2002 levels seems to have been very modest. Furthermore, the Bush administration

emissions intensity
The amount of greenhouse gases emitted per unit of economic output, measured as tons of emissions per million dollars of the gross domestic product.

[35] Susan Solomon et al., eds. *Climate Change 2007: The Physical Science Basis* (New York: Cambridge University Press, 2007), p. 13.

[36] Council on Environmental Quality, "Addressing Global Climate Change," June 11, 2001, at www.whitehouse.gov.

[37] U. S. Department of State, *U.S. Climate Action Report: 2006* (Washington, DC: Department of State, 2007), chap. 4, "Policies and Measures."

plan allows total emissions to rise even as their proportion to economic output falls. A rise of 11 percent over the 2002–2012 period is predicted.

In the absence of strong federal regulation the states have seized the initiative. Nine northeastern states have joined to create a regional cap-and-trade program for CO_2 emissions from power plants. They plan to stabilize emissions by 2015, then reduce the cap by 10 percent between 2015 and 2020. California has passed a law requiring reduction of statewide greenhouse gas emissions to 1990 levels by 2020.[38]

Water

The basic statute for fighting water pollution is the Federal Water Pollution Control Act Amendments of 1972, usually called the Clean Water Act. Congress intended it to be a powerful measure that would stop the deterioration of the nation's lakes, rivers, streams, and estuaries. The act set a goal of eliminating *all* polluting discharges into these waters by 1985. However, the goal was not met and will not soon be met.

The Clean Water Act is effective in reducing, but not eliminating, polluted factory outflows, or effluents. Every industrial plant uses water, and sources of pollution are numerous. In production processes, water is used as a washing, scrubbing, cooling, or mixing medium. It becomes contaminated with a variety of particles and dissolved chemicals. The Clean Water Act prohibits the release of any polluted factory discharge without a permit.

effluent
A treated or untreated wastewater discharge from an industrial facility.

The EPA regulates industrial *effluents* from *point sources*, that is, sites that discharge from a single location, using a permit system called the National Pollution Discharge Elimination System (NPDES). Under the NPDES, each industrial facility must get a permit specifying the volume of one or more substances it can pour into a water body. Effluent limits are based on scientific estimates of how much of a substance the water body can absorb before deteriorating unacceptably and on the ability of available equipment to remove a particular pollutant. The EPA sets water quality criteria for pollutants. Usually there are two standards, one for protecting human health and the other for aquatic life. To give examples, the chloroform standard prohibits chronic exposure of aquatic life to concentrations of more than 1,240 µg/l (micrograms per cubic liter) and exposure of humans to more than 470 µg/l. As noted, permit limits are also based on how much pollution the best control devices can remove from wastewater. These devices range from simple screens for large particles to intricate chemical and biological treatment systems.

point source
A discrete source of effluent such as a factory, mine, ship, or pipeline.

For example, plants that make paperboard out of wastepaper have small amounts of the wood preservative pentachlorophenol (C_6HCl_5O) in their wastewater streams. C_6HCl_5O is so poisonous that swallowing one-tenth of an ounce, about a teaspoon, can be lethal. However, for this substance the EPA has defined the best control technology standard as effluent containing no more than 0.87 pound of C_6HCl_5O for each 1 million pounds of paperboard produced because the best control technology cannot remove more of it. In other words, a paperboard factory can drain almost 14 ounces of C_6HCl_5O into a river or stream every time it makes a million pounds of paperboard. Currently, about 96,000 facilities operate under an NPDES permit.

---

[38] John Byrne et al. "American Policy Conflict in the Greenhouse," *Energy Policy,* September 2007, p. 4555.

While the EPA has limited factory discharges, "nonpoint" effluent, or runoff that enters surface waters from diffuse sources, is largely uncontrolled. Runoff from agriculture—animal wastes, pesticides, and fertilizers—is now the primary cause of impaired water bodies. Although general language in the Clean Water Act permits the EPA to act against any source of water pollution, the law avoided specific language aimed at farmers because of their political power. However, growing pollution from big animal feedlots and poultry farms led the EPA to place several thousand factory farms under permits.

Urban runoff is another major contributor to poor water quality. As urban areas increase in size, more water flows over their streets, collecting pollutants and carrying them to water bodies. The Clean Water Act empowers the EPA to require control measures by cities, including detention ponds, street sweeping, and public education programs. Nonpoint sources are now the biggest contributors to water pollution and efforts to control them are just beginning.

Overall, the quality of surface waters is much improved from 1972 when the Clean Water Act was passed. Then, it was estimated that only 30 to 40 percent of the nation's waters met the law's water quality goals.[39] Today, 60 to 90 percent do. However, progress from now on will be difficult. The current Clean Water Act emphasizes control of point source pollution by industry using end-of-the-pipe equipment. Yet the biggest source of pollution now is copious and little-controlled runoff from farms and cities. Adequate regulation of runoff requires a revision of the law to give the EPA new tools and powers. The existing permit system is ill-suited to control nonpoint pollution.

Land

After Congress passed air and water pollution control laws early in the 1970s, it became apparent that poor handling and disposal of solid hazardous wastes was a major problem. Also, devices that removed air- and waterborne poisons from industrial processes under the new laws produced tons of poisoned sludge, slime, and dust that ended up in poorly contained landfills. Authority over the handling of hazardous waste was inadequate to prevent mismanagement. Responding to the menace, Congress passed two laws.

The Resource Conservation and Recovery Act (RCRA) of 1976 gave the EPA authority to manage hazardous waste "from cradle to grave," that is, from the moment it is created to the moment it is finally destroyed or interred. Firms must label, handle, store, treat, and discard hazardous waste under strict guidelines, keeping meticulous records all the while.

The RCRA is a difficult statute to administer and with which to comply. It demands that regulators keep track of literally all hazardous waste produced anywhere in the country—an exhausting job. It relies on smothering command-and-control regulation and prohibits balancing costs against benefits. One indication of the regulatory burden it imposes is that when it was first implemented, nearly 80 percent of the nation's waste disposal facilities elected to close rather than comply with it. Figure 13.5 illustrates a typical installation of wells required to monitor groundwater quality under a solid-waste disposal site.

[39] Kevin Kane, *How's the Water? The State of the Nation's Water Quality,* Working Paper 171 (St. Louis: Center for the Study of American Business, January 2000), p. 3.

FIGURE 13.5
RCRA Landfill Groundwater Monitoring Requirements

The EPA grants permits to all operators of hazardous waste dumps that comply with standards for physical layout, groundwater monitoring, and emergency planning. The drawing is a cross section of ground below a landfill illustrating minimal RCRA monitoring requirements. Water samples drawn from downgradient wells can detect chemical contamination seeping into the groundwater (saturated zone) from the landfill above.

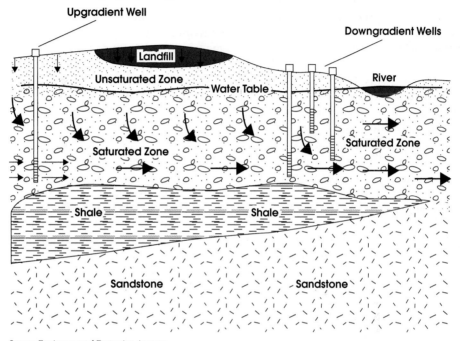

Source: Environmental Protection Agency.

RCRA regulations in the *Code of Federal Regulations* cover 1,763 pages of stupefying detail. For example, in monitoring wells, "[i]f an individual well comparison procedure is used to compare an individual compliance well constituent concentration with background constituent concentrations or a groundwater protection standard, the test shall be done at a Type I error level no less than 0.01 for each testing period."[40] If a pump begins to drip "[t]he first attempt at repair shall be made no later than 5 calendar days after each leak is detected."[41] It is, in the words of one observer, "an amazingly inflexible law with extraordinarily detailed regulations, demanding controls, and a glacially slow permitting system."[42]

Because the law contains no requirement that the benefits of regulation exceed its costs, it has invited many lawsuits by industry. General Motors uses solvents to clean automobile spray painting guns when it changes colors, then recirculates them until, after repeated uses, they go to a waste tank. GM sued when the EPA tried to impose hazardous waste regulations on the recirculation piping. It argued

[40] 40 CFR §258.53(g)(2), July 1, 2006.

[41] 40 CFR §265.1058(c)(2), July 1, 2006.

[42] Robert J. Smith, "RCRA Lives, Alas," *Regulation*, Summer 1991, p. 14.

that the solvents were not a waste while still in use during an industrial process. GM lost when the case was dismissed.[43] Strict enforcement invites litigation over such pinhead technicalities, but there is no question that hazardous waste is much better handled than before the RCRA.

While the RCRA ensured that existing facilities would operate at a high standard, it did nothing about thousands of abandoned toxic waste sites around the country. So Congress passed another law to clean them up. This law is the Comprehensive Environmental Response, Compensation, and Liability Act of 1980, better known as *Superfund,* so-named after the large trust fund it set up to pay for cleanups. This trust fund was generated from special taxes on oil and chemical companies and a small—0.12 percent—addition to the general corporate income tax. However, the taxes expired in 1995. Congress, under pressure from industry, refuses to reinstate them. Corporations believe they are unfair, since they are paid by all companies and fail to distinguish between polluters and exemplary waste handlers. With expiration of the tax the spending power of the program has declined to only about 40 percent of what it was in the late 1980s.[44]

Congress intended Superfund as a temporary measure to be phased out when existing hazardous sites were cleaned. However, the number of sites is higher than predicted and the cleaning process more difficult and expensive than envisioned in 1980. So far, the EPA has identified about 47,000 sites. Early in the program it set up a priority list of sites posing the greatest risk to human health and the environment, usually because of groundwater or drinking water contamination. Since then, 1,569 sites, about 3 percent of the total, have been on this priority list. Cleanup work started at 1,030 sites, however, only 325 have been fully restored and deleted from the list.[45] As completed sites depart the priority list, new ones rotate on from a waiting list.

Far from receding in its activity, the Superfund program now confronts some of the most complex and expensive projects in its history. About 150 priority sites are labeled "mega-sites," where cleanup costs exceed $50 million and the average cost is $140 million. The number of contaminants, the size, how far the contamination has spread, and the location all make mega-sites difficult.

In San Bernardino, California, two plumes of groundwater contaminated by chemicals used in metal plating have moved as far as eight miles under the city. To slow their spread, the EPA dug seven wells that extract water from the leading edge of the underground stream. The wells pump 14,000 gallons per minute through four miles of large water mains laid under city streets for the project. The water goes to a treatment plant, where toxic chemicals are removed using activated charcoal. This mechanism may operate for decades with its cost reaching $450 million.[46]

Superfund
The program to clean up abandoned toxic waste sites set up by the Comprehensive Environmental Response, Compensation, and Liability Act of 1980. It takes its name from the trust fund in which the program's money for cleanup projects is held.

---

[43] *General Motors v. EPA,* 363 F.3d 442 (2003).

[44] Testimony of Katherine N. Probst, "Critical Issues Facing the Superfund Program," Subcommittee on Superfund and Waste Management, U. S. Senate, June 15, 2006, pp. 3–4.

[45] Statement of Susan Parker Bodine, "The Superfund Program," before the Subcommittee on Superfund and Environmental Health, Senate, October 17, 2007, pp. 2–3; "Number of NPL Site Actions and Milestones by Fiscal Year," www.epa.gov/superfund, updated October 26, 2007.

[46] General Accounting Office, *Superfund: Analysis of Costs at Five Superfund Sites,* GAO/RCED-00-22, January 2000, app. I.

FIGURE 13.6
Typical Rotary Kiln Incinerator at a Superfund Site

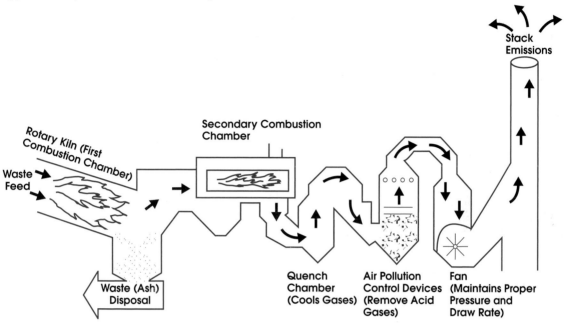

Source: EPA. From: General Accounting Office, *Superfund: EPA Could Further Ensure the Safe Operation of On-Site Incinerators*, GAO/RCED–97–43, March 1997, p. 4.

In New York, 40 miles of the scenic Hudson River will be dredged downstream from a General Electric factory that discharged 1.1 million pounds of polychlorinated biphenyls (PCBs) into the water over 30 years beginning in 1947. PCBs, which are no longer made, are mixtures of chlorinated compounds that do not burn. Because of this property, they were used as coolants and lubricants in electrical equipment. Later, it was discovered that they persist in the environment and in human tissue without breaking down. Even three decades after the discharges ended, the EPA has found more than 40 spots in the river's bed where PCB contamination exceeds 50 parts per million. PCBs are an animal carcinogen and a "probable" human carcinogen. People near the river face a 1 in 1 million lifetime cancer risk if they are exposed to 0.1 microgram of PCBs per liter in drinking water or 0.01 micrograms per cubic meter in the air.[47] These are very tiny amounts, less than 1 millionth of an ounce. To reduce the risk, as much as $700 million will be spent dredging and decontaminating the sediment.

Methods of decontamination and containment differ from site to site. Sometimes, for example, EPA rules require that contaminated dirt be dug up and incinerated at high temperatures. Figure 13.6 shows a diagram of an incinerator. At a rate of 20 tons per hour excavated soil is trucked to a giant revolving kiln, where it is heated to

[47] Environmental Protection Agency, Integrated Risk Information System, "Polychlorinated Biphenyls (PCBs) (CASRN 1336-36-3), June 1, 1997, at www.epa.gov/iris.

1,800° F to break down hazardous organic compounds into simple molecules of CO_2 and H_2O. Then the dirt is backfilled.

Who pays for all this? The law establishes harsh rules of liability for any company that has ever dumped hazardous waste in a Superfund site. In legal terminology, this liability is strict, retroactive, and joint and several. In practical terms, this means that any company that ever dumped hazardous waste on a site can be responsible for the full cleanup cost even if it obeyed the law of years past, was not negligent, and dumped only a small part of the total waste. By 2008, the EPA had spent more than $34 billion fixing contaminated sites, but it had recovered about $26 billion from polluting corporations.

CONCLUDING OBSERVATIONS

Industrial processes damage the environment and cause serious local and global deterioration. The response in the United States and in most of the developed world has been to adopt a series of fairly rigid and expensive regulatory programs. In the United States it is now the largest and most expensive area of regulation. Environmental rules occupy 46 volumes of the *Code of Federal Regulations*, more than any subject and its costs have been estimated as high as $220 billion a year.[48]

Uneven progress has been made in the attack on air, water, and land pollution. Protection for human health and ecosystems has advanced, but there has been too little money, time, and political will to prevent widespread pollution-caused disease and damage to ecosystems.

In the next chapter we discuss methods for determining how regulatory programs can become more efficient and effective and also what voluntary actions corporations are taking to reduce their environmental footprints.

[48] Angela Logomasini, *The Green Regulatory State* (Washington, DC: Competitive Enterprise Institute, Issue Analysis No. 9, 2007), p. 9.

Owls, Loggers, and Old-Growth Forests

In 2007 Jackson County, Oregon, shut its 15 public libraries for six months. The county's readers lost these edifices of learning when the federal government reneged on a promise made by Theodore Roosevelt.

In 1908 Roosevelt seized 2.4 million acres of forested land from the Oregon–California Railroad, which had fraudulently acquired it from the government.[1] This removed large parcels of land from county tax rolls and would have blighted the general prosperity. So

Roosevelt agreed to split funds from timber sales with affected counties. The agreement was formalized in a 1937 law directing that the forests on these former railroad lands be managed for sustained timber yields with 50 percent of the revenues going to 18 counties in northern California and Oregon, including Jackson County.[2]

The pact worked through most of the century as these counties used timber sale money to strengthen their social fabric, building schools and libraries, paving

[1] John Messing, "Public Lands, Politics, and Progressives: The Oregon Land Fraud Trials, 1903–1910," *The Pacific Historical Review,* February 1966.

[2] This was the Oregon and California Railroad and Coos Bay Wagon Road Grant Lands Act.

roads, improving law enforcement, and funding social services. Then, in the 1990s, timber revenues plummeted after the northern spotted owl was declared a threatened species. Forests on the old railroad lands no longer were managed for timber yield as President Roosevelt had promised. Instead, they were turned into species preserves.

For a while, Congress came to the rescue, first with yearly "owl guarantee payments" to timber-dependent counties, and later with annual "safety net" payments. These subsidies never matched revenues from the heydays of logging, but they helped. However, in 2006, President George W. Bush vetoed a bill to continue the safety net payments.

Jackson County lost $23 million from its budget and closed its libraries.[3] It also had to cut back on law enforcement. It no longer monitored all sex offenders and there were fewer jail beds. Other counties made cuts their way. Farther north, Coos County laid off 70 people. To the south, Alpine County, California, which is 92 percent national forest land, closed six schools.

Jackson County no longer has a timber economy. In the 1950s its livelihood was timber sales and it bore the din of 91 sawmills. Today only one remains. The county is more fortunate than some others. It cobbles together a comfortable economy with a university, an internationally known Shakespeare festival, pear orchards, a large mail-order business, and some retirement communities. Still, the loss of timber funds has caused long-term deterioration of county services—and worse. According to one longtime western Oregon resident: "the social and economic welfare of people I know in the past 20 some years has gone straight downhill. I've seen people have to go on welfare. The drinking starts. The divorces."[4]

The cause of this tear in the social fabric is the northern spotted owl, a reclusive, nocturnal bird abiding deep in the forests. With poetic justice, the fate of loggers mirrors that of the owl. Since the 1800s timber cutting and land development have reduced

the creature's habitat by as much as 80 percent, threatening its extinction. In 1973, Congress passed the Endangered Species Act to protect such creatures. Unfortunately for the wood products industry, spotted owls inhabit the most productive timber stands of the Pacific Northwest. So, a great battle has unfolded. The contestants are contrary philosophies about the purpose of forests.

THE NORTHERN SPOTTED OWL

The northern spotted owl (*Strix occidentalis caurina*) is a perch-and-dive predator with a wingspan of 2 feet and a weight of about 1½ pounds. Its body is mottled brown with patches of white. Its habitat ranges from British Columbia in the north to the redwood stands above San Francisco in the south.

Like other owls, the northern spotted owl is anatomically adapted to nighttime activity. It has a large head and a large brain, compared with other birds, and big round eyes. "Indeed," notes one biologist, "the heads of owls are basically little more than brains with raptorial beaks and the largest possible eyes and ears attached."[5] Spotted owls' eyes have rod-rich retinas, endowing them with exceptionally acute black-and-white vision in low-light conditions. They can locate and dive on scampering mice in illuminations as much as 30 times below the lowest reported human visual threshold.

Their hearing is similarly acute. Without benefit of vision, they can locate tree squirrels or mice that make small rustling noises in frequency ranges inaudible to humans. Their brains calculate time lags of microseconds in the arrival of sounds at each ear, enabling them to fly unerringly through darkness to a sound source. The spotted owl, despite its sedentary daytime roosting, has a high metabolism and hunts actively through the night. Its prey is mainly small mammals such as flying squirrels, wood rats, rabbits, mice, and tree voles, but it also kills reptiles and small birds.

Northern spotted owls exhibit a wide range of social behavior. They have courtship rituals, and pairs bond for extended periods. They communicate with postural signals, displays of aggression, and a variety of hoots and calls. They are territorial and

[3] William Yardley, "Timber (and Its Revenues) Decline, and Libraries Suffer," *The New York Times*, May 5, 2007, p. 9; Meredith May, "Largest Library Closure in U.S. Looms," *San Francisco Chronicle*, March 4, 2007, p. A1.

[4] Lynne Vanderlinden, quoted in Jeff Barnard, "Timber Counties Brace for the End of Big Logging Subsidies," Associated Press State & Local Wire, March 10, 2007.

[5] Paul A. Johnsgard, *North American Owls: Biology and Natural History* (Washington, DC: Smithsonian Institution Press, 1988), p. 42.

The northern spotted owl. Source: © Kevin Schafer/CORBIS.

announce their presence with a series of four hoots (described phonetically as "hooo hoo hoo hooo").[6] These low hoots have long wavelengths especially suited for penetrating dense foliage. The territory of a mated spotted owl pair is huge, ranging from 2,955 to 14,211 acres, or roughly 5 to 22 square miles.[7] Reproduction occurs in spring and summer, when females lay an average of two eggs. After hatching, the young owls are cared for by the parents for only 6 months before flying away to establish their own territories.

OLD GROWTH

Spotted owls prefer old-growth forests. Forests develop in stages, during which they undergo changes in composition. Although the definition of an old-growth forest is not precise, it is generally held to be a forest that is 200 or more years old. Such ancient forests are more structurally and biologically complex than younger forests.

[6] This is what ornithologists refer to as its "four-note location call." It has other vocalizations as well, including "barks" and whistles. U.S. Department of the Interior, *Recovery Plan for the Northern Spotted Owl—Draft* (Washington, DC: U.S. Government Printing Office, April 1992), p. 15.

[7] U. S. Fish and Wildlife Service, *2007 Draft Recovery Plan for the Northern Spotted Owl* (Strix occidentalis caurina): *Merged Options 1 and 2* (Portland, OR: Region 1, April 2007), p. 110.

Old-growth forests achieve great natural beauty and inspire comparisons with cathedrals. They have much richer biotic communities than younger forests and are repositories for species that have adapted to ecological niches created under old-growth conditions. The spotted owl is one such species. The dense vegetation protects them from predators such as the red-tailed hawk. A thick, multilayered forest canopy also provides thermal cover, insulating them from extremes of heat and cold. Owls nest in the cavities of standing snags, and fallen snags create conditions that support abundant prey to satisfy their voracious appetites. The spotted owl plays a role in the old-growth ecosystem by culling small mammal and bird populations.

Early studies of northern spotted owls suggested that they lived only in old-growth stands.[8] Biologists believed that the owl was like a canary in a coal mine. If the owl at the top of the forest food chain was in danger of extinction, this was a warning that other species and the old-growth habitat itself were also endangered. Subsequent studies have shown that some northern spotted owls live and breed in younger forests and forests that have been logged.

Some owls do try to nest, roost, and forage in early-succession forests, but ornithologists believe that these are juvenile owls dispersing from old-growth stands. Spotted owls are territorial, live up to 18 years, and maintain large domains in remaining stands of old growth. This makes it difficult for juvenile owls to stake out territories in the limited stands of high structural complexity. Therefore, some young owls leaving nests after breeding season are pushed into younger forests. They forage and breed there, but scientists believe that their reproduction and survival rates are lowered.

LOSS OF OLD GROWTH IMPERILS THE SPOTTED OWL

The expansion of America came at the expense of wilderness. When pilgrims landed at Plymouth Rock, the landmass destined to become the continental

[8] A study in Washington, for example, found that 97 percent of spotted owls lived in old growth, with no known reproductive pairs in second-growth areas. "Proposed Threatened Status for the Northern Spotted Owl," 54 FR 26668, June 23, 1989.

United States had 850 million acres of forest. By the 1920s only 138 million acres of virgin forest remained, roughly 16 percent of what had existed.[9] The rest had been burned, grazed, cut, radically disturbed, or converted to other uses. Reduction of forest area stopped in the 1870s, and, on balance, regrowth now exceeds losses.

As settlers and loggers approached in the 1860s, the northwest coastal forest covered about 94 million acres. Today only about 57 million acres remain, including no more than 17.2 million acres of the late-successional stands that provide spotted owl habitat. Of these 17.2 million acres, 2.8 million acres are in national parks or wilderness areas closed forever to logging. Another 7.5 million acres are on private lands. These are primarily large forest tracts owned by corporations such as Weyerhaeuser, Plumb Creek Timber, and Pacific Lumber. The rest, about 6.9 million acres, are on federal land. Much of the remaining old growth is not contiguous; it is a checkerboard of old stands mixed with younger growth and land converted to other uses.

There are no estimates of northern spotted owl populations before human intrusion in the forests. In 1989 government biologists estimated a population of only 1,550 breeding pairs of owls in the Pacific Northwest.[10] This low count worried scientists who believed that the owl was on the margin of survival as a species.[11]

When species decline to very low numbers, there is danger that even if human impacts are reduced or removed, events in nature, such as random fluctua-tions of climate or food supply, cannot be overcome. When numbers fall, the reproductive pattern of the species is critical. Unfortunately, the spotted owl has a very low reproductive efficiency. Mated pairs lay one to four eggs during the spring breeding season, but do not always breed and, therefore, produce an average of only .50 young per year. After hatching, newborn owls spend about six months in the nest, then disperse into the forest for distances of 10 to 16 miles. Juvenile owls suffer a mortality rate as high as 70 percent in their first year, primarily from starvation and predation. The mortality rate is highest when they cross logged areas during dispersal.[12]

At the time when the owl's precarious situation was discovered, its habitat was being whittled away. In the late 1980s loggers on private lands were cutting down remaining late-succession forest stands at a rate of 8 percent a year. In federal forests the cutting was slower, about 1 to 3 percent a year.[13] At this rate, nearly all old-growth habitat outside the untouchable preserves of national parks would vanish in 50 years.

Federal forests have never been tree museums. By law, they are open to "multiple use" activities such as logging, mining, and recreation. The Forest Service and the Bureau of Land Management, the agencies that manage them, hold timber auctions at which logging companies bid for the right to fell selected timber stands. Once winning bids are picked, timber harvesting proceeds based on precise rules about boundaries, logging techniques, and restoration or replanting. For many years the federal forests of the Pacific Northwest were managed for long-term productivity. In 60 years a replanted forest can be reharvested; a high-density replanting will yield more timber than the original old growth. However, this long-standing yield-management philosophy chewed up owl habitat. Environmentalists with an opposing philosophy came to the rescue.

---

[9] Figures for forest size are from Michael Williams, *Americans and Their Forests: A Historical Geography* (New York: Cambridge University Press, 1989), pp. 3–4.

[10] "Protected Status Proposed for the Northern Spotted Owl," *Endangered Species Technical Bulletin,* July 1989, p. 1.

[11] Two subspecies of spotted owl, the northern spotted owl *(Strix occidentalis caurina)* and the California spotted owl *(Strix occidentalis occidentalis)* mix together at the extremes of their ranges in northern California. Although the California spotted owl is more plentiful, environmental groups have sued the Fish and Wildlife Service demanding that it also be listed as threatened or endangered. The agency has refused to do so. A third subspecies, the Mexican spotted owl *(Strix occidentalis lucida),* lives in the forests of Arizona, Utah, Colorado, Texas, and Mexico. It was listed as threatened in 1993; see U.S. Fish and Wildlife Service, "Final Rule to List the Mexican Spotted Owl as a Threatened Species," 58 FR 14248, March 16, 1993.

[12] Daniel Simberloff, "The Spotted Owl Fracas: Mixing Academic, Applied, and Political Ecology," *Ecology,* August 1987, p. 768; Gary S. Miller et al., "Habitat Selection by Spotted Owls during Natal Dispersal in Western Oregon," *Journal of Wildlife Management* 61, no. 1 (1997), p. 146.

[13] These figures, and others in this section are based on estimates in U. S. Fish and Wildlife Service, *2007 Draft Recovery Plan for the Northern Spotted Owl* (Strix occidentalis caurina): *Merged Options 1 and 2,* pp. 117 and 130.

ENVIRONMENTALISTS CAMPAIGN TO PROTECT THE SPOTTED OWL

In the 1980s environmental groups took up the cause of the northern spotted owl. They believed that the owl had intrinsic, unlimited value as a species; its extinction would be an irrevocable mistake. Equally important, they knew that the owl's use of old growth as habitat made saving owls a convenient pretext for saving ancient forests from the logger's ax. Using the owl, they could invoke the Endangered Species Act and elevate the goal of forest preservation above the economic interests of timber companies, lumber mills, and loggers.

The Endangered Species Act is an exceptionally strong statute. Passed in 1973, it set forth procedures for designating, or "listing," such species. The act defines an *endangered* species as one that is "in danger of extinction throughout all or a significant portion of its range." It also permits listing of a *threatened* species that is "likely to become an endangered species in the future throughout all or a significant portion of its range." Once a species is listed in either category, it is entitled to a great deal of protection. Under threat of civil or criminal penalties, it is illegal to "take"— that is, "to harass, harm, pursue, hunt, shoot, wound, kill, trap, capture, or collect"—any individual of the listed species on public or private lands.

The law also protects geographically defined "critical habitat" of listed species. And it requires that listings be based solely on scientific evidence about species' survival needs; consideration of economic and political consequences is generally prohibited.[14]

In 2008 there were 1,351 species listed as threatened or endangered—607 animals and 744 plants. A listing is ominous. Only 47 species have ever been delisted despite more than 35 years of stringent regulation. Of these, 9 are extinct. Another 19 species recovered. The rest were taken off for a variety of reasons, most because they had been misclassified as a separate species.[15]

At first, the Fish and Wildlife Service declined to list the northern spotted owl as endangered.[16] The agency's biologists believed that evidence of a long-range threat to its survival was insufficient. Angry environmentalists filed a lawsuit. In 1990, bowing to the pressure, it listed the owl as a "threatened" species.[17] This set in motion the powerful devices of the Endangered Species Act. An entire region of the country soon felt the consequences.

The Fish and Wildlife Service adopted protective rules that remain in force today. It mapped the owl's range into 12 provinces extending from the Canadian border in the north to Marin County, California, in the south.[18] Within these provinces it designated 192 sections of critical habitat totaling 6.9 million acres—2.2 million acres in Washington, 3.3 million acres in Oregon, and 1.4 million acres in California. This habitat consisted of late-successional forest that supported the owl's roosting, nesting, and foraging patterns. Within areas of critical habitat, logging was banned near known spotted owl nests. Even if a nest was found empty, a three-year moratorium on logging was required to ensure that it was abandoned. Before activities such as forestry or road maintenance and construction took place in owl territory, the agency had to clear them by issuing a "biological opinion."

These rules applied on federal lands and did not affect logging in the forests owned by big corporations. However, timber harvesting on private lands could not go on without consideration of spotted owls. The Endangered Species Act made it a federal crime punishable by a fine of up to $50,000 and one year in prison to harm them. Washington, Oregon, and California soon adopted rules governing timber harvest on private land. Oregon, for example, prohibited logging a 70-acre area around an adult owl nesting site.

---

[16] The Endangered Species Act is enforced by two agencies. The Fish and Wildlife Service within the Department of the Interior is responsible for the listing and recovery of plants and animals found on land and in freshwater environments and for migratory birds. The National Marine Fisheries Service within the Department of Commerce enforces the law with respect to marine species. Other agencies are bound by its provisions if their actions affect listed species.

[14] For an overview of the statute, see Dale Gobel and Michael Scott et al., *The Endangered Species Act at Thirty*, vols. 1 and 2 (Washington, DC: Island Press, 2005 and 2006).

[15] U. S. Fish and Wildlife Service, "Summary of Listed Species," Threatened and Endangered Species System, http://ecos.fws.gov/tess_public/Boxscore.do, February 2008.

[17] U. S. Fish and Wildlife Service, "Determination of Threatened Status for the Northern Spotted Owl," 55FR 21623, June 26, 1990.

[18] U. S. Fish and Wildlife Service, "Determination of Critical Habitat for the Northern Spotted Owl," 57 FR 1796, January 15, 1992.

For each listed species, the Endangered Species Act requires a recovery plan that serves as a road map to its eventual recovery and delisting. In 1991 a district court in Seattle issued an injunction virtually halting timber sales in federal forests throughout the Pacific Northwest until the Fish and Wildlife Service developed a species recovery plan for the owl.[19] The injunction was a boon for the owls, which could sleep during the day without the annoyance of chainsaws, but it was a disaster for the forest products industry, which depended on timber harvests. In 1990, the year before the injunction, 10.6 billion board feet of timber were cut on federal lands.[20] In 1991 only 4.4 billion board feet were cut before the injunction. In 1992 only 0.7 billion board feet came out of the forests.[21]

HARD TIMES IN THE PACIFIC NORTHWEST

Halted timber sales brought hardship. Hundreds of small-town economies built on jobs created by logging, milling, and related trucking and shipping spiraled downward.

Despair and anger permeated logging towns. In Forks, Washington, where unemployment rose to 20 percent, someone shot a spotted owl and nailed it to a sign. In Oregon, loggers had bumper stickers that read: "IF IT'S HOOTIN', I'M SHOOTIN'," "SAVE A LOGGER/EAT AN OWL," and "I LIKE SPOTTED OWLS . . . FRIED." Northern California suffered too. In Happy Camp, all four sawmills closed and the town collapsed as area timber harvests declined from 50 million board feet to 8 million. The population fell from 2,500 to 1,100, and more than half those remaining were on public assistance.[22]

By now, those trying to save the spotted owl and its old-growth habitat were locked in bitter scientific, legal, political, and personal conflict with those whose livelihood depended on the productivity of national forests. In 1993 President Bill Clinton presided over a "timber summit" in Portland, Oregon, where he listened to the strong and polarized views of scientists, environmentalists, and timber industry representatives. As a result, early in 1994 his administration introduced a new forest management policy named the Northwest Forest Plan (NWFP) to resolve the impasse and move forward.

The NWFP tried to appease both environmentalists and industry. It set up a complex network of reserves on 24.5 million acres of federal forest land in the three states. In particular, it protected large blocks of late successional forest from disturbance and destruction. Logging was proscribed in 80 percent of the plan's territory. The remaining 20 percent would be managed for timber production based on guidelines set up to protect the owl and other endangered species. For example, no logging was permitted in "owl circles" having a radius extending 2.7 miles from known owl nests.

The plan permitted logging 1.1 billion board feet annually in mature and old-growth forests. This harvest level was nearly double that of years since the 1991 district court injunction, but was still almost 90 percent less than the harvests of the late 1980s. Soon after the NWFP was adopted, the Fish and Wildlife Service reported that there were 5,431 forest sites occupied by spotted owls. About a fourth of these were on private lands, the rest were on lands protected by the NWFP.[23]

The NWFP was designed to stay in place for 50 to 100 years, giving the owl time to recover. It spelled permanent loss of tens of thousands of timber jobs, so it committed $1.2 billion over five years to retrain workers, help small businesses, and compensate for lost tax revenues in timber counties.

Despite the broad habitat protection and paltry timber harvest authorized by the NWFP, environmentalists sued to block it. However, it was upheld by a federal court.[24] Even so, little timber cutting took place. At first, delay was caused by convoluted, bureaucratic Forest Service procedures for setting up timber auctions under the NWFP's new rules. Later,

---

[19] *Seattle Audubon Society v. Evans* 771 F. Supp. 1081 (1991).

[20] A board foot is a measure of timber volume. One board foot equals a volume of $12 \times 12 \times 1$ inches.

[21] Department of the Interior memorandum, "The Administration's Response to the Spotted Owl Crisis: Joint Oversight Hearing before the Subcommittee on National Parks and Public Lands of the Committee on Interior and Insular Affairs," U. S. House of Representatives, March 24, 1992, p. 167.

[22] Richard C. Paddock, "Town's Decline Rivals That of the Spotted Owl," *Los Angeles Times,* October 23, 1995, p. A3.

[23] U. S. Fish and Wildlife Service, "Proposed Special Rule for the Conservation of the Northern Spotted Owl on Non-Federal Lands," 60 FR 9495, February 17, 1995.

[24] *Seattle Audubon Society v. Lyons,* 871 F.Supp. 1291(W.D. Wash. 1994).

environmentalists began to challenge timber auctions, suing the agency at every turn to block action. Consequently, the 1.1 billion board feet harvest level was never achieved.

THE ENDANGERED SPECIES ACT ATTACKED

The political climate in the battle for the forests changed in the early 1990s when Republicans gained a congressional majority and began to attack environmental laws. They reserved special ire for the Endangered Species Act.

Private landowners were raising a storm of protest over timber harvest restrictions. Both corporations and small landowners were hurt when they could not harvest the trees they owned. One retired couple had bought a few forest acres, planning to harvest timber stands over time to pay for their retirement, but they were prevented from doing so by the presence of a single spotted owl nest.

As anger about the statute's role in stopping timber harvests rose, sentiment in Congress for changing it grew. To ease pressures for weakening the act, the Clinton administration discovered new flexibility in a provision of the law that permitted *habitat conservation plans* negotiated between the government and private landowners. These plans are binding agreements, entered voluntarily, in which a landowner agrees to take conservation measures, usually beyond the letter of the law, and in return receives permission to log or otherwise use property, even if it means harm to an endangered species or critical habitat in the process.

An early example of one of the plans came in 1995 when the Murray Pacific Company, which owned a 53,000-acre tree farm in Washington populated by spotted owls, agreed to preserve 43 percent of the property as habitat for the owl and four other endangered species. The agreement was detailed and specific; for example, the company was to leave trees outside five cave openings to protect a bat species and had to monitor the temperature of streams and leave more trees standing on their banks to shade them if readings began to rise. In exchange, Murray Pacific received an "incidental take permit" absolving it from blame if, in logging the rest of the property, any members of an endangered species were harassed or killed. Without the plan, Murray Pacific probably would have been denied the right to log its land at all.

Today there are 15 habitat conservation plans allowing "incidental take" of spotted owls. The smallest covers 40 acres and the largest 1.6 million acres. Overall, the plans cover 2.9 million acres of private forest in the owl's range. They have "no-surprise" clauses, guarantees that even if new evidence about an endangered species emerges years later, no additional conservation measures will be required.[25] They also include a "baseline" policy so that if the numbers of an endangered species increase, the landowner is not required to take additional measures to protect them. This removes an incentive for private landowners to drive out or kill endangered species before their presence is reported and the land rendered useless for development or timber harvest.

Environmental groups oppose habitat conservation plans, incidental take permits, and the no-surprises policy, all of which they see as compromising the survival chances of species on the borderline. Incidental take permits allow logging companies to destroy some owl habitat. And the no-surprises policy may turn out to be foolish. Science is just beginning to understand certain species and complex ecosystems. Yet habitat conservation plans are locked into place for decades—some for as long as 100 years. Even if new information about causes of extinction is discovered, landowners cannot be forced to alter their activities.

ENVIRONMENTALISTS BLOCK TIMBER HARVESTS

While habitat conservation plans simplify logging on private timberland, logging in federal forests covered by the Northwest Forest Plan remains severely constrained. Timber harvests have never matched the annual 1.1 billion board feet promised back in 1994. Volume peaked at 885 million board feet in 1997. After this, it plummeted, falling to a low of 148 million board feet in 2000, just 15 percent of the promised sale quantity and 1 percent of what had come out of the woods a decade before. The roadblock is environmentalists who use both the law and tactics of civil disobedience to stop logging.

Environmental activists have brought hundreds of citizen suits over the last decade challenging timber

---

[25] "Habitat Conservation Plan Assurances ('No Surprises') Rule," 63 FR 8859, February 23, 1998.

harvests. Most are based on the presence of endangered species in areas to be logged. Others claim that timber auctions have been inadequately surveyed for the presence of species. Still others press for listing of new species or compliance with legal deadlines to complete recovery plans for previously listed species.

Several groups specialize in this litigation. For example, the Center for Biological Diversity, which calls itself "nature's legal eagles," averaged one new lawsuit every 32 days for years following the adoption of the NWFP.[26] These lawsuits are intended to preserve the forests. Zero harvest is the goal. After a forest fire in Oregon's Ochoco National Forest, environmentalists filed a 104-page appeal when the Forest Service tried to sell 54 trees felled for a fire break—even though they had been on the ground for almost a year.[27] They argued that the trees should be allowed to decay on the forest floor, returning their nutrients to the soil.

A California group developed software enabling it to create so many timber sale appeals that it blocked or slowed the sale of almost 500 million board feet.[28] This lost harvest, logged and floating in a mill pond, would be worth approximately $202 million in today's prices and much more as sawed board.[29]

Activists also use a wide range of protest tactics. They sit in the branches of trees scheduled for harvest and lie in front of logging trucks. They have sabotaged equipment and driven metal spikes into trees that shatter saw blades if the trunks are milled. On private timberland, they trespass and occupy sites slated for logging. All this is illegal once a stand of trees is clear of appeals and ready for logging under government rules. However, activists feel justified by the ethical duty to protect species and forests. "It's against the law to trespass," says one, "but we feel there's a higher law."[30]

---

[26] Tom Knudson, "A Flood of Costly Lawsuits Raises Questions about Motive," *Sacramento Bee,* April 24, 2001, p. A1.

[27] Steve Lundgren, "End of the Line," *The Oregonian,* July 29, 2001, p. A17.

[28] William Wade Keye, "Mill Towns Subsist on Logs from Afar," *Sacramento Bee*, October 28, 2001, p. B6.

[29] The estimate is based on a 2007 in the pond value of $430/mbf (1,000 board feet) in Oregon minus estimated logging costs of $125/mbf.

[30] Eric Bailey, "Two Sides Firmly Rooted over Logging Battle," *Los Angeles Times,* May 29, 2001, p. B8.

A TENUOUS HOLD FOR BOTH OWLS AND LOGGERS

In 2002 a timber industry group, the American Forest Resource Council, sued the Department of the Interior, forcing a review of the spotted owl's status to see if protection under the Endangered Species Act was still needed.[31] The agency set up an expert panel to evaluate evidence.

The panel found no scientific basis for estimating the total owl population. Instead, it focused on long-term studies of owl reproduction and adult survival in 14 areas of Washington, Oregon, and California. As indicated in Exhibit 1, the populations in 9 of the 14 areas were declining. The other five areas were stationary, although there were signs of decline in all but two of these. The panel found it difficult to estimate change in the size of critical habitat. It noted that 515,000 acres, or 2.11 percent of the habitat covered by the Northwest Forest Plan, had been lost to logging over a decade. It also estimated that this loss was offset by the ingrowth of 600,000 acres of late-successional habitat.[32]

Overall, the panel decided that the owl was still threatened with extinction. It no longer faced habitat loss because of logging, but growth of new habitat was insufficient to compensate for losses that had occurred before it was listed as threatened in 1990. In addition, the owl faced several new threats, including habitat destruction from massive forest fires, increased competition from more aggressive barred owls, and the arrival of West Nile virus.

The panel concluded that elevating the status of the northern spotted owl from threatened to endangered was unwarranted. However, slow declines in owl populations, lack of critical habitat expansion, and uncertainties posed by emerging threats suggested that the species was still threatened. It retained its listing.

In 2007 the Fish and Wildlife Service drafted a new recovery plan. It set forth two options, estimating that either one would lead to recovery in 30 years at a cost of about $200 million in government expenditures.

---

[31] *American Forest Resource Council v. Secretary of the Interior*, Civil No. 02-6087-AA (D. Oregon).

[32] U. S. Fish and Wildlife Service, *Northern Spotted Owl Five-Year Review: Summary and Evaluation* (Portland, OR: USFWS, November 2004), pp. 24–26.

EXHIBIT 1

Trends in Northern Spotted Owl Demography in 14 Areas of Population Study in Washington, Oregon, and California

Source: Adapted from U.S. Fish and Wildlife Service, *Northern Spotted Owl Five-Year Review: Summary and Evaluation* (Portland, OR: USFWS, November 2004), table 1.

Owl Population Study Area	Reproduction	Adult Survival	Annual Rate of Change*	Population Change
Washington				
Wenatchee	Stable	Declining	0.917	Declining
Cle Elum	Declining	Declining	0.938	Declining
Rainier	Stable	Declining	0.896	Declining
Olympic	Stable	Declining	0.956	Declining
Oregon				
Coast Ranges	Declining	Stable	0.968	Declining
H. J. Andrews	Stable	Stable	0.978	Declining
Warm Springs	Stable	Stable	0.908	Declining
Tyee	Increasing	Stable	1.005	Stationary
Klamath	Stable	Stable	0.997	Stationary
South Cascades	Declining	Stable	0.974	Stationary
California				
NW California	Declining	Declining	0.985	Declining
Hoopa	Declining	Stable	0.980	Stationary
Simpson	Increasing	Stable	0.970	Declining
Marin	Stable	Stable	NA†	NA

*Estimates of <1 represent a decrease in the number of owls; estimates of >1 represent an increase.
†Sample size too small to make an estimate.

One option proposed continued protection of critical habitat in late-successional forest that was already protected under the Endangered Species Act. However, a second option did not specify areas of critical habitat for protection, recommending instead that federal forest managers have flexibility to identify and protect particular stands based on evolving knowledge of how the owls live.[33] This option rejected locked-in habitat protections and allowed for shrinkage of protected habitat—in effect opening new areas for logging.

Environmentalists disliked this second option. They believed timber interests had influenced the Bush administration to ignore the science of owl preservation. Sure enough, shortly after the plan's release, the Fish and Wildlife Service proposed to reduce designated critical habitat for the owl from 6,887,000 acres to 5,337,839. The reduction, it argued, was based on "improved understanding" of owl behavior and "refinements in mapping

technology."[34] If opened for logging, the 1,549,161 acres removed from protection could produce as much as $2.5 billion of sawtimber.[35] The new draft recovery plan has no legal force. It is only the roadmap for recovery of *Strix occidentalis caurina*, suggesting rather than mandating actions. It does not guarantee recovery for the owl.

While habitat preservation can be planned, other threatening factors elude control. The recovery plan emphasizes the threat posed by the barred owl. Barred owls are not native to the Pacific Northwest. They have migrated from the east until their range now completely overlaps the spotted owl's habitat. Evidence suggests that barred owls, which are larger and eat a wider variety of prey, compete with spotted owls and drive them from their territories.

[33] U. S. Fish and Wildlife Service, *2007 Draft Recovery Plan for the Northern Spotted Owl (Strix occidentalis caurina): Merged Options 1 and 2*, part II, "Recovery Criteria and Recovery Actions (Option 2)."

[34] U. S. Fish and Wildlife Service, "Proposed Revised Designation of Critical Habitat for the Northern Spotted Owl (Strix occidentalis caurina)," 72 FR 32462, June 12, 2007.

[35] Estimate is based on the assumption of 40 mbf (1 mbf = 1,000 board feet)/acre and a 2007 pond value of $430/mbf in Oregon minus estimated logging costs of $125/mbf.

In Olympic National Park, where no logging has ever taken place, wildlife biologists report that "barred owl numbers are through the roof."[36] They have taken over almost two-thirds of spotted owl nests. The spotted owl population there is declining and opponents of owl protection suggest that if such a protected population cannot recover, it is senseless to expect recovery elsewhere. Yet the Endangered Species Act does not permit giving up. So owl protection will continue at the expense of the regional timber economy, pushing along mill closings and job losses in small towns throughout the owl's range.

POSTSCRIPT

Some help, a break in the gloom, may be on the way for Jackson County. To settle another lawsuit by the timber industry the Bureau of Land Management came up with a plan that could nearly triple logging on the 2.4 million acres of old California & Oregon Railroad lands.[37] It proposes to expand the proportion of these lands open to logging from 25 percent to 54 percent and manage them "to achieve a high level of continuous timber production."[38] According to the plan, annual timber yield over the next decade would rise from the current average of 268 million board feet to 727 million board feet, generating $108 million in revenue each year for the 18 railroad land counties, about 94 percent of their historical revenue.

Economic benefits include creation of 3,442 new timber industry jobs paying $137 million in wages. If the plan is rejected, the BLM predicts further loss of 3,770 timber-related jobs, or 42 percent of the 8,948 jobs remaining. Unfortunately for the spotted owl, these benefits will again come at the expense of its habitat. Late-successional reserves would be cut by 36 percent, from 809,400 acres to 521,500 acres. Also, while the BLM now protects "owl activity centers," areas of 250 acres around owl nesting, hunting, and

foraging sites that are off-limits for human interference, these garrisons would be eliminated.

This BLM scheme puts new fire into the battle of competing philosophies about Pacific Northwest forests. Environmentalists reject it and plan to paralyze timber sales with lawsuits. One calls it "the most reckless logging proposal in decades."[39] On the other side, a county commissioner states that "the real problem is this segment of absolutists that will not tolerate any use of federal lands for timber resources."[40] Atlas, the Endangered Species Act seems to be serving neither owls nor loggers well.

Questions

1. Are you in favor of using forests of the Pacific Northwest to preserve the northern spotted owl, even at the cost of lost jobs, mill closures, depleted tax revenues, underfunded libraries, closed schools, and many personal hardships?

2. Should the Fish and Wildlife Service and the Bureau of Land Management be permitted to manage more forest area for timber yield?

3. When government prohibits logging near spotted owl nests on private land, does this violate rights given the landowners by the takings clause of the Fifth Amendment? Should owners of private timberland be compensated by the government for their losses? Would it be fair to shift the burden of species protection to taxpayers?

4. Evaluate the actions of environmental groups. Are the values of activists correct? Do they have an ethical duty found in natural law? Are environmental litigators abusing the privilege of citizen suits?

5. Should enforcement of the Endangered Species Act be made more flexible? Or should it tighten to protect spotted owls and other endangered species more?

6. Do you believe that the northern spotted owl can ever recover and be removed from the list of endangered species? Would its extinction have worldly consequences, or would it be immaterial, registering only in the intangible realm of our thoughts?

[36] Eric Foresman, a U. S. Forest Service biologist, quoted in Michael Milstein, "So Much for Saving the Spotted Owl," *Newhouse News Service*, August 2, 2007.

[37] *American Forest Resource Council v. Clarke,* Civ. No. 94-1031 TPJ (D.D.C.).

[38] Bureau of Land Management, *Draft Environmental Impact Statement for the Revision of Resource Management Plans of the Western Oregon Bureau of Land Management Districts*, vol. 1, BLM/OR/WA/PL-07/046+1792, August 2007, p. xlvi.

[39] Josh Laughlin of Cascadia Wildlands Project, quoted in Susan Palmer, "New Measure Could Nearly Triple Logging in Protected Oregon Area," *The Register Guard*, October 28, 2007, p. A1.

[40] Dennis C. W. Smith, County Commissioner, Jackson County Oregon, quoted in ibid., p. A1.

Chapter Fourteen

Managing Environmental Quality

The Commerce Railyards

Just six miles east of downtown Los Angeles lies a busy, seven-square-mile city of 13,292. On incorporation in 1962, it named itself Commerce to signal that it was a business-friendly community. Over the years the city boomed and today it is a vibrant jumble of factories, businesses, and residential neighborhoods, the whole bisected by two major freeways. Within its borders tight rows of older, modest homes run up to industrial strips and railroad tracks.

The tracks bind four railyards sprawled over a land triangle four miles long and one mile deep. One is operated by Union Pacific Railroad and the other three by BNSF Railway. These are the nation's largest and second-largest railroads in route miles. Around the clock trucks from the south stream in through entrances three lanes wide. They arrive laden with imported goods in cargo containers from the ports of Los Angeles and Long Beach. Inside, cranes lift their loads onto trains that roll to every part of the country.

The area teems with locomotives. Every day 40 long freights run through just the Union Pacific East Yard, pulled by line-haul diesels with 12 to 20 cylinders producing up to 6,000 horsepower. Smaller switch engines rove the metal arteries, building and breaking down the trains. Other locomotives sit being washed, fueled, serviced, and rebuilt.

The railyards saturate Commerce with diesel exhaust. A study by California regulators found that each year they pour out 40 tons of diesel particulate and another 113 tons comes from trucking activity in the vicinity.[1] Exhaust gases and soot billow forth, bred of innumerable explosions within the cylinders of locomotives, trucks, cranes, forklifts, generators, and refrigeration units on railcars. They move on the breezes, infiltrating nearby homes. Residents inhale the vapors, and small poisons soon circulate in their blood. Some become ill. Some die.

---

[1] Ambreen Mahmood et al., *Draft Health Risk Assessment for the Four Commerce Railyards*, California Environmental Protection Agency, Air Resources Board, May 23, 2007, p. 7.

Diesel Exhaust

Diesel exhaust is a complex mix of gases and particles. It has hundreds of components, including at least 40 that cause cancer. Gases include carbon dioxide, oxygen, nitrogen oxides, sulfur dioxide, and hydrocarbon compounds. Among the hydrocarbons are carcinogens such as formaldehyde, acetaldehyde, acrolein, benzene, and 1,3-butadiene. Diesel exhaust also contains tiny spheres of elemental carbon that adsorb organic and inorganic substances during the heat of combustion. These substances come from unburned fuel, lubricating oil, and pyrosynthesis. The inorganic substances are mainly sulfate compounds, including sulfuric acid, but some others, such as arsenic, are carcinogenic. The organic compounds include carcinogens such as nitroarenes and polycyclic aromatic hydrocarbons.

The soot particles are small. The largest are 2.5 micrometers in diameter, but more than 90 percent are less than 0.1 micrometer, or about one-seventieth the diameter of a human hair.[2] Their small size makes them easily respirable. They go deep into the airways where the toxic compounds that coat them undergo reactions with lung tissues and enter the bloodstream.

Acute exposure to diesel exhaust irritates the eyes, throat, and bronchial lining causing phlegm production, coughing, headache, dizziness, chest tightness, bronchitis, and difficulty breathing. Chronic exposure can cause asthma. The Environmental Protection Agency estimates that long-term exposure to diesel exhaust in concentrations greater than 5 micrograms per cubic meter creates a risk of chronic respiratory illness.[3]

On the basis of studies of diesel exhaust exposure and lung cancer in truck drivers, locomotive engineers, and heavy equipment operators, the EPA characterizes diesel exhaust as a "likely" carcinogen.[4] The National Toxicology Program classifies it as "reasonably anticipated to be a human carcinogen." California rates it as a "known" carcinogen. Scientific evidence does not support any safe level of diesel exhaust in the air below which no cancer risk exists.

After emission, diesel exhaust undergoes complex reactions in the atmosphere. Its constituents degrade more rapidly during the day than at night. Most gases break down in a few hours to several days, although some have lifetimes of weeks to months. They contribute to acid rain, global warming, and urban smog. Organic compounds on the particles have half-lives of a few hours to two days. Black soot composed of carbon particles settles to earth over several days.[5] While suspended in the air it absorbs light and reduces visibility.

[2] U.S. Department of Health and Human Services, Public Health Service, National Toxicology Program, *Report on Carcinogens*, 11th ed., February 2005, "Diesel Exhaust Particulates."

[3] Environmental Protection Agency, "Diesel Engine Exhaust (CASRN N.A.)," Integrated Risk Information System, I.B., last revised February 28, 2003.

[4] See, for example, E. Garshick et al., "Lung Cancer in Railroad Workers Exposed to Diesel Exhaust," *Environmental Health Perspectives*, November 2004.

[5] National Center for Environmental Assessment, Office of Research and Development, *Health Assessment Document for Diesel Engine Exhaust* (Washington, DC: Environmental Protection Agency, EPA/600/8-90/057F, May 2002), table 2-20 and p. 2-93.

FIGURE 14.1

Average Elevations in Cancer Risk for Populations Near the Commerce Railyards

Source: Adapted from Figure II-4, A. Mahmood et al., *Draft Health Risk Assessment for the Four Commerce Railyards*.

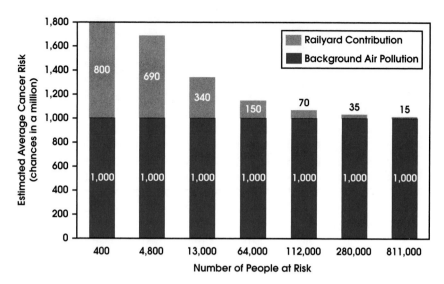

Calculating the Risks

California regulators recently studied the railyards, measuring diesel exhaust emissions, plotting winds, and calculating cancer risks to nearby residents. In a neighborhood of 400 people nestled between two of the railyards they estimated a cancer risk elevation of 800 chances in a million. For another 4,800 people living just beside the railyards they estimated a risk elevation as high as 690 chances in a million. On two small residential islands within a half mile of railyard boundaries another 13,000 people face an elevated risk of up to 500 chances in a million. Floating over the city limits of Commerce, the plume of diesel exhaust falls on another 1.3 million people. Their cancer risk is elevated by 100 chances in a million at roughly one mile, 50 chances in a million at two miles, 25 chances in a million at three miles, and 10 chances in a million at four miles and beyond.[6]

Risk elevation from the railyards must be added to existing background levels. The background cancer risk in Los Angeles is roughly 250,000 per million. Additional risk from inhaling toxic pollutants in the local air basin further elevates this risk by another 1,000 in a million. As Figure 14.1 shows, those living closest to the railyards have an overall risk elevation of 1,800 chances in a million. Public release of these estimates triggered anger in Commerce residents. In the words of one woman whose father died of cancer: "The railroads are a killer."[7]

Controlling the Risk

National emission standards for locomotives were first set in 1997. A decade later the Environmental Protection Agency proposed more stringent standards for locomotives built after 2009, predicting $12 billion in health benefits by 2030.[8] Twice California

[6] Ambreen Mahmood et al., *Draft Health Risk Assessment for the Four Commerce Railyards*, pp. 13–16, 18, and table II-6.

[7] Rosa Zambrano, quoted in Bill Mongelluzzo, "Small Particles, Large Obstacle," *Journal of Commerce*, June 4, 2007, p. 44.

[8] Environmental Protection Agency, *Control of Emissions of Air Pollution from Locomotive Engines and Marine Compression Engines Less than 30 Liters per Cylinder*, 72 FR 15937, April 3, 2007.

regulators reached voluntary agreements with the railroads to take additional emission-reduction measures. Under these agreements Union Pacific claims to have cut overall emissions in Commerce by 28 percent and BNSF claims similar reductions nationwide from accelerating the replacement of older, more polluting locomotives.[9]

The people of Commerce think that progress is too slow. In 2006 the local air district adopted rules limiting the time locomotives could idle. Its rules went beyond federal regulations, so BNSF and Union Pacific sued to overturn them. A federal district judge obliged, holding that federal regulation preempted the local rules "in order to prevent a 'patchwork' of such local regulation from interfering with interstate commerce."[10] "I'm very disappointed," said an environmental activist in Commerce, "[t]he value of one human life should supersede interstate commerce."[11]

In this chapter we begin by explaining how pollution risks such as diesel exhaust are assessed to find out which are most important to regulate. Then, we discuss alternative approaches to regulation with emphasis on new, more flexible initiatives. Finally, we illustrate ways that some innovative companies are seeking to reduce adverse environmental impacts.

REGULATING ENVIRONMENTAL RISK

Environmental regulation is very expensive. In 2004 the total cost of enforcement and compliance was estimated to be $221 billion.[12] This is a large sum. Is the money well spent? It seems to be. According to a government study, for the 10 years from 1996 to 2006 major environmental rules were "responsible for the majority of benefits and costs generated by Federal regulation."[13] The benefits of Environmental Protection Agency rules were estimated at between $99 and $484 billion, while their costs were estimated to be in the range of $39 to $46 billion. Thus, every dollar spent returned between $2.15 and $10.52 in benefits.

risk
A probability existing somewhere between zero and 100 percent that a harm will occur.

If regulatory expenditures are to bring maximum benefit, they must be focused on the highest risks to human health and ecosystems. *Risk* is a probability existing somewhere between zero and absolute certainty that a harm will occur. The probability of any pollution risk can be studied scientifically; then regulators, politicians, and the public must decide what, if anything, should be done to lessen it.

Congress has added about 30 provisions in environmental laws requiring that regulatory decisions be based on risk assessments. Its goal is to focus limited dollars on the greatest hazards. The EPA does many risk assessments, and they have great significance for business. If they show that a pollutant such as the diesel

[9] "Union Pacific Reports Progress in Reducing Los Angeles Area Emissions," news releases, May 23, 2007; and BNSF Railway Company, *Environmental and Hazardous Materials Programs* (Topeka, KA: BNSF, 2007), p. 1.

[10] *Association of American Railroads et al. v. South Coast Air Quality Management District*, No. CV 06-01416-JFW(PLAx), U.S.D.C., C.D. Cal., 2007.

[11] Angelo Logan, head of East Yard Communities for Environmental Justice, in Janet Wilson, "Judge Strikes Down Tough Rules on Diesel," *Los Angeles Times,* May 3, 2007, p. B1.

[12] W. Mark Crain, *Impact of Regulatory Costs on Small Firms* (Washington, DC: Small Business Administration, 2005), p. 29.

[13] Office of Management and Budget, *Draft 2007 Report to Congress on the Costs and Benefits of Federal Regulation* (Washington, DC: OMB, March 9, 2007), p. 7.

exhaust poses relatively high risks, rules can require enormous expenditures to reduce them. Rules proposed for cutting locomotive emissions will cost the railroad industry $4.5 billion by 2040. On the other hand, benefits to the nation are estimated at $5 to $10 billion *each year* by 2030.[14]

ANALYZING HUMAN HEALTH RISKS

risk assessment
The largely scientific process of discovering and weighing dangers posed by a pollutant.

The basic model for analyzing human health risks is shown in Figure 14.2. It separates risk analysis into two parts represented by two circles. In circle A are the elements of *risk assessment,* the largely scientific process of discovering and weighing the dangers posed by a pollutant. In circle B are the elements of *risk management,* the process of deciding which actions to take (or not take) regarding specific risks. We will explain the nature and interaction of these elements.

risk management
The process of deciding which regulatory action to take (or not take) to protect the public from the risk posed by a pollutant.

Risk Assessment

The four basic risk assessment steps shown in circle A in Figure 14.2 are standard at the EPA and other agencies that sometimes evaluate the dangers of pollutants. In fact, they are now the standard worldwide.[15] In theory, risk assessment is a scientific process leading to an objective, quantitative measure of the risks posed by any substance. As we will see, however, science often falls short of this goal. So the EPA and other agencies make a series of precautionary assumptions based on the fear that scientific data, which are often ambiguous or inconclusive, might understate

FIGURE 14.2
Elements of Risk Assessment and Risk Management and Their Sequence

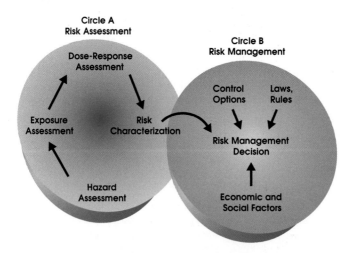

[14] Environmental Protection Agency, *Draft Regulatory Impact Analysis: Control of Emissions of Air Pollution from Locomotive Engines and Marine Compression-Ignition Engines Less than 30 Liters per Cylinder*, EPA420-D-07-001 (March 2007), chap. 7, p. 18 and chap. 6, p. 82.

[15] The most recent statement of these guidelines describes their use in evaluating suspected cancer-causing substances. See Risk Assessment Forum, Environmental Protection Agency, *Guidelines for Carcinogen Risk Assessment*, EPA/630/P-03/001F, March 2005.

risks to human health. As the precautionary assumptions are piled one on top of another, the process grows less rigorous and, in the view of some critics, begins to overstate risks. When risks are overstated regulation of business becomes more expensive and the nation's environmental regulation dollars are not well spent. Nevertheless, risks are often overstated to ensure that public health is protected with a margin of safety.

Hazard Assessment

hazard assessment
The process of establishing a link between a substance, such as a chemical, and human disease. The link is established primarily by animal tests and epidemiological studies.

Hazard assessment establishes a link between a substance, such as a chemical, and human disease. When a substance is thought to pose a risk, the two basic methods of proving it dangerous are animal testing and epidemiological studies.

In animal tests, species such as mice and rats are exposed to high levels of the substance through diet, inhalation, or other means for an appreciable part of their life span. In a cancer study, as many as 1,000 animals may be divided into three groups with different exposure levels. One group is exposed to the maximum dose that the animals can tolerate without dying. The second group receives half this dose. The third group is a control group receiving no exposure. At the end of the test, the animals are dissected and tumors and other abnormalities in organs are counted. If the exposed animals have many tumors, the assumption is that the chemical is an animal carcinogen, and regulators tend then to make the precautionary assumption that it is a human carcinogen as well.

Several problems cast doubt on the validity of animal tests. First, scientists rely heavily on strains of rats and mice genetically disposed to high rates of tumor production. This predisposition raises doubts about whether a substance is a complete carcinogen or simply a tumor promoter in an otherwise susceptible species. EPA guidelines call for summing benign and malignant tumors and basing the assumption of carcinogenicity on the total rather than only on the number of malignant tumors. This is an additional precautionary assumption that may exaggerate risk.

Second, in animals exposed to large amounts of a chemical, tumors can arise from tissue irritation rather than normal carcinogenesis. For example, rats forced to breathe extreme concentrations of formaldehyde exhibit nasal inflammation. Tumors appear in their noses, but some or all of them result from abnormally rapid cell division that magnifies chromosomal abnormalities, not from the carcinogenic properties of formaldehyde. It is scientifically uncertain if a substance that promotes cancer in high doses also promotes it in low doses. Humans, of course, have lower environmental exposures to chemicals than the prodigious doses given to test animals.

And third, animal physiology can be so different from that of humans that disease processes are unique. For example, gasoline vapor causes kidney tumors in male rats, but the biological mechanism causing these tumors is unique to rats; humans lack one protein involved. Even animals differ in their susceptibility to disease. Inhalation of cadmium dust, to which workers in battery factories are exposed, causes high levels of cancer in rats but no cancer in mice. Which result is appropriate for assessing risk to workers? Here EPA guidelines call for making the precautionary assumption that human risk calculations should be based on the reaction of the most sensitive species.

**epidemio-
logical study**
A statistical
survey de-
signed to show
a relationship
between hu-
man mortality
(death) and
morbidity
(sickness) and
environmental
factors such as
chemicals or
radiation.

A second method of identifying hazards is the *epidemiological study,* a statistical survey of human mortality (death) and morbidity (sickness) in a sample population. Epidemiological studies can establish a link between industrial pollutants and health problems. To illustrate, recent studies show the following associations.

- Excessive hearing loss in workers exposed to toluene (TOL-you-een) and noise in a plant manufacturing adhesives. This hearing loss was not found in workers exposed to the same noise levels but without toluene inhalation.[16] Toluene is an inorganic compound used as a solvent in manufacturing paints and glues.
- A 6.5 percent reduction in the time it took to make decisions among workers exposed to 20 parts per million of styrene for eight years.[17] Styrene is used in making plastics, insulation, carpeting, and other products. Styrene inhalation also elevates the risk of losing color vision.
- Reduction in head circumference in babies born to mothers with exposure to chlorpyrifos and pyrethroids, ingredients in household pesticides.[18]
- Elevated mortality from lymphatic cancers among workers exposed to 1,3-butadiene (bue-ta-DIE-een), a chemical used to make synthetic rubber.[19]

Epidemiological studies have the advantage of measuring real human illness, but they have low statistical power and are riddled with uncertainties. In particular, people are exposed to literally thousands of substances, and individual exposures vary. For example, the study of synthetic rubber plant workers, noted above, showed four lymphatic cancers among 364 workers, more in a group that size than the 0.69 predicted by mortality tables for the area's general population. All 364 workers had been exposed to 1,3-butadiene by working at least six months at one of three Union Carbide synthetic rubber plants in West Virginia. The four lymphatic cancers are statistically significant but still a small number. Could exposure to multiple chemicals over the 39-year period covered by the study have caused these cancers?

There are difficulties with epidemiological studies beyond multiple, confounding exposures. Because lung tumors and other cancers have latency periods of up to 40 years, these studies may not detect harm done by recent exposures. Death certificates and diagnoses of disease are frequently inaccurate. Multiple diseases contribute to many deaths. In addition, data from one population may not predict risk for another population. For example, worker populations, on which many epidemiological studies are based, are healthier than the general population, which contains more sensitive older and younger people. In the study at the Union Carbide butadiene units, for example, only 185 of the 365 workers died over the 39 years, compared with 202 deaths that would have been expected in the general

[16] Shu-Ju Chang et al., "Hearing Loss in Workers Exposed to Toluene and Noise," *Environmental Health Perspectives*, August 2006.

[17] Vernon A. Benignus et al., "Human Neurobehavioral Effects of Long-Term Exposure to Styrene: A Meta-Analysis," *Environmental Health Perspectives*, May 2005.

[18] Gertrud S. Berkowitz, "In Utero Pesticide Exposure, Maternal Paraoxonase Activity, and Head Circumference," *Environmental Health Perspectives*, March 2004. Paraoxonase is an enzyme that appears in the blood as a result of pesticide exposure.

[19] Elizabeth Ward et al., "Mortality Study of Workers in 1,3-Butadiene Production Units Identified from a Chemical Workers Cohort," *Environmental Health Perspectives*, June 1995.

FIGURE 14.3
Alternative Assumptions for Extrapolating the Effects of High Doses to Lower-Dose Levels

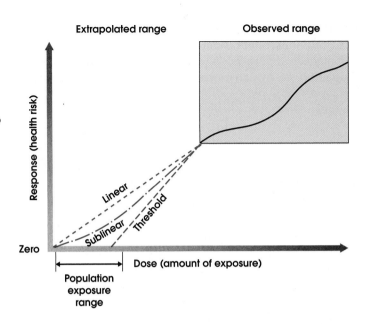

Population exposure range

population. However, though their accuracy is subject to doubt, the results of epidemiological tests can be valuable. Arsenic, for instance, does not cause cancer in lab animals; only epidemiology shows it to be a human carcinogen.

dose-response assessment
A quantitative estimate of how toxic a substance is to humans or animals at varying exposure levels.

extrapolation
To infer the value of an unknown state from the value of another state that is known.

linear dose-response rate
A relationship in which adverse health affects increase or decrease proportionately with the amount of exposure to a toxic substance.

Dose-Response Assessment

A *dose-response assessment* is a quantitative estimate of how toxic a substance is to humans or animals at increasing levels of exposure. The potency of carcinogens, for example, varies widely. Formaldehyde is a strong carcinogen that causes tumors in 50 percent of exposed lab animals at an inhalation dose of 15 parts per million (ppm). Vinyl chloride, on the other hand, is a very weak carcinogen that is benign at less than 50 ppm and, even at the much higher dose of 600 ppm, causes tumors in less than 25 percent of animals.[20]

Public exposures to toxic substances are usually well below the exposures of workers. And the exposures of both workers and the public are far lower than the extreme exposures of animals in high-dose tests. For most chemicals, in fact, regulators use *extrapolation* from high doses to predict the effects on human populations at much lower doses. For many years, the EPA has used a model that assumes a *linear dose-response rate*—that is, that there will be a proportionate decrease in cancers from large exposures to small ones (if, for example, exposure decreases by 25 percent, then cancers will decrease by 25 percent).

Figure 14.3 illustrates the theory of extrapolation from high to low doses with respect to carcinogens. The shaded area covers an observed range of responses at relatively high doses. Epidemiological studies on workers and laboratory experiments with rodents typically produce such data in high-dose ranges. The linear

[20] Louis A. Cox, Jr. and Paolo F. Ricci, "Dealing with Uncertainty: From Health Risk Assessment to Environmental Decision Making," *Journal of Energy Engineering,* August 1992, p. 79.

threshold
An exposure point greater than zero at which a substance begins to pose a health risk. Until this point, or threshold, is reached, exposure to the substance poses no health risk.

extension moving down to zero from the observed range is a prediction made in the absence of experimental data, one that is conservative in protecting public health. It suggests that risks rise substantially over the range of exposure to a human population. Many carcinogens, on the other hand, are less dangerous at low doses, as represented by the sublinear curve extending from the observed range. And still other carcinogens have a *threshold*, that is, they do not produce tumors at very low exposure levels and pose no risk until some threshold exposure amount is exceeded. If the hypothetical substance in Figure 14.3 responded based on the threshold curve as illustrated, there would be little risk of harm to public health within the exposure range shown.

The EPA makes the precautionary assumption that, in the absence of a clear understanding of dose-response relationships at low doses, risk estimates should be based on the linear curve. This invites cautious risk estimates suggesting more regulation to limit human exposure than would be called for based on a sublinear or threshold curve. The higher the inferred risk, the more justification there is for high expenditures to control polluting emissions.

Environmentalists who favor more regulation approve of the linear model. However, industry, which dislikes the expensive regulations it spawns, favors the use of sublinear and threshold models that support less regulation. The EPA has recently suggested willingness to depart from the linear model when rigorous evidence supports the validity of an alternative assumption.

Exposure Assessment

exposure assessment
The study of how much of a substance humans absorb through inhalation, ingestion, or skin absorption.

Exposure assessment is the study of how much of a substance humans absorb through inhalation, ingestion, or skin absorption. The level of a substance in one of the three media—air, water, and land—does not indicate how much of that substance is taken in by humans. Further study is needed to verify intake and concentrations in body tissues.

An example is a study of people pumping gasoline. Gasoline contains five toxic organic compounds that evaporate easily.[21] Pumping gas displaces air in fuel tanks, exposing people to them. To measure this exposure, researchers took blood samples of 60 motorists, both before and after refueling. They found that blood concentrations of all five compounds rose after gas pumping. Benzene, for instance, rose from 0.19 parts per billion (ppb) to 0.54 ppb and toluene from 0.38 ppb to 0.74 ppb. The higher concentrations lasted no longer than 10 minutes. This study confirms that motorists have short-term exposure to carcinogens when they fill up.

To make exposure assessments, researchers measure activities that bring individuals in contact with toxic substances, including such things as how much water people drink, their length of skin contact with water, amounts of soil eaten by children at play, inhalation rates, and consumption of various foods. Because movements and activities differ among people in studied populations, regulators present

---

[21] These are benzene, ethyl benzene, *m-/p*-xylene, *o*-oxylene, and toluene. Lorraine C. Backer et al., "Exposure to Regular Gasoline and Ethanol Oxyfuel during Refueling in Alaska," *Environmental Health Perspectives*, August 1997, p. 850.

their estimates as a distribution of individual exposures. The estimates include both a central estimate (based on mean or median exposure) of the average person's exposure and an upper-end estimate for the most highly exposed persons.

Risk Characterization

risk characterization
A written statement about a substance summarizing the evidence from prior stages of the risk assessment process to reach an overall conclusion about its risk. It includes discussion of the strengths and weaknesses of data and, if the data support it, a quantitative estimate of risk.

Risk characterization is an overall conclusion about the dangers of a substance. It is a detailed, written narrative describing the scientific evidence, including areas of ambiguity. A risk characterization for a carcinogen, for example, discusses the kinds of tumors promoted, human and animal data that suggest cancer causation for pertinent routes of exposure (oral, inhalation, skin absorption), and dose-response levels. Based on the discussion, the narrative ultimately characterizes the risks in quantitative terms.

For example, the EPA estimates the lifetime risk of leukemia from inhalation of benzene in a range from 2.2 to 7.8 in one million for a person exposed to 1 $\mu g/m^3$ (one microgram per cubic meter). That is, in a population of one million people exposed to very low levels of airborne benzene over the 75 years that the EPA calculates as an average lifetime, there will be two to eight extra cases of leukemia.

Such quantitative risk estimates then help to decide what level of abatement should be required of industry. There is no agreement about how high a risk should be before regulators must act to reduce it. Years ago, the Supreme Court addressed the subject of when a risk became "significant" and required regulation. Its plain-spoken explanation has guided regulators ever since.

> Some risks are plainly acceptable and others are plainly unacceptable. If, for example, the odds are one in a billion that a person will die from cancer by taking a drink of chlorinated water, the risk clearly could not be considered significant. On the other hand, if the odds are one in a thousand that regular inhalation of gasoline vapors that are 2 percent benzene will be fatal, a reasonable person might well consider the risk significant and take the appropriate steps to decrease or eliminate it.[22]

At the EPA, a lifetime risk of contracting cancer from a chemical substance or radiation source greater than 1 in 10,000 is generally considered excessive and subject to regulation. The goal of regulation is to reduce such risks to 1 in a million or lower. However, risks that fall between 1 in 10,000 and 1 in a million are usually considered acceptable.[23] With benzene, the EPA estimates that long-term exposures to air concentrations of 0.13 to 0.45 $\mu g/m^3$ pose a 1 in 1,000,000 risk, but when concentrations rise to 13 to 45 $\mu g/m^3$ exposed individuals face a 1 in 10,000 risk.[24] Therefore, if populations living near an oil refinery or a chemical plant were exposed to concentrations above 45 $\mu g/m^3$ the EPA would be inclined to force the facility to reduce air emissions.

Policy guidelines developed from quantitative risk estimates enrage some environmental activists. Asks one: "Would you let me shoot into a crowd of 100,000 people and kill one of them? No? Well, how come Dow Chemical can do it? It's

[22] *Industrial Union Department, AFL-CIO v. American Petroleum Institute*, 488 U.S. 655 (1989).

[23] General Accounting Office, *Radiation Standards: Scientific Basis Inconclusive*, GAO/RCED-00-152, p. 9 and fn. 23.

[24] EPA, Integrated Risk Information System, "Benzene (CASRN 71-43-2)" April 17, 2003, II, C.1.2.

okay for the corporations to do it, but the little guy with a gun goes to jail."[25] However, the alternative to a policy of accepting pollution risks between 1 in 10,000 and 1 in 1,000,000 is to decide that virtually no level of risk is acceptable. Eliminating infinitesimal risks from chemicals in an industrial society is not possible. Efforts to reduce them much below the EPA's acceptable range are often prohibitively expensive. Law enforcement to protect citizens from murderers costs far less.

Risk characterizations are built on scientific calculations of toxicity, potency, and exposure. Yet the precision of these calculations is limited. So risk characterizations tend to be cautiously worded. They also tend to overstate risk. With benzene, for example, the EPA's risk estimates are based on linear extrapolation to low doses because data on human exposures in the range of 1 to 45 $\mu g/m^3$ does not exist. The resulting 1 in 10,000 to 1 in 1,000,000 risk estimates are, therefore, conservative, likely to overstate risk, and likely to impose higher than necessary control costs on business.

Risk Management

Risk management (see again Figure 14.2, circle B) encompasses regulation of pollutants and health risks. Whereas risk assessment in circle A in Figure 14.2 is based on the natural sciences, risk management decisions are based on the social sciences—law, economics, politics, and ethics. We will discuss the elements of risk management.

Control Options

These are alternative methods for reducing most risks. For example, hazardous wastes can be stored in a landfill or broken down into harmless substances by high-temperature incineration. A spectrum of regulatory options also exists, ranging from strict enforcement to voluntary request. Later in the chapter these options are discussed at more length.

Legal Considerations

Environmental laws may be more or less specific about risk reduction required and the methods of achieving it. The Clean Air Act, for example, sets forth the general guideline that regulators should develop criteria for urban air quality that are "reasonably anticipated" to protect public health with "an adequate margin of safety." Further on, the same statute requires the EPA to set standards for hazardous air pollutant emissions based on levels that can be achieved only by the most technologically advanced control devices on the market. The Endangered Species Act prohibits consideration of economic factors in the decision to list a species.

In general, environmental laws tend to dictate regulatory decisions, being so specific that one observer calls them "Congressional handcuffs."[26] However, there

---

[25] Quoted in John A. Hird, *Superfund: The Political Economy of Environmental Risk* (Baltimore: Johns Hopkins University Press, 1994), p. 200.

[26] Kenneth W. Chilton, *Enhancing Environmental Protection while Fostering Economic Growth,* Policy Study No. 151 (St. Louis: Washington University, Center for the Study of American Business, March 1999), p. 22.

is always some latitude for regulators when they set up the specific rules to carry out congressional requirements.

Economic and Social Factors

Risk decisions cannot always be based solely on science. Technical data, such as control device engineering, may open or limit options. Public opinion may define politically acceptable options. Cost–benefit studies can illuminate the economic consequences of regulatory alternatives. We will now discuss cost–benefit analysis at greater length.

COST–BENEFIT ANALYSIS

cost–benefit analysis
The systematic identification, quantification, and monetization of social costs and social benefits so they can be directly compared.

Cost–benefit analysis is the systematic calculation and comparison of the costs and benefits of a proposed regulation. Costs are reductions in human welfare. Benefits are increases in human welfare. Rigorous cost–benefit studies identify costs and benefits, quantify them, and then assign them monetary values so they can be compared using a common denominator. If benefits exceed costs, the regulation increases net social welfare and is desirable, other things being equal.

With environmental regulations, cost calculations typically include factors such as enforcement costs, capital and compliance costs to industry, potential job losses, higher consumer prices, and reduced productivity (for example, lower crop yields from restricting the use of a dangerous, but highly effective pesticide). Benefits accrue from reducing damage to both human health and the environment. Health benefits may include reductions of death and illness, pain and suffering, absenteeism, lost wages, and medical costs. Direct ecological benefits might include greater food and fiber production, recreation opportunities, beautiful scenery, and enhanced ecosystem services (for example, pollination by bees that increases honey yields or soil stability that reduces flooding).

Regulators must submit to the Office of Management and Budget a cost–benefit study to justify any proposed rule with compliance costs of $100 million or more. In practice, these studies are recondite, expensive, and long, running to hundreds of pages. Although they are done to promote efficient decisions, one prominent effect is to complicate and slow regulation.

Advantages

Cost–benefit analysis has several advantages. First, it forces methodical consideration of each impact a policy will have on social welfare. It disciplines thinking, though it does not always result in clear choices. Cost–benefit studies show the net social benefits (or costs) of a regulation in monetary terms. However, this does not dictate a decision because other criteria can be equally or more important, including ethical duties and political consequences.

Second, cost–benefit analysis injects rational calculation into emotional arguments. Environmental risks are not always proportionate to the public alarm they raise. When people are fired up over a new menace, politicians, responding to the alarm, can be hasty to legislate. In some laws Congress has required that public

FIGURE 14.4

Relationship
between
Extent of
Regulation,
Costs, and
Benefits in
Environ-
mental
Regulation

Source: Adapted
from Kenneth W.
Chilton, *Enhancing
Environmental Protec-
tion while Fostering
Economic Growth*,
Policy Study
No. 151 (St. Louis:
Washington Univer-
sity, Center for the
Study of American
Business, March
1999), p. 8.

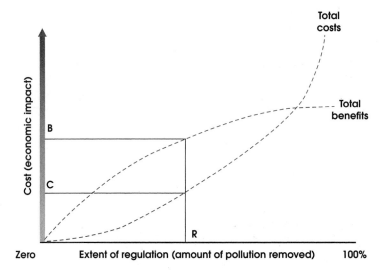

health be protected without consideration of expense and this invites rules costing more than the social value they create. Emotional decisions are not necessarily wrong, but dispassionate ones may better match risks and limited dollars.

Third, cost–benefit analysis that reveals marginal abatement costs helps regulators find the most efficient level of regulation. Figure 14.4 illustrates the typical relationship between environmental regulation and changes in costs and benefits. Initially, at or near zero, pollution controls are very cost-effective. Control equipment rapidly cuts emissions and reduces risks to public health, creating rising benefits. However, as higher levels of control are reached, it is increasingly expensive to remove each additional increment of pollution. New control technologies need to be developed. More complicated equipment that uses more energy must be installed. Yet even as this money is spent, the risk to public health is reduced less and less because falling concentrations of toxics pose fewer dangers. Costs begin to rise more rapidly than benefits, ultimately exceeding them and eventually rising exponentially as 100 percent cleanup, a quixotic goal, is neared.

The ideal level of regulation is at point R in Figure 15.4, the point where benefits most exceed costs (B minus C). At this point, each dollar spent produces maximum benefit. In theory, dollars spent for regulation after point R could be better spent on reducing other, less-regulated environmental risks. In cases such as this, cost–benefit analysis can identify efficient regulatory goals to prevent skyrocketing expenditures for trivial benefits. It provides an artificial but valuable test of efficient resource allocation for regulators not subject to a market mechanism.

Criticisms

As attractive as cost–benefit analysis seems, it has critics. Here are their foremost concerns.

First, fixing precise values of costs and benefits is difficult and controversial. For the method to work, costs and benefits must be quantified and monetized so they can be measured using a common metric. Yet how can the value of a clear sky, fish in a stream, fragrant air, extra years of life, or preserving species for future generations be priced? Their worth is subjective. Assigning dollar amounts to untraded goods such as scenic beauty or human life invites discord. There are ways to do it, but critics dispute their accuracy.

contingent valuation
A method for assigning monetary worth to ecological goods or services that are not traded in markets.

One method of measuring the monetary value of ecosystem goods is *contingent valuation*, a polling process in which people are asked to put a dollar amount on some aspect of nature. Contingent valuation puts a price on these natural features when they are not traded in markets. People in surveys are asked what sum they are willing to pay to protect or improve an ecosystem amenity. The average dollar amount they give is then multiplied by the number of American households (currently 113.2 million) to arrive at a specific dollar figure. For example, people in a survey might be asked how much they would pay from their own pockets to save 2,000 migratory birds that die when they land in ponds polluted by oil drilling. If their answers average $0.15, that sum, multiplied by 113.2 households, equals $16,980,000, which is the monetized value of the birds to human society. Any regulation to protect them should cost less.

The first conspicuous use of contingent valuation was in pricing the value of ecosystems around Prince William Sound after the *Exxon Valdez* oil spill. In another case, the EPA issued a rule requiring that the gargantuan Navajo Generating Station, a coal-burning power plant in Arizona, cut sulfur dioxide emissions by 90 percent at an annual cost of $90 million. The plant sits only 12 miles north of Grand Canyon National Park. The ecological benefit of the rule is a 7 percent improvement of winter visibility in the Grand Canyon, meaning that a person can see about 133 miles instead of only 124. Is this worth $90 million a year? Yes, said the EPA, based on a survey in which a sample of the public was asked how much their households were willing to pay for cleaner Grand Canyon air. This turned out to be from $1.30 to $2.50 per year per household, or $90 to $200 million.[27]

value of a statistical life
The amount that people exposed to pollution are willing to pay to reduce the risk of premature death.

Methods of calculating the *value of a statistical life* are controversial because they clash with public values of fairness and equity. Years ago, environmental regulators estimated the value of a statistical life on the basis of future lifetime earnings. This method was attacked as unfair, because the lives of the poor, homemakers, and retirees had less value than the lives of the rich or of young workers with future earnings potential. One critic noted that such calculations run "directly contrary to the egalitarian principle, with origins deep in the Judeo–Christian heritage, that all persons are equal before the law and God."[28] The method was quickly abandoned.

Today, the EPA uses a "willingness to pay" approach. It values a statistical life as the willingness to pay for reducing risk of premature death in a population exposed to a pollution hazard. It estimates how much people will pay to reduce risk by combining data from surveys that ask people how much they are willing to pay

[27] General Accounting Office, *Navajo Generating Station's Emissions Limit*, GAO/RCED-98-28, January 1998, pp. 1–3 and app. III.

[28] Thomas O. McGarity, "Health Benefits Analysis for Air Pollution Control: An Overview," in John Blodgett, ed., *Health Benefits of Air Pollution Control: A Discussion* (Washington, DC: Library of Congress, Congressional Research Service, February 27, 1989), p. 55.

for reducing the risk of early death with data from studies of the wage premium that workers accept to face added risk in dangerous jobs. The calculation is done this way. If, for example, as a result of controls the risk of early death from an air pollutant is reduced by 1 in 1,000,000 in a town of 2,000,000 people, then two anonymous, or statistical, lives are saved each year. If data from surveys and wage studies shows that individuals are willing to pay $5 to reduce their risk of premature death by 1 in 1,000,000, then the value of each statistical life saved in the town is $5,000,000.[29] Therefore, one benefit of the air pollution controls is $10,000,000 a year, or the monetized value of two statistical lives.

As it turns out, studies tend to value a statistical life at between $5,000,000 and $8,000,000. In recent years environmental regulators have used values ranging from $6.3 to $7 million.[30] Critics believe the willingness-to-pay approach is flawed because workers are not always well informed about risks they face. And women, who are more risk averse than men, are underrepresented in dangerous jobs.[31] Some opponents of life valuation reject all approaches, arguing that the very process of pricing human life mocks its extraordinary and sacred dignity.

Another criticism of cost–benefit approaches is that they compromise ecosystems deserving absolute, not conditional, protection. In American history, the Bill of Rights and the Emancipation Proclamation were never subject to cost–benefit study; the moral rights they set forth were considered absolute. Now, according to some environmentalists, we have a duty to respect nature as we respect humanity, apart from money considerations. Such objections reject the need for efficiency and political compromise in regulation, substituting dogmatic principle in its place. However, it is correct that cost–benefit analysis implies that ethical duties can be balanced against utilitarian benefits to society.

Another difficulty with cost–benefit analysis is that the benefits and costs of a program often fall to separate parties. Purifying factory wastewater raises costs to businesses and consumers. Yet benefits from clean water accrue to shoreline property owners, realtors, and fish. In such cases, weighing diverse cost–benefit effects raises questions of justice.

In sum, there is validity in criticisms of cost–benefit analysis, but it may nonetheless bring more efficient regulation. Dollars for pollution abatement are limited. Decisions about where to spend them are required. One defender of the practice of monetizing human life puts it this way: "It's clearly not a winner when it comes to making yourself look good at public meetings, but it's the right thing to do from a public-safety standpoint."[32]

---

[29] Environmental Protection Agency, *Guidelines for Preparing Economic Analyses*, EPA 240-R-00-003, September 2000, p. 87; and Environmental Protection Agency, *OAQPS Economic Analysis Resource Document*, Office of Air Quality Planning Standards, April 1999, p. 7-16.

[30] See Ike Brannon, "What Is a Life Worth?" *Regulation*, Winter 2004–2005, p. 63; and Ike Brannon, "Treating the Unserious Seriously," *Regulation*, Winter 2005–2006, p. 52.

[31] Frank Ackerman and Lisa Heinzerling, *Priceless: On Knowing the Price of Everything and the Value of Nothing* (New York: New Press, 2004), p. 75.

[32] W. Kip Viscusi, quoted in John J. Fialka, "Balancing Act: Lives vs. Regulations," *The Wall Street Journal*, May 30, 2003, p. A4.

FIGURE 14.5
The Spectrum of Regulatory Options

Command and control	Flexible enforcement	Market incentives	Required disclosure	Voluntary compliance
CONTROL				*FREEDOM*

CONTROL OPTIONS

Legislators and regulators have many options for reducing risks to health and the environment. Figure 14.5 shows a spectrum of choices. Most regulation, by far, takes place on the far left. However, there is growing use of options to the middle and right based on evidence that a balance between control and freedom is most efficient. The regulatory alternatives discussed in this section can work in combination. They are not either/or options. They can reinforce each other as parts of an overall regulatory scheme.

Command-and-Control Regulation

command-and-control regulation
The practice of regulating by setting uniform standards, strictly enforcing rules, and using penalties to force compliance.

One cause of high pollution-abatement costs is heavy reliance on *command-and-control regulation*. Most statutes tell regulators to set uniform standards across industries, apply rigid rules to individual pollution sources, specify cleanup technology, set strict timetables for action, issue permits, and enforce compliance, all with limited or no consideration of costs.

Command-and-control regulation has advantages. It enforces predictable and uniform standards. There is great equity in applying the same rules to all firms in an industry. The record proves that it produces abatements and it comforts the public to know that the EPA is there like an old-fashioned schoolmarm, watching companies like a hawk, slapping wrists, and putting polluters in the dunce's chair.

However, this approach can be inefficient and increase costs without commensurate increases in benefits. The lesson was learned in a milestone case study done by the EPA and Amoco. It focused on regulation at a single refinery. A key finding was that under the EPA's rigid command-and-control approach, cuts in air emissions cost an average $2,100 per ton, but if the refinery had more flexibility in how it achieved these cuts, 90 percent of reductions would cost only $500 per ton.[33] This study was a major stimulus for making regulation more flexible.

Market Incentive Regulation

market incentive regulation
The practice of harnessing market forces to motivate compliance with regulatory goals.

Market incentive regulation gives polluters financial motives to control pollution while also giving them flexibility in how reductions are achieved. This combination usually brings abatement at lower cost and with more creativity. Since the 1990s market incentives have grown in popularity, most of all in Europe, less in the United States. Here we discuss several market approaches.

[33] Caleb Solomon, "What Really Pollutes? A Study of a Refinery Proves an Eye-Opener," *The Wall Street Journal,* March 29, 1993, p. A1.

Environmental Taxes

Taxes can be imposed on polluting emissions or products. They are most used in Europe, where environmental tax revenues average 2 to 2.5 percent of GDP. One example is Ireland's tax on plastic bags. Since 2002, Irish customers have paid retailers a $0.15 tax for each plastic bag they use. This tax reduced bag use from 1.2 billion to 113 million in its first year.[34] More than 90 percent of European green tax revenue comes from levies on the sulfur content in gasoline and diesel fuel and on road use by motor vehicles, but small amounts come from taxing industrial emissions. France, for example, taxes emissions of sulfur dioxide, nitrogen oxides, and volatile organic compounds. Spain, Denmark, Norway, Italy, and Switzerland have similar taxes.

The United States has never moved far down this path, but a few taxes are in place. For example, the EPA enforces an ozone-depletion tax on 20 chemicals. The tax is calculated by multiplying three factors, the number of pounds produced, the monetary tax rate, and a number representing the greater or lesser potential of the molecule for harming the ozone layer. This tax was first introduced in 1990 and since then tax rates have been raised five times to discourage use of these chemicals.

Sometimes taxes are coupled with incentives. The largest such scheme is in China, where regulators apply a combination of emission charges and abatement subsidies along with traditional rule-based regulation. Polluting firms pay taxes based on wastewater discharges, air emissions, and solid waste generation. Then up to 80 percent of the charge can be refunded to the firm for investment in pollution control. More than half a million companies in China are harnessed in this system.[35] Another example of a tax-subsidy tandem is the Swedish government's tax on nitrogen oxide emissions by electric power plants. The tax is collected from all electric companies, then rebated based on emissions per unit of energy produced. In this way the most efficient companies are subsidized by the least efficient ones.

environmental tax reform
The substitution of revenues from taxes on pollution for revenues from taxes on productivity.

More broadly, some countries are experimenting with *environmental tax reform*, or the substitution of revenues from taxes on pollution for revenues from taxes on productivity. Traditionally, the bulk of government revenues comes from income, sales, revenue, and payroll taxes. Environmental tax reform has the greatest support in Europe. Its advocates think that substituting revenue from green taxes for revenue from taxes on productivity pays a double dividend. The switch penalizes ecological harm and also eases the deadweight of taxation on wealth-creating activities.

Emissions Trading

cap and trade
A market-based policy of pollution abatement in which emissions are capped and sources must hold tradeable permits equal to the amount of their discharges.

Emissions trading, an approach often called *cap and trade*, is an alternative to taxation. A cap-and-trade program begins by initially setting an overall limit, or cap, on emissions of a specific pollutant. Then the cap is gradually lowered. At the beginning, the government sets a comfortable cap close to current emissions, trying

[34] Vanessa Houlder et al., "European Countries Become Wary of Eco-Taxes," *Financial Times*, December 9, 2006, p. 4.

[35] Hua Wang and Ming Chen, *How the Chinese System of Charges and Subsidies Affects Pollution Control Efforts by China's Top Industrial Polluters* (Washington, DC: World Bank, Working Paper No. 2198, October 1, 1999).

to avoid a sudden compliance shock to industry. Each company is allocated a number of permits (also called credits or allowances) and is allowed to release only amounts of pollution equal to those covered by the permits. Each permit equals a unit of pollution, for example, one pound or one ton, and is good for a year. Regulators then monitor emissions from each plant. At the end of the year, if a plant's emissions exceed the amount covered by its permits it is fined.

Companies are allowed to trade permits at a market price. If they reduce emissions below their permit allowance, they can sell their unused permits. If emissions exceed their annual allowance, they must buy additional permits. In this way, polluting companies in effect pay a fine and the money goes to cleaner operators.

Total emission reduction comes when, at scheduled intervals, the government retires permits from the market. To reduce emissions by 50 percent over 20 years, for example, the government would eliminate 5 percent of the annual permits every two years. As the emissions cap lowers, companies either reduce their emissions or buy more and more permits at rising market prices.

If the scheme works, those plants that can cut emissions at the lowest cost will act earlier, do relatively more abatement, and make money by selling excess permits to plants that can less cheaply cut emissions. Abatement costs vary for many reasons—type of fuel used, type of industrial process, age of equipment, and level of control already reached. In theory, a cap-and-trade program can achieve the same net reduction in pollution at lower cost than command-and-control rules that ignore differences in marginal abatement costs from firm to firm.

The pioneering large-scale emissions trading scheme is a cap-and-trade program to cut sulfur dioxide emissions from about 3,500 electric generating units in eastern and midwestern states. In 1995 the EPA capped annual SO_2 emissions from these facilities at 14 million tons per year and allocated one-ton permits totaling this amount to utility companies. Then the agency began yearly cap reductions by retiring permits, lowering the ceiling to 10 million tons in 2000 and 9.5 million tons in 2005 on the way to a final cap of 8.95 tons in 2010. Over the life of the program about 190 million one-ton permits to release SO_2 have been traded on an auction market or directly between companies. Their price, set by market forces, rose from a low of $65 in 1996 to about $600 in 2006. This is still far less expensive than the penalty of $3,042 that the EPA assesses for each ton of SO_2 in excess of a generating unit's allocation.[36]

Schemes for trading emissions of CO_2 and other greenhouse gases are a prominent response to the threat of climate change. In 2005 the European Union set up a cap-and-trade mechanism covering CO_2 emissions from about 12,000 power plants, factories, mills, and smelters that altogether emit almost 50 percent of the CO_2 in EU countries. The EU is required under the Kyoto Protocol (see Chapter 13) to reduce its emissions by 2012 to 8 percent less than they were in 1990. The plan is to reduce CO_2 allowances each year to meet this target. So far the scheme is behind schedule because across the entire 27-country region the number of initial allowances given to companies exceeded actual CO_2 emissions, eliminating most

[36] Figures in this paragraph are from Environmental Protection Agency, *Acid Rain Program 2005 Progress Report*, EPA-430-R-06-015, October 2006, pp. 4–5, 8.

of the market incentive for reduction. With this surplus, allowances to emit a metric ton of carbon sank to less than $1. However, a cap reduction in 2007 sent the price flying up to more than $24.

The United Kingdom and Australia have separate and complementary CO_2 emission trading programs. In the United States the Chicago Climate Exchange is a voluntary allowance trading system. About 250 companies have agreed to make an annual 1 percent reduction in their emissions of six greenhouse gases as measured in CO_2 equivalents. After volunteering, they sign a legally binding contract to reduce emissions or, failing that, to purchase contracts equal to the shortfall at the Exchange's market price. One contract equals 100 metric tons of CO_2 equivalent and sold for about $1.85 in 2007. This is a low price, voluntarily paid, and inadequate to force major emission reductions. However, Congress is considering CO_2 reduction measures and if it legislates an effective mandatory cap-and-trade program the price of carbon will rise.

The global market for CO_2 and CO_2 equivalent allowances exceeded $23 billion in 2006 and it is rapidly growing.[37] Almost 80 percent of this market is in the European Union.

carbon offsets
Projects that compensate for all or part of a company's greenhouse gas emissions by eliminating the CO_2 equivalent of those emissions from another source.

In all the greenhouse gas cap-and-trade programs discussed here, companies are allowed to meet their reduction goals by paying for *carbon offsets*, or projects that compensate for all or part of a company's greenhouse gas emissions by eliminating the CO_2 equivalent of those emissions from another source. Such projects include planting trees, paying farmers not to till their soil, and recovering methane from pig farms and waste dumps. In each case, the party buying the offset is credited with the CO_2 equivalent of the global warming gas that is sequestered or trapped. Buying offsets may be less expensive than either direct reduction of factory or power plant emissions or purchase of market-priced allowances.

Clean Development Mechanism
A carbon offset program set up under the Kyoto Protocol. It allows developed countries to meet greenhouse gas reduction pledges by paying for carbon offset projects in developing nations.

Worldwide expenditure for offsets under cap-and-trade programs was $5.5 billion in 2006. The offsets themselves reduced emissions by 518 million metric tons of CO_2 equivalent. About 91 percent of this activity came under the auspices of the *Clean Development Mechanism* (CDM), a carbon offset program set up under the Kyoto Protocol. The CDM allows countries in the developed world to meet their Kyoto pledges by funding offset projects in developing nations.[38]

For example, the Netherlands built a modern landfill in Brazil to capture methane escaping from decomposition of urban rubbish. After capture the methane is simply burned, releasing CO_2 into the atmosphere. However, since methane is a much more potent global warming gas than CO_2, under Kyoto rules the Dutch receive emission reduction credits at a cost of only a little over $4 a ton.[39] This is much cheaper than paying for allowances costing more than $20 a ton on the European carbon market. In such faltering ways does the post-Kyoto world make progress toward its environmental goals.

---

[37] Caran Capoor and Philippe Ambrosi, *State and Trends of the Carbon Market 2007* (Washington, DC: The World Bank, May 2007), p. 3.

[38] Figures in this paragraph are from ibid., pp. 3 and 20.

[39] Jeffrey Ball, "To Cut Pollution, Dutch Pay a Dump in Brazil to Clean Up," *The Wall Street Journal*, August 11, 2005, p. A1.

FIGURE 14.6 **How a Cap-and-Trade System with Offsets Works**

CAP-AND-TRADE MARKET
Say that company A is releasing more CO_2 than its assigned limit, whereas company B is emitting less than its allowance (*left*). Company A can pay company B for its unused permits and thus use them to meet its obligations (*right*).

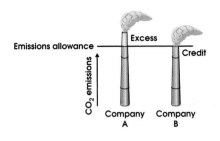
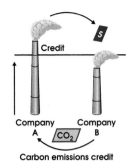

OFFSET EXCHANGE
Imagine that company A is over its emissions allotment. Through Kyoto's clean development mechanism, company A can invest in a carbon reduction project established by company C in a developing nation, which costs less than a similar project in the developed country (*left*). Company A gets the credits it needs at a reduced cost, and company C gets investment money it needs, while less total CO_2 enters the atmosphere than if the developing country had turned to a fossil-fuel energy source (*right*).

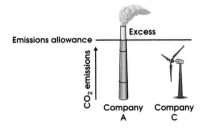
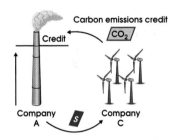

Source: From David G. Victor and Danny Cullenward, "Making Carbon Markets Work," *Scientific American*, December 2007, p. 73. Reprinted with permission of illustrators Ann Sanderson and Logan Parsons.

Some environmentalists ridicule carbon offsets, comparing them with the sale of indulgences by the Church. Catholics who committed a mortal sin owed God seven years of penance. Beginning in the fifteenth century sinners could instead pay a fee to the pope, who would forgive their sins. One, Sixtus IV, promised "complete absolution and remission of all sins" and "preferential treatment for their future sins."[40] Buyers were assured that the Holy Father's action would be accepted by God. An indulgence was convenient. It made the long work of humble contrition unnecessary. Critics charge that carbon offsets are "new indulgences" that allow polluters to "neutralize" their offense against nature without undertaking the difficult process and equipment changes needed to stop their own carbon discharges.[41] Buying offsets may meet legal requirements but it does not stop their own wrong against the heavens and earth.

toxics release inventory
An EPA program that requires facilities handling any of 650 hazardous chemicals to disclose amounts each year that are released or transferred. The information is made public.

Information Disclosure

Information disclosure about environmental performance harnesses market forces by affecting consumer perceptions and equity prices. An example is the *Toxics Release Inventory* (TRI) compiled by the EPA.[42] Each year industrial facilities that

[40] William Manchester, *A World Lit Only by Fire* (Boston: Little, Brown, 1992), p. 133.

[41] Kevin Smith, *The Carbon Neutral Myth: Offset Indulgences for your Climate Sins* (Amsterdam: Transnational Institute, February 2007), p. 6.

[42] The TRI is mandated by the Emergency Planning and Community Right-to-Know Act of 1986. This law was passed after the 1984 gas leak in Bhopal to require that plants and factories report to the public amounts and types of chemicals they store or release.

release or transfer any of 650 toxic pollutants must report the amounts. The data are published, and citizens can comb through them to learn what substances neighboring factories release.

In 2005, facilities reported releasing 2.5 billion pounds of toxics into the environment, a large amount, but less than half that being released when reporting began in 1987. This included 1.5 billion pounds of air emissions, 240 million pounds entering the nation's waters, and 596 million pounds that were spilled, leaked, or dumped on land as unregulated waste.[43]

Among the releases the EPA tracks are 176 substances known or suspected to be carcinogens. Of these, 113 million pounds went into the air, 1.7 million pounds into surface waters, and 308 million pounds fell on the land.[44]

Corporations dislike being listed as leading polluters by volume and there are many examples of reductions exceeding those required by law just to avoid attracting attention.

Voluntary Regulation

voluntary regulation
Regulation without statutory mandate, compulsion, or sanctions.

Another way that regulation is made more flexible, besides the use of market incentives, is to make it voluntary. *Voluntary regulation* is regulation without statutory mandate, compulsion, or sanctions. Corporations participate of their own free will. Its use is widespread. Worldwide there are dozens of voluntary standards negotiated between companies, activists, and governments.

Voluntary regulation is used when the political will for stringent command-and-control rules is absent. Thus, the main focus of voluntary environmental regulation in the United States is reducing global warming emissions, encouraging actions that Congress has had no stomach to decree. Climate Leaders, for example, is a voluntary program set up by the Environmental Protection Agency. Corporations that join this program must set goals for reducing greenhouse emissions and report their progress.[45]

One participant, giant electricity generator American Electric Power, reduced its total greenhouse gas emissions by 4 percent between 2001 and 2006 and pledges to reduce them another 6 percent by 2010. AEP runs 80 generating plants that supply power to millions of customers over 11 states. These plants use so much coal that the company has its own railroad fleet of 7,500 coal cars. A 6 percent greenhouse gas reduction will require eliminating 31 million metric tons of CO_2 emissions by 2010.[46] AEP plans to do this using a combination of measures, from a new technology that captures carbon from pulverized coal to retiring older generating units to offsetting emissions by planting trees.

AEP is one of more than 70 Climate Leaders corporations. Participants must monitor their emissions and report them to the EPA. The pledged emission reductions are expensive, but companies have many reasons for making the effort. Most

[43] Environmental Protection Agency, *2005 TRI Public Data Release eReport: Data Tables and Charts*, March 2007, p. B-1, at www.epa.gov/tri/tridata/tri05/index.htm.

[44] Ibid., p. B-21.

[45] See Environmental Protection Agency, *A Program Guide for Climate Leaders: Setting the Standard for Greenhouse Gas Management*, EPA430-F-05-016, October 2006.

[46] American Electric Power, *Working Together for a Brighter Future: 2006 Corporate Sustainability Report* (Colombus, OH: AEP, April 2007), pp. 13–16.

FIGURE 14.7
The Environ-
mental
Protection
Agency's
Climate
Leaders
Program

Source: EPA.

CLIMATE
LEADERS

ENERGY STAR

Green Power Partnership   WasteWise

Natural Gas STAR   CHP Partnership

Landfill Methane   Coalbed Methane
Outreach Program   Outreach Program

SmartWay Transport   Best Workplaces
                               for Commuters

believe that more greenhouse gas regulation is imminent and want to prepare control strategies now. When they achieve their goals, the EPA gives them awards and favorable publicity.

As shown in Figure 14.7 Climate Leaders is an umbrella for a family of voluntary environmental programs that corporations can enter. Each helps reduce greenhouse gas emissions in one way or another. WasteWise, for example, began in 1994 as a program to encourage waste reduction. Since then, participating "partners" have eliminated 120 million tons of waste and with it millions of tons of CO_2 emissions.[47] In the Green Power Partnership the EPA publicizes companies that buy renewable energy such as electricity from wind power. The Coalbed Methane Outreach Program simply provides technical assistance for mines trying to capture the methane released when underground coal deposits are disturbed.

These voluntary programs work only because there are strong nonregulatory pressures for companies to be environmentally responsible. However, the sum of action under the Climate Leaders umbrella falls far short of profound. Greenhouse gas emissions from industry rise a little more slowly, but they still rise.

MANAGING ENVIRONMENTAL QUALITY

**environ-
mental
management
system**
A set of methods and procedures for aligning corporate strategies, policies, and operations with principles that protect ecosystems.

There are many pressures and incentives for corporations to protect the environment. Except for occasional criminal actions, most do. However, the response ranges from grudging, minimal compliance with government rules to innovative leadership that shrinks a company's environmental footprint. In this section we explain a range of actions that characterize the current efforts of leading companies.

Environmental Management Systems

The most proactive companies establish an *environmental management system* (EMS), which is a set of methods and procedures for aligning corporate strategies,

---

[47] Environmental Protection Agency, *WasteWise 2006 Annual Report*, EPA-530-R-06-010, p. 1.

Core Elements of an Environmental Management System

- An environmental policy
- Planning and strategy that include environmental factors
- Identification of impacts on the environment
- Development of goals and performance measures

- Monitoring and corrective action
- Formal stakeholder involvement
- Employee awards, incentives, and training
- A philosophy of continuous improvement

policies, and operations with principles that protect ecosystems. The core elements of these systems are shown in the box above.

ISO 14001
A standard for an environmental management system created by an international standard-setting body. Certification in meeting this standard allows companies to claim state-of-the-art ecological responsibility.

The leading international model for such systems is *ISO 14001*, a standard for environmental management created by the International Organization for Standardization. Companies that adopt its requirements are certified. The letters ISO reference this international body and the number 14001 indicates its place in a family of environmental standards. Some large companies, for instance, ExxonMobil, design their own systems, but typically firms base them on ISO 14001 and apply for certification by trained third-party auditors. This is especially attractive to smaller firms, because there is a trend for large multinationals to seek suppliers and vendors with a working EMS, and ISO 14001 certification verifies this. Matsushita Electrical Industries (Panasonic), for instance, has a procurement policy to consider a supplier's environmental record along with cost, quality, and delivery and gives priority to companies certified under ISO 14001.[48]

The green procurement trend is responsible for an explosion in worldwide ISO certifications from 257 facilities in 1995 to more than 129,000 in 2007.[49] Many certifications are in developing economies. More facilities in China have adopted ISO 14001 than in the United States. This is one example of the power of large corporations to extend environmental initiatives through global supply chains.

A Range of Actions

Leading companies take a broad range of actions to reduce adverse environmental impacts. Here are some illustrations.

precautionary principle
When industrial activity poses a risk to human health or ecosystems, if that risk is poorly understood, then prudence calls for restraint.

- *Precautionary action.* An idea called the *precautionary principle*, which has taken root among environmentalists, holds that when industrial activity poses a risk, even if the threat is as yet poorly understood, prudence calls for restraint. Recently, advances in methods for detecting chemicals in living tissue led scientists

[48] Matsushita Electric Group, *Green Procurement Standards,* rev. ed., ver. 4 (Osaka: Matsushita Electric Industrial Co., Ltd., April 20, 2006), p. 5.

[49] International Organization for Standardization, *The ISO Survey–2006* (Geneva, International Organization for Standardization, 2007), p. 25.

to discover tiny amounts of the substance perfluorooctane sulfonate (PFO), as little as 0.5 parts per million, in human blood and animal tissue around the world. The source is 3M, which began using the chemical in Scotchgard fabric protector in the late 1950s. Learning this, 3M scientists expressed surprise and disbelief. They examined health data on workers at Scotchgard plants and found no adverse effects. However, 3M decided to take the product off the market in 2000 to avert any possible harm to life. Since it had no substitute for PFO, it lost a $500 million-a-year business until 2006 when a newly formulated Scotchgard was reintroduced. Of course, the company anticipated government action and it was petrified by the lawsuit potential.[50] These pressures enforced the precautionary principle, illustrating again that environmental responsibility by business is most often an adaptation to external pressures.

- *Pollution prevention.* End-of-the-pipe control equipment isolates or neutralizes pollutants after they are generated. Pollution prevention is the modification of industrial processes to eliminate contaminants before they are created. For example, many companies have stopped using solvents to clean production equipment, substituting soap or isopropyl alcohol in their place. This eliminates evaporation of hazardous compounds in solvents and often works just as well and at a lower cost. Simple forms of pollution prevention, such as putting a lid on a tank to stop evaporation or tightening valves to stop leaks, are used by many companies. After such easy steps, however, further progress usually requires complex redesigns of processes and products. These projects are expensive. At many firms they will not be approved, even if they reduce harmful emissions or reduce costs, unless they bring a return on capital invested equal to or greater than alternative investments.

- *Product analysis.* Products can be examined to reduce adverse environmental impacts. Eastman Kodak makes a life-cycle assessment. It looks at factors such as raw materials used, energy consumed, fugitive emissions, and potential for recycling. SC Johnson uses a "greenlist" to rate ingredients for household products. Its chemists have many raw material choices for the surfactants, solvents, propellants, fragrances, and other ingredients that go into brands such as Raid, Off!, Drano, Saran Wrap, and Windex. Before choosing, they look at a scorecard that ranks substances from 0 to 3 based on estimates of toxicity. A 0 means "restricted use" and requires higher management approval, 1 is "acceptable," 2 is "better," and 3 is "best." Chemists try to achieve higher scores as they formulate products. In 2001 the company had an average score of 1.12 and has set a goal of scoring 2.0 by 2011.[51]

- *Environmental marketing.* Some companies see possibilities for revenue creation in green products, services, or marketing appeals. A small company, Planktos Corp., plans to dissolve tons of iron over large areas of ocean to feed plankton.

[50] Both have come to pass. In 2006 the company paid an EPA fine of $1.5 million for 244 illegal releases of PFO in violation of the Toxic Substances Control Act. Six Washington County, Minnesota, residents have sued 3M for allowing PFOs to seep into their drinking water. See Bob Shaw, "3M Suit's Big Issue: Who Got Hurt?" *St. Paul Pioneer Press,* March 24, 2007, p. 1.

[51] SC Johnson & Sons, *2007 Public Report: Doing Our Part* (Racine, WI: SC Johnson, 2007), pp. 14–18.

It will measure their absorption of CO_2, then sell that amount to corporations seeking emissions offsets.[52] Another innovative product is weather-based derivatives offered by Swiss Reinsurance, a colossus of the insurance industry. Buyers can speculate on future temperatures with put and-call options covering specific dates. Businesses now can hedge against global warming losses. Farmers, for example, can protect themselves against crop losses. Wal-Mart recently set a goal of selling 100 million compact fluorescent bulbs a year by 2008. It estimates that this will save consumers $3 billion in electricity costs. Wal-Mart seeks both revenue and reputation enhancement. Although incandescent bulbs are more profitable, it expects to get some of the $3 billion savings back in customer purchases—in effect, stealing revenue from utility corporations. It also hopes to repair an image sullied by charges of irresponsibility.

- *Environmental metrics.* Companies are innovating to find better ways of measuring environmental costs and performance. In the past, costs such as record keeping for hazardous substances or excess energy consumption were hidden in overhead accounts. External costs that companies impose on society by damaging the environment have gone unmeasured and are usually not incorporated into management accounting. For example, in a study of the Financial Times Stock Exchange 100 stock index companies calculated that if they were forced to pay the external costs of their CO_2 emissions, estimated by the British government to be $36 per ton, they would suffer an average 12 percent earnings drop.[53] Some companies are experimenting with accounting methods that reveal such formerly obscured costs. Others are developing innovative ways to measure environmental performance. To reduce consumption of natural resources, SC Johnson tries to use more recycled materials. It tracks its progress by measuring the ratio of virgin packaging to formula weight. DuPont created a metric that measures the ratio of shareholder value added per pound of pollution discharged.[54]

CONCLUDING OBSERVATIONS

In the previous chapter we described how industrial activity harms the environment and explained the basic regulatory approach used to mitigate the damage. In this chapter we look more deeply into the methods of this regulation. We began with a story about railyard diesel exhaust to illustrate one molecular-level danger to human health in modern industrial society. Then we explained how such a danger is scientifically evaluated and how a regulatory approach is then chosen to mitigate it. Finally, we give some illustrations of how companies are greening their operations.

The discussion emphasizes the rationality of science-based regulation and the entry of new, more flexible, market-based approaches to achieving environment-

[52] Matt Richtel, "The Plankton Defense," *The New York Times,* May 1, 2007, p. C1.

[53] Henderson Global Associates, *The Carbon 100: Quantifying the Carbon Emissions, Intensities and Exposures of the FTSE 100* (London: Henderson Global Associates, June 2005), p. 17.

[54] Nicholas Varchaver, "Chemical Reaction," *Fortune,* April 2, 2007, p. 57.

preserving goals. Much progress has been made in protecting both ecosystems and human health. Notwithstanding, the sum of regulatory activity and voluntary business action has been inadequate to avert climate change. The consequences of this failure will fill future chapters.

Harvesting Risk

This is the story of a scavenger. Ascending on shrewdness, Amvac Chemical Corporation has grown from a small Los Angeles pesticide company into a multinational corporation.[1]

It is still growing. Annual revenues are now almost $200 million and CEO Erik Wintemute aspires to reach $1 billion. It has enriched stockholders. Exhibit 1 shows a stellar five-year run from 2001 through 2006 when the value of Amvac's equity rose more than 700 percent.

Amvac's share price floats above indexes because the company follows a singular strategic vision. It stands apart from agrichemical industry giants as they create and market new pesticides. It waits while the big companies build brand names and markets for these molecules. Then, when a product has aged or become less attractive to the original owners, Amvac offers to buy it. Once Amvac has the brand rights, it pushes sales in remaining niche markets or, sometimes, opens new markets by registering additional crop applications or exporting to foreign countries. In this way, as the global behemoths shed shrinking, failing, dangerous, or obsolete product lines, the opportunistic scavenger captures a new stream of revenue.

EXHIBIT 1
Relative Share Price of Amvac and Two Market Indices

Source: American Vanguard Corporation, *Annual Report, Form 10-K* (2006), p. 21.

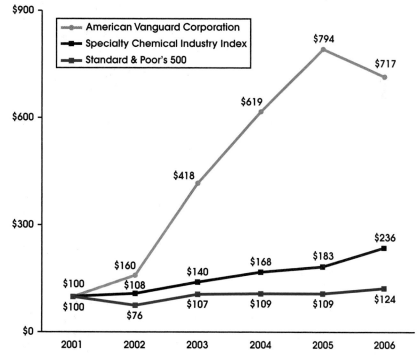

[1] Amvac operates as a subsidiary of a holding company named American Vanguard Corporation and is the company's main business.

Amvac's goal is to acquire one or two niche product lines every year and in recent years it has done so. Big agricultural chemical companies discard pesticides for many reasons. As they integrate businesses after mergers, they may decide to drop redundant brands. When Novartis and AstraZeneca merged their agribusinesses in 2000, Amvac got two vegetable crop insecticides and a herbicide used in cranberry fields. Sometimes big companies cast aside products when sales are inadequate. In the 1990s DuPont created a soil insecticide named Fortress that effectively controls corn rootworms, the most destructive cornfield pests. But sales missed targets. So Amvac bought Fortress in 2000 and with it entry into the midwest corn grower's market. It built a new sales team and within a year Fortress sales that would have disappointed DuPont were adding materially to Amvac's revenues.

In some cases products have matured or become outdated. Larger firms at the forefront of advancing biotechnology are shifting their focus from chemical poisons to genetic lines of insect-resistant seeds. As they do, Amvac has acquired older pesticides, including some organophosphates belonging to a family of pesticides that is on the way out in the industry.

Organophosphate molecules are effective pest killers and still widely used, but they are being superceded by both biotechnology products and by pesticides that better target pests and pose less risk. Some organophosphates are exceptionally dangerous to human health in terms of both acute and long-term exposures. A few are so toxic that they defy safe use, leading to personal injury lawsuits and regulatory crackdowns. Even in these instances Amvac sees opportunity. Faithful to the logic of its niche strategy, it has acquired rights to some of the most poisonous brands even as bigger companies cease their production. Then, it has sought new markets for them while defending them against alarmed regulators. Here are several stories about Amvac pesticides.

DIBROMOCHLOROPROPANE

Dibromochloropropane, or DBCP, is a chemical soil fumigant that kills parasitic worms feeding on fruit and vegetable crops. It belongs to an aging class of organochlorine pesticides developed after World War II. Most of these molecules, which include DDT, are used now only in a few poor countries. They are stable molecules that linger in the environment and accumulate in human tissue. Beginning in the 1960s, DBCP was used in the United States and around the world on cotton, potato, banana, and pineapple crops. Dow and Shell manufactured it until 1977, when it was discovered to cause sterility in men at formulating plants.[2]

Regulators immediately banned DBCP in California. On the day of the ban, Dow and Shell suspended its production and marketing. Although the story of worker infertility got extensive media coverage many farmers still wanted to use DBCP. So Amvac stepped in to fill the void and became its leading maker. Due to bad publicity, domestic sales had fallen, so Amvac supplied foreign markets. It stepped in to replace Dow and Shell as a supplier for Dole Fruit and other companies that used DBCP on large banana plantations in Central America and the Caribbean.

By 1979 the EPA had gathered extensive data on DBCP and concluded that it had no safe uses. The agency proposed a ban. Amvac disputed the evidence and finally persuaded regulators to allow an exception for use on Hawaiian pineapple crops. It agreed to promote safe application and to monitor local groundwater for contamination. In 1983 Amvac applied for a temporary exemption from the regulatory ban in South Carolina so that DBCP could be used in peach orchards. The EPA agreed, basing its decision on university research sponsored by Amvac. Outraged environmentalists stopped the exemption with a lawsuit.[3]

Two years later, Hawaiian wells for drinking water were found contaminated by runoff from pineapple fields and the EPA finally banned all applications of DBCP anywhere in the United States.

By this time evidence of DBCP's dangers was strong and before the end of the decade a substantial body of research backed up the agency's decision. DBCP causes sterility in both animals and humans. Studies showed that men who inhaled small concentrations produced fewer sperm and were more likely to father girls. With longer exposures their testicles atrophied and sperm production fell to zero.

DBCP is so dangerous that current regulations set safe inhalation exposure for workers at one part per billion over an eight-hour day. DBCP also causes cancer in rats and is classified as "reasonably anticipated" to be a human carcinogen. Like other molecules in the

[2] "Helen Dewar, "Workers at Pesticide Plant Found Sterile in California Tests," *Washington Post,* August 5, 1977, p. A3.

[3] Ward Sinclair, "The Return of DBCP," *Washington Post,* February 1, 1983, p. A1.

organochlorine family, it persists in the environment. After application it slowly evaporates from soil or surface water into the air, where it resides for up to three months before breaking down. In soil, it can linger for several years.[4]

DBCP bore a crop of lawsuits for Amvac. The company is named, along with Dow and Shell, in multiple actions involving up to 50,000 banana plantation workers who claim sterility and allege exposure up to 1990, five years after the U.S. ban.[5]

So far Amvac has settled one case, paying $300,000 to 13 Nicaraguan plantation workers.[6] Villagers who drank contaminated water in Hawaii also sued Amvac and the other companies. Researchers found unusual clusters of breast cancer, heart defects, learning disabilities, and infertility among them.[7] Amvac settled its part of the case for $500,000 in 1999.

MEVINPHOS

Mevinphos is an insecticide first developed by Shell in 1954.[8] It protects fruit and vegetable crops against aphids, leaf miners, mites, grasshoppers, cutworms, and caterpillars. It belongs to the organophosphate family of pesticides, which share a common ability to disrupt the transmission of nerve impulses by blocking the action of critical enzymes. Organophosphates are unstable and break down rapidly in the environment. So growers can use them to combat infestations that come just before harvest. Their drawback is an extreme and broad toxicity. They poison any living organism with a nervous system, including humans, fish, and animals. Consequently, large agrichemical companies are moving away from organophosphates to newer molecules that not only are less toxic, but that more narrowly target pests.

After their introduction in the 1950s, organophosphates such as mevinphos were second choice pesticides. Growers preferred to use organochlorines until concerns about the inability of nature to break them down turned the market toward the shorter-lived organophosphates. By the late 1970s mevinphos was being sold in large quantities. DuPont held the rights to it. Amvac manufactured some mevinphos at its Los Angeles factory under contract for DuPont.

As mevinphos was used more widely, concerns about its safety grew. Multiple reports of farm workers sickened by contact with it alarmed regulators. In 1978 the EPA restricted its use, so that only certified applicators could spray it on fields.

In 1988 the leader of the United Farm Workers, César Chávez, held a 36-day hunger strike to protest the use of organophosphate pesticides, including mevinphos, on grapes. He believed that their use recklessly endangered the health of field hands. In fact, subsequent research confirms multiple effects in exposed farm workers. For example, after prolonged exposure they show deficits in coordination, information processing, and other neurologic symptoms.[9] Children of Latina women in agricultural communities show impaired behavioral development.[10]

A few months after Chávez's hunger strike, DuPont ended mevinphos production. Amvac, however, was willing to embrace it. So DuPont sold its exclusive rights to Amvac. Amvac continued to sell mevinphos even as the EPA was gathering further evidence of its dangers. In early 1993 the agency called mevinphos one of the five most dangerous pesticides. It had reports of 600 poisonings and 5 deaths over the previous decade and calculated that the rate of poisonings was 5 to 10 times higher than

[4] U.S. Public Health Service, Agency for Toxic Substances and Disease Registry, *Toxicological Profile for 1,2-Dibromo-3-chloropropane* (Washington, DC: Public Health Service, September 1992); Environmental Protection Agency, *Integrated Risk Information System (IRIS), 1,2-Dibromo-3-chloropropane* (CASRN 96-12-8) at www.epa.gov/iris/subst/0414.htm, updated January 25, 2007.

[5] See, for example, *Delgado v. Shell Oil et al.* 890 F. Supp. 1324 (1995).

[6] T. Christian Miller, "Pesticide Company Settles Sterility Suit for $300,000," *Los Angeles Times,* April 16, 2007, p. 3.

[7] "Malia Zimmerman, "Water Quality Lawsuits Target Chemical and Agriculture Giants," *Pacific Business News,* October 8, 1999, p. 4.

[8] Mevinphos is technically an alpha or beta isomer of 2-carbomethoxy-1-methyl-vinyl dimethyl phosphate. It has been sold under the trade name Phosdrin in at least four formulations. See Department of Pesticide Regulation, *Mevinphos: Risk Characterization Document* (Sacramento: California Environmental Protection Agency, June 30, 1994), p. 5.

[9] Joan Rothlein et al., "Organophosphate Pesticide Exposure and Neurobehavioral Performance in Agricultural and Nonagricultural Hispanic Workers," *Environmental Health Perspectives,* May 2006.

[10] Brenda Eskenazi et al., "Organophosphate Pesticide Exposure and Neurodevelopment in Young Mexican-American Children," *Environmental Health Perspectives,* May 2007.

César Chávez, president of the United Farm Workers, receives a small piece of bread from Ethyl Kennedy, widow of former Attorney General Robert Kennedy. Her symbolic action ended a 36-day hunger strike in 1988 undertaken to protest the exposure of grape pickers to mevinphos and other pesticides.
Source: © Bettmann/CORBIS.

for any other product.[11] Before banning mevinphos, however, it allowed Amvac to suggest risk-reduction measures that might allay its concerns.[12]

Meanwhile, Amvac saw a new market opportunity. Large agrichemical companies had taken several other organophosphate insecticides off the market to placate the EPA. Apple growers in Washington were concerned that they would be unable to fight off ruinous late-season aphid infestations. Amvac believed that mevinphos could be safely used, even though regulators in Washington allowed pesticides to be mixed in open vats before spraying. Other states, for example California, required closed-vat mixing. Amvac negotiated with Washington's regulators, promising to train workers in the use of respirators and safe application.

That summer there were immediate reports of mevinphos poisonings in Washington orchards. In all, there were 26 documented cases. No one died, but seven workers were hospitalized. Martin Martinez, who later sued Amvac, was told to mix a concentrate of mevinphos with water, load a sprayer, and apply it. "My vision started to get blurry," he

said. "I started to get nauseous. I began to vomit."[13] These are classic symptoms of organophosphate poisoning. He was hospitalized for seven days.

Martinez and others had been trained. They were supposed to wear respirators, face shields, and chemical-resistant clothing. However, mevinphos is so toxic that even a slight mistake is very dangerous. Some poisonings took place in very hot weather, when applicators shed articles of clothing. Absorption through skin is rapid. Ten drops of concentrate spilled on flesh is a lethal exposure for a 150-pound person. Inhalation is also dangerous. A 150-pound person who failed to adjust a respirator properly would begin to show effects such as dilation of the pupils after breathing little more than one ten-thousandth of an ounce.[14]

Once inside the body, mevinphos interferes with the regulation of nerve impulses, disrupting the central nervous system and major organs. One of the earliest symptoms of exposure is compromised reasoning ability, which compounds the danger because a worker loses the ability to appreciate an urgent peril. High exposure eventually leads to irregular heart beat, convulsions, unconsciousness, and death. Breathing air with only 10 parts per million of mevinphos over one hour killed 50 percent of rats in one study.[15]

Three orchard workers, including Martinez, sued Amvac alleging that mevinphos was a defectively designed product. It was so unsafe, they argued, that it should never have been marketed for orchard use. At one point, the case went to the Supreme Court of Washington, which handed down a ruling on a point of product liability law. It noted that a pesticide, by its nature, was a dangerous product. Its costs to society could be eliminated only by sacrificing the lethal qualities that made it effective. The question was, when was a pesticide too dangerous, too lethal?

The court ruled that a pesticide could be sold as an unavoidably unsafe product if its advantages greatly outweighed the risks posed by its use.[16] It would be up to a lower court to decide if mevinphos

[11] David Holmstrom, "Control of Farm Chemicals Needs Overhaul," *Christian Science Monitor,* October 6, 1994, p. 7; and *Andrews Litigation Reporter,* "Settlement Reached between Farm Workers and Pesticide Maker," May 31, 2002, p. 1.

[12] Environmental Protection Agency, *R. E. D. Facts: Mevinphos,* EPA-738-F-94-020, September 1994, p. 2.

[13] Arthur C. Gorlick, "Orchard Workers File Lawsuit," *Seattle Post-Intelligencer,* September 13, 1995, p. B4.

[14] Based on a "no observable effect level" in humans of 0.025 mg/kg, see Department of Pesticide Regulation, *Mevinphos: Risk Characterization Document,* p. 1.

[15] Ibid., p. 1.

[16] *Guzman v. Amvac Chemical Corporation,* 141 Wn.2d 493, at 509-10.

passed this test. However, Amvac settled with the orchard workers rather than continue with the suit. It paid them approximately $750,000. According to one of their lawyers, Amvac "was willing to sacrifice farm worker's lives and safety for profits. It had to be held accountable."[17]

Meanwhile, Amvac tried to defend mevinphos before the EPA, but was unable to convince the regulators that it could be safely used. All pesticides must be registered with the EPA for legal use. When the EPA announced it was ready to cancel the registration of mevinphos Amvac voluntarily requested the withdrawal. Today the EPA classifies mevinphos as hazardous waste and bans any agricultural use in the United States. Nevertheless, Amvac sells it in other countries including Mexico, South Africa, and Australia. Once mevinphos was about 25 percent of Amvac's revenues. Now it is less than 1 percent.[18]

DICHLORVOS

Dichlorvos, or DDVP, is another aging member of the organophosphate family abandoned by the big agrichemical firms but still sold by Amvac.[19] It was synthesized in the late 1940s and marketed for the first time by Shell in 1961. It targets a broad range of insect pests, including flies, fleas, ticks, mites, cockroaches, chiggers, caterpillars, moths, and weevils. Like other members of the organophosphate family it disrupts transmission of nervous impulses.

At first DDVP had many agricultural applications. It was used in silos, hoppers, and tobacco warehouses to protect stored crops. In feedlots it was sprayed over animals to control fleas and ticks. Farmers mixed it in feed to deworm horses and pigs. Canning and packing facilities used it to control insects. It was sprayed over wide areas for mosquito control and used as the active ingredient in popular household insecticides. Resin strips impregnated with DDVP were placed in homes, public buildings, buses, aircraft, and ships to control pests such as cockroaches.

By the late 1970s many companies manufactured it, including Amvac. Total annual output in the U.S. rose

as high as 4.2 million pounds.[20] Then, scientific studies began to raise doubts about its safety and by the early 1980s annual use fell below 1 million pounds.

Like all organophosphate pesticides, dichlorvos poisons the nervous system. Acute exposure causes perspiration, nausea, vomiting, diarrhea, headache, and fatigue. Long-term, low exposures can also bring on these symptoms. Very high exposures cause convulsions and loss of consciousness. However, compared with similar pesticides, dichlorvos does not pose exceptional risks from contact during application. The main concern has been that it may cause cancer in humans.

Studies show it to be an animal carcinogen. Rats and mice that inhale or ingest high doses of dichlorvos produce thyroid, adrenal, pituitary, and stomach tumors. Epidemiological studies suggest that dichlorvos can also cause cancer in humans. One showed a significantly elevated risk of leukemia among farmers in Iowa and Minnesota who had used dichlorvos, even when they had used it as long as 20 years in the past. Another showed an elevated rate of non-Hodgkin's leukemia among Nebraska women who had used dichlorvos. Still a third found a "significantly increased risk" for brain cancer among children in homes using Amvac's No-Pest Strips.[21] The statistical power of these and similar studies is weak because they are based on small numbers of people with likely exposures to multiple pesticides. Nevertheless, they have ominous implications.

In 1980 the EPA initiated the first in a series of dichlorvos reviews. By law, the agency must regularly reassess whether a pesticide poses "unreasonable risk to man or the environment taking into account the economic, social, and environmental costs and benefits of [its] use."[22] With this criteria, even very dangerous pesticides can stay on the market if their risks are controlled and outweighed by their utility.

After the first review in 1980, the EPA classified dichlorvos as a "suspected" human carcinogen that acted by mutating genetic material in cells. A second review seven years later led to its classification as a

[17] Co-lead counsel Richard Eymann, quoted in "Precedent-Setting Farm Worker Pesticide Poisoning Suit Settles," *Public Justice,* Summer 2002, p. 11.

[18] T. Christian Miller, "Pesticide Maker Sees Profit When Others See Risk," *Los Angeles Times,* April 8, 2007, p. A1.

[19] Its full name is 2, 2-dichlorovinyl dimethylphosphate.

[20] Renu Gandhi and Suzanne M. Snedeker, "Critical Evaluation of Dichlorvos' Breast Cancer Risk," *Program on Breast Cancer and Environmental Risk Factors in New York State,* Critical Evaluation #7, March 1999, p. 1.

[21] Ibid., p. 3.

[22] Federal Insecticide, Fungicide, and Rodenticide Act of 1947 (as amended), 7 U.S.C §136(bb)(1).

"probable" human carcinogen. This bad news caused the market for it to shrink even more. One by one, agrichemical firms discontinued its sale until only Amvac was left. The company was determined to keep it on the market.

Amvac has a large budget for supporting the registration of its older pesticides in the face of doubts by increasingly skeptical regulators. It budgets around $3 million a year to conduct studies and tests. Its efforts have kept dichlorvos on the market. In the late 1980s, for example, it sponsored human testing in England. Paid volunteers were given capsules of dichlorvos and watched for changes in their brain chemistry. People in the test experienced symptoms of acute dichlorvos poisoning including nausea, nosebleeds, and headaches. Testing was done in England where regulations are more permissive than in the U.S. and the company was less likely to be sued. Although the test was reviewed by a medical ethics committee and complied with international protocols for human testing, environmentalists and some scientists raised an outcry.[23]

Despite Amvac's efforts the EPA in 1995 determined to cancel most uses of dichlorvos. Amvac disagreed and submitted more data, but regulators found it unpersuasive. So Amvac agreed to cancel almost two dozen applications, including aerial spraying and all uses in restaurants and food processing plants.[24]

Meanwhile, Congress in 1996 required the EPA to review all pesticides under a new, tougher standard that required a "reasonable certainty of no harm."[25] The agency finally finished its dichlorvos review in 2006. It allowed continued marketing, but further restricted its uses. Amvac agreed to cancel registration for more applications, including all home uses except for impregnated resin strips.

Dichlorvos can no longer be applied on lawns and turf, in cracks and crevices, and with handheld foggers. In addition, dichlorvos-impregnated pest strips in homes are limited in size. Larger strips containing more than 16 grams can be used only in garages, sheds, and crawl spaces occupied less than four hours a day. They can be used in vacation homes and cabins only if the

dwellings are vacated for four months after use. Smaller strips and flea and tick collars for cats and dogs that contain less than 16 grams of dichlorvos are still in use. According to the EPA, the air concentration of dichlorvos in a room where a dog or cat is wearing one of these collars averages less than one-fortieth of the exposure level at which poisoning symptoms are detectable.[26]

Exposure of the U.S. population to dichlorvos is estimated as slight, 0.0000007 milligrams per kilogram of body weight each day.[27] Even so, regulators believed that dichlorvos residues in food posed a cancer risk to the general population and that there were unacceptable risks to the nervous systems of those who mixed, handled, and applied it. The greatest danger is from skin contact. Based on animal studies, estimates are that short-term absorption of as little as 0.04 ounces of dichlorvos through the skin would cause death in 50 percent of applicators weighing 150 pounds.[28] This makes dichlorvos one of the most toxic pesticides in use. Inhalation toxicity is lower, but still greater than most other pesticides. Current EPA estimates are that inhaling 198 parts per million over an eight-hour period would be fatal to 50 percent of exposed adults. Overall, the EPA believed that these risks outweighed the benefits for all but a few remaining applications.

Meanwhile, other countries have banned DDVP. In 2002, the United Kingdom rejected evidence submitted by Amvac and suspended all uses. Angola, Fiji, Denmark, and Sweden have also banned it. Amvac continues exporting dichlorvos to Australia, Canada, and Mexico.

COSTS AND BENEFITS OF PESTICIDES

Poisonous agrochemicals have high social and environmental costs. Their use on crops and in homes causes tens of thousands of acute exposure injuries each year. Long-term exposure from residues in foods,

---

[23] See John H. Cushman, Jr., "Group Wants Pesticide Companies to End Testing on Humans," *The New York Times,* July 28, 1998, p. A9; and "Correspondence," *Environmental Health Perspectives,* March 2004, pp. A150–A155.

[24] See "Dichlorvos (DDV); Deletion of Certain Uses and Directions," 60 FR 19580-19581, April 19, 1995.

[25] Food Quality Protection Act of 1996.

[26] Ibid., p. 165. This figure is based on a margin of exposure of 39 for infants, who are presumed more sensitive to dichlorvos vapor than adults. Margin of exposure is the ratio of the dose at a "no observable adverse exposure level" to an observed or estimated dose.

[27] Environmental Protection Agency, *Interim Reregistration Eligibility Decision for Dichlorvos (DDVP),* EPA 738-R-06-013, June 2006, app. J, p. 151. There are 31,000 milligrams in one ounce.

[28] Ibid., p. 123.

drinking water, and soil causes an unknown number of chronic illnesses including cancer, birth defects, liver poisoning, and neurological deficits. Many pesticides, especially the older organochlorines and organophosphates, do not discriminate between pests and other forms of life. They kill wildlife and pets along with target insects. An accurate calculation of monetary losses from such problems is infeasible.

Accidents increase the cost burden. Years ago a Southern Pacific freight train derailed on a steep curve above the Sacramento River north of Mt. Shasta in California. One tank car carried 13,000 gallons of metam sodium, a herbicide manufactured by Amvac. The resulting spill virtually sterilized a long stretch of the river, annihilating life right down to the moss on the rocks. It killed 200,000 fish and wiped out a celebrated trout-fishing area.[29] Lawsuits claimed that Amvac failed to identify properly and label its shipment and it agreed to pay $2 million, although it bore no responsibility for the train's derailment.

A later mishap with metam sodium is more typical of accidental exposures. In Arvin, California, 72 workers processing carrots and 178 town residents were sickened when metam sodium manufactured by Amvac drifted from fields where it was being sprayed.[30] The applicator paid a $60,000 fine.

If the costs of pesticide use are great, so are the benefits. The major benefit is availability of a bountiful, affordable food supply. Pesticides control fungal infections, insects, and weeds that would otherwise decimate U.S. crop yields. Without control measures, 50 to 90 percent of fruit and vegetable crops would rot from fungal infections before harvest. To protect them, growers use about 108 million pounds of fungicides annually at a cost of $880 million. Doing so saves an estimated $13 billion in crop value.[31]

Pesticides kill mosquitos, ticks, rats, and other vectors that carry illnesses such as the plague, Lyme disease, and encephalitis. They make human habitations more comfortable by controlling cockroaches, mold, mildew, termites, ants, and spiders.

Herbicides reduce soil erosion, save water, and reduce fuel and labor costs for growers. Their use facilitates increasingly popular no-till agriculture in which farmers poison weeds rather than plowing them under. With less plowing there is less erosion, which means lower water treatment costs, less flood damage, and larger reservoir capacity. Herbicides also kill unwanted growth that competes with crops for water. Without them, crop protection would require as many as 1.1 million hours of hand weeding in peak growing season. The labor force to employ at this job does not exist. Organic farmers, who cannot use herbicides, spend $1,000 per acre weeding their crops compared with only $50 for growers using chemical weed controls. One study estimated the overall benefits of herbicides at $26 billion in 2005.[32]

Finally, pesticides preserve wildlife habitats and protect endangered species. Without their use vastly expanded acreage would be required to grow necessary food crops. More land would be converted from its native state to farms, ranches, plantations, and orchards.

So pesticides clearly have both great costs and great benefits. There are other methods for controlling agricultural pests, but they complement pesticides rather than replace them. Cultivation techniques such as tilling and crop rotation make environmental conditions less favorable for destructive organisms. Biological control methods include release of insect predators such as wasps, lacewings, or lady bugs and the spread of friendly bacteria that compete with damaging strains. In the 1990s, big companies launched bioengineered seeds and their use has soared. Some crops are bred to have insect-resistant traits. Others are genetically manipulated to survive specific herbicides, giving farmers more alternatives for fighting weeds that over time become resistant to popular chemicals.

The rise of biologically based alternatives ended overall growth in pesticide sales, but their use remains constant. Growers applied 495 million pounds of all types in 2004, almost exactly the same amount as in 1990.[33] For the time being, pesticides are still

---

[29] Scott Thurm, "Record Damages for 1991 Rail Spill Settlement," *San Jose Mercury News,* March 15, 1994, p. A1.

[30] Robert Rodriguez, "California Investigates Rise in Pesticide-Caused Illnesses in 2002," *Fresno Bee,* February 27, 2004, p. 1; T. Christian Miller, "Pesticide Maker Sees Profit When Others See Risk," p. A25.

[31] Statement of Jay Vroom, in *Review of the EPA Pesticide Program,* Hearings before the Subcommittee on Conservation, Credit, Rural Development, and Research of the Committee on Agriculture, U.S. House of Representatives, 109th Congress, 2nd Session, September 28, 2006, p. 50.

[32] Ibid., p. 50.

[33] Bureau of the Census, *Statistical Abstract of the United States: 2007,* 126th ed., table 830.

needed to protect the food supply and quality of life to which Americans are accustomed. In the words of an agricultural researcher:

> [S]ome people want a total ban on pesticides, but they must be ready to accept termites in their houses, fleas in their carpets, moldy vegetables, food-borne toxins, food shortages with soaring prices, and outbreaks of long-forgotten diseases.[34]

AMVAC MOVES AHEAD

Amvac now has more than 40 pesticide brands, including five organophosphates. It has grown to 285 employees. It does most of its manufacturing at a Los Angeles plant, but recently purchased a second plant in Alabama from DuPont. The new plant produces organophosphates and also newer classes of pesticides.

Amvac emphasizes profitability. Three directors—its two founding entrepreneurs and the son of one founder, now president and CEO—own 26 percent of its stock.[35] Compensation of its president and CEO is based on four factors: "achieving financial results that equal or exceed" targets, "attracting . . . desirable investors," achieving strategic goals, and creating a strong management team. Revenues nearly doubled during a recent four-year period and export sales have grown to 9 percent of total sales.[36] The company now has foreign sales offices in England, Switzerland, and Mexico. Its strategy is sustained by the ongoing shift to biological pest controls. As long as industry giants continue to discard older pesticides, they create opportunities for Amvac.

Amvac adopted a seven-page Code of Conduct and Ethics in 2006. It states: "[O]ur efforts are focused on achieving the business and personal ethical standards as well as compliance with the laws and regulations that are applicable to our business." It intends its code to "ensure decisions that reflect care for all of our stakeholders."[37] The only specific mention of the environment is this brief section.

> The Company is committed to doing all that it can to assist in minimizing the degradation of our natural environment. Accordingly, employees should always take care in disposing of any waste materials or releasing any discharges into the air or water and comply with all applicable regulations and procedures required by law and by Company Code. If an employee is unclear about what is required, he/she must not dispose of any material or release any discharges until he/she has determined what procedures apply.[38]

Amvac's presence is a lesson in capitalism. Legal opportunities for profit elicit the requisite effort. Actions are justified by their overall utility. Doubtless Amvac's strategic thinkers would be inspired by the words of a Robert Frost poem.

> But a crop is a crop,
> And who's to say where
> The harvest shall stop?[39]

Questions

1. Does Amvac have an ethical strategy? Does it pursue its strategy in an ethical manner?

2. Do you believe that Amvac is faithful to its ethics code? Does the code adequately address the consequences of its operations? What might be added or changed to improve it?

3. Should the law prohibit Amvac and others from exporting pesticides barred from use in the United States?

4. Is the value to society of pesticides such as dibromochloropropane, mevinphos, and dichlorvos great enough to warrant the risks they pose?

5. If economic and market conditions remain favorable for Amvac's strategy, would you buy its stock?

---

[34] Keith S. Delaplane, "Pesticide Usage in the United States: History, Benefits, Risks, and Trends," Cooperative Extension Service, University of Georgia College of Agricultural and Environmental Sciences, *Bulletin 1121*, November 2000, p. 1.

[35] American Vanguard Corporation, Schedule 14-A, Proxy Statement, 2007, pp. 5–13.

[36] Revenues rose from $101 million in 2002 to $194 million in 2006.

[37] American Vanguard Corporation, *Code of Conduct and Ethics*, adopted March 8, 2006, at www.amvac-chemical. com, p. i.

[38] Ibid., p. v.

[39] "Gathering Leaves," in Edward Connery Lathem, ed., *The Poetry of Robert Frost* (New York: Holt, Rinehart and Winston, 1969), p. 235.

Chapter **Fifteen**

Consumerism

Harvey W. Wiley

On a spring day in 1863 a tall, thin boy of 18 left the farm where he had grown up, walking five miles over dirt roads to a nearby town. There he would be the first in his family to attend college. Like the restless America of his era, he was leaving rural roots behind in a journey of hope and ambition. His name was Harvey Washington Wiley. He would become the first modern consumer crusader.

The example of his parents molded Young Harvey's character. His father was a farmer who through self-learning became an evangelical minister and part-time school teacher. A man of Christian virtue, principle, and independent mind, he stood against slavery despite the open anger of neighbors. His mother taught herself to read. Knowledge was so important in the Wiley home that the latest works of science, literature, and commentary were mail-ordered and read aloud to little Harvey.

Harvey got a bachelor's degree from Hanover College, then attended Indiana Medical College, graduating as a physician in 1871. Still hungry for formal education, he enrolled at Harvard and graduated in less than two years with a chemistry degree. He became a professor at the new Purdue University where he was soon absorbed in food chemistry and began working with Indiana state officials to detect adulteration in food products.

With industrialization the nation's food supply was changing. As people moved from farms to cities they depended on businesses to prepare, can, bottle, package, and distribute edibles. It was a time of major advances in science, and the Victorian era had a childlike faith in the powers of modern chemistry. A large, highly competitive food industry applied new food chemistries using preservatives, colorings, flavorings, texturizers, and other additives. With few laws to police dishonorable operators, dangerous, fraudulent, and cheapened products made their way to market. Canned beef was preserved with formaldehyde. Strawberry jam was made from pulped apple skins, hayseeds, and glucose. Ground pepper was sometimes mostly nutshells.[1]

---

[1] W. E. Mason, "Food Adulteration," *North American Review*, April 1900, pp. 548–53.

Working in his campus lab, Wiley pioneered the study of food adulteration. Using new techniques, he detected widespread fraud. His reputation grew and when he was offered the position of Chief Chemist at the Department of Agriculture in 1883, he accepted.

Arriving in Washington, D.C., Wiley, now 39, took charge of the Bureau of Chemistry. This small entity had been set up in 1862 to hunt for contaminated agricultural commodities. He worked tirelessly, uncovering danger, dilution, mislabeling, and cheating in the nation's groceries. Yet he lacked the means to protect public health. Fewer than half the states had pure food laws and those were often contradictory—what was banned in one state was legal in another. Worse, no federal law existed to regulate foodstuffs in interstate commerce.

Wiley agitated for a national pure food law. For more than two decades he worked tirelessly, giving speeches, writing reports, convening meetings of scientists and food producers, and lobbying legislators.

Strong support came from civic groups, physicians, state officials, and food companies that saw a competitive advantage in legislating standards. Devious rivals who mixed cheap ingredients into cans and jars would have to meet the standards or leave the market.[2] The Heinz Company, for example, adopted food purity as an advertising theme. To reassure the public it introduced glass jars and factory tours. Founder H. J. Heinz was intensely religious and often framed business decisions in moral terms. He created a production technique to eliminate preservatives. It required quality ingredients, sterilization, and vacuum seal technology. Although his avowed motive was to safeguard public health, he knew that unscrupulous competitors could not afford his manufacturing method.

Principled opposition to food regulation came from states' rights advocates opposed to any expansion of federal power, no matter how benign of intent. Less honorable opposition came from companies that profited by adulteration. They worked in the shadows of Capitol Hill, buying influence to obstruct passage.

As Wiley labored, 190 protective measures were introduced in Congress. None passed, but support was growing. Wiley himself drafted a bill introduced in 1902. Then he departed from scientific routine, staging a melodramatic experiment that captured the country's imagination. He believed that chemical preservatives harmed consumers, but lacked scientific proof, so he designed a series of "hygienic table trials" in which young men would be fed suspect preservatives and monitored for signs of distress.

Wiley set up a kitchen, dining room, and laboratory in the basement of the Bureau of Chemistry building and advertised for volunteers. A dozen young men, all civil service employees from the Department of Agriculture, signed up. They pledged "on their honor" to take every meal in the basement dining room, to eat or drink nothing (except water) that was not given as part of the trial, to carry around jars for collection of urine and feces to be submitted for lab analysis, to pursue their regular work and sleep schedules, and to submit to weekly doctors' exams.

Wiley first fed the men borax, a then-common preservative. He began by adding half a gram a day to their food. Over two years, he gradually added more. The routine

[2] See Donna J. Wood, *Strategic Uses of Public Policy: Business and Government in the Progressive Era* (Marshfield, MA: Pittman, 1986), chap. 5.

Members of the "poison squad" dining in the basement of the old Bureau of Chemistry building. The Civil Service chef hired to cook their meals had once been chef to the Queen of Bavaria. Source: Courtesy of the Food and Drug Administration History Office.

was 10 days of healthy food followed by 20 days of food dosed with borax. At two grams appetites dropped off and some subjects had bowel problems. At four grams more serious problems emerged. The men had headaches and abdominal pain. Three took to their beds. Wiley stopped the test, believing he had evidence that borax was a human poison.[3]

A *Washington Post* reporter discovered Wiley's experiment, nicknamed the men the "poison squad," and wrote regularly about them. Whether or not Wiley intended the trials as partly grandstanding, the public was captivated. They inspired considerable levity, becoming the grist for comedians and minstrel shows. Yet they also put growing pressure on Congress to pass Wiley's pure food bill.

For five years Wiley tested other preservatives on new ranks of volunteers. He found signs of ill health caused by salicylic acid, formaldehyde, and copper sulfate, none of which are used as preservatives today. Years later, Wiley believed that the experiments had permanently damaged the health of several poison squad members.

In 1906, even as the poison squad continued its work, Congress finally passed the Pure Food and Drug Act "preventing the manufacture, sale, or transportation of adulterated or misbranded or poisonous or deleterious foods, drugs, medicines, and liquors."[4] The dam of obstruction had finally broken under pressure of the acute public indignation about meat packing plants described in Upton Sinclair's novel *The Jungle*. Wiley's years of hard work and the theater of his poison squad, however, had prepared

[3] Harvey W. Wiley, *The History of a Crime Against the Food Law* (Milwaukee: Lee Foundation for Nutritional Research, 1955), chap. II. Originally published in 1929.

[4] Pure Food and Drug Act of 1906, Sec. 1.

Harvey W. Wiley (1845–1930).
Source: Redpath Chautauqua Collection, Special Collections Department, University of Iowa Libraries (Iowa City).

the ground. Recognizing this, Congress gave Wiley's Bureau of Chemistry the power to examine foods for adulteration or misbranding.

The press called the new law the Wiley Act. Its passage seemed to be the final victory in his crusade for public health. Yet appearance deceived. Wiley attempted vigorous enforcement, but his perfectionist standards often dictated overly strict rules. He was uneasy with compromise. Food makers resisted his authority and outflanked him by appealing to his boss, Secretary of Agriculture James Wilson, and to President Theodore Roosevelt. Both grew exasperated with him. Roosevelt thought him a vexing nag. At one White House meeting with Wiley and food manufacturers on the use of saccharine the president became furious with the stubborn chemist. Only an idiot, he told Wiley, would be against all use of saccharine in food.

With time, Wiley's enforcement ability eroded. Secretary Wilson, with Roosevelt's approval, undermined Wiley's independence. Wilson appointed an assistant to Wiley who reported directly to him, not to Wiley. Then he set up a panel of scientists to look over Wiley's shoulder and review his decisions. Defeated and bitter, the aging warrior resigned his post in 1912. Yet he could not leave the field. He continued lecturing and writing about consumer causes. His new bride, a suffragette whom he had married in 1911 at age 66, was active in women's groups such as the Housekeepers' Alliance that fought for consumer causes. He wrote about food for *Good Housekeeping* magazine and set up the Good Housekeeping Seal of Approval standard. He died in 1930.[5]

Harvey Wiley's campaign for pure food came at the time when small, local markets for goods and services were expanding to national size. It was in this era that the idea of a class of people with a well-defined interest in safe, pure, and honest commodities emerged. This class came to be called consumers. Wiley's distinction is to have been its first national champion. Unlike Ralph Nader, he had no basic distrust of big companies and the capitalist system. He believed in fighting for honest firms by driving out shady competition. But he shared with later consumer advocates the goal of using government power to protect consumers from predatory corporations.

America's memory of Dr. Wiley has dimmed, but his work still touches our lives. The law he fought for is the foundation of modern food and drug regulation. The Bureau of Chemistry, by enforcing its provisions, evolved into the current Food and Drug Administration, a powerful agency that protects public health.

[5] "Dr. H. W. Wiley Dies; Pure-Food Expert," *The New York Times,* July 1, 1930, p. 24.

In this chapter we begin by defining and discussing the idea of consumerism. Then we describe the protective shield of statutes, regulations, and consumer law that has risen to protect consumers since Harvey Wiley's era.

CONSUMERISM

consumer
A person who uses products and services in a commercial economy.

A *consumer* is a person who uses products and services in a commercial economy. *Consumerism* is a word with two meanings. In common usage it refers to a movement to promote the rights and powers of consumers in relation to sellers of products and services. It also denotes an exceptionally powerful ideology of pursuit of material goods that shapes social conduct. We will discuss both these themes beginning with the second.

consumerism
A term denoting (1) a movement to promote the rights and powers of consumers in relation to sellers and (2) a powerful ideology in which the pursuit of material goods beyond subsistence shapes social conduct.

Consumerism as an Ideology

In this meaning, consumerism describes a society in which people define their identities by acquiring and displaying material goods beyond what they need for subsistence. Although small pockets of consumerism existed in the distant past, its spread through large populations is relatively recent, happening for the first time in western Europe only about 300 years ago, then advancing from there.[6] Its success is explained by the rise of certain conditions.

Economic progress set the stage. By the 1700s, commercial economies based on currency exchange had replaced subsistence and bartering in western Europe. As economies grew, modest affluence spread in classes below the aristocracy. Expanding overseas trade in colonial empires brought new products, including sugar from the West Indies, porcelain from China, and cotton fabrics from India. Slowly, average people began to spend more for goods and services beyond their basic needs.

As they did, the institutions necessary to support consumerism quickly appeared. Small shops selling goods sprang up in cities. Shopkeepers discovered that their customers' needs were not limited to necessities, but were infinitely expandable. Innovations such as window displays, sale pricing, loss leaders, and print advertising burst forth. Merchants encouraged producers to create a flow of new products, including toys, furniture, books, watches, perfumes, and household decorations.

Enlightenment
A wave of new, challenging ideas based on human reason and scientific inquiry. It swept over western Europe in the eighteenth century.

However, the full bloom of consumerism came only when these economic developments interacted with cultural and social changes. One important change was the declining influence of religion. From the time of its rise in ancient Rome, Christianity sanctified the dignity of the poor and encouraged followers to forsake the life of this world for the goal of otherworldly salvation. This doctrine made no room for any soul living for material pleasure. It would have suffocated rising consumerism. But now this stricture was loosened by the great philosophical current of the *Enlightenment*, a wave of new, challenging ideas that arose early in the 1700s and ran through the century.

[6] Peter N. Stearns, *Consumerism in World History: The Global Transformation of Desire* (London: Routledge, 2001), pp. ix–x.

A key premise of Enlightenment thinking was that the use of human reason and scientific inquiry should supplant passive acceptance of religious dogma as the basis for understanding the world. This view elevated the importance of human ability, separated humanity from deity in a new way, and led to the rise of *individualism*, or the idea that human beings are ends in themselves. In the social realm it paved the way for consumerism as individual choice gained priority over duty to God and individuals could focus on material pleasures with less guilt.

individualism
The idea, arising in the Enlightenment, that human beings are ends in themselves.

Then, the industrial revolution put societies in flux. This was the final element in the alchemy of consumerism. Populations grew. People left ancestral homes in the country to live beside strangers in cities. New occupations emerged. Some merchants and traders became wealthy. Everywhere centuries-old class and status boundaries wore away. As they faded, people replaced them with displays of material goods intended to establish identity and standing in the social hierarchy. If a man no longer wore the insignia of a trade or guild, he could adorn himself with expensive, brilliantly dyed cotton garments to show that his current occupation made him affluent. A newly rich merchant could emulate the aristocracy by building a manor house of his own. People spent more time "shopping." The acquisition of material objects had a new centrality in their lives.

Consumerism Rises in America

Consumerism dawned in America when social and economic forces akin to those in Europe came into play. It took a century for the process to work. Beginning in the early 1800s, a commercial economy arose. The ascetic Puritan theology that oppressed individualism in the northern colonies was fading. The lure of business success in the new land leapt over the boundaries of the tight, authoritarian towns in New England where it could not flourish. Wealth accumulated from foreign trade and in the last half of the century industrial development spread growing affluence.

The full emergence of consumerism in America came with changes around the turn of the twentieth century. The railroads had knitted territory together, forming national markets. The great merger wave of 1896–1904 created businesses with the reach to serve them. Machines and assembly lines made possible mass production of consumer goods. Electricity and other new technologies led to a stream of new products, for example, autos, watches, refrigerators, vacuum cleaners, toasters, and radios. Simultaneously, in large numbers, people left cramped small-town societies and moved to cities with more fluid social currents. Waves of immigrants, people newly adrift from their cultural moorings, arrived.

In this open society characterized by loose social ties, high mobility, and cultural variation, people began to express role and status with the products they bought. Immigrants adopted American culture as they brewed Uncle Sam's Coffee, drank Coca-Cola, or ate a Baby Ruth candy bar, the latter named for the widely loved infant daughter of President Grover Cleveland.[7] Their children

---

[7] Ruth Cleveland was born in 1891 when Grover Cleveland was out of office between his two nonconsecutive terms. A national mourning took place after her tragic death from diphtheria in 1904. The popular Democrat ran for the presidency three times and was elected in 1884, defeated in 1888, and elected again in 1892. The brand was created by the Curtiss Candy Company to honor the deceased "baby Ruth."

FIGURE 15.1
Immigrants and others could display and feel a connection with American culture by using consumer products. This collage of tobacco packaging and advertising images from the late 1800s and early 1900s illustrates powerful symbolism for ideals of liberty and freedom in American culture. Liberty Tobacco was an American Tobacco Company brand, George Washington Greatest American Cut Plug was made by R. J. Reynolds Tobacco Co., and Golden Eagle was made by T. C. Williams Co.

Source: Courtesy Emergence of Advertising in America: Tobacco Advertisements, Special Collections Library, Duke University.

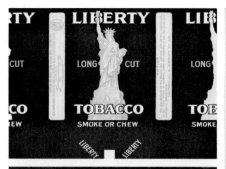

renounced old-country ways by wearing New World clothing styles. Advertising facilitated this social communication through products. It created new national brands and endowed them with social significance, allowing people to declare their membership in groups, their status, and their values by the goods they displayed (see Figure 15.1). The ads conferred on products meanings that were widely shared and understood, even by strangers, in a large and mobile population.

Consumerism in Perspective

Gary Cross, a historian of American commercial culture, defines consumerism as "the belief that goods give meaning to individuals and their roles in society."[8] According to Cross, consumerism, which has never been a formal philosophy, is now the dominant ideology in America. "Americans," says Cross, "define themselves and their relationships with others through the exchange and use of goods."[9] He believes that consumerism expresses a more powerful worldview than political ideologies, religions, or class and ethnic distinctions. If we are unable to appreciate this fully, it is because of its pervasiveness and the lack of a visible alternative.

Acquisitive desire is natural and inevitable in modern society. Purchased objects can fulfill needs beyond subsistence and beyond their practical function. One illustration comes in the story of a home interview conducted by marketers to learn how customers used household insecticides. At one woman's house a roach ran out during the visit. She cursed, sprayed until a puddle formed, then crushed it with the edge of the can, telling her wide-eyed visitors that roaches reminded

[8] Gary Cross, *An All Consuming Society: Why Commercialism Won in Modern America* (New York: Columbia University Press, 2000), p. 1.

[9] Ibid., p. 4.

her of her first husband. It was then, wrote one of the interviewers, we learned that "even a utilitarian product like bug spray can have deeply emotional, even primal meaning."[10]

Marketing research reveals a widespread, profound effort to find love, status, and individuality in products. One researcher's studies for large corporations, for example, show evidence for the following conclusions.[11] The basic purpose of shopping is "reconnecting with life"; it is a social experience, not a hunt for necessities. People buy products to fulfill emotional needs rather than practical ones. For Americans, luxury products are like military stripes, a proof of success that confirms the "goodness" of a person. And, not surprisingly, cars are purchased to express identity, distinctiveness, and personality, not as practical conveyances.

materialism
An emphasis on material objects or money that displaces spiritual, aesthetic, or philosophical values.

These and similar insights invite condemnation by those who reject material possessions as the source of human happiness. *Materialism* is an emphasis on material objects or money that displaces spiritual, aesthetic, or philosophical values. The idea suggests that pursuit of pleasure in external possessions is less worthy than concern for interior virtues, that buying a product creates only false satisfaction. True satisfaction comes only from worship of the divine and character development. Real wisdom is in the cathedral, museum, or library, not the car lot. Despite lack of objective evidence as to their inferiority, material values are subject to perennial ridicule and criticism.

An early signal that the values underlying consumerism would attract critics was the caricature of material society in the work of a maverick economist, Thorstein Veblen. In his 1899 book *The Theory of the Leisure Class,* Veblen challenged conventional economic wisdom that consumers bought goods for their functional utility, seeking the best value for their money. He argued that in the new industrial society people no longer earned their status by conquest in warfare or prowess in hunting. Instead, they acquired property to create what he called "invidious comparison" between themselves and their less successful neighbors.[12] They displayed their status through "conspicuous consumption," or the "unremitting demonstration of the ability to pay."[13]

In one illustration of his thesis, Veblen pointed out that a hand-crafted sterling silver spoon does its job no better than a mass-produced base metal spoon with an identical design. In fact, since silver requires frequent polishing it is inconvenient and costly to own, making it less utilitarian. The most desirable quality of the silver spoon is its greater cost, which confers status on a display-conscious consumer. When the book appeared, it was received as only a satire, which disappointed Veblen. Now, a century later, this and other core insights are widely accepted.

[10] Michael J. Silverstein, *Treasure Hunt: Inside the Mind of the New Consumer* (New York: Portfolio, 2006), p. xiv.

[11] Clotaire Rapaille, *The Culture Code: An Ingenious Way to Understand Why People around the World Buy and Live as They Do* (New York: Broadway Books, 2006).

[12] Thorstein Veblen, *The Theory of the Leisure Class* (New York: Penguin Books, 1979), p. 27. Originally published in 1899.

[13] Ibid., p. 87.

Thorstein Veblen (1857–1929). wrote a satirical but penetrating account of modern consumer society. He outraged economists of his day with the insight that people bought products not for their utility, but to show off.
Source: © Bettmann/ CORBIS.

Since Veblen, consumerism has been a punching bag for social critics. Here are some general complaints. All are based on the belief that material values undermine other, "higher" values.

- Consumerism leads to commodification of all parts of life. Things are judged for their value on the market rather than by some intrinsic value. People are judged for their external possessions rather than their interior qualities.

- Consumption beyond practical needs for emotional reasons encourages unwise, irrational, and unproductive uses of money. In the 1920s a National Thrift Movement emerged to teach children the thrift ethic. It was inspired by the aphorisms of Benjamin Franklin, who cast industriousness and frugality as central character virtues. The movement had Congress declare that Franklin's birthday in January begin a National Thrift Week and its thrift classes were adopted by thousands of schools. Although its organized influence had withered by 1930, its notion of prudent buying lives on as a second-tier cultural value.

- Heavy consumption is profligate with natural resources. It burdens the environment, leading to serious, long-term problems such as global warming.

- Consuming beyond necessity, especially by purchasing luxury items, violates "the idea that God's world is already full and complete."[14] Those who consume

---

[14] James B. Twitchell, *Living It Up: America's Love Affair with Luxury* (New York: Simon & Schuster, 2002), p. 56.

beyond basic needs are guilty of the sins of gluttony and greed. Heavy consumption of frivolous and luxury goods diverts resources from more noble uses, such as ending world poverty.

- Consumerism distorts our values. It "favors laxity and leisure over discipline and denial," it replaces the work ethic with easy credit and compulsive buying.[15] It converts profligacy into social status. It encourages conspicuous, competitive, and imitative consumption in which people buy material goods to show off, outdo others, or try to fit in with peers. These are inferior motives.

- Consumerism is a pathology of corporate capitalism. Beginning with Lenin, socialists have argued that capitalist economies concentrate production in large firms that seek to expand and control their markets.[16] The continually rising returns necessary to satisfy investors require companies to create powerful marketing methods for manipulating consumers.[17] It is this corporate selling that creates the false needs, thoughts, and values underlying consumerism.

Criticism of the values in modern consumerism is persistent.[18] Ralph Nader and other leaders of the consumer movement exhort Americans to be practical in their expenditures, to be vigilant against advertising that tempts them into extravagance, and to put function ahead of excitement in their purchases. A recent best-selling book, *Not Buying It: My Year without Shopping,* describes how the author and a companion elected to satisfy their needs without buying new products for a year.[19] A Yahoo group calling itself The Compact was formed to fight the "negative global environmental and socioeconomic impacts of disposable consumer culture" by not buying any new products for a year.[20] Such appeals come regularly, but they yield few converts. The alternative of simplified, utilitarian living in the mold of the Puritans, Benjamin Franklin, or Henry David Thoreau is now an impractical vision.

Attempts to create sanctuaries from consumerism in American society have also been losing efforts. Blue laws prohibiting stores from opening on Sundays, once pervasive, were an effort to rope off one day of the week and free it of commercialism. Such laws have little coverage now. When radio was new, pioneers of broadcasting such as David Sarnoff at RCA were afraid to air commercials. For the first time, sales pitches came right into the sheltered retreat of the family living room. Would commercials offend listeners? Quickly, the answer came. The vast majority felt no affront.

---

[15] Benjamin R. Barber, "Overselling Capitalism with Consumerism," *The Baltimore Sun*, April 15, 2007, p. A25.

[16] V. I. Lenin, *Imperialism: The Highest Stage of Capitalism* (New York: International Publishers, 1939), originally published in 1917, chap. 1. See also Harry Magdoff and Fred Magdoff, "Approaching Socialism," *Monthly Review,* July–August 2005, who write that consumerism, "the compulsion to purchase more and more, unrelated to basic human needs or happiness" is an "aspect of the culture of capitalism," p. 22.

[17] Michael Dawson, *The Consumer Trap: Big Business Marketing in American Life* (Champaign: University of Illinois Press, 2003).

[18] See, for example, David A. Crocker and Toby Linden, eds., *Ethics of Consumption: The Good Life, Justice, and Global Stewardship* (Lanham, MD: Rowman & Littlefield, 1998).

[19] Judith Levine, *Not Buying It: My Year without Shopping* (New York: Free Press, 2006).

[20] "Welcome to the Compact," at http://groups.yahoo.com/group/thecompact/, accessed June 8, 2007.

More recently, consumer advocates have tried to fence off childhood from the blandishments of materialism. Battles are fought over ads on children's television programs, ads in schools, and ads for tobacco and alcohol suspected of appealing to underage starters. Although there have been some victories with respect to specific products and policies, it is far too late to sequester children from advertising.

The Global Rise of Consumerism

Among young urban dwellers in Vietnam the "attitude of consumerism is now rampant."[21] In China, where "materialism is the new national ideology,"[22] prime minister Wen Jiabao warned that buyers of luxury goods could become "intoxicated with comfort" and sink "into depravity."[23] In Namibia rising debt, excessive spending at Christmas, and a "growing culture of measuring people's success by material possessions" have caused concern.[24] Traveling the globe, the formula for consumerism is activated by economic growth and social change in one nation after another. The ideology has risen in Russia, Asia, Latin America, the Middle East, and even Africa. One historian speculates that it is "the most successful Western influence in world history."[25]

It may, however, be less a Western than a universal phenomenon. Rising like primordial life, it comes when human nature, economic progress, and cultural change interact at a certain moment in a modernizing society. For example, a report by the South African government expressed concern over the growing extent to which consumer goods have become yardsticks for self-identity in that nation. Its explanation is that racial hierarchy determined social status under the old apartheid system. With its end in the early 1990s, people turned to displays of material goods to communicate their social rank.[26]

Once it takes hold, consumerism seems irrepressible, but resistence continues. Western colonialism in Africa left a persistent disdain for Western values and lifestyles, including consumerism. The spread of an Islamic fundamentalism that rejects Western materialism has divided populations in the Middle East. And Catholicism still resists a material focus. Pope John Paul II called the consumer life "improper" and "damaging" because it promotes "having rather than being" and subordinates "interior and spiritual" dimensions of human life to "material and instinctive dimensions."[27] His successor, Pope Benedict XVI now warns against the "commercial pollution" that flows in consumer society.[28]

---

[21] Roger Mitton, "Young Vietnamese Bitten Hard by Consumer Bug," *The Straits Times*, March 26, 2007.

[22] Noreen O'Leary, "The New Superpower: China's Emerging Middle Class, *Adweek,* January 1, 2007.

[23] Quoted in "If You've Got It, Don't Flaunt It," *The Economist*, June 2, 2007, p. 72.

[24] "Namibia: A Nation in Debt," *Africa News*, January 12, 2007.

[25] Stearns, *Consumerism in World History*, p. 73.

[26] David Bruce, "All That Glitters: In Search of Self-Respect," *Business Day*, September 1, 2006, p. 19.

[27] Ioannes Paulus PP.II, Encyclical Letter, *Centesimus annus* (May 1, 1991).

[28] Quoted in Peter Popham, "Brand-Name Products Queue Up for Papal Indulgence," *Sunday Tribune*, April 30, 2006, p. B4. For a discussion of consumerism in Catholic social teaching see Kenneth R. Himes, "Consumerism and Christian Ethics," *Theological Studies* 68 (2007).

Consumerism as a Protective Movement

The second basic meaning of consumerism is a movement to promote the rights and interests of consumers in relation to sellers. It arises because fraud, deception, and greed are universal in markets. In the United States, three national movements have sprung up to protect consumers. The first began in the 1870s when Populist farmers attacked railroads for unfair rates and bad service. The second was the Progressive movement. After 1900 both political parties capitalized on the political power of consumers as a class of citizens with similar interests and grievances. This led to passage of early consumer protection laws such as the Food and Drug Act of 1906. Then consumer issues receded until a new era of progressive activism in the 1960s and 1970s prompted a third wave of legislation to protect and expand consumer rights.[29]

There were several triggers for this modern movement. Popular critics accused business of manipulating consumers. In *The Waste Makers*, for example, Vance Packard attacked corporations for everything from using annual model changes to make automobiles obsolete to designing potato peelers that blended in with the peelings and got thrown away, thereby creating a need for another purchase.[30] Ralph Nader aroused the public about automobile safety in his book *Unsafe at Any Speed* and emerged as the leader of a national movement.[31] President John F. Kennedy responded to rising, widespread consumer discontent with a special message to Congress in 1962 in which he said that consumers had basic rights and these rights had been widely abridged.[32] He listed the rights to make intelligent choices among products and services, to have access to accurate information, to register complaints and be heard, to be offered fair prices and acceptable quality, to have safe and healthful products, and to receive adequate service.

Congress responded to President Kennedy's speech, over the next decade passing more than a dozen consumer protection statutes and setting up four new federal agencies—the Federal Highway Administration (1966) to set highway safety standards, the Federal Railroad Administration (1966) to regulate rail safety, the National Highway Traffic Safety Administration (1970) to protect the public from unsafe automobiles, and the Consumer Product Safety Commission (1972) to guard against unsafe products.

These legislative successes marked the peak of the modern consumer movement. By the mid-1970s the business community had mobilized to block the great dream of the movement's activists, which was to consolidate enforcement of consumer laws, then scattered among many agencies, into one superagency named the Consumer Protection Agency.

[29] According to Elizabeth Cohen in *A Consumer's Republic* (New York: Knopf, 2003), after the Great Depression, politicians elevated the importance of consumers by defining consumer demand as the key to American prosperity.

[30] Vance Packard, *The Waste Makers* (New York: David McKay, 1960), pp. 40–41.

[31] Ralph Nader, *Unsafe at Any Speed* (New York: Pocket Books, 1966).

[32] See "Text of Kennedy's Message to Congress on Protections for Consumers," *The New York Times*, March 16, 1962.

FIGURE 15.2
Spending on
Consumer
Health and
Safety by
Federal
Regulatory
Agencies:
1960–2007
Figures are in
constant (2000)
dollars and
include spend-
ing on a range
of consumer
protection pro-
grams by six
departments
and agencies.
Included are
regulation
of food and
drugs, product
safety, and
chemical
safety. Figures
do not include
environmental
regulation.

Source: Susan
Dudley and Melinda
Warren, *Moderating
Regulatory Growth:
An Analysis of the
U.S. Budget for Fiscal
Years 2006 and 2007*
(Arlington, VA and
St. Louis, MO:
Mercatus Center and
Weidenbaum Center,
May 2006), table A-2.

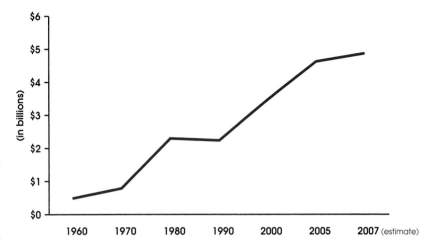

However, conservatives and business lobbies had won a battle for public opinion, convincing Americans that their government was growing too powerful. They claimed that the rising tide of regulatory red tape created costs out of all proportion to benefits and crippled corporations in international competition. In the changed political climate shaped by these views, the Consumer Protection Agency bill was decisively defeated in 1976 despite the support of President Jimmy Carter. Never again was it seriously advanced.

Since then, Congress has not been predisposed to enact many new laws and has not set up another new consumer agency. Nevertheless, there have been some new statutes, and federal agencies steadily mint rules pursuant to existing authority. The result is continuous growth in consumer regulation. Figure 15.2 shows the expansion of spending (in constant 2000 dollars) by agencies that protect consumer health and safety. In fiscal year 1960 existing agencies spent $85 million, but that rose over the years until by fiscal year 2007 it was estimated that the agencies would spend $4.9 billion over the same range of programs. State and local governments have also significantly expanded their regulatory activity. Consumer protection is today a major function of government.

THE CONSUMER'S PROTECTIVE SHIELD

We turn now to an examination of the massive statutory shield that protects consumers from abuses, real and imagined. Every state and local government has extensive consumer protection laws, ranging from requirements for uniform electrical connections to prohibitions against fraudulent billing. More than 50 federal agencies and bureaus also work to protect consumers. Our focus here is on three dominant consumer-protection agencies. A description of the duties of each of these agencies reveals the awesome responsibilities Congress has placed on them.

While each is in need of moderate reforms it is astonishing how effective they are despite changing ideologies in administrations, powerful critics, budget restraints, and too little staff to meet all their statutory mandates.

The Consumer Product Safety Commission (CPSC)

This agency, created by Congress in 1972, is directed by six major statutes that mandate these actions.

- Protect the public against unreasonable risks of injury and death associated with consumer products.
- Help consumers evaluate the safety of products.
- Develop uniform safety standards for products.
- Promote research and investigation into the causes and prevention of product-related deaths, illnesses, and injuries.

The CPSC calculates that in recent years there were an average of about 28,200 deaths and 33.6 million injuries caused by consumer products under its jurisdiction. In its efforts to save lives and make homes safer it often cooperates with business. This collaboration results in voluntary standards created by industries and the CPSC staff. From 1990 through 2007 there were 390 such arrangements. For example, safety standards were set for children's products, including playground equipment, baby walkers, toddler beds, infant carriers, and strollers. The agency also imposed 38 mandatory rules on recalcitrant manufacturers.[33]

The CPSC has also worked with industry to recall thousands of potentially hazardous products. In 2007 it prodded companies to carry out 472 recalls involving 100 million product units.[34] One example is the recall of toys with small magnets. After urging by the CPSC, Mattel recalled 7.3 million Polly Pocket doll play sets. Tiny magnets inside the toys could fall out and be swallowed by children. If more than one magnet was ingested, they could come together causing blocked, perforated, or infected intestines. By the time the recall was complete there were reports of three children with perforated intestines who required surgery.[35] The agency also prodded retailers and toy companies to recall millions of toys manufactured in China because they contained lead or were coated with paint containing excessive amounts of lead.[36]

The CPSC regulates every consumer product except guns, boats, planes, cars, trucks, foods, drugs, cosmetics, tobacco, and pesticides, which are in the province of other agencies. Even with these exclusions, its mandate is enormous since it must oversee 15,000 types of products, work with thousands of manufacturers, and address millions of consumer complaints.

[33] Consumer Product Safety Commission, *2007 Performance and Accountability Report.* (Washington, DC: CPSC, November 2007), p. 3.

[34] Ibid., p. 3.

[35] U. S. Consumer Product Safety Commission, "Additional Reports of Magnets Detaching from Polly Pocket Play Sets Prompts Expanded Recall by Mattell," *News from CPSC*, August 14, 2007.

[36] The CPSC prohibits paint on children's toys in which lead content exceeds 0.06 percent of the weight of the dried paint. See 16 CFR1500.17(6)(ii)(A), January 1, 2007.

From its creation in 1972 by the Nixon administration the agency has faced serious barriers to achieving its mandated goals. The political environment has been difficult. Even President Nixon, who established the agency, was unenthusiastic about it. President Reagan wanted to abolish it but could not. Instead he drastically cut its budget. Funding improved in two succeeding administrations but fell again in the George W. Bush administration. Today it operates with fewer than 450 employees, down from almost 1,000 in the 1980s.

The National Highway Traffic Safety Administration (NHTSA)

Congress created this agency in 1966, giving it authority to do the following.

- Mandate minimum safety standards for automobiles, trucks, and their accessories.
- Establish fuel economy standards.
- Administer grant programs that promote highway safety.
- Conduct research on and develop new vehicle safety technologies.

NHTSA regulations cover virtually every feature of the automobile. No other agency has such extensive controls over a single product. A short list of past rules just to protect occupants of an automobile includes rules on air bags, safety belts, energy-absorbing or collapsible steering columns, penetration-resistant windshields, recessed door handles, breakaway rearview mirrors, padded dashboards, collapsible front ends, crush-resistant passenger compartments, and tire standards.

Although it is a small agency with only about 675 workers, it has formidable powers. One powerful tool is the mandate. For example, the agency has mandated that by 2012 all new vehicles must come with an antirollover technology that senses when a driver has lost control of a vehicle, then brakes to stabilize it. NHTSA claims that its use will save 9,000 lives each year. Another significant power of the NHTSA is the recall. Since its inception "more than 390 million cars, trucks, buses, recreational vehicles, motorcycles, and mopeds, as well as 46 million tires, 66 million pieces of motor vehicle equipment and 42 million child safety seats have been recalled to correct safety defects."[37] Some of these recalls originate from consumer complaints. However, "[m]ost decisions to conduct a recall and remedy a safety defect are made voluntarily by manufacturers prior to any involvement by NHTSA."[38] Automobile companies complain about the costs of the agency's mandates, but there is no doubt that its actions have saved thousands of lives. Some critics believe that less costly alternatives exist to achieve the objectives of the mandates, for example, better lighting on highways, limiting highway speeds, installing breakaway traffic lights and signs, and padding abutments.

The Food and Drug Administration (FDA)

Congress created this agency in the Food and Drug Act of 1906. The original legislation gave it power to regulate in interstate commerce misbranded and adulterated

---

[37] NHTSA, "Motor Vehicle Defects and Recall Campaigns," April 15, 2007, at www.nhtsa.dot.gov.
[38] Ibid.

foods, drinks, and drugs. Since then, Congress has passed 43 more laws expanding its responsibilities. It is a very large agency, with more than 10,000 employees. Here is a sampling of what it is authorized to do.

- Regulate the composition, quality, safety, and labeling of food, food additives, and cosmetics. (This covers all foods in the United States except poultry and meat which the Department of Agriculture regulates.)
- Monitor and enforce regulations through the inspection of food and cosmetics producers' facilities.
- Regulate the composition, quality, safety, efficacy, and labeling of all drugs for human use and establish standards for this purpose.
- Require premarket testing of new drugs and evaluate new drug applications and requests to approve drugs for experimental use.
- Develop standards for the safety and effectiveness of over-the-counter drugs.
- Conduct recalls of products found to violate federal laws and pose hazards to human health.
- Inspect and license manufacturers of biological products.[39]

In discharging such responsibilities the FDA makes decisions that affect every American. Some are life and death decisions. In 1994 the agency ended a 10-year debate over genetically engineered drugs when it approved a bovine growth hormone that increases milk production in cows. It also approved genetically engineered Favr-Savr tomatoes and by that decision opened the door for other genetically modified produce. In 2006 it approved drugs to control blood sugar in patients with type 2 diabetes; new drugs for the treatment of leukemia; drugs to help treat macular degeneration; and new vaccines for cervical cancer, shingles, and influenza. Altogether in 2006 it approved more than 100 new drugs and approved or tentatively approved 525 new applications for generic versions of brand name medications.[40]

These statistical accomplishments contrast with another reality, that of an overwhelmed agency that often has to rely on self-policing by food companies. To illustrate, food import shipments have more than doubled since 2000. At the same time, food import inspections declined to the point where in 2006 samples amounted to slightly over 0.2 percent of total shipments.[41] Contaminated foods can elude this porous network. When discovered, a tainted additive forced a recall of over 100 brands of pet food in 2007, but thousands of cats and dogs still died.[42] David Kessler, former head of the FDA, when testifying before the Congress about this situation said, "Simply, put, our food safety system in

---

[39] Congressional Quarterly, *Federal Regulatory Directory,* 13th ed. (Washington, DC: CQ Press, 2006), passim, pp. 214–15.

[40] Food and Drug Administration, *2006 Accomplishments: Thousands of Safe and Effective Health Care Products Made Available for Patients* (Washington, DC: FDA, 2006), at http://www.fda.gov/oc/accomplishments/healthcare.html.

[41] Alexei Barrionuevo, "Food Imports Often Escape Scrutiny," *The New York Times,* May 1, 2007, p. C1.

[42] Elizabeth Williamson, "FDA Was Aware of Dangers to Food," Washington Post, April 23, 2007, p. A1.

FIGURE 15.3 Federal Agencies Responsible for Ensuring Safe Pizza

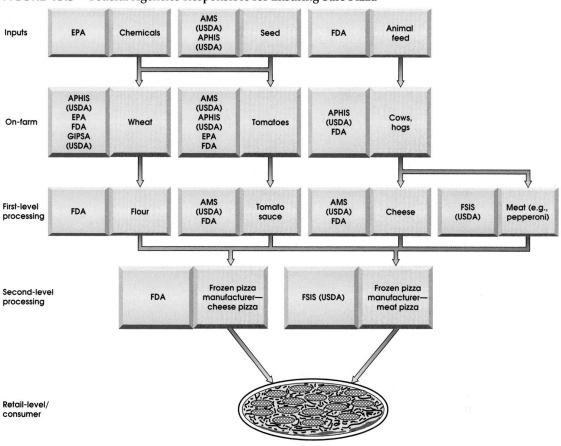

Source: Lawrence J. Dyckman, "Federal Food Safety and Security System," testimony before the Subcommittee on Civil Service and Agency Organization, Committee on Government Reform, House of Representatives, March 30, 2004, p. 5.

Note: AMS—Agriculture Marketing Service
     APHIS—Animal and Plant Health Inspection Service
     GIPSA—Grain Inspection, Packers and Stockyands Administration
     FSIS—Food Safety and Inspection Service

this country is broken,"[43] The FDA has appointed a "food czar" charged with producing a plan of defense against domestic and imported hazards to consumers.[44]

The FDA's jurisdiction is the result of piecemeal legislation enacted from time to time to meet specific challenges. As a consequence the laws often overlap and conflict. Figure 15.3 illustrates the jumble of authority over food safety for pizza. Repeatedly, proposals in Congress to consolidate and clarify FDA authority have failed to pass.

[43] Ricardo Alonso-Zaldivar and Abigail Goldman, "Food Safety Put on New Czar's Plate," *Los Angeles Times,* May 2, 2007, p. A17.
[44] Ibid.

A federal agency with such importance and scope of responsibility, especially with limited resources, is grist for critics. One constant pressure from both companies and individuals is to speed new drug approvals. The agency has responded and improved the time for approvals, but criticism persists. Former Commissioner David Kessler lamented that people want new drugs in a hurry, but if anything goes wrong, they blame the FDA for moving too fast.

Consumer Protection by Other Agencies

Many other agencies also contribute to the consumer's protective shield. The Federal Trade Commission maintains competition and curtails deceptive advertising. The Environmental Protection Agency protects consumers in many ways, for example, by setting drinking water standards. Another important agency that is sometimes classified as a consumer agency is the Occupational Safety and Health Administration. The Food Safety and Inspection Service in the Department of Agriculture has major responsibility over foods.

The Securities and Exchange Commission regulates financial products. The Department of Health and Human Services administers Medicare and other public health programs. The Equal Employment Opportunity Commission protects consumers from housing and loan discrimination. The Federal Deposit Insurance Administration insures funds in about 10,000 banks. The Pension Benefit Guaranty Corporation regulates pension plans and assumes pension liabilities in failing companies. Finally, we note a new agency, the Transportation Security Administration, which is responsible for traveler's safety. Its budget is larger than any other agency in the consumer's protective shield.

PRODUCT LIABILITY LAW

product liability
A doctrine in the law of torts that covers redress for injuries caused by defective products.

Beyond regulation, a major restraint on business is the ability of consumers to file product liability lawsuits when they are harmed. *Product liability* is a doctrine in the body of civil law known as the law of torts. A *tort* is a private wrong committed by one person against another person or her or his property. Under the law of torts injured persons seek compensation from parties they allege to have caused or contributed to their injury. The tort system is designed to provide compensation to victims and to deter future misconduct. Product liability is the branch of tort law that covers redress for injuries caused by defective products.

Product liability was an obscure backwater of the law until the 1960s, when progressive doctrines of consumer rights energized judges and legislatures to expand it. Earlier, consumers had little recourse when they were injured by defective products. Now product liability law is a powerful tool for gaining compensation. Today, manufacturers or other sellers of products can be held liable for defective products under three fundamental theories, namely, negligence, breach of warranty, and strict liability. In practice, product liability cases are often based on all three theories.[45] We will discuss each one.

tort
A private wrong committed by one person against another person or her or his property. An injury to a consumer caused by a manufacturer's defective product is one kind of tort.

negligence
An unintentional failure to act as a reasonable, prudent person exercising ordinary care.

privity
A relationship giving parties a common interest under the law, as in the relationship between parties to a contract.

Negligence

A *tort* involves either an intentional or a negligent action that causes injury. Intentional actions by manufacturers to harm consumers are rare. Ordinarily, the claim is that the manufacturer, component manufacturer, wholesaler, or seller of a product exhibited *negligence*. Under this theory, each of these parties has a duty to do what a reasonable, prudent person exercising ordinary care would do under the same circumstances. Thus, any of the parties in the stream of events leading to the final sale can be held liable and must pay damages if their breach of this duty of ordinary care contributed to an injury. The standard seems logical and fair, but early product liability law was not so generous to consumers.

As the United States turned into a consumer society in the late 1800s and early 1900s, manufacturers were well protected from liability suits brought by individuals who were injured by their products. An injured consumer trying to collect damages faced two formidable obstacles in the law.

One was the entrenched principle of *caveat emptor,* a Latin phrase meaning let the buyer beware. It imposed on buyers the responsibility to inspect carefully and skeptically items they purchased. If they failed to see dangerous defects, the legal presumption was that absent any specified remedy in a formal contract they were at fault, not the manufacturer or seller.

The other obstacle was a narrow interpretation of the doctrine of *privity,* which defined the legal relationship between a consumer and other parties to a sale. Courts held that consumers could sue only the party that sold them the product. This restriction was based on English common law and may have been appropriate in an agrarian America where sellers and product makers were in face-to-face contact.[46] As the distribution chain lengthened and grew impersonal in industrial society, that experience became rare. Yet, under the law, injured buyers had no case against a manufacturer. They had to sue the retailer, the party with whom they had a direct relationship. If retailers lost a suit, they could sue the wholesaler, and the wholesaler, in turn, the manufacturer.

This legal wall protecting manufacturers was broken down by the milestone case of *MacPherson v. Buick Motor Co.* in 1916.[47] Donald MacPherson bought a Buick from a Schenectady dealer. While driving it at 8 miles per hour, defective wood spokes on one wheel disintegrated, causing its collapse. MacPherson was thrown out and injured. He sued Buick for negligence because it had sold the automobile without inspecting the spokes. Buick had purchased the wheel from a company that supplied it with 80,000 wheels, none of which had been defective before. Nevertheless, a future U.S. Supreme Court justice, Benjamin Cardozo, then sitting

[45] See, for example, *Topliff v. Wal-Mart Stores East LP,* 6:04-CV-0297 (GHL), N.D.N.Y. (2007), in which parents unsuccessfully sued after their 5-year-old girl was burned and scarred in a Wal-Mart polyester jogging suit that caught fire and melted in the backdraft of a wood stove.

[46] See *Winterbottom v. Wright,* 15 Eng. Rep. 402 (Eng. 1842) 177.

[47] 217 N.Y. 382 (1916).

on the New York Supreme Court, affirmed a jury verdict for MacPherson, arguing that, as the manufacturer, Buick "was responsible for the finished product" and could reasonably have been expected to discover the defect by inspection. Furthermore, Buick "owed a duty of care and vigilance" that went beyond the immediate buyer, the dealer, to the driver. Because this extension of the negligence doctrine came in the large marketplace of New York, it spread to other states and became the foundation for a more consumer-friendly modern product liability law.

Over the years since *MacPherson* the negligence doctrine has been continuously stretched to favor consumers. For example, in a 1968 case General Motors made a car that was safe to operate, but was held negligent for not designing it to reduce injury in a collision. Erling Larsen had a head-on collision in a Corvair and suffered severe injuries when the steering wheel was pushed back into his head. He sued, arguing that the steering assembly was defective. Though it had not caused the crash, its design exposed him to greater harm than necessary. General Motors responded that its legal duty was to design a safe car, not a car that protected occupants during head-on collisions. In *Larsen v. General Motors* a federal court held that the design of the steering assembly was negligent because other practical designs could have stopped the wheel from moving back toward the driver after impact and it was foreseeable that there would be collisions.[48] Such expansions in the meaning of negligence have reversed the old *caveat emptor* doctrine. Now, let the manufacturer beware.

Warranty

A *warranty* is a contract in which the seller guarantees the nature of the product. If the product does not conform to the standards in the warranty, the buyer is entitled to compensation for any consequent loss or injury. A manufacturer or seller can be held liable for a breach of one or both of two kinds of warranties, express and implied.

An *express warranty* is an explicit claim made by the manufacturer to the buyer. It can be a statement that the product will perform in a specified way, a description of the product, or a picture that shows a model product. In the past, manufacturers often put statements in warranties to limit their liability, but the courts have protected consumers by enlarging the idea of an *implied warranty*, or an unwritten, commonsense warranty arising out of reasonable expectations that a product will both fulfill its ordinary purpose and fulfill the particular purpose of the buyer.

Again, the landmark case involves the automobile industry. Claus Henningsen bought his wife Helen a new 1955 Plymouth as a Mother's Day gift. On the back of the purchase order that he signed, buried in eight inches of fine print, was a statement that in case of a warranty claim for any defect the buyer must return the parts to Chrysler Corporation, postage paid, and that Chrysler would then decide "to its satisfaction" whether there was a defect. Ten days after getting the car, Mrs. Henningsen was driving about 20 miles per hour when a loud noise came from the front. The car veered at 90 degrees to the side, crashing into a brick wall. The steering mechanism in the front end was crushed, making evaluation of

warranty
A contract in which the seller guarantees the nature of the product. The seller must compensate the buyer if the warranty is not fulfilled.

express warranty
An explicit claim made by the manufacturer to the buyer.

implied warranty
An unwritten warranty that a product is adequate to meet a buyer's reasonable expectations that it will fulfill its ordinary purpose and the buyer's particular purpose.

[48] 391 F.2d 495 (8th Cir. 1968).

mechanical defects difficult. Both the dealer and Chrysler Corporation denied any obligation to pay for the damaged car and for medical expenses. In *Henningsen v. Bloomfield Motors* the court said that the limitation on the express warranty was a "sad commentary" on industry practice and could not override an implied warranty that the car was "reasonably suited for ordinary use" by the purchaser.[49] Chrysler had to pay.

Strict Liability

strict liability
The theory that liability exists, even in the absence of negligence, when an activity or product is inherently dangerous.

The doctrine of *strict liability*, or liability without fault, arose in tort law many years ago in England.[50] There it was established that anyone who engaged in a dangerous activity, such as using explosives or keeping ferocious animals, is liable for damages to others, even if the activity is conducted with utmost care. The key to strict liability is that the injured person need not prove negligence to prevail in court. It is presumed that any person engaged in ultrahazardous activities is automatically liable for adverse consequences to society.

The theory of strict liability was gradually extended to product liability and by the 1960s it was firmly entrenched.[51] This furthered the trend toward expansion of manufacturers' liability because injured consumers no longer had to prove negligence or breach of warranty to prevail in cases where there was some inherent danger in the use of a product. The law transferred much of the risk of using such products from consumers to manufacturers.

A landmark case involved William Greenman, who was turning a piece of wood when it flew off the machine, hitting him in the forehead, and causing serious injury. Greenman found evidence that the machine's design was defective and sued the manufacturer, Yuba Power Products, alleging negligence and breach of warranty. A lower court found no evidence of negligence or breach of express warranty, but a jury awarded Greenman $65,000 for breach of implied warranty. On appeal, the manufacturer raised serious issues that might have overturned the verdict, but the California Supreme Court imposed strict liability on the company, holding that all Greenman had to prove was that he was injured by the defective product while using it as it was intended to be used. Proving negligence or breach of warranty was not necessary.[52]

Under strict liability an injured plaintiff must prove only that the manufacturer made a product in a defective condition that made it unreasonably dangerous to the user, that the seller was in the business of selling such products, and that it was unchanged from its manufactured condition when purchased. The "defect" can exist because of poor design, insufficient warning, or even hazards unknown to the manufacturer. It is an inherent danger not anticipated by the buyer and can exist even though the product was carefully made.

This is the legal doctrine that dismantled the asbestos industry. When strict liability was accepted by the courts, sick asbestos workers no longer had to prove

[49] *Henningsen v. Bloomfield Motors, Inc.*, 32 N.J. 358 at 374 and 384.

[50] See *Rylands v. Fletcher,* L.R. 3 H.L. 330 (1868).

[51] See American Law Institute, *Restatement of the Law of Torts,* 2d, ed. vol. 2 (Washington, DC: American Law Institute Publishers, 1965), sec. 402A, pp. 347–48.

[52] *Greenman v. Yuba Power Products, Inc.,* 59 Cal. 2d 57 (1963).

that Johns Manville or other companies were negligent because they already knew about asbestos hazards. All they had to prove was that asbestos was "defective," that is, that it contained an inherently dangerous quality. The asbestos companies were then liable to compensate workers having asbestos disease. As the court stated in *Greenman v. Yuba Power Products*, "[t]he purpose of [strict] liability is to insure that the costs of injuries resulting from defective products are borne by the manufacturers that put such products on the market rather than by the injured persons who are powerless to protect themselves."[53] This idea, now embedded in the law, was another big step away from *caveat emptor*.

Perspectives on Product Liability

Product liability suits are filed in every state and in federal courts, and there is no central reporting of them. Comprehensive statistics about their number, disposition, and jury awards do not exist. However, they are a significant part of an overall tort system that imposes massive costs on business.

The U.S. legal system makes it easier for plaintiffs to win large damage awards from product makers than do the systems of other countries. In Europe, attorneys do not work on a contingency fee basis and most European countries require losers to pay court costs. This discourages low-merit cases. Except in the United Kingdom, lawyers are not permitted to advertise for clients as do American lawyers. And, in addition, awards tend to be much lower, particularly since punitive damages are usually not allowed. In Asia, product liability is a relatively new idea. Chinese product liability laws were introduced only in 1993. And in Japan, only since 1995 have consumers been allowed to sue manufacturers. In short, nowhere else in the world has the legal system created such a favorable environment for product lawsuits as in the United States.

Costs and Benefits of Lawsuits

The tort system is designed to compensate injured parties and deter future wrongdoing by imposing the cost of injuries on persons or corporations whose behavior caused harm. A recent estimate is that this system inflicts an annual economic cost of $865 billion on society, which is about 2.8 percent of GDP, and is the highest in the world and more than triple the 0.9 percent average of other industrial nations.[54]

About a third of this cost is from personal torts, most related to auto accidents; the rest is for commercial torts against businesses including product liability, medical malpractice, and workers compensation.[55]

Much of the cost may be worth it. Because of product liability suits dangerous products such as asbestos, cigarettes, flammable children's pajamas, and some birth control devices have been either taken off the market, had their sales restricted, or been redesigned. Those injured by them have been compensated. While

[53] Ibid., at 63.

[54] Michael Krauss, "Tort-Eating Contest," *The Wall Street Journal*, May 2, 2007, p. A20; Lawrence J. McQuillan, Hovannes Abramyan, and Anthony P. Archie, *Jackpot Justice: The True Cost of America's Tort System* (San Francisco: Pacific Research Institute, 2007), pp. xii–xiii.

[55] Tillingast–Towers Perrin, *U.S. Tort Costs and Cross-Border Perspectives: 2005 Update* (New York: Tillingast–Towers Perrin, 2006), p. 7.

the public may benefit from such lawsuits, others are more problematic. Lawsuit threats and high liability insurance costs regularly cause companies to drop high-risk products such as off-road vehicles, medical implants, football helmets, drugs, and vaccines, some of which are valuable to society. An unknown number of new products and innovations never come to market at all because their liability potential scares manufacturers. In the pharmaceutical industry, funds that might go into research and development of new drugs are regularly diverted to litigation expenses. In other cases, liability insurance and litigation costs are simply passed on to consumers—like an extra tax on the products they buy. Sometimes liability costs even have the perverse effect of reducing safety. Extension ladders for home use now carry such a high price premium for product liability costs that many people just go on using deteriorating older ladders.[56]

Business argues that product liability law has moved beyond equitable victim compensation to become a system that wastefully transfers wealth from corporations, workers, insurers, shareholders, and average consumers to plaintiffs and their attorneys. This is because the system sometimes allows awards to uninjured persons, imposes punitive damages in excess of real compensation, allows awards under strict liability when there has been no negligence, and imposes unnecessary costs as cases drag on for years without resolution. When liability costs higher than the true costs to injured parties are imposed on corporations workers lose jobs and pension benefits, share prices decline, resources are diverted from innovation, and sales of potential new products are foregone.

Occasionally entire industries have been crippled. The general aviation industry is an example. Accident rates for civil aircraft began a steady, uninterrupted decline in the 1940s that has now continued for almost 70 years. Manufacturers worked to design and build safer aircraft because of market forces. No company could survive if buyers thought its planes were more dangerous than those of its competitors. Then, in the 1960s, product liability law changed to permit strict liability and by the 1970s a striking rise in airplane crash lawsuits and liability awards had occurred. Sometimes, crash victims and their relatives prevailed even when accidents were caused by defects unknown or unknowable when the airplanes were made.

Damage to the industry was extensive. One company went bankrupt and others were in financial trouble. The introduction of newly designed planes that might have been safer was delayed. In 1994, Congress passed a law exempting civil aircraft more than 18 years old from product liability claims and this has led to some revival of the industry.[57] In the end, neither the spike in damage awards nor the legislation affected the number of fatal accidents. The rate of decline remained steady and constant. Strict liability rules served only to transfer money from aircraft makers to accident victims and their attorneys and to reduce industry productivity.[58]

---

[56] Michael Krauss, "Tort-Eating Contest," p. A20.

[57] The General Aviation Revitalization Act of 1994, P. L. 103-298, amending the Federal Aviation Act of 1958.

[58] *Economic Report of the President* and *The Annual Report of the Council of Economic Advisors*, 2004 (Washington, DC: U.S. Government Printing Office, 2004), pp. 212–14.

A Look at Two Lawsuits

Despite such examples, product liability law often seems to fulfill its compensation and deterrence functions fairly well. Two well-known cases against McDonald's permit critical analysis of the industry perspective that some product liability lawsuits are frivolous and that jury awards are often excessive.

In *Pelman v. McDonald's Corp.* the guardians of two obese children filed suit seeking to hold McDonald's responsible for the children's weight. They argued that McDonald's products were inherently dangerous because they contained high levels of sugar, salt, fat, and cholesterol. By selling them, McDonald's breached an implied warranty that its food was safe to eat. They claimed that McDonald's was negligent for failing to warn consumers about the dangers of its foods. The case was widely ridiculed as frivolous because it seemed to mock the idea of personal responsibility. But could its legal theories prevail in a court?

A federal district court dismissed the suit because no "reasonable consumer" would find the food dangerous based on its allegations and because there was no proof that the boy's health conditions were directly caused by the products.[59] An appeals court reinstated the case, but only for technical reasons.[60] Since then it has been ongoing. There have been four other decisions on procedural matters, but none allowing the case to go forward for trial on its merits.[61] In fact, courts most often reject meritless claims and this case seems to be an illustration.

In the second case, *Liebeck v. McDonald's Restaurants*, the company was sued by Stella Liebeck, a 79-year-old woman who bought a cup of coffee at a McDonald's in Albuquerque.[62] In the passenger seat of a car, she put the cup between her thighs and tried to pry off the lid. But the cup tipped and scalding coffee burned her. Liebeck sued, arguing that McDonald's had breached an implied warranty of fitness because its coffee, as sold, was simply too hot for consumption. A jury awarded her $160,000 in compensatory damages and hit McDonald's with $2.7 million in punitive damages. In the hands of journalists, disc jockeys, and comics *Liebeck* entered popular culture as an allegory of out-of-control jury awards. But was it?

Stella Liebeck had a major injury. She suffered third-degree burns over 6 percent of her body, spent eight days in the hospital, and had high medical costs. Testimony revealed that McDonald's sold its coffee at a temperature of 180°F, much higher than the 135° to 140° that consumers serve coffee in their homes. At temperatures that high, third-degree burns can occur in as little as 2 seconds, compared to more than 60 seconds at temperatures below about 160°. Moreover, McDonald's was forced to release documents showing more than 700 previous burn claims from customers.

In court, a company representative stated that the coffee tasted better when held at high temperature and that the number of customer burns was so small compared

[59] *Pelman v. McDonald's Corp.*, 237 F. Supp.2d 512 (2003), at 523, 524, and 541.

[60] *Pelman v. McDonald's Corp.*, 396 F. 3d 508 (2005).

[61] See most recently *Pelman v. McDonald's Corp.*, 425 F. Supp. 2d 439 (2006).

[62] No. D-202 CV 93-02419 (D. C. N. M., August 18, 1994). The jury held Liebeck 20 percent accountable for causing her injuries.

with the number of cups served it did not plan to lower the temperature. This may have angered jurors. The $2.7 million in punitive damages they awarded Stella Liebeck was intended to punish the company. However, it was mild punishment, approximating the revenue from two days' coffee sales.[63] Even so, the judge later reduced the award to $480,000, or three times the compensatory award. So, contrary to the popular theory of a runaway jury, the *Liebeck* case reveals a basis for judgment against the corporation and a reasonably limited award.

CONCLUDING OBSERVATIONS

Consumerism is a word with two meanings. It refers both to an ideology and to a protective movement. In this chapter we discuss trends related to both meanings. First, consumerism as a way of life is spreading around the world because the conditions that support it are becoming more common. Where it is already established, it is strengthening its grip. Second, consumers in the United States are now more protected from injury, fraud, and other abuses than in the past because of stronger government regulation and more consumer-friendly common law doctrines. Protections are also growing in other industrialized nations.

These trends seem likely to continue. As the ideology of consumerism tightens its hold, responsible governments will expend more resources on issues raised by shopping for, purchasing, using, and displaying material objects. These issues will be more complex as populations grow, product choices expand, new technologies change products, and marketing becomes more manipulative.

[63] S. Reed Morgan, "McDonald's Burned Itself," *Legal Times*, September 19, 1994, p. 26.

Alcohol Advertising

Anheuser-Busch had high hopes for Spykes. When it was introduced in late 2005, the giant beer company had lost 1 percent of its market share to distilled spirits in each of the previous three years. In 2001 spirits makers had ended their long-standing voluntary policy against aggressive advertising. A wave of liquor ads poured from cable television, then network affiliate channels. At NASCAR races lettering for Jim Beam and Jack Daniels appeared on the cars. More drinkers, notably young adults between 21 and 30 years old, found novelty in new brands, drinks, and mixes marketed by the distillers. Drinking tastes were changing. The taste trend in bars and clubs was moving away from domestic beers such as Anheuser-Busch's Budweiser.

Chairman August A. Busch III believed that the company needed something "fun and new and innovative" to put into the hands of 21- to 30-year-old drinkers.[1] That product was Spykes, a caffeinated malt liquor beverage that was 12 percent alcohol. It came in a 1.7 ounce glass bottle or a 2-ounce plastic one costing $0.75 cents or $1 each. Either way, it had about as much alcohol as in a third of a glass of wine. A lot was done to make Spykes exciting. It included caffeine to capitalize on the popularity of mixing energy drinks with alcohol. There were four flavors—Spicy Lime, Spicy Mango, Hot Melons, and Hot Chocolate. Drinkers could down it as a shot or experiment by mixing the flavors in beer or cocktails.

[1] Quoted in Victor Reklaits, "Anheuser-Busch Unveils Product Aimed at 21- to 30-year-Olds," *Daily Press–Newport*, December 2, 2005, p. 1.

Anheuser-Busch treated Spykes as an experiment. In early 2006 it was test-marketed in eight states and sales were promising. The strategy was to build the brand slowly, by word of mouth at the local level. Marketing literature encouraged distributors to "Spyke up your sales with our new product," an "alternative beverage" for the target audience of "21–27 beer and shot drinkers." Spykes would "open the night up to experimentation and moving outside the beverage 'comfort zone.'"[2] In early 2007 the Spykes rollout reached 32 states.

The company set up a brightly colored Web site with recipes for Spykes. "Try it as a shot. Spice up your beer. Invent a new cocktail. Mix two or more together for a new flavor."[3] Visitors downloaded music mixes, ring tones, screen savers, and instant messaging icons. An interactive feature let users post messages. One exchange of ideas was, "I wonder if it still tastes good if you heat it up lol," which got the response, "I'm gonna try putting one in the microwave. . . lol."[4]

Although there was no national media advertising for Spykes, a few favorable reviews appeared in print. One enthusiastic reporter wrote that it could "turn any beer drinker into a mad scientist."[5] Sales were climbing.

Then there was an astonishing eruption from the precincts of those self-appointed to protect the public from the evils of alcohol. It began with a press release from the Center for Science in the Public Interest, a watchdog group founded by Ralph Nader. In it, George A. Hacker, who heads the group's alcohol projects, unloaded a vicious attack on Spykes, calling it "the latest attempt by Anheuser-Busch to get children interested in alcohol." "This is a shameful ploy to market malt liquor to the Lunchables set," he said. "It's hard to imagine an adult purchasing this beverage, unless they were bringing it for a surprise date with Chris Hansen on Dateline NBC." The evidence that Spykes was intended for underage drinkers included its sweet flavors, the lack of age-verification and "teen-friendly" attractions on the Web site, and its caffeine (because energy drinks are popular with teenagers). Hacker called on the company to "immediately pull Spykes off of shelves, apologize to parents, and hope that in the meantime, no young person wraps his or her car around a tree after being Spyked once too often at the prom."[6]

The Center for Science in the Public Interest is foremost in a coalition of antialcohol groups that closely monitors the alcoholic beverage industry and faults it for social problems caused by drinking. Others in this coalition piled on. The National Center on Addiction and Substance Abuse announced its opposition. Project Extra Mile, which fights underage drinking, expressed concern that minors could hide small Spykes bottles in pockets and purses.[7] Another leading antialcohol group, the Marin Institute, called the product "egregious."[8]

Anheuser-Busch was taken by surprise. "Frankly," said a spokeswoman, "we're perplexed at this criticism. These professional critic groups need to stop the fear mongering and focus on reality."[9]

Concern spread. The Michigan State Police put its officers on special alert for small bottles of Spykes, especially in women's purses. A county coroner in Illinois warned parents to "check your teen on prom night" because Spykes "fit easily into a tux jacket pocket or relatively unobtrusively into a purse for prom night 'fun.'"[10] Although Spykes was not sold there, the town of West Bridgewater, Massachusetts, banned it. And the attorneys general of 28 states sent a letter to Anheuser-Busch stipulating "serious concern" about the nature of Spykes and its marketing. Soon after receiving this letter, the company gave up.

---

[2] "Beer Online Profit Guide" at www.progresivegrocer.com/progresivegrocer/profitguides/beer/v2/news/prodcuts_display.jsp?vnu_content_id=1003019474.

[3] Donna Leinwand, "Beermaker Urged to Pull Spykes," *USA Today,* April 10, 2007, p. A3.

[4] Quoted in Karl Huus, "A Booze Buzz for Teenyboppers?" MSNBC, April 3, 2007.

[5] Chris Sherman, "Spyke Your Beer," *St. Petersburg Times,* February 7, 2007, p. E3.

[6] "CSPI Urges Nationwide Recall of Spykes "Liquid Lunchables," Center for Science in the Public Interest, April 4, www.cspinet.org.2007.

[7] "Jim Osborn, "Tiny Flavored Drink a Worry," *Columbus Telegram,* May 4, 2007, p. 1.

[8] David Lazarus, "Spykes Is No Longer Buzzing," *San Francisco chronicle,* May 27, 2007, p. G1.

[9] Francine Katz, Anheuser-Bush vice president of communications and consumer affairs, quoted in "Anheuser-Busch Product Criticized," *AFX News Limited,* April 6, 2007.

[10] Blog of Dr. Richard Keller, "Live from the Coroner's Office: Spykes," May 4, 2007.

Due to what it called: "unfounded criticism" by "perennial anti-alcohol groups" it announced the end of Spykes on May 18, 2007.[11] Despite victory, the Center for Science in the Public Interest's Hacker did not feel generous toward the company, issuing a short, wary statement in which he accused it of begrudging action and expressed doubts about whether it would "stoop to market kid-friendly drinks" again.[12]

THE ATTACK ON ALCOHOL MARKETING

The story of Spykes is a lesson about a long-standing split in American values. In the late 1800s temperance groups opened a noble crusade against the evils of alcohol. Eventually, they dragged the nation into a brief prohibition era. In 1919 the Eighteenth Amendment banned production and sale of "intoxicating liquors," but the widely evaded ban lasted only until 1933, when the Twenty-First Amendment repealed it. Since then, prohibition attitudes have faded, but not vanished.

In 1939 the first poll on alcohol consumption revealed that 60 percent of American adults were drinkers, and the number has remained approximately that ever since. More recent surveys show that 64 percent of adults drink and 36 percent abstain.[13] About 29 percent are neoprohibitionists who believe that drinking alcohol "can never be justified."[14]

The alcoholic beverage industry must live with these opponents. Although prohibition is a moribund idea, a strong antialcohol movement marches on. Its leaders are activists in church, health, consumer, and citizens' groups such as the Center for Science in the Public Interest and Mothers Against Drunk Driving. Its greatest successes have been getting all states to raise the legal drinking age to 21 and establishing a national drunken-driving standard of .08 blood alcohol content. It now wants to ban or restrict alcoholic beverage advertising. The movement's indictment against alcohol ads is based on four beliefs.

First, advertising increases consumption. Many ads are designed to attract new drinkers and promote additional drinking. Miller Lite's classic "Tastes Great—Less Filling" spots attempted to reposition beer as a competitor to soft drinks, telling consumers that light beer is a low-calorie drink that can be consumed more often than regular beer. The Michelob beer campaign based on the slogan "Put a little weekend in your week" encouraged weekend social drinkers to think of all days of the week as drinking occasions. A recent campaign by the Wine Marketing Council suggests that wine goes with television viewing.

Studies of the effect of advertising on consumption have produced mixed evidence. Generally, national studies find no correlation between overall spending for alcohol ads and consumption. But some studies of local areas show that increased advertising does raise consumption and that advertising bans reduce it.[15] No firm conclusion is possible. This does not deter critics who believe that when alcohol ads saturate the media, they create a climate of undeserved social approval for drinking. George Hacker simply trusts his common sense.

> To pretend, as alcohol marketers do, that the advertisements do not have any effect on consumption is disingenuous at best. . . . [C]onsider that [companies] spend hundreds of millions of dollars advertising their products. One would think they have some faith in that investment. . . . [T]o suggest that it does not help bring in new consumers and encourage current users to consume more begs credulity. Trusting one's eyes and ears makes more sense.[16]

Second, ads encourage underage drinking. Underage alcohol consumption is a serious problem. Survey data show that 42 percent of 12- to 17-year-olds experiment with alcohol. Of these, 18 percent drink at least

[11] Michael J. Owens, vice president of marketing, Anheuser-Busch, quoted in Jeremiah McWilliams, "A-B's Spykes Is Liquidated," *St. Louis Post–Dispatch,* May 18, 2007, p. A1.

[12] Statement of CSPI Alcohol Policies Director George A. Hacker, "Last Call for Anheuser-Busch's Ill-Considered 'Spykes' Drink," CSPI newsroom, May 18, 2007.

[13] Gallup Poll, "Do you have occasion to use alcoholic beverages such as liquor, wine or beer, or are you a total abstainer?" USGALLUP.073106 R20, August 31, 2006.

[14] Princeton Survey Research Associates International, "Pew Forum 10 Nation Survey of Renewalists," USPSRA. 100506RENEW R29F, November 7, 2006.

[15] See Henry Saffer, "Studying the Effects of Alochol Advertising on Consumption," *Alcohol Health & Research World* 20, no. 4 (1996); and Hae-Kyong Bang, "Analyzing the Impact of the Liquor Industry's Lifting of the Ban on Broadcast Advertising," *Journal of Public Policy & Marketing,* Spring 1998.

[16] George Hacker, "Liquor Advertisements on Television: Just Say No," *Journal of Public Policy & Marketing,* Spring 1998, p. 139.

Polygamy Porter, a brand marketed by Wasatch Brewing Co., is a parody of the Mormon custom, now banned, of taking multiple wives. The ad campaign features the slogan "Why have just one!" This kind of appeal is condemned by the antialcohol movement for encouraging more consumption. Source: Courtesy of Wasatch Brewing Company.

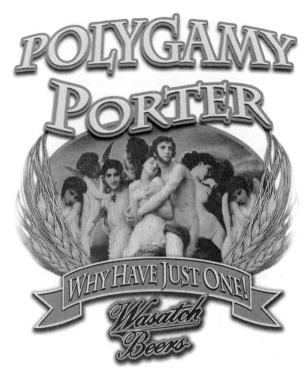

once a month and among them almost two-thirds do binge drinking, defined as having five or more drinks on the same occasion.[17] Overall, this youthful cohort consumes about 20 percent of all alcoholic drinks.[18] Each year some 5,000 underage drinkers die of alcohol-related injuries, most in car crashes, homicides, and suicides. Underage drinking is associated with academic failure, risky sexual behavior, and illicit drug use. New evidence shows that alcohol has pernicious effects on the developing adolescent brain.[19]

There is little evidence that alcohol advertisers target youth in a calculated way, but the ads are nonetheless ever-present. The cumulative mass of alcohol ads is an irresistible lesson that drinking is fun and leads to social acceptance, sexual success, and other parts of the good life. Some studies reveal efficacy with children. Sixth graders in South Dakota who had more exposure to alcohol ads than peers were found more likely to be drinking by the seventh grade.[20] Seventh graders in Los Angeles who watched more television programs with alcohol ads were more frequent and heavier alcohol users in the eighth grade.[21]

Activists claim that the alcoholic beverage industry targets underage drinkers not only with advertising but with products designed to attract youth. These include flavored malt beverages such as Spykes, often called "alcopops," single-serving vodka and tequila cocktails with names such as Yellin Melon Balls and Blue-Dacious Kamikaze, and novelty products such as cups of strawberry gelatin containing vodka.

[17] *Statistical Abstract of the United States: 2007,* 126th ed. (Washington, DC: Bureau of the Census, December 15, 2006), table 194. Data are for 2004.

[18] Leslie B. Snyder et al., "Effects of Alcohol Advertising Exposure on Drinking among Youth," *Archives of Pediatric and Adolescent Medicine,* January 2006, p. 18.

[19] Department of Health and Human Services, *The Surgeon General's Call to Action to Prevent and Reduce Underage Drinking: 2007* (Rockville, MD: Department of HHS, Office of the Surgeon General, 2007), pp. 1–11 and 19–20.

[20] Rebecca L. Collins et al., "Early Adolescent Exposure to Alcohol Advertising and Its Relationship to Underage Drinking," *Journal of Adolescent Health,* April 2007, pp. 531–32.

[21] Alan W. Stacy et al., "Exposure to Televised Alcohol Ads and Subsequent Adolescent Alcohol Use," *American Journal of Health Behavior* 28, no. 6 (2004), p. 498.

Questionable marketing gimmicks include spring break promotions, brand placement in films seen by children, and brand logos on T-shirts and toys. A recent study showed that elementary school children who played with alcohol-themed toys tended to start drinking earlier.[22]

Third, sophisticated lifestyle advertising used by alcohol makers is manipulative because it locks into inner drives. Informational advertising presents details about a product, for example, its price, availability, and quality. In contrast, lifestyle advertising positions a product to fulfill emotional needs. Pictures and copy associate alcohol with fulfillment of desires for popularity, success, sophistication, rebellion, romance, and sexual conquest. The ads endow commodity products such as vodka or lager beer with brand images. Then by drinking that brand, the consumer adopts and projects the brand image. These ads may convey little or no objective information about the beverage, only an emotional theme. Sexual images are a staple of alcohol marketing. However, one study of alcohol ads in magazines during a 14-year period found that other appeals predominated over sexual imagery. In *Life*, for example, prestige and social acceptance were more frequent themes.[23] Whatever the image, critics believe that since lifestyle ads play on emotion, they are highly manipulative. Consumers who respond to them are being tricked into fulfilling inner needs by drinking.

Fourth, alcohol advertising is targeted not only at young drinkers but, sometimes inappropriately, at other groups too. Critics object, for example, to endless ads for malt liquors in inner-city black neighborhoods and in black media. Malt liquor has a higher alcohol content than regular beer, and advertisements for it appeal to drinkers looking for inebriation. United States Beverage Company went against this criticism when it introduced a new brand named Phat Boy with graffiti-style ads for a "new malt liquor with an attitude." Phat Boy came in 40-ounce bottles, each having almost as much alcohol as a six-pack of regular beer. But after an outcry by activists, the company dropped the brand. Hispanics are also targeted. Although nearly 40 percent of Hispanics in the U.S. are under 21 years old, Hispanic neighborhoods are filled with beer billboards. Alcohol companies stage parties, promotions, concerts, and happy hours with Cinco de Mayo themes. Young women are also targeted by companies that have introduced a range of sweet mixed drinks that appeal to their tastes. Anheuser-Busch has a carbonated, alcoholic fruit drink named Peels in flavors such as strawberry with passion and cranberry with peach. Constellation Brands sells a brand of vodka martini called Cocktails by Jenn in Blue Lagoon, Lemon Drop, and Appletini flavors. The drinks come in four packs and each bottle has small metal charms such as a high-heeled shoe, diamond ring, or heart.[24]

ALCOHOL MARKETERS DEFEND THEIR ADVERTISING

Just as the alcohol industry must live with its enemies, it must also live with the stagnating demand characteristic of a mature business. Due to population aging and health consciousness, per capita consumption is in a persistent, long-term decline, revealed by an 11 percent drop between 1985 and 2005. Amid the overall decay, fierce competition exists among the three segments for market share. Since 2000, beer has lost 5 percent of the market while distilled spirits have gained 4.1 percent and wine 0.9 percent. Beer now has a 51 percent market share, distilled spirits 33 percent, and wine 16 percent.[25] Americans still drink a lot of alcohol, about 25 gallons of alcoholic beverages per capita in recent years, an amount the size of a large aquarium and more than the 21 gallons of milk and 24 gallons of coffee they consume.[26] So small fractions of the market equal significant revenues. A fierce struggle over these fractions in a limited, shrinking

[22] Erica Weintraub Austin, "Why Advertisers and Researchers Should Focus on Media Literacy to Respond to the Effects of Alcohol Advertising on Youth," *International Journal of Advertising 25*, no. 4 (2006), p. 542.

[23] Geng Cui, "Advertising of Alcoholic Beverages in African-American and Women's Magazines: Implications for Health Communication," *Howard Journal of Communications*, October 2000, p. 288.

[24] Deborah Ball and Vanessa O'Connell, "As Young Women Drink More, Alcohol Sales, Concerns Rise," *The Wall Street Journal*, February 15, 2006, p. A1.

[25] Distilled Spirits Council of the United States, "2006 Industry Review," at http://www.discus.org/pdf/2006Review-Brief.pdfDiscus ppt.

[26] Department of Agriculture, Economic Research Service, "Beverages: Per Capita Availability, at www.ers.usda.gov, July 2007.

market is the driving force behind the industry's emphasis on clever advertising. It defends its ads with these basic arguments.

First, it says, ads are not the cause of alcohol abuse. As noted, studies fail to show that advertising increases consumption. So commercials and billboards cannot be blamed for car accidents, teen suicides, sexual aggression, spousal abuse, binge drinking, and alcoholism. Alcoholism, for example, is a complex disease caused by personality, family, genetic, and physiological factors rather than by viewing ads. Restraints would only deprive moderate drinkers of product information, not relieve social problems. As an advertising executive once noted, trying to stop problem drinking with an ad ban "makes as little sense as trying to control the Ku Klux Klan by outlawing bed linens."[27]

Ad restrictions would also muzzle a competitive weapon. Because of stagnating demand, most alcohol ads are aimed not at expanding demand but at getting consumers to switch brands. Without advertising, starting a new national brand would be almost impossible and established brands would have an insurmountable advantage. Innovative products such as Spykes would be harder to introduce.

Second, antialcohol groups assume that the public is too stupid to decide responsibly. The idea of curbing ads is condescending. Consumers are intelligent and skeptical. They are not duped by the association of alcohol with attractive images. Does anyone expect brewers and vintners to associate their products with root canals, traffic congestion, or income taxes? The rejection of lifestyle advertising is also condescending. If a consumer used an alcohol brand to feel more sophisticated, popular, or sexual, who is to say that this method of satisfying the person's inner need is wrong? No one would criticize a woman for feeling glamorous while she is wearing perfume, though the perfume is simply a chemical, nonessential to healthy life, and the glamour is created by ad imagery. If advertising endows alcoholic beverages with a quality that satisfies emotional needs in responsible drinkers, it bestows a legitimate benefit. The critics assume there is no merit to a product beyond its utilitarian qualities. What a dull world it would be if all products were marketed and used on this basis.

Third, the beer, wine, and spirits industries have voluntary codes to regulate advertising behavior. The policies in these codes are extensive and specific. For example, the Beer Institute's *Advertising and Marketing Code* prohibits depictions of excessive consumption, intoxication, and drinking while driving. Models in beer ads must be over 25 and "reasonably appear" to be over 21 years old. Beer ads should never show "any symbol, language, music, gesture, or cartoon character intended to appeal primarily to persons below the legal purchase age." No depictions of Santa Claus or sexual promiscuity are permitted.[28] The Wine Institute's *Code of Advertising Standards* has similar guidelines. It also prohibits showing the Easter bunny.[29] The Distilled Spirits Council of the United States' *Code of Good Practice for Distilled Spirits Advertising and Marketing* is similar to the two other codes. It allows "depictions of persons in a social or romantic setting" but forbids advertisers to "depict sexual prowess as a result of beverage alcohol consumption."[30] Each code sets a standard for television, radio, and print ads requiring that at least 70 percent of the audience be 21 years of age or older.

All three codes are backed by mechanisms to investigate complaints of violations. DISCUS, for example, convenes a seven-member review board to look at complaints. But self-regulation has its limits. All the panel members are top executives at distilling companies that belong to DISCUS and the panel's rulings are often gentle. The code seems to forbid strong sexual imagery. One complainant stated that a SKYY Vodka magazine ad in 2006 violated Responsible Content Provision No. 25 of the distiller's code. This section states that "beverage alcohol advertising and marketing materials should not rely upon sexual prowess or sexual success as a selling point for the brand" and "should no contain or depict . . . promiscuity." The complaint alleged a violation due to "the clothing and the position of the female model in the

[27] Eric Clark, *The Want Makers* (New York: Viking Press, 1988), p. 285.

[28] At http://beeresponsible.com/advertising/AdAndMarketingCode.html, January 2006 edition.

[29] At http://www.wineinstitute.org/programs/adcode/adcode.php (revised September 2005).

[30] At http://www.discus.org/responsibility/code/read.asp, undated document.

DISTINCTIVE SINCE 1953

DISTINCTIVE SINCE 1830

Hef says drink responsibly

IMPORTED LONDON DRY GIN 47.3% ALC./VOL., 100% GRAIN NEUTRAL SPIRITS, SCHIEFFELIN & SOMERSET CO., NEW YORK, N.Y. © 2002 GUINNESS UNITED DISTILLERS & VINTNERS AMSTERDAM B.V.

www.tanqueray.com

Although the distiller's advertising code warns advertisers not to "rely upon sexual prowess or sexual success as a selling point," this ad links a brand of gin with Hugh Hefner, mastermind of the *Playboy* philosophy.
Source: Image courtesy of The Advertising Archives.

advertisement insofar as she is wearing a slit, revealing dress and is standing (straddling) between a man's legs in a forward pose with her right leg lifted and bent outside the man's left leg."[31] After deliberation, the review board found no violation, holding that the ad "did not rely upon sexual prowess or sexual success as a selling point . . . and did not depict promiscuity."[32]

The board also lacks enforcement power. The code requires that advertising "not imply illegal activity of any kind." A complaint was lodged against Bong Spirit Vodka, which advertised on the Web using images of its vodka bottle, which is shaped like a bong, a device used for smoking mar-

ijuana. The company argued that its bottle reflected "pop icon imagery" associated with "creative expression" and it was legal to use the word "bong." The review board held that the marketing of distilled spirits in a bong-shaped bottle with the use of the word bong in the brand name inferred illegal activity. It urged the company to change its marketing, but got no response and no sanctions could be imposed.[33]

Fourth, alcohol makers promote responsible consumption. Companies broadcast public service announcements to preach moderation and safe driving. They sponsor designated-driver programs such as Anheuser-Busch's Alert Cab, which gives free taxi rides to restaurant and bar patrons who have been drinking. The Distilled Spirits Council

[31] Distilled Spirits Council of the United States, *Semi-Annual Code Report*, 5th ed., February 2007, at www.discus.org.

[32] Ibid., p. 13.

[33] Ibid., p. 11.

of the United States funds college programs in which students teach each other about moderation, and it trains bartenders to serve drinks responsibly. These efforts, while important, do not get nearly the funding of brand advertising. According to one study by an activist organization, responsibility ads are only 2 percent of the alcohol advertising budget and youths see 239 product ads for every message about safe driving.[34]

Finally, targeting respects diverse audiences. The industry agrees that it targets younger drinkers, minorities, women, and other groups with advertising themes. Young adult drinkers, for example, find value in advertising that informs them of new products and creates images that fulfill their emotional needs. The puzzle faced by companies is that young consumers aged 21–25 share many interests and behaviors with teenagers just below the legal drinking age. Some spillover of appeal is inevitable. Ads aimed at minorities are also legitimate. Market segmentation and the targeted advertising that makes it work are standard in many industries. When toy companies make black or Latina dolls, social critics applaud, but when alcohol companies make products that appeal to minority communities, critics argue that these consumers are too gullible and naive to withstand manipulation, implying that Hispanic or black consumers are not as astute as white consumers. The real problem is that the product is alcohol, not that the ads have ethnic or racial appeal.

RESTRICTING ALCOHOL ADVERTISING

Government regulation of alcohol ads is minimal and over the last 30 years the Supreme Court has weakened that which does exist and raised barriers to any expansion. Two federal agencies have some power over the claims that companies make.

Under a 1935 law, the Bureau of Alcohol, Tobacco and Firearms regulates container labels to prevent false claims, obscene images, and the use of words such as "strong" and "extra strength." Originally, the law prohibited statements of alcohol content on labels

so that companies could not start strength wars. However, in 1995 the Supreme Court held that censoring this information violated bottlers' speech rights, so alcohol content can now be printed on labels.[35] A second agency, the Federal Trade Commission, has the power to stop "deceptive" and "unfair" advertising claims, and now and then it flexes its muscles regarding alcohol ads.

Altogether, the body of government regulation covering alcohol advertising imposes few restraints. Critics want stronger measures. In the 1990s several bills were introduced in Congress to limit alcohol ads, for example, by banning them near schools and playgrounds, in publications with large youth readerships, on college campuses, and during prime-time television hours.[36] The prospect for such measures faded after a 1999 Supreme Court decision that struck down a federal ban on broadcast ads by casinos.[37]

The court has also chipped away at other restrictions. Until 1996 Rhode Island banned price advertising for alcoholic beverages, claiming it was justified in doing so to promote temperance. However, the Supreme Court struck the ban down, saying that price advertising is protected by the First Amendment's free-speech guarantee.[38]

Recently, a series of aggressive class action lawsuits sought to regulate the alcohol industry through the courts. In these actions, parents of underage drinkers accused more than 100 companies of defrauding them by attracting their sons and daughters to spend family money illegally on alcohol. The parents alleged injury from a complicated scheme including marketing "alcopops," ads with themes that appeal to youth, distributing promotional items, using cartoons, sponsoring spring break events, and setting up sham self-regulatory codes. They sought to recover the money their underage children spent and stop the ongoing seduction of youth. However, courts have now dismissed most of these lawsuits for insufficient evidence

[34] *Drowned Out: Alcohol Industry 'Responsibility' Advertising on Television, 2001–2005,* Center on Alcohol Marketing and Youth, Georgetown University, Washington, DC, 2005, p. 1.

[35] *Rubin v. Coors Brewing Company,* 514 U.S. 618 (1995).

[36] See, for example, the "Voluntary Alcohol Advertising Standards for Children Act," H.R. 1292, 105th Congress., 1st Sess. (1997), introduced by Representative Joseph P. Kennedy II (D-Massachusetts).

[37] *Greater New Orleans Broadcasting Association, Inc. v. U.S.,* 527 U.S. 173 (1999).

[38] *44 Liquormart v. Rhode Island,* 517 U.S. 484 (1996).

that company actions caused underage alcohol abuse.[39]

Some nations go further than the United States in restricting alcohol advertising. India and Thailand ban it completely. Ireland prohibits distilled spirits ads on television and radio and prohibits beer and wine ads before sports events. France bans alcohol ads on television and restricts ad content in other media. Norway, Sweden, Denmark, and Finland prohibit advertising of beverages with more than a certain alcohol content ranging from 2.2 to 3.5 percent, less than regular beer or wine. Italy, Spain, and Portugal restrict alcohol advertising before 8:00, 9:30, and 10:00 p.m. respectively. Greece limits the number of television and radio ads per brand per day. The U.K. prohibits television ads using personalities that appeal to those under 18 years old. Such restrictions may not be permissible in the United States because of constitutional protections for free speech.

ARE RESTRICTIONS ON ALCOHOL AND TOBACCO ADS CONSTITUTIONAL?

Images and statements in advertising are speech. Therefore, proposals for muzzling liquor, beer, and wine companies raise constitutional issues. The First Amendment protects all speech from government curbs, but courts have distinguished *noncommercial* speech from *commercial* speech. The former is speech in the broad marketplace of ideas, encompassing political, scientific, and artistic expression. Such speech is broadly protected. The latter is speech intended to stimulate business transactions, including advertising. This kind of speech receives less protection.

The right of free speech is assumed to be a fundamental barrier against tyranny and is not restricted lightly. Courts will not permit censorship of noncommercial speech unless it poses an imminent threat to public welfare, as it would, for example, if a speaker

incited violence or a writer tried to publish military secrets.

With respect to commercial speech, however, various restrictions are allowed. For example, ads for securities offerings can appear only in the austere format of a legal notice and tobacco ads are barred on radio and TV. Would courts approve additional restrictions on alcoholic beverage advertising?

The most important legal guidelines for weighing restraints on commercial speech are those set forth by the Supreme Court in 1980 in the *Central Hudson* case.[40] Here the Court struck down a New York regulation banning advertising by public utilities, a regulation intended to help conserve energy. Justice Lewis Powell, writing for the majority, set forth a four-part test to decide when commercial speech could be restricted.

- The ad in question should promote a lawful product and must be accurate. If an ad is misleading or suggests illegal activity, it does not merit protection.
- The government interest in restricting the particular commercial speech must be substantial, not trivial or unimportant.
- The advertising restriction must directly further the interest of the government. In other words, it should demonstrably help the government reach its public policy goal.
- The suppression of commercial speech must not be more extensive than is necessary to achieve the government's purpose.

All government actions to ban or restrict alcohol ads could be challenged by industry and would have to pass the four-part *Central Hudson* test to survive.

A PERSPECTIVE ON ALCOHOL ADVERTISING

Alcohol advertising is controversial. The Prohibition Party argument that it promotes an immoral, sinful, and unhealthy habit has few advocates today. However, underage drinking is an important social problem and sometimes leads to unnecessary tragedy. The mainstream campaign to limit alcohol advertising is now focused on protecting children and

[39] See, for example, *Hakki v. Zima Company*, 03-0009183 (Sup Ct. Dist. Col., November 14, 2003); *Eisenberg v. Anheuser-Busch, Inc.*, 1:04 CV 1081 (N.D. Ohio February 1, 2006); *Alston v. Advanced Brands & Importing*, 05-72629 (E.D. Mich., S.D, May 19, 2006); and *Bertovich v. Advanced Brands & Importing Co.*, 5:05CV74 (N.D. West Virginia, August 16, 2006).

[40] *Central Hudson Gas & Electric Corp. v. Public Service Commission*, 447 U.S. 557.

teenagers. Its militants believe that appeals in alcohol ads intentionally or negligently spill over to influence underage drinkers. Evidence is strong that children and teenagers are attracted to some of these ads. But proof that they cause underage consumption is elusive.

Some critics think alcohol marketers are so sophisticated that they could precisely limit appeals to adult drinkers without any spillover to those under 21. Belief in this much command of an audience is perhaps wishful. Skepticism about the ability of alcohol ads to influence anyone may be equally reasonable. Miller Brewing developed a series of "Catfight" commercials for Miller Lite that won the 2003 grand prize for sexism from the Advertising Women of New York, but sales fell 2.5 percent while they ran.[41] When Allied Domecq tried to reposition its Kahlúa brand with drinkers aged 21 to 29, it ran youth-oriented print ads with brazen sexual imagery. The effort was a complete failure.[42]

[41]See Christopher Lawton, "Miller, Coors Still Bet Sex Sells Beer," *The Wall Street Journal,* June 6, 2003, p. B3; and Suzanne Vranica, "Sirius Ad Is Best Bet for Most Sexist," *The Wall Street Journal,* November 11, 2004, p. B5.

Questions

1. Was Spykes a bad product? Do you think Anheuser-Busch did the right thing by stopping its sale?

2. Do alcoholic beverage companies fulfill their ethical duty to be informative and truthful in advertising? Do they generally uphold their ethical duty to minimize potential harm to society from underage drinking?

3. Are some beer, wine, or spirits ads misleading? What examples can you give? What is misleading in them? Do some ads contain images and themes that go too far in appealing to an audience under the legal drinking age? Can you give examples?

4. Do you believe there is a need for more restrictions on alcohol advertising? If so, what limits are needed? Explain how a ban or any restrictions could meet the Central Hudson guidelines.

[42] Robert Guy Matthews, "Spirits Makers Aim to Juice Up Their Old-School Beverages," *The Wall Street Journal,* November 11, 2004, p. B5.

Chapter Sixteen

The Changing Workplace

Ford Motor Company

The history of the Ford Motor Company is told in the changing experiences of its workers. Their story illustrates how powerful forces discussed in this chapter act to change the workplace.

Henry Ford (1863–1947) was a brilliant inventor. After incorporating the Ford Motor Company in 1903, he designed one car after another, naming each chassis after a letter of the alphabet. In 1908, he began selling the Model T, a utilitarian, crank-started auto that came only in black. An early Model T cost $850, but Ford introduced the first moving auto assembly line and, by 1924, mass output lowered the price to $290. The assembly line was a new, revolutionary technology that changed work at Ford, turning assemblers from craftsmen into interchangeable parts like those in the cars they put together.

Ford sold 15.5 million Model Ts before production ended in 1927. Despite a warning in the form of fast-dropping market share in the mid-1920s, Ford failed utterly to anticipate a sea change in the auto market. The company clung to the spartan Model T even as consumers turned to the styling changes, closed body design, and brand hierarchy offered by General Motors. Finally, Ford had to suspend production, stilling its great River Rouge assembly plant for seven months while the Model A was hurriedly designed. More than 100,000 idled workers felt the sting of hardship that came from competition not well met.

Henry Ford was an obstinate man, obsessed with power, iron-willed, dictatorial, and cynical about human nature. He spied on his employees in their homes to see if they smoked or drank. Believing that workers were motivated by fear, he created a tense atmosphere marked by arbitrary and capricious dismissals. Managers knew they had been fired when they came to work and found their desks chopped into splinters. Sometimes two managers were given the same duties and the one failing to thrive in the competition was fired. In his autobiography, Ford wrote that a "great business is really too big to be human."[1] As the firm grew, his authoritarian style became

---

[1] Henry Ford, *My Life and Work* (Garden City, NY: Doubleday, 1923), p. 263.

Model Ts pass along the first moving assembly line at Ford Motor Company's Highland Avenue plant in Detroit. The photograph was taken in 1913. Source: © National Archives/CORBIS.

embedded in its informal culture. Independent managers left, and he was surrounded by sycophants who would have jumped into the Detroit River if he had asked. They, in turn, were ruthless and autocratic with their subordinates.[2]

This atmosphere made conditions attractive for early labor organizers. The first efforts came in 1913. Ford fought unions, calling them "the worst things that ever struck the earth."[3] He hired thugs and underworld figures to work at his plants, spying on workers and intimidating anyone who abetted the union cause. This strategy was successful until Congress passed the landmark National Labor Relations Act in 1935, protecting the right of unions to organize. Under the new law, Ford Motor Company was found guilty of unfair labor practices at nine plants. Ford's lawyers delayed the inevitable for a few years, but in 1941 its workers, by a vote of 97 percent to 3 percent, voted to unionize. Federal regulation had been too powerful a force for Ford's campaign of fear to overcome.

Even after the unions, authoritarianism remained firmly entrenched. In 1945 Henry Ford himself felt its barb when he was ousted in a coup engineered by family members. He was replaced by his grandson, Henry Ford II, who also proved to be an autocrat.

In the early 1980s Ford again suffered the harsh discipline of the market. Three years of disastrous losses awakened it to heightened international competition. Japanese auto companies had captured 20 percent of American sales. The company studied the Japanese and decided to emulate thier focus on work teams and continuous quality improvement. It set out to make a world-class sedan using the Japanese carmakers' methods.

[2] Anne Jardim, *The First Henry Ford: A Study in Personality and Business Leadership* (Cambridge, MA: MIT Press, 1970), pp. 114–15.

[3] Quoted in Keith Sward, *The Legend of Henry Ford* (New York: Rinehart & Company, 1948), p. 370.

In Japanese management philosophy, competing personalities and individualism are thought to hamper productivity. So Ford tried to change its corporate culture. Over the years, it had tended to select autocrats for management positions. A study of 2,000 Ford managers classified 76 percent as "noncreative types who are comfortable with strong authority" (as compared with 38 percent of the population).[4] To bring change, thousands of managers went to workshops on participative management.

Ford was rewarded for its efforts with the new Taurus sedan in 1985. It was a quick success and became the best-selling car in America between 1993 and 1995. In 1994 the company made an extraordinary profit of $5.3 billion. Yet in that year, a new Ford chairman, Alexander Trotman, initiated a radical change program to prepare the company for an even more competitive global car market.

He reorganized the way work was done, redrawing the company's organization-chart, destroying fiefdom's of independence in foreign operations and centralizing control at U.S. headquarters. He tried to shred bureaucracy and instill teamwork. Layers vanished as 25,000 managers left hierarchical slots and moved into teams. Tasks were defined in meetings instead of by superiors. Committees decided on promotions. The company invested in more automation. Many jobs were eliminated. Workers felt considerable anxiety over these changes.

Although Ford's profits rose for a time, the upheaval failed to make it a dominant global competitor. Its market share continued to slip and profits became sporadic. In 1999 Trotman was replaced by a new CEO, Jacques Nasser. Nasser, a man of relentless energy who functioned on three hours of sleep, had visions of turning Ford into a high-flying company like General Electric. He pushed methods like those Jack Welch used at GE, vowing to remake Ford's culture yet again.

Ford earned a record profit in 1999, but more trouble lay ahead. In 2000 tire failures on Ford Explorers caused hundreds of deaths and injuries. Ford suffered big losses and its market share slipped further. Nasser did not survive the crisis and in 2001 William Clay "Bill" Ford, Jr., the great-grandson of Henry Ford, took over. Soon he announced another restructuring in which Ford shed four car models and 35,000 employees. Suppliers were pressured to cut their prices. They laid off employees and outsourced work to low-wage factories in Mexico and China. Then Ford began sending engineering work to India, where automotive design cost $60 an hour instead of up to $800 an hour in Detroit.[5]

This was not enough to stem financial losses and in 2006, after Toyota passed Ford to become the number 2 carmaker in America, Bill Ford announced yet another reorganization, closing 10 U.S. plants and moving production to Mexico, where assembly workers average $3.50 an hour compared with $27 in the United States. To save remaining jobs, Ford's unions agreed to concessions such as weekend work with no overtime pay. When this effort faltered Bill Ford gave up, stepping aside in 2007 for a new CEO, Alan Mulally, a talented manager from Boeing. Mulally announced the need for still one more reorganization. Morale at the company is low.

---

[4] Melinda G. Builes and Paul Ingrassia, "Ford's Leaders Push Radical Shift in Culture as Competition Grows," *The Wall Street Journal,* December 3, 1985, p. A1.

[5] "Second Wave: Design Outsourcing Set to Hit Indian Shores," *Financial Express,* December 28, 2004, p. 1.

The basic problem at Ford is the relentless pressure of global competition on a dysfunctional culture that proves impervious to change. Unlike his father and great-grandfather, Bill Ford was considered a good-natured man, but he lacked a corrective answer for an atmosphere in which managers who fear for their careers refuse to take risks. As a result, Ford could not overcome its two great strategic weaknesses—high costs and lack of innovation. This failure leaves its workers exposed to the unforgiving discipline that global forces impose on weak companies. In this chapter we take a systematic look at these forces.

EXTERNAL FORCES SHAPING THE WORKPLACE

Those who work today are caught up in the turbulence of six environmental forces: (1) demographic change, (2) technological change, (3) structural change, (4) competitive pressures, (5) reorganization of work, and (6) government intervention. These forces are interconnected. A discussion of each follows.

Demographic Change

Population dynamics slowly but continuously alter labor forces. Out of a 2008 population of 304 million Americans, about half, or 154 million, made up the civilian labor force as either working or unemployed (the rest are retired, disabled, students, homemakers, children under age 16, or not counted because they received unreported wages). This is the third-largest labor force in the world, though it pales in comparison to China's 795 million and India's 507 million.[6]

Table 16.1 gives three snapshots of the American labor force, showing its size and composition in 2006, then a medium-range 2016 and a long-range 2050 projections. The figures reveal three important trends.

TABLE 16.1
Three Snapshots of the American Labor Force (in thousands)

Source: Bureau of Labor Statistics database.

	2006		2016		2050		Percentage Change 2006–2050
Total labor force	151,428		164,232		194,757		
Men*	81,255	53.7%	87,781	53.4%	103,183	53.0%	−0.7%
Women	70,173	46.3	76,450	46.6	91,574	47.0	0.7
White	123,834	81.8	130,665	79.6	142,371	73.1	−8.7
Black	17,314	11.4	20,121	12.3	26,809	13.8	2.4
Hispanic	20,694	13.7	26,889	16.4	47,317	24.3	10.6
Asian	6,727	4.4	8,741	5.3	16,124	8.3	3.9
Other groups†	3,443	2.3	4,705	2.9	9,453	4.9	2.6
Average age	40.8		42.1		41.6		

*Numerical and percentage totals exceed 100 percent because Hispanics may also be classified in other racial categories.
†Includes American Indians, Alaska Natives, Native Hawaiians, Pacific Islanders, and those reporting two or more races.

[6] Central Intelligence Agency, *World Factbook,* "China" and "India," at www.cia.gov/library, accessed March 2008.

First, growth is slowing. Historically, the American labor force grew rapidly and continuously. It continues to grow, but more slowly now because the general population is growing more slowly. In the 1970s, as the baby-boom generation entered, labor force growth peaked at 2.6 percent a year, but by 2006 growth fell to 1.2 percent and the deceleration is projected to continue, with annual growth falling to 0.8 percent by 2016 and 0.6 percent by 2050.[7] This slowing is caused by a past fall in the fertility rate among American women. The rate is

replacement fertility rate The number of children a woman must have on average to ensure that one daughter survives to reproductive age.

now stable at about 2.05, or just below the *replacement fertility rate* of 2.1. Growth in the population, which is eventually reflected in the labor force, continues because of reductions in mortality and net international immigration.

Second, the labor force is growing more diverse in gender, race, and ethnicity. This is a long-term trend. Table 16.1 shows that all components of the labor force are projected to increase in sheer numbers. Yet they are increasing at different rates and their relative proportions will change. Decade by decade the ebbs and flows of these differential movements create modest changes, but as the far-right column shows, by 2050 cumulative changes in race and ethnicity will be dramatic, with changes in gender less so.

By 2050 whites will decline as a percentage of the labor force by 8.7 percent and men by 0.7 percent. The largest increase will be the 10.6 percent expansion of Hispanics. Asians will increase at a more rapid rate and nearly double their proportion in the labor force, moving from 4.4 percent in 2006 to 8.3 percent in 2050. However, their overall numbers will remain small. Blacks will increase modestly by 2.4 percent. The proportion of the sexes will change little. Since the 1950s women have increased their participation more rapidly than men. Now, however, this trend is slowing and although it will continue through 2050 the percentage of women in the labor force will rise by only 0.7 percent.

Third, the workforce is aging. High fertility rates following World War II created a baby-boom generation born between 1946 and 1964. As this generation entered the labor market in the 1970s, the median age of the workforce dropped, reaching a low of 34.6 years in 1980. The baby boomers are now a bulge of workers in their midforties to early sixties. As they age, the median age of the workforce rises, and it is predicted to reach 42.1 years in 2016, then fall only slightly after 2020 as baby boomers retire.[8] Because the nation's fertility rate has declined since the baby-boom years, generational cohorts of workers following the baby boomers are smaller and the average age will decline only slightly as these aging mainstays of the labor force retire during the 2010s and 2020s. As they retire, shortages of skilled and experienced workers may arise.

Graying of the workforce is more rapid in other developed nations. It is caused by increases in life expectancy combined with declines in fertility. Life expectancy

---

[7]Mitra Toossi, "A New Look at Long-Term Labor Force Projections to 2050," *Monthly Labor Review,* November 2006, table 2.

[8] Figures in this paragraph are based on tables in Mitra Toossi, "A New Look at Long-Term Labor Force Projections to 2050" and "Labor Force Projections to 2016: More Workers in Their Golden Years," *Monthly Labor Review*, November 2007.

has increased markedly in most nations. In the United States it rose from 47 in 1900 to 78 in 2004.[9] Birth rates have fallen in the developed world and are now below the replacement rate in many nations. In Japan, for example, the fertility rate of 1.3 births per woman is far below the replacement rate of 2.1. The populations of these nations are predicted to experience long-term decline. The Japanese labor force began to shrink in 1996 and is expected to fall by 17 percent from its current levels by 2030.[10]

While Japan and Europe confront population declines and aging labor forces, many developing countries have explosively growing, youthful populations. Since the 1970s the United States has absorbed a huge wave of immigrants, most from these nations. It currently takes in about 1 million legal immigrants each year and an estimated 500,000 undocumented immigrants. About 9.3 million undocumented immigrants reside in the United States and 6 million of these are estimated to be in the workforce.[11] The influx of immigrants shapes the American labor force by accelerating its growth, increasing its diversity, and slowing the rise in average age.

Since the fertility rate in the United States has fallen to 2.05, slightly below the replacement rate, continued immigration will prevent the population declines facing Europe and Japan. Immigration gives the United States a long-run competitive advantage in labor costs. Japan and some European countries have tight immigration laws. The Japanese want to preserve racial purity and have difficulty integrating non-Japanese into their workplaces.[12] Many European nations are strongly ethnocentric and do not welcome immigrants. Immigration, however, brings an influx of younger workers who are less costly and more adaptable.

Technological Change

The greatest story of technology shaping the labor force is not about the computer, but the mechanical harvester. When the United States was an agrarian nation fall harvests absorbed enormous amounts of labor. Gangs of men crossed grain fields swinging sickles and scythes. Behind them came women and children to bundle the cuttings. In the 1850s Cyrus McCormick began to manufacture horse-drawn mechanical harvesters, each ridden by a single farmer, that mowed and mechanically baled tall crops. Over the last three harvests of the Civil War, farmers bought 160,000 of McCormick's harvesters. The Commissioner of Agriculture estimated that each reaper freed five men for service in the Union Army, a factor in its victory.[13] With the war over, the men returned to work in factories, not fields, a sud-

---

[9] Robert A. Rosenblatt, "U.S. Not as Gray as 31 Other Countries," *Los Angeles Times*, December 15, 2001, p. A17; and *Statistical Abstract of the United States 2007,* table 98.

[10] Michiyo Nakamoto, "A Labor Force in Decline," *Financial Times,* November 6, 2006, p. 3.

[11] Government Accountability Office, *Workforce Challenges and Opportunities for the 21st Century: Changing Labor Force Dynamics and the Role of Government Policies,* GAO-04-845SP, June 2004, p. 5.

[12] Yuka Hayashi and Sebastian Moffet, "Cautiously, an Aging Japan Warms to Foreign Workers," *The Wall Street Journal,* May 25, 2007, p. A1.

[13] T. A. Heppenheimer, "Cyrus H. McCormick and Company," *American Heritage,* June 2001, p. 10.

den, unprecedented conversion of 7.6 percent of the labor force that stimulated industrial growth.[14]

Technological change has many impacts on work. It affects the number and type of jobs available. Invention of the airplane, for example, created new job titles such as pilot and flight attendant. Webmasters, or employees who design and update Web sites, emerged with the rise of the Internet. New machines are used by management to raise productivity and reduce costs. Robots in auto manufacturing made American companies more competitive in cost and quality with Japanese automakers. Computers have reduced the need for clerical workers and middle managers who existed primarily to collect, analyze, and report information.

Automation has a turbulent impact on employment. It has long been feared. When running for president in 1960, John F. Kennedy warned that automation posed "the dark menace of industrial dislocation."[15] Two years later an industry–labor group compared its effects on the economy to that of a hydrogen bomb. It displaces jobs in traditional occupations. Yet, the number of jobs available in the United States has continuously increased, absorbing new entrants in the growing labor force. This is projected to continue.

Automation causes significant job loss in less-skilled manufacturing and service occupations. In coal mining, for example, mechanization has eliminated 344,000 pick-and-shovel jobs, 83 percent, since 1950. The movement to robotics in the 1980s put almost 40,000 robots on U.S. assembly lines and eliminated two-thirds of all assembly-line jobs by 1990. In service industries, the blows have been equally telling. Automated phones have eliminated 239,000 telephone operators, 67 percent, since 1950.[16] Between 1987 and 1998, 20 percent of these jobs were lost, even as the average number of daily conversations increased by more than 600 percent.[17]

Structural Change

structural change
Any shift in the proportions of agricultural, goods-producing, and service occupations in an economy.

Structural change is caused by processes of job creation and job destruction that continuously alter the mix of productive work in every economy. The American job landscape is shaped by the three long-term structural trends shown in Figure 16.1. Their action is similar in all industrialized nations.

First, the *agricultural sector* has declined from predominance to near insignificance in numbers. In early colonial America, farming occupied 90 percent of Americans. By 2006 it employed only 1.4 percent as fewer and larger farms delivered

agricultural sector
The economic sector that includes farming, fishing, and forestry occupations.

[14] Based on an estimate of 800,000 agricultural workers as a percentage of the 1860 labor force of 10,532,750.

[15] Quoted in Brink Lindsey, "10 Truths about Trade," *Reason,* July 2004, p. 31.

[16] Figures for coal mining and telephone operator employment are for the years 1950 to 2002, from U.S. Census Bureau, *Statistical Abstract of the United States: 1956,* 77th ed., and *2003,* 123rd ed. (Washington, DC, 1956 and 2003); for 1950, tables 910 and 257; for 2003, tables 889 and 615.

[17] Stephen Franklin, "Telephone Operators Are among Those Being Displaced by Technology," *San Jose Mercury News,* September 6, 1998; U.S. Census Bureau, *Statistical Abstract of the United States: 2000,* 120th ed. (Washington, DC, 2000), table 917.

FIGURE 16.1   **Historical Trend Lines for Employment by Major Industry Sector, 1800 to 2012 (Projection)**

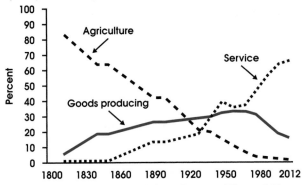

Sources: Bureau of Labor Statistics, U.S. Census Bureau; and Herman E. Kroose, *American Economic Development*, 2d ed. (Englewood Cliffs, NJ: Prentice Hall, 1966), p. 27. Post-1985 figures reflect some reclassification of industries.

goods-producing sector
The economic sector that includes manufacturing, mining, and construction.

the nation's food supply using automated methods to grow crops and raise animals.[18] The Bureau of Labor Statistics predicts that the number of agricultural workers will fall a little more, to 1.2 percent of the labor force, by 2016.

Second, the percentage of workers employed in the *goods-producing sector*, which rose through most of the nation's early history, is now in long-term decline. In 1950 goods-producing jobs occupied 34 percent of workers, but by 2006 this kind of employment had declined to only 14.9 percent of the labor force. By 2016 these occupations are predicted to slump further to 13.1 percent. There are many reasons for the decline of goods-producing work as a percentage of the overall labor force, but the two most significant are productivity growth, primarily through automation, and relocation of work to lower-wage countries. Though fewer people are employed in goods-producing occupations today than in the past, it is a myth that the United States is losing its productive capacity. Over the decade between 1996 and 2006 employment in manufacturing fell by 26 percent in absolute numbers. At the same time, manufacturing output increased by 45 percent, from $3.6 trillion to $5.3 trillion.[19] So even as fewer Americans go to work at factories their output is surging.

service sector
The sector of occupations that add value to manufactured goods.

Third, there is explosive growth in the *service sector,* which includes jobs in retailing, transportation, health care, and other occupations that add value to manufactured goods. For example, a surgeon adds value to a scalpel, a desk clerk to the mattress in a hotel room. Growth in this sector is caused by growth in goods

[18] Historical sector employment figures in this section are from U.S. Census Bureau, *Statistical Abstract of the United States: 1956,* 77th ed. (Washington, DC: Government Printing Office, 1956), table 987. Current figures and projections are from Eric B. Figueroa and Rose A. Woods, "Industry Output and Employment Projections to 2016," *Monthly Labor Review,* November 2007, table 1. Sector employment percentages do not total 100 percent; the missing increment includes private household wage and salary earners and nonagricultural self-employed not included in the three sectors by the Bureau of Labor Statistics.

[19] Eric B. Figueroa and Rose A. Woods, "Industry Output and Employment Projections to 2016," tables 1 and 2.

TABLE 16.2
Comparative
Employment
Structures in
Seven
Developed
Nations

Source: Central Intelligence Agency, *World Factbook*, at www.cia.gov/library/publications, "Field Listing—Labor Force—by Occupation," extracted January 7, 2008. Percentages are for various years 1999–2006.

	Agriculture	Industry	Services
Australia	4%	21%	75%
France	4	24	72
Germany	3	33	64
Italy	5	32	63
Japan	5	28	67
Sweden	2	24	74
United Kingdom	1	18	81

production and trade. Service jobs have risen from 40 percent of the workforce in 1950 to 76 percent in 2006 and are predicted to rise to 78.3 percent by 2016. The nation's fastest-growing occupation, network systems and data communications analyst, exemplifies this explosive growth. It employed 119,000 people in 2000 and rose to 262,000 in 2006, an increase of 120 percent.[20]

The direction of these three trends is remarkably similar in all developed nations. Table 16.2 shows how they have shaped occupational structures elsewhere. The seven nations in the table all experienced long-term job losses in agriculture and industry and steep growth in service sector employment. Nations that have not yet industrialized tend to have large agricultural sectors. Among low-income countries, the agricultural sector averages 20 percent of GDP as opposed to just 2 percent in developed countries.[21]

Structural change is a critical factor in the decline of labor unions. Before the wave of protective legislation passed in the 1930s, unions represented only 5 percent of industrial workers, but this tripled to 15 percent by 1940 and reached a zenith of 25 percent in the 1950s.[22] Unions raised wages and increased benefits for blue-collar workers. These improvements rippled through the entire manufacturing sector because nonunionized companies had to approximate the welfare levels of union workers if they wished to prevent unionization.

In the 1970s, however, union membership in the private sector began a long slide as structural change eroded its base of factory workers. Employment shifted to service industries and to industries employing knowledge workers, who are difficult for industrial unions to organize, and to low-wage countries where unions are illegal or weak. By 2007 unions represented only 7.5 percent of private sector employees in the United States.[23] The upward push on wages and benefits that unions provide for both members and nonmembers has weakened commensurately.

Today, the United States has lower union representation of the private labor force than most other developed economies. In western Europe, although union membership has declined for two decades, roughly a third to a half of all workers

---

[20] U.S. Department of Labor, *Bureau of Labor Statistics News*, December 4, 2007, table 6.

[21] World Bank, *World Development Report 2008* (Washington, DC: World Bank, 2007), table 4. Figures in this paragraph and in table 16.2 are value-added as a percent of GDP in 2006.

[22] U.S. Bureau of the Census, *Statistical Abstract of the United States: 1956* (Washington, DC: U.S. Government Printing Office, 1956), table 271.

[23] Bureau of Labor Statistics, "Union Members in 2007," *BLS News Release,* January 25, 2008, p. 1.

remain unionized. This is one reason that labor costs are much higher in many European nations than in the United States.

Competitive Pressures

Recent trends have intensified competition for American companies. Customers demand higher quality, better service, and faster new-product development. In the United States deregulation of large industries such as airlines, telecommunications, trucking, and electric utilities has stirred formerly complacent rivals. In both domestic and foreign markets, corporations are increasingly challenged by global competitors. Foreign trade grew from just 9 percent of the U.S. economy in 1960 to 29 percent in 2006 and is predicted to rise to 34 percent by 2016.[24] Foreign competitors have many advantages, including lower labor costs, a strong dollar, and, sometimes, higher worker productivity.

In a global labor market workers in developed countries are exposed to competition from pools of low-cost workers. In less affluent, less industrialized countries, wages are lower for many reasons, including oversupply of labor compared with demand, low living standards, local currency valuations, labor policies of regimes where workers have limited political power, and wage competition among countries seeking to attract jobs.

By global standards, American workers are extremely expensive. In 2005 the average hourly compensation for a manufacturing worker in the United States was $23.65. This was not the highest in the world. That distinction went to heavily unionized workers in Norway making $39.14 an hour. Average compensation in the original 15 European Union nations was $27.52.[25] However, in the industrializing economies of Asia and Latin America an hour of labor costs far less. Table 16.3 shows the huge wage gap between developed and developing economies.

TABLE 16.3 International Wage Comparison The table shows hourly compensation for manufacturing workers in U.S. dollars. Compensation includes wages, insurance, labor taxes, and paid leave.

Source: Bureau of Labor Statistics. Figures are for 2005, except Sri Lanka (2004) and China (2004).

Sri Lanka	$ 0.52
China	0.67
Mexico	2.63
Brazil	4.09
Taiwan	6.38
Singapore	7.66
Korea	13.56
Japan	21.76
France	24.63
United Kingdom	25.66
United States	23.65
Germany	33.00
Norway	39.14

[24] Betty W. Su, "The U.S. Economy to 2016: Slower Growth as Boomers Begin to Retire," *Monthly Labor Review,* November 2007, table 2.

[25] Bureau of Labor Statistics, "Hourly Compensation Costs for Production Workers in Manufacturing: 33 Countries or Areas, 22 Manufacturing Industries, 1992–2005," April 30, 2007, p. 8, at www.bls.gov.

Given this wage variation, companies in some industries can no longer afford to do low-skilled manufacturing in the United States and contract to have it done in a foreign country. Or they find ways to increase the productivity of domestic labor by reducing employees to a minimum and applying technology to enlarge their output. Either way, there are generally fewer jobs for American workers in the occupation affected. Similar wage competition now exists in globalizing service industries.

Reorganization of Work

business process
Any sequence of action that adds value to a product or service.

Corporations alter *business processes*—sequences of actions that add value to products and services—as they adjust to environmental changes, primarily competition. A key driver of competition and, therefore, change in business processes, is a changing relationship with time and space. Digitized communication and modern transport are both faster and cheaper than in the past. Both factors lead companies to reorganize their work flows to cut costs, speed product cycles, and increase productivity. These reorganizations cause workforce turbulence. This turbulence, which is the creative force of the economy on display, is widely feared by workers who lose jobs.

For most of the twentieth century, manufacturing occurred near markets for products. As transport costs have fallen, manufacturers more often separate production from consumption by sending their manufacturing to low-cost countries, then shipping products back to customers. There are many examples. One story is how the prime contractor on a new six-story Salt Lake City public library underbid its competitors by sending part of the construction work to Mexico. It hired a Mexico City company with lower labor costs to manufacture 2,000 massive concrete panels that make up the building, saving $1 million although the panels had to be trucked 2,350 miles to the job site.[26]

Because of abundant and inexpensive bandwidth in fiber optic cable, service work that formerly had to be done within companies can now also be sent to low-cost foreign locations. At first, only simple, routine tasks such as customer service, telemarketing, accounting, and document management were outsourced. But increasingly complex tasks such as software development, financial analysis, and marketing research are going offshore. The redesign of the 10,200-room Tropicana Casino & Resort in Las Vegas is being done 8,000 miles from Las Vegas by dozens of Indian architects making about $15,000 a year.[27] DuPont sends much of its legal work to the Philippines, where attorneys with years of experience handle it for $30,000 annual salaries. A newly hired attorney in New York doing the same work would make $150,000 a year.[28]

outsourcing
The transfer of work from within a company to an outside supplier.

Trade in services between nations is growing, creating fears about job loss from *outsourcing*. Outsourcing occurs when a company sends work of any kind to an outside supplier rather than pay its own employees to do it. It may be manufacturing or service work. Usually, outsourcing is done to cut labor costs, although outside suppliers may have expertise or achieve economies of scale that a company would find expensive to duplicate. Outsourcing can move work to either a domestic or a

---

[26] Joel Millman, "Blueprint for Outsourcing," *The Wall Street Journal*, March 3, 2004, p. B1.

[27] Pete Engardio, "Blueprint from India," *BusinessWeek*, April 2, 2007, p. 44.

[28] Pete Engardio, "Let's Offshore the Lawyers," *BusinessWeek*, September 18, 2006, p. 42.

offshoring

The transfer of work from a domestic to a foreign location or to a foreign supplier.

foreign contractor. When work moves to a foreign country, this is called *offshoring*. Offshoring also occurs when reorganized work remains within the company but moves from the home country to a foreign location.

Offshoring has fueled attacks on corporations for destroying well-paying jobs in developed nations out of greed. Statistics on outsourcing lack the power to rigorously define the trend, but suggest that media and scholarly attention may exaggerate its importance. In a recent one-year period, for example, 937,652 workers lost their jobs in mass layoffs. However, only 31,089 or 3.3 percent were laid off because their work moved out of the company and of these only 2,037, less than 2 one-hundredths of 1 percent, lost their jobs because the work moved to a foreign company.[29] These figures are not definitive because they do not register layoffs of fewer than 50 persons and they cannot measure jobs never added to domestic roles because they were created overseas.

Some predict that the current trickle of offshoring will grow to a flood. A few economists believe that the current ability to outsource fragments of productive work to distant corners of the globe represents a fundamental change equal in importance to the industrial revolution.[30] For example, Alan S. Binder analyzed 817 occupations for susceptibility to foreign migration and concluded that 30 to 40 million jobs are in danger of being shipped out of the American economy in the next decade.[31]

Nevertheless, outsourcing is so far a minor eddy in the churning tides of job gain and job loss that sweep over American workers. Figure 16.2 shows that between 1993

FIGURE 16.2

Quarterly Private Sector Job Gains and Job Losses: 1993–2007

Source: Bureau of Labor Statistics, "Business Employment Dynamics," series extracted December 15, 2007.

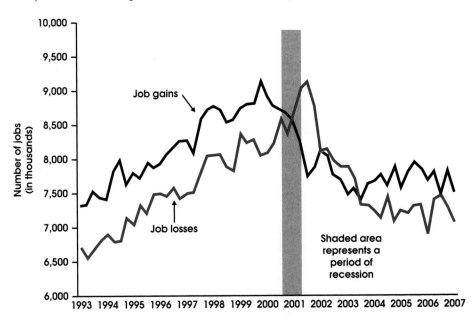

[29] Figures are from Bureau of Labor Statistics Mass Layoffs Statistics Program data on extended mass layoffs for the fourth quarter of 2006 through the third quarter of 2007 at www.bls.gov/mls/home.

[30] Alan S. Binder, "Offshoring: The Next Industrial Revolution," *Foreign Affairs,* March/April 2006.

[31] Cited in David Wessel and Bob Davis, "Pain from Free Trade Spurs Second Thoughts," *The Wall Street Journal,* March 28, 2007, p. A1.

and 2007, except for a period of recession and recovery, each quarter more jobs were created than lost. Each year the economy creates millions of new jobs while eliminating millions of old ones, but averages an annual gain of about 1.5 million new jobs. This dynamic of job creation and job loss reshapes the structure of the economy.

GOVERNMENT INTERVENTION

All governments intervene in labor markets, but there is wide variation. We first discuss how labor regulation has developed in the United States. Then we explain the alternative model in Japan and Europe. Last, we explain the trade-offs in labor regulation that all governments face.

Development of Labor Regulation in the United States

employment contract
The agreement by which an employee exchanges his or her labor in return for specific pay and working conditions. It is an abstract concept, but may also be set forth in writing.

Historically, a strong laissez-faire current in American economic philosophy made governments at all levels reluctant to interfere with the *employment contract,* or the agreement by which an employee exchanges his or her labor in return for specific pay and working conditions. Today, government intervention is extensive and growing, but this is a twentieth-century trend.

Before 1860, the number of persons employed as wage earners in factories, mines, railroads, and other workplaces was relatively small. With industrialization, the number rapidly grew. Between 1860 and 1890, the number of wage earners rose from 1.33 million to 4.25 million, a 320 percent increase.[32] This rise, which would continue into the 1930s, created a new class interest, and it was an aggrieved one. In the hardhearted wisdom of the day, employers treated workers as simply production costs to be minimized; there was relentless downward pressure on wages and reluctance to improve working conditions.

Liberty of Contract

liberty of contract
The freedom of employers and workers to negotiate the employment contract— including wages, hours, duties, and conditions— without government interference.

Before the 1930s, government intervention on behalf of workers was very limited, consisting mostly of feeble state safety regulations and laws to limit working hours. In the late 1800s and early 1900s, strong majorities on the Supreme Court upheld the *liberty of contract* doctrine. This doctrine was that employers and workers should be free of government intervention to negotiate all aspects of the employment contract, including wages, hours, duties, and conditions.[33] For many years, the Court struck down state and federal laws inconsistent with this theoretical freedom. Such laws were regarded as "meddlesome interferences with the rights of the individual."[34]

The great flaw in the liberty of contract doctrine was that it assumed equal bargaining power for all parties, whereas employers unquestionably predominated.

[32] Arthur M. Schlesinger, *Political and Social Growth of the United States: 1852–1933* (New York: Macmillan, 1935), p. 203.

[33] The liberty of contract majority first emerged in *Allgeyer v. Louisiana,* 106 U.S. 578 (1897), where Justice Rufus W. Peckham grounded it in the due process clause of the Fourteenth Amendment, which says that no state can "deprive any person of life, liberty, or property, without due process of law."

[34] Justice Peckham, writing for a 5–4 majority in *Lockner v. New York,* 198 U.S. 61 (1905). The decision struck down an 1897 New York State law limiting bakery employees to 60-hour weeks.

Turn-of-the-century cartoonist Art Young drew this cynical view of the lopsided employment contract in the days before labor unions and laws protecting worker rights.
Source: Cartoon by Art Young.

For employers, liberty of contract was the liberty to exploit. Employees could be fired at will and had to accept virtually any working conditions. Unchallenged dominion of employers opened the door to the negligent treatment of workers that fueled the labor union movement, a social movement to empower workers. Employers resisted demands for kinder treatment of workers and bitterly fought the rise of unions.

Waves of Regulation

It was not until the 1930s that government regulation of the workplace began to redress the huge power imbalance favoring employers. One major step was the Norris-LaGuardia Anti-Injunction Act of 1932, which struck down a type of employer–employee agreement called, in the colorful language of unionists, a "yellow dog contract." These were agreements that workers would not join unions. Employers virtually extorted signatures on them when workers were hired, and hapless applicants had little choice but to sign if they wanted the job—and jobs were scarce in the 1930s. If union organizing began, companies went to court, where judges enforced the agreements. The Norris–LaGuardia Act outlawed yellow dog contracts, overturning a 1908 Supreme Court decision that upheld them under the liberty of contract doctrine.[35]

The new law encouraged unions. It was soon followed by the National Labor Relations Act of 1935, which guaranteed union organizing and bargaining rights, and by other laws that fleshed out a body of rules for labor relations. After the 1930s, employers still dominated the employment contract, but unions increasingly checked company power over wages and working conditions.

Figure 16.3 shows how this first wave of federal workplace regulation in the 1930s, which established union rights, was followed by two subsequent waves. A second wave, between 1963 and 1974, moved federal law into new areas, protecting civil rights, worker health and safety, and pension rights. A third wave, between 1986 and 1996, again broadened federal authority to address additional, and somewhat narrower, employment issues. During this period, Congress enacted the following laws.

- A provision in the Comprehensive Omnibus Budget Reconciliation Act of 1986 allows separated workers to continue in group health plans for up to 18 months at their own expense.

- The Immigrant Reform and Control Act of 1986 protects work rights of legal aliens and prohibits hiring illegal aliens.

- The Worker Adjustment and Retraining Act of 1988 requires companies with more than 100 workers to give 60 days' notice prior to plant closings or large layoffs.

- The Employee Polygraph Protection Act of 1988 prohibits the use of lie detectors to screen job applicants and narrows grounds for using the tests to detect employee theft or sabotage.

- The Drug-Free Workplace Act of 1988 requires companies with federal contracts to take measures against drug abuse.

- The Americans with Disabilities Act of 1990 prohibits discrimination against the disabled and requires employers to make reasonable accommodations for people with substantial physical or mental impairments.

- The Family and Medical Leave Act of 1993 gives workers the right to take up to 12 weeks of unpaid leave for family reasons such as childbirth or illness.

- The Health Insurance Portability and Accountability Act of 1996 guarantees that preexisting medical problems will continue to be covered by health insurance when workers switch jobs.

Altogether, approximately 200 federal workplace laws have been enacted since the 1930s, including amendments to original statutes, so only the major ones are shown in Figure 16.3. These laws are rooted in the dominant perspective of 1930s reformers that the relationship between labor and management is antagonistic. Based on this model, a broad and complex regulatory structure has been created over more than 80 years to counterbalance the perceived weakness of workers in the employment contract with corporations. It has greatly improved the lives of workers. No more dramatic example of a beneficial regulation exists than the decline in workplace fatalities

---

[35] *Adair v. United States,* 291 U.S. 293 (1908).

FIGURE 16.3   A Chronology of Major Workplace Regulations

This figure shows the historical march of major statutes (and one executive order) regulating labor–management and employer–employee relations. Note the existence of three rough clusters or waves of intervention.

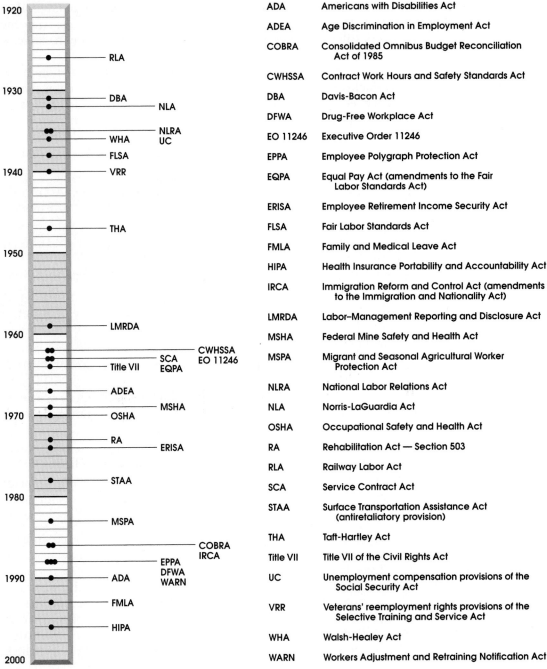

ADA	Americans with Disabilities Act
ADEA	Age Discrimination in Employment Act
COBRA	Consolidated Omnibus Budget Reconciliation Act of 1985
CWHSSA	Contract Work Hours and Safety Standards Act
DBA	Davis-Bacon Act
DFWA	Drug-Free Workplace Act
EO 11246	Executive Order 11246
EPPA	Employee Polygraph Protection Act
EQPA	Equal Pay Act (amendments to the Fair Labor Standards Act)
ERISA	Employee Retirement Income Security Act
FLSA	Fair Labor Standards Act
FMLA	Family and Medical Leave Act
HIPA	Health Insurance Portability and Accountability Act
IRCA	Immigration Reform and Control Act (amendments to the Immigration and Nationality Act)
LMRDA	Labor–Management Reporting and Disclosure Act
MSHA	Federal Mine Safety and Health Act
MSPA	Migrant and Seasonal Agricultural Worker Protection Act
NLRA	National Labor Relations Act
NLA	Norris-LaGuardia Act
OSHA	Occupational Safety and Health Act
RA	Rehabilitation Act — Section 503
RLA	Railway Labor Act
SCA	Service Contract Act
STAA	Surface Transportation Assistance Act (antiretaliatory provision)
THA	Taft-Hartley Act
Title VII	Title VII of the Civil Rights Act
UC	Unemployment compensation provisions of the Social Security Act
VRR	Veterans' reemployment rights provisions of the Selective Training and Service Act
WHA	Walsh-Healey Act
WARN	Workers Adjustment and Retraining Notification Act

Source: Adapted from General Accounting Office, "Testimony: Rethinking the Federal Role in Worker Protection and Workforce Development," 1995, p. 5.

FIGURE 16.4
After OSHA: Declining Workplace Fatalities, Rising Labor Force

Sources: Bureau of Labor Statistics, Census of Fatal Occupational Injuries.

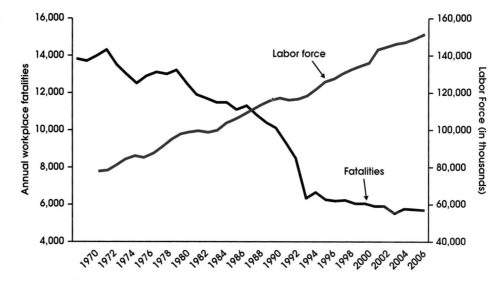

after creation of the Occupational Safety and Health Administration in 1970. Through the 1950s and the 1960s the number of injuries and deaths for workers was slowly rising.[36] As Figure 16.4 shows, since 1970 the number of fatalities has dropped markedly even as the size of the labor force increased by 75 percent.

Federal regulations are only part of the growing web of regulation that fetters employers. State courts and legislatures have created additional rules. Legislatures in many states enact laws that go beyond federal requirements, turning the states into "policy laboratories" that experiment with the cutting edges of employment law.[37] For example, Vermont gives workers 24 hours of leave to attend school functions and go to medical appointments. Louisiana bans employment discrimination based on the sickle cell trait. Each year more states adopt laws banning discrimination based on genetic test results.

Federal laws typically apply only to firms with more than a specified number of employees—often as many as 50 or 100. Many states enact laws that extend the same employee protections to smaller firms. The federal Family and Medical Leave Act, for example, entitles employees of firms with 50 or more workers to take as long as 12 weeks of unpaid leave for family matters such as adoption, illness, or birth. But Oregon lowers the size of the company to 25 workers and Vermont to 15. The federal law requiring 60-day advance notification of plant closings applies only to companies with 100 or more workers, but in Hawaii, employers with 50 or more workers must give 45-day notice. These state actions enhance worker protections.

State courts have added additional worker protections. While federal courts often decide issues of constitutionality and statutory interpretation, they have not expanded workplace rights beyond the statutes. State courts, on the other hand,

---

[36] Charles Noble, *Liberalism at Work: The Rise and Fall of OSHA* (Philadelphia: Temple University Press, 1986), pp. 61–63.

[37] Kirstin Downey Grimsleyz, "Where Congress Fears to Tread," *Washington Post National Weekly Edition,* August 21, 2000, p. 18.

have used doctrines of common law to establish new employee rights in the absence of legislation. A leading example of the power of state courts is how, in recent years, they have revised the doctrine of employment-at-will, shriveling perhaps the most fundamental right of an employer—the right to hire and fire.

Erosion of the Employment-at-Will Doctrine

In the United States, there is a body of common law, or law derived from judicial decisions, that governs employer–employee relationships. In general, this law holds that employers and employees may enter voluntary employment contracts and that either party may freely end these agreements anytime.

While employed, an employee must act "solely and entirely" for the employer's benefit in all work-related matters or be liable for termination and damages. Furthermore, when a conflict arises between an employee and an employer, the employee must conform to the employer's rules. The common law in this area is derived from paternalistic English common law that, in turn, was influenced by Roman law that framed employment in terms of a master–servant relationship. Under this body of law, employers have had extensive rights to restrict employee freedom and arbitrarily fire workers.

Until recently, an extreme interpretation of the employment contract prevailed. It resounds in the oft-quoted statement by a Tennessee judge in 1884: "All may dismiss their employees at will be they many or few, for good cause, for no cause, or even for cause morally wrong without being thereby guilty of legal wrong."[38] *Employment-at-will*, therefore, was traditionally defined as an employment contract that could be ended by either party without notice and for any reason—or for no reason.

employment-at-will
A theory in law that an employment contract can be ended by either the employer or the employee without notice and for any reason.

With the rise of government intervention since the 1930s, absolute discharge rights have been eroded. Federal and state laws take away the right to fire employees for many reasons, including union activity, pregnancy, physical disability, race, sex, national origin, and religious belief. In addition, state courts have introduced three common-law exceptions to firing at will.

First, employees cannot be fired for complying with public policy. In *Petermann v. International Brotherhood of Teamsters*, a supervisor requested a California worker to dissemble in testimony before a legislative committee probing unions.[39] The worker answered questions honestly anyway and was fired. The court struck down the firing, declaring an overriding public interest in ensuring truthful testimony to lawmakers. In another case, *Sabine Pilot Service, Inc. v. Hauck,* a deckhand was ordered to pump oily bilge water into the ocean off the Texas coast. The worker read a placard posted on the ship stating that this was illegal, phoned the Coast Guard for confirmation, and refused to do it any more. He was fired. A Texas court held that an employer could not fire a worker for refusing to disobey the law.[40] This exception to firing at will is recognized in 43 states.[41]

[38] *Payne v. Western & Atlantic R.R. Co.,* 81 Tenn. 507 (1884).

[39] 344 Cal. App. 2d 25 (1959).

[40] 687 S.W.2d 733 (Tex. 1985).

[41] Charles J. Muhl, "The Employment-at-Will Doctrine: Three Major Exceptions," *Monthly Labor Review,* January 2001, p. 4.

A second check on freedom to fire is recognized where an implied contract exists. Daniel Foley worked at Chase Manhattan Bank, and his superiors made oral statements that his job was secure. For seven years he got regular promotions and raises. One day, Foley learned that the FBI was investigating his supervisor for embezzling money at a former job, so he told a vice president. Shortly, the supervisor fired Foley. However, a California court ruled that Foley had been promised permanent employment if his performance was satisfactory. It held, in *Foley v. Interactive Data Corp.,* that the company had violated an implied contract.[42] Following this decision, companies began to avoid hinted promises of job tenure, such as references to "permanent" employees in brochures and handbooks. Courts in 38 states have adopted this exception.

Third, courts in 11 states limit the employer's ability to fire when an implied covenant of good faith is breached. These courts accept that such a covenant is present in all employer–employee relations. The test of any firing is whether it meets an implied duty to be fair and just. Unfair and malicious dismissals fail to pass. In *Cleary v. American Airlines*, for example, the company fired an 18-year employee, giving no reason.[43] Although company policy contained a statement that the firm reserved the right to fire an employee for any reason, a California court was convinced that the purpose of the firing was to avoid paying Cleary a sales commission. It awarded him punitive damages.

Of the three exceptions to employment-at-will, the implied covenant of good faith exception departs most from the vision of unrestricted dismissal. Indeed, it defies the amoral core of employment-at-will. Those courts adopting it reject the old notion of employer–employee equality, believing that employers overmatch the power of employees and have a duty of fairness in actions that determine the livelihoods of their workers. In a case where Kmart Corporation fired an employee to avoid paying retirement benefits, a Nevada court, holding the firing in "bad faith," noted that:

> We have become a nation of employees. We are dependent upon others for our means of livelihood, and most of our people have become completely dependent upon wages. If they lose their jobs they lose every resource except for the relief supplied by the various forms of social security. Such dependence of the mass of the people upon others for all of their income is something new in the world. For our generation, the substance of life is in another man's hands.[44]

Only three states fail to take up any of the new exceptions, and only six states embrace all of them. The great majority have adopted one or two, and the overall trend is toward greater restriction on the employer's ability to fire. One state, Montana, now has a law that permits employers to discharge workers only for "good cause."

Work and Worker Protection in Japan and Europe

The level of benefits and protections in the United States is high but not exceptional. Elsewhere in the developed world, workers benefit from similar and even greater

[42] 205 Cal. App. 3d 344 (1985).
[43] 168 Cal. Reptr. 722 (1980).
[44] Quoted in Muhl, "The Employment-at-Will Doctrine: Three Major Exceptions," p. 10, citing 103 Nev. 49, 732 P.2d 1364 (1987).

welfare guarantees. Cultural differences are evident in how worker rights are supported, but every nation with strong welfare measures has high labor costs.

Japanese workers are among the world's most expensive. In 2005 average hourly compensation for a manufacturing worker in Japan was $21.76, or just $1.89 less than an American counterpart. The fringe benefits of regular employees in the large companies that employ about 40 percent of the Japanese workforce typically include company housing, meals, child education expenses, and paid vacations. Japanese males, called salarymen, enjoy virtual lifetime employment in major firms. Protection against job loss is not, however, extended to women. These benefits are provided voluntarily by paternalistic Japanese companies.

Japanese history and culture in part explain why companies are so generous. Japan's long feudal period shaped cultural patterns based on values derived from the spread of ancient Chinese culture to the islands, including belief in rigid status hierarchies, strong duties of loyalty owed to rulers, emphasis on group rather than individual welfare, and the belief that a paternalistic government should provide for citizen welfare. Later, these values molded the relationship between modern workers and the industrial corporation. Just as the feudal Japanese vassal owed fealty to a lord, workers were asked to give loyalty to their company and place work group interests above individual interests.

Japanese workers are very committed. They work long hours. Most salarymen will not leave the office at night until their boss does and the boss is reluctant to leave before his subordinates. Vacations are often neglected and holiday credits accumulate. Sick leave is seldom used. One explanation for this hard work, in addition to cultural values, is that career ladders in large corporations have frequent small promotion and salary steps.[45]

Japanese salarymen sometimes work themselves to illness or death. A stereotypical case is that of Kazumi Kanaya, a Toyota Motors manager who crumpled at the office one day and lapsed into a permanent coma. Kanaya worked 12 hours a day every day, seldom taking a day off in spite of gout so painful that he needed a cane to walk. Although his wife pushed him to get medical attention, he argued that his work schedule precluded it. Near the end, he was in charge of an important sales office at Toyota, and the company culture dictated extraordinary efforts. He worked seven days a week, often staying until after 10:00 P.M. His collapse was caused by untreated meningitis.[46] Such overwork is not blamed on unreasonable employers. It is regarded as exceptional dedication and as a duty called forth by the beneficence of the company toward its workers.

Estimates of incidents of mortality from working too hard range from 10,000 to 30,000 each year. Such deaths are so common that a word, *karoshi*, appeared in the Japanese language to denote death from the pressure and fatigue of overwork. In 1986 the Japanese worker compensation system recognized karoshi as a syndrome marked by emotional and physical stress accumulated during six months or more

karoshi
A Japanese word denoting death from the stress of overwork.

[45] Toyohiro Kono and Stewart Clegg, *Trends in Japanese Management: Continuing Strengths, Current Problems and Changing Priorities* (New York: Palgrave, 2001), p. 280.
[46] Darius Mehri, "Death by Overwork: Corporate Pressure on Employees Takes a Fatal Toll in Japan," *Multinational Monitor,* June 2000, p. 26.

of overwork. However, few claims are filed and in 2006 only about 150 overwork deaths were compensated.[47]

In the United States, worker rights and social protections were wrested from employers by pugnacious labor unions. In Japan, however, the centuries-old Confucian tradition of harmony in relationships prevented a similar labor–management fissure from developing. Unions never grew strong and unified. Most today are company unions, and they rarely strike or make strident demands. Likewise, no adversarial relationship arises between companies and government agencies enforcing worker rights in Japan as often happens in the United States. Japanese workers have far fewer legislated rights than U.S. and European workers.

social welfare model
A form of industry–labor–government cooperation in which government strongly regulates the labor market to secure expansive rights and high benefits for workers.

Industrialized nations in Europe also give high wages and comprehensive benefits to workers. This is reflected in average hourly compensation for manufacturing workers of $27.52 across Europe, including $39.14 in Norway, $35.47 in Denmark, and $33.00 in Germany.[48] In the aftermath of World War II, these countries and others in Europe adopted, in similar versions, a *social welfare model* of industrial relations to protect their populations against any repeat of the ravages of depression and unemployment experienced in the 1930s. Governments took over major industries and ran them to ensure full employment. Lavish welfare packages for workers were legislated in European parliaments. Socialist parties supported the creation of powerful unions that could negotiate wages and benefits over entire industries.

Forces of global competition now strain this model. European workers are so expensive to employ that job-creating investments go elsewhere. Germany is an example. The benefits and protections achieved by German workers are exceptional. At a Volkswagen plant in Wolfsburg, for example, they get $69 an hour and work 33 hours a week.[49] The average German worker gets 35 vacation days a year, compared with 16 for an American counterpart. Retail stores must close on Sundays to give employees the day off.

Workers are entitled to generous government pensions, health insurance, annual sick leave of up to four weeks, a six-month notice before firing, and unemployment checks of up to 60 percent of their previous wages for up to a year.[50] However, workers must support this generous welfare state. The average payroll tax to support federal programs is 40 percent of a paycheck.[51] By law, worker's spouses who get a job are taxed at an even higher rate. Such measures explain why Germany has one of the highest labor costs in the world and struggles to keep its unemployment rate below 10 percent. Its detailed, voluminous labor laws are enforced by a huge bureaucracy, the Bundesagentur für Arbeit, which at 90,000 employees is the country's largest federal agency.

[47] Leo Lewis, "Downside of Japanese Recovery Is Death by Overwork," *The Times,* May 18, 2007, p. 69.

[48] Bureau of Labor Statistics, "Hourly Compensation Costs for Production Workers in Manufacturing: 33 Countries or Areas, 22 Manufacturing Industries, 1992–2005," December 14, 2007, p. 8, at www.bls.gov.

[49] Stephen Power and Almut Schoenfeld, "VW's 28-Hour Workweek Goes Kaputt in Wolfsburg," *The Wall Street Journal*, February 5, 2007, p. B1.

[50] Mark Landler, "Where to Be Jobless in Europe," *New York Times*, October 9, 2005, p. 4.

[51] "Waiting for a Wunder: A Survey of Germany," *The Economist*, February 11, 2006, p. 8.

Other European nations are equally or more generous. Between 2000 and 2002 a socialist government in France, over the objections of employers, established a 35-hour workweek. Its purpose was to create more jobs by mandating shorter hours, forcing companies to hire more people to maintain output. Like their German counterparts, French employees are expensive. In France, a motorman on the state railway gets $90,000 a year and free health care for working a 25-hour week and can retire at age 50.[52] French employers pay an average of 47 percent of each employee's wages in social taxes, the second-highest total in the world (Belgium is the highest at 55 percent and the rate is only 8 percent in the United States).[53] Laid-off workers must be paid by their former employers for nine months while they seek new jobs.

Such expensive labor discourages investments that create more jobs. Between 2000 and 2007 unemployment averaged 8.5 percent in the European Union, as opposed to 5 percent in the United States.[54] As a result, there are many proposals for reform. European governments have reprivatized industries, but they have had less success rolling back social supports for workers in the face of opposition by large unions and socialist parties. For example, because companies are reluctant to hire expensive workers, youth unemployment in France has recently run as high as 23 percent. To encourage hiring, the government changed the law so employers could fire employees under the age of 26 for any reason during a two-year probationary period. This reform inspired more than 1 million youths and union members to protest in the streets, some violently.[55]

In much of Europe, the result of lavish social safety nets and protections for workers is persistent, high unemployment and slowed economic growth. However, most countries have attempted reforms, with modest success, and more reform is coming.

Labor Regulation in Perspective

core labor standards
A set of four standards to protect basic worker rights on which there is broad international agreement.

The bare minimum for labor market regulation is compliance with four *core labor standards* set forth in international labor conventions. They call on nations at any stage of economic development to (1) eliminate all forced or compulsory labor, (2) abolish child labor, (3) eliminate employment discrimination, and (4) guarantee the right of collective bargaining.[56] These standards are widely accepted, though not yet universally enforced. Most nations move beyond them, providing added rights and protections for workers. Worker welfare is an important goal, but experience teaches that

[52] Sebastian Rotella, "France's Economic Model Showing Signs of Stress," *Los Angeles Times,* October 17, 2005, p. C1.

[53] World Bank, *Doing Business 2007: How to Reform* (Washington, DC: World Bank, 2006), pp. 19, 85.

[54] Bureau of Labor Statistics, "Unemployment Rates in the European Union and Selected Member Countries, Civilian Labor Force Basis (1), Seasonally Adjusted, 1995–2007," and "Unemployment Rates in Ten Countries, Civilian Labor Force Basis, Approximating U.S. Concepts, Seasonally Adjusted, 1995–2007," at www.bls.gov.

[55] Andrew Higgins, "Liberté, Précarité: Labor Law Ignites Anxiety in France," *The Wall Street Journal,* March 29, 2006, p. A1.

[56] See, for example, International Labor Organization and Asian Development Bank, *Core Labor Standards Handbook* (Manila, Philippines: Asian Development Bank, October 2006), pp. 12–15.

FIGURE 16.5
The Trade-off in Labor Regulation

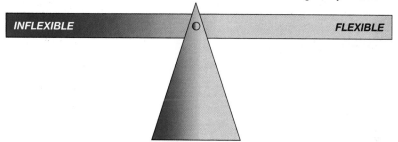

Worker Protection Goals
- Job security
- Collective bargaining
- High wages
- Limited hours
- Pensions
- Health and safety
- Nondiscrimination

Competitiveness Goals
- Create jobs
- Allow restructuring
- Adopt new technology
- Adjust to changing demand
- Encourage investment
- Allow turnover
- Reduce regulatory burden

INFLEXIBLE   FLEXIBLE

striking the right balance between too much and too little is difficult. When Slovakia turned over state-run enterprises to private owners, it tried to protect workers by adopting a labor code that made firings nearly impossible. The new owners promptly moved operations across the border to the Czech Republic.[57]

Workers must be protected, but they are hurt in the end if companies cannot allocate labor to its most productive uses. Firms must respond quickly to changing technologies and competition. If they are slowed by rules that obstruct the reorganization of work they grow less competitive and, in the end, hire fewer workers at lower wages. Research suggests that in heavily regulated labor markets job growth is slower, unemployment lasts longer, companies invest less in new technology, firm size is smaller, and the labor force is less skilled.[58]

Figure 16.5 illustrates trade-offs in labor regulation and suggests that a balance must be struck between worker welfare and competitiveness. When a nation puts more weight on the left side of the balance by protecting workers, its labor market becomes more inflexible. When it moves to the right, by loosening constraints on the treatment of workers, its labor market turns more flexible. *Labor flexibility* is the ability to make quick and smooth shifts of workers into and out of jobs, companies, or industries as business conditions change.

Trade-offs are unavoidable. If a nation tries to create good jobs for low-skilled workers by adopting a high minimum wage, employers will hire fewer unskilled workers, leaving many without any job. As the minimum wage drops, more jobs appear, but the worker's standard of living falls. In some nations expensive safety regulations discourage hiring and leave many workers in the informal sector where they are not protected by any rules at all. If rules are too strict, they will be bypassed,

labor flexibility
The ability to make quick and smooth shifts of workers into and out of jobs, companies, or industries as business conditions change.

---

[57] World Bank, *Doing Business 2007: How to Reform*, p. 20.

[58] See, for example, Rita Almeida, "Enforcement of Regulation, Informal Labor, Firm Size, and Firm Performance," at http://siteresources.worldbank.org; and World Bank, *Doing Business 2004: Understanding Regulation* (New York: Oxford University Press, 2004), chapter 3.

FIGURE 16.6   **Country Scores on the World Bank Rigidity of Employment Index**

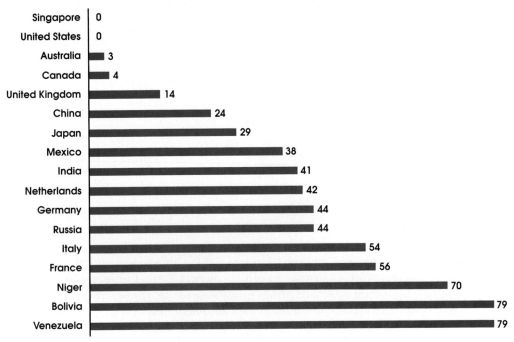

Source: World Bank, *Doing Business 2008* (Washington, DC: World Bank 2007), table 4.3.

frustrating both workers and employers. Similar trade-offs are present with rules that set work hours, limit dismissals, mandate union participation in company decisions, and tax employers for social benefits provided by the government.

Around the world countries differ greatly in labor market flexibility. Figure 16.6 shows how selected countries rank on the World Bank's Rigidity of Employment Index, a composite of 16 measures of labor regulation that runs from 0, highest flexibility, to 100, least flexibility. The figure shows that the United States, with a score of zero, has one of the most flexible labor markets. The social welfare states of Europe are much less flexible. Least flexible of all are some less-developed economies, including Bolivia and Venezuela, which have the most rigid labor codes anywhere.

In theory, greater labor flexibility benefits both workers and employers by making a nation's industries competitive in global markets. "The best protection for workers," argues the World Bank, "is to make labor rules flexible so that the economy will have more jobs . . . and transitions from one job to another are easy."[59] In practice, reforms that increase flexibility often weaken unions and can, at least temporarily, lead to painful adjustments for some workers. In 2006 Australia adopted a reform law advocated by corporations. It eliminated restrictions on overtime and night work and freed companies with fewer than 100 employees from complying

[59] World Bank, *Doing Business 2007: How to Reform*, p. 22.

with unfair dismissal laws. Australian unions held major protests and publicized stories of workers who were unfairly fired. Meanwhile, the World Bank recalculated the country's rigidity of employment index number, lowering it from 17 to 3. An editorial in the pro-labor *Multinational Monitor* argued that "flexibility is all for employers, not workers," calling it "a corporate con" that should be seen "as a fancy and obscure term for enhanced employer power over workers."[60]

CONCLUDING OBSERVATIONS

Six forces changing the workplace—demography, technology, structural shift, competition, reorganization of work, and government regulation—create both uncertainty and opportunity. They vary in the degree to which they can be managed. Demographic and structural changes are uncontrollable but also slow and predictable. Technological change, which can be rapid and unpredictable, is a disruptive force but it has always created new jobs to replace the ones it destroys. Competition and work reorganization are reshaping labor markets everywhere as great corporations rush to automate and send work to low-wage countries. Finally, government regulation, especially policies of labor flexibility, holds the key to global competitiveness. Regulation is an art that needs to be used with judgment.

How will workers fare in the currents of change? Experience suggests that fortunes will be mixed. Yet it is likely that if the global economy runs hot, prosperity will allow more protections and long-run job gains will outweigh short-run dislocations.

[60] "The Labor Flexibility Con," *Multinational Monitor*, July/August 2006, p. 6. See also, Graham Matthews, "No Choices: Australia's Unions Confront Labor Law 'Reform,'" *Multinational Monitor*, July/August 2006.

Workplace Drug Testing

Nancy Clark, a nurse, was working in a Pennsylvania hospital when she admitted alcohol addiction to her supervisor. She agreed to enter a state monitoring program. For five years she averaged three recovery meetings a week instead of the required two. Each weekday morning, with not one missed day, she called in to see if she had to give a random urine sample that day. She paid $120 a month to be in the program. She became a leader in local church activities. All in all, she seemed to be a model recovering alcoholic.

Then the program introduced a new kind of urine test to screen for alcohol use. Prior tests detected alcohol in the urine, but often failed to expose even regular drinking because the body rapidly metabolizes alcohol. Cunning subjects simply abstained for several hours before giving a urine sample. The new test screened for a chemical, ethyl glucuronide (EtG), that the body produces as it metabolizes alcohol. And it could expose minute quantities in urine for up to three days after alcohol use.

Suddenly, Nancy Clark failed an EtG test. The state of Pennsylvania suspended her license and she lost her job. She is fighting the suspension, claiming that she never relapsed and the test result is false. A polygraph test showed her to be truthful.[1]

The EtG test detects infinitesimal levels of ethyl glucuronide, about one molecule in 10 billion urine molecules. Alcohol is present in a variety of consumer

[1] Kevin Helliker, "A Test for Alcohol—and Its Flaws," *The Wall Street Journal*, August 12, 2006, p. A1.

products besides alcoholic beverages, including cosmetics, over-the-counter medications, ice cream, mouthwash, laundry detergents, pesticides, and baked goods. An overripe piece of fruit contains alcohol. Many hospitals use alcohol-based hand sanitizers to kill germs. One brand, Purell, is 62 percent alcohol. Could Nancy Clark have encountered alcohol this way?

Drug testing is a complex issue with scientific, economic, social, ethical, and legal dimensions. It raises many questions. Who should be tested? What tests should be given? How should they be administered? What should be done when tests are positive? A fundamental problem is striking the balance between the right of employers to protect their property and the right of employees to be free of intrusions on their privacy.

THE RISE OF TESTING

Use of alcohol and drugs at work is timeless. Testing by employers began only in the 1980s with the initiative coming mainly from the federal government. In 1981 a plane crashed on the *USS Nimitz* killing 14 sailors. Forensic tests found that several members of the flight deck crew had used marijuana. This led President Ronald Reagan to begin a "zero tolerance" policy for drug abuse in the military and the Navy began the first random drug testing. In 1986 President Reagan issued Executive Order 12564, stating that as the nation's largest employer the federal government "can and should show the way toward achieving drug-free workplaces."[2] The order required all federal agencies to test employees in safety-sensitive positions for illegal drugs.

Drug and alcohol use then blazed forth as a problem in the private sector. Early in 1987 a Conrail engineer who was smoking marijuana with his brakeman rolled a string of locomotives beyond a warning light and into the path of a high-speed train with 500 passengers. The wreck killed 16 and injured 176. In 1989 the tanker *Exxon Valdez* struck a rock formation, spilling millions of gallons of crude oil into Alaska's Prince William Sound. After the accident, its captain was found inebriated. The costs were enormous. Along with the sound's ecosystem, the economic and social fabric of the area collapsed. Exxon spent $3.5 billion to clean up the oil and settle lawsuits and still faces more than $4 billion in punitive damages.

Such accidents led to passage of the Omnibus Transportation Employee Testing Act of 1991, requiring the Department of Transportation to test employees in safety-sensitive transportation jobs for drug and alcohol use. The Department of Energy, the Department of Defense, and the Nuclear Regulatory Commission now require some private-sector drug testing. The Occupational Safety and Health Act encourages drug testing because it requires employers to provide safe working environments. The Drug-Free Workplace Act of 1988 requires federal contractors to maintain drug-free workplaces.

In addition, many states adopted drug-free workplace laws for their employees and encouraged private employers to do the same. Ohio, for example, gives grants of up to $20,000 to companies to defray the expense of setting up testing programs and then gives 20 percent discounts on worker compensation premiums.[3]

Following this combination of conspicuous accidents and new laws there was rapid expansion of drug testing in public and private workplaces. Federal testing programs now cover 1.8 million civilian employees in 120 agencies. They require testing of both job applicants and current employees for marijuana, cocaine, opiates, amphetamines, and phencyclidine.[4] In 1983 only six Fortune 500 firms tested employees for drugs. In a recent survey, 43 percent of workers reported that their companies test job applicants and 30 percent said they were subject to random testing.[5]

---

[3] Dalia Fahmy, "Aiming for a Drug-Free Workplace," *New York Times*, May 10, 2007, p. C6.

[4] Statement by Robert L. Stephenson, Director Division of Workplace Programs, Center for Substance Abuse Prevention, Substance Abuse and Mental Health Services Administration, on Products Used to Thwart Detection in Drug Testing Programs, before the House Transportation and Infrastructure Subcommittee on Highways and Transit, United States House of Representatives, Thursday, November 01, 2007, at www.hhs.gov/asl/testify/2007/10/t20071101b.html. Current federal testing guidelines are in Department of Health and Human Services, "Mandatory Guidelines for Federal Workplace Drug Testing Programs," 69 FR 19644, April 13, 2004.

[5] Sharon L. Larson et al., *Worker Substance Use and Workplace Policies and Programs* (Washington, DC: Department of Health and Human Services, Substance Abuse and Mental Health Services Administration, June 2007), p. 3. Figures are for 2002–2004 combined.

[2] Executive Order 12564, "Drug Free Federal Workplace," 51 FR 32889, September 15, 1986.

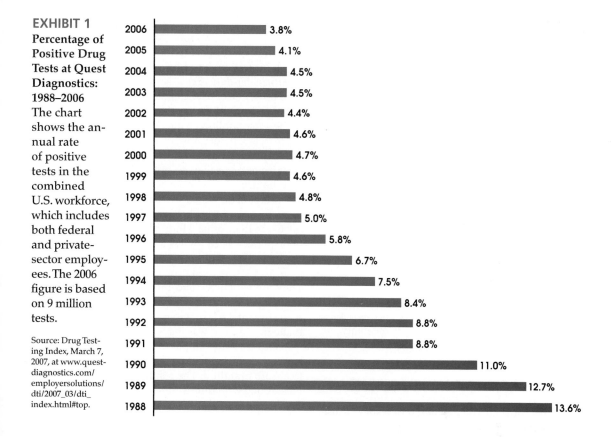

EXHIBIT 1

Percentage of Positive Drug Tests at Quest Diagnostics: 1988–2006

The chart shows the annual rate of positive tests in the combined U.S. workforce, which includes both federal and private-sector employees. The 2006 figure is based on 9 million tests.

Source: Drug Testing Index, March 7, 2007, at www.questdiagnostics.com/employersolutions/dti/2007_03/dti_index.html#top.

Year	Percentage
2006	3.8%
2005	4.1%
2004	4.5%
2003	4.5%
2002	4.4%
2001	4.6%
2000	4.7%
1999	4.6%
1998	4.8%
1997	5.0%
1996	5.8%
1995	6.7%
1994	7.5%
1993	8.4%
1992	8.8%
1991	8.8%
1990	11.0%
1989	12.7%
1988	13.6%

There is no question that testing reduces drug use by workers. Exhibit 1 shows the declining rate of positive drug tests over 18 years at Quest Diagnostics, the largest commercial testing company. Companies that use random testing are often able to reduce their abuse problem to less than 1 percent of employees.[6] However, substance-abusing workers gravitate toward employers who do not test. Percentages in Exhibit 1 are based only on companies and government agencies that do testing. They do not reveal the situation in workplaces with no testing.

COSTS OF DRUG ABUSE

Millions of Americans abuse drugs and alcohol. They also work. In 2005 there were 19.7 million illicit drug users and 15.4 million heavy alcohol users. Of these, about 75 percent of the drug users and 80 percent of the drinkers were employed. Illicit drug users were 8.2 percent of all full-time employees and heavy drinkers were 8.4 percent. An estimated 3.1 percent of drug users took illegal drugs either before coming to work or while on the job. An estimated 7.1 percent of the heavy drinkers drank while working.[7]

The cost is huge. It includes an estimated $82 billion in lost productivity,[8] higher insurance premiums and claims, higher absentee and sick leave rates, loss of trained workers who leave or die, the administrative costs of antidrug programs, extra plant security, property damage, declines in employee morale, lawsuits, and property theft.

[6] Clyde E. Witt, "Just Say Yes: Drug Testing in the Workplace," *Material Handling Management*, May 1, 2006, p. 36.

[7] Department of Labor, Office of the Assistant Secretary for Policy, "General Workplace Impact," at www.dol.gov/asp. Figures are for 2005.

[8] Dalia Fahmy, "Aiming for a Drug-Free Workplace," p. C6.

BEHAVIOR PATTERNS

Substance-abusing employees often exhibit one or both of two pernicious effects. The first, distortion of time, is the inability to follow normal time patterns for job activities. The second, lack of motivation, is seen as lack of interest in normal performance standards. Both effects stem from imbalances of brain chemistry caused by the chronic presence of drugs and their breakdown products in the blood and other tissues.[9]

Trained supervisors suspect drug abuse when employees show patterns of behavior such as these.

- Frequent tardiness and absences from work, especially on Mondays and Fridays and near holidays.
- Poor concentration, forgetfulness, missed deadlines, and frequent mistakes.
- Mood changes, including a wide range of states that interfere with personal relationships such as depression, withdrawal, hostility, and overexcitability.
- Risk taking and frequent accidents.

OBSERVATION AND TESTING

Companies must choose what kind of testing to use. A variety of methods to uncover the presence of illicit drugs and alcohol exist.

Employee searches may include searches of lockers, workstations, desks, and purses. They seldom include body searches, which anger workers and invite litigation. Drug-sniffing dogs are effective in finding contraband. However, searches alone are a limited deterrent. For example, clever employees hide drugs in common areas to conceal individual ownership.

Surveillance can detect drug use, but has many pitfalls. Keeping undercover agents a secret is difficult. Spying undermines employee morale. Surveillance agents can make mistakes, such as striking an employee, that can result in expensive lawsuits.

Written drug tests are available from vendors of employment tests. They ask job applicants and employees if they have used drugs, what kind, and how often. Their validity is suspect, but they are the least expensive type of drug or alcohol test.

Polygraphs, or lie detectors, were used frequently in the past, but no more. Accuracy of the results is open to debate. Furthermore, the Employee Polygraph Protection Act of 1988 severely limits their use.

Fitness-for-duty exams, sometimes called performance tests, detect psychomotor impairment. One test, called "Cleared-for-Duty," evaluates eye movements as the subject follows a moving light for 90 seconds.[10] It predicts whether a worker would pass a roadside sobriety test. Fitness-for-duty exams measure current impairment, but they do not show the cause, which may be drugs, alcohol, emotional upset, or fatigue from staying up with a sick baby all night. Advocates of performance tests believe they are less physically intrusive than other kinds of tests. Critics fear that poor performance invites an employer to ask intrusive questions about private, off-work behavior.

Blood tests are used primarily for alcohol detection. They are expensive and intrusive. Because of legal challenges, employers now rarely use them. Their main advantage is that they can establish the approximate time a drug was ingested.

Saliva tests are simple to administer. A subject is handed a swab and asked to put it in his or her mouth to absorb oral fluid. The results are available in minutes. Along with fitness-for-duty exams, they are useful for finding out if an employee is under the influence at the moment. If a test is positive, a second, more sophisticated test gives confirmation. Oral tests are good at detecting cocaine and heroin, but poor at detecting marijuana, which does not pass into saliva. They cannot detect alcohol. At about $20 the tests are inexpensive.

Hair analysis tests can detect illicit drug use for up to 90 days. If the hair sample is shorter than 1½ inches, the test can detect drug use only for a shorter period. Hair testing is relatively noninvasive and difficult for devious employees to defeat. However, it takes two to three days before drug residues appear in hair so it cannot expose very recent drug use. And it is expensive, costing about $115 to $150 a test.

Urine tests are the most common testing method, constituting about 90 percent of all tests. They are inexpensive and accurate, but difficult to administer and relatively invasive. Before discussing urine testing in more detail, the options about whom to test and the drugs to be tested for should be noted.

[9] William F. Banta and Forest Tennant, Jr., *Complete Handbook for Combating Substance Abuse in the Workplace* (Lexington, MA: Lexington Books, 1989), p. 45.

[10] "AcuNetx Details Recent Developments," *Physician Law Weekly*, January 17, 2007, p. 445.

WHOM TO TEST, WHAT TO TEST FOR

Employers have options about whom to test. Here are some major ones.

- *Those in safety-sensitive positions.* This might refer to national security but can also include those who could jeopardize their own safety or the safety of others, for example, when operating machinery. The Department of Transportation requires employers to conduct random testing of airline pilots, truck drivers, ship captains, bus drivers, railroad engineers, and others for drugs and alcohol. Its rules cover more than 12 million workers. Some companies test people handling substantial amounts of money or carrying firearms.

- *Those who provide cause.* When employees are frequently absent on Mondays or take periodic unexpected absences, have an accident, display erratic behavior, or show inconsistent job performance, they may be singled out for testing.

- *Those who have gone through rehabilitation or treatment programs.* Many employers require random testing of these workers as long as they remain with the company.

- *Those who apply for employment.* Job applicants who abuse drugs or alcohol come to employers who do not test. Therefore, screening applicants is a useful protection.

- *All employees at random.* Random testing makes it harder for employees who use drugs to escape detection, since they cannot arrange to be free of drugs for irregular tests that come by surprise.

Guidelines of the Federal Drug-Free Workplace Program call for chemical analysis of urine to detect marijuana, cocaine, opiates, amphetamines, and phencyclidine (PCP) or their metabolic by-products. Many employers add other drugs to this list, including barbiturates, benzodiazepines, methadone, methaqualone, and propoxyphene. Many also test for alcohol, the most commonly abused drug.

URINE TESTING

The federal government and most corporations outsource urine testing. Job applicants and employees visit certified collection sites to give specimens, which are then sent to laboratories. Both collection sites and laboratories must comply with federal standards. Initial screening is done with an *immunoassay test*. This is an inexpensive screening test costing about $20 to $66. The price varies based on how much business the client gives the testing company. Immunoassay tests can be done quickly with modest laboratory equipment and technician training. However, they are not 100 percent accurate. For example, they can register a false positive if a person has recently used some common over-the-counter drugs.

If an initial screening test is positive, a second and much more accurate test is used to confirm the result. Federal guidelines call for a confirming test with a *mass spectrometer*, a device that converts molecules in the urine to ions that are then exposed to an electronic or magnetic field within a vacuum and sorted by mass and charge. The results are reported on a printed graph. This test is more expensive than the screening test, but it is exceedingly accurate. Mass spectrometers are so sensitive they can detect minute amounts of cocaine and a by-product, cinnomolycocaine, in the urine of people who drink just one cup of coca leaf tea.

Urine tests, correctly administered, are nearly 100 percent accurate. However, clever substance abusers regularly defeat them. To avoid the nuisance and unfairness of many false positives employers set thresholds for target substances so that they will not falsely accuse persons exposed to side-stream smoke from marijuana or who have taken legal medications. Drinking large amounts of water before a test or adding tap water to a vial of urine can dilute concentrations of residues and metabolites below the threshold. Cheaters also use household products to mask telltale traces. Table salt, bleach, laundry soap, ammonia, vinegar, and drain cleaner adulterate samples, preventing accurate analysis. Specially formulated products that claim to cleanse the urine of toxins or adulterate samples are sold by entrepreneurs familiar with lab procedures. They change the formulas as often as every six months to keep ahead of evolving lab detection methods. Internet sites and head shops also market synthetic urine and devices with hidden pouches and tubes so that workers can slip clean urine into test sites.

One government agency counted 400 products designed to defeat not only urine tests, but blood, saliva, and hair tests. It found 79 videos on YouTube demonstrating how to use them.[11] Making and selling products to falsify tests is illegal in some, but not all, states.[12] Since they are manufactured and marketed underground their effectiveness is unproven.

Procedures are set up to prevent subjects from beating the tests, but they are imperfectly followed. A study of collection sites used by trucking companies to meet Department of Transportation testing requirements found protocol flaws at almost every one. Undercover investigators documented repeated errors. They were able to use false identification. They were not always required to empty their pockets and frequently had access to water sources in bathrooms when they filled sample vials. Lack of careful observation by staff at the collection sites allowed them to put adulterants in samples. At some locations bottles of bleach and drain cleaner were left in collection areas.

Even without lapses in test protocol, sample collectors may not directly observe subjects as they urinate. In the privacy of a stall, resourceful workers could use concealed substances to falsify tests. Investigators believed that "a drug user could easily pass a [Department of Transportation] drug test and continue to work in his or her safety-sensitive commercial transportation job—driving children to school or transporting hazardous materials, for example."[13]

A shortcoming of urine testing is that it cannot show whether an employee is "high" or impaired at the moment. Methamphetamine and heroin can be detected 2 to 3 days after last use, cocaine 2 to 10 days, and marijuana up to 2 months after last use. This means that a person who used cocaine at a party Saturday night could be nailed by a drug test Tuesday morning when feeling hale and working productively. Yet if a colleague took LSD that morning and was hallucinating, the LSD would not be detected by the immunoassay test used for screening.

[11] Statement by Robert L. Stephenson before the House Transportation and Infrastructure Subcommittee on Highways and Transit, p. 3.

[12] Government Accountability Office, *Drug Tests: Products to Defraud Drug Use Screening Tests Are Widely Available,* GAO-05-653T, May 17, 2005, pp. 3–4.

[13] Government Accountability Office, *Drug Testing: Undercover Tests Reveal Significant Vulnerabilities in DOT's Drug Testing Program,* GAO-08-225T, November 1, 2007, p. 20.

WHY CORPORATIONS FAVOR DRUG TESTING

There are many persuasive factors. First, testing is needed to comply with certain laws and contract requirements. Federal law mandates testing. Beyond Department of Transportation requirements, the Drug-Free Workplace Act of 1988 requires companies with federal contracts of more than $25,000 to have policies for stopping drug abuse. Many states and some cities have laws permitting drug and alcohol testing, Mississippi requires it of employers in its worker's compensation program and California requires it of state contractors. Thus, complying with the law is a major stimulus for testing.

Second, testing has beneficial results. Insurance costs are reduced, productivity increases, and the company protects itself from an influx of addled workers rejected by companies with testing policies.

Third, in urinalysis corporations have a practical, accurate tool. Although urine tests are intrusive, they are less so than alternatives such as polygraphs, searches through handbags and desks, undercover investigations, entry and exit searches, and video monitoring. When done correctly, urine tests are reliable. Good programs follow the "rule of two," in which two positive results are required before any disciplinary action. The first screening test, if positive, must be followed by a more sophisticated spectrometry test on the same urine sample. Cutoff levels for positive results can be set reasonably high to avoid unnecessarily stigmatizing innocent employees. Using proper procedures for specimen collection and laboratory analysis minimizes errors.

Fourth, there is a social responsibility argument for drug testing. As employers screen applicants and employees, it becomes harder for drug abusers to make a living. Workers have no right to use marijuana, cocaine, hallucinogens, PCP, heroin, and designer drugs on or off the job. Their use is illegal and leads to crime, illness, broken families, and failed health. Thus, business is helping society by combating drug use. From an individual standpoint, if companies can catch a drug-using employee early, it might save his or her career. Many companies refer those who test positive to treatment programs instead of firing them.

WHY SOME EMPLOYEES OPPOSE DRUG TESTING

As compelling as these arguments are, drug testing in general and urine testing in particular raise difficult questions. Critics point out that the right of an employer to protect assets and property must be balanced against the rights of individual employees to a reasonable amount of privacy. Opponents make telling points.

First, urine testing is intrusive and an invasion of privacy. To avoid false positive results based on the presence of other drugs in the urine, employees are asked to list all prescription and over-the-counter drugs taken in the last 30 days. This reveals their private, off-duty lives and medical histories. Also, chemical analysis of urine (or blood) can reveal more than drug use. Employers could test it and discover medical conditions such as pregnancy, clinical depression, diabetes, and epilepsy. For all these reasons, civil libertarians believe urine testing smacks of Big Brother.

Second, urine testing is inherently demeaning whether a sample is taken with visual or passive supervision. An author of a law journal article put it this way: "[I]n our culture the excretory functions are shielded by more or less absolute privacy, so much so that situations in which this privacy is violated are experienced as extremely distressing, as detracting from one's dignity and self-esteem."[14]

Third, the tests are unjust because they violate ethical standards of fair treatment. Testing is a dragnet; many innocent people are tested for each drug user detected. A presumption of guilt is placed on everyone, and workers must prove their innocence. If there is an overriding safety justification to prohibit drug abuse—for example, among bus drivers or railroad engineers—then it may be prudent. But indiscriminate testing of applicants and employees who are not in critical safety-related positions is an evil greater than the drug abuse it seeks to remedy.

Fourth, urine tests are imperfect. Inaccuracies arise from lab errors, mixed-up specimens, and false positives that are due to legal drugs in the body. Errors are too frequent and cast suspicion on employees or cost them their jobs. If scrupulous collection and laboratory procedures are followed, testing is very accurate. But not all companies and labs are that scrupulous.

Fifth, drug tests can be misleading and cannot meet reasonable evidentiary standards. The ACLU says "they cannot detect impairment and, thus, in no way enhance an employer's ability to evaluate or predict job performance."[15] The ACLU adds, "Even a confirmed 'positive' provides no evidence of present intoxication or impairment; it merely indicates that a person may have taken a drug at some time in the past."[16] Emphasis should be placed on employee assistance programs and not drug testing, says the ACLU.

DRUG TESTING AND THE LAW

Legal precedent on drug testing is relatively new and still developing, but the clear trend is to uphold it where it is part of a previously announced and carefully formulated policy. Here is a short briefing on legal issues.

Since the Bill of Rights in the U.S. Constitution restrains only government actions, public employees are protected by these provisions, but employees in private businesses are not. This is a major legal difference; public employers must meet stricter guidelines for testing. The Fourth Amendment guarantees protection to public employees against "unreasonable searches and seizures," and courts have generally held that urine tests and other forms of testing, such as blood tests for HIV antibodies, are a form of search and seizure. The Fifth Amendment guarantees due process of law and protects against self-incrimination. Public employers must guard against firings that violate these rights.[17] Since 1988 federal agencies have adhered to testing guidelines issued by the Department of Health and Human Services. These guidelines attempt to elevate due process for government employees to an impeccable level and stipulate testing procedures in detail.[18]

There have been many court challenges to federal urine-testing programs. Those programs that have reached the Supreme Court have been upheld. Yet the decisions also show that some of the justices had

[14] Charles Fried, "Privacy," *Yale Law Journal*, January 1968, p. 487.

[15] American Civil Liberties Union, *Drug Testing in the Workplace*, Briefing Paper No. 5, undated, p. 1.
[16] Ibid., p.1.
[17] These rights are extended to state, county, and local employees through the Fourteenth Amendment.
[18] National Institute on Drug Abuse, *Comprehensive Procedure for Drug Testing in the Workplace*.

grave misgivings about drug testing and did not believe it is permitted by the Fourth Amendment.

In *Skinner v. Railway Labor Executives' Association,* the Court was asked to decide whether railroad workers could be forced to submit to mandatory urine and blood tests for drugs.[19] In a 7–2 decision, the Court held that the clear public interest in railroad safety outweighed the privacy rights of employees. But in a strong dissent, Justice Thurgood Marshall compared the decision with the Court's 1940s decisions upholding the assignment of Japanese to relocation camps during World War II and noted that "when we allow fundamental freedoms to be sacrificed in the name of real or perceived exigency, we invariably come to regret it."[20]

A second case decided by the Supreme Court, *National Treasury Employees Union v. Von Raab,* involved a urine-testing program of the U.S. Customs Service.[21] It required applicants for positions in which they would interdict drugs, carry guns, or work with classified material of interest to criminals to submit to urine tests. In a 5–4 decision, the majority argued that the national drug crisis, together with the special gravity of drug enforcement work, justified weighing the public interest in drug-free customs agents more heavily than the interference with the agents' civil liberties. Thus, testing was "reasonable" under the Fourth Amendment. Justice Antonin Scalia, writing in dissent, warned that the Court was too cavalier in sacrificing basic constitutional privacy rights. He quoted these famous lines written by Justice Louis Brandeis in 1928: "The greatest dangers to liberty lurk in insidious encroachment by men of zeal, well-meaning but without understanding."[22]

In 1995 the Court decided a third case and remained divided about the issue. In a 6–3 decision in *Vernonia School District v. Acton,* it upheld the requirement that all student athletes in an Oregon high school submit to urine testing. The majority in *Vernonia* was willing to balance the privacy right of individuals against the legitimate needs of government agencies, in this case, the "substantial need of teachers and administrators for freedom to maintain order in the schools."[23] Writing in dissent, however, Justice Sandra Day O'Connor argued that random drug testing such as that of the high school athletes intruded on privacy where individual grounds for suspicion of wrongdoing did not exist. The Founding Fathers, she stated, clearly intended the Fourth Amendment to prohibit general searches of the population such as this and, therefore, such random drug tests were unconstitutional.

Even though the Court approved testing in all three situations that came before it, the cases revealed an undercurrent of discomfort and opposition. Nevertheless, they established a settled precedent for testing. Since 1995 the Court has decided only one other drug-testing case. In *Board of Education v. Earls* in 2002 it expanded its *Vernonia* ruling to allow random testing of Oklahoma high school students in extracurricular activities such as clubs, bands, and choirs.[24]

In the end, private employers are generally free to test, provided they have a well-written company policy conforming to federal regulations and the laws of states and cities in which they operate. However, there is such a tangle of rules on testing and privacy that compliance is complicated for corporations with geographically dispersed locations. Many states, for example, Georgia, Illinois, and Ohio, encourage drug testing. Iowa, Rhode Island, and Vermont prohibit random testing. Vermont and Minnesota forbid companies to fire workers the first time they are caught.[25] And in Vermont if employees are tested owners and managers must also submit to tests.

Questions

1. Should urine testing, or other types of testing, be permitted among public and private employees to prevent drug and alcohol abuse? Why or why not?

2. If you believe that urine testing in some form might be acceptable, write down the outlines of a sound testing program. Who should be tested?

[19] 57 LW 4324 (1989).

[20] At 57 LW 4324 (1989); the relocation camp cases are *Hirabayashi v. United States,* 320 U.S. 81 (1943); and *Korematsu v. United States,* 320 U.S. 323 U.S. 214 (1944).

[21] 49 U.S. 656 (1989).

[22] In *Olmstead v. United States,* 227 U.S. 479 (1928).

[23] *Vernonia School District v. Acton,* 115 S.Ct. 2391 (1995).

[24] 122 S.Ct. 2559 (2002). In one other case the Court prohibited a company from discharging a truck driver who twice tested positive for marijuana, but did so in a narrow ruling about the validity of an arbitration agreement. The justices did not reach the conduct of the drug-testing program in their decision. See *Eastern Associated Coal Corp. v. United Mine Workers of America,* 531 U.S. 57 (2000).

[25] Dalia Fahmy, "Aiming for a Drug-Free Workplace," p. C6.

Employees? Job applicants? Should there be random testing? Should people in all job categories be tested?

3. As a manager with responsibility for conducting a testing program, what would be your response to the following situations?

   a. An employee who tests positive for marijuana on a Monday morning but has a spotless 10-year work record.

   b. An airline pilot who refuses a random test.

   c. A job applicant who tests positive for cocaine use.

   d. An employee who tests positive for cocaine use.

   e. An employee who comes to your office the night before an announced urinalysis and admits that he regularly uses a hallucinogenic drug off the job.

   f. A productive worker who gives no outward sign of drug use but who is named as a drug abuser at work in an anonymous tip.

   g. An employee involved in a serious work accident who refuses to take an immunoassay test based on her belief in the right to privacy.

   h. The recommendation of the union that management be given the same tests as workers.

Chapter Seventeen

Civil Rights in the Workplace

The Employment Non-Discrimination Act of 2007

Anyone, even a noncitizen, who works in a corporation on American soil, or any American who works for an American corporation on foreign soil, is broadly protected against workplace discrimination. It is unlawful for a company to discriminate against or allow harassment of workers based on race, color, national origin, sex, or religion. These protections apply to all individuals of any race or ethnicity including whites, blacks, Asians, Native Hawaiians, Pacific Islanders, Latinos, Arabs, and those of two or more races. Moreover, employees cannot be subject to bias or retaliation because of marriage to or association with individuals of any race, nationality, ethnicity, or religious background. Women are protected against unfair job actions based on pregnancy. Employers are required to make reasonable accommodations for physical and mental disability. Persons over 40 years old are shielded from age bias.

The consequences of these legal protections are remarkable, even amazing. A citizen of China or Mexico working in a New York garment factory, with or without work authorization, is protected against ethnic jokes and teasing about accents and English fluency. A deaf person or a person blind in one eye must be given a chance to work as a truck driver. A person cannot be fired simply for being diagnosed with paranoid schizophrenia. A woman who has just delivered a baby cannot be told to take time off from work. Overall, the laws prohibit *almost* all kinds of workplace discrimination based on personal attributes.

Brooke Waits was hired by Cellular Sales of Texas. Her job was to track inventory in stores throughout Texas and Oklahoma. To reduce theft of valuable electronic equipment she set up a new inventory control system. She worked hard. In her words, "I went to work to be a rock star."[1] The job was part of her. She put in hours each morning before the office day. Her supervisor regularly praised her. She was also uneasy.

Men in the office joked about gay and lesbian people. A co-worker said her walk was masculine. Away from work, Waits was open about being a lesbian, but she

---

[1] Testimony of Brooke Waits, Hearing on "The Employment Non-Discrimination Act of 2007 (H.R. 2015)," U. S. House of Representatives, Health, Employment, Labor, and Pensions Subcommittee, 110th Congress, 1st Session, September 5, 2007, CQ Transcriptions, p. 31

Congressman Barney Frank (D-Mass.), chairman of the House Financial Services Committee and lead sponsor of the Employee Non-Discrimination Act of 2007. Source: © AP Photo/Susan Walsh.

sensed that revealing herself would estrange her from the others. She wavered, then hesitation turned to hiding and she was caught in a game of daily deceptions. She avoided stories about her personal life. She avoided pronouns. When the others talked about activities with their husbands and wives, she called her girlfriend her "better half."

Almost a year passed. One morning, her supervisor picked up Waits's cell phone and saw a picture of her kissing her girlfriend. That day the atmosphere froze.

I dreaded coming to work the next day and, to my dismay, my manager was already there three hours earlier than she usually arrived. As I passed her office door, she called me in, stood up, and without the slightest hesitation, told me that she was going to have to let me go. When I asked why, she told me that they needed someone more dependable in the position. . . . When I defended myself, she simply repeated, "I'm sorry. We just need to let you go."[2]

Testifying before Congress, Waits said "I do not believe that anyone should be exposed to a workplace where they have to worry about being who they are costing them their livelihood."[3]

In fact, the federal laws that forbid so many acts of bias lay useless and silent in the face of Waits's humiliation. Nineteen states protect gay, lesbian, and bisexual workers against workplace discrimination for sexual orientation. Eleven states also protect transsexual individuals against gender identification bias. Waits's misfortune was to work in Texas, a state offering no protection to lesbian workers.

Since the 1970s, supporters in Congress have tried to pass a law protecting victims of bias such as Waits. The latest effort is a bill entitled the Employment Non-Discrimination Act of 2007. This bill would make it illegal to refuse to hire, to fire, or to take any adverse job action against anyone "because of such individual's actual or perceived sexual orientation."[4] According to its lead sponsor, Rep. Barney Frank (D-Mass.), "[t]he principle of the bill is very simple . . . you should be judged by your job performance only."[5]

To mollify opponents the bill does not include rights for transsexuals, a compromise that cost it the support of gay groups. It prohibits affirmative action for gays,

[2] Ibid., p. 32.

[3] Ibid., p. 32.

[4] H.R. 3685, "Employment Non-Discrimination Act of 2007," 110th Congress 1st Session, sec. 4 (a)(1)(2).

[5] Testimony of Congressman Barney Frank, Hearing on "The Employment Non-Discrimination Act of 2007 (H.R. 2015)," U. S. House of Representatives, Health, Employment, Labor, and Pensions Subcommittee, 110th Congress, 1st Session, September 5, 2007, CQ Transcriptions, p. 21.

lesbians, and bisexuals. It exempts the armed forces and religious organizations from compliance. It allows employers to enforce dress codes and grooming standards. And companies are not required to give medical benefits to unmarried partners. Nonetheless, resistence was massive.

Opponents raised many arguments. Some said its wording was too vague. How could employers refute accusations of unfair treatment based on a person's "perceived" sexual orientation? Others believed it would require Christian or Muslim bookstores to violate their religious beliefs by hiring gays. Also, the government would have to decide which employers were exempt from the law for religious reasons, breaching the Constitution's requirement for separation of church and state. Proponents of traditional marriage and family values thought that activist judges might later use the bill's wording to redefine the institution of marriage.

Beneath these cultivated objections were others more basic. Some Christians, believing that homosexuality affronts God, opposed creating a new protected class and then assisting its members to promote a sinful lifestyle. A letter on the bill printed in the *Washington Post* said, "engaging in homosexual practices is not only a choice but a vice."[6] To such critics Representative Frank had this reply:

> People have their rights to their opinions. People have a right to be racist. People have a right to dislike certain religions. What you don't have a right to do . . . is, in your economic interactions with people, be prejudiced against them on that.[7]

Late in 2007 the Employment Non-Discrimination Act passed in the House of Representatives by a 235–184 roll call vote. It is not yet law and faces an uphill battle for approval in the Senate and a presidential signature. However, it was the first time in more than three decades of trying that such a measure passed in either chamber of Congress.

This story is part of the long history of struggle for civil rights protections in the workplace. In this chapter we discuss this history, explaining the evolution of laws and methods used to fight employment discrimination over the years. We then explain how these laws function today. The chapter also explores the topics of women in management and diversity in organizations.

A SHORT HISTORY OF WORKPLACE CIVIL RIGHTS

The American nation was founded on noble ideals of justice, liberty, and human rights. Yet for most of the country's history, business practice openly diverged from these ideals and discrimination on the basis of race, color, sex, national origin, religion, and other grounds was common and widespread. Significant protection from employment discrimination has existed for little more than 40 years of the 230 years since independence.

---

[6] Chris Stevenson, "A Matter of Belief," *Washington Post,* May 8, 2007, p. 24.

[7] Testimony of Congressman Barney Frank, Hearing on "The Employment Non-Discrimination Act of 2007 (H.R. 2015)," p. 22.

The Colonial Era

Employment discrimination in America can be dated from 1619 when European slave traders first brought African natives to the New Worlds' shores. When the colonies declared their independence from England in 1776, there were 500,000 slaves, mostly in the southern colonies. In the northern colonies, there was considerable anguish about slavery because it clashed with the ideals of those who had recently escaped from religious persecution and government tyranny in Europe. The Declaration of Independence expresses the founders' ideals.

> We hold these truths to be self-evident, that all men are created equal, that they are endowed by their Creator with certain unalienable Rights, that among these are Life, Liberty, and the pursuit of Happiness.

natural rights
Rights to which all human beings are entitled. Governments cannot grant them or take them away.

civil rights
Rights bestowed by governments on their citizens.

These "unalienable" rights are *natural rights,* that is, rights to which a person is entitled simply because he or she is human and that cannot be taken away by government. Natural rights exist on a higher plane than *civil rights,* which are rights bestowed by governments on their citizens. Natural rights are a standard against which the actions of governments and employers must be measured and can be found wanting.

This statement in the Declaration distills a body of doctrine known as the American Creed, which historian Arthur M. Schlesinger, Jr., defines as incorporating "the ideals of the essential dignity and equality of all human beings, of inalienable rights to freedom, justice, and opportunity."[8] In the language of the time, the phrase "all men" was a reference to free, white males. Thomas Jefferson included in the original draft a strong statement condemning slavery as a "cruel war against human nature itself, violating its most sacred rights of life & liberty."[9] But this offended slave owners and had to be deleted to preserve unity in the coming revolution against England.

Despite the limited inclusiveness of the Declaration's language, its statement of natural rights, notes Schlesinger, challenged whites to live up to its ideals and, if anything, "meant even more to blacks than to whites, since it was the great means of pleading their unfulfilled rights."[10]

The U.S. Constitution reflected this bifurcated view of civil rights. When it was ratified in 1789, it sanctioned the practice of slavery in five clauses. Article 1, section 2, for example, counted slaves as three-fifths of a person for purposes of apportioning seats in the House of Representatives.[11] Yet the Bill of Rights contained ringing phrases protecting a wide range of fundamental rights.

Civil War and Reconstruction

Beginning at about the time the Constitution was ratified, an antislavery movement originated in a small sect within the Church of England. This movement

---

[8] Arthur M. Schlesinger, Jr., *The Disuniting of America* (New York: Norton, 1992), p. 27.

[9] Edward S. Corwin and J. W. Peltason, *Understanding the Constitution,* 4th ed. (New York: Holt, Rinehart and Winston, 1967), p. 4.

[10] Schlesinger, *The Disuniting of America,* p. 39.

[11] See also Article I, section 9, limiting taxation of slaves; Article I, section 9, prohibiting Congress from ending the slave trade before 1808; Article IV, section 2, requiring return of fugitive slaves to owners; and Article V, prohibiting amendment of Article 1, section 9, before 1808.

grew rapidly, and in a century's time, its moral arguments largely swept slavery from the world stage.[12] In the United States, the issue of slavery rose to a crisis in the Civil War fought between 1861 and 1865. In 1863 President Abraham Lincoln issued the Emancipation Proclamation that freed an estimated 4 million slaves. Following the war, Congress passed three constitutional amendments designed to protect the rights of former slaves especially in the South.

- The *Thirteenth Amendment* in 1865 abolished slavery.
- The *Fourteenth Amendment* in 1868 was intended to prevent southern states from passing discriminatory laws. It reads, in part: "No State shall make or enforce any law which shall abridge the privileges or immunities of citizens of the United States; nor shall any State deprive any person of life, liberty, or property, without due process of law; nor deny to any person within its jurisdiction the equal protection of the laws."
- The *Fifteenth Amendment* in 1870 prohibited race discrimination in voting.

These amendments were supplemented by a series of civil rights acts passed by Congress, most notably one in 1866 to protect blacks against employment discrimination and another in 1875 to protect them from discrimination in transportation and accommodations. Altogether, these amendments and statutes created a formidable legal machinery to implement the rights to which blacks were entitled under the American Creed. If this machinery had been allowed to function, a century of painful employment discrimination against blacks and other groups might have been prevented. But it was not to be.

There was tremendous resistance to the new laws in the South, but at first much enforcement was possible because of the continuing presence of the Union Army, an occupying force that kept a temporary lid on southern resistance to black rights, which was formidable and violent. Because the troops protected voting rights, for example, 16 blacks were elected to Congress and about 600 to state legislatures. But the presidential election of 1876 ended the era of southern rehabilitation.

In the race, the Republican candidate Rutherford B. Hayes lost the popular vote to his Democratic opponent Samuel J. Tilden, but the vote was close in the electoral college and returns from three southern states were contested. Hayes agreed to an "understanding" that if the electoral votes from these southern states were cast for him, he would withdraw the remaining federal troops. History records that Hayes won the election and the soldiers left. An important check on racism went with them.

racism
The belief that each race has distinctive cultural characteristics and that one's own race is superior to other races.

White racism reasserted itself in the South in many ways. *Racism,* defined broadly, is the belief that each race has distinctive cultural characteristics and that one's own race is superior to other races. It persists when myths and stereotypes about inferiorities are expressed in institutions of education, government, religion, and business. Racism leads to social discrimination, or the apportioning of resources based on group membership rather than individual merit. It insulates the power of a privileged group—for example, white Americans—from challenge.

---

[12] Thomas Sowell, *Race and Culture: A World View* (New York: Basic Books, 1994), pp. 210–14.

Jim Crow laws
Measures enacted in the South from 1877 to the 1950s legalizing segregation in public places, buses, trains, restaurants, schools, and businesses. The term *Jim Crow*, taken from a song in a nineteenth-century minstrel show, came to stand for the practice of discrimination or segregation.

Southern states adopted segregationist statutes called *Jim Crow laws.* These laws institutionalized the idea that whites were superior to blacks by creating segregated schools, restrooms, and water fountains; in literacy tests that disenfranchised blacks; in restrictive covenants, or deeds, that prevented whites from selling property to blacks in certain neighborhoods; and in discriminatory hiring that kept blacks in menial occupations.

Other Groups Face Employment Discrimination

Other groups in the United States faced extensive and institutionalized employment discrimination as well. Native Americans were widely treated as an inferior race. In the nineteenth century, the federal government spent uncounted millions of dollars to destroy their societies and segregate them on reservations.

A large population of roughly 90,000 Hispanics suddenly became residents of United States territory when Mexico ceded Texas in 1845 and other tracts of southwestern land in 1848. Soon these Mexican Americans were victims of a range of discriminatory actions. They were legally stripped of extensive land holdings and exploited in a labor market where discrimination confined them to lesser occupations. They suffered great violence; more Hispanics were killed in the Southwest between 1850 and 1930 than blacks were lynched in the South.[13]

Beginning in 1851, Chinese laborers began to enter the country. They settled in western states and many owned placer mines. In 1863 several thousand began working on the construction of the Central Pacific Railroad. Some started businesses such as laundries and restaurants. By the 1870s there were 100,000 Chinese in western states; in California there were 75,000, about 10 percent of the population. Although they faced prejudice, their presence was tolerated until economic depression set in and the white majority felt they were competing for jobs and customers. Then economic and racial discrimination began in earnest.

Special taxes passed by state legislatures were used to confiscate their mines and ruin their commercial businesses. Some towns ordered all Chinese to leave. San Francisco passed an ordinance requiring city licenses for all laundries, then denied licenses to Chinese laundries.[14] The California state constitution, adopted in 1874, prohibited Chinese from voting and made it illegal for corporations to hire them. Finally, Congress banned the immigration of Chinese laborers in 1882.

The earliest Japanese immigrants found similar inhospitality. By 1880 there were only 124 Japanese in the United States, but their numbers increased rapidly as employers sought replacements for the cheap Chinese labor supply that had been cut off. By 1890 about 100,000 Japanese immigrants had arrived, most in California. Japanese laborers were typically paid 7 to 10 cents an hour less than whites. Like the Chinese, they ultimately threatened white labor and soon faced violent prejudice in cities. They turned to agricultural work in California's fertile inland valleys, but powerful white farmers resented their presence. California

---

[13] John P. Fernandez, *Managing a Diverse Work Force* (Lexington, MA: Lexington Books, 1991), p. 165.

[14] In *Yick Wo v. Hopkins,* 118 U.S. 356 (1886), the Supreme Court struck down the ordinance as a violation of the equal protection clause of the Fourteenth Amendment. Had the Court followed up on this precedent, it could have struck down Jim Crow laws in the South.

passed laws prohibiting Japanese land ownership, and in 1924 Congress banned further Japanese immigration.

Although employers wanted to utilize Japanese labor, social attitudes frequently made this impossible. For example, in 1925 Pacific Spruce Corporation brought 35 Japanese to the small lumber town of Toledo, Oregon, to work in its sawmill. A mob of 500 men, women, and children swarmed the mill and the company had to load the Japanese on trucks that took them to Portland.[15]

As this brief sketch on nineteenth- and early twentieth-century employment discrimination shows, neither the American Creed nor the fine legal mechanism put in place after the Civil War worked to stop racism. Why not? The former was eclipsed by broad public prejudice. The latter had to be enforced against the grain of southern racism and was, in any case, soon dismantled by the Supreme Court in two landmark cases—the *Civil Rights Cases* and *Plessy v. Ferguson*.

The *Civil Rights Cases*

The Civil Rights Act of 1875 was passed to prevent racial discrimination in "inns, public conveyances on land or water, theaters and other places of public amusement."[16] The law set a fine of up to $1,000 or imprisonment up to one year for violation. Still, there was widespread discrimination against freed slaves by business and soon a series of cases reached the Supreme Court. Two cases involved inns in Kansas and Missouri that had refused rooms to blacks. And in one case, the Memphis and Charleston Railroad Company in Tennessee had refused to allow a woman "of African descent" to ride in the ladies' car of a train. These cases were consolidated into one opinion by the Supreme Court in 1883 and called the *Civil Rights Cases.*[17]

The Civil Rights Act of 1875 was based on the Fourteenth Amendment, and in the Court's opinion, Justice Joseph P. Bradley focused on its wording. Because the amendment reads that "no state" shall discriminate, Bradley held that it did not prohibit what he referred to as a "private wrong." If race discrimination was not supported by state laws, it was a private matter between companies and their customers or employees and the Fourteenth Amendment did not prohibit it. For this reason, Congress lacked the authority to regulate race bias among private parties; therefore, the Civil Rights Act of 1875 was unconstitutional.

The *Civil Rights Cases* so narrowed the meaning of the Fourteenth Amendment that it became irrelevant to a broad range of economic and social bias. Congress and the courts could no longer use it to strike down much of the most brazen race discrimination. It was not necessarily a wrong decision; in fact, many constitutional scholars believe that the Court made a reasonable decision for that day given the clear reference to state action in the Fourteenth Amendment. But in dissent, Justice John Marshall Harlan argued that "the substance and spirit of the recent Amendments of the Constitution have been sacrificed by a subtle and ingenious verbal criticism."[18]

---

[15] Herman Feldman, *Racial Factors in American Industry* (New York: Harper, 1931), pp. 89–90.

[16] An Act to Protect all Citizens in their Civil and Legal Rights, 18 Stat. At L., 335, section 1.

[17] 109 U.S. 835 (1883).

[18] 109 U.S. 844.

Plessy v. Ferguson

Southern states had passed so-called Jim Crow laws that sanctioned race segregation. If the Fourteenth Amendment could not prohibit private individuals from depriving each other of basic rights, did it not still clearly prohibit states from enacting laws that abused the former slaves? The answer was no.

One such law was the Separate Car Act passed by Louisiana in 1890. This statute required all Louisiana railroads to "provide equal but separate accommodations for the white, and colored races, by providing two or more passenger coaches for each passenger train, or by dividing the passenger coaches by a partition so as to secure separate accommodations."[19] This law, like other Jim Crow laws, was based on the *police power* of the state, a presumed power inherent in the sovereignty of every government, to protect citizens from nuisances and dangers that might harm public safety, health, and morals.

police power
An inherent power of state governments to regulate economic and social relationships for the welfare of all citizens.

On June 7, 1892, Homer Plessy, who was seven-eighths Caucasian and one-eighth African, bought a first-class ticket on the East Louisiana railroad to travel from New Orleans to Covington. Boarding the train, he took a vacant seat in the white coach. He was asked by the conductor to move to the "nonwhite" coach. Plessy refused and was taken to a New Orleans jail.

Plessy brought suit, claiming he was entitled to "equal protection of the laws" as stated in the Fourteenth Amendment. In 1896, in *Plessy v. Ferguson*, the Supreme Court disagreed, holding that as long as separate accommodations for blacks were equal to those of whites, blacks were not deprived of any rights. Justice Henry B. Brown, writing for the majority, argued that laws requiring race separation "do not necessarily imply the inferiority of either race to the other" and were a valid exercise of police power by state legislatures because they enhanced "comfort, and the preservation of the public peace and good order."[20]

separate but equal
The belief, prevalent in the South, that racially segregated facilities were not inherently unequal.

This ruling completed the destruction of the Fourteenth Amendment as a mechanism to guarantee civil rights. The Court's interpretation legitimized the *separate but equal* doctrine, or the belief that segregation of races was not inherently unequal. The separate but equal doctrine, which became the foundation for legal apartheid in the South, stood for 58 years until reversed in 1954 by the Court in its famous school desegregation case, *Brown v. Board of Education*.[21]

Plessy is in retrospect notorious and some say one of the worst decisions ever made by the Court because of its consequences. The justices missed an opportunity to read the Fourteenth Amendment in a way that would protect blacks from the schemes of white racists. They must have thought that a decision striking down Jim Crow would be unpopular and widely disobeyed and may have sought to prevent the Court from being weakened by disregard for its opinions. As in the *Civil Rights Cases*, Justice Harlan was a lone dissenter who kept the light of the American Creed flickering by lecturing the majority. He wrote:

---

[19] Act 111 of 1890, quoted in Richard Epstein, *Forbidden Grounds: The Case Against Employment Discrimination Laws* (Cambridge, MA: Harvard University Press, 1992), pp. 99–100.

[20] *Plessy v. Ferguson,* 163 U.S. 540 (1896), at 544 and 550. John H. Ferguson was the judge who denied Plessy's constitutional claim in the New Orleans Criminal Court.

[21] 347 U.S. 483.

After the *Plessy* decision, Jim Crow laws became entrenched throughout the South. The water fountains in this photograph taken in North Carolina in 1950 symbolize a much larger universe of discrimination, including employment discrimination. Source: © Elliott Erwitt/ Magnum Photos.

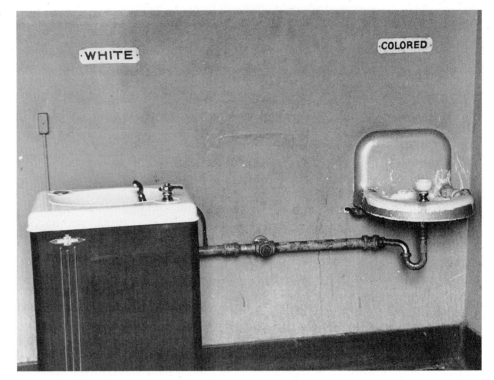

Our Constitution is color-blind and neither knows nor tolerates classes among citizens. In respect of civil rights, all citizens are equal before the law. The humblest is the peer of the most powerful. The law regards man as man, and takes no account of his . . . color when his civil rights as guaranteed by the supreme law of the land are involved.[22]

Long Years of Discrimination

The nation's civil rights laws were now hopelessly crippled. Southern legislatures were emboldened by *Plessy.* Now needing no special moral justification, Jim Crow laws spread. Black workers faced the most blatant discrimination. They were not allowed to hold jobs such as streetcar conductor or cashier where they would have any authority over whites. Labor unions refused to admit blacks, and a few that did limited them to low-pay occupations. The Brotherhood of Locomotive Engineers, for example, barred blacks from being locomotive engineers. In South Carolina, a law prohibited blacks and whites from working in the same room or using the same plant entrances in the cotton textile industry. Such customs spread to the North. A study of economic opportunity for blacks in Buffalo, New York, told the following tale.

[22] 163 U.S. 537.

A [black] man tells of being made a moulder in a foundry, later to be replaced by a white worker and reduced to the grade of moulder's helper, and finally dismissed when he made a complaint. Another man was given a chance to try out for a skilled-labor job in a stone-cutting concern and, having made good, was given the position temporarily, losing it, however, a few days later when the superintendent "came down through the shop" and, seeing him so employed, told the foreman to put another man on the work.[23]

THE CIVIL RIGHTS ACT OF 1964

This kind of open discrimination continued in the South. A study of 175 firms in New Orleans in 1943 found that almost all of them hired blacks, but then 93 percent segregated their workforces and 79 percent segregated job categories.[24] In the North, many companies refused to hire blacks at all. A study of 14 plants in Chicago in 1952, for example, found that 10 of them, or 71 percent, excluded blacks.[25]

In the late 1950s and early 1960s, a new civil rights movement arose. Under the leadership of blacks such as Martin Luther King, this movement was nonviolent and again focused on making America live up to the ideals in the American Creed. "The American people are infected with racism—that is the peril," said King. "Paradoxically, they are also infected with democratic ideals—that is the hope."[26]

The pressures of this movement led to many social reforms, among them passage of the Civil Rights Act of 1964, which is today the cornerstone of the structure of laws and regulations enforcing equal opportunity. Its Title VII prohibits discrimination in any aspect of employment. It reads, in part:

It shall be an unlawful employment practice for an employer:

1. To fail or refuse to hire or to discharge any individual, or otherwise to discriminate against any individual with respect to his compensation, terms, conditions, or privileges of employment, because of such individual's race, color, religion, sex, or national origin.

2. To limit or classify his employees or applicants for employment in any way which would deprive any individual of employment opportunities or otherwise adversely affect his status as an employee, because of such individual's race, color, religion, sex, or national origin. [Section 703(a)]

Title VII also created the Equal Employment Opportunity Commission (EEOC), an independent regulatory commission, to enforce its provisions. All companies with 15 or more employees fall under the jurisdiction of Title VII

---

[23] Quoted in Feldman, *Racial Factors in American Industry,* p. 36.

[24] Logan Wilson and Harlan Gilmore, "White Employers and Negro Workers," *American Sociological Review,* December 1943, pp. 698–700.

[25] Lewis M. Killian, "The Effects of Southern White Workers on Race Relations in Northern Plants," *American Sociological Review,* June 1952, p. 329.

[26] Quoted in Lani Guinier, "[E]racing Democracy: The Voting Rights Cases," *Harvard Law Review,* November 1994, p. 109.

and must report annually to the EEOC the number of minorities and women in various job categories.[27] If bias exists, employees can file charges with the EEOC. The agency then attempts to resolve charges through conciliation or voluntary settlement, but if that fails, it can sue in a federal court. In 2006 there were 56,155 charges filed under Title VII leading to the recovery of $127 million in monetary benefits to workers suffering discrimination.[28]

The overall purpose of Title VII, which is clear from the congressional debates that preceded its passage, was to remove discriminatory barriers to hiring and advancement and create a level playing field for all workers. As originally enacted, it did not require that minority workers be hired simply because they belonged to protected groups. It did not require employers to redress racially imbalanced workforces or change established seniority systems. No whites would be fired, lose their seniority, or be adversely affected. Simply put, from the day the law went into effect, all bias was to end. Job decisions could be made only on merit.

Disparate Treatment and Disparate Impact

disparate treatment
Unequal treatment of employees based on race, color, religion, sex, or national origin.

Title VII made overt, blatant employment discrimination illegal. It enforced a legal theory of *disparate treatment.* Disparate treatment exists if an employer gives less favorable treatment to employees because of their race, color, religion, sex, or national origin. For example, a retail store that refused to promote black warehouse workers to sales positions, preferring white salespeople to serve predominantly white customers, would be guilty of this kind of discrimination. Disparate treatment violates the plain meaning of Title VII.

Although the intention of Title VII was to create a level playing field by prohibiting all discrimination, given the entrenched prejudices of employers in the 1960s, expecting that bigotry would instantly vanish was futile. The statute would need to evolve, and it did.

disparate impact
Discrimination caused by policies that apply to everyone and seem neutral but have the effect of disadvantaging a protected group. Such policies are illegal unless strongly job related and indispensable to conduct of the business.

When Title VII went into effect, employers could no longer engage in outwardly visible displays of discrimination. "Whites only" signs came down from windows and discrimination went underground where it was disguised but just as invidious. Instead of openly revealing prejudicial motives, employers hid them. Minority job applicants were simply rejected without comment or were found less qualified in some way. Or employers introduced job requirements that appeared merit based but were in fact pretexts for discrimination. Female applicants had to meet height, weight, and strength requirements that favored men. Southern blacks were given tests that favored better-educated whites.

This kind of discrimination was hard to eradicate under the existing provisions of Title VII because employers would not admit a discriminatory motive and claimed that their job criteria were neutral and merit based. The flaw in Title VII was that it contained no weapon to fight *disparate impact.* Disparate impact exists

[27] A 1972 law extended coverage of Title VII to federal, state, and local government employees, so today Title VII covers most workers. Workers at firms with fewer than 15 employees can sue under state and local civil rights laws or, for race discrimination, may seek remedy under the Civil Rights Act of 1866.

[28] U.S. Equal Employment Opportunity Commission, "Title VII of the Civil Rights Act of 1964 Charges: FY 1997–FY 2006," www.eeoc.gov/stats/vii.html, accessed January 2008.

where an employment policy is apparently neutral in its impact on all employees but, in fact, is not job related and prevents individuals in protected categories from being hired or from advancing.

To combat disparate impact, the court initially used a case-by-case judicial test for discrimination. First, the applicant or employee made a charge alleging bias. Then the employer had to set forth a reason why it was a *business necessity* to engage in the practice. Then the burden of proof shifted back to the employee to prove that the employer's reason was phony, which was frequently hard to do.[29] This back-and-forth dance in which each individual case was separately considered was awkward and time consuming for the courts and placed the difficult burden of proving the employer's secret motive on individual plaintiffs who lacked the legal resources of corporations. Some other way to fight hidden employer racism was needed. The Supreme Court would create it.

business necessity
A legal defense a company can use to fight a disparate impact charge. It must show the practice in question was job-related and essential. To rebut this defense, a plaintiff can show that another practice was equally good and less discriminatory.

The *Griggs* Case

The Duke Power Company had a steam-generating plant in Draper, North Carolina, where workers had been segregated by race for many years. The plant was organized into five divisions and blacks had been allowed to work only in the lowest-paying labor department. The company had openly discriminated, but when Title VII took effect, it rescinded its race-based policies and opened all jobs to blacks.

However, it also instituted a new policy that required a high school diploma to move up from the labor department to the coal-handling, operations, maintenance, or laboratory and test departments. Now black workers could apply for formerly white-only jobs that paid more only if they had finished high school. Alternatively, they could take an intelligence test and a mechanical aptitude test, and if they scored at the same level as the average high school graduate, they could meet the high school diploma requirement. But since blacks in the area were less educated, this requirement frustrated their ambitions. Instead of rejecting blacks for being black, Duke Power now rejected them for lacking education. Black workers filed suit, alleging that the education and testing requirements had the effect of screening them out and were, in any case, unrelated to the ability, for example, to shovel coal in the coal-handling department.

80 percent rule
A statistical test for disparate impact. The test is failed when, for example, blacks or women are selected at a rate less than 80 percent of the rate at which white male applicants are selected.

In *Griggs v. Duke Power,* decided in 1971, the Supreme Court held that diploma requirements and tests that screened out blacks or other protected classes were illegal unless employers could show that they were related to job performance or justified by business necessity. They were unlawful even if no discrimination was intended. The *Griggs* decision, and the legal theory of disparate impact it created, was necessary for Title VII to work. If employers had been permitted to use sinuous evasions and substitute proxies for direct racial bias, Title VII would have been ineffective.

In 1978 the EEOC defined illegal disparate impact for employers with a guideline known as the *80 percent rule.*

---

[29] This sequence was set up in *McDonnell Douglas v. Green,* 411 U.S. 792 (1973).

> A selection rate for any race, sex, or ethnic group which is less than four-fifths (4/5) or (eighty percent) of the rate for the group with the highest rate will generally be regarded . . . as evidence of adverse impact.[30]

This rule is met if a company has hired minorities at the rate of at least 80 percent of the rate at which it hires from the demographic group (usually white males) that provides most of its employees. If, for example, it hires 20 percent of all white applicants, it must then hire at least 16 percent (80 percent of 20 percent) of black applicants. If it hires less than 16 percent of blacks, this statistical evidence defines unlawful disparate impact. The company is now on the defensive. It must show that the employment practices it uses, such as tests or applicant screening criteria, are a business necessity. Using the business necessity defense, it must prove that the test or practice is "essential," and the need for it is "compelling."[31]

With the addition of the theory of disparate impact by the judiciary, Title VII had evolved beyond its original meaning and could be used to strike down a broader range of discrimination. Title VII finally gave blacks and others a potent legal mechanism to get the civil rights on the job that Congress had tried to give them during the Reconstruction era. In a sense, broken promises were repaired. There is little in Title VII that would have been needed if, a century before, the Supreme Court had given good-faith construction to Reconstruction-era laws.

AFFIRMATIVE ACTION

affirmative action
Policies that seek out, encourage, and sometimes give preferential treatment to employees in groups protected by Title VII.

Affirmative action is a phrase describing a range of policies to seek out, encourage, and sometimes give preferential treatment to employees in the groups protected by Title VII. The broad use of affirmative action was rejected when Title VII was drafted and its congressional backers assured the business community that blacks and others would not have to be given preference over whites. Title VII was designed as a stop sign to end discrimination, not as a green light to engineer racially balanced workforces. Yet no sooner had President Lyndon Johnson signed it than civil rights groups argued that its philosophy of equal opportunity was too weak; blacks and others were so disadvantaged by past rejection that they lacked the seniority and credentials of whites. They could not compete equally in a merit system, and preferential treatment was needed to get justice.

Executive Order 11246

The origin of most affirmative action in corporations is Executive Order 11246, issued by President Johnson in 1965.[32] It requires all companies with federal contracts of $50,000 or more and 50 or more employees, criteria that include almost every Fortune 500 company, to have a written affirmative action plan. This plan must specify the policies, procedures, and actions being used to recruit minorities

[30] U.S. Department of Labor, "Uniform Guidelines on Employee Selection Procedures," 43 FR 38295, August 25, 1978.

[31] Epstein, *Forbidden Grounds,* p. 212, citing *Williams v. Colorado Springs School District,* 641 F2d 835 (1981), at 842.

[32] "Equal Employment Opportunity," 30 FR 12319, September 24, 1954.

and women and eliminate discrimination. Each company must analyze its workforce at every major location, using census data to learn if it is employing minorities and women in the same proportion as they are present in the area labor force. American Indians, Alaskan Natives, Asians, Native Hawaiians or other Pacific Islanders, Blacks, Hispanics, or persons of "two or more races" are considered minorities. The analysis focuses on employment in 10 major job categories to see if, in each one, minorities and women are employed in the same proportion as they are present in the local.[33] If protected groups are underrepresented, companies must set up goals and timetables for hiring, retention, and promotion.

Executive Order 11246 is enforced by the Office of Federal Contract Compliance Programs (OFCCP), an agency in the Department of Labor. The OFCCP, with one exception, does not establish rigid hiring goals for companies. The exception is in the construction industry, where, since 1980 it has mandated a goal of 6.9 percent females. In other industries, however, it requires contractors to set hiring goals and make a "good faith" effort to achieve them. Adequate progress is usually defined as a final hiring total that meets the 80 percent rule.

The OFCCP conducts zealous compliance reviews. It uses statistical tools to target companies where discrimination is most likely to be uncovered. Then, teams descend on a facility, looking around, interviewing employees and managers, and auditing all kinds of records from interview notes to payroll slips. It is common for inspections to uncover violations. Between 2005 and 2007 more than 11 percent resulted in fines or other actions.[34]

THE SUPREME COURT CHANGES TITLE VII

From the beginning, affirmative action was controversial. Philosophically, it challenges the American Creed in several ways. It affronts the ideal of equality of opportunity by substituting equality of result. It affronts the ideal of achievement based on merit. And it affronts the ideal of individual rights before the law by substituting group preferences. When affirmative action first started, it posed more than a philosophical problem. Corporations were alarmed by its potential for generating lawsuits. If they failed to remedy race and sex imbalances in their workforces, they faced penalties for violating federal laws. If they used affirmative action to increase numbers of minorities and women, they feared reverse discrimination suits by white males.

Affirmative action was bound to provoke fierce legal challenges, and the Supreme Court used these attacks to read revolutionary changes into Title VII. The first high-profile challenge came from Allan Bakke, a white male denied admission to the medical school at the University of California at Davis. In the entering class, 16 places out of 100 had been reserved for minority students. Bakke argued

---

[33] These job categories are executives and senior officials, first- and mid-level managers, professionals, technicians, sales workers, administrative support workers, craft workers, operatives, laborers and helpers, and service workers.

[34] U.S. Department of Labor, "OFCCP Once Again Produces Record Financial Remedies for a Record Number of Workers in FY 07," http://www.dol.gov/esa/ofccp/enforc07.pdf, January 8, 2008.

that he was better qualified than some minority students admitted and he had suffered illegal race discrimination under Title VII because he was white. In *Regents of the University of California v. Bakke,* the Supreme Court ruled in his favor.[30] In a muddled, divided, and verbose opinion, the justices forbade strict quotas. Yet they also held that race and ethnicity could be one factor considered in admissions. This kept affirmative action alive but failed to resolve the dilemma of employers, who still feared reverse discrimination lawsuits.

Then a second case arose from a Kaiser Aluminum and Chemical Corporation plant in Louisiana. The Kaiser plant was near New Orleans where 39 percent of the workforce was black. Few blacks worked at the plant before passage of Title VII, and even with it, by 1974, only 18 percent of the plant's workers were black. Moreover, less than 2 percent of skilled crafts workers were black because Kaiser required previous craft experience and seniority. Blacks had little of either since crafts unions excluded them. Kaiser had federal contracts and, to comply with Executive Order 11246, it adopted an affirmative action plan in 1974 to raise percentages of black workers. One goal was to bring blacks into skilled craft positions, so the plan reserved 50 percent of crafts-training openings for them. This was clearly a race-based quota.

In 1974 a white laboratory analyst, Brian Weber, who had worked for Kaiser for 10 years, applied for a crafts-training program that would place him in a more skilled job and raise his yearly pay from $17,000 to $25,000. To pick the trainees, Kaiser set up dual seniority ladders—one for blacks and another for whites. Names were picked alternately in descending order from the top of each ladder, starting with the black ladder, until positions were filled, with the result that seven blacks and six whites were chosen. Weber was too low on the white ladder and was not selected, whereas two blacks with less seniority than Weber were chosen (see Figure 17.1). This was a classic case of reverse discrimination.

Weber brought suit, claiming that the selection procedure violated the clear language in Title VII that prohibited making employment decisions based on race. He claimed that his Fourteenth Amendment rights to equal treatment under the law had been abridged. Justice William J. Brennan delivered the opinion of the Court in 1979 in *United Steelworkers of America v. Weber,* ruling that Kaiser's affirmative action plan embodied the "spirit of the law," which was to overcome the effects of past discrimination against blacks.[35]

The Court also established important criteria for judging the legality of affirmative action programs that it would frequently use in later years. First, a plan must be designed to break down historic patterns of race or sex discrimination. Second, the plan must not create an absolute bar to the advance of white employees. In the *Weber* case, for example, some whites were still admitted to training. Third, the plan must not require the discharge of white workers. And finally, the plan should be flexible and temporary, so that it ends when goals are met.

The *Weber* decision added an entirely new meaning to Title VII. Henceforth, Title VII no longer stood guard over a neutral playing field. Now, it permitted the very thing that its drafters assured the nation it would not do—it permitted

[35] 443 U.S. 193.

FIGURE 17.1

Selection of Crafts Trainees at Kaiser

Kaiser and the union selected 13 crafts trainees. All candidates met minimum qualifications, but black applicants number 6 and 7 had less seniority than whites number 7, 8, and 9.

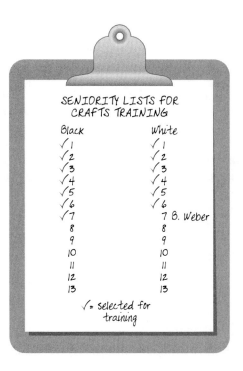

SENIORITY LISTS FOR
CRAFTS TRAINING

Black	White
✓ 1	✓ 1
✓ 2	✓ 2
✓ 3	✓ 3
✓ 4	✓ 4
✓ 5	✓ 5
✓ 6	✓ 6
✓ 7	7 B. Weber
8	8
9	9
10	10
11	11
12	12
13	13

✓ = selected for
training

race-conscious preferential treatment for members of protected groups. A strong dissent in *Weber* by future Chief Justice William Rehnquist attacked the majority for adding this meaning to Title VII in contravention of its language, which clearly forbade *all* race discrimination, including that against whites. He referred to Brennan's opinion as "a tour de force reminiscent not of jurists such as Hale, Holmes, or Hughes, but of escape artists such as Houdini."[36]

The *Weber* case squarely raised the issue of reverse discrimination and confirmed that affirmative action plans were legal even if they adversely affected whites. After *Weber*, companies no longer worried about lawsuits by angry white workers. Affirmative action spread.

In the 1980s a liberal majority on the Court established generous boundaries for affirmative action. It held, for example, that seniority systems could not be overridden during layoffs to retain recently hired blacks.[37] In several other cases, it confirmed its decision in *Weber* by upholding affirmative action plans with hiring quotas for blacks.[38] It also upheld affirmative action to increase percentages of women in skilled crafts work.[39] Throughout, a minority of conservative justices vigorously dissented from the opinions of the liberal majority.

[36] 47 LW 4859.

[37] *Firefighters Local Union No. 178 v. Stotts,* 467 U.S. 561 (1984); and *Wygant v. Jackson Board of Education,* 476 U.S. 267 (1986).

[38] *Local 28 v. EEOC,* 478 U.S. 421 (1986); *Local No. 93 v. City of Cleveland,* 478 U.S. 450 (1986); and *United States v. Paradise,* 480 U.S. 149 (1987).

[39] *Johnson v. Transportation Agency, Santa Clara County, California,* 480 U.S. 616 (1987).

By 1988, however, President Ronald Reagan, an opponent of affirmative action, had appointed three new associate justices and a conservative bloc of five justices emerged to dominate the liberals on affirmative action cases.[40] As cases came before the court, this group began to whittle away at race-conscious preferences, making affirmative action more difficult to carry out.[41] Its advocates were infuriated, and soon Congress sent a clear message to the Supreme Court by passing the Civil Rights Act of 1991. This statute reversed a number of decisions to restore broad grounds for affirmative action.

Since 1991, through retirements and appointments, a majority of justices have in one case or another declared an inclination to end affirmative action on constitutional grounds. Yet the policy has survived every major test. In *Adarand v. Peña*, a cobbled-together majority saved the day by setting up a "strict scrutiny" test that made affirmative action programs more difficult to justify.[42] In *Grutter v. Bollinger*, a bare five-to-four majority agreed that the University of Michigan Law School's affirmative action program met this test.[43] The future is uncertain, but if the conservative bloc retains its strength, new tests of affirmative action are likely to result in a decision that racial preferences in employment violate the equal protection clause in the Fourteenth Amendment.

The Affirmative Action Debate

The legal debate about affirmative action parallels a broader debate in society. This debate revolves around three basic ethical considerations.

First, there are *utilitarian* considerations. Utilitarian ethics require calculations about the overall benefit to society, as opposed to the costs, of affirmative action. Advocates argue that preferential treatment policies benefit everyone by making fuller use of talent. Critics say that affirmative action has been ineffective or that its meager benefits are outweighed by the fairness problems it raises.

Research on the effectiveness of affirmative action is mixed, but suggests that, overall, it works. A recent study of 708 companies over 31 years found that after they set up a plan "the odds for [the presence of] white men in management decline by 8 percent; the odds for white women rise by 9 percent; and the odds for black men rise by 4 percent."[44] However, such statistics cannot resolve the utilitarian argument about whether affirmative action, on the whole, is a net benefit or cost to society.

---

[40] This bloc included Chief Justice William Rehnquist and Justices Anthony Kennedy, Sandra Day O'Connor, Antonin Scalia, and Byron White. These five joined to dominate the liberals William Brennan, Thurgood Marshall, Harry Blackmun, and John Paul Stevens. Kennedy, O'Connor, and Scalia were Reagan appointees.

[41] See, for example, *City of Richmond v. J. A. Croson Co.*, 488 U.S. 469 (1989) requiring more proof of past discrimination to justify affirmative action; *Wards Cove Packing Company v. Atonio*, 490 U.S. 642 (1989), raising the burden of proof in disparate impact cases; and *Martin v. Wilks*, 490 U.S. 755 (1989), allowing whites passed over for promotion because of affirmative action to bring discrimination lawsuits.

[42] 132 L.Ed.2d 158 (1995).

[43] 59 U.S. 306 (2003).

[44] Alexandra Kalev, Frank Dobbin, and Erin Kelly, "Best Practices or Best Guesses? Assessing the Efficacy of Corporate Affirmative Action and Diversity Policies," *American Sociological Review*, August 2006, p. 604.

Second, ethical theories of *justice* raise questions about the ultimate fairness of affirmative action. Norms of distributive justice require that fair criteria be used to assign benefits and burdens. It is widely believed that economic rewards should be distributed based on merit, not on race, ethnicity, or sex. On the other hand, norms of compensatory justice require that payment be made to compensate for past wrongs. Past and current discrimination has handicapped women and minorities and placed them at a disadvantage. Thus, discrimination in favor of blacks may be justified to compensate for past deprivation. In 1963 President Lyndon Johnson used a colorful analogy to make this point.

> Imagine a 100-yard dash in which one of the two runners has his legs shackled together. He has progressed 10 yards, while the unshackled runner has gone 50 yards. How do they rectify the situation? Do they merely remove the shackles and allow the race to proceed? Then they could say that "equal opportunity" now prevailed. But one of the runners would still be 40 yards ahead of the other. Would it not be the better part of justice to allow the previously shackled runner to make up the 40-yard gap or to start the race all over again?[45]

With affirmative action, however, the penalty for past injustices falls on the current generation of white males—the least racist of any generation. Retributive justice requires that punishment be proportional to the crime committed. By what proof can it be shown that this generation should inherit the guilt of past generations?

And third, affirmative action may be debated in light of ethical theories of *rights*. Advocates of affirmative action argue that it is appropriate to mint a new civil right for women and minorities, the right to preferential treatment, and to exercise it until equality prevails. Discrimination in favor of protected groups is benevolent of intention, unlike the evil race discrimination of bigoted whites in the past. Opponents of the right to preferences argue that they destroy a more fundamental right—the right of all individuals to equal treatment before the law. Affirmative action can result in rewards being taken from persons who did not discriminate and given to persons who suffered no discrimination.

There is no easy solution to the contradictory appeals of these ethical arguments. Affirmative action is a complex policy with important benefits but also highly visible drawbacks. As a broad public policy, it is aging and past its prime. Four forces work to weaken it. First, the Supreme Court has narrowed its use. Second, the value of nondiscrimination, though hardly universal, is much stronger in the United States today than it was in the 1960s, when racism was more widespread. The nation now is closer to the ideal of equal treatment. Third, expansion of affirmative action weakened its justification. Originally, it was introduced to overcome lingering effects of black slavery and Jim Crow laws in the South. Strong action was warranted to roll back this heritage of bigotry. Then over the years the same preferences were extended to other groups, including Hispanics, Asians, Pacific Islanders, women, and recent immigrants who fall into protected categories. There has been less consensus about their need for this advantage. Fourth, racial categories are

---

[45] Quoted in Robert A. Fullinwider, *The Reverse Discrimination Controversy: A Moral and Legal Analysis* (Totowa, NJ: Rowman and Littlefield, 1980), p. 95.

Other Important Antidiscrimination Laws

The problem of employment discrimination is so longstanding that, in addition to Title VII and Executive Order 11246, other laws have been passed to protect women, ethnic or racial minorities, and other disadvantaged groups. They include these:

The Civil Rights Act of 1866 was passed after the Civil War to protect the employment rights of freed slaves. It provides that "All persons . . . shall have the same right . . . to make and enforce contracts . . . as is enjoyed by white citizens."[46] Soon after its passage, the Supreme Court narrowly interpreted it to protect only state employees. For nearly a century, it remained on the books as an emasculated law, but it was revived by the Supreme Court in 1968.[47] Since then, it has been widely used by civil rights attorneys. It protects millions of workers in firms with fewer than 15 employees against all forms of racial discrimination in employment. Employees of such small firms are not covered by Title VII.

The Equal Pay Act of 1963 prohibits pay differentials between male and female employees with equal or substantially equal duties in similar working conditions. It does not override pay differences that stem from legitimate seniority or merit systems. It also covers nonwage benefits.

The Age Discrimination in Employment Act of 1967 protects people over age 40. After that age, it is illegal to discriminate against people in hiring and job decisions because of their age. As the workforce ages, age bias complaints are the fastest-growing kind of discrimination charge. The average charge is brought by a white male in his fifties, dismissed in corporate downsizing, believing that his age was the reason.

The Vietnam-Era Veterans' Readjustment Assistance Act of 1974 requires federal contractors to develop affirmative action programs for hiring, training, and promoting Vietnam veterans.

The Pregnancy Discrimination Act of 1978 prohibits employment discrimination based on pregnancy, childbirth, or related medical conditions. If a woman can still work, she cannot be made to resign or go on leave for any pregnancy-related condition, including having an abortion. If she is temporarily unable to perform her regular duties, the employer must try modifying her work assignments or grant leave with or without pay.

The Americans with Disabilities Act of 1990 protects workers with mental and physical impairments, including those with AIDS, from job discrimination and extends to them the protections granted to women and ethnic, racial, and religious minorities in Title VII. In interviews, employers can ask only about the ability to do specific work. Companies must make "reasonable accommodations" for disabled workers, including, for instance, provision of devices that allow deaf workers to communicate visually and readers for blind workers. Companies must also try to accommodate persons with mental illnesses such as major depression, manic depression, schizophrenia, and obsessive compulsive disorder. For example, employers have been required to install soundproofing and set up room dividers for schizophrenic workers who have heightened sensitivity to noise and visual distractions. However, companies are not required to make accommodations imposing an "undue burden" on the business.

The Civil Rights Act of 1991 amended five existing civil rights laws, including Title VII, to extend their coverage in employment situations. It encouraged civil rights lawsuits. Employment discrimination cases are difficult to prove, the evidence is often subtle or hidden in voluminous employment records, and they can take years to complete. Before this law, awards were limited to reinstatement and back pay, so the attorneys trying them were, in effect, low-paid crusaders. Then the 1991 act allowed plaintiffs in class actions to recover up to $300,000 in pain and suffering in addition to back pay and permitted their lawyers to bill losing corporations double their fees. The

---

[46] 42 U.S.C. Sec. 1981, rev. stat. 1977.

[47] *Jones v. Alfred H. Mayer Co.*, 392 U.S. 409 (1968). This case overturned the *Civil Rights Cases.*

result was that more lawyers were attracted to bias litigation.

No federal law provides specific protection against employment discrimination based on sexual orientation or gender identity. Gay, lesbian, bisexual, and transsexual victims can bring charges only if they are framed as sex discrimination under Title VII, although courts have broadened the meaning of sex discrimination to include same-sex sexual harassment and harassment based on variation-from-sex stereotypes.[48] Also, 20 states and 276 cities have laws and ordinances banning sexual orientation discrimination.

[48] See *Oncale v. Sundowner Offshore Services,* 523 U.S. 75 (1998); and *Nichols v. Azteca Restaurant Enterprises,* 256 F.3d 864 (9th Cir. 2001).

blurring. In the 2000 census 7 million Americans declined to check boxes for traditional racial categories, preferring to be classified as multiracial.[49] Cumulatively, these changes weaken the case for affirmative action, and long ago public opinion began to move against it. Still, much life remains in this old warhorse of a policy, and it may continue to exist in some form for many years.

WOMEN AT WORK

Around the world more women work than ever before. Everywhere they face age-old social and cultural barriers to economic equality with men. These barriers are wearing away now, but very slowly. In 2006 there were 1.2 billion women in a global labor force of 3.1 billion, making them 40 percent of the total.

Women participate in paid labor at a lower rate than men. Worldwide only 52 percent of females are economically active outside the home compared with 79 percent of males.[50] Participation rates are high in the least-developed countries, where poverty pushes women into paid labor. The rate averages 67 percent in East Asia and 63 percent in Sub-Saharan Africa. China has the highest participation rate at 76 percent. At 70 percent the United States has the second-highest participation rate among high-income nations, just behind Finland with 73 percent.

The lowest rates are in the Middle East and North Africa, where patriarchal religious and cultural values discourage women from work outside the home. In Oman, only 23 percent of women enter the labor force, in Egypt, only 22 percent. Saudi Arabia, at 15 percent, has the world's lowest participation rate.[51] The main barrier in that country is a requirement, enforced by moral police, that women be segregated from men to prevent immorality. The Prophet Muhammad is quoted as saying, "A man is not secluded with a woman but that Satan is the third party to

[49] Peter H. Schuck, "Affirmative Action: Don't Mend It or End It—Bend It," *Brookings Review,* Winter 2002, pp. 25–26.

[50] International Labor Office, *Global Employment Trends for Women: Brief,* March 2007, Annex, tables 1 and 2.

[51] All participation rate figures in this section are from World Bank, *World Development Indicators* 2006 (Washington, DC: World Bank, 2006), table 2.2.

them."[52] Therefore, employers must set up separate work sections for women. At a three-story mall in Riyadh women can work as salespersons, but they are confined to a single floor. Such segregation discourages employers. When women cannot drive or work with an unrelated man typical work processes become inefficient.

Wherever women work, they are more likely than men to be in low-productivity jobs in agriculture and services. They are paid lower wages and salaries than men. They are more likely to be unemployed. And they are less likely to reach positions of high power, status, and income. This lack of advancement is caused by cultural values that give higher status to men leading to women getting less education, having fewer legal rights, and facing unequal distribution of household responsibilities.

Gender Attitudes at Work

Historically, men and women have been socialized into distinct sex roles. Men were traditionally thought to be aggressive, forceful, logical, self-reliant, and dominant; they were the warriors and breadwinners. Women were objects of sexual desire and homemakers; they were expected to be kind, helpful, submissive, and emotional. For centuries, these stereotypes dominated perceptions of the sexes, and they were carried from family and social life into the workplace, where they defined male–female relationships.

In the 1960s, however, a worldwide woman's movement came to challenge male domination in Eastern and Western cultures. Arguing that women could do men's jobs, its advocates attacked cultural impediments to equality. Because of this movement, two competing values began to clash in the workplace. The new feminist perspective asserted that women were entitled to the same jobs, rights, ambitions, and status achievements as men. Yet deeply rooted traditional sex-role stereotypes remained. Men who believed in them still thought that women were too emotional to manage well; lacked ambition, logic, and toughness; and could not sustain career drive because of family obligations.

In the United States, as in much of the developed West, belief in the traditional stereotype has eroded but proves durable. Back in 1965 only 27 percent of male executives in a survey said they "would feel comfortable working for a woman." Twenty years later, when the survey was given again, that number rose to 47 percent. And given again after the passage of still another 20 years, it rose further to 71 percent.[53] Thus, after 40 years of effort by women to advance into upper management almost a third of the men still felt uncomfortable with women's leadership skills.

A recent survey by Catalyst, a group devoted to advancing female leadership, illustrates the survival of traditional attitudes in both men and women. The responses of 296 male and female corporate leaders, one-third CEOs, revealed that both sexes believed male leaders had "take charge" traits such as delegating

---

[52] Quoted in Karen Elliot House, "For Saudi Women, a Whiff of Change," *The Wall Street Journal,* April 7–8, 2007, p. A1.

[53] Dawn S. Carlson, K. Michele Kacmar, and Dwayne Whitten, "What Men Think They Know about Executive Women," *Harvard Business Review,* September 2006, p. 28.

responsibility to others and problem solving. Both sexes saw female leaders as having more "caretaker traits," including giving praise, helping others develop skills, and building relationships. Catalyst concluded that gender stereotypes were "alive and well" in both sexes, "posing an invisible and powerful threat to women leaders."[54]

Subtle Discrimination

Most workplace cultures are based on masculine values. Women can find them difficult to navigate.

For one thing, women are expected by men to behave according to traditional male–female stereotypes. Men holding these attitudes are conditioned to see women in the role of mothers, lovers, wives, or daughters; they consciously or unconsciously expect female co-workers to act similarly. One female executive explains how this hurts women.

> Women are put into this box that I call the four-H club. What the four H's stand for are a woman's hair, hips, hemline and husband. You rarely hear any of these for a man—and of course you expect his wife to be at home. So there's this unconscious bias stuff swimming around when people are interviewing others for positions. They think to themselves, "This woman can't travel," or "She's married, she's not going to want to move," or "She's going to want to have kids so therefore won't be available."[55]

In blue-collar settings, sexism can be blatant; some men openly express biases. In managerial settings, it is usually subtle, even unintentional. Men may assume that women are secretaries. One woman CEO, invited to participate in a meeting of business and political leaders in Washington, describes being repeatedly skipped over in the conversation because the men at the table assumed she was an office assistant. "Happens all the time," she noted.[56] Men also discount or ignore women's ideas. They make women uncomfortable with locker-room humor and macho behavior.

> EMC Corp. sells software and data-storage devices to corporations. It favors former college athletes in its sales force, but there are some women. Sales tactics are very aggressive. Over time a sales culture of masculine recreation and entertainment with clients formed. The entertainment included frequent trips to strip clubs. One sales-woman was told that she was unqualified to work on a big Motorola account because she did not "smoke, drink, swear, hunt, fish and tolerate strip clubs."[57]

Masculine cultures underlie many kinds of differential treatment. The norms in these cultures are not openly sexist. They can be nearly invisible, manifest only as

---

[54] Catalyst, *Women "Take Care," Men "Take Charge:" Stereotyping of U.S. Business Leaders Exposed* (New York: Catalyst, 2005), pp. 1,4.

[55] Michele Coleman Mayes, senior vice president, Allstate Corp., quoted in "View From the Top," *The Wall Street Journal*, November 19, 2007, p. R6.

[56] Carol Bartz, former CEO of Autodesk, quoted in Julie Creswell, "How Suite It Isn't: A Dearth of Female Bosses," *New York Times,* December 17, 2006, sec. 3, p. 1.

[57] Quoted in William M. Bulkeley, "A Data-Storage Titan Confronts Bias Claims," *The Wall Street Journal,"* September 12, 2007, p. A16.

practices that seem innocent and neutral. The problems they cause are often unintended. One main problem for women is the traditional career path. According to one study, men typically rise in a smooth trajectory, making especially rapid progress in their thirties. Their success in achieving promotions and their rising status is based on uninterrupted hard work. Women, on the other hand, achieve progress roughly equal to men's in their twenties, but face a deepening conflict in their thirties, the peak childbearing and child-rearing years. Many women interrupt their progress with leaves that average 1.2 years.[58] Throughout their careers, women also do more of the routine work in the home than men.

> At one global retailing corporation dominated by men in the top ranks, a culture of flexible operations had grown up in which meetings were held spontaneously, often at the last minute or late in the day. Important decisions were made quickly. This culture was highly successful because it facilitated fast reaction to markets and minimized bureaucratic inefficiencies. However, it was hard on women who bore heavier responsibilities for households and children than the men. When a meeting suddenly was called for the early evening, some women could not stay, and if they did not they were left out of critical decisions and unable to defend their turf.[59]

Success in this kind of workaholic atmosphere requires the ambitious to invest in face time at the office and not divide their time with responsibilities away from work. Thus, flexible working hours and telecommuting, often introduced for working mothers, may fail because they violate workplace norms. At one firm telecommuting was "jokingly referred to as 'Mom's day off,'" and women were afraid to sign up for fear of career damage.[60]

Deborah Tannen studied the linguistic styles of men and women at work.[61] According to Tannen, men and women learn different ways of speaking in childhood. Boys are taught by peers and cultural cues to use words in ways that build status and emphasize power over other boys. Girls, on the other hand, use language to build rapport and empathy with their playmates. Unlike boys, girls will ostracize a playmate who brags and asserts superiority in a group.

Later in life, these conversation styles carry over into the workplace, where they can place women at a disadvantage. In meetings, women may be reluctant to interrupt or criticize the ideas of another, whereas men push themselves into the conversation and engage in ritual challenges over the validity of ideas. Men hear women make self-effacing or apologetic remarks and conclude that they lack self-confidence. Tannen thinks that the female linguistic style makes it harder to make a firm impression in male-dominated groups, so women are more often interrupted

---

[58] Sylvia Ann Hewlett and Carolyn Buck Luce, "Off-Ramps and On-Ramps: Keeping Talented Women on the Road to Success," *Harvard Business Review,* March 2005, p. 46.

[59] Debra E. Meyerson and Joyce K. Fletcher," "A Modest Manifesto for Shattering the Glass Ceiling," *Harvard Business Review,* January–February 2000, pp. 128–29.

[60] Louise Marie Roth, "Women on Wall Street: Despite Diversity Measures, Wall Street Remains Vulnerable to Sex Discrimination Charges," *Academy of Management Perspectives,* February 2007, p. 31.

[61] Deborah Tannen, "The Power of Talk: Who Gets Heard and Why," *Harvard Business Review,* September–October 1995.

in meetings and their ideas may be pushed aside. Tannen recommends demonstrative speech, but many women report that men can react negatively to an "unfeminine," assertive tone. A former prime minister of Canada explains this.

> I don't have a traditionally female way of speaking … I'm quite assertive. If I didn't speak the way I do, I wouldn't have been seen as a leader. But my way of speaking may have grated on people who were not used to hearing it from a woman. It was the right way for a leader to speak, but it wasn't the right way for a woman to speak.[62]

Harassment

sexual harassment
Annoying or persecuting behavior in the workplace that asserts power over a person because of their sexual identity. It is illegal under Title VII of the Civil Rights Act of 1964.

Many women experience *sexual harassment* at some time in their careers. In a landmark book, *Sexual Shakedown*, Lin Farley defined this form of harassment as "unsolicited nonreciprocal male behavior that asserts a woman's sex role over her function as a worker."[63] Various forms of harassment exist, including women harassing men and same-sex harassment; however, the strong, background presence of gender stereotypes assures that the major workplace problem is sexual harassment of women by men.

Sexual harassment of women encompasses a wide range of behaviors. It can be very subtle, as when older men treat younger women like daughters, an approach that diminishes the authority of a female manager. More direct forms of harassment are staring, touching, joking, and gratuitous discussions of sex. The most serious forms include demands for sexual favors or physical assaults.

Men are motivated to harass by gender distinctions. Some harassment is based on romantic motives, but this is the least common. More often it is intended to reinforce male power and status in work settings. Hostile, intimidating behavior based on sex-role distinctions is designed to frighten or humiliate a woman, putting her in the stereotyped role of submissive female, thereby subordinating her. The message is, "You're only a woman, that's the way I see you. And at that level you're vulnerable to me and any man."[64]

Research by social psychologist Jennifer Berdahl suggests that the women most likely to be harassed are those that violate traditional gender ideals by exhibiting masculine behaviors. Women who have more typically feminine behaviors are less likely targets.[65] According to Berdahl, men use sex-based harassment to maintain their social status, which is based on being male. In every society, and in male-dominated corporate cultures, "being male is associated with higher status than being female."[66] Maintaining social status is a deep drive because such status is the basis for self-esteem, income, influence, and job security.

[62] Kim Cameron, quoted in Alice H. Eagly and Linda L. Carli, "Women and the Labyrinth of Leadership," *Harvard Business Review,* September 2007, pp. 65–66.

[63] Lin Farley, *Sexual Shakedown* (New York: McGraw-Hill, 1978), pp. 14–15.

[64] Cynthia Cockburn, *In the Way of Women: Men's Resistance to Sex Equality in Organizations* (Ithaca, NY: ILR Press, 1991), p. 142.

[65] Jennifer L. Berdahl, "The Sexual Harassment of Uppity Women," *Journal of Applied Psychology 92,* no. 2 (2007), p. 433.

[66] Jennifer L. Berdahl, "Harassment Based on Sex: Protecting Social Status in the Context of Gender Hierarchy," *Academy of Management Review,* April 2007, p. 645.

FIGURE 17.2
The EEOC
Guidelines
on Sexual
Harassment

Source: 29 CFR
1604.11(a).

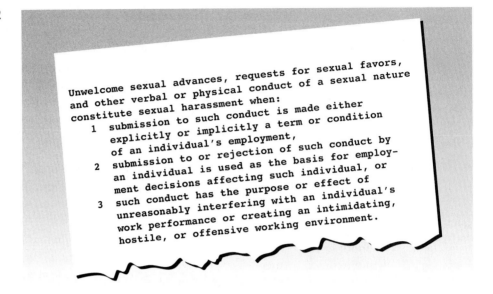

Unwelcome sexual advances, requests for sexual favors, and other verbal or physical conduct of a sexual nature constitute sexual harassment when:

1 submission to such conduct is made either explicitly or implicitly a term or condition of an individual's employment,

2 submission to or rejection of such conduct by an individual is used as the basis for employment decisions affecting such individual, or

3 such conduct has the purpose or effect of unreasonably interfering with an individual's work performance or creating an intimidating, hostile, or offensive working environment.

Men use sex-based harassment to define and enforce gender distinctions, doing so to defend against threats to their status by women who display masculine qualities. When, for example, a woman becomes an assertive leader, a man may devalue her to subordinate female status by calling her a "bitch." A woman in a traditionally male job may threaten men who define their status by their ability to do strenuous or skilled labor. Male co-workers may try to reassert their superior male status by sex-based intimidation as with a woman at a Chrysler plant who found crude phalluses made of rubber sealant coming down the assembly line to her station.[67] Similar race- or ethnicity-based harassment is used to defend white status against the perceived incursions of minority workers.

In 1980 the EEOC issued guidelines (see Figure 17.2) making sexual harassment a form of sex discrimination under Title VII. The guidelines define two situations where harassment is illegal. One is the *quid pro quo*, when submission to sexual activity is required to get or keep a job. The other is a *hostile environment*, where sexually offensive conduct is so pervasive that it becomes unreasonably difficult to work.

The range of conduct that can create a hostile environment has expanded to become very broad, but is not subject to precise definition. At first, courts often held that coarse language, innuendo, and pinups were part of some work environments and that Title VII could not magically dignify the manners of male workers throughout America.[68] Then, in a landmark case, a female welder named Lois Robinson, one of only seven women among 1,010 skilled craftsworkers in a Florida shipyard, complained that suggestive and lewd pinups, drawings, and cartoons created a hostile working environment. A Florida court agreed with her, holding that even if men enjoyed this decor, it nevertheless created an abusive climate for Robinson.[69]

quid pro quo
A situation, defined as illegal, when submission to sexual activity is required to get or keep a job.

hostile environment
A situation, defined as illegal, where sexually offensive conduct is pervasive in a workplace, making work unreasonably difficult for an affected individual.

[67] *Donnie M. Wilson v. Chrysler Corporation,* 172 F.3d 500 (1999).
[68] See, for example, *Rabidue v. Osceola Refinery Co.,* 805 F.2d 611 (CA–6 1986).
[69] *Robinson v. Jacksonville Shipyards,* 760 F.Supp. 1486 (M.D. Fla. 1991), at 1524.

In 1993 the Supreme Court set up a test for hostile environments. Teresa Harris, a manager in a Nashville company that rented forklifts, filed an EEOC complaint about the behavior of the company president, Charles Hardy. Over several years, Hardy had engaged in a pattern of vulgar and demeaning behavior that targeted Harris as a woman. He made derogatory remarks such as "You're a woman, what do you know?" and "We need a man as the rental manager." He made her serve coffee in meetings. He asked Harris and other female employees to fish coins out of his front pants pockets and sometimes threw objects on the floor, asking the women to pick them up while he commented on their breasts and clothing. He proposed negotiating Harris's raise at a Holiday Inn and suggested that she try giving sexual favors to get forklift rentals. When Harris complained and threatened to quit, Hardy apologized and she stayed, but his boorishness resumed.

Other women at the company testified that Hardy's behavior was all part of a ribald, joking atmosphere that everyone understood and enjoyed. Did Forklift Systems contain a hostile working environment? A lower court did not think so, ruling that although it was a close call and Hardy was a vulgar man, there was no proof that his conduct created a situation so intimidating that it interfered with Harris's ability to do her job.[70] However, when the case reached the Supreme Court, the justices created new criteria for defining a hostile environment.

In *Harris v. Forklift Systems,* they held that the guideline was whether sexual harassment created "an environment that a reasonable person would find hostile or abusive." There was no "mathematically precise test" for what constituted a hostile environment, but harassing conduct should be examined with respect to its "frequency" and "severity," whether it is "physically threatening or humiliating," and whether it "unreasonably interferes" with work.[71] The Supreme Court sent the *Harris* case back to a lower court for rehearing based on these criteria, and, a year later, that court ordered the company to set up a sexual harassment policy and to pay Harris's attorney fees. Forklift Systems appealed, but the litigants ultimately made a nonpublic, out-of-court settlement to end the case.

Since the *Harris* decision, the Supreme Court has expanded the law of sexual harassment. In two 1998 decisions it made corporations liable for damages when their employees create a hostile environment.[72] They can escape liability only if management proves that it tried hard to prevent and remedy harassment and, in addition, that the aggrieved employee neglected to make a complaint.[73] Now, most companies have formal policies prohibiting sexual harassment and have set up complaint channels.

---

[70] *Harris v. Forklift Systems, Inc.,* No. 3–89–0557 (M.D. Tenn. 1990).

[71] 510 U.S. 23 (1993).

[72] See *Burlington Industries v. Ellerth,* 524 U.S. 742 (1998) and *Faragher v. City of Boca Raton,* 524 U.S. 775 (1998). As a result of these cases, the EEOC issued new guidelines for employers. See EEOC, "Enforcement Guidance: Vicarious Employer Liability for Unlawful Harassment by Supervisors," Notice 915.002, June 18, 1999. These guidelines cover all forms of harassment prohibited under Title VII, including that based on race, ethnicity, national origin, and religion as well as sexual harassment.

[73] See *Pennsylvania State Police v. Suders,* 124 S. Ct. 2342 (2004).

Occupational Segregation

Women are more likely to work in some jobs than others. Within corporations and the economy as a whole, traditionally female jobs generally are lower in status and pay than typically male jobs. Women also have less occupational diversity than do men.

In the 1960s two-thirds of all women worked in clerical, sales, or low-level service occupations such as domestic worker. Another 15 percent worked in the professions, mainly as teachers and nurses. Since then, women have entered nontraditional occupations. They flow most freely into growing occupations where demand for labor reduces barriers to entry, including sex discrimination. They have moved in large numbers into management positions in service industries becoming, for example, 68 percent of the managers in health care organizations. Because jobs in the manufacturing sector have not been expanding since the 1960s, women have had far less success moving into skilled blue-collar occupations. Women are only 3 percent of supervisors and managers in the construction trades.

Table 17.1 shows the occupations with the largest and smallest percentages of women. The 10 female-dominated job categories on the left have the largest ratio of women to men. The 10 jobs on the right are the least feminized among the 84 traditionally male occupations in manufacturing, construction, and precision craft work tracked by the Bureau of Labor Statistics. Of these, 50 occupations, or 60 percent, have fewer than 5 percent women. Although women are moving into these nontraditional occupations, they do so in very small numbers.

About 5.6 million women work in management occupations, where they are 37 percent of all managers. Yet they have not moved into the highest-paying, most prestigious positions. Within all corporations, women are only 23 percent of chief executives and 29 percent of general managers. Even this proportionately low upper-echelon presence falls precipitously within the aristocracies of the Fortune 500. There, in 2007, women were only 15.4 percent of corporate officers, 14.8 percent of directors, 6.7 percent of the officers in the top-five highest-paid positions, and 2 percent of CEOs.[74] These numbers lead some to say that

TABLE 17.1
The 10 Occupations with the Largest and the 10 with the Smallest Percentages of Women

Source: U.S. Department of Labor, *Women in the Labor Force: A Databook* (Washington, DC: U.S. Bureau of Labor Statistics, May 2005), table 11. Figures are for 2004.

Highest Percentage of Women*		Lowest Percentage of Women*	
Dental hygienists	98.6	Loggers	0.2
Preschool and kindergarten teachers	97.7	Auto body repairers	0.6
Secretaries and administrative assistants	96.9	Concrete masons	0.7
Speech language pathologists	95.3	Electrical power line installers	0.9
Licensed vocational nurses	94.2	Bus and truck mechanics	0.9
Child care workers	94.2	Tool and die makers	0.9
Hairdressers	93.4	Roofers	1.1
Receptionists	92.7	Home appliance repairers	1.5
Payroll clerks	92.4	Dredge, shovel, and loader operators	1.5
Teacher assistants	92.3	Crane and tower operators	1.5

*Refers to women as a percentage of all workers in the occupation.

[74] Catalyst, "2007 Catalyst Census Finds Women Gained Ground as Board Chairs," *Press Room*, December 10, 2007.

glass ceiling
An invisible barrier of sex discrimination thwarting the advance of women to top corporate positions.

women have hit a *glass ceiling,* or an invisible barrier of sex discrimination thwarting career advancement to the highest levels. Although the image of a glass ceiling is now conventional, to the extent that it implies a single barrier stopping women's promotion to the very highest levels, it is misleading. In fact, the low representation of women at the top is the cumulative result of a series of abrasions, impediments, and disadvantages that complicate women's careers from the beginning. It has been suggested that the metaphor of a glass ceiling should be replaced by that of a labyrinth, or a "complex journey toward a goal" filled with twists, turns, blind alleys, and obstacles in which "the odds are stacked higher against women with each step."[75]

Compensation

Women earn less than men, however, the gap is narrowing. Before the Equal Pay Act of 1963, newspapers openly ran help-wanted ads with separate male and female pay scales for identical jobs, and in that year, across all occupations, the average woman earned only 59 cents for every dollar earned by a man. Since passage of the Equal Pay Act, which forbids pay differences based on sex, the gap has steadily narrowed. By 2006 women earned 81 cents for every dollar earned by a man.

As the gap has narrowed, women's earnings have steadily grown, while men's have stagnated. Figure 17.3 shows the trend in average weekly earnings in all occupations for both men and women over the past quarter century. Adjusted for inflation, men's earnings in 2006 were $7 a week less than they were 27 years

FIGURE 17.3
The Narrowing Gap in Weekly Earnings

Source: Bureau of labor Statistics, *Highlights of Women's Earnings in 2006,* Report 1000, September 2007, table 12.

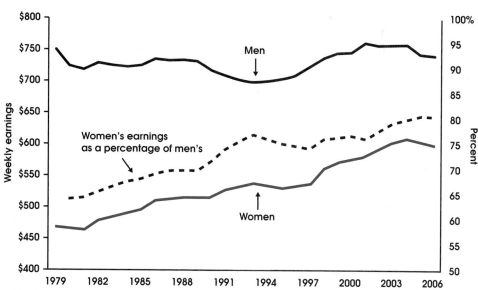

Note: The trend lines represent median weekly earnings of full-time wage and salary workers between 1979 and 2006 in constant (2006) dollars.

[75] Alice H. Eagly and Linda L. Carli, "Women and the Labyrinth of Leadership," pp. 64–65.

earlier, while women made $132 a week more, an increase of 28 percent.[76] An underlying factor that explains the better fortune of women is long-term structural change in the economy. Women hold a higher percentage of jobs in rapidly growing service occupations, while men predominate in the static manufacturing and construction sectors where there has been no job growth. Other factors are gains in women's educational levels and their progress toward equal opportunity because of new laws and declining sexist bias. Although closing, the gender wage gap is persistent. There are three reasons.

First, occupational segregation places many women in female-dominated occupations that tend to be lower paying than male-dominated ones. One study found that in occupations where more than 90 percent of jobs were held by women, the women earned 29 percent less than in predominantly male occupations. As the percentage of women in the occupation fell, the wage gap narrowed, falling to only 14 percent when the occupation was only 30 percent female.[77] Women continue to choose female-dominated occupations because they see other women in them, because cultural stereotyping feminizes certain occupational roles, because some traditionally female jobs better accommodate career interruptions, and because barriers to entry are low.

Second, women pay a heavy earnings penalty for childbearing and child rearing, activities that interrupt careers. Because women in their 20s and 30s often leave work, employers sometimes hesitate to invest heavily in training them, their seniority lags, and men leap ahead. The statistic cited above, that women now make 81 percent of men's earnings, is based on comparisons of earnings for men and women working full time for a year. It does not account for women who work only part time or part of the year. An analysis of the actual earnings histories for a group of 2,826 similar men and women aged 26 to 59 who were followed for 15 years revealed that the women made only 38 percent of what the men did.[78] So the estimate that women's earnings are 19 percent lower than men's in a recent year fails to reflect the depth of earnings gaps that grow over careers.

Third, the earnings gap reflects elements of sex discrimination. It narrows when men and women of similar age, occupational experience, and educational background are compared. Still, it does not disappear. In one study of men and women holding degrees in 130 professional fields, women were paid equally with or made more than men in only 11 fields employing just 2 percent of the women. In all the remaining fields, women averaged only 73 percent of men's pay.[79] Nothing in the statistical analysis of key factors that affect earnings, besides sex, accounts for this shortfall.

[76] Bureau of Labor Statistics, *Highlights of Women's Earnings in 2006,* Report 1000, September 2007, table 12.

[77] Stephanie Boraas and William M. Rodgers III, "How Does Gender Play a Role in the Earnings Gap? An Update," *Monthly Labor Review,* March 2003, p. 10.

[78] Stephen J. Rose and Heidi Hartmann, *Still a Man's Labor Market: The Long-Term Earning's Gap* (Washington, DC: Institute for Women's Policy Research, 2004), p. 10.

[79] Daniel E. Hecker, "Earnings of College Graduates: Women Compared with Men," *Monthly Labor Review,* March 1998, p. 63. See also Daniel H. Weinberg, "Earnings by Gender: Evidence from Census 2000," *Monthly Labor Review,* July/August 2007.

Its cause defies explanation by a range of statistical indicators and is either sex discrimination or another unmeasured factor, for example, the hesitance of women found in some studies to engage in competition, show ambition, or negotiate for salary.[80] Even in the most heavily female occupations men still earn more than women. For example, women's earnings are only 90 percent of men's salaries for elementary and middle school teachers, 86 percent for maids and housekeepers, and 83 percent for receptionists.[81] No research pinpoints factors apart from bias or the unknown as causes for these discrepancies.

The pay gap between men and women is worldwide, although on average it is narrower outside the United States. Within the European Union, women earn 15 percent less than men.[82] The International Labor Office reports that "in most economies women still earn 90 percent or less of what their male co-workers earn."[83] Usually, wage gaps are highest in rich, developed nations because high-paying occupations dominated by men have expanded. The gaps are smaller in developing nations where men and women still crowd into agricultural and low-skill occupations.

CORPORATE EFFORTS TO PROMOTE DIVERSITY

diversity management
Programs to increase worker heterogeneity and make corporate cultures more friendly to employees of any race, ethnicity, gender, age, religion, sexual orientation, or disability.

Employers are now heavily regulated. While most companies, particularly small ones, simply try to comply with all the laws and regulations, many large firms go beyond compliance to promote workforce diversity. *Diversity management* refers to programs that increase worker heterogeneity and change corporate cultures, making them hospitable to employees regardless of race, ethnicity, gender, age, religion, sexual orientation, or disability.

Diversity management is a broader effort than affirmative action. Affirmative action is compliance-oriented hiring of individuals from a narrow range of racial and ethnic categories. Once hired, the law requires nondiscrimination and, sometimes, promotion to fill quotas, but there is no requirement that people's differences be indulged. Women and minorities must often assimilate into white and male cultures with low tolerance for differences. Protected individuals get in, but to prosper and advance they must mirror the values and behavior of the dominant group.

Diversity management, on the other hand, is based on the belief that people in a wide range of identity groupings have dissimilar backgrounds and social experiences. Their behavior does not always conform to the norms of a single corporate culture. One woman raised in Taiwan was taught to be modest and

---

[80] See, for example, Uri Gneezy et al., "Performance in Competitive Environments: Gender Differences," *Quarterly Journal of Economics,* August 2003; Anna Fels, "Do Women Lack Ambition?" *Harvard Business Review,* April 2004; and Linda Babcock and Sara Lashever, *Women Don't Ask: Negotiation and the Gender Divide* (Princeton, NJ: Princeton University Press, 2003).

[81] Bureau of Labor Statistics, *Highlights of Women's Earnings in 2006,* table 18.

[82] European Commission, *Equal Pay: Exchange of Good Practices* (Luxembourg: Office for Official Publications of the European Communities, January 2007), p. 5

[83] International Labor Office, *Global Employment Trends for Women: Brief,* p. 11.

never boast, in keeping with the Chinese proverb that "the loudest duck gets shot." Hired by General Electric, she entered an atmosphere charged with ambition and competition. As part of General Electric's diversity program she was coached on how to be aggressive.[84]

Sometimes feelings of isolation arise for minority individuals. Another Asian woman complained that co-workers talked only about "American culture stories." She began to avoid having lunch with them and they invited her to join them less frequently.[85] A black executive felt anger that he was addressed in more familiar ways than his white counterparts.[86] A Hispanic manager complained that colleagues held stereotyped attitudes toward Mexican workers and assumed that she would take siestas and be lazy.[87] Such experiences diminish an employee's sense of being valued and supported.

Advocates promote diversity management using two arguments. First, it is an ethical action needing no justification beyond its inherent goodness. Second, it can strengthen businesses in several ways.

- *It lowers costs of recruiting, turnover, absenteeism, and lawsuits.* Minorities and women have higher turnover and absenteeism than whites and males because of the presence of hurdles the corporation fails to see and remove. Less frustration raises both tenure and productivity and can prevent discrimination charges.

- *It improves understanding of markets and customers.* PepsiCo believes that its diversity efforts inspired profitable new products, including guacamole-flavored Doritos chips aimed at Hispanics and Mountain Dew Code Red, aimed at blacks.[88]

- *It reduces friction and leads to creativity and better decisions in groups and teams.* Research does not confirm this. There is some evidence that diverse teams make better decisions because they consider more perspectives. However, team members may have more trouble learning to work together.[89] Some studies have associated diversity with better corporate performance, but overall the evidence is thin.[90]

To succeed, a diversity management program must be part of the corporate management system.

---

[84] Lisa Takeuchi Cullen, "Pathways to Power," *Time,* December 2005, p. A3.

[85] Catalyst, *Advancing Asian Women in the Workplace: What Managers Need to Know* (New York: Catalyst, 2003), p. 14.

[86] Robin J. Ely, Debra E. Meyerson, and Martin N. Davidson, "Rethinking Political Correctness," *Harvard Business Review,* September 2006, p. 81.

[87] Catalyst, *Advancing Latinas in the Workplace: What Managers Need to Know* (New York: Catalyst, 2003), p. 15.

[88] Carol Hymowitz, "The New Diversity," *The Wall Street Journal,* November 14, 2005, p. R3.

[89] Jennifer A. Chatman and Francis J. Flynn, "The Influence of Demographic Heterogeneity on the Emergence and Consequences of Cooperative Norms in Work Teams," *Academy of Management Journal,* October 2001.

[90] Lois Joy, et al., "The Bottom Line: Corporate Performance and Women's Representation on Boards," at www.catalyst.org; and Pamela Tudor, "Adding Value with Diversity," at www.tudorconsulting.net, p. 10.

- *Leadership* is critical. Without it, diversity efforts will not be seen as central to business strategy. Taylor Cox, Jr., a diversity management consultant, tells how leaders go wrong. Managers commit to attending meetings about diversity tasks but change their plans when operations make competing demands on their time. A manager picked to open a diversity training session welcomed attendees and then said, "I'm sorry you have to be here today and sit through all of this."[91] When asked at a diversity meeting whether anyone in the company had been promoted or passed over because of performance on diversity, a senior vice president of human resources could not think of anyone. Glen Hiner of Owens Corning, Inc., set a different example. When he came into the company, he stated at the first meeting with senior executives, "We are too white and too male, and that will change." He followed this by taking large and small actions, from appointing women and minorities to high positions to requiring a statement about the dignity of individuals printed on all business cards.[92]

- *Change in the organization structure* creates focal points for diversity efforts. Leadership can come from steering committees, task forces, or directors. In large companies, local coordinators in business units often report to these corporate entities. Many companies also encourage *affinity groups*, or networks of employees by race, culture, ethnicity, gender, sexual orientation, age, disability, or other diverse categories. Participation in such groups can reduce an individual's sense of isolation within a dominant organization culture. Affinity groups create a forum for mentoring, coaching, exchanging ideas, and advising the company. At IBM locations around the world there are 181 such groups. At PepsiCo each top executive must sponsor one group.

affinity group
A networking group formed by employees who personify an attribute associated with bias and social isolation.

- *Training programs* are very popular. They are designed to overcome stereotypes and biases by teaching employees about differences based on gender, ethnicity, and cultural background. Often they use short cases or videos to invite discussion of common misunderstandings and coach more sensitive behavior. Some studies suggest that training is effective in shifting values.[93] Others have found that it can awaken biases rather than eliminate them.[94] A long-term evaluation of diversity training in hundreds of corporations concluded that it was the least effective of seven methods for increasing diversity.[95]

- *Mentors* can be assigned to women and minorities to overcome isolation in firms where the hierarchy is predominantly white and male. At General Electric

[91] Taylor Cox, Jr., *Creating the Multicultural Organization* (San Francisco: Jossey-Bass, 2001), p. 41.

[92] Marc Bendick, Jr., Mary Lou Egan, and Suzanne M. Lofhjelm, "Workforce Diversity Training: From Antidiscrimination Compliance to Organizational Development," *Human Resource Planning,* January 2001, p. 10.

[93] Kenneth P. DeMeuse, "A Longitudinal Evaluation of Senior Managers' Perceptions and Attitudes of a Workplace Diversity Training Program," *Human Resource Planning* 30, no. 2 (2007).

[94] Deborah L. Kidder et al.,"Backlash toward Diversity Initiatives: Examining the Impact of Diversity Program Justification, Personal, and Group Outcomes." *International Journal of Conflict Management* 15, no. 1 (2004).

[95] Alexandra Kalev, Frank Dobbin, and Erin Kelly, "Best Practices or Best Guesses? Assessing the Efficacy of Corporate Affirmative Action and Diversity Policies," p. 602.

diversity officers assign not just one mentor, but a "personal board of directors" to advise individuals. A recent study of successful managers in large companies found that high-potential minorities were often demoralized by midcareer. They tended to move up more slowly than high-potential whites, who were put on fast tracks earlier. As whites got key assignments and promotions, the minority managers grew discouraged. A key to their ultimate success was the support of mentors who opened doors for them.[96] The use of mentoring requires sensitivity to cultural backgrounds. Some blacks want to advance solely on merit and see mentoring as selling out. Latinos and women may see mentoring as phony because they have been socialized to value relationships for their intrinsic good, not for some instrumental value.[97]

- *Data collection* is needed to define issues and measure progress. Because of the pervasive philosophy in business that what gets measured gets done, many companies quantify diversity goals. The Quaker Oats Company created a statistic called the "best-practices index" that registers points for every program and action taken in each of its plants. Its diversity administrator argues: "Most CEOs may not know a lot about diversity, but they understand numbers. They can tell the difference between a facility with 1,000 points on the best-practices index, and a facility with 500 points."[98]

- *Policy changes* establish new rules. Following a public relations disaster when tapes of executives making racially biased remarks were leaked to the press and a $115 million settlement of a race discrimination lawsuit, Texaco set up a program to reform its corporate culture. Many policies changed as a result. One example is a new rule that no human resource committee meeting can take place unless attended by a minority or a woman. If such a person is sick or delayed, the meeting is postponed.[99]

- *Reward systems* encourage managers to achieve diversity goals. Diversity can be one element of performance reviews. Division managers at ExxonMobil are required at annual reviews to present career development plans for 10 females and 10 minority males. At Lockheed each business unit is ranked using a mathematical "diversity maturity model" that includes surveys of employees. Part of each manager's bonus is tied to the unit's score.[100]

Resistance to diversity projects comes from white males who feel blamed for problems and perceive a losing game in which the advance of others precludes their success and from some women and minorities hoping to deemphasize their differences and assimilate into the dominant company culture. Yet, growing diversity in workforces and labor markets ensures that these programs will remain

---

[96] David A. Thomas, "The Truth about Mentoring Minorities: Race Matters," *Harvard Business Review,* April 2001, pp. 99–107.

[97] Kathryn Tyler, "Cross-Cultural Connections," *HRMagazine,* 52, no. 10, October 2007, p. 77.

[98] I. Charles Mathews, vice president of diversity management, cited in Margaret A. Hart, *Managing Diversity for Sustained Competitiveness* (New York: The Conference Board, 1997), p. 8.

[99] Kenneth Labich, "No More Crude at Texaco," *Fortune,* September 6, 1999, p. 208.

[100] Jill Dutt, "Taking an Engineer's Approach at Lockheed Martin," *Washington Post,* May 1, 2006, p. D1.

strong because there is a business rationale for them. Nondiscrimination has moved from a social responsibility, to a legal duty, to a business imperative. In the end, it may be the latter consideration that closes any remaining gap between the promises of natural rights in the Declaration of Independence and their neglect in practice.

CONCLUDING OBSERVATIONS

Workplace discrimination has existed throughout American history. The first national effort to end it began during the Civil War, with the Emancipation Proclamation freeing slaves, and included constitutional amendments and civil rights laws passed after the war. This visionary effort was defeated by social values contrary to the laws.

In the 1960s, a second effort to eradicate discrimination began with passage of the Civil Rights Act of 1964. Since then, more laws and thousands of agency and court decisions have greatly reduced, but not eliminated, job bias against minorities and women. Today, the accumulated corpus of antidiscrimination law is massive, complex, and controversial where it embodies preferential treatment. But overall, and unlike the Reconstruction-era effort, it works. Along with government, corporations are taking many actions—both voluntary and legally mandated—to make progress.

Yet more needs to be done. There is widespread evidence of continuing discrimination. Research on wage gaps, studies of job applications, and the continued existence of discrimination suits attest to it.

Adarand v. Peña

This is the story of an affirmative action case that made its way to the U.S. Supreme Court. When the Court announced that it would hear *Adarand v. Peña,* there was considerable speculation about the outcome. The plaintiff, a white male, argued that preferential treatment for minority and female contractors was unconstitutional. Would the justices agree?

In due course, the nine-member Court issued a lengthy (21,800 words) split decision, showing itself to be as fractured as the public in its thinking. It divided 5 to 4, with six separate opinions—a majority opinion, two concurring opinions, and three dissents. The result? Affirmative action lived on but became harder to justify. With the support of affirmative action foes in the legal community, Adarand Constructors tried to carry the case farther, refusing to give up until the Court killed affirmative action in all its forms. The case bounced around the federal court system for another six years until fizzling out in 2001 when the Supreme Court dismissed it.

THE GUARDRAIL SUBCONTRACT

In 1987 Congress appropriated a huge sum, more than $16 billion, to the Department of Transportation (DOT) for highway construction across the nation.[1] Ten percent, or $1.6 billion, was earmarked for small businesses run by "socially and economically disadvantaged individuals."[2]

---

[1] The Surface Transportation and Uniform Relocation Assistance Act of 1987, P.L. 100–17.

[2] Section 106(c)(1).

Socially disadvantaged persons were defined as "those who have been subjected to racial or ethnic prejudice or cultural bias" and *economically disadvantaged persons* were defined as those "whose ability to compete in the free enterprise system has been impaired due to diminished capital and credit opportunites as compared to others in the same business area who are not socially disadvantaged."[3]

It was to be presumed that black, Hispanic, Asian Pacific, subcontinent Asian, and Native American persons and women were both socially and economically handicapped. Any small business with 51 percent or greater ownership by persons in these categories could be certified as a *disadvantaged business enterprise,* or DBE. Then, Congress put monetary incentives to hire DBEs into the highway construction law. The story here illustrates how these incentives worked.

In 1989 Mountain Gravel & Construction Company received a $1 million prime contract to build highways in the San Juan National Forest of southwest Colorado. It requested bids from subcontractors to install 4.7 miles of guardrails. Two small companies that specialize in guardrail installation responded. Adarand Constructors, Inc., a white-owned company, submitted the low bid, and Gonzales Construction Company, a firm certified as a DBE, submitted a bid that was $1,700 higher.

Ordinarily, Mountain Gravel would have chosen the low bidder, but the prime contract provided that it would be paid a bonus, up to 10 percent of the guardrail subcontract, if it picked a DBE.

On this subcontract, the bonus payment was approximately $10,000, so even by accepting a bid $1,700 above the low bid, Mountain Gravel came out $8,300 ahead. Gonzales Construction, the high bidder, got the nod.

The part of the prime contract that caused Mountain Gravel to reject Adarand Constructors's low bid was called a *subcontractor compensation clause.* It provided that a sum equal to 10 percent of the subcontract would be paid to Mountain Gravel, up to a maximum of 1.5 percent of the dollar amount of the prime contract, if one DBE subcontractor was used. If two DBE subcontractors had been used, the extra payment could have been as much as 2 percent of the prime contract.

Losing the guardrail job angered Randy Pech, the white male co-owner and general manager of

Adarand Constructors. "It was very discouraging to run a legitimate, honest business," said Pech, "to go to a lot of trouble of bidding on a project—to know you did a great job and come in the low bid—and then find out they can't use you because they have to meet their 'goals.'"[4] Pech's lawyer, William Pendley, spoke more bluntly about the subcontractor compensation clause. "It works like a bribe," he said.[5]

This was not the first time Adarand Constructors had faced this situation. It was one of only five Colorado contractors specializing in guardrails. The other four, Cruz Construction, Ideal Fencing, C&K, and Gonzales Construction, were minority-owned and, by virtue of that, designated as DBEs. These four competitors were all stable businesses at least 10 years old, and on nonfederal highway projects, they sometimes beat Adarand Constructors with lower bids. Yet when federal highway dollars were being spent, Adarand Constructors frequently lost—even with the lowest bid.

Later it would be documented that because of the subcontractor compensation clause, prime contractors had rejected the company's low bids five times to favor its DBE competitors. Mountain Gravel's bid estimator verified that Adarand Constructors's low bid on the 4.7 mile guardrail job would have been accepted if the extra payment had not existed. Fed up, Randy Pech sued the federal government.

In his suit, Pech claimed that the subcontractor compensation clause violated his constitutional right to equal treatment under the law. This right is found in the Fifth Amendment of the Constitution, which reads: "No person shall . . . be deprived of life, liberty, or property, without due process of law." Although this wording does not literally state that citizens are entitled to equal treatment, the Supreme Court has held that its meaning protects citizens from arbitrary or unequal treatment by the federal government in the same way that the Fourteenth Amendment prohibits states fom denying "equal protection of the laws" to their citizens. Pech did not seek monetary damages, but requested an injunction, or a court-ordered halt, to any future use of

---

[3] Section 106(c)(2)(B).

[4] Marlene Cimons, "Businessman Who Brought Lawsuit Praises Ruling by Justices," *Los Angeles Times,* June 13, 1995, p. A15.

[5] David G. Savage, "'Colorblind' Constitution Faces a New Test," *Los Angeles Times,* January 16, 1995, p. A17.

contract clauses providing extra payments on sub-contracts given to DBEs.

Things got off to a bad start for Pech when the U.S. District Court for the District of Colorado ruled against him.[6] The court held that it was within the power of Congress, when it enacted the highway bill, to use race- and gender-based preferences to compensate for the harmful effects of past discrimination. Pech appealed to the Tenth Circuit Court of Appeals, but, two years later, it affirmed the district court's decision.[7] Pech then took the next step and appealed to the Supreme Court, which agreed to decide the case. Because the lawsuit named Transportation Secretary Federico Peña as a defendant, it was entitled *Adarand v. Peña*.

THE CONSTITUTION AND RACE

The Court was being asked to decide whether classifying citizens by race in order to treat them differently was constitutionally respectable. This was not a new question; neither was it one that has ever been resolved with clarity. Affirmative action has deeply divided the Court, but it is not the first race-based classification scheme to raise constitutional problems.

Between 1884 and 1893, the Court decided a series of challenges to exclusionary laws passed by Congress stopping the immigration of Chinese laborers and restricting the civil rights of resident Chinese. At first, the justices struck down laws that treated Chinese differently from American citizens.[8] Eventually, however, the Court went along with a wave of public hysteria over the Chinese and in key decisions upheld laws that denied them equal treatment.[9]

A few years later, in 1896, the Court had an opportunity to strike down the Jim Crow laws of the old South in *Plessy v. Ferguson* but failed to do so. Instead, it upheld the Louisiana statute requiring segregation of whites and nonwhites in separate railroad cars and fixed in place the infamous "separate but equal" doctrine. In a lone dissent that rang across decades, Justice John Marshall Harlan called the Constitution "color blind" and said that race was not a valid criterion for making law.

> In respect of civil rights, common to all citizens, the Constitution of the United States does not, I think, permit any public authority to know the race of those entitled to be protected in the enjoyment of such rights. . . . [T]he common government of all shall not permit the seeds of race hate to be planted under the sanction of law.[10]

During World War II, the Court was once again called upon to decide the question of a race-based government action. In early 1942, President Franklin Roosevelt issued an executive order, which Congress ratified, requiring the relocation of 70,000 persons of Japanese descent, both American citizens and resident aliens, from homes on the West Coast to inland evacuation camps.

This policy was challenged as depriving the Japanese Americans of their Fifth Amendment guarantee of equal protection of the laws. However, the Court once again upheld a racial classification scheme. In the majority opinion, Justice Black conceded that "all legal restrictions which curtail the civil rights of a single racial group are immediately suspect" and must be subjected "to the most rigid scrutiny."[11] Nevertheless, the evacuation order passed this "rigid scrutiny," because the president and Congress were taking emergency actions in time of war to prevent sabotage and avert grave danger. In dissent, Justice Frank Murphy argued that the evacuation "goes over 'the very brink of constitutional power' and falls into the ugly abyss of racism."[12]

In 1954 the Court finally reversed its decision in *Plessy*. In the landmark school desegregation case *Brown v. Board of Education*, it agreed that under the "separate but equal" doctrine, the states had provided grossly unequal schools for blacks.[13] During oral arguments in the case, Thurgood Marshall, destined to be the first black Supreme Court justice, invoked the principle of a color-blind Constitution. A unanimous Court struck down "separate but equal" as a violation of the equal protection clause in the Fourteenth Amendment.

---

[6] *Adarand Constructors, Inc. v. Samuel K. Skinner,* 790 F.Supp. 240 (D.Colo. 1992). Then-Secretary of Transportation Skinner was named as the defendant.

[7] *Adarand Constructors, Inc. v. Federico Peña,* 16 F.3d 1537 (10th Cir. 1994). By this time, Peña was Secretary of Transportation.

[8] *Chew Heong v. United States,* 112 U.S. 536 (1884); and *United States v. Jung Ah Lung,* 124 U.S. 621 (1888).

[9] *Lee Joe v. United States,* 149 U.S. 698 (1893).

[10] 163 U.S. 554, 560.

[11] *Korematsu v. United States,* 323 U.S. 214.

[12] 323 U.S. 242.

[13] 347 U.S. 483.

The *Brown* decision, however, did not mean that the Court saw a completely color-blind Constitution. In the 1970s, suits by whites who had suffered reverse discrimination as a result of affirmative action began to reach its docket. In the first such cases, a divided Court upheld affirmative action, but was obviously troubled by it and tried to define its limits. There was also an ideological split among the justices, with a liberal bloc condoning race-based affirmative action and a conservative bloc inclined to severely limit or prohibit it.

THE FULLILOVE CASE

In 1980 the Court heard for the first time a challenge to a set-aside program for minority businesses. In the Public Works Employment Act of 1977, Congress authorized $4 billion for public works projects such as dams, bridges, and highways. At least 10 percent of this sum was set aside for businesses owned by "minority group members," who were defined as "Negroes, Spanish-speaking, Orientals, Indians, Eskimos, and Aleuts."[14]

The law was challenged by several associations of white contractors, who claimed to have lost business and argued that the set-aside violated their constitutional rights to equal protection. But in *Fullilove v. Klutznick*, the Court held that Congress could use racial classification schemes to strike at racist practices used by prime contractors on federal projects.[15]

Over the years, courts have developed standards for testing the constitutional validity of laws that classify citizens. All such laws must withstand one of three levels of scrutiny by a skeptical judiciary.

The lowest level is *ordinary scrutiny,* which requires that government prove its classification scheme is "reasonably" related to a "legitimate interest." For example, classifying citizens by income for purposes of tax collection would pass this minimum test.

The second level is *intermediate scrutiny,* a heightened standard requiring that the law be "substantially related" to an "important government objective." In the past, intermediate scrutiny was typically used for laws related to gender, for example, the law drafting men for military service but not women.

The final, and most exacting, level of scrutiny, called *strict scrutiny,* is reserved for racial classifications regarded as pernicious and undesirable. When strict scrutiny is used, it is presumed that the law in question is unconstitutional unless it passes a specific two-part test. The government must prove that it serves a "compelling" government interest and is "narrowly tailored," that is, not more extensive than it needs to be to serve its purpose. There are no fixed definitions of the words "reasonably," "substantially related," and "compelling," but they represent an escalating standard of proof.

The majority opinion in *Fullilove* showed that neither Chief Justice Warren Burger nor the five other justices who joined and concurred with him were particularly alarmed about race-based set-asides for minority contractors. The chief justice subjected the minority business program in the Public Works Employment Act to only an intermediate level of scrutiny.

THE CROSON AND METRO CASES

After *Fullilove,* nine years passed before the Court looked at set-asides again. In 1989 the Court struck down an affirmative action plan used by the city of Richmond, Virginia, requiring that 30 percent of construction work be awarded to minority contractors. In *Richmond v. Croson,* the Court held that because the city's plan was a suspect racial classification, it should be subject to strict scrutiny.[16] And when the two tests required by strict scrutiny were applied, the plan could not pass constitutional muster.

First, although the population of Richmond was 50 percent black and less than 1 percent of city contracts were awarded to black firms, the city had not proved a "compelling" interest because it had never conducted studies to show that this statistical discrepancy was caused by race discrimination. Without proof of past discrimination, no "compelling" justification for raced-based remedial action existed.

And second, the plan was not "narrowly tailored"; in addition to giving preference to black contractors, it entitled Hispanic, Asian, Native American, Eskimo, and Aleut contractors located anywhere in the United States to take advantage of preferential bidding rules. This scheme of inclusion was too broad. The Court

[14] Section 103(f)(2).

[15] 448 U.S. 448.

[16] *City of Richmond v. J. A. Croson Co.,* 488 U.S. 469 (1989).

ruled that for white contractors, the Richmond plan violated the Fourteenth Amendment guarantee of equal protection under the law.[17]

In the wake of the *Croson* decision, more than 200 set-aside plans around the country were dropped or changed for fear that they would be challenged and struck down. In Richmond, the percentage of contract dollars awarded to minority businesses plummeted from 30 percent to "the low single digits."[18]

A year later, in 1990, the Court confronted a case in which white-owned broadcasters challenged a congressional statute requiring that the Federal Communications Commission give certain preferences to minority radio and television companies when it issued broadcast licenses. Congress declared that its purpose was to promote diversity in programming. In *Metro Broadcasting v. FCC,* a five-member majority of the Court composed of four remaining liberals and the usually conservative Justice Byron White held that "benign race-conscious measures" undertaken by Congress to compensate victims of discrimination need be subject only to the standard of "intermediate scrutiny."[19] Creating diversity in broadcasting was an "important governmental objective," and preferences for nonwhite and female broadcasters were "substantially related" to achieving this objective. In dissent, Justice Anthony M. Kennedy sought to refocus the Court on the mistake made in the *Plessy* case. "I regret," he wrote, "that after a century of judicial opinions we interpret the Constitution to do no more than move us from 'separate but equal' to 'unequal but benign.'"[20]

TWO LINES OF PRECEDENT

This was where matters stood until 1994, when *Adarand* came before the Court. The Supreme Court likes to follow precedent and generally adheres to the rule of *stare decisis* (STARE-ray da-SEE-sis), a Latin

term meaning to stand as decided. The judicial system is based on the principle that once a matter of law is settled, courts should follow the established path. Judges believe that this should be the case even though a court would decide the question differently if it were new. *Stare decisis* preserves one of the law's primary virtues, its predictability.

However, two different precedents had been established for minority preferences in contracting. In *Croson,* the Court had applied strict scrutiny to a city plan and declared it unconstitutional. But *Adarand* was not about a city plan; it involved a plan enacted by Congress. Traditionally, the Supreme Court recognizes that Congress represents the will of the American people and thus its actions deserve great deference. The line of precedent closest to the issue in *Adarand* was that emerging from *Fullilove* and *Metro.* In both cases, the Court had applied only intermediate scrutiny to congressional affirmative action plans and in both cases the plans were upheld. This result was consistent with the Court's studied deference toward Congress.

THE DECISION

Attorneys for each side in *Adarand v. Peña* presented 30 minutes of oral argument before the nine justices on January 17, 1995.[21] On June 12, 1995, the Supreme Court released a 5–4 decision in favor of Adarand Constructors.[22] The majority opinion, written by Justice Sandra Day O'Connor, departed from the line of precedent running from *Fullilove* and *Metro* and instead returned to *Croson* and ruled that the Department of Transportation plan giving preferences in bidding to minority subcontractors would have to withstand the test of strict scrutiny. It held that the plan was a race classification and presumed to be unconstitutional unless it was "narrowly tailored" to meet a "compelling government interest." Justice O'Connor wrote as follows.

> [W]e hold today that all racial classifications, imposed by whatever federal, state, or local governmental actor, must be analyzed by a reviewing court under strict scrutiny. In other words, such classifications are constitutional only if they are narrowly tailored measures that further compelling governmental

[17] The Fourteenth Amendment protects American citizens from unjust actions by state governments. It reads: "No State shall . . . deny to any person within its jurisdiction the equal protection of the laws." The City of Richmond, being chartered by the state of Virginia, was therefore a governmental actor falling under the reach of the Fourteenth Amendment.

[18] Paul M. Barrett and Michael K. Frisby, "Affirmative-Action Advocates Seeking Lessons from States to Help Preserve Federal Programs," *The Wall Street Journal,* December 7, 1994, p. A18.

[19] 497 U.S. 547.

[20] 497 U.S. 637–38.

[21] This oral argument can be heard in CSPAN's recorded archives at www.cspan.org/guide/courts/historic/oa072598.htm.

[22] 132 L. Ed. 2d 158, 515 U.S. 200 (1995).

interests. To the extent that *Metro Broadcasting* is inconsistent with that holding it is overruled.[23]

She justified departing from the *Fullilove* and *Metro* precedents by citing Justice Felix Frankfurter, who 55 years earlier had written that *"stare decisis* is . . . not a mechanical formula of adherence to the latest decision, however recent and questionable, when such adherence involves collision with a prior doctrine more embracing in its scope, intrinsically sounder, and verified by experience."[24] The Court's longstanding, deep suspicion of any race classification, wrote O'Connor, should override the recent efforts of some liberal justices to apply more lax scrutiny to forms of discrimination they called "benign."

However, the majority was unwilling to say that no scheme of race-conscious preferences could withstand strict scrutiny. Using affirmative action might still be possible for the government. O'Connor wrote:

> Finally, we wish to dispel the notion that strict scrutiny is "strict in theory, but fatal in fact ...." The unhappy persistence of both the practice and the lingering effects of racial discrimination against minority groups in this country is an unfortunate reality, and government is not disqualified from acting in response to it.[25]

This completed the majority opinion. The Court did not uphold or strike down the Transportation Department's subcontractor bidding clauses. Instead, it remanded, or returned, the case to the Tenth Circuit Court of Appeals to be redecided using the strict scrutiny test instead of the lesser test of intermediate scrutiny.[26] The result of this tougher review would determine whether the equal protection rights of Randy Pech at Adarand Constructors had been violated. Thus, as in many cases that come before the high court, the justices avoided deciding the specific question and decided only matters of law.

JUSTICE SCALIA CONCURS

Justice Antonin Scalia, a conservative and longtime foe of affirmative action, wrote a concurring opinion in which he agreed with the application of strict scrutiny but took the extreme position that "government can never have a 'compelling interest' in discriminating on the basis of race in order to 'make up' for past racial discrimination in the opposite direction."[27] He elaborated:

> Individuals who have been wronged by unlawful racial discrimination should be made whole; but under our Constitution there can be no such thing as either a creditor or a debtor race. The concept of racial entitlement—even for the most admirable and benign of purposes—is to reinforce and preserve for future mischief the way of thinking that produced race slavery, race privilege and race hatred. In the eyes of government, we are just one race here. It is American.[28]

Justice Scalia concluded that it was very unlikely and probably impossible that the Department of Transportation program could pass the strict scrutiny test.

JUSTICE THOMAS CONCURS

Justice Clarence Thomas, the Court's only black member, agreed with the majority opinion, but wrote separately to underscore the principle that the Constitution requires all races to be treated equally. In his eyes, there was no moral difference between a law designed to subjugate a race and a law passed to give it benefits.

> That these programs may have been motivated, in part, by good intentions cannot provide refuge from the principle that under our Constitution, the government may not make distinctions on the basis of race. As far as the Constitution is concerned, it is irrelevant whether a government's racial classifications are drawn by those who wish to oppress a race or by those who have a sincere desire to help those thought to be disadvantaged.[29]

Thomas also argued that affirmative action degrades the very individuals it tries to help.

> So-called "benign" discrimination teaches many that because of chronic and apparently immutable handicaps, minorities cannot compete with them without their patronizing indulgence. Inevitably such programs engender attitudes of superiority or,

---

[23] 132 L. Ed. 2d 182.

[24] 132 L. Ed. 2d 184, citing *Helvering v. Hallock,* 390 U.S. 106, at 119.

[25] 132 L. Ed. 2d 188.

[26] 16 F.3d 1537, vacated and remanded.

[27] 132 L. Ed. 2d 190.

[28] Ibid.

[29] Ibid.

The nine Supreme Court justices who decided the *Adarand* cases. Front row, left to right, are Antonin Scalia, John Paul Stevens, William Rehnquist (Chief Justice), Sandra Day O'Connor, and Anthony Kennedy. Back row, left to right, are Ruth Bader Ginsburg, David Souter, Clarence Thomas, and Steven Breyer. Source: © Reuters/CORBIS.

alternatively, provoke resentment among those who believe that they have been wronged by the government's use of race. These programs stamp minorities with a badge of inferiority and may cause them to develop dependencies or to adopt an attitude that they are "entitled" to preferences.[30]

THE DISSENTERS

Three separate dissenting opinions were written, joined in by four justices. In the first, Justice Stevens, joined by Justice Ginsburg, objected to the departure of the majority from established precedent and argued that the Court had a duty to uphold the intermediate scrutiny standard. Stevens also disagreed with the majority that all discrimination was the same in principle.

> There is no moral or constitutional equivalence between a policy that is designed to perpetuate a caste system and one that seeks to eradicate racial subordination. Invidious discrimination is an engine of oppression, subjugating a disfavored group to enhance or maintain the power of the majority. Remedial race-based preferences reflect the opposite impulse: a desire to foster equality in society. No sensible conception of the Government's constitutional obligation to "govern impartially" . . . should ignore this distinction. . . . The consistency that the

Court espouses would disregard the difference between a "No Trespassing" sign and a welcome mat.[31]

A second dissent by Justice Souter, in which Justices Ginsburg and Breyer joined, objected to the Court's departure from the *Fullilove* and *Metro* precedents. He argued that more deference was owed to Congress and affirmed his approval for laws that try to redress persistent racism.

The third dissenting opinion came from Justice Ginsburg, joined by Justice Breyer. She wrote to underscore the lingering effects of "a system of racial cast" in American life. According to Ginsburg:

> White and African-American consumers still encounter different deals. People of color looking for housing still face discriminatory treatment by landlords, real estate agents, and mortgage lenders. Minority entrepreneurs sometimes fail to gain contracts though they are the low bidders, and they are sometimes refused work even after winning contracts. Bias both conscious and unconscious, reflecting traditional and unexamined habits of thought, keeps up barriers that must come down if equal opportunity and nondiscrimination are ever genuinely to become this country's law and practice.
>
> Given this history and its practical consequences, Congress surely can conclude that a carefully designed affirmative action program may help to realize, finally, the "equal protection of the laws" the Fourteenth Amendment has promised since 1868.[32]

THE CASE MOVES ON

The Supreme Court elected to decide principles of law. It declined to settle the specific question of whether the subcontractor compensation clause was constitutional. Therefore, it sent the case back to the Tenth Circuit, with instructions to decide the constitutionality question. The Tenth Circuit, in turn, sent the case down to the U.S. District Court in Colorado where it had originated in 1992.

In 1997, almost two years after the Supreme Court's decision, the district court issued an opinion. Judge John L. Kane Jr. applied the strict scrutiny test to the subcontractor compensation clause, and the result invalidated the clause. The clause passed the part of the test requiring the government to show a

---

[30] 132 L. Ed. 2d 191.

[31] 132 L. Ed. 2d 192, 193.
[32] 132 L. Ed. 2d 212.

compelling interest. Judge Kane stated that there was sufficient evidence of bias in contracting before Congress when it passed the law.

However, the clause failed the test of narrow tailoring. Judge Kane held that basing social and economic disadvantage solely on race was unfair. Under the existing criteria for selecting DBEs, a multimillionaire who immigrated from Hong Kong and became a U.S. citizen one day before applying would automatically qualify, but a poor white man who had lived in the United States his entire life could not. So the set-aside program was overinclusive and unconstitutional. Since Colorado was administering the program for the federal government, Judge Kane issued an injunction ordering the state to stop using the objectionable regulation.[33]

Pech and his company had won, but defenders of affirmative action wanted to put up a fight. The Department of Transportation appealed the decision back to the Tenth Circuit. Then Colorado refused to comply with Judge Kane's ruling. Governor Roy Romer argued, disingenuously, that a federal court order did not apply to a state government.

Adarand Constructors immediately sued the state to force its obedience. When the case came before Judge Kane, Colorado argued that it had changed its contracting program. It no longer used the subcontractor compensation clause, and it allowed all contractors, including white males, to get DBE status if they could show disadvantage.

Judge Kane was furious at the recalcitrance of Colorado officials. Instead of retrying the entire issue, he declared that Adarand Constructors had suffered years of discrimination and financial hardship at the hands of a government enforcing an unfair, unconstitutional law. He decreed that the company was eligible for DBE status.[34] Pech applied for it, and it was granted by Colorado in 1998.

Meanwhile, the *Adarand* decision had sparked a national debate. The federal government had approximately 160 preference programs for businesses certified as disadvantaged. In the year that *Adarand* was decided, $10 billion in contracts earmarked for minority and female vendors was distributed through various preference schemes. Opponents of affirma-

tive action felt that, because of the decision, such practices should cease.

There was no doubt that *Adarand* cast a shadow over these arrangements, but their supporters had no intention of conceding defeat. Instead, President Clinton promised to "mend, not end" affirmative action. What he had in mind was revising preferential treatment rules so that the programs would withstand legal challenge.

Congressional opponents of affirmative action started a floor fight trying to kill a 10 percent set-aside provision in a new highway funding bill. In March 1998 strident debate erupted in the Senate over an amendment to delete the set-aside, but the amendment was defeated, leaving more than $17 billion of new highway funds earmarked for DBEs.[35]

In 1999 the Department of Transportation issued revised rules for awarding federal highway contracts to DBEs.[36] They stated that the 10 percent of highway funding reserved for DBEs was not a "quota" or a "set-aside" but an "aspirational goal at the national level." The DBE participation level in each state receiving highway funds could be higher or lower. To meet DBE goals, the states were required to first use "race-neutral" measures, that is, to do things to help all small businesses, including both DBEs and white-male-owned companies.

These measures did not require race–gender classifications and included, for example, training and advice in bidding and contract work, bonding assistance, and breaking large contracts into pieces that small businesses could more easily handle. However, if such methods did not fully achieve DBE goals and "egregious" discrimination existed, then "race-conscious" methods that gave preferences to DBEs, including set-asides on which only DBEs could bid, could be used.

The states were required to do studies pinpointing discrimination, so that there would be a compelling rationale for race-conscious actions if they were needed. The rules also tightened qualifications for persons designated as "economically disadvantaged." This status was from now on denied to persons with a net worth of $750,000 or more (calculated as personal net worth minus the value of a primary

[33] *Adarand Constructors, Inc. v. Peña*, 965 F. Supp. 1556 (D. Colo. 1997).

[34] *Adarand Constructors, Inc. v. Romer*, Civ. No. 97–K–1351 (June 26, 1997).

[35] Amendment No. 1708, 144 Cong. Rec. S1395.

[36] Department of Transportation, "Participation by Disadvantaged Business Enterprises in Department of Transportation Program," 64 FR 5096–5148, December 9, 1999.

Who Is Disadvantaged?

Any person who is a citizen and falls into one of the following categories is presumed to be socially and economically disadvantaged (beginning in 1999, persons with a net worth of $750,000 or more were disqualified). If the person has 51 percent ownership or greater in a company applying for a federal highway construction contract, that company qualifies as a "disadvantaged business enterprise" and can receive preferential treatment on federal highway contracts.

Black. Includes persons having origins in any black racial groups in Africa.

Hispanic. Includes persons of Mexican, Puerto Rican, Cuban, Dominican, Central or South American, or other Spanish or Portuguese culture or origin, regardless of race.

Native American. Includes American Indians, Eskimos, Aleuts, or Native Hawaiians.

Asian-Pacific Americans. Includes persons whose origins are from Japan, China, Taiwan, Korea, Burma (Myanmar), Vietnam, Laos, Cambodia (Kampuchea), Thailand, Malaysia, Indonesia, the Philippines, Brunei, Samoa, Guam, the U.S. Trust Territories of the Pacific Islands (Republic of Palau), the Commonwealth of the Northern Marianas Islands, Macao, Fiji, Tonga, Kirbati, Juvalu, Nauru, Federated States of Micronesia, or Hong Kong.

Women. All women are included.

Source: 49 CFR §26.5 (2000); 64 FR 5128, February 2, 1999.

---

residence and the ownership interest in the contracting business). The rules allowed white males to apply for socially or economically disadvantaged status. However, unlike minorities and women who are still automatically included (unless worth more than $750,000), the burden is on white males to prove that they have suffered financial hardship from discrimination.

These changes significantly scaled back affirmative action in highway programs. Later, President Clinton issued an executive order that introduced similarly constricted affirmative action methods in all federal contracting.[37]

ADARAND KEEPS GOING

Although the use of preferences was being scaled back, through it all Pech persisted in the belief that any race- and sex-based preferences at all were unconstitutional. The case continued its odyssey through the federal courts.

The Department of Transportation had appealed Judge Kane's 1997 ruling that the subcontractor compensation clause was unconstitutional. In 1999 the Tenth Circuit ruled that the case was now moot because Colorado had changed its contracting guidelines and no longer used the bonus clause. In addition, the court noted that Colorado had classified Adarand Constructors as a DBE.[38] Adarand, which argued that the Colorado guidelines were still unconstitutional, appealed to the Supreme Court. In 2000 the Supreme Court reversed the Tenth Circuit's decision and sent the case back with instructions to decide the constitutionality of the Colorado contracting guidelines.[39]

Later that year, the Tenth Circuit responded, deciding that although the original Colorado highway contracting rules had been unconstitutional, the states' new rules were narrowly tailored to meet a compelling government interest, and therefore, constitutional. Again, Adarand Constructors appealed the decision to the Supreme Court, which took the case under review. It argued that the Tenth Circuit had erred in its constitutional analysis because no rules that used race or sex as a criterion for awarding government funds could pass the strict scrutiny standard. In its brief, it argued the arbitrariness of the rules:

---

[37] Executive Order 13170, "Increasing Opportunities and Access for Disadvantaged Businesses," October 6, 2000.

[38] *Adarand Constructors, Inc. v. Slater,* 169 F.3d 1292 (10th Cir. 1999).

[39] *Adarand Constructors, Inc. v. Slater,* 528 U.S. 216 (2000).

EXHIBIT 1 The *Adarand* Odyssey.

This diagram shows the path of the case as it moved through levels of the federal court system over nine years. Twice the Supreme Court remanded the case, that is, sent it back to a lower court for deliberation consistent with legal principles it set forth. Name changes occurred as each new Secretary of Transportation was named as the defendant.

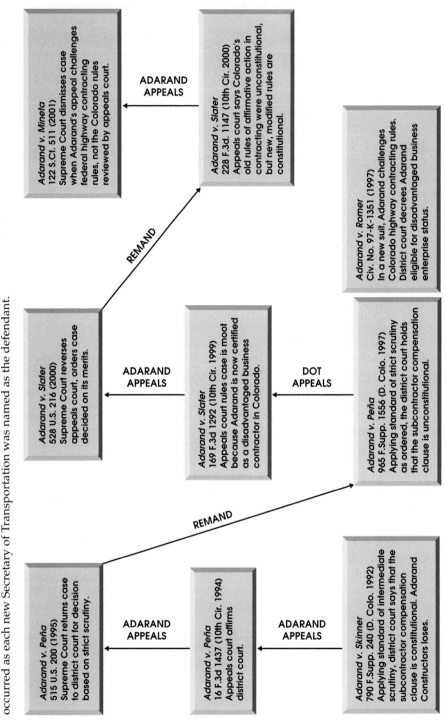

Adarand v. Mineta
122 S.Ct. 511 (2001)
Supreme Court dismisses case when Adarand's appeal challenges federal highway contracting rules, not the Colorado rules reviewed by appeals court.

Adarand v. Slater
228 F.3d. 1147 (10th Cir. 2000)
Appeals court says Colorado's old rules of affirmative action in contracting were unconstitutional, but new, modified rules are constitutional.

ADARAND APPEALS

REMAND

Adarand v. Romer
Civ. No. 97-K-1351 (1997)
In a new suit, Adarand challenges Colorado highway contracting rules. District court decrees Adarand eligible for disadvantaged business enterprise status.

Adarand v. Slater
528 U.S. 216 (2000)
Supreme Court reverses appeals court, orders case decided on its merits.

Adarand v. Slater
169 F.3d 1292 (10th Cir. 1999)
Appeals court rules case is moot because Adarand is now certified as a disadvantaged business contractor in Colorado.

Adarand v. Peña
965 F.Supp. 1556 (D. Colo. 1997)
Applying standard of strict scrutiny as ordered, the district court holds that the subcontractor compensation clause is unconstitutional.

ADARAND APPEALS

DOT APPEALS

REMAND

Adarand v. Peña
515 U.S. 200 (1995)
Supreme Court returns case to district court for decision based on strict scrutiny.

Adarand v. Peña
16 F.3d 1437 (10th Cir. 1994)
Appeals court affirms district court.

Adarand v. Skinner
790 F.Supp. 240 (D. Colo. 1992)
Applying standard of intermediate scrutiny, district court says that the subcontractor compensation clause is constitutional. Adarand Constructors loses.

ADARAND APPEALS

ADARAND APPEALS

582

[E]very single legally admitted permanent resident or citizen of the United States who happens to be female or who can trace his origins to any of 42 specifically designated countries is automatically presumed to have attempted to enter the American highway construction business and to have experienced racial prejudice that somehow hindered that attempt.[40]

Adarand Constructors urged the Court to adopt the position of Justice John Marshall Harlan that the Constitution is color-blind. It believed that both Congress and the states continued to "trample the constitutional rights of countless innocent individuals."[41] Conservative foes of affirmative action cheered the case on. John O'Sullivan, writing in the *National Review,* articulated their view.

> Today, . . . preferences bestow benefits on something like 65 percent of Americans by extracting a sacrifice from the remaining 35 percent who happen to be white males. Their injustice is now real and concentrated. In other words, they are now plainly and undeniably [victims of] an official program of negative discrimination against a minority: the sole remaining example of institutionalized racism in the United States.[42]

Adarand was a major challenge to affirmative action, but there would be no decision on it. In late 2001 the Supreme Court, after hearing oral arguments, dismissed the case without a decision, saying that it should never have accepted it in the first place. The reason was something of a technicality. In an unsigned opinion, a unanimous Court explained that in the case Adarand Constructors was not challenging the Tenth Circuit's decision about Colorado's contracting rules. Instead, it was arguing that federal guidelines were unconstitutional. The Tenth Circuit decision had not addressed federal guidelines. Therefore, since the Supreme Court was "a court of final review and not first review," it declined to take up the merits of Adarand's arguments and the case was "dismissed as improvidently granted."[43]

With this dismissal the litigation epic of the *Adarand* case, shown in Exhibit 1, came to sudden end. The merits of its final appeal are still up for debate, if not for a formal decision.

While the *Adarand* decision lives on, making affirmative action in government contracting harder to justify, minority contractors continue to struggle. For example, in 1996 California voters passed a proposition banning affirmative action in state contracting. Over the next 10 years, the dollar amount of contracts awarded to minority-owned contractors by the California Department of Transportation fell more than 50 percent and two-thirds of these contractors went out of business.[44]

Questions

1. What constitutional issue is raised in the Adarand litigation?

2. After the Supreme Court's 1995 decision in *Adarand v. Peña* what requirements did an affirmative action program have to meet to be constitutional?

3. Was the decision of the Court majority correct? Why or why not?

4. In a concurring opinion, Justice Scalia said that race classifications by government were never legitimate. In dissenting opinions, Justices Stevens, Souter, and Ginsburg argued that race-conscious remedies were justified. What were their arguments? With whom do you agree? Why?

5. Following Adarand v. Peña, the district court held that the affirmative action program in federal highway contracts was unconstitutional. Do you agree with this decision? Why or why not?

6. Do you believe that the Department of Transportation's current rules for helping DBEs get highway construction contracts pass the strict scrutiny requirement?

[40] Petitioner's Brief on the Merits, June 11, 2001, p. 11.

[41] Ibid., pp. 19–20.

[42] John O'Sullivan, "Preferred Members," *National Review,* September 3, 2001, p. 20.

[43] *Adarand Constructors, Inc. v. Mineta,* 122 S. Ct. 511, at 514 and 515. Norman Mineta, a new Secretary of Transportation, was now the respondent.

[44] Monique W. Morris et al., *Free to Compete: Measuring the Impact of Proposition 209 on Minority Business Enterprises* (Berkley, CA: Discrimination Research Center, 2006), p. 42.

Corporate Governance

Backdating with Dr. McGuire

On March 18, 2006, an article entitled "The Perfect Payday" appeared in *The Wall Street Journal*.[1] It focused on dates that companies picked to award stock options, a rather arcane topic.

Stock options are a form of executive compensation. An option is the right to buy a share of company stock at a fixed price on a later date. That price is usually the market price on the day the option is awarded. After a set time, the executive holding the option can buy a share of stock at that price.

An executive holding options is motivated to ensure that when they become exercisable the company's stock price will be higher than it was on the day the options were granted. The bigger the spread between the price of the option and the current price, the more the holder profits. Suppose an executive gets options on a day when the stock is worth $50 a share and is allowed to exercise them after a wait of one year. If the stock has risen to $60 the executive can pocket $10 a share. If, on the other hand, the stock was worth $40 a share on the day the options were granted, the executive can pocket $20 a share. Therefore, the so-called exercise price, or the price on the day options are granted, is very important.

Relying on statistical analysis of grant dates the *Journal* found that at some companies stock options were granted repeatedly on days when share prices hit historic lows. One example was a striking series of favorable coincidences at UnitedHealth Group, a Minneapolis-based health care corporation. Twelve separate option grants went to William W. McGuire, M.D., its chairman and chief executive, on days when the stock fell to yearly or quarterly lows. According to the *Journal*, the odds against picking this series of dates by chance were 1 in 200 million, lower than the odds for winning the Powerball lottery. The *Journal* also noted that Dr. McGuire had already made $450 million selling some of his options. He still held options with unrealized gains of $1.6 billion.

Had UnitedHealth used hindsight to pick the dates? If it had, it was using a practice called backdating, where options are granted on one date, but priced as if they

---

[1] Charles Forcelle and James Bandler, "The Perfect Payday," *The Wall Street Journal,* March 18, 2006, p. A1.

William W. McGuire, M.D., Chairman and Chief Executive Officer of UnitedHealth Group.
Source: © AP Photo/Eric Miller.

had been granted on a historical date when the market price was lower. Backdating is legal if it is revealed to shareholders. It is illegal if hidden. Since options create a compensation expense for the company, improper dating leads to incorrect financial statements. After reading the *Journal* article, regulators at the Securities and Exchange Commission grew suspicious and told the company they were looking into the matter. Meanwhile, UnitedHealth's board of directors engaged a law firm to investigate how options had been handled.

Dr. McGuire, a former pulmonary surgeon, seemed untroubled. He was a star at UnitedHealth, where he had been chairman and CEO since 1991. During his tenure the share price had risen by 8,500 percent.[2] "To my knowledge," he told analysts in a conference call, "every member of management in this company believed at the time that we followed appropriate practices. We sleep with a good conscience."[3]

Two weeks later, Dr. McGuire stood before shareholders at UnitedHealth's annual meeting. He apologized for allowing the options issue to arise and conceded that

[2] UnitedHealth Group, "UnitedHealth Group Board Announces a Series of Actions," press release, October 14, 2006, p. 1.

[3] Quoted in James Bandler, Charles Forelle, and Vanessa Fuhrmans, "CEO Aims to Halt Stock-Based Pay at UnitedHealth," *The Wall Street Journal,* April 19, 2006, p. A1.

FIGURE 18.1
United Health-
Group Share
Price: 1999

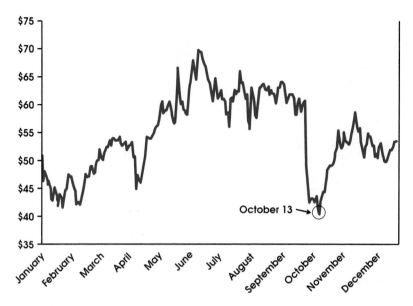

"[w]ith perfect hindsight we perhaps should have moved to make adjustments in our options program." In the audience, a retired schoolteacher owning 800 shares rose to call McGuire's options "obscene." "I grant you many more sleepless nights so you might make better decisions for this company in the future," he said. Other shareholders burst into applause.[4]

The ensuing investigation by the law firm was thorough, involving 80 interviews and a review of 4 million documents with more than 26 million pages. It looked into 29 option grants, giving special scrutiny to two enormous 1999 grants received by Dr. McGuire.

In the first grant, he received 1,000,000 options as part of an employment agreement negotiated with a five-member committee of the board of directors. Investigators determined that talks between Dr. McGuire and the committee started in September 1999, with the committee finally approving the grants at a meeting on November 5, a day when shares sold at $52.56. The grant was not official until the full board approved it and Dr. McGuire signed the agreement in December, when the share price was still above $50. However, the options were dated October 13 and priced at $40. As shown in Figure 18.1, October 13 was the day that UnitedHealth's shares hit their yearly low, closing at $40.13.

When investigators asked Dr. McGuire why the options were dated October 13, he responded that he and a member of the committee had reached a verbal agreement about granting them on that date. When interviewed, the committee member could

[4] "Apology Issued on Stock Options," *New York Times,* May 3, 2006, p. C7.

not recall the conversation and said that, in any case, he had no authority to bind the full committee.

In the second grant, the board's compensation committee approved 750,000 options for Dr. McGuire at a meeting on October 26, 1999, a day when United-Health's shares closed at $49. However, the grant date was set as October 13, 1999, and the options were priced at $40. Again, the date coincided with the yearly low.

In interviews, Dr. McGuire told investigators that grant dates were usually set in a memo, phone call, meeting, or discussion with members of the board's compensation committee. He denied that they were picked with the benefit of hindsight. Yet investigators had trouble finding evidence of such communications around many of the 29 grant dates they studied. The first written mention often came weeks or months after a grant date and the date always seemed to coincide with prices at or near yearly and quarterly lows. Moreover, this improbable series of coincidences abruptly ended when a new law, the Sarbanes-Oxley Act, went into effect in 2002. It requires companies to notify the Securities and Exchange Commission within two days of an options grant. After the new law, no more quarterly grants were dated on the days of market lows.

In their final report, the investigators concluded that most of the 29 grants they looked into were "likely backdated" because of inadequate controls and lack of "an appropriate tone at the top."[5] In no case was backdating disclosed to shareholders. On the day the report came out the UnitedHealth board forced Dr. McGuire to resign. Subsequently, the company restated its financial results from 1994 through 2005 because of errors in accounting for option-based compensation.

Dr. McGuire's troubles were not over. Late in 2007 the SEC announced it had settled enforcement actions against him. The agency believed that most of the 44 million options he received during his tenure at UnitedHealth were illegally backdated. He paid a $7 million fine and disgorged $11 million in wrongful gains. He was barred from serving as an officer or director of a public company for 10 years.[6] In a settlement with UnitedHealth, he agreed to return approximately $600 million in cash and options to the company. He was allowed to keep options worth more than $800 million.[7]

This is a tale of greed with a dose of justice at the end. It is also a story of the flawed relationship among one company's share owners, managers, and directors. As such, it is a fitting introduction to the subject of corporate governance, or the study of how these three entities coexist in an imperfect alliance. In this chapter we define corporate governance, describe its operation, and discuss related issues, including especially, executive compensation.

[5] *Report of Wilmer Cutler Pickering Hale and Dorr LLP to the Special Committee of the Board of Directors of UnitedHealth Group, Inc,* October 15, 2006, p. 13.

[6] U.S. Securities and Exchange Commission, "Former UnitedHealth Group CEO/Chairman Settles Stock Options Backdating Case for $468 Million," Litigation Release No. 20387, December 6, 2007, p. 2.

[7] Eric Dash, "Former Chief Will Forfeit $418 Million," *New York Times,* December 7, 2007, p. C1.

FIGURE 18.2
The Power Triangle
Corporate governance is the exercise of authority over members of a corporate community. It is based on rules that define power relationships among shareholders, boards of directors, and managers.

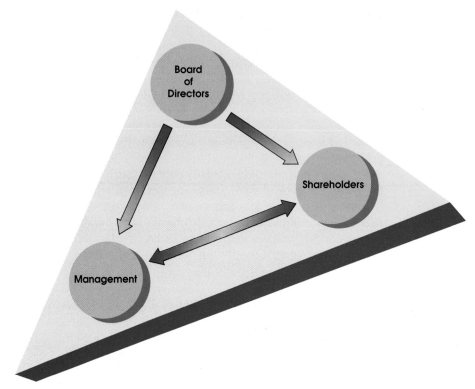

WHAT IS CORPORATE GOVERNANCE?

corporate governance
The exercise of authority over the members of a corporate community based on formal structures, rules, and processes.

Corporate governance is the exercise of authority over the members of a corporate community based on formal structures, rules, and processes. This authority is exercised in accordance with a body of rules that define the rights and powers of shareholders, boards of directors, and managers (see Figure 18.2). These rules come from multiple sources including state charters or articles of incorporation, state and federal laws, stock exchange listing standards, and governance policies written by corporations. Fundamentally, they define how power is distributed among these parties and how disputes are settled.[8]

The nature of corporate governance has changed dramatically over time. From the rise of market economies in the 1700s until the mid-1800s most companies were small and run by their owners. However, as industrial capitalism created expansive economies, these small companies grew into big corporations that could no longer be capitalized or managed by one or two owner–proprietors. Soon ownership was dispersed among a multitude of shareholders. Shareholding turned into a relatively passive form of ownership because many owners had little specific

---

[8] For a discussion of theories of corporate governance see Thomas Clarke, *Theories of Corporate Governance* (New York: Routledge, 2004).

knowledge of the business. So power to create strategy and take action passed to ranks of expert managers acting as agents of the owners.

With this transition, boards of directors evolved to perform the critical role of monitoring hired managers for the shareholders. Shareholders were largely unqualified and unknowledgeable to manage what they owned. Hired managers had the competence to run a complex corporation, but they needed day-to-day freedom from the crowd of owners to be effective. Yet they still needed supervision, because as salaried employees they lacked the same incentive to maximize profits as the owners. They might even be tempted to make their continued employment and larger salaries the top priority. It became the job of the board to balance, mediate, and reconcile the competing powers and interests of owners and managers. Thus emerged the basic structure of modern corporate governance.

THE CORPORATE CHARTER

corporate charter
The document that authorizes formation of a corporation.

The *corporate charter* is the document that authorizes formation of a corporation. Charters are also called articles of incorporation. U.S. corporations are chartered by the state in which they incorporate.[9] At the Constitutional Convention of 1787, the Founders debated a federal chartering power but decided that state controls were adequate to regulate the more geographically limited corporate activity of that time.

Corporate charters specify the rights and responsibilities of stockholders, directors, and officers. Fundamentally, they lodge control over the property of the enterprise in stockholders who own shares of the company's equity and vote those shares in naming a board of directors to oversee the firm. State incorporation laws give directors a *fiduciary responsibility* to shareholders, that is, as the entity entrusted with the owner's property, they are legally bound to manage that property in the owner's interests. They are responsible for appointing officers to run the day-to-day affairs of the company. The charters may also include provisions about such matters as par value and issuance of stock, calling annual meetings of shareholders, declaring dividends, electing and removing officers, and proposing amendments to the charter.

fiduciary responsibility
The legal duty of a representative to manage property in the interest of the owner.

The legal line of power in state charters and incorporation laws runs from the state, to shareholders, to directors, to managers. However, this legal theory of power in corporate governance diverges from the reality as widely practiced. The theory is shown on the left side of Figure 18.3. The reality, as shown to the right, is that CEOs often dominate boards of directors and both together dominate shareholders.

All 50 states have general incorporation laws and compete with one another to attract the incorporation fees of large corporations. For more than a century,

---

[9] A few quasi-public enterprises chartered by the federal government, such as the Tennessee Valley Authority, are exceptions.

FIGURE 18.3   Flow of Authority in Corporate Governance

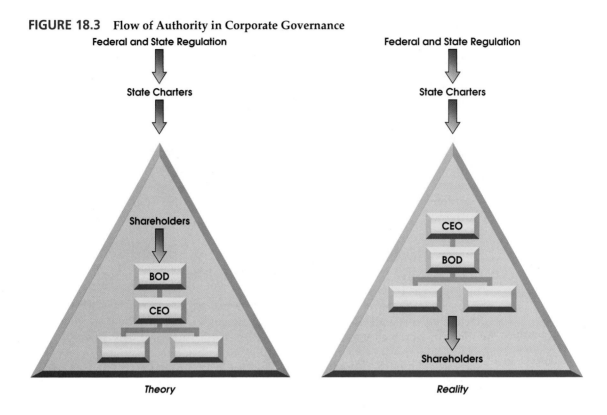

Delaware has been the victor in this competition. It charters about half the largest corporations in the United States and most newly chartered ones. About 17 percent of its state tax revenues come from chartering fees.[10] The attraction of Delaware, although costs of incorporating there are higher than in most states, is that its corporate laws are business-friendly. To maintain its addiction to corporate revenue it has repeatedly innovated more flexible and enabling rules. For other states to remain competitive with Delaware, they must match or come near to its standards.

It has been said that Delaware will not be underregulated. For example, when the personal liability of directors for their decisions began to expand in the 1980s, several states experimented with changes in their corporation laws to limit such exposure. Delaware reacted by allowing amendments to its charters that limited directors' liability. Within a year, 35 other states had adopted the same approach.[11] Besides its business-friendly approach, Delaware also has a special Chancery Court, which handles only business cases and is very accommodating to corporate interests.

---

[10] Roberta Romano, "The States as a Laboratory: Legal Innovation and State Competition for Corporate Charters," *Yale Journal on Regulation*, summer 2006, p. 212.

[11] Ibid., p. 221.

FEDERAL REGULATION OF GOVERNANCE

For more than 200 years corporate governance laws have been primarily the province of states. However, the Supreme Court, in decisions made over many years, has said that while states have the authority to create domestic corporations and to regulate them, the Commerce Clause in the Constitution empowers Congress to regulate corporations if it chooses. In the past, the federal government rarely took an interest in specific aspects of corporate governance. Over the years, the state competition for incorporation fees has led to the buildup of a flexible and permissive governance environment. Federal intervention generally comes in reaction to conspicuous failures of governance and imposes mandatory rules and restrictions.

Extensive intervention into corporate governance came in the 1930s when the country was in the worst economic depression in its history. To deal with widespread distress President Franklin D. Roosevelt created new federal agencies to protect bank depositors, investors, and farmers. When hostile takeover bids from corporate raiders began to surprise managers and shareholders in the 1960s, Congress passed a law regulating acquisitions and tender offers. More recently, a cluster of turn-of-the-century scandals highlighted weaknesses in corporate governance. This led to another incursion into state authority—the Sarbanes-Oxley Act passed in 2002. Before discussing this law we illuminate governance failures at Enron and several other companies to explain what inspired it.

The Failure of Corporate Governance at Enron

Spectacular business scandals are recurrent in United States history. However, not since the revelations of corporate misdeeds in the 1930s has there been a wave of business scandals such as that of recent years. Enron's failure in 2001 lit the investigative searchlight that revealed illegal actions in many prominent firms. Government regulators uncovered multiple instances of juggling accounting records to inflate sales and profits, hiding debt, concealing excessive CEO perks and compensation in vague footnotes, ignoring standard accounting and financial practices, and shredding documents to destroy incriminating records.

Enron enjoyed admiration and respect among investors, managers of other companies, and the public. This was reflected in the rise of its share price from $19.10 in 1999 to a high of $90.80 in 2000. Until the 1990s the company was one of the world's largest natural gas, oil, and electricity producers. Then its business model changed radically as it evolved into the world's largest energy trading company. It also created limited partnerships and exotic financial entities, numbering in the hundreds, dealing with commodities and services.

In its 2000 *Annual Report* Enron announced an astronomical increase in profits from $1 million in 1996 to $1.1 billion in 2000. This bright picture clouded in October 2001 when the company announced a $544 million after-tax charge against revenues. A month later it said it was revising its financial statements from 1997 to

2001 to reduce net income by more than $1 billion. The reason was that it had been reporting false income from unusual trading arrangements. Cash flow declined to the point where Enron could not meet its obligations and on December 2, 2001, it filed for bankruptcy. About $60 billion in market value and $2 billion of pension savings were wiped out.[12] There were mass layoffs.

Enron had a board of distinguished directors (see the box). Following the bankruptcy filing it set up a Special Investigative Committee to scrutinize the partnerships created by Andrew S. Fastow, the company's chief financial officer. The committee's report showed how the board had approved Fastow's partnerships although they created a conflict of interest.[13] The problem was that in some partnerships he was both a manager for Enron and an investor in an outside entity that engaged in financial transactions, such as the buying and selling of assets, with Enron. Which interest would be his priority, Enron's or his own?

The rules of the Financial Accounting Standards Board, which sets guidelines for accounting practices, are that if an outside investor, in this case Fastow, puts in 3 percent or more of the capital in a partnership, the corporation, even if it provides the other 97 percent, does not have to declare the partnership a subsidiary. Therefore, assets and debt in the partnership can be withheld from the corporation's balance sheet. Using this device, Enron hid losses and debt totaling hundreds of millions of dollars.[14]

The directors had recognized that it was a conflict of interest for Fastow to be an outside investor in the partnerships, but rationalized that it was a modest problem considering the great potential gain for Enron. They thought it could be handled with controls specified by the board. These controls required the approval of both top executives and the board on partnership deals. This policy was a mistake. It gave a green light to expansion of the partnerships beyond anything envisioned by the board.

The controls on Fastow were never properly implemented. The Special Investigative Committee found that board members "were severely hampered by the fact that significant information was withheld from them."[15] It reached the obvious conclusion that proliferation of the partnerships had exposed the company to enormous risks. At the same time, Fastow had orchestrated side deals netting him more than $30 million as an individual.

---

[12] There are many books and articles written about the Enron debacle. One of the best and most thorough is Kurt Eichenwald, *Conspiracy of Fools* (New York: Broadway Books, 2005). Two other informative books are Rebecca Smith and John R. Emshwiller, *24 Days* (New York: HarperBusiness, 2003) and Bethany McLean and Peter Elkind, *The Smartest Guys in the Room* (New York: Portfolio, 2003).

[13] William C. Powers, Jr., chair; Raymond S. Troubh; and Herbert S. Winokur, Jr., *Report of Investigation by the Special Investigative Committee of the Board of Directors of Enron Corp.,* February 1, 2002. Powers was dean of the University of Texas School of Law. Powers and Troubh were appointed to the board after the committee was formed. Winokur had been a member of the board before Enron's bankruptcy.

[14] John R. Emshwiller and Rebecca Smith, "Murky Waters: A Primer on Enron Partnerships," *The Wall Street Journal,* January 21, 2002, p. C14.

[15] Powers, Troubh, and Winokur, *Report of Investigation,* p. 159.

Enron's Board of Directors

In 2001, the year that Enron filed for bankruptcy, its board consisted of the 14 members below, including one female, one black, and two Asian directors. Two members, Lay and Skilling, were officers of Enron. The other 12 were nonemployee directors.

ROBERT A. BELFER, 65
Chairman and CEO
Belco Oil & Gas Corp.

NORMAN P. BLAKE, JR., 59
Chairman, President, and CEO
Comdisco, Inc.

RONNIE C. CHAN, 51
Chairman
Hang Lung Group

JOHN H. DUNCAN, 73
Investor

DR. WENDY L. GRAMM, 56
Director, Mercatus Center Regulatory Studies
Program, George Mason University and
wife of U.S. Senator Phil Gramm (R-Tex.)

DR. ROBERT K. JAEDICKE, 72
Professor (Emeritus) of Accounting
Stanford University

KENNETH L. LAY, 58
Chairman of the Board

CHARLES A. LeMAISTRE, 77
President (Emeritus)
University of Texas M. D. Anderson Cancer Center

JOHN MENDELSOHN, 64
President
University of Texas M.D. Anderson
Cancer Center

PAULO V. FERRAZ PEREIRA, 46
Executive Vice President
Group Bozano

FRANK SAVAGE, 62
Chairman
Alliance Capital Management International

JEFFREY K. SKILLING, 47
President and CEO
Enron Corporation

JOHN WAKEHAM, 68
United Kingdom Secretary of State (ret.)
and former Member of Parliament

HERBERT S. WINOKUR, JR., 57
Chairman and CEO
Capricorn Holdings, Inc

In the previous year, each nonemployee director received an average cash payment of $79,107, including an annual fee and additional fees for attending meetings or chairing one of the five board committees (executive, audit, finance, compensation, or nominating). In addition, each nonemployee director received grants of Enron stock and stock options valued at $836,517. At the time of the 2001 annual shareholder's meeting the nonemployee directors owned a total of $670 million in Enron shares. The 14 directors also served on the boards of 25 other companies.

Source: Enron Corp., *Proxy Statement*, March 27, 2001, pp. 1–12.

The Special Investigative Committee did not place sole blame for Enron's failure on its directors, but it accused the board of failing to exercise its oversight responsibility. It found that the board "was denied important information that might have led it to take action, but the board also did not fully appreciate the significance of some specific information that came before it."[16] Partnership arrangements involving substantial sums and risk were presented to the board and it failed to give them the scrutiny they deserved. Some intricate deals received only 10 or 15 minutes of attention at board meetings. The board cannot be faulted, said the Special Investigative Committee, for not acting if it had no or insufficient information. It could be faulted, however, for limited scrutiny and probing.

The board had approved procedures for management appraisal of partnerships. For example, it directed its audit committee to conduct annual reviews of all partnership transactions. The audit committee, however, failed to probe deeply into the bizarre transactions being generated. The board gave Enron's chief accounting officer the responsibility of reviewing and approving all transactions between Enron and its partnerships. Here again, the review was inadequate. What it came down to, concluded the Special Investigative Committee, was that top management was not "watching the store."

Indeed, a fundamental cause of the catastrophe was the change in culture wrought by the two top officers, Chairman of the Board Kenneth L. Lay and CEO Jeffrey K. Skilling. They fostered and permitted a freewheeling climate that tolerated junior officers engaging in illegal activities. With Lay as its chairman and Skilling a member, the board failed to establish strong norms of ethics and compliance. Enron became the classic illustration of a Wild West corporate culture characterized by reckless financial deals, avarice, and deceit. A sense of social responsibility and ethical behavior seemed absent. Enron had a 65-page "Code of Ethics" given to all employees. It contains page after page of laudable advice, such as obey the law, treat customers fairly and honestly, and avoid conflicts of interest. However, such behavior was not promoted.

In 2006, a federal jury found Lay and Skilling guilty of conspiracy and fraud in the Enron collapse. It believed that both had repeatedly lied publicly about the company's financial health while all along profiting from the sale of millions of shares of their Enron stock. Lay's death voided his conviction. Skilling was found guilty of 19 counts of fraud, deception, and conspiracy and sentenced to 24 years and 4 months in jail. Fastow pleaded guilty to conspiracy to commit wire fraud and securities fraud. Because of his willingness to testify against former top executives he was given a comparatively light prison sentence of 6 years. None of Enron's outside directors went to jail. However, 10 members of the board agreed to pay $13 million from their own pockets to settle a civil suit against them by Enron employees charging that they failed in their oversight of company retirement plans.[17]

[16] Ibid., p. 148.
[17] *Newby, et al. v. Enron Corp.*, 235 F. Supp. 2d 594 (2002).

Other Corporate Governance Scandals

The failures of the Enron board were echoed in other fraud and conspiracy scandals.

- At Tyco International the board slumbered while CEO L. Dennis Kozlowski diverted as much as $125 million in corporate funds to his personal use and conspired with his CFO Mark H. Swartz to misrepresent the company's financial condition and boost its stock price. On conviction for grand larceny, falsifying accounting records, and conspiracy, both received prison sentences of $8\frac{1}{3}$ to 25 years. Kozlowski was ordered to pay $97 million in restitution and a $70 million fine. He also lost his wife, who on her only visit to him in a New York state prison told him she wanted a divorce.[18]

- At Adelphia Communications, directors dozed as founder John J. Rigas and his son Timothy concealed $2.3 billion in off-balance-sheet debt, stole $100 million from the company, and lied to investors about its financial condition. John Rigas was sentenced to 15 years in federal prison, his son Timothy to 20 years, and another son, John, Jr., to 10 months home confinement. The Rigas family, including those not facing criminal charges, relinquished 95 percent of its net worth, or $1.5 billion, to settle civil fraud charges by the SEC.[19] At sentencing, the judge told the elder Rigas that he had "set Adelphia on a track of lying, of cheating, of defrauding," then heard Rigas announce that "in my heart and conscience, I'll go to my grave really and truly believing I did nothing."[20]

- At WorldCom, in a story told more fully in Chapter 7, CEO Bernard J. Ebbers and CFO Scott D. Sullivan concealed falling revenues and rising expenses in an $11 billion accounting fraud. Ebbers was sentenced to 25 years in prison, Sullivan to 5 years. Accused of negligent oversight, 11 of WorldCom's directors agreed to pay 20 percent of their aggregate net worth, about $20.3 million, in restitution to defrauded investors.[21] As with the Enron directors, this came from their own pockets.

In each of these instances the corporations declared bankruptcy. In each case the directors failed in their duty to protect shareholders from self-interested, predatory managers. Their failure inspired a range of corporate governance reforms aimed at sharpening boardroom vigilance. The centerpiece of these reforms is the Sarbanes-Oxley Act of 2002.

The Sarbanes-Oxley Act

Sarbanes-Oxley Act of 2002
A federal statute designed to prevent financial fraud. It enacted new regulations on auditing, financial reporting, and legal compliance.

On signing the *Sarbanes-Oxley Act of 2002* into law President George W. Bush said that it embodied "the most far-reaching reforms of American business

[18] Steve Dunleavy, "On Her First Prison Visit, My Wife Told Me, 'I Want a Divorce': Koz," *The New York Post*, October 30, 2006, p. 6.

[19] Jerry Zremski, "Rigases Agree to Forfeit 95% of Assets," *Buffalo News*, April 26, 2005, p. A1.

[20] Quoted in Dean Starkman, "Rigases Given Prison Terms," *Washington Post*, June 21, 2005, p. D1.

[21] Daniel Akst, "Fining the Directors Misses the Mark," *New York Times*, August 21, 2005, sec. 3, p. 6.

practice since the time of Franklin Delano Roosevelt."[22] There has been little disagreement. The law holds management responsible for accurate financial reports and strengthens the power and responsibility of board of directors' audit committees. While it touches on the role and structure of boards, its primary focus is on accounting rules. This intent is clear in the formal title of the act—the Public Company Accounting Reform and Investor Protection Act of 2002. However, it is better known by its short title, the Sarbanes-Oxley Act of 2002, after its congressional sponsors, Sen. Paul Sarbanes (D-Maryland), and Rep. Michael Oxley (R-Ohio). Space permits noting only a few of the act's provisions, as follows:

- Creates a five-member oversight board, the Public Company Accounting Oversight Board, giving it authority over practices of accounting firms. The Board reports to the Securities and Exchange Commission.
- Prescribes rules to improve auditing. For example, outside auditors are prohibited from accepting certain types of consulting fees when auditing the books of a company. Accounting firm auditors must be rotated every five years, and each company must create an audit committee composed of outside directors, one of whom must be a finance "specialist."
- Mandates a system run by the audit committee of the board of directors to protect whistleblowers.
- Requires the CEO and the CFO to sign and certify the accuracy of annual and quarterly financial statements. If they sign reports not in conformance with the law, they face substantial fines and long jail sentences. Corporations must also demonstrate that they have accurate financial reporting systems with strong controls.
- Stipulates that corporate executives must forfeit profits from the sale of stock and bonuses when company earnings are being restated because of securities fraud.
- Prohibits corporate executives from receiving loans unavailable to outsiders.
- Establishes heavy criminal penalties for violating its provisions. The maximum penalty for securities fraud, for example, is 25 years in jail.
- Allows the SEC to bar individual offenders from serving as directors or officers of a company.

The business community immediately complained that the new law would be extremely burdensome. A survey commissioned by the Big Four accounting firms in 2005 found that the average cost of implementing it in 90 firms ranged from a few hundred thousand dollars for small companies to $7.8 million for larger firms.[23] For some small firms the costs have been crippling. Larger firms find the costs onerous.

---

[22] Stephen M. Bainbridge "The Creeping Federalization of Corporation Law," *Regulation,* spring 2003, p. 28.
[23] Deborah Solomon, "At What Price?" *The Wall Street Journal,* October 17, 2005, p. R3.

Most compliance costs are related to Section 404 of the act. This section requires annual reports to contain an internal control report to "(1) state the responsibility of management for establishing and maintaining an adequate internal control structure and procedures for financial reporting; and (2) contain an assessment . . . of the effectiveness of the internal control structure and procedures of the issuer for financial reporting." In addition, the public accounting firm auditing the report must attest to the accuracy of the assessment.

Other institutions also responded to popular demands for reform by adding new rules. These include the New York Stock Exchange, the National Association of Corporate Directors, and the Financial Accounting Standards Board. Robert F. Felton, a director at McKinsey & Company, noted in 2004, "Arguably, the past few years have seen more corporate-governance reform than the previous several decades. Yet McKinsey surveys show that many directors and institutional investors clearly agree that too little reform has taken place to meaningfully improve board governance."[24] Others strongly disagree. John A. Thain, CEO of the New York Stock Exchange, told the Economic Club of New York that reform has "gone far enough."[25]

BOARDS OF DIRECTORS

The basic requirement for a board of directors is to manage affairs of the corporation as found in the charter. There is no set number for board membership. In 2005 the average board had 11 members and that number has not changed for publicly traded companies in a decade according to Korn/Ferry International.[26] The number varies by industry. Bank boards, for example, have on average 14 members. Most other industries have 10 to 12 members. Most small firms and many large ones have fewer board members.

Directors in large corporations are chosen after being nominated by the board and approved by a majority vote of shareholders. In the past, nominees for the board were usually suggested by the CEO and approved by the board. This is still the practice in some companies, especially smaller ones. Most boards now have nominating committees or corporate governance committees that take on this responsibility. CEOs still play a prominent role in nomination. Once approved by the full board, the names of nominees are presented to the shareholders for their approval or disapproval at the company's annual shareholder's meeting. Rarely do shareholders in larger companies unite to challenge the board's recommendations, so nomination is tantamount to election.

Requirements for being a director are flexible. At McGraw-Hill, the board seeks "qualities of intellect, integrity and judgment" and then considers a range of other factors including "diversity, background, senior management experience and an

---

[24] Robert F. Felton, "What Directors and Investors Want from Governance Reform," *McKinsey Quarterly,* summer 2004, supplement, p. 2.

[25] Louis Lavelle, "Governance: Backlash in the Executive Suite,"*BusinessWeek,* June 14, 2004, p. 36.

[26] Korn/Ferry International, *32nd Annual Board of Directors Study* (New York: Korn/Ferry International, 2006), p. 10.

understanding of marketing, finance, technology, international business matters, government regulation and public policy."[27]

inside directors
Directors who are employees of the company.

Directors who are employees of the company are called *inside directors*. They usually come from the ranks of top executives. Those who are not employed by the company are *outside directors*. They are most often top executives of other corporations who are sought out to bring expertise to board deliberations. When these outsiders have no important business dealings with the company other than being on its board, they are called *independent directors*. Listing standards of the New York Stock Exchange, which are an important source of governance rules, require that companies have a majority of independent directors to ensure that board deliberations are not marred by conflicts of interest.

outside directors
Directors who are not employees of the company.

independent directors
Outside directors who do not have business dealings with a corporation that would impair their impartiality.

Boards are divided into committees. The committees most frequently found on boards as reported by Korn/Ferry are audit (100 percent), compensation (100 percent), nominating (97 percent), corporate governance (90 percent), stock options (81 percent), director compensation (48 percent), executive (46 percent), succession planning (36 percent), finance (30 percent), corporate responsibility (17 percent), and investment (15 percent). Other committees sometimes found are public affairs, employee pensions and benefits, human resources, environmental affairs, science and technology, corporate philanthropy, and legal compliance. Specific committee responsibilities vary from company to company.[28]

Duties of Directors

State incorporation laws require corporations to place themselves under the general direction of a board of directors. These laws impose two lofty duties on directors. First is the duty to represent the interests of stockholders. Second is the duty to exercise due diligence in the oversight of corporate activity.[29] Directors violate these duties if they act in self-interested ways or if they are negligent in seeking information or making decisions. In practice, directors do not make day-to-day management decisions. Instead, boards exercise a very broad oversight, taking responsibility for "the overall picture, not the daily business decisions, the forest, not the trees."[30] Following is a short list of specific board functions.

1. Review and approve the corporation's goals and strategies.
2. Select the CEO, evaluate his or her performance, and remove the CEO if necessary.
3. Give advice and counsel to management.
4. Create governance policies for the firm, including compensation policies.

---

[27] The McGraw-Hill Companies, *Proxy Statement: 2007 Annual Meeting of Shareholders*, March 19, 2007, p. 15.

[28] Korn/Ferry International, *32nd Annual Board of Directors Study*, p. 14.

[29] Robert A. G. Monks and Nell Minow, *Corporate Governance*, 3d ed. (Malden, MA: Blackwell Publishing, 2004), p. 200.

[30] Ibid., p. 201.

5. Evaluate the performance of individual directors, board committees, and the board as a whole.
6. Nominate candidates to be presented to the stockholders for election as directors.
7. Exercise oversight of ethics and compliance programs.

These duties are critical. According to a blue-ribbon commission that was created to study the role of directors, "[o]nly a strong, diligent and independent board of directors that understands the key issues, provides wise counsel and asks management the tough questions is capable of ensuring that the interests of share owners as well as other constituencies are being properly served."[31] If such a board had existed at Enron that name would not today symbolize corporate disgrace.

Compensation of Outside Board Members

Inside directors are compensated as full-time employees of the firm. Compensation of outside directors is determined by compensation committees on boards. Outsiders are usually paid an annual retainer supplemented with additional payments for chairing or serving on board committees. Directors of large companies also receive pensions and perquisites such as life insurance policies.

Compensation varies substantially among industries. For example, the annual compensation of individual directors in the aerospace industry ranged from $29,000 to $200,000. In the computer hardware industry the range was from $32,000 to $200,000. In the electric and electronic machinery industry the range was from $6,000 to $195,000. More than 90 percent of companies allow or require directors to take part of their annual compensation in company stock.[32]

Suggestions for Improving Board Performance

McKinsey & Company researchers surveyed 150 U.S. directors in 300 public companies to get their evaluation of board performance and suggestions for improvement. Here are a few results. Directors were asked to what extent recent reforms improved board performance. Twenty eight percent said a lot, 41 percent said moderately, 22 percent said a little, and 8 percent said not at all. Asked how much additional reform is needed 22 percent said a lot, 28 percent said a moderate amount, 26 percent said a little, and 23 percent said none.[33]

A perennial question is whether or not the CEO should serve simultaneously as the board chairman. The primary purpose of the board is to safeguard the shareholders by maintaining detached, impartial oversight on management. The board also evaluates the CEO. Critics argue that it is, therefore, a conflict of interest for

---

[31] The Conference Board, *Commission on Public Trust and Private Enterprise* (New York: The Conference Board, January 2003), p. 18.

[32] All numbers are from *Directors' Compensation and Board Practices in 2006* (New York: The Conference Board, October 2006), p. 9.

[33] Robert F. Felton, "What Directors and Investors Want from Governance Reform," p. 2.

the CEO to chair the board. The McKinsey survey found that 72 percent of the directors favored a split.[34]

In defense of combining the two roles in one person, it is usually argued that the CEO is most knowledgeable about the company's affairs and can best determine what matters to bring before the board. To mute criticism, companies that combine the board chair and CEO positions often appoint a *lead director,* or an independent director who chairs regular meetings of the independent board majority without the CEO and other inside directors being present.

lead director
An independent director who chairs regular board meetings of other independent directors.

Directors were asked how well they were informed about what is happening in the companies on whose boards they serve. Thirty percent said moderately, 56 percent said partially, and 14 percent said not at all. This is a revealing but understandable response. Many directors are absorbed with the management of their own companies. Many are given thick packages of materials to be covered in the coming board meetings. They have difficulty in finding the time to read and study the contents.[35]

Correspondents were asked what were the major impediments to improving board performance. In descending order of importance the directors responded directors' motivation, time commitment, resistence from CEOs, lack of director independence, resistence from directors, insufficient pressure from investors, and insufficient regulatory pressure.[36]

INSTITUTIONAL INVESTORS AND GOVERNANCE

institutional investors
Organizational investors that buy shares in publicly traded corporations.

Institutional investors are organizations that buy shares in publicly traded corporations. They include insurance companies, banks, pension funds, mutual funds, hedge funds, and private equity funds. The growth of pension and mutual fund assets has given institutional investors new power in corporate governance. Their total assets rose from $70 billion in 1980 to more than $5.5 trillion in 2006. The equity investments of these funds rose from $258 billion in 1980 to $2.7 trillion in 2006.[37] The proportion of equities held by institutions has increased sharply since the 1950s, as shown in Figure 18.4. The big stock holdings of these institutions give them the power to influence corporate governance, and they have used it.

Fund managers were passive investors up to the 1980s. In the early 1980s Jesse Unruh, treasurer of the State of California's two largest pension funds, decided it was about time for these funds to exert their power to protect their investments from the financial predators then exploiting the corporate equities market. His concern led to formation of the Council of Institutional Investors by 31 pension fund managers who controlled approximately $200 billion of assets, most of which

[34] Ibid., p. 2.

[35] Ibid., p. 2.

[36] Ibid., p. 2.

[37] Board of Governors of the Federal Reserve System, *Guide to the Flow of Funds Accounts* (Washington, DC, 2007).

FIGURE 18.4 **Percent of Equity Held by Institutions**

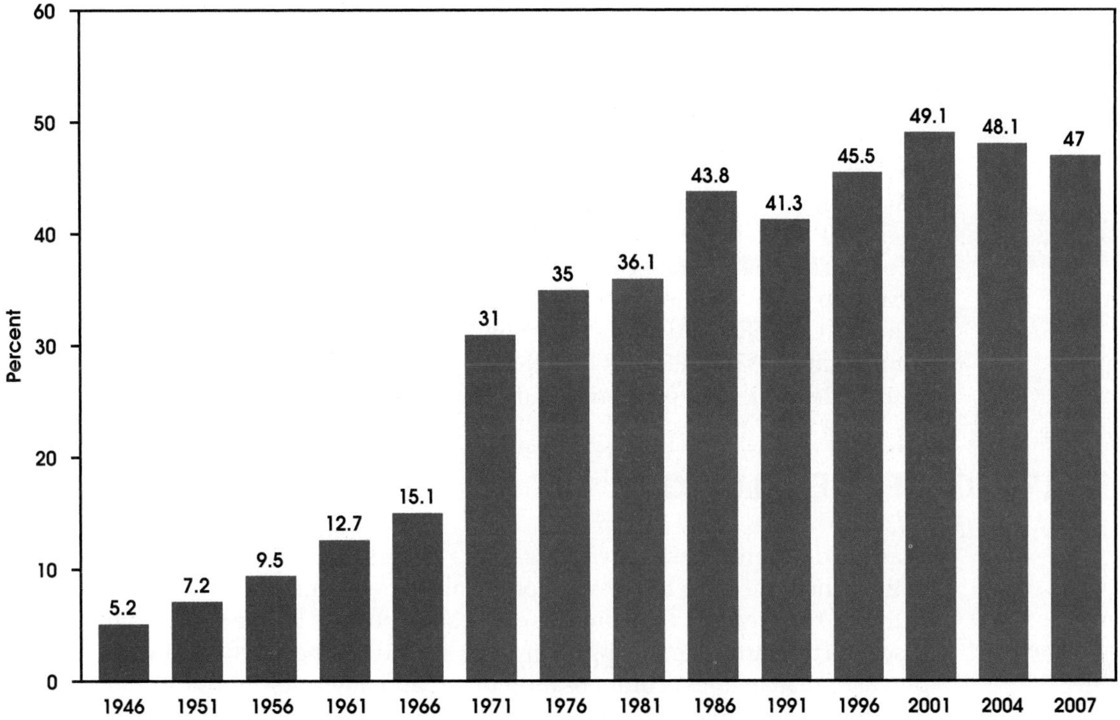

Source: Board of Governors of the Federal Reserve System.

was invested in equities. The council endorsed a Shareholders Bill of Rights demanding a voice in "fundamental decisions which could affect corporate performance and growth."[38] Since then these funds, especially the California Public Employees' Retirement System (CalPERS), the largest state pension fund, and TIAA-CREF, the largest private pension fund, have been increasingly active in corporate governance issues.

With their activism, these funds raise important governance issues. For example: should pension fund managers seek to influence corporate governance? If not, why not? If so, in what way? If pension fund managers are not satisfied with the management of the companies whose stock they hold, the shares can be sold. This is easy when the fund owns only a small number of shares. But when a massive pension fund such as CalPERS or TIAA-CREF owns a substantial number of a large company's shares it is essentially an owner–investor. This is so because selling the number of shares required to liquidate such a position could significantly depress the price per share. In the end, it may be less costly for an institutional owner to pressure management for better performance, if the long-term promise is bright.

[38] Debra Whitefield, "Unruh Calls for Pension Funds to Flex Muscles," *Los Angeles Times,* February 3, 1985, p. E3.

CalPERS' activism has evolved. Its earliest initiatives dealt with actions taken by companies to ward off corporate raiders.[39] Since 1993, the fund has identified each year a list of about 10 companies in its portfolio whose shares are under-performing market indexes. This is called the "focus list." The fund specifies why each stock on the list is targeted. Merely publicizing the list puts managers under some duress to improve their stock's performance. But in addition, CalPERS urges the boards of these companies, sometimes privately and sometimes publicly, to enhance returns to stockholders.

CalPERS has issued a list of standards for a model corporate board called the "Corporate Governance Principles and Guidelines." Pressure upon corporate boards to follow these principles is an important part of the fund's activism. Another CalPERS initiative raises concerns about what it sees as excess officer compensation. The fund has also threatened to sell its investments in companies that are delinquent in protecting human rights and the environment.

SHAREHOLDER RESOLUTIONS

proxy statement
A document sent to share-holders before the annual meeting that sets forth mat-ters requiring their vote.

Shareholders, either as individuals or organized funds, can advance resolutions at the annual meeting to be voted on by all shareholders. Resolutions are printed in the *proxy statement,* a document sent to shareholders before the annual meeting. It sets forth matters requiring their vote, including the election of directors, approval of management compensation plans, and any resolutions. SEC regulations governing shareholder proposals are found in Rule 14a-8.[40] The rule stipulates that a company must include a shareholder's proposal in its proxy statement if it meets specified requirements, including the following.

- Stockholders must own $2,000 or more of the company's shares for at least one year.
- The resolution cannot exceed 500 words.
- The resolution must be sent to the company for approval at least 120 days before the annual meeting.
- If accepted for inclusion in the proxy statement the shareholder must appear at the annual meeting to present the resolution.
- A shareholder may submit only one resolution per shareholder meeting.
- If a resolution receives less than 3 percent of the vote, it cannot be presented again at the next shareholder meeting.

All owners of common stock are entitled to one vote for each share they own. Voting may take place at the meeting, by mail, or by Internet. The format of the annual meeting is governed by the bylaws of the corporation.

---

[39] So-called corporate raiders invested enough stock in a targeted company to control it. Then they either forced the company to pay enough to get the raider to go away or actually took over control of the company to liquidate it and reap profits in the sale.

[40] 17 CFR §240.14a-8 (2007).

A company can reject a proposed shareholder resolution for any of 13 reasons described in Rule 14a-8. For example, it can reject a proposal if it violates a state law, contains false or misleading statements, deals with a matter beyond the company's power to effect, or is contrary to technical SEC proxy rules. The SEC must approve any rejection.

Each year hundreds of shareholder resolutions pass through this carefully orchestrated process and appear on proxy statements along with resolutions prepared by management. They cover a wide range of topics and their focus has changed over time. At first, in the 1970s and 1980s, shareholder groups focused on corporate social responsibilities, for example, automobile safety, doing business in apartheid South Africa, and antinuclear policies. In recent years, most proposals have focused on corporate governance issues, especially methods for the election of directors and limits on executive compensation.

Almost universally, such proposals are followed with a statement that, "the Board of Directors recommends a vote AGAINST this proposal." This is accompanied by an explanation of why the company's management wants shareholders to reject it. Most shareholder proposals fail to get a majority vote when opposed by the company. Since companies oppose most of them, only a handful get a majority vote. Few receive even double-digit affirmation. Rule 14a-8 allows proposals to be resubmitted the following year if they receive 3 percent or more of the vote cast, a third year if they receive more than 6 percent, and a fourth year if they receive more than 10 percent. Even if a proposal receives a majority vote, it is not binding. However, it puts strong pressure on both directors and management and usually results in action.

EXECUTIVE COMPENSATION

The perception of widespread, excessively generous pay and benefits for top managers is an old story. President Franklin D. Roosevelt railed against the "entrenched greed" of executives. High CEO pay in Roosevelt's era was modest compared with today's top compensation. For example, in 1929 Eugene G. Grace, president of Bethlehem Steel, the highest-paid executive, received a salary of $12,000 and a bonus of $1.6 million. Twenty years later, in 1949, Louis B. Mayer, first vice president of Lowe's Inc., a major movie studio, got $509,622. This was in contrast to the average pay of $2,612 for workers. Twenty years later, in 1968, James M. Roche, chairman of General Motors, got $795,000. The average worker then was paid $5,602.[41] Translated into current dollars these sums would be much larger, but still far below today's highest compensation figures.

Components of Executive Compensation

A compensation committee of the board of directors sets the pay of top corporate officers. New York Stock Exchange listing standards require that this committee, usually of three to five members, be composed entirely of independent directors,

---

[41]"Executive Pay, Up, Up, and Away," *BusinessWeek,* April 19, 1999, center insert.

so the CEO cannot be on it. Its members, of course, may be sympathetic friends of the CEO. Nevertheless, the committee must create a defensible plan. At most companies the compensation scheme reflects three beliefs. First, overall compensation must be competitive so that managerial talent is attracted and retained. Second, compensation should be based on both individual and company performance. And third, compensation should align the interests of executives with the interests of shareholders in long-term value creation. These goals are typically achieved by using some combination of the following elements.

Base Salary   The annual base salary is usually set near the median salary for leaders at similar firms. At Sherwin Williams, for example, it is based on a survey of two groups of comparable companies, one of 24 peer companies and the other of 35 Fortune 500 companies with revenues between $6 and $10 billion.[42] Base salaries are often around $1 million, the amount that the Internal Revenue Service allows as tax deductible.

Annual Cash Incentives   Most large companies make an annual bonus part of the compensation package. Criteria for earning the bonus vary. At McGraw-Hill the CEO receives a sliding-scale bonus based on how close the company comes to a target of 10 percent growth in earnings per share.[43] At Abbott Laboratories the CEO's yearly bonus is based on whether the company hits multiple financial goals including consolidated net earnings, profitability, sales, and earnings per share.[44] To the extent that these goals are met, the CEO can earn a maximum of .0015 percent of adjusted consolidated net earnings. Financial targets are typically the basis of annual cash incentives. If targets are missed bonuses go down and, when companies do poorly, the bonus columns in compensation tables often contain goose eggs.

Long-Term Stock-Based Incentives   Compensation in stock is designed to align manager's incentives with the interests of shareholders. There are several frequently used types of stock awards.

stock option
The right to buy the company's stock at a fixed price in the future and under conditions determined by the board of directors.

First, s*tock options* give an executive the right to buy the company's stock at a fixed price in the future and under conditions determined by the board of directors. Options are usually priced at the closing market price on the day they are granted. The holder of the options then can buy these shares from the company at a specified future date, called the vesting date, and must sell them before a later expiration date. At United Parcel Service, for example, option shares vest and can only be exercised (purchased) five years after they are granted and must be exercised within 10 years or they expire. Thus, if UPS grants options to the CEO for 1,000 shares at $70 a share and the price rises to $100 after five years, the CEO may buy them from the company for $70,000, then sell them for $100,000, making a $30,000 profit (minus fees and taxes). However, if after five years the shares have fallen to $50, they are said to be "under water" and they are worthless. The CEO will not exercise the options.

[42] Sherwin Williams Company, *Proxy Statement,* March 8, 2007, p. 17.

[43] McGraw-Hill Companies, *Proxy Statement: 2007 Annual Meeting of Shareholders,* p. 26.

[44] Abbott Laboratories, *Proxy Statement,* March 19, 2007, p. 14.

performance shares
Shares of company stock awarded after a fixed period of years if individual and company performance goals are met.

restricted stock
A grant of stock with restrictions. It cannot be sold until certain conditions are met, most often the lapse of a time period or meeting a performance goal.

Second, *performance shares* are shares awarded after a fixed period of years only if individual or company performance goals are met. These shares may be awarded in part or not at all depending on how closely performance matches goals. Typically, the time from grant to award is at least three years. General Electric awards its top executives "performance share units" that convert into shares of GE stock after five years. Half the shares are granted if cash flow from operating activities grows an average of 10 percent a year during the interim. The other half are granted if total return to shareholders exceeds that of the Standard & Poor's 500 index.[45] If these goals are not met, the "units" are canceled, unlike options that can be exercised any time between vesting and expiration.

Third, *restricted stock* is a grant of stock with restrictions on transaction that are removed when a specified condition is met. Usually, the recipient receives dividends and can vote the shares, but cannot sell them until the restriction is lifted. Any specified condition can be a restriction. Often, it is tenure at the company. In this way, restricted stock is used to lock in promising talent or key executives. If, for example, the shares vest in 10 years, then the executive must stay with the company to eventually realize their price value. At Procter & Gamble the rules are firm. During the vesting period restricted stock is forfeited immediately when the employment of an executive ends "for any reason other than death."[46] Restrictions can also be based on performance goals. The cost basis of restricted stock for the recipient is zero. Its value is the market price on the day restrictions are lifted (plus the stream of dividends since the day it was awarded). Unlike stock options, restricted stock is not worthless if the market price is below the grant price when it vests.[47]

Options, performance shares, and restricted stock are all used to create a long-term performance incentive. They also align manager's and shareholder's interests by promoting stock ownership of top executives. GE requires its CEO to hold shares worth six times his annual base salary of $3.3 million. The CEO, Jeffrey R. Immelt, exceeds this by holding 6,313,224 shares worth approximately $221 million.

Retirement Plans Companies provide generous pensions for top executives. Each year they credit top executives' pension funds with a sum calculated as a percent of the person's salary. This sum is held by the company to cover future pension payments, however, it is reported as part of the executive's total compensation. For large companies with highly paid executives the increased value of a pension can be significant. At GE, it adds more than $1 million a year to CEO Immelt's compensation.

Perquisites Acknowledging the needs and lifestyles of top executives, companies often provide extra benefits. Among the most common are annual physical exams, parking, security services, financial planning, tax preparation, life insurance policies,

[45] General Electric Company, *Notice of 2007 Annual Meeting and Proxy Statement,* February 28, 2007, p. 17.
[46] The Procter & Gamble Company, *Notice of Annual Meeting and Proxy Statement,* August 28, 2007, p. 44.
[47] As an example, suppose a manager is awarded both options and restricted stock on a day when shares sell at $20. Five years later, on a day when the price is $18, both the options and the restricted shares vest. The options are worthless, because to exercise them the manager must buy the shares at $20. The restricted stock, on the other hand, is transferred to the manager at its current value. It can be sold immediately for $18 a share.

FIGURE 18.5 How Emerson Electric Co. Compensates Its Executives

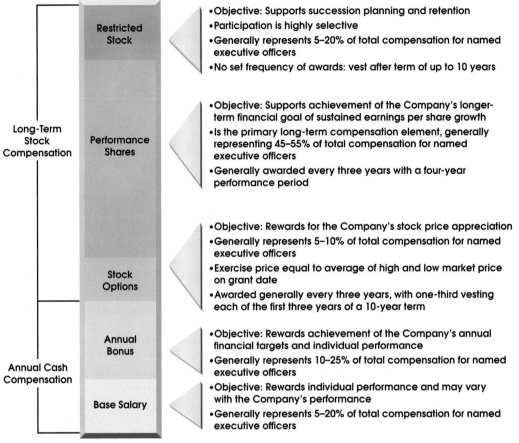

Source: Emerson Electric Co., *Notice of Annual Meeting of Stockholders,* December 14, 2007, p. 16.

club memberships, personal use of aircraft, and leased cars. SEC rules require that the dollar value of such extras be reported to shareholders.

At each company, compensation committees choose among basic components of executive compensation, picking combinations that fit their compensation philosophy. Figure 18.5 show how Emerson Electric uses a flexible combination of compensation elements to reward and retain its top executives. Each executive is compensated based on factors such as their level of responsibility, promise, performance, and length of service. Although the base pay of top executives can be generous, very large compensations usually result from incentive payouts. With stock options, these payouts can come 1 to 10 years after the shares are awarded, sometimes making it seem that compensation is out of step with current performance.

Criticisms of CEO Compensation

There are multiple criticisms of CEO compensation. Here we discuss some of the most important.

First, critics are outraged by extraordinary payouts. For example, Lee R. Raymond, who retired as CEO of ExxonMobil in 2006, received more than $400 million in his last year. Raymond spent 43 years with the company and was considered an effective leader. While his total compensation was one of the highest ever paid to an executive there were other examples of very high pay that year. Ray Irani, CEO of Occidental Petroleum, in 2006 received $315 million; Kenneth Lewis, CEO of Bank of America, received $91.6 million; John Chambers, CEO of Cisco Systems received $69.7 million; and Larry Ellison, CEO of Oracle, received $63.1.[48] In 2006, the average compensation of top executives was much more modest. A study of 350 of the largest U.S. corporations reported that median direct compensation was $6,008,368. Of 185 chief executives who cashed in options, the median amount was $3,299,193.[49]

Second, some compensation packages given to newly hired CEOs have raised eyebrows. For instance, when Ford Motor Company recruited Alan Mulally from Boeing to be its CEO in 2006 it paid him $28.2 million for the last four months in the year, including an $18.5 million signing bonus and $8.6 million in stock awards and options.[50] For the year, Ford posted a loss of $5.8 billion.

Third, critics deplore handsome golden handshakes received by some CEOs when they leave under fire. One example is Robert Nardelli, former CEO of Home Depot, who left with a package of $210 million after the company's shares slid from above $50 to $41 over his six-year tenure. Another is Henry McKinnell, who departed Pfizer with a pay package of $213 million after the company lost $137 billion in market value under his direction.[51]

Fourth, critics charge that on too many compensation committees the members are CEOs of other corporations, cronies of the CEO, or consultants who have profited from business with the company. In such cases, it is alleged, the bias is clearly in favor of boosting CEO compensation. Furthermore, as Lucian A. Bebchuk and Jesse Fried, two compensation scholars, explain in their book *Pay Without Performance,* the greater the power of the CEO the fatter his compensation.[52]

Fifth, critics complain that boards of directors are not approving compensation of CEOs in conformance with the interests of shareholders. The conventional assumption is that directors evaluate compensation packages primarily if not solely in the interest only of stockholders. That is incorrect say Bebchuk and Fried.

> Directors have had and continue to have various economic incentives to support, or
> at least go along with, arrangements favorable to the company's top executives.
> Social and psychological factors—collegiality, team spirit, a natural desire to avoid

[48] Joann S. Lublin, "Ten Ways to Restore Investor Confidence in Compensation," *The Wall Street Journal,* April 9, 2007, p. R3.

[49] Joann S. Lublin, "The Pace of Pay Gains: A Survey Overview," *The Wall Street Journal,* April 9, 2007, p. R1.

[50] Ford Motor Company, *Notice of 2007 Annual Meeting of Shareholders and Proxy Statement,* April 5, 2007, p. 45.

[51] Eric Dash, "An Ousted Chief's Going Away Pay Is Seen by Many as Typically Excessive," *New York Times,* January 4, 2007, p. C4.

[52] Lucian A. Bebchuk and Jesse Fried, *Pay Without Performance* (Cambridge, MA: Harvard University Press, 2004).

conflict within the board, friendship and loyalty, and cognitive dissonance—exert additional pressure in that direction. . . . In addition, limitations on time and resources have made it difficult for even well-intentioned directors to do their pay-setting job properly.[53]

Sixth, critics assert that companies are too lavish in stock option grants. Stock options are given for many reasons. They are often given when a company is created. For instance, at the time of Microsoft's creation and in the early days, Microsoft's founders, Bill Gates and Paul Allen, received millions of options instead of salary. Today these are worth billions of dollars. Options are also used as inducements in executive recruiting. They are given for good performance. The result is that executives accumulate thousands, and sometimes, millions of options. When a CEO leaves, for whatever reason, the exercise of accumulated options can be substantial.

backdating

Setting the exercise price of stock options at the price on a date before the date they were granted.

Seventh, critics complain about misuse of options. One problem is *backdating*, or setting the exercise price of stock options at the price on a date before the date they were granted. As explained, an option gives the owner the right to buy the stock in the future at a set price, called the exercise price. Normally the price is the closing stock market price on the day of issuance. Backdating occurs when the company, at the time of the grant or retroactively, fixes the grant date as a part date when the price of the stock was lower. In plain terms, companies search the past for troughs in share prices, then pretend the options were granted at those low points (see the box).

Backdating is criticized for giving executives unearned rewards. Individuals cannot buy shares in a company, then decide to value their cost at the price they sold for on an earlier day. Backdating is legal if disclosed to shareholders, but illegal if concealed. The practice of backdating options took off in the 1990s in Silicon Valley. Among high-technology companies it was common to reward employees and entice talented people with generous stock options. Executives saw that the value of their options would rise if the grant date was replaced with an earlier date when the company's stock was low.

spring loading

Granting options shortly before good news causes a share price rise.

A related practice is *spring loading*, or the granting of options shortly before the release of good news, already known to the company but not yet to the public, causes share prices to rise. Shareholders sued Tyson Foods in Delaware's Chancery Court for issuing four grants of spring-loaded options between 1999 and 2003. For example, four days before Tyson announced favorable earnings in 2003 its board's compensation committee granted a total of 940,000 option shares to three top executives. After the announcement the share price rose $0.92, giving the options an instant $864,800 lift. The judge declared the grants illegal.[54] However, they were defended by a commissioner of the SEC, Paul S. Atkins, who argued that the compensation committee should be allowed to exercise a "business judgment" in which it determines that it can issue fewer options to get the same result when it anticipates a rise in the share price.[55]

---

[53] Lucian A. Bebchuk and Jesse M. Fried, "Pay Without Performance: Overview of the Issues," *Academy of Management Perspectives,* February 2006, p. 9.

[54] *In re Tyson Foods, Inc. Consolidated Shareholder Litigation,* Del. Ch., No. 116-N (2007).

[55] Quoted in Floyd Norris, "Option Lies May Be Costly for Directors," *New York Times,* February 16, 2007, p. 1.

Backdating: A Hypothetical Example

1. On June 1, 2008, a CEO gets an option grant to purchase 1,000 shares of his company's stock which can be exercised in two years. The shares are priced at $30, the closing price on the New York Stock Exchange that day.

2. On June 1, 2010, when the options vest, the stock is selling for $29 a share. At this point the stock option is worthless.

3. The company decides to backdate the options to May 1, 2008, when the shares closed at $22.

4. The executive now decides to exercise the options, buying 1,000 shares from the company at $22 for $22,000, then selling them on the open market for $29 a share or $29,000. This nets a profit before taxes and brokerage fees of $7,000.

5. The value of the options is reported by the corporation as a cost, reducing net income. The lost value, in theory, reduces shareholder value.

Finally, critics complain that the spread between executive pay and the pay of the average worker is widening. Calculations of different analysts vary but they all see the gap widening over the years. For example, one study concluded that in 1965 CEOs of the largest companies were paid 24 times an average worker's pay. By 2004 the gap grew to 431 times the pay of an average worker.[56] Thereafter, there was a slight decline but still it was 411 in 2006.[57] In 2006, according to another survey, the average pay of a CEO of a Standard & Poor's company was $29.1 million.[58] The average worker received $33,200.[59]

In Defense of CEO Pay

First, Congress has considerable responsibility for the boom in stock options, not corporations. Congress became concerned about high executive salaries and responded in 1993 by legislating that only $1 million of the annual salary and benefits paid to a top executive could be deducted as a business expense. The provision in the law did not apply to performance-based compensation, pensions, and existing contracts. Unexercised stock options and performance grants were not charged as costs to the company. The result was an explosive growth of stock options to pay executives beyond $1 million annual salaries. Currently, option grants must be charged as expenses. The result has been a decline in option grants.

Second, stock options became a large part of compensation during a period marked by long rises in stock markets. Bull markets in stock prices since the 1980s

---

[56] Democratic Staff of the Financial Services Committee, U.S. House of Representatives, October 24, 2006, at http://financialservices.house.gov/ExecCompvsWorkers.html.

[57] Institute for Policy Studies–United for a Fair Economy, in "2006 Trends in CEO Pay," AFL-CIO, 2007.

[58] "The Boss's Pay, The WSJ/Mercer 2006 CEO Compensation Survey," *The Wall Street Journal,* April 9, 2007, p. R6.

[59] Abid Aslam, "U.S. Pay Gap Widens between CEOs and Workers," CommonDreams.org,News Center, April 12, 2005, p. 1.

were opportunities for executives to exercise options granted earlier at much lower prices. When these options were exercised, compensation figures rose significantly.

Third, defenders say many large compensation packages were justified by stockholder gains during their tenure. This clearly applied to former CEOs Lee Raymond of ExxonMobil and Jack Welch of General Electric. The price of their companies' stock rose significantly over long periods while they were in office. Arguably they, and CEOs like them, devised and executed the strategies that produced rising equity. Their achievements should be rewarded accordingly.

Fourth, boards believe that if they do not pay their CEOs what executives in comparable companies get, they stand to lose them, and that would be more costly than high compensation. Anyway, they say, the compensation is not out of line with comparable professionals, such as top lawyers and Wall Street investment bankers.

Finally, most managers never get the dramatically high salaries that attract criticism. Indeed, some argue that more than a few top executives are underpaid. This is especially true in smaller businesses. Even casual observation of executive pay shows that it generally varies with company size and revenues. The larger the company and the greater the revenues the larger the top executive compensation. Conversely the smaller the company and its revenues the lower is executive compensation.

Suggested Compensation Reforms

The list of suggestions for compensation reform is long. Here are a few.

First, the SEC should require more data on compensation in reports to shareholders. Under new rules mandated in 2006, the first major change since 1992, corporations must provide more detailed information about total pay and benefits of the top-five officers. They must include the value of executive perks such as airplane use and country club dues. The new rules require comprehensive information about options and pensions. Details of commitments to pay executives when they leave the company must also be disclosed.[60] Corporations, however, can still obscure the exact nature of compensation with complicated explanations only financial experts can fully understand.

Second, pay and performance relationships should be revealed. This means telling shareholders how much of an executive's compensation is for performance and how much is due to other factors, such as stock market booms. Making these calculations is difficult but estimates could be included in public statements.

Third, bonuses should be tied to long-term performance. "Rewarding executives for short-term improvements," say Bebchuk and Fried, "is not an effective way to provide beneficial incentives and indeed might create incentives to manipulate short-term accounting results."[61]

Fourth, shareholders should be able to vote on executive compensation. In 2007, a proposal to allow shareholders an advisory vote on senior executive compensation

---

[60] For details see Jonathan Peterson and Kathy M. Kristof, "More Data on Pay at the Top Is Mandated," *Los Angeles Times,* July 27, 2006, p. C1.

[61] Bebchuk and Fried, *Pay Without Performance,* p. 21.

received 50.18 percent of the vote at Verizon Communication. The company's directors then adopted a policy requiring such a vote. The first one will come at its 2009 annual meeting. Also in 2007, a bill requiring public companies to put executive pay packages before shareholders for a nonbinding vote passed the House of Representatives.[62] Managers generally are opposed to such a requirement, arguing that it would intrude unnecessarily on management prerogatives. They also argue that current SEC rules give shareholders all the information they need to make informed decisions about their investments.

CONCLUDING OBSERVATIONS

In this chapter we discuss the key parties in corporate governance–share owners, boards of directors, and management. Despite well-defined legal bonds, there are many tensions between them. Their relationships evolve. Today these relationships are generally healthy, but problems remain, especially for boards of directors. Turn-of-the-century scandals revealed lax oversight of financial strategies and reporting by many boards. Many shareholders believe that boards have allowed management compensation to exceed reason. Recently, the practice of corporate governance has been elevated by requirements in the postscandal Sarbanes-Oxley Act of 2002 and overhauls of corporate governance policies urged by share owners. Overall, the outlook is for more pressures and regulations that tighten board oversight.

[62] H. R. 1257, the Shareholder Vote on Compensation Act, sponsored by Rep. Barney Frank (D-Mass.), passed on April 20, 2007, by a 269 to 134 vote. The Senate has taken no action.

High Noon at Hewlett-Packard

In the beginning there was a garage. As legend has it, this humble structure in Palo Alto gave birth to giant Hewlett-Packard Company. It was there that Bill Hewlett and David Packard, both recent graduates of Stanford, spent years tinkering before coming up with their first successful product, a precision oscillator. The two partners went public with their company in 1949.

As it grew they ran it using a home-grown philosophy that came to be called the HP Way. At its core the HP Way emphasized the worth of each employee. It inspired a nonhierarchical, decentralized, and participative company in which the creativity of each scientist and engineer could be freed. The HP Way seeded an egalitarian spirit that now infuses tech companies throughout Silicon Valley.

For many years Hewlett-Packard was the bright star in the Silicon Valley firmament. But as the twentieth century approached it no longer blazed with innovation. Its aging cofounder's hands had lifted from the controls. Despite booming markets, its earnings were lackluster, its share price stagnant. Eventually, its board of directors saw the need for a new CEO.

CARLY FIORINA

The choice was Carleton S. Fiorina, called Carly by friends and associates. Fiorina was the first woman to head a corporation as large as Hewlett-Packard. She came from a position as a group president at Lucent Technologies. Her mandate from the HP board was to "shake things up."

Immediately, Fiorina became a celebrity. It frustrated her when the media categorized her as "Carly

EXHIBIT 1
The Hewlett-Packard Board in 1999

When Carly Fiorina arrived at Hewlett-Packard this was the board of directors. There were 13 members, 9 outside directors and, including herself, 4 inside directors. Four of the outside directors were related to the cofounders by birth or marriage. The board had five committees: Audit, Compensation, Executive, Finance and Investment, and Organization Review and Nominating. Each director was paid a $100,000 retainer, of which 75 percent was paid in HP stock. Individual directors were paid $5,000 for serving as committee chairs and a fee of $1,200 for each full board meeting attended.

Philip M. Condit, 57
Chairman and CEO, Boeing Company

Patricia C. Dunn, 46
Chair, Barclays Global Investors

John B. Fery, 69
Retired Chairman and CEO, Boise Cascade

Carleton S. Fiorina, 45
CEO, Hewlett-Packard Company

Jean-Paul G. Gimon, 63
General Representative, Credit Lyonnais and
son-in-law of HP cofounder William R. Hewlett

Sam Ginn, 62
Chairman, Vodafone AirTouch

Richard A. Hackborn, 62
Retired Executive Vice President, Hewlett-Packard

Walter B. Hewlett, 55
Chairman, The William and Flora Hewlett Foundation

George A. Keyworth, 60
Chairman, Progress & Freedom Association

Susan Packard Orr, 53
Chair, The David and Lucile Packard Foundation

David Woodly Packard, 58
Founder, Packard Humanities Institute

Lewis E. Platt, 58 (Chairman)
Former CEO, Hewlett-Packard

Robert P. Wayman, 54
Executive Vice President and Chief Financial Officer, Hewlett-Packard

Fiorina, female CEO" and reporters focused on her as a woman rather than on her mission at HP.[1]

> From the first . . . both the language and the intensity of the coverage were different for me than for any other CEO. It was more personal, with much commentary about my personality and my physical appearance, my dress, my hair or my shoes. . . .

There was a persistent rumor . . . that I'd built a pink marble bathroom in my office.[2]

After taking the helm at HP in 1999 she was called both a "bimbo" and a "bitch" in Silicon Valley chat rooms. She learned that her actions would be interpreted through a gender lens. When male CEOs fired people, they were called firm and commanding;

[1] Carly Fiorina, *Tough Choices: A Memoir* (New York: Portfolio, 2006), p. 171.

[2] Ibid., p. 172.

she was labeled vengeful. Such interpretations made her job "infinitely more difficult."[3]

Fiorina believed that HP had been poorly managed for years. She set to work galvanizing its managers. One problem was that in the HP culture decisions were decentralized. This was faithful to the HP Way, which taught that employees were the primary source of wisdom. But it slowed operations. Fiorina began to restructure processes so that everything went through her. The first sign of trouble came in November 2000, when Lewis Platt, the former CEO who continued as chairman of the board, requested that Fiorina leave a board meeting so the other directors could talk.[4] He told them that she was moving too fast with her plans for change.

Although the board affirmed its support for her, Fiorina was troubled. She responded by regularly inviting the directors to management meetings and setting up a Web site where they could find any data available to other HP employees. At board meetings she started going around the table asking each director to speak and state what action they would take on important issues. After each meeting she summarized points of agreement and disagreement in writing, along with action steps. This detail mentality may have irritated some directors.

TENSION ON THE BOARD

Fiorina had a strong view about the boards' role in corporate governance. The directors were there to give advice and counsel to management. Their duty was to see the big picture and ensure that major strategies were aligned with the stockholders' interests. However, the day-to-day work of running the enterprise was management's job—her job.

> The management team's job is to manage the company and produce results. A board meets six or eight times a year and cannot possibly know enough of the details of a business to manage it. And yet a board must represent the company's owners and this means knowing enough to ask the right questions.[5]

As time went on, she believed that some influential board members failed to draw a line between

their broad oversight role and her daily management role. One was Richard Hackborn, a retired HP executive who had worked closely with the cofounders over the years. Another was George Keyworth, a former science adviser to President Ronald Reagan with a doctorate in physics. Both were technologists who, she felt, lacked appreciation for problems of execution. They were filled with suggestions and sometimes wanted to change projects and budgets in midstream. They met with employees. They even suggested that Fiorina fire certain managers. Among other ideas, they proposed the acquisition of Compaq Computer Corporation. This was an opportunity to expand market share and achieve operating economies, but the combination would be difficult. It would require laying off tens of thousands of people in both companies and blending distinctive cultures.

After considerable debate, the full HP board unanimously agreed to the $22 billion acquisition. Just before the announcement in late 2001, HP's intentions were leaked to the media, obviously by a well-informed insider. Now HP was placed on the defensive. Reaction in the business press and among investors was immediately hostile due to the conventional wisdom that such huge combinations usually failed. HP's share price fell. The identity of the leaker was never discovered.

Then board member Walter Hewlett, the cofounder's son, surprised Fiorina by changing his mind and opposing the acquisition. He was soon joined by David Packard, son of the other cofounder. Together, the two controlled more than 16 percent of HP shares. Both disliked the dilution of their ownership in the company that would come from issuing millions of new shares to make the acquisition.

Hewlett stopped attending board meetings and, with Packard, launched a battle to garner enough votes to stop the deal. He persuaded one board member, Sam Ginn, to change his mind. Ginn then came to a board meeting and pressed the other directors to reverse course. They held firm. Finally, after a bitter fight, HP's shareholders approved the acquisition by a slight 3 percent margin of shares voted.[6] The merger was completed in 2001 and 2002. However, a consequence of the internecine battle was that investors remained skeptical about it for years.

---

[3] Ibid., p. 173.

[4] Platt's resignation as CEO had been amicable. He would resign as chairman and retire from the company on December 31, 1999. Fiorina was then elected chairman.

[5] Carly Fiorina, *Tough* Choices, p. 210.

[6] A week after the meeting Walter Hewlett filed a lawsuit in the Delaware Chancery Court alleging that HP had bought the vote of Deutsche Bank. In April, the court dismissed the lawsuit and Hewlett did not further contest the vote.

Carly Fiorina discusses the plan to buy Compaq at a 2001 news conference. Source: © AP Photo/Paul Sakuma.

Fiorina's problems with the board continued. As time passed, expectations from the Compaq merger were far from being met. Earnings targets were missed. HP's share price languished. The board was unhappy about this news. Fiorina continued to believe that the board was intruding on her role as chief executive by nosing into operational details. One change on the board came when two CEOs, Sam Ginn and Phil Condit, retired in early 2004. That left only two other CEOs with operating experience. These were the kind of board members most valued by Fiorina because she felt that they respected her management prerogatives. It proved difficult to recruit others in their mold, however, because after the passage of the Sarbanes-Oxley Act in 2002 the leaders of large corporations cut back on outside board memberships to focus more on time-consuming governance requirements in their own firms.

Then there was the abrasion of the board's technology committee. It was formed in 2002 at the suggestion of director Tom Perkins. Perkins had moved

to the HP board from the Compaq board in 2001. He was a formidable presence, combining a long history at HP with a keen mind for strategy. He had been hired by Hewlett and Packard in 1957 and ran the company's research labs for more than a decade until they put him in charge of their new computer division. Perkins built the HP computer business, then left in 1972 to cofound what became the nation's leading venture capital firm, Kleiner, Perkins, Caufield & Byers.

This partnership provided seed capital for Silicon Valley start-ups. Its spectacular successes were Genentech, AOL, Netscape, Amazon, and Google. Perkins became a billionaire, soon adopting an extraordinary lifestyle of mansions and fast cars. His sailing ship, the *Maltese Falcon* is, at 289 feet, the longest private yacht in the world. After his first wife died of cancer, he married, then divorced, celebrity romance novelist Danielle Steel. According to Perkins, they remain deeply in love, but they cannot live together because "it would be easier to merge General Motors and General Electric. You know, we lead big, complicated lives."[7]

Perkins was joined on the technology committee by George Keyworth and Dick Hackborn, the inventor of laser printing. All three were fascinated with scientific details and soaring possibilities for new products. All three were dominating directors. Under their lead, the committee began to function as a board-within-a-board. It often met the day before a regular board meeting and its agenda ranged over all aspects of HP's business. It was a breeding ground for projects and suggestions. Most of them were rejected by Fiorina, who believed that the "disruptive" technologists lacked appreciation for the obstacles to achieving financial results from their ideas. In her view, "[t]hey thought because they understood technology, they understood everything."[8] As their suggestions were spurned, the committee members grew restive.

Another conflict also arose. The technologists became impatient with Patricia Dunn's leadership of the audit committee. Dunn was a determined force. The proof was in her career. She grew up in Las Vegas, where her mother was a model and showgirl and her father booked entertainment at hotels. When

<hr/>

[7] "Conversation with Tom Perkins," *The Charlie Rose Show,* December 5, 2007, transcript, p. 12.

[8] Carly Fiorina, *Tough Choices,* p. 280.

HP Director Tom Perkins at the window of his San Francisco office in 2006. Source: © AP Photo/Eric Risberg.

she was 11, her father died. When the time for college came, she won a scholarship to the University of Oregon, but had to drop out and work as a cook and housekeeper to support herself and her mother. Later she attended UC Berkeley on a scholarship, making a three-bus commute and graduating with a journalism degree.[9]

Soon she took a temporary secretarial position at Wells Fargo Bank in San Francisco. She stayed on and after the bank was acquired by Barclays Global Investors she rose to become that company's CEO from 1995 to 2002. She came to the HP board in 1998. In 2001 she was diagnosed with breast cancer and a year later with melanoma, causing her to step down as CEO. She retained her position as chairman of the board at Barclays.

On the audit committee she focused on governance procedures. She was methodical and organized. Keyworth and others saw an obsession with details that blocked her appreciation of the big picture. Her strength was the minutia of legal compliance, not the spirited, free-wheeling strategy debate the technologists thrived on. They worried that the board was moving in the wrong direction. It needed an infusion of imagination.

Perkins felt that it had become what he called a "compliance board," or a board focused on obeying laws and rules, where meeting time was consumed with boring hours of reports by lawyers and committees. Such boards could be filled with big company executives who were familiar with governance rules, if not necessarily with a company's unique business. In contrast, Perkins wanted a "guidance board," or a board of knowledgeable insiders and industry experts that takes an active role in the company, not only reviewing strategy, but becoming deeply involved in its management.[10] A compliance board plodded along checking boxes. A guidance board could better jolt HP from its slumber.

Perkins and his technology committee colleagues wanted to add Silicon Valley friends with scientific and entrepreneurial backgrounds to the board. Fiorina resisted these nominations. She continued to favor candidates with big-company operating experience, ideally, CEOs of other large corporations. These were the directors likely to share her view that the board should stay at arms' length from management's actions. Tension over the role of the board and its composition hung in the air. This was not eased when Tom Perkins retired in 2003 after reaching the mandatory retirement age for HP directors of 72.

Throughout 2004 other directors were becoming troubled by HP's performance. During Fiorina's tenure, revenues and profits had climbed, largely because the company grew much bigger with the Compaq merger. However, the merger was not living up to expectations. Talented managers from both companies were jumping to competitors. HP had lost market share in computers to Dell and in network servers to both Dell and IBM. Its profit margins in key business segments were falling. HP's share price was just over $40 when Fiorina was named CEO in 1999. Through 2004 it traded below $20. She had centralized management so that almost every decision went through her, and she resisted efforts by board members to enter into the management process.

Late in the year, several directors proposed bringing Perkins back, arguing that the board needed another member with technology expertise. Keyworth told Fiorina that Perkins missed being on the board. She countered that his return was a breach of HP's governance policy. In the post-Enron climate of re-

[9] George Anders and Alan Murray, "Inside Story of Feud That Plunged HP into Crisis," *The Sunday Times,* October 15, 2006, p. B18.

[10] Tom Perkins, "The 'Compliance' Board," *The Wall Street Journal,* March 2, 2007, p. A11.

form, disregard of the retirement rule would look bad. Moreover, what the board really needed was another big-company chief executive with operating expertise. Yet in a momentary lapse of resolve, she agreed to Perkins's return. It was a slip she would regret.

FIORINA'S FALL

In January 2005 the board met again. Perkins had been invited to attend this meeting as a visitor. His official reappointment would take longer to meet the letter of HP's governance policy. However, several members requested that the board vote immediately to appoint him. Fiorina countered that his formal confirmation must wait. He had not studied statements of operating results that needed approval that day. If all voting directors were not well versed on the financials, requirements of the Sarbanes-Oxley Act would be sacrificed. She got her way.

Although not yet officially appointed, Perkins nevertheless stayed in the meeting and immediately began to play an advocacy role. He strongly suggested actions, including acquisition of another software firm and altering the roles of specific top executives. Fiorina rebuffed the advice, telling Perkins and his allies that it was her prerogative as CEO to make such decisions. According to Perkins, "she made it very clear . . . that our opinions were less than welcome on operational and organizational specifics."[11]

As the meeting wore on, the board proposed a reorganization to delegate some of Fiorina's duties to other executives. She opposed the plan. If the board held her accountable for results, then it should let her make her own decisions about how to achieve them. But by the end of the meeting she had agreed to combine two product groups under a new manager and yielded to ground rules for evaluating other changes over the coming months.

Days later, *The Wall Street Journal* published a front-page story about the meeting quoting "people close to the situation," phrasing that could refer only to two or more directors.[12] According to the article, the HP board was still supportive of Fiorina, but very concerned about the company's ragged financial performance, an exodus of managers to competing firms, and weak market performance. Of Fiorina, one source said she "has tremendous abilities," but "she shouldn't be running everything every day. She is very hands on and that slows things down."[13]

"It is hard to convey how violated I felt," said Fiorina.[14] This leak was a profound breach of confidentiality. If directors are to fulfill their oversight role, they must be able to trust the others present. If they fear that remarks will become public they might not engage in the kind of open, honest, and unreserved deliberations that best serve share owners. She immediately convened a conference call with the entire board. After scolding them for the breach, she asked the board's nominating and governance committee to investigate. It engaged an attorney to interview each board member, not only to ask about the leak, but to solicit their views about the overall effectiveness of the board and how it could improve its functioning.

Fiorina was certain that Tom Perkins and his technology committee friend Keyworth were the sources because they were the ones pushing hardest for the reorganization described in the article.[15] In the investigation, only Perkins admitted speaking to a reporter, insisting that he had not initiated the story, but responded only when he was called to confirm its contents. He claimed he had only tried to ward off some damaging details. No other director admitted involvement. The attorney's report also described the board as "dysfunctional" due to personality conflicts and the tendency of a few dominating members to divert the agenda to long discussions on side topics.

After this, the directors stopped communicating with Fiorina. A special February 8 board meeting was set up in a hotel to keep it out of the media. When Fiorina arrived Patricia Dunn immediately called the group to order, though Fiorina, as chairman of the board, would ordinarily preside. Dunn asked if Fiorina had anything to say. Fiorina read a 30-minute statement defining and defending her role as CEO. She was asked to leave the room while the board met in executive session.

After she left, the directors broke into "turbulent" debate, with Perkins and Keyworth pushing hard for her removal.[16] Three hours later, a majority had

---

[11] Tom Perkins, *Valley Boy: The Education of Tom Perkins* (New York: Gotham Books, 2007), p. 4.

[12] Pui-Wing Tam, "Hewlett-Packard Board Considers a Reorganization," *The Wall Street Journal,* January 24, 2005, p. A1.

[13] Ibid., p. 1.

[14] Carly Fiorina, *Tough Choices,* p. 290.

[15] James B. Stewart, "The Kona Files," *The New Yorker,* February 19–26, 2007, p. 155.

[16] Tom Perkins, *Valley Boy,* p. 6.

EXHIBIT 2
The Hewlett-Packard Board in Early 2005

This is the board that fired Carly Fiorina on February 8. One director, Sanford Litvak, had abruptly resigned on February 2. He was replaced on February 7 by Tom Perkins. Since 1999 the board had shrunk to nine members due largely to resignations by representatives of the Hewlett and Packard families in protest over the Compaq merger. Finding replacements in the new governance climate created by the Sarbanes-Oxley Act proved difficult. By now each director was paid a $200,000 retainer. The board had voted in 2004 to double its compensation. Directors who chaired committees were paid an additional $10,000.

Lawrence T. Babbio, Jr., 60
Vice Chairman and President, Verizon Communications

Patricia C. Dunn, 51 (Non-executive Chairman)
Chair, Barclays Global Investors

Richard A. Hackborn, 67
Retired Executive Vice President, Hewlett-Packard

George A. Keyworth, 60
Chairman, Progress & Freedom Association,

Robert E. Knowling, Jr., 49
Former Chairman and CEO, Simdesk Technologies

Thomas J. Perkins, 73
Partner, Kleiner Perkins Caufield & Byers

Robert L. Ryan, 61
Senior Vice President and CFO, Medtronic

Lucille S. Salhany, 58
President and CEO, JHMedia

Robert P. Wayman, 59
Interim CEO, Hewlett-Packard

formed behind Fiorina's immediate replacement. She was summoned. On her return, only two board members remained at the conference table, Dunn and Robert Knowling, the retired CEO of Simdesk Technologies. "The Board has decided to make a change," said Knowling. "I'm very sorry, Carly."[17] She left with a bonus package of $21 million, HP shares worth $18.2 million, and a pension of $200,000 a year.[18] Yet in that hour her star fell to earth. She felt devastated.[19]

[17] Carly Fiorina, *Tough Choices*, p. 303.
[18] Pui-Wing Tam and Joann S. Lublin, "H-P Gave Fiorina $1.57 Million in Bonus Payments Last Year," *The Wall Street Journal*, February 14, 2005, p. B2; and Carol J. Loomis, "How the HP Board KO'd Carly," *Fortune*, March 7, 2005, p. 99.
[19] Carly Fiorina, *Tough Choices*, p. 303.

PATRICIA DUNN ASCENDANT

In the following days, the board named Robert P. Wayman, HP's long-time chief financial officer, to be interim CEO and picked Patricia Dunn to be its non-executive chairman. In this position Dunn would preside at board meetings but would not play an active role in managing the company. Separation of the board chairmanship from the CEO position was Tom Perkin's idea and reflected his belief that a strong board should not be dominated by the same person who is the company's top manager. It also gave the board more power over management.

Dunn's influence had risen during the period when Perkins and Keyworth emerged as the leading antagonists toward Fiorina. At first Dunn was neutral, but at some point she moved over to join the two influential directors in their campaign for change.[20] In addition, Dunn had been diagnosed the year before with advanced ovarian cancer and endured surgery and chemotherapy. Both Perkins and Keyworth had lost wives to cancer. They were sympathetic and liked her fortitude. Perkins even proposed that Dunn receive an additional $100,000 for serving as chairman. She declined to accept it.

The immediate task for the board was to find a new CEO. Dunn, Perkins, and Keyworth headed the search. Within two months they had hired Mark Hurd from NCR Corporation. Hurd would prove to be an excellent choice. Meanwhile, seven directors had approached Dunn, telling her that identifying the source of leaks and ending them was critical to maintaining trust and integrity on the board. All told, there had been 10 unauthorized leaks. They asked her to make renewed investigation a top priority.[21]

Dunn turned to the interim CEO, Bob Wayman for advice. He sent her to an HP security manager, who in turn referred her to a security firm in Boston that was under contract with HP. A new investigation was opened. Dunn named it Project Kona after a spot in Hawaii where she and her husband own a vacation home.

As the investigation began, other events eroded the comity between Dunn and Perkins. Perkins believed that since he had initiated her elevation to the chairmanship she would be deferential toward him. In this he erred. Early on he came to a board meeting with a sweeping agenda of strategy issues he wanted discussed. Dunn, however, had retreated into her armor of focus on details. She announced her discovery of many inconsistencies between HP's director's handbook and its bylaws. The meeting would be about harmonizing the two. Perkins was taken aback. This button-down approach assaulted his venture capitalist DNA. He had not read the handbook and had no intention ever of doing so.

Vacancies existed on the board. As chairman of the nominating and governance committee Perkins found nominees, but Dunn was lukewarm. Again a difference of philosophy was the cause. Perkins submitted the names of Silicon Valley comrades who shared his values. Dunn wanted top executives from large, established corporations. When she suggested the president of PepsiCo, Perkins mocked him as "Sugar Daddy."[22]

Other abrasions angered Perkins, including a comment by Dunn in the presence of Hewlett-Packard managers that his new novel, *Sex and the Single Zillionaire* was not her kind of reading.[23] The two frequently quarreled. However, he thought they had an agreement that if the leak investigation bore fruit the matter would be handled by the two of them talking privately with the offending director. He wanted to extract an apology and a promise never again to talk with the press, then close the matter and go on. Again, he misjudged.

In the background, the leak investigation continued. One day the head of the Boston security firm told Dunn and HP's general counsel that his investigators had gotten the phone numbers of reporters who had written stories based on leaks. They were now going to obtain phone records using a technique called "pretexting." Investigators would call phone companies, pretending to be the reporters, and ask for records of their calls. Then they would get the directors' phone records the same way and check for calls back and forth. The HP counsel asked if this was legal. The security firm manager said yes. When the phone records were obtained, however, no evidence incriminated any director. The investigation had failed.

Nothing further was done until early in 2006 when another leak appeared. A CNET reporter published a story about the company's annual management retreat in January 2006. In it "a source" was quoted as saying that "[b]y the time the lectures were done at 10 P.M., we were pooped and went to bed."[24] The story also revealed that HP was considering certain kinds of software acquisitions, but it contained no specifics and no confidential information.

Because of this new leak, Dunn launched a second round of investigation labeled Kona II. This time it was run by an HP lawyer with in-house investigators. Again, pretexting was used to obtain the phone records of both reporters and HP directors. Comparing these

---

[20] James B. Stewart, "The Kona Files," p. 156.

[21] U.S. House of Representatives, Subcommittee on Oversight and Investigations of the Committee on Energy and Commerce, *Hewlett-Packard's Pretexting Scandal*, 109th Congress, 2d Sess., September 28, 2006, pp. 90, 129.

[22] James B. Stewart, "The Kona Files," p. 157.

[23] New York: Harper, 2007. Perkins had given Dunn an early draft of the book.

[24] Dawn Kawamoto, "HP Outlines Long-Term Strategy," C/NET News.com, January 23, 2006.

Patricia Dunn at a 2005 news conference. Source: © AP Photo/Paul Sakuma.

phone records, they discovered two brief calls between Dawn Kawamoto, the reporter who wrote the January story, and Perkin's ally, director George Keyworth.

Trying to catch the conspirators in the act, they launched a sting operation. They fabricated a disgruntled HP manager who sent Kawamoto fake e-mails offering to reveal something sensational. A tracking program was embedded, so that if she sought to forward them to Keyworth or another director for confirmation the investigators would know. However, she simply invited the employee to call her. The HP investigators also staked out the homes of Kawamoto and Keyworth. No contact between them was observed.

In weekly meetings the investigative team kept Dunn informed. Questions about the legality of the tactics being used were raised by former police officers in HP's security department, but company attorneys told Dunn that all actions were legal. She said, "Throughout the process I asked and was assured—by both H-P's internal security department and the company's top lawyers, both verbally and in writing—that the work being undertaken to investigate and discover these leaks was legal, proper and consistent with the H-P way of performing investigations."[25]

Dunn and Perkins continued to abrade each other. After the regular board meeting in March, Dunn requested that Perkins and two others remain in the meeting room for a moment. The two disagree on what happened next. According to Perkins, Dunn told the others that he was out to get her and burst into tears. Dunn denies the statement, saying she told Perkins that his disruptive outbursts in meetings were counterproductive.[26]

Results of the leak investigation were revealed at the May 18, 2006, board meeting. That morning, just before the board convened, director Robert Ryan, an executive with Medtronic, who was now chair of the audit committee, met with Keyworth. When asked about Dawn Kawamoto's CNET article, Keyworth admitted to having lunch with her and discussing the retreat. He considered it a friendly lunch, not a press contact, and said he was surprised by the article. He felt that it was positive and harmless and told Ryan that if anyone had just asked him, he would have divulged the conversation. He was amazed to learn that this piece was the focus of a major investigation.

Meanwhile, Dunn took Perkins aside moments before the meeting and informed him about Keyworth. When she said that the matter had to go before the full board he was startled and irate. In the meeting, Ryan summarized a report from the HP lawyer in charge of the investigation. Keyworth was contrite. "I apologize for any discussion I had with the reporter in question that may have resulted in any of my colleagues on this board losing trust with me."[27] He added, "I would have told you all about this. Why didn't you ask? I thought I was just helping the company through a rough patch with the press. Aren't directors supposed to do that?"[28] He was asked to leave the room.

With Keyworth outside, Perkins spoke up. He argued that his friend's intention was innocent and the leak inconsequential. He believed that once again Dunn was focused on the trivia of process, "the 'sin' of the leak itself," rather than its substance.[29] When a motion was made to ask for Keyworth's resignation, he grew "incandescent," and directed most of his fury at Dunn. After 90 minutes of dispute a vote was

---

[25] Patricia Dunn, "The H-P Investigation," *The Wall Street Journal*, October 11, 2006, p. A14.

[26] James B. Stewart, "The Kona Files," p. 162.

[27] Ibid, p. 163.

[28] Tom Perkins, *Valley Boy,* p. 15.

[29] Ibid., p. 15.

taken by secret ballot. The motion passed. At that, Perkins said simply, "I resign," and walked out.[30] When Keyworth reentered he was asked to resign, but refused, noting that he had been elected by HP share owners and his legal obligation was to serve until they removed him.

THE END OF DUNN

It was Perkins's final meeting as an HP director, but he was not through with the company. He sought to have the minutes of the meeting rewritten to include his remarks that the investigatory tactics were illegal. When he discovered that his home telephone records had been deceitfully obtained, he wrote a letter to the board saying that the investigation had violated the law. He demanded that it forward a copy of the letter to the Securities and Exchange Commission. When his demands were rejected, he instructed his lawyer to contact not only the SEC, but U.S. Attorney's offices in Manhattan and San Francisco, the California Attorney General, the Federal Communications Commission, and the Federal Trade Commission. This caused an explosion in the press, removing the cloak from an investigation that could not survive the light.

Within months, Dunn agreed to step down as chairman. Individual board members told her they did not believe she was involved in anything improper or illegal. But she had become a lightning rod for criticism of HP and its board. CEO Mark Hurd and other directors urged her to remain on the board as a member. Soon, however, it was plain that she would be a major distraction. Finally, the board asked her to resign and she did so on September 22. She was asked not to speak at the press conference where her retirement was announced. Two HP attorneys who played a leading role in the investigations also resigned.

The next week, Dunn testified at a congressional hearing where she was flayed by members of the House Committee on Energy and Commerce. "What were you thinking?" asked Rep. John Dingell (D-Mich.).[31] "[I]s all of this really the HP way?"

inquired Rep. Jan Schakowsky (D-Ill.).[32] In her testimony Dunn repeatedly fell back on assurances by HP lawyers and managers that the investigation was legal, at one point saying, "I do not accept personal responsibility for what happened."[33]

On October 4, she was charged by the State of California with four felony counts of wire fraud, identity theft, and conspiracy, charges that carried a potential sentence of 12 years in a state prison. Three investigators were also charged. All pleaded not guilty.

Dunn's defense was that she had consistently questioned investigation tactics and been assured that they were legal. Therefore, state prosecutors could not prove she intended to commit a crime, a necessary factor for conviction. Moreover, no federal or state law was specific in making pretexting a crime.[34] Five months later a California Superior Court judge dropped the case against her and agreed to dismiss charges against the others in exchange for 96 hours of community service.[35] Dunn's health was a factor in the judge's decision, but the main reason was the tenuous nature of the charges.

Whether Dunn intended to commit a crime or not, Perkins is convinced that she pursued the investigation on the likelihood that he and Keyworth would be incriminated and forced to resign, thereby removing two of her political enemies. He states that at one point he decided to seek her resignation as chair, but claims he was talked out of it by Keyworth.[36]

In the end he brought her down, doing on the outside what he did not do on the inside. His actions put Hewlett-Packard at the center of a scandal, made it the subject of late-night jokes, and ended careers. As a director, he was unruly, challenging, and stubborn. Those who would condemn him, however, should entertain this question. What would happen if he were put in a time machine and returned to the 1990s for service on Enron's board?

---

[30] Ibid., p. 16.

[31] U.S. House of Representatives, Subcommittee on Oversight and Investigations of the Committee on Energy and Commerce, *Hewlett-Packard's Pretexting Scandal*, 109th Congress, 2d Sess., September 28, 2006, p. 13.

[32] Ibid., p. 96.

[33] Ibid., p. 120.

[34] As a result of the scandal, Congress passed the Telephone Records and Privacy Protection Act of 2006 (P. L. 109-476) to criminalize pretexting. More than a dozen states have passed similar laws.

[35] Matt Richtel, "H.P. Chairwoman and 3 Others Cleared in Spying Case," *New York Times,* March 15, 2007, p. C1.

[36] Perkins, *Valley Boy,* p. 15.

Questions

1. Over the time covered here, did Hewlett-Packard's board of directors fulfill its duties to the company's share owners? Explain how it met or did not meet basic duties.

2. What different perspectives on the role of the board are revealed in this story?

3. Was Carly Fiorina treated fairly by the board? Why or why not?

4. Were the leak investigations overseen by Patricia Dunn useful and important? Were they ethical?

5. Should George Keyworth have been asked to resign? Why or why not?

6. How do you appraise the behavior of Tom Perkins? Was he a model director or a renegade?

7. What could have been taken to improve the functioning of the HP board?

8. Did gender play any role in the fortunes of Fiorina and Dunn?

Index